The Oxford

French Dictionary

Revised Edition

FRENCH–ENGLISH
ENGLISH–FRENCH

FRANÇAIS–ANGLAIS
ANGLAIS–FRANÇAIS

Michael Janes
Dora Carpenter
Edwin Carpenter

Word games prepared
by Natalie Pomier

Oxford   New York

OXFORD UNIVERSITY PRESS

1998

Oxford University Press, Great Clarendon Street, Oxford, OX2 6DP
Oxford New York
Athens Auckland Bangkok Bogota Bombay Buenos Aires
Calcutta Cape Town Dar es Salaam Delhi
Florence Hong Kong Istanbul Karachi
Kuala Lumpur Madras Madrid Melbourne
Mexico City Nairobi Paris Singapore
Taipei Tokyo Toronto Warsaw
and associated companies in
Berlin Ibadan

Oxford is a trade mark of Oxford University Press

© Oxford University Press 1998

First published 1986 as The Oxford French dictionary
Second edition first published 1993
First issued as an Oxford University Press paperback 1989
Second edition first published 1994
Two-color edition first published 1995
Revised edition published 1998

British Library Cataloguing in Publication Data
Data available

Library of Congress Cataloging in Publication Data
Data available

ISBN 0-19-8601905

10 9 8 7 6 5 4 3 2 1

Typeset by Pentacor PLC
Printed in Spain by
Mateu Cromo Artes Graficas S.A.
Madrid

The Oxford–Hachette Language Program

The Oxford–Hachette Language Program is the result of a unique partnership between two of the world's foremost reference publishers, and marks the start of a new age of bilingual dictionaries. The Program has produced the only French dictionaries to be written using the evidence of scores of millions of words of English and French, drawn from every type of written and spoken language. Each dictionary provides a more accurate, up-to-date, and complete picture of real language than has ever been possible before.

The Bank of French

Capturing current French as it is truly used is the primary aim of The Bank of French, a unique 13 million word database of current French. The Bank shapes every dictionary entry and translation to meet the needs of today's users, highlighting important constructions, illustrating difficult meanings, and focusing attention on common usage.

The richest choice of words

Combining a comprehensive vocabulary with the full variety of idiomatic and colloquial French is a distinctive element of the Oxford–Hachette Language Program. The Program has captured standard, regional, and world French. In addition, variant pronunciations and the degree of formality for words, from formal right through to taboo, are signaled whenever necessary.

The library of French Literature

From Racine and Balzac to Gide and Camus, a library of the works of many of the greatest of France's playwrights, poets, and novelists has been included in the Bank of French, enabling the editors of the Program to analyze and describe the vocabulary and usage of literary French – historical and contemporary – to assist readers and students of French literature.

The British National Corpus

Every English entry has been shaped by direct evidence from the British National Corpus, an unrivaled balanced collection of 100 million words of text representing every kind of writing and speech in English.

Total Language Accessibility

For over 150 years Oxford's hallmarks of integrity and authority have been adapted to meet the changing needs of dictionary users. Oxford–Hachette's range of French dictionaries are an integral part of this tradition and offer an unequaled range of carefully designed benefits to ensure maximum language accessibility.

Rapid Access Design

Oxford's new quick-access page designs and typography have been specially created to ensure exceptional clarity and accessibility. Paper and binding styles are carefully selected for their durability. Entries are written in clear, jargon-free language without confusing abbreviations.

Unrivaled practical help

Extended treatment of the core vocabulary offers the user step-by-step guidance on how to select, construct, and translate a given word correctly. Unrivaled practical grammatical help has been built into every dictionary within the range. Generous numbers of examples are carefully selected to illustrate the many different nuances of meaning and context. A clear, efficient system of translation signposting guides the user to the most appropriate translation.

Supplementary Information

All the dictionaries in the Oxford–Hachette range offer valuable additional help and information, which can include regular and irregular verb tables, thematic vocabulary boxes, political and cultural information, guides to effective communication (how to write letters, CVs, book holidays, or take minutes), two colour texts, and pronunciation guidance.

Business, technical, and computing vocabulary

The editors of The Oxford-Hachette Language Program have provided the widest and most accurate representation of the language of every notable specialist field. All translations were checked by a skilled team of specialist translators before being included.

Contents

Preface

The Oxford Color French Dictionary is a dictionary designed for be-
ginners of French. This revised edition includes word games
specifically designed to build key skills in using your dictionary
more effectively, and to improve knowledge of French vocabulary usage in a fun and entertaining way. You will find answers
to all puzzles and games at the end of the section.

Acknowledgments

The Oxford Color French Dictionary is based on the second edition of *The Oxford Paperback French Dictionary*. It remains largely the work of Michael Jane, the compiler of the first edition, but some entries have been substantially revised and we have been able to incorporate a large proportion of new material. We hope to have kept to the aim of the original: to provide users requiring a compact dictionary with the maximum amount of useful material.

Dora Latiri-Carpenter
Edwin Carpenter

Introduction

As an aid to easy reference all main headwords, compounds, and derivatives in this dictionary appear in blue. When you look up a word, you will find a pronunciation, a grammatical part of speech, and the translation. Sometimes more than one translation is given, and the material in brackets in *italics* is included to help you choose the right one. For example, under **cabin** you will see (*hut*) and (*in ship, aircraft*). When a word has more than one part of speech, this can affect the translation. For example **praise** is translated one way when it is a verb (*v.t.*) and another when it is a noun (*n.*).

A swung dash (∼) represents the entry word, or the part of it that comes before a vertical bar (as in **libert|y**). You will see it in examples using the entry word and words based on it. For example, under **good** you will find **as ∼ as** and **∼ -looking**.

Translations are given in their basic form. You will find tables at the end showing verb forms. Irregular verbs are marked on the French to English side with †. This side also shows the plurals of nouns and the feminine forms of adjectives when they do not follow the normal rules.

Abbreviations • Abréviations

abbreviation	*abbr., abrév.*	abréviation
adjective(s)	*a. (adjs.)*	adjectif(s)
adverb(s)	*adv(s).*	adverbe(s)
American	*Amer.*	américain
anatomy	*anat.*	anatomie
approximately	*approx.*	approximativement
archaeology	*archaeol., archéol.*	archéologie
architecture	*archit.*	architecture
motoring	*auto.*	automobile
auxiliary	*aux.*	auxiliaire
aviation	*aviat.*	aviation
botany	*bot.*	botanique
computing	*comput.*	informatique
commerce	*comm.*	commerce
conjunction(s)	*conj(s).*	conjonction(s)
cookery	*culin.*	culinaire
electricity	*electr., électr.*	électricité
feminine	*f.*	féminin
familiar	*fam.*	familier
figurative	*fig.*	figuré
geography	*geog., géog.*	géographie
geology	*geol., géol.*	géologie
grammar	*gram.*	grammaire
humorous	*hum.*	humoristique
interjection(s)	*int(s).*	interjection(s)
invariable	*invar.*	invariable
legal, law	*jurid.*	juridique
language	*lang.*	langue
masculine	*m.*	masculin
medicine	*med., méd.*	médecine
military	*mil.*	militaire
music	*mus.*	musique
noun(s)	*n(s).*	nom(s)
nautical	*naut.*	nautique

oneself	*o.s.*	se, soi-même
proprietary term	*P.*	marque déposée
pejorative	*pej., péj.*	péjoratif
philosophy	*phil.*	philosophie
photography	*photo.*	photographie
plural	*pl.*	pluriel
politics	*pol.*	politique
possessive	*poss.*	possessif
past participle	*p.p.*	participe passé
prefix	*pref., préf.*	préfixe
preposition(s)	*prep(s)., prép(s).*	préposition(s)
present participle	*pres. p.*	participe présent
pronoun	*pron.*	pronom
relative pronoun	*pron. rel.*	pronom relatif
psychology	*psych.*	psychologie
past tense	*p.t.*	passé
something	*qch.*	quelque chose
someone	*qn.*	quelqu'un
railway	*rail.*	chemin de fer
religion	*relig.*	religion
relative pronoun	*rel. pron.*	pronom relatif
school, scholastic	*schol., scol.*	scolaire
singular	*sing.*	singulier
slang	*sl.*	argot
someone	*s.o.*	quelqu'un
something	*sth.*	quelque chose
technical	*techn.*	technique
television	*TV*	télévision
university	*univ.*	université
auxiliary verb	*v. aux.*	verb auxiliaire
intransitive verb	*v.i.*	verbe intransitif
pronominal verb	*v. pr.*	verbe pronominal
transitive verb	*v.t.*	verbe transitif

Pronunciation of French

Phonetic symbols

Vowels

i vie	ɑ bas	y vêtu	ɛ̃ matin
e pré	ɔ mort	ø peu	ɑ̃ sans
ɛ lait	o mot	œ peur	ɔ̃ bon
a plat	u genou	ə de	œ̃ lundi

Consonants and semi-consonants

p payer	f feu	m main	j yeux
b bon	v vous	n nous	w oui
t terre	s sale	l long	ɥ huile
d dans	z zéro	r rue	
k cou	ʃ chat	ɲ agneau	
g gant	ʒ je	ŋ camping	

Notes: ' before the pronunciation of a word beginning with *h* indicates no liaison or elision.

An asterisk immediately following an apostrophe in some words like **qu'*** shows that this form of the word is used before a vowel or mute 'h'.

Proprietary terms

This dictionary includes some words which have, or are asserted to have, proprietary status as trade marks or otherwise. Their inclusion does not imply that they have acquired for legal purposes a non-proprietary or general significance, nor any other judgement concerning their legal status. In cases where the editorial staff have some evidence that a word has proprietary status this is indicated in the entry for that word by the symbol P., but no judgement concerning the legal status of such words is made or implied thereby.

Français · Anglais
French · English

A

a /a/ *voir* avoir.

à /a/ *prép.* (*à* + *le* = *au*, *à* + *les* = *aux*) in, at; (*direction*) to; (*temps*) at; (*jusqu'à*) to, till; (*date*) on; (*époque*) in; (*moyen*) by, on; (*prix*) for; (*appartenance*) of; (*mesure*) by. **donner**/*etc.* **à qn.**, give/*etc.* to s.o. **apprendre**/*etc.* **à faire**, learn/*etc.* to do. **l'homme à la barbe**, the man with the beard. **à la radio**, on the radio. **c'est à moi**/*etc.*, it is mine/*etc.* **c'est à vous**/*etc.* **de**, it is up to you/*etc.* to; (*en jouant*) it is your/*etc.* turn to. **à six km d'ici**, six km. away. **dix km à l'heure**, ten km. an *ou* per hour. **il a un crayon à la main**, he's got a pencil in his hand.

abaissement /abɛsmã/ *n.m.* (*baisse*) drop, fall.

abaisser /abese/ *v.t.* lower; (*levier*) pull *ou* push down; (*fig.*) humiliate. **s'~** *v. pr.* go down, drop; (*fig.*) humiliate o.s. **s'~ à**, stoop to.

abandon /abãdɔ̃/ *n.m.* abandonment, desertion; (*sport*) withdrawal; (*naturel*) abandon. **à l'~**, in a state of neglect. **~ner** /-ɔne/ *v.t.* abandon, desert; (*renoncer à*) give up, abandon; (*céder*) give (**à**, to). **s'~ner à**, give o.s. up to.

abasourdir /abazurdir/ *v.t.* stun.

abat-jour /abaʒur/ *n.m. invar.* lampshade.

abats /aba/ *n.m. pl.* offal.

abattement /abatmã/ *n.m.* dejection; (*faiblesse*) exhaustion; (*comm.*) allowance.

abattis /abati/ *n.m. pl.* giblets.

abattoir /abatwar/ *n.m.* slaughter-house, abattoir.

abattre† /abatr/ *v.t.* knock down; (*arbre*) cut down; (*animal*) slaughter; (*avion*) shoot down; (*affaiblir*) weaken; (*démoraliser*) dishearten. **s'~** *v. pr.* come down, fall (down). **se laisser ~**, let things get one down.

abbaye /abei/ *n.f.* abbey.

abbé /abe/ *n.m.* priest; (*supérieur d'une abbaye*) abbot.

abcès /apsɛ/ *n.m.* abscess.

abdi|quer /abdike/ *v.t./i.* abdicate. **~cation** *n.f.* abdication.

abdom|en /abdɔmɛn/ *n.m.* abdomen. **~inal** (*m. pl.* **~inaux**) *a.* abdominal.

abeille /abɛj/ *n.f.* bee.

aberrant, ~e /abɛrɑ̃, -t/ *a.* absurd.

aberration /abɛrasjɔ̃/ *n.f.* aberration; (*idée*) absurd idea.

abêtir /abetir/ *v.t.* make stupid.

abhorrer /abɔre/ *v.t.* loathe, abhor.

abîme /abim/ *n.m.* abyss.

abîmer /abime/ *v.t.* damage, spoil. **s'~** *v. pr.* get damaged *ou* spoilt.

abject /abʒɛkt/ *a.* abject.

abjurer /abʒyre/ *v.t.* abjure.

ablation /ablasjɔ̃/ *n.f.* removal.

ablutions /ablysjɔ̃/ *n.f. pl.* ablutions.

aboiement /abwamã/ *n.m.* bark (ing). **~s**, barking.

abois (aux) /(oz)abwa/ *adv.* at bay.

abol|ir /abɔlir/ *v.t.* abolish. **~ition** *n.f.* abolition.

abominable /abɔminabl/ *a.* abominable.

abond|ant, ~ante /abɔ̃dɑ̃, -t/ *a.* abundant, plentiful. **~amment** *adv.* abundantly. **~ance** *n.f.* abundance; (*prospérité*) affluence.

abonder /abɔ̃de/ *v.i.* abound (**en**, in). **~ dans le sens de qn.**, completely agree with s.o.

abonn|er (s') /(s)abɔne/ *v. pr.* subscribe (**à**, to). **~é, ~ée** *n.m.*, *f.* subscriber; season-ticket holder. **~ement** *n.m.* (*à un journal*) subscription; (*de bus, théâtre, etc.*) season-ticket.

abord /abɔr/ *n.m.* access. **~s**, surroundings. **d'~**, first.

abordable /abɔrdabl/ *a.* (*prix*) reasonable; (*personne*) approachable.

abordage /abɔrdaʒ/ *n.m.* (*accident: naut.*) collision. **prendre à l'~**, (*navire*) board, attack.

2

aborder /abɔrde/ v.t. approach; (*lieu*) reach; (*problème etc.*) tackle. ● v.i. reach land.

aborigène /abɔriʒɛn/ n.m. aborigine, aboriginal.

aboutir /abutir/ v.i. succeed, achieve a result. ~ **à**, end (up) in, lead to. **n'~ à rien**, come to nothing.

aboutissement /abutismã/ n.m. outcome.

aboyer /abwaje/ v.i. bark.

abrasi|f, ~ve /abrazif, -v/ a. & n.m. abrasive.

abrégé /abreʒe/ n.m. summary.

abréger /abreʒe/ v.t. (*texte*) shorten, abridge; (*mot*) abbreviate, shorten; (*visite*) cut short.

abreuv|er /abrœve/ v.t. water; (*fig.*) overwhelm (**de**, with). **s'~er** v. pr. drink. **~oir** n.m. watering-place.

abréviation /abrevjasjɔ̃/ n.f. abbreviation.

abri /abri/ n.m. shelter. **à l'~**, under cover. **à l'~ de** sheltered from.

abricot /abriko/ n.m. apricot.

abriter /abrite/ v.t. shelter; (*recevoir*) house. **s'~** v. pr. (take) shelter.

abroger /abrɔʒe/ v.t. repeal.

abrupt /abrypt/ a. steep, sheer; (*fig.*) abrupt.

abruti, ~e /abryti/ n.m., f. (*fam.*) idiot.

abrutir /abrytir/ v.t. make ou drive stupid, dull the mind of.

absence /apsɑ̃s/ n.f. absence.

absent, ~e /apsɑ̃, -t/ a. absent, away; (*chose*) missing. ● n.m., f. absentee. **il est toujours ~**, he's still away. **d'un air ~**, absently. **~éisme** /-teism/ n.m. absenteeism. **~éiste** /-teist/ n.m./f. absentee.

absenter (s') /(s)apsɑ̃te/ v. pr. go ou be away; (*sortir*) go out, leave.

absolu /apsɔly/ a. absolute. **~ment** adv. absolutely.

absolution /apsɔlysjɔ̃/ n.f. absolution.

absor|ber /apsɔrbe/ v.t. absorb; (*temps etc.*) take up. **~bant, ~bante** a. (*travail etc.*) absorbing; (*matière*) absorbent. **~ption** n.f. absorption.

absoudre /apsudr/ v.t. absolve.

absten|ir (s') /(s)apstanir/ v. pr. abstain. **s'~ir de**, refrain from. **~tion** /-ɑ̃sjɔ̃/ n.f. abstention.

abstinence /apstinɑ̃s/ n.f. abstinence.

abstr|aire /apstrɛr/ v.t. abstract. **~action** n.f. abstraction. **faire ~action de**, disregard. **~ait, ~aite** a. & n.m. abstract.

absurd|e /apsyrd/ a. absurd. **~ité** n.f. absurdity.

abus /aby/ n.m. abuse, misuse; (*injustice*) abuse. **~ de confiance**, breach of trust. **~ sexuel**, sexual abuse.

abuser /abyze/ v.t. deceive. ● v.i. go too far. **s'~** v. pr. be mistaken. **~ de**, abuse, misuse; (*profiter de*) take advantage of; (*alcool etc.*) over-indulge in.

abusi|f, ~ve /abyzif, -v/ a. excessive; (*usage*) mistaken.

acabit /akabi/ n.m. **du même ~**, of that sort.

académicien, ~ne /akademisjɛ̃, -jɛn/ n.m., f. academician.

académ|ie /akademi/ n.f. academy; (*circonscription*) educational district. **A~ie**, Academy. **~ique** a. academic.

acajou /akaʒu/ n.m. mahogany.

acariâtre /akarjɑtr/ a. cantankerous.

accablement /akabləmɑ̃/ n.m. despondency.

accabl|er /akable/ v.t. overwhelm. **~er d'impôts**, burden with taxes. **~er d'injures**, heap insults upon. **~ant, ~ante** a. (*chaleur*) oppressive.

accalmie /akalmi/ n.f. lull.

accaparer /akapare/ v.t. monopolize; (*fig.*) take up all the time of.

accéder /aksede/ v.i. **~ à**, reach; (*pouvoir, requête, trône, etc.*) accede to.

accélér|er /akselere/ v.i. (*auto.*) accelerate. ● v.t., **s'~er** v. pr. speed up. **~ateur** n.m. accelerator. **~ation** n.f. acceleration; speeding up.

accent /aksɑ̃/ n.m. accent; (*sur une syllabe*) stress, accent; (*ton*) tone. **mettre l'~ sur**, stress.

accentu|er /aksɑ̃tɥe/ v.t. (*lettre, syllabe*) accent; (*fig.*) emphasize, accentuate. **s'~uer** v. pr. become more pronounced, increase. **~uation** n.f. accentuation.

accept|er /aksɛpte/ v.t. accept. **~er de**, agree to. **~able** a. acceptable. **~ation** n.f. acceptance.

acception /aksɛpsjɔ̃/ n.f. meaning.

accès /aksɛ/ n.m. access; (*porte*) entrance; (*de fièvre*) attack; (*de colère*) fit; (*de joie*) (out)burst. **les ~ de,** (*voies*) the approaches to. **facile d'~,** easy to get to.

accessible /aksesibl/ *a.* accessible; (*personne*) approachable.

accession /aksesjɔ̃/ *n.f.* ~ **à,** accession to.

accessit /aksesit/ *n.m.* honourable mention.

accessoire /akseswar/ *a.* secondary. ● *n.m.* accessory; (*théâtre*) prop.

accident /aksidɑ̃/ *n.m.* accident. ~ **de train/d'avion,** train/plane crash. **par ~,** by accident. **~é** /-te/ *a.* damaged *ou* hurt (in an accident); (*terrain*) uneven, hilly.

accidentel, ~le /aksidɑ̃tɛl/ *a.* accidental.

acclam|er /aklame/ *v.t.* cheer, acclaim. **~ations** *n.f. pl.* cheers.

acclimat|er /aklimate/ *v.t.,* **s'~er** *v. pr.* acclimatize; (*Amer.*) acclimate. **~ation** *n.f.* acclimatization; (*Amer.*) acclimation.

accolade /akɔlad/ *n.f.* embrace; (*signe*) brace, bracket.

accommodant, ~e /akɔmɔdɑ̃, -t/ *a.* accommodating.

accommodement /akɔmɔdmɑ̃/ *n.m.* compromise.

accommoder /akɔmɔde/ *v.t.* adapt (**à,** to); (*cuisiner*) prepare; (*assaisonner*) flavour. **s'~ de,** put up with.

accompagn|er /akɔ̃paɲe/ *v.t.* accompany. **s'~er de,** be accompanied by. **~ateur, ~atrice** *n.m., f.* (*mus.*) accompanist; (*guide*) guide. **~ement** *n.m.* (*mus.*) accompaniment.

accompli /akɔ̃pli/ *a.* accomplished.

accompl|ir /akɔ̃plir/ *v.t.* carry out, fulfil. **s'~ir** *v. pr.* be carried out, happen. **~issement** *n.m.* fulfilment.

accord /akɔr/ *n.m.* agreement; (*harmonie*) harmony; (*mus.*) chord. **être d'~,** agree (**pour,** to). **se mettre d'~,** come to an agreement, agree. **d'~!,** all right!, OK!

accordéon /akɔrdeɔ̃/ *n.m.* accordion.

accord|er /akɔrde/ *v.t.* grant; (*couleurs etc.*) match; (*mus.*) tune. **s'~er** *v. pr.* agree. **s'~er avec,** (*s'entendre avec*) get on with. **~eur** *n.m.* tuner.

accoster /akɔste/ *v.t.* accost; (*navire*) come alongside.

accotement /akɔtmɑ̃/ *n.m.* roadside, verge; (*Amer.*) shoulder.

accoter (s') /(s)akɔte/ *v. pr.* lean (**à,** against).

accouch|er /akuʃe/ *v.i.* give birth (**de,** to); (*être en travail*) be in labour. ● *v.t.* deliver. **~ement** *n.m.* childbirth; (*travail*) labour. (*médecin*) **~eur** *n.m.* obstetrician. **~euse** *n.f.* midwife.

accoud|er (s') /(s)akude/ *v. pr.* lean (one's elbows) on. **~oir** *n.m.* armrest.

accoupl|er /akuple/ *v.t.* couple; (*faire copuler*) mate. **s'~er** *v. pr.* mate. **~ement** *n.m.* mating; coupling.

accourir /akurir/ *v.i.* run up.

accoutrement /akutrəmɑ̃/ *n.m.* (strange) garb.

accoutumance /akutymɑ̃s/ *n.f.* habituation; (*méd.*) addiction.

accoutum|er /akutyme/ *v.t.* accustom. **s'~er** *v. pr.* get accustomed. **~é a** *a.* customary.

accréditer /akredite/ *v.t.* give credence to; (*personne*) accredit.

accro /akro/ *n.m./f.* (*drogué*) addict; (*amateur*) fan.

accroc /akro/ *n.m.* tear, rip; (*fig.*) hitch.

accroch|er /akrɔʃe/ *v.t.* (*suspendre*) hang up; (*attacher*) hook, hitch; (*déchirer*) catch; (*heurter*) hit; (*attirer*) attract. **s'~er** *v. pr.* cling, hang on; (*se disputer*) clash. **~age** *n.m.* hanging; hooking; (*auto.*) collision; (*dispute*) clash; (*mil.*) encounter.

accroissement /akrwasmɑ̃/ *n.m.* increase (**de,** in).

accroître /akrwatr/ *v.t.,* **s'~** *v. pr.* increase.

accroup|ir (s') /(s)akrupir/ *v. pr.* squat. **~i** *a.* squatting.

accru /akry/ *a.* increased, greater.

accueil /akœj/ *n.m.* reception, welcome.

accueill|ir† /akœjir/ *v.t.* receive, welcome; (*aller chercher*) meet. **~ant, ~ante** *a.* friendly.

aculer /akyle/ *v.t.* corner. **~ à,** force *ou* drive into *ou* against *ou* close to.

accumul|er /akymyle/ *v.t.,* **s'~er** *v. pr.* accumulate, pile up. **~ateur** *n.m.* accumulator. **~ation** *n.f.* accumulation.

accus /aky/ *n.m. pl.* (*fam.*) battery.

accusation /akyzasjɔ̃/ *n.f.* accusation; (*jurid.*) charge. **l'~,** (*magistrat*) the prosecution.

accus|er /akyze/ *v.t.* accuse (**de,** of); (*blâmer*) blame (**de,** for); (*jurid.*) charge (**de,** with); (*fig.*) show, emphasize. **~er reception de,**

acknowledge receipt of. **~ateur**, **~atrice** *a.* incriminating; *n.m.*, *f.* accuser. **~é**, **~ée** *a.* marked; *n.m.*, *f.* accused.

acerbe /asɛrb/ *a.* bitter.

acéré /asere/ *a.* sharp.

achalandé /aʃalɑ̃de/ *a.* **bien ~**, well-stocked.

acharn|é /aʃarne/ *a.* relentless, ferocious. **~ement** *n.m.* relentlessness.

acharner (s') /(s)aʃarne/ *v. pr.* **s'~ sur**, set upon; (*poursuivre*) hound. **s'~ à faire**, keep on doing.

achat /aʃa/ *n.m.* purchase. **~s**, shopping. **faire l'~ de**, buy.

acheminer /aʃmine/ *v.t.* dispatch, convey. **s'~ vers**, head for.

achet|er /aʃte/ *v.t.* buy. **~er à**, buy from; (*pour*) buy for. **~eur**, **~euse** *n.m.*, *f.* buyer; (*client de magasin*) shopper.

achèvement /aʃɛvmɑ̃/ *n.m.* completion.

achever /aʃve/ *v.t.* finish (off). **s'~** *v. pr.* end.

acid|e /asid/ *a.* acid, sharp. ● *n.m.* acid. **~ité** *n.f.* acidity. **~ulé** *a.* slightly acid.

acier /asje/ *n.m.* steel. **aciérie** *n.f.* steelworks.

acné /akne/ *n.f.* acne.

acolyte /akɔlit/ *n.m.* (*péj.*) associate.

acompte /akɔ̃t/ *n.m.* deposit, part-payment.

à-côté /akote/ *n.m.* side-issue. **~s**, (*argent*) extras.

à-coup /aku/ *n.m.* jolt, jerk. **par ~s**, by fits and starts.

acoustique /akustik/ *n.f.* acoustics. ● *a.* acoustic.

acqu|érir† /akerir/ *v.t.* acquire, gain; (*biens*) purchase, acquire. **~éreur** *n.m.* purchaser. **~isition** /-izisjɔ̃/ *n.f.* acquisition; purchase.

acquiescer /akjese/ *v.i.* acquiesce, agree.

acquis, **~e** /aki, -z/ *n.m.* experience. ● *a.* acquired; (*fait*) established; (*faveurs*) secured. **~ à**, (*projet*) in favour of.

acquit /aki/ *n.m.* receipt. **par ~ de conscience**, for peace of mind.

acquitt|er /akite/ *v.t.* acquit; (*dette*) settle. **s'~er de**, (*promesse*, *devoir*) carry out. **s'~er envers**, repay. **~ement** *n.m.* acquittal; settlement.

âcre /akr/ *a.* acrid.

acrobate /akrɔbat/ *n.m./f.* acrobat.

acrobatie /akrɔbasi/ *n.f.* acrobatics. **~ aérienne**, aerobatics. **acrobatique** /-tik/ *a.* acrobatic.

acte /akt/ *n.m.* act, action, deed; (*théâtre*) act; (*de naissance*, *mariage*) certificate. **~s**, (*compte rendu*) proceedings. **prendre ~ de**, note.

acteur /aktœr/ *n.m.* actor.

acti|f, **~ve** /aktif, -v/ *a.* active. ● *n.m.* (*comm.*) assets. **avoir à son ~f**, have to one's credit *ou* name. **~vement** *adv.* actively.

action /aksjɔ̃/ *n.f.* action; (*comm.*) share; (*jurid.*) action. **~naire** /-jɔnɛr/ *n.m./f.* shareholder.

actionner /aksjɔne/ *v.t.* work, activate.

activer /aktive/ *v.t.* speed up; (*feu*) boost. **s'~** *v. pr.* hurry, rush.

activiste /aktivist/ *n.m./f.* activist.

activité /aktivite/ *n.f.* activity. **en ~**, active.

actrice /aktris/ *n.f.* actress.

actualiser /aktɥalize/ *v.t.* update.

actualité /aktɥalite/ *n.f.* topicality. **l'~**, current events. **les ~s**, news. **d'~**, topical.

actuel, **~le** /aktɥɛl/ *a.* present; (*d'actualité*) topical. **~lement** *adv.* at the present time.

acuité /akɥite/ *n.f.* acuteness.

acupunct|ure /akypɔ̃ktyr/ *n.f.* acupuncture. **~eur** *n.m.* acupuncturist.

adage /adaʒ/ *n.m.* adage.

adapt|er /adapte/ *v.t.* adapt; (*fixer*) fit. **s'~er** *v. pr.* adapt (o.s.); (*techn.*) fit, **~ateur**, **~atrice** *n.m.*, *f.* adapter; *n.m.* (*électr.*) adapter. **~ation** *n.f.* adaptation.

additif /aditif/ *n.m.* (*note*) rider; (*substance*) additive.

addition /adisjɔ̃/ *n.f.* addition; (*au café etc.*) bill; (*Amer.*) check. **~nel**, **~nelle** /-jɔnɛl/ *a.* additional. **~ner** /-jɔne/ *v.t.* add; (*totaliser*) add (up).

adepte /adɛpt/ *n.m./f.* follower.

adéquat, **~e** /adekwa, -t/ *a.* suitable.

adhérent, **~e** /aderɑ̃, -t/ *n.m.*, *f.* member.

adhé|rer /adere/ *v.i.* adhere, stick (à, to). **~rer à**, (*club etc.*) be a member of; (*s'inscrire à*) join. **~rence** *n.f.* adhesion. **~sif**, **~sive** *a.* & *n.m.* adhesive. **~sion** *n.f.* membership; (*accord*) adherence.

adieu (*pl.* **~x**) /adjø/ *int.* & *n.m.* goodbye, farewell.

adipeu|x, ~se /adipø, -z/ *a.* fat; (*tissu*) fatty.

adjacent, ~e /adʒasɑ̃, -t/ *a.* adjacent.

adjectif /adʒɛktif/ *n.m.* adjective.

adjoindre† /adʒwɛ̃dr/ *v.t.* add, attach; (*personne*) appoint. **s'~** *v. pr.* appoint.

adjoint, ~e /adʒwɛ̃, -t/ *n.m., f. & a.* assistant. **~ au maire,** deputy mayor.

adjudant /adʒydɑ̃/ *n.m.* warrant-officer.

adjuger /adʒyʒe/ *v.t.* award; (*aux enchères*) auction. **s'~** *v. pr.* take.

adjurer /adʒyre/ *v.t.* beseech.

admettre† /admɛtr/ *v.t.* let in, admit; (*tolérer*) allow; (*reconnaître*) admit; (*candidat*) pass.

administrati|f, ~ve /administratif, -v/ *a.* administrative.

administr|er /administre/ *v.t.* run, manage; (*justice, biens, antidote, etc.*) administer. **~ateur, ~atrice** *n.m., f.* administrator, director. **~ation** *n.f.* administration. **A~ation,** Civil Service.

admirable /admirabl/ *a.* admirable.

admirati|f, ~ve /admiratif, -v/ *a.* admiring.

admir|er /admire/ *v.t.* admire. **~ateur, ~atrice** *n.m., f.* admirer. **~ation** *n.f.* admiration.

admissible /admisibl/ *a.* admissible; (*candidat*) eligible.

admission /admisjɔ̃/ *n.f.* admission.

adolescen|t, ~te /adɔlesɑ̃, -t/ *n.m., f.* adolescent. **~ce** *n.f.* adolescence.

adonner (s') /(s)adɔne/ *v. pr.* **s'~ à,** devote o.s. to; (*vice*) take to.

adopt|er /adɔpte/ *v.t.* adopt. **~ion** /-psjɔ̃/ *n.f.* adoption.

adopti|f, ~ve /adɔptif, -v/ *a.* (*enfant*) adopted; (*parents*) adoptive.

adorable /adɔrabl/ *a.* delightful, adorable.

ador|er /adɔre/ *v.t.* adore; (*relig.*) worship, adore. **~ation** *n.f.* adoration; worship.

adosser /adɔse/ *v.t.* **s'~** *v. pr.* lean back (**à, contre,** against).

adouci|r /adusir/ *v.t.* soften; (*boisson*) sweeten; (*personne*) mellow; (*chagrin*) ease. **s'~r** *v. pr.* soften; mellow; ease; (*temps*) become milder. **~ssant** *n.m.* (fabric) softener.

adresse /adrɛs/ *n.f.* address; (*habileté*) skill.

adresser /adrese/ *v.t.* send; (*écrire l'adresse sur*) address; (*remarque etc.*) address. **~ la parole à,** speak to. **s'~ à,** address; (*aller voir*) go and ask *ou* see; (*bureau*) enquire at; (*viser, intéresser*) be directed at.

adroit, ~e /adrwa, -t/ *a.* skilful, clever. **~ement** /-tmã/ *adv.* skilfully, cleverly.

aduler /adyle/ *v.t.* adulate.

adulte /adylt/ *n.m./f.* adult. ● *a.* adult; (*plante, animal*) fully-grown.

adultère /adyltɛr/ *a.* adulterous. ● *n.m.* adultery.

advenir /advənir/ *v.i.* occur.

adverbe /advɛrb/ *n.m.* adverb.

adversaire /advɛrsɛr/ *n.m.* opponent, adversary.

adverse /advɛrs/ *a.* opposing.

adversité /advɛrsite/ *n.f.* adversity.

aérateur /aeratœr/ *n.m.* ventilator.

aér|er /aere/ *v.t.* air; (*texte*) lighten. **s'~er** *v. pr.* get some air. **~ation** *n.f.* ventilation. **~é** *a.* airy.

aérien, ~ne /aerjɛ̃, -jɛn/ *a.* air; (*photo*) aerial; (*câble*) overhead; (*fig.*) airy.

aérobic /aerɔbik/ *m.* aerobics.

aérodrome /aerɔdrom/ *n.m.* aerodrome.

aérodynamique /aerɔdinamik/ *a.* streamlined, aerodynamic.

aérogare /aerɔgar/ *n.f.* air terminal.

aéroglisseur /aerɔglisœr/ *n.m.* hovercraft.

aérogramme /aerɔgram/ *n.m.* air-mail letter; (*Amer.*) aerogram.

aéronautique /aerɔnotik/ *a.* aeronautical. ● *n.f.* aeronautics.

aéronavale /aerɔnaval/ *n.f.* Fleet Air Arm; (*Amer.*) Naval Air Force.

aéroport /aerɔpɔr/ *n.m.* airport.

aéroporté /aerɔpɔrte/ *a.* airborne.

aérosol /aerɔsɔl/ *n.m.* aerosol.

aérospat|ial (*m. pl.* **~iaux**) /aerɔspasjal, -jo/ *a.* aerospace.

affable /afabl/ *a.* affable.

affaibl|ir /afeblir/ *v.t.,* **s'~ir** *v. pr.* weaken. **~issement** *n.m.* weakening.

affaire /afɛr/ *n.f.* matter, affair; (*histoire*) affair; (*transaction*) deal; (*occasion*) bargain; (*firme*) business; (*jurid.*) case. **~s,** affairs; (*comm.*) business; (*effets*) belongings. **avoir ~ à,** (have to) deal with. **c'est mon ~, ce sont mes ~s,** that is my business. **faire l'~,** do the job. **tirer**

qn. d'~, help s.o. out. **se tirer d'~**, manage.

affair|er (s') /(s)afere/ *v. pr.* bustle about. **~é** *a.* busy.

affaiss|er (s') /(s)afese/ *v. pr.* (*sol*) sink, subside; (*poutre*) sag; (*personne*) collapse. **~ement** /-ɛsmɑ̃/ *n.m.* subsidence.

affaler (s') /(s)afale/ *v. pr.* slump (down), collapse.

affam|er /afame/ *v.t.* starve. **~é** *a.* starving.

affect|é /afɛkte/ *a.* affected. **~ation** [1] *n.f.* affectation.

affect|er /afɛkte/ *v.t.* (*feindre, émouvoir*) affect; (*destiner*) assign; (*nommer*) appoint, post. **~ation** [2] *n.f.* assignment; appointment, posting.

affecti|f, **~ve** /afɛktif, -v/ *a.* emotional.

affection /afɛksjɔ̃/ *n.f.* affection; (*maladie*) ailment. **~ner** /-jɔne/ *v.t.* be fond of.

affectueu|x, **~se** /afɛktɥø, -z/ *a.* affectionate.

affermir /afɛrmir/ *v.t.* strengthen.

affiche /afiʃ/ *n.f.* (public) notice; (*publicité*) poster; (*théâtre*) bill.

affich|er /afiʃe/ *v.t.* (*annonce*) put up; (*événement*) announce; (*sentiment etc, comput.*) display. **~age** *n.m.* billposting; (*électronique*) display.

affilée (d') /(d)afile/ *adv.* in a row, at a stretch.

affiler /afile/ *v.t.* sharpen.

affil|ier (s') /(s)afilje/ *v. pr.* become affiliated. **~iation** *n.f.* affiliation.

affiner /afine/ *v.t.* refine.

affinité /afinite/ *n.f.* affinity.

affirmati|f, **~ve** /afirmatif, -v/ *a.* affirmative. ● *n.f.* affirmative.

affirm|er /afirme/ *v.t.* assert. **~ation** *n.f.* assertion.

affleurer /aflœre/ *v.i.* appear on the surface.

affliction /afliksjɔ̃/ *n.f.* affliction.

afflig|er /afliʒe/ *v.t.* grieve. **~é** *a.* distressed. **~é de**, afflicted with.

affluence /aflyɑ̃s/ *n.f.* crowd(s).

affluent /aflyɑ̃/ *n.m.* tributary.

affluer /aflye/ *v.i.* flood in; (*sang*) rush.

afflux /afly/ *n.m.* influx, flood; (*du sang*) rush.

affol|er /afɔle/ *v.t.* throw into a panic. **s'~er** *v. pr.* panic. **~ant**, **~ante** *a.* alarming. **~ement** *n.m.* panic.

affranch|ir /afrɑ̃ʃir/ *v.t.* stamp; (*à la machine*) frank; (*esclave*) emancipate; (*fig.*) free. **~issement** *n.m.* (*tarif*) postage.

affréter /afrete/ *v.t.* charter.

affreu|x, **~se** /afrø, -z/ *a.* (*laid*) hideous; (*mauvais*) awful. **~sement** *adv.* awfully, hideously.

affriolant, **~e** /afrijɔlɑ̃, -t/ *a.* enticing.

affront /afrɔ̃/ *n.m.* affront.

affront|er /afrɔ̃te/ *v.t.* confront. **s'~er** *v. pr.* confront each other. **~ement** *n.m.* confrontation.

affubler /afyble/ *v.t.* rig out (**de**, in).

affût /afy/ *n.m.* **à l'~**, on the watch (**de**, for).

affûter /afyte/ *v.t.* sharpen.

afin /afɛ̃/ *prép. & conj.* **~ de/que**, in order to/that.

africain, **~e** /afrikɛ̃, -ɛn/ *a. & n.m.*, *f.* African.

Afrique /afrik/ *n.f.* Africa. **~ du Sud**, South Africa.

agacer /agase/ *v.t.* irritate, annoy.

âge /ɑʒ/ *n.m.* age. **quel ~ avez-vous?**, how old are you? **~ adulte**, adulthood. **~ mûr**, middle age. **d'un certain ~**, past one's prime.

âgé /aʒe/ *a.* elderly. **~ de cinq ans** *etc.*, five years/*etc.* old.

agence /aʒɑ̃s/ *n.f.* agency, bureau, office; (*succursale*) branch. **~ d'intérim**, employment agency. **~ de voyages**, travel agency.

agenc|er /aʒɑ̃se/ *v.t.* organize, arrange. **~ement** *n.m.* organization.

agenda /aʒɛ̃da/ *n.m.* diary; (*Amer.*) datebook.

agenouiller (s') /(s)aʒnuje/ *v. pr.* kneel (down).

agent /aʒɑ̃/ *n.m.* agent; (*fonctionnaire*) official. **~ (de police)**, policeman. **~ de change**, stockbroker.

agglomération /aglɔmerasjɔ̃/ *n.f.* built-up area, town.

aggloméré /aglɔmere/ *n.m.* (*bois*) chipboard.

agglomérer /aglɔmere/ *v.t.*, **s'~** *v. pr.* pile up.

agglutiner /aglytine/ *v.t.*, **s'~** *v. pr.* stick together.

aggraver /agrave/ *v.t.*, **s'~** *v. pr.* worsen.

agil|e /aʒil/ *a.* agile, nimble. **~ité** *n.f.* agility.

agir /aʒir/ *v.i.* act. **il s'agit de faire**, it is a matter of doing; (*il faut*) it is necessary to do. **dans ce livre il s'agit de,** this book is about. **dont il s'agit,** in question.

agissements /aʒismɑ̃/ *n.m. pl.* (*péj.*) dealings.

agité /aʒite/ *a.* restless, fidgety; (*troublé*) agitated; (*mer*) rough.

agit|er /aʒite/ *v.t.* (*bras etc.*) wave; (*liquide*) shake; (*troubler*) agitate; (*discuter*) debate. **s'~er** *v. pr.* bustle about; (*enfant*) fidget; (*foule, pensées*) stir. **~ateur, ~atrice** *n.m., f.* agitator. **~ation** *n.f.* bustle; (*trouble*) agitation.

agneau (*pl.* **~x**) /aɲo/ *n.m.* lamb.

agonie /aɡɔni/ *n.f.* death throes.

agoniser /aɡɔnize/ *v.i.* be dying.

agraf|e /aɡraf/ *n.f.* hook; (*pour papiers*) staple. **~er** *v.t.* hook (up); staple. **~euse** *n.f.* stapler.

agrand|ir /aɡrɑ̃dir/ *v.t.* enlarge. **s'~ir** *v. pr.* expand, grow. **~issement** *n.m.* extension; (*de photo*) enlargement.

agréable /aɡreabl/ *a.* pleasant. **~ment** /-əmɑ̃/ *adv.* pleasantly.

agré|er /aɡree/ *v.t.* accept. **~er à,** please. **~é** *a.* authorized.

agrég|ation /aɡreɡɑsjɔ̃/ *n.f.* agrégation (*highest examination for recruitment of teachers*). **~é, ~ée** /-ʒe/ *n.m., f.* agrégé (*teacher who has passed the agrégation*).

agrément /aɡremɑ̃/ *n.m.* charm; (*plaisir*) pleasure; (*accord*) assent.

agrémenter /aɡremɑ̃te/ *v.t.* embellish (**de,** with).

agrès /aɡrɛ/ *n.m. pl.* (gymnastics) apparatus.

agress|er /aɡrese/ *v.t.* attack. **~eur** /-ɛsœr/ *n.m.* attacker; (*mil.*) aggressor. **~ion** /-ɛsjɔ̃/ *n.f.* attack; (*mil.*) aggression.

agressi|f, ~ve /aɡresif, -v/ *a.* aggressive. **~vité** *n.f.* aggressiveness.

agricole /aɡrikɔl/ *a.* agricultural; (*ouvrier etc.*) farm.

agriculteur /aɡrikyltœr/ *n.m.* farmer.

agriculture /aɡrikyltyr/ *n.f.* agriculture, farming.

agripper /aɡripe/ *v.t.,* **s'~ à,** grab, clutch.

agroalimentaire /aɡrɔalimɑ̃tɛr/ *n.m.* food industry.

agrumes /aɡrym/ *n.m. pl.* citrus fruit(s).

aguerrir /aɡerir/ *v.t.* harden.

aguets (aux) /(oz)aɡɛ/ *adv.* on the look-out.

aguicher /aɡiʃe/ *v.t.* entice.

ah /a/ *int.* ah, oh.

ahur|ir /ayrir/ *v.t.* dumbfound. **~issement** *n.m.* stupefaction.

ai /e/ *voir* **avoir**.

aide /ɛd/ *n.f.* help, assistance, aid. ● *n.m./f.* assistant. **à l'~ de,** with the help of. **~ familiale,** home help. **~-mémoire** *n.m. invar.* handbook of facts. **~ sociale,** social security; (*Amer.*) welfare. **~-soignant, ~-soignante** *n.m., f.* auxiliary nurse. **venir en ~ à,** help.

aider /ede/ *v.t./i.* help, assist. **~ à faire,** help to do. **s'~ de,** use.

aïe /aj/ *int.* ouch, ow.

aïeul, ~e /ajœl/ *n.m., f.* grandparent.

aïeux /ajø/ *n.m. pl.* forefathers.

aigle /ɛɡl/ *n.m.* eagle.

aigr|e /ɛɡr/ *a.* sour, sharp; (*fig.*) sharp. **~e-doux, ~e-douce** *a.* bitter-sweet. **~eur** *n.f.* sourness; (*fig.*) sharpness. **~eurs d'estomac,** heartburn.

aigrir /eɡrir/ *v.t.* embitter; (*caractère*) sour. **s'~** *v. pr.* turn sour; (*personne*) become embittered.

aigu, ~ë /eɡy/ *a.* acute; (*objet*) sharp; (*voix*) shrill. (*mus.*) **les ~s,** the high notes.

aiguillage /eɡɥijaʒ/ *n.m.* (*rail.*) points; (*rail., Amer.*) switches.

aiguille /eɡɥij/ *n.f.* needle; (*de montre*) hand; (*de balance*) pointer.

aiguill|er /eɡɥije/ *v.t.* shunt; (*fig.*) steer. **~eur** *n.m.* pointsman; (*Amer.*) switchman. **~eur du ciel,** air traffic controller.

aiguillon /eɡɥijɔ̃/ *n.m.* (*dard*) sting; (*fig.*) spur. **~ner** /-jɔne/ *v.t.* spur on.

aiguiser /eɡ(ɥ)ize/ *v.t.* sharpen; (*fig.*) stimulate.

ail (*pl.* **~s**) /aj/ *n.m.* garlic.

aile /ɛl/ *n.f.* wing.

ailé /ele/ *a.* winged.

aileron /ɛlrɔ̃/ *n.m.* (*de requin*) fin.

ailier /elje/ *n.m.* winger; (*Amer.*) end.

aille /aj/ *voir* **aller** [1].

ailleurs /ajœr/ *adv.* elsewhere. **d'~,** besides, moreover. **par ~,** moreover, furthermore. **partout ~,** everywhere else.

ailloli /ajɔli/ *n.m.* garlic mayonnaise.

aimable /ɛmabl/ *a.* kind. **~ment** /-əmɑ̃/ *adv.* kindly.

aimant [1] /ɛmɑ̃/ *n.m.* magnet. **~er** /-te/ *v.t.* magnetize.

aimant [2], **~e** /ɛmɑ̃, -t/ *a.* loving.

aimer /eme/ *v.t.* like; (*d'amour*) love. **j'aimerais faire,** I'd like to do. **~ bien,** quite like. **~ mieux** *ou* **autant,** prefer.

aine /ɛn/ *n.f.* groin.

aîné, ~e /ene/ *a.* eldest; (*entre deux*) elder. ● *n.m., f.* eldest (child); elder (child). **~s** *n.m. pl.* elders. **il est mon ~,** he is older than me *ou* my senior.

ainsi /ɛ̃si/ *adv.* thus; (*donc*) so. **~ que,** as well as; (*comme*) as. **et ~ de suite,** and so on. **pour ~ dire,** so to speak, as it were.

air /ɛr/ *n.m.* air; (*mine*) look, air; (*mélodie*) tune. **~ conditionné,** air-conditioning. **avoir l'~ de,** look like. **avoir l'~ de faire,** appear to be doing. **en l'~,** (up) in the air; (*promesses etc.*) empty.

aire /ɛr/ *n.f.* area. **~ d'atterrissage,** landing-strip.

aisance /ɛzɑ̃s/ *n.f.* ease; (*richesse*) affluence.

aise /ɛz/ *n.f.* joy. ● *a.* **bien ~ de/ que,** delighted about/that. **à l'~,** (*sur un siège*) comfortable; (*pas gêné*) at ease; (*fortuné*) comfortably off. **mal à l'~,** uncomfortable; ill at ease. **aimer ses ~s,** like one's comforts. **se mettre à l'~,** make o.s. comfortable.

aisé /eze/ *a.* easy; (*fortuné*) well-off. **~ment** *adv.* easily.

aisselle /ɛsɛl/ *n.f.* armpit.

ait /ɛ/ *voir* avoir.

ajonc /aʒɔ̃/ *n.m.* gorse.

ajourn|er /aʒurne/ *v.t.* postpone; (*assemblée*) adjourn. **~ement** *n.m.* postponement; adjournment.

ajout /aʒu/ *n.m.* addition.

ajouter /aʒute/ *v.t.* **s'~** *v. pr.* add (**à,** to). **~ foi à,** lend credence to.

ajust|er /aʒyste/ *v.t.* adjust; (*coup*) aim; (*cible*) aim at; (*adapter*) fit. **s'~er** *v. pr.* fit. **~age** *n.m.* fitting. **~é** *a.* close-fitting. **~ement** *n.m.* adjustment. **~eur** *n.m.* fitter.

alambic /alɑ̃bik/ *n.m.* still.

alanguir (s') /(s)alɑ̃gir/ *v. pr.* grow languid.

alarme /alarm/ *n.f.* alarm. **donner l'~,** sound the alarm.

alarmer /alarme/ *v.t.* alarm. **s'~** *v. pr.* become alarmed (**de,** at).

alarmiste /alarmist/ *a. & n.m.* alarmist.

albâtre /albɑtr/ *n.m.* alabaster.

albatros /albatros/ *n.m.* albatross.

album /albɔm/ *n.m.* album.

albumine /albymin/ *n.f.* albumin.

alcali /alkali/ *n.m.* alkali.

alcool /alkɔl/ *n.m.* alcohol; (*eau de vie*) brandy. **~ à brûler,** methylated spirit. **~ique** *a. & n.m./f.* alcoholic. **~isé** *a.* (*boisson*) alcoholic. **~isme** *n.m.* alcoholism.

alcootest /alkɔtɛst/ *n.m.* (P.) breath test; (*appareil*) breathalyser.

alcôve /alkov/ *n.f.* alcove.

aléa /alea/ *n.m.* hazard.

aléatoire /aleatwar/ *a.* uncertain; (*comput.*) random.

alentour /alɑ̃tur/ *adv.* around. **~s** *n.m. pl.* surroundings. **aux ~s de,** round about.

alerte /alɛrt/ *a.* agile. ● *n.f.* alert. **~ à la bombe,** bomb scare.

alerter /alɛrte/ *v.t.* alert.

algarade /algarad/ *n.f.* altercation.

alg|èbre /alʒɛbr/ *n.f.* algebra. **~ébrique** *a.* algebraic.

Alger /alʒe/ *n.m./f.* Algiers.

Algérie /alʒeri/ *n.f.* Algeria.

algérien, ~ne /alʒerjɛ̃, -jɛn/ *a. & n.m., f.* Algerian.

algue /alg/ *n.f.* seaweed. **les ~s,** (*bot.*) algae.

alias /aljas/ *adv.* alias.

alibi /alibi/ *n.m.* alibi.

alién|é, ~e /aljene/ *n.m., f.* insane person.

alién|er /aljene/ *v.t.* alienate; (*céder*) give up. **s'~er** *v. pr.* alienate. **~ation** *n.f.* alienation.

aligner /aliɲe/ *v.t.* (*objets*) line up, make lines of; (*chiffres*) string together. **~ sur,** bring into line with. **s'~** *v. pr.* line up. **s'~ sur,** align o.s. on. **alignement** /-əmɑ̃/ *n.m.* alignment.

aliment /alimɑ̃/ *n.m.* food. **~aire** /-tɛr/ *a.* food; (*fig.*) bread-and-butter.

aliment|er /alimɑ̃te/ *v.t.* feed; (*fournir*) supply; (*fig.*) sustain. **~ation** *n.f.* feeding; supply(ing); (*régime*) diet; (*aliments*) groceries.

alinéa /alinea/ *n.m.* paragraph.

aliter (s') /(s)alite/ *v. pr.* take to one's bed.

allaiter /alete/ *v.t.* feed. **~ au biberon,** bottle-feed. **~ au sein,** breast-feed; (*Amer.*) nurse.

allant /alɑ̃/ *n.m.* verve, drive.

allécher /aleʃe/ *v.t.* tempt.

allée /ale/ *n.f.* path, lane; (*menant à une maison*) drive(way). **~s et venues**, comings and goings.

allégation /alegɑsjɔ̃/ *n.f.* allegation.

allég|er /aleʒe/ *v.t.* make lighter; (*poids*) lighten; (*fig.*) alleviate. **~é** *a.* (*diététique*) light.

allègre /alɛgr/ *a.* gay; (*vif*) lively, jaunty.

allégresse /alegrɛs/ *n.f.* gaiety.

alléguer /alege/ *v.t.* put forward.

Allemagne /alman/ *n.f.* Germany. **~ de l'Ouest**, West Germany.

allemand, ~e /almã, -d/ *a. & n.m., f.* German. ● *n.m.* (*lang.*) German.

aller† [1] /ale/ (*aux. être*) go. **s'en ~** *v. pr.* go away. **~ à**, (*convenir à*) suit; (*s'adapter à*) fit. **~ faire**, be going to do. **comment allez-vous?**, (**comment**) **ça va?**, how are you? **ça va!**, all right! **il va bien**, he is well. **il va mieux**, he's better. **allez-y!**, go on! **allez!**, come on! **allons-y!**, let's go!

aller [2] /ale/ *n.m.* outward journey; **~ (simple)**, single (ticket); (*Amer.*) one-way (ticket). **~ (et) retour**, return journey; (*Amer.*) round trip; (*billet*) return (ticket); (*Amer.*) round trip (ticket).

allerg|ie /alɛrʒi/ *n.f.* allergy. **~ique** *a.* allergic.

alliage /aljaʒ/ *n.m.* alloy.

alliance /aljãs/ *n.f.* alliance; (*bague*) wedding-ring; (*mariage*) marriage.

allié, ~e /alje/ *n.m., f.* ally; (*parent*) relative (by marriage).

allier /alje/ *v.t.* combine (*pol.*) ally. **s'~** *v. pr.* combine, (*pol.*) become allied; (*famille*) become related (**à**, to).

alligator /aligator/ *n.m.* alligator.

allô /alo/ *int.* hallo, hello.

allocation /alɔkɑsjɔ̃/ *n.f.* allowance. **~ (de) chômage**, unemployment benefit. **~s familiales**, family allowance.

allocution /alɔkysjɔ̃/ *n.f.* speech.

allongé /alɔ̃ʒe/ *a.* elongated.

allongement /alɔ̃ʒmã/ *n.m.* lengthening.

allonger /alɔ̃ʒe/ *v.t.* lengthen; (*bras, jambe*) stretch (out). **s'~** *v. pr.* get longer; (*s'étendre*) stretch (o.s.) out.

allouer /alwe/ *v.t.* allocate.

allum|er /alyme/ *v.t.* light; (*radio, lampe, etc.*) turn on; (*pièce*) switch the light(s) on in; (*fig.*) arouse. **s'~er** *v. pr.* (*lumière*) come on. **~age** *n.m.*

lighting; (*auto.*) ignition. **~e-gaz** *n.m. invar.* gas lighter.

allumette /alymɛt/ *n.f.* match.

allure /alyr/ *n.f.* speed, pace; (*démarche*) walk; (*prestance*) bearing; (*air*) look. **à toute ~**, at full speed. **avoir de l'~**, have style.

allusion /alyzjɔ̃/ *n.f.* allusion (**à**, to); (*implicite*) hint (**à**, at). **faire ~ à**, allude to; hint at.

almanach /almana/ *n.m.* almanac.

aloi /alwa/ *n.m.* **de bon ~**, sterling; (*gaieté*) wholesome.

alors /alɔr/ *adv.* then. ● *conj.* so, then. **~ que**, when, while; (*tandis que*) whereas. **ça ~!**, well! **et ~?**, so what?

alouette /alwɛt/ *n.f.* lark.

alourdir /alurdir/ *v.t.* weigh down.

aloyau (*pl.* **~x**) /alwajo/ *n.m.* sirloin.

alpage /alpaʒ/ *n.m.* mountain pasture.

Alpes /alp/ *n.f. pl.* **les ~**, the Alps.

alpestre /alpɛstr/ *a.* alpine.

alphabet /alfabɛ/ *n.m.* alphabet. **~ique** *a.* alphabetical.

alphabétiser /alfabetize/ *v.t.* teach to read and write.

alphanumérique /alfanymerik/ *a.* alphanumeric.

alpin, ~e /alpɛ̃, -in/ *a.* alpine.

alpinis|te /alpinist/ *n.m./f.* mountaineer. **~me** *n.m.* mountaineering.

altér|er /altere/ *v.t.* falsify; (*abîmer*) spoil; (*donner soif à*) make thirsty. **s'~er** *v. pr.* deteriorate. **~ation** *n.f.* deterioration.

alternati|f, ~ve /altɛrnatif, -v/ *a.* alternating. ● *n.f.* alternative. **~vement** *adv.* alternately.

altern|er /altɛrne/ *v.t./i.* alternate. **~ance** *n.f.* alternation. **en ~ance**, alternately. **~é** *a.* alternate.

Altesse /altɛs/ *n.f.* Highness.

alt|ier, ~ière /altje, -jɛr/ *a.* haughty.

altitude /altityd/ *n.f.* altitude, height.

alto /alto/ *n.m.* viola.

aluminium /alyminjɔm/ *n.m.* aluminium; (*Amer.*) aluminum.

alvéole /alveɔl/ *n.f.* (*de ruche*) cell.

amabilité /amabilite/ *n.f.* kindness.

amadouer /amadwe/ *v.t.* win over.

amaigr|ir /amegrir/ *v.t.* make thin(ner). **~issant, ~issante** *a.* (*régime*) slimming.

amalgam|e /amalgam/ *n.m.* combination. **~er** *v.t.* combine, amalgamate.

amande /amɑ̃d/ *n.f.* almond; (*d'un fruit à noyau*) kernel.

amant /amɑ̃/ *n.m.* lover.

amarr|e /amar/ *n.f.* (mooring) rope. **~es,** moorings. **~er** *v.t.* moor.

amas /amɑ/ *n.m.* heap, pile.

amasser /amɑse/ *v.t.* amass, gather; (*empiler*) pile up. **s'~** *v. pr.* pile up; (*gens*) gather.

amateur /amatœr/ *n.m.* amateur. **~ de,** lover of. **d'~,** amateur; (*péj.*) amateurish. **~isme** *n.m.* amateurism.

amazone (en) /(ɑ̃n)amazon/ *adv.* side-saddle.

Amazonie /amazɔni/ *n.f.* Amazonia.

ambages (sans) /(sɑ̃z)ɑ̃baʒ/ *adv.* in plain language.

ambassade /ɑ̃basad/ *n.f.* embassy.

ambassa|deur, ~drice /ɑ̃basadœr, -dris/ *n.m., f.* ambassador.

ambiance /ɑ̃bjɑ̃s/ *n.f.* atmosphere.

ambiant, ~e /ɑ̃bjɑ̃, -t/ *a.* surrounding.

ambigu, ~ë /ɑ̃bigy/ *a.* ambiguous. **~ïté** /-ɥite/ *n.f.* ambiguity.

ambitieu|x, ~se /ɑ̃bisjø, -z/ *a.* ambitious.

ambition /ɑ̃bisjɔ̃/ *n.f.* ambition. **~ner** /-jɔne/ *v.t.* have as one's ambition (**de,** to).

ambivalent, ~e /ɑ̃bivalɑ̃, -t/ *a.* ambivalent.

ambre /ɑ̃br/ *n.m.* amber.

ambulanc|e /ɑ̃bylɑ̃s/ *n.f.* ambulance. **~ier, ~ière** *n.m., f.* ambulance driver.

ambulant, ~e /ɑ̃bylɑ̃, -t/ *a.* itinerant.

âme /ɑm/ *n.f.* soul. **~ sœur,** soul mate.

amélior|er /ameljɔre/ *v.t.,* **s'~er** *v. pr.* improve. **~ation** *n.f.* improvement.

aménag|er /amenaʒe/ *v.t.* (*arranger*) fit out; (*transformer*) convert; (*installer*) fit up; (*territoire*) develop. **~ement** *n.m.* fitting out; conversion; fitting up; development; (*modification*) adjustment.

amende /amɑ̃d/ *n.f.* fine. **faire ~ honorable,** make an apology.

amend|er /amɑ̃de/ *v.t.* improve; (*jurid.*) amend. **s'~er** *v. pr.* mend one's ways. **~ement** *n.m.* (*de texte*) amendment.

amener /amne/ *v.t.* bring; (*causer*) bring about. **~ qn. à faire,** cause sb. to do. **s'~** *v. pr.* (*fam.*) come along.

amenuiser (s') /(s)amənɥize/ *v. pr.* dwindle.

amer, amère /amɛr/ *a.* bitter.

américain, ~e /amerikɛ̃, -ɛn/ *a. & n.m., f.* American.

Amérique /amerik/ *n.f.* America. **~ centrale/latine,** Central/ Latin America. **~ du Nord/Sud,** North/ South America.

amertume /amɛrtym/ *n.f.* bitterness.

ameublement /amœbləmɑ̃/ *n.m.* furniture.

ameuter /amøte/ *v.t.* draw a crowd of; (*fig.*) stir up.

ami, ~e /ami/ *n.m., f.* friend; (*de la nature, des livres, etc.*) lover. ● *a.* friendly.

amiable /amjabl/ *a.* amicable. **à l'~** *adv.* amicably; *a.* amicable.

amiante /amjɑ̃t/ *n.m.* asbestos.

amic|al (*m. pl.* **~aux**) /amikal, -o/ *a.* friendly. **~alement** *adv.* in a friendly manner.

amicale /amikal/ *n.f.* association.

amidon /amidɔ̃/ *n.m.* starch. **~ner** /-ɔne/ *v.t.* starch.

amincir /amɛ̃sir/ *v.t.* make thinner. **s'~** *v. pr.* get thinner.

amir|al (*pl.* **~aux**) /amiral, -o/ *n.m.* admiral.

amitié /amitje/ *n.f.* friendship. **~s,** kind regards. **prendre en ~,** take a liking to.

ammoniac /amɔnjak/ *n.m.* (*gaz*) ammonia.

ammoniaque /amɔnjak/ *n.f.* (*eau*) ammonia.

amnésie /amnezi/ *n.f.* amnesia.

amnistie /amnisti/ *n.f.* amnesty.

amniocentèse /amnjɔsɛtɛz/ *n.f.* amniocentesis.

amocher /amɔʃe/ *v.t.* (*fam.*) mess up.

amoindrir /amwɛ̃drir/ *v.t.* diminish.

amollir /amɔlir/ *v.t.* soften.

amonceler /amɔ̃sle/ *v.t.,* **s'~** *v.pr.* pile up.

amont (en) /(ɑ̃n)amɔ̃/ *adv.* upstream.

amorc|e /amɔrs/ *n.f.* bait; (*début*) start; (*explosif*) fuse, cap; (*de pistolet d'enfant*) cap. **~er** *v.t.* start; (*hameçon*) bait; (*pompe*) prime.

amorphe /amɔrf/ *a.* (*mou*) listless.

amortir /amɔrtir/ *v.t.* (*choc*) cushion; (*bruit*) deaden; (*dette*) pay off; (*objet acheté*) make pay for itself.

amortisseur /amɔrtisœr/ *n.m.* shock absorber.

amour /amur/ *n.m.* love. **pour l'~de**, for the sake of. **~-propre** *n.m.* self-respect.

amouracher (s') /(s)amuraʃe/ *v. pr.* become infatuated (**de**, with).

amoureu|x, ~se /amurø, -z/ *a.* (*ardent*) amorous; (*vie*) love. ● *n.m., f.* lover. **~x de qn.**, in love with s.o.

amovible /amɔvibl/ *a.* removable.

ampère /ɑ̃pɛr/ *n.m.* amp(ere).

amphibie /ɑ̃fibi/ *a.* amphibious.

amphithéâtre /ɑ̃fiteatr/ *n.m.* amphitheatre; (*d'université*) lecture hall.

ample /ɑ̃pl/ *a.* ample; (*mouvement*) broad. **~ment** /-əmɑ̃/ *adv.* amply.

ampleur /ɑ̃plœr/ *n.f.* extent, size; (*de vêtement*) fullness.

ampli /ɑ̃pli/ *n.m.* amplifier.

amplif|ier /ɑ̃plifje/ *v.t.* amplify; (*fig.*) expand, develop. **s'~ier** *v.pr.* expand, develop. **~icateur** *n.m.* amplifier.

ampoule /ɑ̃pul/ *n.f.* (*électrique*) bulb; (*sur la peau*) blister; (*de médicament*) phial.

ampoulé /ɑ̃pule/ *a.* turgid.

amput|er /ɑ̃pyte/ *v.t.* amputate; (*fig.*) reduce. **~ation** *n.f.* amputation; (*fig.*) reduction.

amuse-gueule /amyzgœl/ *n.m. invar.* appetizer.

amus|er /amyze/ *v.t.* amuse; (*détourner l'attention de*) distract. **s'~er** *v. pr.* enjoy o.s.; (*jouer*) play. **~ant, ~ante** *a.* (*blague*) funny; (*soirée*) enjoyable, entertaining. **~ement** *n.m.* amusement; (*passe-temps*) diversion. **~eur** *n.m.* (*péj.*) entertainer.

amygdale /amidal/ *n.f.* tonsil.

an /ɑ̃/ *n.m.* year. **avoir dix/etc. ans**, be ten/etc. years old.

anachronisme /anakrɔnism/ *n.m.* anachronism.

analgésique /analʒezik/ *a.* & *n.m.* analgesic.

analog|ie /analɔʒi/ *n.f.* analogy. **~ique** *a.* analogical, (*comput.*) analogue.

analogue /analɔg/ *a.* similar.

analphabète /analfabɛt/ *a.* & *n.m./f.* illiterate.

analy|se /analiz/ *n.f.* analysis; (*de sang*) test. **~ser** *v.t.* analyse. **~ste** *n.m./f.* analyst. **~tique** *a.* analytical.

ananas /anana(s)/ *n.m.* pineapple.

anarch|ie /anarʃi/ *n.f.* anarchy. **~ique** *a.* anarchic. **~iste** *n.m./f.* anarchist.

anatom|ie /anatɔmi/ *n.f.* anatomy. **~ique** *a.* anatomical.

ancestral (*m. pl.* **~aux**) /ɑ̃sɛstral, -o/ *a.* ancestral.

ancêtre /ɑ̃sɛtr/ *n.m.* ancestor.

anche /ɑ̃ʃ/ *n.f.* (*mus.*) reed.

anchois /ɑ̃ʃwa/ *n.m.* anchovy.

ancien, ~ne /ɑ̃sjɛ̃, -jɛn/ *a.* old; (*de jadis*) ancient; (*meuble*) antique; (*précédent*) former, ex-, old; (*dans une fonction*) senior. ● *n.m., f.* senior; (*par l'âge*) elder. **~ combattant**, ex-serviceman. **~nement** /-jɛnmɑ̃/ *adv.* formerly. **~neté** /-jɛnte/ *n.f.* age; seniority.

ancr|e /ɑ̃kr/ *n.f.* anchor. **jeter/lever l'~e**, cast/weigh anchor. **~er** *v.t.* anchor; (*fig.*) fix. **s'~er** *v.pr.* anchor.

andouille /ɑ̃duj/ *n.f.* sausage filled with chitterlings; (*idiot: fam.*) nitwit.

âne /ɑn/ *n.m.* donkey, ass; (*imbécile*) ass.

anéantir /aneɑ̃tir/ *v.t.* destroy; (*exterminer*) annihilate; (*accabler*) overwhelm.

anecdot|e /anɛkdɔt/ *n.f.* anecdote. **~ique** *a.* anecdotal.

aném|ie /anemi/ *n.f.* anaemia. **~ié, ~ique** *adjs.* anaemic.

ânerie /ɑnri/ *n.f.* stupidity; (*parole*) stupid remark.

ânesse /ɑnɛs/ *n.f.* she-ass.

anesthés|ie /anɛstezi/ *n.f.* (*opération*) anaesthetic. **~ique** *a.* & *n.m.* (*substance*) anaesthetic.

ang|e /ɑ̃ʒ/ *n.m.* angel. **aux ~es**, in seventh heaven. **~élique** *a.* angelic.

angélus /ɑ̃ʒelys/ *n.m.* angelus.

angine /ɑ̃ʒin/ *n.f.* throat infection.

anglais, ~e /ɑ̃glɛ, -z/ *a.* English. ● *n.m., f.* Englishman, Englishwoman. ● *n.m.* (*lang.*) English.

angle /ɑ̃gl/ *n.m.* angle; (*coin*) corner.

Angleterre /ɑ̃glətɛr/ *n.f.* England.

anglicisme /ɑ̃glisism/ *n.m.* anglicism.

angliciste /ɑ̃glisist/ *n.m./f.* English specialist.

anglo- /ɑ̃glo/ *préf.* Anglo-.

anglophone /ɑ̃glɔfɔn/ *a.* English-speaking. ● *n.m./f.* English speaker.

anglo-saxon, ~ne /ɑ̃glɔsaksɔ̃, -ɔn/ *a.* & *n.m., f.* Anglo-Saxon.

angoiss|e /ɑ̃gwas/ *n.f.* anxiety. **~ant, ~ante** *a.* harrowing. **~é** *a.* anxious. **~er** *v.t.* make anxious.

anguille /ɑ̃gij/ *n.f.* eel.

anguleux, **~se** /ɑ̃gylø, -z/ *a.* (*traits*) angular.

anicroche /anikrɔʃ/ *n.f.* snag.

anim|al (*pl.* **~aux**) /animal, -o/ *n.m.* animal. ● *a.* (*m. pl.* **~aux**) animal.

anima|teur, **~trice** /animatœr, -tris/ *f.* organizer, leader; (*TV*) host, hostess.

anim|é /anime/ *a.* lively; (*affairé*) busy, (*être*) animate. **~ation** *n.f.* liveliness; (*affairement*) activity; (*cinéma*) animation.

animer /anime/ *v.t.* liven up; (*mener*) lead; (*mouvoir, pousser*) drive; (*encourager*) spur on. **s'~** *v. pr.* liven up.

animosité /animozite/ *n.f.* animosity.

anis /anis/ *n.m.* (*parfum, boisson*) aniseed.

ankylos|er (s') /(s)ɑ̃kiloze/ *v. pr.* go stiff. **~é** *a.* stiff.

anneau (*pl.* **~x**) /ano/ *n.m.* ring; (*de chaîne*) link.

année /ane/ *n.f.* year.

annexe /anɛks/ *a.* attached; (*question*) related. (*bâtiment*) adjoining. ● *n.f.* annexe; (*Amer.*) annex.

annex|er /anɛkse/ *v.t.* annex; (*document*) attach. **~ion** *n.f.* annexation.

annihiler /aniile/ *v.t.* annihilate.

anniversaire /aniversɛr/ *n.m.* birthday; (*d'un événement*) anniversary. ● *a.* anniversary.

annonc|e /anɔ̃s/ *n.f.* announcement; (*publicitaire*) advertisement; (*indice*) sign. **~er** *v.t.* announce; (*dénoter*) indicate. **s'~er bien/mal**, look good/bad. **~eur** *n.m.* advertiser; (*speaker*) announcer.

Annonciation /anɔ̃sjasjɔ̃/ *n.f.* **l'~**, the Annunciation.

annuaire /anɥɛr/ *n.m.* year-book. ● **(téléphonique)**, (telephone) directory.

annuel, **~le** /anɥɛl/ *a.* annual, yearly. **~lement** *adv.* annually, yearly.

annuité /anɥite/ *n.f.* annual payment.

annulaire /anylɛr/ *n.m.* ringfinger.

annul|er /anyle/ *v.t.* cancel; (*contrat*) nullify; (*jugement*) quash. **s'~er** *v. pr.* cancel each other out. **~ation** *n.f.* cancellation.

anodin, **~e** /anɔdɛ̃, -in/ *a.* insignificant; (*blessure*) harmless.

anomalie /anɔmali/ *n.f.* anomaly.

ânonner /anɔne/ *v.t./i.* mumble, drone.

anonymat /anɔnima/ *n.m.* anonymity.

anonyme /anɔnim/ *a.* anonymous.

anorak /anɔrak/ *n.m.* anorak.

anorexie /anɔreksi/ *n.f.* anorexia.

anorm|al (*m. pl.* **~aux**) /anɔrmal, -o/ *a.* abnormal.

anse /ɑ̃s/ *n.f.* handle; (*baie*) cove.

antagonis|me /ɑ̃tagɔnism/ *n.m.* antagonism. **~te** *n.m./f.* antagonist; *a.* antagonistic.

antan (d') /(d)ɑ̃tɑ̃/ *a.* of long ago.

antarctique /ɑ̃tarktik/ *a.* & *n.m.* Antarctic.

antenne /ɑ̃tɛn/ *n.f.* aerial; (*Amer.*) antenna; (*d'insecte*) antenna; (*succursale*) agency; (*mil.*) outpost; (*auto., méd.*) emergency unit. **à l'~**, on the air. **sur l'~ de**, on the wavelength of.

antérieur /ɑ̃terjœr/ *a.* previous, earlier; (*placé devant*) front. **~ à**, prior to. **~ement** *adv.* earlier. **~ement à**, prior to. **antériorité** /-jɔrite/ *n.f.* precedence.

anthologie /ɑ̃tɔlɔʒi/ *n.f.* anthology.

anthropolo|gie /ɑ̃trɔpɔlɔʒi/ *n.f.* anthropology. **~gue** *n.m./f.* anthropologist.

anthropophage /ɑ̃trɔpɔfaʒ/ *a.* cannibalistic. ● *n.m./f.* cannibal.

anti- /ɑ̃ti/ *préf.* anti-.

antiadhési|f, **~ve** /ɑ̃tiadezif, -v/ *a.* non-stick.

antiaérien, **~ne** /ɑ̃tiaerjɛ̃, -jɛn/ *a.* anti-aircraft. **abri ~**, air-raid shelter.

antiatomique /ɑ̃tiatɔmik/ *a.* **abri ~**, fall-out shelter.

antibiotique /ɑ̃tibjɔtik/ *n.m.* antibiotic.

anticancéreu|x, **~se** /ɑ̃tikɑ̃serø, -z/ *a.* (anti-)cancer.

antichambre /ɑ̃tiʃɑ̃br/ *n.f.* waiting-room, antechamber.

anticipation /ɑ̃tisipasjɔ̃/ *n.f.* **d'~**, (*livre, film*) science fiction. **par ~**, in advance.

anticipé /ɑ̃tisipe/ *a.* early.

anticiper /ɑ̃tisipe/ *v.t./i.* **~ (sur)**, anticipate.

anticonceptionnel, **~le** /ɑ̃tikɔ̃sɛpsjɔnɛl/ *a.* contraceptive.

anticorps /ɑ̃tikɔr/ *n.m.* antibody.

anticyclone /ɑ̃tisiklon/ n.m. anticyclone.

antidater /ɑ̃tidate/ v.t. backdate, antedate.

antidote /ɑ̃tidɔt/ n.m. antidote.

antigel /ɑ̃tiʒɛl/ n.m. antifreeze.

antihistaminique /ɑ̃tiistaminik/ a. & n.m. antihistamine.

antillais, ~e /ɑ̃tijɛ, -z/ a. & n.m., f. West Indian.

Antilles /ɑ̃tij/ n.f. pl. **les ~,** the West Indies.

antilope /ɑ̃tilɔp/ n.f. antelope.

antimite /ɑ̃timit/ n.m. moth repellent.

antipath|ie /ɑ̃tipati/ n.f. antipathy. **~ique** a. unpleasant.

antipodes /ɑ̃tipɔd/ n.m. pl. antipodes. **aux ~ de,** (fig.) poles apart from.

antiquaire /ɑ̃tikɛr/ n.m./f. antique dealer.

antiqu|e /ɑ̃tik/ a. ancient. **~ité** n.f. antiquity; (objet) antique.

antirouille /ɑ̃tiruj/ a. & n.m. rustproofing.

antisémit|e /ɑ̃tisemit/ a. antiSemitic. **~isme** n.m. anti- Semitism.

antiseptique /ɑ̃tisɛptik/ a. & n.m. antiseptic.

antithèse /ɑ̃titɛz/ n.f. antithesis.

antivol /ɑ̃tivɔl/ n.m. anti-theft lock ou device.

antre /ɑ̃tr/ n.m. den.

anus /anys/ n.m. anus.

anxiété /ɑ̃ksjete/ n.f. anxiety.

anxieu|x /ɑ̃ksjø, -z/ a. anxious. ● n.m., f. worrier.

août /u(t)/ n.m. August.

apais|er /apeze/ v.t. calm down, (douleur, colère) soothe (faim) appease. **s'~er** v. pr. (tempête) die down. **~ement** n.m. appeasement; soothing. **~ements** n.m. pl. reassurances.

apanage /apanaʒ/ n.m. **l'~ de,** the privilege of.

aparté /aparte/ n.m. private exchange; (théâtre) aside. **en ~,** in private.

apath|ie /apati/ n.f. apathy. **~ique** a. apathetic.

apatride /apatrid/ n.m./f. stateless person.

apercevoir† /apɛrsəvwar/ v.t. see. **s'~ de,** notice. **s'~ que,** notice ou realize that.

aperçu /apɛrsy/ n.m. general view ou idea; (intuition) insight.

apéritif /aperitif/ n.m. aperitif.

à-peu-près /apøprɛ/ n.m. invar. approximation.

apeuré /apœre/ a. scared.

aphone /afɔn/ a. voiceless.

aphte /aft/ n.m. mouth ulcer.

apit|oyer /apitwaje/ v.t. move (to pity). **s'~oyer sur,** feel pity for. **~oiement** n.m. pity.

aplanir /aplanir/ v.t. level; (fig.) smooth out.

aplatir /aplatir/ v.t. flatten (out). **s'~** v. pr. (s'allonger) lie flat; (s'humilier) grovel; (tomber: fam.) fall flat on one's face.

aplomb /aplɔ̃/ n.m. balance; (fig.) self-possession. **d'~,** (en équilibre) steady, balanced.

apogée /apɔʒe/ n.m. peak.

apologie /apɔlɔʒi/ n.f. vindication.

a posteriori /aposterjɔri/ adv. after the event.

apostolique /apɔstɔlik/ a. apostolic.

apostroph|e /apɔstrɔf/ n.f. apostrophe; (appel) sharp address. **~er** v.t. address sharply.

apothéose /apɔteoz/ n.f. final triumph.

apôtre /apotr/ n.m. apostle.

apparaître† /aparɛtr/ v.i. appear. **il apparaît que,** it appears that.

apparat /apara/ n.m. pomp. **d'~,** ceremonial.

appareil /aparɛj/ n.m. apparatus; (électrique) appliance; (anat.) system; (téléphonique) phone; (dentaire) brace; (auditif) hearing-aid; (avion) plane; (culin.) mixture. **l'~ du parti,** the party machinery. **c'est Gabriel à l'~,** it's Gabriel on the phone. **~(-photo),** camera. **~ électroménager,** household electrical appliance.

appareiller¹ /apareje/ v.i. (navire) cast off, put to sea.

appareiller² /apareje/ v.t. (assortir) match.

apparemment /aparamɑ̃/ adv. apparently.

apparence /aparɑ̃s/ n.f. appearance. **en ~,** outwardly; (apparemment) apparently.

apparent, ~e /aparɑ̃, -t/ a. apparent; (visible) conspicuous.

apparenté /aparɑ̃te/ a. related; (semblable) similar.

appariteur /aparitœr/ n.m. (univ.) attendant, porter.

apparition /aparisjɔ̃/ *n.f.* appearance; (*spectre*) apparition.

appartement /apartəmɑ̃/ *n.m.* flat; (*Amer.*) apartment.

appartenance /apartənɑ̃s/ *n.f.* membership (**à,** of), belonging (**à,** to).

appartenir† /apartənir/ *v.i.* belong (**à,** to) **il lui/vous/***etc.* **appartient de,** it is up to him/you/*etc.* to.

appât /apɑ/ *n.m.* bait; (*fig.*) lure. **~er** /-te/ *v.t.* lure.

appauvrir /apovrir/ *v.t.* impoverish. **s'~** *v. pr.* grow impoverished.

appel /apɛl/ *n.m.* call; (*jurid.*) appeal; (*mil.*) call-up. **faire ~,** appeal. **faire ~ à,** (*recourir à*) call on; (*invoquer*) appeal to; (*évoquer*) call up; (*exiger*) call for him. **faire l'~,** (*scol.*) call the register; (*mil.*) take a roll-call. **~ d'offres,** (*comm.*) invitation to tender. **faire un ~ de phares,** flash one's headlights.

appelé /aple/ *n.m.* conscript.

appel|er /aple/ *v.t.* call; (*nécessiter*) call for. **s'~er** *v. pr.* be called. **~é à,** (*désigné à*) marked out for. **en ~er à,** (*recourir à*) appeal to. **il s'appelle,** his name is. **~lation** /apelasjɔ̃/ *n.f.* designation.

appendic|e /apɛ̃dis/ *n.m.* appendix. **~ite** *n.f.* appendicitis.

appentis /apɑ̃ti/ *n.m.* lean-to.

appesantir /apəzɑ̃tir/ *v.t.* weigh down. **s'~** *v. pr.* grow heavier. **s'~ sur,** dwell upon.

appétissant, ~e /apetisɑ̃, -t/ *a.* appetizing.

appétit /apeti/ *n.m.* appetite.

applaud|ir /aplodir/ *v.t./i.* applaud. **~ir à,** applaud. **~issements** *n.m. pl.* applause.

applique /aplik/ *n.f.* wall lamp.

appliqué /aplike/ *a.* painstaking.

appliquer /aplike/ *v.t.* apply; (*loi*) enforce. **s'~ à,** apply o.s. (**à,** to). **s'~ à,** (*concerner*) apply to. **applicable** /-abl/ *a.* applicable. **application** /-asjɔ̃/ *n.f.* application.

appoint /apwɛ̃/ *n.m.* contribution. **d'~,** extra. **faire l'~,** give the correct money.

appointements /apwɛ̃təmɑ̃/ *n.m. pl.* salary.

apport /apɔr/ *n.m.* contribution.

apporter /apɔrte/ *v.t.* bring.

apposer /apoze/ *v.t.* affix.

appréciable /apresjabl/ *a.* appreciable.

appréc|ier /apresje/ *v.t.* appreciate; (*évaluer*) appraise. **~iation** *n.f.* appreciation; appraisal.

appréhen|der /apreɑ̃de/ *v.t.* dread, fear; (*arrêter*) apprehend. **~sion** *n.f.* apprehension.

apprendre† /aprɑ̃dr/ *v.t./i.* learn; (*être informé de*) hear of. **~ qch. à qn.,** teach s.o. sth.; (*informer*) tell s.o. sth. **~ à faire,** learn to do. **~ à qn. à faire,** teach s.o. to do. **~ que,** learn that; (*être informé*) hear that.

apprenti, ~e /aprɑ̃ti/ *n.m., f.* apprentice.

apprentissage /aprɑ̃tisaʒ/ *n.m.* apprenticeship; (*d'un sujet*) learning.

apprêté /aprete/ *a.* affected.

apprêter /aprete/ *v.t.,* **s'~** *v. pr.* prepare.

apprivoiser /aprivwaze/ *v.t.* tame.

approba|teur, ~trice /aprobatœr, -tris/ *a.* approving.

approbation /aprobasjɔ̃/ *n.f.* approval.

approchant, ~e /aprɔʃɑ̃, -t/ *a.* close, similar.

approche /aprɔʃ/ *n.f.* approach.

approché /aprɔʃe/ *a.* approximate.

approcher /aprɔʃe/ *v.t.* (*objet*) move near(er) (**de,** to); (*personne*) approach. ● *v.i.* **~ (de),** approach. **s'~ de,** approach, move near(er) to.

approfond|ir /aprɔfɔ̃dir/ *v.t.* deepen; (*fig.*) go into thoroughly. **~i** *a.* thorough.

approprié /aprɔprije/ *a.* appropriate.

approprier (s') /(s)aprɔprije/ *v. pr.* appropriate.

approuver /apruve/ *v.t.* approve; (*trouver louable*) approve of; (*soutenir*) agree with.

approvisionn|er /aprɔvizjɔne/ *v.t.* supply. **s'~er** *v. pr.* stock up. **~ement** *n.m.* supply.

approximati|f, ~ve /aprɔksimatif, -v/ *a.* approximate. **~vement** *adv.* approximately.

approximation /aprɔksimasjɔ̃/ *n.f.* approximation.

appui /apɥi/ *n.m.* support; (*de fenêtre*) sill; (*pour objet*) rest. **à l'~ de,** in support of. **prendre ~,** support o.s. on.

appuie-tête /apɥitɛt/ *n.m.* headrest.

appuyer /apɥije/ *v.t.* lean, rest; (*presser*) press; (*soutenir*) support, back. ● *v.i.* **~ sur,** press (on); (*fig.*) stress. **s'~** *v. pr.* lean on; (*compter sur*) rely on.

âpre /ɑpr/ a. harsh, bitter. **~ au gain**, grasping.

après /aprɛ/ prép. after; (au-delà de) beyond. ● adv. after(wards); (plus tard) later. **~ avoir fait**, after doing. **~ qu'il est parti**, after he left. **~ coup**, after the event. **~ tout**, after all. **d'~**, (selon) according to. **~-demain** adv. the day after tomorrow. **~-guerre** n.m. postwar period. **~-midi** n.m./f. invar. afternoon. **~-rasage** n.m. aftershave. **~-ski** n.m. moonboot. **~-vente** a. after-sales.

a priori /aprijɔri/ adv. in principle, without going into the matter. ● n.m. preconception.

à-propos /apropo/ n.m. timeliness; (fig.) presence of mind.

apte /apt/ a. capable (**à**, of).

aptitude /aptityd/ n.f. aptitude, ability.

aquarelle /akwarɛl/ n.f. water-colour, aquarelle.

aquarium /akwarjɔm/ n.m. aquarium.

aquatique /akwatik/ a. aquatic.

aqueduc /akdyk/ n.m. aqueduct.

arabe /arab/ a. Arab; (lang.) Arabic; (désert) Arabian. ● n.m./f. Arab. ● n.m. (lang.) Arabic.

Arabie /arabi/ n.f. **~ Séoudite**, Saudi Arabia.

arable /arabl/ a. arable.

arachide /araʃid/ n.f. peanut.

araignée /areɲe/ n.f. spider.

arbitraire /arbitrɛr/ a. arbitrary.

arbitr|e /arbitr/ n.m. referee; (cricket, tennis) umpire; (maître) arbiter; (jurid.) arbitrator. **~age** n.m. arbitration; (sport) refereeing. **~er** v.t. (match) referee; (jurid.) arbitrate.

arborer /arbɔre/ v.t. display; (vêtement) sport.

arbre /arbr/ n.m. tree; (techn.) shaft.

arbrisseau (pl. **~x**) /arbriso/ n.m. shrub.

arbuste /arbyst/ n.m. bush.

arc /ark/ n.m. (arme) bow; (voûte) arch. **~ de cercle**, arc of a circle.

arcade /arkad/ n.f. arch. **~s**, arcade, arches.

arc-boutant (pl. **arcs-boutants**) /arkbutã/ n.m. flying buttress.

arc-bouter (s') /(s)arkbute/ v. pr. lean (for support), brace o.s.

arceau (pl. **~x**) /arso/ n.m. hoop; (de voûte) arch.

arc-en-ciel (pl. **arcs-en-ciel**) /arkɑ̃sjɛl/ n.m. rainbow.

archaïque /arkaik/ a. archaic.

arche /arʃ/ n.f. arch. **~ de Noé**, Noah's ark.

archéolo|gie /arkeɔlɔʒi/ n.f. archaeology. **~gique** a. archaeological. **~gue** n.m./f. archaeologist.

archer /arʃe/ n.m. archer.

archet /arʃɛ/ n.m. (mus.) bow.

archétype /arketip/ n.m. archetype.

archevêque /arʃəvɛk/ n.m. archbishop.

archi- /arʃi/ préf. (fam.) tremendously.

archipel /arʃipɛl/ n.m. archipelago.

architecte /arʃitɛkt/ n.m. architect.

architecture /arʃitɛktyr/ n.f. architecture.

archiv|es /arʃiv/ n.f. pl. archives. **~iste** n.m./f. archivist.

arctique /arktik/ a. & n.m. Arctic.

ardemment /ardamã/ adv. ardently.

ard|ent, ~ente /ardã, -t/ a. burning; (passionné) ardent; (foi) fervent. **~eur** n.f. ardour; (chaleur) heat.

ardoise /ardwaz/ n.f. slate.

ardu /ardy/ a. arduous.

are /ar/ n.m. are (= 100 square metres).

arène /arɛn/ n.f. arena. **~(s)**, (pour courses de taureaux) bullring.

arête /arɛt/ n.f. (de poisson) bone; (bord) ridge.

argent /arʒã/ n.m. money; (métal) silver. **~ comptant**, cash. **prendre pour ~ comptant**, take at face value. **~ de poche**, pocket money.

argenté /arʒãte/ a. silver(y); (métal) (silver-)plated.

argenterie /arʒãtri/ n.f. silverware.

argentin, ~e /arʒãtɛ̃, -in/ a. & n.m., f. Argentinian, Argentine.

Argentine /arʒãtin/ n.f. Argentina.

argil|e /arʒil/ n.f. clay. **~eux, ~euse** a. clayey.

argot /argo/ n.m. slang. **~ique** /-ɔtik/ a. (terme) slang; (style) slangy.

arguer /argɥe/ v.i. **~ de**, put forward as a reason.

argument /argymã/ n.m. argument. **~er** /-te/ v.i. argue.

aride /arid/ a. arid, barren.

aristocrate /aristɔkrat/ n.m./f. aristocrat.

aristocrat|ie /aristɔkrasi/ n.f. aristocracy. **~ique** /-atik/ a. aristocratic.

arithmétique /aritmetik/ *n.f.* arithmetic. ● *a.* arithmetical.

armateur /armatœr/ *n.m.* ship-owner.

armature /armatyr/ *n.f.* framework; (*de tente*) frame.

arme /arm/ *n.f.* arm, weapon. ~**s**, (*blason*) arms. ~ **à feu**, firearm.

armée /arme/ *n.f.* army. ~ **de l'air**, Air Force. ~ **de terre**, Army.

armement /arməmã/ *n.m.* arms.

armer /arme/ *v.t.* arm; (*fusil*) cock; (*navire*) equip; (*renforcer*) reinforce; (*photo*) wind on. ~ **de**, (*garnir de*) fit with. **s'~ de**, arm o.s. with.

armistice /armistis/ *n.m.* armistice.

armoire /armwar/ *n.f.* cupboard; (*penderie*) wardrobe; (*Amer.*) closet.

armoiries /armwari/ *n.f. pl.* (coat of) arms.

armure /armyr/ *n.f.* armour.

arnaque /arnak/ *n.f.* (*fam.*) swindling. **c'est de l'~**, it's a swindle *ou* con (*fam.*). ~**r** *v.t.* swindle, con (*fam.*).

arnica /arnika/ *n.f.* (*méd.*) arnica.

aromate /aromat/ *n.m.* herb, spice.

aromatique /aromatik/ *a.* aromatic.

aromatisé /aromatize/ *a.* flavoured.

arôme /arom/ *n.m.* aroma.

arpent|er /arpãte/ *v.t.* pace up and down; (*terrain*) survey. ~**eur** *n.m.* surveyor.

arqué /arke/ *a.* arched; (*jambes*) bandy.

arraché (à l') /(al)arafe/ *adv.* with a struggle, after a hard struggle.

arrache-pied (d') /(d)arafpje/ *adv.* relentlessly.

arrach|er /arafe/ *v.t.* pull out *ou* off; (*plante*) pull *ou* dig up; (*cheveux, page*) tear *ou* pull out; (*par une explosion*) blow off. ~**er à**, (*enlever à*) snatch from; (*fig.*) force *ou* wrest from. **s'~er qch.**, fight over sth. ~**age** /-aʒ/ *n.m.* pulling *ou* digging up.

arraisonner /arezone/ *v.t.* inspect.

arrangeant, ~e /arãʒã, -t/ *a.* obliging.

arrangement /arãʒmã/ *n.m.* arrangement.

arranger /arãʒe/ *v.t.* arrange, fix up; (*réparer*) put right; (*régler*) sort out; (*convenir à*) suit. **s'~** *v. pr.* (*se mettre d'accord*) come to an arrangement; (*se débrouiller*) manage (**pour**, to).

arrestation /arɛstasjɔ̃/ *n.f.* arrest.

arrêt /arɛ/ *n.m.* stopping (**de**, of); (*lieu*) stop; (*pause*) pause; (*jurid.*) decree. ~**s**, (*mil.*) arrest. **à l'~**, stationary. **faire un ~**, (make a) stop. **sans ~**, without stopping. ~ **maladie**, sick leave. ~ **de travail**, (*grève*) stoppage; (*méd.*) sick leave. **rester** *ou* **tomber en ~**, stop short.

arrêté /arete/ *n.m.* order.

arrêter /arete/ *v.t./i.* stop; (*date, regard*) fix; (*appareil*) turn off; (*appréhender*) arrest. **s'~** *v. pr.* stop. (**s'**)~ **de faire**, stop doing.

arrhes /ar/ *n.f. pl.* deposit.

arrière /arjɛr/ *n.m.* back, rear; (*football*) back. ● *a. invar.* back, rear. **à l'~**, in *ou* at the back. **en ~**, behind; (*marcher*) backwards. **en ~ de**, behind. ~**-boutique** *n.f.* back room (of the shop). ~**-garde** *n.f.* rearguard. ~**-goût** *n.m.* aftertaste. ~**-grand-mère** *n.f.* great-grandmother. ~**-grand-père** (*pl.* ~**-grands-pères**) *n.m.* great-grandfather. ~**-pays** *n.m.* backcountry. ~**-pensée** *n.f.* ulterior motive. ~**-plan** *n.m.* background.

arriéré /arjere/ *a.* backward. ● *n.m.* arrears.

arrimer /arime/ *v.t.* rope down; (*cargaison*) stow.

arrivage /arivaʒ/ *n.m.* consignment.

arrivant, ~e /arivã, -t/ *n.m., f.* new arrival.

arrivée /arive/ *n.f.* arrival; (*sport*) finish.

arriver /arive/ *v.i.* (*aux. être*) arrive, come; (*réussir*) succeed; (*se produire*) happen. ~ **à**, (*atteindre*) reach. ~ **à faire**, manage to do. **en ~ à faire**, get to the stage of doing. **il arrive que**, it happens that. **il lui arrive de faire**, he (sometimes) does.

arriviste /arivist/ *n.m./f.* self-seeker.

arrogan|t, ~te /arɔgã, -t/ *a.* arrogant. ~**ce** *n.f.* arrogance.

arroger (s') /(s)arɔʒe/ *v. pr.* assume (without justification).

arrondir /arɔ̃dir/ *v.t.* (make) round; (*somme*) round off. **s'~** *v. pr.* become round(ed).

arrondissement /arɔ̃dismã/ *n.m.* district.

arros|er /aroze/ *v.t.* water; (*repas*) wash down; (*rôti*) baste; (*victoire*) celebrate with a drink. ~**age** *n.m.* watering. ~**oir** *n.m.* watering-can.

arsen|al (*pl.* **~aux**) /arsənal, -o/ *n.m.* arsenal; (*naut.*) dockyard.

arsenic /arsənik/ *n.m.* arsenic.

art /ar/ *n.m.* art. **~s et métiers**, arts and crafts. **~s ménagers**, domestic science.

artère /artɛr/ *n.f.* artery. (**grande**) **~**, main road.

artériel, ~le /arterjɛl/ *a.* arterial.

arthrite /artrit/ *n.f.* arthritis.

arthrose /artroz/ *n.f.* osteoarthritis.

artichaut /artiʃo/ *n.m.* artichoke.

article /artikl/ *n.m.* article; (*comm.*) item, article. **à l'~ de la mort**, at death's door. **~ de fond**, feature (article). **~s d'ameublement**, furnishings. **~s de voyage**, travel requisites *ou* goods.

articul|er /artikyle/ *v.t., s'~er v. pr.* articulate. **~ation** *n.f.* articulation. (*anat.*) joint.

artifice /artifis/ *n.m.* contrivance.

artificiel, ~le /artifisjɛl/ *a.* artificial. **~lement** *adv.* artificially.

artill|erie /artijri/ *n.f.* artillery. **~eur** *n.m.* gunner.

artisan /artizɑ̃/ *n.m.* artisan, craftsman. **l'~ de**, (*fig.*) the architect of. **~al** (*m. pl.* **~aux**) /-anal, -o/ *a.* of *ou* by craftsmen, craft; (*amateur*) home-made. **~at** /-ana/ *n.m.* craft; (*classe*) artisans.

artist|e /artist/ *n.m./f.* artist. **~ique** *a.* artistic.

as[1] /a/ *voir* avoir.

as[2] /ɑs/ *n.m.* ace.

ascendant[1], **~e** /asɑ̃dɑ̃, -t/ *a.* ascending, upward.

ascendant[2] /asɑ̃dɑ̃/ *n.m.* influence. **~s**, ancestors.

ascenseur /asɑ̃sœr/ *n.m.* lift; (*Amer.*) elevator.

ascension /asɑ̃sjɔ̃/ *n.f.* ascent. **l' A~**, Ascension.

ascète /asɛt/ *n.m./f.* ascetic.

ascétique /asetik/ *a.* ascetic.

aseptique /asɛptik/ *a.* aseptic.

aseptis|er /asɛptize/ *v.t.* disinfect; (*stériliser*) sterilize. **~é** (*péj.*) sanitized.

asiatique /azjatik/ *a.* & *n.m./f.*, **Asiate** /azjat/ *n.m./f.* Asian.

Asie /azi/ *n.f.* Asia.

asile /azil/ *n.m.* refuge; (*pol.*) asylum; (*pour malades, vieillards*) home.

aspect /aspɛ/ *n.m.* appearance; (*fig.*) aspect. **à l'~ de**, at the sight of.

asperge /aspɛrʒ/ *n.f.* asparagus.

asperg|er /aspɛrʒe/ *v.t.* spray. **~sion** *n.f.* spray(ing).

aspérité /asperite/ *n.f.* bump, rough edge.

asphalt|e /asfalt/ *n.m.* asphalt. **~er** *v.t.* asphalt.

asphyxie /asfiksi/ *n.f.* suffocation.

asphyxier /asfiksje/ *v.t., s'~ v. pr.* suffocate, asphyxiate; (*fig.*) stifle.

aspic /aspik/ *n.m.* (*serpent*) asp.

aspirateur /aspiratœr/ *n.m.* vacuum cleaner.

aspir|er /aspire/ *v.t.* inhale; (*liquide*) suck up. ● *v.i.* **~er à**, aspire to. **~ation** *n.f.* inhaling; suction; (*ambition*) aspiration.

aspirine /aspirin/ *n.f.* aspirin.

assagir /asaʒir/ *v.t., s'~ v. pr.* sober down.

assaill|ir /asajir/ *v.t.* assail. **~ant** *n.m.* assailant.

assainir /asenir/ *v.t.* clean up.

assaisonn|er /asɛzɔne/ *v.t.* season. **~ement** *n.m.* seasoning.

assassin /asasɛ̃/ *n.m.* murderer; (*pol.*) assassin.

assassin|er /asasine/ *v.t.* murder; (*pol.*) assassinate. **~at** *n.m.* murder; (*pol.*) assassination.

assaut /aso/ *n.m.* assault, onslaught. **donner l'~ à, prendre d'~**, storm.

assécher /aseʃe/ *v.t.* drain.

assemblée /asɑ̃ble/ *n.f.* meeting; (*gens réunis*) gathering; (*pol.*) assembly.

assembl|er /asɑ̃ble/ *v.t.* assemble, put together; (*réunir*) gather. **s'~er** *v. pr.* gather, assemble. **~age** *n.m.* assembly; (*combinaison*) collection; (*techn.*) joint. **~eur** *n.m.* (*comput.*) assembler.

assener /asene/ *v.t.* (*coup*) deal.

assentiment /asɑ̃timɑ̃/ *n.m.* assent.

asseoir† /aswar/ *v.t.* sit (down), seat; (*affermir*) establish; (*baser*) base. **s'~** *v. pr.* sit (down).

assermenté /asɛrmɑ̃te/ *a.* sworn.

assertion /asɛrsjɔ̃/ *n.f.* assertion.

asservir /asɛrvir/ *v.t.* enslave.

assez /ase/ *adv.* enough; (*plutôt*) quite, fairly. **~ grand/rapide** *etc.*, big/fast/*etc.* enough (**pour**, to). **~ de**, enough. **j'en ai ~ (de)**, I've had enough (of).

assid|u /asidy/ *a.* (*zèle*) assiduous; (*régulier*) regular. **~u auprès de**, attentive to. **~uité** /-ɥite/ *n.f.* assiduousness; regularity. **~ûment** *adv.* assiduously.

assiéger /asjeʒe/ *v.t.* besiege.

assiette /asjɛt/ *n.f.* plate; (*équilibre*) seat. **~ anglaise**, assorted cold meats. **~ creuse/plate**, soup-/dinner-plate. **ne pas être dans son ~**, feel out of sorts.

assiettée /asjete/ *n.f.* plateful.

assigner /asiɲe/ *v.t.* assign; (*limite*) fix.

assimil|er /asimile/ *v.t.*, **s'~er** *v. pr.* assimilate. **~er à**, liken to; (*classer*) class as. **~ation** *n.f.* assimilation; likening; classification.

assis, ~e /asi, -z/ *voir* asseoir. ● *a.* sitting (down), seated.

assise /asiz/ *n.f.* (*base*) foundation. **~s**, (*tribunal*) assizes; (*congrès*) conference, congress.

assistance /asistãs/ *n.f.* audience; (*aide*) assistance. **l'A~ (publique)**, government child care service.

assistant, ~e /asistã, -t/ *n.m., f.* assistant; (*univ.*) assistant lecturer. **~s**, (*spectateurs*) members of the audience. **~ social, ~e sociale**, social worker.

assist|er /asiste/ *v.t.* assist. ● *v.i.* **~er à**, attend, be (present) at; (*scène*) witness. **~é par ordinateur**, computer-assisted.

association /asɔsjɑsjɔ̃/ *n.f.* association.

associé, ~e /asɔsje/ *n.m., f.* partner, associate. ● *a.* associate.

associer /asɔsje/ *v.t.* associate; (*mêler*) combine (**à**, with). **~ qn. à**, (*projet*) involve s.o. in; (*bénéfices*) give s.o. a share of. **s'~** *v. pr.* (*sociétés, personnes*) become associated, join forces (**à**, with); (*s'harmoniser*) combine (**à**, with). **s'~ à**, (*joie de qn.*) share in; (*opinion de qn.*) share, (*projet*) take part in.

assoiffé /aswafe/ *a.* thirsty.

assombrir /asɔ̃brir/ *v.t.* darken; (*fig.*) make gloomy. **s'~** *v. pr.* darken; become gloomy.

assommer /asɔme/ *v.t.* knock out; (*tuer*) kill; (*animal*) stun; (*fig.*) overwhelm; (*ennuyer: fam.*) bore.

Assomption /asɔ̃psjɔ̃/ *n.f.* Assumption.

assorti /asɔrti/ *a.* matching; (*objets variés*) assorted.

assort|ir /asɔrtir/ *v.t.* match (**à**, with, to). **~ir de**, accompany with. **s'~ir** (**à**), match. **~iment** *n.m.* assortment.

assoup|ir (s') /(s)asupir/ *v. pr.* doze off; (*s'apaiser*) subside. **~i** *a.* dozing.

assouplir /asuplir/ *v.t.* make supple; (*fig.*) make flexible.

assourdir /asurdir/ *v.t.* (*personne*) deafen; (*bruit*) deaden.

assouvir /asuvir/ *v.t.* satisfy.

assujettir /asyʒetir/ *v.t.* subject, subdue. **~ à**, subject to.

assumer /asyme/ *v.t.* assume.

assurance /asyrãs/ *n.f.* (self-) assurance; (*garantie*) assurance; (*contrat*) insurance. **~-maladie** *n.f.* health insurance. **~s sociales**, National Insurance. **~-vie** *n.f.* life assurance *ou* insurance.

assuré, ~e /asyre/ *a.* certain, assured; (*sûr de soi*) (self-)confident, assured. ● *n.m., f.* insured. **~ment** *adv.* certainly.

assurer /asyre/ *v.t.* ensure; (*fournir*) provide; (*exécuter*) carry out; (*comm.*) insure; (*stabiliser*) steady; (*frontières*) make secure. **~ à qn. que**, assure s.o. that. **~ qn. de**, assure s.o. of. **~ la gestion de**, manage. **s'~ de/que**, make sure of/that. **s'~ qch.**, (*se procurer*) secure *ou* ensure sth. **assureur** /-œr/ *n.m.* insurer.

astérisque /asterisk/ *n.m.* asterisk.

asthm|e /asm/ *n.m.* asthma. **~atique** *a. & n.m./f.* asthmatic.

asticot /astiko/ *n.m.* maggot.

astiquer /astike/ *v.t.* polish.

astre /astr/ *n.m.* star.

astreignant, ~e /astrɛɲã, -t/ *a.* exacting.

astreindre /astrɛ̃dr/ *v.t.* **~ qn. à qch.**, force sth. on s.o. **~ à faire**, force to do.

astringent, ~e /astrɛ̃ʒã, -t/ *a.* astringent.

astrolo|gie /astrɔlɔʒi/ *n.f.* astrology. **~gue** *n.m./f.* astrologer.

astronaute /astronot/ *n.m./f.* astronaut.

astronom|ie /astronɔmi/ *n.f.* astronomy. **~e** *n.m./f.* astronomer. **~ique** *a.* astronomical.

astuce /astys/ *n.f.* smartness; (*truc*) trick; (*plaisanterie*) wisecrack.

astucieu|x, ~se /astysjø, -z/ *a.* smart, clever.

atelier /atəlje/ *n.m.* workshop; (*de peintre*) studio.

athé|e /ate/ *n.m./f.* atheist. ● *a.* atheistic. **~isme** *n.m.* atheism .

athl|ète /atlɛt/ *n.m./f.* athlete. **~étique** *a.* athletic. **~étisme** *n.m.* athletics.

atlantique /atlɑ̃tik/ *a.* Atlantic. ● *n.m.* **A~,** Atlantic (Ocean).

atlas /atlɑs/ *n.m.* atlas.

atmosph|ère /atmosfɛr/ *n.f.* atmosphere. **~érique** *a.* atmospheric.

atome /atom/ *n.m.* atom.

atomique /atomik/ *a.* atomic.

atomiseur /atomizœr/ *n.m.* spray.

atout /atu/ *n.m.* trump (card); (*avantage*) great asset.

âtre /ɑtr/ *n.m.* hearth.

atroc|e /atros/ *a.* atrocious. **~ité** *n.f.* atrocity.

atroph|ie /atrofi/ *n.f.* atrophy. **~ié** *a.* atrophied.

attabler (s') /(s)atable/ *v. pr.* sit down at table.

attachant, ~e /ataʃɑ̃, -t/ *a.* likeable.

attache /ataʃ/ *n.f.* (*agrafe*) fastener; (*lien*) tie.

attach|é /ataʃe/ *a.* être **~é à,** (*aimer*) be attached to. ● *n.m., f.* (*pol.*) attaché. **~é-case** *n.m.* attaché case. **~ement** *n.m.* attachment.

attacher /ataʃe/ *v.t.* tie (up); (*ceinture, robe, etc.*) fasten; (*étiquette*) attach. **~ à,** (*attribuer à*) attach to. ● *v.i.* (*culin.*) stick. **s'~ à,** (*se lier à*) become attached to; (*se consacrer à*) apply o.s. to.

attaque /atak/ *n.f.* attack. **~ (cérébrale),** stroke. **il va en faire une ~,** he'll have a fit. **~ à main armée,** armed attack.

attaqu|er /atake/ *v.t./i., s'~er à,* attack; (*problème, sujet*) tackle. **~ant, ~ante** *n.m., f.* attacker; (*football*) striker; (*football, Amer.*) forward.

attardé /atarde/ *a.* backward; (*idées*) outdated; (*en retard*) late.

attarder (s') /(s)atarde/ *v. pr.* linger.

atteindre† /atɛ̃dr/ *v.t.* reach; (*blesser*) hit; (*affecter*) affect.

atteint, ~e /atɛ̃, -t/ *a.* **~ de,** suffering from.

atteinte /atɛ̃t/ *n.f.* attack (à, on). **porter ~ à,** make an attack on.

attel|er /atle/ *v.t.* (*cheval*) harness; (*remorque*) couple. **s'~er à,** get down to. **~age** *n.m.* harnessing; coupling; (*bêtes*) team.

attelle /atɛl/ *n.f.* splint.

attenant, ~e /atnɑ̃, -t/ *a.* **~ (à),** adjoining.

attendant (en) /(ɑ̃n)atɑ̃dɑ̃/ *adv.* meanwhile.

attendre /atɑ̃dr/ *v.t.* wait for; (*bébé*) expect; (*être le sort de*) await; (*escompter*) expect. ● *v.i.* wait. **~ que qn. fasse,** wait for s.o. to do. **s'~ à,** expect.

attendr|ir /atɑ̃drir/ *v.t.* move (to pity). **s'~ir** *v. pr.* be moved to pity. **~issant, ~issante** *a.* moving.

attendu /atɑ̃dy/ *a.* (*escompté*) expected; (*espéré*) long-awaited. **~ que,** considering that.

attentat /atɑ̃ta/ *n.m.* murder attempt. **~ (à la bombe),** (bomb) attack.

attente /atɑ̃t/ *n.f.* wait(ing); (*espoir*) expectation.

attenter /atɑ̃te/ *v.i.* **~ à,** make an attempt on; (*fig.*) violate.

attenti|f, ~ve /atɑ̃tif, -v/ *a.* attentive; (*scrupuleux*) careful. **~f à,** mindful of; (*soucieux*) careful of. **~vement** *adv.* attentively.

attention /atɑ̃sjɔ̃/ *n.f.* attention; (*soin*) care. **~ (à)!,** watch out (for)! **faire ~ à,** (*professeur*) pay attention to; (*marche*) mind. **faire ~ à faire,** be careful to do. **~né** /-jɔne/ *a.* considerate.

attentisme /atɑ̃tism/ *n.m.* wait-and-see policy.

atténuer /atenɥe/ *v.t.* (*violence*) tone down; (*douleur*) ease; (*faute*) mitigate. **s'~** *v. pr.* subside.

atterrer /atere/ *v.t.* dismay.

atterr|ir /aterir/ *v.i.* land. **~issage** *n.m.* landing.

attestation /atɛstasjɔ̃/ *n.f.* certificate.

attester /atɛste/ *v.t.* testify to. **~ que,** testify that.

attifé /atife/ *a.* (*fam.*) dressed up.

attirail /atiraj/ *n.m.* (*fam.*) gear.

attirance /atirɑ̃s/ *n.f.* attraction.

attirant, ~e /atirɑ̃, -t/ *a.* attractive.

attirer /atire/ *v.t.* draw, attract; (*causer*) bring. **s'~** *v. pr.* bring upon o.s.; (*amis*) win.

attiser /atize/ *v.t.* (*feu*) poke; (*sentiment*) stir up.

attitré /atitre/ *a.* accredited; (*habituel*) usual.

attitude /atityd/ *n.f.* attitude; (*maintien*) bearing.

attraction /atraksjɔ̃/ *n.f.* attraction.

attrait /atrɛ/ *n.m.* attraction.

attrape-nigaud /atrapnigo/ *n.m.* (*fam.*) con.

attraper /atrape/ v.t. catch; (*habitude, style*) pick up; (*duper*) take in; (*gronder: fam.*) tell off.

attrayant, **~e** /atrɛjɑ̃, -t/ a. attractive.

attrib|uer /atribɥe/ v.t. award; (*donner*) assign; (*imputer*) attribute. **s'~uer** v. pr. claim. **~ution** n.f. awarding; assignment. **~utions** n.f. pl. attributions.

attrister /atriste/ v.t. sadden.

attroup|er (s') /(s)atrupe/ v. pr. gather. **~ement** n.m. crowd.

au /o/ voir à.

aubaine /obɛn/ n.f. (stroke of) good fortune.

aube /ob/ n.f. dawn, daybreak.

aubépine /obepin/ n.f. hawthorn.

auberg|e /obɛrʒ/ n.f. inn. **~e de jeunesse**, youth hostel. **~iste** n.m./ f. innkeeper.

aubergine /obɛrʒin/ n.f. aubergine; (*Amer.*) egg-plant.

aucun, ~e /okœ̃, okyn/ a. no, not any; (*positif*) any. ● pron. none, not any; (*positif*) any. **~ des deux**, neither of the two. **d'~s**, some. **~ement** /okynmɑ̃/ adv. not at all.

audace /odas/ n.f. daring; (*impudence*) audacity.

audacieu|x, ~se /odasjø, -z/ a. daring.

au-delà /odla/ adv., **~ de** prép. beyond.

au-dessous /odsu/ adv., **~ de** prép. below; (*couvert par*) under.

au-dessus /odsy/ adv., **~ de** prép. above.

au-devant (de) /odvɑ̃(də)/ prép. **aller ~ de qn.**, go to meet s.o.

audience /odjɑ̃s/ n.f. audience; (*d'un tribunal*) hearing; (*intérêt*) attention.

Audimat /odimat/ n.m. (P.) **l'~**, the TV ratings.

audiotypiste /odjotipist/ n.m./f. audio typist.

audio-visuel, ~le /odjovizɥɛl/ a. audio-visual.

audi|teur, ~trice /oditœr, -tris/ n.m., f. listener.

audition /odisjɔ̃/ n.f. hearing; (*théâtre, mus.*) audition. **~ner** /-jone/ v.t./i. audition.

auditoire /oditwar/ n.m. audience.

auditorium /oditɔrjɔm/ n.m. (*mus., radio*) recording studio.

auge /oʒ/ n.f. trough.

augment|er /ogmɑ̃te/ v.t./i. increase; (*employé*) increase the pay of. **~ation** n.f. increase. **~ation (de salaire)**, (pay) rise; (*Amer.*) raise.

augure /ogyr/ n.m. (*devin*) oracle. **être de bon/mauvais ~**, be a good/ bad sign.

auguste /ogyst/ a. august.

aujourd'hui /oʒurdɥi/ adv. today.

aumône /omon/ n.f. alms.

aumônier /omonje/ n.m. chaplain.

auparavant /oparavɑ̃/ adv. before (-hand).

auprès (de) /oprɛ(də)/ prép. by, next to; (*comparé à*) compared with; (*s'adressant à*) to.

auquel, ~le /okɛl/ voir lequel.

aura, aurait /ora, orɛ/ voir avoir.

auréole /oreɔl/ n.f. halo.

auriculaire /orikyler/ n.m. little finger.

aurore /orɔr/ n.f. dawn.

ausculter /oskylte/ v.t. examine with a stethoscope.

auspices /ospis/ n.m. pl. auspices.

aussi /osi/ adv. too, also; (*comparaison*) as; (*tellement*) so. ● conj. (*donc*) therefore. **~ bien que**, as well as.

aussitôt /osito/ adv. immediately. **~ que**, as soon as. **~ arrivé/levé/**etc., as soon as one has arrived/got up/ etc.

aust|ère /ostɛr/ a. austere. **~érité** n.f. austerity.

austral (m. pl. ~s) /ostral/ a. southern.

Australie /ostrali/ n.f. Australia.

australien, ~ne /ostraljɛ̃, -jɛn/ a. & n.m., f. Australian.

autant /otɑ̃/ adv. (*travailler, manger, etc.*) as much (que, as). **~ (de)**, (*quantité*) as much (que, as); (*nombre*) as many (que, as); (*tant*) so much; so many. **~ faire**, one had better do. **d'~ plus que**, all the more since. **en faire ~**, do the same. **pour ~**, for all that.

autel /otɛl/ n.m. altar.

auteur /otœr/ n.m. author. **l'~ du crime**, the person who committed the crime.

authentifier /otɑ̃tifje/ v.t. authenticate.

authenti|que /otɑ̃tik/ a. authentic. **~cité** n.f. authenticity.

auto /oto/ n.f. car. **~s tamponneuses**, dodgems, bumper cars.

auto- /oto/ préf. self-, auto-.

autobiographie /otɔbjɔgrafi/ *n.f.* autobiography.

autobus /otɔbys/ *n.m.* bus.

autocar /otɔkar/ *n.m.* coach.

autochtone /otɔktɔn/ *n.m./f.* native.

autocollant, ~e /otɔkɔlã, -t/ *a.* self-adhesive. ● *n.m.* sticker.

autocratique /otɔkratik/ *a.* autocratic.

autocuiseur /otɔkµizœr/ *n.* pressure cooker.

autodéfense /otodefãs/ *n.f.* self-defence.

autodidacte /otɔdidakt/ *a.* & *n.m./f.* self-taught (person).

auto-école /otɔekɔl/ *n.f.* driving school.

autographe /otɔgraf/ *n.m.* autograph.

automate /otɔmat/ *n.m.* automaton, robot.

automatique /otɔmatik/ *a.* automatic. **~ment** *adv.* automatically.

automat|iser /otɔmatize/ *v.t.* automate. **~ion** /-masjõ/ *n.f.* **~isation** *n.f.* automation.

automne /otɔn/ *n.m.* autumn; (*Amer.*) fall.

automobil|e /otɔmɔbil/ *a.* motor, car. ● *n.f.* (motor) car. **l'~e**, (*sport*) motoring. **~iste** *n.m./f.* motorist.

autonom|e /otɔnɔm/ *a.* autonomous. **~ie** *n.f.* autonomy.

autopsie /otɔpsi/ *n.f.* post-mortem, autopsy.

autoradio /otɔradjo/ *n.m.* car radio.

autorail /otɔraj/ *n.m.* railcar.

autorisation /otɔrizasjõ/ *n.f.* permission, authorization; (*permis*) permit.

autoris|er /otɔrize/ *v.t.* authorize, permit; (*rendre possible*) allow (of). **~é** *a.* (*opinions*) authoritative.

autoritaire /otɔriter/ *a.* authoritarian.

autorité /otɔrite/ *n.f.* authority. **faire ~**, be authoritative.

autoroute /otɔrut/ *n.f.* motorway; (*Amer.*) highway.

auto-stop /otɔstɔp/ *n.m.* hitch-hiking. **faire de l'~**, hitch-hike. **prendre en ~**, give a lift to. **~peur, ~peuse** *n.m.*, *f.* hitch-hiker.

autour /otur/ *adv.*, **~ de** *prép.* around. **tout ~**, all around.

autre /otr/ *a.* other. **un ~ jour/etc.**, another day/etc. ● *pron.* **un ~, une ~**, another (one). **l'~** the other

(one). **les ~s**, the others; (*autrui*) others. **d'~s**, (some) others. **l'un l'~**, each other. **l'un et l'~**, both of them. **~ chose/part**, sth./somewhere else. **qn./rien d'~**, s.o./nothing else. **quoi d'~?**, what else? **d'~ part**, on the other hand. **vous ~s Anglais**, you English. **d'un jour/etc. à l'~**, (*bientôt*) any day/etc. now. **entre ~s**, among other things.

autrefois /otrəfwa/ *adv.* in the past.

autrement /otrəmã/ *adv.* differently; (*sinon*) otherwise; (*plus*) far more. **~ dit**, in other words.

Autriche /otriʃ/ *n.f.* Austria.

autrichien, ~ne /otriʃjɛ̃, -jɛn/ *a.* & *n.m.*, *f.* Austrian.

autruche /otryʃ/ *n.f.* ostrich.

autrui /otrµi/ *pron.* others.

auvent /ovã/ *n.m.* canopy.

aux /o/ *voir* à.

auxiliaire /oksiljer/ *a.* auxiliary. ● *n.m./f.* (*assistant*) auxiliary. ● *n.m.* (*gram.*) auxiliary.

auxquel|s, ~les /okel/ *voir* lequel.

aval (en) /(ãn)aval/ *adv.* downstream.

avalanche /avalãʃ/ *n.f.* avalanche.

avaler /avale/ *v.t.* swallow.

avance /avãs/ *n.f.* advance; (*sur un concurrent*) lead. **~ (de fonds)**, advance. **à l'~, d'~**, in advance. **en ~**, early; (*montre*) fast. **en ~ (sur)**, (*menant*) ahead (of).

avancement /avãsmã/ *n.m.* promotion.

avanc|er /avãse/ *v.i.* move forward, advance; (*travail*) make progress; (*montre*) be fast; (*faire saillie*) jut out. ● *v.t.* (*argent*) advance; (*montre*) put forward. **s'~er** *v. pr.* move forward, advance; (*se hasarder*) commit o.s. **~é, ~ée** *a.* advanced; *n.f.* projection.

avanie /avani/ *n.f.* affront.

avant /avã/ *prép* & *adv.* before. ● *a. invar.* front. ● *n.m.* front; (*football*) forward. **~ de faire**, before doing. **~ qu'il (ne) fasse**, before he does. **en ~**, (*mouvement*) forward. **en ~ (de)**, (*position, temps*) in front (of). **~ peu**, before long. **~ tout**, above all. **bien ~ dans**, very deep(ly) *ou* far into. **~-bras** *n.m. invar.* forearm. **~-centre** *n.m.* centre-forward. **~-coureur** *a. invar.* precursory, foreshadowing. **~-dernier, ~-dernière** *a.* & *n.m.*, *f.* last but one. **~-garde** *n.f.* (*mil.*) vanguard; (*fig.*)

avant-garde. **~-goût** *n.m.* foretaste. **~-guerre** *n.f.* pre-war period. **~-hier** /-tjer/ *adv.* the day before yesterday. **~-poste** *n.m.* outpost. **~-première** *n.f.* preview. **~-propos** *n.m.* foreword. **~-veille** *n.f.* two days before.

avantag|e /avɑ̃taʒ/ *n.m.* advantage; (*comm.*) benefit. **~er** *v.t.* favour; (*embellir*) show off to advantage.

avantageu|x, ~se /avɑ̃taʒø, -z/ *a.* attractive.

avar|e /avar/ *a.* miserly. ● *n.m./f.* miser. **~e de**, sparing of. **~ice** *n.f.* avarice.

avarié /avarje/ *a.* (*aliment*) spoiled.

avaries /avari/ *n.f. pl.* damage.

avatar /avatar/ *n.m.* (*fam.*) misfortune.

avec /avɛk/ *prép.* with; (*envers*) towards. ● *adv.* (*fam.*) with it *ou* them.

avenant, ~e /avnɑ̃, -t/ *a.* pleasing.

avenant (à l') /(al)avnɑ̃/ *adv.* in a similar style.

avènement /avɛnmɑ̃/ *n.m.* advent; (*d'un roi*) accession.

avenir /avnir/ *n.m.* future. **à l'~,** in future. **d'~,** with (future) prospects.

aventur|e /avɑ̃tyr/ *n.f.* adventure; (*sentimentale*) affair. **~eux, ~euse** *a.* adventurous; (*hasardeux*) risky. **~ier, ~ière** *n.m., f.* adventurer.

aventurer (s') /(s)avɑ̃tyre/ *v. pr.* venture.

avenue /avny/ *n.f.* avenue.

avérer (s') /(s)avere/ *v. pr.* prove (to be).

averse /avɛrs/ *n.f.* shower.

aversion /avɛrsjɔ̃/ *n.f.* aversion.

avert|ir /avɛrtir/ *v.t.* inform; (*mettre en garde, menacer*) warn. **~i** *a.* informed. **~issement** *n.m.* warning.

avertisseur /avɛrtisœr/ *n.m.* (*auto.*) horn. **~ d'incendie**, fire-alarm.

aveu (*pl.* **~x**) /avø/ *n.m.* confession. **de l'~ de**, by the admission of.

aveugl|e /avœgl/ *a.* blind. ● *n.m./f.* blind man, blind woman. **~ement** *n.m.* blindness. **~ément** *adv.* blindly. **~er** *v.t.* blind.

aveuglette (à l') /(al)avœglɛt/ *adv.* (*à tâtons*) blindly.

avia|teur, ~trice /avjatœr, -tris/ *n.m., f.* aviator.

aviation /avjɑsjɔ̃/ *n.f.* flying; (*industrie*) aviation; (*mil.*) air force. **d'~,** air.

avid|e /avid/ *a.* greedy (**de**, for); (*anxieux*) eager (**de**, for). **~e de faire**, eager to do. **~ité** *n.f.* greed; eagerness.

avilir /avilir/ *v.t.* degrade.

avion /avjɔ̃/ *n.m.* plane, aeroplane, aircraft; (*Amer.*) airplane. **~ à réaction**, jet.

aviron /avirɔ̃/ *n.m.* oar. **l'~,** (*sport*) rowing.

avis /avi/ *n.m.* opinion; (*renseignement*) notification; (*comm.*) advice. **à mon ~,** in my opinion. **changer d'~,** change one's mind. **être d'~ que**, be of the opinion that.

avisé /avize/ *a.* sensible. **bien/mal ~ de**, well-/ill-advised to.

avis|er /avize/ *v.t.* notice; (*informer*) advise. ● *v.i.* decide what to do (**à**, about). **s'~ de**, suddenly realize. **s'~ de faire**, take it into one's head to do.

aviver /avive/ *v.t.* revive.

avocat¹, ~e /avɔka, -t/ *n.m., f.* barrister; (*Amer.*) attorney; (*fig.*) advocate. **~ de la défense**, counsel for the defence.

avocat² /avɔka/ *n.m.* (*fruit*) avocado (pear).

avoine /avwan/ *n.f.* oats.

avoir† /avwar/ *v. aux.* have. ● *v.t.* have; (*obtenir*) get; (*duper: fam.*) take in. ● *n.m.* assets. **je n'ai pas de café**, I haven't (got) any coffee; (*Amer.*) I don't have any coffee. **est-ce que tu as du café?**, have you (got) any coffee?; (*Amer.*) do you have any coffee? **~ à faire**, have to do. **tu n'as qu'à l'appeler**, all you have to do is call her. **~ chaud/faim/etc.**, be hot/hungry/etc. **~ dix/etc. ans**, be ten/etc. years old. **~ lieu**, take place. **~ lieu de**, have good reason to. **en ~ contre qn.,** have a grudge against s.o. **en ~ assez**, have had enough. **en ~ pour une minute/etc.**, be busy for a minute/etc. **il en a pour cent francs**, it will cost him one hundred francs. **qu'est-ce que vous avez?**, what is the matter with you? **on m'a eu!**, I've been had.

avoisin|er /avwazine/ *v.t.* border on. **~ant, ~ante** *a.* neighbouring.

avort|er /avɔrte/ *v.i.* (*projet etc.*) miscarry. **(se faire) ~er**, have an abortion. **~é** *a.* abortive. **~ement** *n.m.* (*méd.*) abortion.

avou|er /avwe/ v.t. confess (to). ● v.i. confess. **~é** a. avowed; n.m. solicitor; (Amer.) attorney.

avril /avril/ n.m. April.

axe /aks/ n.m. axis; (essieu) axle; (d'une politique) main line(s), basis. **~ (routier),** main road.

axer /akse/ v.t. centre.

axiome /aksjom/ n.m. axiom.

ayant /ɛjã/ voir avoir.

azimuts /azimyt/ n.m. pl. **dans tous les ~,** (fam.) all over the place.

azote /azɔt/ n.m. nitrogen.

azur /azyr/ n.m. sky-blue.

B

ba-ba /beaba/ n.m. **le ~ (de),** the basics (of).

baba /baba/ n.m. **~ (au rhum),** rum baba. **en rester ~,** (fam.) be flabbergasted.

babil /babi(l)/ n.m. babble. **~ler** /-ije/ v.i. babble.

babines /babin/ n.f. pl. **se lécher les ~,** lick one's chops.

babiole /babjɔl/ n.f. knick-knack.

bâbord /babɔr/ n.m. port (side).

babouin /babwɛ̃/ n.m. baboon.

baby-foot /babifut/ n.m. invar. table football.

baby-sitt|er /bebisitœr/ n.m./f. baby-sitter. **~ing** n.m. **faire du ~ing,** babysit.

bac [1] /bak/ n.m. = **baccalauréat.**

bac [2] /bak/ n.m. (bateau) ferry; (récipient) tub; (plus petit) tray.

baccalauréat /bakalɔrea/ n.m. school leaving certificate.

bâch|e /baʃ/ n.f. tarpaulin. **~er** v.t. cover (with a tarpaulin).

bachel|ier, ~ière /baʃəlje, -jɛr/ n.m., f. holder of the baccalauréat.

bachot /baʃo/ n.m. (fam.) = **baccalauréat. ~er** /-ɔte/ v.i. cram (for an exam).

bâcler /bakle/ v.t. botch (up).

bactérie /bakteri/ n.f. bacterium.

badaud, ~e /bado, -d/ n.m., f. (péj.) onlooker.

badigeon /badiʒɔ̃/ n.m. whitewash. **~ner** /-ɔne/ v.t. whitewash; (barbouiller) daub.

badin, ~e /badɛ̃, -in/ a. light-hearted.

badiner /badine/ v.i. joke (**sur, avec,** about).

badminton /badmintɔn/ n.m. badminton.

baffe /baf/ n.f. (fam.) slap.

baffle /bafl/ n.m. speaker.

bafouer /bafwe/ v.t. scoff at.

bafouiller /bafuje/ v.t./i. stammer.

bâfrer /bafre/ v.i. (fam.) gobble. **se ~** v.pr. stuff o.s.

bagage /bagaʒ/ n.m. bag; (fig.) (store of) knowledge. **~s,** luggage, baggage. **~s à main,** hand luggage.

bagarr|e /bagar/ n.f. fight. **~er** v.i., **se ~er** v. pr. fight.

bagatelle /bagatɛl/ n.f. trifle; (somme) trifling amount.

bagnard /baɲar/ n.m. convict.

bagnole /baɲɔl/ n.f. (fam.) car.

bagou(t) /bagu/ n.m. **avoir du ~,** have the gift of the gab.

bagu|e /bag/ n.f. (anneau) ring. **~er** v.t. ring.

baguette /bagɛt/ n.f. stick; (de chef d'orchestre) baton; (chinoise) chopstick; (magique) wand; (pain) stick of bread. **~ de tambour,** drumstick.

baie /bɛ/ n.f. (géog.) bay; (fruit) berry. **~ (vitrée),** picture window.

baign|er /beɲe/ v.t. bathe; (enfant) bath. ● v.i. **~er dans,** soak in; (être enveloppé dans) be steeped in. **se ~er** v. pr. go swimming (ou) bathing. **~é de,** bathed in; (sang) soaked in. **~ade** /beɲad/ n.f. bathing, swimming. **~eur, ~euse** /beɲœr, -øz/ n.m., f. bather.

baignoire /beɲwar/ n.f. bath(-tub).

bail (pl. **baux** /baj, bo/ n.m. lease.

bâill|er /baje/ v.i. yawn; (être ouvert) gape. **~ement** n.m. yawn.

bailleur /bajœr/ n.m. **~ de fonds,** (comm.) backer.

bâillon /bajɔ̃/ n.m. gag. **~ner** /bajone/ v.t. gag.

bain /bɛ̃/ n.m. bath; (de mer) bathe. **~(s) de soleil,** sunbathing. **~-marie** (pl. **~s-marie**) n.m. double boiler. **~ de bouche,** mouthwash. **mettre qn. dans le ~,** (compromettre) drop s.o. in it; (au courant) put s.o. in the picture. **se remettre dans le ~,** get back into the swim of things. **prendre un ~ de foule,** mingle with the crowd.

baiser /beze/ n.m. kiss. ● v.t. (main) kiss; (fam.) screw.

baisse /bɛs/ n.f. fall, drop. **en ~,** falling.

baisser /bese/ *v.t.* lower; (*radio, lampe, etc.*) turn down. ● *v.i.* go down, fall; (*santé, forces*) fail. **se ~** *v. pr.* bend down.

bajoues /baʒu/ *n.f. pl.* chops.

bakchich /bakʃiʃ/ *n.m.* (*fam.*) bribe.

bal (*pl.* **~s**) /bal/ *n.m.* dance; (*habillé*) ball; (*lieu*) dance-hall. **~ costumé**, fancy-dress ball.

balad|**e** /balad/ *n.f.* stroll; (*en auto*) drive. **~er** *v.t.* take for a stroll. **se ~er** *v. pr.* (go for a) stroll; (*excursionner*) wander around. **se ~er (en auto)**, go for a drive.

baladeur /baladœr/ *n.m.* personal stereo.

balafr|**e** /balafr/ *n.f.* gash; (*cicatrice*) scar. **~er** *v.t.* gash.

balai /bale/ *n.m.* broom. **~-brosse** *n.m.* garden broom.

balance /balɑ̃s/ *n.f.* scales. **la B~**, Libra.

balancer /balɑ̃se/ *v.t.* swing; (*doucement*) sway; (*lancer: fam.*) chuck; (*se débarrasser de: fam.*) chuck out. ● *v.i.*, **se ~** *v. pr.* swing; sway. **se ~ de**, (*fam.*) not care about.

balancier /balɑ̃sje/ *n.m.* (*d'horloge*) pendulum; (*d'équilibriste*) pole.

balançoire /balɑ̃swar/ *n.f.* swing; (*bascule*) see-saw.

balay|**er** /baleje/ *v.t.* sweep (up); (*chasser*) sweep away; (*se débarrasser de*) sweep aside. **~age** *n.m.* sweeping; (*cheveux*) highlights. **~eur, ~euse** *n.m., f.* road sweeper.

balbut|**ier** /balbysje/ *v.t./i.* stammer. **~iement** *n.m.* stammering.

balcon /balkɔ̃/ *n.m.* balcony; (*théâtre*) dress circle.

baleine /balɛn/ *n.f.* whale.

balis|**e** /baliz/ *n.f.* beacon; (*bouée*) buoy; (*auto.*) (road) sign. **~er** *v.t.* mark out (with beacons); (*route*) signpost.

balistique /balistik/ *a.* ballistic.

balivernes /balivɛrn/ *n.f. pl.* balderdash.

ballade /balad/ *n.f.* ballad.

ballant, ~e /balɑ̃, -t/ *a.* dangling.

ballast /balast/ *n.m.* ballast.

balle /bal/ *n.f.* (*projectile*) bullet; (*sport*) ball; (*paquet*) bale.

ballerine /balrin/ *n.f.* ballerina.

ballet /balɛ/ *n.m.* ballet.

ballon /balɔ̃/ *n.m.* balloon; (*sport*) ball. **~ de football**, football.

ballonné /balɔne/ *a.* bloated.

ballot /balo/ *n.m.* bundle; (*nigaud: fam.*) idiot.

ballottage /balɔtaʒ/ *n.m.* second ballot (*due to indecisive result*).

ballotter /balɔte/ *v.t./i.* shake about, toss.

balnéaire /balneɛr/ *a.* seaside.

balourd, ~e /balur, -d/ *n.m., f.* oaf. ● *a.* oafish.

balustrade /balystrad/ *n.f.* railing(s).

bambin /bɑ̃bɛ̃/ *n.m.* tot.

bambou /bɑ̃bu/ *n.m.* bamboo.

ban /bɑ̃/ *n.m.* round of applause. **~s**, (*de mariage*) banns. **mettre au ~ de**, cast out from. **publier les ~s**, have the banns called.

banal (*m. pl.* **~s**) /banal/ *a.* commonplace, banal. **~ité** *n.f.* banality.

banane /banan/ *n.f.* banana.

banc /bɑ̃/ *n.m.* bench; (*de poissons*) shoal. **~ des accusés**, dock. **~ d'essai**, test bed; (*fig.*) testing-ground.

bancaire /bɑ̃kɛr/ *a.* banking; (*chèque*) bank.

bancal (*m. pl.* **~s**) /bɑ̃kal/ *a.* wobbly; (*raisonnement*) shaky.

bandage /bɑ̃daʒ/ *n.m.* bandage. **~ herniaire**, truss.

bande[1] /bɑ̃d/ *n.f.* (*de papier etc.*) strip; (*rayure*) stripe; (*de film*) reel; (*radio*) band; (*pansement*) bandage. **~ (magnétique)**, tape. **~ dessinée**, comic strip. **~ sonore**, sound-track. **par la ~**, indirectly.

bande[2] /bɑ̃d/ *n.f.* (*groupe*) bunch, band, gang.

bandeau (*pl.* **~x**) /bɑ̃do/ *n.m.* headband; (*sur les yeux*) blindfold.

bander /bɑ̃de/ *v.t.* bandage; (*arc*) bend; (*muscle*) tense. **~ les yeux à**, blindfold.

banderole /bɑ̃drɔl/ *n.f.* banner.

bandit /bɑ̃di/ *n.m.* bandit. **~isme** /-tism/ *n.m.* crime.

bandoulière (en) /(ɑ̃)bɑ̃duljɛr/ *adv.* across one's shoulder.

banjo /bɑ̃(d)ʒo/ *n.m.* banjo.

banlieu|**e** /bɑ̃ljø/ *n.f.* suburbs. **de ~e**, suburban. **~sard, ~sarde** /-zar, -zard/ *n.m., f.* (suburban) commuter.

bannière /banjɛr/ *n.f.* banner.

bannir /banir/ *v.t.* banish.

banque /bɑ̃k/ *n.f.* bank; (*activité*) banking. **~ d'affaires**, merchant bank.

banqueroute /bɑ̃krut/ *n.f.* (*fraudulent*) bankruptcy.

banquet /bɑ̃kɛ/ n.m. dinner; (fastueux) banquet.

banquette /bɑ̃kɛt/ n.f. seat.

banquier /bɑ̃kje/ n.m. banker.

bapt|ême /batɛm/ n.m. baptism; christening. **~iser** v.t. baptize, christen; (appeler) christen.

baquet /bakɛ/ n.m. tub.

bar /bar/ n.m. (lieu) bar.

baragouin /baragwɛ̃/ n.m. gibberish, gabble. **~er** /-wine/ v.t./i. gabble; (langue) speak a few words of.

baraque /barak/ n.f. hut, shed; (boutique) stall; (maison: fam.) house. **~ments** n.m. pl. huts.

baratin /baratɛ̃/ n.m. (fam.) sweet ou smooth talk. **~er** /-ine/ v.t. (fam.) chat up; (Amer.) sweet-talk.

barbar|e /barbar/ a. barbaric. ● n.m./f. barbarian. **~ie** n.f. (cruauté) barbarity.

barbe /barb/ n.f. beard. **~ à papa**, candy-floss; (Amer.) cotton candy. **la ~!**, (fam.) blast (it)! **quelle ~!**, (fam.) what a bore!

barbecue /barbəkju/ n.m. barbecue.

barbelé /barbəle/ a. **fil ~**, barbed wire.

barber /barbe/ v.t. (fam.) bore.

barbiche /barbiʃ/ n.f. goatee.

barbiturique /barbityrik/ n.m. barbiturate.

barboter¹ /barbɔte/ v.i. paddle, splash.

barboter² /barbɔte/ v.t. (voler: fam.) pinch.

barbouill|er /barbuje/ v.t. (peindre) daub; (souiller) smear; (griffonner) scribble. **avoir l'estomac ~é ou se sentir ~é** feel liverish.

barbu /barby/ a. bearded.

barda /barda/ n.m. (fam.) gear.

barder /barde/ v.i. **ça va ~**, (fam.) sparks will fly.

barème /barɛm/ n.m. list, table; (échelle) scale.

baril /baril/ n.m. barrel; (de poudre) keg.

bariolé /barjɔle/ a. motley.

barman /barman/ n.m. barman; (Amer.) bartender.

baromètre /barɔmɛtr/ n.m. barometer.

baron, ~ne /barɔ̃, -ɔn/ n.m., f. baron, baroness.

baroque /barɔk/ a. (fig.) weird; (archit., art) baroque.

baroud /barud/ n.m. **~ d'honneur**, gallant last fight.

barque /bark/ n.f. (small) boat.

barrage /baraʒ/ n.m. dam; (sur route) road-block.

barre /bar/ n.f. bar; (trait) line, stroke; (naut.) helm.

barreau (pl. ~x) /baro/ n.m. bar; (d'échelle) rung. **le ~**, (jurid.) the bar.

barrer /bare/ v.t. block; (porte) bar; (rayer) cross out; (naut.) steer. **se ~** v. pr. (fam.) hop it.

barrette /barɛt/ n.f. (hair-)slide.

barricad|e /barikad/ n.f. barricade. **~er** v.t. barricade. **se ~er** v. pr. barricade o.s.

barrière /barjɛr/ n.f. (porte) gate; (clôture) fence; (obstacle) barrier.

barrique /barik/ n.f. barrel.

baryton /baritɔ̃/ n.m. baritone.

bas, basse /bɑ, bɑs/ a. low; (action) base. ● n.m. bottom; (chaussette) stocking. ● n.f. (mus.) bass. ● adv. low. **à ~**, down with. **au ~ mot**, at the lowest estimate. **en ~**, down below; (dans une maison) downstairs. **en ~ âge**, young. **en ~ de**, at the bottom of. **plus ~**, further ou lower down. **~-côté** n.m. (de route) verge; (Amer.) shoulder. **~ de casse** n.m. invar. lower case. **~ de laine**, nest-egg. **~-fonds** n.m. pl. (eau) shallows; (fig.) dregs. **~ morceaux**, (viande) cheap cuts. **~-relief** n.m. low relief. **~-ventre** n.m. lower abdomen. **mettre ~**, give birth (to).

basané /bazane/ a. tanned.

bascule /baskyl/ n.f. (balance) scales. **cheval/fauteuil à ~**, rocking-horse/-chair.

basculer /baskyle/ v.t./i. topple over; (benne) tip up.

base /bɑz/ n.f. base; (fondement) basis; (pol.) rank and file. **de ~**, basic.

baser /bɑze/ v.t. base. **se ~ sur**, base o.s. on.

basilic /bazilik/ n.m. basil.

basilique /bazilik/ n.f. basilica.

basket(-ball) /baskɛt(bol)/ n.m. basketball.

basque /bask/ a. & n.m./f. Basque.

basse /bɑs/ voir bas.

basse-cour (pl. **basses-cours**) /baskur/ n.f. farmyard.

bassement /bɑsmɑ̃/ adv. basely.

bassesse /bɑsɛs/ n.f. baseness; (action) base act.

bassin /basɛ̃/ n.m. bowl; (*pièce d'eau*) pond; (*rade*) dock; (*géog.*) basin; (*anat.*) pelvis. ~ **houiller**, coalfield.

basson /basɔ̃/ n.m. bassoon.

bastion /bastjɔ̃/ n.m. bastion.

bat /ba/ *voir* battre.

bât /bɑ/ n.m. là où le ~ **blesse**, where the shoe pinches.

bataill|e /batɑj/ n.f. battle; (*fig.*) fight. ~**er** v.i. fight.

bataillon /batɑjɔ̃/ n.m. battalion.

bâtard, ~**e** /batar, -d/ n.m., f. bastard. ● a. (*solution*) hybrid.

bateau (pl. ~**x**) /bato/ n.m. boat. ~-**mouche** (pl. ~**x-mouches**) n.m. sightseeing boat.

bâti /bɑti/ a. **bien** ~, well-built.

batifoler /batifole/ v.i. fool about.

bâtiment /bɑtimɑ̃/ n.m. building; (*navire*) vessel; (*industrie*) building trade.

bâtir /bɑtir/ v.t. build; (*coudre*) baste.

bâtisse /bɑtis/ n.f. (*péj.*) building.

bâton /bɑtɔ̃/ n.m. stick. **à** ~**s rompus**, jumping from subject to subject. ~ **de rouge**, lipstick.

battage /bataʒ/ n.m. (*publicité*: *fam.*) (hard) plugging.

battant /batɑ̃/ n.m. (*vantail*) flap. **porte à deux** ~**s**, double door.

battement /batmɑ̃/ n.m. (*de cœur*) beat(ing); (*temps*) interval.

batterie /batri/ n.f. (*mil.*, *électr.*) battery; (*mus.*) drums. ~ **de cuisine**, pots and pans.

batteur /batœr/ n.m. (*mus.*) drummer; (*culin.*) whisk.

battre† /batr/ v.t./i. beat; (*blé*) thresh; (*cartes*) shuffle; (*parcourir*) scour; (*faire du bruit*) bang. **se** ~ v. pr. fight. ~ **des ailes**, flap its wings. ~ **des mains**, clap. ~ **en retraite**, beat a retreat. ~ **la semelle**, stamp one's feet. ~ **pavillon britannique/** *etc.*, fly the British/*etc.* flag. ~ **son plein**, be in full swing.

battue /baty/ n.f. (*chasse*) beat; (*de police*) search.

baume /bom/ n.m. balm.

bavard, ~**e** /bavar, -d/ a. talkative. ● n.m., f. chatterbox.

bavard|er /bavarde/ v.i. chat; (*jacasser*) chatter, gossip. ~**age** n.m. chatter, gossip.

bav|e /bav/ n.f. dribble, slobber; (*de limace*) slime. ~**er** v.i. dribble, slobber. ~**eux**, ~**euse** a. dribbling; (*omelette*) runny.

bav|ette /bavɛt/ n.f., ~**oir** n.m. bib. **tailler une** ~**ette**, (*fam.*) have a chat.

bavure /bavyr/ n.f. smudge; (*erreur*) mistake. ~ **policière**, (*fam.*)police cock-up. **sans** ~, flawless(ly).

bazar /bazar/ n.m. bazaar; (*objets*: *fam.*) clutter.

bazarder /bazarde/ v.t. (*vendre*: *fam.*) get rid of, flog.

BCBG abrév. (*bon chic bon genre*) posh.

BD abrév. (*bande dessinée*) comic strip.

béant, ~**e** /beɑ̃, -t/ a. gaping.

béat, ~**e** /bea, -t/ a. (*hum.*) blissful; (*péj.*) smug. ~**itude** /-tityd/ n.f. (*hum.*) bliss.

beau *ou* **bel***, **belle** (m. pl. ~**x**) /bo, bɛl/ a. fine, beautiful; (*femme*) beautiful; (*homme*) handsome; (*grand*) big. ● n.f. beauty; (*sport*) deciding game. **au** ~ **milieu**, right in the middle. **bel et bien**, well and truly. **de plus belle**, more than ever. **faire le** ~, sit up and beg. **on a** ~ **essayer/insister/**etc., however much one tries/insists/*etc.*, it is no use trying/insisting/*etc.* ~**x-arts** n.m. pl. fine arts. ~**x-fils** (pl. ~**x-fils**) n.m. son-in-law; (*remariage*) stepson. ~**-frère** (pl. ~**x-frères**) n.m. brother-in-law. ~**-père** (pl. ~**x-pères**) n.m. father-in-law; stepfather. ~**x-parents** n.m. pl. parents-in-law.

beaucoup /boku/ adv. a lot, very much. ● pron. many (people). ~ **de**, (*nombre*) many; (*quantité*) a lot of. **pas** ~ **(de)**, not many; (*quantité*) not much. ~ **plus/**etc., much more/*etc.* ~ **trop**, much too much. **de** ~, by far.

beauté /bote/ n.f. beauty. **en** ~, magnificently. **tu es en** ~, you are looking good.

bébé /bebe/ n.m. baby. ~**-éprouvette**, test-tube baby.

bec /bɛk/ n.m. beak; (*de plume*) nib; (*de bouilloire*) spout; (*de casserole*) lip; (*bouche*: fam.) mouth. ~**-de-cane** (pl. ~**s-de-cane**) door-handle. ~ **de gaz**, gas lamp (*in street*).

bécane /bekan/ n.f. (*fam.*) bike.

bécasse /bekɑs/ n.f. woodcock.

bêche /bɛʃ/ n.f. spade.

bêcher /beʃe/ v.t. dig.

bécoter /bekɔte/ v.t., **se** ~ v. pr. (*fam.*) kiss.

becquée /beke/ *n.f.* **donner la ~ à,** (*oiseau*) feed; (*fig.*) spoonfeed.

bedaine /bədɛn/ *n.f.* paunch.

bedeau (*pl.* **~x**) /bədo/ *n.m.* beadle.

bedonnant, ~e /bədɔnɑ̃, -t/ *a.* paunchy.

beffroi /befrwa/ *n.m.* belfry.

bégayer /begeje/ *v.t./i.* stammer.

bègue /bɛg/ *n.m./f.* stammerer. **être ~,** stammer.

bégueule /begœl/ *a.* prudish.

béguin /begɛ̃/ *n.m.* **avoir le ~ pour,** (*fam.*) have a crush on.

beige /bɛʒ/ *a.* & *n.m.* beige.

beignet /bɛɲɛ/ *n.m.* fritter.

bel /bɛl/ *voir* beau.

bêler /bele/ *v.i.* bleat.

belette /bəlɛt/ *n.f.* weasel.

belge /bɛlʒ/ *a.* & *n.m./f.* Belgian.

Belgique /bɛlʒik/ *n.f.* Belgium.

bélier /belje/ *n.m.* ram. **le B~,** Aries.

belle /bɛl/ *voir* beau.

belle-fille (*pl.* **~s-filles**) /bɛlfij/ *n.f.* daughter-in-law; (*remariage*) stepdaughter. **~-mère** (*pl.* **~s-mères**) *n.f.* mother-in-law; stepmother. **~-sœur** (*pl.* **~-sœurs**) *n.f.* sister-in-law.

belligérant, ~e /beliʒerɑ̃, -t/ *a.* & *n.m.* belligerent.

belliqueu|x, ~se /belikø, -z/ *a.* warlike.

belote /bəlɔt/ *n.f.* belote (*card game*).

belvédère /bɛlvedɛr/ *n.m.* (*lieu*) viewing spot, viewpoint.

bémol /bemɔl/ *n.m.* (*mus.*) flat.

bénédiction /benediksjɔ̃/ *n.f.* blessing.

bénéfice /benefis/ *n.m.* (*gain*) profit; (*avantage*) benefit.

bénéficiaire /benefisjɛr/ *n.m./f.* beneficiary.

bénéficier /benefisje/ *v.i.* **~ de,** benefit from; (*jouir de*) enjoy, have.

bénéfique /benefik/ *a.* beneficial.

Bénélux /benelyks/ *n.m.* Benelux.

benêt /bənɛ/ *n.m.* simpleton.

bénévole /benevɔl/ *a.* voluntary.

bén|in, ~igne /benɛ̃, -iɲ/ *a.* mild, slight; (*tumeur*) benign.

bén|ir /benir/ *v.t.* bless. **~it, ~ite** *a.* (*eau*) holy; (*pain*) consecrated.

bénitier /benitje/ *n.m.* stoup.

benjamin, ~e /bɛ̃ʒamɛ̃, -in/ *n.m.*, *f.* youngest child.

benne /bɛn/ *n.f.* (*de grue*) scoop; (*amovible*) skip. **~ (basculante),** dump truck.

benzine /bɛ̃zin/ *n.f.* benzine.

béotien, ~ne /beɔsjɛ̃, -jɛn/ *n.m.*, *f.* philistine.

béquille /bekij/ *n.f.* crutch; (*de moto*) stand.

bercail /bɛrkaj/ *n.m.* fold.

berceau (*pl.* **~x**) /bɛrso/ *n.m.* cradle.

bercer /bɛrse/ *v.t.* (*balancer*) rock; (*apaiser*) lull; (*leurrer*) delude.

berceuse /bɛrsøz/ *n.f.* lullaby.

béret /berɛ/ *n.m.* beret.

berge /bɛrʒ/ *n.f.* (*bord*) bank.

berg|er, ~ère /bɛrʒe, -ɛr/ *n.m.*, *f.* shepherd, shepherdess. **~erie** *n.f.* sheep-fold.

berlingot /bɛrlɛ̃go/ *n.m.* boiled sweet; (*emballage*) carton.

berne (en) /(ɑ̃)bɛrn/ *adv.* at half-mast.

berner /bɛrne/ *v.t.* hoodwink.

besogne /bəzɔɲ/ *n.f.* task, job, chore.

besoin /bəzwɛ̃/ *n.m.* need. **avoir ~ de,** need. **au ~,** if need be.

best|ial (*m. pl.* **~iaux**) /bɛstjal, -jo/ *a.* bestial.

bestiaux /bɛstjo/ *n.m. pl.* livestock.

bestiole /bɛstjɔl/ *n.f.* creepy-crawly.

bétail /betaj/ *n.m.* farm animals.

bête[1] /bɛt/ *n.f.* animal. **~ noire,** pet hate, pet peeve. **~ sauvage,** wild beast. **chercher la petite ~,** be overfussy.

bête[2] /bɛt/ *a.* stupid. **~ment** *adv.* stupidly.

bêtise /betiz/ *n.f.* stupidity; (*action*) stupid thing.

béton /betɔ̃/ *n.m.* concrete. **~ armé,** reinforced concrete. **~nière** /-ɔnjɛr/ *n.f.* cement-mixer, concrete-mixer.

betterave /bɛtrav/ *n.f.* beetroot. **~ sucrière,** sugar-beet.

beugler /bøgle/ *v.i.* bellow, low; (*radio*) blare.

beur /bœr/ *n.m./f.* & *a.* (*fam.*) young French North African.

beurr|e /bœr/ *n.m.* butter. **~er** *v.t.* butter. **~ier** *n.m.* butter-dish. **~é,** *a.* buttered; (*fam.*) drunk.

bévue /bevy/ *n.f.* blunder.

biais /bjɛ/ *n.m.* (*fig.*) expedient; (*côté*) angle. **de ~, en ~,** at an angle. **de ~,** (*fig.*) indirectly.

biaiser /bjeze/ *v.i.* hedge.

bibelot /biblo/ *n.m.* curio.

biberon /bibrɔ̃/ *n.m.* (*feeding-*) bottle. **nourrir au ~,** bottle-feed.

bible /bibl/ *n.f.* bible. **la B~,** the Bible.

bibliographie /biblijɔgrafi/ *n.f.* bibliography.

bibliophile /biblijɔfil/ *n.m./f.* book-lover.

biblioth|èque /biblijɔtɛk/ *n.f.* library; (*meuble*) bookcase; **~écaire** *n.m./f.* librarian.

biblique /biblik/ *a.* biblical.

bic /bik/ *n.m.* (P.) biro (P.).

bicarbonate /bikarbɔnat/ *n.m.* **~ (de soude)**, bicarbonate (of soda).

biceps /bisɛps/ *n.m.* biceps.

biche /biʃ/ *n.f.* doe.

bichonner /biʃɔne/ *v.t.* doll up.

bicoque /bikɔk/ *n.f.* shack.

bicyclette /bisiklɛt/ *n.f.* bicycle.

bide /bid/ *n.m.* (*ventre: fam.*) belly; (*théâtre: fam.*) flop.

bidet /bidɛ/ *n.m.* bidet.

bidon /bidɔ̃/ *n.m.* can. ● *a. invar.* (*fam.*) phoney. **c'est pas du ~**, (*fam.*) it's the truth, for real.

bidonville /bidɔ̃vil/ *n.f.* shanty town.

bidule /bidyl/ *n.m.* (*fam.*) thing.

bielle /bjɛl/ *n.f.* connecting rod.

bien /bjɛ̃/ *adv.* well; (*très*) quite, very. ● *n.m.* good; (*patrimoine*) possession. ● *a. invar.* good; (*passable*) all right; (*en forme*) well; (*à l'aise*) comfortable; (*beau*) attractive; (*respectable*) nice, respectable. ● *conj.* **~ que**, (al)though. **~ soit/que ça ait**, although it is/it has. **~ du**, (*quantité*) a lot of, much. **~ des**, (*nombre*) many. **il l'a ~ fait**, (*intensif*) he did it. **ce n'est pas ~ de**, it is not right to. **~ sûr**, of course. **~s de consommation**, consumer goods. **~-aimé**, **~aimée** *a.* & *n.m.*, *f.* beloved. **~-être** *n.m.* well-being. **~-fondé** *n.m.* soundness. **~-pensant**, **~-pensante** *a.* & *n.m.*, *f.* (*péj.*) right-thinking.

bienfaisan|t, **-te** /bjɛ̃fəzɑ̃, -t/ *a.* beneficial. **~ce** *n.f.* charity. **fête de ~ce**, fête.

bienfait /bjɛ̃fɛ/ *n.m.* (kind) favour; (*avantage*) benefit.

bienfai|teur, **~trice** /bjɛ̃fɛtœr, -tris/ *n.m.*, *f.* benefactor.

bienheureu|x, **~se** /bjɛ̃nœrø, -z/ *a.* happy, blessed.

bienséan|t, **~te** /bjɛ̃seɑ̃, -t/ *a.* proper. **~ce** *n.f.* propriety.

bientôt /bjɛ̃to/ *adv.* soon. **à ~**, see you soon.

bienveillan|t, **~te** /bjɛ̃vɛjɑ̃, -t/ *a.* kind(ly). **~ce** *n.f.* kind(li)ness.

bienvenu, **~e** /bjɛ̃vny/ *a.* welcome. ● *n.f.* welcome. ● *n.m.*, *f.* **être le ~**,

être la ~e, be welcome. **souhaiter la ~e à**, welcome.

bière /bjɛr/ *n.f.* beer; (*cercueil*) coffin. **~ blonde**, lager. **~ brune**, stout, brown ale. **~ pression**, draught beer.

biffer /bife/ *v.t.* cross out.

bifteck /biftɛk/ *n.m.* steak.

bifur|quer /bifyrke/ *v.i.* branch off, fork. **~cation** *n.f.* fork, junction.

bigam|e /bigam/ *a.* bigamous. ● *n.m./f.* bigamist. **~ie** *n.f.* bigamy.

bigarré /bigare/ *a.* motley.

big-bang /bigbɑ̃g/ *n.m.* big bang.

bigot, **~e** /bigo, -ɔt/ *n.m.*, *f.* religious fanatic. ● *a.* over-pious.

bigoudi /bigudi/ *n.m.* curler.

bijou (*pl.* **~x**) /biʒu/ *n.m.* jewel. **~terie** *n.f.* (*boutique*) jeweller's shop; (*comm.*) jewellery. **~tier**, **~tière** *n.m.*, *f.* jeweller.

bikini /bikini/ *n.m.* bikini.

bilan /bilɑ̃/ *n.m.* outcome; (*d'une catastrophe*) (casualty) toll; (*comm.*) balance sheet. **faire le ~ de**, assess. **~ de santé**, check-up.

bile /bil/ *n.f.* bile. **se faire de la ~**, (*fam.*) worry.

bilieu|x, **~se** /biljø, -z/ *a.* bilious; (*fig.*) irascible.

bilingue /bilɛ̃g/ *a.* bilingual.

billard /bijar/ *n.m.* billiards; (*table*) billiard-table.

bille /bij/ *n.f.* (*d'enfant*) marble; (*de billard*) billiard-ball.

billet /bijɛ/ *n.m.* ticket; (*lettre*) note; (*article*) column. **~ (de banque)**, (bank)note. **~ d'aller et retour**, return ticket; (*Amer.*) round trip ticket. **~ de faveur**, complimentary ticket. **~ aller simple**, single ticket; (*Amer.*) one-way ticket.

billetterie /bijɛtri/ *n.f.* cash dispenser.

billion /biljɔ̃/ *n.m.* billion (= 10^{12}); (*Amer.*) trillion.

billot /bijo/ *n.m.* block.

bimensuel, **~le** /bimɑ̃sɥɛl/ *a.* fortnightly, bimonthly.

bin|er /bine/ *v.t.* hoe. **~ette** *n.f.* hoe; (*fam.*) face.

biochimie /bjoʃimi/ *n.f.* biochemistry.

biodégradable /bjodegradabl/ *a.* biodegradable.

biograph|ie /bjografi/ *n.f.* biography. **~e** *n.m./f.* biographer.

biolog|ie /bjɔlɔʒi/ *n.f.* biology. **~ique** *a.* biological. **~iste** *n.m./f.* biologist.

bipède /bipɛd/ *n.m.* biped.

bis [1], **bise** /bi, biz/ *a.* greyish brown.

bis [2] /bis/ *a.invar.* (*numéro*) A, a. ● *n.m. & int.* encore.

bisbille (en) /(ɑ̃)bisbij/ *adv.* (*fam.*) at loggerheads (**avec**, with).

biscornu /biskɔrny/ *a.* crooked; (*bizarre*) weird.

biscotte /biskɔt/ *n.f.* rusk.

biscuit /biskɥi/ *n.m.* (*salé*) biscuit; (*Amer.*) cracker; (*sucré*) biscuit; (*Amer.*) cookie. **~ de Savoie**, sponge-cake.

bise [1] /biz/ *n.f.* (*fam.*) kiss.

bise [2] /biz/ *n.f.* (*vent*) north wind.

bison /bizɔ̃/ *n.m.* (American) buffalo, bison.

bisou /bizu/ *n.m.* (*fam.*) kiss.

bisser /bise/ *v.t.* encore.

bistouri /bisturi/ *n.m.* lancet.

bistre /bistr/ *a. & n.m.* blackish brown.

bistro(t) /bistro/ *n.m.* café, bar.

bit /bit/ *n.m.* (*comput.*) bit.

bitume /bitym/ *n.m.* asphalt.

bizarre /bizar/ *a.* odd, peculiar. **~ment** *adv.* oddly. **~rie** *n.f.* peculiarity.

blafard, **~e** /blafar, -d/ *a.* pale.

blagu|e /blag/ *n.f.* joke. **~ à tabac**, tobacco-pouch. **~er** *v.i.* joke; *v.t.* tease. **~eur**, **~euse** *n.m.*, *f.* joker; *a.* jokey.

blaireau (*pl.* **~x**) /blɛro/ *n.m.* shaving-brush; (*animal*) badger.

blâm|e /blɑm/ *n.m.* rebuke, blame. **~able** *a.* blameworthy. **~er** *v.t.* rebuke, blame.

blanc, **blanche** /blɑ̃, blɑ̃ʃ/ *a.* white; (*papier*, *page*) blank. ● *n.m.* white; (*espace*) blank. ● *n.m.*, *f.* white man, white woman. ● *n.f.* (*mus.*) minim. **~ (de poulet)**, breast, white meat (of the chicken). **le ~**, (*linge*) whites. **laisser en ~**, leave blank.

blancheur /blɑ̃ʃœr/ *n.f.* whiteness.

blanch|ir /blɑ̃ʃir/ *v.t.* whiten; (*linge*) launder; (*personne*: *fig.*) clear; (*culin.*) blanch. **~ir (à la chaux)**, whitewash. ● *v.i.* turn white. **~issage** *n.m.* laundering. **~isserie** *n.f.* laundry. **~isseur**, **~isseuse** *n.m.*, *f.* laundryman, laundress.

blasé /blaze/ *a.* blasé.

blason /blazɔ̃/ *n.m.* coat of arms.

blasph|ème /blasfɛm/ *n.m.* blasphemy. **~ématoire** *a.* blasphemous. **~émer** *v.t./i.* blaspheme.

blatte /blat/ *n.f.* cockroach.

blazer /blɛzœr/ *n.m.* blazer.

blé /ble/ *n.m.* wheat.

bled /blɛd/ *n.m.* (*fam.*) dump, hole.

blême /blɛm/ *a.* (sickly) pale.

bless|er /blese/ *v.t.* wound, hurt; (*par balle*) wound; (*offenser*) hurt, wound. **se ~er** *v. pr.* injure ou hurt o.s. **~ant**, **~ante** /blɛsɑ̃, -t/ *a.* hurtful. **~é**, **~ée** *n.m.*, *f.* casualty, injured person.

blessure /blesyr/ *n.f.* wound.

blet, **~te** /blɛ, blɛt/ *a.* over-ripe.

bleu /blø/ *a.* blue; (*culin.*) very rare. **~ marine**, navy blue. ● *n.m.* blue; (*contusion*) bruise. **~(s)**, (*vêtement*) overalls. **~ir** *v.t./i.* turn blue.

bleuet /bløɛ/ *n.m.* cornflower.

bleuté /bløte/ *a.* slightly blue.

blind|er /blɛ̃de/ *v.t.* armour (-plate); (*fig.*) harden. **~é** *a.* armoured; (*fig.*) immune (**contre**, to); *n.m.* armoured car, tank.

blizzard /blizar/ *n.m.* blizzard.

bloc /blɔk/ *n.m.* block; (*de papier*) pad; (*système*) unit; (*pol.*) bloc. **à ~**, hard, tight. **en ~**, all together. **~-notes** (*pl.* **~s-notes**) *n.m.* note-pad.

blocage /blɔkaʒ/ *n.m.* (*des prix*) freeze, freezing; (*des roues*) locking; (*psych.*) block.

blocus /blɔkys/ *n.m.* blockade.

blond, **~e** /blɔ̃, -d/ *a.* fair, blond. ● *n.m.*, *f.* fair-haired ou blond man ou woman. **~eur** /-dœr/ *n.f.* fairness.

bloqu|er /blɔke/ *v.t.* block; (*porte, machine*) jam; (*freins*) slam on; (*roues*) lock; (*prix, crédits*) freeze; (*grouper*) put together. **se ~** *v. pr.* jam; (*roues*) lock.

blottir (se) /(sə)blɔtir/ *v. pr.* snuggle, huddle.

blouse /bluz/ *n.f.* smock.

blouson /bluzɔ̃/ *n.m.* lumber-jacket; (*Amer.*) windbreaker.

blue-jean /bludʒin/ *n.m.* jeans.

bluff /blœf/ *n.m.* bluff. **~er** *v.t./i.* bluff.

blush /blœʃ/ *n.m.* blusher.

boa /bɔa/ *n.m.* boa.

bobard /bɔbar/ *n.m.* (*fam.*) fib.

bobine /bɔbin/ *n.f.* reel; (*sur machine*) spool; (*électr.*) coil.

bobo /bɔbo/ *n.m.* (*fam.*) sore, cut. **avoir ~**, have a pain.

bocage /bɔkaʒ/ *n.m.* grove.

boc|al (*pl.* **~aux**) /bɔkal, -o/ *n.m.* jar.

bock /bɔk/ *n.m.* beer glass; (*contenu*) glass of beer.

body /bɔdi/ *n.m.* leotard.

bœuf (*pl.* ~s) /bœf, bø/ *n.m.* ox; (*viande*) beef. ~s, oxen.

bogue /bɔg/ *n.m.* (*comput.*) bug.

bohème /bɔɛm/ *a. & n.m./f.* unconventional.

boire† /bwar/ *v.t./i.* drink; (*absorber*) soak up. ~ **un coup**, have a drink.

bois ¹ /bwa/ *voir* boire.

bois ² /bwa/ *n.m.* (*matériau, forêt*) wood. **de** ~, **en** ~, wooden.

boisé /bwaze/ *a.* wooded.

bois|er /bwaze/ *v.t.* (*chambre*) panel. ~**eries** *n.f. pl.* panelling.

boisson /bwasɔ̃/ *n.f.* drink.

boit /bwa/ *voir* boire.

boîte /bwat/ *n.f.* box; (*de conserves*) tin, can; (*firme: fam.*) firm. ~ **à gants**, glove compartment. ~ **aux lettres**, letter-box. ~ **de nuit**, night-club. ~ **postale**, post-office box. ~ **de vitesses**, gear box.

boiter /bwate/ *v.i.* limp; (*meuble*) wobble.

boiteu|x, ~se /bwatø, -z/ *a.* lame; (*meuble*) wobbly; (*raisonnement*) shaky.

boîtier /bwatje/ *n.m.* case.

bol /bɔl/ *n.m.* bowl. **un** ~ **d'air**, a breath of fresh air. **avoir du** ~, (*fam.*) be lucky.

bolide /bɔlid/ *n.m.* racing car.

Bolivie /bɔlivi/ *n.f.* Bolivia.

bolivien, ~ne /bɔlivjɛ̃, -jɛn/ *a. & n.m., f.* Bolivian.

bombance /bɔ̃bɑ̃s/ *n.f.* **faire** ~, (*fam.*) revel.

bombard|er /bɔ̃barde/ *v.t.* bomb; (*par obus*) shell; (*nommer: fam.*) appoint unexpectedly (as). ~**er qn. de**, (*fig.*) bombard s.o. with. ~**ement** *n.m.* bombing; shelling. ~**ier** *n.m.* (*aviat.*) bomber.

bombe /bɔ̃b/ *n.f.* bomb; (*atomiseur*) spray, aerosol.

bombé /bɔ̃be/ *a.* rounded; (*route*) cambered.

bomber /bɔ̃be/ *v.t.* ~ **la poitrine**, throw out one's chest.

bon, bonne /bɔ̃, bɔn/ *a.* good; (*qui convient*) right; (*prudent*) wise. ~ **à/ pour**, (*approprié*) fit to/for. **tenir** ~, stand firm. ● *n.m.* (*billet*) voucher, coupon; (*comm.*) bond. **du** ~, some good. **pour de** ~, for good. **à quoi** ~?, what's the good *ou* point? **bonne année**, happy New Year. ~ **anniversaire**, happy birthday. ~ **appétit/voyage**, enjoy your meal/trip.

bonne chance/nuit, good luck/ night. **bonne femme**, (*péj.*) woman. **bonne-maman** (*pl.* **bonnes-mamans**) *n.f.* (*fam.*) granny. ~**-papa** (*pl.* ~**s-papas**) *n.m.* (*fam.*) grand-dad. ~ **sens**, common sense. ~ **vivant**, bon viveur. **de bonne heure**, early.

bonbon /bɔ̃bɔ̃/ *n.m.* sweet; (*Amer.*) candy. ~**nière** /-ɔnjɛr/ *n.f.* sweet box; (*Amer.*) candy box.

bonbonne /bɔ̃bɔn/ *n.f.* demijohn; (*de gaz*) canister.

bond /bɔ̃/ *n.m.* leap. **faire un** ~, leap in the air; (*de surprise*) jump.

bonde /bɔ̃d/ *n.f.* plug; (*trou*) plug-hole.

bondé /bɔ̃de/ *a.* packed.

bondir /bɔ̃dir/ *v.i.* leap; (*de surprise*) jump.

bonheur /bɔnœr/ *n.m.* happiness; (*chance*) (good) luck. **au petit** ~, haphazardly. **par** ~, luckily.

bonhomme ¹ (*pl.* **bonshommes**) /bɔnɔm, bɔ̃zɔm/ *n.m.* fellow. ~ **de neige**, snowman.

bonhom|me ² /bɔnɔm/ *a. invar.* good-hearted. ~**ie** *n.f.* good-heartedness.

bonifier (se) /(sə)bɔnifje/ *v. pr.* improve.

boniment /bɔnimɑ̃/ *n.m.* smooth talk.

bonjour /bɔ̃ʒur/ *n.m. & int.* hallo, hello, good morning *ou* afternoon.

bon marché /bɔ̃marʃe/ *a. invar.* cheap. ● *adv.* cheap(ly).

bonne ¹ /bɔn/ *a.f. voir* bon.

bonne ² /bɔn/ *n.f.* (*domestique*) maid. ~ **d'enfants**, nanny.

bonnement /bɔnmɑ̃/ *adv.* **tout** ~, quite simply.

bonnet /bɔnɛ/ *n.m.* hat; (*de soutien-gorge*) cup. ~ **de bain**, swimming cap.

bonneterie /bɔnɛtri/ *n.f.* hosiery.

bonsoir /bɔ̃swar/ *n.m. & int.* good evening; (*en se couchant*) good night.

bonté /bɔ̃te/ *n.f.* kindness.

bonus /bɔnys/ *n.m.* (*auto.*) no claims bonus.

boom /bum/ *n.m.* (*comm.*) boom.

boots /buts/ *n.m. pl.* ankle boots.

bord /bɔr/ *n.m.* edge; (*rive*) bank. **à** ~ (**de**), on board. **au** ~ **de la mer**, at the seaside. **au** ~ **des larmes**, on the verge of tears. ~ **de la route**, roadside. ~ **du trottoir**, kerb; (*Amer.*) curb.

bordeaux /bɔrdo/ *n.m. invar.* Bordeaux (wine), claret. ● *a. invar.* maroon.

bordée /bɔrde/ *n.f.* ~ **d'injures,** torrent of abuse.

bordel /bɔrdɛl/ *n.m.* brothel; (*désordre: fam.*) shambles.

border /bɔrde/ *v.t.* line, border; (*tissu*) edge; (*personne, lit*) tuck in.

bordereau (*pl.* ~**x**) /bɔrdəro/ *n.m.* (*liste*) note, slip; (*facture*) invoice.

bordure /bɔrdyr/ *n.f.* border. **en ~ de,** on the edge of.

borgne /bɔrɲ/ *a.* one-eyed; (*fig.*) shady.

borne /bɔrn/ *n.f.* boundary marker. ~ **(kilométrique),** (*approx.*) milestone. ~**s,** limits.

borné /bɔrne/ *a.* narrow; (*personne*) narrow-minded.

borner /bɔrne/ *v.t.* confine. **se ~** *v. pr.* confine o.s. **(à,** to).

bosquet /bɔskɛ/ *n.m.* grove.

bosse /bɔs/ *n.f.* bump; (*de chameau*) hump. **avoir la ~ de,** (*fam.*) have a gift for. **avoir roulé sa ~,** have been around.

bosseler /bɔsle/ *v.t.* emboss; (*endommager*) dent.

bosser /bɔse/ *v.i.* (*fam.*) work (hard). ● *v.t.* (*fam.*) work (hard) at.

bossu, ~**e** /bɔsy/ *n.m., f.* hunchback.

botani|que /bɔtanik/ *n.f.* botany. ● *a.* botanical. ~**ste** *n.m./f.* botanist.

bott|e /bɔt/ *n.f.* boot; (*de fleurs, légumes*) bunch; (*de paille*) bundle, bale. ~**s de caoutchouc,** wellingtons. ~**ier** *n.m.* boot-maker.

botter /bɔte/ *v.t.* (*fam.*) **ça me botte,** I like the idea.

Bottin /bɔtɛ̃/ *n.m.* (P.) phone book.

bouc /buk/ *n.m.* (billy-)goat; (*barbe*) goatee. ~ **émissaire,** scapegoat.

boucan /bukɑ̃/ *n.m.* (*fam.*) din.

bouche /buʃ/ *n.f.* mouth. ~ **bée,** open-mouthed. ~ **d'égout,** manhole. ~ **d'incendie,** (fire) hydrant. ~ **de métro,** entrance to the underground *ou* subway (*Amer.*). ~**-à-bouche** *n.m.* mouth-to-mouth resuscitation.

bouché /buʃe/ *a.* **c'est ~,** (*profession, avenir*) it's a dead end.

bouchée /buʃe/ *n.f.* mouthful.

boucher¹ /buʃe/ *v.t.* block; (*bouteille*) cork. **se ~** *v. pr.* get blocked. **se ~ le nez,** hold one's nose.

bouch|er², ~**ère** /buʃe, -ɛr/ *n.m., f.* butcher. ~**erie** *n.f.* butcher's (shop); (*carnage*) butchery.

bouche-trou /buʃtru/ *n.m.* stopgap.

bouchon /buʃɔ̃/ *n.m.* stopper; (*en liège*) cork; (*de bidon, tube*) cap; (*de pêcheur*) float; (*de circulation: fig.*) hold-up.

boucle /bukl/ *n.f.* (*de ceinture*) buckle; (*forme*) loop; (*de cheveux*) curl. ~ **d'oreille,** ear-ring.

boucl|er /bukle/ *v.t.* fasten; (*terminer*) finish off; (*enfermer: fam.*) shut up; (*encercler*) seal off; (*budget*) balance. ● *v.i.* curl. ~**é** *a.* (*cheveux*) curly.

bouclier /buklije/ *n.m.* shield.

bouddhiste /budist/ *a. & n.m./f.* Buddhist.

boud|er /bude/ *v.i.* sulk. ● *v.t.* steer clear of. ~**erie** *n.f.* sulkiness. ~**eur,** ~**euse** *a. & n.m., f.* sulky (person).

boudin /budɛ̃/ *n.m.* black pudding.

boudoir /budwar/ *n.m.* boudoir.

boue /bu/ *n.f.* mud.

bouée /bwe/ *n.f.* buoy. ~ **de sauvetage,** lifebuoy.

boueu|x, ~**se** /bwø, -z/ *a.* muddy. ● *n.m.* dustman; (*Amer.*) garbage collector.

bouff|e /buf/ *n.f.* (*fam.*) food, grub. ~**er** *v.t./i.* (*fam.*) eat; (*bâfrer*) gobble.

bouffée /bufe/ *n.f.* puff, whiff; (*méd.*) flush; (*d'orgueil*) fit.

bouff|i† /bufi/ *a.* bloated.

bouffon, ~**ne** /bufɔ̃, -ɔn/ *a.* farcical. ● *n.m.* buffoon.

bouge /buʒ/ *n.m.* hovel; (*bar*) dive.

bougeoir /buʒwar/ *n.m.* candlestick.

bougeotte /buʒɔt/ *n.f.* **la ~,** (*fam.*) the fidgets.

bouger /buʒe/ *v.t./i.* move; (*agir*) stir. **se ~** *v. pr.* (*fam.*) move.

bougie /buʒi/ *n.f.* candle; (*auto.*) spark(ing)-plug.

bougon, ~**ne** /bugɔ̃, -ɔn/ *a.* grumpy. ~**ner** /-ɔne/ *v.i.* grumble.

bouillabaisse /bujabɛs/ *n.f.* bouillabaisse.

bouillie /buji/ *n.f.* porridge; (*pour bébé*) baby food; (*péj.*) mush. **en ~,** crushed, mushy.

bouill|ir† /bujir/ *v.i.* boil. ● *v.t.* **(faire)** ~**ir,** boil. ~**ant,** ~**ante** *a.* boiling; (*très chaud*) boiling hot.

bouilloire /bujwar/ *n.f.* kettle.

bouillon /bujɔ̃/ *n.m.* (*aliment*) stock. **~ cube**, stock cube. **~ner** /-jɔne/ *v.i.* bubble.

bouillotte /bujɔt/ *n.f.* hot-water bottle.

boulang|er, **~ère** /bulɑ̃ʒe, -ɛr/ *n.m., f.* baker. **~erie** *n.f.* bakery. **~erie-pâtisserie** *n.f.* baker's and confectioner's shop.

boule /bul/ *n.f.* ball; (*de machine à écrire*) golf ball. **~s**, (*jeu*) bowls. **jouer aux ~s**, play bowls. **une ~ dans la gorge**, lump in one's throat. **~ de neige**, snowball. **faire ~ de neige**, snowball.

bouleau (*pl.* **~x**) /bulo/ *n.m.* (silver) birch.

bouledogue /buldɔg/ *n.m.* bulldog.

boulet /bulɛ/ *n.m.* (*de canon*) cannon-ball; (*de forçat: fig.*) ball and chain.

boulette /bulɛt/ *n.f.* (*de papier*) pellet; (*aliment*) meat ball.

boulevard /bulvar/ *n.m.* boulevard.

boulevers|er /bulvɛrse/ *v.t.* turn upside down; (*pays, plans*) disrupt; (*émouvoir*) distress, upset. **~ant**, **ante** *a.* deeply moving. **~ement** *n.m.* upheaval.

boulier /bulje/ *n.m.* abacus.

boulimie /bulimi/ *n.f.* compulsive eating; (*méd.*) bulimia.

boulon /bulɔ̃/ *n.m.* bolt.

boulot[1] /bulo/ *n.m.* (*travail: fam.*) work.

boulot[2], **~te** /bulo, -ɔt/ *a.* (*rond: fam.*) dumpy.

boum /bum/ *n.m. & int.* bang. ● *n.f.* (*réunion: fam.*) party.

bouquet /bukɛ/ *n.m.* (*de fleurs*) bunch, bouquet; (*d'arbres*) clump. **c'est le ~!**, (*fam.*) that's the last straw!

bouquin /bukɛ̃/ *n.m.* (*fam.*) book. **~er** /-ine/ *v.t./i.* (*fam.*) read. **~iste** /-inist/ *n.m./f.* second-hand bookseller.

bourbeu|x, **~se** /burbø, -z/ *a.* muddy.

bourbier /burbje/ *n.m.* mire.

bourde /burd/ *n.f.* blunder.

bourdon /burdɔ̃/ *n.m.* bumble-bee.

bourdonn|er /burdɔne/ *v.i.* buzz. **~ement** *n.m.* buzzing.

bourg /bur/ *n.m.* (market) town.

bourgade /burgad/ *n.f.* village.

bourgeois, **~e** /burʒwa, -z/ *a. & n.m., f.* middle-class (person); (*péj.*)

bourgeois. **~ie** /-zi/ *n.f.* middle class(es).

bourgeon /burʒɔ̃/ *n.m.* bud. **~ner** /-ɔne/ *v.i.* bud.

bourgogne /burgɔɲ/ *n.m.* burgundy. ● *n.f.* **la B~**, Burgundy.

bourlinguer /burlɛ̃ge/ *v.i.* (*fam.*) travel about.

bourrade /burad/ *n.f.* prod.

bourrage /buraʒ/ *n.m.* **~ de crâne**, brainwashing.

bourrasque /burask/ *n.f.* squall.

bourrati|f, **~ve** /buratif, -v/ *a.* filling, stodgy.

bourreau (*pl.* **~x**) /buro/ *n.m.* executioner. **~ de travail**, workaholic.

bourrelet /burlɛ/ *n.m.* weather-strip, draught excluder; (*de chair*) roll of fat.

bourrer /bure/ *v.t.* cram (**de**, with); (*pipe*) fill. **~ de**, (*nourriture*) stuff with. **~ de coups**, thrash. **~ le crâne à qn.**, fill s.o.'s head with nonsense.

bourrique /burik/ *n.f.* ass.

bourru /bury/ *a.* surly.

bours|e /burs/ *n.f.* purse; (*subvention*) grant. **la B~e**, the Stock Exchange. **~ier**, **~ière** *a.* Stock Exchange; *n.m., f.* holder of a grant.

boursoufl|er /bursufle/ *v.t.*, **se ~** *v. pr.* puff up, swell.

bouscul|er /buskyle/ *v.t.* (*pousser*) jostle; (*presser*) rush; (*renverser*) knock over. **~ade** *n.f.* rush; (*cohue*) crush.

bouse /buz/ *n.f.* (cow) dung.

bousiller /buzije/ *v.t.* (*fam.*) mess up.

boussole /busɔl/ *n.f.* compass.

bout /bu/ *n.m.* end; (*de langue, bâton*) tip; (*morceau*) bit. **à ~**, exhausted. **à ~ de souffle**, out of breath. **à ~ portant**, point-blank. **au ~ de**, (*après*) after. **~ filtre**, filter-tip. **venir à ~ de**, (*finir*) manage to finish.

boutade /butad/ *n.f.* jest; (*caprice*) whim.

boute-en-train /butɑ̃trɛ̃/ *n.m. invar.* joker, live wire.

bouteille /butɛj/ *n.f.* bottle.

boutique /butik/ *n.f.* shop; (*de mode*) boutique.

bouton /butɔ̃/ *n.m.* button; (*pustule*) pimple; (*pousse*) bud; (*de porte, radio, etc.*) knob. **~ de manchette**, cuff-link. **~-d'or** *n.m.* (*pl.* **~s-d'or**) buttercup. **~ner** /-ɔne/ *v.t.* button (up). **~nière** /-ɔnjɛr/ *n.f.* buttonhole. **~-pression** (*pl.* **~s-pression**) *n.m.* press-stud; (*Amer.*) snap.

boutonneu|x, **~se** /butɔnø, -z/ *a.* pimply.

bouture /butyr/ *n.f.* (*plante*) cutting.

bovin, **~e** /bɔvɛ̃, -in/ *a.* bovine. **~s** *n.m. pl.* cattle.

bowling /boliŋ/ *n.m.* bowling; (*salle*) bowling-alley.

box (*pl.* **~** *ou* **boxes**) /bɔks/ *n.m.* lock-up garage; (*de dortoir*) cubicle; (*d'écurie*) (loose) box; (*jurid.*) dock.

box|e /bɔks/ *n.f.* boxing. **~er** *v.t./i.* box. **~eur** *n.m.* boxer.

boyau (*pl.* **~x**) /bwajo/ *n.m.* gut; (*corde*) catgut; (*galerie*) gallery; (*de bicyclette*) tyre; (*Amer.*) tire.

boycott|er /bɔjkɔte/ *v.t.* boycott. **~age** *n.m.* boycott.

BP *abrév.* (*boîte postale*) PO Box.

bracelet /braslɛ/ *n.m.* bracelet; (*de montre*) strap.

braconn|er /brakɔne/ *v.i.* poach. **~ier** *n.m.* poacher.

brad|er /brade/ *v.t.* sell off. **~erie** *n.f.* open-air sale.

braguette /bragɛt/ *n.f.* fly.

braille /braj/ *n.m. & a.* Braille.

brailler /brɑje/ *v.t./i.* bawl.

braire /brɛr/ *v.i.* bray.

braise /brɛz/ *n.f.* embers.

braiser /breze/ *v.t.* braise.

brancard /brɑ̃kar/ *n.m.* stretcher; (*bras*) shaft. **~ier** /-dje/ *n.m.* stretcher-bearer.

branch|e /brɑ̃ʃ/ *n.f.* branch. **~ages** *n.m. pl.* (cut) branches.

branché /brɑ̃ʃe/ *a.* (*fam.*) trendy.

branch|er /brɑ̃ʃe/ *v.t.* connect; (*électr.*) plug in. **~ement** *n.m.* connection.

branchies /brɑ̃ʃi/ *n.f. pl.* gills.

brandir /brɑ̃dir/ *v.t.* brandish.

branle /brɑ̃l/ *n.m.* **mettre en ~**, set in motion. **se mettre en ~**, get started. **~-bas (de combat)** *n.m. invar.* bustle.

branler /brɑ̃le/ *v.i.* be shaky. ● *v.t.* shake.

braquer /brake/ *v.t.* aim; (*regard*) fix; (*roue*) turn; (*banque*: *fam.*) hold up. **~ qn. contre**, turn s.o. against. ● *v.i.* (*auto.*) turn (the wheel). ● *v. pr.* **se ~**, dig one's heels in.

bras /brɑ/ *n.m.* arm. ● *n.m. pl.* (*fig.*) labour, hands. **à ~-le-corps** *adv.* round the waist. **~ dessus bras dessous**, arm in arm. **~ droit**,

(*fig.*) right-hand man. **en ~ de chemise**, in one's shirtsleeves.

brasier /brazje/ *n.m.* blaze.

brassard /brasar/ *n.m.* arm-band.

brasse /brɑs/ *n.f.* (breast-)stroke; (*mesure*) fathom.

brassée /brɑse/ *n.f.* armful.

brass|er /brase/ *v.t.* mix; (*bière*) brew; (*affaires*) handle a lot of. **~age** *n.m.* mixing; brewing. **~erie** *n.f.* brewery; (*café*) brasserie. **~eur** *n.m.* brewer. **~eur d'affaires**, big businessman.

brassière /brasjɛr/ *n.f.* (baby's) vest.

bravache /bravaʃ/ *n.m.* braggart.

bravade /bravad/ *n.f.* **par ~**, out of bravado.

brave /brav/ *a.* brave; (*bon*) good. **~ment** *adv.* bravely.

braver /brave/ *v.t.* defy.

bravo /bravo/ *int.* bravo. ● *n.m.* cheer.

bravoure /bravur/ *n.f.* bravery.

break /brɛk/ *n.m.* estate car; (*Amer.*) station-wagon.

brebis /brəbi/ *n.f.* ewe. **~ galeuse**, black sheep.

brèche /brɛʃ/ *n.f.* gap, breach. **être sur la ~**, be on the go.

bredouille /brəduj/ *a.* empty-handed.

bredouiller /brəduje/ *v.t./i.* mumble.

bref, brève /brɛf, -v/ *a.* short, brief. ● *adv.* in short. **en ~**, in short.

Brésil /brezil/ *n.m.* Brazil.

brésilien, **~ne** /breziljɛ̃, -jɛn/ *a. & n.m., f.* Brazilian.

Bretagne /brətaɲ/ *n.f.* Brittany.

bretelle /brətɛl/ *n.f.* (shoulder-) strap; (*d'autoroute*) access road. **~s**, (*pour pantalon*) braces; (*Amer.*) suspenders.

breton, **~ne** /brətɔ̃, -ɔn/ *a. & n.m., f.* Breton.

breuvage /brœvaʒ/ *n.m.* beverage.

brève /brɛv/ *voir* bref.

brevet /brəvɛ/ *n.m.* diploma. **~ (d'invention)**, patent.

brevet|er /brəvte/ *v.t.* patent. **~é** *a.* patented.

bribes /brib/ *n.f. pl.* scraps.

bric-à-brac /brikabrak/ *n.m. invar.* bric-à-brac.

bricole /brikɔl/ *n.f.* trifle.

bricol|er /brikɔle/ *v.i.* do odd (do-it-yourself) jobs. ● *v.t.* fix (up). **~age** *n.m.* do-it-yourself (jobs). **~eur**, **~euse** *n.m., f.* handyman, handy-woman.

brid|e /brid/ *n.f.* bridle. **tenir en ~e,** keep in check. **~er** *v.t.* (*cheval*) bridle; (*fig.*) keep in check, bridle; (*culin.*) truss.

bridé /bride/ *a.* **yeux ~s,** slit eyes.

bridge /bridʒ/ *n.m.* (*cartes*) bridge.

briève|ment /brijɛvmã/ *adv.* briefly. **~té** *n.f.* brevity.

brigad|e /brigad/ *n.f.* (*de police*) squad; (*mil.*) brigade; (*fig.*) team. **~ier** *n.m.* (*de police*) sergeant.

brigand /brigã/ *n.m.* robber. **~age** /-daʒ/ *n.m.* robbery.

briguer /brige/ *v.t.* seek (after).

brill|ant, ~ante /brijã, -t/ *a.* (*couleur*) bright; (*luisant*) shiny; (*remarquable*) brilliant. ● *n.m.* (*éclat*) shine; (*diamant*) diamond. **~amment** *adv.* brilliantly.

briller /brije/ *v.i.* shine.

brim|er /brime/ *v.t.* bully, harass. **se sentir brimé,** feel put down. **~ade** *n.f.* vexation.

brin /brɛ̃/ *n.m.* (*de corde*) strand; (*de muguet*) sprig. **~ d'herbe,** blade of grass. **un ~ de,** a bit of.

brindille /brɛ̃dij/ *n.f.* twig.

bringuebaler /brɛ̃gbale/ *v.i.* (*fam.*) wobble about.

brio /brijo/ *n.m.* brilliance. **avec ~,** brilliantly.

brioche /brijoʃ/ *n.f.* brioche (*small round sweet cake*); (*ventre: fam.*) paunch.

brique /brik/ *n.f.* brick.

briquer /brike/ *v.t.* polish.

briquet /brikɛ/ *n.m.* (cigarette-)lighter.

brisant /brizã/ *n.m.* reef.

brise /briz/ *n.f.* breeze.

bris|er /brize/ *v.t.* break. **se ~er** *v. pr.* break. **~e-lames** *n.m. invar.* breakwater. **~eur de grève** *n.m.* strikebreaker.

britannique /britanik/ *a.* British. ● *n.m./f.* Briton. **les B~s,** the British.

broc /bro/ *n.m.* pitcher.

brocant|e /brokãt/ *n.f.* second-hand goods. **~eur, ~euse** *n.m.,* *f.* second-hand goods dealer.

broche /broʃ/ *n.f.* brooch; (*culin.*) spit. **à la ~,** spit-roasted.

broché /broʃe/ *a.* paperback(ed).

brochet /broʃɛ/ *n.m.* (*poisson*) pike.

brochette /broʃɛt/ *n.f.* skewer.

brochure /broʃyr/ *n.f.* brochure, booklet.

brod|er /brode/ *v.t.* embroider. ● *v.i.* (*fig.*) embroider the truth. **~erie** *n.f.* embroidery.

broncher /brõʃe/ *v.i.* **sans ~,** without turning a hair.

bronch|es /brõʃ/ *n.f. pl.* bronchial tubes. **~ite** *n.f.* bronchitis.

bronze /brõz/ *n.m.* bronze.

bronz|er /brõze/ *v.i.,* **se ~er** *v. pr.* get a (sun-)tan. **~age** *n.m.* (sun-)tan. **~é** *a.* (sun-)tanned.

brosse /bros/ *n.f.* brush. **~ à dents,** toothbrush. **~ à habits,** clothes-brush. **en ~,** (*coiffure*) in a crew cut.

brosser /brose/ *v.t.* brush; (*fig.*) paint. **se ~ les dents/les cheveux,** brush one's teeth/hair.

brouette /bruɛt/ *n.f.* wheelbarrow.

brouhaha /bruaa/ *n.m.* hubbub.

brouillard /brujar/ *n.m.* fog.

brouille /bruj/ *n.f.* quarrel.

brouill|er /bruje/ *v.t.* mix up; (*vue*) blur; (*œufs*) scramble; (*radio*) jam; (*amis*) set at odds. **se ~er** *v. pr.* become confused; (*ciel*) cloud over; (*amis*) fall out. **~on**[1], **~onne** *a.* untidy.

brouillon[2] /brujõ/ *n.m.* (*rough*) draft.

broussailles /brusaj/ *n.f. pl.* undergrowth.

brousse /brus/ *n.f.* **la ~,** the bush.

brouter /brute/ *v.t./i.* graze.

broutille /brutij/ *n.f.* trifle.

broyer /brwaje/ *v.t.* crush; (*moudre*) grind.

bru /bry/ *n.f.* daughter-in-law.

bruin|e /bruin/ *n.f.* drizzle. **~er** *v.i.* drizzle.

bruire /bruir/ *v.i.* rustle.

bruissement /bruismã/ *n.m.* rustling.

bruit /brui/ *n.m.* noise; (*fig.*) rumour.

bruitage /bruitaʒ/ *n.m.* sound effects.

brûlant, ~e /brylã, -t/ *a.* burning (hot); (*sujet*) red-hot; (*ardent*) fiery.

brûlé /bryle/ *a.* (*démasqué: fam.*) blown. ● *n.m.* burning. **ça sent le ~,** I can smell sth. burning.

brûle-pourpoint (à) /(a)brylpurpwɛ̃/ *adv.* point-blank.

brûl|er /bryle/ *v.t./i.* burn; (*essence*) use (up); (*signal*) go through *ou* past (without stopping); (*dévorer: fig.*) consume. **se ~er** *v. pr.* burn o.s. **~eur** *n.m.* burner.

brûlure /brylyr/ *n.f.* burn. **~s d'estomac,** heartburn.

brum|e /brym/ *n.f.* mist. **~eux,
~euse** *a.* misty; (*idées*) hazy.

brun, ~e /brœ̃, bryn/ *a.* brown,
dark. ● *n.m.* brown. ● *n.m., f.*
dark-haired person. **~ir** /brynir/
v.i. turn brown; (*se bronzer*) get a
tan.

brunch /brœnʃ/ *n.m.* brunch.

brushing /brœʃiŋ/ *n.m.* blow-dry.

brusque /brysk/ *a.* (*soudain*) sudden, abrupt; (*rude*) abrupt. **~ment**
/-əmã/ *adv.* suddenly, abruptly.

brusquer /bryske/ *v.t.* rush.

brut /bryt/ *a.* (*diamant*) rough; (*soie*)
raw; (*pétrole*) crude; (*comm.*) gross.

brut|al (*m. pl.* **~aux**) /brytal, -o/ *a.*
brutal. **~aliser** *v.t.* treat roughly *ou*
violently, manhandle. **~alité** *n.f.*
brutality.

brute /bryt/ *n.f.* brute.

Bruxelles /brysɛl/ *n.m./f.* Brussels.

bruy|ant, ~ante /brɥijã, -t/ *a.* noisy.
~amment *adv.* noisily.

bruyère /bryjɛr/ *n.f.* heather.

bu /by/ *voir* boire.

bûche /byʃ/ *n.f.* log. **~ de Noël,**
Christmas log. **(se) ramasser une
~,** (*fam.*) come a cropper.

bûcher[1] /byʃe/ *n.m.* (*supplice*) stake.

bûch|er[2] /byʃe/ *v.t./i.* (*fam.*) slog
away (at). **~eur, ~euse** *n.m., f.*
(*fam.*) slogger.

bûcheron /byʃrɔ̃/ *n.m.* woodcutter.

budg|et /bydʒɛ/ *n.m.* budget.
~étaire *a.* budgetary.

buée /bɥe/ *n.f.* mist, condensation.

buffet /byfɛ/ *n.m.* sideboard;
(*réception, restaurant*) buffet.

buffle /byfl/ *n.m.* buffalo.

buis /bɥi/ *n.m.* (*arbre, bois*) box.

buisson /bɥisɔ̃/ *n.m.* bush.

buissonnière /bɥisonjɛr/ *a.f.* **faire
l'école ~,** play truant.

bulbe /bylb/ *n.m.* bulb.

bulgare /bylgar/ *a. & n.m./f.* Bulgar-
ian.

Bulgarie /bylgari/ *n.f.* Bulgaria.

bulldozer /byldozɛr/ *n.m.* bulldozer.

bulle /byl/ *n.f.* bubble.

bulletin /byltɛ̃/ *n.m.* bulletin, report;
(*scol.*) report; (*billet*) ticket. **~ d'information,** news bulletin. **~ météorologique,** weather report. **~
(de vote),** ballot-paper. **~ de salaire,** pay-slip. **~-réponse** *n.m.* (*pl.*
~s-réponses) reply slip.

buraliste /byralist/ *n.m./f.* tobacconist; (*à la poste*) clerk.

bureau (*pl.* **~x**) /byro/ *n.m.* office;
(*meuble*) desk; (*comité*) board. **~ de
location,** booking-office; (*théâtre*)
box-office. **~ de poste,** post office.
~ de tabac, tobacconist's (shop). **~
de vote,** polling station.

bureaucrate /byrokrat/ *n.m./f.* bureaucrat.

bureaucrat|ie /byrokrasi/ *n.f.* bur-
eaucracy. **~ique** /-tik/ *a.* bureau-
cratic.

bureautique /byrotik/ *n.f.* office
automation.

burette /byrɛt/ *n.f.* (*de graissage*)
oilcan.

burin /byrɛ̃/ *n.m.* (cold) chisel.

burlesque /byrlɛsk/ *a.* ludicrous;
(*théâtre*) burlesque.

bus /bys/ *n.m.* bus.

busqué /byske/ *a.* hooked.

buste /byst/ *n.m.* bust.

but /by(t)/ *n.m.* target; (*dessein*) aim,
goal; (*football*) goal. **avoir pour ~
de,** aim to. **de ~ en blanc,** point-
blank. **dans le ~ de,** with the
intention of.

butane /bytan/ *n.m.* butane, Calor
gas (P.).

buté /byte/ *a.* obstinate.

buter /byte/ *v.i.* **~ contre,** knock
against; (*problème*) come up
against. ● *v.t.* antagonize. **se ~** *v.
pr.* (*s'entêter*) become obstinate.

buteur /bytœr/ *n.m.* striker.

butin /bytɛ̃/ *n.m.* booty, loot.

butiner /bytine/ *v.i.* gather nectar.

butoir /bytwar/ *n.m.* **~ (de porte),**
doorstop.

butor /bytɔr/ *n.m.* (*péj.*) lout.

butte /byt/ *n.f.* mound. **en ~ à,**
exposed to.

buvard /byvar/ *n.m.* blotting-paper.

buvette /byvɛt/ *n.f.* (refreshment)
bar.

buveu|r, ~se /byvœr, -øz/ *n.m., f.*
drinker.

C

c' /s/ *voir* ce[1].

ça /sa/ *pron.* it, that; (*pour désigner*)
that; (*plus près*) this. **ça va?,** (*fam.*)
how's it going? **ça va!,** (*fam.*) all
right! **où ça?,** (*fam.*) where? **quand
ça?,** (*fam.*) when? **c'est ça,** that's
right.

çà /sa/ *adv.* **çà et là,** here and there.

caban|e /kaban/ *n.f.* hut; (*à outils*) shed. **~on** *n.m.* hut; (*en Provence*) cottage.

cabaret /kabarɛ/ *n.m.* night-club.

cabas /kabɑ/ *n.m.* shopping bag.

cabillaud /kabijo/ *n.m.* cod.

cabine /kabin/ *n.f.* (*à la piscine*) cubicle; (*à la plage*) (beach) hut; (*de bateau*) cabin; (*de pilotage*) cockpit; (*de camion*) cab; (*d'ascenseur*) cage. **~ (téléphonique),** phone-booth, phone-box.

cabinet /kabinɛ/ *n.m.* (*de médecin*) surgery; (*Amer.*) office; (*d'avocat*) office; (*clientèle*) practice; (*pol.*) Cabinet; (*pièce*) room. **~s,** (*toilettes*) toilet. **~ de toilette,** bathroom.

câble /kɑbl/ *n.m.* cable; (*corde*) rope.

câbler /kɑble/ *v.t.* cable.

cabosser /kabɔse/ *v.t.* dent.

cabot|age /kabotaʒ/ *n.m.* coastal navigation. **~eur** *n.m.* coaster.

cabotin, **~e** /kabɔtɛ̃, -in/ *n.m., f.* (*théâtre*) ham; (*fig.*) play-actor. **~age** /-inaʒ/ *n.m.* ham acting; (*fig.*) play-acting.

cabrer /kabre/ *v.t.,* **se ~** *v. pr.* (*cheval*) rear up. **se ~ contre,** rebel against.

cabri /kabri/ *n.m.* kid.

cabriole /kabrijɔl/ *n.f.* (*culbute*) somersault. **faire des ~s,** caper about.

cacahuète /kakaɥɛt/ *n.f.* peanut.

cacao /kakao/ *n.m.* cocoa.

cachalot /kaʃalo/ *n.m.* sperm whale.

cache /kaʃ/ *n.m.* mask; (*photo.*) lens cover.

cachemire /kaʃmir/ *n.m.* cashmere.

cach|er /kaʃe/ *v.t.* hide, conceal (**à,** from). **se ~er** *v. pr.* hide; (*se trouver caché*) be hidden. **~e-cache** *n.m. invar.* hide-and-seek. **~e-nez** *n.m. invar.* scarf. **~e-pot** *n.m.* cache-pot.

cachet /kaʃɛ/ *n.m.* seal; (*de la poste*) postmark; (*comprimé*) tablet; (*d'artiste*) fee; (*fig.*) style.

cacheter /kaʃte/ *v.t.* seal.

cachette /kaʃɛt/ *n.f.* hiding-place. **en ~,** in secret.

cachot /kaʃo/ *n.m.* dungeon.

cachott|eries /kaʃɔtri/ *n.f. pl.* secrecy. **faire des ~eries,** be secretive. **~ier, ~ière** *a.* secretive.

cacophonie /kakɔfɔni/ *n.f.* cacophony.

cactus /kaktys/ *n.m.* cactus.

cadavérique /kadaverik/ *a.* (*teint*) deathly pale.

cadavre /kadavr/ *n.m.* corpse.

caddie /kadi/ *n.m.* trolley.

cadeau (*pl.* **~x**) /kado/ *n.m.* present, gift. **faire un ~ à qn.,** give s.o. a present.

cadenas /kadnɑ/ *n.m.* padlock. **~ser** /-ase/ *v.t.* padlock.

cadenc|e /kadɑ̃s/ *n.f.* rhythm, cadence; (*de travail*) rate. **en ~e,** in time. **~é** *a.* rhythmic(al).

cadet, **~te** /kadɛ, -t/ *a.* youngest; (*entre deux*) younger. ● *n.m., f.* youngest (child); younger (child).

cadran /kadrɑ̃/ *n.m.* dial. **~ solaire,** sundial.

cadre /kadr/ *n.m.* frame; (*milieu*) surroundings; (*limites*) scope; (*contexte*) framework. ● *n.m./f.* (*personne: comm.*) executive. **les ~s,** (*comm.*) the managerial staff.

cadrer /kadre/ *v.i.* **~ avec,** tally with. ● *v.t.* (*photo*) centre.

cadu|c, ~que /kadyk/ *a.* obsolete.

cafard /kafar/ *n.m.* (*insecte*) cockroach. **avoir le ~,** (*fam.*) be feeling low. **~er** /-de/ *v.i.* (*fam.*) tell tales.

caf|é /kafe/ *n.m.* coffee; (*bar*) café. **~é au lait,** white coffee. **~etière** *n.f.* coffee-pot.

caféine /kafein/ *n.f.* caffeine.

cafouiller /kafuje/ *v.i.* (*fam.*) bumble, flounder.

cage /kaʒ/ *n.f.* cage; (*d'escalier*) well; (*d'ascenseur*) shaft.

cageot /kaʒo/ *n.m.* crate.

cagibi /kaʒibi/ *n.m.* storage room.

cagneu|x, ~se /kaɲø, -z/ *a.* knock-kneed.

cagnotte /kaɲɔt/ *n.f.* kitty.

cagoule /kagul/ *n.f.* hood.

cahier /kaje/ *n.m.* notebook; (*scol.*) exercise-book.

cahin-caha /kaɛ̃kaa/ *adv.* **aller ~,** (*fam.*) jog along.

cahot /kao/ *n.m.* bump, jolt. **~er** /kaote/ *v.t./i.* bump, jolt. **~eux, ~euse** /kaotø, -z/ *a.* bumpy.

caïd /kaid/ *n.m.* (*fam.*) big shot.

caille /kɑj/ *n.f.* quail.

cailler /kɑje/ *v.t./i.,* **se ~** *v. pr.* (*sang*) clot; (*lait*) curdle.

caillot /kɑjo/ *n.m.* (blood) clot.

caillou (*pl.* **~x**) /kɑju/ *n.m.* stone; (*galet*) pebble. **~teux, ~teuse** *a.* stony. **~tis** *n.m.* gravel.

caisse /kɛs/ n.f. crate, case; (tiroir, machine) till; (guichet) pay-desk; (bureau) office; (mus.) drum. ~ enregistreuse, cash register. ~ d'épargne, savings bank. ~ de retraite, pension fund.

caiss|ier, ~ière /kesje, -jɛr/ n.m., f. cashier.

cajol|er /kaʒɔle/ v.t. coax. ~eries n.f. pl. coaxing.

cake /kɛk/ n.m. fruit-cake.

calamité /kalamite/ n.f. calamity.

calandre /kalɑ̃dr/ n.f. radiator grill.

calanque /kalɑ̃k/ n.f. creek.

calcaire /kalkɛr/ a. (sol) chalky; (eau) hard.

calciné /kalsine/ a. charred.

calcium /kalsjɔm/ n.m. calcium.

calcul /kalkyl/ n.m. calculation; (scol.) arithmetic; (différentiel) calculus. ~ biliaire, gallstone.

calcul|er /kalkyle/ v.t. calculate. ~ateur n.m. (ordinateur) computer, calculator. ~atrice n.f. (ordinateur) calculator. ~ette n.f. (pocket) calculator.

cale /kal/ n.f. wedge; (de navire) hold. ~ sèche, dry dock.

calé /kale/ a. (fam.) clever.

caleçon /kalsɔ̃/ n.m. underpants; (de femme) leggings. ~ de bain, (bathing) trunks.

calembour /kalɑ̃bur/ n.m. pun.

calendrier /kalɑ̃drije/ n.m. calendar; (fig.) timetable.

calepin /kalpɛ̃/ n.m. notebook.

caler /kale/ v.t. wedge; (moteur) stall. ● v.i. stall.

calfeutrer /kalføtre/ v.t. stop up the cracks of.

calibr|e /kalibr/ n.m. calibre; (d'un œuf, fruit) grade. ~er v.t. grade.

calice /kalis/ n.m. (relig.) chalice; (bot.) calyx.

califourchon (à) /(a)kalifurʃɔ̃/ adv. astride. ● prép. à ~ sur, astride.

câlin, ~e /kɑlɛ̃, -in/ a. endearing, cuddly. ~er v.t./-ine/ v.t. cuddle.

calmant /kalmɑ̃/ n.m. sedative.

calm|e /kalm/ a. calm ● n.m. calm(ness). du ~e!, calm down! ~er v.t., se ~er v. pr. (personne) calm (down); (diminuer) ease.

calomn|ie /kalɔmni/ n.f. slander; (écrite) libel. ~ier v.t. slander; libel. ~ieux, ~ieuse a. slanderous, libellous.

calorie /kalɔri/ n.f. calorie.

calorifuge /kalɔrifyʒ/ a. (heat-)insulating. ● n.m. lagging.

calot /kalo/ n.m. (mil.) forage-cap.

calotte /kalɔt/ n.f. (relig.) skullcap; (tape. fam.) slap.

calqu|e /kalk/ n.m. tracing; (fig.) exact copy. ~er v.t. trace; (fig.) copy. ~er sur, model on.

calvaire /kalvɛr/ n.m. (croix) calvary; (fig.) suffering.

calvitie /kalvisi/ n.f. baldness.

camarade /kamarad/ n.m./f. friend; (pol.) comrade. ~ de jeu, playmate. ~rie n.f. good companionship.

cambiste /kɑ̃bist/ n.m./f. foreign exchange dealer.

cambouis /kɑ̃bwi/ n.m. (engine) oil.

cambrer /kɑ̃bre/ v.t. arch. se ~ v. pr. arch one's back.

cambriol|er /kɑ̃brijɔle/ v.t. burgle. ~age n.m. burglary. ~eur, ~euse n.m., f. burglar.

cambrure /kɑ̃bryr/ n.f. curve.

came /kam/ n.f. arbe à ~s, camshaft.

camée /kame/ n.m. cameo.

camelot /kamlo/ n.m. street vendor.

camelote /kamlɔt/ n.f. junk.

camembert /kamɑ̃bɛr/ n.m. Camembert (cheese).

caméra /kamera/ n.f. (cinéma, télévision) camera.

caméra|man (pl. ~men) /kameraman, -mɛn/ n.m. cameraman.

camion /kamjɔ̃/ n.m. lorry, truck. ~-citerne n.m. tanker. ~nage /-jɔnaʒ/ n.m. haulage. ~nette /-jɔnɛt/ n.f. van. ~neur /-jɔnœr/ n.m. lorry ou truck driver; (entrepreneur) haulage contractor.

camisole /kamizɔl/ n.f. ~ (de force), strait-jacket.

camoufl|er /kamufle/ v.t. camouflage. ~age n.m. camouflage.

camp /kɑ̃/ n.m. camp; (sport) side.

campagn|e /kɑ̃paɲ/ n.f. country (side); (mil., pol.) campaign. ~ard, ~arde a. country; n.m., f. countryman, countrywoman.

campanile /kɑ̃panil/ n.m. belltower.

camp|er /kɑ̃pe/ v.i. camp. ● v.t. plant boldly; (esquisser) sketch. se ~er v. pr. plant o.s. ~ement n.m. encampment. ~eur, ~euse n.m., f. camper.

camphre /kɑ̃fr/ n.m. camphor.

camping /kɑ̃piŋ/ n.m. camping. faire du ~, go camping. ~-car n.m. camper-van; (Amer.) motorhome.

~-gaz *n.m. invar.* (P.) camping-gaz. **(terrain de) ~,** campsite.

campus /kãpys/ *n.m.* campus.

Canada /kanada/ *n.m.* Canada.

canadien, ~ne /kanadjɛ̃, -jɛn/ *a. & n.m., f.* Canadian. ● *n.f.* fur-lined jacket.

canaille /kanɑj/ *n.f.* rogue.

can|al (*pl.* **~aux**) /kanal, -o/ *n.m.* (*artificiel*) canal; (*bras de mer*) channel; (*techn., TV*) channel. **par le ~al de,** through.

canalisation /kanalizɑsjɔ̃/ *n.f.* (*tuyaux*) main(s).

canaliser /kanalize/ *v.t.* (*eau*) canalize; (*fig.*) channel.

canapé /kanape/ *n.m.* sofa.

canard /kanar/ *n.m.* duck; (*journal: fam.*) rag.

canari /kanari/ *n.m.* canary.

cancans /kãkã/ *n.m. pl.* malicious gossip.

canc|er /kãsɛr/ *n.m.* cancer. **le C~er,** Cancer. **~éreux, ~éreuse** *a.* cancerous. **~érigène** *a.* carcinogenic.

cancre /kãkr/ *n.m.* dunce.

cancrelat /kãkrəla/ *n.m.* cockroach.

candélabre /kãdelabr/ *n.m.* candelabrum.

candeur /kãdœr/ *n.f.* naïvety.

candidat, ~e /kãdida, -t/ *n.m., f.* candidate; (*à un poste*) applicant, candidate (*à,* for). **~ure** /-tyr/ *n.f.* application; (*pol.*) candidacy. **poser sa ~ure** pour, apply for.

candide /kãdid/ *a.* naïve.

cane /kan/ *n.f.* (female) duck. **~ton** *n.m.* duckling.

canette /kanɛt/ *n.f.* (*de bière*) bottle.

canevas /kanva/ *n.m.* canvas; (*plan*) framework, outline.

caniche /kaniʃ/ *n.m.* poodle.

canicule /kanikyl/ *n.f.* hot summer days.

canif /kanif/ *n.m.* penknife.

canin, ~e /kanɛ̃, -in/ *a.* canine. ● *n.f.* canine (tooth).

caniveau (*pl.* **~x**) /kanivo/ *n.m.* gutter.

cannabis /kanabis/ *n.m.* cannabis.

canne /kan/ *n.f.* (walking-)stick. **~ à pêche,** fishing-rod. **~ à sucre,** sugar-cane.

cannelle /kanɛl/ *n.f.* cinnamon.

cannibale /kanibal/ *a. & n.m./f.* cannibal.

canoë /kanɔe/ *n.m.* canoe; (*sport*) canoeing.

canon /kanɔ̃/ *n.m.* (big) gun; (*d'une arme*) barrel; (*principe, règle*) canon. **~nade** /-ɔnad/ *n.f.* gunfire. **~nier** /-ɔnje/ *n.m.* gunner.

canot /kano/ *n.m.* boat. **~ de sauvetage,** lifeboat. **~ pneumatique,** rubber dinghy.

canot|er /kanɔte/ *v.i.* boat. **~age** *n.m.* boating. **~ier** *n.m.* boater.

cantate /kãtat/ *n.f.* cantata.

cantatrice /kãtatris/ *n.f.* opera singer.

cantine /kãtin/ *n.f.* canteen.

cantique /kãtik/ *n.m.* hymn.

canton /kãtɔ̃/ *n.m.* (*en France*) district; (*en Suisse*) canton.

cantonade (à la) /(ala)kãtɔnad/ *adv.* for all to hear.

cantonner /kãtɔne/ *v.t.* (*mil.*) billet. **se ~ dans,** confine o.s. to.

cantonnier /kãtɔnje/ *n.m.* roadman, road mender.

canular /kanylar/ *n.m.* hoax.

caoutchou|c /kautʃu/ *n.m.* rubber; (*élastique*) rubber band. **~c mousse,** foam rubber. **~té** *a.* rubberized. **~teux, ~teuse** *a.* rubbery.

cap /kap/ *n.m.* cape, headland; (*direction*) course. **doubler** *ou* **franchir le ~ de,** go beyond (the point of). **mettre le ~ sur,** steer a course for.

capable /kapabl/ *a.* able, capable. **~ de qch.,** capable of sth. **~ de faire,** able to do, capable of doing.

capacité /kapasite/ *n.f.* ability; (*contenance*) capacity.

cape /kap/ *n.f.* cape. **rire sous ~,** laugh up one's sleeve.

capillaire /kapilɛr/ *a.* (*lotion, soins*) hair. **(vaisseau) ~,** capillary.

capilotade (en) /(ã)kapilɔtad/ *adv.* (*fam.*) reduced to a pulp.

capitaine /kapitɛn/ *n.m.* captain.

capit|al, ~ale (*m. pl.* **~aux**) /kapital, -o/ *a.* major, fundamental; (*peine, lettre*) capital. ● *n.m.* (*pl.* **~aux**) (*comm.*) capital; (*fig.*) stock. **~aux,** (*comm.*) capital. ● *n.f.* (*ville, lettre*) capital.

capitalis|te /kapitalist/ *a. & n.m./f.* capitalist. **~me** *n.m.* capitalism.

capiteu|x, ~se /kapitø, -z/ *a.* heady.

capitonné /kapitɔne/ *a.* padded.

capitul|er /kapityle/ *v.i.* capitulate. **~ation** *n.f.* capitulation.

capor|al (*pl.* **~aux**) /kapɔral, -o/ *n.m.* corporal.

capot /kapo/ *n.m.* (*auto.*) bonnet; (*auto.*, *Amer.*) hood.

capote /kapɔt/ *n.f.* (*auto.*) hood; (*auto.*, *Amer.*) (convertible) top; (*fam.*) condom.

capoter /kapɔte/ *v.i.* overturn.

câpre /kɑpr/ *n.f.* (*culin.*) caper.

capric|e /kapris/ *n.m.* whim, caprice. **~ieux, ~ieuse** *a.* capricious; (*appareil*) temperamental.

Capricorne /kaprikɔrn/ *n.m.* **le ~,** Capricorn.

capsule /kapsyl/ *n.f.* capsule; (*de bouteille*) cap.

capter /kapte/ *v.t.* (*eau*) tap; (*émission*) pick up; (*fig.*) win, capture.

capti|f, ~ve /kaptif, -v/ *a. & n.m., f.* captive.

captiver /kaptive/ *v.t.* captivate.

captivité /kaptivite/ *n.f.* captivity.

captur|e /kaptyr/ *n.f.* capture. **~er** *v.t.* capture.

capuch|e /kapyʃ/ *n.f.* hood. **~on** *n.m.* hood; (*de stylo*) cap.

caquet /kakɛ/ *n.m.* **rabattre le ~ à qn.,** take s.o. down a peg or two.

caquet|er /kakte/ *v.i.* cackle. **~age** *n.m.* cackle.

car[1] /kar/ *conj.* because, for.

car[2] /kar/ *n.m.* coach; (*Amer.*) bus.

carabine /karabin/ *n.f.* rifle.

caracoler /karakɔle/ *v.i.* prance.

caract|ère /karaktɛr/ *n.m.* (*nature, lettre*) character. **~ères d'imprimerie,** block letters. **~ériel, ~érielle** *a.* character; *n.m., f.* disturbed child.

caractérisé /karakterize/ *a.* well-defined.

caractériser /karakterize/ *v.t.* characterize. **se ~ par,** be characterized by.

caractéristique /karakteristik/ *a. & n.f.* characteristic.

carafe /karaf/ *n.f.* carafe; (*pour le vin*) decanter.

caraïbe /karaib/ *a.* Caribbean. **les C~s,** the Caribbean.

carambol|er (se) /(sə)karɑ̃bɔle/ *v. pr.* (*voitures*) smash into each other. **~age** *n.m.* multiple smash-up.

caramel /karamɛl/ *n.m.* caramel. **~iser** *v.t./i.* caramelize.

carapace /karapas/ *n.f.* shell.

carat /kara/ *n.m.* carat.

caravane /karavan/ *n.f.* (*auto.*) caravan; (*auto.*, *Amer.*) trailer; (*convoi*) caravan.

carbone /karbɔn/ *n.m.* carbon; (*double*) carbon (copy). **(papier) ~,** carbon (paper).

carboniser /karbɔnize/ *v.t.* burn (to ashes).

carburant /karbyrɑ̃/ *n.m.* (motor) fuel.

carburateur /karbyratœr/ *n.m.* carburettor; (*Amer.*) carburetor.

carcan /karkɑ̃/ *n.m.* (*contrainte*) yoke.

carcasse /karkas/ *n.f.* carcass; (*d'immeuble, de voiture*) frame.

cardiaque /kardjak/ *a.* heart. ● *n.m./f.* heart patient.

cardigan /kardigɑ̃/ *n.m.* cardigan.

cardin|al (*m. pl. ~aux*) /kardinal, -o/ *a.* cardinal. ● *n.m.* (*pl. ~aux*) cardinal.

Carême /karɛm/ *n.m.* Lent.

carence /karɑ̃s/ *n.f.* inadequacy; (*manque*) deficiency.

caressant, ~e /karɛsɑ̃, -t/ *a.* endearing.

caress|e /karɛs/ *n.f.* caress. **~er** /-ese/ *v.t.* caress, stroke; (*espoir*) cherish.

cargaison /kargɛzɔ̃/ *n.f.* cargo.

cargo /kargo/ *n.m.* cargo boat.

caricatur|e /karikatyr/ *n.f.* caricature. **~al** (*m. pl. ~aux*) *a.* caricature-like.

car|ie /kari/ *n.f.* cavity. **la ~ie (dentaire),** tooth decay. **~ié** *a.* (*dent*) decayed.

carillon /karijɔ̃/ *n.m.* chimes; (*horloge*) chiming clock. **~ner** /-jɔne/ *v.i.* chime, peal.

caritati|f, ~ve /karitatif, -v/ *a.* **association ~ve,** charity.

carlingue /karlɛ̃g/ *n.f.* (*d'avion*) cabin.

carnage /karnaʒ/ *n.m.* carnage.

carnass|ier, ~ière /karnasje, -jɛr/ *a.* flesh-eating.

carnaval (*pl. ~s*) /karnaval/ *n.m.* carnival.

carnet /karnɛ/ *n.m.* notebook; (*de tickets etc.*) book. **~ de chèques,** cheque-book. **~ de notes,** school report.

carotte /karɔt/ *n.f.* carrot.

carotter /karɔte/ *v.t.* (*argot*) swindle. **~ qch. à qn.,** (*argot*) wangle sth. from s.o.

carpe /karp/ *n.f.* carp.

carpette /karpɛt/ *n.f.* rug.

carré /kare/ *a.* (*forme, mesure*) square; (*fig.*) straightforward. ● *n.m.* square; (*de terrain*) patch.

carreau (*pl.* **~x**) /karo/ *n.m.* (window) pane; (*par terre, au mur*) tile; (*dessin*) check; (*cartes*) diamonds. **à ~x**, check(ed).

carrefour /karfur/ *n.m.* crossroads.

carrel|er /karle/ *v.t.* tile. **~age** *n.m.* tiling; (*sol*) tiles.

carrelet /karlɛ/ *n.m.* (*poisson*) plaice.

carrément /karemã/ *adv.* straight; (*dire*) straight out.

carrer (se) /(sə)kare/ *v. pr.* settle firmly (**dans,** in).

carrière /karjɛr/ *n.f.* career; (*terrain*) quarry.

carrossable /karɔsabl/ *a.* suitable for vehicles.

carrosse /karɔs/ *n.m.* (horse-drawn) coach.

carross|erie /karɔsri/ *n.f.* (*auto.*) body(work). **~ier** *n.m.* (*auto.*) bodybuilder.

carrure /karyr/ *n.f.* build; (*fig.*) calibre.

cartable /kartabl/ *n.m.* satchel.

carte /kart/ *n.f.* card; (*géog.*) map; (*naut.*) chart; (*au restaurant*) menu. **~s,** (*jeu*) cards. **à la ~,** (*manger*) à la carte. **~ blanche,** a free hand. **~ de crédit,** credit card. **~ des vins,** wine list. **~ de visite,** (business) card. **~ grise,** (car) registration card. **~ postale,** postcard.

cartel /kartɛl/ *n.m.* cartel.

cartilage /kartilaʒ/ *n.m.* cartilage.

carton /kartɔ̃/ *n.m.* cardboard; (*boîte*) (cardboard) box. **~ à dessin,** portfolio. **faire un ~,** (*fam.*) take a pot-shot. **~nage** /-ɔnaʒ/ *n.m.* cardboard packing. **~-pâte** *n.m.* pasteboard. **en ~-pâte,** cardboard.

cartonné /kartɔne/ *a.* (*livre*) hardback.

cartouch|e /kartuʃ/ *n.f.* cartridge; (*de cigarettes*) carton. **~ière** *n.f.* cartridge-belt.

cas /kɑ/ *n.m.* case. **au ~ où,** in case. **~ urgent,** emergency. **en aucun ~,** on no account. **en ~ de,** in the event of, in case of. **en tout ~,** in any case. **faire ~ de,** set great store by. **~ de conscience,** matter of conscience.

casan|ier, **~ière** /kazanje, -jɛr/ *a.* home-loving.

casaque /kazak/ *n.f.* (*de jockey*) shirt.

cascade /kaskad/ *n.f.* waterfall; (*fig.*) spate.

cascad|eur, **~euse** /kaskadœr, -øz/ *n.m., f.* stuntman, stuntgirl.

case /kɑz/ *n.f.* hut; (*compartiment*) pigeon-hole; (*sur papier*) square.

caser /kaze/ *v.t.* (*mettre*) put; (*loger*) put up; (*dans un travail*) find a job for; (*marier: péj.*) marry off.

caserne /kazɛrn/ *n.f.* barracks.

cash /kaʃ/ *adv.* **payer ~,** pay (in) cash.

casier /kazje/ *n.m.* pigeon-hole, compartment; (*meuble*) cabinet; (*à bouteilles*) rack. **~ judiciaire,** criminal record.

casino /kazino/ *n.m.* casino.

casqu|e /kask/ *n.m.* helmet; (*chez le coiffeur*) (hair-)drier. **~ (à écouteurs),** headphones. **~é** *a.* wearing a helmet.

casquette /kaskɛt/ *n.f.* cap.

cassant, **~e** /kasã, -t/ *a.* brittle; (*brusque*) curt.

cassation /kasasjɔ̃/ *n.f.* **cour de ~,** appeal court.

casse /kɑs/ *n.f.* (*objets*) breakages. **mettre à la ~,** scrap.

cass|er /kase/ *v.t./i.* break; (*annuler*) annul. **se ~er** *v. pr.* break. **~er la tête à,** (*fam.*) give a headache to. **~e-cou** *n.m. invar.* daredevil. **~e-croûte** *n.m. invar.* snack. **~e-noisettes** *ou* **~e-noix** *n.m. invar.* nutcrackers. **~e-pieds** *n.m./f. invar.* (*fam.*) pain (in the neck). **~e-tête** *n.m. invar.* (*problème*) headache; (*jeu*) brain teaser.

casserole /kasrɔl/ *n.f.* saucepan.

cassette /kasɛt/ *n.f.* casket; (*de magnétophone*) cassette; (*de video*) video tape.

cassis[1] /kasi(s)/ *n.m.* black currant.

cassis[2] /kasi(s)/ *n.m.* (*auto.*) dip.

cassoulet /kasulɛ/ *n.m.* stew (of beans and meat).

cassure /kasyr/ *n.f.* break.

caste /kast/ *n.f.* caste.

castor /kastɔr/ *n.m.* beaver.

castr|er /kastre/ *v.t.* castrate. **~ation** *n.f.* castration.

cataclysme /kataklism/ *n.m.* cataclysm.

catalogu|e /katalɔg/ *n.m.* catalogue. **~er** *v.t.* catalogue; (*personne: péj.*) label.

catalyseur /katalizœr/ *n.m.* catalyst.

cataphote /katafɔt/ *n.m.* reflector.

cataplasme /kataplasm/ *n.m.* poultice.

catapult|e /katapylt/ *n.f.* catapult. **~er** *v.t.* catapult.

cataracte /katarakt/ *n.f.* cataract.

catastroph|e /katastrɔf/ *n.f.* disaster, catastrophe. **~ique** *a.* catastrophic.

catch /katʃ/ *n.m.* (all-in) wrestling. **~eur, ~euse** *n.m., f.* (all-in) wrestler.

catéchisme /kateʃism/ *n.m.* catechism.

catégorie /kategɔri/ *n.f.* category.

catégorique /kategɔrik/ *a.* categorical.

cathédrale /katedral/ *n.f.* cathedral.

catholi|que /katɔlik/ *a.* Catholic. **~cisme** *n.m.* Catholicism. **pas très ~que,** a bit fishy.

catimini (en) /(ɑ̃)katimini/ *adv.* on the sly.

cauchemar /koʃmar/ *n.m.* nightmare.

cause /koz/ *n.f.* cause; (*jurid.*) case. **à ~ de,** because of. **en ~,** (*en jeu, concerné*) involved. **pour ~ de,** on account of.

caus|er /koze/ *v.t.* cause. ● *v.i.* chat. **~erie** *n.f.* talk. **~ette** *n.f.* **faire la ~ette,** have a chat.

caustique /kostik/ *a.* caustic.

caution /kosjɔ̃/ *n.f.* surety; (*jurid.*) bail; (*appui*) backing; (*garantie*) deposit. **sous ~,** on bail.

cautionn|er /kosjone/ *v.t.* guarantee; (*soutenir*) back.

cavalcade /kavalkad/ *n.f.* (*fam.*) stampede, rush.

cavalerie /kavalri/ *n.f.* (*mil.*) cavalry; (*au cirque*) horses.

caval|ier, ~ière /kavalje, -jɛr/ *a.* offhand. ● *n.m., f.* rider; (*pour danser*) partner. ● *n.m.* (*échecs*) knight.

cave[1] /kav/ *n.f.* cellar.

cave[2] /kav/ *a.* sunken.

caveau (*pl.* **~x**) /kavo/ *n.m.* vault.

caverne /kavɛrn/ *n.f.* cave.

caviar /kavjar/ *n.m.* caviare.

cavité /kavite/ *n.f.* cavity.

CD (*abrév.*) (*compact disc*) CD.

ce[1], **c'**[*] /sə, s/ *pron.* it, that. **c'est,** it *ou* that is. **ce sont,** they are. **c'est moi,** it's me. **c'est un chanteur/une chanteuse/***etc.***,** he/she is a singer/ *etc.* **ce qui, ce que,** what. **ce que c'est bon/***etc.***!,** how good/*etc.* it is! **tout ce qui, tout ce que,** everything that.

ce[2] *ou* **cet*** , **cette** (*pl.* **ces**) /sə, sɛt, se/ *a.* that; (*proximité*) this. **ces,** those; (*proximité*) these.

CE *abrév.* (Communauté européenne) EC.

ceci /səsi/ *pron.* this.

cécité /sesite/ *n.f.* blindness.

céder /sede/ *v.t.* give up. ● *v.i.* (*se rompre*) give way; (*se soumettre*) give in.

cédille /sedij/ *n.f.* cedilla.

cèdre /sɛdr/ *n.m.* cedar.

CEE *abrév.* (Communauté économique européenne) EEC.

ceinture /sɛ̃tyr/ *n.f.* belt; (*taille*) waist; (*de bus, métro*) circle (line). **~ de sauvetage,** lifebelt. **~ de sécurité,** seat-belt.

ceinturer /sɛ̃tyre/ *v.t.* seize round the waist; (*entourer*) surround.

cela /səla/ *pron.* it, that; (*pour désigner*) that. **~ va de soi,** it is obvious.

célèbre /selɛbr/ *a.* famous.

célébr|er /selebre/ *v.t.* celebrate. **~ation** *n.f.* celebration (**de,** of).

célébrité /selebrite/ *n.f.* fame; (*personne*) celebrity.

céleri /sɛlri/ *n.m.* (*en branches*) celery. **~(-rave),** celeriac.

céleste /selɛst/ *a.* celestial.

célibat /seliba/ *n.m.* celibacy.

célibataire /selibatɛr/ *a.* unmarried. ● *n.m.* bachelor. ● *n.f.* unmarried woman.

celle, celles /sɛl/ *voir* celui.

cellier /selje/ *n.m.* store-room (*for wine*).

cellophane /selɔfan/ *n.f.* (P.) Cellophane (P.).

cellul|e /selyl/ *n.f.* cell. **~aire** *a.* cell. **fourgon** *ou* **voiture ~aire,** prison van.

celui, celle (*pl.* **ceux, celles**) /səlɥi, sɛl, sø/ *pron.* the one. **~ de mon ami,** my friend's. **~-ci,** this (one). **~-là,** that (one). **ceux-ci,** these (ones). **ceux-là,** those (ones).

cendr|e /sɑ̃dr/ *n.f.* ash. **~é** *a.* (*couleur*) ashen. **blond ~é,** ash blond.

cendrier /sɑ̃drije/ *n.m.* ashtray.

censé /sɑ̃se/ *a.* **être ~ faire,** be supposed to do.

censeur /sɑ̃sœr/ *n.m.* censor; (*scol.*) assistant headmaster.

censur|e /sɑ̃syr/ *n.f.* censorship. **~er** *v.t.* censor; (*critiquer*) censure.

cent (*pl.* **~s**) /sɑ̃/ (*generally* /sɑ̃t/ *pl.* /sɑ̃z/ *before vowel*) *a. & n.m.* (a) hundred. **~ un** /sɑ̃œ̃/ *a* hundred and one.

centaine /sɑ̃tɛn/ *n.f.* hundred. **une ~ (de)**, (about) a hundred.

centenaire /sɑ̃tnɛr/ *n.m.* (*anniversaire*) centenary.

centième /sɑ̃tjɛm/ *a.* & *n.m./f.* hundredth.

centigrade /sɑ̃tigrad/ *a.* centigrade.

centilitre /sɑ̃tilitr/ *n.m.* centilitre.

centime /sɑ̃tim/ *n.m.* centime.

centimètre /sɑ̃timɛtr/ *n.m.* centimetre; (*ruban*) tape-measure.

centr|al, ~ale (*m. pl.* **~aux**) /sɑ̃tral, -o/ *a.* central. ● *n.m.* (*pl.* **~aux**). **~al (téléphonique)**, (telephone) exchange. ● *n.f.* power-station. **~aliser** *v.t.* centralize.

centr|e /sɑ̃tr/ *n.m.* centre. **~e-ville** *n.m.* town centre. **~er** *v.t.* centre.

centuple /sɑ̃typl/ *n.m.* **le ~ (de)**, a hundredfold. **au ~**, a hundredfold.

cep /sɛp/ *n.m.* vine stock.

cépage /sepaʒ/ *n.m.* (variety of) vine.

cèpe /sɛp/ *n.m.* (edible) boletus.

cependant /səpɑ̃dɑ̃/ *adv.* however.

céramique /seramik/ *n.f.* ceramic; (*art*) ceramics.

cerceau (*pl.* **~x**) /sɛrso/ *n.m.* hoop.

cercle /sɛrkl/ *n.m.* circle; (*cerceau*) hoop. **~ vicieux**, vicious circle.

cercueil /sɛrkœj/ *n.m.* coffin.

céréale /sereal/ *n.f.* cereal.

cérébr|al (*m. pl.* **~aux**) /serebral, -o/ *a.* cerebral.

cérémonial (*pl.* **~s**) /seremɔnjal/ *n.m.* ceremonial.

cérémon|ie /seremɔni/ *n.f.* ceremony. **~ie(s)**, (*façons*) fuss. **~ieux, ~ieuse** *a.* ceremonious.

cerf /sɛr/ *n.m.* stag.

cerfeuil /sɛrfœj/ *n.m.* chervil.

cerf-volant (*pl.* **cerfs-volants**) /sɛrvɔlɑ̃/ *n.m.* kite.

ceris|e /sriz/ *n.f.* cherry. **~ier** *n.m.* cherry tree.

cerne /sɛrn/ *n.m.* ring.

cern|er /sɛrne/ *v.t.* surround; (*question*) define. **les yeux ~és**, with rings under one's eyes.

certain, ~e /sɛrtɛ̃, -ɛn/ *a.* certain; (*sûr*) certain, sure (**de**, of; **que**, that). ● *pron.* **~s**, certain people. **d'un ~ âge**, past one's prime. **un ~ temps**, some time.

certainement /sɛrtɛnmɑ̃/ *adv.* certainly.

certes /sɛrt/ *adv.* indeed.

certificat /sɛrtifika/ *n.m.* certificate.

certif|ier /sɛrtifje/ *v.t.* certify. **~ier qch. à qn.**, assure s.o. of sth. **~ié** *a.* (*professeur*) qualified.

certitude /sɛrtityd/ *n.f.* certainty.

cerveau (*pl.* **~x**) /sɛrvo/ *n.m.* brain.

cervelas /sɛrvəla/ *n.m.* saveloy.

cervelle /sɛrvɛl/ *n.f.* (*anat.*) brain; (*culin.*) brains.

ces /se/ *voir* ce³.

césarienne /sezarjɛn/ *n.f.* Caesarean (section).

cessation /sesasjɔ̃/ *n.f.* suspension.

cesse /sɛs/ *n.f.* **n'avoir de ~ que**, have no rest until. **sans ~**, incessantly.

cesser /sese/ *v.t./i.* stop. **~ de faire**, stop doing.

cessez-le-feu /seselfø/ *n.m. invar.* cease-fire.

cession /sesjɔ̃/ *n.f.* transfer.

c'est-à-dire /sɛtadir/ *conj.* that is (to say).

cet, cette /sɛt/ *voir* ce².

ceux /sø/ *voir* celui.

chacal (*pl.* **~s**) /ʃakal/ *n.m.* jackal.

chacun, ~e /ʃakœ̃, -yn/ *pron.* each (one), every one; (*tout le monde*) everyone.

chagrin /ʃagrɛ̃/ *n.m.* sorrow. **avoir du ~**, be distressed. **~er** /-ine/ *v.t.* distress.

chahut /ʃay/ *n.m.* row, din. **~er** /-te/ *v.i.* make a row; *v.t.* be rowdy with. **~eur, ~euse** /- tœr, -tøz/ *n.m.*, *f.* rowdy.

chaîn|e /ʃɛn/ *n.f.* chain; (*de télévision*) channel. **~e de montagnes**, mountain range. **~e de montage/fabrication**, assembly/production line. **~e hi-fi**, hi-fi system. **en ~e**, (*accidents*) multiple. **~ette** *n.f.* (small) chain. **~on** *n.m.* link.

chair /ʃɛr/ *n.f.* flesh. **bien en ~**, plump. **en ~ et en os**, in the flesh. **~ à saucisses**, sausage meat. **la ~ de poule**, goose-flesh. ● *a. invar.* (*couleur*) **~**, flesh-coloured.

chaire /ʃɛr/ *n.f.* (*d'église*) pulpit; (*univ.*) chair.

chaise /ʃɛz/ *n.f.* chair. **~ longue**, deck-chair.

chaland /ʃalɑ̃/ *n.m.* barge.

châle /ʃɑl/ *n.m.* shawl.

chalet /ʃalɛ/ *n.m.* chalet.

chaleur /ʃalœr/ *n.f.* heat; (*moins intense*) warmth; (*d'un accueil, d'une couleur*) warmth. **~eux, ~euse** *a.* warm.

challenge /ʃalɑ̃ʒ/ *n.m.* contest.

chaloupe /ʃalup/ *n.f.* launch, boat.

chalumeau (*pl.* ~x) /ʃalymo/ *n.m.* blowlamp; (*Amer.*) blowtorch.

chalut /ʃaly/ *n.m.* trawl-net ~ier /-tje/ *n.m.* trawler.

chamailler (se) /(sə)ʃamɑje/ *v. pr.* squabble.

chambarder /ʃābarde/ *v.t.* (*fam.*) turn upside down.

chambre /ʃābr/ *n.f.* (bed)room; (*pol., jurid.*) chamber. **faire ~ à part,** sleep in different rooms. **~ à air,** inner tube. **~ d'amis,** spare *ou* guest room. **~ à coucher,** bedroom. **~ à un lit/deux lits,** single/double room. **~ forte,** strong-room.

chambrer /ʃābre/ *v.t.* (*vin*) bring to room temperature.

chameau (*pl.* ~x) /ʃamo/ *n.m.* camel.

chamois /ʃamwa/ *n.m.* chamois. **peau de ~,** chamois leather.

champ /ʃā/ *n.m.* field. **~ de bataille,** battlefield. **~ de courses,** race-course.

champagne /ʃāpaɲ/ *n.m.* champagne.

champêtre /ʃāpɛtr/ *a.* rural.

champignon /ʃāpiɲɔ̃/ *n.m.* mushroom; (*moisissure*) fungus. **~ de Paris,** button mushroom.

champion, ~ne /ʃāpjɔ̃, -jɔn/ *n.m., f.* champion. **~nat** /-jɔna/ *n.m.* championship.

chance /ʃās/ *n.f.* (good) luck; (*possibilité*) chance. **avoir de la ~,** be lucky. **quelle ~!,** what luck!

chanceler /ʃāsle/ *v.i.* stagger; (*fig.*) falter.

chancelier /ʃāsəlje/ *n.m.* chancellor.

chanceu|x, ~se /ʃāsø, -z/ *a.* lucky.

chancre /ʃākr/ *n.m.* canker.

chandail /ʃādaj/ *n.m.* sweater.

chandelier /ʃādəlje/ *n.m.* candlestick.

chandelle /ʃādɛl/ *n.f.* candle. **dîner aux ~s,** candlelight dinner.

change /ʃāʒ/ *n.m.* (foreign) exchange.

changeant, ~e /ʃāʒā, -t/ *a.* changeable.

changement /ʃāʒmā/ *n.m.* change. **~ de vitesses** (*dispositif*) gears.

changer /ʃāʒe/ *v.t./i.* change. **se ~** *v. pr.* change (one's clothes). **~ de nom/voiture,** change one's name/car. **~ de place/train,** change places/trains. **~ de direction,** change direction. **~ d'avis** *ou* **d'idée,** change one's mind. **~ de vitesses,** change gear.

changeur /ʃāʒœr/ *n.m.* **~ automatique,** (money) change machine.

chanoine /ʃanwan/ *n.m.* canon.

chanson /ʃāsɔ̃/ *n.f.* song.

chant /ʃā/ *n.m.* singing; (*chanson*) song; (*religieux*) hymn.

chantage /ʃātaʒ/ *n.m.* blackmail. **~ psychologique,** emotional blackmail.

chant|er /ʃāte/ *v.t./i.* sing. **si cela vous ~e,** (*fam.*) if you feel like it. **faire ~,** (*délit*) blackmail. **~eur** *n.m.,* f. singer.

chantier /ʃātje/ *n.m.* building site. **~ naval,** shipyard. **mettre en ~,** get under way, start.

chantonner /ʃātɔne/ *v.t./i.* hum.

chanvre /ʃāvr/ *n.m.* hemp.

chao|s /kao/ *n.m.* chaos. **~tique** /kaɔtik/ *a.* chaotic.

chaparder /ʃaparde/ *v.t.* (*fam.*) filch.

chapeau (*pl.* ~x) /ʃapo/ *n.m.* hat. **~!,** well done!

chapelet /ʃaplɛ/ *n.m.* rosary; (*fig.*) string.

chapelle /ʃapɛl/ *n.f.* chapel. **~ ardente,** chapel of rest.

chapelure /ʃaplyr/ *n.f.* breadcrumbs.

chaperon /ʃaprɔ̃/ *n.m.* chaperon. **~ner** /-ɔne/ *v.t.* chaperon.

chapiteau (*pl.* ~x) /ʃapito/ *n.m.* (*de cirque*) big top; (*de colonne*) capital.

chapitre /ʃapitr/ *n.m.* chapter; (*fig.*) subject.

chapitrer /ʃapitre/ *v.t.* reprimand.

chaque /ʃak/ *a.* every, each.

char /ʃar/ *n.m.* (*mil.*) tank; (*de carnaval*) float; (*charrette*) cart; (*dans l'antiquité*) chariot.

charabia /ʃarabja/ *n.m.* (*fam.*) gibberish.

charade /ʃarad/ *n.f.* riddle.

charbon /ʃarbɔ̃/ *n.m.* coal. **~ de bois,** charcoal. **~nages** /-ɔnaʒ/ *n.m. pl.* coal-mines.

charcut|erie /ʃarkytri/ *n.f.* pork-butcher's shop; (*aliments*) (cooked) pork meats. **~ier, ~ière** *n.m., f.* pork-butcher.

chardon /ʃardɔ̃/ *n.m.* thistle.

charge /ʃarʒ/ *n.f.* load, burden; (*mil., électr., jurid.*) charge; (*mission*) responsibility. **~s,** expenses; (*de locataire*) service charges. **être à la ~ de,** be the responsibility of. **~s sociales,** social security contributions. **prendre en ~,** take charge of; (*transporter*) give a ride to.

chargé /ʃarʒe/ *a.* (*journée*) busy; (*langue*) coated. ● *n.m., f.* ~ **de mission.** head of mission. ~ **d'affaires,** chargé d'affaires, ~ **de cours,** lecturer.

charger /ʃarʒe/ *v.t.* load; (*attaquer*) charge; (*batterie*) charge. ● *v.i.* (*attaquer*) charge. **se** ~ **de,** take charge *ou* care of. ~ **qn. de,** weigh. s.o. down with; (*tâche*) entrust s.o. with. ~ **qn. de faire,** instruct s.o. to do.

chargement /-əmɑ̃/ *n.m.* loading; (*objets*) load.

chariot /ʃarjo/ *n.m.* (*à roulettes*) trolley; (*charrette*) cart.

charitable /ʃaritabl/ *a.* charitable.

charité /ʃarite/ *n.f.* charity. **faire la** ~, give to charity. **faire la** ~ **à,** give to.

charlatan /ʃarlatɑ̃/ *n.m.* charlatan.

charmant, ~e /ʃarmɑ̃, -t/ *a.* charming.

charm|e /ʃarm/ *n.m.* charm. **~er** *v.t.* charm. **~eur, ~euse** *n.m., f.* charmer.

charnel, ~le /ʃarnɛl/ *a.* carnal.

charnier /ʃarnje/ *n.m.* mass grave.

charnière /ʃarnjɛr/ *n.f.* hinge. **à la** ~ **de,** at the meeting point between.

charnu /ʃarny/ *a.* fleshy.

charpent|e /ʃarpɑ̃t/ *n.f.* framework; (*carrure*) build. **~é** *a.* built.

charpentier /ʃarpɑ̃tje/ *n.m.* carpenter.

charpie (en) /(ɑ̃)ʃarpi/ *adv.* in(to) shreds.

charretier /ʃartje/ *n.m.* carter.

charrette /ʃarɛt/ *n.f.* cart.

charrier /ʃarje/ *v.t.* carry.

charrue /ʃary/ *n.f.* plough.

charte /ʃart/ *n.f.* charter.

charter /ʃartɛr/ *n.m.* charter flight.

chasse /ʃas/ *n.f.* hunting; (*au fusil*) shooting; (*poursuite*) chase; (*recherche*) hunt. ~ **(d'eau),** (toilet) flush. ~ **sous-marine,** underwater fishing.

châsse /ʃas/ *n.f.* shrine, reliquary.

chass|er /ʃase/ *v.t./i.* hunt; (*faire partir*) chase away; (*odeur, employé*) get rid of. ~**e-neige** *n.m. invar.* snow-plough. **~eur, ~euse** *n.m., f.* hunter; *n.m.* page-boy; (*avion*) fighter.

châssis /ʃasi/ *n.m.* frame; (*auto.*) chassis.

chaste /ʃast/ *a.* chaste. **~té** /-əte/ *n.f.* chastity.

chat, ~te /ʃa, ʃat/ *n.m., f.* cat.

châtaigne /ʃatɛɲ/ *n.f.* chestnut.

châtaignier /ʃatɛɲe/ *n.m.* chestnut tree.

châtain /ʃatɛ̃/ *a. invar.* chestnut (brown).

château (*pl.* ~x) /ʃato/ *n.m.* castle; (*manoir*) manor. ~ **d'eau,** water-tower. ~ **fort,** fortified castle.

châtelain, ~e /ʃatlɛ̃, -ɛn/ *n.m., f.* lord of the manor, lady of the manor.

châtier /ʃatje/ *v.t.* chastise; (*style*) refine.

châtiment /ʃatimɑ̃/ *n.m.* punishment.

chaton /ʃatɔ̃/ *n.m.* (*chat*) kitten.

chatouill|er /ʃatuje/ *v.t.* tickle. **~ement** *n.m.* tickling.

chatouilleu|x, ~se /ʃatujø, -z/ *a.* ticklish; (*susceptible*) touchy.

chatoyer /ʃatwaje/ *v.i.* glitter.

châtrer /ʃatre/ *v.t.* castrate.

chatte /ʃat/ *voir* chat.

chaud, ~e /ʃo, ʃod/ *a.* warm; (*brûlant*) hot; (*vif. fig.*) warm. ● *n.m.* heat. **au** ~, in the warm(th). **avoir** ~, be warm; be hot. **il fait** ~, it is warm; it is hot. **pour te tenir** ~, to keep you warm. **~ement** /-dmɑ̃/ *adv.* warmly; (*disputé*) hotly.

chaudière /ʃodjɛr/ *n.f.* boiler.

chaudron /ʃodrɔ̃/ *n.m.* cauldron.

chauffage /ʃofaʒ/ *n.m.* heating. ~ **central,** central heating.

chauffard /ʃofar/ *n.m.* (*péj.*) reckless driver.

chauff|er /ʃofe/ *v.t./i.* heat (up). **se** ~ *v. pr.* warm o.s. (up). **~e-eau** *n.m. invar.* water-heater.

chauffeur /ʃofœr/ *n.m.* driver; (*aux gages de qn.*) chauffeur.

chaum|e /ʃom/ *n.m.* (*de toit*) thatch.

chaussée /ʃose/ *n.f.* road(way).

chauss|er /ʃose/ *v.t.* (*chaussures*) put on; (*enfant*) put shoes on (to). **se** ~**er** *v. pr.* put one's shoes on. **~er bien,** (*aller*) fit well. **~er du 35/etc.,** take a size 35/*etc.* shoe. **~e-pied** *n.m.* shoehorn. **~eur** *n.m.* shoemaker.

chaussette /ʃosɛt/ *n.f.* sock.

chausson /ʃosɔ̃/ *n.m.* slipper; (*de bébé*) bootee. ~ **(aux pommes),** (apple) turnover.

chaussure /ʃosyr/ *n.f.* shoe. **~s de ski,** ski boots. **~s de marche,** hiking boots.

chauve /ʃov/ *a.* bald.

chauve-souris (*pl.* **chauves-souris**) /ʃovsuri/ *n.f.* bat.

chauvin, **~e** /ʃovɛ̃, -in/ *a.* chauvinistic. ● *n.m.*, *f.* chauvinist. **~isme** /-inism/ *n.m.* chauvinism.

chaux /ʃo/ *n.f.* lime.

chavirer /ʃavire/ *v.t./i.* (*bateau*) capsize.

chef /ʃɛf/ *n.m.* leader, head; (*culin.*) chef; (*de tribu*) chief. **~ d'accusation**, (*jurid.*) charge. **~ d'équipe**, foreman; (*sport*) captain. **~ d'État**, head of State. **~ de famille**, head of the family. **~ de file**, (*pol.*) leader. **~ de gare**, station-master. **~ d'orchestre**, conductor. **~ de service**, department head. **~-lieu** (*pl.* **~s-lieux**) *n.m.* county town.

chef-d'œuvre (*pl.* **chefs-d'œuvre**) /ʃedœvr/ *n.m.* masterpiece.

cheik /ʃɛk/ *n.m.* sheikh.

chemin /ʃmɛ̃/ *n.m.* path, road; (*direction*, *trajet*) way. **beaucoup de ~ à faire**, a long way to go. **~ de fer**, railway. **en ou par ~ de fer**, by rail. **~ de halage**, towpath. **~ vicinal**, by-road. **se mettre en ~**, start out.

cheminée /ʃmine/ *n.f.* chimney; (*intérieur*) fireplace; (*encadrement*) mantelpiece; (*de bateau*) funnel.

cheminer /ʃmine/ *v.i.* plod; (*fig.*) progress. **~ement** *n.m.* progress.

cheminot /ʃmino/ *n.m.* railwayman; (*Amer.*) railroad man.

chemis|e /ʃmiz/ *n.f.* shirt; (*dossier*) folder; (*de livre*) jacket. **~e de nuit**, night-dress. **~ette** *n.f.* short-sleeved shirt.

chemisier /ʃmizje/ *n.m.* blouse.

chen|al (*pl.* **~aux**) /ʃənal, -o/ *n.m.* channel.

chêne /ʃɛn/ *n.m.* oak.

chenil /ʃni(l)/ *n.m.* kennels.

chenille /ʃnij/ *n.f.* caterpillar.

chenillette /ʃnijɛt/ *n.f.* tracked vehicle.

cheptel /ʃɛptɛl/ *n.m.* livestock.

chèque /ʃɛk/ *n.m.* cheque. **~ de voyage**, traveller's cheque.

chéquier /ʃekje/ *n.m.* cheque-book.

cher, **chère** /ʃɛr/ *a.* (*coûteux*) dear, expensive; (*aimé*) dear. ● *adv.* (*coûter*, *payer*) a lot (of money). ● *n.m.*, *f.* **mon ~**, **ma chère**, my dear.

chercher /ʃɛrʃe/ *v.t.* look for; (*aide*, *paix*, *gloire*) seek. **aller ~**, go and get

ou fetch, go for. **~ à faire**, attempt to do. **~ la petite bête**, be finicky.

chercheu|r, **~se** /ʃɛrʃœr, -øz/ *n.m.*, *f.* research worker.

chèrement /ʃɛrmã/ *adv.* dearly.

chéri, **~e** /ʃeri/ *a.* beloved. ● *n.m.*, *f.* darling.

chérir /ʃerir/ *v.t.* cherish.

cherté /ʃɛrte/ *n.f.* high cost.

chétif, **~ve** /ʃetif, -v/ *a.* puny.

chev|al (*pl.* **~aux**) /ʃval, -o/ *n.m.* horse. **~al (vapeur)**, horsepower. **à ~al**, on horseback. **à ~al sur**, straddling. **faire du ~al**, ride (a horse). **~al-d'arçons** *n.m. invar.* (*gymnastique*) horse.

chevaleresque /ʃvalrɛsk/ *a.* chivalrous.

chevalerie /ʃvalri/ *n.f.* chivalry.

chevalet /ʃvalɛ/ *n.m.* easel.

chevalier /ʃvalje/ *n.m.* knight.

chevalière /ʃvaljɛr/ *n.f.* signet ring.

chevalin, **~e** /ʃvalɛ̃, -in/ *a.* (*boucherie*) horse; (*espèce*) equine.

chevauchée /ʃvoʃe/ *n.f.* (horse) ride.

chevaucher /ʃvoʃe/ *v.t.* straddle. ● *v.i.*, **se ~** *v. pr.* overlap.

chevelu /ʃvəly/ *a.* hairy.

chevelure /ʃvəlyr/ *n.f.* hair.

chevet /ʃvɛ/ *n.m.* **au ~ de**, at the bedside of.

cheveu (*pl.* **~x**) /ʃvø/ *n.m.* (*poil*) hair. **~x**, (*chevelure*) hair. **avoir les ~x longs**, have long hair.

cheville /ʃvij/ *n.f.* ankle; (*fiche*) peg, pin; (*pour mur*) (wall) plug.

chèvre /ʃɛvr/ *n.f.* goat.

chevreau (*pl.* **~x**) /ʃvro/ *n.m.* kid.

chevreuil /ʃvrœj/ *n.m.* roe(-deer); (*culin.*) venison.

chevron /ʃvrɔ̃/ *n.m.* (*poutre*) rafter. **à ~s**, herring-bone.

chevronné, **~e** /ʃvrɔne/ *a.* experienced, seasoned.

chevrotant, **~e** /ʃvrɔtã, -t/ *a.* quavering.

chewing-gum /ʃwiŋgɔm/ *n.m.* chewing-gum.

chez /ʃe/ *prép.* at *ou* to the house of; (*parmi*) among; (*dans le caractère ou l'œuvre de*) in. **~ le boucher/***etc.*, at the butcher's/ *etc.* **~ soi**, at home; (*avec direction*) home. **~-soi** *n.m. invar.* home.

chic /ʃik/ *a. invar.* smart; (*gentil*) kind. **sois ~**, do me a favour. ● *n.m.* style. **avoir le ~ pour**, have the knack of. **~ (alors)!**, great!

chicane /ʃikan/ *n.f.* zigzag. **chercher ~ à qn**, needle s.o.

chiche /ʃiʃ/ *a.* mean (**de**, with). **~ (que je le fais)!**, (*fam.*) I bet you I will, can, *etc.*

chichis /ʃiʃi/ *n.m. pl.* (*fam.*) fuss.

chicorée /ʃikɔre/ *n.f.* (*frisée*) endive; (*à café*) chicory.

chien, ~ne /ʃjɛ̃, ʃjɛn/ *n.m.* dog. ● *n.f.* dog, bitch. **~ de garde**, watchdog. **~-loup** *n.m.* (*pl.* **~s-loups**) wolfhound.

chiffon /ʃifɔ̃/ *n.m.* rag.

chiffonner /ʃifɔne/ *v.t.* crumple; (*préoccuper: fam.*) bother.

chiffonnier /ʃifɔnje/ *n.m.* rag-and-bone man.

chiffre /ʃifr/ *n.m.* figure; (*code*) code. **~s arabes/romains**, Arabic/roman numerals. **~ d'affaires**, turnover.

chiffrer /ʃifre/ *v.t.* set a figure to, assess; (*texte*) encode. **se ~ à**, amount to.

chignon /ʃiɲɔ̃/ *n.m.* bun, chignon.

Chili /ʃili/ *n.m.* Chile.

chilien, ~ne /ʃiljɛ̃, -jɛn/ *a. & n.m., f.* Chilean.

chim|ère /ʃimɛr/ *n.f.* fantasy. **~érique** *a.* fanciful.

chim|ie /ʃimi/ *n.f.* chemistry. **~ique** *a.* chemical. **~iste** *n.m./f.* chemist.

chimpanzé /ʃɛ̃pɑ̃ze/ *n.m.* chimpanzee.

Chine /ʃin/ *n.f.* China.

chinois, ~e /ʃinwa, -z/ *a. & n.m., f.* Chinese. ● *n.m.* (*lang.*) Chinese.

chiot /ʃjo/ *n.m.* pup(py).

chiper /ʃipe/ *v.t.* (*fam.*) swipe.

chipoter /ʃipɔte/ *v.i.* (*manger*) nibble; (*discuter*) quibble.

chips /ʃips/ *n.m. pl.* crisps; (*Amer.*) chips.

chiquenaude /ʃiknod/ *n.f.* flick.

chiromanc|ie /kirɔmɑ̃si/ *n.f.* palmistry. **~ien, ~ienne** *n.m., f.* palmist.

chirurgic|al (*m. pl.* **~aux**) /ʃiryrʒikal, -o/ *a.* surgical.

chirurg|ie /ʃiryrʒi/ *n.f.* surgery. **~ie esthétique**, plastic surgery. **~ien** *n.m.* surgeon.

chlore /klɔr/ *n.m.* chlorine.

choc /ʃɔk/ *n.m.* (*heurt*) impact, shock; (*émotion*) shock; (*collision*) crash; (*affrontement*) clash; (*méd.*) shock.

chocolat /ʃɔkɔla/ *n.m.* chocolate; (*à boire*) drinking chocolate. **~ au lait**,

milk chocolate. **~ chaud**, hot chocolate.

chœur /kœr/ *n.m.* (*antique*) chorus; (*chanteurs, nef*) choir. **en ~**, in chorus.

chois|ir /ʃwazir/ *v.t.* choose, select. **~i** *a.* carefully chosen; (*passage*) selected.

choix /ʃwa/ *n.m.* choice, selection. **au ~**, according to preference. **de ~**, choice. **de premier ~**, top quality.

choléra /kɔlera/ *n.m.* cholera.

chômage /ʃomaʒ/ *n.m.* unemployment. **en ~**, unemployed. **mettre en ~ technique**, lay off.

chôm|er /ʃome/ *v.i.* be unemployed; (*usine*) lie idle. **~eur, ~euse** *n.m., f.* unemployed person. **les ~eurs**, the unemployed.

chope /ʃɔp/ *n.f.* tankard.

choper /ʃɔpe/ *v.t.* (*fam.*) catch.

choquer /ʃɔke/ *v.t.* shock; (*commotionner*) shake.

choral, ~e (*m. pl.* **~s**) /kɔral/ *a.* choral. ● *n.f.* choir, choral society.

chorégraph|ie /kɔregrafi/ *n.f.* choreography. **~e** *n.m./f.* choreographer.

choriste /kɔrist/ *n.m./f.* (*à l'église*) chorister; (*opéra, etc.*) member of the chorus *ou* choir.

chose /ʃoz/ *n.f.* thing. **(très) peu de ~**, nothing much.

chou (*pl.* **~x**) /ʃu/ *n.m.* cabbage. **~ (à la crème)**, cream puff. **~x de Bruxelles**, Brussels sprouts. **mon petit ~**, (*fam.*) my little dear.

choucas /ʃuka/ *n.m.* jackdaw.

chouchou, ~te /ʃuʃu, -t/ *n.m., f.* pet, darling. **le ~ du prof.**, the teacher's pet.

choucroute /ʃukrut/ *n.f.* sauerkraut.

chouette[1] /ʃwɛt/ *n.f.* owl.

chouette[2] /ʃwɛt/ *a.* (*fam.*) super.

chou-fleur (*pl.* **choux-fleurs**) /ʃuflœr/ *n.m.* cauliflower.

choyer /ʃwaje/ *v.t.* pamper.

chrétien, ~ne /kretjɛ̃, -jɛn/ *a. & n.m., f.* Christian.

Christ /krist/ *n.m.* **le ~**, Christ.

christianisme /kristjanism/ *n.m.* Christianity.

chrom|e /krom/ *n.m.* chromium, chrome. **~é** *a.* chromium-plated.

chromosome /krɔmozom/ *n.m.* chromosome.

chronique /krɔnik/ *a.* chronic. ● *n.f.* (*rubrique*) column; (*nouvelles*) news; (*annales*) chronicle.

~eur *n.m.* columnist; (*historien*) chronicler.

chronologie /krɔnɔlɔʒi/ *n.f.* chronology. **~ique** *a.* chronological.

chronomètre /krɔnɔmɛtr/ *n.m.* stopwatch. **~étrer** *v.t.* time.

chrysanthème /krizɑ̃tɛm/ *n.m.* chrysanthemum.

chuchoter /ʃyʃɔte/ *v.t./i.* whisper. **~ement** *n.m.* whisper(ing).

chuinter /ʃɥɛ̃te/ *v.i.* hiss.

chut /ʃyt/ *int.* shush.

chute /ʃyt/ *n.f.* fall; (*déchet*) scrap. **~ (d'eau)**, waterfall. **~ du jour**, nightfall. **~ de pluie**, rainfall. **la ~ des cheveux**, hair loss.

chuter /ʃyte/ *v.i.* fall.

Chypre /ʃipr/ *n.f.* Cyprus.

-ci /si/ *adv.* (*après un nom précédé de ce, cette, etc.*) **cet homme-ci**, this man. **ces maisons-ci**, these houses.

ci- /si/ *adv.* here. **ci-après**, hereafter. **ci-contre**, opposite. **ci-dessous**, below. **ci-dessus**, above. **ci-gît**, here lies. **ci-inclus, ci-incluse, ci-joint, ci-jointe**, enclosed.

cible /sibl/ *n.f.* target.

cibou|le /sibul/ *n.f.*, **~ette** *n.f.* chive(s).

cicatrice /sikatris/ *n.f.* scar.

cicatriser /sikatrize/ *v.t.*, **se ~** *v. pr.* heal (up).

cidre /sidr/ *n.m.* cider.

ciel (*pl.* **cieux, ciels**) /sjɛl, sjø/ *n.m.* sky; (*relig.*) heaven. **cieux**, (*relig.*) heaven.

cierge /sjɛrʒ/ *n.m.* candle.

cigale /sigal/ *n.f.* cicada.

cigare /sigar/ *n.m.* cigar.

cigarette /sigarɛt/ *n.f.* cigarette.

cigogne /sigɔɲ/ *n.f.* stork.

cil /sil/ *n.m.* (eye)lash.

ciller /sije/ *v.i.* blink.

cime /sim/ *n.f.* peak, tip.

ciment /simɑ̃/ *n.m.* cement. **~er** /-te/ *v.t.* cement.

cimetière /simtjɛr/ *n.m.* cemetery. **~ de voitures**, breaker's yard.

cinéaste /sineast/ *n.m./f.* film-maker.

ciné-club /sineklœb/ *n.m.* film society.

cinéma /sinema/ *n.m.* cinema. **~tographique** *a.* cinema.

cinémathèque /sinematɛk/ *n.f.* film library; (*salle*) film theatre.

cinéphile /sinefil/ *n.m./f.* film lover.

cinétique /sinetik/ *a.* kinetic.

cinglant, ~e /sɛ̃glɑ̃, -t/ *a.* biting.

cinglé /sɛ̃gle/ *a.* (*fam.*) crazy.

cingler /sɛ̃gle/ *v.t.* lash.

cinq /sɛ̃k/ *a. & n.m.* five. **~ième** *a. & n.m./f.* fifth.

cinquantaine /sɛ̃kɑ̃tɛn/ *n.f.* **une ~ (de)**, about fifty.

cinquant|e /sɛ̃kɑ̃t/ *a. & n.m.* fifty. **~ième** *a. & n.m./f.* fiftieth.

cintre /sɛ̃tr/ *n.m.* coat-hanger; (*archit.*) curve.

cintré /sɛ̃tre/ *a.* (*chemise*) fitted.

cirage /siraʒ/ *n.m.* (wax) polish.

circoncision /sirkɔ̃sizjɔ̃/ *n.f.* circumcision.

circonférence /sirkɔ̃ferɑ̃s/ *n.f.* circumference.

circonflexe /sirkɔ̃flɛks/ *a.* circumflex.

circonscription /sirkɔ̃skripsjɔ̃/ *n.f.* district. **~ (électorale)**, constituency.

circonscrire /sirkɔ̃skrir/ *v.t.* confine; (*sujet*) define.

circonspect /sirkɔ̃spɛkt/ *a.* circumspect.

circonstance /sirkɔ̃stɑ̃s/ *n.f.* circumstance; (*occasion*) occasion. **~s atténuantes**, mitigating circumstances.

circonstancié /sirkɔ̃stɑ̃sje/ *a.* detailed.

circonvenir /sirkɔ̃vnir/ *v.t.* circumvent.

circuit /sirkɥi/ *n.m.* circuit; (*trajet*) tour, trip.

circulaire /sirkylɛr/ *a. & n.f.* circular.

circul|er /sirkyle/ *v.i.* circulate; (*train, automobile, etc.*) travel; (*piéton*) walk. **faire ~er**, (*badauds*) move on. **~ation** *n.f.* circulation; (*de véhicules*) traffic.

cire /sir/ *n.f.* wax.

ciré /sire/ *n.m.* oilskin; waterproof.

cir|er /sire/ *v.t.* polish, wax. **~euse** *n.f.* (*appareil*) floor-polisher.

cirque /sirk/ *n.m.* circus; (*arène*) amphitheatre; (*désordre: fig.*) chaos.

cirrhose /siroz/ *n.f.* cirrhosis.

cisaille(s) /sizaj/ *n.f.* (*pl.*) shears.

ciseau (*pl.* **~x**) /sizo/ *n.m.* chisel. **~x**, scissors.

ciseler /sizle/ *v.t.* chisel.

citadelle /sitadɛl/ *n.f.* citadel.

citadin, ~e /sitadɛ̃, -in/ *n.m., f.* city dweller. ● *a.* city.

cité /site/ *n.f.* city. **~ ouvrière**, (workers') housing estate. **~ universitaire**, (university) halls of residence. **~-dortoir** *n.f.* (*pl.* **~s-dortoirs**) dormitory town.

cit|er /site/ *v.t.* quote, cite; (*jurid.*) summon. **~ation** *n.f.* quotation; (*jurid.*) summons.

citerne /sitɛrn/ *n.f.* tank.

cithare /sitar/ *n.f.* zither.

citoyen, ~ne /sitwajɛ̃, -jɛn/ *n.m., f.* citizen. **~neté** /-jɛnte/ *n.f.* citizenship.

citron /sitrɔ̃/ *n.m.* lemon. **~ vert**, lime. **~nade** /-ɔnad/ *n.f.* lemon squash *ou* drink, (still) lemonade.

citrouille /sitruj/ *n.f.* pumpkin.

civet /sive/ *n.m.* stew. **~ de lièvre/ lapin**, jugged hare/rabbit.

civette /sivɛt/ *n.f.* (*culin.*) chive(s).

civière /sivjɛr/ *n.f.* stretcher.

civil /sivil/ *a.* civil; (*non militaire*) civilian; (*poli*) civil. ● *n.m.* civilian. **dans le ~**, in civilian life. **en ~**, in plain clothes.

civilisation /sivilizasjɔ̃/ *n.f.* civilization.

civiliser /sivilize/ *v.t.* civilize. **se ~** *v. pr.* become civilized.

civi|que /sivik/ *a.* civic. **~sme** *n.m.* civic sense.

clair /klɛr/ *a.* clear; (*éclairé*) light, bright; (*couleur*) light; (*liquide*) thin. ● *adv.* clearly. ● *n.m.* **~ de lune**, moonlight. **le plus ~ de**, most of. **~ement** *adv.* clearly.

claire-voie (à) /(a)klɛrvwa/ *adv.* with slits to let the light through.

clairière /klɛrjɛr/ *n.f.* clearing.

clairon /klɛrɔ̃/ *n.m.* bugle. **~ner** /-ɔne/ *v.t.* trumpet (forth).

clairsemé /klɛrsəme/ *a.* sparse.

clairvoyant, ~e /klɛrvwajɑ̃, -t/ *a.* clear-sighted.

clamer /klame/ *v.t.* utter aloud.

clameur /klamœr/ *n.f.* clamour.

clan /klɑ̃/ *n.m.* clan.

clandestin, ~e /klɑ̃dɛstɛ̃, -in/ *a.* secret; (*journal*) underground. **passager ~**, stowaway.

clapet /klapɛ/ *n.m.* valve.

clapier /klapje/ *n.m.* (rabbit) hutch.

clapot|er /klapɔte/ *v.i.* lap. **~is** *n.m.* lapping.

claquage /klakaʒ/ *n.m.* strained muscle.

claque /klak/ *n.f.* slap. **en avoir sa ~ (de)**, (*fam.*) be fed up (with).

claqu|er /klake/ *v.i.* bang; (*porte*) slam, bang; (*fouet*) snap, crack; (*se casser*: *fam.*) conk out; (*mourir*: *fam.*) snuff it. ● *v.t.* (*porte*) slam, bang; (*dépenser*: *fam.*) blow; (*fatiguer*: *fam.*) tire out. **~er des doigts**,

snap one's fingers. **~er des mains**, clap one's hands. **il claque des dents**, his teeth are chattering. **~ement** *n.m.* bang(ing); slam(ming); snap(ping).

claquettes /klakɛt/ *n.f. pl.* tap-dancing.

clarifier /klarifje/ *v.t.* clarify.

clarinette /klarinɛt/ *n.f.* clarinet.

clarté /klarte/ *n.f.* light, brightness; (*netteté*) clarity.

classe /klɑs/ *n.f.* class; (*salle*: *scol.*) class(-room). **aller en ~**, go to school. **~ ouvrière/moyenne**, working/middle class. **faire la ~**, teach.

class|er /klɑse/ *v.t.* classify; (*par mérite*) grade; (*papiers*) file; (*affaire*) close. **se ~er premier/dernier**, come first/last. **~ement** *n.m.* classification; grading; filing; (*rang*) place, grade; (*de coureur*) placing.

classeur /klɑsœr/ *n.m.* filing cabinet; (*chemise*) file.

classif|ier /klasifje/ *v.t.* classify. **~ication** *n.f.* classification.

classique /klasik/ *a.* classical; (*de qualité*) classic(al); (*habituel*) classic. ● *n.m.* classic; (*auteur*) classical author.

clause /kloz/ *n.f.* clause.

claustration /klostrasjɔ̃/ *n.f.* confinement.

claustrophobie /klostrɔfɔbi/ *n.f.* claustrophobia.

clavecin /klavsɛ̃/ *n.m.* harpsichord.

clavicule /klavikyl/ *n.f.* collar-bone.

clavier /klavje/ *n.m.* keyboard.

claviste /klavist/ *n.m./f.* keyboarder.

clé, clef /kle/ *n.f.* key; (*outil*) spanner; (*mus.*) clef. ● *a. invar.* key. **~ anglaise**, (monkey-)wrench. **~ de contact**, ignition key. **~ de voûte**, keystone. **prix ~s en main**, (*voiture*) on-the-road price.

clémen|t, ~te /klemɑ̃, -t/ *a.* (*doux*) mild; (*indulgent*) lenient. **~ce** *n.f.* mildness; leniency.

clémentine /klemɑ̃tin/ *n.f.* clementine.

clerc /klɛr/ *n.m.* (*de notaire etc.*) clerk; (*relig.*) cleric.

clergé /klɛrʒe/ *n.m.* clergy.

cléric|al (*m. pl.* **~aux**) /klerikal, -o/ *a.* clerical.

cliché /kliʃe/ *n.m.* cliché; (*photo.*) negative.

client, ~e /klijɑ̃, -t/ *n.m., f.* customer; (*d'un avocat*) client; (*d'un* *médecin*) patient; (*d'hôtel*) guest. **~èle** /-tɛl/ *n.f.* customers, clientele; (*d'un avocat*) clientele, clients, practice; (*d'un médecin*) practice, patients; (*soutien*) custom.

cligner /kliɲe/ *v.i.* **~ des yeux**, blink. **~ de l'œil**, wink.

clignot|er /kliɲɔte/ *v.i.* blink; (*lumière*) flicker; (*comme signal*) flash. **~ant** *n.m.* (*auto.*) indicator; (*auto.*, *Amer.*) directional signal.

climat /klima/ *n.m.* climate. **~ique** /-tik/ *a.* climatic.

climatis|ation /klimatizɑsjɔ̃/ *n.f.* air-conditioning. **~é** *a.* air-conditioned.

clin d'œil /klɛ̃dœj/ *n.m.* wink. **en un ~**, in a flash.

clinique /klinik/ *a.* clinical. ● *n.f.* (private) clinic.

clinquant, ~e /klɛ̃kɑ̃, -t/ *a.* showy.

clip /klip/ *n.m.* video.

clique /klik/ *n.f.* clique; (*mus.*, *mil.*) band.

cliquet|er /klikte/ *v.i.* clink. **~is** *n.m.* clink(ing).

clitoris /klitɔris/ *n.m.* clitoris.

clivage /klivaʒ/ *n.m.* cleavage.

clochard, ~e /klɔʃar, -d/ *n.m.*, *f.* tramp.

cloch|e[1] /klɔʃ/ *n.f.* bell. **~ à fromage**, cheese-cover. **~ette** *n.f.* bell.

cloche[2] /klɔʃ/ *n.f.* (*fam.*) idiot.

cloche-pied (à) /(a)klɔʃpje/ *adv.* hopping on one foot.

clocher[1] /klɔʃe/ *n.m.* bell-tower; (*pointu*) steeple. **de ~**, parochial.

clocher[2] /klɔʃe/ *v.i.* (*fam.*) be wrong.

cloison /klwazɔ̃/ *n.f.* partition; (*fig.*) barrier. **~ner** /-ɔne/ *v.t.* partition; (*personne*) cut off.

cloître /klwatr/ *n.m.* cloister.

cloîtrer (se) /(sə)klwatre/ *v. pr.* shut o.s. away.

clopin-clopant /klɔpɛ̃klɔpɑ̃/ *adv.* hobbling.

cloque /klɔk/ *n.f.* blister.

clore /klɔr/ *v.t.* close.

clos, ~e /klo, -z/ *a.* closed.

clôtur|e /klotyr/ *n.f.* fence; (*fermeture*) closure. **~er** *v.t.* enclose; (*festival, séance, etc.*) close.

clou /klu/ *n.m.* nail; (*furoncle*) boil; (*de spectacle*) star attraction. **~ de girofle**, clove. **les ~s**, (*passage*) zebra *ou* pedestrian crossing. **~er** *v.t.* nail down; (*fig.*) pin down. **être ~é au lit**, be confined to one's bed. **~er le bec à qn.**, shut s.o. up.

clouté /klute/ *a.* studded.

clown /klun/ *n.m.* clown.

club /klœb/ *n.m.* club.

coaguler /kɔagyle/ *v.t./i.*, **se ~** *v. pr.* coagulate.

coaliser (se) /(sə)kɔalize/ *v. pr.* join forces.

coalition /kɔalisjɔ̃/ *n.f.* coalition.

coasser /kɔase/ *v.i.* croak.

cobaye /kɔbaj/ *n.m.* guinea-pig.

coca /kɔka/ *n.m.* (P.) Coke.

cocagne /kɔkaɲ/ *n.f.* **pays de ~**, land of plenty.

cocaïne /kɔkain/ *n.f.* cocaine.

cocarde /kɔkard/ *n.f.* rosette.

cocard|ier, ~ière /kɔkardje, -jɛr/ *a.* chauvinistic.

cocasse /kɔkas/ *a.* comical.

coccinelle /kɔksinɛl/ *n.f.* ladybird; (*Amer.*) ladybug; (*voiture*) beetle.

cocher[1] /kɔʃe/ *v.t.* tick (off), check.

cocher[2] /kɔʃe/ *n.m.* coachman.

cochon, ~ne /kɔʃɔ̃, -ɔn/ *n.m.* pig. ● *n.m.*, *f.* (*personne*: *fam.*) pig. ● *a.* (*fam.*) filthy. **~nerie** /-ɔnri/ *n.f.* (*saleté*: *fam.*) filth; (*marchandise*: *fam.*) rubbish.

cocktail /kɔktɛl/ *n.m.* cocktail; (*réunion*) cocktail party.

cocon /kɔkɔ̃/ *n.m.* cocoon.

cocorico /kɔkɔriko/ *n.m.* cock-a-doodle-doo.

cocotier /kɔkɔtje/ *n.m.* coconut palm.

cocotte /kɔkɔt/ *n.f.* (*marmite*) casserole. **~ minute**, (P.) pressure-cooker. **ma ~**, (*fam.*) my sweet, my dear.

cocu /kɔky/ *n.m.* (*fam.*) cuckold.

code /kɔd/ *n.m.* code. **~s, phares ~**, dipped headlights. **~ de la route**, Highway Code. **se mettre en ~**, dip one's headlights.

coder /kɔde/ *v.t.* code.

codifier /kɔdifje/ *v.t.* codify.

coéquip|ier, ~ière /kɔekipje, -jɛr/ *n.m.*, *f.* team-mate.

cœur /kœr/ *n.m.* heart; (*cartes*) hearts. **~ d'artichaut**, artichoke heart. **~ de palmier**, heart of palm. **à ~ ouvert**, (*opération*) open-heart; (*parler*) freely. **avoir bon ~**, be kind-hearted. **de bon ~**, with a good heart. **par ~**, by heart. **avoir mal au ~**, feel sick. **je veux en avoir le ~ net**, I want to be clear in my own mind (about it).

coexist|er /kɔɛgziste/ *v.i.* coexist. **~ence** *n.f.* coexistence.

coffre /kɔfr/ *n.m.* chest; (*pour argent*) safe; (*auto.*) boot; (*auto.*, *Amer.*) trunk. **~-fort** (*pl.* **~s-forts**) *n.m.* safe.

coffrer /kɔfre/ *v.t.* (*fam.*) lock up.

coffret /kɔfrɛ/ *n.m.* casket, box.

cognac /kɔɲak/ *n.m.* cognac.

cogner /kɔɲe/ *v.t./i.* knock. **se ~** *v. pr.* knock o.s.

cohabit|er /kɔabite/ *v.i.* live together. **~ation** *n.f.* living together.

cohérent, ~e /kɔerɑ̃, -t/ *a.* coherent.

cohésion /kɔezjɔ̃/ *n.f.* cohesion.

cohorte /kɔɔrt/ *n.f.* troop.

cohue /kɔy/ *n.f.* crowd.

coi, coite /kwa, -t/ *a.* silent.

coiffe /kwaf/ *n.f.* head-dress.

coiff|er /kwafe/ *v.t.* do the hair of; (*chapeau*) put on; (*surmonter*) cap. **~er qn. d'un chapeau**, put a hat on s.o. **se ~er** *v. pr.* do one's hair. **~é de**, wearing. **bien/mal ~é**, with tidy/untidy hair. **~eur, ~euse** *n.m.*, *f.* hairdresser; *n.f.* dressing-table.

coiffure /kwafyr/ *n.f.* hairstyle; (*chapeau*) hat; (*métier*) hairdressing.

coin /kwɛ̃/ *n.m.* corner; (*endroit*) spot; (*cale*) wedge; (*pour graver*) die. **~ du feu**, by the fireside. **dans le ~**, locally. **du ~**, local. **le boulanger du ~**, the local baker.

coincer /kwɛ̃se/ *v.t.* jam; (*caler*) wedge; (*attraper*. *fam.*) catch. **se ~** *v. pr.* get jammed.

coïncid|er /kɔɛ̃side/ *v.i.* coincide. **~ence** *n.f.* coincidence.

coing /kwɛ̃/ *n.m.* quince.

coït /kɔit/ *n.m.* intercourse.

coite /kwat/ *voir* coi.

coke /kɔk/ *n.m.* coke.

col /kɔl/ *n.m.* collar; (*de bouteille*) neck; (*de montagne*) pass. **~ roulé**, polo-neck; (*Amer.*) turtle-neck. **~ de l'utérus**, cervix.

coléoptère /kɔleɔptɛr/ *n.m.* beetle.

colère /kɔlɛr/ *n.f.* anger; (*accès*) fit of anger. **en ~**, angry. **se mettre en ~**, lose one's temper.

colér|eux, ~euse /kɔlerø, -z/, **~ique** *adjs.* quick-tempered.

colibri /kɔlibri/ *n.m.* humming-bird.

colifichet /kɔlifiʃɛ/ *n.m.* trinket.

colimaçon (en) /(ɑ̃)kɔlimasɔ̃/ *adv.* spiral.

colin /kɔlɛ̃/ *n.m.* (*poisson*) hake.

colin-maillard /kɔlɛ̃majar/ *n.m.* **jouer à ~**, play blind man's buff.

colique /kɔlik/ *n.f.* diarrhoea; (*méd.*) colic.

colis /kɔli/ *n.m.* parcel.

collabor|er /kɔlabɔre/ *v.i.* collaborate (à, on). **~er à**, (*journal*) contribute to. **~ateur, ~atrice** *n.m.*, *f.* collaborator; contributor. **~ation** *n.f.* collaboration (à, on); contribution (à, to).

collant, ~e /kɔlɑ̃, -t/ *a.* skin-tight; (*poisseux*) sticky. ● *n.m.* (*bas*) tights; (*de danseur*) leotard.

collation /kɔlasjɔ̃/ *n.f.* light meal.

colle /kɔl/ *n.f.* glue; (*en pâte*) paste; (*problème*: *fam.*) poser; (*scol.*, *argot*) detention.

collect|e /kɔlɛkt/ *n.f.* collection. **~er** *v.t.* collect.

collecteur /kɔlɛktœr/ *n.m.* (*égout*) main sewer.

collecti|f, ~ve /kɔlɛktif, -v/ *a.* collective; (*billet*, *voyage*) group. **~vement** *adv.* collectively.

collection /kɔlɛksjɔ̃/ *n.f.* collection.

collectionn|er /kɔlɛksjɔne/ *v.t.* collect. **~eur, ~euse** *n.m.*, *f.* collector.

collectivité /kɔlɛktivite/ *n.f.* community.

coll|ège /kɔlɛʒ/ *n.m.* (*secondary*) school; (*assemblée*) college. **~égien, ~égienne** *n.m.*, *f.* schoolboy, schoolgirl.

collègue /kɔlɛg/ *n.m./f.* colleague.

coll|er /kɔle/ *v.t.* stick; (*avec colle liquide*) glue; (*affiche*) stick up; (*mettre*: *fam.*) stick; (*scol.*, *argot*) keep in; (*par une question*: *fam.*) stump. ● *v.i.* stick (à, to); (*être collant*) be sticky. **~er à**, (*convenir à*) fit, correspond to. **être ~é à**, (*examen*: *fam.*) fail.

collet /kɔlɛ/ *n.m.* (*piège*) snare. **~ monté**, prim and proper. **prendre qn. au ~**, collar s.o.

collier /kɔlje/ *n.m.* necklace; (*de chien*) collar.

colline /kɔlin/ *n.f.* hill.

collision /kɔlizjɔ̃/ *n.f.* (*choc*) collision; (*lutte*) clash. **entrer en ~ (avec)**, collide (with).

colloque /kɔlɔk/ *n.m.* symposium.

collyre /kɔlir/ *n.m.* eye drops.

colmater /kɔlmate/ *v.t.* seal; (*trou*) fill in.

colombe /kɔlɔ̃b/ *n.f.* dove.

Colombie /kɔlɔ̃bi/ *n.f.* Colombia.

colon /kɔlɔ̃/ *n.m.* settler.

colonel /kɔlɔnɛl/ *n.m.* colonel.

colon|ial, **~iale** (*m. pl.* **~iaux**) /kɔlɔnjal, -jo/ *a.* & *n.m.*, *f.* colonial.

colonie /kɔlɔni/ *n.f.* colony. **~ de vacances**, children's holiday camp.

coloniser /kɔlɔnize/ *v.t.* colonize.

colonne /kɔlɔn/ *n.f.* column. **~ vertébrale**, spine. **en ~ par deux**, in double file.

color|er /kɔlɔre/ *v.t.* colour; (*bois*) stain. **~ant** *n.m.* colouring. **~ation** *n.f.* (*couleur*) colour(ing).

colorier /kɔlɔrje/ *v.t.* colour (in).

coloris /kɔlɔri/ *n.m.* colour.

coloss|al (*m. pl.* **~aux**) /kɔlɔsal, -o/ *a.* colossal.

colosse /kɔlɔs/ *n.m.* giant.

colport|er /kɔlpɔrte/ *v.t.* hawk. **~eur**, **~euse** *n.m.*, *f.* hawker.

colza /kɔlza/ *n.m.* rape(-seed).

coma /kɔma/ *n.m.* coma. **dans le ~**, in a coma.

combat /kɔ̃ba/ *n.m.* fight; (*sport*) match. **~s**, fighting.

combati|f, **~ve** /kɔ̃batif, -v/ *a.* eager to fight; (*esprit*) fighting.

combatt|re† /kɔ̃batr/ *v.t./i.* fight. **~ant**, **~ante** *n.m.*, *f.* fighter; (*mil.*) combatant.

combien /kɔ̃bjɛ̃/ *adv.* ~ (**de**), (*quantité*) how much; (*nombre*) how many; (*temps*) how long. **~ il a changé!**, (*comme*) how he has changed! **~y a-t-il d'ici à ...?**, how far is it to ...?

combinaison /kɔ̃binɛzɔ̃/ *n.f.* combination; (*manigance*) scheme; (*de femme*) slip; (*bleu de travail*) boiler suit; (*Amer.*) overalls; (*de plongée*) wetsuit. **~ d'aviateur**, flying-suit.

combine /kɔ̃bin/ *n.f.* trick; (*fraude*) fiddle.

combiné /kɔ̃bine/ *n.m.* (*de téléphone*) receiver.

combiner /kɔ̃bine/ *v.t.* (*réunir*) combine; (*calculer*) devise.

comble¹ /kɔ̃bl/ *a.* packed.

comble² /kɔ̃bl/ *n.m.* height. **~s**, (*mansarde*) attic, loft. **c'est le ~!**, that's the (absolute) limit!

combler /kɔ̃ble/ *v.t.* fill; (*perte, déficit*) make good; (*désir*) fulfil; (*personne*) gratify. **~ qn. de cadeaux/** *etc.*, lavish gifts/*etc.* on s.o.

combustible /kɔ̃bystibl/ *n.m.* fuel.

combustion /kɔ̃bystjɔ̃/ *n.f.* combustion.

comédie /kɔmedi/ *n.f.* comedy. **~ musicale**, musical. **jouer la ~**, put on an act.

comédien, **~ne** /kɔmedjɛ̃, -jɛn/ *n.m.*, *f.* actor, actress.

comestible /kɔmɛstibl/ *a.* edible. **~s** *n.m. pl.* foodstuffs.

comète /kɔmɛt/ *n.f.* comet.

comique /kɔmik/ *a.* comical; (*genre*) comic. ● *n.m.* (*acteur*) comic; (*comédie*) comedy; (*côté drôle*) comical aspect.

comité /kɔmite/ *n.m.* committee.

commandant /kɔmɑ̃dɑ̃/ *n.m.* commander; (*armée de terre*) major. **~ (de bord)**, captain. **~ en chef**, Commander-in-Chief.

commande /kɔmɑ̃d/ *n.f.* (*comm.*) order. **~s**, (*d'avion etc.*) controls.

command|er /kɔmɑ̃de/ *v.t.* command; (*acheter*) order. ● *v.i.* be in command. **~er à**, (*maîtriser*) control. **~er à qn. de**, command s.o. to. **~ement** *n.m.* command; (*relig.*) commandment.

commando /kɔmɑ̃do/ *n.m.* commando.

comme /kɔm/ *conj.* as. ● *prép.* like. ● *adv.* (*exclamation*) how. **~ ci comme ça**, so-so. **~ d'habitude**, **~ à l'ordinaire**, as usual. **~ il faut**, proper(ly). **~ pour faire**, as if to do. **~ quoi**, to the effect that. **qu'avez-vous ~ amis/etc.?**, what have you in the way of friends/*etc.*? **~ c'est bon!**, it's so good! **~ il est mignon!** isn't he sweet!

commémor|er /kɔmemɔre/ *v.t.* commemorate. **~ation** *n.f.* commemoration.

commenc|er /kɔmɑ̃se/ *v.t.* begin, start. **~er à faire**, begin *ou* start to do. **~ement** *n.m.* beginning, start.

comment /kɔmɑ̃/ *adv.* how. **~?**, (*répétition*) pardon?; (*surprise*) what? **~ est-il?**, what is he like? **le ~ et le pourquoi**, the whys and wherefores.

commentaire /kɔmɑ̃tɛr/ *n.m.* comment; (*d'un texte*) commentary.

comment|er /kɔmɑ̃te/ *v.t.* comment on. **~ateur**, **~atrice** *n.m.*, *f.* commentator.

commérages /kɔmeraʒ/ *n.m. pl.* gossip.

commerçant, **~e** /kɔmɛrsɑ̃, -t/ *a.* (*rue*) shopping; (*personne*) business-minded. ● *n.m.*, *f.* shopkeeper.

commerce /kɔmɛrs/ *n.m.* trade, commerce; (*magasin*) business. **faire du ~**, trade.

commerc|ial (*m. pl.* **~iaux**) /kɔmɛrsjal, -jo/ *a.* commercial. **~ialiser** *v.t.* market. **~ialisable** *a.* marketable.

commère /kɔmɛr/ *n.f.* gossip.

commettre /kɔmɛtr/ *v.t.* commit.

commis /kɔmi/ *n.m.* (*de magasin*) assistant; (*de bureau*) clerk.

commissaire /kɔmisɛr/ *n.m.* (*sport*) steward. **~ (de police),** (police) superintendent. **~-priseur** (*pl.* **~spriseurs**) *n.m.* auctioneer.

commissariat /kɔmisarja/ *n.m.* **~ (de police),** police station.

commission /kɔmisjɔ̃/ *n.f.* commission; (*course*) errand; (*message*) message. **~s,** shopping. **~naire** /-jɔnɛr/ *n.m.* errand-boy.

commod|e /kɔmɔd/ *a.* handy; (*facile*) easy. **pas ~e,** (*personne*) a difficult customer. ● *n.f.* chest (of drawers). **~ité** *n.f.* convenience.

commotion /kɔmosjɔ̃/ *n.f.* **~ (cérébrale),** concussion. **~né** /-jɔne/ *a.* shaken.

commuer /kɔmɥe/ *v.t.* commute.

commun, ~e /kɔmœ̃, -yn/ *a.* common; (*effort, action*) joint; (*frais, pièce*) shared. ● *n.f.* (*circonscription*) commune. **~s** *n.m. pl.* outhouses, outbuildings. **avoir** *ou* **mettre en ~,** share. **le ~ des mortels,** ordinary mortals. **~al** (*m. pl.* **~aux**) /-ynal, -o/ *a.* of the commune, local. **~ément** /-ynemɑ̃/ *adv.* commonly.

communauté /kɔmynote/ *n.f.* community. **~ des biens** (*entre époux*) shared estate.

commune /kɔmyn/ *voir* commun.

communiant, ~e /kɔmynjɑ̃, -t/ *n.m., f.* (*relig.*) communicant.

communicati|f, ~ve /kɔmynikatif, -v/ *a.* communicative.

communication /kɔmynikasjɔ̃/ *n.f.* communication; (*téléphonique*) call. **~ interurbaine,** long-distance call.

commun|ier /kɔmynje/ *v.i.* (*relig.*) receive communion; (*fig.*) commune. **~ion** *n.f.* communion.

communiqué /kɔmynike/ *n.m.* communiqué.

communiquer /kɔmynike/ *v.t.* pass on, communicate; (*mouvement*) impart. ● *v.i.* communicate. **se ~ à,** spread to.

communis|te /kɔmynist/ *a. & n.m./f.* communist. **~me** *n.m.* communism.

commutateur /kɔmytatœr/ *n.m.* (*électr.*) switch.

compact /kɔ̃pakt/ *a.* dense; (*voiture*) compact.

compact disc /kɔ̃paktdisk/ *n.m.* (P.) compact disc.

compagne /kɔ̃paɲ/ *n.f.* companion.

compagnie /kɔ̃paɲi/ *n.f.* company. **tenir ~ à,** keep company.

compagnon /kɔ̃paɲɔ̃/ *n.m.* companion; (*ouvrier*) workman. **~ de jeu,** playmate.

comparaître /kɔ̃parɛtr/ *v.i.* (*jurid.*) appear (**devant,** before).

compar|er /kɔ̃pare/ *v.t.* compare. **~er qch./qn. à** *ou* **et** compare sth./ s.o. with *ou* and; **se ~er** *v. pr.* be compared. **~able** *a.* comparable. **~aison** *n.f.* comparison; (*littéraire*) simile. **~atif, ~ative** *a. & n.m.* comparative. **~é** *a.* comparative.

comparse /kɔ̃pars/ *n.m./f.* (*péj.*) stooge.

compartiment /kɔ̃partimɑ̃/ *n.m.* compartment. **~er** /-te/ *v.t.* divide up.

comparution /kɔ̃parysjɔ̃/ *n.f.* (*jurid.*) appearance.

compas /kɔ̃pa/ *n.m.* (pair of) compasses; (*boussole*) compass.

compassé /kɔ̃pase/ *a.* stilted.

compassion /kɔ̃pasjɔ̃/ *n.f.* compassion.

compatible /kɔ̃patibl/ *a.* compatible.

compatir /kɔ̃patir/ *v.i.* sympathize. **~ à,** share in.

compatriote /kɔ̃patrijot/ *n.m./f.* compatriot.

compens|er /kɔ̃pɑ̃se/ *v.t.* compensate for, make up for. **~ation** *n.f.* compensation.

compère /kɔ̃pɛr/ *n.m.* accomplice.

compéten|t, ~te /kɔ̃petɑ̃, -t/ *a.* competent. **~ce** *n.f.* competence.

compétiti|f, ~ve /kɔ̃petitif, -v/ *a.* competitive.

compétition /kɔ̃petisjɔ̃/ *n.f.* competition; (*sportive*) event. **de ~,** competitive.

complainte /kɔ̃plɛ̃t/ *n.f.* lament.

complaire (se) /(sə)kɔ̃plɛr/ *v. pr.* **se ~ dans,** delight in.

complaisan|t, ~te /kɔ̃plɛzɑ̃, -t/ *a.* kind; (*indulgent*) indulgent. **~ce** *n.f.* kindness; indulgence.

complément /kɔ̃plemɑ̃/ *n.m.* complement; (*reste*) rest. **~ (d'objet),** (*gram.*) object. **~ d'information,** further information. **~aire** /-tɛr/ *a.*

complementary; (*renseignements*) supplementary.

compl|et [1], **~ète** /kɔ̃plɛ, -t/ a. complete; (*train, hôtel, etc.*) full. **~ètement** adv. completely.

complet [2] /kɔ̃plɛ/ n.m. suit.

compléter /kɔ̃plete/ v.t. complete; (*agrémenter*) complement. **se ~** v. pr. complement each other.

complex|e [1] /kɔ̃plɛks/ a. complex. **~ité** n.f. complexity.

complex|e [2] /kɔ̃plɛks/ n.m. (*sentiment, bâtiments*) complex. **~é** a. hung up.

complication /kɔ̃plikasjɔ̃/ n.f. complication; (*complexité*) complexity.

complic|e /kɔ̃plis/ n.m. accomplice. **~ité** n.f. complicity.

compliment /kɔ̃plimɑ̃/ n.m. compliment. **~s,** (*félicitations*) congratulations. **~er** /-te/ v.t. compliment.

compliqu|er /kɔ̃plike/ v.t. complicate. **se ~er** v. pr. become complicated. **~é** a. complicated.

complot /kɔ̃plo/ n.m. plot. **~er** /-ɔte/ v.t./i. plot.

comporter [1] /kɔ̃pɔrte/ v.t. contain; (*impliquer*) involve.

comport|er [2] (se) /(sə)kɔ̃pɔrte/ v. pr. behave; (*joueur*) perform. **~ement** n.m. behaviour; (*de joueur*) performance.

composé /kɔ̃poze/ a. compound; (*guindé*) affected. ● n.m. compound.

compos|er /kɔ̃poze/ v.t. make up, compose; (*chanson, visage*) compose; (*numéro*) dial. ● v.i. (*scol.*) take an exam; (*transiger*) compromise. **se ~er de,** be made up *ou* composed of. **~ant** n.m., **~ante** n.f. component.

composi|teur, **~trice** /kɔ̃pozitœr, -tris/ n.m., f. (*mus.*) composer.

composition /kɔ̃pozisjɔ̃/ n.f. composition; (*examen*) test, exam.

composter /kɔ̃pɔste/ v.t. (*billet*) punch.

compot|e /kɔ̃pɔt/ n.f. stewed fruit. **~e de pommes,** stewed apples. **~ier** n.m. fruit dish.

compréhensible /kɔ̃preɑ̃sibl/ a. understandable.

compréhensi|f, **~ve** /kɔ̃preɑ̃sif, -v/ a. understanding.

compréhension /kɔ̃preɑ̃sjɔ̃/ n.f. understanding, comprehension.

comprendre† /kɔ̃prɑ̃dr/ v.t. understand; (*comporter*) comprise. **ça se comprend,** that is understandable.

compresse /kɔ̃prɛs/ n.f. compress.

compression /kɔ̃prɛsjɔ̃/ n.f. (*physique*) compression; (*réduction*) reduction. **~ de personnel,** staff cuts.

comprimé /kɔ̃prime/ n.m. tablet.

comprimer /kɔ̃prime/ v.t. compress; (*réduire*) reduce.

compris, **~e** /kɔ̃pri, -z/ a. included; (*d'accord*) agreed. **~ entre,** (contained) between. **service (non) ~,** service (not) included, (not) including service. **tout ~,** (all) inclusive. **y ~,** including.

compromettre /kɔ̃prɔmɛtr/ v.t. compromise.

compromis /kɔ̃prɔmi/ n.m. compromise.

comptab|le /kɔ̃tabl/ a. accounting. ● n.m. accountant. **~ilité** n.f. accountancy; (*comptes*) accounts; (*service*) accounts department.

comptant /kɔ̃tɑ̃/ adv. (*payer*) (in) cash; (*acheter*) for cash.

compte /kɔ̃t/ n.m. count; (*facture, à la banque, comptabilité*) account; (*nombre exact*) right number. **demander/rendre des ~s,** ask for/ give an explanation. **à bon ~,** cheaply. **s'en tirer à bon ~,** get off lightly. **à son ~,** (*travailler*) for o.s., on one's own. **faire le ~ de,** count. **pour le ~ de,** on behalf of. **sur le ~ de,** about. **~ à rebours,** countdown. **~-gouttes** n.m. invar. (*méd.*) dropper. **au ~-gouttes,** (*fig.*) in dribs and drabs. **~ rendu,** report; (*de film, livre*) review. **~-tours** n.m. invar. rev counter.

compter /kɔ̃te/ v.t. count; (*prévoir*) reckon; (*facturer*) charge for; (*avoir*) have; (*classer*) consider. ● v.i. (*calculer, importer*) count. **~ avec,** reckon with. **~ faire,** expect to do. **~ parmi,** be considered among. **~ sur,** rely on.

compteur /kɔ̃tœr/ n.m. meter. **~ de vitesse,** speedometer.

comptine /kɔ̃tin/ n.f. nursery rhyme.

comptoir /kɔ̃twar/ n.m. counter; (*de café*) bar.

compulser /kɔ̃pylse/ v.t. examine.

comt|e, **~esse** /kɔ̃t, -ɛs/ n.m., f. count, countess.

comté /kɔ̃te/ n.m. county.

con, conne /kɔ̃, kɔn/ *a.* (*argot*) bloody foolish. ● *n.m.*, *f.* (*argot*) bloody fool.

concave /kɔ̃kav/ *a.* concave.

concéder /kɔ̃sede/ *v.t.* grant, concede.

concentr|er /kɔ̃sɑ̃tre/ *v.t.*, **se ~er** *v. pr.* concentrate. **~ation** *n.f.* concentration. **~é** *a.* concentrated; (*lait*) condensed; (*personne*) absorbed; *n.m.* concentrate.

concept /kɔ̃sɛpt/ *n.m.* concept.

conception /kɔ̃sɛpsjɔ̃/ *n.f.* conception.

concerner /kɔ̃sɛrne/ *v.t.* concern. **en ce qui me concerne**, as far as I am concerned.

concert /kɔ̃sɛr/ *n.m.* concert. **de ~**, in unison.

concert|er /kɔ̃sɛrte/ *v.t.* organize, prepare. **se ~er** *v. pr.* confer. **~é** *a.* (*plan etc.*) concerted.

concerto /kɔ̃sɛrto/ *n.m.* concerto.

concession /kɔ̃sesjɔ̃/ *n.f.* concession; (*terrain*) plot.

concessionnaire /kɔ̃sesjɔnɛr/ *n.m./f.* (authorized) dealer.

concevoir† /kɔ̃svwar/ *v.t.* (*imaginer*, *engendrer*) conceive; (*comprendre*) understand.

concierge /kɔ̃sjɛrʒ/ *n.m./f.* caretaker.

concile /kɔ̃sil/ *n.m.* council.

concil|ier /kɔ̃silje/ *v.t.* reconcile. **se ~ier** *v. pr.* (*s'attirer*) win (over). **~iation** *n.f.* conciliation.

concis, ~e /kɔ̃si, -z/ *a.* concise. **~ion** /-zjɔ̃/ *n.f.* concision.

concitoyen, ~ne /kɔ̃sitwajɛ̃, -jɛn/ *n.m.*, *f.* fellow citizen.

concl|ure† /kɔ̃klyr/ *v.t./i.* conclude. **~ure à**, conclude in favour of. **~uant, ~uante** *a.* conclusive. **~usion** *n.f.* conclusion.

concocter /kɔ̃kɔkte/ *v.t.* (*fam.*) cook up.

concombre /kɔ̃kɔ̃br/ *n.m.* cucumber.

concorde /kɔ̃kɔrd/ *n.f.* concord.

concord|er /kɔ̃kɔrde/ *v.i.* agree. **~ance** *n.f.* agreement; (*analogie*) similarity. **~ant, ~ante** *a.* in agreement.

concourir /kɔ̃kurir/ *v.i.* compete. **~ à**, contribute towards.

concours /kɔ̃kur/ *n.m.* competition; (*examen*) competitive examination; (*aide*) aid; (*de circonstances*) combination.

concr|et, ~ète /kɔ̃krɛ, -t/ *a.* concrete. **~ètement** *adv.* in concrete terms.

concrétiser /kɔ̃kretize/ *v.t.* give concrete form to. **se ~** *v. pr.* materialize.

conçu /kɔ̃sy/ *a.* **bien/mal ~**, (*appartement etc.*) well/badly planned.

concubinage /kɔ̃kybinaʒ/ *n.m.* cohabitation.

concurrenc|e /kɔ̃kyrɑ̃s/ *n.f.* competition. **faire ~e à**, compete with. **jusqu'à ~e de**, up to. **~er** *v.t.* compete with.

concurrent, ~e /kɔ̃kyrɑ̃, -t/ *n.m.*, *f.* competitor; (*scol.*) candidate. ● *a.* competing.

condamn|er /kɔ̃dane/ *v.t.* (*censurer*, *obliger*) condemn; (*jurid.*) sentence; (*porte*) block up. **~ation** *n.f.* condemnation; (*peine*) sentence. **~é** *a.* (*fichu*) without hope, doomed.

condens|er /kɔ̃dɑ̃se/ *v.t.*, **se ~er** *v. pr.* condense. **~ation** *n.f.* condensation.

condescendre /kɔ̃desɑ̃dr/ *v.i.* condescend (**à**, to).

condiment /kɔ̃dimɑ̃/ *n.m.* condiment.

condisciple /kɔ̃disipl/ *n.m.* classmate, schoolfellow.

condition /kɔ̃disjɔ̃/ *n.f.* condition. **~s**, (*prix*) terms. **à ~ de ou que**, provided (that). **sans ~**, unconditional(ly). **~nel, ~nelle** /-jɔnɛl/ *a.* conditional. **~nel** *n.m.* conditional (tense).

conditionnement /kɔ̃disjɔnmɑ̃/ *n.m.* conditioning; (*emballage*) packaging.

conditionner /kɔ̃disjɔne/ *v.t.* condition; (*emballer*) package.

condoléances /kɔ̃dɔleɑ̃s/ *n.f. pl.* condolences.

conduc|teur, ~trice /kɔ̃dyktœr, -tris/ *n.m.*, *f.* driver.

conduire† /kɔ̃dɥir/ *v.t.* lead; (*auto.*) drive; (*affaire*) conduct. ● *v.i.* drive. **se ~** *v. pr.* behave. **~ à**, (*accompagner à*) take to.

conduit /kɔ̃dɥi/ *n.m.* (*anat.*) duct.

conduite /kɔ̃dɥit/ *n.f.* conduct; (*auto.*) driving; (*tuyau*) main. **~ à droite**, (*place*) right-hand drive.

cône /kon/ *n.m.* cone.

confection /kɔ̃fɛksjɔ̃/ *n.f.* making. **de ~**, ready-made. **la ~**, the clothing industry. **~ner** /-jɔne/ *v.t.* make.

confédération /kɔ̃federɑsjɔ̃/ *n.f.* confederation.

conférenc|e /kɔ̃ferɑ̃s/ *n.f.* conference; (*exposé*) lecture. **~e au sommet**, summit conference. **~ier**, **~ière** *n.m.*, *f.* lecturer.

conférer /kɔ̃fere/ *v.t.* give; (*décerner*) confer.

confess|er /kɔ̃fese/ *v.t.*, **se ~er** *v. pr.* confess. **~eur** *n.m.* confessor. **~ion** *n.f.* confession; (*religion*) denomination. **~ionnal** (*pl.* **~ionnaux**) *n.m.* confessional. **~ionnel**, **~ionnelle** *a.* denominational.

confettis /kɔ̃feti/ *n.m. pl.* confetti.

confiance /kɔ̃fjɑ̃s/ *n.f.* trust. **avoir ~ en**, trust.

confiant, **~e** /kɔ̃fjɑ̃, -t/ *a.* (*assuré*) confident; (*sans défiance*) trusting. **~ en** *ou* **dans**, confident in.

confiden|t, **~te** /kɔ̃fidɑ̃, -t/ *n.m.*, *f.* confidant, confidante. **~ce** *n.f.* confidence.

confidentiel, **~le** /kɔ̃fidɑ̃sjɛl/ *a.* confidential.

confier /kɔ̃fje/ *v.t.* **~ à qn.**, entrust s.o. with; (*secret*) confide to s.o. **se ~ à**, confide in.

configuration /kɔ̃figyrɑsjɔ̃/ *n.f.* configuration.

confiner /kɔ̃fine/ *v.t.* confine. ● *v.i.* **~ à**, border on. **se ~** *v. pr.* confine o.s. (**à**, **dans**, to).

confins /kɔ̃fɛ̃/ *n.m. pl.* confines.

confirm|er /kɔ̃firme/ *v.t.* confirm. **~ation** *n.f.* confirmation.

confis|erie /kɔ̃fizri/ *n.f.* sweet shop. **~eries**, confectionery. **~eur**, **~euse** *n.m.*, *f.* confectioner.

confis|quer /kɔ̃fiske/ *v.t.* confiscate. **~cation** *n.f.* confiscation.

confit, **~e** /kɔ̃fi, -t/ *a.* (*culin.*) candied. **fruits ~s**, crystallized fruits. ● *n.m.* **~ d'oie**, goose liver conserve.

confiture /kɔ̃fityr/ *n.f.* jam.

conflit /kɔ̃fli/ *n.m.* conflict.

confondre /kɔ̃fɔ̃dr/ *v.t.* confuse, mix up; (*consterner*, *étonner*) confound. **se ~** *v. pr.* merge. **se ~ en excuses**, apologize profusely.

confondu /kɔ̃fɔ̃dy/ *a.* (*déconcerté*) overwhelmed, confounded.

conforme /kɔ̃fɔrm/ *a.* **~ à**, in accordance with.

conformément /kɔ̃fɔrmemɑ̃/ *adv.* **~ à**, in accordance with.

conform|er /kɔ̃fɔrme/ *v.t.* adapt. **se ~er à**, conform to. **~ité** *n.f.* conformity.

conformis|te /kɔ̃fɔrmist/ *a. & n.m./f.* conformist. **~me** *n.m.* conformism.

confort /kɔ̃fɔr/ *n.m.* comfort. **tout ~**, with all mod cons. **~able** /-tabl/ *a.* comfortable.

confrère /kɔ̃frɛr/ *n.m.* colleague.

confrérie /kɔ̃freri/ *n.f.* brotherhood.

confront|er /kɔ̃frɔ̃te/ *v.t.* compare; (*textes*) collate. **se ~er à** *v. pr.* confront. **~ation** *n.f.* confrontation.

confus, **~e** /kɔ̃fy, -z/ *a.* confused; (*gêné*) embarrassed.

confusion /kɔ̃fyzjɔ̃/ *n.f.* confusion; (*gêné*) embarrassment.

congé /kɔ̃ʒe/ *n.m.* holiday; (*arrêt momentané*) time off; (*mil.*) leave; (*avis de départ*) notice. **~ de maladie**, sick-leave. **~ de maternité**, maternity leave. **jour de ~**, day off. **prendre ~ de**, take one's leave of.

congédier /kɔ̃ʒedje/ *v.t.* dismiss.

congeler /kɔ̃ʒle/ *v.t.* freeze. **les ~elés**, frozen food. **~élateur** *n.m.* freezer.

congénère /kɔ̃ʒenɛr/ *n.m./f.* fellow creature.

congénit|al (*m. pl.* **~aux**) /kɔ̃ʒenital, -o/ *a.* congenital.

congère /kɔ̃ʒer/ *n.f.* snow-drift.

congestion /kɔ̃ʒɛstjɔ̃/ *n.f.* congestion. **~ cérébrale**, stroke, cerebral haemorrhage. **~ner** /-jɔne/ *v.t.* congest; (*visage*) flush.

congrégation /kɔ̃gregɑsjɔ̃/ *n.f.* congregation.

congrès /kɔ̃grɛ/ *n.m.* congress.

conifère /kɔnifɛr/ *n.m.* conifer.

conique /kɔnik/ *a.* conic(al).

conjecture /kɔ̃ʒɛktyr/ *n.f.* conjecture. **~er** *v.t./i.* conjecture.

conjoint, **~e**[1] /kɔ̃ʒwɛ̃, -t/ *n.m.*, *f.* spouse.

conjoint, **~e**[2] /kɔ̃ʒwɛ̃, -t/ *a.* joint. **~ement** /-tmɑ̃/ *adv.* jointly.

conjonction /kɔ̃ʒɔ̃ksjɔ̃/ *n.f.* conjunction.

conjonctivite /kɔ̃ʒɔ̃ktivit/ *n.f.* conjunctivitis.

conjoncture /kɔ̃ʒɔ̃ktyr/ *n.f.* circumstances; (*économique*) economic climate.

conjugaison /kɔ̃ʒygɛzɔ̃/ *n.f.* conjugation.

conjug|al (*m. pl.* **~aux**) /kɔ̃ʒygal, -o/ *a.* conjugal.

conjuguer /kɔ̃ʒyge/ *v.t.* (*gram.*) conjugate; (*efforts*) combine. **se ~** *v. pr.* (*gram.*) be conjugated.

conjur|er /kɔ̃ʒyre/ *v.t.* (*éviter*) avert; (*implorer*) entreat. **~ation** *n.f.* conspiracy. **~é, ~ée** *n.m., f.* conspirator.

connaissance /kɔnɛsɑ̃s/ *n.f.* knowledge; (*personne*) acquaintance. **~s,** (*science*) knowledge. **faire la ~ de,** meet; (*personne connue*) get to know. **perdre ~,** lose consciousness. **sans ~,** unconscious.

connaisseur /kɔnɛsœr/ *n.m.* connoisseur.

connaître† /kɔnɛtr/ *v.t.* know; (*avoir*) have. **se ~** *v. pr.* (*se rencontrer*) meet. **faire ~,** make known. **s'y ~ à ou en,** know (all) about.

conne|cter /kɔnɛkte/ *v.t.* connect. **~xion** *n.f.* connection.

connerie /kɔnri/ *n.f.* (*argot*) (*remarque*) rubbish. **faire une ~,** do sth. stupid. **dire une ~,** talk rubbish. **quelle ~!,** how stupid!

connivence /kɔnivɑ̃s/ *n.f.* connivance.

connotation /kɔnɔtasjɔ̃/ *n.f.* connotation.

connu /kɔny/ *a.* well-known.

conquér|ir /kɔ̃kerir/ *v.t.* conquer. **~ant, ~ante** *n.m., f.* conqueror.

conquête /kɔ̃kɛt/ *n.f.* conquest.

consacrer /kɔ̃sakre/ *v.t.* devote; (*relig.*) consecrate; (*sanctionner*) establish. **se ~** *v. pr.* devote o.s. (**à,** to).

consciemment /kɔ̃sjamɑ̃/ *adv.* consciously.

conscience /kɔ̃sjɑ̃s/ *n.f.* conscience; (*perception*) consciousness. **avoir/prendre ~ de,** be/become aware of. **perdre ~,** lose consciousness. **avoir bonne/mauvaise ~,** have a clear/guilty conscience.

consciencieu|x, ~se /kɔ̃sjɑ̃sjø, -z/ *a.* conscientious.

conscient, ~e /kɔ̃sjɑ̃, -t/ *a.* conscious. **~ de,** aware *ou* conscious of.

conscrit /kɔ̃skri/ *n.m.* conscript.

consécration /kɔ̃sekrasjɔ̃/ *n.f.* consecration.

consécuti|f, ~ve /kɔ̃sekytif, -v/ *a.* consecutive. **~f à,** following upon. **~vement** *adv.* consecutively.

conseil /kɔ̃sɛj/ *n.m.* (piece of) advice; (*assemblée*) council, committee; (*séance*) meeting; (*personne*) consultant. **~ d'administration,** board of directors. **~ des ministres,** Cabinet. **~ municipal,** town council.

conseiller[1] /kɔ̃seje/ *v.t.* advise. **~ à qn. de,** advise s.o. to. **~ qch. à qn.,** recommend sth. to s.o.

conseill|er[2], **~ère** /kɔ̃seje, -ɛjɛr/ *n.m., f.* adviser, counsellor. **~er municipal,** town councillor.

consent|ir /kɔ̃sɑ̃tir/ *v.i.* agree (**à,** to). ● *v.t.* grant. **~ement** *n.m.* consent.

conséquence /kɔ̃sekɑ̃s/ *n.f.* consequence. **en ~,** consequently; (*comme il convient*) accordingly.

conséquent, ~e /kɔ̃sekɑ̃, -t/ *a.* logical; (*important; fam.*) sizeable. **par ~,** consequently.

conserva|teur, ~trice /kɔ̃sɛrvatœr, -tris/ *a.* conservative. ● *n.m., f.* (*pol.*) conservative. ● *n.m.* (*de musée*) curator. **~tisme** *n.m.* conservatism.

conservatoire /kɔ̃sɛrvatwar/ *n.m.* academy.

conserve /kɔ̃sɛrv/ *n.f.* tinned *ou* canned food. **en ~,** tinned, canned.

conserv|er /kɔ̃sɛrve/ *v.t.* keep; (*en bon état*) preserve; (*culin.*) preserve. **se ~er** *v. pr.* (*culin.*) keep. **~ation** *n.f.* preservation.

considérable /kɔ̃siderabl/ *a.* considerable.

considération /kɔ̃siderasjɔ̃/ *n.f.* consideration; (*respect*) regard. **prendre en ~,** take into consideration.

considérer /kɔ̃sidere/ *v.t.* consider; (*respecter*) esteem. **~ comme,** consider to be.

consigne /kɔ̃siɲ/ *n.f.* (*de gare*) left luggage (office); (*Amer.*) (baggage) checkroom; (*scol.*) detention; (*somme*) deposit; (*ordres*) orders. **~ automatique,** (left-luggage) lockers; (*Amer.*) (baggage) lockers.

consigner /kɔ̃siɲe/ *v.t.* (*comm.*) charge a deposit on; (*écrire*) record; (*élève*) keep in; (*soldat*) confine.

consistan|t, ~te /kɔ̃sistɑ̃, -t/ *a.* solid; (*épais*) thick. **~ce** *n.f.* consistency; (*fig.*) solidity.

consister /kɔ̃siste/ *v.i.* **~ en/dans,** consist of/in. **~ à faire,** consist in doing.

consœur /kɔ̃sœr/ *n.f.* colleague; fellow member.

consol|er /kɔ̃sɔle/ *v.t.* console. **se ~er** *v. pr.* be consoled (**de,** for). **~ation** *n.f.* consolation.

consolider /kɔ̃sɔlide/ v.t. strengthen; (fig.) consolidate.

consomma|teur, ~trice /kɔ̃sɔmatœr, -tris/ n.m., f. (comm.) consumer; (dans un café) customer.

consommé [1] /kɔ̃sɔme/ a. consummate.

consommé [2] /kɔ̃sɔme/ n.m. (bouillon) consommé.

consomm|er /kɔ̃sɔme/ v.t. consume; (user) use, consume; (mariage) consummate. ● v.i. drink. **~ation** n.f. consumption; consummation; (boisson) drink. **de ~ation,** (comm.) consumer.

consonne /kɔ̃sɔn/ n.f. consonant.

consortium /kɔ̃sɔrsjɔm/ n.m. consortium.

conspir|er /kɔ̃spire/ v.i. conspire. **~ateur, ~atrice** n.m., f. conspirator. **~ation** n.f. conspiracy.

conspuer /kɔ̃spɥe/ v.t. boo.

const|ant, ~ante /kɔ̃stɑ̃, -t/ a. constant. ● n.f. constant. **~amment** /-amɑ̃/ adv. constantly. **~ance** n.f. constancy.

constat /kɔ̃sta/ n.m. (official) report.

constat|er /kɔ̃state/ v.t. note; (certifier) certify. **~ation** n.f. observation, statement of fact.

constellation /kɔ̃stelɑsjɔ̃/ n.f. constellation.

constellé /kɔ̃stele/ a. **~ de,** studded with.

constern|er /kɔ̃stɛrne/ v.t. dismay. **~ation** n.f. dismay.

constip|é /kɔ̃stipe/ a. constipated; (fig.) stilted. **~ation** n.f. constipation.

constitu|er /kɔ̃stitɥe/ v.t. make up, constitute; (organiser) form; (être) constitute. **se ~er prisonnier,** give o.s. up. **~é de,** made up of.

constituti|f, ~ve /kɔ̃stitytif, -v/ a. constituent.

constitution /kɔ̃stitysjɔ̃/ n.f. formation; (d'une équipe) composition; (pol., méd.) constitution. **~nel, ~nelle** /-jɔnɛl/ a. constitutional.

constructeur /kɔ̃stryktœr/ n.m. manufacturer.

constructi|f, ~ve /kɔ̃stryktif, -v/ a. constructive.

constru|ire† /kɔ̃strɥir/ v.t. build; (système, phrase, etc.) construct. **~uction** n.f. building; (structure) construction.

consul /kɔ̃syl/ n.m. consul. **~aire** a. consular. **~at** n.m. consulate.

consult|er /kɔ̃sylte/ v.t. consult. ● v.i. (médecin) hold surgery; (Amer.) hold office hours. **se ~er** v. pr. confer. **~ation** n.f. consultation; (réception: méd.) surgery; (Amer.) office.

consumer /kɔ̃syme/ v.t. consume. **se ~** v. pr. be consumed.

contact /kɔ̃takt/ n.m. contact; (toucher) touch. **au ~ de,** on contact with; (personne) by contact with, by seeing. **mettre/couper le ~,** (auto.) switch on/off the ignition. **prendre ~ avec,** get in touch with. **~er** v.t. contact.

contag|ieux, ~ieuse /kɔ̃taʒjø, -z/ a. contagious. **~ion** n.f. contagion.

container /kɔ̃tɛnɛr/ n.m. container.

contamin|er /kɔ̃tamine/ v.t. contaminate. **~ation** n.f. contamination.

conte /kɔ̃t/ n.m. tale. **~ de fées,** fairy tale.

contempl|er /kɔ̃tɑ̃ple/ v.t. contemplate. **~ation** n.f. contemplation.

contemporain, ~e /kɔ̃tɑ̃pɔrɛ̃, -ɛn/ a. & n.m., f. contemporary.

contenance /kɔ̃tnɑ̃s/ n.f. (contenu) capacity; (allure) bearing; (sangfroid) composure.

conteneur /kɔ̃tnœr/ n.m. container.

contenir† /kɔ̃tnir/ v.t. contain; (avoir une capacité de) hold. **se ~** v. pr. contain o.s.

content, ~e /kɔ̃tɑ̃, -t/ a. pleased (de, with). **~ de faire,** pleased to do.

content|er /kɔ̃tɑ̃te/ v.t. satisfy. **se ~er de,** content o.s. with. **~ement** n.m. contentment.

contentieux /kɔ̃tɑ̃sjø/ n.m. matters in dispute; (service) legal department.

contenu /kɔ̃tny/ n.m. (de contenant) contents; (de texte) content.

conter /kɔ̃te/ v.t. tell, relate.

contestataire /kɔ̃tɛstatɛr/ n.m./f. protester.

conteste (sans) /(sɑ̃)kɔ̃tɛst/ adv. indisputably.

contest|er /kɔ̃tɛste/ v.t. dispute; (s'opposer) protest against. ● v.i. protest. **~able** a. debatable. **~ation** n.f. dispute; (opposition) protest.

conteu|r, ~se /kɔ̃tœr, -øz/ n.m., f. story-teller.

contexte /kɔ̃tɛkst/ n.m. context.

contigu, **~ë** /kɔ̃tigy/ *a.* adjacent (**à**, to).

continent /kɔ̃tinɑ̃/ *n.m.* continent. **~al** (*m. pl.* **~aux**) /-tal, -to/ *a.* continental.

contingences /kɔ̃tɛ̃ʒɑ̃s/ *n.f. pl.* contingencies.

contingent /kɔ̃tɛ̃ʒɑ̃/ *n.m.* (*mil.*) contingent; (*comm.*) quota.

continu /kɔ̃tiny/ *a.* continuous.

continuel, **~le** /kɔ̃tinɥɛl/ *a.* continual. **~lement** *adv.* continually.

contin|uer /kɔ̃tinɥe/ *v.t.* continue. ● *v.i.* continue, go on. **~uer à** *ou* **de faire,** carry on *ou* go on *ou* continue doing. **~uation** *n.f.* continuation.

continuité /kɔ̃tinɥite/ *n.f.* continuity.

contorsion /kɔ̃tɔrsjɔ̃/ *n.f.* contortion. **se ~ner** *v. pr.* wriggle.

contour /kɔ̃tur/ *n.m.* outline, contour. **~s**, (*d'une route etc.*) twists and turns, bends.

contourner /kɔ̃turne/ *v.t.* go round; (*difficulté*) get round.

contracepti|f, **~ve** /kɔ̃traseptif, -v/ *a.* & *n.m.* contraceptive.

contraception /kɔ̃trasepsjɔ̃/ *n.f.* contraception.

contract|er /kɔ̃trakte/ *v.t.* (*maladie, dette*) contract; (*muscle*) tense, contract; (*assurance*) take out. **se ~er** *v. pr.* contract. **~é** *a.* tense. **~ion** /-ksjɔ̃/ *n.f.* contraction.

contractuel, **~le** /kɔ̃traktɥɛl/ *n.m.,f.* (*agent*) traffic warden.

contradiction /kɔ̃tradiksjɔ̃/ *n.f.* contradiction.

contradictoire /kɔ̃tradiktwar/ *a.* contradictory; (*débat*) open.

contraignant, **~e** /kɔ̃trɛɲɑ̃, -t/ *a.* restricting.

contraindre† /kɔ̃trɛ̃dr/ *v.t.* compel.

contraint, **~e** /kɔ̃trɛ̃, -t/ *a.* constrained. ● *n.f.* constraint.

contraire /kɔ̃trɛr/ *a.* & *n.m.* opposite. **~ à,** contrary to. **au ~,** on the contrary. **~ment** *adv.* **~ment à,** contrary to.

contralto /kɔ̃tralto/ *n.m.* contralto.

contrar|ier /kɔ̃trarje/ *v.t.* annoy; (*action*) frustrate. **~iété** *n.f.* annoyance.

contrast|e /kɔ̃trast/ *n.m.* contrast. **~er** *v.i.* contrast.

contrat /kɔ̃tra/ *n.m.* contract.

contravention /kɔ̃travɑ̃sjɔ̃/ *n.f.* (parking)ticket. **en ~,** in contravention (**à,** of).

contre /kɔ̃tr(ə)/ *prép.* against; (*en échange de*) for. **par ~,** on the other hand. **tout ~,** close by. **~-attaque** *n.f.,* **~-attaquer** *v.t.* counter-attack. **~-balancer** *v.t.* counterbalance. **~-courant** *n.m.* **aller à ~-courant de,** swim against the current of. **~-indiqué** *a.* (*méd.*) contra-indicated; (*déconseillé*) not recommended. **à ~-jour** *adv.* against the (sun)light. **~-offensive** *n.f.* counter-offensive. **prendre le ~-pied,** do the opposite; (*opinion*) take the opposite view. **à ~-pied** *adv.* (*sport*) on the wrong foot. **~-plaqué** *n.m.* plywood. **~-révolution** *n.f.* counter-revolution. **~-torpilleur** *n.m.* destroyer.

contreband|e /kɔ̃trəbɑ̃d/ *n.f.* contraband. **faire la ~e de, passer en ~e,** smuggle. **~ier** *n.m.* smuggler.

contrebas (en) /(ɑ̃)kɔ̃trəba/ *adv.* & *prép.* **en ~ (de),** below.

contrebasse /kɔ̃trəbas/ *n.f.* double-bass.

contrecarrer /kɔ̃trəkare/ *v.t.* thwart.

contrecœur (à) /(a)kɔ̃trəkœr/ *adv.* reluctantly.

contrecoup /kɔ̃trəku/ *n.m.* consequence.

contredire† /kɔ̃trədir/ *v.t.* contradict. **se ~** *v. pr.* contradict o.s.

contrée /kɔ̃tre/ *n.f.* region, land.

contrefaçon /kɔ̃trəfasɔ̃/ *n.f.* (*objet imité, action*) forgery.

contrefaire /kɔ̃trəfɛr/ *v.t.* (*falsifier*) forge; (*parodier*) mimic; (*déguiser*) disguise.

contrefait, **~e** /kɔ̃trəfɛ, -t/ *a.* deformed.

contreforts /kɔ̃trəfɔr/ *n.m. pl.* foot-hills.

contremaître /kɔ̃trəmɛtr/ *n.m.* foreman.

contrepartie /kɔ̃trəparti/ *n.f.* compensation. **en ~,** in exchange, in return.

contrepoids /kɔ̃trəpwa/ *n.m.* counterbalance.

contrer /kɔ̃tre/ *v.t.* counter.

contresens /kɔ̃trəsɑ̃s/ *n.m.* misinterpretation; (*absurdité*) nonsense. **à ~,** the wrong way.

contresigner /kɔ̃trəsiɲe/ *v.t.* countersign.

contretemps /kɔ̃trətɑ̃/ *n.m.* hitch. **à ~**, at the wrong time.

contrevenir /kɔ̃trəvnir/ *v.i.* **~ à**, contravene.

contribuable /kɔ̃tribɥabl/ *n.m./f.* taxpayer.

contribuer /kɔ̃tribɥe/ *v.t.* contribute (**à**, towards).

contribution /kɔ̃tribysjɔ̃/ *n.f.* contribution. **~s**, (*impôts*) taxes; (*administration*) tax office.

contrit, **~e** /kɔ̃tri, -t/ *a.* contrite.

contrôl|e /kɔ̃trol/ *n.m.* check; (*des prix, d'un véhicule*) control; (*poinçon*) hallmark; (*scol.*) test. **~e continu**, continuous assessment. **~e de soi-même**, self-control. **~e des changes**, exchange control. **~e des naissances** birth-control. **~er** *v.t.* check; (*surveiller, maîtriser*) control. **se ~er** *v. pr.* control o.s.

contrôleu|r, **~se** /kɔ̃trolœr, -øz/ *n.m., f.* (bus) conductor *ou* conductress; (*de train*) (ticket) inspector.

contrordre /kɔ̃trɔrdr/ *n.m.* change of orders.

controvers|e /kɔ̃trɔvɛrs/ *n.f.* controversy. **~é** *a.* controversial.

contumace (par) /(par)kɔ̃tymas/ *adv.* in one's absence.

contusion /kɔ̃tyzjɔ̃/ *n.f.* bruise. **~né** /-jɔne/ *a.* bruised.

convaincre† /kɔ̃vɛ̃kr/ *v.t.* convince. **~ qn. de faire**, persuade s.o. to do.

convalescen|t, **~te** /kɔ̃valesɑ̃, -t/ *a. & n.m., f.* convalescent. **~ce** *n.f.* convalescence. **être en ~ce**, convalesce.

convenable /kɔ̃vnabl/ *a.* (*correct*) decent, proper; (*approprié*) suitable.

convenance /kɔ̃vnɑ̃s/ *n.f.* **à sa ~**, to one's satisfaction. **les ~s**, the proprieties.

convenir† /kɔ̃vnir/ *v.i.* be suitable. **~ à qch.**, suit. **~ de/que**, (*avouer*) admit (to)/that. **~ de qch.**, (*s'accorder sur*) agree on sth. **~ de faire**, agree to do. **il convient de**, it is advisable to; (*selon les bienséances*) it would be right to.

convention /kɔ̃vɑ̃sjɔ̃/ *n.f.* convention. **~s**, (*convenances*) convention. **de ~**, conventional. **~ collective**, industrial agreement. **~né** *a.* (*prix*) official; (*médecin*) health service (*not private*). **~nel**, **~nelle** /-jɔnɛl/ *a.* conventional.

convenu /kɔ̃vny/ *a.* agreed.

converger /kɔ̃vɛrʒe/ *v.i.* converge.

convers|er /kɔ̃vɛrse/ *v.i.* converse. **~ation** *n.f.* conversation.

conver|tir /kɔ̃vɛrtir/ *v.t.* convert (**à**, to; **en**, into). **se ~tir** *v. pr.* be converted, convert. **~sion** *n.f.* conversion. **~tible** *a.* convertible.

convexe /kɔ̃vɛks/ *a.* convex.

conviction /kɔ̃viksjɔ̃/ *n.f.* conviction.

convier /kɔ̃vje/ *v.t.* invite.

convive /kɔ̃viv/ *n.m./f.* guest.

conviv|ial (*m. pl.* **~iaux**) /kɔ̃vivjal, -jo/ *a.* convivial; (*comput.*) user-friendly.

convocation /kɔ̃vɔkasjɔ̃/ *n.f.* summons to attend; (*d'une assemblée*) convening; (*document*) notification to attend.

convoi /kɔ̃vwa/ *n.m.* convoy; (*train*) train. **~ (funèbre)**, funeral procession.

convoit|er /kɔ̃vwate/ *v.t.* desire, covet, envy. **~ise** *n.f.* desire, envy.

convoquer /kɔ̃vɔke/ *v.t.* (*assemblée*) convene; (*personne*) summon.

convoy|er /kɔ̃vwaje/ *v.t.* escort. **~eur** *n.m.* escort ship. **~eur de fonds**, security guard.

convulsion /kɔ̃vylsjɔ̃/ *n.f.* convulsion.

cool /kul/ *a. invar.* cool, laidback.

coopérati|f, **~ve** /kɔɔperatif, -v/ *a.* co-operative. ● *n.f.* co-operative (society).

coopér|er /kɔɔpere/ *v.i.* co-operate (**à**, in). **~ation** *n.f.* co-operation. **la C~ation**, civilian national service.

coopter /kɔɔpte/ *v.t.* co-opt.

coordination /kɔɔrdinasjɔ̃/ *n.f.* co-ordination.

coordonn|er /kɔɔrdɔne/ *v.t.* co-ordinate. **~ées** *n.f. pl.* co-ordinates; (*adresse: fam.*) particulars.

copain /kɔpɛ̃/ *n.m.* (*fam.*) pal; (*petit ami*) boyfriend.

copeau (*pl.* **~x**) /kɔpo/ *n.m.* (*lamelle de bois*) shaving.

cop|ie /kɔpi/ *n.f.* copy; (*scol.*) paper. **~ier** *v.t./i.* copy. **~ier sur**, (*scol.*) copy *ou* crib from.

copieu|x, **~se** /kɔpjø, -z/ *a.* copious.

copine /kɔpin/ *n.f.* (*fam.*) pal; (*petite amie*) girlfriend.

copiste /kɔpist/ *n.m./f.* copyist.

coproduction /kɔprɔdyksjɔ̃/ *n.f.* co-production.

copropriété /kɔprɔprijete/ *n.f.* co-ownership.

copulation /kɔpylasjɔ̃/ *n.f.* copulation.

coq /kɔk/ *n.m.* cock. ~-à-l'âne *n.m. invar.* abrupt change of subject.

coque /kɔk/ *n.f.* shell; (*de bateau*) hull.

coquelicot /kɔkliko/ *n.m.* poppy.

coqueluche /kɔklyʃ/ *n.f.* whooping cough.

coquet, ~te /kɔkɛ, -t/ *a.* flirtatious; (*élégant*) pretty; (*somme: fam.*) tidy. ~terie /-tri/ *n.f.* flirtatiousness.

coquetier /kɔktje/ *n.m.* egg-cup.

coquillage /kɔkijaʒ/ *n.m.* shellfish; (*coquille*) shell.

coquille /kɔkij/ *n.f.* shell; (*faute*) misprint. ~ **Saint-Jacques**, scallop.

coquin, ~e /kɔkɛ̃, -in/ *a.* naughty. ● *n.m., f.* rascal.

cor /kɔr/ *n.m.* (*mus.*) horn; (*au pied*) corn.

cor|ail (*pl.* ~**aux**) /kɔraj, -o/ *n.m.* coral.

Coran /kɔrɑ̃/ *n.m.* Koran.

corbeau (*pl.* ~**x**) /kɔrbo/ *n.m.* (*oiseau*) crow.

corbeille /kɔrbɛj/ *n.f.* basket. ~ **à papier**, waste-paper basket.

corbillard /kɔrbijar/ *n.m.* hearse.

cordage /kɔrdaʒ/ *n.m.* rope. ~**s**, (*naut.*) rigging.

corde /kɔrd/ *n.f.* rope; (*d'arc, de violon, etc.*) string. ~ **à linge**, washing line. ~ **à sauter**, skipping-rope. ~ **raide**, tightrope. ~**s vocales**, vocal cords.

cordée /kɔrde/ *n.f.* roped party.

cord|ial (*m. pl.* ~**iaux**) /kɔrdjal, -jo/ *a.* warm, cordial. ~**ialité** *n.f.* warmth.

cordon /kɔrdɔ̃/ *n.m.* string, cord. ~-**bleu** (*pl.* ~**s-bleus**) *n.m.* first-rate cook. ~ **de police**, police cordon.

cordonnier /kɔrdɔnje/ *n.m.* shoe mender.

Corée /kɔre/ *n.f.* Korea.

coreligionnaire /kɔrəliʒjɔnɛr/ *n.m./ f.* person of the same religion.

coriace /kɔrjas/ *a.* (*aliment*) tough. ● *a. & n.m.* tenacious and tough (person).

corne /kɔrn/ *n.f.* horn.

cornée /kɔrne/ *n.f.* cornea.

corneille /kɔrnɛj/ *n.f.* crow.

cornemuse /kɔrnəmyz/ *n.f.* bagpipes.

corner[1] /kɔrne/ *v.t.* (*page*) make dog-eared. ● *v.i.* (*auto.*) hoot; (*auto., Amer.*) honk.

corner[2] /kɔrnɛr/ *n.m.* (*football*) corner.

cornet /kɔrnɛ/ *n.m.* (*paper*) cone; (*crème glacée*) cornet, cone.

corniaud /kɔrnjo/ *n.m.* (*fam.*) nitwit.

corniche /kɔrniʃ/ *n.f.* cornice; (*route*) cliff road.

cornichon /kɔrniʃɔ̃/ *n.m.* gherkin.

corollaire /kɔrɔlɛr/ *n.m.* corollary.

corporation /kɔrpɔrasjɔ̃/ *n.f.* professional body.

corporel, ~le /kɔrpɔrɛl/ *a.* bodily; (*châtiment*) corporal.

corps /kɔr/ *n.m.* body; (*mil., pol.*) corps. ~ **à corps**, hand to hand. ~ **électoral**, electorate. ~ **enseignant**, teaching profession. **faire ~ avec**, form part of.

corpulen|t, ~te /kɔrpylɑ̃, -t/ *a.* stout. ~**ce** *n.f.* stoutness.

correct /kɔrɛkt/ *a.* proper, correct; (*exact*) correct; (*tenue*) decent. ~**ement** *adv.* properly; correctly; decently.

correc|teur, ~trice /kɔrɛktœr, -tris/ *n.m., f.* (*d'épreuves*) proof-reader; (*scol.*) examiner. ~**teur d'ortho-graphe**, spelling checker.

correction /kɔrɛksjɔ̃/ *n.f.* correction; (*punition*) beating.

corrélation /kɔrelasjɔ̃/ *n.f.* correlation.

correspondan|t, ~te /kɔrɛspɔ̃dɑ̃, -t/ *a.* corresponding. ● *n.m., f.* correspondent; (*au téléphone*) caller. ~**ce** *n.f.* correspondence; (*de train, d'au-tobus*) connection. **vente par ~ce**, mail order.

correspondre /kɔrɛspɔ̃dr/ *v.i.* (*s'accorder, écrire*) correspond; (*chambres*) communicate.

corrida /kɔrida/ *n.f.* bullfight.

corridor /kɔridɔr/ *n.m.* corridor.

corrig|er /kɔriʒe/ *v.t.* correct; (*de-voir*) mark, correct; (*punir*) beat; (*guérir*) cure. **se ~er de**, cure o.s. of. ~**é** *n.m.* (*scol.*) correct version, model answer.

corroborer /kɔrɔbɔre/ *v.t.* corroborate.

corro|der /kɔrɔde/ *v.t.* corrode. ~**sion** /-ozjɔ̃/ *n.f.* corrosion.

corromp|re[†] /kɔrɔ̃pr/ *v.t.* corrupt; (*soudoyer*) bribe. ~**u** *a.* corrupt.

corrosi|f, ~ve /kɔrozif, -v/ *a.* corrosive.

corruption /kɔrypsjɔ̃/ *n.f.* corruption.

corsage /kɔrsaʒ/ n.m. bodice; (*chemisier*) blouse.

corsaire /kɔrsɛr/ n.m. pirate.

Corse /kɔrs/ n.f. Corsica.

corse /kɔrs/ a. & n.m./f. Corsican.

corsé /kɔrse/ a. (*vin*) full-bodied; (*scabreux*) spicy.

corset /kɔrsɛ/ n.m. corset.

cortège /kɔrtɛʒ/ n.m. procession.

cortisone /kɔrtizon/ n.f. cortisone.

corvée /kɔrve/ n.f. chore.

cosaque /kɔzak/ n.m. Cossack.

cosmétique /kɔsmetik/ n.m. cosmetic.

cosmique /kɔsmik/ a. cosmic.

cosmonaute /kɔsmonot/ n.m./f. cosmonaut.

cosmopolite /kɔsmɔpɔlit/ a. cosmopolitan.

cosmos /kɔsmos/ n.m. (*espace*) (outer) space; (*univers*) cosmos.

cosse /kɔs/ n.f. (*de pois*) pod.

cossu /kɔsy/ a. (*gens*) well-to-do; (*demeure*) opulent.

costaud, **~e** /kɔsto, -d/ a. (*fam.*) strong. ● n.m. (*fam.*) strong man.

costum|e /kɔstym/ n.m. suit; (*théâtre*) costume. **~é** a. dressed up.

cote /kɔt/ n.f. (classification) mark; (*en Bourse*) quotation; (*de cheval*) odds (**de**, on); (*de candidat, acteur*) rating. **~ d'alerte**, danger level.

côte /kot/ n.f. (*littoral*) coast; (*pente*) hill; (*anat.*) rib; (*de porc*) chop. **~ à côte**, side by side. **la C~ d'Azur**, the (French) Riviera.

côté /kote/ n.m. side; (*direction*) way. **à ~ de**, nearby; (*voisin*) nextdoor. **à ~ de**, next to; (*comparé à*) compared to; (*cible*) wide of. **aux ~s de**, by the side of. **de ~**, aside; (*regarder*) sideways. **mettre de ~**, put aside. **de ce ~**, this way. **de chaque ~**, on each side. **de tous les ~s**, on every side; (*partout*) everywhere. **du ~ de**, towards; (*proximité*) near; (*provenance*) from.

coteau (*pl.* **~x**) /kɔto/ n.m. hill.

côtelette /kotlɛt/ n.f. chop.

coter /kɔte/ v.t. (*comm.*) quote; (*apprécier, noter*) rate.

coterie /kɔtri/ n.f. clique.

côt|ier, **~ière** /kotje, -jɛr/ a. coastal.

cotis|er /kɔtize/ v.i. pay one's contributions (**à**, to); (*à un club*) pay one's subscription. **se ~er** v. pr. club together. **~ation** n.f. contribution(s); subscription.

coton /kɔtɔ̃/ n.m. cotton. **~ hydrophile**, cotton wool.

côtoyer /kotwaje/ v.t. skirt, run along; (*fréquenter*) rub shoulders with; (*fig.*) verge on.

cotte /kɔt/ n.f. (*d'ouvrier*) overalls.

cou /ku/ n.m. neck.

couchage /kuʃaʒ/ n.m. sleeping arrangements.

couchant /kuʃã/ n.m. sunset.

couche /kuʃ/ n.f. layer; (*de peinture*) coat; (*de bébé*) nappy. **~s**, (*méd.*) childbirth. **~s sociales**, social strata.

coucher /kuʃe/ n.m. **~ (du soleil)**, sunset. ● v.t. put to bed; (*loger*) put up; (*étendre*) lay down. ● **~ (par écrit)**, set down. ● v.i. sleep. **se ~** v. pr. go to bed; (*s'étendre*) lie down; (*soleil*) set. **couché** a. in bed; (*étendu*) lying down.

couchette /kuʃɛt/ n.f. (*rail.*) couchette; (*naut.*) bunk.

coucou /kuku/ n.m. cuckoo.

coude /kud/ n.m. elbow; (*de rivière etc.*) bend. **~ à coude**, side by side.

cou-de-pied (*pl.* **cous-de-pied**) /kudpje/ n.m. instep.

coudoyer /kudwaje/ v.t. rub shoulders with.

coudre† /kudr/ v.t./i. sew.

couenne /kwan/ n.f. (*de porc*) rind.

couette /kwɛt/ n.f. duvet, continental quilt.

couffin /kufɛ̃/ n.m. Moses basket.

couiner /kwine/ v.i. squeak.

coulant, **~e** /kulã, -t/ a. (*indulgent*) easy-going; (*fromage*) runny.

coulée /kule/ n.f. **~ de lave**, lava flow.

couler[1] /kule/ v.i. flow, run; (*fromage, nez*) run; (*fuir*) leak. ● v.t. (*sculpture, métal*) cast; (*vie*) pass, lead. **se ~** v. pr. (*se glisser*) slip.

couler[2] /kule/ v.t./i. (*bateau*) sink.

couleur /kulœr/ n.f. colour; (*peinture*) paint; (*cartes*) suit. **~s**, (*teint*) colour. **de ~**, (*homme, femme*) coloured. **en ~s**, (*télévision, film*) colour.

couleuvre /kulœvr/ n.f. (grass *ou* smooth) snake.

coulis /kuli/ n.m. (*culin.*) coulis.

couliss|e /kulis/ n.f. (*de tiroir etc.*) runner. **~es**, (*théâtre*) wings. **à ~e**, (*porte, fenêtre*) sliding. **~er** v.i. slide.

couloir /kulwar/ *n.m.* corridor; (*de bus*) gangway; (*sport*) lane.

coup /ku/ *n.m.* blow; (*choc*) knock; (*sport*) stroke; (*de crayon, chance, cloche*) stroke; (*de fusil, pistolet*) shot; (*fois*) time; (*aux échecs*) move. **à ~ sûr**, definitely. **après ~**, after the event. **boire un ~**, have a drink. **~ de chiffon**, wipe (with a rag). **~ de coude**, nudge. **~ de couteau**, stab. **~ d'envoi**, kick-off. **~ d'état** (*pol.*) coup. **~ de feu**, shot. **~ de fil**, phone call. **~ de filet**, haul. **~ de frein**, sudden braking. **~ de grâce**, coup de grâce. **~ de main**, helping hand. **avoir le ~ de main**, have the knack. **~ d'œil**, glance. **~ de pied**, kick. **~ de poing**, punch. **~ de sang**, (*méd.*) stroke. **~ de soleil**, sunburn. **~ de sonnette**, ring (on a bell). **~ de téléphone**, (tele)phone call. **~ de tête**, wild impulse. **~ de théâtre**, dramatic event. **~ de tonnerre**, thunderclap. **~ de vent**, gust of wind. **~ franc**, free kick. **~ sur coup**, in rapid succession. **d'un seul ~**, in one go. **du premier ~**, first go. **sale ~**, dirty trick. **sous le ~ de**, under the influence of. **sur le ~**, immediately. **tenir le coup**, take it.

coupable /kupabl/ *a.* guilty. ● *n.m./ f.* culprit.

coupe[1] /kup/ *n.f.* cup; (*de champagne*) goblet; (*à fruits*) dish.

coupe[2] /kup/ *n.f.* (*de vêtement etc.*) cut; (*dessin*) section. **~ de cheveux**, haircut.

coupé /kupe/ *n.m.* (*voiture*) coupé.

coup|er /kupe/ *v.t./i.* cut; (*arbre*) cut down; (*arrêter*) cut off; (*voyage*) break; (*appétit*) take away; (*vin*) water down. **~er par**, take a short cut via. **se ~er** *v. pr.* cut o.s.; (*routes*) intersect. **~er la parole à**, cut short. **~e-papier** *n.m. invar.* paper-knife.

couperosé /kuproze/ *a.* blotchy.

couple /kupl/ *n.m.* couple.

coupler /kuple/ *v.t.* couple.

couplet /kuplɛ/ *n.m.* verse.

coupole /kupɔl/ *n.f.* dome.

coupon /kupɔ̃/ *n.m.* (*étoffe*) remnant; (*billet, titre*) coupon.

coupure /kupyr/ *n.f.* cut; (*billet de banque*) note; (*de presse*) cutting. **~ (de courant)**, power cut.

cour /kur/ *n.f.* (court)yard; (*de roi*) court; (*tribunal*) court. **~ (de ré-**

création), playground. **~ martiale**, court martial. **faire la ~ à**, court.

courag|e /kuraʒ/ *n.m.* courage. **~eux, ~euse** *a.* courageous.

couramment /kuramɑ̃/ *adv.* frequently; (*parler*) fluently.

courant[1], **~e** /kurɑ̃, -t/ *a.* standard, ordinary; (*en cours*) current.

courant[2] /kurɑ̃/ *n.m.* current; (*de mode, d'idées*) trend. **~ d'air**, draught. **dans le ~ de**, in the course of. **être/mettre au ~ de**, know/tell about; (*à jour*) be/bring up to date on.

courbatur|e /kurbatyr/ *n.f.* ache. **~é** *a.* aching.

courbe /kurb/ *n.f.* curve. ● *a.* curved.

courber /kurbe/ *v.t./i.*, **se ~** *v. pr.* bend.

coureu|r, ~se /kurœr, -øz/ *n.m., f.* (*sport*) runner. **~r automobile**, racing driver. ● *n.m.* womanizer.

courge /kurʒ/ *n.f.* marrow; (*Amer.*) squash.

courgette /kurʒɛt/ *n.f.* courgette; (*Amer.*) zucchini.

courir† /kurir/ *v.i.* run; (*se hâter*) rush; (*nouvelles etc.*) go round. ● *v.t.* (*risque*) run; (*danger*) face; (*épreuve sportive*) run *ou* compete in; (*fréquenter*) do the rounds of; (*filles*) chase.

couronne /kurɔn/ *n.f.* crown; (*de fleurs*) wreath.

couronn|er /kurɔne/ *v.t.* crown. **~ement** *n.m.* coronation, crowning; (*fig.*) crowning achievement.

courrier /kurje/ *n.m.* post, mail; (*à écrire*) letters; (*de journal*) column.

courroie /kurwa/ *n.f.* strap; (*techn.*) belt.

courroux /kuru/ *n.m.* wrath.

cours /kur/ *n.m.* (*leçon*) class; (*série de leçons*) course; (*prix*) price; (*cote*) rate; (*déroulement, d'une rivière*) course; (*allée*) avenue. **au ~ de**, in the course of. **avoir ~**, (*monnaie*) be legal tender; (*fig.*) be current; (*scol.*) have a lesson. **~ d'eau**, river, stream. **~ du soir**, evening class. **~ magistral**, (*univ.*) lecture. **en ~**, current; (*travail*) in progress. **en ~ de route**, on the way.

course /kurs/ *n.f.* run(ning); (*épreuve de vitesse*) race; (*entre rivaux: fig.*) race; (*de projectile*) flight; (*voyage*) journey; (*commission*) errand. **~s,**

(*achats*) shopping; (*de chevaux*) races.

cours|ier /kursje, -jɛr/ *n.m.*, *f.* messenger.

court [1] /kur, -t/ *a.* short. ● *adv.* short. **à ~ de**, short of. **pris de ~**, caught unawares. **~-circuit** (*pl.* **~s-circuits**) *n.m.* short circuit.

court [2] /kur/ *n.m.* **~ (de tennis)**, (tennis) court.

court|ier /kurtje, -jɛr/ *n.m.*, *f.* broker.

courtisan /kurtizã/ *n.m.* courtier.

courtisane /kurtizan/ *n.f.* courtesan.

courtiser /kurtize/ *v.t.* court.

courtois, **~e** /kurtwa, -z/ *a.* courteous. **~ie** /-zi/ *n.f.* courtesy.

couscous /kuskus/ *n.m.* couscous.

cousin, **~e** /kuzɛ̃, -in/ *n.m.*, *f.* cousin. **~ germain**, first cousin.

coussin /kusɛ̃/ *n.m.* cushion.

coût /ku/ *n.m.* cost.

couteau (*pl.* **~x**) /kuto/ *n.m.* knife. **~ à cran d'arrêt**, flick-knife.

coutellerie /kutɛlri/ *n.f.* (*magasin*) cutlery shop.

coût|er /kute/ *v.t./i.* cost. **~e que coûte**, at all costs. **au prix ~ant**, at cost (price). **~eux**, **~euse** *a.* costly.

coutum|e /kutym/ *n.f.* custom. **~ier**, **~ière** *a.* customary.

coutur|e /kutyr/ *n.f.* sewing; (*métier*) dressmaking; (*points*) seam. **~ier** *n.m.* fashion designer. **~ière** *n.f.* dressmaker.

couvée /kuve/ *n.f.* brood.

couvent /kuvã/ *n.m.* convent; (*de moines*) monastery.

couver /kuve/ *v.t.* (*œufs*) hatch; (*personne*) pamper; (*maladie*) be coming down with, be sickening for. ● *v.i.* (*feu*) smoulder; (*mal*) be brewing.

couvercle /kuvɛrkl/ *n.m.* (*de marmite, boite*) lid; (*d'objet allongé*) top.

couvert [1], **~e** /kuvɛr, -t/ *a.* covered (**de**, with); (*habillé*) covered up; (*ciel*) overcast. ● *n.m.* (*abri*) cover. **à ~**, (*mil.*) under cover. **à ~ de**, (*fig.*) safe from.

couvert [2] /kuvɛr/ *n.m.* (*à table*) place-setting; (*prix*) cover charge. **~s**, (*couteaux etc.*) cutlery. **mettre le ~**, lay the table.

couverture /kuvɛrtyr/ *n.f.* cover; (*de lit*) blanket; (*toit*) roofing. **~ chauffante**, electric blanket.

couveuse /kuvøz/ *n.f.* **~ (artificielle)**, incubator.

couvreur /kuvrœr/ *n.m.* roofer.

couvr|ir† /kuvrir/ *v.t.* cover. **se ~ir** *v. pr.* (*s'habiller*) put one's hat on; (*se coiffer*) put one's hat on; (*ciel*) become overcast. **~e-chef** *n.m.* hat. **~e-feu** (*pl.* **~e-feux**) *n.m.* curfew. **~e-lit** *n.m.* bedspread.

cow-boy /koboj/ *n.m.* cowboy.

crabe /krab/ *n.m.* crab.

crachat /kraʃa/ *n.m.* spit(tle).

cracher /kraʃe/ *v.i.* spit; (*radio*) crackle. ● *v.t.* spit (out).

crachin /kraʃɛ̃/ *n.m.* drizzle.

crack /krak/ *n.m.* (*fam.*) wizard, ace, prodigy.

craie /krɛ/ *n.f.* chalk.

craindre† /krɛ̃dr/ *v.t.* be afraid of, fear; (*être sensible à*) be easily damaged by.

crainte /krɛ̃t/ *n.f.* fear. **de ~ de/que**, for fear of/that.

crainti|f, **~ve** /krɛ̃tif, -v/ *a.* timid.

cramoisi /kramwazi/ *a.* crimson.

crampe /krãp/ *n.f.* cramp.

crampon /krãpɔ̃/ *n.m.* (*de chaussure*) stud.

cramponner (se) /(sə)krãpɔne/ *v. pr.* **se ~ à**, cling to.

cran /krã/ *n.m.* (*entaille*) notch; (*trou*) hole; (*courage: fam.*) pluck.

crâne /krɑn/ *n.m.* skull.

crâner /krɑne/ *v.i.* (*fam.*) swank.

crapaud /krapo/ *n.m.* toad.

crapul|e /krapyl/ *n.f.* villain. **~eux**, **~euse** *a.* sordid, foul.

craqu|er /krake/ *v.i.* crack, snap; (*plancher*) creak; (*couture*) split; (*fig.*) break down; (*céder*) give in. ● *v.t.* **~er une allumette**, strike a match. **~ement** *n.m.* crack(ing), snap(ping); creak(ing); striking.

crass|e /kras/ *n.f.* grime. **~eux**, **~euse** *a.* grimy.

cratère /krater/ *n.m.* crater.

cravache /kravaʃ/ *n.f.* horsewhip.

cravate /kravat/ *n.f.* tie.

crawl /krol/ *n.m.* (*nage*) crawl.

crayeu|x, **~se** /krɛjø, -z/ *a.* chalky.

crayon /krɛjɔ̃/ *n.m.* pencil. **~ (de couleur)**, crayon. **~ à bille**, ball-point pen. **~ optique**, light pen.

créanc|ier, **~ière** /kreãsje, -jɛr/ *n.m.*, *f.* creditor.

créa|teur, **~trice** /kreatœr, -tris/ *a.* creative. ● *n.m.*, *f.* creator.

création /kreasjɔ̃/ *n.f.* creation; (*comm.*) product.

créature /kreatyr/ *n.f.* creature.

crèche /krɛʃ/ *n.f.* day nursery; (*relig.*) crib.

crédibilité /kredibilite/ *n.f.* credibility.

crédit /kredi/ *n.m.* credit; (*banque*) bank. **~s**, funds. **à ~**, on credit. **faire ~**, give credit (à, to). **~er** /-te/ *v.t.* credit. **~eur, ~euse** /-tœr, -tøz/ *a.* in credit.

credo /kredo/ *n.m.* creed.

crédule /kredyl/ *a.* credulous.

créer /kree/ *v.t.* create.

crémation /kremasjɔ̃/ *n.f.* cremation.

crème /krɛm/ *n.f.* cream; (*dessert*) cream dessert. ● *a. invar.* cream. ● *n.m.* **(café) ~**, white coffee. **~ anglaise**, fresh custard. **~ à raser**, shaving-cream.

crémeu|x, ~se /kremø, -z/ *a.* creamy.

crém|ier, ~ière /kremje, -jɛr/ *n.m., f.* dairyman, dairywoman. **~erie** /krɛmri/ *n.f.* dairy.

créneau (*pl.* **~x**) /kreno/ *n.m.* (*trou, moment*) slot; (*dans le marché*) gap; **faire un ~**, park between two cars.

créole /kreɔl/ *n.m./f.* Creole.

crêpe [1] /krɛp/ *n.f.* (*galette*) pancake. **~rie** *n.f.* pancake shop.

crêpe [2] /krɛp/ *n.m.* (*tissu*) crêpe; (*matière*) crêpe (rubber).

crépit|er /krepite/ *v.i.* crackle. **~ement** *n.m.* crackling.

crépu /krepy/ *a.* frizzy.

crépuscule /krepyskyl/ *n.m.* twilight, dusk.

crescendo /kreʃendo/ *adv. & n.m. invar.* crescendo.

cresson /kresɔ̃/ *n.m.* (water)cress.

crête /krɛt/ *n.f.* crest; (*de coq*) comb.

crétin, ~e /kretɛ̃, -in/ *n.m., f.* cretin.

creuser /krøze/ *v.t.* dig; (*évider*) hollow out; (*fig.*) go deeply into. **se ~ (la cervelle)**, (*fam.*) rack one's brains.

creuset /krøzɛ/ *n.m.* (*lieu*) melting-pot.

creu|x, ~se /krø, -z/ *a.* hollow; (*heures*) off-peak. ● *n.m.* hollow; (*de l'estomac*) pit.

crevaison /krəvɛzɔ̃/ *n.f.* puncture.

crevasse /krəvas/ *n.f.* crack; (*de glacier*) crevasse; (*de la peau*) chap.

crevé /krəve/ *a.* (*fam.*) worn out.

crève-cœur /krɛvkœr/ *n.m. invar.* heart-break.

crever /krəve/ *v.t./i.* burst; (*pneu*) puncture burst; (*exténuer*: *fam.*)

exhaust; (*mourir*: *fam.*) die; (*œil*) put out.

crevette /krəvɛt/ *n.f.* **~ (grise)**, shrimp. **~ (rose)**, prawn.

cri /kri/ *n.m.* cry; (*de douleur*) scream, cry.

criant, ~e /krijɑ̃, -t/ *a.* glaring.

criard, ~e /krijar, -d/ *a.* (*couleur*) garish; (*voix*) bawling.

crible /kribl/ *n.m.* sieve, riddle.

criblé /krible/ *a.* **~ de**, riddled with.

cric /krik/ *n.m.* (*auto.*) jack.

crier /krije/ *v.i.* (*fort*) shout, cry (out); (*de douleur*) scream; (*grincer*) creak. ● *v.t.* (*ordre*) shout (out).

crim|e /krim/ *n.m.* crime; (*meurtre*) murder. **~inalité** *n.f.* crime. **~inel, ~inelle** *a.* criminal; *n.m., f.* criminal; (*assassin*) murderer.

crin /krɛ̃/ *n.m.* horsehair.

crinière /krinjɛr/ *n.f.* mane.

crique /krik/ *n.f.* creek.

criquet /krikɛ/ *n.m.* locust.

crise /kriz/ *n.f.* crisis; (*méd.*) attack; (*de colère*) fit. **~ cardiaque**, heart attack. **~ de foie**, bilious attack.

crisp|er /krispe/ *v.t.*, **se ~er** *v. pr.* tense; (*poings*) clench. **~ation** *n.f.* tenseness; (*spasme*) twitch. **~é** *a.* tense.

crisser /krise/ *v.i.* crunch; (*pneu*) screech.

crist|al (*pl.* **~aux**) /kristal, -o/ *n.m.* crystal.

cristallin, ~e /kristalɛ̃, -in/ *a.* (*limpide*) crystal-clear.

cristalliser /kristalize/ *v.t./i.*, **se ~** *v. pr.* crystallize.

critère /kritɛr/ *n.m.* criterion.

critique /kritik/ *a.* critical. ● *n.f.* criticism; (*article*) review. ● *n.m.* critic. **la ~**, (*personnes*) the critics.

critiquer /kritike/ *v.t.* criticize.

croasser /krɔase/ *v.i.* caw.

croc /kro/ *n.m.* (*dent*) fang; (*crochet*) hook.

croc-en-jambe (*pl.* **crocs-en-jambe**) /krɔkɑ̃ʒɑ̃b/ *n.m.* = **croche-pied**.

croche /krɔʃ/ *n.f.* quaver. **double ~**, semiquaver.

croche-pied /krɔʃpje/ *n.m.* **faire un ~ à**, trip up.

crochet /krɔʃɛ/ *n.m.* hook; (*détour*) detour; (*signe*) square bracket; (*tricot*) crochet. **faire au ~**, crochet.

crochu /krɔʃy/ *a.* hooked.

crocodile /krɔkɔdil/ *n.m.* crocodile.

crocus /krɔkys/ *n.m.* crocus.

croire† /krwar/ *v.t./i.* believe (**à, en,** in); (*estimer*) think, believe (**que,** that).

croisade /krwazad/ *n.f.* crusade.

croisé /krwaze/ *a.* (*veston*) double-breasted. ● *n.m.* crusader.

croisée /krwaze/ *n.f.* window. **~ des chemins,** crossroads.

crois|er¹ /krwaze/ *v.t.,* **se ~er** *v. pr.* cross; (*passant, véhicule*) pass (each other). (**se**) **~er les bras,** fold one's arms. (**se**) **~er les jambes,** cross one's legs. **~ement** *n.m.* crossing; passing; (*carrefour*) crossroads.

crois|er² /krwaze/ *v.i.* (*bateau*) cruise. **~eur** *n.m.* cruiser. **~ière** *n.f.* cruise.

croissan|t¹, **~te** /krwasɑ̃, -t/ *a.* growing. **~ce** *n.f.* growth.

croissant² /krwasɑ̃/ *n.m.* crescent; (*pâtisserie*) croissant.

croître† /krwatr/ *v.i.* grow; (*lune*) wax.

croix /krwa/ *n.f.* cross. **~ gammée,** swastika. **C~-Rouge,** Red Cross.

croque-monsieur /krɔkməsjø/ *n.m. invar.* toasted ham and cheese sandwich.

croque-mort /krɔkmɔr/ *n.m.* (*fam.*) undertaker's assistant.

croqu|er /krɔke/ *v.t./i.* crunch; (*dessiner*) sketch. **chocolat à ~er,** plain chocolate. **~ant, ~ante** *a.* crunchy.

croquet /krɔke/ *n.m.* croquet.

croquette /krɔkɛt/ *n.f.* croquette.

croquis /krɔki/ *n.m.* sketch.

crosse /krɔs/ *n.f.* (*de fusil*) butt; (*d'évêque*) crook.

crotte /krɔt/ *n.f.* droppings.

crotté /krɔte/ *a.* muddy.

crottin /krɔtɛ̃/ *n.m.* (horse) dung.

crouler /krule/ *v.i.* collapse; (*être en ruines*) crumble.

croupe /krup/ *n.f.* rump; (*de colline*) brow. **en ~,** pillion.

croupier /krupje/ *n.m.* croupier.

croupir /krupir/ *v.i.* stagnate.

croustill|er /krustije/ *v.i.* be crusty. **~ant, ~ante** *a.* crusty; (*fig.*) spicy.

croûte /krut/ *n.f.* crust; (*de fromage*) rind; (*de plaie*) scab. **en ~,** (*culin.*) en croûte.

croûton /krutɔ̃/ *n.m.* (*bout de pain*) crust; (*avec potage*) croûton.

croyable /krwajabl/ *a.* credible.

croyan|t, ~te /krwajɑ̃, -t/ *n.m., f.* believer. **~ce** *n.f.* belief.

CRS *abrév.* (*Compagnies républicaines de sécurité*) French state security police.

cru¹ /kry/ *voir* croire.

cru² /kry/ *a.* raw; (*lumière*) harsh; (*propos*) crude. ● *n.m.* vineyard; (*vin*) wine.

crû /kry/ *voir* croître.

cruauté /kryote/ *n.f.* cruelty.

cruche /kryʃ/ *n.f.* pitcher.

cruc|ial (*m. pl.* **~iaux**) /krysjal, -jo/ *a.* crucial.

cruc|ifier /krysifje/ *v.t.* crucify. **~ifixion** *n.f.* crucifixion.

crucifix /krysifi/ *n.m.* crucifix.

crudité /krydite/ *n.f.* (*de langage*) crudeness. **~s,** (*culin.*) raw vegetables.

crue /kry/ *n.f.* rise in water level. **en ~,** in spate.

cruel, ~le /kryɛl/ *a.* cruel.

crûment /krymɑ̃/ *adv.* crudely.

crustacés /krystase/ *n.m. pl.* shellfish.

crypte /kript/ *n.f.* crypt.

Cuba /kyba/ *n.m.* Cuba.

cubain, ~e /kybɛ̃, -ɛn/ *a. & n.m., f.* Cuban.

cub|e /kyb/ *n.m.* cube. ● *a.* (*mètre etc.*) cubic. **~ique** *a.* cubic.

cueill|ir† /kœjir/ *v.t.* pick, gather; (*personne: fam.*) pick up. **~ette** *n.f.* picking, gathering.

cuill|er, ~ère /kɥijɛr/ *n.f.* spoon. **~er à soupe,** soup-spoon; (*mesure*) tablespoonful. **~erée** *n.f.* spoonful.

cuir /kɥir/ *n.m.* leather. **~ chevelu,** scalp.

cuirassé /kɥirase/ *n.m.* battleship.

cuire /kɥir/ *v.t./i.* cook; (*picoter*) smart. **~ (au four),** bake. **faire ~,** cook.

cuisine /kɥizin/ *n.f.* kitchen; (*art*) cookery, cooking; (*aliments*) cooking. **faire la ~,** cook.

cuisin|er /kɥizine/ *v.t./i.* cook; (*interroger: fam.*) grill. **~ier, ~ière** *n.m., f.* cook; *n.f.* (*appareil*) cooker, stove.

cuisse /kɥis/ *n.f.* thigh; (*de poulet, mouton*) leg.

cuisson /kɥisɔ̃/ *n.m.* cooking.

cuit, ~e /kɥi, -t/ *a.* cooked. **bien ~,** well done *ou* cooked. **trop ~,** overdone.

cuivr|e /kɥivr/ *n.m.* copper. **~e (jaune),** brass. **~es,** (*mus.*) brass. **~é** *a.* coppery.

cul /ky/ *n.m.* (*derrière*: *fam.*) back-side, bum.

culasse /kylas/ *n.f.* (*auto.*) cylinder head; (*arme*) breech.

culbut|e /kylbyt/ *n.f.* somersault; (*chute*) tumble. **~er** *v.i.* tumble; *v.t.* knock over.

cul-de-sac (*pl.* **culs-de-sac**) /kydsak/ *n.m.* cul-de-sac.

culinaire /kyliner/ *a.* culinary; (*recette*) cooking.

culminer /kylmine/ *v.i.* reach the highest point.

culot [1] /kylo/ *n.m.* (*audace*: *fam.*) nerve, cheek.

culot [2] /kylo/ *n.m.* (*fond*: *techn.*) base.

culotte /kylɔt/ *n.f.* (*de femme*) knickers; (*Amer.*) panties. **~ (de cheval)**, (riding) breeches. **~ courte**, short trousers.

culpabilité /kylpabilite/ *n.f.* guilt.

culte /kylt/ *n.m.* cult, worship; (*religion*) religion; (*protestant*) service.

cultivé /kyltive/ *a.* cultured.

cultiv|er /kyltive/ *v.t.* cultivate; (*plantes*) grow. **~ateur**, **~atrice** *n.m.*, *f.* farmer.

culture /kyltyr/ *n.f.* cultivation; (*de plantes*) growing; (*agriculture*) farming; (*éducation*) culture. **~s**, (*terrains*) lands under cultivation. **~ physique**, physical training.

culturel, **~le** /kyltyrel/ *a.* cultural.

cumuler /kymyle/ *v.t.* (*fonctions*) hold simultaneously.

cupide /kypid/ *a.* grasping.

cure /kyr/ *n.f.* (course of) treatment, cure.

curé /kyre/ *n.m.* (parish) priest.

cur|er /kyre/ *v.t.* clean. **se ~er les dents/ongles**, clean one's teeth/nails. **~e-dent** *n.m.* toothpick. **~e-pipe** *n.m.* pipe-cleaner.

curieu|x, **~se** /kyrjø, -z/ *a.* curious. ● *n.m.*, *f.* (*badaud*) onlooker. **~sement** *adv.* curiously.

curiosité /kyrjozite/ *n.f.* curiosity; (*objet*) curio; (*spectacle*) unusual sight.

curriculum vitae /kyrikylɔm vite/ *n.m. invar.* curriculum vitae.

curseur /kyrsœr/ *n.m.* cursor.

cutané /kytane/ *a.* skin.

cuve /kyv/ *n.f.* tank.

cuvée /kyve/ *n.f.* (*de vin*) vintage.

cuvette /kyvɛt/ *n.f.* bowl; (*de lavabo*) (wash-)basin; (*des cabinets*) pan, bowl.

CV /seve/ *n.m.* CV.

cyanure /sjanyr/ *n.m.* cyanide.

cybernétique /sibɛrnetik/ *n.f.* cybernetics.

cycl|e /sikl/ *n.m.* cycle. **~ique** *a.* cyclic(al).

cyclis|te /siklist/ *n.m./f.* cyclist. ● *a.* cycle. **~me** *n.m.* cycling.

cyclomoteur /syklɔmɔtœr/ *n.m.* moped.

cyclone /siklon/ *n.m.* cyclone.

cygne /siɲ/ *n.m.* swan.

cylindr|e /silɛ̃dr/ *n.m.* cylinder. **~ique** *a.* cylindrical.

cylindrée /silɛ̃dre/ *n.f.* (*de moteur*) capacity.

cymbale /sɛ̃bal/ *n.f.* cymbal.

cystite /sistit/ *n.f.* cystitis.

cyni|que /sinik/ *a.* cynical. ● *n.m.* cynic. **~sme** *n.m.* cynicism.

cyprès /siprɛ/ *n.m.* cypress.

cypriote /siprijɔt/ *a.* & *n.m./f.* Cypriot.

D

d' /d/ *voir* de.

d'abord /dabɔr/ *adv.* first; (*au début*) at first.

dactylo /daktilo/ *n.f.* typist. **~-(graphie)** *n.f.* typing. **~graphe** *n.f.* typist. **~graphier** *v.t.* type.

dada /dada/ *n.m.* hobby-horse.

dahlia /dalja/ *n.m.* dahlia.

daigner /deɲe/ *v.t.* deign.

daim /dɛ̃/ *n.m.* (fallow) deer; (*cuir*) suede.

dall|e /dal/ *n.f.* paving stone, slab. **~age** *n.m.* paving.

daltonien, **~ne** /daltɔnjɛ̃, -jɛn/ *a.* colour-blind.

dame /dam/ *n.f.* lady; (*cartes*, *échecs*) queen. **~s**, (*jeu*) draughts; (*jeu*: *Amer.*) checkers.

damier /damje/ *n.m.* draught-board; (*Amer.*) checker-board. **à ~**, chequered.

damn|er /dɑne/ *v.t.* damn. **~ation** *n.f.* damnation.

dancing /dɑ̃siŋ/ *n.m.* dance-hall.

dandiner (se) /(sə)dɑ̃dine/ *v. pr.* waddle.

Danemark /danmark/ *n.m.* Denmark.

danger /dɑ̃ʒe/ *n.m.* danger. **en ~**, in danger. **mettre en ~**, endanger.

dangereu|x, ~se /dɑ̃ʒrø, -z/ *a.* dangerous.

danois, ~e /danwa, -z/ *a.* Danish. ● *n.m.*, *f.* Dane. ● *n.m.* (*lang.*) Danish.

dans /dɑ̃/ *prép.* in; (*mouvement*) into; (*à l'intérieur de*) inside, in; (*approximation*) about. **~ dix jours,** in ten days' time. **prendre/boire/***etc.* **~,** take/drink/*etc.* out of *ou* from.

dans|e /dɑ̃s/ *n.f.* dance; (*art*) dancing. **~er** *v.t./i.* dance. **~eur, ~euse** *n.m.*, *f.* dancer.

dard /dar/ *n.m.* (*d'animal*) sting.

darne /darn/ *n.f.* steak (*of fish*).

dat|e /dat/ *n.f.* date. **~e limite,** deadline; **~e limite de vente,** sell-by date; **~e de péremption,** expiry date. **~er** *v.t./i.* date. **à ~er de,** as from.

datt|e /dat/ *n.f.* (*fruit*) date. **~ier** *n.m.* date-palm.

daube /dob/ *n.f.* casserole.

dauphin /dofɛ̃/ *n.m.* (*animal*) dolphin.

davantage /davɑ̃taʒ/ *adv.* more; (*plus longtemps*) longer. **~ de,** more. **~ que,** more than; longer than.

de, d'* /də, d/ *prép.* (*de + le = du, de + les = des*) of; (*provenance*) from; (*moyen, manière*) with; (*agent*) by. ● *article* some; (*interrogation*) any, some. **le livre de mon ami,** my friend's book. **un pont de fer,** an iron bridge. **dix mètres de haut,** ten metres high. **du pain,** (some) bread; **une tranche de pain,** a slice of bread. **des fleurs,** (some) flowers.

dé /de/ *n.m.* (*à jouer*) dice; (*à coudre*) thimble. **dés,** (*jeu*) dice.

dealer /dilər/ *n.m.* (*drug*) dealer.

débâcle /debakl/ *n.f.* (*mil.*) rout.

déball|er /debale/ *v.t.* unpack; (*montrer, péj.*) spill out. **~age** *n.m.* unpacking.

débarbouiller /debarbuje/ *v.t.* wash the face of. **se ~** *v. pr.* wash one's face.

débarcadère /debarkadɛr/ *n.m.* landing-stage.

débardeur /debardœr/ *n.m.* docker; (*vêtement*) tank top.

débarqu|er /debarke/ *v.t./i.* disembark, land; (*arriver: fam.*) turn up. **~ement** *n.m.* disembarkation.

débarras /debara/ *n.m.* junk room. **bon ~!,** good riddance!

débarrasser /debarase/ *v.t.* clear (**de,** of). **~ qn. de,** take from s.o.; (*défaut, ennemi*) rid s.o. of. **se ~ de,** get rid of, rid o.s. of.

débat /deba/ *n.m.* debate.

débattre†¹ /debatr/ *v.t.* debate. ● *v.i.* **~ de,** discuss.

débattre†² (se) /(sə)debatr/ *v. pr.* struggle (to get free).

débauch|e /deboʃ/ *n.f.* debauchery; (*fig.*) profusion. **~er¹** *v.t.* debauch.

débaucher² /deboʃe/ *v.t.* (*licencier*) lay off.

débile /debil/ *a.* weak; (*fam.*) stupid. ● *n.m./f.* moron.

débit /debi/ *n.m.* (rate of) flow; (*de magasin*) turnover; (*élocution*) delivery; (*de compte*) debit. **~ de tabac,** tobacconist's shop; **~ de boissons,** licensed premises.

débi|ter /debite/ *v.t.* cut up; (*fournir*) produce; (*vendre*) sell; (*dire: péj.*) spout; (*compte*) debit. **~teur, ~trice** *n.m.*, *f.* debtor; *a.* (*compte*) in debit.

débl|ayer /debleje/ *v.t.* clear. **~aiement, ~ayage** *n.m.* clearing.

déblo|quer /debloke/ *v.t.* (*prix, salaires*) free. **~cage** *n.m.* freeing.

déboires /debwar/ *n.m. pl.* disappointments.

déboiser /debwaze/ *v.t.* clear (of trees).

déboîter /debwate/ *v.i.* (*véhicule*) pull out. ● *v.t.* (*membre*) dislocate.

débord|er /deborde/ *v.i.* overflow. ● *v.t.* (*dépasser*) extend beyond. **~er de,** (*joie etc.*) be overflowing with. **~é** *a.* snowed under (**de,** with). **~ement** *n.m.* overflowing.

débouché /debuʃe/ *n.m.* opening; (*carrière*) prospect; (*comm.*) outlet; (*sortie*) end, exit.

déboucher /debuʃe/ *v.t.* (*bouteille*) uncork; (*évier*) unblock. ● *v.i.* emerge (**de,** from). **~ sur,** (*rue*) lead into.

débourser /deburse/ *v.t.* pay out.

déboussolé /debusole/ *a.* (*fam.*) disorientated, disoriented.

debout /dəbu/ *adv.* standing; (*levé, éveillé*) up. **être ~, se tenir ~,** be standing, stand. **se mettre ~,** stand up.

déboutonner /debutɔne/ *v.t.* unbutton. **se ~** *v. pr.* unbutton o.s.; (*vêtement*) come undone.

débraillé /debraje/ *a.* slovenly.

débrancher /debrɑ̃ʃe/ *v.t.* unplug, disconnect.

débray|er /debreje/ v.i. (auto.) de-
clutch; (faire grève) stop work.
~age /debrɛjaʒ/ n.m. (pédale)
clutch; (grève) stoppage.

débris /debri/ n.m. pl. fragments;
(détritus) rubbish, debris.

débrouill|er /debruje/ v.t. disentan-
gle; (problème) sort out. **se ~er** v.
pr. manage. **~ard, ~arde** a. (fam.)
resourceful.

débroussailler /debrusaje/ v.t. clear
(of brushwood).

début /deby/ n.m. beginning. **faire
ses ~s,** (en public) make one's
début.

début|er /debyte/ v.i. begin; (dans un
métier ou art) start out. **~ant,
~ante** n.m., f. beginner.

déca /deka/ n.m. decaffeinated coffee.

décaféiné /dekafeine/ a. decaffeinated. ● n.m. **du ~,** decaffeinated coffee.

deçà (en) /(ɑ̃)dəsa/ adv. this side.
● prép. **en ~ de,** this side of.

décacheter /dekaʃte/ v.t. open.

décade /dekad/ n.f. ten days; (décennie) decade.

décaden|t, ~te /dekadɑ̃, -t/ a.
decadent. **~ce** n.f. decadence.

décalcomanie /dekalkɔmani/ n.f.
transfer; (Amer.) decal.

décal|er /dekale/ v.t. shift. **~age** n.m.
(écart) gap. **~age horaire,** time
difference.

décalquer /dekalke/ v.t. trace.

décamper /dekɑ̃pe/ v.i. clear off.

décanter /dekɑ̃te/ v.t. allow to settle.
se ~ v. pr. settle.

décap|er /dekape/ v.t. scrape down;
(surface peinte) strip. **~ant** n.m.
chemical agent; (pour peinture)
paint stripper.

décapotable /dekapɔtabl/ a. convertible.

décapsul|er /dekapsyle/ v.t. take the
cap off. **~eur** n.m. bottle- opener.

décarcasser (se) /(sə)dekarkase/ v.
pr. (fam.) work o.s. to death.

décathlon /dekatlɔ̃/ n.m. decathlon.

décéd|er /desede/ v.i. die. **~é** a.
deceased.

décel|er /desle/ v.t. detect; (dé-
montrer) reveal. **~able** a. detect-
able.

décembre /desɑ̃br/ n.m. December.

décennie /deseni/ n.f. decade.

décen|t, ~te /desɑ̃, -t/ a. decent.
~emment /-amɑ̃/ adv. decently.
~ence n.f. decency.

décentralis|er /desɑ̃tralize/ v.t.
decentralize. **~ation** n.f. decentrali-
zation.

déception /desɛpsjɔ̃/ n.f. disappointment.

décerner /deserne/ v.t. award.

décès /desɛ/ n.m. death.

décev|oir† /desvwar/ v.t. disappoint.
~ant, ~ante a. disappointing.

déchaîn|er /deʃene/ v.t. (violence
etc.) unleash; (enthousiasme) arouse
a good deal of. **se ~er** v. pr. erupt.
~ement /-ɛnmɑ̃/ n.m. (de passions)
outburst.

décharge /deʃarʒ/ n.f. (salve) volley
of shots. **~ (électrique),** electrical
discharge. **~ (publique),** rubbish
tip.

décharg|er /deʃarʒe/ v.t. unload;
(arme, accusé) discharge. **~er de,**
release from. **se ~er** v. pr. (batterie,
pile) go flat. **~ement** n.m. unload-
ing.

décharné /deʃarne/ a. bony.

déchausser (se) /(sə)deʃose/ v. pr.
take off one's shoes; (dent) work
loose.

dèche /dɛʃ/ n.f. (fam.) **dans la ~,**
broke.

déchéance /deʃeɑ̃s/ n.f. decay.

déchet /deʃɛ/ n.m. (reste) scrap;
(perte) waste. **~s,** (ordures) refuse.

déchiffrer /deʃifre/ v.t. decipher.

déchiqueter /deʃikte/ v.t. tear to
shreds.

déchir|ant, ~ante /deʃirɑ̃, -t/ a.
heart-breaking. **~ement** n.m.
heart-break; (conflit) split.

déchir|er /deʃire/ v.t. tear; (lacérer)
tear up; (arracher) tear off ou out;
(diviser) tear apart; (oreilles: fig.)
split. **se ~er** v. pr. tear. **~ure** n.f.
tear.

déch|oir /deʃwar/ v.i. demean o.s.
~oir de, (rang) lose. **~oir from. ~u**
a. fallen.

décibel /desibɛl/ n.m. decibel.

décid|er /deside/ v.t. decide on; (per-
suader) persuade. **~er que/de,** decide that/to. ● v.i. decide. **~er de
qch.,** decide on sth. **se ~er** v. pr.
make up one's mind (**à,** to). **~é** a.
(résolu) determined; (fixé, marqué)
decided. **~ément** adv. really.

décim|al, ~ale (m. pl. **~aux**) /de-
simal, -o/ a. & n.f. decimal.

décimètre /desimɛtr/ n.m. decimetre.

décisi|f, ~ve /desizif, -v/ a. decisive.

décision /desizjɔ̃/ n.f. decision.

déclar|er /deklare/ v.t. declare; (naissance) register. **se ~er** v. pr. (feu) break out. **~er forfait**, (sport) withdraw. **~ation** n.f. declaration; (commentaire politique) statement. **~ation d'impôts**, tax return.

déclasser /deklase/ v.t. (coureur) relegate; (hôtel) downgrade.

déclench|er /deklɑ̃ʃe/ v.t. (techn.) release, set off; (lancer) launch; (provoquer) trigger off. **se ~er** v. pr. (techn.) go off. **~eur** n.m. (photo.) trigger.

déclic /deklik/ n.m. click; (techn.) trigger mechanism.

déclin /deklɛ̃/ n.m. decline.

déclin|er[1] /dekline/ v.i. decline. **~aison** n.f. (lang.) declension.

décliner[2] /dekline/ v.t. (refuser) decline; (dire) state.

déclivité /deklivite/ n.f. slope.

décocher /dekɔʃe/ v.t. (coup) fling; (regard) shoot.

décoder /dekɔde/ v.t. decode.

décoiffer /dekwafe/ v.t. (ébouriffer) disarrange the hair of.

décoincer /dekwɛ̃se/ v.t. free.

décoll|er[1] /dekɔle/ v.i. (avion) take off. **~age** n.m. take-off.

décoller[2] /dekɔle/ v.t. unstick.

décolleté /dekɔlte/ a. low-cut. ● n.m. low neckline.

décolor|er /dekɔlɔre/ v.t. fade; (cheveux) bleach. **se ~er** v. pr. fade. **~ation** n.f. bleaching.

décombres /dekɔ̃br/ n.m. pl. rubble.

décommander /dekɔmɑ̃de/ v.t. cancel.

décompos|er /dekɔ̃poze/ v.t. break up; (substance) decompose; (visage) contort. **se ~er** v. pr. (pourrir) decompose. **~ition** n.f. decomposition.

décompt|e /dekɔ̃t/ n.m. deduction; (détail) breakdown. **~er** v.t. deduct.

déconcerter /dekɔ̃sɛrte/ v.t. disconcert.

décongel|er /dekɔ̃ʒle/ v.t. thaw. **~ation** n.f. thawing.

décongestionner /dekɔ̃ʒɛstjɔne/ v.t. relieve congestion in.

déconseill|er /dekɔ̃seje/ v.t. **~er qch. à qn.**, advise s.o. against sth. **~é à**, not advisable, inadvisable.

décontenancer /dekɔ̃tnɑ̃se/ v.t. disconcert.

décontract|er (se) /(sə)dekɔ̃trakte/ v.t., se **~** v. pr. relax. **~é à**. relaxed.

déconvenue /dekɔ̃vny/ n.f. disappointment.

décor /dekɔr/ n.m. (paysage, théâtre) scenery; (cinéma) set; (cadre) setting; (de maison) décor.

décorati|f, ~ve /dekɔratif, -v/ a. decorative.

décor|er /dekɔre/ v.t. decorate. **~ateur, ~atrice** n.m., f. (intérieur) decorator. **~ation** n.f. decoration.

décortiquer /dekɔrtike/ v.t. shell; (fig.) dissect.

découdre (se) /(sə)dekudr/ v. pr. come unstitched.

découler /dekule/ v.i. **~ de**, follow from.

découp|er /dekupe/ v.t. cut up; (viande) carve; (détacher) cut out. **se ~er sur**, stand out against. **~age** n.m. (image) cut-out.

décourag|er /dekuraʒe/ v.t. discourage. **se ~er** v. pr. become discouraged. **~ement** n.m. discouragement. **~é à**. discouraged.

décousu /dekuzy/ a. (vêtement) falling apart; (idées etc.) disjointed.

découvert, ~e /dekuvɛr, -t/ a. (tête etc.) bare; (terrain) open. ● n.m. (de compte) overdraft. ● n.f. discovery. **à ~**, exposed; (fig.) openly. **à la ~e de**, in search of.

découvrir† /dekuvrir/ v.t. discover; (enlever ce qui couvre) uncover; (voir) see; (montrer) reveal. **se ~** v. pr. uncover o.s.; (ciel) clear.

décrasser /dekrase/ v.t. clean.

décrépit, ~e /dekrepi, -t/ a. decrepit. **~ude** n.f. decay.

décret /dekrɛ/ n.m. decree. **~er** /-ete/ v.t. decree.

décrié /dekrije/ v.t. decried.

décrire† /dekrir/ v.t. describe.

décrisp|er (se) /(sə)dekrispe/ v. pr. become less tense. **~ation** n.f. lessening of tension.

décroch|er /dekrɔʃe/ v.t. unhook; (obtenir: fam.) get. ● v.i. (abandonner: fam.) give up. **~er (le téléphone)**, pick up the phone. **~é à**. (téléphone) off the hook.

décroître /dekrwatr/ v.i. decrease.

décrue /dekry/ n.f. going down (of river water).

déçu /desy/ a. disappointed.

décupl|e /dekypl/ n.m. **au ~e**, tenfold. **le ~e de**, ten times. **~er** v.t./i. increase tenfold.

dédaign|er /dedeɲe/ v.t. scorn. **~er de faire**, consider it beneath one to do. **~eux**, **~euse** /dedɛɲø, -z/ a. scornful.

dédain /dedɛ̃/ n.m. scorn.

dédale /dedal/ n.m. maze.

dedans /dədɑ̃/ adv. & n.m. inside. **au ~ (de)**, inside. **en ~**, on the inside.

dédicac|e /dedikas/ n.f. dedication, inscription. **~er** v.t. dedicate, inscribe.

dédier /dedje/ v.t. dedicate.

dédommag|er /dedɔmaʒe/ v.t. compensate (**de**, for). **~ement** n.m. compensation.

dédouaner /dedwane/ v.t. clear through customs.

dédoubler /deduble/ v.t. split into two. **~ un train**, put on a relief train.

déd|uire† /dedɥir/ v.t. deduct; (conclure) deduce. **~uction** n.f. deduction; **~uction d'impôts** tax deduction.

déesse /deɛs/ n.f. goddess.

défaillance /defajɑ̃s/ n.f. weakness; (évanouissement) black-out; (panne) failure.

défaill|ir /defajir/ v.i. faint; (forces etc.) fail. **~ant**, **~ante** a. (personne) faint; (candidat) defaulting.

défaire† /defɛr/ v.t. undo; (valise) unpack; (démonter) take down; (débarrasser) rid. **se ~** v. pr. come undone. **se ~ de**, rid o.s. of.

défait, **~e**[1] /defɛ, -t/ a. (cheveux) ruffled; (visage) haggard.

défaite[2] /defɛt/ n.f. defeat.

défaitisme /defetizm/ n.m. defeatism.

défaitiste /defetist/ a. & n.m./f. defeatist.

défalquer /defalke/ v.t. (somme) deduct.

défaut /defo/ n.m. fault, defect; (d'un verre, diamant, etc.) flaw; (carence) lack; (pénurie) shortage. **à ~ de**, for lack of. **en ~**, at fault. **faire ~**, (argent etc.) be lacking. **par ~**, (jurid.) in one's absence.

défav|eur /defavœr/ n.f. disfavour. **~orable** a. unfavourable.

défavoriser /defavɔrize/ v.t. put at a disadvantage.

défection /defɛksjɔ̃/ n.f. desertion. **faire ~**, desert.

défect|ueux, **~ueuse** /defɛktɥø, -z/ a. faulty, defective. **~uosité** n.f. faultiness; (défaut) fault.

défendre /defɑ̃dr/ v.t. defend; (interdire) forbid. **~ à qn. de**, forbid s.o. to. **se ~** v. pr. defend o.s.; (se débrouiller) manage; (se protéger) protect o.s. **se ~ de**, (refuser) refrain from.

défense /defɑ̃s/ n.f. defence; (d'éléphant) tusk. **~ de fumer**/etc., no smoking/etc.

défenseur /defɑ̃sœr/ n.m. defender.

défensi|f, **~ve** /defɑ̃sif, -v/ a. & n.f. defensive.

déféren|t, **~te** /deferɑ̃, -t/ a. deferential. **~ce** n.f. deference.

déférer /defere/ v.t. (jurid.) refer. ● v.i. **~ à**, (avis etc.) defer to.

déferler /defɛrle/ v.i. (vagues) break; (violence etc.) erupt.

défi /defi/ n.m. challenge; (refus) defiance. **mettre au ~**, challenge.

déficeler /defisle/ v.t. untie.

déficience /defisjɑ̃s/ n.f. deficiency.

déficient /defisjɑ̃/ a. deficient.

déficit /defisit/ n.m. deficit. **~aire** a. in deficit.

défier /defje/ v.t. challenge; (braver) defy. **se ~ de**, mistrust.

défilé[1] /defile/ n.m. procession; (mil.) parade; (fig.) (continual) stream. **~ de mode**, fashion parade.

défilé[2] /defile/ n.m. (géog.) gorge.

défiler /defile/ v.i. march (past); (visiteurs) stream; (images) flash by. **se ~** v. pr. (fam.) sneak off.

défini /defini/ a. definite.

définir /definir/ v.t. define.

définissable /definisabl/ a. definable.

définiti|f, **~ve** /definitif, -v/ a. final; (permanent) definitive. **en ~ve**, in the final analysis. **~vement** adv. definitively, permanently.

définition /definisjɔ̃/ n.f. definition; (de mots croisés) clue.

déflagration /deflagrasjɔ̃/ n.f. explosion.

déflation /deflɑsjɔ̃/ n.f. deflation. **~niste** /-jɔnist/ a. deflationary.

défoncer /defɔ̃se/ v.t. (porte etc.) break down; (route, terrain) dig up; (lit) break the springs of. **se ~** v. pr. (fam.) work like mad; (drogué) get high.

déform|er /defɔrme/ v.t. put out of shape; (membre) deform; (faits, pensée) distort. **~ation** n.f. loss of shape; deformation; distortion.

défouler (se) /(sə)defule/ v. pr. let off steam.

défraîchir (se) /(sə)defreʃir/ v. pr. become faded.

défrayer /defreje/ v.t. (payer) pay the expenses of.

défricher /defriʃe/ v.t. clear (for cultivation).

défroisser /defrwase/ v.t. smooth out.

défunt, ~e /defœ̃, -t/ a. (mort) late. ● n.m., f. deceased.

dégagé /degaʒe/ a. clear; (ton) free and easy.

dégag|er /degaʒe/ v.t. (exhaler) give off; (désencombrer) clear; (délivrer) free; (faire ressortir) bring out.
● v.i. (football) kick the ball (down the pitch ou field). **se ~er** v. pr. free o.s.; (ciel, rue) clear; (odeur etc.) emanate. **~ement** n.m. giving off; clearing; freeing; (espace) clearing; (football) clearance.

dégainer /degene/ v.t./i. draw.

dégarnir /degarnir/ v.t. clear, empty. **se ~** v. pr. clear, empty; (crâne) go bald.

dégâts /dega/ n.m. pl. damage.

dégel /deʒɛl/ n.m. thaw. **~er** /deʒle/ v.t./i. thaw (out). **(faire) ~er,** (culin.) thaw.

dégénér|er /deʒenere/ v.i. degenerate. **~é, ~ée** a. & n.m., f. degenerate.

dégingandé /deʒɛ̃gɑ̃de/ a. gangling.

dégivrer /deʒivre/ v.t. (auto.) de-ice; (réfrigérateur) defrost.

déglacer /deglase/ v.t. (culin.) deglaze.

déglingu|er /deglɛ̃ge/ (fam.) v.t. knock about. **se ~er** v. pr. fall to bits. **~é** adj. falling to bits.

dégonfl|er /degɔ̃fle/ v.t. let down, deflate. **se ~er** v. pr. (fam.) get cold feet. **~é** a. (pneu) flat; (lâche: fam.) yellow.

dégorger /degɔrʒe/ v.i. **faire ~,** (culin.) soak.

dégouliner /deguline/ v.i. trickle.

dégourdi /degurdi/ a. smart.

dégourdir /degurdir/ v.t. (membre, liquide) warm up. **se ~ les jambes,** stretch one's legs.

dégoût /degu/ n.m. disgust.

dégoût|er /degute/ v.t. disgust. **~er qn. de qch.,** put s.o. off sth. **~ant, ~ante** a. disgusting. **~é** a. disgusted. **~é de,** sick of. **faire le ~é,** look disgusted.

dégradant /degradɑ̃/ a. degrading.

dégrader /degrade/ v.t. degrade; (abîmer) damage. **se ~** v. pr. (se détériorer) deteriorate.

dégrafer /degrafe/ v.t. unhook.

degré /dəgre/ n.m. degree; (d'escalier) step.

dégressi|f, ~ve /degresif, -v/ a. gradually lower.

dégrèvement /degrɛvmɑ̃/ n.m. **~ fiscal ou d'impôts,** tax reduction.

dégrever /degrəve/ v.t. reduce the tax on.

dégringol|er /degrɛ̃gɔle/ v.i. tumble (down). ● v.t. rush down. **~ade** n.f. tumble.

dégrossir /degrosir/ v.t. (bois) trim; (projet) rough out.

déguerpir /degerpir/ v.i. clear off.

dégueulasse /degœlas/ a. (argot) disgusting, lousy.

dégueuler /degœle/ v.t. (argot) throw up.

déguis|er /degize/ v.t. disguise. **se ~er** v. pr. disguise o.s.; (au carnaval etc.) dress up. **~ement** n.m. disguise; (de carnaval etc.) fancy dress.

dégust|er /degyste/ v.t. taste, sample; (savourer) enjoy. **~ation** n.f. tasting, sampling.

déhancher (se) /(sə)deɑ̃ʃe/ v. pr. sway one's hips.

dehors /dəɔr/ adv. & n.m. outside. ● n.m. pl. (aspect de qn.) exterior. **au ~ (de),** outside. **en ~ de,** outside; (hormis) apart from. **jeter/ mettre/etc. ~,** throw/put/etc. out.

déjà /deʒa/ adv. already; (avant) before, already.

déjà-vu /deʒavy/ n.m. inv. déjà vu.

déjeuner /deʒœne/ v.i. (have) lunch; (le matin) (have) breakfast. ● n.m. lunch. **(petit) ~,** breakfast.

déjouer /deʒwe/ v.t. thwart.

delà /dəla/ adv. & prép. **au ~ (de), en ~ (de), par ~,** beyond.

délabrer (se) /(sə)delabre/ v. pr. become dilapidated.

délacer /delase/ v.t. undo.

délai /delɛ/ n.m. time-limit; (attente) wait; (sursis) extension (of time). **sans ~,** without delay. **dans les plus brefs ~s,** as soon as possible.

délaisser /delese/ v.t. desert.

délass|er /delase/ v.t., **se ~er** v. pr. relax. **~ement** n.m. relaxation.

délation /delasjɔ̃/ n.f. informing.

délavé /delave/ a. faded.

délayer /deleje/ v.t. mix (with liquid); (*idée*) drag out.

delco /dɛlko/ n.m. (P., *auto.*) distributor.

délecter (se) /(sə)delɛkte/ v. pr. se ~ de, delight in.

délégation /delegɑsjɔ̃/ n.f. delegation.

délégu|er /delege/ v.t. delegate. ~é, ~ée n.m., f. delegate.

délibéré /delibere/ a. deliberate; (*résolu*) determined. ~ment adv. deliberately.

délibér|er /delibere/ v.i. deliberate. ~ation n.f. deliberation.

délicat, ~e /delika, -t/ a. delicate; (*plein de tact*) tactful; (*exigeant*) particular. ~ement /-tmɑ̃/ adv. delicately; tactfully. ~esse /-tɛs/ n.f. delicacy; tact. ~esses /-tɛs/ n.f. pl. (kind) attentions.

délice /delis/ n.m. delight. ~s n.f. pl. delights.

délicieu|x, ~se /delisjø, -z/ a. (*au goût*) delicious; (*charmant*) delightful.

délié /delje/ a. fine, slender; (*agile*) nimble.

délier /delje/ v.t. untie; (*délivrer*) free. se ~ v. pr. come untied.

délimit|er /delimite/ v.t. determine, demarcate. ~ation n.f. demarcation.

délinquan|t, ~te /delɛ̃kɑ̃, -t/ a. & n.m., f. delinquent. ~ce n.f. delinquency.

délire /delir/ n.m. delirium; (*fig.*) frenzy.

délir|er /delire/ v.i. be delirious (**de**, with); (*déraisonner*) rave. ~ant, ~ante a. delirious; (*frénétique*) frenzied; (*fam.*) wild.

délit /deli/ n.m. offence, crime.

délivr|er /delivre/ v.t. free, release; (*pays*) deliver; (*remettre*) issue. ~ance n.f. release; deliverance; issue.

déloger /delɔʒe/ v.t. force out.

déloy|al (m. pl. ~aux) /delwajal, -jo/ a. disloyal; (*procédé*) unfair.

delta /dɛlta/ n.m. delta.

deltaplane /dɛltaplan/ n.m. hang-glider.

déluge /delyʒ/ n.m. flood; (*pluie*) downpour.

démagogie /demagɔʒi/ n.m. demagogy.

démagogue /demagɔg/ n.m./f. demagogue.

demain /dmɛ̃/ adv. tomorrow.

demande /dmɑ̃d/ n.f. request; (*d'emploi*) application; (*exigence*) demand. ~ en mariage, proposal (of marriage).

demandé /dmɑ̃de/ a. in demand.

demander /dmɑ̃de/ v.t. ask for; (*chemin, heure*) ask; (*emploi*) apply for; (*nécessiter*) require. ~ que/si, ask that/if. ~ qch. à qn., ask for sth. ~ à qn. de, ask s.o. to. ~ en mariage, propose to. se ~ si/où/ etc., wonder if/where/etc.

demandeu|r, ~se /dmɑ̃dœr, -øz/ n.m., f. les ~rs d'emploi job seekers.

démang|er /demɑ̃ʒe/ v.t./i. itch. ~eaison n.f. itch(ing).

démanteler /demɑ̃tle/ v.t. break up.

démaquill|er (se) /(sə)demakije/ v. pr. remove one's make-up. ~ant n.m. make-up remover.

démarcation /demarkɑsjɔ̃/ n.f. demarcation.

démarchage /demarʃaʒ/ n.m. door-to-door selling.

démarche /demarʃ/ n.f. walk, gait; (*procédé*) step. faire des ~s auprès de, make approaches to.

démarcheu|r, ~se /demarʃœr, -øz/ n.m., f. (door-to-door) canvasser.

démarr|er /demare/ v.i. (*moteur*) start (up); (*partir*) move off; (*fig.*) get moving. ● v.t. (*fam.*) get moving. ~age n.m. start. ~eur n.m. starter.

démasquer /demaske/ v.t. unmask.

démêlant /demelɑ̃/ n.m. conditioner.

démêler /demele/ v.t. disentangle.

démêlés /demele/ n.m. pl. trouble.

déménag|er /demenaʒe/ v.i. move (house). ● v.t. (*meubles*) remove. ~ement n.m. move; (*de meubles*) removal. ~eur n.m. removal man; (*Amer.*) furniture mover.

démener (se) /(sə)demne/ v. pr. move about wildly; (*fig.*) exert o.s.

dément, ~te /demɑ̃, -t/ a. insane. ● n.m., f. lunatic. ~ce n.f. insanity.

démenti /demɑ̃ti/ n.m. denial.

démentir /demɑ̃tir/ v.t. refute; (*ne pas être conforme à*) belie. ~ que, deny that.

démerder (se) /(sə)demɛrde/ (*fam.*) manage.

démesuré /demzyre/ a. inordinate.

démettre /demɛtr/ v.t. (*poignet etc.*) dislocate. ~ qn. de, dismiss s.o. from. se ~ v. pr. resign (**de**, from).

demeure /dəmœr/ *n.f.* residence. **mettre en ~ de**, order to.

demeurer /dəmœre/ *v.i.* live; (*rester*) remain.

demi, **~e** /dmi/ *a.* half(-). ● *n.m.*, *f.* half. ● *n.m.* (*bière*) (half-pint) glass of beer; (*football*) half-back. ● *n.f.* (*à l'horloge*) half-hour. ● *adv.* **à ~**, half; (*ouvrir, fermer*) half-way. **à la ~e**, at half-past. **une heure et ~e**, an hour and a half; (*à l'horloge*) half past one. **une ~-journée/-livre/etc.**, half a day/pound/*etc.*, a half-day/-pound/*etc.* **~-cercle** *n.m.* semicircle. **~-finale** *n.f.* semifinal. **~-frère** *n.m.* stepbrother. **~-heure** *n.f.* half-hour, half an hour. **~-jour** *n.m.* half-light. **~-mesure** *n.f.* half-measure. **à ~-mot** *adv.* without having to express every word. **~-pension** *n.f.* half-board. **~-pensionnaire** *n.m./f.* day-boarder. **~-sel** *a. invar.* slightly salted. **~-sœur** *n.f.* stepsister. **~-tarif** *n.m.* half-fare. **~-tour** *n.m.* about turn; (*auto.*) U-turn. **faire ~-tour**, turn back.

démis, **~e** /demi, -z/ *a.* dislocated. **~ de ses fonctions**, removed from his post.

démission /demisjɔ̃/ *n.f.* resignation. **~ner** /-jɔne/ *v.i.* resign.

démobiliser /demɔbilize/ *v.t.* demobilize.

démocrate /demɔkrat/ *n.m./f.* democrat. ● *a.* democratic.

démocrat|ie /demɔkrasi/ *n.f.* democracy. **~ique** /-atik/ *a.* democratic.

démodé /demɔde/ *a.* old-fashioned.

démographi|e /demɔgrafi/ *n.f.* demography. **~que** *a.* demographic.

demoiselle /dəmwazɛl/ *n.f.* young lady; (*célibataire*) spinster. **~ d'honneur**, bridesmaid.

démol|ir /demɔlir/ *v.t.* demolish. **~ition** *n.f.* demolition.

démon /demɔ̃/ *n.m.* demon. **le D~**, the Devil.

démoniaque /demɔnjak/ *a.* fiendish.

démonstra|teur, **~trice** /demɔ̃strater, -tris/ *n.m.*, *f.* demonstrator. **~tion** /-asjɔ̃/ *n.f.* demonstration; (*de force*) show.

démonstrati|f, **~ve** /demɔ̃stratif, -v/ *a.* demonstrative.

démonter /demɔ̃te/ *v.t.* take apart, dismantle; (*installation*) take down; (*fig.*) disconcert. **se ~** *v. pr.* come apart.

démontrer /demɔ̃tre/ *v.t.* show, demonstrate.

démoraliser /demɔralize/ *v.t.* demoralize.

démuni /demyni/ *a.* impoverished. **~ de**, without.

démunir /demynir/ *v.t.* **~ de**, deprive of. **se ~ de**, part with.

démystifier /demistifje/ *v.t.* enlighten.

dénaturer /denatyre/ *v.t.* (*faits etc.*) distort.

dénégation /denegasjɔ̃/ *n.f.* denial.

dénicher /denife/ *v.t.* (*trouver*) dig up; (*faire sortir*) flush out.

dénigr|er /denigre/ *v.t.* denigrate. **~ement** *n.m.* denigration.

dénivellation /denivɛlasjɔ̃/ *n.f.* (*pente*) slope.

dénombrer /denɔ̃bre/ *v.t.* count; (*énumérer*) enumerate.

dénomination /denɔminasjɔ̃/ *n.f.* designation.

dénommé, **~e** /denɔme/ *n. m.*, *f.* **le ~ X**, the said X.

dénonc|er /denɔ̃se/ *v.t.* denounce; (*scol.*) tell on. **se ~er** *v. pr.* give o.s. up. **~iateur**, **~iatrice** *n.m.*, *f.* informer; (*scol.*) tell-tale. **~iation** *n.f.* denunciation.

dénoter /denɔte/ *v.t.* denote.

dénouement /denumɑ̃/ *n.m.* outcome; (*théâtre*) dénouement.

dénouer /denwe/ *v.t.* unknot, undo. **se ~** *v. pr.* (*nœud*) come undone.

dénoyauter /denwajote/ *v.t.* stone; (*Amer.*) pit.

denrée /dɑ̃re/ *n.f.* foodstuff.

dens|e /dɑ̃s/ *a.* dense. **~ité** *n.f.* density.

dent /dɑ̃/ *n.f.* tooth; (*de roue*) cog. **faire ses ~s**, teethe. **~aire** /-tɛr/ *a.* dental.

dentelé /dɑ̃tle/ *a.* jagged.

dentelle /dɑ̃tɛl/ *n.f.* lace.

dentier /dɑ̃tje/ *n.m.* denture.

dentifrice /dɑ̃tifris/ *n.m.* toothpaste.

dentiste /dɑ̃tist/ *n.m./f.* dentist.

dentition /dɑ̃tisjɔ̃/ *n.f.* teeth.

dénud|er /denyde/ *v.t.* bare. **~é** *a.* bare.

dénué /denɥe/ *a.* **~ de**, devoid of.

dénuement /denymɑ̃/ *n.m.* destitution.

déodorant /deɔdɔrɑ̃/ *a.m.* & *n.m.* (**produit**) deodorant.

déontologi|e /deɔ̃tɔlɔʒi/ *n.f.* code of practice. **~que** *a.* ethical.

dépann|er /depane/ v.t. repair; (fig.) help out. **~age** n.m. repair. **de ~age**, (service etc.) breakdown. **~euse** n.f. breakdown lorry; (Amer.) wrecker.

dépareillé /depareje/ a. odd, not matching.

départ /depar/ n.m. departure; (sport) start. **au ~**, at the outset.

départager /departaʒe/ v.t. settle the matter between.

département /departəmɑ̃/ n.m. department.

dépassé /depase/ a. outdated.

dépass|er /depase/ v.t. go past, pass; (véhicule) overtake; (excéder) exceed; (rival) surpass; (dérouter: fam.) be beyond. ● v.i. stick out; (véhicule) overtake. **~ement** n.m. overtaking.

dépays|er /depeize/ v.t. disorientate, disorient. **~ant**, **~e** a. disorientating. **~ement** n.m. disorientation; (changement) change of scenery.

dépêch|e /depɛʃ/ n.f. dispatch. **~er**[1] /-eʃe/ v.t. dispatch.

dépêcher[2] **(se)** /(sə)depeʃe/ v. pr. hurry (up).

dépeindre /depɛ̃dr/ v.t. depict.

dépendance /depɑ̃dɑ̃s/ n.f. dependence; (bâtiment) outbuilding.

dépendre /depɑ̃dr/ v.t. take down. ● v.i. depend (**de**, on). **~ de**, (appartenir à) belong to.

dépens (aux) /(o)depɑ̃/ prép. **aux ~ de**, at the expense of.

dépens|e /depɑ̃s/ n.f. expense; expenditure. **~er** v.t./i. spend; (énergie etc.) expend. **se ~er** v. pr. exert o.s.

dépens|ier, **~ière** /depɑ̃sje, -jɛr/ a. **être ~ier**, be a spendthrift.

dépérir /deperir/ v.i. wither.

dépêtrer (se) /(sə) depetre/ v. pr. get o.s. out (**de**, of).

dépeupler /depœple/ v.t. depopulate. **se ~** v. pr. become depopulated.

déphasé /defaze/ a. (fam.) out of touch.

dépilatoire /depilatwar/ a. & n.m. depilatory.

dépist|er /depiste/ v.t. detect; (criminel) track down; (poursuivant) throw off the scent. **~age** n.m. detection.

dépit /depi/ n.m. resentment. **en ~ de**, despite. **en ~ du bon sens**,

against all common sense. **~é** /-te/ a. vexed.

déplacé /deplase/ a. out of place.

déplac|er /deplase/ v.t. move. **se ~** v. pr. move; (voyager) travel. **~ement** n.m. moving; travel(-ling).

déplaire /deplɛr/ v.i. **~ à**, (irriter) displease. **ça me déplaît**, I dislike that.

déplaisant, **~e** /deplɛzɑ̃, -t/ a. unpleasant, disagreeable.

déplaisir /deplɛzir/ n.m. displeasure.

dépliant /deplijɑ̃/ n.m. leaflet.

déplier /deplije/ v.t. unfold.

déplor|er /deplore/ v.t. (trouver regrettable) deplore; (mort) lament. **~able** a. deplorable.

dépl|oyer /deplwaje/ v.t. (ailes, carte) spread; (courage) display; (armée) deploy. **~oiement** n.m. display; deployment.

déport|er /deporte/ v.t. (exiler) deport; (dévier) carry off course. **~ation** n.f. deportation.

déposer /depoze/ v.t. put down; (laisser) leave; (passager) drop; (argent) deposit; (installation) dismantle; (plainte) lodge; (armes) lay down; (roi) depose. ● v.i. (jurid.) testify. **se ~** v. pr. settle.

dépositaire /depozitɛr/ n.m./f. (comm.) agent.

déposition /depozisjɔ̃/ n.f. (jurid.) statement.

dépôt /depo/ n.m. (garantie, lie) deposit; (entrepôt) warehouse; (d'autobus) depot; (d'ordures) dump. **laisser en ~**, give for safe keeping.

dépotoir /depotwar/ n.m. rubbish dump.

dépouille /depuj/ n.f. skin, hide. **~ (mortelle)**, mortal remains. **~s**, (butin) spoils.

dépouiller /depuje/ v.t. go through; (votes) count; (écorcher) skin. **~ de**, strip of.

dépourvu /depurvy/ a. **~ de**, devoid of. **prendre au ~**, catch unawares.

dépréc|ier /depresje/ v.t., **se ~ier** v. pr. depreciate. **~iation** n.f. depreciation.

déprédations /depredasjɔ̃/ n.f. pl. damage.

dépr|imer /deprime/ v.t. depress. **~ession** n.f. depression. **~ession nerveuse**, nervous breakdown.

depuis /dəpɥi/ prép. since; (durée) for; (à partir de) from. ● adv. (ever) since. **~ que**, since. **~ quand attendez-vous?**, how long have you been waiting?

députation /depytɑsjɔ̃/ *n.f.* deputation.

député, ~e /depyte/ *n.m., f.* Member of Parliament.

déraciné, ~e /derasine/ *a. & n.m., f.* rootless (person).

déraciner /derasine/ *v.t.* uproot.

dérailler /deraje/ *v.i.* be derailed; (*fig., fam.*) be talking nonsense. **faire ~er**, derail. **~ement** *n.m.* derailment. **~eur** *n.m.* (*de vélo*) gear mechanism, *dérailleur*.

déraisonnable /derɛzɔnabl/ *a.* unreasonable.

dérang|er /derɑ̃ʒe/ *v.t.* (*gêner*) bother, disturb; (*dérégler*) upset, disrupt. **se ~er** *v. pr.* put o.s. out. **ça vous ~e si . . .?**, do you mind if . . .? **~ement** *n.m.* bother; (*désordre*) disorder, upset. **en ~ement**, out of order.

dérap|er /derape/ *v.i.* skid; (*fig.*) get out of control. **~age** *n.m.* skid.

déréglé /deregle/ *a.* (*vie*) dissolute; (*estomac*) upset; (*pendule*) (that is) not running properly.

dérégler /deregle/ *v.t.* put out of order. **se ~** *v. pr.* go wrong.

dérision /derizjɔ̃/ *n.f.* mockery. **par ~**, derisively. **tourner en ~**, mock.

dérisoire /derizwar/ *a.* derisory.

dérivatif /derivatif/ *n.m.* distraction.

dériv|e /deriv/ *n.f.* **aller à la ~e**, drift. **~er**[1] *v.i.* (*bateau*) drift; *v.t.* (*détourner*) divert.

dériv|er /derive/ *v.i.* **~er de**, derive from. **~é** *a.* derived; *n.m.* derivative; (*techn.*) by-product.

dermatolo|gie /dɛrmatɔlɔʒi/ *n.f.* dermatology. **~gue** /-g/ *n.m./f.* dermatologist.

dern|ier, ~ière /dɛrnje, -jɛr/ *a.* last; (*nouvelles, mode*) latest; (*étage*) top. ● *n.m., f.* last (one). **ce ~ier**, the latter. **en ~ier**, last. **le ~ier cri**, the latest fashion.

dernièrement /dɛrnjɛrmɑ̃/ *adv.* recently.

dérobé /derɔbe/ *a.* hidden. **à la ~e**, stealthily.

dérober /derɔbe/ *v.t.* steal; (*cacher*) hide (**à**, from). **se ~** *v. pr.* slip away. **se ~ à**, (*obligation*) shy away from; (*se cacher à*) hide from.

dérogation /derɔgɑsjɔ̃/ *n.f.* exemption.

déroger /derɔʒe/ *v.i.* **~ à**, go against.

dérouiller (se) /(sə)deruje/ *v.t. pr.* **~ les jambes** to stretch one's legs.

déroul|er /derule/ *v.t.* (*fil etc.*) unwind. **se ~er** *v. pr.* unwind; (*avoir lieu*) take place; (*récit, paysage*) unfold. **~ement** *n.m.* (*d'une action*) development.

déroute /derut/ *n.f.* (*mil.*) rout.

dérouter /derute/ *v.t.* disconcert.

derrière /dɛrjɛr/ *prép. & adv.* behind. ● *n.m.* back, rear; (*postérieur*) behind. **de ~**, back, rear; (*pattes*) hind. **par ~**, (from) behind, at the back *ou* rear.

des /de/ *voir* de.

dès /dɛ/ *prép.* (right) from, from the time of. **~ lors**, from then on. **~ que**, as soon as.

désabusé /dezabyze/ *a.* disillusioned.

désaccord /dezakɔr/ *n.m.* disagreement. **~é** /-de/ *a.* out of tune.

désaffecté /dezafɛkte/ *a.* disused.

désaffection /dezafɛksjɔ̃/ *n.f.* alienation (**pour**, from).

désagréable /dezagreabl/ *a.* unpleasant.

désagréger (se) /(sə)dezagreʒe/ *v. pr.* disintegrate.

désagrément /dezagremɑ̃/ *n.m.* annoyance.

désaltérant /dezalterɑ̃/ *a.* thirst-quenching, refreshing.

désaltérer /dezaltere/ *v.i., se ~* *v. pr.* quench one's thirst.

désamorcer /dezamɔrse/ *v.t.* (*situation, obus*) defuse.

désappr|ouver /dezapruve/ *v.t.* disapprove of. **~obation** *n.f.* disapproval.

désarçonner /dezarsɔne/ *v.t.* disconcert, throw; (*jockey*) unseat, throw.

désarmant /dezarmɑ̃/ *a.* disarming.

désarm|er /dezarme/ *v.t./i.* disarm. **~ement** *n.m.* (*pol.*) disarmament.

désarroi /dezarwa/ *n.m.* confusion.

désarticulé /dezartikyle/ *a.* dislocated.

désastr|e /dezastr/ *n.m.* disaster. **~eux, ~euse** *a.* disastrous.

désavantag|e /dezavɑ̃taʒ/ *n.m.* disadvantage. **~er** *v.t.* put at a disadvantage. **~eux, ~euse** *a.* disadvantageous.

désaveu (*pl.* **~x**) /dezavø/ *n.m.* repudiation.

désavouer /dezavwe/ *v.t.* repudiate.

désaxé, **~e** /dezakse/ *a. & n.m.*, *f.* unbalanced (person).

descendan|t, **~te** /desᾱdᾱ, -t/ *n.m.*, *f.* descendant. **~ce** *n.f.* descent; (*enfants*) descendants.

descendre /desᾱdr/ *v.i.* (*aux. être*) go down; (*venir*) come down; (*passager*) get off *ou* out; (*nuit*) fall. **~ de**, (*être issu de*) be descended from. **~ à l'hôtel**, go to a hotel. ● *v.t.* (*aux. avoir*) (*escalier etc.*) go *ou* come down; (*objet*) take down; (*abattre*, *fam.*) shoot down.

descente /desᾱt/ *n.f.* descent; (*pente*) (downward) slope; (*raid*) raid. **~ de lit**, bedside rug.

descripti|f, **~ve** /dεskriptif, -v/ *a.* descriptive.

description /dεskripsjɔ̃/ *n.f.* description.

désemparé /dezᾱpare/ *a.* distraught.

désemplir /dezᾱplir/ *v.i.* **ne pas ~**, be always crowded.

désendettement /dezᾱdεtmᾱ/ *n.m.* getting out of debt.

désenfler /dezᾱfle/ *v.i.* go down.

déséquilibre /dezekilibr/ *n.m.* imbalance. **en ~**, unsteady.

déséquilibr|er /dezekilibre/ *v.t.* throw off balance. **~é**, **~ée** *a. & n.m.*, *f.* unbalanced (person).

désert [1] **~e** /dezεr, -t/ *a.* deserted.

désert [2] /dezεr/ *n.m.* desert. **~ique** /-tik/ *a.* desert.

déserter /dezεrte/ *v.t./i.* desert. **~eur** *n.m.* deserter. **~ion** /-εrsjɔ̃/ *n.f.* desertion.

désespér|er /dezεspere/ *v.i.*, **se ~er** *v. pr.* despair. **~er de**, despair of. **~ant**, **~ante** *a.* utterly disheartening. **~é** *a.* in despair; (*état*, *cas*) hopeless; (*effort*) desperate. **~ément** *adv.* desperately.

désespoir /dezεspwar/ *n.m.* despair. **au ~**, in despair. **en ~ de cause**, as a last resort.

déshabill|er /dezabije/ *v.t.* **se ~er** *v. pr.* undress, get undressed. **~é** *a.* undressed; *n.m.* négligée.

déshabituer (se) /(sə)dezabitɥe/ *v. pr.* **se ~ de**, get out of the habit of.

désherb|er /dezεrbe/ *v.t.* weed. **~ant** *n.m.* weed-killer.

déshérit|er /dezerite/ *v.t.* disinherit. **~é** *a.* (*région*) deprived. **les ~és** *n.m. pl.* the underprivileged.

déshonneur /dezɔnœr/ *n.m.* dishonour.

déshonor|er /dezɔnɔre/ *v.t.* dishonour. **~ant**, **~ante** *a.* dishonourable.

déshydrater /dezidrate/ *v.t.*, **se ~** *v. pr.* dehydrate.

désigner /deziɲe/ *v.t.* (*montrer*) point to *ou* out; (*élire*) appoint; (*signifier*) indicate.

désillusion /dezilyzjɔ̃/ *n.f.* disillusionment.

désincrust|er /dezɛ̃kryste/ *v. pr.* (*chaudière*) descale; (*peau*) exfoliate. **~ant à produit** **~ant**, (*skin*) scrub.

désinence /dezinᾱs/ *n.f.* (*gram.*) ending.

désinfect|er /dezɛ̃fεkte/ *v.t.* disinfect. **~ant** *n.m.* disinfectant.

désinfection /dezɛ̃fεksjɔ̃/ *n.f.* disinfection.

désintégrer /dezɛ̃tegre/ *v.t.*, **se ~** *v. pr.* disintegrate.

désintéressé /dezɛ̃terese/ *a.* disinterested.

désintéresser (se) /(sə)dezɛ̃terese/ *v. pr.* **se ~ de**, lose interest in.

désintoxication /dezɛ̃tɔksikasjɔ̃/ *n.f.* detoxification. **cure de ~**, detoxification course.

désintoxiquer /dezɛ̃tɔksike/ *v.t.* cure of an addiction; (*régime*) purify.

désinvolt|e /dezɛ̃vɔlt/ *a.* casual. **~ure** *n.f.* casualness.

désir /dezir/ *n.m.* wish, desire; (*convoitise*) desire.

désirer /dezire/ *v.t.* want; (*convoiter*) desire. **~ faire**, want *ou* wish to do.

désireu|x, **~se** /dezirø, -z/ *a.* **~x de**, anxious to.

désist|er (se) /(sə)deziste/ *v. pr.* withdraw. **~ement** *n.m.* withdrawal.

désobéir /dezɔbeir/ *v.i.* **~ (à)**, disobey.

désobéissan|t, **~te** /dezɔbeisᾱ, -t/ *a.* disobedient. **~ce** *n.f.* disobedience.

désobligeant, **~e** /dezɔbliʒᾱ, -t/ *a.* disagreeable, unkind.

désodé /desɔde/ *a.* sodium-free.

désodorisant /dezɔdɔrizᾱ/ *n.m.* air freshener.

désœuvr|é /dezœvre/ *a.* idle. **~ement** *n.m.* idleness.

désolé /dezɔle/ *a.* (*région*) desolate.

désol|er /dezɔle/ *v.t.* distress. **être ~é**, (*regretter*) be sorry. **~ation** *n.f.* distress.

désopilant, **~e** /dezɔpilã, -t/ a. hilarious.

désordonné /dezɔrdɔne/ a. untidy; (*mouvements*) uncoordinated.

désordre /dezɔrdr/ n.m. disorder; (*de vêtements, cheveux*) untidiness. **mettre en ~**, make untidy.

désorganiser /dezɔrganize/ v.t. disorganize.

désorienté /dezɔrjãte/ a. disorientated.

désorienter /dezɔrjãte/ v.t. disorientate, disorient.

désormais /dezɔrmɛ/ adv. from now on.

désosser /dezɔse/ v.t. bone.

despote /dɛspɔt/ n.m. despot.

desquels, desquelles /dekɛl/ voir lequel.

dessécher /deseʃe/ v.t., **se ~** v. pr. dry out *ou* up.

dessein /desɛ̃/ n.m. intention. **à ~**, intentionally.

desserrer /desere/ v.t. loosen. **sans ~ les dents**, without opening his/her mouth. **se ~** v. pr. come loose.

dessert /desɛr/ n.m. dessert.

desserte /desɛrt/ n.f. (*transports*) service, servicing.

desservir /desɛrvir/ v.t./i. clear away; (*autobus*) provide a service to, serve.

dessin /desɛ̃/ n.m. drawing; (*motif*) design; (*contour*) outline. **~ animé**, (*cinéma*) cartoon. **~ humoristique**, cartoon.

dessiner /desine/ v.t./i. draw; (*fig.*) outline. **se ~** v. pr. appear, take shape. **~ateur, ~atrice** n.m., f. artist; (*industriel*) draughtsman.

dessoûler /desule/ v.t./i. sober up.

dessous /dsu/ adv. underneath.
● *n.m.* under-side, underneath.
● *n.m. pl.* underclothes. **du ~**, bottom; (*voisins*) downstairs. **en ~, par ~**, underneath. **~-de-plat** n.m. invar. (heat-resistant) table-mat. **~-de-table** n.m. invar. backhander.

dessus /dsy/ adv. on top (of it), on it.
● *n.m.* top. **du ~**, top; (*voisins*) upstairs. **en ~**, above. **par ~**, over (it). **avoir le ~**, get the upper hand. **~-de-lit** n.m. invar. bedspread.

destabiliser /destabilize/ v.t. destabilize. **~ation** n.f. destabilization.

destin /destɛ̃/ n.m. (*sort*) fate; (*avenir*) destiny.

destinataire /dɛstinatɛr/ n.m./f. addressee.

destination /dɛstinasjɔ̃/ n.f. destination; (*emploi*) purpose. **à ~ de**, (going) to.

destinée /dɛstine/ n.f. (*sort*) fate; (*avenir*) destiny.

destiner /dɛstine/ v.t. **~er à**, intend for; (*vouer*) destine for; (*affecter*) earmark for. **être ~é à faire**, be intended to do; (*condamné, obligé*) be destined to do. **se ~er à**, (*carrière*) intend to take up.

destituer /dɛstitɥe/ v.t. dismiss (from office). **~ution** n.f. dismissal.

destructeur, ~trice /dɛstryktœr, -tris/ a. destructive.

destruction /dɛstryksjɔ̃/ n.f. destruction.

désuet, ~uète /dezɥɛ, -t/ a. outdated.

désunir /dezynir/ v.t. divide.

détachant /detaʃã/ n.m. stain-remover.

détaché /detaʃe/ a. detached. **~ement** n.m. detachment.

détacher /detaʃe/ v.t. untie; (*ôter*) remove, detach; (*déléguer*) send (on assignment *ou* secondment). **se ~** v. pr. come off, break away; (*nœud etc.*) come undone; (*ressortir*) stand out.

détail /detaj/ n.m. detail; (*de compte*) breakdown; (*comm.*) retail. **au ~**, (*vendre etc.*) retail. **de ~**, (*prix etc.*) retail. **en ~**, in detail.

détaillé /detaje/ a. detailed.

détailler /detaje/ v.t. (*articles*) sell in small quantities, split up. **~ant, ~ante** n.m., f. retailer.

détaler /detale/ v.i. (*fam.*) make tracks, run off.

détartrant /detartrã/ n.m. descaler.

détaxer /detakse/ v.t. reduce the tax on.

détecter /detɛkte/ v.t. detect. **~eur** n.m. detector. **~ion** /-ksjɔ̃/ n.f. detection.

détective /detɛktiv/ n.m. detective.

déteindre /detɛ̃dr/ v.i. (*couleur*) run (sur, on to). **~ sur**, (*fig.*) rub off on.

détendre /detãdr/ v.t. slacken; (*ressort*) release; (*personne*) relax. **se ~re** v. pr. become slack, slacken; be released; relax. **~u** a. (*calme*) relaxed.

détenir† /detnir/ v.t. hold; (*secret, fortune*) possess.

détente /detãt/ *n.f.* relaxation; (*pol.*) détente; (*saut*) spring; (*gâchette*) trigger; (*relâchement*) release.

déten|teur, ~trice /detãtœr, -tris/ *n.m., f.* holder.

détention /detãsjõ/ *n.f.* ~ **préventive**, custody.

détenu, ~e /detny/ *n.m., f.* prisoner.

détergent /detɛrʒã/ *n.m.* detergent.

détérior|er /deterjore/ *v.t.* damage. **se ~er** *v. pr.* deteriorate. **~ation** *n.f.* damaging; deterioration.

détermin|er /determine/ *v.t.* determine. **se ~er** *v. pr.* make up one's mind (**à**, to). **~ation** *n.f.* determination. **~é** *a.* (*résolu*) determined; (*précis*) definite.

déterrer /detere/ *v.t.* dig up.

détersif /detɛrsif/ *n.m.* detergent.

détestable /detɛstabl/ *a.* foul.

détester /detɛste/ *v.t.* hate. **se ~** *v. pr.* hate each other.

déton|er /detone/ *v.i.* explode, detonate. **~ateur** *n.m.* detonator. **~ation** *n.f.* explosion, detonation.

détonner /detone/ *v.i.* clash.

détour /detur/ *n.m.* bend; (*crochet*) detour; (*fig.*) roundabout means.

détourné /deturne/ *a.* roundabout.

détourn|er /deturne/ *v.t.* divert; (*tête, yeux*) turn away; (*avion*) hijack; (*argent*) embezzle. **se ~er de**, stray from. **~ement** *n.m.* hijack(ing); embezzlement.

détrac|teur, ~trice /detraktœr, -tris/ *n.m., f.* critic.

détraquer /detrake/ *v.t.* break, put out of order; (*estomac*) upset. **se ~** *v. pr.* (*machine*) go wrong.

détresse /detrɛs/ *n.f.* distress.

détriment /detrimã/ *n.m.* detriment.

détritus /detrity(s)/ *n.m. pl.* rubbish.

détroit /detrwa/ *n.m.* strait.

détromper /detrõpe/ *v.t.* undeceive, enlighten.

détruire† /detrɥir/ *v.t.* destroy.

dette /dɛt/ *n.f.* debt.

deuil /dœj/ *n.m.* mourning; (*perte*) bereavement. **porter le ~**, be in mourning.

deux /dø/ *a. & n.m.* two. **~ fois**, twice. **tous (les) ~**, both. **~- pièces** *n.m. invar.* (*vêtement*) two-piece; (*logement*) two-room flat *or* apartment. **~-points** *n.m. invar.* (*gram.*) colon. **~-roues** *n.m. invar.* two-wheeled vehicle.

deuxième /døzjɛm/ *a. & n.m./f.* second. **~ment** *adv.* secondly.

dévaler /devale/ *v.t./i.* hurtle down.

dévaliser /devalize/ *v.t.* rob, clean out.

dévaloriser /devalorize/ *v.t.*, **se ~** *v. pr.* reduce in value.

dévalorisant, ~e /devalorizã, -t/ *a.* demeaning.

déval|uer /devalɥe/ *v.t.*, **se ~uer** *v. pr.* devalue. **~uation** *n.f.* devaluation.

devancer /dəvãse/ *v.t.* be *ou* go ahead of; (*arriver*) arrive ahead of; (*prévenir*) anticipate.

devant /dəvã/ *prép.* in front of; (*distance*) ahead of; (*avec mouvement*) past; (*en présence de*) before; (*face à*) in the face of. ● *adv.* in front; (*à distance*) ahead. ● *n.m.* front. **prendre les ~s**, take the initiative. **de ~**, front. **par ~**, at *ou* from the front, in front. **aller au ~ de qn.**, go to meet sb. **aller au ~ des désirs de qn.**, anticipate sb.'s wishes.

devanture /dəvãtyr/ *n.f.* shop front; (*étalage*) shop-window.

dévaster /devaste/ *v.t.* devastate.

déveine /devɛn/ *n.f.* bad luck.

développ|er /devlope/ *v.t.*, **se ~er** *v. pr.* develop. **~ement** *n.m.* development; (*de photos*) developing.

devenir† /dəvnir/ *v.i.* (*aux. être*) become. **qu'est-il devenu?**, what has become of him?

dévergondé /devɛrgõde/ *a.* shameless.

déverser /devɛrse/ *v.t.*, **se ~** *v. pr.* empty out, pour out.

dévêtir /devetir/ *v.t.*, **se ~** *v. pr.* undress.

déviation /devjasjõ/ *n.f.* diversion.

dévier /devje/ *v.t.* divert; (*coup*) deflect. ● *v.i.* (*ballon, balle*) veer; (*personne*) deviate.

devin /dəvɛ̃/ *n.m.* fortune-teller.

deviner /dəvine/ *v.t.* guess; (*apercevoir*) distinguish.

devinette /dəvinɛt/ *n.f.* riddle.

devis /dəvi/ *n.m.* estimate.

dévisager /devizaʒe/ *v.t.* stare at.

devise /dəviz/ *n.f.* motto. **~s**, (*monnaie*) (foreign) currency.

dévisser /devise/ *v.t.* unscrew.

dévitaliser /devitalize/ *v.t.* (*dent*) kill the nerve in.

dévoiler /devwale/ *v.t.* reveal.

devoir¹ /dəvwar/ *n.m.* duty; (*scol.*) homework; (*fait en classe*) exercise.

devoir†² /dvwar/ *v.t.* owe. ● *v. aux.*
~ **faire**, (*nécessité*) must do, have
(got) to do; (*intention*) be due to do.
~ **être**, (*probabilité*) must be. **vous
devriez**, you should. **il aurait dû**, he
should have.

dévolu /devɔly/ *n.m.* **jeter son** ~ **sur**,
set one's heart on. ● *a.* ~ **à**, allotted
to.

dévorer /devɔre/ *v.t.* devour.

dévot, ~**e** /devo, -ɔt/ *a.* devout.

dévotion /devosjɔ̃/ *n.f.* (*relig.*) devotion.

dévouer (se) /(sə)devwe/ *v. pr.* devote o.s. (**à**, to); (*se sacrifier*) sacrifice o.s. ~**é** *a.* devoted. ~**ement** /-
vumɑ̃/ *n.m.* devotion.

dextérité /dɛksterite/ *n.f.* skill.

diabète /djabɛt/ *n.m.* diabetes.
~**étique** *a. & n.m./f.* diabetic.

diable /djɑbl/ *n.m.* devil. ~**olique** *a.*
diabolical.

diagnostic /djagnɔstik/ *n.m.* diagnosis. ~**quer** *v.t.* diagnose.

diagonal, ~**ale** (*m. pl.* ~**aux**) /dja-
gɔnal, -o/ *a. & n.f.* diagonal. **en** ~**ale**,
diagonally.

diagramme /djagram/ *n.m.* diagram;
(*graphique*) graph.

dialecte /djalɛkt/ *n.m.* dialect.

dialogue /djalɔg/ *n.m.* dialogue. ~**er**
v.i. (*pol.*) have a dialogue.

diamant /djamɑ̃/ *n.m.* diamond.

diamètre /djamɛtr/ *n.m.* diameter.

diapason /djapazɔ̃/ *n.m.* tuning-fork.

diaphragme /djafragm/ *n.m.* diaphragm.

diapo /djapo/ *n.f.* (colour) slide.

diapositive /djapozitiv/ *n.f.* (colour)
slide.

diarrhée /djare/ *n.f.* diarrhoea.

dictat|eur /diktatœr/ *n.m.* dictator.
~**ure** *n.f.* dictatorship.

dict|er /dikte/ *v.t.* dictate. ~**ée** *n.f.*
dictation.

diction /diksjɔ̃/ *n.f.* diction.

dictionnaire /diksjɔnɛr/ *n.m.* dictionary.

dicton /diktɔ̃/ *n.m.* saying.

dièse /djɛz/ *n.m.* (*mus.*) sharp.

diesel /djezɛl/ *n.m. & a. invar.* diesel.

diète /djɛt/ *n.f.* (*régime*) diet.

diététicien, ~**ne** /djetetisjɛ̃, -jɛn/
n.m., *f.* dietician.

diététique /djetetik/ *n.f.* dietetics.
● *a.* **produit** *ou* **aliment** ~, dietary
product.

dieu (*pl.* ~**x**) /djø/ *n.m.* god. **D**~,
God.

diffamatoire /difamatwar/ *a.* defa-
matory.

diffam|er /difame/ *v.t.* slander; (*par
écrit*) libel. ~**ation** *n.f.* slander;
libel.

différé (en) /(ɑ̃)difere/ *adv.* (*émission*) recorded.

différemment /diferamɑ̃/ *adv.* differently.

différence /diferɑ̃s/ *n.f.* difference. **à
la** ~ **de**, unlike.

différencier /diferɑ̃sje/ *v.t.* differentiate. **se** ~ **de**, (*différer de*)
differ from.

différend /diferɑ̃/ *n.m.* difference (of
opinion).

différent, ~**e** /diferɑ̃, -t/ *a.* different
(**de**, from).

différentiel, ~**le** /diferɑ̃sjɛl/ *a. &
n.m.* differential.

différer¹ /difere/ *v.t.* postpone.

différer² /difere/ *v.i.* differ (**de**,
from).

difficile /difisil/ *a.* difficult. ~**ment**
adv. with difficulty.

difficulté /difikylte/ *n.f.* difficulty.

difform|e /diform/ *a.* deformed. ~**ité**
n.f. deformity.

diffus, ~**e** /dify, -z/ *a.* diffuse.

diffus|er /difyze/ *v.t.* broadcast;
(*lumière, chaleur*) diffuse. ~**ion** *n.f.*
broadcasting; diffusion.

dig|érer /diʒere/ *v.t.* digest;
(*endurer: fam.*) stomach. ~**este,
~estible** *adjs.* digestible. ~**estion**
n.f. digestion.

digesti|f, ~**ve** /diʒɛstif, -v/ *a.*
digestive. ● *n.m.* after-dinner liqueur.

digit|al (*m. pl.* ~**aux**) /diʒital, -o/ *a.*
digital.

digne /diɲ/ *a.* (*noble*) dignified; (*honnête*) worthy. ~ **de**, worthy of. ~ **de
foi**, trustworthy.

dignité /diɲite/ *n.f.* dignity.

digression /digresjɔ̃/ *n.f.* digression.

digue /dig/ *n.f.* dike.

diktat /diktat/ *n.m.* diktat.

dilapider /dilapide/ *v.t.* squander.

dilat|er /dilate/ *v.t.*, **se** ~**er** *v. pr.*
dilate. ~**ation** /-asjɔ̃/ *n.f.* dilation.

dilemme /dilɛm/ *n.m.* dilemma.

dilettante /diletɑ̃t/ *n.m.*, *f.* amateur.

diluant /dilɥɑ̃/ *n.m.* thinner.

diluer /dilɥe/ *v.t.* dilute.

diluvien, ~**ne** /dilyvjɛ̃, -ɛn/ *a.*
(*pluie*) torrential.

dimanche /dimɑ̃ʃ/ *n.m.* Sunday.

dimension /dimɑ̃sjɔ̃/ n.f. (taille) size; (mesure) dimension.

dimin|uer /diminɥe/ v.t. reduce, decrease; (plaisir, courage, etc.) lessen; (dénigrer) lessen. ● v.i. decrease. ~ution n.f. decrease (de, in).

diminutif /diminytif/ n.m. diminutive; (surnom) pet name ou form.

dinde /dɛ̃d/ n.f. turkey.

dindon /dɛ̃dɔ̃/ n.m. turkey.

dîn|er /dine/ n.m. dinner. ● v.i. have dinner. ~eur, ~euse n.m., f. diner.

dingue /dɛ̃g/ a. (fam.) crazy.

dinosaure /dinozɔr/ n.m. dinosaur.

diocèse /djɔsɛz/ n.m. diocese.

diphtérie /difteri/ n.f. diphtheria.

diphtongue /diftɔ̃g/ n.f. diphthong.

diplomate /diplɔmat/ n.m. diplomat. ● a. diplomatic.

diplomat|ie /diplɔmasi/ n.f. diplomacy. ~ique /-atik/ a. diplomatic.

diplôm|e /diplom/ n.m. certificate, diploma; (univ.) degree. ~é a. qualified.

dire† /dir/ v.t. say; (secret, vérité, heure) tell; (penser) think. ~ que, say that. ~ à qn. que/de, tell s.o. that/to. se ~ v. pr. (mot) be said; (fatigué etc.) say that one is. **ça me/vous/etc. dit de faire**, I/you/etc. feel like doing. **on dirait que,** it would seem that, it seems that. **dis/dites donc!,** hey! ● n.m. **au ~ de, selon les ~s de,** according to.

direct /dirɛkt/ a. direct. **en ~,** (émission) live. ~ement adv. directly.

direc|teur, ~trice /dirɛktœr, -tris/ n.m., f. director; (chef de service) manager, manageress; (d'école) headmaster, headmistress.

direction /dirɛksjɔ̃/ n.f. (sens) direction; (de société etc.) management; (auto.) steering. **en ~ de,** (going) to.

directive /dirɛktiv/ n.f. instruction.

dirigeant, ~e /diriʒɑ̃, -t/ n.m., f. (pol.) leader; (comm.) manager. ● a. (classe) ruling.

diriger /diriʒe/ v.t. run, manage, direct; (véhicule) steer; (orchestre) conduct; (braquer) aim; (tourner) turn. se ~ v. pr. guide o.s. **se ~ vers,** make one's way to.

dirigis|me /diriʒism/ n.m. interventionism. ~te /-ist/ a. & n.m./f. interventionist.

dis /di/ voir **dire**.

discern|er /disɛrne/ v.t. discern. ~ement n.m. discernment.

disciple /disipl/ n.m. disciple.

disciplin|e /disiplin/ n.f. discipline. ~aire a. disciplinary. ~er v.t. discipline.

discontinu /diskɔ̃tiny/ a. intermittent.

discontinuer /diskɔ̃tinɥe/ v.i. **sans ~,** without stopping.

discordant, ~e /diskɔrdɑ̃, -t/ a. discordant.

discorde /diskɔrd/ n.f. discord.

discothèque /diskɔtɛk/ n.f. record library; (club) disco(thèque).

discount /diskunt/ n.m. discount.

discourir /diskurir/ v.i. (péj.) hold forth, ramble on.

discours /diskur/ n.m. speech.

discréditer /diskredite/ v.t. discredit.

discr|et, ~ète /diskrɛ, -t/ a. discreet. ~ètement adv. discreetly.

discrétion /diskresjɔ̃/ n.f. discretion. **à ~,** as much as one desires.

discrimination /diskriminɑsjɔ̃/ n.f. discrimination.

discriminatoire /diskriminatwar/ a. discriminatory.

disculper /diskylpe/ v.t. exonerate. **se ~** v. pr. prove o.s. innocent.

discussion /diskysjɔ̃/ n.f. discussion; (querelle) argument.

discuté /diskyte/ a. controversial.

discut|er /diskyte/ v.t. discuss; (contester) question. ● v.i. (parler) talk; (répliquer) argue. ~er de, discuss. ~able a. debatable.

disette /dizɛt/ n.f. (food) shortage.

diseuse /dizøz/ n.f. **~ de bonne aventure,** fortune-teller.

disgrâce /disgrɑs/ n.f. disgrace.

disgracieu|x, ~se /disgrasjø, -z/ a. ungainly.

disjoindre /disʒwɛdr/ v.t. take apart. **se ~** v. pr. come apart.

dislo|quer /disloke/ v.t. (membre) dislocate; (machine etc.) break (apart). **se ~quer** v. pr. (parti, cortège) break up; (meuble) come apart. ~cation n.f. (anat.) dislocation.

dispar|aître† /disparɛtr/ v.i. disappear; (mourir) die. **faire ~aître,** get rid of. ~ition n.f. disappearance; (mort) death. ~u, ~ue a. (soldat etc.) missing; n.m., f. missing person; (mort) dead person.

disparate /disparat/ a. ill-assorted.

disparité /disparite/ n.f. disparity.

dispensaire /dispɑ̃sɛr/ n.m. clinic.

dispense /dispɑ̃s/ n.f. exemption.

dispenser /dispãse/ v.t. exempt (**de**, from). **se ~ de (faire)**, avoid (doing).

disperser /dispɛrse/ v.t. (éparpiller) scatter; (répartir) disperse. **se ~** v. pr. disperse.

disponib|le /dispɔnibl/ a. available. **~ilité** n.f. availability.

dispos, ~e /dispo, -z/ a. frais et ~, fresh and alert.

disposé /dispoze/ a. **bien/mal ~**, in a good/bad mood. **~ à**, prepared to. **~ envers**, disposed towards.

disposer /dispoze/ v.t. arrange. **~ à**, (engager à) incline to. ● v.i. **~ de**, have at one's disposal. **se ~ à**, prepare to.

dispositif /dispozitif/ n.m. device; (plan) plan of action. **~ anti-parasite**, suppressor.

disposition /dispozisjɔ̃/ n.f. arrangement; (humeur) mood; (tendance) tendency. **~s**, (préparatifs) arrangements; (aptitude) aptitude. **à la ~ de**, at the disposal of.

disproportionné /dispropɔrsjɔne/ a. disproportionate.

dispute /dispyt/ n.f. quarrel.

disputer /dispyte/ v.t. (match) play; (course) run in; (prix) fight for; (gronder: fam.) tell off. **se ~** v. pr. quarrel; (se battre pour) fight over; (match) be played.

disquaire /diskɛr/ n.m./f. record dealer.

disqualif|ier /diskalifje/ v.t. disqualify. **~ication** n.f. disqualification.

disque /disk/ n.m. (mus.) record; (sport) discus; (cercle) disc, disk. **~ dur**, hard disk.

disquette /diskɛt/ n.f. (floppy) disk.

dissection /disɛksjɔ̃/ n.f. dissection.

dissemblable /disãblabl/ a. dissimilar.

disséminer /disemine/ v.t. scatter.

disséquer /diseke/ v.t. dissect.

dissertation /disɛrtasjɔ̃/ n.f. (scol.) essay.

disserter /disɛrte/ v.i. **~ sur**, comment upon.

dissiden|t, ~te /disidã, -t/ a. & n.m., f. dissident. **~ce** n.f. dissidence.

dissimul|er /disimyle/ v.t. conceal (**à**, from). **se ~er** v. pr. conceal o.s. **~ation** n.f. concealment; (fig.) deceit.

dissipé /disipe/ a. (élève) unruly.

dissip|er /disipe/ v.t. (fumée, crainte) dispel; (fortune) squander; (personne) lead into bad ways. **se ~er** v. pr. disappear. **~ation** n.f. squandering; (indiscipline) misbehaviour.

dissolution /disɔlysjɔ̃/ n.f. dissolution.

dissolvant /disɔlvã/ n.m. solvent; (pour ongles) nail polish remover.

dissonant, ~e /disɔnã, -t/ a. discordant.

dissoudre† /disudr/ v.t., **se ~** v. pr. dissolve.

dissua|der /disɥade/ v.t. dissuade (**de**, from). **~sion** /-ɥazjɔ̃/ n.f. dissuasion. **force de ~sion**, deterrent force.

dissuasi|f, ~ve /disɥazif, -v/ a. dissuasive.

distance /distãs/ n.f. distance; (écart) gap. **à ~**, at ou from a distance.

distancer /distãse/ v.t. leave behind.

distant, ~e /distã, -t/ a. distant.

distendre /distãdr/ v.t., **se ~** v. pr. distend.

distill|er /distile/ v.t. distil. **~ation** n.f. distillation.

distillerie /distilri/ n.f. distillery.

distinct, ~e /distɛ̃(kt), -ɛ̃kt/ a. distinct. **~ement** /-ɛ̃ktəmã/ adv. distinctly.

distinctif, ~ve /distɛ̃ktif, -v/ a. distinctive.

distinction /distɛ̃ksjɔ̃/ n.f. distinction.

distingué /distɛ̃ge/ a. distinguished.

distinguer /distɛ̃ge/ v.t. distinguish.

distraction /distraksjɔ̃/ n.f. absent-mindedness; (oubli) lapse; (passe-temps) distraction.

distraire† /distrɛr/ v.t. amuse; (rendre inattentif) distract. **se ~** v. pr. amuse o.s.

distrait, ~e /distrɛ, -t/ a. absent-minded. **~ement** a. absent-mindedly.

distrayant, ~e /distrɛjã, -t/ a. entertaining.

distrib|uer /distribɥe/ v.t. hand out, distribute; (répartir, amener) distribute; (courrier) deliver. **~uteur** n.m. (auto., comm.) distributor. **~uteur (automatique)**, vending-machine; (de billets) (cash) dispenser. **~ution** n.f. distribution; (du courrier) delivery; (acteurs) cast.

district /distrikt/ n.m. district.

dit[1], **dites** /di, dit/ *voir* dire.

dit[2], **~e** /di, dit/ *a.* (*décidé*) agreed; (*surnommé*) called.

diurétique /djyretik/ *a. & n.m.* diurétic.

diurne /djyrn/ *a.* diurnal.

divaguer /divage/ *v.i.* rave. **~ations** *n.f. pl.* ravings.

divan /divã/ *n.m.* divan.

divergen|t, ~te /divɛrʒã, -t/ *a.* divergent. **~ce** *n.f.* divergence.

diverger /divɛrʒe/ *v.i.* diverge.

divers, ~e /divɛr, -s/ *a.* (*varié*) diverse; (*différent*) various. **~e- ment** /-səmã/ *adv.* variously.

diversifier /divɛrsifje/ *v.t.* diversify.

diversion /divɛrsjɔ̃/ *n.f.* diversion.

diversité /divɛrsite/ *n.f.* diversity.

divis|er /divize/ *v.t.*, **se ~er** *v. pr.* divide. **~ion** *n.f.* division.

divertir /divɛrtir/ *v.t.* amuse. **se ~ir** *v. pr.* amuse o.s. **~issement** *n.m.* amusement.

dividende /dividãd/ *n.m.* dividend.

divin, ~e /divɛ̃, -in/ *a.* divine.

divinité /divinite/ *n.f.* divinity.

divorc|e /divɔrs/ *n.m.* divorce. **~ée** *a.* divorced; *n.m., f.* divorcee. **~er** *v.i.* **~er (d'avec)**, divorce.

divulguer /divylge/ *v.t.* divulge.

dix /dis/ (/di/ *before consonant*, /diz/ *before vowel*) *a. & n.m.* ten. **~ième** /dizjɛm/ *a. & n.m./f.* tenth.

dix-huit /dizɥit/ *a. & n.m.* eighteen. **~ième** *a. & n.m./f.* eighteenth.

dix-neuf /diznœf/ *a. & n.m.* nineteen. **~vième** *a. & n.m./f.* nine-teenth.

dix-sept /disɛt/ *a. & n.m.* seventeen. **~ième** *a. & n.m./f.* seventeenth.

dizaine /dizɛn/ *n.f.* (about) ten.

docile /dɔsil/ *a.* docile.

docilité /dɔsilite/ *n.f.* docility.

dock /dɔk/ *n.m.* dock.

docker /dɔkɛr/ *n.m.* docker.

doct|eur /dɔktœr/ *n.m.* doctor. **~oresse** *n.f.* (*fam.*) lady doctor.

doctorat /dɔktɔra/ *n.m.* doctorate.

doctrin|e /dɔktrin/ *n.f.* doctrine. **~aire** *a.* doctrinaire.

document /dɔkymã/ *n.m.* document. **~aire** /-tɛr/ *a. & n.m.* documentary.

documentaliste /dɔkymãtalist/ *n.m./f.* information officer.

document|er /dɔkymãte/ *v.t.* document. **se ~er** *v. pr.* collect information. **~ation** *n.f.* information, literature. **~é** *a.* well-documented.

dodo /dodo/ *n.m.* **faire ~**, (*langage enfantin*) go to byebyes.

dodu /dody/ *a.* plump.

dogm|e /dɔgm/ *n.m.* dogma. **~atique** *a.* dogmatic.

doigt /dwa/ *n.m.* finger. **un ~ de**, a drop of. **à deux ~s de**, a hair's breadth away from. **~ de pied**, toe.

doigté /dwate/ *n.m.* (*mus.*) fingering, touch; (*adresse*) tact.

dois, doit /dwa/ *voir* devoir[2].

Dolby /dɔlbi/ *n.m. & a.* (P.) Dolby (P.).

doléances /dɔleãs/ *n.f. pl.* grie-vances.

dollar /dɔlar/ *n.m.* dollar.

domaine /dɔmɛn/ *n.m.* estate, do-main; (*fig.*) domain.

dôme /dom/ *n.m.* dome.

domestique /dɔmɛstik/ *a.* domestic. ● *n.m./f.* servant.

domestiquer /dɔmɛstike/ *v.t.* domes-ticate.

domicile /dɔmisil/ *n.m.* home. **à ~**, at home; (*livrer*) to the home.

domicilié /dɔmisilje/ *a.* resident.

domin|er /dɔmine/ *v.t./i.* dominate; (*surplomber*) tower over, dominate; (*équipe*) dictate the game (to). **~ant, ~ante** *a.* dominant; *n.f.* dominant feature. **~ation** *n.f.* domination.

domino /dɔmino/ *n.m.* domino.

dommage /dɔmaʒ/ *n.m.* (*tort*) harm. **~(s)**, (*dégâts*) damage. **c'est ~**, it's a pity. **quel ~**, what a shame. **~s-intérêts** *n.m. pl.* (*jurid.*) damages.

dompt|er /dɔ̃te/ *v.t.* tame. **~eur, ~euse** *n.m., f.* tamer.

don /dɔ̃/ *n.m.* (*cadeau, aptitude*) gift.

dona|teur, ~trice /dɔnatœr, -tris/ *n.m., f.* donor.

donation /dɔnasjɔ̃/ *n.f.* donation.

donc /dɔ̃k/ *conj.* so, then; (*par con-séquent*) so, therefore.

donjon /dɔ̃ʒɔ̃/ *n.m.* (*tour*) keep.

donné /dɔne/ *a.* (*fixé*) given; (*pas cher*: *fam.*) dirt cheap. **étant ~ que**, given that.

données /dɔne/ *n.f. pl.* (*de science*) data; (*de problème*) facts.

donner /dɔne/ *v.t.* give; (*vieilles af-faires*) give away; (*distribuer*) give out; (*récolte etc.*) produce; (*film*) show; (*pièce*) put on. ● *v.i.* **~ sur**, look out on to. **~ dans**, (*piège*) fall into. **ça donne soif/faim**, it makes one thirsty/ hungry. **~ à réparer/ etc.**, take to be repaired/*etc.* **~ lieu à**, give rise to. **se ~ à**, devote o.s. to. **se**

~ **du mal**, go to a lot of trouble (**pour faire**, to do).

donneu|r, **~se** /dɔnœr, -øz/ *n.m.*, *f.* (*de sang*) donor.

dont /dõ/ *pron. rel.* (*chose*) whose, of which; (*personne*) whose; (*partie d'un tout*) of whom; (*chose*) of which; (*provenance*) from which; (*manière*) in which. **le père ~ la fille**, the father whose daughter. **ce ~**, what. **~ il a besoin**, which he needs. **l'enfant ~ il est fier**, the child is proud of. **trois enfants ~ deux sont jumeaux**, three children, two of whom are twins.

dopage /dɔpaʒ/ *n.m.* doping.

doper /dɔpe/ *v.t.* dope. **se ~** *v. pr.* take dope.

doré /dɔre/ *a.* (*couleur d'or*) golden; (*avec dorure*) gold. **la bourgeoisie ~e** the affluent middle class.

dorénavant /dɔrenavã/ *adv.* henceforth.

dorer /dɔre/ *v.t.* gild; (*culin.*) brown.

dorloter /dɔrlɔte/ *v.t.* pamper.

dorm|ir† /dɔrmir/ *v.i.* sleep; (*être endormi*) be asleep. **~eur**, **~euse** *n.m.*, *f.* sleeper. **il dort debout**, he can't keep awake. **une histoire à ~ir debout**, a cock-and-bull story.

dortoir /dɔrtwar/ *n.m.* dormitory.

dorure /dɔryr/ *n.f.* gilding.

dos /do/ *n.m.* back; (*de livre*) spine. **à ~ de**, riding on. **de ~**, from behind. **~ crawlé**, backstroke.

dos|e /doz/ *n.f.* dose. **~age** *n.m.* (*mélange*) mixture. **faire le ~age de**, measure out; balance. **~er** *v.t.* measure out; (*équilibrer*) balance.

dossard /dɔsar/ *n.m.* (*sport*) number.

dossier /dɔsje/ *n.m.* (*documents*) file; (*de chaise*) back.

dot /dɔt/ *n.f.* dowry.

doter /dɔte/ *v.t.* ~ **de**, equip with.

douan|e /dwan/ *n.f.* customs. **~ier**, **~ière** *a.* customs; *n.m.*, *f.* customs officer.

doubl|e /dubl/ *a. & adv.* double. ● *n.m.* (*copie*) duplicate; (*sosie*) double. **le ~e (de)**, twice as much *ou* as many (as). **le ~e messieurs**, the men's doubles. **~e décimètre**, ruler. **~ement¹** *adv.* doubly.

doubl|er /duble/ *v.t./i.* (*dépasser*) overtake; (*vêtement*) line; (*film*) dub; (*classe*) repeat; (*cap*) round. **~ement²** *n.m.* doubling. **~ure** *n.f.* (*étoffe*) lining; (*acteur*) understudy.

douce /dus/ *voir* doux.

douceâtre /dusɑtr/ *a.* sickly sweet.

doucement /dusmã/ *adv.* gently.

douceur /dusœr/ *n.f.* (*mollesse*) softness; (*de climat*) mildness; (*de personne*) gentleness; (*joie, plaisir*) sweetness. **~s**, (*friandises*) sweet things. **en ~**, smoothly.

douch|e /duʃ/ *n.f.* shower. **~er** *v.t.* give a shower to. **se ~er** *v. pr.* have *ou* take a shower.

doudoune /dudun/ *n.f.* (*fam.*) anorak.

doué /dwe/ *a.* gifted. **~ de**, endowed with.

douille /duj/ *n.f.* (*électr.*) socket.

douillet, **~te** /dujɛ, -t/ *a.* cosy, comfortable; (*personne: péj.*) soft.

doul|eur /dulœr/ *n.f.* pain; (*chagrin*) grief. **~oureux**, **~oureuse** *a.* painful. **la ~oureuse** *n.f.* the bill.

doute /dut/ *n.m.* doubt. **sans ~**, no doubt. **sans aucun ~**, without doubt.

douter /dute/ *v.i.* ~ **de**, doubt. **se ~ de**, suspect.

douteu|x, **~se** /dutø, -z/ *a.* doubtful.

Douvres /duvr/ *n.m./f.* Dover.

doux, **douce** /du, dus/ *a.* (*moelleux*) soft; (*sucré*) sweet; (*clément, pas fort*) mild; (*pas brusque, bienveillant*) gentle.

douzaine /duzɛn/ *n.f.* about twelve; (*douze*) dozen. **une ~ d'œufs/etc.**, a dozen eggs/etc.

douz|e /duz/ *a. & n.m.* twelve. **~ième** *a. & n.m./f.* twelfth.

doyen, **~ne** /dwajẽ, -jɛn/ *n.m.*, *f.* dean; (*en âge*) most senior person.

dragée /draʒe/ *n.f.* sugared almond.

dragon /dragõ/ *n.m.* dragon.

dragu|e /drag/ *n.f.* (*bateau*) dredger. **~er** *v.t.* (*rivière*) dredge; (*filles: fam.*) chat up, try to pick up.

drain /drẽ/ *n.m.* drain.

drainer /drene/ *v.t.* drain.

dramatique /dramatik/ *a.* dramatic; (*tragique*) tragic. ● *n.f.* (television) drama.

dramatiser /dramatize/ *v.t.* dramatize.

dramaturge /dramatyrʒ/ *n.m./f.* dramatist.

drame /dram/ *n.m.* drama.

drap /dra/ *n.m.* sheet; (*tissu*) (woollen) cloth. **~-housse** /draus/ *n.m.* fitted sheet.

drapeau (*pl.* **~x**) /drapo/ *n.m.* flag.

draper /drape/ *v.t.* drape.

dress|er /drese/ v.t. put up, erect; (*tête*) raise; (*animal*) train; (*liste etc.*) draw up. **se ~er** v. pr. (*bâtiment etc.*) stand; (*personne*) draw o.s. up. **~er l'oreille**, prick up one's ears. **~age** /dresaʒ/ n.m. training. **~eur, ~euse** /dresœr, -øz/ n.m., f. trainer.

dribbler /drible/ v.t./i. (*sport*) dribble.

drille /drij/ n.m. **un joyeux ~**, a cheery character.

drive /drajv/ n.m. (*comput.*) drive.

drogue /drɔg/ n.f. drug. **la ~**, drugs.

drogu|er /drɔge/ v.t. (*malade*) drug heavily, dose up; (*victime*) drug. **se ~er** v. pr. take drugs. **~é, ~ée** n.m., f. drug addict.

drogu|erie /drɔgri/ n.f. hardware and chemist's shop; (*Amer.*) drugstore. **~iste** n.m./f. owner of a *droguerie*.

droit [1] **, ~e** /drwa, -t/ a. (*non courbe*) straight; (*loyal*) upright; (*angle*) right. ● adv. straight. ● n.f. straight line.

droit [2] **~e** /drwa, -t/ a. (*contraire de gauche*) right. **à ~e**, on the right; (*direction*) (to the) right. **la ~e**, the right (side); (*pol.*) the right (wing). **~ier, ~ière** /-tje, -tjɛr/ a. & n.m., f. right-handed (person).

droit [3] /drwa/ n.m. right. **~(s)**, (*taxe*) duty; (*d'inscription*) fee(s). **le ~**, (*jurid.*) law. **avoir ~ à**, be entitled to. **avoir le ~ de**, be allowed to. **être dans son ~**, be in the right. **~ d'auteur**, copyright. **~s d'auteur**, royalties.

drôle /drol/ a. funny. **~ d'air**, funny look. **~ment** adv. funnily; (*extrêmement*: fam.) dreadfully.

dromadaire /drɔmadɛr/ n.m. dromedary.

dru /dry/ a. thick. **tomber ~**, fall thick and fast.

drugstore /drœgstɔr/ n.m. drugstore.

du /dy/ voir **de**.

dû, due /dy/ voir **devoir** [2]. ● a. due. ● n.m. due; (*argent*) dues. **~ à**, due to.

duc, duchesse /dyk, dyʃɛs/ n.m., f. duke, duchess.

duel /dɥɛl/ n.m. duel.

dune /dyn/ n.f. dune.

duo /dɥo/ n.m. (*mus.*) duet; (*fig.*) duo.

dup|e /dyp/ n.f. dupe. **~er** v.t. dupe.

duplex /dyplɛks/ n.m. split-level apartment; (*Amer.*) duplex; (*émission*) link-up.

duplicata /dyplikata/ n.m. invar. duplicate.

duplicité /dyplisite/ n.f. duplicity.

duquel /dykɛl/ voir **lequel**.

dur /dyr/ a. hard; (*sévère*) harsh, hard; (*viande*) tough, hard; (*col, brosse*) stiff. ● adv. hard. ● n.m. tough guy. **~ d'oreille**, hard of hearing.

durable /dyrabl/ a. lasting.

durant /dyrɑ̃/ prép. during; (*mesure de temps*) for.

durc|ir /dyrsir/ v.t./i., **se ~ir** v. pr. harden. **~issement** n.m. hardening.

dure /dyr/ n.f. **à la ~**, the hard way.

durée /dyre/ n.f. length; (*période*) duration.

durement /dyrmɑ̃/ adv. harshly.

durer /dyre/ v.i. last.

dureté /dyrte/ n.f. hardness; (*sévérité*) harshness.

duvet /dyvɛ/ n.m. down; (*sac*) (down-filled) sleeping-bag.

dynami|que /dinamik/ a. dynamic. **~sme** n.m. dynamism.

dynamit|e /dinamit/ n.f. dynamite. **~er** v.t. dynamite.

dynamo /dinamo/ n.f. dynamo.

dynastie /dinasti/ n.f. dynasty.

dysenterie /disɑ̃tri/ n.f. dysentery.

E

eau (pl. **~x**) /o/ n.f. water. **~ courante/dormante**, running/still water. **~ de Cologne**, eau-de-Cologne. **~ dentifrice**, mouthwash. **~ de toilette**, eau de toilette. **~-de-vie** (pl. **~x-de-vie**) n.f. brandy. **~ douce/salée**, fresh/salt water. **~-forte** (pl. **~x-fortes**) n.f. etching. **~ potable**, drinking water. **~ de Javel**, bleach. **~ minérale**, mineral water. **~ gazeuse**, fizzy water. **~ plate**, still water. **~x usées**, dirty water. **tomber à l'~** (*fig.*) fall through. **prendre l'~**, take in water.

ébahi /ebai/ a. dumbfounded.

ébattre (s') /(s)ebatr/ v. pr. frolic.

ébauch|e /eboʃ/ n.f. outline. **~er** v.t. outline. **s'~er** v. pr. form.

ébène /ebɛn/ n.f. ebony.

ébéniste /ebenist/ n.m. cabinet-maker.

éberlué /ebɛrlɥe/ a. flabbergasted.

éblou|ir /ebluir/ *v.t.* dazzle. **~is- sement** *n.m.* dazzle, dazzling; (*ma- laise*) dizzy turn.

éboueur /ebwœr/ *n.m.* dustman; (*Amer.*) garbage collector.

ébouillanter /ebujɑ̃te/ *v.t.* scald.

éboul|er (s') /(s)ebule/ *v. pr.* crum- ble, collapse. **~ement** *n.m.* land- slide. **~is** *n.m. pl.* fallen rocks and earth.

ébouriffé /eburife/ *a.* dishevelled.

ébranler /ebrɑ̃le/ *v.t.* shake. **s'~** *v. pr.* move off.

ébrécher /ebreʃe/ *v.t.* chip.

ébriété /ebrijete/ *n.f.* intoxication.

ébrouer (s') /(s)ebrue/ *v. pr.* shake o.s.

ébruiter /ebrɥite/ *v.t.* spread about.

ébullition /ebylisjɔ̃/ *n.f.* boiling. en **~,** boiling.

écaille /ekaj/ *n.f.* (*de poisson*) scale; (*de peinture, roc*) flake; (*matière*) tortoiseshell.

écailler /ekaje/ *v.t.* (*poisson*) scale. **s'~** *v. pr.* flake (off).

écarlate /ekarlat/ *a. & n.f.* scarlet.

écarquiller /ekarkije/ *v.t.* **~ les yeux,** open one's eyes wide.

écart /ekar/ *n.m.* gap; (*de prix etc.*) difference; (*embardée*) swerve; (*de conduite*) lapse (**de,** in). **à l'~,** out of the way. **tenir à l'~,** (*participant*) keep out of things. **à l'~ de,** away from.

écarté /ekarte/ *a.* (*lieu*) remote. **les jambes ~es,** (with) legs apart. **les bras ~s,** with one's arms out.

écartement /ekartəmɑ̃/ *n.m.* gap.

écarter /ekarte/ *v.t.* (*objets*) move apart; (*ouvrir*) open; (*éliminer*) dismiss. **~ qch. de,** move sth. away from. **~ qn. de,** keep s.o. away from. **s'~** *v. pr.* (*s'éloigner*) move away; (*quitter son chemin*) move aside. **s'~ de,** stray from.

ecchymose /ekimoz/ *n.f.* bruise.

ecclésiastique /eklezjastik/ *a.* ec- clesiastical. ● *n.m.* clergyman.

écervelé, ~e /esɛrvəle/ *a.* scatter- brained. ● *n.m., f.* scatter-brain.

échafaud|age /eʃafodaʒ/ *n.m.* scaf- folding; (*amas*) heap. **~er** *v.t.* (*pro- jets*) construct.

échalote /eʃalɔt/ *n.f.* shallot.

échang|e /eʃɑ̃ʒ/ *n.m.* exchange. **en ~e (de),** in exchange (for). **~er** *v.t.* exchange (**contre,** for).

échangeur /eʃɑ̃ʒœr/ *n.m.* (*auto.*) interchange.

échantillon /eʃɑ̃tijɔ̃/ *n.m.* sample. **~nage** /-jɔnaʒ/ *n.m.* range of sam- ples.

échappatoire /eʃapatwar/ *n.f.* (cle- ver) way out.

échappée /eʃape/ *n.f.* (*sport*) break- away.

échappement /eʃapmɑ̃/ *n.m.* ex- haust.

échapper /eʃape/ *v.i.* **~ à,** escape; (*en fuyant*) escape (from). **s'~** *v. pr.* escape. **~ des mains de** *ou* **à,** slip out of the hands of. **l'~ belle,** have a narrow *ou* lucky escape.

écharde /eʃard/ *n.f.* splinter.

écharpe /eʃarp/ *n.f.* scarf; (*de maire*) sash. **en ~,** (*bras*) in a sling.

échasse /eʃas/ *n.f.* stilt.

échassier /eʃasje/ *n.m.* wader.

échaud|er /eʃode/ *v.t.* **se faire ~er, être ~é,** get one's fingers burnt.

échauffer /eʃofe/ *v.t.* heat; (*fig.*) excite. **s'~** *v. pr.* warm up.

échauffourée /eʃofure/ *n.f.* (*mil.*) skirmish; (*bagarre*) scuffle.

échéance /eʃeɑ̃s/ *n.f.* due date (for payment); (*délai*) deadline; (*obliga- tion*) (financial) commitment.

échéant (le cas) /(lakaz)eʃeɑ̃/ *adv.* if the occasion arises, possibly.

échec /eʃɛk/ *n.m.* failure. **~s,** (*jeu*) chess. **~ et mat,** checkmate. **en ~,** in check.

échelle /eʃɛl/ *n.f.* ladder; (*dimension*) scale.

échelon /eʃlɔ̃/ *n.m.* rung; (*de fonc- tionnaire*) grade; (*niveau*) level.

échelonner /eʃlone/ *v.t.* spread out, space out.

échevelé /eʃəvle/ *a.* dishevelled.

échine /eʃin/ *n.f.* backbone.

échiquier /eʃikje/ *n.m.* chessboard.

écho /eko/ *n.m.* echo. **~s,** (*dans la presse*) gossip.

échographie /ekɔɡrafi/ *n.f.* ultra- sound (scan).

échoir /eʃwar/ *v.i.* (*dette*) fall due; (*délai*) expire.

échoppe /eʃɔp/ *n.f.* stall.

échouer[1] /eʃwe/ *v.i.* fail.

échouer[2] /eʃwe/ *v.t.* (*bateau*) ground. ● *v.i.*, **s'~** *v. pr.* run aground.

éclabouss|er /eklabuse/ *v.t.* splash. **~ure** *n.f.* splash.

éclair /eklɛr/ *n.m.* (flash of) lightning; (*fig.*) flash; (*gâteau*) éclair. ● *a. invar.* lightning.

éclairage /eklɛraʒ/ n.m. lighting; (*point de vue*) light. ~**iste** /-aʒist/ n.m. lighting technician.

éclaircie /eklɛrsi/ n.f. sunny interval.

éclaircir /eklɛrsir/ v.t. make lighter; (*mystère*) clear up. s'~**ir** v. pr. (*ciel*) clear; (*mystère*) become clearer. ~**issement** n.m. clarification.

éclairer /eklere/ v.t. light (up); (*personne*) give some light to; (*fig.*) enlighten; (*situation*) throw light on. ● v.i. give light. s'~ v. pr. become clearer. s'~ **à la bougie**, use candle-light.

éclaireur, ~se /eklɛrœr, -øz/ n.m., f. (boy) scout, (girl) guide. ● n.m. (*mil.*) scout.

éclat /ekla/ n.m. fragment; (*de lumière*) brightness; (*de rire*) (out-)burst; (*splendeur*) brilliance.

éclatant, ~e /eklatɑ̃, -t/ a. brilliant.

éclater /eklate/ v.i. burst; (*exploser*) go off; (*verre*) shatter; (*guerre*) break out; (*groupe*) split up. ~ **de rire**, burst out laughing. ~**ement** n.m. bursting; (*de bombe*) explosion; (*scission*) split.

éclipse /eklips/ n.f. eclipse.

éclipser /eklipse/ v.t. eclipse. s'~ v. pr. slip away.

éclore /eklɔr/ v.i. (*œuf*) hatch; (*fleur*) open. ~**osion** n.f. hatching; opening.

écluse /eklyz/ n.f. (*de canal*) lock.

écœurant, ~e /ekœrɑ̃, -t/ a. (*gâteau*) sickly; (*fig.*) disgusting.

écœurer /ekœre/ v.t. sicken.

école /ekɔl/ n.f. school. ~ **maternelle/primaire/secondaire**, nursery/primary/secondary school. ~ **normale**, teachers' training college.

écolier, ~ière /ekɔlje, -jɛr/ n.m., f. schoolboy, schoolgirl.

écolo /ekɔlo/ a. & n.m./f. (*fam.*) green.

écologie /ekɔlɔʒi/ n.f. ecology. ~**ique** a. ecological, green.

écologiste /ekɔlɔʒist/ n.m./f. ecologist.

éconduire /ekɔ̃dɥir/ v.t. dismiss.

économat /ekɔnɔma/ n.m. bursary.

économe /ekɔnɔm/ a. thrifty. ● n.m./f. bursar.

économie /ekɔnɔmi/ n.f. economy. ~**ies**, (*argent*) savings. **une ~ie de**, (*gain*) a saving of. ~**ie politique**, economics. ~**ique** a. (*pol.*) economic; (*bon marché*) economical.

~iser v.t./i. save. ~**iste** n.m./f. economist.

écoper /ekɔpe/ v.t. bail out. ~ **(de)**, (*fam.*) get.

écorce /ekɔrs/ n.f. bark; (*de fruit*) peel.

écorcher /ekɔrʃe/ v.t. graze; (*animal*) skin. s'~**er** v. pr. graze o.s. ~**ure** n.f. graze.

écossais, ~e /ekɔsɛ, -z/ a. Scottish. ● n.m., f. Scot.

Écosse /ekɔs/ n.f. Scotland.

écosser /ekɔse/ v.t. shell.

écosystème /ekɔsistɛm/ n.m. ecosystem.

écouler [1] /ekule/ v.t. dispose of, sell.

écouler [2] **(s')** /(s)ekule/ v. pr. flow (out), run (off); (*temps*) pass. ~**ement** n.m. flow.

écourter /ekurte/ v.t. shorten.

écoute /ekut/ n.f. listening. **à l'~ (de)**, listening in (to). **aux ~s**, attentive. **heures de grande ~**, peak time. ~**s téléphoniques**, phone tapping.

écouter /ekute/ v.t. listen to; (*radio*) listen (in) to. ● v.i. listen. ~**eur** n.m. earphones; (*de téléphone*) receiver.

écran /ekrɑ̃/ n.m. screen. ~ **total**, sun-block.

écrasant, ~e /ekrazɑ̃, -t/ a. overwhelming.

écraser /ekraze/ v.t. crush; (*piéton*) run over. s'~ v. pr. crash (**contre**, into).

écrémé /ekreme/ a. **lait ~**, skimmed milk. **lait demi-~**, semi-skimmed milk.

écrevisse /ekrəvis/ n.f. crayfish.

écrier (s') /(s)ekrije/ v. pr. exclaim.

écrin /ekrɛ̃/ n.m. case.

écrire† /ekrir/ v.t./i. write; (*orthographier*) spell. s'~ v. pr. (*mot*) be spelt.

écrit /ekri/ n.m. document; (*examen*) written paper. **par ~**, in writing.

écriteau (*pl.* ~**x**) /ekrito/ n.m. notice.

écriture /ekrityr/ n.f. writing. ~**s**, (*comm.*) accounts. **l'É~ (sainte)**, the Scriptures.

écrivain /ekrivɛ̃/ n.m. writer.

écrou /ekru/ n.m. nut.

écrouer /ekrue/ v.t. imprison.

écrouler (s') /(s)ekrule/ v. pr. collapse.

écru /ekry/ a. (*couleur*) natural; (*tissu*) raw.

Écu /eky/ n.m. *invar.* ecu.

écueil /ekœj/ *n.m.* reef; (*fig.*) danger.

éculé /ekyle/ *a.* (*soulier*) worn at the heel; (*fig.*) well-worn.

écume /ekym/ *n.f.* foam; (*culin.*) scum.

écum|er /ekyme/ *v.t.* skim; (*piller*) plunder. ● *v.i.* foam. **~oire** *n.f.* skimmer.

écureuil /ekyrœj/ *n.m.* squirrel.

écurie /ekyri/ *n.f.* stable.

écuy|er, ~ère /ekɥije, -jɛr/ *n.m., f.* (horse) rider.

eczéma /ɛgzema/ *n.m.* eczema.

édenté /edɑ̃te/ *a.* toothless.

édifice /edifis/ *n.m.* building.

édif|ier /edifje/ *v.t.* construct; (*porter à la vertu, éclairer*) edify. **~ication** *n.f.* construction; edification.

édit /edi/ *n.m.* edict.

édi|ter /edite/ *v.t.* publish; (*annoter*) edit. **~teur, ~trice** *n.m., f.* publisher; editor.

édition /edisjɔ̃/ *n.f.* edition; (*industrie*) publishing.

édifor|ial (*pl.* **~iaux**) /editɔrjal, -jo/ *n.m.* editorial.

édredon /edrədɔ̃/ *n.m.* eiderdown.

éducateur, ~trice /edykatœr, -tris/ *n.m., f.* teacher.

éducati|f, ~ve /edykatif, -v/ *a.* educational.

éducation /edykɑsjɔ̃/ *n.f.* education; (*dans la famille*) upbringing; (*manières*) manners. **~ physique**, physical education.

édulcorant /edylkɔrɑ̃/ *n.m. & a.* (**produit**) **~**, sweetener.

éduquer /edyke/ *v.t.* educate; (*à la maison*) bring up.

effacé /efase/ *a.* (*modeste*) unassuming. **~ement** *n.m.* unassuming manner; (*suppression*) erasure.

effacer /efase/ *v.t.* (*gommer*) rub out; (*par lavage*) wash out; (*souvenir etc.*) erase. **s'~** *v. pr.* fade; (*s'écarter*) step aside.

effar|er /efare/ *v.t.* alarm. **~ement** *n.m.* alarm.

effaroucher /efaruʃe/ *v.t.* scare away.

effecti|f¹, ~ve /efɛktif, -v/ *a.* effective. **~vement** *adv.* effectively; (*en effet*) indeed.

effectif² /efɛktif/ *n.m.* size, strength. **~s**, numbers.

effectuer /efɛktɥe/ *v.t.* carry out, make.

efféminé /efemine/ *a.* effeminate.

effervescen|t, ~te /efɛrvesɑ̃, -t/ *a.* **comprimé ~t,** effervescent tablet. **~ce** *n.f.* excitement.

effet /efɛ/ *n.m.* effect; (*impression*) impression. **~s,** (*habits*) clothes, things. **en ~,** indeed. **faire de l'~,** have an effect, be effective. **faire bon/mauvais ~,** make a good/bad impression.

efficac|e /efikas/ *a.* effective; (*personne*) efficient. **~ité** *n.f.* effectiveness; efficiency.

effigie /efiʒi/ *n.f.* effigy.

effilocher (s') /(s)efilɔʃe/ *v. pr.* fray.

efflanqué /eflɑ̃ke/ *a.* emaciated.

effleurer /eflœre/ *v.t.* touch lightly; (*sujet*) touch on; (*se présenter à*) occur to.

effluves /eflyv/ *n.m. pl.* exhalations.

effondr|er (s') /(s)efɔ̃dre/ *v. pr.* collapse. **~ement** *n.m.* collapse.

efforcer (s') /(s)efɔrse/ *v. pr.* try (hard) (**de,** to).

effort /efɔr/ *n.m.* effort.

effraction /efraksjɔ̃/ *n.f.* **entrer par ~,** break in.

effray|er /efreje/ *v.t.* frighten; (*décourager*) put off. **s'~er** *v. pr.* be frightened. **~ant, ~ante** *a.* frightening; (*fig.*) frightful.

effréné /efrene/ *a.* wild.

effriter (s') /(s)efrite/ *v. pr.* crumble.

effroi /efrwa/ *n.m.* dread.

effronté /efrɔ̃te/ *a.* impudent.

effroyable /efrwajabl/ *a.* dreadful.

effusion /efyzjɔ̃/ *n.f.* **~ de sang,** bloodshed.

ég|al, ~ale (*m. pl.* **~aux**) /egal, -o/ *a.* equal; (*surface, vitesse*) even. ● *n. m., f.* equal. **ça m'est/lui est ~al,** it is all the same to me/him. **sans égal,** matchless. **d'~ à égal,** between equals.

également /egalmɑ̃/ *adv.* equally; (*aussi*) as well.

égaler /egale/ *v.t.* equal.

égaliser /egalize/ *v.t./i.* (*sport*) equalize; (*niveler*) level out; (*cheveux*) trim.

égalit|é /egalite/ *n.f.* equality; (*de surface, d'humeur*) evenness. **à ~é (de points),** equal. **~aire** *a.* egalitarian.

égard /egar/ *n.m.* regard. **~s,** consideration. **à cet ~,** in this respect. **à l'~ de,** with regard to; (*envers*) towards. **eu ~ à,** in view of.

égar|er /egare/ *v.t.* mislay; (*tromper*) lead astray. **s'~er** *v. pr.* get lost; (*se* *tromper*) go astray. **~ement** *n.m.* loss; (*affolement*) confusion.

égayer /egeje/ *v.t.* (*personne*) cheer up; (*pièce*) brighten up.

égide /eʒid/ *n.f.* aegis.

églantier /eglɑ̃tje/ *n.m.* wild rose (-bush).

églefin /eglǝfɛ̃/ *n.m.* haddock.

église /egliz/ *n.f.* church.

égoïs|te /egoist/ *a.* selfish. ● *n.m./f.* egoist. **~me** *n.m.* selfishness, egoism.

égorger /egɔrʒe/ *v.t.* slit the throat of.

égosiller (s') /(s)egozije/ *v. pr.* shout one's head off.

égout /egu/ *n.m.* sewer.

égout|ter /egute/ *v.t./i.*, **s'~er** *v. pr.* (*vaisselle*) drain. **~oir** *n.m.* draining-board; (*panier*) dish drainer.

égratign|er /egratiɲe/ *v.t.* scratch. **~ure** *n.f.* scratch.

égrener /egrǝne/ *v.t.* (*raisins*) pick off; (*notes*) sound one by one.

Égypte /eʒipt/ *n.f.* Egypt.

égyptien, ~ne /eʒipsjɛ̃, -jɛn/ *a. & n.m., f.* Egyptian.

eh /e/ *int.* hey. **eh bien**, well.

éjacul|er /eʒakyle/ *v.i.* ejaculate. **~ation** *n.f.* ejaculation.

éjectable *a.* **siège ~,** ejector seat.

éjecter /eʒɛkte/ *v.t.* eject.

élabor|er /elabɔre/ *v.t.* elaborate. **~ation** *n.f.* elaboration.

élaguer /elage/ *v.t.* prune.

élan[1] /elɑ̃/ *n.m.* (*sport*) run-up; (*vitesse*) momentum; (*fig.*) surge.

élan[2] /elɑ̃/ *n.m.* (*animal*) moose.

élancé /elɑ̃se/ *a.* slender.

élancement /elɑ̃smɑ̃/ *n.m.* twinge.

élancer (s') /(s)elɑ̃se/ *v. pr.* leap forward, dash; (*se dresser*) soar.

élarg|ir /elarʒir/ *v.t.*, **s'~ir** *v. pr.* widen. **~issement** *n.m.* widening.

élasti|que /elastik/ *a.* elastic. ● *n.m.* elastic band; (*tissu*) elastic. **~cité** *n.f.* elasticity.

élec|teur, ~trice /elɛktœr, -tris/ *n.m., f.* voter, elector.

élection /elɛksjɔ̃/ *n.f.* election.

élector|al (*m. pl.* **~aux**) /elɛktɔral, -o/ *a.* (*réunion etc.*) election; (*collège*) electoral.

électorat /elɛktɔra/ *n.m.* electorate, voters.

électricien /elɛktrisjɛ̃/ *n.m.* electrician.

électricité /elɛktrisite/ *n.f.* electricity.

électrifier /elɛktrifje/ *v.t.* electrify.

électrique /elɛktrik/ *a.* electric (al).

électrocuter /elɛktrɔkyte/ *v.t.* electrocute.

électroménager /elɛktrɔmenaʒe/ *n.m.* **l'~,** household appliances.

électron /elɛktrɔ̃/ *n.m.* electron.

électronique /elɛktrɔnik/ *a.* electronic. ● *n.f.* electronics.

électrophone /elɛktrɔfɔn/ *n.m.* record-player.

élég|ant, ~ante /elegɑ̃, -t/ *a.* elegant. **~amment** *adv.* elegantly. **~ance** *n.f.* elegance.

élément /elemɑ̃/ *n.m.* element; (*meuble*) unit. **~aire** /-tɛr/ *a.* elementary.

éléphant /elefɑ̃/ *n.m.* elephant.

élevage /ɛlvaʒ/ *n.m.* (stock-)breeding.

élévation /elevasjɔ̃/ *n.f.* raising; (*hausse*) rise; (*plan*) elevation.

élève /elɛv/ *n.m./f.* pupil.

élevé /ɛlve/ *a.* high; (*noble*) elevated. **bien ~,** well-mannered.

élever /ɛlve/ *v.t.* raise; (*enfants*) bring up, raise; (*animal*) breed. **s'~** *v. pr.* rise; (*dans le ciel*) soar up. **s'~ à,** amount to.

éleveu|r, ~se /ɛlvœr, -øz/ *n.m., f.* (stock-)breeder.

éligible /eliʒibl/ *a.* eligible.

élimé /elime/ *a.* worn thin.

élimin|er /elimine/ *v.t.* eliminate. **~ation** *n.f.* elimination. **~atoire** *a.* eliminating; *n.f.* (*sport*) heat.

élire† /elir/ *v.t.* elect.

élite /elit/ *n.f.* élite.

elle /ɛl/ *pron.* she; (*complément*) her; (*chose*) it. **~-même** *pron.* herself; itself.

elles /ɛl/ *pron.* they; (*complément*) them. **~-mêmes** *pron.* themselves.

ellip|se /elips/ *n.f.* ellipse. **~tique** *a.* elliptical.

élocution /elɔkysjɔ̃/ *n.f.* diction.

élog|e /elɔʒ/ *n.m.* praise. **faire l'~e de,** praise. **~ieux, ~ieuse** *a.* laudatory.

éloigné /elwaɲe/ *a.* distant. **~ de,** far away from. **parent ~,** distant relative.

éloign|er /elwaɲe/ *v.t.* take away *ou* remove (**de,** from); (*personne aimée*) estrange (**de,** from); (*danger*) ward off; (*visite*) put off. **s'~er** *v. pr.* go *ou* move away (**de,** from); (*affectivement*) become estranged (**de,** from). **~ement** *n.m.* removal; (*distance*) distance; (*oubli*) estrangement.

élongation /elɔ̃gasjɔ̃/ *n.f.* strained muscle.

éloquen|t, ~te /elɔkɑ̃, -t/ *a.* eloquent. **~ce** *n.f.* eloquence.

élu, ~e /ely/ *a.* elected. ● *n.m., f.* (*pol.*) elected representative.

élucider /elyside/ *v.t.* elucidate.

éluder /elyde/ *v.t.* elude.

émacié /emasje/ *a.* emaciated.

ém|ail (*pl.* **~aux**) /emaj, -o/ *n.m.* enamel.

émaillé /emaje/ *a.* enamelled. **~ de,** studded with.

émancip|er /emɑ̃sipe/ *v.t.* emancipate. **s'~er** *v. pr.* become emancipated. **~ation** *n.f.* emancipation.

éman|er /emane/ *v.i.* emanate. **~ation** *n.f.* emanation.

émarger /emarʒe/ *v.t.* initial.

emball|er /ɑ̃bale/ *v.t.* pack, wrap; (*personne*: *fam.*) enthuse. **s'~er** *v. pr.* (*moteur*) race; (*cheval*) bolt; (*personne*) get carried away. **~age** *n.m.* package, wrapping.

embarcadère /ɑ̃barkadɛr/ *n.m.* landing-stage.

embarcation /ɑ̃barkasjɔ̃/ *n.f.* boat.

embardée /ɑ̃barde/ *n.f.* swerve.

embargo /ɑ̃bargo/ *n.m.* embargo.

embarqu|er /ɑ̃barke/ *v.t.* embark; (*charger*) load; (*emporter*: *fam.*) cart off. ● *v.i.,* **s'~er** *v. pr.* board, embark. **s'~er dans,** embark upon. **~ement** *n.m.* embarkation; loading.

embarras /ɑ̃bara/ *n.m.* obstacle; (*gêne*) embarrassment; (*difficulté*) difficulty.

embarrasser /ɑ̃barase/ *v.t.* clutter (up); (*gêner dans les mouvements*) hinder; (*fig.*) embarrass. **s'~ de,** burden o.s. with.

embauch|e /ɑ̃boʃ/ *n.f.* hiring; (*emploi*) employment. **~er** *v.t.* hire, take on.

embauchoir /ɑ̃boʃwar/ *n.m.* shoe tree.

embaumer /ɑ̃bome/ *v.t./i.* (make) smell fragrant; (*cadavre*) embalm.

embellir /ɑ̃belir/ *v.t.* brighten up; (*récit*) embellish.

embêt|er /ɑ̃bete/ *v.t.* (*fam.*) annoy. **s'~er** *v. pr.* (*fam.*) get bored. **~ant, ~ante** *a.* (*fam.*) annoying. **~ement** /ɑ̃bɛtmɑ̃/ *n.m.* (*fam.*) annoyance.

emblée (d') /(d)ɑ̃ble/ *adv.* right away.

emblème /ɑ̃blɛm/ *n.m.* emblem.

embobiner /ɑ̃bɔbine/ *v.t.* (*fam.*) get round.

emboîter /ɑ̃bwate/ *v.t.,* **s'~** *v. pr.* fit together. **(s')~ dans,** fit into. **~ le pas à qn.,** (*imiter*) follow suit.

embonpoint /ɑ̃bɔ̃pwɛ̃/ *n.m.* stoutness.

embouchure /ɑ̃buʃyr/ *n.f.* (*de fleuve*) mouth; (*mus.*) mouthpiece.

embourber (s') /(s)ɑ̃burbe/ *v. pr.* get bogged down.

embourgeoiser (s') /(s)ɑ̃burʒwaze/ *v. pr.* become middle-class.

embout /ɑ̃bu/ *n.m.* tip.

embouteillage /ɑ̃buteja3/ *n.m.* traffic jam.

emboutir /ɑ̃butir/ *v.t.* (*heurter*) crash into.

embranchement /ɑ̃brɑ̃ʃmɑ̃/ *n.m.* (*de routes*) junction.

embraser /ɑ̃braze/ *v.t.* set on fire, fire. **s'~** *v. pr.* flare up.

embrass|er /ɑ̃brase/ *v.t.* kiss; (*adopter, contenir*) embrace. **s'~er** *v. pr.* kiss. **~ades** *n.f. pl.* kissing.

embrasure /ɑ̃brazyr/ *n.f.* opening.

embray|er /ɑ̃breje/ *v.i.* let in the clutch. **~age** /ɑ̃brejaʒ/ *n.m.* clutch.

embrigader /ɑ̃brigade/ *v.t.* enrol.

embrocher /ɑ̃brɔʃe/ *v.t.* (*viande*) spit.

embrouiller /ɑ̃bruje/ *v.t.* mix up; (*fils*) tangle. **s'~** *v. pr.* get mixed up.

embroussaillé /ɑ̃brusaje/ *a.* (*poils, chemin*) bushy.

embryon /ɑ̃brijɔ̃/ *n.m.* embryo. **~naire** /-jɔnɛr/ *a.* embryonic.

embûches /ɑ̃byʃ/ *n.f. pl.* traps.

embuer /ɑ̃bɥe/ *v.t.* mist up.

embuscade /ɑ̃byskad/ *n.f.* ambush.

embusquer (s') /(s)ɑ̃byske/ *v. pr.* lie in ambush.

éméché /emeʃe/ *a.* tipsy.

émeraude /emrod/ *n.f.* emerald.

émerger /emɛrʒe/ *v.i.* emerge; (*fig.*) stand out.

émeri /ɛmri/ *n.m.* emery.

émerveill|er /emɛrveje/ *v.t.* amaze. **s'~er de,** marvel at, be amazed at. **~ement** /-vɛjmɑ̃/ *n.m.* amazement, wonder.

émett|re† /emɛtr/ *v.t.* give out; (*message*) transmit; (*timbre, billet*) issue; (*opinion*) express. **~eur** *n.m.* transmitter.

émeut|e /emøt/ *n.f.* riot. **~ier, ~ière** *n.m., f.* rioter.

émietter /emjete/ *v.t.,* **s'~** *v. pr.* crumble.

émigrant, **~e** /emigrã, -t/ *n.m.*, *f.* emigrant.

émigr|er /emigre/ *v.i.* emigrate. **~ation** *n.f.* emigration.

émincer /emɛ̃se/ *v.t.* cut into thin slices.

émin|ent, **~ente** /eminã, -t/ *a.* eminent. **~emment** /-amã/ *adv.* eminently. **~ence** *n.f.* eminence; (*colline*) hill. **~ence grise**, éminence grise.

émissaire /emisɛr/ *n.m.* emissary.

émission /emisjɔ̃/ *n.f.* emission; (*de message*) transmission; (*de timbre*) issue; (*programme*) broadcast.

emmagasiner /ãmagazine/ *v.t.* store.

emmanchure /ãmãʃyr/ *n.f.* armhole.

emmêler /ãmele/ *v.t.* tangle. **s'~** *v. pr.* get mixed up.

emménager /ãmenaʒe/ *v.i.* move in. **~ dans**, move into.

emmener /ãmne/ *v.t.* take; (*comme prisonnier*) take away.

emmerder /ãmɛrde/ *v.t.* (*argot*) bother. **s'~** *v. pr.* (*argot*) get bored.

emmitoufler /ãmitufle/ *v.t.*, **s'~** *v. pr.* wrap up (warmly).

émoi /emwa/ *n.m.* excitement.

émoluments /emɔlymã/ *n.m. pl.* remuneration.

émonder /emɔ̃de/ *v.t.* prune.

émoti|f, **~ve** /emɔtif, -v/ *a.* emotional.

émotion /emosjɔ̃/ *n.f.* emotion; (*peur*) fright. **~nel**, **~nelle** /-jɔnɛl/ *a.* emotional.

émousser /emuse/ *v.t.* blunt.

émouv|oir /emuvwar/ *v.t.* move. **s'~oir** *v. pr.* be moved. **~ant**, **~ante** *a.* moving.

empailler /ãpaje/ *v.t.* stuff.

empaqueter /ãpakte/ *v.t.* package.

emparer (s') /(s)ãpare/ *v. pr.* **s'~ de**, seize.

empâter (s') /(s)ãpate/ *v. pr.* fill out, grow fatter.

empêchement /ãpɛʃmã/ *n.m.* hitch, difficulty.

empêcher /ãpeʃe/ *v.t.* prevent. **~ de faire**, prevent *ou* stop (from) doing. **il ne peut pas s'~ de penser**, he cannot help thinking. **(il) n'empêche que**, still.

empêch|eur, **~euse** /ãpeʃœr, -øz/ *n.m.*, *f.* **~eur de tourner en rond**, spoilsport.

empeigne /ãpɛɲ/ *n.f.* upper.

empereur /ãprœr/ *n.m.* emperor.

empeser /ãpəze/ *v.t.* starch.

empester /ãpɛste/ *v.t.* make stink, stink out; (*essence etc.*) stink of. ● *v.i.* stink.

empêtrer (s') /(s)ãpetre/ *v. pr.* become entangled.

emphase /ãfaz/ *n.f.* pomposity.

empiéter /ãpjete/ *v.i.* **~ sur**, encroach upon.

empiffrer (s') /(s)ãpifre/ *v. pr.* (*fam.*) gorge o.s.

empiler /ãpile/ *v.t.*, **s'~** *v. pr.* pile (up).

empire /ãpir/ *n.m.* empire; (*fig.*) control.

empirer /ãpire/ *v.i.* worsen.

empirique /ãpirik/ *a.* empirical.

emplacement /ãplasmã/ *n.m.* site.

emplâtre /ãplatr/ *n.m.* (*méd.*) plaster.

emplettes /ãplɛt/ *n.f. pl.* purchase. **faire des ~**, do one's shopping.

emplir /ãplir/ *v.t.*, **s'~** *v. pr.* fill.

emploi /ãplwa/ *n.m.* use; (*travail*) job. **~ du temps**, timetable. **l'~**, (*pol.*) employment.

employ|er /ãplwaje/ *v.t.* use; (*personne*) employ. **s'~er** *v. pr.* be used. **s'~er à**, devote o.s. to. **~é**, **~ée** *n.m.*, *f.* employee. **~eur**, **~euse** *n.m.*, *f.* employer.

empocher /ãpɔʃe/ *v.t.* pocket.

empoigner /ãpwaɲe/ *v.t.* grab. **s'~** *v. pr.* come to blows.

empoisonn|er /ãpwazɔne/ *v.t.* poison; (*empuantir*) stink out; (*embêter*: *fam.*) annoy. **~ement** *n.m.* poisoning.

emport|é /ãpɔrte/ *a.* quicktempered. **~ement** *n.m.* anger.

emporter /ãpɔrte/ *v.t.* take (away); (*entraîner*) carry away; (*prix*) carry off; (*arracher*) tear off. **~ un chapeau**/*etc.*, (*vent*) blow off a hat/*etc.* **s'~** *v. pr.* lose one's temper. **l'~**, get the upper hand (**sur**, of). **plat à ~**, take-away.

empoté /ãpɔte/ *a.* silly.

empourpré /ãpurpre/ *a.* crimson.

empreint, **~e** /ãprɛ̃, -t/ *a.* **~ de**, marked with. ● *n.f.* mark. **~e (digitale)**, fingerprint. **~e de pas**, footprint.

empress|er (s') /(s)ãprese/ *v. pr.* **s'~er auprès de**, be attentive to. **s'~er de**, hasten to. **~é** *a.* eager, attentive. **~ement** /ãprɛsmã/ *n.m.* eagerness.

emprise /ãpriz/ *n.f.* influence.

emprisonn|er /ɑ̃prizɔne/ v.t. imprison. **~ement** n.m. imprisonment.

emprunt /ɑ̃prœ̃/ n.m. loan. **faire un ~**, take out a loan.

emprunté /ɑ̃prœ̃te/ a. awkward.

emprunt|er /ɑ̃prœ̃te/ v.t. borrow (**à**, from); (route) take; (fig.) assume. **~eur, ~euse** n.m., f. borrower.

ému /emy/ a. moved; (apeuré) nervous; (joyeux) excited.

émulation /emylɑsjɔ̃/ n.f. emulation.

émule /emyl/ n.m./f. imitator.

émulsion /emylsjɔ̃/ n.f. emulsion.

en¹ /ɑ̃/ prép. in; (avec direction) to; (manière, état) in, on; (moyen de transport) by; (composition) made of. **en cadeau/médecin/etc.**, as a present/doctor/etc. **en guerre**, at war. **en faisant**, by ou on ou while doing.

en² /ɑ̃/ pron. of it, of them; (moyen) with it; (cause) from it; (lieu) from there. **en avoir/vouloir/etc.**, have/want/etc. some. **ne pas en avoir/vouloir/etc.**, not have/want/etc. any. **où en êtes-vous?**, where are you up to?, how far have you got? **j'en ai assez**, I've had enough. **en êtes-vous sûr?**, are you sure?

encadr|er /ɑ̃kɑdre/ v.t. frame; (entourer d'un trait) circle; (entourer) surround. **~ement** n.m. framing; (de porte) frame.

encaiss|er /ɑ̃kese/ v.t. (argent) collect; (chèque) cash; (coups: fam.) take. **~eur** n.m. debt-collector.

encart /ɑ̃kar/ n.m. **~ publicitaire**, (advertising) insert.

en-cas /ɑ̃ka/ n.m. (stand-by) snack.

encastré /ɑ̃kastre/ a. built-in.

encaustiqu|e /ɑ̃kostik/ n.f. wax polish. **~er** v.t. wax.

enceinte¹ /ɑ̃sɛ̃t/ a./f. pregnant. **~ de 3 mois**, 3 months pregnant.

enceinte² /ɑ̃sɛ̃t/ n.f. enclosure. **~ (acoustique)**, loudspeaker.

encens /ɑ̃sɑ̃/ n.m. incense.

encercler /ɑ̃sɛrkle/ v.t. surround.

enchaîn|er /ɑ̃ʃene/ v.t. chain (up); (coordonner) link (up). ● v.i. continue. **s'~er** v. pr. be linked (up). **~ement** /ɑ̃ʃɛnmɑ̃/ n.m. (suite) chain; (liaison) link(ing).

enchant|er /ɑ̃ʃɑ̃te/ v.t. delight; (ensorceler) enchant. **~é** a. (ravi) delighted. **~ement** n.m. delight; (magie) enchantment.

enchâsser /ɑ̃ʃase/ v.t. set.

enchère /ɑ̃ʃɛr/ n.f. bid. **mettre ou vendre aux ~s**, sell by auction.

enchevêtrer /ɑ̃ʃvetre/ v.t. tangle. **s'~** v. pr. become tangled.

enclave /ɑ̃klav/ n.f. enclave.

enclencher /ɑ̃klɑ̃ʃe/ v.t. engage.

enclin, ~e /ɑ̃klɛ̃, -in/ a. **~ à**, inclined to.

enclore /ɑ̃klɔr/ v.t. enclose.

enclos /ɑ̃klo/ n.m. enclosure.

enclume /ɑ̃klym/ n.f. anvil.

encoche /ɑ̃kɔʃ/ n.f. notch.

encoignure /ɑ̃kɔɲyr/ n.f. corner.

encoller /ɑ̃kɔle/ v.t. paste.

encolure /ɑ̃kɔlyr/ n.f. neck.

encombre /ɑ̃kɔ̃br/ n.m. **sans ~**, without any problems.

encombr|er /ɑ̃kɔ̃bre/ v.t. clutter (up); (gêner) hamper. **s'~er de**, burden o.s. with. **~ant, ~ante** a. cumbersome. **~ement** n.m. congestion; (auto.) traffic jam; (volume) bulk.

encontre de (à l') /(al)ɑ̃kɔ̃trədə/ prép. against.

encore /ɑ̃kɔr/ adv. (toujours) still; (de nouveau) again; (de plus) more; (aussi) also. **~ mieux/plus grand/etc.**, even better/larger/etc. **~ une heure/un café/etc.**, another hour/ coffee/etc. **pas ~**, not yet. **si ~**, if only.

encourag|er /ɑ̃kuraʒe/ v.t. encourage. **~ement** n.m. encouragement.

encourir /ɑ̃kurir/ v.t. incur.

encrasser /ɑ̃krase/ v.t. clog up (with dirt).

encr|e /ɑ̃kr/ n.f. ink. **~er** v.t. ink.

encrier /ɑ̃krije/ n.m. ink-well.

encroûter (s') /(s)ɑ̃krute/ v. pr. become doggedly set in one's ways. **s'~ dans**, sink into.

encyclopéd|ie /ɑ̃siklɔpedi/ n.f. encyclopaedia. **~ique** a. encyclopaedic.

endetter /ɑ̃dete/ v.t., **s'~** v. pr. get into debt.

endeuiller /ɑ̃dœje/ v.t. plunge into mourning.

endiablé /ɑ̃djable/ a. wild.

endiguer /ɑ̃dige/ v.t. dam; (fig.) check.

endimanché /ɑ̃dimɑ̃ʃe/ a. in one's Sunday best.

endive /ɑ̃div/ n.f. chicory.

endocrinolo|gie /ãdɔkrinɔlɔʒi/ *n.f.* endocrinology. **~gue** *n.m./f.* endocrinologist.

endoctrin|er /ãdɔktrine/ *v.t.* indoctrinate. **~ement** *n.m.* indoctrination.

endommager /ãdɔmaʒe/ *v.t.* damage.

endorm|ir /ãdɔrmir/ *v.t.* send to sleep; (*atténuer*) allay. **s'~ir** *v. pr.* fall asleep. **~i** *a.* asleep; (*apathique*) sleepy.

endosser /ãdɔse/ *v.t.* (*vêtement*) put on; (*assumer*) assume; (*comm.*) endorse.

endroit /ãdrwa/ *n.m.* place; (*de tissu*) right side. **à l'~**, the right way round, right side out.

end|uire /ãdɥir/ *v.t.* coat. **~uit** *n.m.* coating.

endurance /ãdyrãs/ *n.f.* endurance.

endurant, ~e /ãdyrã, -t/ *a.* tough.

endurci /ãdyrsi/ *a.* **célibataire ~**, confirmed bachelor.

endurcir /ãdyrsir/ *v.t.* harden. **s'~** *v. pr.* become hard(ened).

endurer /ãdyre/ *v.t.* endure.

énerg|ie /enɛrʒi/ *n.f.* energy; (*techn.*) power. **~étique** *a.* energy. **~ique** *a.* energetic.

énervant, ~e /enɛrvã, -t/ *a.* irritating, annoying.

énerver /enɛrve/ *v.t.* irritate. **s'~** *v. pr.* get worked up.

enfance /ãfãs/ *n.f.* childhood. **la petite ~**, infancy.

enfant /ãfã/ *n.m./f.* child. **~ en bas âge**, infant. **~illage** /-tijaʒ/ *n.m.* childishness. **~in, ~ine** /-tɛ̃, -tin/ *a.* childlike; (*puéril*) childish; (*jeu, langage*) children's.

enfanter /ãfãte/ *v.t./i.* give birth (to).

enfer /ãfɛr/ *n.m.* hell.

enfermer /ãfɛrme/ *v.t.* shut up. **s'~** *v. pr.* shut o.s. up.

enferrer (s') /(s)ãfere/ *v. pr.* become entangled.

enfiévré /ãfjevre/ *a.* feverish.

enfilade /ãfilad/ *n.f.* string, row.

enfiler /ãfile/ *v.t.* (*aiguille*) thread; (*anneaux*) string; (*vêtement*) slip on; (*rue*) take; (*insérer*) insert.

enfin /ãfɛ̃/ *adv.* at last, finally; (*en dernier lieu*) finally; (*somme toute*) after all; (*résignation, conclusion*) well.

enflammer /ãflame/ *v.t.* set fire to; (*méd.*) inflame. **s'~** *v. pr.* catch fire.

enfl|er /ãfle/ *v.t./i.*, **s'~er** *v. pr.* swell. **~é** *a.* swollen. **~ure** *n.f.* swelling.

enfoncer /ãfõse/ *v.t.* (*épingle etc.*) push *ou* drive in; (*chapeau*) push down; (*porte*) break down; (*mettre*) thrust, put. ● *v.i.*, **s'~** *v. pr.* sink (**dans**, into).

enfouir /ãfwir/ *v.t.* bury.

enfourcher /ãfurʃe/ *v.t.* mount.

enfourner /ãfurne/ *v.t.* put in the oven.

enfreindre /ãfrɛ̃dr/ *v.t.* infringe.

enfuir† (s') /(s)ãfɥir/ *v. pr.* run off.

enfumer /ãfyme/ *v.t.* fill with smoke.

engagé /ãgaʒe/ *a.* committed.

engageant, ~e /ãgaʒã, -t/ *a.* attractive.

engag|er /ãgaʒe/ *v.t.* (*lier*) bind, commit; (*embaucher*) take on; (*commencer*) start; (*introduire*) insert; (*entraîner*) involve; (*encourager*) urge; (*investir*) invest. **s'~er** *v. pr.* (*promettre*) commit o.s.; (*commencer*) start; (*soldat*) enlist; (*concurrent*) enter. **s'~er à faire**, undertake to do. **s'~er dans**, (*voie*) enter. **~ement** *n.m.* (*promesse*) promise; (*pol., comm.*) commitment; (*début*) start; (*inscription: sport*) entry.

engelure /ãʒlyr/ *n.f.* chilblain.

engendrer /ãʒãdre/ *v.t.* beget; (*causer*) generate.

engin /ãʒɛ̃/ *n.m.* machine; (*outil*) instrument; (*projectile*) missile. **~ explosif**, explosive device.

englober /ãglɔbe/ *v.t.* include.

engloutir /ãglutir/ *v.t.* swallow (up). **s'~** *v. pr.* (*navire*) be engulfed.

engorger /ãgɔrʒe/ *v.t.* block.

engoue|r (s') /(s)ãgwe/ *v. pr.* **s'~er de**, become infatuated with. **~ement** /-umã/ *n.m.* infatuation.

engouffrer /ãgufre/ *v.t.* devour. **s'~ dans**, rush into (with force).

engourd|ir /ãgurdir/ *v.t.* numb. **s'~ir** *v. pr.* go numb. **~i** *a.* numb.

engrais /ãgrɛ/ *n.m.* manure; (*chimique*) fertilizer.

engraisser /ãgrese/ *v.t.* fatten. **s'~** *v. pr.* get fat.

engrenage /ãgrənaʒ/ *n.m.* gears; (*fig.*) chain (of events).

engueuler /ãgœle/ *v.t.* (*argot*) curse, swear at, hurl abuse at.

enhardir (s') /(s)ãardir/ *v. pr.* become bolder.

énième /ɛnjɛm/ *a.* (*fam.*) umpteenth.

énigm|e /enigm/ *n.f.* riddle, enigma. **~atique** *a.* enigmatic.

enivrer /ɑ̃nivre/ v.t. intoxicate. **s'~** v. pr. get drunk.

enjamb|er /ɑ̃ʒɑ̃be/ v.t. step over; (pont) span. **~ée** n.f. stride.

enjeu (pl. **~x**) /ɑ̃ʒø/ n.m. stake(s).

enjôler /ɑ̃ʒole/ v.t. wheedle.

enjoliver /ɑ̃ʒolive/ v.t. embellish.

enjoliveur /ɑ̃ʒolivœr/ n.m. hub-cap.

enjoué /ɑ̃ʒwe/ a. cheerful.

enlacer /ɑ̃lase/ v.t. entwine.

enlaidir /ɑ̃ledir/ v.t. make ugly. ● v.i. grow ugly.

enlèvement /ɑ̃lɛvmɑ̃/ n.m. removal; (rapt) kidnapping.

enlever /ɑ̃lve/ v.t. (emporter) take (away), remove (**à**, from); (vêtement) take off, remove; (tache, organe) take out, remove; (kidnapper) kidnap; (gagner) win.

enliser (s') /(s)ɑ̃lize/ v. pr. get bogged down.

enluminure /ɑ̃lyminyr/ n.f. illumination.

enneig|é /ɑ̃neʒe/ a. snow-covered. **~ement** /ɑ̃nɛʒmɑ̃/ n.m. snow conditions.

ennemi /ɛnmi/ n.m. & a. enemy. **~ de**, (fig.) hostile to. **l'~ public numéro un**, public enemy number one.

ennui /ɑ̃nɥi/ n.m. boredom; (tracas) trouble, worry. **il a des ~s**, he's got problems.

ennuyer /ɑ̃nɥije/ v.t. bore; (irriter) annoy; (préoccuper) worry. **s'~** v. pr. get bored.

ennuyeu|x, **~se** /ɑ̃nɥijø, -z/ a. boring; (fâcheux) annoying.

énoncé /enɔ̃se/ n.m. wording, text; (gram.) utterance.

énoncer /enɔ̃se/ v.t. express, state.

enorgueillir (s') /(s)ɑ̃nɔrgœjir/ v. pr. **s'~ de**, pride o.s. on.

énorm|e /enɔrm/ a. enormous. **~ément** adv. enormously. **~ément de**, an enormous amount of. **~ité** n.f. enormous size; (atrocité) enormity; (bévue) enormous blunder.

enquérir (s') /(s)ɑ̃kerir/ v. pr. **s'~ de**, enquire about.

enquêt|e /ɑ̃kɛt/ n.f. investigation; (jurid.) inquiry; (sondage) survey. **mener l'~**, lead the inquiry. **~er /-ete/** v.i. **~er (sur)**, investigate. **~eur**, **~euse** n.m., f. investigator.

enquiquin|er /ɑ̃kikine/ v.t. (fam.) bother. **~ant**, **~ante** a. irritating. **c'est ~ant**, it's a nuisance.

enraciné /ɑ̃rasine/ a. deep-rooted.

enrag|er /ɑ̃raʒe/ v.i. be furious. **faire ~er**, annoy. **~é** a. furious; (chien) mad; (fig.) fanatical. **~eant**, **~eante** a. infuriating.

enrayer /ɑ̃reje/ v.t. check.

enregistr|er /ɑ̃rʒistre/ v.t. note, record; (mus.) record. **(faire) ~er**, (bagages) register, check in. **~ement** n.m. recording; (des bagages) registration.

enrhumer (s') /(s)ɑ̃ryme/ v. pr. catch a cold.

enrich|ir /ɑ̃riʃir/ v.t. enrich. **s'~ir** v. pr. grow rich(er). **~issement** n.m. enrichment.

enrober /ɑ̃robe/ v.t. coat (**de**, with).

enrôler /ɑ̃role/ v.t., **s'~** v. pr. enlist, enrol.

enrouer (s') /(s)ɑ̃rwe/ v. pr. become hoarse. **~é** a. hoarse.

enrouler /ɑ̃rule/ v.t., **s'~** v. pr. wind. **s'~ dans une couverture**, roll o.s. up in a blanket.

ensabler /ɑ̃sable/ v.t., **s'~** v. pr. (port) silt up.

ensanglanté /ɑ̃sɑ̃glɑ̃te/ a. bloodstained.

enseignant, **~e** /ɑ̃sɛɲɑ̃, -t/ n.m., f. teacher. ● a. teaching.

enseigne /ɑ̃sɛɲ/ n.f. sign.

enseignement /ɑ̃sɛɲmɑ̃/ n.m. teaching; (instruction) education.

enseigner /ɑ̃seɲe/ v.t./i. teach. **~ qch. à qn.**, teach s.o. sth.

ensemble /ɑ̃sɑ̃bl/ adv. together. ● n.m. unity; (d'objets) set; (mus.) ensemble; (vêtements) outfit. **dans l'~**, on the whole. **d'~**, (idée etc.) general. **l'~ de**, (totalité) all of, the whole of.

ensemencer /ɑ̃smɑ̃se/ v.t. sow.

enserrer /ɑ̃sere/ v.t. grip (tightly).

ensevelir /ɑ̃svəlir/ v.t. bury.

ensoleill|é /ɑ̃soleje/ a. sunny. **~ement** /ɑ̃solɛjmɑ̃/ n.m. (period of) sunshine.

ensommeillé /ɑ̃someje/ a. sleepy.

ensorceler /ɑ̃sɔrsəle/ v.t. bewitch.

ensuite /ɑ̃sɥit/ adv. next, then; (plus tard) later.

ensuivre (s') /(s)ɑ̃sɥivr/ v. pr. follow. **et tout ce qui s'ensuit**, and so on.

entaill|e /ɑ̃taj/ n.f. notch; (blessure) gash. **~er** v.t. notch; gash.

entamer /ɑ̃tame/ v.t. start; (inciser) cut into; (ébranler) shake.

entass|er /ɑ̃tase/ v.t., **s'~** v. pr. pile up. **(s')~er dans**, cram (together) into. **~ement** n.m. (tas) pile.

entendement /ɑ̃tɑ̃dmɑ̃/ *n.m.*
understanding. **ça dépasse l'~,** it
defies one's understanding.

entendre /ɑ̃tɑ̃dr/ *v.t.* hear; (*comprendre*) understand; (*vouloir*) intend, mean; (*vouloir dire*) mean. **s'~**
v. pr. (*être d'accord*) agree. **~ dire
que,** hear that. **~ parler de,** hear of.
s'~ (bien), get on (**avec,** with).
(**cela**) **s'entend,** of course.

entendu /ɑ̃tɑ̃dy/ *a.* (*convenu*)
agreed; (*sourire, air*) knowing. **bien
~,** of course. (**c'est**) **~!,** all right!

entente /ɑ̃tɑ̃t/ *n.f.* understanding. **à
double ~,** with a double meaning.

entériner /ɑ̃terine/ *v.t.* ratify.

enterr|er /ɑ̃tere/ *v.t.* bury. **~ement**
/ɑ̃tɛrmɑ̃/ *n.m.* burial, funeral.

entêtant, ~e /ɑ̃tɛtɑ̃, -t/ *a.* heady.

en-tête /ɑ̃tɛt/ *n.m.* heading. **à ~,**
headed.

entêt|é /ɑ̃tete/ *a.* stubborn. **~ement**
/ɑ̃tɛtmɑ̃/ *n.m.* stubbornness.

entêter (s') /(s)ɑ̃tete/ *v. pr.* persist (**à,
dans,** in).

enthousias|me /ɑ̃tuzjasm/ *n.m.*
enthusiasm. **~mer** *v.t.* enthuse.
s'~mer pour, enthuse over. **~te** *a.*
enthusiastic.

enticher (s') /(s)ɑ̃tiʃe/ *v. pr.* **s'~ de,**
become infatuated with.

ent|ier, ~ière /ɑ̃tje, -jɛr/ *a.* whole;
(*absolu*) absolute; (*entêté*) un-
yielding. ● *n.m.* whole. **en ~ier,**
entirely. **~ièrement** *adv.* entirely.

entité /ɑ̃tite/ *n.f.* entity.

entonner /ɑ̃tone/ *v.t.* start singing.

entonnoir /ɑ̃tɔnwar/ *n.m.* funnel;
(*trou*) crater.

entorse /ɑ̃tɔrs/ *n.f.* sprain. **~ à,** (*loi*)
infringement of.

entortiller /ɑ̃tɔrtije/ *v.t.* wrap (up);
(*enrouler*) wind, wrap; (*duper*) deceive.

entourage /ɑ̃turaʒ/ *n.m.* circle of
family and friends; (*bordure*) surround.

entourer /ɑ̃ture/ *v.t.* surround (**de,**
with); (*réconforter*) rally round. **~
de,** (*écharpe etc.*) wrap round.

entracte /ɑ̃trakt/ *n.m.* interval.

entraide /ɑ̃trɛd/ *n.f.* mutual aid.

entraider (s') /(s)ɑ̃trede/ *v. pr.* help
each other.

entrailles /ɑ̃traj/ *n.f. pl.* entrails.

entrain /ɑ̃trɛ̃/ *n.m.* zest, spirit.

entraînant, ~e /ɑ̃trenɑ̃, -t/ *a.* rous-
ing.

entraînement /ɑ̃trenmɑ̃/ *n.m.*
(*sport*) training.

entraîn|er /ɑ̃trene/ *v.t.* carry away *ou*
along; (*emmener, influencer*) lead;
(*impliquer*) entail; (*sport*) train;
(*roue*) drive. **~eur** /ɑ̃trenœr/ *n.m.*
trainer.

entrav|e /ɑ̃trav/ *n.f.* hindrance. **~er**
v.t. hinder.

entre /ɑ̃tr(ə)/ *prép.* between; (*parmi*)
among(st). **~ autres,** among other
things. **l'un d'~ nous/vous/eux,**
one of us/you/them.

entrebâillé /ɑ̃trəbaje/ *a.* ajar.

entrechoquer (s') /(s)ɑ̃trəʃɔke/ *v.
pr.* knock against each other.

entrecôte /ɑ̃trəkot/ *n.f.* rib steak.

entrecouper /ɑ̃trəkupe/ *v.t.* **~ de,**
intersperse with.

entrecroiser (s') /(s)ɑ̃trəkrwaze/ *v.
pr.* (*routes*) intersect.

entrée /ɑ̃tre/ *n.f.* entrance; (*accès*)
admission, entry; (*billet*) ticket; (*culin.*) first course; (*de données: techn.*)
input. **~ interdite,** no entry.

entrefaites (sur ces) /(syrsez)-
ɑ̃trəfɛt/ *adv.* at that moment.

entrefilet /ɑ̃trəfilɛ/ *n.m.* paragraph.

entrejambe /ɑ̃trəʒɑ̃b/ *n.m.* crotch.

entrelacer (s') /ɑ̃trəlase/ *v.t.,* **s'~** *v. pr.*
intertwine.

entremêler /ɑ̃trəmele/ *v.t.,* **s'~** *v. pr.*
(inter)mingle.

entremets /ɑ̃trəmɛ/ *n.m.* dessert.

entremetteu|r, ~se /ɑ̃trəmɛtœr,
-øz/ *n.m., f.* (*péj.*) go-between.

entre|mettre (s') /(s)ɑ̃trəmɛtr/ *v. pr.*
intervene. **~mise** *n.f.* intervention.
par l'~mise de, through.

entreposer /ɑ̃trəpoze/ *v.t.* store.

entrepôt /ɑ̃trəpo/ *n.m.* warehouse.

entreprenant, ~e /ɑ̃trəprənɑ̃, -t/ *a.*
(*actif*) enterprising; (*séducteur*) forward.

entreprendre† /ɑ̃trəprɑ̃dr/ *v.t.* start
on; (*personne*) buttonhole. **~ de
faire,** undertake to do.

entrepreneur /ɑ̃trəprənœr/ *n.m.* **~
(de bâtiments),** (building) contractor.

entreprise /ɑ̃trəpriz/ *n.f.* undertaking; (*société*) firm.

entrer /ɑ̃tre/ *v.i.* (*aux. être*) go in,
enter; (*venir*) come in, enter. **~
dans,** go *ou* come into, enter; (*club*)
join. **~ en collision,** collide (**avec,**
with). **faire ~,** (*personne*) show in.
laisser ~, let in.

entresol /ɑ̃trəsɔl/ *n.m.* mezzanine.

entre-temps /ɑ̃trətɑ̃/ *adv.* meanwhile.

entretenir† /ɑ̃trətnir/ *v.t.* maintain; (*faire durer*) keep alive. ~ **qn. de,** converse with s.o. about. **s'~** *v. pr.* speak (**de,** about; **avec,** to).

entretien /ɑ̃trətjɛ̃/ *n.m.* maintenance; (*discussion*) talk; (*audience pour un emploi*) interview.

entrevoir /ɑ̃trəvwar/ *v.t.* make out; (*brièvement*) glimpse.

entrevue /ɑ̃trəvy/ *n.f.* interview.

entrouvrir /ɑ̃truvrir/ *v.t.* half-open.

énumér|er /enymere/ *v.t.* enumerate. **~ation** *n.f.* enumeration.

envah|ir /ɑ̃vair/ *v.t.* invade, overrun; (*douleur, peur*) overcome. **~isseur** *n.m.* invader.

enveloppe /ɑ̃vlɔp/ *n.f.* envelope; (*emballage*) covering; (*techn.*) casing.

envelopper /ɑ̃vlɔpe/ *v.t.* wrap (up); (*fig.*) envelop.

envenimer /ɑ̃vnime/ *v.t.* embitter. **s'~** *v. pr.* become embittered.

envergure /ɑ̃vɛrgyr/ *n.f.* wing-span; (*importance*) scope; (*qualité*) calibre.

envers /ɑ̃vɛr/ *prép.* toward(s), to. ● *n.m.* (*de tissu*) wrong side. **à l'~,** upside down; (*pantalon*) back to front; (*chaussette*) inside out.

enviable /ɑ̃vjabl/ *a.* enviable. **peu ~,** unenviable.

envie /ɑ̃vi/ *n.f.* desire, wish; (*jalousie*) envy. **avoir ~ de,** want, feel like. **avoir ~ de faire,** want to do, feel like doing.

envier /ɑ̃vje/ *v.t.* envy.

envieu|x, ~se /ɑ̃vjø, -z/ *a. & n.m., f.* envious (person).

environ /ɑ̃virɔ̃/ *adv.* (*round*) about. **~s** *n.m. pl.* surroundings. **aux ~s de,** round about.

environnement /ɑ̃virɔnmɑ̃/ *n.m.* environment.

environn|er /ɑ̃virɔne/ *v.t.* surround. **~ant, ~ante** *a.* surrounding.

envisager /ɑ̃vizaʒe/ *v.t.* consider. **~ de faire,** consider doing.

envoi /ɑ̃vwa/ *n.m.* dispatch; (*paquet*) consignment.

envol /ɑ̃vɔl/ *n.m.* flight; (*d'avion*) take-off.

envol|er (s') /(s)ɑ̃vɔle/ *v. pr.* fly away; (*avion*) take off; (*papiers*) blow away.

envoûter /ɑ̃vute/ *v.t.* bewitch.

envoyé, ~e /ɑ̃vwaje/ *n.m., f.* envoy; (*de journal*) correspondent.

envoyer† /ɑ̃vwaje/ *v.t.* send; (*lancer*) throw. **~ promener qn.,** give s.o. the brush-off.

enzyme /ɑ̃zim/ *n.f.* enzyme.

épagneul, ~e /epaɲœl/ *n.m., f.* spaniel.

épais, ~se /epɛ, -s/ *a.* thick. **~seur** /-sœr/ *n.f.* thickness.

épaissir /epesir/ *v.t./i.,* **s'~** *v. pr.* thicken.

épanch|er (s') /(s)epɑ̃ʃe/ *v. pr.* pour out one's feelings; (*liquide*) pour out. **~ement** *n.m.* outpouring.

épanoui /epanwi/ *a.* (*joyeux*) beaming, radiant.

épan|ouir (s') /(s)epanwir/ *v. pr.* (*fleur*) open out; (*visage*) beam; (*personne*) blossom. **~ouissement** *n.m.* (*éclat*) blossoming, full bloom.

épargne /eparɲ/ *n.f.* saving; (*somme*) savings. **caisse d'~,** savings bank.

épargn|er /eparɲe/ *v.t./i.* save; (*ne pas tuer*) spare. **~er qch. à qn.,** spare s.o. sth. **~ant, ~ante** *n.m., f.* saver.

éparpiller /eparpije/ *v.t.* scatter. **s'~** *v. pr.* scatter; (*fig.*) dissipate one's efforts.

épars, ~e /epar, -s/ *a.* scattered.

épat|er /epate/ *v.t.* (*fam.*) amaze. **~ant, ~ante** *a.* (*fam.*) amazing.

épaule /epol/ *n.f.* shoulder.

épauler /epole/ *v.t.* (*arme*) raise; (*aider*) support.

épave /epav/ *n.f.* wreck.

épée /epe/ *n.f.* sword.

épeler /ɛple/ *v.t.* spell.

éperdu /epɛrdy/ *a.* wild, frantic. **~ment** *adv.* wildly, frantically.

éperon /eprɔ̃/ *n.m.* spur. **~ner** /-ɔne/ *v.t.* spur (on).

épervier /epɛrvje/ *n.m.* sparrowhawk.

éphémère /efemɛr/ *a.* ephemeral.

éphéméride /efemerid/ *n.f.* tear-off calendar.

épi /epi/ *n.m.* (*de blé*) ear. **~ de cheveux,** tuft of hair.

épic|e /epis/ *n.f.* spice. **~é** *a.* spicy. **~er** *v.t.* spice.

épic|ier, ~ière /episje, -jɛr/ *n.m., f.* grocer. **~erie** *n.f.* grocery shop; (*produits*) groceries.

épidémie /epidemi/ *n.f.* epidemic.

épiderme /epidɛrm/ *n.m.* skin.

épier /epje/ *v.t.* spy on.

épilep|sie /epilɛpsi/ n.f. epilepsy. **~tique** a. & n.m./f. epileptic.

épiler /epile/ v.t. remove unwanted hair from; (sourcils) pluck.

épilogue /epilɔg/ n.m. epilogue; (fig.) outcome.

épinard /epinar/ n.m. (plante) spinach. **~s**, (nourriture) spinach.

épin|e /epin/ n.f. thorn, prickle; (d'animal) prickle, spine. **~e dorsale**, backbone. **~eux, ~euse** a. thorny.

épingl|e /epɛ̃gl/ n.f. pin. **~e de nourrice, ~e de sûreté**, safety-pin. **~er** v.t. pin; (arrêter: fam.) nab.

épique /epik/ a. epic.

épisod|e /epizɔd/ n.m. episode. **à ~es**, serialized. **~ique** a. occasional.

épitaphe /epitaf/ n.f. epitaph.

épithète /epitɛt/ n.f. epithet.

épître /epitr/ n.f. epistle.

éploré /eplɔre/ a. tearful.

épluche-légumes /eplyʃlegym/ n.m. invar. (potato) peeler.

épluch|er /eplyʃe/ v.t. peel; (examiner: fig.) scrutinize. **~age** n.m. peeling; (fig.) scrutiny. **~ure** n.f. piece of peel ou peeling. **~ures** n.f. pl. peelings.

épong|e /epɔ̃ʒ/ n.f. sponge. **~er** v.t. (liquide) sponge up; (surface) sponge (down); (front) mop; (dettes) wipe out.

épopée /epɔpe/ n.f. epic.

époque /epɔk/ n.f. time, period. **à l'~**, at the time. **d'~**, period.

épouse /epuz/ n.f. wife.

épouser [1] /epuze/ v.t. marry.

épouser [2] /epuze/ v.t. (forme, idée) assume, embrace, adopt.

épousseter /epuste/ v.t. dust.

époustouflant, ~e /epustuflɑ̃, -t/ a. (fam.) staggering.

épouvantable /epuvɑ̃tabl/ a. appalling.

épouvantail /epuvɑ̃taj/ n.m. scarecrow.

épouvant|e /epuvɑ̃t/ n.f. terror. **~er** v.t. terrify.

époux /epu/ n.m. husband. **les ~**, the married couple.

éprendre (s') /(s)eprɑ̃dr/ v. pr. **s'~ de**, fall in love with.

épreuve /eprœv/ n.f. test; (sport) event; (malheur) ordeal; (photo.) print; (d'imprimerie) proof. **mettre à l'~**, put to the test.

éprouvé /epruve/ a. (well-)proven.

éprouv|er /epruve/ v.t. test; (ressentir) experience; (affliger) distress. **~ant, ~ante** a. testing.

éprouvette /epruvɛt/ n.f. test-tube. **bébé-~**, test-tube baby.

épuis|er /epɥize/ v.t. (fatiguer, user) exhaust. **s'~er** v. pr. become exhausted. **~é** a. exhausted; (livre) out of print. **~ement** n.m. exhaustion.

épuisette /epɥizɛt/ n.f. fishing-net.

épur|er /epyre/ v.t. purify; (pol.) purge. **~ation** n.f. purification; (pol.) purge.

équat|eur /ekwatœr/ n.m. equator. **~orial** (m. pl. **~oriaux**) a. equatorial.

équation /ekwɑsjɔ̃/ n.f. equation.

équerre /ekɛr/ n.f. (set) square. **d'~**, square.

équilibr|e /ekilibr/ n.m. balance. **être** ou **se tenir en ~e**, (personne) balance; (objet) be balanced. **~é** a. well-balanced. **~er** v.t. balance. **s'~er** v. pr. (forces etc.) counterbalance each other.

équilibriste /ekilibrist/ n.m./f. tightrope walker.

équinoxe /ekinɔks/ n.m. equinox.

équipage /ekipaʒ/ n.m. crew.

équipe /ekip/ n.f. team. **~ de nuit/ jour**, night/day shift.

équipé /ekipe/ a. **bien/mal ~**, well/ poorly equipped.

équipée /ekipe/ n.f. escapade.

équipement /ekipmɑ̃/ n.m. equipment. **~s**, (installations) amenities, facilities.

équiper /ekipe/ v.t. equip (de, with). **s'~** v. pr. equip o.s.

équip|ier, ~ière /ekipje, -jɛr/ n.m., f. team member.

équitable /ekitabl/ a. fair. **~ment** /-əmɑ̃/ adv. fairly.

équitation /ekitɑsjɔ̃/ n.f. (horse-)riding.

équité /ekite/ n.f. equity.

équivalen|t, ~te /ekivalɑ̃, -t/ a. equivalent. **~ce** n.f. equivalence.

équivaloir /ekivalwar/ v.i. **~ à**, be equivalent to.

équivoque /ekivɔk/ a. equivocal; (louche) questionable. ● n.f. ambiguity.

érable /erabl/ n.m. maple.

érafl|er /erafle/ v.t. scratch. **~ure** n.f. scratch.

éraillé /eraje/ a. (voix) raucous.

ère /ɛr/ n.f. era.

érection /erɛksjɔ̃/ *n.f.* erection.

éreinter /erɛte/ *v.t.* exhaust; (*fig.*) criticize severely.

ergoter /ɛrgɔte/ *v.i.* quibble.

ériger /eriʒe/ *v.t.* erect. **(s')~ en,** set (o.s.) up as.

ermite /ɛrmit/ *n.m.* hermit.

éroder /erɔde/ *v.t.* erode.

érosion /erozjɔ̃/ *n.f.* erosion.

éroti|que /erɔtik/ *a.* erotic. **~sme** *n.m.* eroticism.

errer /ɛre/ *v.i.* wander.

erreur /ɛrœr/ *n.f.* mistake, error. **dans l'~,** mistaken. **par ~,** by mistake. **~ judiciaire,** miscarriage of justice.

erroné /erɔne/ *a.* erroneous.

ersatz /ɛrzats/ *n.m.* ersatz.

érudit, ~e /erydi, -t/ *a.* scholarly. ● *n.m., f.* scholar. **~ion** /-sjɔ̃/ *n.f.* scholarship.

éruption /erypsjɔ̃/ *n.f.* eruption; (*méd.*) rash.

es /ɛ/ *voir* être.

escabeau (*pl.* **~x**) /ɛskabo/ *n.m.* step-ladder; (*tabouret*) stool.

escadre /ɛskadr/ *n.f.* (*naut.*) squadron.

escadrille /ɛskadrij/ *n.f.* (*aviat.*) flight, squadron.

escadron /ɛskadrɔ̃/ *n.m.* (*mil.*) squadron.

escalad|e /ɛskalad/ *n.f.* climbing; (*pol., comm.*) escalation. **~er** *v.t.* climb.

escalator /ɛskalatɔr/ *n.m.* (P.) escalator.

escale /ɛskal/ *n.f.* (*d'avion*) stopover; (*port*) port of call. **faire ~ à,** (*avion, passager*) stop over at; (*navire, passager*) put in at.

escalier /ɛskalje/ *n.m.* stairs. **~ mécanique** *ou* **roulant,** escalator.

escalope /ɛskalɔp/ *n.f.* escalope.

escamotable /ɛskamɔtabl/ *a.* (*techn.*) retractable.

escamoter /ɛskamɔte/ *v.t.* make vanish; (*éviter*) dodge.

escargot /ɛskargo/ *n.m.* snail.

escarmouche /ɛskarmuʃ/ *n.f.* skirmish.

escarpé /ɛskarpe/ *a.* steep.

escarpin /ɛskarpɛ̃/ *n.m.* pump.

escient /ɛsjɑ̃/ *n.m.* **à bon ~,** with good reason.

esclaffer (s') /(s)ɛsklafe/ *v. pr.* guffaw, burst out laughing.

esclandre /ɛsklɑ̃dr/ *n.m.* scene.

esclav|e /ɛsklav/ *n.m./f.* slave. **~age** *n.m.* slavery.

escompte /ɛskɔ̃t/ *n.m.* discount.

escompter /ɛskɔ̃te/ *v.t.* expect; (*comm.*) discount.

escort|e /ɛskɔrt/ *n.f.* escort. **~er** *v.t.* escort. **~eur** *n.m.* escort (ship).

escouade /ɛskwad/ *n.f.* squad.

escrim|e /ɛskrim/ *n.f.* fencing. **~eur, ~euse** *n.m., f.* fencer.

escrimer (s') /(s)ɛskrime/ *v. pr.* struggle.

escroc /ɛskro/ *n.m.* swindler.

escroqu|er /ɛskrɔke/ *v.t.* swindle. **~er qch. à qn.,** swindle s.o. out of sth. **~erie** *n.f.* swindle.

espace /ɛspas/ *n.m.* space. **~s verts,** gardens, parks.

espacer /ɛspase/ *v.t.* space out. **s'~** *v. pr.* become less frequent.

espadrille /ɛspadrij/ *n.f.* rope sandals.

Espagne /ɛspaɲ/ *n.f.* Spain.

espagnol, ~e /ɛspaɲɔl/ *a.* Spanish. ● *n.m., f.* Spaniard. ● *n.m.* (*lang.*) Spanish.

espagnolette /ɛspaɲɔlɛt/ *n.f.* (window) catch.

espèce /ɛspɛs/ *n.f.* kind, sort; (*race*) species. **~s,** (*argent*) cash. **~ d'idiot/de brute/etc.!,** you idiot/ brute/*etc.*!

espérance /ɛsperɑ̃s/ *n.f.* hope.

espérer /ɛspere/ *v.t.* hope for. **~ faire/que,** hope to do/that. ● *v.i.* hope. **~ en,** have faith in.

espiègle /ɛspjɛgl/ *a.* mischievous.

espion, ~ne /ɛspjɔ̃, -jɔn/ *n.m., f.* spy.

espionn|er /ɛspjɔne/ *v.t./i.* spy (on). **~age** *n.m.* espionage, spying.

esplanade /ɛsplanad/ *n.f.* esplanade.

espoir /ɛspwar/ *n.m.* hope.

esprit /ɛspri/ *n.m.* spirit; (*intellect*) mind; (*humour*) wit. **perdre l'~,** lose one's mind. **reprendre ses ~s,** come to. **vouloir faire de l'~,** try to be witty.

Esquimau, ~de (*m. pl.* **~x**) /ɛskimo, -d/ *n.m., f.* Eskimo.

esquinter /ɛskɛ̃te/ *v.t.* (*fam.*) ruin.

esquiss|e /ɛskis/ *n.f.* sketch; (*fig.*) suggestion. **~er** *v.t.* sketch; (*geste etc.*) make an attempt at.

esquiv|e /ɛskiv/ *n.f.* (*sport*) dodge. **~er** *v.t.* dodge. **s'~er** *v. pr.* slip away.

essai /esɛ/ *n.m.* testing; (*épreuve*) test, trial; (*tentative*) try; (*article*) essay. **à l'~,** on trial.

essaim /esɛ̃/ *n.m.* swarm. **~er** /eseme/ *v.i.* swarm; (*fig.*) spread.

essayage /esɛjaʒ/ *n.m.* (*de vêtement*) fitting. **salon d'~**, fitting room.

essayer /eseje/ *v.t./i.* try; (*vêtement*) try (on); (*voiture etc.*) try (out). **~ de faire**, try to do.

essence [1] /esɑ̃s/ *n.f.* (*carburant*) petrol; (*Amer.*) gas.

essence [2] /esɑ̃s/ *n.f.* (*nature, extrait*) essence.

essentiel, ~le /esɑ̃sjɛl/ *a.* essential. ● *n.m.* **l'~**, the main thing; (*quantité*) the main part. **~lement** *adv.* essentially.

essieu (*pl.* **~x**) /esjø/ *n.m.* axle.

essor /esɔr/ *n.m.* expansion. **prendre son ~**, expand.

essorer /esɔre/ *v.t.* (*linge*) spin-dry; (*en tordant*) wring. **~euse** *n.f.* spindrier.

essouffler *v.t.* make breathless. **s'~** *v. pr.* get out of breath.

essuyer [1] /esɥije/ *v.t.* wipe. **s'~uyer** *v. pr.* dry *ou* wipe o.s. **~uie-glace** *n.m. invar.* windscreen wiper; (*Amer.*) windshield wiper. **~uie-mains** *n.m. invar.* hand-towel.

essuyer [2] /esɥije/ *v.t.* (*subir*) suffer.

est [1] /ɛ/ *voir* être.

est [2] /ɛst/ *n.m.* east. ● *a. invar.* east; (*partie*) eastern; (*direction*) easterly.

estampe /ɛstɑ̃p/ *n.f.* print.

estampille /ɛstɑ̃pij/ *n.f.* stamp.

esthète /ɛstɛt/ *n.m./f.* aesthete.

esthéticienne /ɛstetisjɛn/ *n.f.* beautician.

esthétique /ɛstetik/ *a.* aesthetic.

estimable /ɛstimabl/ *a.* worthy.

estimation /ɛstimasjɔ̃/ *n.f.* valuation.

estime /ɛstim/ *n.f.* esteem.

estimer /ɛstime/ *v.t.* (*objet*) value; (*calculer*) estimate; (*respecter*) esteem; (*considérer*) consider. **~ation** *n.f.* valuation; (*calcul*) estimation.

estival (*m. pl.* **~aux**) /ɛstival, -o/ *a.* summer. **~ant, ~ante** *n.m., f.* summer visitor, holiday-maker.

estomac /ɛstɔma/ *n.m.* stomach.

estomaqué /ɛstɔmake/ *a.* (*fam.*) stunned.

estomper (s') /(s)ɛstɔpe/ *v. pr.* become blurred.

estrade /ɛstrad/ *n.f.* platform.

estragon /ɛstragɔ̃/ *n.m.* tarragon.

estropier /ɛstrɔpje/ *v.t.* cripple; (*fig.*) mangle. **~ié, ~iée** *n.m., f.* cripple.

estuaire /ɛstɥɛr/ *n.m.* estuary.

estudiantin, ~e /ɛstydjɑ̃tɛ̃, -in/ *a.* student.

esturgeon /ɛstyrʒɔ̃/ *n.m.* sturgeon.

et /e/ *conj.* and. **et moi/lui**/*etc.*?, what about me/him/*etc.*?

étable /etabl/ *n.f.* cow-shed.

établi [1] /etabli/ *a.* established. **un fait bien ~**, a well-established fact.

établi [2] /etabli/ *n.m.* work-bench.

établir /etablir/ *v.t.* establish; (*liste, facture*) draw up; (*personne, camp, record*) set up. **s'~** *v. pr.* (*personne*) establish o.s. **s'~ épicier**/*etc.*, set (o.s.) up as a grocer/*etc.* **s'~ à son compte**, set up on one's own.

établissement /etablismɑ̃/ *n.m.* (*bâtiment, institution*) establishment.

étage /etaʒ/ *n.m.* floor, storey; (*de fusée*) stage. **à l'~**, upstairs. **au premier ~**, on the first floor.

étager (s') /(s)etaʒe/ *v. pr.* rise at different levels.

étagère /etaʒɛr/ *n.f.* shelf; (*meuble*) shelving unit.

étai /etɛ/ *n.m.* prop, buttress.

étain /etɛ̃/ *n.m.* pewter.

étais, était /etɛ/ *voir* être.

étal (*pl.* **~s**) /etal/ *n.m.* stall.

étalage /etalaʒ/ *n.m.* display; (*vitrine*) shop-window. **faire ~ de**, show off **~iste** *n.m./f.* windowdresser.

étaler /etale/ *v.t.* spread; (*journal*) spread (out); (*vacances*) stagger; (*exposer*) display. **s'~** *v. pr.* (*s'étendre*) stretch out; (*tomber*. *fam.*) fall flat. **s'~ sur**, (*paiement*) be spread over.

étalon /etalɔ̃/ *n.m.* (*cheval*) stallion; (*modèle*) standard.

étanche /etɑ̃ʃ/ *a.* watertight; (*montre*) waterproof.

étancher /etɑ̃ʃe/ *v.t.* (*soif*) quench; (*sang*) stem.

étang /etɑ̃/ *n.m.* pond.

étant /etɑ̃/ *voir* être.

étape /etap/ *n.f.* stage; (*lieu d'arrêt*) stopover.

état /eta/ *n.m.* state; (*liste*) statement; (*métier*) profession; (*nation*) State. **en bon/mauvais ~**, in good/bad condition. **en ~ de**, in a position to. **hors d'~ de**, not in a position to. **en ~ de marche**, in working order. **~ civil**, civil status. **~-major** (*pl.* **~s-majors**) *n.m.* (*officiers*) staff.

faire ~ de, (*citer*) mention. **être dans tous ses ~s,** be in a state. **~ des lieux,** inventory.

étatisé /etatize/ *a.* State-controlled.

États-Unis /etazyni/ *n.m. pl.* **(d'Amérique),** United States (of America).

étau (*pl.* **~x**) /eto/ *n.m.* vice.

étayer /eteje/ *v.t.* prop up.

été¹ /ete/ *voir* être.

été² /ete/ *n.m.* summer.

étein|dre† /etɛ̃dr/ *v.t.* put out, extinguish; (*lumière, radio*) turn off. **s'~dre** *v. pr.* (*feu*) go out; (*mourir*) die. **~t, ~te** /etɛ̃, -t/ *a.* (*feu*) out; (*volcan*) extinct.

étendard /etɑ̃dar/ *n.m.* standard.

étendre /etɑ̃dr/ *v.t.* spread; (*journal, nappe*) spread out; (*bras, jambes*) stretch (out); (*linge*) hang out; (*agrandir*) extend. **s'~** *v. pr.* (*s'allonger*) stretch out; (*se propager*) spread; (*plaine etc.*) stretch. **s'~ sur,** (*sujet*) dwell on.

étendu, ~e /etɑ̃dy/ *a.* extensive. ● *n.f.* area; (*d'eau*) stretch; (*importance*) extent.

éternel, ~le /etɛrnɛl/ *a.* eternal. **~lement** *adv.* eternally.

éterniser (s') /(s)etɛrnize/ *v. pr.* (*durer*) drag on.

éternité /etɛrnite/ *n.f.* eternity.

étern|uer /etɛrnɥe/ *v.i.* sneeze. **~uement** /-ymɑ̃/ *n.m.* sneeze.

êtes /ɛt/ *voir* être.

éthique /etik/ *a.* ethical. ● *n.f.* ethics.

ethn|ie /ɛtni/ *n.f.* ethnic group. **~ique** *a.* ethnic.

éthylisme /etilism/ *n.m.* alcoholism.

étinceler /etɛ̃sle/ *v.i.* sparkle.

étincelle /etɛ̃sɛl/ *n.f.* spark.

étioler (s') /(s)etjɔle/ *v. pr.* wilt.

étiqueter /etikte/ *v.t.* label.

étiquette /etikɛt/ *n.f.* label; (*protocole*) etiquette.

étirer /etire/ *v.t.,* **s'~** *v. pr.* stretch.

étoffe /etɔf/ *n.f.* fabric.

étoffer /etɔfe/ *v.t.,* **s'~** *v. pr.* fill out.

étoil|e /etwal/ *n.f.* star. **à la belle ~e,** in the open. **~e de mer,** starfish. **~é** *a.* starry.

étonn|er /etɔne/ *v.t.* amaze. **s'~er** *v. pr.* be amazed (**de,** at). **~ant, ~ante** *a.* amazing. **~ement** *n.m.* amazement.

étouffée /etufe/ *n.f.* **cuire à l'~,** braise.

étouff|er /etufe/ *v.t./i.* suffocate; (*sentiment, révolte*) stifle; (*feu*) smother; (*bruit*) muffle. **on ~e,** it is stifling. **s'~er** *v. pr.* suffocate; (*en mangeant*) choke. **~ant, ~ante** *a.* stifling.

étourd|i, ~ie /eturdi/ *a.* unthinking, scatter-brained. ● *n.m., f.* scatter-brain. **~erie** /-dri/ *n.f.* thoughtlessness; (*acte*) thoughtless act.

étourd|ir /eturdir/ *v.t.* stun; (*griser*) make dizzy. **~issant, ~issante** *a.* stunning. **~issement** *n.m.* (*syncope*) dizzy spell.

étourneau (*pl.* **~x**) /eturno/ *n.m.* starling.

étrang|e /etrɑ̃ʒ/ *a.* strange. **~ment** *adv.* strangely. **~té** *n.f.* strangeness.

étrang|er, ~ère /etrɑ̃ʒe, -ɛr/ *a.* strange, unfamiliar; (*d'un autre pays*) foreign. ● *n.m., f.* foreigner; (*inconnu*) stranger. **à l'~er,** abroad. **de l'~er,** from abroad.

étrangler /etrɑ̃gle/ *v.t.* strangle; (*col*) stifle. **s'~** *v. pr.* choke.

être† /ɛtr/ *v.i.* be. ● *v. aux.* (*avec aller, sortir, etc.*) have. **~ donné/fait par,** (*passif*) be given/done by. ● *n.m.* (*personne, créature*) being. **~ humain,** human being. **~ médecin/tailleur/***etc.***,** be a doctor/a tailor/*etc.* **~ à qn.,** be the s.o.'s. **c'est à faire,** it needs to be *ou* should be done. **est-ce qu'il travaille?,** is he working?, does he work? **vous travaillez, n'est-ce pas?,** you are working, aren't you? **il est deux heures/***etc.***,** it is two o'clock/*etc.* **nous sommes le six mai,** it is the sixth of May.

étrein|dre /etrɛ̃dr/ *v.t.* grasp; (*ami*) embrace. **~te** /-ɛ̃t/ *n.f.* grasp; embrace.

étrenner /etrene/ *v.t.* use for the first time.

étrennes /etrɛn/ *n.f. pl.* (*cadeau*) New Year's gift.

étrier /etrije/ *n.m.* stirrup.

étriqué /etrike/ *a.* tight; (*fig.*) small-minded.

étroit, ~e /etrwa, -t/ *a.* narrow; (*vêtement*) tight; (*liens, surveillance*) close. **à l'~,** cramped. **~ement** /-tmɑ̃/ *adv.* closely. **~esse** /-tɛs/ *n.f.* narrowness.

étude /etyd/ *n.f.* study; (*bureau*) office. **(salle d')~,** (*scol.*) prep room; (*scol., Amer.*) study hall. **à l'~,**

under consideration. **faire des ~s (de)**, study.

étudiant, ~e /etydjɑ̃, -t/ *n.m., f.* student.

étudier /etydje/ *v.t./i.* study.

étui /etɥi/ *n.m.* case.

étuve /etyv/ *n.f.* steamroom. **quelle ~!**, it's like a hothouse in here.

étuvée /etyve/ *n.f.* **cuire à l'~**, braise.

etymologie /etimɔlɔʒi/ *n.f.* etymology.

eu, eue /y/ *voir* avoir.

eucalyptus /økaliptys/ *n.m.* eucalyptus.

euphémisme /øfemism/ *n.m.* euphemism.

euphorie /øfɔri/ *n.f.* euphoria.

Europe /ørɔp/ *n.f.* Europe.

européen, ~ne /ørɔpeɛ̃, -eɛn/ *a. & n.m., f.* European.

euthanasie /øtanazi/ *n.f.* euthanasia.

eux /ø/ *pron.* they; (*complément*) them. **~-mêmes** *pron.* themselves.

évac|uer /evakɥe/ *v.t.* evacuate. **~uation** *n.f.* evacuation.

évad|er (s') /(s)evade/ *v. pr.* escape. **~é, ~ée** *a.* escaped; *n.m., f.* escaped prisoner.

éval|uer /evalɥe/ *v.t.* assess. **~uation** *n.f.* assessment.

évang|ile /evɑ̃ʒil/ *n.m.* gospel. **l'Évangile**, the Gospel. **~élique** *a.* evangelical.

évan|ouir (s') /(s)evanwir/ *v. pr.* faint; (*disparaître*) vanish. **~ouissement** *n.m.* (*syncope*) fainting fit.

évapor|er /evapɔre/ *v.t.i.*, **s'~er** *v. pr.* evaporate. **~ation** *n.f.* evaporation.

évasi|f, ~ve /evazif, -v/ *a.* evasive.

évasion /evazjɔ̃/ *n.f.* escape; (*par le rêve etc.*) escapism.

éveil /evɛj/ *n.m.* awakening. **donner l'~ à**, arouse the suspicions of. **en ~**, alert.

éveill|er /eveje/ *v.t.* awake(n); (*susciter*) arouse. **s'~er** *v. pr.* awake(n); be aroused. **~é** *a.* awake; (*intelligent*) alert.

événement /evɛnmɑ̃/ *n.m.* event.

éventail /evɑ̃taj/ *n.m.* fan; (*gamme*) range.

éventaire /evɑ̃tɛr/ *n.m.* stall, stand.

éventé /evɑ̃te/ *a.* (*gâté*) stale.

éventrer /evɑ̃tre/ *v.t.* (*sac etc.*) rip open.

éventualité /evɑ̃tɥalite/ *n.f.* possibility. **dans cette ~**, in that event.

éventuel, ~le /evɑ̃tɥɛl/ *a.* possible. **~lement** *adv.* possibly.

évêque /evɛk/ *n.m.* bishop.

évertuer (s') /(s)evɛrtɥe/ *v. pr.* **s'~ à**, struggle hard to.

éviction /eviksjɔ̃/ *n.f.* eviction.

évidemment /evidamɑ̃/ *adv.* obviously; (*bien sûr*) of course.

évidence /evidɑ̃s/ *n.f.* obviousness; (*fait*) obvious fact. **être en ~**, be conspicuous. **mettre en ~**, (*fait*) highlight.

évident, ~e /evidɑ̃, -t/ *a.* obvious, evident.

évider /evide/ *v.t.* hollow out.

évier /evje/ *n.m.* sink.

évincer /evɛ̃se/ *v.t.* oust.

éviter /evite/ *v.t.* avoid (**de faire**, doing). **~ à qn.**, (*dérangement etc.*) spare s.o.

évoca|teur ~trice /evɔkatœr, -tris/ *a.* evocative.

évocation /evɔkasjɔ̃/ *n.f.* evocation.

évolué /evɔlɥe/ *a.* highly developed.

évol|uer /evɔlɥe/ *v.i.* develop; (*se déplacer*) move, manœuvre; (*Amer.*) maneuver. **~ution** *n.f.* development; (*d'une espèce*) evolution; (*déplacement*) movement.

évoquer /evɔke/ *v.t.* call to mind, evoke.

ex- /ɛks/ *préf.* ex-.

exacerber /ɛgzasɛrbe/ *v.t.* exacerbate.

exact, ~e /ɛgza(kt), -akt/ *a.* exact, accurate; (*correct*) correct; (*personne*) punctual. **~ement** /-ktamɑ̃/ *adv.* exactly. **~itude** /-ktityd/ *n.f.* exactness; punctuality.

ex aequo /ɛgzeko/ *adv.* (*classer*) equal. **être ~**, be equally placed.

exagéré /ɛgzaʒere/ *a.* excessive.

exagér|er /ɛgzaʒere/ *v.t./i.* exaggerate; (*abuser*) go too far. **~ation** *n.f.* exaggeration.

exaltation /ɛgzaltɑsjɔ̃/ *n.f.* elation.

exalté, ~e /ɛgzalte/ *n.m., f.* fanatic.

exalter /ɛgzalte/ *v.t.* excite; (*glorifier*) exalt.

examen /ɛgzamɛ̃/ *n.m.* examination; (*scol.*) exam(ination).

examin|er /ɛgzamine/ *v.t.* examine. **~ateur, ~atrice** *n.m., f.* examiner.

exaspér|er /ɛgzaspere/ *v.t.* exasperate. **~ation** *n.f.* exasperation.

exaucer /ɛgzose/ v.t. grant; (*personne*) grant the wish(es) of.

excavateur /ɛkskavatœr/ n.m. digger.

excavation /ɛkskavɑsjɔ̃/ n.f. excavation.

excédent /ɛksedɑ̃/ n.m. surplus. ~ de bagages, excess luggage. ~ de la balance commerciale, trade surplus. ~aire /-tɛr/ a. excess, surplus.

excéder¹ /ɛksede/ v.t. (*dépasser*) exceed.

excéder² /ɛksede/ v.t. (*agacer*) irritate.

excellen|t, ~te /ɛkselɑ̃, -t/ a. excellent. ~ce n.f. excellence.

exceller /ɛksele/ v.i. excel (dans, in).

excentri|que /ɛksɑ̃trik/ a. & n.m./f. eccentric. ~cité n.f. eccentricity.

excepté /ɛksɛpte/ a. & prép. except.

excepter /ɛksɛpte/ v.t. except.

exception /ɛksɛpsjɔ̃/ n.f. exception. à l'~ de, except for. d'~, exceptional. faire ~, be an exception. ~nel, ~nelle /-jɔnɛl/ a. exceptional. ~nellement /-jɔnɛlmɑ̃/ adv. exceptionally.

excès /ɛksɛ/ n.m. excess. ~ de vitesse, speeding.

excessi|f, ~ve /ɛksesif, -v/ a. excessive. ~vement adv. excessively.

excitant /ɛksitɑ̃/ n.m. stimulant.

excit|er /ɛksite/ v.t. excite; (*encourager*) exhort (à, to); (*irriter: fam.*) annoy. ~ation n.f. excitement.

exclam|er (s') /(s)ɛksklame/ v. pr. exclaim. ~ation n.f. exclamation.

exclu|re† /ɛksklyr/ v.t. exclude; (*expulser*) expel; (*empêcher*) preclude. ~sion n.f. exclusion.

exclusi|f, ~ve /ɛksklyzif, -v/ a. exclusive. ~vement adv. exclusively. ~vité n.f. (*comm.*) exclusive rights. en ~vité à, (*film*) (showing) exclusively at.

excrément(s) /ɛkskremɑ̃/ n.m. (pl.). excrement.

excroissance /ɛkskrwasɑ̃s/ n.f. (out)growth, excrescence.

excursion /ɛkskyrsjɔ̃/ n.f. excursion; (à pied) hike.

excuse /ɛkskyz/ n.f. excuse. ~s, apology. faire des ~s, apologize.

excuser /ɛkskyze/ v.t. excuse. s'~ v. pr. apologize (de, for). je m'excuse, (fam.) excuse me.

exécrable /ɛgzekrabl/ a. abominable.

exécrer /ɛgzekre/ v.t. loathe.

exécut|er /ɛgzekyte/ v.t. carry out, execute; (*mus.*) perform; (*tuer*) execute. ~ion /-sjɔ̃/ n.f. execution; (*mus.*) performance.

exécuti|f, ~ve /ɛgzekytif, -v/ a. & n.m. (*pol.*) executive.

exemplaire /ɛgzɑ̃plɛr/ a. exemplary. ● n.m. copy.

exemple /ɛgzɑ̃pl/ n.m. example. par ~, for example. donner l'~, set an example.

exempt, ~e /ɛgzɑ̃, -t/ a. ~ de, exempt from.

exempt|er /ɛgzɑ̃te/ v.t. exempt (de, from). ~ion /-psjɔ̃/ n.f. exemption.

exercer /ɛgzɛrse/ v.t. exercise; (*influence, contrôle*) exert; (*métier*) work at; (*former*) train, exercise. s'~ (à), practise.

exercice /ɛgzɛrsis/ n.m. exercise; (*mil.*) drill; (de métier) practice. en ~, in office; (*médecin*) in practice.

exhaler /ɛgzale/ v.t. emit.

exhausti|f, ~ve /ɛgzostif, -v/ a. exhaustive.

exhiber /ɛgzibe/ v.t. exhibit.

exhibitionniste /ɛgzibisjɔnist/ n.m./f. exhibitionist.

exhorter /ɛgzɔrte/ v.t. exhort (à, to).

exigence /ɛgziʒɑ̃s/ n.f. demand.

exig|er /ɛgziʒe/ v.t. demand. ~eant, ~eante a. demanding.

exigu, ~ë /ɛgzigy/ a. tiny.

exil /ɛgzil/ n.m. exile. ~é, ~ée n.m., f. exile. ~er v.t. exile. s'~er v. pr. go into exile.

existence /ɛgzistɑ̃s/ n.f. existence.

exist|er /ɛgziste/ v.i. exist. ~ant, ~ante a. existing.

exode /ɛgzɔd/ n.m. exodus.

exonér|er /ɛgzɔnere/ v.t. exempt (de, from). ~ation n.f. exemption.

exorbitant, ~e /ɛgzɔrbitɑ̃, -t/ a. exorbitant.

exorciser /ɛgzɔrsize/ v.t. exorcize.

exotique /ɛgzɔtik/ a. exotic.

expansi|f, ~ve /ɛkspɑ̃sif, -v/ a. expansive.

expansion /ɛkspɑ̃sjɔ̃/ n.f. expansion.

expatr|ier (s') /(s)ɛkspatrije/ v. pr. leave one's country. ~ié, ~iée n.m., f. expatriate.

expectative /ɛkspɛktativ/ n.f. dans l'~, still waiting.

expédient, ~e /ɛkspedjɑ̃, -t/ a. & n.m. expedient. vivre d'~s, live by one's wits. user d'~s, resort to expedients.

expéd|ier /ɛkspedje/ v.t. send, dispatch; (*tâche: péj.*) dispatch. **~iteur**, **~itrice** n.m., f. sender. **~ition** n.f. dispatch; (*voyage*) expedition.

expéditi|f, **~ve** /ɛkspeditif, -v/ a. quick.

expérience /ɛksperjɑ̃s/ n.f. experience; (*scientifique*) experiment.

expérimenté /ɛksperimɑ̃te/ a. experienced.

expériment|er /ɛksperimɑ̃te/ v.t. test, experiment with. **~al** (m. pl. **~aux**) a. experimental. **~ation** n.f. experimentation.

expert, **~e** /ɛkspɛr, -t/ a. expert. ● n.m. expert; (*d'assurances*) valuer; (*Amer.*) appraiser. **~-comptable** (pl. **~s-comptables**) n.m. accountant.

expertis|e /ɛkspɛrtiz/ n.f. expert appraisal. **~er** v.t. appraise.

expier /ɛkspje/ v.t. atone for.

expir|er /ɛkspire/ v.i. breathe out; (*finir, mourir*) expire. **~ation** n.f. expiry.

explicati|f, **~ve** /ɛksplikatif, -v/ a. explanatory.

explication /ɛksplikasjɔ̃/ n.f. explanation; (*fig.*) discussion; (*scol.*) commentary. **~ de texte**, (*scol.*) literary commentary.

explicite /ɛksplisit/ a. explicit.

expliquer /ɛksplike/ v.t. explain. **s'~** v. pr. explain o.s.; (*discuter*) discuss things; (*être compréhensible*) be understandable.

exploit /ɛksplwa/ n.m. exploit.

exploitant /ɛksplwatɑ̃/ n.m. **~ (agricole)**, farmer.

exploit|er /ɛksplwate/ v.t. (*personne*) exploit; (*ferme*) run; (*champs*) work. **~ation** n.f. exploitation; running; working; (*affaire*) concern. **~eur**, **~euse** n.m., f. exploiter.

explor|er /ɛksplɔre/ v.t. explore. **~ateur**, **~atrice** n.m., f. explorer. **~ation** n.f. exploration.

explos|er /ɛksploze/ v.i. explode. **faire ~er**, explode; (*bâtiment*) blow up. **~ion** n.f. explosion.

explosi|f, **~ve** /ɛksplozif, -v/ a. & n.m. explosive.

export|er /ɛkspɔrte/ v.t. export. **~ateur**, **~atrice** n.m., f. exporter; a. exporting. **~ation** n.f. export.

exposant, **~e** /ɛkspozɑ̃, -t/ n.m., f. exhibitor.

exposé /ɛkspoze/ n.m. talk (*sur*, on); (*d'une action*) account. **faire l'~ de**

la situation, give an account of the situation.

expos|er /ɛkspoze/ v.t. display, show; (*expliquer*) explain; (*soumettre, mettre en danger*) endanger; (*vie*) endanger. **~é au nord**/*etc.*, facing north/*etc.* **s'~er à**, expose o.s. to.

exposition /ɛkspozisjɔ̃/ n.f. display; (*salon*) exhibition. **~ à**, exposure to.

exprès [1] /ɛksprɛ/ adv. specially; (*délibérément*) on purpose.

expr|ès [2], **~esse** /ɛksprɛs/ a. express. **~essément** adv. expressly.

exprès [3] /ɛksprɛs/ a. invar. & n.m. **lettre ~**, express letter. **(par) ~**, sent special delivery.

express /ɛksprɛs/ a. & n.m. invar. (*café*) **~**, espresso. **(train) ~**, fast train.

expressi|f, **~ve** /ɛkspresif, -v/ a. expressive.

expression /ɛkspresjɔ̃/ n.f. expression. **~ corporelle**, physical expression.

exprimer /ɛksprime/ v.t. express. **s'~** v. pr. express o.s.

expuls|er /ɛkspylse/ v.t. expel; (*locataire*) evict; (*joueur*) send off. **~ion** n.f. expulsion; eviction.

expurger /ɛkspyrʒe/ v.t. expurgate.

exquis, **~e** /ɛkski, -z/ a. exquisite.

extase /ɛkstaz/ n.f. ecstasy.

extasier (s') /(s)ɛkstazje/ v. pr. **s'~ sur**, be ecstatic about.

extensible /ɛkstɑ̃sibl/ a. expandable, extendible. **tissu ~**, stretch fabric.

extensi|f, **~ve** /ɛkstɑ̃sif, -v/ a. extensive.

extension /ɛkstɑ̃sjɔ̃/ n.f. extension; (*expansion*) expansion.

exténuer /ɛkstenɥe/ v.t. exhaust.

extérieur /ɛksterjœr/ a. outside; (*signe, gaieté*) outward; (*politique*) foreign. ● n.m. outside, exterior; (*de personne*) exterior. **à l'~ (de)**, outside. **~ement** adv. outwardly.

extérioriser /ɛksterjɔrize/ v.t. show, externalize.

extermin|er /ɛkstɛrmine/ v.t. exterminate. **~ation** n.f. extermination.

externe /ɛkstɛrn/ a. external. ● n.m./f. (*scol.*) day pupil.

extincteur /ɛkstɛ̃ktœr/ n.m. fire extinguisher.

extinction /ɛkstɛ̃ksjɔ̃/ n.f. extinction. **~ de voix**, loss of voice.

extirper /ɛkstirpe/ v.t. eradicate.

extor|quer /ɛkstɔrke/ v.t. extort. **~sion** n.f. extortion.

extra /ɛkstra/ a. invar. first-rate. ● n.m. invar. (repas) (special) treat.

extra- /ɛkstra/ préf. extra-.

extrad|er /ɛkstrade/ v.t. extradite. **~ition** n.f. extradition.

extr|aire† /ɛkstrɛr/ v.t. extract. **~action** n.f. extraction.

extrait /ɛkstrɛ/ n.m. extract.

extraordinaire /ɛkstraɔrdinɛr/ a. extraordinary.

extravagan|t, ~te /ɛkstravagã, -t/ a. extravagant. **~ce** n.f. extravagance.

extraverti, ~e /ɛkstravɛrti/ n.m., f. extrovert.

extrême /ɛkstrɛm/ a. & n.m. extreme. **E~-Orient** n.m. Far East. **~ment** adv. extremely.

extrémiste /ɛkstremist/ n.m., f. extremist.

extrémité /ɛkstremite/ n.f. extremity, end; (misère) dire straits. **~s,** (excès) extremes.

exubéran|t, ~te /ɛgzyberã, -t/ a. exuberant. **~ce** n.f. exuberance.

exulter /ɛgzylte/ v.i. exult.

exutoire /ɛgzytwar/ n.m. outlet.

F

F abrév. (franc, francs) franc, francs.
fable /fabl/ n.f. fable.
fabrique /fabrik/ n.f. factory.
fabri|quer /fabrike/ v.t. make; (industriellement) manufacture; (fig.) make up. **~cant, ~cante** n.m., f. manufacturer. **~cation** n.f. making; manufacture.
fabul|er /fabyle/ v.i. fantasize. **~ation** n.f. fantasizing.
fabuleu|x, ~se /fabylø, -z/ a. fabulous.
fac /fak/ n.f. (fam.) university.
façade /fasad/ n.f. front; (fig.) façade.
face /fas/ n.f. face; (d'un objet) side. **en ~ (de), d'en ~,** opposite. **en ~ de,** (fig.) faced with. **~ à,** facing; (fig.) faced with. **faire ~ à,** face.
facétie /fasesi/ n.f. joke.
facette /fasɛt/ n.f. facet.
fâch|er /faʃe/ v.t. anger. **se ~er** v. pr. get angry; (se brouiller) fall out. **~é** a. angry; (désolé) sorry.

fâcheu|x, ~se /faʃø, -z/ a. unfortunate.

facil|e /fasil/ a. easy; (caractère) easygoing. **~ement** adv. easily. **~ité** n.f. easiness; (aisance) ease; (aptitude) ability; (possibilité) facility. **~ités de paiement,** easy terms.

faciliter /fasilite/ v.t. facilitate.

façon /fasɔ̃/ n.f. way; (de vêtement) cut. **~s,** (chichis) fuss. **de cette ~,** in this way. **de ~ à,** so as to. **de toute ~,** anyway.

façonner /fasɔne/ v.t. shape; (faire) make.

facteur[1] /faktœr/ n.m. postman.

facteur[2] /faktœr/ n.m. (élément) factor.

factice /faktis/ a. artificial.

faction /faksjɔ̃/ n.f. faction. **de ~,** (mil.) on guard.

factur|e /faktyr/ n.f. bill; (comm.) invoice. **~er** v.t. invoice.

facultati|f, ~ve /fakyltatif, -v/ a. optional.

faculté /fakylte/ n.f. faculty; (possibilité) power; (univ.) faculty.

fade /fad/ a. insipid.

fagot /fago/ n.m. bundle of firewood.

fagoter /fagɔte/ v.t. (fam.) rig out.

faibl|e /fɛbl/ a. weak; (espoir, quantité, écart) slight; (revenu, intensité) low. ● n.m. weakling; (penchant, défaut) weakness. **~e d'esprit,** feeble-minded. **~esse** n.f. weakness. **~ir** v.i. weaken.

faïence /fajãs/ n.f. earthenware.

faille /faj/ n.f. (géog.) fault; (fig.) flaw.

faillir /fajir/ v.i. **j'ai failli acheter/** etc., I almost bought/etc.

faillite /fajit/ n.f. bankruptcy; (fig.) collapse.

faim /fɛ̃/ n.f. hunger. **avoir ~,** be hungry.

fainéant, ~e /feneã, -t/ a. idle. ● n.m., f. idler.

faire† /fɛr/ v.t. make; (activité) do; (rêve, chute, etc.) have; (dire) say. **ça fait 20 F,** that's 20 F. **ça fait 3 ans,** it's been 3 years. ● v.i. do; (paraître) look. **se ~,** v. pr. (petit etc.) make o.s.; (amis, argent) make; (illusions) have; (devenir) become. **~ du rugby/du violon/etc.,** play rugby/the violin/etc. **~ construire/ punir/etc.,** have ou get built/punished/etc. **~ pleurer/tomber/ etc.,** make cry/fall/etc. **se ~ tuer/etc.,** get killed/*etc.* **se ~ couper les cheveux**, have one's hair cut. **il fait beau/ chaud**/*etc.*, it is fine/hot/*etc.* **~ l'idiot**, play the fool. **ne ~ que pleurer**/*etc.*, (*faire continuellement*) do nothing but cry/*etc.* **ça ne fait rien**, it doesn't matter. **se ~ à**, get used to. **s'en ~**, worry. **ça se fait**, that is done. **~-part** *n.m. invar.* announcement.

fais, fait [1] /fɛ/ *voir* faire.

faisable /fəzabl/ *a.* feasible.

faisan /fəzɑ̃/ *n.m.* pheasant.

faisandé /fəzɑ̃de/ *a.* high.

faisceau (*pl.* **~x**) /fɛso/ *n.m.* (*rayon*) beam; (*fagot*) bundle.

fait [2], **~e** /fɛ, fɛt/ *a.* done; (*fromage*) ripe. **~ pour**, made for. **tout ~**, ready made. **c'est bien ~ pour toi**, it serves you right.

fait [3] /fɛ/ *n.m.* fact; (*événement*) event. **au ~ (de)**, informed (of). **de ce ~**, therefore. **du ~ de**, on account of. **~ divers**, (trivial) news item. **~ nouveau**, new development. **sur le ~**, in the act.

faîte /fɛt/ *n.m.* top; (*fig.*) peak.

faites /fɛt/ *voir* faire.

faitout /fɛtu/ *n.m.* stew-pot.

falaise /falɛz/ *n.f.* cliff.

falloir† /falwar/ *v.i.* **il faut qch./qn.**, we, you, *etc.* need sth./so. **il lui faut du pain**, he needs bread. **il faut rester**, we, you, *etc.* have to *ou* must stay. **il faut que j'y aille**, I have to *ou* must go. **il faudrait que tu partes**, you should leave. **il aurait fallu le faire**, we, you, *etc.* should have done it. **il s'en faut de beaucoup que je sois**, I am far from being. **comme il faut**, properly; *a.* proper.

falot, ~e /falo, -ɔt/ *a.* grey.

falsifier /falsifje/ *v.t.* falsify.

famélique /famelik/ *a.* starving.

fameu|x, ~se /famø, -z/ *a.* famous; (*excellent: fam.*) first-rate. **~sement** *adv.* (*fam.*) extremely.

famil|ial (*m. pl.* **~iaux**) /familjal, -jo/ *a.* family.

familiar|iser /familjarize/ *v.t.* familiarize (**avec**, with). **se ~iser** *v. pr.* familiarize o.s. **~isé** *a.* familiar. **~ité** *n.f.* familiarity.

famil|ier, ~ière /familje, -jɛr/ *a.* familiar; (*amical*) informal. ● *n.m.* regular visitor. **~ièrement** *adv.* informally.

famille /famij/ *n.f.* family. **en ~**, with one's family.

famine /famin/ *n.f.* famine.

fanati|que /fanatik/ *a.* fanatical. ● *n.m./f.* fanatic. **~sme** *n.m.* fanaticism.

faner (se) /(sə)fane/ *v. pr.* fade.

fanfare /fɑ̃far/ *n.f.* brass band; (*musique*) fanfare.

fanfaron, ~ne /fɑ̃farɔ̃, -ɔn/ *a.* boastful. ● *n.m., f.* boaster.

fanion /fanjɔ̃/ *n.m.* pennant.

fantaisie /fɑ̃tezi/ *n.f.* imagination, fantasy; (*caprice*) whim. **(de) ~**, (*boutons etc.*) fancy.

fantaisiste /fɑ̃tezist/ *a.* unorthodox.

fantasme /fɑ̃tasm/ *n.m.* fantasy.

fantasque /fɑ̃task/ *a.* whimsical.

fantastique /fɑ̃tastik/ *a.* fantastic.

fantoche /fɑ̃tɔʃ/ *a.* puppet.

fantôme /fɑ̃tom/ *n.m.* ghost. ● *a.* (*péj.*) bogus.

faon /fɑ̃/ *n.m.* fawn.

faramineu|x, ~se /faraminø, -z/ *a.* astronomical.

farce [1] /fars/ *n.f.* (practical) joke; (*théâtre*) farce. **~eur, ~euse** *n.m., f.* joker.

farce [2] /fars/ *n.f.* (*hachis*) stuffing. **~ir** *v.t.* stuff.

fard /far/ *n.m.* make-up. **piquer un ~**, blush. **~er** /-de/ *v.t.*, **se ~er** *v. pr.* make up.

fardeau (*pl.* **~x**) /fardo/ *n.m.* burden.

farfelu, ~e /farfəly/ *a. & n.m., f.* eccentric.

farin|e /farin/ *n.f.* flour. **~eux, ~euse** *a.* floury. **les ~eux** *n.m. pl.* starchy food.

farouche /faruʃ/ *a.* shy; (*peu sociable*) unsociable; (*violent*) fierce. **~ment** *adv.* fiercely.

fascicule /fasikyl/ *n.m.* volume.

fascin|er /fasine/ *v.t.* fascinate. **~ation** *n.f.* fascination.

fascis|te /faʃist/ *a. & n.m./f.* fascist. **~me** *n.m.* fascism.

fasse /fas/ *voir* faire.

faste /fast/ *n.m.* splendour.

fast-food /fastfud/ *n.m.* fast-food place.

fastidieu|x, ~se /fastidjø, -z/ *a.* tedious.

fat|al (*m. pl.* **~als**) /fatal/ *a.* inevitable; (*mortel*) fatal. **~alement** *adv.* inevitably. **~alité** *n.f.* (*destin*) fate.

fataliste /fatalist/ *n.m./f.* fatalist.

fatidique /fatidik/ *a.* fateful.

fatigant, **~e** /fatigã, -t/ *a.* tiring; (*ennuyeux*) tiresome.

fatigue /fatig/ *n.f.* fatigue, tiredness.

fatigu|er /fatige/ *v.t.* tire; (*yeux, moteur*) strain. ● *v.i.* (*moteur*) labour. **se ~er** *v. pr.* get tired, tire (**de**, of). **~é** *a.* tired.

fatras /fatra/ *n.m.* jumble.

faubourg /fobur/ *n.m.* suburb.

fauché /foʃe/ *a.* (*fam.*) broke.

faucher /foʃe/ *v.t.* (*herbe*) mow; (*voler: fam.*) pinch. **~** **qn.**, (*véhicule, tir*) mow s.o. down.

faucille /fosij/ *n.f.* sickle.

faucon /fokõ/ *n.m.* falcon, hawk.

faudra, faudrait /fodra, fodrɛ/ *voir* falloir.

faufiler (se) /(sə)fofile/ *v. pr.* edge one's way.

faune /fon/ *n.f.* wildlife, fauna.

faussaire /fosɛr/ *n.m.* forger.

fausse /fos/ *voir* faux².

faussement /fosmã/ *adv.* falsely, wrongly.

fausser /fose/ *v.t.* buckle; (*fig.*) distort. **~** **compagnie à**, sneak away from.

fausseté /foste/ *n.f.* falseness.

faut /fo/ *voir* falloir.

faute /fot/ *n.f.* mistake; (*responsabilité*) fault; (*délit*) offence; (*péché*) sin. **en ~**, at fault. **~ de**, for want of. **~ de quoi**, failing which. **sans faute**, without fail. **~ de frappe**, typing error. **~ de goût**, bad taste. **~ professionelle**, professional misconduct.

fauteuil /fotœj/ *n.m.* armchair; (*de président*) chair; (*théâtre*) seat. **~ roulant**, wheelchair.

fauti|f, **~ve** /fotif, -v/ *a.* guilty; (*faux*) faulty. ● *n.m.*, *f.* guilty party.

fauve /fov/ *a.* (*couleur*) fawn. ● *n.m.* wild cat.

faux¹ /fo/ *n.f.* scythe.

faux², **fausse** /fo, fos/ *a.* false; (*falsifié*) fake, forged; (*numéro, calcul*) wrong; (*voix*) out of tune. **c'est ~!**, that is wrong! **~** **témoignage**, perjury. **faire ~ bond à qn.**, stand s.o. up. ● *adv.* (*chanter*) out of tune. ● *n.m.* forgery. **fausse alerte**, false alarm. **fausse couche**, miscarriage. **~-filet** *n.m.* sirloin. **~ frais**, *n.m. pl.* incidental expenses. **~-monnayeur** *n.m.* forger.

faveur /favœr/ *n.f.* favour. **de ~**, (*régime*) preferential. **en ~ de**, in favour of.

favorable /favorabl/ *a.* favourable.

favori, **~te** /favori, -t/ *a. & n.m.*, *f.* favourite. **~tisme** *n.m.* favouritism.

favoriser /favorize/ *v.t.* favour.

fax /faks/ *n.m.* fax. **~er** *v.t.* fax.

fébrile /febril/ *a.* feverish.

fécond, **~e** /fekõ, -d/ *a.* fertile. **~er** /-de/ *v.t.* fertilize. **~ité** /-dite/ *n.f.* fertility.

fédér|al (*m. pl.* **~aux**) /federal, -o/ *a.* federal.

fédération /federasjõ/ *n.f.* federation.

fée /fe/ *n.f.* fairy.

féer|ie /fe(e)ri/ *n.f.* magical spectacle. **~ique** *a.* magical.

feindre† /fɛ̃dr/ *v.t.* feign. **~ de**, pretend to.

feinte /fɛ̃t/ *n.f.* feint.

fêler /fele/ *v.t., se ~** *v. pr.* crack.

félicit|er /felisite/ *v.t.* congratulate (**de**, on). **~ations** *n.f. pl.* congratulations (**pour**, on).

félin, **~e** /felɛ̃, -in/ *a. & n.m.* feline.

fêlure /felyr/ *n.f.* crack.

femelle /fəmɛl/ *a. & n.f.* female.

fémin|in, **~ine** /feminɛ̃, -in/ *a.* feminine; (*sexe*) female; (*mode, équipe*) women's. ● *n.m.* feminine. **~ité** *n.f.* femininity.

féministe /feminist/ *n.m./f.* feminist.

femme /fam/ *n.f.* woman; (*épouse*) wife. **~ au foyer**, housewife. **~ de chambre**, chambermaid. **~ de ménage**, cleaning lady.

fémur /femyr/ *n.m.* thigh-bone.

fendiller /fãdije/ *v.t., se ~** *v. pr.* crack.

fendre /fãdr/ *v.t.* (*couper*) split; (*fissurer*) crack; (*foule*) push through. **se ~** *v. pr.* crack.

fenêtre /fənɛtr/ *n.f.* window.

fenouil /fənuj/ *n.m.* fennel.

fente /fãt/ *n.f.* (*ouverture*) slit, slot; (*fissure*) crack.

féod|al (*m. pl.* **~aux**) /feodal, -o/ *a.* feudal.

fer /fɛr/ *n.m.* iron. **~ (à repasser)**, iron. **~ à cheval**, horseshoe. **~-blanc** (*pl.* **~s-blancs**) *n.m.* tinplate. **~ de lance**, spearhead. **~ forgé**, wrought iron.

fera, ferait /fəra, fərɛ/ *voir* faire.

férié /ferje/ *a.* **jour ~**, public holiday.

ferme¹ /fɛrm/ *a.* firm. ● *adv.* (*travailler*) hard. **~ment** /-əmã/ *adv.* firmly.

ferme² /fɛrm/ *n.f.* farm; (*maison*) farm(house).

fermé /fɛrme/ a. closed; (*gaz, radio, etc.*) off.

ferment /fɛrmɑ̃/ n.m. ferment.

ferment|er /fɛrmɑ̃te/ v.i. ferment. **~ation** n.f. fermentation.

fermer /fɛrme/ v.t./i. close, shut; (*cesser d'exploiter*) close *ou* shut down; (*gaz, robinet*) turn off. **se ~** v. pr. close, shut.

fermeté /fɛrməte/ n.f. firmness.

fermeture /fɛrmətyr/ n.f. closing; (*dispositif*) catch. **~ annuelle,** annual closure. **~ éclair,** (P.) zip (-fastener); (*Amer.*) zipper.

ferm|ier, ~ière /fɛrmje, -jɛr/ n.m. farmer. ● n.f. farmer's wife. ● a. farm.

fermoir /fɛrmwar/ n.m. clasp.

féroc|e /feros/ a. ferocious. **~ité** n.f. ferocity.

ferraille /fɛrɑj/ n.f. scrap-iron.

ferré /fɛre/ a. (*canne*) steel-tipped.

ferrer /fɛre/ v.t. (*cheval*) shoe.

ferronnerie /fɛrɔnri/ n.f. ironwork.

ferroviaire /fɛrɔvjɛr/ a. rail(way).

ferry(-boat) /fɛri(bot)/ n.m. ferry.

fertil|e /fɛrtil/ a. fertile. **~e en,** (*fig.*) rich in. **~iser** v.t. fertilize. **~ité** n.f. fertility.

féru, ~e /fery/ a. **~ de,** passionate about.

ferv|ent, ~ente /fɛrvɑ̃, -t/ a. fervent. ● n.m., f. enthusiast (**de,** of). **~eur** n.f. fervour.

fesse /fɛs/ n.f. buttock.

fessée /fese/ n.f. spanking.

festin /fɛstɛ̃/ n.m. feast.

festival (*pl.* **~s**) /fɛstival/ n.m. festival.

festivités /fɛstivite/ n.f. pl. festivities.

festoyer /fɛstwaje/ v.i. feast.

fêtard /fɛtar/ n.m. merry-maker.

fête /fɛt/ n.f. holiday; (*religieuse*) feast; (*du nom*) name-day; (*réception*) party; (*en famille*) celebration; (*foire*) fair; (*folklorique*) festival. **~ des Mères,** Mother's Day. **~ foraine,** fun-fair. **faire la ~,** make merry. **les ~s (de fin d'année),** the Christmas season.

fêter /fɛte/ v.t. celebrate; (*personne*) give a celebration for.

fétiche /fetiʃ/ n.m. fetish; (*fig.*) mascot.

fétide /fetid/ a. fetid.

feu[1] (*pl.* **~x**) /fø/ n.m. fire; (*lumière*) light; (*de réchaud*) burner. **~x (rouges),** (traffic) lights. **à ~ doux/**

vif, on a low/high heat. **du ~,** (*pour cigarette*) a light. **au ~!,** fire! **~ d'artifice,** firework display. **~ de joie,** bonfire. **~ rouge/vert/orange,** red/green/amber *ou* yellow (*Amer.*). **~ de position,** sidelight. **mettre le ~ à,** set fire to. **prendre ~,** catch fire. **jouer avec le ~,** play with fire. **ne pas faire long ~,** not last.

feu[2] /fø/ a. invar. (*mort*) late.

feuillage /fœjaʒ/ n.m. foliage.

feuille /fœj/ n.f. leaf; (*de papier, bois, etc.*) sheet; (*formulaire*) form.

feuillet /fœjɛ/ n.m. leaf.

feuilleter /fœjte/ v.t. leaf through.

feuilleton /fœjtɔ̃/ n.m. (*à suivre*) serial; (*histoire complète*) series.

feuillu /fœjy/ a. leafy.

feutre /føtr/ n.m. felt; (*chapeau*) felt hat; (*crayon*) felt-tip (pen).

feutré /føtre/ a. (*bruit*) muffled.

fève /fɛv/ n.f. broad bean.

février /fevrije/ n.m. February.

fiable /fjabl/ a. reliable.

fiançailles /fjɑ̃saj/ n.f. pl. engagement.

fianc|er (se) /(sə)fjɑ̃se/ v. pr. become engaged (**avec,** to). **~é, ~ée** a. engaged; n.m. fiancé; n.f. fiancée.

fiasco /fjasko/ n.m. fiasco.

fibre /fibr/ n.f. fibre. **~ de verre,** fibreglass.

ficeler /fisle/ v.t. tie up.

ficelle /fisɛl/ n.f. string.

fiche /fiʃ/ n.f. (index) card; (*formulaire*) form, slip; (*électr.*) plug.

ficher[1] /fiʃe/ v.t. (*enfoncer*) drive (**dans,** into).

ficher[2] /fiʃe/ v.t. (*faire: fam.*) do; (*donner: fam.*) give; (*mettre: fam.*) put. **se ~ de,** (*fam.*) make fun of. **~ le camp,** (*fam.*) clear off. **il s'en fiche,** (*fam.*) he couldn't care less.

fichier /fiʃje/ n.m. file.

fichu /fiʃy/ a. (*mauvais: fam.*) rotten; (*raté: fam.*) done for. **mal ~,** (*fam.*) terrible.

ficti|f, ~ve /fiktif, -v/ a. fictitious.

fiction /fiksjɔ̃/ n.f. fiction.

fidèle /fidɛl/ a. faithful. ● n.m./f. (*client*) regular; (*relig.*) believer. **~s,** (*à l'église*) congregation. **~ment** adv. faithfully.

fidélité /fidelite/ n.f. fidelity.

fier[1], **fière** /fjɛr/ a. proud (**de,** of). **fièrement** adv. proudly. **~té** n.f. pride.

fier[2] **(se)** /(sə)fje/ v. pr. **se ~ à,** trust.

fièvre /fjɛvr/ n.f. fever.

fiévreu|x, **~se** /fjevrø, -z/ a. feverish.

figé /fiʒe/ a. fixed, set; (*manières*) stiff.

figer /fiʒe/ v.t./i., **se ~** v. pr. congeal. **~ sur place**, petrify.

fignoler /fiɲɔle/ v.t. refine (upon), finish off meticulously.

figu|e /fig/ n.f. fig. **~ier** n.m. fig-tree.

figurant, **~e** /figyrã, -t/ n.m., f. (*cinéma*) extra.

figure /figyr/ n.f. face; (*forme, personnage*) figure; (*illustration*) picture.

figuré /figyre/ a. (*sens*) figurative. **au ~**, figuratively.

figurer /figyre/ v.i. appear. ● v.t. represent. **se ~** v. pr. imagine.

fil /fil/ n.m. thread; (*métallique, électrique*) wire; (*de couteau*) edge; (*à coudre*) cotton. **au ~ de**, with the passing of. **au ~ de l'eau**, with the current. **~ de fer**, wire. **au bout du ~**, on the phone.

filament /filamã/ n.m. filament.

filature /filatyr/ n.f. (textile) mill; (*surveillance*) shadowing.

file /fil/ n.f. line; (*voie: auto.*) lane. **~ (d'attente)**, queue; (*Amer.*) line. **en ~ indienne**, in single file. **se mettre en ~**, line up.

filer /file/ v.t. spin; (*suivre*) shadow. **~ qch. à qn.**, (*fam.*) slip s.o. sth. ● v.i. (*bas*) ladder, run; (*liquide*) run; (*aller vite: fam.*) speed along, fly by; (*partir: fam.*) dash off. **~ doux**, do as one's told. **~ à l'anglaise**, take French leave.

filet /file/ n.m. net; (*d'eau*) trickle; (*de viande*) fillet. **~ (à bagages)**, (luggage) rack. **~ à provisions**, string bag (*for shopping*).

fil|ial, **~iale** (*m. pl.* **~iaux**) /filjal, -jo/ a. filial. ● n.f. subsidiary (company).

filière /filjɛr/ n.f. (official) channels; (*de trafiquants*) network. **passer par** *ou* **suivre la ~**, (*employé*) work one's way up.

filigrane /filigran/ n.m. watermark. **en ~**, between the lines.

filin /filɛ̃/ n.m. rope.

fille /fij/ n.f. girl; (*opposé à fils*) daughter. **~-mère** (*pl.* **~s-mères**) n.f. (*péj.*) unmarried mother.

fillette /fijɛt/ n.f. little girl.

filleul /fijœl/ n.m. godson. **~e** n.f. god-daughter.

film /film/ n.m. film. **~ d'épouvante/muet/parlant**, horror-si-

lent/talking film. **~ dramatique**, drama. **~er** v.t. film.

filon /filɔ̃/ n.m. (*géol.*) seam; (*situation*) source of wealth.

filou /filu/ n.m. crook.

fils /fis/ n.m. son.

filtr|e /filtr/ n.m. filter. **~er** v.t./i. filter; (*personne*) screen.

fin [1] /fɛ̃/ n.f. end. **à la ~**, finally. **en ~ de compte**, all things considered. **~ de semaine**, weekend. **mettre ~ à**, put an end to. **prendre ~**, come to an end.

fin [2], **fine** /fɛ̃, fin/ a. fine; (*tranche, couche*) thin; (*taille*) slim; (*plat*) exquisite; (*esprit, vue*) sharp. ● adv. (*couper*) finely. **~es herbes**, herbs.

fin|al, **~ale** (*m. pl.* **~aux** *ou* **~als**) /final, -o/ a. final. ● n.f. (*sport*) final; (*gram.*) final syllable. ● n.m. (*pl.* **~aux** *ou* **~als**) (*mus.*) finale. **~alement** adv. finally; (*somme toute*) after all.

finaliste /finalist/ n.m./f. finalist.

financ|e /finãs/ n.f. finance. **~er** v.t. finance. **~ier**, **~ière** a. financial; n.m. financier.

finesse /fines/ n.f. fineness; (*de taille*) slimness; (*acuité*) sharpness. **~s**, (*de langue*) niceties.

fini /fini/ a. finished; (*espace*) finite. ● n.m. finish.

finir /finir/ v.t./i. finish, end; (*arrêter*) stop; (*manger*) finish (up). **en ~ avec**, have done with. **~ par faire**, end up doing. **ça va mal ~**, it will turn out badly.

finition /finisjɔ̃/ n.f. finish.

finlandais, **~e** /fɛ̃lɑdɛ, -z/ a. Finnish. ● n.m., f. Finn.

finlande /fɛ̃lɑd/ n.f. Finland.

finnois, **~e** /finwa, -z/ a. Finnish. ● n.m. (*lang.*) Finnish.

fiole /fjɔl/ n.f. phial.

firme /firm/ n.f. firm.

fisc /fisk/ n.m. tax authorities. **~al** (*m. pl.* **~aux**) a. tax, fiscal. **~alité** n.f. tax system.

fission /fisjɔ̃/ n.f. fission.

fissur|e /fisyr/ n.f. crack. **~er** v.t., **se ~er** v. pr. crack.

fiston /fistɔ̃/ n.m. (*fam.*) son.

fixation /fiksasjɔ̃/ n.f. fixing; (*complexe*) fixation.

fixe /fiks/ a. fixed; (*stable*) steady. **à heure ~**, at a set time. **menu à prix ~**, set menu.

fix|er /fikse/ *v.t.* fix. **~er (du regard)**, stare at. **se ~er** *v. pr.* (*s'installer*) settle down. **être ~é**, (*personne*) have made up one's mind.

flacon /flakɔ̃/ *n.m.* bottle.

flageolet /flaʒɔlɛ/ *n.m.* (*haricot*) (dwarf) kidney bean.

flagrant, **~e** /flagrɑ̃, -t/ *a.* flagrant. **en ~ délit**, in the act.

flair /flɛr/ *n.m.* (sense of) smell; (*fig.*) intuition. **~er** /flere/ *v.t.* sniff at; (*fig.*) sense.

flamand, **~e** /flamɑ̃, -d/ *a.* Flemish. ● *n.m.* (*lang.*) Flemish. ● *n.m.*, *f.* Fleming.

flamant /flamɑ̃/ *n.m.* flamingo.

flambant /flɑ̃bɑ̃/ *adv.* **~ neuf**, brand-new.

flambé, **~e** /flɑ̃be/ *a.* (*culin.*) flambé.

flambeau (*pl.* **~x**) /flɑ̃bo/ *n.m.* torch.

flambée /flɑ̃be/ *n.f.* blaze; (*fig.*) explosion.

flamber /flɑ̃be/ *v.i.* blaze; (*prix*) shoot up. ● *v.t.* (*aiguille*) sterilize; (*volaille*) singe.

flamboyer /flɑ̃bwaje/ *v.i.* blaze.

flamme /flam/ *n.f.* flame; (*fig.*) ardour. **en ~s**, ablaze.

flan /flɑ̃/ *n.m.* custard-pie.

flanc /flɑ̃/ *n.m.* side; (*d'animal, d'armée*) flank.

flancher /flɑ̃ʃe/ *v.i.* (*fam.*) give in.

Flandre(s) /flɑ̃dr/ *n.f.* (*pl.*) Flanders.

flanelle /flanɛl/ *n.f.* flannel.

flân|er /flɑne/ *v.i.* stroll. **~erie** *n.f.* stroll.

flanquer /flɑ̃ke/ *v.t.* flank; (*jeter: fam.*) chuck; (*donner: fam.*) give. **~ à la porte**, kick out.

flaque /flak/ *n.f.* (*d'eau*) puddle; (*de sang*) pool.

flash (*pl.* **~es**) /flaʃ/ *n.m.* (*photo.*) flash; (*information*) news flash.

flasque /flask/ *a.* flabby.

flatt|er /flate/ *v.t.* flatter. **se ~er de**, pride o.s. on. **~erie** *n.f.* flattery. **~eur**, **~euse** *a.* flattering; *n.m.*, *f.* flatterer.

fléau (*pl.* **~x**) /fleo/ *n.m.* (*désastre*) scourge; (*personne*) bane.

flèche /flɛʃ/ *n.f.* arrow; (*de clocher*) spire. **monter en ~**, spiral. **partir en ~**, shoot off.

flécher /fleʃe/ *v.t.* mark *ou* signpost (with arrows).

fléchette /fleʃɛt/ *n.f.* dart.

fléchir /fleʃir/ *v.t.* bend; (*personne*) move. ● *v.i.* (*faiblir*) weaken; (*poutre*) sag, bend.

flegmatique /flɛgmatik/ *a.* phlegmatic.

flemm|e /flɛm/ *n.f.* (*fam.*) laziness. **j'ai la ~e de faire**, I can't be bothered doing. **~ard**, **~arde** *a.* (*fam.*) lazy; *n.m.*, *f.* (*fam.*) lazybones.

flétrir /fletrir/ *v.t.*, **se ~** *v. pr.* wither.

fleur /flœr/ *n.f.* flower. **à ~ de terre/ d'eau**, just above the ground/water. **à ~s**, flowery. **~ de l'âge**, prime of life. **en ~s**, in flower.

fleur|ir /flœrir/ *v.i.* flower; (*arbre*) blossom; (*fig.*) flourish. ● *v.t.* adorn with flowers. **~i** *a.* flowery.

fleuriste /flœrist/ *n.m./f.* florist.

fleuve /flœv/ *n.m.* river.

flexible /flɛksibl/ *a.* flexible.

flexion /flɛksjɔ̃/ *n.f.* (*anat.*) flexing.

flic /flik/ *n.m.* (*fam.*) cop.

flipper /flipœr/ *n.m.* pinball (machine).

flirter /flœrte/ *v.i.* flirt.

flocon /flɔkɔ̃/ *n.m.* flake.

flopée /flɔpe/ *n.f.* (*fam.*) **une ~ de**, masses of.

floraison /flɔrɛzɔ̃/ *n.f.* flowering.

flore /flɔr/ *n.f.* flora.

florissant, **~e** /flɔrisɑ̃, -t/ *a.* flourishing.

flot /flo/ *n.m.* flood, stream. **être à ~**, be afloat. **les ~s**, the waves.

flottant, **~e** /flɔtɑ̃, -t/ *a.* (*vêtement*) loose; (*indécis*) indecisive.

flotte /flɔt/ *n.f.* fleet; (*pluie: fam.*) rain; (*eau: fam.*) water.

flottement /flɔtmɑ̃/ *n.m.* (*incertitude*) indecision.

flott|er /flɔte/ *v.i.* float; (*drapeau*) flutter; (*nuage, parfum, pensées*) drift; (*pleuvoir: fam.*) rain. **~eur** *n.m.* float.

flou /flu/ *a.* out of focus; (*fig.*) vague.

fluctu|er /flyktɥe/ *v.i.* fluctuate. **~uation** *n.f.* fluctuation.

fluet, **~te** /flɥɛ, -t/ *a.* thin.

fluid|e /flɥid/ *a. & n.m.* fluid. **~ité** *n.f.* fluidity.

fluor /flyɔr/ *n.m.* (*pour les dents*) fluoride.

fluorescent, **~e** /flyɔrɛsɑ̃, -t/ *a.* fluorescent.

flût|e /flyt/ *n.f.* flute; (*verre*) champagne glass. **~iste** *n.m./f.* flautist; (*Amer.*) flutist.

fluvial (*m. pl.* **~iaux**) /flyvjal, -jo/ *a.* river.

flux /fly/ *n.m.* flow. **~ et reflux**, ebb and flow.

FM /ɛfɛm/ *abrév. f.* FM.

foc /fɔk/ *n.m.* jib.

fœtus /fetys/ *n.m.* foetus.

foi /fwa/ *n.f.* faith. **être de bonne/ mauvaise ~**, be acting in good/bad faith. **ma ~!**, well (indeed)! **digne de ~**, reliable.

foie /fwa/ *n.m.* liver. **~ gras**, foie gras.

foin /fwɛ̃/ *n.m.* hay. **faire tout un ~**, (*fam.*) make a fuss.

foire /fwar/ *n.f.* fair. **faire la ~**, (*fam.*) make merry.

fois /fwa/ *n.f.* time. **une ~**, once. **deux ~**, twice. **à la ~**, at the same time. **des ~**, (*parfois*) sometimes. **une ~ pour toutes**, once and for all.

foison /fwazɔ̃/ *n.f.* abundance. **à ~**, in abundance. **~ner** /-ɔne/ *v.i.* abound (**de**, in).

fol /fɔl/ *voir* fou.

folâtrer /fɔlɑtre/ *v.i.* frolic.

folichon, ~ne /fɔliʃɔ̃, -ɔn/ *a.* **pas ~**, (*fam.*) not much fun.

folie /fɔli/ *n.f.* madness; (*bêtise*) foolish thing, folly.

folklor|e /fɔlklɔr/ *n.m.* folklore. **~ique** *a.* folk; (*fam.*) picturesque.

folle /fɔl/ *voir* fou.

follement /fɔlmɑ̃/ *adv.* madly.

fomenter /fɔmɑ̃te/ *v.t.* foment.

fonc|er¹ /fɔ̃se/ *v.t./i.* darken. **~é** *a.* dark.

foncer² /fɔ̃se/ *v.i.* (*fam.*) dash along. **~ sur**, (*fam.*) charge at.

fonc|ier, ~ière /fɔ̃sje, -jɛr/ *a.* fundamental; (*comm.*) real estate. **~ièrement** *adv.* fundamentally.

fonction /fɔ̃ksjɔ̃/ *n.f.* function; (*emploi*) position. **~s**, (*obligations*) duties. **en ~ de**, according to. **~ publique**, civil service. **voiture de ~**, company car.

fonctionnaire /fɔ̃ksjɔnɛr/ *n.m./f.* civil servant.

fonctionnel, ~le /fɔ̃ksjɔnɛl/ *a.* functional.

fonctionn|er /fɔ̃ksjɔne/ *v.i.* work. **faire ~er**, work. **~ement** *n.m.* working.

fond /fɔ̃/ *n.m.* bottom; (*de salle, magasin, etc.*) back; (*essentiel*) basis; (*contenu*) content; (*plan*) background. **à ~**, thoroughly. **au ~**, basically. **de ~**, (*bruit*) background;

(*sport*) long-distance. **de ~ en comble**, from top to bottom. **au** *ou* **dans le ~**, really.

fondament|al (*m. pl.* **~aux**) /fɔ̃damɑ̃tal, -o/ *a.* fundamental.

fondation /fɔ̃dɑsjɔ̃/ *n.f.* foundation.

fond|er /fɔ̃de/ *v.t.* found; (*baser*) base (**sur**, on). **(bien) ~é**, well-founded. **~é à**, justified in. **se ~er sur**, be guided by, place one's reliance on. **~ateur, ~atrice** *n.m., f.* founder.

fonderie /fɔ̃dri/ *n.f.* foundry.

fond|re /fɔ̃dr/ *v.t./i.* melt; (*dans l'eau*) dissolve; (*mélanger*) merge. **se ~** *v. pr.* merge. **faire ~**, melt; dissolve. **~ en larmes**, burst into tears. **~ sur**, swoop on.

fondrière /fɔ̃drijɛr/ *n.f.* pot-hole.

fonds /fɔ̃/ *n.m.* fund. ● *n.m. pl.* (*capitaux*) funds. **~ de commerce**, business.

fondu /fɔ̃dy/ *a.* melted; (*métal*) molten.

font /fɔ̃/ *voir* faire.

fontaine /fɔ̃tɛn/ *n.f.* fountain; (*source*) spring.

fonte /fɔ̃t/ *n.f.* melting; (*fer*) cast iron. **~ des neiges**, thaw.

foot /fut/ *n.m.* (*fam.*) football.

football /futbol/ *n.m.* football. **~eur** *n.m.* footballer.

footing /futiŋ/ *n.m.* fast walking.

forage /fɔraʒ/ *n.m.* drilling.

forain /fɔrɛ̃/ *n.m.* fairground entertainer. **(marchand) ~**, stallholder (*at a fair or market*).

forçat /fɔrsa/ *n.m.* convict.

force /fɔrs/ *n.f.* force; (*physique*) strength; (*hydraulique etc.*) power. **~s**, (*physiques*) strength. **à ~ de**, by sheer force of. **de ~**, **par la ~**, by force. **~ de dissuasion**, deterrent. **~ de frappe**, strike force, deterrent. **~ de l'âge**, prime of life. **~s de l'ordre**, police (force).

forcé /fɔrse/ *a.* forced; (*inévitable*) inevitable.

forcément /fɔrsemɑ̃/ *adv.* necessarily; (*évidemment*) obviously.

forcené, ~e /fɔrsane/ *a.* frenzied. ● *n.m., f.* maniac.

forceps /fɔrsɛps/ *n.m.* forceps.

forcer /fɔrse/ *v.t.* force (**à faire**, to do); (*voix*) strain. ● *v.i.* (*exagérer*) overdo it. **se ~** *v. pr.* force o.s.

forcir /fɔrsir/ *v.i.* fill out.

forer /fɔre/ *v.t.* drill.

forest|ier, ~ière /fɔrɛstje, -jɛr/ *a.* forest.

foret /fɔrɛ/ *n.m.* drill.

forêt /fɔrɛ/ *n.f.* forest.

forfait /fɔrfɛ/ *n.m.* (*comm.*) inclusive price. **~aire** /-tɛr/ *a.* (*prix*) inclusive.

forge /fɔrʒ/ *n.f.* forge.

forger /fɔrʒe/ *v.t.* forge; (*inventer*) make up.

forgeron /fɔrʒərɔ̃/ *n.m.* blacksmith.

formaliser (se) /(sə)fɔrmalize/ *v. pr.* take offence (**de**, at).

formalité /fɔrmalite/ *n.f.* formality.

format /fɔrma/ *n.m.* format.

formater /fɔrmate/ *v.t.* (*comput.*) format.

formation /fɔrmasjɔ̃/ *n.f.* formation; (*de médecin etc.*) training; (*culture*) education. **~ permanente** *ou* **~ continue**, continuing education. **~ professionnelle**, professional training.

forme /fɔrm/ *n.f.* form; (*contour*) shape, form. **~s**, (*de femme*) figure. **en ~**, (*sport*) in good shape, on form. **en ~ de**, in the shape of. **en bonne et due ~**, in due form.

formel, **~le** /fɔrmɛl/ *a.* formal; (*catégorique*) positive. **~lement** *adv.* positively.

former /fɔrme/ *v.t.* form; (*instruire*) train. **se ~** *v. pr.* form.

formidable /fɔrmidabl/ *a.* fantastic.

formulaire /fɔrmylɛr/ *n.m.* form.

formul|e /fɔrmyl/ *n.f.* formula; (*expression*) expression; (*feuille*) form. **~e de politesse**, polite phrase, letter ending. **~er** *v.t.* formulate.

fort[1], **~e** /fɔr, -t/ *a.* strong; (*grand*) big; (*pluie*) heavy; (*bruit*) loud; (*pente*) steep; (*élève*) clever. ● *adv.* (*frapper*) hard; (*parler*) loud; (*très*) very; (*beaucoup*) very much. ● *n.m.* strong point. **au plus ~ de**, at the height of. **c'est une ~e tête**, she/ he's headstrong.

fort[2] /fɔr/ *n.m.* (*mil.*) fort.

forteresse /fɔrtərɛs/ *n.f.* fortress.

fortifiant /fɔrtifjɑ̃/ *n.m.* tonic.

fortif|ier /fɔrtifje/ *v.t.* fortify. **~ication** *n.f.* fortification.

fortiori /fɔrtjɔri/ **a ~**, even more so.

fortuit, **~e** /fɔrtɥi, -t/ *a.* fortuitous.

fortune /fɔrtyn/ *n.f.* fortune. **de ~**, (*improvisé*) makeshift. **faire ~**, make one's fortune.

fortuné /fɔrtyne/ *a.* wealthy.

fosse /fos/ *n.f.* pit; (*tombe*) grave. **~ d'aisances**, cesspool. **~ d'orchestre**, orchestral pit. **~ septique**, septic tank.

fossé /fose/ *n.m.* ditch; (*fig.*) gulf.

fossette /fosɛt/ *n.f.* dimple.

fossile /fosil/ *n.m.* fossil.

fossoyeur /foswajœr/ *n.m.* gravedigger.

fou *ou* **fol***, **folle** /fu, fɔl/ *a.* mad; (*course*, *regard*) wild; (*énorme*: *fam.*) tremendous. **~ de**, crazy about. ● *n.m.* madman; (*bouffon*) jester. ● *n.f.* madwoman; (*fam.*) gay. **le ~ rire**, the giggles.

foudre /fudr/ *n.f.* lightning.

foudroy|er /fudrwaje/ *v.t.* strike by lightning; (*maladie etc.*) strike down; (*atterrer*) stagger. **~ant**, **~ante** *a.* staggering; (*mort*, *maladie*) violent.

fouet /fwɛ/ *n.m.* whip; (*culin.*) whisk.

fouetter /fwete/ *v.t.* whip; (*crème etc.*) whisk.

fougère /fuʒɛr/ *n.f.* fern.

fougu|e /fug/ *n.f.* ardour. **~eux**, **~euse** *a.* ardent.

fouill|e /fuj/ *n.f.* search; (*archéol.*) excavation. **~er** *v.t./i.* search; (*creuser*) dig. **~er dans**, (*tiroir*) rummage through.

fouillis /fuji/ *n.m.* jumble.

fouine /fwin/ *n.f.* beech-marten.

fouiner /fwine/ *v.i.* nose about.

foulard /fular/ *n.m.* scarf.

foule /ful/ *n.f.* crowd. **une ~ de**, (*fig.*) a mass of.

foulée /fule/ *n.f.* stride. **il l'a fait dans la ~**, he did it while he was at it.

fouler /fule/ *v.t.* press; (*sol*) tread. **se ~ le poignet/le pied** sprain one's wrist/foot. **ne pas se ~**, (*fam.*) not strain o.s.

foulure /fulyr/ *n.f.* sprain.

four /fur/ *n.m.* oven; (*de potier*) kiln; (*théâtre*) flop. **~ à micro-ondes**, microwave oven. **~ crématoire**, crematorium.

fourbe /furb/ *a.* deceitful.

fourbu /furby/ *a.* exhausted.

fourche /furʃ/ *n.f.* fork; (*à foin*) pitchfork.

fourchette /furʃɛt/ *n.f.* fork; (*comm.*) margin.

fourchu /furʃy/ *a.* forked.

fourgon /furgɔ̃/ *n.m.* van; (*wagon*) wagon. **~ mortuaire**, hearse.

fourgonnette /furgɔnɛt/ *n.f.* (small) van.

fourmi /furmi/ *n.f.* ant. **avoir des ~s**, have pins and needles.

fourmiller /furmije/ *v.i.* swarm (**de**, with).

fournaise /furnɛz/ *n.f.* (*feu, endroit*) furnace.

fourneau (*pl.* ~**x**) /furno/ *n.m.* stove.

fournée /furne/ *n.f.* batch.

fourni /furni/ *a.* (*épais*) thick.

fourn|ir /furnir/ *v.t.* supply, provide; (*client*) supply; (*effort*) put in. ~**ir à qn.**, supply s.o. with. **se** ~**ir chez**, shop at. ~**isseur** *n.m.* supplier. ~**iture** *n.f.* supply.

fourrage /furaʒ/ *n.m.* fodder.

fourré /fure/ *n.m.* thicket.

fourré [2] /fure/ *a.* (*vêtement*) fur-lined; (*gâteau etc.*) filled (*with jam, cream, etc.*).

fourreau (*pl.* ~**x**) /furo/ *n.m.* sheath.

fourr|er /fure/ *v.t.* (*mettre: fam.*) stick. ~**e-tout** *n.m. invar.* (*sac*) holdall.

fourreur /furœr/ *n.m.* furrier.

fourrière /furjɛr/ *n.f.* (*lieu*) pound.

fourrure /furyr/ *n.f.* fur.

fourvoyer (se) /(sə)furvwaje/ *v. pr.* go astray.

foutaise /futɛz/ *n.f.* (*argot*) rubbish.

foutre /futr/ *v.t.* (*argot*) = **ficher** [2].

foutu, ~**e** /futy/ *a.* (*argot*) = **fichu**.

foyer /fwaje/ *n.m.* home; (*âtre*) hearth; (*club*) club; (*d'étudiants*) hostel; (*théâtre*) foyer; (*photo.*) focus; (*centre*) centre.

fracas /fraka/ *n.m.* din; (*de train*) roar; (*d'objet qui tombe*) crash.

fracass|er /frakase/ *v.t.*, **se** ~**er** *v. pr.* smash. ~**ant**, ~**ante** *a.* (*bruyant, violent*) shattering.

fraction /fraksjɔ̃/ *n.f.* fraction. ~**ner** /-jɔne/ *v.t.*, **se** ~**ner** *v. pr.* split (up).

fractur|e /fraktyr/ *n.f.* fracture. ~**er** *v.t.* (*os*) fracture; (*porte etc.*) break open.

fragil|e /fraʒil/ *a.* fragile. ~**ité** *n.f.* fragility.

fragment /fragmã/ *n.m.* bit, fragment. ~**aire** /-tɛr/ *a.* fragmentary. ~**er** /-te/ *v.t.* split, fragment.

fraîche /frɛʃ/ *voir* **frais** [1].

fraîchement /frɛʃmã/ *adv.* (*récemment*) freshly; (*avec froideur*) coolly.

fraîcheur /frɛʃœr/ *n.f.* coolness; (*nouveauté*) freshness.

fraîchir /freʃir/ *v.i.* freshen.

frais [1], **fraîche** /frɛ, -ʃ/ *a.* fresh; (*temps, accueil*) cool; (*peinture*) wet. ● *adv.* (*récemment*) newly. ● *n.m.* **mettre au** ~, put in a cool

place. **prendre le** ~, take a breath of cool air. ~ **et dispos**, fresh. **il fait** ~, it is cool.

frais [2] /frɛ/ *n.m. pl.* expenses; (*droits*) fees. ~ **généraux**, (*comm.*) overheads, running expenses. ~ **de scolarité**, school fees.

frais|e /frɛz/ *n.f.* strawberry. ~**ier** *n.m.* strawberry plant.

frambois|e /frãbwaz/ *n.f.* raspberry. ~**ier** *n.m.* raspberry bush.

fran|c [1], ~**che** /frã, -ʃ/ *a.* frank; (*regard*) open; (*net*) clear; (*cassure*) clean; (*libre*) free; (*véritable*) downright. ~**c-maçon** (*pl.* ~**cs-maçons**) *n.m.* Freemason. ~**c-maçonnerie** *n.f.* Freemasonry. ~**parler** *n.m. inv.* outspokenness.

franc [2] /frã/ *n.m.* franc.

français, ~**e** /frãsɛ, -z/ *a.* French. ● *n.m., f.* Frenchman, French-woman. ● *n.m.* (*lang.*) French.

France /frãs/ *n.f.* France.

franche /frãʃ/ *a.f. voir* **franc** [1].

franchement /frãʃmã/ *adv.* frankly; (*nettement*) clearly; (*tout à fait*) really.

franchir /frãʃir/ *v.t.* (*obstacle*) get over; (*traverser*) cross; (*distance*) cover; (*limite*) exceed.

franchise /frãʃiz/ *n.f.* frankness; (*douanière*) exemption (from duties).

franco /frãko/ *adv.* postage paid.

franco- /frãko/ *préf.* Franco-.

francophone /frãkɔfɔn/ *a.* French-speaking. ● *n.m./f.* French speaker.

frange /frãʒ/ *n.f.* fringe.

franquette (à la bonne) /(alabɔn)frãkɛt/ *adv.* informally.

frappant, ~**e** /frapã, -t/ *a.* striking.

frappe /frap/ *n.f.* (*de courrier etc.*) typing; (*de dactylo*) touch.

frappé, ~**e** /frape/ *a.* chilled.

frapp|er /frape/ *v.t./i.* strike; (*battre*) hit, strike; (*monnaie*) mint; (*à la porte*) knock, bang. ~**é de panique**, panic-stricken.

frasque /frask/ *n.f.* escapade.

fratern|el, ~**elle** /fratɛrnɛl/ *a.* brotherly. ~**iser** *v.i.* fraternize. ~**ité** *n.f.* brotherhood.

fraude /frod/ *n.f.* fraud; (*à un examen*) cheating.

frauder /frode/ *v.t./i.* cheat.

frauduleu|x, ~**se** /frodylø, -z/ *a.* fraudulent.

frayer /freje/ v.t. open up. se ~ un passage, force one's way (dans, through).

frayeur /frɛjœr/ n.f. fright.

fredonner /frədɔne/ v.t. hum.

free-lance /frilɑ̃s/ a. & n.m./f. free-lance.

freezer /frizœr/ n.m. freezer.

frégate /fregat/ n.f. frigate.

frein /frɛ̃/ n.m. brake. **mettre un ~ à**, curb. ~ **à main**, hand brake.

frein|er /frene/ v.t. slow down; (modérer, enrayer) curb. ● v.i. (auto.) brake. ~**age** /frenaʒ/ n.m. braking.

frelaté /frəlate/ a. adulterated.

frêle /frɛl/ a. frail.

frelon /frəlɔ̃/ n.m. hornet.

freluquet /frəlyke/ n.m. (fam.) weed.

frémir /fremir/ v.i. shudder, shake; (feuille, eau) quiver.

frêne /frɛn/ n.m. ash.

fréné|sie /frenezi/ n.f. frenzy. ~**tique** a. frenzied.

fréqu|ent, ~ente /frekɑ̃ -t/ a. frequent. ~**emment** /-amɑ̃/ adv. frequently. ~**ence** n.f. frequency.

fréquenté /frekɑ̃te/ a. crowded.

fréquent|er /frekɑ̃te/ v.t. frequent; (école) attend; (personne) see. ~**ation** n.f. frequenting. ~**ations** n.f. pl. acquaintances.

frère /frɛr/ n.m. brother.

fresque /frɛsk/ n.f. fresco.

fret /frɛt/ n.m. freight.

frétiller /fretije/ v.i. wriggle.

fretin /frətɛ̃/ n.m. **menu ~**, small fry.

friable /frijabl/ a. crumbly.

friand, ~e /frijɑ̃, -d/ a. ~ **de**, fond of.

friandise /frijɑ̃diz/ n.f. sweet; (Amer.) candy; (gâteau) cake.

fric /frik/ n.m. (fam.) money.

fricassée /frikase/ n.f. casserole.

friche (en) /(ɑ̃)friʃ/ adv. fallow. **être en ~**, lie fallow.

friction /friksjɔ̃/ n.f. friction; (massage) rub-down. ~**ner** /-jɔne/ v.t. rub (down).

frigidaire /friʒidɛr/ n.m. (P.) refrigerator.

frigid|e /friʒid/ a. frigid. ~**ité** n.f. frigidity.

frigo /frigo/ n.m. (fam.) fridge.

frigorif|ier /frigɔrifje/ v.t. refrigerate. ~**ique** a. (vitrine etc.) refrigerated.

frileu|x, ~se /frilø, -z/ a. sensitive to cold.

frime /frim/ n.f. (fam.) show off. ~**r** v.i. (fam.) putting on a show.

frimousse /frimus/ n.f. (sweet) face.

fringale /frɛ̃gal/ n.f. (fam.) ravenous appetite.

fringant, ~e /frɛ̃gɑ̃, -t/ a. dashing.

fringues /frɛ̃g/ n.f. pl. (fam.) togs.

frip|er /fripe/ v.t., **se** ~ v. pr. crumple.

fripon, ~ne /fripɔ̃, -ɔn/ n.m., f. rascal. ● a. rascally.

fripouille /fripuj/ n.f. rogue.

frire /frir/ v.t./i. fry. **faire ~**, fry.

frise /friz/ n.f. frieze.

fris|er /frize/ v.t./i. (cheveux) curl; (personne) curl the hair of. ~**é** a. curly.

frisquet /friske/ a.m. (fam.) chilly.

frisson /frisɔ̃/ n.m. (de froid) shiver; (de peur) shudder. ~**ner** /-ɔne/ v.i. shiver; shudder.

frit, ~e /fri, -t/ a. fried. ● n.f. chip. **avoir la ~e**, (fam.) feel good.

friteuse /fritøz/ n.f. (deep)fryer.

friture /frityr/ n.f. fried fish; (huile) (frying) oil ou fat.

frivol|e /frivɔl/ a. frivolous. ~**ité** n.f. frivolity.

froid, ~e /frwa, -d/ a. & n.m. cold. **avoir/prendre ~**, be/catch cold. **il fait ~**, it is cold. ~**ement** /-dmɑ̃/ adv. coldly; (calculer) coolly. ~**eur** /-dœr/ n.f. coldness.

froisser /frwase/ v.t. crumple; (fig.) offend. **se** ~ v. pr. crumple; (fig.) take offence. **se** ~ **un muscle**, strain a muscle.

frôler /frole/ v.t. brush against; skim; (fig.) come close to.

fromag|e /frɔmaʒ/ n.m. cheese. ~**er**, ~**ère** a. cheese; n.m., f. cheese maker; (marchand) cheesemonger.

froment /frɔmɑ̃/ n.m. wheat.

froncer /frɔ̃se/ v.t. gather. ~ **les sourcils**, frown.

fronde /frɔ̃d/ n.f. sling; (fig.) revolt.

front /frɔ̃/ n.m. forehead; (mil., pol.) front. **de ~**, at the same time; (de face) head-on; (côte à côte) abreast. **faire ~ à**, face up to. ~**al** (m. pl. ~**aux**) /-tal, -to/ a. frontal.

frontali|er, ère /frɔ̃talje, -ɛr/ a. border. **(travailleur) ~er**, commuter from across the border.

frontière /frɔ̃tjɛr/ n.f. border, frontier.

frott|er /frote/ v.t./i. rub; (allumette) strike. ~**ement** n.m. rubbing.

frottis /frɔti/ n.m. ~ **vaginal**, smear test.

frouss|e /frus/ *n.f.* (*fam.*) fear. **avoir la ~e**, (*fam.*) be scared. **~ard, ~arde** *n.m.*, *f.* (*fam.*) coward.

fructifier /fryktifje/ *v.i.* **faire ~**, put to work.

fructueu|x, **~se** /fryktɥø, -z/ *a.* fruitful.

frug|al (*m. pl.* **~aux**) /frygal, -o/ *a.* frugal. **~alité** *n.f.* frugality.

fruit /frɥi/ *n.m.* fruit. **des ~s**, (some) fruit. **~s de mer**, seafood. **~é /-te/** *a.* fruity. **~ier**, **~ière** /-tje, -tjɛr/ *a.* fruit; *n.m.*, *f.* fruiterer.

fruste /fryst/ *a.* coarse.

frustr|er /frystre/ *v.t.* frustrate. **~ant**, **~ante** *a.* frustrating. **~ation** *n.f.* frustration.

fuel /fjul/ *n.m.* fuel oil.

fugiti|f, **~ve** /fyʒitif, -v/ *a.* (*passager*) fleeting. ● *n.m.*, *f.* fugitive.

fugue /fyg/ *n.f.* (*mus.*) fugue. **faire une ~**, run away.

fuir† /fɥir/ *v.i.* flee, run away; (*eau, robinet, etc.*) leak. ● *v.t.* (*éviter*) shun.

fuite /fɥit/ *n.f.* flight; (*de liquide, d'une nouvelle*) leak. **en ~**, on the run. **mettre en ~**, put to flight. **prendre la ~**, take (to) flight.

fulgurant, **~e** /fylgyrɑ̃, -t/ *a.* (*vitesse*) lightning.

fumée /fyme/ *n.f.* smoke; (*vapeur*) steam.

fum|er /fyme/ *v.t./i.* smoke. **~e-cigarette** *n.m. invar.* cigarette-holder. **~é** *a.* (*poisson, verre*) smoked. **~eur**, **~euse** *n.m.*, *f.* smoker.

fumet /fymɛ/ *n.m.* aroma.

fumeu|x, **~se** /fymø, -z/ *a.* (*confus*) hazy.

fumier /fymje/ *n.m.* manure.

fumiste /fymist/ *n.m./f.* (*fam.*) shirker.

funambule /fynɑ̃byl/ *n.m./f.* tight-rope walker.

funèbre /fynɛbr/ *a.* funeral; (*fig.*) gloomy.

funérailles /fynerɑj/ *n.f. pl.* funeral.

funéraire /fynerɛr/ *a.* funeral.

funeste /fynɛst/ *a.* fatal.

funiculaire /fynikylɛr/ *n.m.* funicular.

fur /fyr/ *n.m.* **au ~ et à mesure**, as one goes along, progressively. **au ~ et à mesure que**, as.

furet /fyrɛ/ *n.m.* ferret.

fureter /fyrte/ *v.i.* nose (about).

fureur /fyrœr/ *n.f.* fury; (*passion*) passion. **avec ~**, furiously; passionately. **mettre en ~**, infuriate. **faire ~**, be all the rage.

furibond, **~e** /furibɔ̃, -d/ *a.* furious.

furie /fyri/ *n.f.* fury; (*femme*) shrew.

furieu|x, **~se** /fyrjø, -z/ *a.* furious.

furoncle /fyrɔ̃kl/ *n.m.* boil.

furti|f, **~ve** /fyrtif, -v/ *a.* furtive.

fusain /fyzɛ̃/ *n.m.* (*crayon*) charcoal; (*arbre*) spindle-tree.

fuseau (*pl.* **~x**) /fyzo/ *n.m.* ski trousers; (*pour filer*) spindle. **~ horaire**, time zone.

fusée /fyze/ *n.f.* rocket.

fuselage /fyzlaʒ/ *n.m.* fuselage.

fuselé /fyzle/ *a.* slender.

fusible /fyzibl/ *n.m.* fuse.

fuser /fyze/ *v.i.* issue forth.

fusil /fyzi/ *n.m.* rifle, gun; (*de chasse*) shotgun. **~ mitrailleur**, machine-gun.

fusill|er /fyzije/ *v.t.* shoot. **~ade** *n.f.* shooting.

fusion /fyzjɔ̃/ *n.f.* fusion; (*comm.*) merger. **~ner** /-jɔne/ *v.t./i.* merge.

fut /fy/ *voir* être.

fût /fy/ *n.m.* (*tonneau*) barrel; (*d'arbre*) trunk.

futé /fyte/ *a.* cunning.

futil|e /fytil/ *a.* futile. **~ité** *n.f.* futility.

futur /fytyr/ *a. & n.m.* future. **~e femme/maman**, wife-/mother-to-be.

fuyant, **~e** /fɥijɑ̃, -t/ *a.* (*front, ligne*) receding; (*personne*) evasive.

fuyard, **~e** /fɥijar, -d/ *n.m.*, *f.* runaway.

G

gabardine /gabardin/ *n.f.* gabardine; raincoat.

gabarit /gabari/ *n.m.* dimension; (*patron*) template; (*fig.*) calibre.

gâcher /gaʃe/ *v.t.* (*gâter*) spoil; (*gaspiller*) waste.

gâchette /gaʃɛt/ *n.f.* trigger.

gâchis /gaʃi/ *n.m.* waste.

gadoue /gadu/ *n.f.* sludge.

gaff|e /gaf/ *n.f.* blunder. **faire ~e**, (*fam.*) be careful (**à**, of). **~er** *v.i.* blunder.

gag /gag/ *n.m.* gag.

gage /gaʒ/ *n.m.* pledge; (*de jeu*) forfeit. **~s**, (*salaire*) wages. **en ~**

de, as a token of. **mettre en ~**, pawn.

gageure /gaʒyr/ *n.f.* wager (against all the odds).

gagn|er /gaɲe/ *v.t.* (*match, prix, etc.*) win; (*argent, pain*) earn; (*temps, terrain*) gain; (*atteindre*) reach; (*convaincre*) win over. ● *v.i.* win; (*fig.*) gain. **~er sa vie**, earn one's living. **~ant, ~ante**, *a.* winning; *n.m., f.* winner. **~e-pain** *n.m. invar.* job.

gai /ge/ *a.* cheerful; (*ivre*) merry. **~ement** *adv.* cheerfully. **~eté** *n.f.* cheerfulness. **~etés** *n.f. pl.* delights.

gaillard, ~e /gajar, -d/ *a.* hale and hearty; (*grivois*) coarse. ● *n.m.* hale and hearty fellow; (*type: fam.*) fellow.

gain /gɛ̃/ *n.m.* (*salaire*) earnings; (*avantage*) gain; (*économie*) saving. **~s**, (*comm.*) profits; (*au jeu*) winnings.

gaine /gɛn/ *n.f.* (*corset*) girdle; (*étui*) sheath.

gala /gala/ *n.m.* gala.

galant, ~e /galɑ̃, -t/ *a.* courteous; (*scène, humeur*) romantic.

galaxie /galaksi/ *n.f.* galaxy.

galb|e /galb/ *n.m.* curve. **~é** *a.* shapely.

gale /gal/ *n.f.* (*de chat etc.*) mange.

galéjade /galeʒad/ *n.f.* (*fam.*) tall tale.

galère /galɛr/ *n.f.* (*navire*) galley. **c'est la ~!**, (*fam.*) what an ordeal!

galérer /galere/ *v.i.* (*fam.*) have a hard time.

galerie /galri/ *n.f.* gallery; (*théâtre*) circle; (*de voiture*) roof-rack.

galet /galɛ/ *n.m.* pebble.

galette /galɛt/ *n.f.* flat cake.

galeu|x, ~se /galø, -z/ *a.* (*animal*) mangy.

galipette /galipɛt/ *n.f.* somersault.

Galles /gal/ *n.f. pl.* **le pays de ~**, Wales.

gallois, ~e /galwa, -z/ *a.* Welsh. ● *n.m., f.* Welshman, Welshwoman. ● *n.m.* (*lang.*) Welsh.

galon /galɔ̃/ *n.m.* braid; (*mil.*) stripe. **prendre du ~**, be promoted.

galop /galo/ *n.m.* gallop. **aller au ~**, gallop. **~ d'essai**, trial run. **~er** /-ɔpe/ *v.i.* (*cheval*) gallop; (*personne*) run.

galopade /galɔpad/ *n.f.* wild rush.

galopin /galɔpɛ̃/ *n.m.* (*fam.*) rascal.

galvaudé /galvode/ *a.* worthless.

gambad|e /gɑ̃bad/ *n.f.* leap. **~er** *v.i.* leap about.

gamelle /gamɛl/ *n.f.* (*de soldat*) mess bowl *ou* tin; (*d'ouvrier*) food-box.

gamin, ~e /gamɛ̃, -in/ *a.* playful. ● *n.m., f.* (*fam.*) kid.

gamme /gam/ *n.f.* (*mus.*) scale; (*série*) range. **haut de ~**, up-market, top of the range. **bas de ~**, down-market, bottom of the range.

gang /gɑ̃g/ *n.m.* gang.

ganglion /gɑ̃glijɔ̃/ *n.m.* swelling.

gangrène /gɑ̃grɛn/ *n.f.* gangrene.

gangster /gɑ̃gstɛr/ *n.m.* gangster; (*escroc*) crook.

gant /gɑ̃/ *n.m.* glove. **~ de toilette**, face-flannel, face-cloth. **~é** /gɑ̃te/ *a.* (*personne*) wearing gloves.

garag|e /garaʒ/ *n.m.* garage. **~iste** *n.m.* garage owner; (*employé*) garage mechanic.

garant, ~e /garɑ̃, -t/ *n.m., f.* guarantor. ● *n.m.* guarantee. **se porter ~ de**, guarantee, vouch for.

garant|ie /garɑ̃ti/ *n.f.* guarantee; (*protection*) safeguard. **~ies**, (*de police d'assurance*) cover. **~ir** *v.t.* guarantee; (*protéger*) protect (**de**, from).

garce /gars/ *n.f.* (*fam.*) bitch.

garçon /garsɔ̃/ *n.m.* boy; (*célibataire*) bachelor. **~ (de café)**, waiter. **~ d'honneur**, best man.

garçonnière /garsɔnjɛr/ *n.f.* bachelor flat.

garde [1] /gard/ *n.f.* guard; (*d'enfants, de bagages*) care; (*service*) duty; (*infirmière*) nurse. **de ~**, on duty. **~ à vue**, (*police*) custody. **mettre en ~**, warn. **prendre ~**, be careful (**à**, of). (**droit de**) **~**, custody (**de**, of).

garde [2] /gard/ *n.m.* (*personne*) guard; (*de propriété, parc*) warden. **~ champêtre**, village policeman. **~ du corps**, bodyguard.

gard|er /garde/ *v.t.* (*conserver, maintenir*) keep; (*vêtement*) keep on; (*surveiller*) look after; (*défendre*) guard. **se ~er** *v. pr.* (*denrée*) keep. **~er le lit**, stay in bed. **se ~er de faire**, be careful not to do. **~e-à-vous** *int.* (*mil.*) attention. **~e-boue** *n.m. invar.* mudguard. **~e-chasse** (*pl.* **~es-chasses**) *n.m.* gamekeeper. **~e-fou** *n.m.* railing. **~e-manger** *n.m. invar.* (*food*) safe; (*placard*) larder. **~e-robe** *n.f.* wardrobe.

garderie /gardəri/ *n.f.* crèche.

gardien, ~ne /gardjɛ̃, -jɛn/ n.m., f. (de prison, réserve) warden; (d'immeuble) caretaker; (de musée) attendant; (garde) guard. **~ de but**, goalkeeper. **~ de la paix**, policeman. **~ de nuit**, night watchman. **~ne d'enfants**, childminder.

gare [1] /gar/ n.f. (rail.) station. **~ routière**, coach station; (Amer.) bus station.

gare [2] /gar/ int. **~ (à toi)**, watch out!

garer /gare/ v.t., se **~** v. pr. park.

gargariser (se) /(sə)gargarize/ v. pr. gargle.

gargarisme /gargarism/ n.m. gargle.

gargouille /garguj/ n.f. (water-)spout; (sculptée) gargoyle.

gargouiller /garguje/ v.i. gurgle.

garnement /garnəmɑ̃/ n.m. rascal.

garn|ir /garnir/ v.t. fill; (décorer) decorate; (couvrir) cover; (tissu) line; (culin.) garnish. **~i** a. (plat) served with vegetables. **bien ~i**, (rempli) well-filled.

garnison /garnizɔ̃/ n.f. garrison.

garniture /garnityr/ n.f. (légumes) vegetables; (ornement) trimming; (de voiture) trim.

garrot /garo/ n.m. (méd.) tourniquet.

gars /ga/ n.m. (fam.) fellow.

gas-oil /gazɔjl/ n.m. diesel oil.

gaspill|er /gaspije/ v.t. waste. **~age** n.m. waste.

gastrique /gastrik/ a. gastric.

gastronom|e /gastrɔnɔm/ n.m./f. gourmet. **~ie** n.f. gastronomy.

gâteau (pl. **~x**) /gato/ n.m. cake. **~ sec**, biscuit; (Amer.) cookie. **un papa ~**, a doting dad.

gâter /gate/ v.t. spoil. **se ~** v. pr. (dent, viande) go bad; (temps) get worse.

gâterie /gatri/ n.f. little treat.

gâteu|x, ~se /gatø, -z/ a. senile.

gauche [1] /goʃ/ a. left. **à ~e**, on the left; (direction) to the left. **la ~e**, the left (side); (pol.) the left (wing). **~er, ~ère** a. & n.m., f. left-handed (person). **~iste** a. & n.m./f. (pol.) leftist.

gauche [2] /goʃ/ a. (maladroit) awkward. **~rie** n.f. awkwardness.

gaufre /gofr/ n.f. waffle.

gaufrette /gofrɛt/ n.f. wafer.

gaulois, ~e /golwa, -z/ a. Gallic; (fig.) bawdy. ● n.m., f. Gaul.

gausser (se) /(sə)gose/ v. pr. se **~ de**, deride, scoff at.

gaver /gave/ v.t. force-feed; (fig.) cram. **se ~ de**, gorge o.s. with.

gaz /gaz/ n.m. invar. gas. **~ lacrymogène**, tear-gas.

gaze /gaz/ n.f. gauze.

gazelle /gazɛl/ n.f. gazelle.

gaz|er /gaze/ v.i. (fam.) **ça ~e**, it's going all right.

gazette /gazɛt/ n.f. newspaper.

gazeu|x, ~se /gazø, -z/ a. (boisson) fizzy.

gazoduc /gazɔdyk/ n.m. gas pipeline.

gazomètre /gazɔmɛtr/ n.m. gasometer.

gazon /gazɔ̃/ n.m. lawn, grass.

gazouiller /gazuje/ v.i. (oiseau) chirp; (bébé) babble.

geai /ʒɛ/ n.m. jay.

géant, ~e /ʒeɑ̃, -t/ a. & n.m., f. giant.

geindre /ʒɛ̃dr/ v.i. groan.

gel /ʒɛl/ n.m. frost; (pâte) gel; (comm.) freezing.

gélatine /ʒelatin/ n.f. gelatine.

gel|er /ʒəle/ v.t./i. freeze. **on gèle**, it's freezing. **~é** a. frozen; (membre abîmé) frost-bitten. **~ée** n.f. frost; (culin.) jelly. **~ée blanche**, hoarfrost.

gélule /ʒelyl/ n.f. (méd.) capsule.

Gémeaux /ʒemo/ n.m. pl. Gemini.

gém|ir /ʒemir/ v.i. groan. **~issement** n.m. groan(ing).

gênant, ~e /ʒɛnɑ̃, -t/ a. embarrassing; (irritant) annoying.

gencive /ʒɑ̃siv/ n.f. gum.

gendarme /ʒɑ̃darm/ n.m. policeman, gendarme. **~rie** /-əri/ n.f. police force; (local) police station.

gendre /ʒɑ̃dr/ n.m. son-in-law.

gène /ʒɛn/ n.m. gene.

gêne /ʒɛn/ n.f. discomfort; (confusion) embarrassment; (dérangement) trouble. **dans la ~**, in financial straits.

généalogie /ʒenealɔʒi/ n.f. genealogy.

gên|er /ʒene/ v.t. bother, disturb; (troubler) embarrass; (encombrer) hamper; (bloquer) block. **~é** a. embarrassed.

génér|al (m. pl. **~aux**) /ʒeneral, -o/ a. general. ● n.m. (pl. **~aux**) general. **en ~al**, in general. **~alement** adv. generally.

généralis|er /ʒeneralize/ v.t./i. generalize. **se ~er** v. pr. become general. **~ation** n.f. generalization.

généraliste /ʒeneralist/ n.m./f. general practitioner, GP.

généralité /ʒeneralite/ *n.f.* majority. **~s,** general points.

génération /ʒenerɑsjõ/ *n.f.* generation.

génératrice /ʒeneratris/ *n.f.* generator.

généreu|x, **~se** /ʒenerø, -z/ *a.* generous. **~sement** *adv.* generously.

générique /ʒenerik/ *n.m.* (*cinéma*) credits. ● *a.* generic.

générosité /ʒenerozite/ *n.f.* generosity.

genêt /ʒənɛ/ *n.m.* (*plante*) broom.

génétique /ʒenetik/ *a.* genetic. ● *n.f.* genetics.

Genève /ʒənɛv/ *n.m./f.* Geneva.

gén|ial (*m. pl.* **~iaux**) /ʒenjal, -jo/ *a.* brilliant; (*fam.*) fantastic.

génie /ʒeni/ *n.m.* genius. **~ civil,** civil engineering.

genièvre /ʒənjɛvr/ *n.m.* juniper.

génisse /ʒenis/ *n.f.* heifer.

génit|al (*m. pl.* **~aux**) /ʒenital, -o/ *a.* genital.

génocide /ʒenɔsid/ *n.m.* genocide.

génoise /ʒenwaz/ *n.f.* sponge (cake).

genou (*pl.* **~x**) /ʒnu/ *n.m.* knee. **à ~x,** kneeling. **se mettre à ~x,** kneel.

genre /ʒãr/ *n.m.* sort, kind; (*attitude*) manner; (*gram.*) gender. **~ de vie,** life-style.

gens /ʒã/ *n.m./f. pl.* people.

genti|l, **~lle** /ʒãti, -j/ *a.* kind, nice; (*agréable*) nice; (*sage*) good. **~llesse** /-jɛs/ *n.f.* kindness. **~ment** *adv.* kindly.

géograph|ie /ʒeɔɡrafi/ *n.f.* geography. **~e** *n.m./f.* geographer. **~ique** *a.* geographical.

geôl|ier, **~ière** /ʒolje, -jɛr/ *n.m.,* *f.* gaoler, jailer.

géolo|gie /ʒeɔlɔʒi/ *n.f.* geology. **~gique** *a.* geological. **~gue** *n.m./f.* geologist.

géomètre /ʒeɔmɛtr/ *n.m.* surveyor.

géométr|ie /ʒeɔmetri/ *n.f.* geometry. **~ique** *a.* geometric.

géranium /ʒeranjɔm/ *n.m.* geranium.

géran|t, **~te** /ʒerã, -t/ *n.m.,* *f.* manager, manageress. **~t d'immeuble,** landlord's agent. **~ce** *n.f.* management.

gerbe /ʒɛrb/ *n.f.* (*de fleurs, d'eau*) spray; (*de blé*) sheaf.

gercé /ʒɛrse/ *a.* chapped.

ger|cer /ʒɛrse/ *v.t./i.,* **se ~cer** *v. pr.* chap. **~çure** *n.f.* chap.

gérer /ʒere/ *v.t.* manage.

germain, **~e** /ʒɛrmɛ̃, -ɛn/ *a.* **cousin ~,** first cousin.

germanique /ʒɛrmanik/ *a.* Germanic.

germ|e /ʒɛrm/ *n.m.* germ. **~er** *v.i.* germinate.

gésier /ʒezje/ *n.m.* gizzard.

gestation /ʒɛstasjõ/ *n.f.* gestation.

geste /ʒɛst/ *n.m.* gesture.

gesticul|er /ʒɛstikyle/ *v.i.* gesticulate. **~ation** *n.f.* gesticulation.

gestion /ʒɛstjõ/ *n.f.* management.

geyser /ʒezɛr/ *n.m.* geyser.

ghetto /ɡeto/ *n.m.* ghetto.

gibecière /ʒibsjɛr/ *n.f.* shoulder-bag.

gibet /ʒibɛ/ *n.m.* gallows.

gibier /ʒibje/ *n.m.* (*animaux*) game.

giboulée /ʒibule/ *n.f.* shower.

gicl|er /ʒikle/ *v.i.* squirt. **faire ~er,** squirt. **~ée** *n.f.* squirt.

gifl|e /ʒifl/ *n.f.* slap (in the face). **~er** *v.t.* slap.

gigantesque /ʒiɡãtɛsk/ *a.* gigantic.

gigot /ʒiɡo/ *n.m.* leg (of lamb).

gigoter /ʒiɡɔte/ *v.i.* (*fam.*) wriggle.

gilet /ʒilɛ/ *n.m.* waistcoat; (*cardigan*) cardigan. **~ de sauvetage,** life-jacket.

gin /dʒin/ *n.m.* gin.

gingembre /ʒɛ̃ʒãbr/ *n.m.* ginger.

gingivite /ʒɛ̃ʒivit/ *n.f.* gum infection.

girafe /ʒiraf/ *n.f.* giraffe.

giratoire /ʒiratwar/ *a.* **sens ~,** roundabout.

giroflée /ʒirɔfle/ *n.f.* wallflower.

girouette /ʒirwɛt/ *n.f.* weathercock, weather-vane.

gisement /ʒizmã/ *n.m.* deposit.

gitan, **~e** /ʒitã, -an/ *n.m.,* *f.* gypsy.

gîte /ʒit/ *n.m.* (*maison*) home; (*abri*) shelter. **~ rural,** holiday cottage.

givr|e /ʒivr/ *n.m.* (hoar-)frost. **~er** *v.t.,* **se ~er** *v. pr.* frost (up).

givré /ʒivre/ *a.* (*fam.*) nuts.

glace /ɡlas/ *n.f.* ice; (*crème*) ice-cream; (*vitre*) window; (*miroir*) mirror; (*verre*) glass.

glac|er /ɡlase/ *v.t.* freeze; (*gâteau, boisson*) ice; (*papier*) glaze; (*pétrifier*) chill. **se ~er** *v. pr.* freeze. **~é** *a.* (*vent, accueil*) icy.

glac|ial (*m. pl.* **~iaux**) /ɡlasjal, -jo/ *a.* icy.

glacier /ɡlasje/ *n.m.* (*géog.*) glacier; (*vendeur*) ice-cream man.

glacière /glasjɛr/ n.f. icebox.

glaçon /glasɔ̃/ n.m. (pour boisson) ice-cube; (péj.) cold fish.

glaïeul /glajœl/ n.m. gladiolus.

glaise /glɛz/ n.f. clay.

gland /glɑ̃/ n.m. acorn; (ornement) tassel.

glande /glɑ̃d/ n.f. gland.

glander /glɑ̃de/ v.i. (fam.) laze around.

glaner /glane/ v.t. glean.

glapir /glapir/ v.i. yelp.

glas /gla/ n.m. knell.

glauque /glok/ a. (fig.) gloomy.

glissant, **~e** /glisɑ̃, -t/ a. slippery.

gliss|er /glise/ v.i. slide; (sur l'eau) glide; (déraper) slip; (véhicule) skid. ● v.t., se **~er** v. pr. slip (dans, into). **~ade** n.f. sliding; (endroit) slide. **~ement** n.m. sliding; gliding; (fig.) shift. **~ement de terrain**, landslide.

glissière /glisjɛr/ n.f. groove. **à ~**, (porte, système) sliding.

glob|al (m. pl. **~aux**) /glɔbal, -o/ a. (entier, général) overall. **~alement** adv. as a whole.

globe /glɔb/ n.m. globe. **~ oculaire**, eyeball. **~ terrestre**, globe.

globule /glɔbyl/ n.m. (du sang) corpuscle.

gloire /glwar/ n.f. glory.

glorieu|x, **~se** /glɔrjø, -z/ a. glorious. **~sement** adv. gloriously.

glorifier /glɔrifje/ v.t. glorify.

glose /gloz/ n.f. gloss.

glossaire /glɔsɛr/ n.m. glossary.

glouss|er /gluse/ v.i. chuckle; (poule) cluck. **~ement** n.m. chuckle; cluck.

glouton, **~ne** /glutɔ̃, -ɔn/ a. gluttonous. ● n.m., f. glutton.

gluant, **~e** /glyɑ̃, -t/ a. sticky.

glucose /glykoz/ n.m. glucose.

glycérine /gliserin/ n.f. glycerine.

glycine /glisin/ n.f. wisteria.

gnome /gnom/ n.m. gnome.

go /go/ **tout de go**, straight out.

GO (abrév. grandes ondes) long wave.

goal /gol/ n.m. goalkeeper.

gobelet /gɔblɛ/ n.m. tumbler, mug.

gober /gɔbe/ v.t. swallow (whole). **je ne peux pas le ~**, (fam.) I can't stand him.

godasse /gɔdas/ n.f. (fam.) shoe.

godet /gɔdɛ/ n.m. (small) pot.

goéland /gɔelɑ̃/ n.m. (sea)gull.

goélette /gɔelɛt/ n.f. schooner.

gogo (à) /(a)gogo/ adv. (fam.) galore, in abundance.

goguenard, **~e** /gɔgnar, -d/ a. mocking.

goguette (en) /(ɑ̃)gɔgɛt/ adv. (fam.) having a binge ou spree.

goinfr|e /gwɛ̃fr/ n.m. (glouton: fam.) pig. **se ~er** v. pr. (fam.) stuff o.s. like a pig (**de**, with).

golf /gɔlf/ n.m. golf; golf course.

golfe /gɔlf/ n.m. gulf.

gomm|e /gɔm/ n.f. rubber; (Amer.) eraser; (résine) gum. **~er** v.t. rub out.

gond /gɔ̃/ n.m. hinge. **sortir de ses ~s**, go mad.

gondol|e /gɔ̃dɔl/ n.f. gondola. **~ier** n.m. gondolier.

gondoler (se) /(sə)gɔ̃dɔle/ v. pr. warp; (rire: fam.) split one's sides.

gonfl|er /gɔ̃fle/ v.t./i. swell; (ballon, pneu) pump up, blow up; (exagérer) inflate. **se ~er** v. pr. swell. **~é** a. swollen. **il est ~é**, (fam.) he's got a nerve. **~ement** n.m. swelling.

gorge /gɔrʒ/ n.f. throat; (poitrine) breast; (vallée) gorge.

gorgée /gɔrʒe/ n.f. sip, gulp.

gorg|er /gɔrʒe/ v.t. fill (**de**, with). **se ~er** v. pr. gorge o.s. (**de**, with). **~é de**, full of.

gorille /gɔrij/ n.m. gorilla; (garde: fam.) bodyguard.

gosier /gozje/ n.m. throat.

gosse /gɔs/ n.m./f. (fam.) kid.

gothique /gɔtik/ a. Gothic.

goudron /gudrɔ̃/ n.m. tar. **~ner** /-ɔne/ v.t. tar; (route) surface. **à faible teneur en ~**, low tar.

gouffre /gufr/ n.m. gulf, abyss.

goujat /guʒa/ n.m. lout, boor.

goulot /gulo/ n.m. neck. **boire au ~**, drink from the bottle.

goulu, **~e** /guly/ a. gluttonous. ● n.m., f. glutton.

gourde /gurd/ n.f. (à eau) flask; (idiot: fam.) chump.

gourdin /gurdɛ̃/ n.m. club, cudgel.

gourer (se) /(sə)gure/ v. pr. (fam.) make a mistake.

gourmand, **~e** /gurmɑ̃, -d/ a. greedy. ● n.m., f. glutton. **~ise** /-diz/ n.f. greed; (mets) delicacy.

gourmet /gurmɛ/ n.m. gourmet.

gourmette /gurmɛt/ n.f. chain bracelet.

gousse /gus/ n.f. **~ d'ail**, clove of garlic.

goût /gu/ n.m. taste.

goûter /gute/ *v.t.* taste; (*apprécier*) enjoy. ● *v.i.* have tea. ● *n.m.* tea, snack. ~ **à** *ou* **de**, taste.

goutt|e /gut/ *n.f.* drop; (*méd.*) gout. ~**er** *v.i.* drip.

goutte-à-goutte /gutagut/ *n.m.* drip.

gouttelette /gutlɛt/ *n.f.* droplet.

gouttière /gutjɛr/ *n.f.* gutter.

gouvernail /guvɛrnaj/ *n.m.* rudder; (*barre*) helm.

gouvernante /guvɛrnɑ̃t/ *n.f.* governess.

gouvernement /guvɛrnəmɑ̃/ *n.m.* government. ~**al** (*m. pl.* ~**aux**) /-tal, -to/ *a.* government.

gouvern|er /guvɛrne/ *v.t./i.* govern. ~**eur** *n.m.* governor.

grâce /grɑs/ *n.f.* (*charme*) grace; (*faveur*) favour; (*jurid.*) pardon; (*relig.*) grace. ~ **à**, thanks to.

gracier /grasje/ *v.t.* pardon.

gracieu|x, ~se /grasjø, -z/ *a.* graceful; (*gratuit*) free. ~**sement** *adv.* gracefully; free (of charge).

gradation /gradɑsjɔ̃/ *n.f.* gradation.

grade /grad/ *n.m.* rank. **monter en** ~, be promoted.

gradé /grade/ *n.m.* non-commissioned officer.

gradin /gradɛ̃/ *n.m.* tier, step. **en** ~**s**, terraced.

gradué /gradɥe/ *a.* graded, graduated.

graduel, ~le /gradɥɛl/ *a.* gradual.

grad|uer /gradɥe/ *v.t.* increase gradually. ~**uation** *n.f.* graduation.

graffiti /grafiti/ *n.m. pl.* graffiti.

grain /grɛ̃/ *n.m.* grain; (*naut.*) squall; (*de café*) bean; (*de poivre*) peppercorn. ~ **de beauté**, beauty spot. ~ **de raisin**, grape.

graine /grɛn/ *n.f.* seed.

graissage /grɛsaʒ/ *n.m.* lubrication.

graiss|e /grɛs/ *n.f.* fat; (*lubrifiant*) grease. ~**er** *v.t.* grease. ~**eux, ~euse** *a.* greasy.

gramm|aire /gramɛr/ *n.f.* grammar. ~**atical** (*m. pl.* ~**aticaux**) *a.* grammatical.

gramme /gram/ *n.m.* gram.

grand, ~e /grɑ̃, -d/ *a.* big, large; (*haut*) tall; (*mérite, distance, ami*) great; (*bruit*) loud; (*plus âgé*) big. ● *adv.* (*ouvrir*) wide. ~ **ouvert**, wide open. **voir** ~, think big. ● *n.m., f.* (*adulte*) grown-up; (*enfant*) older child. **au** ~ **air**, in the open air. **au** ~ **jour**, in broad day-

light; (*fig.*) in the open. **de** ~**e envergure**, large-scale. **en** ~**e partie**, largely. ~**-angle**, *n.m.* wide angle. ~**e banlieue**, outer suburbs. **G~e-Bretagne** *n.f.* Great Britain. **pas** ~**-chose**, not much. ~ **ensemble**, housing estate. ~**es lignes**, (*rail.*) main lines. ~ **magasin**, department store. ~**-mère** (*pl.* ~**s-mères**) *n.f.* grandmother. ~**s-parents** *n.m. pl.* grandparents. ~**père** (*pl.* ~**s-pères**) *n.m.* grandfather. ~**e personne**, grown-up. ~ **public**, general public. ~**-rue** *n.f.* high street. ~**e surface**, hypermarket. ~**es vacances**, summer holidays.

grandeur /grɑ̃dœr/ *n.f.* greatness; (*dimension*) size. **folie des** ~**s**, delusions of grandeur.

grandiose /grɑ̃djoz/ *a.* grandiose.

grandir /grɑ̃dir/ *v.i.* grow; (*bruit*) grow louder. ● *v.t.* make taller.

grange /grɑ̃ʒ/ *n.f.* barn.

granit /granit/ *n.m.* granite.

granulé /granyle/ *n.m.* granule.

graphique /grafik/ *a.* graphic. ● *n.m.* graph.

graphologie /grafɔlɔʒi/ *n.f.* graphology.

grappe /grap/ *n.f.* cluster. ~ **de raisin**, bunch of grapes.

grappin /grapɛ̃/ *n.m.* **mettre le** ~ **sur**, get one's claws into.

gras, ~se /grɑ, -s/ *a.* fat; (*aliment*) fatty; (*surface*) greasy; (*épais*) thick; (*caractères*) bold. ● *n.m.* (*culin.*) fat. **faire la** ~**se matinée**, sleep late. ~**sement payé**, highly paid.

gratification /gratifikɑsjɔ̃/ *n.f.* bonus, satisfaction.

gratifi|er /gratifje/ *v.t.* favour, reward (**de**, with). ~**ant, ~ante** *a.* rewarding.

gratin /gratɛ̃/ *n.m.* baked dish with cheese topping; (*élite: fam.*) upper crust.

gratis /gratis/ *adv.* free.

gratitude /gratityd/ *n.f.* gratitude.

gratt|er /grate/ *v.t./i.* scratch; (*avec un outil*) scrape. **se** ~**er** *v. pr.* scratch o.s. **ça me** ~**e**, (*fam.*) it itches. ~**-ciel** *n.m. invar.* skyscraper. ~**-papier** *n.m. invar.* (*péj.*) pen pusher.

gratuit, ~e /gratɥi, -t/ *a.* free; (*acte*) gratuitous. ~**ement** /-tmɑ̃/ *adv.* free (of charge).

gravats /grava/ *n.m. pl.* rubble.

grave /grav/ *a.* serious; (*solennel*) grave; (*voix*) deep; (*accent*) grave. **~ment** *adv.* seriously; gravely.

grav|er /grave/ *v.t.* engrave; (*sur bois*) carve. **~eur** *n.m.* engraver.

gravier /gravje/ *n.m.* gravel.

gravir /gravir/ *v.t.* climb.

gravitation /gravitasjɔ̃/ *n.f.* gravitation.

gravité /gravite/ *n.f.* gravity.

graviter /gravite/ *v.i.* revolve.

gravure /gravyr/ *n.f.* engraving; (*de tableau, photo*) print, plate.

gré /gre/ *n.m.* (*volonté*) will; (*goût*) taste. **à son ~,** (*agir*) as one likes. **de bon ~,** willingly. **bon ~ mal gré,** like it or not. **je vous en saurais ~,** I'll be grateful for that.

grec, ~que /grɛk/ *a. & n.m., f.* Greek. ● *n.m.* (*lang.*) Greek.

Grèce /grɛs/ *n.f.* Greece.

greff|e /grɛf/ *n.f.* graft; (*d'organe*) transplant. **~er** /grefe/ *v.t.* graft; transplant.

greffier /grefje/ *n.m.* clerk of the court.

grégaire /greger/ *a.* gregarious.

grêle[1] /grɛl/ *a.* (*maigre*) spindly; (*voix*) shrill.

grêl|e[2] /grɛl/ *n.f.* hail. **~er** /grele/ *v.i.* hail. **~on** *n.m.* hailstone.

grelot /grəlo/ *n.m.* (little) bell.

grelotter /grəlɔte/ *v.i.* shiver.

grenade[1] /grənad/ *n.f.* (*fruit*) pomegranate.

grenade[2] /grənad/ *n.f.* (*explosif*) grenade.

grenat /grəna/ *a. invar.* dark red.

grenier /grənje/ *n.m.* attic; (*pour grain*) loft.

grenouille /grənuj/ *n.f.* frog.

grès /grɛ/ *n.m.* sandstone; (*poterie*) stoneware.

grésiller /grezije/ *v.i.* sizzle; (*radio*) crackle.

grève[1] /grɛv/ *n.f.* strike. **se mettre en ~,** go on strike. **~ du zèle,** work-to-rule; (*Amer.*) rule-book slow-down. **~ de la faim,** hunger strike. **~ sauvage,** wildcat strike.

grève[2] /grɛv/ *n.f.* (*rivage*) shore.

gréviste /grevist/ *n.m./f.* striker.

gribouill|er /gribuje/ *v.t./i.* scribble. **~is** /-ji/ *n.m.* scribble.

grief /grijɛf/ *n.m.* grievance.

grièvement /grijɛvmɑ̃/ *adv.* seriously.

griff|e /grif/ *n.f.* claw; (*de couturier*) label. **~er** *v.t.* scratch, claw.

griffonner /grifɔne/ *v.t./i.* scrawl.

grignoter /griɲɔte/ *v.t./i.* nibble.

gril /gril/ *n.m.* grill, grid(iron).

grillade /grijad/ *n.f.* (*viande*) grill.

grillage /grijaʒ/ *n.m.* wire netting.

grille /grij/ *n.f.* railings; (*portail*) (metal) gate; (*de fenêtre*) bars; (*de cheminée*) grate; (*fig.*) grid.

grill|er /grije/ *v.t./i.* burn; (*ampoule*) blow; (*feu rouge*) go through. **(faire) ~er,** (*pain*) toast; (*viande*) grill; (*café*) roast. **~e-pain** *n.m. invar.* toaster.

grillon /grijɔ̃/ *n.m.* cricket.

grimac|e /grimas/ *n.f.* (funny) face; (*de douleur, dégoût*) grimace.

grimer /grime/ *v.t.*, **se ~** *v. pr.* make up.

grimper /grɛ̃pe/ *v.t./i.* climb.

grinc|er /grɛ̃se/ *v.i.* creak. **~er des dents,** grind one's teeth. **~ement** *n.m.* creak(ing).

grincheu|x, ~se /grɛ̃ʃø, -z/ *a.* grumpy.

gripp|e /grip/ *n.f.* influenza, flu. **être ~é,** have (the) flu; (*mécanisme*) be seized up *ou* jammed.

gris, ~e /gri, -z/ *a.* grey; (*saoul*) tipsy.

grisaille /grizaj/ *n.f.* greyness, gloom.

grisonner /grizɔne/ *v.i.* go grey.

grisou /grizu/ *n.m.* **coup de ~,** firedamp explosion.

grive /griv/ *n.f.* (*oiseau*) thrush.

grivois, ~e /grivwa, -z/ *a.* bawdy.

grog /grɔg/ *n.m.* grog.

grogn|er /grɔɲe/ *v.i.* growl; (*fig.*) grumble. **~ement** *n.m.* growl; grumble.

grognon, ~ne /grɔɲɔ̃, -ɔn/ *a.* grumpy.

groin /grwɛ̃/ *n.m.* snout.

grommeler /grɔmle/ *v.t./i.* mutter.

grond|er /grɔ̃de/ *v.i.* rumble; (*chien*) growl; (*conflit etc.*) be brewing. ● *v.t.* scold. **~ement** *n.m.* rumbling; growling.

groom /grum/ *n.m.* page(-boy).

gros, ~se /gro, -s/ *a.* big, large; (*gras*) fat; (*important*) great; (*épais*) thick; (*lourd*) heavy. ● *n.m.*, *f.* fat man, fat woman. ● *n.m.* **le ~ de,** the bulk of. **de ~,** (*comm.*) wholesale. **en ~,** roughly; (*comm.*) wholesale. **~ bonnet,** (*fam.*) bigwig. **~ lot,** jackpot. **~ mot,** rude word. **~ plan,** close-up. **~ titre,** headline. **~se caisse,** big drum.

groseille /grozɛj/ *n.f.* (red *ou* white) currant. ~ **à maquereau**, gooseberry.

grosse /gros/ *voir* gros.

grossesse /grosɛs/ *n.f.* pregnancy.

grosseur /grosœr/ *n.f.* (*volume*) size; (*enflure*) lump.

gross|ier, ~**ière** /grosje, -jɛr/ *a.* coarse, rough; (*imitation, instrument*) crude; (*vulgaire*) coarse; (*insolent*) rude; (*erreur*) gross. ~**ièrement** *adv.* (*sommairement*) roughly; (*vulgairement*) coarsely. ~**ièreté** *n.f.* coarseness; crudeness; rudeness; (*mot*) rude word.

grossir /grosir/ *v.t./i.* swell; (*personne*) put on weight; (*au microscope*) magnify; (*augmenter*) grow; (*exagérer*) magnify.

grossiste /grosist/ *n.m./f.* wholesaler.

grosso modo /grosomodo/ *adv.* roughly.

grotesque /grotɛsk/ *a.* grotesque; (*ridicule*) ludicrous.

grotte /grot/ *n.f.* cave, grotto.

grouill|er /gruje/ *v.i.* be swarming (**de**, with). ~**ant**, ~**ante** *a.* swarming.

groupe /grup/ *n.m.* group; (*mus.*) band. ~ **électrogène**, generating set. ~ **scolaire**, school block.

group|er /grupe/ *v.t.*, **se** ~**er** *v. pr.* group (together). ~**ement** *n.m.* grouping.

grue /gry/ *n.f.* (*machine, oiseau*) crane.

grumeau (*pl.* ~**x**) /grymo/ *n.m.* lump.

gruyère /gryjɛr/ *n.m.* gruyère (cheese).

gué /ge/ *n.m.* ford. **passer** *ou* **traverser à** ~, ford.

guenon /gənɔ̃/ *n.f.* female monkey.

guépard /gepar/ *n.m.* cheetah.

guêp|e /gɛp/ *n.f.* wasp. ~**ier** /gepje/ *n.m.* wasp's nest; (*fig.*) trap.

guère /gɛr/ *adv.* (**ne**) ~, hardly. **il n'y a** ~ **d'espoir**, there is no hope.

guéridon /geridɔ̃/ *n.m.* pedestal table.

guérill|a /gerija/ *n.f.* guerrilla warfare. ~**ero** /-jero/ *n.m.* guerrilla.

guér|ir /gerir/ *v.t.* (*personne, maladie, mal*) cure (**de**, of); (*plaie, membre*) heal. ● *v.i.* get better; (*blessure*) heal. ~**ir de**, recover from. ~**ison** *n.f.* curing; healing; (*de personne*)

recovery. ~**isseur**, ~**isseuse** *n.m.*, *f.* healer.

guérite /gerit/ *n.f.* (*mil.*) sentry-box.

guerre /gɛr/ *n.f.* war. **en** ~, at war. **faire la** ~, wage war (**à**, against). ~ **civile**, civil war. ~ **d'usure**, war of attrition.

guerr|ier, ~**ière** /gɛrje, -jɛr/ *a.* warlike. ● *n.m., f.* warrior.

guet /gɛ/ *n.m.* watch. **faire le** ~, be on the watch. ~**-apens** /gɛtapɑ̃/ *n.m. invar.* ambush.

guetter /gete/ *v.t.* watch; (*attendre*) watch out for.

gueule /gœl/ *n.f.* mouth; (*figure: fam.*) face. **ta** ~!, (*fam.*) shut up!

gueuler /gœle/ *v.i.* (*fam.*) bawl.

gueuleton /gœltɔ̃/ *n.m.* (*repas: fam.*) blow-out, slap-up meal.

gui /gi/ *n.m.* mistletoe.

guichet /giʃɛ/ *n.m.* window, counter; (*de gare*) ticket-office (window); (*de théâtre*) box-office (window).

guide /gid/ *n.m.* guide. ● *n.f.* (*fille scout*) girl guide. ~**s** *n.f. pl.* (*rênes*) reins.

guider /gide/ *v.t.* guide.

guidon /gidɔ̃/ *n.m.* handlebars.

guignol /giɲɔl/ *n.m.* puppet; (*personne*) clown; (*spectacle*) puppet-show.

guili-guili /giligili/ *n.m.* (*fam.*) tickle. **faire** ~ **à**, tickle.

guillemets /gijmɛ/ *n.m. pl.* quotation marks, inverted commas. **entre** ~, in inverted commas.

guilleret, ~**te** /gijrɛ, -t/ *a.* sprightly, jaunty.

guillotin|e /gijotin/ *n.f.* guillotine. ~**er** *v.t.* guillotine.

guimauve /gimov/ *n.f.* marshmallow. **c'est de la** ~, (*fam.*) it's mush.

guindé /gɛ̃de/ *a.* stilted.

guirlande /girlɑ̃d/ *n.f.* garland.

guise /giz/ *n.f.* **à sa** ~, as one pleases. **en** ~ **de**, by way of.

guitar|e /gitar/ *n.f.* guitar. ~**iste** *n.m./f.* guitarist.

gus /gys/ *n.m.* (*fam.*) bloke.

guttur|al (*m. pl.* ~**aux**) /gytyral, -o/ *a.* guttural.

gym /ʒim/ *n.f.* gym.

gymnas|e /ʒimnaz/ *n.m.* gym (nasium). ~**te** /-ast/ *n.m./f.* gymnast. ~**tique** /-astik/ *n.f.* gymnastics.

gynécolo|gie /ʒinekɔlɔʒi/ *n.f.* gynaecology. ~**gique** *a.* gynaeco-

logical. **~gue** *n.m./f.* gynaecologist.
gypse /ʒips/ *n.m.* gypsum.

H

habile /abil/ *a.* skilful, clever. **~té**
n.f. skill.
habilité /abilite/ *a.* **~ à faire,** entitled to do.
habill|er /abije/ *v.t.* dress (**de,** in);
(*équiper*) clothe; (*recouvrir*) cover
(**de,** with). **s'~er** *v. pr.* dress (o.s.),
get dressed; (*se déguiser*) dress up.
~é *a.* (*costume*) dressy. **~ement**
n.m. clothing.
habit /abi/ *n.m.* dress, outfit; (*de
cérémonie*) tails. **~s,** clothes.
habitable /abitabl/ *a.* (in)habitable.
habitant, ~e /abitã, -t/ *n.m., f.* (*de
maison*) occupant; (*de pays*) inhabitant.
habitat /abita/ *n.m.* housing conditions; (*d'animal*) habitat.
habitation /abitasjõ/ *n.f.* living; (*logement*) house.
habit|er /abite/ *v.i.* live. ● *v.t.* live in;
(*planète, zone*) inhabit. **~é a.** (*terre*)
inhabited.
habitude /abityd/ *n.f.* habit. **avoir
l'~ de faire,** be used to doing. **d'~,**
usually. **comme d'~,** as usual.
habitué, ~e /abitɥe/ *n.m., f.* regular
visitor; (*client*) regular.
habituel, ~le /abitɥɛl/ *a.* usual.
~lement *adv.* usually.
habituer /abitɥe/ *v.t.* **~ à,** accustom
to. **s'~ à,** get used to.
hache /ʼaʃ/ *n.f.* axe.
haché /ʼaʃe/ *a.* (*viande*) minced;
(*phrases*) jerky.
hacher /ʼaʃe/ *v.t.* mince; (*au couteau*)
chop.
hachette /ʼaʃɛt/ *n.f.* hatchet.
hachis /ʼaʃi/ *n.m.* minced meat;
(*Amer.*) ground meat.
hachisch /ʼaʃiʃ/ *n.m.* hashish.
hachoir /ʼaʃwar/ *n.m.* (*appareil*)
mincer; (*couteau*) chopper;
(*planche*) chopping board.
hagard, ~e /ʼagar, -d/ *a.* wild(-look-
ing).
haie /ʼɛ/ *n.f.* hedge; (*rangée*) row.
course de ~s, hurdle race.
haillon /ʼɑjõ/ *n.m.* rag.

hain|e /ʼɛn/ *n.f.* hatred. **~eux, ~euse**
a. full of hatred.
haïr /ʼair/ *v.t.* hate.
hâl|e /ʼɑl/ *n.m.* (sun-)tan. **~é** *a.*
(sun-)tanned.
haleine /alɛn/ *n.f.* breath. **hors d'~,**
out of breath. **travail de longue ~,**
long job.
hal|er /ʼale/ *v.t.* tow. **~age** *n.m.* tow-
ing.
haleter /ʼalte/ *v.i.* pant.
hall /ʼol/ *n.m.* hall; (*de gare*) concourse.
halle /ʼal/ *n.f.* (covered) market. **~s,**
(main) food market.
hallucination /alysinasjõ/ *n.f.* hallucination.
halo /ʼalo/ *n.m.* halo.
halte /ʼalt/ *n.f.* stop; (*repos*) break;
(*escale*) stopping place. ● *int.* stop;
(*mil.*) halt. **faire ~,** stop.
halt|ère /ʼalter/ *n.m.* dumb-bell.
~érophilie *n.f.* weight-lifting.
hamac /ʼamak/ *n.m.* hammock.
hamburger /ʼãburgœr/ *n.m.* hamburger.
hameau (*pl.* **~x**) /ʼamo/ *n.m.* hamlet.
hameçon /amsõ/ *n.m.* (fish-)hook.
hanche /ʼãʃ/ *n.f.* hip.
hand-ball /ʼãdbal/ *n.m.* handball.
handicap /ʼãdikap/ *n.m.* handicap.
~é, ~ée *a.* & *n.m., f.* handicapped
(person). **~er** *v.t.* handicap.
hangar /ʼãgar/ *n.m.* shed; (*pour
avions*) hangar.
hanneton /ʼantõ/ *n.m.* May-bug.
hanter /ʼãte/ *v.t.* haunt.
hantise /ʼãtiz/ *n.f.* obsession (**de,**
with).
happer /ʼape/ *v.t.* snatch, catch.
haras /ʼara/ *n.m.* stud-farm.
harasser /ʼarase/ *v.t.* exhaust.
harcèlement /ʼarsɛlmã/ *n.m.* **~
sexuel,** sexual harassment.
harceler /ʼarsəle/ *v.t.* harass.
hardi /ʼardi/ *a.* bold. **~esse** /-djɛs/ *n.f.*
boldness. **~ment** *adv.* boldly.
hareng /ʼarã/ *n.m.* herring.
hargn|e /ʼarɲ/ *n.f.* (aggressive) bad
temper. **~eux, ~euse** *a.* bad-
tempered.
haricot /ʼariko/ *n.m.* bean. **~ vert,**
French *ou* string bean; (*Amer.*)
green bean.
harmonica /armɔnika/ *n.m.* harmonica.
harmon|ie /armɔni/ *n.f.* harmony.
~ieux, ~ieuse *a.* harmonious.

harmoniser /armɔnize/ v.t., s'~ v. pr. harmonize.

harnacher /'arnaʃe/ v.t. harness.

harnais /'arnɛ/ n.m. harness.

harp|e /'arp/ n.f. harp. ~**iste** n.m./f. harpist.

harpon /'arpɔ̃/ n.m. harpoon. ~**ner** /-ɔne/ v.t. harpoon; (arrêter: fam.) detain.

hasard /'azar/ n.m. chance; (coïncidence) coincidence. ~**s**, (risques) hazards. **au** ~, (choisir etc.) at random; (flâner) aimlessly. ~**eux**, ~**euse** /-dø, -z/ a. risky.

hasarder /'azarde/ v.t. risk; (remarque) venture. **se** ~ **dans**, risk going into. **se** ~ **à faire**, risk doing.

hâte /'ɑt/ n.f. haste. **à la** ~, **en** ~, hurriedly. **avoir** ~ **de**, be eager to.

hâter /'ɑte/ v.t. hasten. **se** ~ v. pr. hurry (**de**, to).

hâti|f, ~**ve** /'ɑtif, -v/ a. hasty; (précoce) early.

hauss|e /'os/ n.f. rise (**de**, in). ~**e des prix**, price rises. **en** ~**e**, rising. ~**er** v.t. raise; (épaules) shrug. **se** ~**er** v. pr. stand up, raise o.s. up.

haut /'o, 'ot/ a. high; (de taille) tall. ● adv. high; (parler) loud(ly); (lire) aloud. ● n.m. top. **à** ~**e voix**, aloud. **des** ~**s et des bas**, ups and downs. **en** ~, (regarder, jeter) up; (dans une maison) upstairs. **en** ~ (**de**), at the top (of). ~ **en couleur**, colourful. **plus** ~, further up, higher up; (dans un texte) above. **en** ~ **lieu**, in high places. ~-**de-forme** (pl. ~**s-de-forme**) n.m. top hat. ~-**fourneau** (pl. ~**s-fourneaux**) n.m. blast-furnace. ~-**le-cœur** n.m. invar. nausea. ~-**parleur** n.m. loudspeaker.

hautain, ~**e** /'otɛ̃, -ɛn/ a. haughty.

hautbois /'obwa/ n.m. oboe.

hautement /'otmɑ̃/ adv. highly.

hauteur /'otœr/ n.f. height; (colline) hill; (arrogance) haughtiness. **à la** ~, (fam.) up to it. **à la** ~ **de**, level with; (tâche, situation) equal to.

hâve /'av/ a. gaunt.

havre /'avr/ n.m. haven.

Haye (La) /(la)'ɛ/ n.f. The Hague.

hayon /'ajɔ̃/ n.m. (auto.) rear opening, tail-gate.

hebdo /ɛbdo/ n.m. (fam.) weekly.

hebdomadaire /ɛbdomadɛr/ a. & n.m. weekly.

héberg|er /eberʒe/ v.t. accommodate, take in. ~**ement** n.m. accommodation.

hébété /ebete/ a. dazed.

hébraïque /ebraik/ a. Hebrew.

hébreu (pl. ~**x**) /ebrø/ a.m. Hebrew. ● n.m. (lang.) Hebrew. **c'est de l'**~!, it's double Dutch.

hécatombe /ekatɔ̃b/ n.f. slaughter.

hectare /ɛktar/ n.m. hectare (=10,000 square metres).

hégémonie /eʒemɔni/ n.f. hegemony.

hein /'ɛ̃/ int. (fam.) eh.

hélas /'elɑs/ int. alas. ● adv. sadly.

héler /'ele/ v.t. hail.

hélice /elis/ n.f. propeller.

hélicoptère /elikɔptɛr/ n.m. helicopter.

helvétique /ɛlvetik/ a. Swiss.

hématome /ematom/ n.m. bruise.

hémisphère /emisfɛr/ n.m. hemisphere.

hémorragie /emɔraʒi/ n.f. haemorrhage.

hémorroïdes /emɔroid/ n.f. pl. piles, haemorrhoids.

henn|ir /'enir/ v.i. neigh. ~**issement** n.m. neigh.

hépatite /epatit/ n.f. hepatitis.

herbage /ɛrbaʒ/ n.m. pasture.

herb|e /ɛrb/ n.f. grass; (méd., culin.) herb. **en** ~**e**, green; (fig.) budding. ~**eux**, ~**euse** a. grassy.

herbicide /ɛrbisid/ n.m. weed-killer.

héréditlé /eredite/ n.f. heredity. ~**aire** a. hereditary.

héré|sie /erezi/ n.f. heresy. ~**tique** a. heretical; n.m./f. heretic.

hériss|er /'erise/ v.t., **se** ~**er** v. pr. bristle. ~**er qn.**, ruffle s.o. ~**é à**, bristling (**de**, with).

hérisson /'erisɔ̃/ n.m. hedgehog.

héritage /eritaʒ/ n.m. inheritance; (spirituel etc.) heritage.

hérit|er /erite/ v.t./i. inherit (**de**, from). ~**er de qch.**, inherit sth. ~**ier**, ~**ière** n.m., f. heir, heiress.

hermétique /ɛrmetik/ a. airtight; (fig.) unfathomable. ~**ment** adv. hermetically.

hermine /ɛrmin/ n.f. ermine.

hernie /ɛrni/ n.f. hernia.

héroïne[1] /erɔin/ n.f. (femme) heroine.

héroïne[2] /erɔin/ n.f. (drogue) heroin.

héroïque /erɔik/ a. heroic. ~**sme** n.m. heroism.

héron /'erɔ̃/ *n.m.* heron.

héros /'ero/ *n.m.* hero.

hésit|er /ezite/ *v.i.* hesitate (**à**, to). **en ~ant**, hesitantly. **~ant**, **~ante** *a.* hesitant. **~ation** *n.f.* hesitation.

hétéro /etero/ *n.m. & a.* (*fam.*) straight.

hétéroclite /eterɔklit/ *a.* heterogeneous.

hétérogène /eterɔʒɛn/ *a.* heterogeneous.

hétérosexuel, **~le** /eterɔseksɥɛl/ *n.m.*, *f. & a.* heterosexual.

hêtre /'ɛtr/ *n.m.* beech.

heure /œr/ *n.f.* time; (*mesure de durée*) hour; (*scol.*) period. **quelle ~ est-il?**, what time is it? **il est dix/** *etc.* **~s**, it is ten/*etc.* o'clock. **à l'~**, (*venir*, *être*) on time. **d'~ en heure**, hourly. **~ avancée**, late hour. **~ d'affluence**, **~ de pointe**, rush-hour. **~ indue**, ungodly hour. **~s creuses**, off-peak periods. **~s supplémentaires**, overtime.

heureusement /œrøzmã/ *adv.* fortunately, luckily.

heureu|x, **~se** /œrø, -z/ *a.* happy; (*chanceux*) lucky, fortunate.

heurt /'œr/ *n.m.* collision; (*conflit*) clash.

heurter /'œrte/ *v.t.* (*cogner*) hit; (*mur etc.*) bump into, hit; (*choquer*) offend. **se ~ à**, bump into, hit; (*fig.*) come up against.

hexagone /ɛgzagon/ *n.m.* hexagon. **l'~**, France.

hiberner /ibɛrne/ *v.i.* hibernate.

hibou (*pl.* **~x**) /'ibu/ *n.m.* owl.

hideu|x, **~se** /'idø, -z/ *a.* hideous.

hier /jɛr/ *adv.* yesterday. **~ soir**, last night, yesterday evening.

hiérarch|ie /jerarʃi/ *n.f.* hierarchy. **~ique** *a.* hierarchical.

hi-fi /'ifi/ *a. invar. & n.f.* (*fam.*) hi-fi.

hilare /ilar/ *a.* merry.

hilarité /ilarite/ *n.f.* laughter.

hindou, **~e** /ɛ̃du/ *a. & n.m.*, *f.* Hindu.

hippi|que /ipik/ *a.* horse, equestrian. **~sme** *n.m.* horse-riding.

hippodrome /ipodrom/ *n.m.* race-course.

hippopotame /ipopotam/ *n.m.* hippopotamus.

hirondelle /irɔ̃dɛl/ *n.f.* swallow.

hirsute /irsyt/ *a.* shaggy.

hisser /'ise/ *v.t.* hoist, haul. **se ~** *v. pr.* raise o.s.

histoire /istwar/ *n.f.* (*récit*, *mensonge*) story; (*étude*) history; (*affaire*) business. **~(s)**, (*chichis*) fuss. **~s**, (*ennuis*) trouble.

historien, **~ne** /istɔrjɛ̃, -jɛn/ *n.m.*, *f.* historian.

historique /istɔrik/ *a.* historical.

hiver /ivɛr/ *n.m.* winter. **~nal** (*m. pl.* **~naux**) *a.* winter; (*glacial*) wintry. **~ner** *v.i.* winter.

H.L.M. /'aʃɛlɛm/ *n.m./f.* (=**habitation à loyer modéré**) block of council flats; (*Amer.*) (government-sponsored) low-cost apartment building.

hocher /'ɔʃe/ *v.t.* **~ la tête**, (*pour dire oui*) nod; (*pour dire non*) shake one's head.

hochet /'ɔʃɛ/ *n.m.* rattle.

hockey /'ɔkɛ/ *n.m.* hockey. **~ sur glace**, ice hockey.

hold-up /'ɔldœp/ *n.m. invar.* (*attaque*) hold-up.

hollandais, **~e** /'ɔlɑ̃dɛ, -z/ *a.* Dutch. ● *n.m.*, *f.* Dutchman, Dutchwoman. ● *n.m.* (*lang.*) Dutch.

Hollande /'ɔlɑ̃d/ *n.f.* Holland.

hologramme /ɔlɔgram/ *n.m.* hologram.

homard /'ɔmar/ *n.m.* lobster.

homéopathie /ɔmeopati/ *n.f.* homoeopathy.

homicide /ɔmisid/ *n.m.* homicide. **~ involontaire**, manslaughter.

hommage /ɔmaʒ/ *n.m.* tribute. **~s**, (*salutations*) respects. **rendre ~ à**, pay tribute.

homme /ɔm/ *n.m.* man; (*espèce*) man(kind). **~ d'affaires**, businessman. **~ de la rue**, man in the street. **~ d'État**, statesman. **~ de paille**, stooge. **~-grenouille** (*pl.* **~s-grenouilles**) *n.m.* frogman. **~ politique**, politician.

homogène /ɔmɔʒɛn/ *a.* homogeneous. **~énéité** *n.f.* homogeneity.

homologue /ɔmɔlɔg/ *n.m./f.* counterpart.

homologué /ɔmɔlɔge/ *a.* (*record*) officially recognized; (*tarif*) official.

homologuer /ɔmɔlɔge/ *v.t.* recognize (officially), validate.

homonyme /ɔmɔnim/ *n.m.* (*personne*) namesake.

homosex|uel, **~uelle** /ɔmɔseksɥɛl/ *a. & n.m.*, *f.* homosexual. **~ualité** *n.f.* homosexuality.

Hongrie /'ɔ̃gri/ *n.f.* Hungary.

hongrois /ˈɔ̃grwa, -z/ *a. & n.m., f.* Hungarian.

honnête /ɔnɛt/ *a.* honest; (*satisfaisant*) fair. **~ment** *adv.* honestly; fairly. **~té** *n.f.* honesty.

honneur /ɔnœr/ *n.m.* honour; (*mérite*) credit. **d'~**, (*invité, place*) of honour; (*membre*) honorary. **en l'~ de**, in honour of. **en quel ~?**, (*fam.*) why? **faire ~ à**, (*équipe, famille*) bring credit to.

honorable /ɔnɔrabl/ *a.* honourable; (*convenable*) respectable. **~ment** /-əmɑ̃/ *adv.* honourably; respectably.

honoraire /ɔnɔrɛr/ *a.* honorary. **~s** *n.m. pl.* fees.

honorer /ɔnɔre/ *v.t.* honour; (*faire honneur à*) do credit to. **s'~ de**, pride o.s. on.

honorifique /ɔnɔrifik/ *a.* honorary.

hont|e /ˈɔ̃t/ *n.f.* shame. **avoir ~e**, be ashamed (**de**, of). **faire ~e à**, make ashamed. **~eux, ~euse** *a.* (*personne*) ashamed (**de**, of); (*action*) shameful. **~eusement** *adv.* shamefully.

hôpit|al (*pl.* **~aux**) /ɔpital, -o/ *n.m.* hospital.

hoquet /ɔkɛ/ *n.m.* hiccup. **le ~**, (the) hiccups.

horaire /ɔrɛr/ *a.* hourly. ● *n.m.* timetable. **~ flexible**, flexitime.

horizon /ɔrizɔ̃/ *n.m.* horizon; (*perspective*) view.

horizont|al (*m. pl.* **~aux**) /ɔrizɔ̃tal, -o/ *a.* horizontal. **~alement** *adv.* horizontally.

horloge /ɔrlɔʒ/ *n.f.* clock.

horlog|er, ~ère /ɔrlɔʒe, -ɛr/ *n.m., f.* watchmaker.

hormis /ˈɔrmi/ *prép.* save.

hormon|al (*m. pl.* **~aux**) /ɔrmɔnal, -no/ *a.* hormonal. **hormone**.

hormone /ɔrmɔn/ *n.f.* hormone.

horoscope /ɔrɔskɔp/ *n.m.* horoscope.

horreur /ɔrœr/ *n.f.* horror. **avoir ~ de**, detest.

horrible /ɔribl/ *a.* horrible. **~ment** /-əmɑ̃/ *adv.* horribly.

horrifier /ɔrifje/ *v.t.* horrify.

hors /ˈɔr/ *prép.* **~ de**, out of; (*à l'extérieur de*) outside. **~-bord** *n.m. invar.* speedboat. **~ d'atteinte**, out of reach. **~ d'haleine**, out of breath. **~-d'œuvre** *n.m. invar.* hors-d'œuvre. **~ de prix**, exorbitant. **~ de soi**, beside o.s. **~-jeu** *a. invar.* offside. **~-la-loi** *n.m. invar.* outlaw.

~ pair, outstanding. **~-taxe** *a. invar.* duty-free.

hortensia /ɔrtɑ̃sja/ *n.m.* hydrangea.

horticulture /ɔrtikyltyr/ *n.f.* horticulture.

hospice /ɔspis/ *n.m.* home.

hospital|ier, ~ière [1] /ɔspitalje, -jɛr/ *a.* hospitable. **~ité** *n.f.* hospitality.

hospital|ier, ~ière [2] /ɔspitalje, -jɛr/ *a.* (*méd.*) hospital. **~iser** *v.t.* take to hospital.

hostie /ɔsti/ *n.f.* (*relig.*) host.

hostil|e /ɔstil/ *a.* hostile. **~ité** *n.f.* hostility.

hosto /ɔsto/ *n.m.* (*fam.*) hospital.

hôte /ot/ *n.m.* (*maître*) host; (*invité*) guest.

hôtel /otɛl/ *n.m.* hotel. **~ (particulier)**, (private) mansion. **~ de ville**, town hall. **~ier, ~ière** /otəlje, -jɛr/ *a.* hotel; *n.m., f.* hotelier. **~lerie** *n.f.* hotel business; (*auberge*) country hotel.

hôtesse /otɛs/ *n.f.* hostess. **~ de l'air**, air hostess.

hotte /ˈɔt/ *n.f.* basket; (*de cuisinière*) hood.

houblon /ublɔ̃/ *n.m.* **le ~**, hops.

houill|e /uj/ *n.f.* coal. **~e blanche**, hydroelectric power. **~er, ~ère** *a.* coal; *n.f.* coalmine.

houl|e /ul/ *n.f.* (*de mer*) swell. **~eux, ~euse** *a.* stormy.

houligan /uligan/ *n.m.* hooligan.

houppette /ˈupɛt/ *n.f.* powder-puff.

hourra /ˈura/ *n.m. & int.* hurrah.

housse /ˈus/ *n.f.* dust-cover.

houx /ˈu/ *n.m.* holly.

hovercraft /ɔverkraft/ *n.m.* hovercraft.

hublot /ˈyblo/ *n.m.* porthole.

huche /ˈyʃ/ *n.f.* **~ à pain**, breadbin.

huer /ˈɥe/ *v.t.* boo. **huées** /ɥe/ *n.f. pl.* boos.

huil|e /ɥil/ *n.f.* oil; (*personne: fam.*) bigwig. **~er** *v.t.* oil. **~eux, ~euse** *a.* oily.

huis /ˈɥi/ *n.m.* **à ~ clos**, in camera.

huissier /ɥisje/ *n.m.* (*appariteur*) usher; (*jurid.*) bailiff.

huit /ˈɥi(t)/ *a.* eight. ● *n.m.* eight. **~ jours**, a week. **lundi en ~**, a week on Monday. **~aine** /ˈɥiten/ *n.f.* (*semaine*) week. **~ième** /ˈɥitjɛm/ *a. & n.m./f.* eighth.

huître /ɥitr/ *n.f.* oyster.

humain, ~e /ymɛ̃, ymɛn/ *a.* human; (*compatissant*) humane. **~ement** /ymɛnmɑ̃/ *adv.* humanly; humanely.

humanitaire /ymanitɛr/ *a.* humanitarian.

humanité /ymanite/ *n.f.* humanity.

humble /œbl/ *a.* humble.

humecter /ymɛkte/ *v.t.* moisten.

humer /'yme/ *v.t.* smell.

humeur /ymœr/ *n.f.* mood; (*tempérament*) temper. **de bonne/mauvaise ~,** in a good/bad mood.

humid|e /ymid/ *a.* damp; (*chaleur, climat*) humid; (*lèvres, yeux*) moist. **~ité** *n.f.* humidity.

humil|ier /ymilje/ *v.t.* humiliate. **~iation** *n.f.* humiliation.

humilité /ymilite/ *n.f.* humility.

humorist|e /ymɔrist/ *n.m./f.* humorist. **~ique** *a.* humorous.

humour /ymur/ *n.m.* humour; (*sens*) sense of humour.

huppé /'ype/ *a.* (*fam.*) high-class.

hurl|er /'yrle/ *v.t./i.* howl. **~ement** *n.m.* howl(ing).

hurluberlu /yrlybɛrly/ *n.m.* scatterbrain.

hutte /'yt/ *n.f.* hut.

hybride /ibrid/ *a.* & *n.m.* hybrid.

hydratant, ~e /idratɑ̃, -t/ *a.* (*lotion*) moisturizing.

hydrate /idrat/ *n.m.* **~ de carbone,** carbohydrate.

hydraulique /idrolik/ *a.* hydraulic.

hydravion /idravjɔ̃/ *n.m.* seaplane.

hydro-electrique /idrɔelɛktrik/ *a.* hydroelectric.

hydrogène /idrɔʒɛn/ *n.m.* hydrogen.

hyène /'jɛn/ *n.f.* hyena.

hyg|iène /iʒjɛn/ *n.f.* hygiene. **~iénique** /iʒjenik/ *a.* hygienic.

hymne /imn/ *n.m.* hymn. **~ national,** national anthem.

hyper- /ipɛr/ *préf.* hyper-.

hypermarché /ipɛrmarʃe/ *n.m.* (*supermarché*) hypermarket.

hypermétrope /ipɛrmetrɔp/ *a.* long-sighted.

hypertension /ipɛrtɑ̃sjɔ̃/ *n.f.* high blood-pressure.

hypno|se /ipnoz/ *n.f.* hypnosis. **~tique** /-ɔtik/ *a.* hypnotic. **~tisme** /-ɔtism/ *n.m.* hypnotism.

hypnotis|er /ipnɔtize/ *v.t.* hypnotize. **~eur** *n.m.* hypnotist.

hypocrisie /ipɔkrizi/ *n.f.* hypocrisy.

hypocrite /ipɔkrit/ *a.* hypocritical. ● *n.m./f.* hypocrite.

hypoth|èque /ipɔtɛk/ *n.f.* mortgage. **~équer** *v.t.* mortgage.

hypoth|èse /ipɔtɛz/ *n.f.* hypothesis. **~étique** *a.* hypothetical.

hystér|ie /isteri/ *n.f.* hysteria. **~ique** *a.* hysterical.

I

iceberg /isbɛrg/ *n.m.* iceberg.

ici /isi/ *adv.* (*espace*) here; (*temps*) now. **d'~ demain,** by tomorrow. **d'~ là,** in the meantime. **d'~ peu,** shortly. **~ même,** in this very place.

icône /ikon/ *n.f.* icon.

idé|al (*m. pl.* **~aux**) /ideal, -o/ *a.* ideal. ● *n.m.* (*pl.* **~aux**) ideal. **~aliser** *v.t.* idealize.

idéalis|te /idealist/ *a.* idealistic. ● *n.m./f.* idealist. **~me** *n.m.* idealism.

idée /ide/ *n.f.* idea; (*esprit*) mind. **~ fixe,** obsession. **~ reçue,** conventional opinion.

identif|ier /idɑ̃tifje/ *v.t.,* **s'~ier** *v. pr.* identify (**à,** with). **~ication** *n.f.* identification.

identique /idɑ̃tik/ *a.* identical.

identité /idɑ̃tite/ *n.f.* identity.

idéolog|ie /ideɔlɔʒi/ *n.f.* ideology. **~ique** *a.* ideological.

idiom|e /idjom/ *n.m.* idiom. **~atique** /idjɔmatik/ *a.* idiomatic.

idiot, ~e /idjo, idjɔt/ *a.* idiotic. ● *n.m., f.* idiot. **~ie** /idjɔsi/ *n.f.* idiocy; (*acte, parole*) idiotic thing.

idiotisme /idjɔtism/ *n.m.* idiom.

idolâtrer /idɔlatre/ *v.t.* idolize.

idole /idɔl/ *n.f.* idol.

idyll|e /idil/ *n.f.* idyll. **~ique** *a.* idyllic.

if /if/ *n.m.* (*arbre*) yew.

igloo /iglu/ *n.m.* igloo.

ignare /iɲar/ *a.* ignorant. ● *n.m./f.* ignoramus.

ignifugé /iɲifyʒe/ *a.* fireproof.

ignoble /iɲɔbl/ *a.* vile.

ignoran|t, ~te /iɲɔrɑ̃, -t/ *a.* ignorant. ● *n.m., f.* ignoramus. **~ce** *n.f.* ignorance.

ignorer /iɲɔre/ *v.t.* not know; (*personne*) ignore.

il /il/ *pron.* he; (*chose*) it. **il est vrai/***etc.* **que,** it is true/*etc.* that. **il neige/pleut/***etc.,* it is snowing/raining/*etc.* **il y a,** there is; (*pluriel*) there are; (*temps*) ago; (*durée*) for. **il y a 2 ans,** 2 years ago. **il y a plus d'une heure que j'attends,** I've been waiting for over an hour.

île /il/ *n.f.* island. ~ **déserte**, desert island. ~**s anglo-normandes**, Channel Islands. ~**s Britanniques**, British Isles.

illég|al (*m. pl.* ~**aux**) /ilegal, -o/ *a.* illegal. ~**alité** *n.f.* illegality.

illégitim|e /ileʒitim/ *a.* illegitimate. ~**ité** *n.f.* illegitimacy.

illettré, ~e /iletre/ *a. & n.m., f.* illiterate.

illicite /ilisit/ *a.* illicit.

illimité /ilimite/ *a.* unlimited.

illisible /ilizibl/ *a.* illegible; (*livre*) unreadable.

illogique /iloʒik/ *a.* illogical.

illumin|er /ilymine/ *v.t., s'~er v. pr.* light up. ~**ation** *n.f.* illumination. ~**é** *a.* (*monument*) floodlit.

illusion /ilyzjõ/ *n.f.* illusion. **se faire des** ~**s**, delude o.s. ~**ner** /-jɔne/ *v.t.* delude. ~**niste** /-jɔnist/ *n.m./f.* conjuror.

illusoire /ilyzwar/ *a.* illusory.

illustre /ilystr/ *a.* illustrious.

illustr|er /ilystre/ *v.t.* illustrate. **s'~er** *v. pr.* become famous. ~**ation** *n.f.* illustration. ~**é** *a.* illustrated; *n.m.* illustrated magazine.

îlot /ilo/ *n.m.* island; (*de maisons*) block.

ils /il/ *pron. fine.*

imag|e /imaʒ/ *n.f.* picture; (*métaphore*) image; (*reflet*) reflection. ~**é** *a.* full of imagery.

imaginaire /imaʒinɛr/ *a.* imaginary.

imaginat|if, ~ve /imaʒinatif, -v/ *a.* imaginative.

imagin|er /imaʒine/ *v.t.* imagine; (*inventer*) think up. **s'~er** *v. pr.* imagine (**que**, that). ~**ation** *n.f.* imagination.

imbattable /ɛ̃batabl/ *a.* unbeatable.

imbécil|e /ɛ̃besil/ *a.* idiotic. ● *n.m./f.* idiot. ~**lité** *n.f.* idiocy; (*action*) idiotic thing.

imbib|er /ɛ̃bibe/ *v.t.* soak (**de**, with). **être** ~**é**, (*fam.*) be sozzled. **s'~er** *v. pr.* become soaked.

imbriqué /ɛ̃brike/ *a.* (*lié*) linked.

imbroglio /ɛ̃brɔglio/ *n.m.* imbroglio.

imbu /ɛ̃by/ *a.* ~ **de**, full of.

imbuvable /ɛ̃byvabl/ *a.* undrinkable; (*personne: fam.*) insufferable.

imit|er /imite/ *v.t.* imitate; (*personnage*) impersonate; (*faire comme*) do the same as; (*document*) copy. ~**ateur**, ~**atrice** *n.m., f.* imitator; impersonator. ~**ation** *n.f.* imitation; impersonation.

immaculé /imakyle/ *a.* spotless.

immangeable /ɛ̃mɑ̃ʒabl/ *a.* inedible.

immatricul|er /imatrikyle/ *v.t.* register. (**se**) **faire** ~**er**, register. ~**ation** *n.f.* registration.

immature /imatyr/ *a.* immature.

immédiat, ~e /imedja, -t/ *a.* immediate. ● *n.m.* **dans l'**~, for the moment. ~**ement** /-tmɑ̃/ *adv.* immediately.

immens|e /imɑ̃s/ *a.* immense. ~**ément** *adv.* immensely. ~**ité** *n.f.* immensity.

immer|ger /imɛrʒe/ *v.t.* immerse. **s'~ger** *v. pr.* submerge. ~**sion** *n.f.* immersion.

immeuble /imœbl/ *n.m.* block of flats, building. ~ (**de bureaux**), (office) building *ou* block.

immigr|er /imigre/ *v.i.* immigrate. ~**ant, ~ante** *a. & n.m., f.* immigrant. ~**ation** *n.f.* immigration. ~**é, ~ée** *a. & n.m., f.* immigrant.

imminen|t, ~te /iminɑ̃, -t/ *a.* imminent. ~**ce** *n.f.* imminence.

immiscer (s') /(s)imise/ *v. pr.* interfere (**dans**, in).

immobil|e /imɔbil/ *a.* still, motionless. ~**ité** *n.f.* stillness; (*inaction*) immobility.

immobil|ier, ~ière /imɔbilje, -jɛr/ *a.* property. **agence** ~**ière**, estate agent's office; (*Amer.*) real estate office. **agent** ~**ier**, estate agent; (*Amer.*) real estate agent. **l'**~**ier**, property; (*Amer.*) real estate.

immobilis|er /imɔbilize/ *v.t.* immobilize; (*stopper*) stop. **s'~er** *v. pr.* stop. ~**ation** *n.f.* immobilization.

immodéré /imɔdere/ *a.* immoderate.

immoler /imɔle/ *v.t.* sacrifice.

immonde /imɔ̃d/ *a.* filthy.

immondices /imɔ̃dis/ *n.f. pl.* refuse.

immor|al (*m. pl.* ~**aux**) /imɔral, -o/ *a.* immoral. ~**alité** *n.f.* immorality.

immortaliser /imɔrtalize/ *v.t.* immortalize.

immort|el, ~elle /imɔrtɛl/ *a.* immortal. ~**alité** *n.f.* immortality.

immuable /imyabl/ *a.* unchanging.

immunis|er /imynize/ *v.t.* immunize. ~**é contre**, (*à l'abri de*) immune to.

immunité /imynite/ *n.f.* immunity.

impact /ɛ̃pakt/ *n.m.* impact.

impair[1] /ɛ̃pɛr/ *a.* (*numéro*) odd.

impair[2] /ɛ̃pɛr/ *n.m.* blunder.

impardonnable /ɛ̃pardɔnabl/ *a.* unforgivable.

imparfait, ~e /ɛ̃parfɛ, -t/ *a. & n.m.* imperfect.

impart|ial (*m. pl.* **~iaux**) /ɛ̃parsjal, -jo/ *a.* impartial. **~ialité** *n.f.* impartiality.

impasse /ɛ̃pɑs/ *n.f.* (*rue*) dead end; (*situation*) deadlock.

impassible /ɛ̃pasibl/ *a.* impassive.

impat|ient, ~iente /ɛ̃pasjɑ̃, -t/ *a.* impatient. **~iemment** /-jamɑ̃/ *adv.* impatiently. **~ience** *n.f.* impatience.

impatienter /ɛ̃pasjɑ̃te/ *v.t.* annoy. **s'~** *v. pr.* lose patience (**contre**, with).

impayable /ɛ̃pɛjabl/ *a.* (killingly) funny, hilarious.

impayé /ɛ̃peje/ *a.* unpaid.

impeccable /ɛ̃pekabl/ *a.* impeccable.

impénétrable /ɛ̃penetrabl/ *a.* impenetrable.

impensable /ɛ̃pɑ̃sabl/ *a.* unthinkable.

impérati|f, ~ve /ɛ̃peratif, -v/ *a.* imperative. ● *n.m.* requirement; (*gram.*) imperative.

impératrice /ɛ̃peratris/ *n.f.* empress.

imperceptible /ɛ̃pɛrsɛptibl/ *a.* imperceptible.

imperfection /ɛ̃pɛrfɛksjɔ̃/ *n.f.* imperfection.

impér|ial (*m. pl.* **~iaux**) /ɛ̃perjal, -jo/ *a.* imperial. **~ialisme** *n.m.* imperialism.

impériale /ɛ̃perjal/ *n.f.* upper deck.

impérieu|x, ~se /ɛ̃perjø, -z/ *a.* imperious; (*pressant*) pressing.

impérissable /ɛ̃perisabl/ *a.* undying.

imperméable /ɛ̃pɛrmeabl/ *a.* impervious (**à**, to); (*manteau, tissu*) waterproof. ● *n.m.* raincoat.

impersonnel, ~le /ɛ̃pɛrsɔnɛl/ *a.* impersonal.

impertinen|t, ~te /ɛ̃pɛrtinɑ̃, -t/ *a.* impertinent. **~ce** *n.f.* impertinence.

imperturbable /ɛ̃pɛrtyrbabl/ *a.* unshakeable.

impét|ueux, ~ueuse /ɛ̃petɥø, -z/ *a.* impetuous. **~uosité** *n.f.* impetuosity.

impitoyable /ɛ̃pitwajabl/ *a.* merciless.

implacable /ɛ̃plakabl/ *a.* implacable.

implant /ɛ̃plɑ̃/ *n.m.* implant.

implant|er /ɛ̃plɑ̃te/ *v.t.* establish. **s'~** *v. pr.* become established. **~ation** *n.f.* establishment.

implication /ɛ̃plikasjɔ̃/ *n.f.* implication.

implicite /ɛ̃plisit/ *a.* implicit.

impliquer /ɛ̃plike/ *v.t.* imply (**que**, that). **~ dans**, implicate in.

implorer /ɛ̃plɔre/ *v.t.* implore.

impoli /ɛ̃pɔli/ *a.* impolite. **~tesse** *n.f.* impoliteness; (*remarque*) impolite remark.

impondérable /ɛ̃pɔ̃derabl/ *a. & n.m.* imponderable.

impopulaire /ɛ̃pɔpylɛr/ *a.* unpopular.

importance /ɛ̃pɔrtɑ̃s/ *n.f.* importance; (*taille*) size; (*ampleur*) extent. **sans ~**, unimportant.

important, ~e /ɛ̃pɔrtɑ̃, -t/ *a.* important; (*en quantité*) considerable, sizeable, big. ● *n.m.* l'**~**, the important thing.

import|er [1] /ɛ̃pɔrte/ *v.t.* (*comm.*) import. **~ateur, ~atrice** *n.m., f.* importer; *a.* importing. **~ation** *n.f.* import.

import|er [2] /ɛ̃pɔrte/ *v.i.* matter, be important (**à**, to). **il ~e que**, it is important that. **n'~e, peu ~e**, it does not matter. **n'~e comment**, anyhow. **n'~e où**, anywhere. **n'~e qui**, anybody. **n'~e quoi**, anything.

importun, ~e /ɛ̃pɔrtœ̃, -yn/ *a.* troublesome. ● *n.m., f.* nuisance. **~er** /-yne/ *v.t.* trouble.

imposant, ~e /ɛ̃pozɑ̃, -t/ *a.* imposing.

imposer /ɛ̃poze/ *v.t.* impose (**à**, on); (*taxer*) tax. **s'~** *v. pr.* be essential; (*se faire reconnaitre*) stand out. **en ~ à qn.**, impress s.o.

imposition /ɛ̃pozisjɔ̃/ *n.f.* taxation. **~ des mains**, laying-on of hands.

impossibilité /ɛ̃pɔsibilite/ *n.f.* impossibility. **dans l'~ de**, unable to.

impossible /ɛ̃pɔsibl/ *a. & n.m.* impossible. **faire l'~**, do the impossible.

impost|eur /ɛ̃pɔstœr/ *n.m.* impostor. **~ure** *n.f.* imposture.

impôt /ɛ̃po/ *n.m.* tax. **~s**, (*contributions*) tax(ation), taxes. **~ sur le revenu**, income tax.

impotent, ~e /ɛ̃pɔtɑ̃, -t/ *a.* crippled. ● *n.m., f.* cripple.

impraticable /ɛ̃pratikabl/ *a.* (*route*) impassable.

imprécis, ~e /ɛ̃presi, -z/ *a.* imprecise. **~ion** /-zjɔ̃/ *n.f.* imprecision.

imprégner /ɛ̃preɲe/ *v.t.* fill (**de**, with); (*imbiber*) impregnate (**de**, with). **s'~ de**, become filled with;

(*s'imbiber*) become impregnated with.

imprenable /ɛ̃prənabl/ *a.* impregnable.

impresario /ɛ̃presarjo/ *n.m.* manager.

impression /ɛ̃presjɔ̃/ *n.f.* impression; (*de livre*) printing.

impressionn|er /ɛ̃presjone/ *v.t.* impress. ~**able** *a.* impressionable. ~**ant**, ~**ante** *a.* impressive.

imprévisible /ɛ̃previzibl/ *a.* unpredictable.

imprévoyant, ~**e** /ɛ̃prevwajɑ̃, -t/ *a.* improvident.

imprévu /ɛ̃prevy/ *a.* unexpected. ● *n.m.* unexpected incident.

imprim|er /ɛ̃prime/ *v.t.* print; (*marquer*) imprint; (*transmettre*) impart. ~**ante** *n.f.* (*d'un ordinateur*) printer. ~**é** *a.* printed; *n.m.* (*formulaire*) printed form. ~**erie** *n.f.* (*art*) printing; (*lieu*) printing works. ~**eur** *n.m.* printer.

improbable /ɛ̃prɔbabl/ *a.* unlikely, improbable.

impromptu /ɛ̃prɔ̃pty/ *a. & adv.* impromptu.

impropr|e /ɛ̃prɔpr/ *a.* incorrect. ~**e à**, unfit for. ~**iété**, *n.f.* incorrectness; (*erreur*) error.

improvis|er /ɛ̃prɔvize/ *v.t./i.* improvise. ~**ation** *n.f.* improvisation.

improviste (à l') /(a)ɛ̃prɔvist/ *adv.* unexpectedly.

imprud|ent, ~**ente** /ɛ̃prydɑ̃, -t/ *a.* careless. **il est ~ent de,** it is unwise to. ~**emment** /-amɑ̃/ *adv.* carelessly. ~**ence** *n.f.* carelessness; (*acte*) careless action.

impud|ent, ~**te** /ɛ̃pydɑ̃, -t/ *a.* impudent. ~**ce** *n.f.* impudence.

impudique /ɛ̃pydik/ *a.* immodest.

impuissan|t, ~**te** /ɛ̃pɥisɑ̃, -t/ *a.* helpless; (*méd.*) impotent. ~**t à,** powerless to. ~**ce** *n.f.* helplessness; (*méd.*) impotence.

impulsi|f, ~**ve** /ɛ̃pylsif, -v/ *a.* impulsive.

impulsion /ɛ̃pylsjɔ̃/ *n.f.* (*poussée*, *influence*) impetus; (*instinct*, *mouvement*) impulse.

impunément /ɛ̃pynemɑ̃/ *adv.* with impunity.

impuni /ɛ̃pyni/ *a.* unpunished.

impunité /ɛ̃pynite/ *n.f.* impunity.

impur /ɛ̃pyr/ *a.* impure. ~**eté** *n.f.* impurity.

imput|er /ɛ̃pyte/ *v.t.* ~**er à,** impute to. ~**able** *a.* ascribable (à, to).

inabordable /inabɔrdabl/ *a.* (*prix*) prohibitive.

inacceptable /inakseptabl/ *a.* unacceptable; (*scandaleux*) outrageous.

inaccessible /inaksesibl/ *a.* inaccessible.

inaccoutumé /inakutyme/ *a.* unaccustomed.

inachevé /inaʃve/ *a.* unfinished.

inacti|f, ~**ve** /inaktif, -v/ *a.* inactive.

inaction /inaksjɔ̃/ *n.f.* inactivity.

inadapté, ~**e** /inadapte/ *n.m.*, *f.* (*psych.*) maladjusted person.

inadéquat, ~**e** /inadekwa, -t/ *a.* inadequate.

inadmissible /inadmisibl/ *a.* unacceptable.

inadvertance /inadvɛrtɑ̃s/ *n.f.* **par ~,** by mistake.

inaltérable /inalterabl/ *a.* stable, that does not deteriorate; (*sentiment*) unfailing.

inanimé /inanime/ *a.* (*évanoui*) unconscious; (*mort*) lifeless; (*matière*) inanimate.

inaperçu /inapɛrsy/ *a.* unnoticed.

inappréciable /inapresjabl/ *a.* invaluable.

inapte /inapt/ *a.* unsuited (à, to). ~ **à faire,** incapable of doing.

inarticulé /inartikyle/ *a.* inarticulate.

inassouvi /inasuvi/ *a.* unsatisfied.

inattendu /inatɑ̃dy/ *a.* unexpected.

inattenti|f, ~**ve** /inatɑ̃tif, -v/ *a.* inattentive (à, to).

inattention /inatɑ̃sjɔ̃/ *n.f.* inattention.

inaugur|er /inɔgyre/ *v.t.* inaugurate. ~**ation** *n.f.* inauguration.

inaugur|al (*m. pl.* ~**aux**) /inɔgyral, -o/ *a.* inaugural.

incalculable /ɛ̃kalkylabl/ *a.* incalculable.

incapable /ɛ̃kapabl/ *a.* incapable (**de qch.,** of sth.). ~ **de faire,** unable to do, incapable of doing. ● *n.m./f.* incompetent.

incapacité /ɛ̃kapasite/ *n.f.* incapacity. **dans l' ~ de,** unable to.

incarcérer /ɛ̃karsere/ *v.t.* incarcerate.

incarn|er /ɛ̃karne/ *v.t.* embody. ~**ation** *n.f.* embodiment, incarnation. ~**é** *a.* (*ongle*) ingrowing.

incartade /ɛ̃kartad/ n.f. indiscretion, misdeed, prank.

incassable /ɛ̃kasabl/ a. unbreakable.

incendiaire /ɛ̃sɑ̃djɛr/ a. incendiary, (*propos*) inflammatory. ● n.m./f. arsonist.

incend|ie /ɛ̃sɑ̃di/ n.m. fire. ~ie criminel, arson. ~ier v.t. set fire to.

incert|ain, ~aine /ɛ̃sɛrtɛ̃, -ɛn/ a. uncertain; (*contour*) vague. ~itude n.f. uncertainty.

incessamment /ɛ̃sɛsamɑ̃/ adv. shortly.

incessant, ~e /ɛ̃sɛsɑ̃, -t/ a. incessant.

incest|e /ɛ̃sɛst/ n.m. incest. ~ueux, ~ueuse a. incestuous.

inchangé /ɛ̃ʃɑ̃ʒe/ a. unchanged.

incidence /ɛ̃sidɑ̃s/ n.f. effect.

incident /ɛ̃sidɑ̃/ n.m. incident. ~ technique, technical hitch.

incinér|er /ɛ̃sinere/ v.t. incinerate; (*mort*) cremate. ~ateur n.m. incinerator.

incis|er /ɛ̃size/ v.t. (*abcès etc.*) lance. ~ion n.f. lancing; (*entaille*) incision.

incisi|f, ~ve /ɛ̃sizif, -v/ a. incisive.

incit|er /ɛ̃site/ v.t. incite (à, to). ~ation n.f. incitement.

inclinaison /ɛ̃klinɛzɔ̃/ n.f. incline; (*de la tête*) tilt.

inclination[1] /ɛ̃klinasjɔ̃/ n.f. (*penchant*) inclination.

inclin|er /ɛ̃kline/ v.t. tilt, lean; (*courber*) bend; (*inciter*) encourage (à, to). ● v.i. ~er à, be inclined to. s'~er v. pr. (*se courber*) bow down; (*céder*) give in; (*chemin*) slope. ~er la tête, (*approuver*) nod; (*révérence*) bow. ~ation[2] n.f. (*de la tête*) nod; (*du buste*) bow.

incl|ure /ɛ̃klyr/ v.t. include; (*enfermer*) enclose. **jusqu'au lundi ~us**, up to and including Monday. ~usion n.f. inclusion.

incognito /ɛ̃kɔɲito/ adv. incognito.

incohéren|t, ~te /ɛ̃kɔerɑ̃, -t/ a. incoherent. ~ce n.f. incoherence.

incollable /ɛ̃kɔlabl/ a. **il est ~**, he can't be stumped.

incolore /ɛ̃kɔlɔr/ a. colourless; (*crème, verre*) clear.

incomber /ɛ̃kɔ̃be/ v.i. **il vous/etc. incombe de**, it is your/etc. responsibility to.

incombustible /ɛ̃kɔ̃bystibl/ a. incombustible.

incommode /ɛ̃kɔmɔd/ a. awkward.

incommoder /ɛ̃kɔmɔde/ v.t. inconvenience.

incomparable /ɛ̃kɔ̃parabl/ a. incomparable.

incompatib|le /ɛ̃kɔ̃patibl/ a. incompatible. ~ilité n.f. incompatibility.

incompéten|t, ~te /ɛ̃kɔ̃petɑ̃, -t/ a. incompetent. ~ce n.f. incompetence.

incompl|et, ~ète /ɛ̃kɔ̃plɛ, -t/ a. incomplete.

incompréhensible /ɛ̃kɔ̃preɑ̃sibl/ a. incomprehensible.

incompréhension /ɛ̃kɔ̃preɑ̃sjɔ̃/ n.f. lack of understanding.

incompris, ~e /ɛ̃kɔ̃pri, -z/ a. misunderstood.

inconcevable /ɛ̃kɔ̃svabl/ a. inconceivable.

inconciliable /ɛ̃kɔ̃siljabl/ a. irreconcilable.

inconditionnel, ~le /ɛ̃kɔ̃disjɔnɛl/ a. unconditional.

inconduite /ɛ̃kɔ̃dɥit/ n.f. loose behaviour.

inconfort /ɛ̃kɔ̃fɔr/ n.m. discomfort. ~able /-tabl/ a. uncomfortable.

incongru /ɛ̃kɔ̃gry/ a. unseemly.

inconnu, ~e /ɛ̃kɔny/ a. unknown (à, to). ● n.m., f. stranger. ● n.m. l'~, the unknown. ● n.f. unknown (quantity).

inconsc|ient, ~iente /ɛ̃kɔ̃sjɑ̃, -t/ a. unconscious (de, of); (*fou*) mad. ● n.m. (*psych.*) subconscious. ~iemment /-jamɑ̃/ adv. unconsciously. ~ience n.f. unconsciousness; (*folie*) madness.

inconsidéré /ɛ̃kɔ̃sidere/ a. thoughtless.

inconsistant, ~e /ɛ̃kɔ̃sistɑ̃, -t/ a. (*fig.*) flimsy.

inconsolable /ɛ̃kɔ̃sɔlabl/ a. inconsolable.

inconstan|t, ~te /ɛ̃kɔ̃stɑ̃, -t/ a. fickle. ~ce n.f. fickleness.

incontest|able /ɛ̃kɔ̃tɛstabl/ a. indisputable. ~é a. undisputed.

incontinen|t, ~te /ɛ̃kɔ̃tinɑ̃, -t/ a. incontinent. ~ce n.f. incontinence.

incontrôlable /ɛ̃kɔ̃trolabl/ a. unverifiable.

inconvenan|t, ~te /ɛ̃kɔ̃vnɑ̃, -t/ a. improper. ~ce n.f. impropriety.

inconvénient /ɛ̃kɔ̃venjɑ̃/ n.m. disadvantage; (*risque*) risk; (*objection*) objection.

incorpor|er /ɛ̃kɔrpɔre/ v.t. incorporate; (mil.) enlist. ~ation n.f. incorporation; (mil.) enlistment.

incorrect /ɛ̃kɔrɛkt/ a. (faux) incorrect; (malséant) improper; (impoli) impolite.

incorrigible /ɛ̃kɔriʒibl/ a. incorrigible.

incrédul|e /ɛ̃kredyl/ a. incredulous. ~ité n.f. incredulity.

increvable /ɛ̃krəvabl/ a. (fam.) tireless.

incriminer /ɛ̃krimine/ v.t. incriminate.

incroyable /ɛ̃krwajabl/ a. incredible.

incroyant, ~e /ɛ̃krwajɑ̃, -t/ n.m., f. non-believer.

incrust|er /ɛ̃kryste/ v.t. (décorer) inlay (de, with). s'~er (invité: péj.) take root. ~ation n.f. inlay.

incubateur /ɛ̃kybatœr/ n.m. incubator.

inculp|er /ɛ̃kylpe/ v.t. charge (de, with). ~ation n.f. charge. ~é, ~ée n.m., f. accused.

inculquer /ɛ̃kylke/ v.t. instil (à, into).

inculte /ɛ̃kylt/ a. uncultivated; (personne) uneducated.

incurable /ɛ̃kyrabl/ a. incurable.

incursion /ɛ̃kyrsjɔ̃/ n.f. incursion.

incurver /ɛ̃kyrve/ v.t., s'~ v. pr. curve.

Inde /ɛ̃d/ n.f. India.

indécen|t, ~te /ɛ̃desɑ̃, -t/ a. indecent. ~ce n.f. indecency.

indéchiffrable /ɛ̃deʃifrabl/ a. indecipherable.

indécis, ~e /ɛ̃desi, -z/ a. indecisive; (qui n'a pas encore pris de décision) undecided. ~ion /-izjɔ̃/ n.f. indecision.

indéfendable /ɛ̃defɑ̃dabl/ a. indefensible.

indéfini /ɛ̃defini/ a. indefinite; (vague) undefined. ~ment adv. indefinitely. ~ssable a. indefinable.

indélébile /ɛ̃delebil/ a. indelible.

indélicat, ~e /ɛ̃delika, -t/ a. (malhonnête) unscrupulous.

indemne /ɛ̃dɛmn/ a. unharmed.

indemniser /ɛ̃dɛmnize/ v.t. compensate (de, for).

indemnité /ɛ̃dɛmnite/ n.f. indemnity; (allocation) allowance. ~s de licenciement, redundancy payment.

indéniable /ɛ̃denjabl/ a. undeniable.

indépend|ant, ~ante /ɛ̃depɑ̃dɑ̃, -t/ a. independent. ~amment adv. independently. ~amment de, apart from. ~ance n.f. independence.

indescriptible /ɛ̃dɛskriptibl/ a. indescribable.

indésirable /ɛ̃dezirabl/ a. & n.m./f. undesirable.

indestructible /ɛ̃dɛstryktibl/ a. indestructible.

indétermination /ɛ̃detɛrminasjɔ̃/ n.f. indecision.

indéterminé /ɛ̃detɛrmine/ a. unspecified.

index /ɛ̃dɛks/ n.m. forefinger; (liste) index. ~er v.t. index.

indic /ɛ̃dik/ (fam.) grass.

indica|teur, ~trice /ɛ̃dikatœr, -tris/ n.m., f. (police) informer. ● n.m. (livre) guide; (techn.) indicator. ~teur des chemins de fer, railway timetable. ~teur des rues, street directory.

indicati|f, ~ve /ɛ̃dikatif, -v/ a. indicative (de, of). ● n.m. (radio) signature tune; (téléphonique) dialling code; (gram.) indicative.

indication /ɛ̃dikasjɔ̃/ n.f. indication; (renseignement) information; (directive) instruction.

indice /ɛ̃dis/ n.m. sign; (dans une enquête) clue; (des prix) index; (de salaire) rating.

indien, ~ne /ɛ̃djɛ̃, -jɛn/ a. & n.m., f. Indian.

indifféremment /ɛ̃diferamɑ̃/ adv. equally.

indifféren|t, ~te /ɛ̃diferɑ̃, -t/ a. indifferent (à, to). ça m'est ~t, it makes no difference to me. ~ce n.f. indifference.

indigène /ɛ̃diʒɛn/ a. & n.m./f. native.

indigen|t, ~te /ɛ̃diʒɑ̃, -t/ a. poor. ~ce n.f. poverty.

indigeste /ɛ̃diʒɛst/ a. indigestible. ~ion n.f. indigestion.

indignation /ɛ̃diɲasjɔ̃/ n.f. indignation.

indign|e /ɛ̃diɲ/ a. unworthy (de, of); (acte) vile. ~ité n.f. unworthiness; (acte) vile act.

indigner /ɛ̃diɲe/ s'~ v. pr. become indignant (de, at).

indiqu|er /ɛ̃dike/ v.t. show, indicate; (renseigner sur) point out, tell; (déterminer) give, state, appoint. ~er du doigt, point to ou out ou at. ~é a. (heure) appointed; (opportun) appropriate; (conseillé) recommended.

indirect /ɛ̃dirɛkt/ a. indirect.

indiscipliné /ɛ̃disipline/ a. unruly.

indiscr|et, **~ète** /ɛ̃diskrɛ, -t/ a. inquisitive. **~étion** n.f. indiscretion; inquisitiveness.

indiscutable /ɛ̃diskytabl/ a. unquestionable.

indispensable /ɛ̃dispɑ̃sabl/ a. indispensable. **il est ~ qu'il vienne**, it is essential that he comes.

indispos|er /ɛ̃dispoze/ v.t. make unwell. **~er** (*mécontenter*) antagonize. **~é** a. unwell. **~ition** n.f. indisposition.

indistinct, **~e** /ɛ̃distɛ̃(kt), -ɛ̃kt/ a. indistinct. **~ement** /-ɛ̃ktəmɑ̃/ adv. indistinctly; (*également*) without distinction.

individ|u /ɛ̃dividy/ n.m. individual. **~ualiste** n.m./f. individualist.

individuel, **~le** /ɛ̃dividɥɛl/ a. individual; (*opinion*) personal. **chambre ~le**, single room. **maison ~le**, private house. **~lement** adv. individually.

indivisible /ɛ̃divizibl/ a. indivisible.

indolen|t, **~te** /ɛ̃dɔlɑ̃, -t/ a. indolent. **~ce** n.f. indolence.

indolore /ɛ̃dɔlɔr/ a. painless.

Indonésie /ɛ̃dɔnezi/ n.f. Indonesia.

Indonésien, **~ne** /ɛ̃dɔnezjɛ̃, -jɛn/ a. & n.m., f. Indonesian.

indu, **~e** /ɛ̃dy/ a. **à une heure ~e**, at some ungodly hour.

induire /ɛ̃dɥir/ v.t. infer (**de**, from). **~ en erreur**, mislead.

indulgen|t, **~te** /ɛ̃dylʒɑ̃, -t/ a. indulgent; (*clément*) lenient. **~ce** n.f. indulgence; leniency.

industr|ie /ɛ̃dystri/ n.f. industry. **~ialisé** a. industrialized.

industriel, **~le** /ɛ̃dystrijɛl/ a. industrial. ● n.m. industrialist. **~lement** adv. industrially.

inébranlable /inebrɑ̃labl/ a. unshakeable.

inédit, **~e** /inedi, -t/ a. unpublished; (*fig.*) original.

inefficace /inefikas/ a. ineffective.

inég|al (m. pl. **~aux**) /inegal, -o/ a. unequal; (*irrégulier*) uneven. **~alé** a. unequalled. **~alable** a. matchless. **~alité** n.f. (*injustice*) inequality; (*irrégularité*) unevenness; (*différence*) difference (**de**, between).

inéluctable /inelyktabl/ a. inescapable.

inep|te /inɛpt/ a. inept, absurd. **~ie** /inɛpsi/ n.f. ineptitude.

inépuisable /inepɥizabl/ a. inexhaustible.

inert|e /inɛrt/ a. inert; (*mort*) lifeless. **~ie** /inɛrsi/ n.f. inertia.

inespéré /inɛspere/ a. unhoped for.

inestimable /inɛstimabl/ a. priceless.

inévitable /inevitabl/ a. inevitable.

inexact, **~e** /inɛgza(kt), -akt/ a. (*imprécis*) inaccurate; (*incorrect*) incorrect.

inexcusable /inɛkskyzabl/ a. unforgivable.

inexistant, **~e** /inɛgzistɑ̃, -t/ a. nonexistent.

inexorable /inɛgzɔrabl/ a. inexorable.

inexpérience /inɛksperjɑ̃s/ n.f. inexperience.

inexpli|cable /inɛksplikabl/ a. inexplicable. **~qué** a. unexplained.

in extremis /inɛkstremis/ adv. & a. (*par nécessité*) (taken/done etc.) as a last resort; (*au dernier moment*) (at the) last minute.

inextricable /inɛkstrikabl/ a. inextricable.

infaillible /ɛ̃fajibl/ a. infallible.

infâme /ɛ̃fɑm/ a. vile.

infamie /ɛ̃fami/ n.f. infamy; (*action*) vile action.

infanterie /ɛ̃fɑ̃tri/ n.f. infantry.

infantile /ɛ̃fɑ̃til/ a. infantile.

infantilisme /ɛ̃fɑ̃tilism/ n.m. infantilism. **faire de l'~**, be childish.

infarctus /ɛ̃farktys/ n.m. coronary (thrombosis).

infatigable /ɛ̃fatigabl/ a. tireless.

infatué /ɛ̃fatɥe/ a. **~ de sa personne**, full of himself.

infect /ɛ̃fɛkt/ a. revolting.

infect|er /ɛ̃fɛkte/ v.t. infect. **s'~er** v. pr. become infected. **~ion** /-ksjɔ̃/ n.f. infection.

infectieu|x, **~se** /ɛ̃fɛksjø, -z/ a. infectious.

inférieur, **~e** /ɛ̃ferjœr/ a. (*plus bas*) lower; (*moins bon*) inferior (**à**, to). ● n.m., f. inferior. **~ à**, (*plus petit que*) smaller than.

infériorité /ɛ̃ferjɔrite/ n.f. inferiority.

infern|al (m. pl. **~aux**) /ɛ̃fɛrnal, -o/ a. infernal.

infester /ɛ̃fɛste/ v.t. infest.

infid|èle /ɛ̃fidɛl/ a. unfaithful. **~élité** n.f. unfaithfulness; (*acte*) infidelity.

infiltr|er (s') /(s)ɛ̃filtre/ v. pr. **s'~er** (**dans**), (*personnes, idées, etc.*) infiltrate; (*liquide*) percolate. **~ation** *n.f.* infiltration.

infime /ɛ̃fim/ *a.* tiny, minute.

infini /ɛ̃fini/ *a.* infinite. ● *n.m.* infinity. **à l'~,** endlessly. **~ment** *adv.* infinitely.

infinité /ɛ̃finite/ *n.f.* **une ~ de,** an infinite amount of.

infinitésimal /ɛ̃finitezimal/ *a.* infinitesimal.

infinitif /ɛ̃finitif/ *n.m.* infinitive.

infirm|e /ɛ̃firm/ *a. & n.m./f.* disabled (person). **~ité** *n.f.* disability.

infirmer /ɛ̃firme/ *v.t.* invalidate.

infirm|erie /ɛ̃firməri/ *n.f.* sickbay, infirmary. **~ier** *n.m.* (male) nurse. **~ière** *n.f.* nurse. **~ière-chef,** sister.

inflammable /ɛ̃flamabl/ *a.* (in)flammable.

inflammation /ɛ̃flamɑsjɔ̃/ *n.f.* inflammation.

inflation /ɛ̃flɑsjɔ̃/ *n.f.* inflation.

inflexible /ɛ̃flɛksibl/ *a.* inflexible.

inflexion /ɛ̃flɛksjɔ̃/ *n.f.* inflexion.

infliger /ɛ̃fliʒe/ *v.t.* inflict; (*sanction*) impose.

influen|ce /ɛ̃flyɑ̃s/ *n.f.* influence. **~çable** *a.* easily influenced. **~cer** *v.t.* influence.

influent, ~e /ɛ̃flyɑ̃, -t/ *a.* influential.

influer /ɛ̃flye/ *v.i.* **~ sur,** influence.

info /ɛ̃fo/ *n.f.* (some) news. **les ~s,** the news.

informa|teur, ~trice /ɛ̃fɔrmatœr, -tris/ *n.m., f.* informant.

informaticien, ~ne /ɛ̃fɔrmatisjɛ̃, -jɛn/ *n.m., f.* computer scientist.

information /ɛ̃fɔrmɑsjɔ̃/ *n.f.* information; (*jurid.*) inquiry. **une ~,** (some) information; (*nouvelle*) (some) news. **les ~s,** the news.

informati|que /ɛ̃fɔrmatik/ *n.f.* computer science; (*techniques*) data processing. **~ser** *v.t.* computerize.

informe /ɛ̃fɔrm/ *a.* shapeless.

informer /ɛ̃fɔrme/ *v.t.* inform (**de,** about, of). **s'~** *v. pr.* enquire (**de,** about).

infortune /ɛ̃fɔrtyn/ *n.f.* misfortune.

infraction /ɛ̃fraksjɔ̃/ *n.f.* offence. **~ à,** breach of.

infranchissable /ɛ̃frɑ̃ʃisabl/ *a.* impassable; (*fig.*) insuperable.

infrarouge /ɛ̃fraruʒ/ *a.* infra-red.

infrastructure /ɛ̃frastryktyr/ *n.f.* infrastructure.

infructueu|x, ~se /ɛ̃fryktɥø, -z/ *a.* fruitless.

infus|er /ɛ̃fyze/ *v.t./i.* infuse, brew. **~ion** *n.f.* herb-tea, infusion.

ingénier (s') /(s)ɛ̃ʒenje/ *v. pr.* **s'~ à,** strive to.

ingénieur /ɛ̃ʒenjœr/ *n.m.* engineer.

ingén|ieux, ~ieuse /ɛ̃ʒenjø, -z/ *a.* ingenious. **~iosité** *n.f.* ingenuity.

ingénu /ɛ̃ʒeny/ *a.* naïve.

ingér|er (s') /(s)ɛ̃ʒere/ *v. pr.* **s'~er dans,** interfere in. **~ence** *n.f.* interference.

ingrat, ~e /ɛ̃gra, -t/ *a.* ungrateful; (*pénible*) thankless; (*disgracieux*) unattractive. **~itude** /-tityd/ *n.f.* ingratitude.

ingrédient /ɛ̃gredjɑ̃/ *n.m.* ingredient.

ingurgiter /ɛ̃gyrʒite/ *v.t.* swallow.

inhabité /inabite/ *a.* uninhabited.

inhabituel, ~le /inabitɥel/ *a.* unusual.

inhalation /inalɑsjɔ̃/ *n.f.* inhaling.

inhérent, ~e /inerɑ̃, -t/ *a.* inherent (**à, in**).

inhibition /inibisjɔ̃/ *n.f.* inhibition.

inhospital|ier, ~ière /inɔspitalje, -jɛr/ *a.* inhospitable.

inhumain, ~e /inymɛ̃, -ɛn/ *a.* inhuman.

inhum|er /inyme/ *v.t.* bury. **~ation** *n.f.* burial.

inimaginable /inimaʒinabl/ *a.* unimaginable.

inimitié /inimitje/ *n.f.* enmity.

ininterrompu /inɛ̃tɛrɔ̃py/ *a.* continuous, uninterrupted.

inique /inik/ *a.* iniquitous. **~ité** *n.f.* iniquity.

init|ial (*m. pl.* **~iaux**) /inisjal, -jo/ *a.* initial. **~ialement** *adv.* initially.

initiale /inisjal/ *n.f.* initial.

initialis|er /inisjalize/ (*comput.*) format. **~ation** *n.f.* formatting.

initiative /inisjativ/ *n.f.* initiative.

init|ier /inisje/ *v.t.* initiate (**à, into**). **s'~ier** *v. pr.* become initiated (**à, into**). **~iateur, ~iatrice** *n.m., f.* initiator. **~iation** *n.f.* initiation.

inject|er /ɛ̃ʒekte/ *v.t.* inject. **~é de sang,** bloodshot. **~ion** /-ksjɔ̃/ *n.f.* injection.

injur|e /ɛ̃ʒyr/ *n.f.* insult. **~ier** *v.t.* insult. **~ieux, ~ieuse** *a.* insulting.

injust|e /ɛ̃ʒyst/ *a.* unjust, unfair. **~ice** *n.f.* injustice.

inlassable /ɛ̃lɑsabl/ *a.* tireless.

inné /ine/ *a.* innate, inborn.

innocen|t, ~te /inɔsɑ̃, -t/ *a. & n.m., f.* innocent. **~ce** *n.f.* innocence.

innocenter /inɔsɑ̃te/ *v.t.* (*disculper*) clear, prove innocent.

innombrable /inɔ̃brabl/ *a.* countless.

innov|er /inɔve/ *v.i.* innovate. **~ateur, ~atrice** *n.m.,* f. innovator. **~ation** *n.f.* innovation.

inoccupé /inɔkype/ *a.* unoccupied.

inoculer /inɔkyle/ *v.t.* inoculate.

inodore /inɔdɔr/ *a.* odourless.

inoffensi|f, ~ve /inɔfɑ̃sif, -v/ *a.* harmless.

inond|er /inɔ̃de/ *v.t.* flood; (*mouiller*) soak; (*envahir*) inundate (**de**, with). **~é de soleil**, bathed in sunlight. **~ation** *n.f.* flood; (*action*) flooding.

inopérant, ~e /inɔperɑ̃, -t/ *a.* inoperative.

inopiné /inɔpine/ *a.* unexpected.

inopportun, ~e /inɔpɔrtœ̃, -yn/ *a.* inopportune.

inoubliable /inublijabl/ *a.* unforgettable.

inouï /inwi/ *a.* incredible.

inox /inɔks/ *n.m.* (P.) stainless steel.

inoxydable /inɔksidabl/ *a.* **acier ~**, stainless steel.

inqualifiable /ɛ̃kalifjabl/ *a.* unspeakable.

inqu|iet, ~iète /ɛ̃kjɛ, -jɛt/ *a.* worried. ● *n.m.,* f. worrier.

inquiét|er /ɛ̃kjete/ *v.t.* worry. **s'~er** worry (**de**, about). **~ant, ~ante** *a.* worrying.

inquiétude /ɛ̃kjetyd/ *n.f.* anxiety, worry.

inquisition /ɛ̃kizisjɔ̃/ *n.f.* inquisition.

insaisissable /ɛ̃sezisabl/ *a.* indefinable.

insalubre /ɛ̃salybr/ *a.* unhealthy.

insanité /ɛ̃sanite/ *n.f.* insanity.

insatiable /ɛ̃sasjabl/ *a.* insatiable.

insatisfaisant, ~e /ɛ̃satisfəzɑ̃, -t/ *a.* unsatisfactory.

insatisfait, ~e /ɛ̃satisfɛ, -t/ *a.* (*mécontent*) dissatisfied; (*frustré*) unfulfilled.

inscription /ɛ̃skripsjɔ̃/ *n.f.* inscription; (*immatriculation*) enrolment.

inscrire† /ɛ̃skrir/ *v.t.* write (down); (*graver, tracer*) inscribe; (*personne*) enrol; (*sur une liste*) put down. **s'~** *v. pr.* put one's name down. **s'~ à**, (*école*) enrol at; (*club, parti*) join; (*examen*) enter for. **s'~ dans le cadre de**, come within the framework of.

insecte /ɛ̃sɛkt/ *n.m.* insect.

insecticide /ɛ̃sɛktisid/ *n.m.* insecticide.

insécurité /ɛ̃sekyrite/ *n.f.* insecurity.

insensé /ɛ̃sɑ̃se/ *a.* mad.

insensib|le /ɛ̃sɑ̃sibl/ *a.* insensitive (**à**, to); (*graduel*) imperceptible. **~ilité** *n.f.* insensitivity.

inséparable /ɛ̃separabl/ *a.* inseparable.

insérer /ɛ̃sere/ *v.t.* insert. **s'~ dans**, be part of.

insidieu|x, ~se /ɛ̃sidjø, -z/ *a.* insidious.

insigne /ɛ̃siɲ/ *n.m.* badge. **~(s)**, (*d'une fonction*) insignia.

insignifian|t, ~te /ɛ̃siɲifjɑ̃, -t/ *a.* insignificant. **~ce** *n.f.* insignificance.

insinuation /ɛ̃sinɥasjɔ̃/ *n.f.* insinuation.

insinuer /ɛ̃sinɥe/ *v.t.* insinuate. **s'~ dans**, penetrate.

insipide /ɛ̃sipid/ *a.* insipid.

insistan|t, ~te /ɛ̃sistɑ̃, -t/ *a.* insistent. **~ce** *n.f.* insistence.

insister /ɛ̃siste/ *v.i.* insist (**pour faire**, on doing). **~ sur**, stress.

insolation /ɛ̃sɔlasjɔ̃/ *n.f.* (*méd.*) sunstroke.

insolen|t, ~te /ɛ̃sɔlɑ̃, -t/ *a.* insolent. **~ce** *n.f.* insolence.

insolite /ɛ̃sɔlit/ *a.* unusual.

insoluble /ɛ̃sɔlybl/ *a.* insoluble.

insolvable /ɛ̃sɔlvabl/ *a.* insolvent.

insomnie /ɛ̃sɔmni/ *n.f.* insomnia.

insonoriser /ɛ̃sɔnɔrize/ *v.t.* soundproof.

insoucian|t, ~te /ɛ̃susjɑ̃, -t/ *a.* carefree. **~ce** *n.f.* unconcern.

insoumission /ɛ̃sumisjɔ̃/ *n.f.* rebelliousness.

insoupçonnable /ɛ̃supsɔnabl/ *a.* undetectable.

insoutenable /ɛ̃sutnabl/ *a.* unbearable; (*argument*) untenable.

inspec|ter /ɛ̃spɛkte/ *v.t.* inspect. **~teur, ~trice** *n.m.,* f. inspector. **~tion** /-ksjɔ̃/ *n.f.* inspection.

inspirer /ɛ̃spire/ *v.t.* inspire. ● *v.i.* breathe in. **~er à qn.**, inspire s.o. with. **s'~er de**, be inspired by. **~ation** *n.f.* inspiration; (*respiration*) breath.

instab|le /ɛ̃stabl/ *a.* unstable; (*temps*) unsettled; (*meuble, équilibre*) unsteady. **~ilité** *n.f.* instability; unsteadiness.

install|er /ɛ̃stale/ *v.t.* install; (*gaz, meuble*) put in; (*étagère*) put up;

(*équiper*) fit out. **s'~er** *v. pr.* settle (down); (*emménager*) settle in. **s'~er comme,** set o.s. up as. **~ation** *n.f.* installation; (*de local*) fitting out; (*de locataire*) settling in. **~ations** *n.f. pl.* (*appareils*) fittings.

instance /ɛ̃stɑ̃s/ *n.f.* authority; (*prière*) entreaty. **avec ~,** with insistence. **en ~,** pending. **en ~ de,** in the course of, on the point of.

instant /ɛ̃stɑ̃/ *n.m.* moment, instant. **à l'~,** this instant.

instantané /ɛ̃stɑ̃tane/ *a.* instantaneous; (*café*) instant.

instar /ɛ̃star/ *n.m.* **à l'~ de,** like.

instaur|er /ɛ̃store/ *v.t.* institute. **~ation** *n.f.* institution.

instiga|teur, ~trice /ɛ̃stigatœr, -tris/ *n.m., f.* instigator. **~tion** /-asjɔ̃/ instigation.

instinct /ɛ̃stɛ̃/ *n.m.* instinct. **d'~,** instinctively.

instincti|f, ~ve /ɛ̃stɛ̃ktif, -v/ *a.* instinctive. **~vement** *adv.* instinctively.

instit /ɛ̃stit/ *n.m./f.* (*fam.*) teacher.

instituer /ɛ̃stitɥe/ *v.t.* establish.

institut /ɛ̃stity/ *n.m.* institute. **~ de beauté,** beauty parlour. **~ universitaire de technologie,** polytechnic, technical college.

institu|teur, ~trice /ɛ̃stitytœr, -tris/ *n.m., f.* primary-school teacher.

institution /ɛ̃stitysjɔ̃/ *n.f.* institution; (*école*) private school.

instructi|f, ~ve /ɛ̃stryktif, -v/ *a.* instructive.

instruction /ɛ̃stryksjɔ̃/ *n.f.* education; (*document*) directive. **~s,** (*ordres, mode d'emploi*) instructions.

instruire† /ɛ̃strɥir/ *v.t.* teach, educate. **~ de,** inform of. **s'~** *v. pr.* educate o.s. **s'~ de,** enquire about.

instruit, ~e /ɛ̃strɥi, -t/ *a.* educated.

instrument /ɛ̃strymɑ̃/ *n.m.* instrument; (*outil*) implement.

insu /ɛ̃sy/ *n.m.* **à l'~ de,** without the knowledge of.

insubordination /ɛ̃sybɔrdinasjɔ̃/ *n.f.* insubordination.

insuffisan|t, ~te /ɛ̃syfizɑ̃, -t/ *a.* inadequate; (*en nombre*) insufficient. **~ce** *n.f.* inadequacy.

insulaire /ɛ̃sylɛr/ *a.* island. ● *n.m./f.* islander.

insuline /ɛ̃sylin/ *n.f.* insulin.

insult|e /ɛ̃sylt/ *n.f.* insult. **~er** *v.t.* insult.

insupportable /ɛ̃sypɔrtabl/ *a.* unbearable.

insurg|er (s') /(s)ɛ̃syrʒe/ *v. pr.* rebel. **~é, ~ée** *a. & n.m., f.* rebel.

insurmontable /ɛ̃syrmɔ̃tabl/ *a.* insurmountable.

insurrection /ɛ̃syrɛksjɔ̃/ *n.f.* insurrection.

intact /ɛ̃takt/ *a.* intact.

intangible /ɛ̃tɑ̃ʒibl/ *a.* intangible.

intarissable /ɛ̃tarisabl/ *a.* inexhaustible.

intégr|al (*m. pl. ~aux*) /ɛ̃tegral, -o/ *a.* complete; (*édition*) unabridged. **~alement** *adv.* in full. **~alité** *n.f.* whole. **dans son ~alité,** in full.

intégrant, ~e /ɛ̃tegrɑ̃, -t/ *a.* **faire partie ~e de,** be part and parcel of.

intègre /ɛ̃tegr/ *a.* upright.

intégr|er /ɛ̃tegre/ *v.t.,* **s'~er** *v. pr.* integrate. **~ation** *n.f.* integration.

intégri|ste /ɛ̃tegrist/ *a.* fundamentalist. **~sme** /-sm/ *n.m.* fundamentalism.

intégrité /ɛ̃tegrite/ *n.f.* integrity.

intellect /ɛ̃telɛkt/ *n.m.* intellect. **~uel, ~uelle** *a. & n.m., f.* intellectual.

intelligence /ɛ̃teliʒɑ̃s/ *n.f.* intelligence; (*compréhension*) understanding; (*complicité*) complicity.

intellig|ent, ~ente /ɛ̃teliʒɑ̃, -t/ *a.* intelligent. **~emment** /-amɑ̃/ *adv.* intelligently.

intelligible /ɛ̃teliʒibl/ *a.* intelligible.

intempéries /ɛ̃tɑ̃peri/ *n.f. pl.* severe weather.

intempesti|f, ~ve /ɛ̃tɑ̃pɛstif, -v/ *a.* untimely.

intenable /ɛ̃tnabl/ *a.* unbearable; (*enfant*) impossible.

intendan|t, ~te /ɛ̃tɑ̃dɑ̃, -t/ *n.m.* (*mil.*) quartermaster. ● *n.m., f.* (*scol.*) bursar. **~ce** *n.f.* (*scol.*) bursar's office.

intens|e /ɛ̃tɑ̃s/ *a.* intense; (*circulation*) heavy. **~ément** *adv.* intensely. **~ifier** *v.t.,* **s'~ifier** *v. pr.* intensify. **~ité** *n.f.* intensity.

intensi|f, ~ve /ɛ̃tɑ̃sif, -v/ *a.* intensive.

intenter /ɛ̃tɑ̃te/ *v.t.* **~ un procès** *ou* **une action,** institute proceedings (**à, contre,** against).

intention /ɛ̃tɑ̃sjɔ̃/ *n.f.* intention (**de faire,** of doing). **à l'~ de qn.,** for s.o. **~né** /-jɔne/ *a.* **bien/mal ~né,** well-/ill-intentioned.

intentionnel, ~le /ētɑ̃sjɔnɛl/ a. intentional.

inter- /ɛ̃tɛr/ préf. inter-.

interaction /ɛ̃tɛraksjɔ̃/ n.f. interaction.

intercaler /ɛ̃tɛrkale/ v.t. insert.

intercéder /ɛ̃tɛrsede/ v.i. intercede **(en faveur de,** on behalf of).

intercept|er /ɛ̃tɛrsɛpte/ v.t. intercept. **~ion** /-sjɔ̃/ n.f. interception.

interchangeable /ɛ̃tɛrʃɑ̃ʒabl/ a. interchangeable.

interdiction /ɛ̃tɛrdiksjɔ̃/ n.f. ban. **~ de fumer,** no smoking.

interdire† /ɛ̃tɛrdir/ v.t. forbid; (officiellement) ban, prohibit. **~ à qn. de faire,** forbid s.o. to do.

interdit, ~e /ɛ̃tɛrdi, -t/ a. (étonné) nonplussed.

intéressant, ~e /ɛ̃terɛsɑ̃, -t/ a. interesting; (avantageux) attractive.

intéressé, ~e /ɛ̃terese/ a. (en cause) concerned; (pour profiter) self-interested. ● n.m., f. person concerned.

intéresser /ɛ̃terese/ v.t. interest; (concerner) concern. **s'~ à,** be interested in.

intérêt /ɛ̃terɛ/ n.m. interest; (égoïsme) self-interest. **~(s),** (comm.) interest. **vous avez ~ à,** it is in your interest to.

interférence /ɛ̃tɛrferɑ̃s/ n.f. interference.

intérieur /ɛ̃terjœr/ a. inner, inside; (vol, politique) domestic; (vie, calme) inner. ● n.m. interior; (de boite, tiroir) inside. **à l'~ (de),** inside; (fig.) within. **~ement** adv. inwardly.

intérim /ɛ̃terim/ n.m. interim. **assurer l'~,** deputize (de, for). **par ~,** acting. **faire de l'~,** temp. **~aire** a. temporary, interim.

interjection /ɛ̃tɛrʒɛksjɔ̃/ n.f. interjection.

interlocu|teur, ~trice /ɛ̃tɛrlɔkytœr, -tris/ n.m., f. **son ~teur,** the person one is speaking to.

interloqué /ɛ̃tɛrlɔke/ a. **être ~,** be taken aback.

intermède /ɛ̃tɛrmɛd/ n.m. interlude.

intermédiaire /ɛ̃tɛrmedjɛr/ a. intermediate. ● n.m./f. intermediary.

interminable /ɛ̃tɛrminabl/ a. endless.

intermittence /ɛ̃tɛrmitɑ̃s/ n.f. **par ~,** intermittently.

intermittent, ~e /ɛ̃tɛrmitɑ̃, -t/ a. intermittent.

internat /ɛ̃tɛrna/ n.m. boarding-school.

internation|al (m. pl. **~aux**) /ɛ̃tɛrnasjɔnal, -o/ a. international.

interne /ɛ̃tɛrn/ a. internal. ● n.m./f. (scol.) boarder.

intern|er /ɛ̃tɛrne/ v.t. (pol.) intern; (méd.) confine. **~ement** n.m. (pol.) internment.

interpell|er /ɛ̃tɛrpɛle/ v.t. shout to; (apostropher) shout at; (interroger) question. **~ation** n.f. (pol.) questioning.

interphone /ɛ̃tɛrfɔn/ n.m. intercom.

interposer (s') /(s)ɛ̃tɛrpoze/ v. pr. intervene.

interpr|ète /ɛ̃tɛrprɛt/ n.m./f. interpreter; (artiste) performer. **~étariat** n.m. interpreting.

interprét|er /ɛ̃tɛrprete/ v.t. interpret; (jouer) play; (chanter) sing. **~ation** n.f. interpretation; (d'artiste) performance.

interroga|teur, ~trice /ɛ̃tɛrɔgatœr, -tris/ a. questioning.

interrogati|f, ~ve /ɛ̃tɛrɔgatif, -v/ a. interrogative.

interrogatoire /ɛ̃tɛrɔgatwar/ n.m. interrogation.

interro|ger /ɛ̃tɛrɔʒe/ v.t. question; (élève) test. **~gateur, ~gatrice** a. questioning. **~gation** n.f. question; (action) questioning; (épreuve) test.

interr|ompre† /ɛ̃tɛrɔ̃pr/ v.t. break off, interrupt; (personne) interrupt. **s'~ompre** v. pr. break off. **~upteur** n.m. switch. **~uption** n.f. interruption; (arrêt) break.

intersection /ɛ̃tɛrsɛksjɔ̃/ n.f. intersection.

interstice /ɛ̃tɛrstis/ n.m. crack.

interurbain /ɛ̃tɛryrbɛ̃/ n.m. long-distance telephone service.

intervalle /ɛ̃tɛrval/ n.m. space; (temps) interval. **dans l'~,** in the meantime.

interven|ir† /ɛ̃tɛrvənir/ v.i. intervene; (survenir) occur; (méd.) operate. **~tion** /-vɑ̃sjɔ̃/ n.f. intervention; (méd.) operation.

intervertir /ɛ̃tɛrvertir/ v.t. invert.

interview /ɛ̃tɛrvju/ n.f. interview. **~er** /-ve/ v.t. interview.

intestin /ɛ̃tɛstɛ̃/ n.m. intestine.

intim|e /ɛ̃tim/ a. intimate; (fête, vie) private; (dîner) quiet. ● n.m./f. intimate friend. **~ement** adv.

intimately. **~ité** *n.f.* intimacy; (*vie privée*) privacy.
intimid|er /ɛ̃timide/ *v.t.* intimidate. **~ation** *n.f.* intimidation.
intituler /ɛ̃tityle/ *v.t.* entitle. **s'~** *v. pr.* be entitled.
intolérable /ɛ̃tɔlerabl/ *a.* intolerable.
intoléran|t, ~te /ɛ̃tɔlerã, -t/ *a.* intolerant. **~ce** *n.f.* intolerance.
intonation /ɛ̃tɔnasjɔ̃/ *n.f.* intonation.
intox /ɛ̃tɔks/ *n.f.* (*fam.*) brainwashing.
intoxi|quer /ɛ̃tɔsike/ *v.t.* poison; (*pol.*) brainwash. **~cation** *n.f.* poisoning; (*pol.*) brainwashing.
intraduisible /ɛ̃tradɥizibl/ *a.* untranslatable.
intraitable /ɛ̃tretabl/ *a.* inflexible.
intransigean|t, ~te /ɛ̃trãsiʒã, -t/ *a.* intransigent. **~ce** *n.f.* intransigence.
intransiti|f, ~ve /ɛ̃trãzitif, -v/ *a.* intransitive.
intraveineu|x, ~se /ɛ̃travɛnø, -z/ *a.* intravenous.
intrépide /ɛ̃trepid/ *a.* fearless.
intrigu|e /ɛ̃trig/ *n.f.* intrigue; (*théâtre*) plot. **~er** *v.t./i.* intrigue.
intrinsèque /ɛ̃trɛ̃sɛk/ *a.* intrinsic.
introduction /ɛ̃trɔdyksjɔ̃/ *n.f.* introduction.
introduire† /ɛ̃trɔdɥir/ *v.t.* introduce, bring in; (*insérer*) put in, insert. **~ qn.**, show s.o. in. **s'~ dans**, get into, enter.
introspecti|f, ~ve /ɛ̃trɔspɛktif, -v/ *a.* introspective.
introuvable /ɛ̃truvabl/ *a.* that cannot be found.
introverti, ~e /ɛ̃trɔvɛrti/ *n.m., f.* introvert. ● *a.* introverted.
intrus, ~e /ɛ̃try, -z/ *n.m., f.* intruder. **~ion** /-zjɔ̃/ *n.f.* intrusion.
intuiti|f, ~ve /ɛ̃tɥitif, -v/ *a.* intuitive.
intuition /ɛ̃tɥisjɔ̃/ *n.f.* intuition.
inusable /inyzabl/ *a.* hard-wearing.
inusité /inyzite/ *a.* little used.
inutil|e /inytil/ *a.* useless; (*vain*) needless. **~ement** *adv.* needlessly. **~ité** *n.f.* uselessness.
inutilisable /inytilizabl/ *a.* unusable.
invalid|e /ɛ̃valid/ *a. & n.m./f.* disabled (person). **~ité** *n.f.* disablement.
invariable /ɛ̃varjabl/ *a.* invariable.
invasion /ɛ̃vazjɔ̃/ *n.f.* invasion.
invectiv|e /ɛ̃vɛktiv/ *n.f.* invective. **~er** *v.t.* abuse.

invend|able /ɛ̃vãdabl/ *a.* unsaleable. **~u** *a.* unsold.
inventaire /ɛ̃vãtɛr/ *n.m.* inventory. **faire l'~ de**, take stock of.
invent|er /ɛ̃vãte/ *v.t.* invent. **~eur** *n.m.* inventor. **~ion** /ɛ̃vãsjɔ̃/ *n.f.* invention.
inventi|f, ~ve /ɛ̃vãtif, -v/ *a.* inventive.
inverse /ɛ̃vɛrs/ *a.* opposite; (*ordre*) reverse. ● *n.m.* reverse. **~ment** /-əmã/ *adv.* conversely.
invers|er /ɛ̃vɛrse/ *v.t.* reverse, invert. **~ion** *n.f.* inversion.
investigation /ɛ̃vɛstigasjɔ̃/ *n.f.* investigation.
invest|ir /ɛ̃vɛstir/ *v.t.* invest. **~issement** *n.m.* (*comm.*) investment.
investiture /ɛ̃vɛstityr/ *n.f.* nomination.
invétéré /ɛ̃vetere/ *a.* inveterate.
invincible /ɛ̃vɛ̃sibl/ *a.* invincible.
invisible /ɛ̃vizibl/ *a.* invisible.
invit|er /ɛ̃vite/ *v.t.* invite (à, to). **~ation** *n.f.* invitation. **~é, ~ée** *n.m., f.* guest.
invivable /ɛ̃vivabl/ *a.* unbearable.
involontaire /ɛ̃vɔlɔ̃tɛr/ *a.* involuntary.
invoquer /ɛ̃vɔke/ *v.t.* call upon, invoke; (*alléguer*) plead.
invraisembl|able /ɛ̃vrɛsãblabl/ *a.* improbable; (*incroyable*) incredible. **~ance** *n.f.* improbability.
invulnérable /ɛ̃vylnerabl/ *a.* invulnerable.
iode /jɔd/ *n.m.* iodine.
ion /jɔ̃/ *n.m.* ion.
ira, irait /ira, irɛ/ *voir* aller[1].
Irak /irak/ *n.m.* Iraq. **~ien, ~ienne** *a. & n.m., f.* Iraqi.
Iran /irã/ *n.m.* Iran. **~ien, ~ienne** /iranjɛ̃, -jɛn/ *a. & n.m., f.* Iranian.
irascible /irasibl/ *a.* irascible.
iris /iris/ *n.m.* iris.
irlandais, ~e /irlãdɛ, -z/ *a.* Irish. ● *n.m., f.* Irishman, Irishwoman.
Irlande /irlãd/ *n.f.* Ireland.
iron|ie /irɔni/ *n.f.* irony. **~ique** *a.* ironic(al).
irraisonné /irɛzɔne/ *a.* irrational.
irrationnel, ~le /irasjɔnɛl/ *a.* irrational.
irréalisable /irealizabl/ *a.* (*projet*) unworkable.
irrécupérable /irekyperabl/ *a.* irretrievable, beyond recall.
irréel, ~le /ireɛl/ *a.* unreal.

irréfléchi /irefleʃi/ *a.* thoughtless.

irréfutable /irefytabl/ *a.* irrefutable.

irrégul|ier, **~ière** /iregylje, -jɛr/ *a.* irregular. **~arité** *n.f.* irregularity.

irrémédiable /iremedjabl/ *a.* irreparable.

irremplaçable /irũplasabl/ *a.* irreplaceable.

irréparable /ireparabl/ *a.* beyond repair.

irréprochable /ireprɔʃabl/ *a.* flawless.

irrésistible /irezistibl/ *a.* irresistible; (*drôle*) hilarious.

irrésolu /irezɔly/ *a.* indecisive.

irrespirable /irɛspirabl/ *a.* stifling.

irresponsable /irɛspõsabl/ *a.* irresponsible.

irréversible /irevɛrsibl/ *a.* irreversible.

irrévocable /irevɔkabl/ *a.* irrevocable.

irrigation /irigasjõ/ *n.f.* irrigation.

irriguer /irige/ *v.t.* irrigate.

irrit|er /irite/ *v.t.* irritate. **s'~er de**, be annoyed at. **~able** *a.* irritable. **~ation** *n.f.* irritation.

irruption /irypsjõ/ *n.f.* **faire ~ dans**, burst into.

Islam /islam/ *n.m.* Islam.

islamique /islamik/ *a.* Islamic.

islandais, **~e** /islãdɛ, -z/ *a.* Icelandic. ● *n.m., f.* Icelander. ● *n.m.* (*lang.*) Icelandic.

Islande /islãd/ *n.f.* Iceland.

isolé /izɔle/ *a.* isolated. **~ment** *adv.* in isolation.

isol|er /izɔle/ *v.t.* isolate; (*électr.*) insulate. **s'~er** *v. pr.* isolate o.s. **~ant** *n.m.* insulating material. **~ation** *n.f.* insulation. **~ement** *n.m.* isolation.

isoloir /izɔlwar/ *n.m.* polling booth.

Isorel /izɔrɛl/ *n.m.* (P.) hardboard.

isotope /izɔtɔp/ *n.m.* isotope.

Israël /israɛl/ *n.m.* Israel.

israélien, **~ne** /israeljɛ̃, -jɛn/ *a. & n.m., f.* Israeli.

israélite /israelit/ *a.* Jewish. ● *n.m./ f.* Jew, Jewess.

issu /isy/ *a.* **être ~ de**, come from.

issue /isy/ *n.f.* exit; (*résultat*) outcome; (*fig.*) solution. **à l'~ de**, at the conclusion of. **rue** *ou* **voie sans ~**, dead end.

isthme /ism/ *n.m.* isthmus.

Italie /itali/ *n.f.* Italy.

italien, **~ne** /italjɛ̃, -jɛn/ *a. & n.m., f.* Italian. ● *n.m.* (*lang.*) Italian.

italique /italik/ *n.m.* italics.

itinéraire /itinerɛr/ *n.m.* itinerary, route.

itinérant, **~e** /itinerã, -t/ *a.* itinerant.

I.U.T. /iyte/ *n.m.* (*abrév.*) polytechnic.

I.V.G. /iveʒe/ *n.f.* (*abrév.*) abortion.

ivoire /ivwar/ *n.m.* ivory.

ivr|e /ivr/ *a.* drunk. **~esse** *n.f.* drunkenness. **~ogne** *n.m.* drunk(ard).

J

j' /ʒ/ *voir* je.

jacasser /ʒakase/ *v.i.* chatter.

jachère (en) /(ã)ʒaʃɛr/ *adv.* fallow.

jacinthe /ʒasɛ̃t/ *n.f.* hyacinth.

jade /ʒad/ *n.m.* jade.

jadis /ʒadis/ *adv.* long ago.

jaillir /ʒajir/ *v.i.* (*liquide*) spurt (out); (*lumière*) stream out; (*apparaître, fuser*) burst forth.

jais /ʒɛ/ *n.m.* (**noir**) **de ~**, jet-black.

jalon /ʒalõ/ *n.m.* (*piquet*) marker. **~ner** /-ɔne/ *v.t.* mark (out).

jalou|x, **~se** /ʒalu, -z/ *a.* jealous. **~ser** *v.t.* be jealous of. **~sie** *n.f.* jealousy; (*store*) (venetian) blind.

jamais /ʒamɛ/ *adv.* ever. (**ne**) **~**, never. **il ne boit ~**, he never drinks. **à ~**, for ever. **si ~**, if ever.

jambe /ʒãb/ *n.f.* leg.

jambon /ʒãbõ/ *n.m.* ham. **~neau** (*pl.* **~neaux**) /-ɔno/ *n.m.* knuckle of ham.

jante /ʒãt/ *n.f.* rim.

janvier /ʒãvje/ *n.m.* January.

Japon /ʒapõ/ *n.m.* Japan.

japonais, **~e** /ʒapɔnɛ, -z/ *a. & n.m., f.* Japanese. ● *n.m.* (*lang.*) Japanese.

japper /ʒape/ *v.i.* yelp.

jaquette /ʒakɛt/ *n.f.* (*de livre, femme*) jacket; (*d'homme*) morning coat.

jardin /ʒardɛ̃/ *n.m.* garden. **~ d'enfants**, nursery (school). **~ public**, public park.

jardin|er /ʒardine/ *v.i.* garden. **~age** *n.m.* gardening. **~ier**, **~ière** *n.m., f.* gardener; *n.f.* (*meuble*) plant-stand. **~ière de légumes**, mixed vegetables.

jargon /ʒargõ/ *n.m.* jargon.

jarret /ʒarɛ/ *n.m.* back of the knee.

jarretelle /ʒartɛl/ *n.f.* suspender; (*Amer.*) garter.

jarretière /ʒartjɛr/ *n.f.* garter.

jaser /ʒaze/ *v.i.* jabber.

jasmin /ʒasmɛ̃/ *n.m.* jasmine.

jatte /ʒat/ *n.f.* bowl.

jaug|e /ʒoʒ/ *n.f.* capacity; (*de navire*) tonnage; (*compteur*) gauge. **~er** *v.t.* gauge.

jaun|e /ʒon/ *a.* & *n.m.* yellow; (*péj.*) scab. **~e d'œuf,** (egg) yolk. **rire ~e,** laugh on the other side of one's face. **~ir** *v.t./i.* turn yellow.

jaunisse /ʒonis/ *n.f.* jaundice.

javelot /ʒavlo/ *n.m.* javelin.

jazz /dʒaz/ *n.m.* jazz.

J.C. /ʒezykri/ *n.m.* (*abrév.*) **500 avant/après ~,** 500 B.C./A.D.

je, j' */ʒə, ʒ/ pron.* I.

jean /dʒin/ *n.m.* jeans.

jeep /(d)ʒip/ *n.f.* jeep.

jerrycan /ʒerikan/ *n.m.* jerrycan.

jersey /ʒɛrze/ *n.m.* jersey.

Jersey /ʒɛrze/ *n.f.* Jersey.

Jésus /ʒezy/ *n.m.* Jesus.

jet [1] /ʒɛ/ *n.m.* throw; (*de liquide, vapeur*) jet. **~ d'eau,** fountain.

jet [2] /dʒɛt/ *n.m.* (*avion*) jet.

jetable /ʒətabl/ *a.* disposable.

jetée /ʒte/ *n.f.* pier.

jeter /ʒte/ *v.t.* throw; (*au rebut*) throw away; (*regard, ancre, lumière*) cast; (*cri*) utter; (*bases*) lay. **~ un coup d'œil,** have *ou* take a look (à, at). **se ~ contre,** (*heurter*) bash into. **se ~ dans,** (*fleuve*) flow into. **se ~ sur,** (*se ruer sur*) rush at.

jeton /ʒtɔ̃/ *n.m.* token; (*pour compter*) counter.

jeu (*pl.* **~x**) /ʒø/ *n.m.* game; (*amusement*) play; (*au casino etc.*) gambling; (*théâtre*) acting; (*série*) set; (*de lumière, ressort*) play. **en ~,** (*honneur*) at stake; (*forces*) at work. **~ de cartes,** (*paquet*) pack of cards. **~ d'échecs,** (*boîte*) chess set. **~ de mots,** pun. **~ télévisé,** television quiz.

jeudi /ʒødi/ *n.m.* Thursday.

jeun (à) /(a)ʒœ̃/ *adv.* **être/rester à ~,** be/stay without food; **comprimé à prendre à ~,** tablet to be taken on an empty stomach.

jeune /ʒœn/ *a.* young. ● *n.m./f.* young person. **~ fille,** girl. **~s mariés,** newlyweds. **les ~s,** young people.

jeûn|e /ʒøn/ *n.m.* fast. **~er** *v.i.* fast.

jeunesse /ʒœnɛs/ *n.f.* youth; (*apparence*) youthfulness. **la ~,** (*jeunes*) the young.

joaill|ier, ~ière /ʒɔalje, -jɛr/ *n.m., f.* jeweller. **~erie** *n.f.* jewellery; (*magasin*) jeweller's shop.

job /dʒɔb/ *n.m.* (*fam.*) job.

jockey /ʒɔkɛ/ *n.m.* jockey.

joie /ʒwa/ *n.f.* joy.

joindre† /ʒwɛ̃dr/ *v.t.* join (**à,** to); (*contacter*) contact; (*mains, pieds*) put together; (*efforts*) combine; (*dans une enveloppe*) enclose. **se ~ à,** join.

joint, ~e /ʒwɛ̃, -t/ *a.* (*efforts*) joint; (*pieds*) together. ● *n.m.* joint; (*ligne*) join; (*de robinet*) washer. **~ure** -tyr/ *n.f.* joint; (*ligne*) join.

joker /ʒɔkɛr/ *n.m.* (*carte*) joker.

joli /ʒɔli/ *a.* pretty, nice; (*somme, profit*) nice. **c'est du ~!,** (*ironique*) charming! **c'est bien ~ mais,** that is all very well but. **~ment** *adv.* prettily; (*très: fam.*) awfully.

jonc /ʒɔ̃/ *n.m.* (bul)rush.

jonch|er /ʒɔ̃ʃe/ *v.t.,* **~é de,** littered with.

jonction /ʒɔ̃ksjɔ̃/ *n.f.* junction.

jongl|er /ʒɔ̃gle/ *v.i.* juggle. **~eur, ~euse** *n.m., f.* juggler.

jonquille /ʒɔ̃kij/ *n.f.* daffodil.

Jordanie /ʒɔrdani/ *n.f.* Jordan.

joue /ʒu/ *n.f.* cheek.

jou|er /ʒwe/ *v.t./i.* play; (*théâtre*) act; (*au casino etc.*) gamble; (*fonctionner*) work; (*film, pièce*) put on; (*cheval*) back; (*être important*) count. **~er à ou de,** play. **~er la comédie,** put on an act. **bien ~é!,** well done!

jouet /ʒwɛ/ *n.m.* toy; (*personne, fig.*) plaything; (*victime*) victim.

joueu|r, ~se /ʒwœr, -øz/ *n.m., f.* player; (*parieur*) gambler.

joufflu /ʒufly/ *a.* chubby-cheeked; (*visage*) chubby.

joug /ʒu/ *n.m.* yoke.

jouir /ʒwir/ *v.i.* (*sexe*) come. **~ de,** enjoy.

jouissance /ʒwisɑ̃s/ *n.f.* pleasure; (*usage*) use (**de qch.,** of sth.).

joujou (*pl.* **~x**) /ʒuʒu/ *n.m.* (*fam.*) toy.

jour /ʒur/ *n.m.* day; (*opposé à nuit*) day(time); (*lumière*) daylight; (*aspect*) light; (*ouverture*) gap. **de nos ~s,** nowadays. **du ~ au lendemain,** overnight. **il fait ~,** it is (day)light. **~ chômé ou férié,** public holiday. **~ de fête,** holiday. **~ ouvrable, ~**

de travail, working day. **mettre à ~,** update. **mettre au ~,** uncover. **au grand ~,** in the open. **donner le ~,** give birth. **voir le ~,** be born. **vivre au ~ le jour,** live from day to day.

journal (*pl.* **~aux**) /ʒurnal, -o/ *n.m.* (news)paper; (*spécialisé*) journal; (*intime*) diary; (*radio*) news. **~al de bord,** log-book.

journal|ier, **~ière** /ʒurnalje, -jɛr/ *a.* daily.

journalis|te /ʒurnalist/ *n.m./f.* journalist. **~me** *n.m.* journalism.

journée /ʒurne/ *n.f.* day.

journellement /ʒurnɛlmɑ̃/ *adv.* daily.

jov|ial (*m. pl.* **~iaux**) /ʒɔvjal, -jo/ *a.* jovial.

joyau (*pl.* **~x**) /ʒwajo/ *n.m.* gem.

joyeu|x, **~se** /ʒwajø, -z/ *a.* merry, joyful. **~x anniversaire,** happy birthday. **~sement** *adv.* merrily.

jubilé /ʒybile/ *n.m.* jubilee.

jubil|er /ʒybile/ *v.i.* be jubilant. **~ation** *n.f.* jubilation.

jucher /ʒyʃe/ *v.t.,* **se ~** *v. pr.* perch.

judaï|que /ʒydaik/ *a.* Jewish. **~sme** *n.m.* Judaism.

judas /ʒyda/ *n.m.* peep-hole.

judiciaire /ʒydisjɛr/ *a.* judicial.

judicieu|x, **~se** /ʒydisjø, -z/ *a.* judicious.

judo /ʒydo/ *n.m.* judo.

juge /ʒyʒ/ *n.m.* judge; (*arbitre*) referee. **~ de paix,** Justice of the Peace. **~ de touche,** linesman.

jugé (au) /(o)ʒyʒe/ *adv.* by guesswork.

jugement /ʒyʒmɑ̃/ *n.m.* judgement; (*criminel*) sentence.

jugeote /ʒyʒɔt/ *n.f.* (*fam.*) gumption, common sense.

juger /ʒyʒe/ *v.t./i.* judge; (*estimer*) consider (**que,** that). **~ de,** judge.

juguler /ʒygyle/ *v.t.* stifle, check.

jui|f, **~ve** /ʒɥif, -v/ *a.* Jewish. ● *n.m., f.* Jew, Jewess.

juillet /ʒɥijɛ/ *n.m.* July.

juin /ʒɥɛ̃/ *n.m.* June.

jules /ʒyl/ *n.m.* (*fam.*) guy.

jum|eau, **~elle** (*m. pl.* **~eaux**) /ʒymo, -ɛl/ *a. & n.m.,* *f.* twin. **~elage** *n.m.* twinning. **~eler** *v.t.* (*villes*) twin.

jumelles /ʒymɛl/ *n.f. pl.* binoculars.

jument /ʒymɑ̃/ *n.f.* mare.

jungle /ʒœ̃gl/ *n.f.* jungle.

junior /ʒynjɔr/ *n.m./f. & a.* junior.

junte /ʒœ̃t/ *n.f.* junta.

jupe /ʒyp/ *n.f.* skirt.

jupon /ʒypɔ̃/ *n.m.* slip, petticoat.

juré, **~e** /ʒyre/ *n.m.,* *f.* juror. ● *a.* sworn.

jurer /ʒyre/ *v.t.* swear (**que,** that). ● *v.i.* (*pester*) swear; (*contraster*) clash (**avec,** with). **~ de qch./de faire,** swear to sth./to do.

juridiction /ʒyridiksjɔ̃/ *n.f.* jurisdiction; (*tribunal*) court of law.

juridique /ʒyridik/ *a.* legal.

juriste /ʒyrist/ *n.m./f.* legal expert.

juron /ʒyrɔ̃/ *n.m.* swear-word.

jury /ʒyri/ *n.m.* jury.

jus /ʒy/ *n.m.* juice; (*de viande*) gravy. **~ de fruit,** fruit juice.

jusque /ʒysk(ə)/ *prép.* **jusqu'à,** (up) to, as far as; (*temps*) until, till; (*limite*) up to; (*y compris*) even. **jusqu'à ce que,** until. **jusqu'à présent,** until now. **jusqu'en,** until. **jusqu'où?,** how far? **~ dans, ~ sur,** as far as.

juste /ʒyst/ *a.* fair, just; (*légitime*) just; (*correct, exact*) right; (*vrai*) true; (*vêtement*) tight; (*quantité*) on the short side. **le ~ milieu,** the happy medium. ● *adv.* rightly, correctly; (*chanter*) in tune; (*seulement, exactement*) just. **(un peu) ~,** (*calculer, mesurer*) a bit fine *ou* close. **au ~,** exactly. **c'était ~,** (*presque raté*) it was a close thing.

justement /ʒystəmɑ̃/ *adv.* just; (*avec justice ou justesse*) justly.

justesse /ʒystɛs/ *n.f.* accuracy. **de ~,** just, narrowly.

justice /ʒystis/ *n.f.* justice; (*autorités*) law; (*tribunal*) court.

justif|ier /ʒystifje/ *v.t.* justify. ● *v.i.* **~ier de,** prove. **se ~ier** *v. pr.* justify o.s. **~iable** *a.* justifiable. **~ication** *n.f.* justification.

juteu|x, **~se** /ʒytø, -z/ *a.* juicy.

juvénile /ʒyvenil/ *a.* youthful.

juxtaposer /ʒykstapoze/ *v.t.* juxtapose.

K

kaki /kaki/ *a. invar. & n.m.* khaki.

kaléidoscope /kaleidɔskɔp/ *n.m.* kaleidoscope.

kangourou /kɑ̃guru/ *n.m.* kangaroo.

karaté /karate/ *n.m.* karate.

kart /kart/ *n.m.* go-cart.

kascher /kaʃɛr/ *a. invar.* kosher.

képi /kepi/ *n.m.* kepi.

kermesse /kɛrmɛs/ *n.f.* fair; (*de charité*) fête.

kérosène /kerozɛn/ *n.m.* kerosene, aviation fuel.

kibboutz /kibuts/ *n.m.* kibbutz.

kidnapp|er /kidnape/ *v.t.* kidnap. **~eur, ~euse** *n.m., f.* kidnapper.

kilo /kilo/ *n.m.* kilo.

kilogramme /kilɔgram/ *n.m.* kilogram.

kilohertz /kilɔɛrts/ *n.m.* kilohertz.

kilom|ètre /kilɔmɛtr/ *n.m.* kilometre. **~étrage** *n.m.* (*approx.*) mileage.

kilowatt /kilɔwat/ *n.m.* kilowatt.

kinésithérapie /kineziterapi/ *n.f.* physiotherapy.

kiosque /kjɔsk/ *n.m.* kiosk. **~ à musique**, bandstand.

kit /kit/ *n.m.* **meubles en ~**, flat-pack furniture.

kiwi /kiwi/ *n.m.* (*fruit, bird*) kiwi.

klaxon /klaksɔn/ *n.m.* (P.) (*auto.*) horn. **~ner** /-e/ *v.i.* sound one's horn.

knock-out /nɔkaut/ *n.m.* knock-out.

ko /kao/ *n.m.* (*comput.*) k.

K.O. /kao/ *a. invar.* (knocked) out.

k-way /kawe/ *n.m. invar.* (P.) cagoule.

kyste /kist/ *n.m.* cyst.

L

l', la /l, la/ *voir* le.

là /la/ *adv.* there; (*ici*) here; (*chez soi*) in; (*temps*) then. **c'est là que**, this is where. **là où**, where. **là-bas** *adv.* over there. **là-dedans** *adv.* inside, in there. **là-dessous** *adv.* underneath, under there. **là-dessus** *adv.* on there. **là-haut** *adv.* up there; (*à l'étage*) upstairs.

-là /la/ *adv.* (*après un nom précédé de ce, cette, etc.*) **cet homme-là**, that man. **ces maisons-là**, those houses.

label /label/ *n.m.* (*comm.*) seal.

labeur /labœr/ *n.m.* toil.

labo /labo/ *n.m.* (*fam.*) lab.

laboratoire /labɔratwar/ *n.m.* laboratory.

laborieu|x, ~se /labɔrjø, -z/ *a.* laborious; (*personne*) industrious; (*dur*) heavy going. **classes/masses ~ses**, working classes/masses.

labour /labur/ *n.m.* ploughing; (*Amer.*) plowing. **~er** *v.t./i.* plough; (*Amer.*) plow; (*déchirer*) rip at. **~eur** *n.m.* ploughman; (*Amer.*) plowman.

labyrinthe /labirɛ̃t/ *n.m.* maze.

lac /lak/ *n.m.* lake.

lacer /lase/ *v.t.* lace up.

lacérer /lasere/ *v.t.* tear (up).

lacet /lase/ *n.m.* (shoe-)lace; (*de route*) sharp bend, zigzag.

lâche /laʃ/ *a.* cowardly; (*détendu*) loose. ● *n.m./f.* coward. **~ment** *adv.* in a cowardly way.

lâcher /laʃe/ *v.t.* let go of; (*abandonner*) give up; (*laisser*) leave; (*libérer*) release; (*parole*) utter; (*desserrer*) loosen. ● *v.i.* give way. **~ prise**, let go.

lâcheté /laʃte/ *n.f.* cowardice.

laconique /lakɔnik/ *a.* laconic.

lacrymogène /lakrimɔʒɛn/ *a.* **gaz ~**, tear gas. **grenade ~**, tear gas grenade.

lacté /lakte/ *a.* milk.

lacune /lakyn/ *n.f.* gap.

ladite /ladit/ *voir* ledit.

lagune /lagyn/ *n.f.* lagoon.

laïc /laik/ *n.m.* layman.

laid, ~e /lɛ, lɛd/ *a.* ugly; (*action*) vile. **~eur** /lɛdœr/ *n.f.* ugliness.

lain|e /lɛn/ *n.f.* wool. **de ~e**, woollen. **~age** *n.m.* woollen garment.

laïque /laik/ *a.* secular; (*habit, personne*) lay. ● *n.m./f.* layman, laywoman.

laisse /lɛs/ *n.f.* lead, leash.

laisser /lese/ *v.t.* leave. ● **~ qn. faire**, let s.o. do. **~ qch. à qn.**, let s.o. have sth., leave s.o. sth. **~ tomber**, drop. **se ~ aller**, let o.s. go. **~-aller** *n.m. invar.* carelessness. **laissez-passer** *n.m. invar.* pass.

lait /lɛ/ *n.m.* milk. **frère/sœur de ~**, foster-brother/-sister. **~age** /lɛtaʒ/ *n.m.* milk product. **~eux, ~euse** /lɛtø, -z/ *a.* milky.

lait|ier, ~ière /letje, letjɛr/ *a.* dairy. ● *n.m., f.* dairyman, dairywoman. ● *n.m.* (*livreur*) milkman. **~erie** /lɛtri/ *n.f.* dairy.

laiton /lɛtɔ̃/ *n.m.* brass.

laitue /lety/ *n.f.* lettuce.

laïus /lajys/ *n.m.* (*péj.*) big speech.

lama /lama/ *n.m.* llama.

lambeau (*pl.* ~x) /lɑ̃bo/ *n.m.* shred. **en ~x**, in shreds.

lambris /lɑ̃bri/ *n.m.* panelling.

lame /lam/ *n.f.* blade; (*lamelle*) strip; (*vague*) wave. ~ **de fond**, ground swell.

lamelle /lamɛl/ *n.f.* (thin) strip.

lamentable /lamᾶtabl/ *a.* deplorable.

lament|er (se) /(sə)lamᾶte/ *v. pr.* moan. **~ation(s)** *n.f.* (*pl.*) moaning.

laminé /lamine/ *a.* laminated.

lampadaire /lᾶpadɛr/ *n.m.* standard lamp; (*de rue*) street lamp.

lampe /lᾶp/ *n.f.* lamp; (*de radio*) valve; (*Amer.*) vacuum tube. ~ **(de poche)**, torch; (*Amer.*) flashlight. ~ **de chevet**, bedside lamp.

lampion /lᾶpjɔ̃/ *n.m.* (Chinese) lantern.

lance /lᾶs/ *n.f.* spear; (*de tournoi*) lance; (*tuyau*) hose. ~ **d'incendie**, fire hose.

lancée /lᾶse/ *n.f.* **continuer sur sa ~**, keep going.

lanc|er /lᾶse/ *v.t.* throw; (*avec force*) hurl; (*navire, idée, personne*) launch; (*émettre*) give out; (*regard*) cast; (*moteur*) start. **se ~er** *v. pr.* (*sport*) gain momentum; (*se précipiter*) rush. **se ~er dans**, launch into. ● *n.m.* throw; (*action*) throwing. **~ement** *n.m.* throwing; (*de navire*) launching. **~e-missiles** *n.m. invar.* missile launcher. **~e-pierres** *n.m. invar.* catapult.

lancinant, ~e /lᾶsinᾶ, -t/ *a.* haunting; (*douleur*) throbbing.

landau /lᾶdo/ *n.m.* pram; (*Amer.*) baby carriage.

lande /lᾶd/ *n.f.* heath, moor.

langage /lᾶgaʒ/ *n.m.* language.

langoureu|x, ~se /lᾶgurø, -z/ *a.* languid.

langoust|e /lᾶgust/ *n.f.* (spiny) lobster. **~ine** *n.f.* (Norway) lobster.

langue /lᾶg/ *n.f.* tongue; (*idiome*) language. **il m'a tiré la ~**, he stuck out his tongue out at me. **de ~ anglaise/française**, English-/French-speaking. ~ **maternelle**, mother tongue.

languette /lᾶgɛt/ *n.f.* tongue.

langueur /lᾶgœr/ *n.f.* languor.

langu|ir /lᾶgir/ *v.i.* languish; (*conversation*) flag. **faire ~ir qn.**, keep s.o. waiting. **se ~ir de**, miss. **~issant, ~issante** *a.* languid.

lanière /lanjɛr/ *n.f.* strap.

lanterne /lᾶtɛrn/ *n.f.* lantern; (*électrique*) lamp; (*de voiture*) sidelight.

laper /lape/ *v.t./i.* lap.

lapider /lapide/ *v.t.* stone.

lapin /lapɛ̃/ *n.m.* rabbit. **poser un ~ à qn.**, stand s.o. up.

laps /laps/ *n.m.* ~ **de temps**, lapse of time.

lapsus /lapsys/ *n.m.* slip (of the tongue).

laquais /lakɛ/ *n.m.* lackey.

laqu|e /lak/ *n.f.* lacquer. **~er** *v.t.* lacquer.

laquelle /lakɛl/ *voir* lequel.

larcin /larsɛ̃/ *n.m.* theft.

lard /lar/ *n.m.* (pig's) fat; (*viande*) bacon.

large /larʒ/ *a.* wide, broad; (*grand*) large; (*non borné*) broad; (*généreux*) generous. ● *adv.* (*mesurer*) broadly; (*voir*) big. ● *n.m. de* ~, (*mesure*) wide. **le ~**, (*mer*) the open sea. **au ~ de**, (*en face de: naut.*) off. ~ **d'esprit**, broad-minded. **~ment** /-əmᾶ/ *adv.* widely; (*ouvrir*) wide; (*amplement*) amply; (*généreusement*) generously; (*au moins*) easily.

largesse /larʒɛs/ *n.f.* generosity.

largeur /larʒœr/ *n.f.* width, breadth; (*fig.*) breadth.

larguer /large/ *v.t.* drop. ~ **les amarres**, cast off.

larme /larm/ *n.f.* tear; (*goutte: fam.*) drop.

larmoyant, ~e /larmwajᾶ, -t/ *a.* tearful.

larron /larɔ̃/ *n.m.* thief.

larve /larv/ *n.f.* larva.

larvé /larve/ *a.* latent.

laryngite /larɛ̃ʒit/ *n.f.* laryngitis.

larynx /larɛ̃ks/ *n.m.* larynx.

las, ~se /lɑ, lɑs/ *a.* weary.

lasagnes /lazaɲ/ *n.f. pl.* lasagne.

lasci|f, ~ve /lasif, -v/ *a.* lascivious.

laser /lazer/ *n.m.* laser.

lasse /lɑs/ *voir* las.

lasser /lɑse/ *v.t.* weary. **se ~** *v. pr.* weary (**de**, of).

lassitude /lɑsityd/ *n.f.* weariness.

lasso /laso/ *n.m.* lasso.

latent, ~e /latᾶ, -t/ *a.* latent.

latér|al (*m. pl.* **~aux**) /lateral, -o/ *a.* lateral.

latex /latɛks/ *n.m.* latex.

latin, ~e /latɛ̃, -in/ *a. & n.m., f.* Latin. ● *n.m.* (*lang.*) Latin.

latitude /latityd/ *n.f.* latitude.

latrines /latrin/ *n.f. pl.* latrine(s).

latte /lat/ *n.f.* lath; (*de plancher*) board.

lauréat, ~e /lɔrea, -t/ *a.* prize-winning. ● *n.m., f.* prize-winner.

laurier /lɔrje/ *n.m.* laurel; (*culin.*) bay-leaves.

lavable /lavabl/ *a.* washable.

lavabo /lavabo/ *n.m.* wash-basin. ~s, toilet(s).

lavage /lavaʒ/ *n.m.* washing. ~ de cerveau, brainwashing.

lavande /lavɑ̃d/ *n.f.* lavender.

lave /lav/ *n.f.* lava.

lav|er /lave/ *v.t.* wash; (*injure etc.*) avenge. se ~er *v. pr.* wash (o.s.). (se) ~er de, clear (o.s.) of. ~e-glace *n.m.* windscreen washer. ~eur de carreaux, window-cleaner. ~e-vaisselle *n.m. invar.* dishwasher.

laverie /lavri/ *n.f.* ~ (automatique), launderette; (*Amer.*) laundromat.

lavette /lavɛt/ *n.f.* dishcloth; (*péj.*) wimp.

lavoir /lavwar/ *n.m.* wash-house.

laxati|f, ~ve /laksatif, -v/ *a. & n.m.* laxative.

laxisme /laksism/ *n.m.* laxity.

layette /lɛjɛt/ *n.f.* baby clothes.

le *ou* **l'***, **la** *ou* **l'*** (*pl.* **les**) /lə, l/, /la, le/ *article* the; (*mesure*) a, per. ● *pron.* (*homme*) him; (*femme*) her; (*chose, animal*) it. **les** *pron.* them. **aimer le thé/la France**, like tea/France. **le matin**, in the morning. **il sort le mardi**, he goes out on Tuesdays. **levez le bras**, raise your arm. **je le connais**, I know him. **je le sais**, I know (it).

lécher /leʃe/ *v.t.* lick.

lèche-vitrines /lɛʃvitrin/ *n.m.* faire du ~, go window-shopping.

leçon /ləsɔ̃/ *n.f.* lesson. faire la ~ à, lecture.

lec|teur, ~trice /lɛktœr, -tris/ *n.m.,f.* reader; (*univ.*) foreign language assistant. ~teur de cassettes, cassette player. ~teur de disquettes, (disk) drive.

lecture /lɛktyr/ *n.f.* reading.

ledit, ladite (*pl.* **lesdit(e)s**) /lədi, ladit, ledi(t)/ *a.* the aforesaid.

lég|al (*m. pl.* ~aux) /legal, -o/ *a.* legal. ~alement *adv.* legally. ~aliser *v.t.* legalize. ~alité *n.f.* legality; (*loi*) law.

légation /legasjɔ̃/ *n.f.* legation.

légend|e /leʒɑ̃d/ *n.f.* (*histoire, inscription*) legend. ~aire *a.* legendary.

lég|er, ~ère /leʒe, -ɛr/ *a.* light; (*bruit, faute, maladie*) slight; (*café, argument*) weak; (*imprudent*) thoughtless; (*frivole*) fickle. **à la**

~ère, thoughtlessly. ~èrement /-ɛrmɑ̃/ *adv.* lightly; (*agir*) thoughtlessly; (*un peu*) slightly. ~èreté /-ɛrte/ *n.f.* lightness; thoughtlessness.

légion /leʒjɔ̃/ *n.f.* legion. une ~ de, a crowd of. ~naire /-jɔner/ *n.m.* (*mil.*) legionnaire.

législati|f, ~ve /leʒislatif, -v/ *a.* legislative.

législation /leʒislasjɔ̃/ *n.f.* legislation.

législature /leʒislatyr/ *n.f.* term of office.

légitim|e /leʒitim/ *a.* legitimate. en état de ~e défense, acting in self-defence. ~ité *n.f.* legitimacy.

legs /lɛg/ *n.m.* legacy.

léguer /lege/ *v.t.* bequeath.

légume /legym/ *n.m.* vegetable.

lendemain /lɑ̃dmɛ̃/ *n.m.* le ~, the next day, the day after; (*fig.*) the future. le ~ de, the day after. le ~ matin/soir, the next morning/evening.

lent, ~e /lɑ̃, lɑ̃t/ *a.* slow. ~ement /lɑ̃tmɑ̃/ *adv.* slowly. ~eur /lɑ̃tœr/ *n.f.* slowness.

lentille ¹ /lɑ̃tij/ *n.f.* (*plante*) lentil.

lentille ² /lɑ̃tij/ *n.f.* (*verre*) lens; ~s de contact, (contact) lenses.

léopard /leopar/ *n.m.* leopard.

lèpre /lɛpr/ *n.f.* leprosy.

lequel, laquelle (*pl.* **lesquel(le)s**) /ləkɛl, lakɛl, lekɛl/ *pron.* (*à + lequel = auquel, à + lesquel(le)s = auxquel(le)s; de + lequel = duquel, de + lesquel(le)s = desquel(le)s*) which; (*interrogatif*) which (one); (*personne*) who; (*complément indirect*) whom.

les /le/ *voir* le.

lesbienne /lɛsbjɛn/ *n.f.* lesbian.

léser /leze/ *v.t.* wrong.

lésiner /lezine/ *v.i.* ne pas ~ sur, not stint on.

lésion /lezjɔ̃/ *n.f.* lesion.

lesquels, lesquelles /lekɛl/ *voir* lequel.

lessive /lesiv/ *n.f.* washing-powder; (*linge, action*) washing.

lest /lɛst/ *n.m.* ballast. jeter du ~, (*fig.*) climb down. ~er *v.t.* ballast.

leste /lɛst/ *a.* nimble; (*grivois*) coarse.

léthargie /letarʒi/ *n.f.* lethargy. ~ique *a.* lethargic.

lettre /lɛtr/ *n.f.* letter. à la ~, literally. en toutes ~s, in full. ~

exprès, express letter. **les ~s**, (*univ.*) (the) arts.

lettré /letre/ *a.* well-read.

leucémie /løsemi/ *n.f.* leukaemia.

leur /lœr/ *a.* (*f. invar.*) their. ● *pron.* (to) them. **le ~, la ~, les ~s**, theirs.

leurr|e /lœr/ *n.m.* illusion; (*duperie*) deception. **~er** *v.t.* delude.

levain /ləvɛ̃/ *n.m.* leaven.

levé /ləve/ *a.* (*debout*) up.

levée /ləve/ *n.f.* lifting; (*de courrier*) collection; (*de troupes, d'impôts*) levying.

lever /ləve/ *v.t.* lift (up), raise; (*interdiction*) lift; (*séance*) close; (*armée, impôts*) levy. ● *v.i.* (*pâte*) rise. **se ~** *v. pr.* get up; (*soleil, rideau*) rise; (*jour*) break. ● *n.m.* **au ~**, on getting up. **~ du jour**, daybreak. **~ du rideau**, (*théâtre*) curtain (up). **~ du soleil**, sunrise.

levier /ləvje/ *n.m.* lever.

lèvre /lɛvr/ *n.f.* lip.

lévrier /levrije/ *n.m.* greyhound.

levure /ləvyr/ *n.f.* yeast. **~ alsacienne** *ou* **chimique**, baking powder.

lexicographie /lɛksikɔgrafi/ *n.f.* lexicography.

lexique /lɛksik/ *n.m.* vocabulary; (*glossaire*) lexicon.

lézard /lezar/ *n.m.* lizard.

lézard|e /lezard/ *n.f.* crack. **se ~er** *v. pr.* crack.

liaison /ljɛzɔ̃/ *n.f.* connection; (*transport*) link; (*contact*) contact; (*gram., mil.*) liaison; (*amoureuse*) affair.

liane /ljan/ *n.f.* creeper.

liasse /ljas/ *n.f.* bundle, wad.

Liban /libɑ̃/ *n.m.* Lebanon.

libanais, ~e /libanɛ, -z/ *a. & n.m., f.* Lebanese.

libell|er /libele/ *v.t.* (*chèque*) write; (*lettre*) draw up. **~é à l'ordre de**, made out to.

libellule /libelyl/ *n.f.* dragonfly.

libér|al (*m. pl.* **~aux**) /liberal, -o/ *a.* liberal. **les professions ~ales** the professions. **~alement** *adv.* liberally. **~alisme** *n.m.* liberalism. **~alité** *n.f.* liberality.

libér|er /libere/ *v.t.* (*personne*) free, release; (*pays*) liberate, free. **se ~er** *v. pr.* free o.s. **~ateur, ~atrice** *a.* liberating; *n.m., f.* liberator. **~ation** *n.f.* release; (*de pays*) liberation.

liberté /libɛrte/ *n.f.* freedom, liberty; (*loisir*) free time. **en ~ provisoire**, on bail. **être/mettre en ~**, be/set free.

libertin, ~e /libɛrtɛ̃, -in/ *a. & n.m., f.* libertine.

librair|e /librɛr/ *n.m./f.* bookseller. **~ie** /-eri/ *n.f.* bookshop.

libre /libr/ *a.* free; (*place, pièce*) vacant, free; (*passage*) clear; (*école*) private (*usually religious*). **~ de qch./de faire**, free from sth./to do. **~-échange** *n.m.* free trade. **~ment** /-əmɑ̃/ *adv.* freely. **~-service** (*pl.* **~s-services**) *n.m.* self-service.

Libye /libi/ *n.f.* Libya.

libyen, ~ne /libjɛ̃, -jɛn/ *a. & n.m., f.* Libyan.

licence /lisɑ̃s/ *n.f.* licence; (*univ.*) degree.

licencié, ~e /lisɑ̃sje/ *n.m., f.* **~ ès lettres/sciences**, Bachelor of Arts/Science.

licenc|ier /lisɑ̃sje/ *v.t.* make redundant, (*pour faute*) dismiss. **~iements** *n.m. pl.* redundancies.

licencieu|x, ~se /lisɑ̃sjø, -z/ *a.* licentious, lascivious.

lichen /likɛn/ *n.m.* lichen.

licite /lisit/ *a.* lawful.

licorne /likɔrn/ *n.f.* unicorn.

lie /li/ *n.f.* dregs.

liège /ljɛʒ/ *n.m.* cork.

lien /ljɛ̃/ *n.m.* (*rapport*) link; (*attache*) bond, tie; (*corde*) rope.

lier /lje/ *v.t.* tie (up), bind; (*relier*) link; (*engager, unir*) bind. **~ conversation**, strike up a conversation. **se ~ avec**, make friends with. **ils sont très liés**, they are very close.

lierre /ljɛr/ *n.m.* ivy.

lieu (*pl.* **~x**) /ljø/ *n.m.* place. **~x**, (*locaux*) premises; (*d'un accident*) scene. **au ~ de**, instead of. **avoir ~**, take place. **tenir ~ de**, serve as. **en premier ~**, firstly. **en dernier ~**, lastly. **~ commun**, commonplace.

lieutenant /ljøtnɑ̃/ *n.m.* lieutenant.

lièvre /ljɛvr/ *n.m.* hare.

ligament /ligamɑ̃/ *n.m.* ligament.

ligne /liɲ/ *n.f.* line; (*trajet*) route; (*formes*) lines; (*de femme*) figure. **en ~**, (*joueurs etc.*) lined up; (*personne au téléphone*) on the phone.

lignée /liɲe/ *n.f.* ancestry, line.

ligoter /ligɔte/ *v.t.* tie up.

ligu|e /lig/ *n.f.* league. **se ~er** *v. pr.* form a league (**contre**, against).

lilas /lila/ *n.m. & a. invar.* lilac.

limace /limas/ *n.f.* slug.

limande /limɑ̃d/ *n.f.* (*poisson*) dab.

lim|e /lim/ *n.f.* file. **~e à ongles**, nail file. **~er** *v.t.* file.

limier /limje/ *n.m.* bloodhound; (*policier*) sleuth.

limitation /limitasjɔ̃/ *n.f.* limitation. **~ de vitesse**, speed limit.

limit|e /limit/ *n.f.* limit; (*de jardin, champ*) boundary. ● *a.* (*vitesse, âge*) maximum. **cas ~e**, borderline case. **date ~e**, deadline. **~er** *v.t.* limit; (*délimiter*) form the border of.

limoger /limɔʒe/ *v.t.* dismiss.

limon /limɔ̃/ *n.m.* stilt.

limonade /limɔnad/ *n.f.* lemonade.

limpid|e /lɛ̃pid/ *a.* limpid, clear. **~ité** *n.f.* clearness.

lin /lɛ̃/ *n.m.* (*tissu*) linen.

linceul /lɛ̃sœl/ *n.m.* shroud.

linéaire /lineɛr/ *a.* linear.

linge /lɛ̃ʒ/ *n.m.* linen; (*lessive*) washing; (*torchon*) cloth. **~ (de corps)**, underwear. **~rie** *n.f.* underwear.

lingot /lɛ̃go/ *n.m.* ingot.

linguiste /lɛ̃gɥist/ *n.m./f.* linguist.

linguistique /lɛ̃gɥistik/ *a.* linguistic. ● *n.f.* linguistics.

lino /lino/ *n.m.* lino.

linoléum /linɔleɔm/ *n.m.* linoleum.

lion, ~ne /ljɔ̃, ljɔn/ *n.m.*, *f.* lion, lioness. **le L~**, leo.

lionceau (*pl.* **~x**) /ljɔ̃so/ *n.m.* lion cub.

liquéfier /likefje/ *v.t.*, **se ~** *v. pr.* liquefy.

liqueur /likœr/ *n.f.* liqueur.

liquide /likid/ *a.* & *n.m.* liquid. (*argent*) **~**, ready money. **payer en ~**, pay cash.

liquid|er /likide/ *v.t.* liquidate; (*vendre*) sell. **~ation** *n.f.* liquidation; (*vente*) (clearance) sale.

lire[1] /lir/ *v.t./i.* read.

lire[2] /lir/ *n.f.* lira.

lis[1] /li/ *voir* lire[1].

lis[2] /lis/ *n.m.* (*fleur*) lily.

lisible /lizibl/ *a.* legible; (*roman etc.*) readable.

lisière /lizjɛr/ *n.f.* edge.

liss|e /lis/ *a.* smooth. **~er** *v.t.* smooth.

liste /list/ *n.f.* list. **~ électorale**, register of voters.

listing /listiŋ/ *n.m.* printout.

lit[1] /li/ *voir* lire[1].

lit[2] /li/ *n.m.* (*de personne, fleuve*) bed. **se mettre au ~**, get into bed. **~ de camp**, camp-bed. **~ d'enfant**, cot. **~ d'une personne**, single bed.

litanie /litani/ *n.f.* litany.

litchi /litʃi/ *n.m.* litchi.

literie /litri/ *n.f.* bedding.

litière /litjɛr/ *n.f.* (*paille*) litter.

litige /litiʒ/ *n.m.* dispute.

litre /litr/ *n.m.* litre.

littéraire /literɛr/ *a.* literary.

littér|al (*m. pl.* **~aux**) /literal, -o/ *a.* literal. **~alement** *adv.* literally.

littérature /literatyr/ *n.f.* literature.

littor|al (*pl.* **~aux**) /litɔral, -o/ *n.m.* coast.

liturg|ie /lityrʒi/ *n.f.* liturgy. **~ique** *a.* liturgical.

livide /livid/ *a.* (*blême*) pallid.

livraison /livrɛzɔ̃/ *n.f.* delivery.

livre[1] /livr/ *n.m.* book. **~ de bord**, log-book. **~ de compte**, books. **~ de poche**, paperback.

livre[2] /livr/ *n.f.* (*monnaie, poids*) pound.

livrée /livre/ *n.f.* livery.

livr|er /livre/ *v.t.* deliver; (*abandonner*) give over (**à**, to); (*secret*) give away. **~é à soi-même**, left to o.s. **se ~er à**, give o.s. over to; (*actes, boisson*) indulge in; (*se confier à*) confide in; (*effectuer*) carry out.

livret /livrɛ/ *n.m.* book; (*mus.*) libretto. **~ scolaire**, school report (book).

livreu|r, ~se /livrœr, -øz/ *n.m.*, *f.* delivery boy *ou* girl.

lobe /lɔb/ *n.m.* lobe.

loc|al[1] (*m. pl.* **~aux**) /lɔkal, -o/ *a.* local. **~alement** *adv.* locally.

loc|al[2] (*pl.* **~aux**) /lɔkal, -o/ *n.m.* premises. **~aux**, premises.

localisé /lɔkalize/ *a.* localized.

localité /lɔkalite/ *n.f.* locality.

locataire /lɔkatɛr/ *n.m./f.* tenant; (*de chambre, d'hôtel*) lodger.

location /lɔkasjɔ̃/ *n.f.* (*de maison*) renting; (*de voiture*) hiring, renting; (*de place*) booking, reservation; (*guichet*) booking office; (*théâtre*) box office; (*par propriétaire*) renting out; hiring out. **en ~**, (*voiture*) on hire, rented.

lock-out /lɔkaut/ *n.m. invar.* lockout.

locomotion /lɔkɔmosjɔ̃/ *n.f.* locomotion.

locomotive /lɔkɔmɔtiv/ *n.f.* engine, locomotive.

locution /lɔkysjɔ̃/ *n.f.* phrase.

logarithme /lɔgaritm/ *n.m.* logarithm.

loge /lɔʒ/ *n.f.* (*de concierge*) lodge; (*d'acteur*) dressing-room; (*de spectateur*) box.

logement /lɔʒmɑ̃/ *n.m.* accommodation; (*appartement*) flat; (*habitat*) housing.

loge|r /lɔʒe/ *v.t.* accommodate. ● *v.i.*, **se ~er** *v. pr.* live. **trouver à se ~er**, find accommodation. **être ~é**, live. **se ~er dans**, (*balle*) lodge itself in.

logeu|r, ~se /lɔʒœr, -øz/ *n.m., f.* landlord, landlady.

logiciel /lɔʒisjel/ *n.m.* software.

logique /lɔʒik/ *a.* logical. ● *n.f.* logic. **~ment** *adv.* logically.

logis /lɔʒi/ *n.m.* dwelling.

logistique /lɔʒistik/ *n.f.* logistics.

logo /lɔgo/ *n.m.* logo.

loi /lwa/ *n.f.* law.

loin /lwɛ̃/ *adv.* far (away). **au ~**, far away. **de ~**, from far away; (*de beaucoup*) by far. **~ de là**, far from it. **plus ~**, further. **il revient de ~**, (*fig.*) he had a close shave.

lointain, ~e /lwɛ̃tɛ̃, -ɛn/ *a.* distant. ● *n.m.* distance.

loir /lwar/ *n.m.* dormouse.

loisir /lwazir/ *n.m.* (spare) time. **~s**, spare time; (*distractions*) spare time activities. **à ~**, at one's leisure.

londonien, ~ne /lɔ̃dɔnjɛ̃, -jɛn/ *a., n.m., f.* Londoner. ● *a.* London.

Londres /lɔ̃dr/ *n.m./f.* London.

long, ~ue /lɔ̃, lɔ̃g/ *a.* long. ● *n.m.* de **~**, (*mesure*) long. **à la ~ue**, in the end. **à ~ terme**, long-term. **de ~ en large**, back and forth. **~ à faire**, a long time doing. **(tout) le ~ de**, (all) along.

longer /lɔ̃ʒe/ *v.t.* go along; (*limiter*) border.

longévité /lɔ̃ʒevite/ *n.f.* longevity.

longiligne /lɔ̃ʒiliɲ/ *a.* tall and slender.

longitude /lɔ̃ʒityd/ *n.f.* longitude.

longtemps /lɔ̃tɑ̃/ *adv.* a long time. **avant ~**, before long. **trop ~**, too long. **ça prendra ~**, it will take a long time.

longue /lɔ̃g/ *voir* long.

longuement /lɔ̃gmɑ̃/ *adv.* at length.

longueur /lɔ̃gœr/ *n.f.* length. **~s**, (*de texte etc.*) over-long parts. **à ~ de journée**, all day long. **~ d'onde**, wavelength.

longue-vue /lɔ̃gvy/ *n.f.* telescope.

look /luk/ *n.m.* (*fam.*) look, image.

lopin /lɔpɛ̃/ *n.m.* **~ de terre**, patch of land.

loquace /lɔkas/ *a.* talkative.

loque /lɔk/ *n.f.* **~s**, rags. **~ (humaine)**, (human) wreck.

loquet /lɔkɛ/ *n.m.* latch.

lorgner /lɔrɲe/ *v.t.* eye.

lors de /lɔrdə/ *prép.* at the time of.

lorsque /lɔrsk(ə)/ *conj.* when.

losange /lɔzɑ̃ʒ/ *n.m.* diamond.

lot /lo/ *n.m.* prize; (*portion, destin*) lot.

loterie /lɔtri/ *n.f.* lottery.

lotion /lɔsjɔ̃/ *n.f.* lotion.

lotissement /lɔtismɑ̃/ *n.m.* (*à construire*) building plot; (*construit*) (housing) development.

louable /lwabl/ *a.* praiseworthy.

louange /lwɑ̃ʒ/ *n.f.* praise.

louche[1] /luʃ/ *a.* shady, dubious.

louche[2] /luʃ/ *n.f.* ladle.

loucher /luʃe/ *v.i.* squint.

louer[1] /lwe/ *v.t.* (*maison*) rent; (*voiture*) hire, rent; (*place*) book, reserve; (*propriétaire*) rent out; hire out. **à ~**, to let, for rent (*Amer.*).

louer[2] /lwe/ *v.t.* (*approuver*) praise (**de**, for). **se ~ de**, congratulate o.s. on.

loufoque /lufɔk/ *a.* (*fam.*) crazy.

loup /lu/ *n.m.* wolf.

loupe /lup/ *n.f.* magnifying glass.

louper /lupe/ *v.t.* (*fam.*) miss.

lourd, ~e /lur, -d/ *a.* heavy; (*chaleur*) close; (*faute*) gross. **~ de conséquences**, with dire consequences. **~ement** /-dəmɑ̃/ *adv.* heavily. **~eur** /-dœr/ *n.f.* heaviness.

lourdaud, ~e /lurdo, -d/ *a.* loutish. ● *n.m., f.* lout, oaf.

loutre /lutr/ *n.f.* otter.

louve /luv/ *n.f.* she-wolf.

louveteau (*pl.* **~x**) /luvto/ *n.m.* wolf cub; (*scout*) Cub (Scout).

louvoyer /luvwaje/ *v.i.* (*fig.*) sidestep the issue; (*naut.*) tack.

loy|al (*m. pl.* **~aux**) /lwajal, -o/ *a.* loyal; (*honnête*) fair. **~alement** *adv.* loyally; fairly. **~auté** *n.f.* loyalty; fairness.

loyer /lwaje/ *n.m.* rent.

lu /ly/ *voir* lire[1].

lubie /lybi/ *n.f.* whim.

lubrif|ier /lybrifje/ *v.t.* lubricate. **~iant** *n.m.* lubricant.

lubrique /lybrik/ *a.* lewd.

lucarne /lykarn/ *n.f.* skylight.

lucid|e /lysid/ *a.* lucid. **~ité** *n.f.* lucidity.

lucrati|f, ~ve /lykratif, -v/ *a.* lucrative. **à but non ~f**, non-profit-making.

lueur /lɥœr/ *n.f.* (faint) light, glimmer; (*fig.*) glimmer, gleam.

luge /lyʒ/ *n.f.* toboggan.

lugubre /lygybr/ *a.* gloomy.

lui /lɥi/ *pron.* him; (*sujet*) he; (*chose*) it; (*objet indirect*) (to) him; (*femme*) (to) her; (*chose*) (to) it. ~-même *pron.* himself; itself.

luire† /lɥir/ *v.i.* shine; (*reflet humide*) glisten; (*reflet chaud, faible*) glow.

lumbago /lɔ̃bago/ *n.m.* lumbago.

lumière /lymjɛr/ *n.f.* light. ~s, (*connaissances*) knowledge. **faire (toute) la ~ sur,** clear up.

luminaire /lyminɛr/ *n.m.* lamp.

lumineu|x, ~se /lyminø, -z/ *a.* luminous; (*éclairé*) illuminated; (*source, rayon*) (of) light; (*vif*) bright.

lunaire /lynɛr/ *a.* lunar.

lunatique /lynatik/ *a.* temperamental.

lunch /lœnʃ/ *n.m.* buffet lunch.

lundi /lœdi/ *n.m.* Monday.

lune /lyn/ *n.f.* moon. **~ de miel,** honeymoon.

lunette /lynɛt/ *n.f.* ~s, glasses; (*de protection*) goggles. **~ arrière,** (*auto.*) rear window. **~s de soleil,** sun-glasses.

luron /lyrɔ̃/ *n.m.* **gai** *ou* **joyeux ~,** (*fam.*) quite a lad.

lustre /lystr/ *n.m.* (*éclat*) lustre; (*objet*) chandelier.

lustré /lystre/ *a.* shiny.

luth /lyt/ *n.m.* lute.

lutin /lytɛ̃/ *n.m.* goblin.

lutrin /lytrɛ̃/ *n.m.* lectern.

lutt|e /lyt/ *n.f.* fight, struggle; (*sport*) wrestling. **~er** *v.i.* fight, struggle; (*sport*) wrestle. **~eur, ~euse** *n.m., f.* fighter; (*sport*) wrestler.

luxe /lyks/ *n.m.* luxury. **de ~,** luxury; (*produit*) de luxe.

Luxembourg /lyksɑ̃bur/ *n.m.* Luxemburg.

lux|er /lykse/ *v.t.* **se ~er le genou,** dislocate one's knee. **~ation** *n.f.* dislocation.

luxueu|x, ~se /lyksɥø, -z/ *a.* luxurious.

luxure /lyksyr/ *n.f.* lust.

luxuriant, ~e /lyksyrjɑ̃, -t/ *a.* luxuriant.

luzerne /lyzɛrn/ *n.f.* (*plante*) lucerne, alfalfa.

lycée /lise/ *n.m.* (secondary) school. **~n, ~nne** /-ɛ̃, -ɛn/ *n.m., f.* pupil (at secondary school).

lynch|er /lɛ̃ʃe/ *v.t.* lynch. **~age** *n.m.* lynching.

lynx /lɛ̃ks/ *n.m.* lynx.

lyophilis|er /ljofilize/ *v.t.* freeze-dry. **~é** *a.* freeze-dried.

lyre /lir/ *n.f.* lyre.

lyri|que /lirik/ *a.* (*poésie*) lyric; (*passionné*) lyrical. **artiste/théâtre ~que,** opera singer/-house. **~sme** *n.m.* lyricism.

lys /lis/ *n.m.* lily.

M

m' /m/ *voir* me.

ma /ma/ *voir* mon.

maboul /mabul/ *a.* (*fam.*) mad.

macabre /makabr/ *a.* gruesome, macabre.

macadam /makadam/ *n.m.* (*goudronné*) Tarmac (P.).

macaron /makarɔ̃/ *n.m.* (*gâteau*) macaroon; (*insigne*) badge.

macaronis /makarɔni/ *n.m. pl.* macaroni.

macédoine /masedwan/ *n.f.* mixed vegetables. **~ de fruits,** fruit salad.

macérer /masere/ *v.t./i.* soak; (*dans du vinaigre*) pickle.

mâchefer /maʃfɛr/ *n.m.* clinker.

mâcher /maʃe/ *v.t.* chew. **ne pas ~ ses mots,** not mince one's words.

machiavélique /makjavelik/ *a.* machiavellian.

machin /maʃɛ̃/ *n.m.* (*chose: fam.*) thing; (*personne: fam.*) what's-his-name.

machin|al (*m. pl.* ~aux) /maʃinal, -o/ *a.* automatic. **~alement** *adv.* automatically.

machinations /maʃinasjɔ̃/ *n.f. pl.* machinations.

machine /maʃin/ *n.f.* machine; (*d'un train, navire*) engine. **~ à écrire,** typewriter. **~ à laver/coudre,** washing-/sewing-machine. **~ à sous,** fruit machine; (*Amer.*) slot-machine. **~-outil** (*pl.* ~s-outils) *n.f.* machine tool. **~rie** *n.f.* machinery.

machiner /maʃine/ *v.t.* plot.

machiniste /maʃinist/ *n.m.* (*théâtre*) stage-hand; (*conducteur*) driver.

macho /ma(t)ʃo/ *n.m.* (*fam.*) macho.

mâchoire /maʃwar/ *n.f.* jaw.

mâchonner /maʃone/ *v.t.* chew at.

maçon /masɔ̃/ *n.m.* builder; (*poseur de briques*) bricklayer. **~nerie** /-ɔnri/ *n.f.* brickwork; (*pierres*) stonework, masonry.

maçonnique /masɔnik/ *a.* Masonic.

macrobiotique /makrɔbjɔtik/ *a.* macrobiotic.

maculer /makyle/ *v.t.* stain.

Madagascar /madagaskar/ *n.f.* Madagascar.

madame (*pl.* **mesdames**) /madam, medam/ *n.f.* madam. **M~ ou Mme Dupont**, Mrs Dupont. **bonsoir, mesdames**, good evening, ladies.

madeleine /madlɛn/ *n.f.* madeleine (*small shell-shaped sponge-cake*).

mademoiselle (*pl.* **mesdemoiselles**) /madmwazɛl, medmwazɛl/ *n.f.* miss. **M~ ou Mlle Dupont**, Miss Dupont. **bonsoir, mesdemoiselles**, good evening, ladies.

madère /madɛr/ *n.m.* (*vin*) Madeira.

madone /madɔn/ *n.f.* madonna.

madrigal (*pl.* **~aux**) /madrigal, -o/ *n.m.* madrigal.

maestro /maestro/ *n.m.* maestro.

maf(f)ia /mafja/ *n.f.* Mafia.

magasin /magazɛ̃/ *n.m.* shop, store; (*entrepôt*) warehouse; (*d'une arme etc.*) magazine.

magazine /magazin/ *n.m.* magazine; (*émission*) programme.

Maghreb /magrɛb/ *n.m.* North Africa. **~in, ~ine** *a.* & *n.m.*, *f.* North African.

magicien, ~ne /maʒisjɛ̃, -jɛn/ *n.m.*, *f.* magician.

magie /maʒi/ *n.f.* magic.

magique /maʒik/ *a.* magic; (*mystérieux*) magical.

magistral (*m. pl.* **~aux**) /maʒistral, -o/ *a.* masterly; (*grand: hum.*) colossal. **~ement** *adv.* in a masterly fashion.

magistrat /maʒistra/ *n.m.* magistrate.

magistrature /maʒistratyr/ *n.f.* judiciary.

magnanime /mananim/ *a.* magnanimous. **~ité** *n.f.* magnanimity.

magnat /magna/ *n.m.* tycoon, magnate.

magner (se) /(sə)maɲe/ *v. pr.* (*argot*) hurry.

magnésie /maɲezi/ *n.f.* magnesia.

magnétique /maɲetik/ *a.* magnetic. **~ser** *v.t.* magnetize. **~sme** *n.m.* magnetism.

magnétophone /maɲetɔfɔn/ *n.m.* tape recorder. **~ à cassettes**, cassette recorder.

magnétoscope /maɲetɔskɔp/ *n.m.* video-recorder.

magnifique /maɲifik/ *a.* magnificent. **~cence** *n.f.* magnificence.

magnolia /maɲɔlja/ *n.m.* magnolia.

magot /mago/ *n.m.* (*fam.*) hoard (of money).

magouiller /maguje/ *v.i.* (*fam.*) scheming. **~eur, ~euse** *n.m.*, *f.* (*fam.*) schemer. **~e** *n.f.* (*fam.*) scheming.

magret /magrɛ/ *n.m.* **~ de canard**, steaklet of duck.

mai /mɛ/ *n.m.* May.

maigre /mɛgr/ *a.* thin; (*viande*) lean; (*yaourt*) low-fat; (*fig.*) poor, meagre. **faire ~e**, abstain from meat. **~ement** *adv.* poorly. **~eur** *n.f.* thinness; leanness; (*fig.*) meagreness.

maigrir /megrir/ *v.i.* get thin(ner); (*en suivant un régime*) slim. ● *v.t.* make thin(ner).

maille /maj/ *n.f.* stitch; (*de filet*) mesh. **~ filée**, ladder, run.

maillet /majɛ/ *n.m.* mallet.

maillon /majɔ̃/ *n.m.* link.

maillot /majo/ *n.m.* (*de sport*) jersey. **~ (de corps)**, vest. **~ (de bain)**, (swimming) costume.

main /mɛ̃/ *n.f.* hand. **avoir la ~ heureuse**, be lucky. **donner la ~ à qn.**, hold s.o.'s hand. **en ~s propres**, in person. **en bonnes ~**, in good hands. **~ courante**, handrail. **~-d'œuvre** (*pl.* **~s- d'œuvre**) *n.f.* labour; (*ensemble d'ouvriers*) labour force. **~-forte** *n.f. invar.* assistance. **se faire la ~**, get the hang of it. **perdre la ~**, lose one's touch. **sous la ~**, to hand. **vol/attaque à ~ armée**, armed robbery/attack.

mainmise /mɛ̃miz/ *n.f.* **~ sur**, complete hold on.

maint, ~e /mɛ̃, mɛ̃t/ *a.* many a. **~s**, many. **à ~es reprises**, on many occasions.

maintenant /mɛ̃tnɑ̃/ *adv.* now; (*de nos jours*) nowadays.

maintenir† /mɛ̃tnir/ *v.t.* keep, maintain; (*soutenir*) hold up; (*affirmer*) maintain. **se ~** *v. pr.* (*continuer*) persist; (*rester*) remain.

maintien /mɛ̃tjɛ̃/ *n.m.* (*attitude*) bearing; (*conservation*) maintenance.

maire /mɛr/ *n.m.* mayor.

mairie /meri/ *n.f.* town hall; (*administration*) town council.

mais /mɛ/ *conj.* but. ~ **oui**, ~ **si**, of course. ~ **non**, definitely not.

maïs /mais/ *n.m.* (*à cultiver*) maize; (*culin.*) sweetcorn; (*Amer.*) corn.

maison /mɛzɔ̃/ *n.f.* house; (*foyer*) home; (*immeuble*) building. ~ (**de commerce**), firm. ● *a. invar.* (*culin.*) home-made. **à la** ~, at home. **rentrer** *ou* **aller à la** ~, go home. ~ **des jeunes**, youth centre. ~ **de repos**, ~ **de convalescence**, convalescent home. ~ **de retraite**, old people's home. ~ **mère**, parent company.

maisonnée /mɛzɔne/ *n.f.* household.

maisonnette /mɛzɔnɛt/ *n.f.* small house, cottage.

maître /mɛtr/ *n.m.* master. ~ (**d'école**), schoolmaster. ~ **de**, in control of. **se rendre** ~ **de**, gain control of; (*incendie*) bring under control. ~ **assistant/de conférences**, junior/senior lecturer. ~ **chanteur**, blackmailer. ~ **d'hôtel**, head waiter; (*domestique*) butler. ~ **nageur**, swimming instructor.

maîtresse /mɛtrɛs/ *n.f.* mistress. ~ (**d'école**), schoolmistress. ● *a.f.* (*idée, poutre, qualité*) main. ~ **de**, in control of.

maîtris|e /metriz/ *n.f.* mastery; (*univ.*) master's degree. ~**e** (**de soi**), self-control. ~**er** *v.t.* master; (*incendie*) control; (*personne*) subdue. **se** ~**er** *v. pr.* control o.s.

maïzena /maizena/ *n.f.* (P.) cornflour.

majesté /maʒɛste/ *n.f.* majesty.

majestueu|x, ~**se** /maʒɛstɥø -z/ *a.* majestic. ~**sement** *adv.* majestically.

majeur /maʒœr/ *a.* major; (*jurid.*) of age. ● *n.m.* middle finger. **en** ~ **partie**, mostly. **la** ~**e partie de**, most of.

major|er /maʒɔre/ *v.t.* increase. ~**ation** *n.f.* increase (**de**, in).

majorit|é /maʒɔrite/ *n.f.* majority. **en** ~**é**, chiefly. ~**aire** *a.* majority. **être** ~**aire**, be in the majority.

Majorque /maʒɔrk/ *n.f.* Majorca.

majuscule /maʒyskyl/ *a.* capital. ● *n.f.* capital letter.

mal[1] /mal/ *adv.* badly; (*incorrectement*) wrong(ly). ~ (**à l'aise**), uncomfortable. **aller** ~, (*malade*) be bad. **c'est** ~ **de**, it is wrong *ou* bad to. ~ **entendre/comprendre**, not hear/understand properly. ~ **famé**, of ill repute. ~ **fichu**, (*personne: fam.*) feeling lousy. ~ **en point**, in a bad state. **pas** ~, not bad; quite a lot.

mal[2] (*pl.* **maux**) /mal, mo/ *n.m.* evil; (*douleur*) pain, ache; (*maladie*) disease; (*effort*) trouble; (*dommage*) harm; (*malheur*) misfortune. **avoir** ~ **à la tête/aux dents/à la gorge**, have a headache/a toothache/a sore throat. **avoir le** ~ **de mer/du pays**, be seasick/homesick. **faire du** ~ **à**, hurt, harm. **se donner du** ~ **pour faire qch.**, go to a lot of trouble to do sth.

malade /malad/ *a.* sick, ill; (*bras, gorge*) bad; (*plante*) diseased. **tu es complètement** ~**!**, (*fam.*) you're mad. ● *n.m./f.* sick person; (*d'un médecin*) patient.

maladie /maladi/ *n.f.* illness, disease.

maladi|f, ~**ve** /maladif, -v/ *a.* sickly; (*peur*) morbid.

maladresse /maladrɛs/ *n.f.* clumsiness; (*erreur*) blunder.

maladroit, ~**e** /maladrwa, -t/ *a. & n.m., f.* clumsy (person).

malais, ~**e**[1] /malɛ, -z/ *a. & n.m., f.* Malay.

malaise[2] /malɛz/ *n.m.* feeling of faintness *ou* dizziness; (*fig.*) uneasiness, malaise.

malaisé /maleze/ *a.* difficult.

malaria /malarja/ *n.f.* malaria.

Malaysia /malɛzja/ *n.f.* Malaysia.

malaxer /malakse/ *v.t.* (*pétrir*) knead; (*mêler*) mix.

malchanc|e /malʃɑ̃s/ *n.f.* misfortune. ~**eux**, ~**euse** *a.* unlucky.

malcommode /malkɔmɔd/ *a.* awkward.

mâle /mɑl/ *a.* male; (*viril*) manly. ● *n.m.* male.

malédiction /malediksjɔ̃/ *n.f.* curse.

maléfice /malefis/ *n.m.* evil spell.

maléfique /malefik/ *a.* evil.

malencontreu|x, ~**se** /malɑ̃kɔ̃trø, -z/ *a.* unfortunate.

malentendant, ~**e** *a. & n.m., f.* hard of hearing.

malentendu /malɑ̃tɑ̃dy/ *n.m.* misunderstanding.

malfaçon /malfasɔ̃/ *n.f.* fault.

malfaisant, ~e /malfəzã, -t/ *a.* harmful.

malfaiteur /malfɛtœr/ *n.m.* criminal.

malformation /malfɔrmasjɔ̃/ *n.f.* malformation.

malgache /malgaʃ/ *a. & n.m./f.* Malagasy.

malgré /malgre/ *prép.* in spite of, despite. **~ tout,** after all.

malhabile /malabil/ *a.* clumsy.

malheur /malœr/ *n.m.* misfortune; (*accident*) accident. **faire un ~,** be a big hit.

malheureu|x, ~se /malœrø, -z/ *a.* unhappy; (*regrettable*) unfortunate; (*sans succès*) unlucky; (*insignifiant*) wretched. ● *n.m., f.* (*poor*) wretch. **~sement** *adv.* unfortunately.

malhonnête /malɔnɛt/ *a.* dishonest. **~té** *n.f.* dishonesty; (*action*) dishonest action.

malic|e /malis/ *n.f.* mischievousness; (*méchanceté*) malice. **~ieux, ~ieuse a.** mischievous.

mal|in, ~igne /malɛ̃, -iɲ/ *a.* clever, smart; (*méchant*) malicious; (*tumeur*) malignant; (*difficile: fam.*) difficult. **~ignité** *n.f.* malignancy.

malingre /malɛ̃gr/ *a.* puny.

malintentionné /malɛ̃tãsjɔne/ *a.* malicious.

malle /mal/ *n.f.* (*valise*) trunk; (*auto.*) boot; (*auto., Amer.*) trunk.

malléable /maleabl/ *a.* malleable.

mallette /malɛt/ *n.f.* (small) suitcase.

malmener /malməne/ *v.t.* manhandle, handle roughly.

malnutrition /malnytrisjɔ̃/ *n.f.* malnutrition.

malodorant, ~e /malɔdɔrã, -t/ *a.* smelly, foul-smelling.

malotru /malɔtry/ *n.m.* boor.

malpoli /malpɔli/ *a.* impolite.

malpropre /malprɔpr/ *a.* dirty. **~té** /-ǝte/ *n.f.* dirtiness.

malsain, ~e /malsɛ̃, -ɛn/ *a.* unhealthy.

malt /malt/ *n.m.* malt.

maltais, ~e /maltɛ, -z/ *a. & n.m., f.* Maltese.

Malte /malt/ *n.f.* Malta.

maltraiter /maltrete/ *v.t.* ill-treat.

malveillan|t, ~te /malvɛjã, -t/ *a.* malevolent. **~ce** *n.f.* malevolence.

maman /mamã/ *n.f.* mum(my), mother.

mamelle /mamɛl/ *n.f.* teat.

mamelon /mamlɔ̃/ *n.m.* (*anat.*) nipple; (*colline*) hillock.

mamie /mami/ *n.f.* (*fam.*) granny.

mammifère /mamifɛr/ *n.m.* mammal.

mammouth /mamut/ *n.m.* mammoth.

manche¹ /mãʃ/ *n.f.* sleeve; (*sport, pol.*) round. **la M~,** the Channel.

manche² /mãʃ/ *n.m.* (*d'un instrument*) handle. **~ à balai,** broomstick.

manchette /mãʃɛt/ *n.f.* cuff; (*de journal*) headline.

manchot¹, **~e** /mãʃo, -ɔt/ *a. & n.m., f.* one-armed (person); (*sans bras*) armless (person).

manchot² /mãʃo/ *n.m.* (*oiseau*) penguin.

mandarin /mãdarɛ̃/ *n.m.* (*fonctionnaire*) mandarin.

mandarine /mãdarin/ *n.f.* tangerine, mandarin (orange).

mandat /mãda/ *n.m.* (*postal*) money order; (*pol.*) mandate; (*procuration*) proxy; (*de police*) warrant. **~aire** /-tɛr/ *n.m.* (*représentant*) representative. **~er** /-te/ *v.t.* (*pol.*) delegate.

manège /manɛʒ/ *n.m.* riding-school; (*à la foire*) merry-go-round; (*manœuvre*) wiles, ploy.

manette /manɛt/ *n.f.* lever; (*comput.*) joystick.

mangeable /mãʒabl/ *a.* edible.

mangeoire /mãʒwar/ *n.f.* trough.

mang|er /mãʒe/ *v.t./i.* (*fortune*) go through; (*ronger*) eat into. ● *n.m.* food. **donner à ~ à,** feed. **~eur, ~euse** *n.m., f.* eater.

mangue /mãg/ *n.f.* mango.

maniable /manjabl/ *a.* easy to handle.

maniaque /manjak/ *a.* fussy. ● *n.m./f.* fuss-pot; (*fou*) maniac. **un ~ de,** a maniac for.

manie /mani/ *n.f.* habit; obsession.

man|ier /manje/ *v.t.* handle. **~iement** *n.m.* handling.

manière /manjɛr/ *n.f.* way, manner. **~s,** (*politesse*) manners; (*chichis*) fuss. **de cette ~,** in this way. **de ~ à,** so as to. **de toute ~,** anyway, in any case.

maniéré /manjere/ *a.* affected.

manif /manif/ *n.f.* (*fam.*) demo.

manifestant, ~e /manifɛstã, -t/ *n.m., f.* demonstrator.

manifeste /manifɛst/ *a.* obvious. ● *n.m.* manifesto.

manifest|er[1] /manifɛste/ *v.t.* show, manifest. **se ~er** *v. pr.* (*sentiment*) show itself; (*apparaître*) appear. **~ation**[1] *n.f.* expression, demonstration, manifestation; (*de maladie*) appearance.

manifest|er[2] /manifɛste/ *v.i.* (*pol.*) demonstrate. **~ation**[2] *n.f.* (*pol.*) demonstration; (*événement*) event.

maniganc|e /manigɑ̃s/ *n.f.* little plot. **~er** *v.t.* plot.

manipul|er /manipyle/ *v.t.* handle; (*péj.*) manipulate. **~ation** *n.f.* handling; (*péj.*) manipulation.

manivelle /manivɛl/ *n.f.* crank.

manne /man/ *n.f.* (*aubaine*) godsend.

mannequin /mankɛ̃/ *n.m.* (*personne*) model; (*statue*) dummy.

manœuvr|e[1] /manœvr/ *n.f.* manœuvre. **~er** *v.t./i.* manœuvre; (*machine*) operate.

manœuvre[2] /manœvr/ *n.m.* (*ouvrier*) labourer.

manoir /manwar/ *n.m.* manor.

manque /mɑ̃k/ *n.m.* lack (**de**, of); (*vide*) gap. **~s**, (*défauts*) faults. **~ à gagner**, loss of profit. **en (état de) ~**, having withdrawal symptoms.

manqué /mɑ̃ke/ *a.* (*écrivain etc.*) failed. **garçon ~**, tomboy.

manquement /mɑ̃kmɑ̃/ *n.m.* **~ à**, breach of.

manquer /mɑ̃ke/ *v.t.* miss; (*gâcher*) spoil; (*examen*) fail. ● *v.i.* be short *ou* lacking; (*absent*) be absent; (*en moins*, *disparu*) be missing; (*échouer*) fail. **~ à**, (*devoir*) fail in. **~ de**, be short of, lack. **il/ça lui manque**, he misses him/it. **~ (de) faire**, (*faillir*) nearly do. **ne pas ~ de**, not fail to.

mansarde /mɑ̃sard/ *n.f.* attic.

manteau (*pl.* **~x**) /mɑ̃to/ *n.m.* coat.

manucur|e /manykyr/ *n.m./f.* manicurist. **~er** *v.t.* manicure.

manuel, ~le /manɥɛl/ *a.* manual. ● *n.m.* (*livre*) manual. **~lement** *adv.* manually.

manufactur|e /manyfaktyr/ *n.f.* factory. **~é** *a.* manufactured.

manuscrit, ~e /manyskri, -t/ *a.* handwritten. ● *n.m.* manuscript.

manutention /manytɑ̃sjɔ̃/ *n.f.* handling.

mappemonde /mapmɔ̃d/ *n.f.* world map; (*sphère*) globe.

maquereau (*pl.* **~x**) /makro/ *n.m.* (*poisson*) mackerel; (*fam.*) pimp.

maquette /makɛt/ *n.f.* (scale) model; (*mise en page*) paste-up.

maquill|er /makije/ *v.t.* make up; (*truquer*) fake. **se ~er** *v. pr.* make (o.s.) up. **~age** *n.m.* make-up.

maquis /maki/ *n.m.* (*paysage*) scrub; (*mil.*) Maquis, underground.

maraîch|er, ~ère /mareʃe, -ɛʃɛr/ *n.m., f.* market gardener; (*Amer.*) truck farmer. **cultures ~ères**, market gardening.

marais /marɛ/ *n.m.* marsh.

marasme /marasm/ *n.m.* slump.

marathon /maratɔ̃/ *n.m.* marathon.

marbre /marbr/ *n.m.* marble.

marc /mar/ *n.m.* (*eau-de-vie*) marc. **~ de café**, coffee-grounds.

marchand, ~e /marʃɑ̃, -d/ *n.m., f.* trader; (*de charbon, vins*) merchant. ● *a.* (*valeur*) market. **~ de couleurs**, ironmonger; (*Amer.*) hardware merchant. **~ de journaux**, newsagent. **~ de légumes**, greengrocer. **~ de poissons**, fishmonger.

marchand|er /marʃɑ̃de/ *v.t.* haggle over. ● *v.i.* haggle. **~age** *n.m.* haggling.

marchandise /marʃɑ̃diz/ *n.f.* goods.

marche /marʃ/ *n.f.* (*démarche, trajet*) walk; (*rythme*) pace; (*mil., mus.*) march; (*d'escalier*) step; (*sport*) walking; (*de machine*) working; (*de véhicule*) running. **en ~**, (*train etc.*) moving. **faire ~ arrière**, (*véhicule*) reverse. **mettre en ~**, start (up). **se mettre en ~**, start moving.

marché /marʃe/ *n.m.* market; (*contrat*) deal. **faire son ~**, do one's shopping. **~ aux puces**, flea market. **M~ commun**, Common Market. **~ noir**, black market.

marchepied /marʃəpje/ *n.m.* (*de train, camion*) step.

march|er /marʃe/ *v.i.* walk; (*aller*) go; (*fonctionner*) work, run; (*prospérer*) go well; (*consentir: fam.*) agree. **~er (au pas)**, (*mil.*) march. **faire ~er qn.**, pull s.o.'s leg. **~eur, ~euse** *n.m., f.* walker.

mardi /mardi/ *n.m.* Tuesday. **M~ gras**, Shrove Tuesday.

mare /mar/ *n.f.* (*étang*) pond; (*flaque*) pool.

marécag|e /marekaʒ/ *n.m.* marsh. **~eux, ~euse** *a.* marshy.

maréch|al (*pl.* **~aux**) /mareʃal, -o/ *n.m.* marshal. **~al-ferrant** (*pl.* **~aux-ferrants**) blacksmith.

marée /mare/ *n.f.* tide; (*poissons*) fresh fish. ~ **haute/basse,** high/ low tide. ~ **noire,** oil-slick.

marelle /marɛl/ *n.f.* hopscotch.

margarine /margarin/ *n.f.* margarine.

marge /marʒ/ *n.f.* margin. **en ~ de,** (*à l'écart de*) on the fringe(s) of. ~ **bénéficiaire,** profit margin.

margin|al, ~ale (*m. pl.* ~**aux**) /marʒinal, -o/ *a.* marginal. ● *n.m., f.* drop-out.

marguerite /margərit/ *n.f.* daisy; (*qui imprime*) daisy-wheel.

mari /mari/ *n.m.* husband.

mariage /marjaʒ/ *n.m.* marriage; (*cérémonie*) wedding.

marié, ~e /marje/ *a.* married. ● *n.m.* (bride)groom. ● *n.f.* bride. **les ~s,** the bride and groom.

marier /marje/ *v.t.* marry. **se ~** *v. pr.* get married, marry. **se ~ avec,** marry, get married to.

marin, ~e /marɛ̃, -in/ *a.* sea. ● *n.m.* sailor. ● *n.f.* navy. ~**e marchande,** merchant navy.

mariner /marine/ *v.t./i.* marinate. **faire ~,** (*fam.*) keep hanging around.

marionnette /marjɔnɛt/ *n.f.* puppet; (*à fils*) marionette.

maritalement /maritalmɑ̃/ *adv.* as husband and wife.

maritime /maritim/ *a.* maritime, coastal; (*droit, agent*) shipping.

mark /mark/ *n.m.* mark.

marmaille /marmaj/ *n.f.* (*enfants: fam.*) brats.

marmelade /marməlad/ *n.f.* stewed fruit. ~ **(d'oranges),** marmelade.

marmite /marmit/ *n.f.* (cooking-)pot.

marmonner /marmɔne/ *v.t./i.* mumble.

marmot /marmo/ *n.m.* (*fam.*) kid.

marmotter /marmɔte/ *v.t./i.* mumble.

Maroc /marɔk/ *n.m.* Morocco.

marocain, ~e /marɔkɛ̃, -ɛn/ *a. & n.m., f.* Moroccan.

maroquinerie /marɔkinri/ *n.f.* (*magasin*) leather goods shop.

marotte /marɔt/ *n.f.* fad, craze.

marquant, ~e /markɑ̃, -t/ *a.* (*remarquable*) outstanding; (*qu'on n'oublie pas*) significant.

marque /mark/ *n.f.* mark; (*de produits*) brand, make. **à vos ~s!,** (*sport*) on your marks! **de ~,** (*comm.*) brand-name; (*fig.*)

important. ~ **de fabrique,** trade mark. ~ **déposée,** registered trade mark.

marqué /marke/ *a.* marked.

marquer /marke/ *v.t.* mark; (*indiquer*) show; (*écrire*) note down; (*point, but*) score; (*joueur*) mark; (*animal*) brand. ● *v.i.* (*trace*) leave a mark; (*événement*) stand out.

marqueterie /markɛtri/ *n.f.* marquetry.

marquis, ~e ¹ /marki, -z/ *n.m., f.* marquis, marchioness.

marquise ² /markiz/ *n.f.* (*auvent*) glass awning.

marraine /marɛn/ *n.f.* godmother.

marrant, ~e /marɑ̃, -t/ *a.* (*fam.*) funny.

marre /mar/ *n.m.* **en avoir ~,** (*fam.*) be fed up (**de,** with).

marrer (se) /(sə)mare/ *v. pr.* (*fam.*) laugh, have a (good) laugh.

marron /marɔ̃/ *n.m.* chestnut; (*couleur*) brown; (*coup: fam.*) thump. ● *a. invar.* brown. ~ **d'Inde,** horsechestnut.

mars /mars/ *n.m.* March.

marsouin /marswɛ̃/ *n.m.* porpoise.

marteau (*pl.* ~**x**) /marto/ *n.m.* hammer. ~ **(de porte),** (door) knocker. ~ **piqueur** *ou* **pneumatique,** pneumatic drill. **être ~,** (*fam.*) mad.

marteler /martəle/ *v.t.* hammer.

mart|ial (*m. pl.* ~**iaux**) /marsjal, -jo/ *a.* martial.

martien, ~ne /marsjɛ̃, -jɛn/ *a. & n.m., f.* Martian.

martyr, ~e ¹ /martir/ *n.m., f.* martyr. ● *a.* martyred. ~**iser** *v.t.* martyr; (*fig.*) batter.

martyre ² /martir/ *n.m.* (*souffrance*) martyrdom.

marxis|te /marksist/ *a. & n.m./f.* Marxist. ~**me** *n.m.* Marxism.

mascara /maskara/ *n.m.* mascara.

mascarade /maskarad/ *n.f.* masquerade.

mascotte /maskɔt/ *n.f.* mascot.

masculin, ~e /maskylɛ̃, -in/ *a.* masculine; (*sexe*) male; (*mode, équipe*) men's. ● *n.m.* masculine. ~**ité** /-inite/ *n.f.* masculinity.

maso /mazo/ *n.m./f.* (*fam.*) masochist. ● *a. invar.* masochistic.

masochis|te /mazɔʃist/ *n.m./f.* masochist. ● *a.* masochistic. ~**me** *n.m.* masochism.

masqu|e /mask/ *n.m.* mask. **~er** *v.t.* (*cacher*) hide, conceal (**à**, from); (*lumière*) block (off).

massacr|e /masakr/ *n.m.* massacre. **~er** *v.t.* massacre; (*abîmer: fam.*) spoil.

massage /masaʒ/ *n.m.* massage.

masse /mas/ *n.f.* (*volume*) mass; (*gros morceau*) lump, mass; (*outil*) sledge-hammer. **en ~**, (*vendre*) in bulk; (*venir*) in force; (*production*) mass. **la ~**, (*foule*) the masses. **une ~ de**, (*fam.*) masses of.

masser¹ /mase/ *v.t.*, **se ~** *v. pr.* (*gens, foule*) mass.

mass|er² /mase/ *v.t.* (*pétrir*) massage. **~eur, ~euse** *n.m., f.* masseur, masseuse.

massi|f, ~ve /masif, -v/ *a.* massive; (*or, argent*) solid. ● *n.m.* (*de fleurs*) clump; (*géog.*) massif. **~vement** *adv.* (*en masse*) in large numbers.

massue /masy/ *n.f.* club, bludgeon.

mastic /mastik/ *n.m.* putty.

mastiquer /mastike/ *v.t.* (*mâcher*) chew.

masturb|er (se) /(sə)mastyrbe/ *v. pr.* masturbate. **~ation** *n.f.* masturbation.

masure /mazyr/ *n.f.* hovel.

mat /mat/ *a.* (*couleur*) matt; (*bruit*) dull. **être ~**, (*aux échecs*) be checkmate.

mât /mɑ/ *n.m.* mast; (*pylône*) pole.

match /matʃ/ *n.m.* match; (*Amer.*) game. (**faire**) **~ nul**, tie, draw. **~ aller**, first leg. **~ retour**, return match.

matelas /matla/ *n.m.* mattress. **~ pneumatique**, air mattress.

matelassé /matlase/ *a.* padded; (*tissu*) quilted.

matelot /matlo/ *n.m.* sailor.

mater /mate/ *v.t.* (*personne*) subdue; (*réprimer*) stifle.

matérialiser (se) /(sə)materjalize/ *v. pr.* materialize.

matérialiste /materjalist/ *a.* materialistic. ● *n.m./f.* materialist.

matériaux /materjo/ *n.m. pl.* materials.

matériel, ~le /materjɛl/ *a.* material. ● *n.m.* equipment, materials; (*d'un ordinateur*) hardware.

maternel, ~le /matɛrnɛl/ *a.* motherly, maternal; (*rapport de parenté*) maternal. ● *n.f.* nursery school.

maternité /matɛrnite/ *n.f.* maternity hospital; (*état de mère*) motherhood.

mathémati|que /matematik/ *a.* mathematical. ● *n.f. pl.* mathematics. **~cien, ~cienne** *n.m., f.* mathematician.

maths /mat/ *n.f. pl.* (*fam.*) maths.

matière /matjɛr/ *n.f.* matter; (*produit*) material; (*sujet*) subject. **en ~ de**, as regards. **~ plastique**, plastic. **~s grasses**, fat. **à 0% de ~s grasses**, fat free. **~s premières**, raw materials.

matin /matɛ̃/ *n.m.* morning. **de bon ~**, early in the morning.

matin|al (*m. pl.* **~aux**) /matinal, -o/ *a.* morning; (*de bonne heure*) early. **être ~**, be up early.

matinée /matine/ *n.f.* morning; (*spectacle*) matinée.

matou /matu/ *n.m.* tom-cat.

matraqu|e /matrak/ *n.f.* (*de police*) truncheon; (*Amer.*) billy (club). **~er** *v.t.* club, beat; (*message*) plug.

matrice /matris/ *n.f.* (*techn.*) matrix.

matrimon|ial (*m. pl.* **~iaux**) /matrimɔnjal, -jo/ *a.* matrimonial.

maturité /matyrite/ *n.f.* maturity.

maudire† /modir/ *v.t.* curse.

maudit, ~e /modi, -t/ *a.* (*fam.*) damned.

maugréer /mogree/ *v.i.* grumble.

mausolée /mozole/ *n.m.* mausoleum.

maussade /mosad/ *a.* gloomy.

mauvais, ~e /mɔvɛ, -z/ *a.* bad; (*erroné*) wrong; (*malveillant*) evil; (*désagréable*) nasty, bad; (*mer*) rough. ● *n.m.* **il fait ~**, the weather is bad. **le ~ moment**, the wrong time. **~e herbe**, weed. **~e langue**, gossip. **~e passe**, tight spot. **~ traitements**, ill-treatment.

mauve /mov/ *a. & n.m.* mauve.

mauviette /movjɛt/ *n.f.* weakling.

maux /mo/ *voir* **mal²**.

maxim|al (*m. pl.* **~aux**) /maksimal, -o/ *a.* maximum.

maxime /maksim/ *n.f.* maxim.

maximum /maksimɔm/ *a. & n.m.* maximum. **au ~**, as much as possible; (*tout au plus*) at most.

mayonnaise /majɔnɛz/ *n.f.* mayonnaise.

mazout /mazut/ *n.m.* (fuel) oil.

me, m'* /mə, m/ *pron.* me; (*indirect*) (to) me; (*réfléchi*) myself.

méandre /meɑ̃dr/ *n.m.* meander.

mec /mɛk/ *n.m.* (*fam.*) bloke, guy.

mécanicien /mekanisjɛ̃/ *n.m.* mechanic; (*rail.*) train driver.

mécani|que /mekanik/ *a.* mechanical; (*jouet*) clockwork. **problème** ~**que**, engine trouble. ● *n.f.* mechanics; (*mécanisme*) mechanism. ~**ser** *v.t.* mechanize.

mécanisme /mekanism/ *n.m.* mechanism.

méch|ant, ~ante /meʃɑ̃, -t/ *a.* (*cruel*) wicked; (*désagréable*) nasty; (*enfant*) naughty; (*chien*) vicious; (*sensationnel: fam.*) terrific. ● *n.m., f.* (*enfant*) naughty child. ~**amment** *adv.* wickedly. ~**anceté** *n.f.* wickedness; (*action*) wicked action.

mèche /mɛʃ/ *n.f.* (*de cheveux*) lock; (*de bougie*) wick; (*d'explosif*) fuse. **de ~ avec**, in league with.

méconnaissable /mekɔnɛsabl/ *a.* unrecognizable.

méconn|aître /mekɔnɛtr/ *v.t.* be ignorant of; (*mésestimer*) underestimate. ~**aissance** *n.f.* ignorance. ~**u** *a.* unrecognized.

mécontent, ~e /mekɔ̃tɑ̃, -t/ *a.* dissatisfied (**de,** with); (*irrité*) annoyed (**de,** at, with). ~**ement** /-tmɑ̃/ *n.m.* dissatisfaction; annoyance. ~**er** /-te/ *v.t.* dissatisfy; (*irriter*) annoy.

médaill|e /medaj/ *n.f.* medal; (*insigne*) badge; (*bijou*) medallion. ~**é, ~ée** *n.m., f.* medal holder.

médaillon /medajɔ̃/ *n.m.* medallion; (*bijou*) locket.

médecin /medsɛ̃/ *n.m.* doctor.

médecine /medsin/ *n.f.* medicine.

média /medja/ *n.m.* medium. **les ~s,** the media.

média|teur, ~trice /medjatœr, -tris/ *n.m., f.* mediator.

médiation /medjasjɔ̃/ *n.f.* mediation.

médiatique /medjatik/ *a.* **événement/personnalité ~,** media event/personality.

médic|al (*m. pl.* ~**aux**) /medikal, -o/ *a.* medical.

médicament /medikamɑ̃/ *n.m.* medicine.

médicin|al (*m. pl.* ~**aux**) /medisinal, -o/ *a.* medicinal.

médico-lég|al (*m. pl.* ~**aux**) /medikɔlegal, -o/ *a.* forensic.

médiév|al (*m. pl.* ~**aux**) /medjeval, -o/ *a.* medieval.

médiocr|e /medjɔkr/ *a.* mediocre, poor. ~**ement** *adv.* (*peu*) not very;

(*mal*) in a mediocre way. ~**ité** *n.f.* mediocrity.

médire /medir/ *v.i.* ~ **de,** speak ill of.

médisance /medizɑ̃s/ *n.f.* ~(**s**), malicious gossip.

méditati|f, ~ve /meditatif, -v/ *a.* (*pensif*) thoughtful.

médit|er /medite/ *v.t./i.* meditate. ~**er de,** plan to. ~**ation** *n.f.* meditation.

Méditerranée /mediterane/ *n.f.* **la ~,** the Mediterranean.

méditerranéen, ~ne /mediteraneɛ̃, -ɛn/ *a.* Mediterranean.

médium /medjɔm/ *n.m.* (*personne*) medium.

méduse /medyz/ *n.f.* jellyfish.

meeting /mitiŋ/ *n.m.* meeting.

méfait /mefɛ/ *n.m.* misdeed. **les ~s de,** (*conséquences*) the ravages of.

méfian|t, ~te /mefjɑ̃, -t/ *a.* distrustful. ~**ce** *n.f.* distrust.

méfier (se) /(sə)mefje/ *v. pr.* be wary *ou* careful. **se ~ de,** distrust, be wary of.

mégarde (par) /(par)megard/ *adv.* by accident, accidentally.

mégère /meʒɛr/ *n.f.* (*femme*) shrew.

mégot /mego/ *n.m.* (*fam.*) cigarette-end.

meilleur, ~e /mɛjœr/ *a. & adv.* better (**que,** than). **le ~ livre/***etc.***,** the best book/*etc.* **mon ~ ami/***etc.***,** my best friend/*etc.* ~ **marché,** cheaper. ● *n.m., f.* **le ~/la ~,** the best (one).

mélancol|ie /melɑ̃kɔli/ *n.f.* melancholy. ~**ique** *a.* melancholy.

mélang|e /melɑ̃ʒ/ *n.m.* mixture, blend. ~**er** *v.t.*, **se ~er** *v. pr.* mix, blend; (*embrouiller*) mix up.

mélasse /melas/ *n.f.* treacle; (*Amer.*) molasses.

mêlée /mele/ *n.f.* scuffle; (*rugby*) scrum.

mêler /mele/ *v.t.* mix (**à,** with); (*qualités*) combine; (*embrouiller*) mix up. ~ **à,** (*impliquer dans*) involve in. **se ~** *v. pr.* mix; combine. **se ~ à,** (*se joindre à*) join. **se ~** *v. pr.* meddle in. **mêle-toi de ce qui te regarde,** mind your own business.

méli-mélo /melimelo/ *n.m.* (*pl.* **mélis-mélos**) jumble.

mélo /melo/ (*fam.*) *n.m.* melodrama. ● *a. invar.* melodramatic.

mélod|ie /melɔdi/ *n.f.* melody. ~**ieux, ~ieuse** *a.* melodious. ~**ique** *a.* melodic.

mélodram|e /melɔdram/ *n.m.* melodrama. **~atique** *a.* melodramatic.

mélomane /melɔman/ *n.m./f.* music lover.

melon /mlɔ̃/ *n.m.* melon. **(chapeau) ~,** bowler (hat).

membrane /mãbran/ *n.f.* membrane.

membre[1] /mãbr/ *n.m.* limb.

membre[2] /mãbr/ *n.m.* (*adhérent*) member.

même /mɛm/ *a.* same. **ce livre/etc. ~,** this very book/*etc.* **la bonté/etc. ~,** kindness/*etc.* itself. ● *pron.* **le ~/la ~,** the same (one). ● *adv.* even. **à ~,** (*sur*) directly on. **à ~ de,** in a position to. **de ~,** (*aussi*) too; (*de la même façon*) likewise. **de ~ que,** just as. **en ~ temps,** at the same time.

mémé /meme/ *n.f.* (*fam.*) granny.

mémo /memo/ *n.m.* memo.

mémoire /memwar/ *n.f.* memory. ● *n.m.* (*requête*) memorandum; (*univ.*) dissertation. **~s,** (*souvenirs écrits*) memoirs. **à la ~ de,** to the memory of. **de ~,** from memory. **~ morte/vive,** (*comput.*) ROM/RAM.

mémorable /memɔrabl/ *a.* memorable.

memorandum /memɔrɑ̃dɔm/ *n.m.* memorandum.

menac|e /mənas/ *n.f.* threat. **~er** *v.t.* threaten (**de faire,** to do).

ménage /menaʒ/ *n.m.* (married) couple; (*travail*) housework. **se mettre en ~,** set up house. **scène de ~,** scene. **dépenses du ~,** household expenditure.

ménagement /menaʒmɑ̃/ *n.m.* care and consideration.

ménag|er[1], **~ère** /menaʒe, -ɛr/ *a.* household, domestic. **travaux ~ers,** housework. ● *n.f.* housewife.

ménager[2] /menaʒe/ *v.t.* treat with tact; (*utiliser*) be sparing in the use of; (*organiser*) prepare (carefully).

ménagerie /menaʒri/ *n.f.* menagerie.

mendiant, ~e /mɑ̃djɑ̃, -t/ *n.m., f.* beggar.

mendicité /mɑ̃disite/ *n.f.* begging.

mendier /mɑ̃dje/ *v.t.* beg for. ● *v.i.* beg.

menées /məne/ *n.f. pl.* schemings.

mener /məne/ *v.t.* lead; (*entreprise, pays*) run. ● *v.i.* lead. **~ à,** (*accompagner à*) take to. **~ à bien,** see through.

meneur /mənœr/ *n.m.* (*chef*) (ring)leader. **~ de jeu,** compère; (*Amer.*) master of ceremonies.

méningite /menɛ̃ʒit/ *n.f.* meningitis.

ménopause /menɔpoz/ *n.f.* menopause.

menotte /mənɔt/ *n.f.* (*fam.*) hand. **~s,** handcuffs.

mensonge /mɑ̃sɔ̃ʒ/ *n.m.* lie; (*action*) lying. **~er, ~ère** *a.* untrue.

menstruation /mɑ̃stryasjɔ̃/ *n.f.* menstruation.

mensualité /mɑ̃syalite/ *n.f.* monthly payment.

mensuel, ~le /mɑ̃sɥɛl/ *a. & n.m.* monthly. **~lement** *adv.* monthly.

mensurations /mɑ̃syrasjɔ̃/ *n.f. pl.* measurements.

ment|al (*m. pl.* **~aux**) /mɑ̃tal, -o/ *a.* mental.

mentalité /mɑ̃talite/ *n.f.* mentality.

menteu|r, ~se /mɑ̃tœr, -øz/ *n.m., f.* liar. ● *a.* untruthful.

menthe /mɑ̃t/ *n.f.* mint.

mention /mɑ̃sjɔ̃/ *n.f.* mention; (*annotation*) note; (*scol.*) grade. **~ bien,** (*scol.*) distinction. **~ner** /-jɔne/ *v.t.* mention.

mentir† /mɑ̃tir/ *v.i.* lie.

menton /mɑ̃tɔ̃/ *n.m.* chin.

mentor /mɛ̃tɔr/ *n.m.* mentor.

menu[1] /məny/ *n.m.* (*carte*) menu; (*repas*) meal.

menu[2] /məny/ *a.* (*petit*) tiny; (*fin*) fine; (*insignifiant*) minor. ● *adv.* (*couper*) fine.

menuis|ier /mənɥizje/ *n.m.* carpenter, joiner. **~erie** *n.f.* carpentry, joinery.

méprendre (se) /(sə)meprɑ̃dr/ *v. pr.* **se ~ sur,** be mistaken about.

mépris /mepri/ *n.m.* contempt, scorn (**de,** for). **au ~ de,** in defiance of.

méprisable /meprizabl/ *a.* despicable.

méprise /mepriz/ *n.f.* mistake.

mépris|er /meprize/ *v.t.* scorn, despise. **~ant, ~ante** *a.* scornful.

mer /mɛr/ *n.f.* sea; (*marée*) tide. **en haute ~,** on the open sea.

mercenaire /mɛrsənɛr/ *n.m. & a.* mercenary.

merci /mɛrsi/ *int.* thank you, thanks (**de, pour,** for). ● *n.f.* mercy. **~ beaucoup, ~ bien,** thank you very much.

merc|ier, ~ière /mɛrsje, -jɛr/ *n.m., f.* haberdasher; (*Amer.*) notions merchant. **~erie** *n.f.* haberdashery; (*Amer.*) notions store.

mercredi /mɛrkrədi/ *n.m.* Wednesday. **~ des Cendres**, Ash Wednesday.

mercure /mɛrkyr/ *n.m.* mercury.

merde /mɛrd/ *n.f.* (*fam.*) shit. **être dans la ~**, be in a mess.

mère /mɛr/ *n.f.* mother. **~ de famille**, mother.

méridien /meridjɛ̃/ *n.m.* meridian.

méridion|al, **~ale** (*m. pl. ~aux*) /meridjɔnal, -o/ *a.* southern. ● *n.m.*, *f.* southerner.

meringue /mərɛ̃g/ *n.f.* meringue.

mérite /merit/ *n.m.* merit. **il n'a aucun ~**, that's as it should be. **il a du ~**, it's very much to his credit.

mérit|er /merite/ *v.t.* deserve. **~ant**, **~ante** *a.* deserving.

méritoire /meritwar/ *a.* commendable.

merlan /mɛrlɑ̃/ *n.m.* whiting.

merle /mɛrl/ *n.m.* blackbird.

merveille /mɛrvɛj/ *n.f.* wonder, marvel. **à ~**, wonderfully. **faire des ~s**, work wonders.

merveilleu|x, **~se** /mɛrvɛjø, -z/ *a.* wonderful, marvellous. **~sement** *adv.* wonderfully.

mes /me/ *voir* mon.

mésange /mezɑ̃ʒ/ *n.f.* tit(mouse).

mésaventure /mezavɑ̃tyr/ *n.f.* misadventure.

mesdames /medam/ *voir* madame.

mesdemoiselles /medmwazɛl/ *voir* mademoiselle.

mésentente /mezɑ̃tɑ̃t/ *n.f.* disagreement.

mesquin, **~e** /mɛskɛ̃, -in/ *a.* mean. **~erie** /-inri/ *n.f.* meanness.

mess /mɛs/ *n.m.* (*mil.*) mess.

messag|e /mesaʒ/ *n.m.* message. **~er**, **~ère** *n.m.*, *f.* messenger.

messe /mɛs/ *n.f.* (*relig.*) mass.

Messie /mesi/ *n.m.* Messiah.

messieurs /mesjø/ *voir* monsieur.

mesure /məzyr/ *n.f.* measurement; (*quantité, étalon*) measure; (*disposition*) measure, step; (*cadence*) time; (*modération*) moderation. **à ~ que**, as. **dans la ~ où**, in so far as. **dans une certaine ~**, to some extent. **en ~ de**, in a position to.

mesuré /məzyre/ *a.* measured; (*personne*) moderate.

mesurer /məzyre/ *v.t.* measure; (*juger*) assess; (*argent, temps*) ration. **se ~ avec**, pit o.s. against.

met /mɛ/ *voir* mettre.

métabolisme /metabɔlism/ *n.m.* metabolism.

mét|al (*pl. ~aux*) /metal, -o/ *n.m.* metal. **~allique** *a.* (*objet*) metal; (*éclat etc.*) metallic.

métallurg|ie /metalyrʒi/ *n.f.* (*industrie*) steel *ou* metal industry. **~iste** *n.m.* steel *ou* metal worker.

métamorphos|e /metamɔrfoz/ *n.f.* metamorphosis. **~er** *v.t.*, **se ~er** *v. pr.* transform.

métaphor|e /metafɔr/ *n.f.* metaphor. **~ique** *a.* metaphorical.

météo /meteo/ *n.f.* (*bulletin*) weather forecast.

météore /meteɔr/ *n.m.* meteor.

météorolog|ie /meteɔrɔlɔʒi/ *n.f.* meteorology; (*service*) weather bureau. **~ique** *a.* weather; (*études etc.*) meteorological.

méthod|e /metɔd/ *n.f.* method; (*ouvrage*) course, manual. **~ique** *a.* methodical.

méticuleu|x, **~se** /metikylø, -z/ *a.* meticulous.

métier /metje/ *n.m.* job; (*manuel*) trade; (*intellectuel*) profession; (*expérience*) skill. **~ (à tisser)**, loom. **remettre sur le ~**, keep going back to the drawing-board.

métis, **~se** /metis/ *a. & n.m.*, *f.* half-caste.

métrage /metraʒ/ *n.m.* length. **court ~**, short film. **long ~**, full-length film.

mètre /mɛtr/ *n.m.* metre; (*règle*) rule. **~ ruban**, tape-measure.

métreur /metrœr/ *n.m.* quantity surveyor.

métrique /metrik/ *a.* metric.

métro /metro/ *n.m.* underground; (*à Paris*) Métro.

métropol|e /metrɔpɔl/ *n.f.* metropolis; (*pays*) mother country. **~itain**, **~itaine** *a.* metropolitan.

mets[1] /mɛ/ *n.m.* dish.

mets[2] /mɛ/ *voir* mettre.

mettable /metabl/ *a.* wearable.

metteur /metœr/ *n.m.* **~ en scène**, (*théâtre*) producer; (*cinéma*) director.

mettre† /mɛtr/ *v.t.* put; (*vêtement*) put on; (*radio, chauffage, etc.*) put *ou* switch on; (*table*) lay; (*pendule*) set; (*temps*) take; (*installer*) put in; (*supposer*) suppose. **se ~** *v. pr.* put o.s.; (*objet*) go; (*porter*) wear. **~ bas**, give birth. **~ qn. en boîte**, pull s.o.'s

leg. ~ **en cause** *ou* **en question,**
question. ~ **en colère,** make angry.
~ **en valeur,** highlight. (*un bien*)
exploit. **se ~ à,** (*entrer dans*) get *ou*
go into. **se ~ à faire,** start doing. **se
~ à l'aise,** make o.s. comfortable. **se
~ à table,** sit down at the table. **se
~ au travail,** set to work. **(se) ~ en
ligne,** line up. **se ~ dans tous ses
états,** get into a state. **se ~ du sable
dans les yeux,** get sand in one's
eyes.

meuble /mœbl/ *n.m.* piece of
furniture. **~s,** furniture.

meublé /møble/ *n.m.* furnished flat-
let.

meubler /møble/ *v.t.* furnish; (*fig.*)
fill. **se ~** *v. pr.* buy furniture.

meugl|er /møgle/ *v.i.* moo. **~e-
ment(s)** *n.m.* (*pl.*) mooing.

meule /møl/ *n.f.* (*de foin*) haystack;
(*à moudre*) millstone.

meun|ier, ~ière /mønje, -jɛr/ *n.m.,
f.* miller.

meurs, meurt /mœr/ *voir* mourir.

meurtr|e /mœrtr/ *n.m.* murder. **~ier,
~ière** *a.* deadly; *n.m.* murderer; *n.f.*
murderess.

meurtr|ir /mœrtrir/ *v.t.* bruise.
~issure *n.f.* bruise.

meute /møt/ *n.f.* (*troupe*) pack.

mexicain, ~e /mɛksikɛ̃, -ɛn/ *a. &
n.m., f.* Mexican.

Mexique /mɛksik/ *n.m.* Mexico.

mi- /mi/ *préf.* mid-, half-. **à mi-chemin,** half-way. **à mi-côte,** half-way
up the hill. **la mi-juin**/*etc.*, mid-
June/*etc.*

miaou /mjau/ *n.m.* mew.

miaul|er /mjole/ *v.i.* mew. **~ement**
n.m. mew.

miche /miʃ/ *n.f.* round loaf.

micro /mikro/ *n.m.* microphone,
mike; (*comput.*) micro.

micro- /mikro/ *préf.* micro-.

microbe /mikrɔb/ *n.m.* germ.

microfilm /mikrɔfilm/ *n.m.* microfilm.

micro-onde /mikrɔɔ̃d/ *n.f.* microwave. **un (four à) ~s,** microwave
(oven).

microphone /mikrɔfɔn/ *n.m.* microphone.

microplaquette /mikrɔplakɛt/ *n.f.*
(micro)chip.

microprocesseur /mikrɔprɔsɛsœr/
n.m. microprocess.

microscop|e /mikrɔskɔp/ *n.m.*
microscope. **~ique** *a.* microscopic.

microsillon /mikrɔsijɔ̃/ *n.m.* long-
playing record.

midi /midi/ *n.m.* twelve o'clock, midday, noon; (*déjeuner*) lunch-time;
(*sud*) south. **le M~,** the South of
France.

mie /mi/ *n.f.* soft part (of the loaf). **un
pain de ~,** a sandwich loaf.

miel /mjɛl/ *n.m.* honey.

mielleu|x, ~se /mjɛlø, -z/ *a.* unctu-
ous.

mien, ~ne /mjɛ̃, mjɛn/ *pron.* **le ~, la
~ne, les ~(ne)s,** mine.

miette /mjɛt/ *n.f.* crumb; (*fig.*) scrap.
en ~s, in pieces.

mieux /mjø/ *adv. & a. invar.* better
(**que,** than). **le** *ou* **la** *ou* **les ~,** (the)
best. ● *n.m.* best; (*progrès*) im-
provement. **faire de son ~,** do one's
best. **tu ferais ~ de faire,** you
would be better off doing. **le ~
serait de,** the best thing would be to.

mièvre /mjɛvr/ *a.* genteel and insipid.

mignon, ~ne /miɲɔ̃, -ɔn/ *a.* pretty.

migraine /migrɛn/ *n.f.* headache.

migration /migrasjɔ̃/ *n.f.* migration.

mijoter /miʒɔte/ *v.t./i.* simmer;
(*tramer: fam.*) cook up.

mil /mil/ *n.m.* a thousand.

milic|e /milis/ *n.f.* militia. **~ien** *n.m.*
militiaman.

milieu (*pl.* **~x**) /miljø/ *n.m.* middle;
(*environnement*) environment;
(*groupe*) circle; (*voie*) middle way;
(*criminel*) underworld. **au ~ de,** in
the middle of. **en plein** *ou* **au beau
~ de,** right in the middle (of).

militaire /militɛr/ *a.* military.
● *n.m.* soldier.

milit|er /milite/ *v.i.* be a militant.
~er pour, militate in favour of.
~ant, ~ante *n.m., f.* militant.

milk-shake /milkʃɛk/ *n.m.* milk
shake.

mille[1] /mil/ *a. & n.m. invar.* a
thousand. **deux ~,** two thousand.
dans le ~, bang on target.

mille[2] /mil/ *n.m.* ~ **(marin),** (nautical) mile.

millénaire /milenɛr/ *n.m.* millennium.

mille-pattes /milpat/ *n.m. invar.*
centipede.

millésime /milezim/ *n.m.* year.

millésimé /milezime/ *a.* **vin ~,** vintage wine.

millet /mijɛ/ *n.m.* millet.

milliard /miljar/ n.m. thousand million, billion. **~aire** /-dɛr/ n.m./f. multimillionaire.

millier /milje/ n.m. thousand. **un ~ (de)**, about a thousand.

millimètre /milimɛtr/ n.m. millimetre.

million /miljɔ̃/ n.m. million. **deux ~s (de)**, two million. **~naire** /-jɔnɛr/ n.m./f. millionaire.

mim|e /mim/ n.m./f. (personne) mime. ● int. (art) mime. **~er** v.t. mime; (singer) mimic.

mimique /mimik/ n.f. (expressive) gestures.

mimosa /mimoza/ n.m. mimosa.

minable /minabl/ a. shabby.

minaret /minarɛ/ n.m. minaret.

minauder /minode/ v.i. simper.

minc|e /mɛ̃s/ a. thin; (svelte, insignifiant) slim. ● int. dash (it). **~ir** v.i. get slimmer. **ça te ~it**, it makes you look slimmer. **~eur** n.f. thinness; slimness.

mine¹ /min/ n.f. expression; (allure) appearance. **avoir bonne ~**, look well. **faire ~ de**, make as if to.

mine² /min/ n.f. (exploitation, explosif) mine; (de crayon) lead. **~ de charbon**, coal-mine.

miner /mine/ v.t. (saper) undermine; (garnir d'explosifs) mine.

minerai /minrɛ/ n.m. ore.

minér|al (m. pl. **~aux**) /mineral, -o/ a. mineral. ● n.m. (pl. **~aux**) mineral.

minéralogique /mineralɔʒik/ a. **plaque ~**, number/license (Amer.) plate.

minet, ~te /minɛ, -t/ n.m., f. (chat: fam.) puss(y).

mineur¹, **~e** /minœr/ a. minor; (jurid.) under age. ● n.m., f. (jurid.) minor.

mineur² /minœr/ n.m. (ouvrier) miner.

mini- /mini/ préf. mini-.

miniature /minjatyr/ n.f. & a. miniature.

minibus /minibys/ n.m. minibus.

min|ier, ~ière /minje, -jɛr/ a. mining.

minim|al (m. pl. **~aux**) /minimal, -o/ a. minimum.

minime /minim/ a. minor. ● n.m./f. (sport) junior.

minimiser /minimize/ v.t. minimize.

minimum /minimɔm/ a. & n.m. minimum. **au ~**, (pour le moins) at the very least.

mini-ordinateur /miniɔrdinatœr/ n.m. minicomputer.

minist|ère /ministɛr/ n.m. ministry; (gouvernement) government. **~ère de l'Intérieur**, Home Office; (Amer.) Department of the Interior. **~ériel, ~érielle** a. ministerial, government.

ministre /ministr/ n.m. minister. **~ de l'Intérieur**, Home Secretary; (Amer.) Secretary of the Interior.

Minitel /minitel/ n.m. (P.) Minitel (telephone videotext system).

minorer /minɔre/ v.t. reduce.

minorit|é /minɔrite/ n.f. minority. **~aire** a. minority. **être ~aire**, be in the minority.

minuit /minɥi/ n.m. midnight.

minuscule /minyskyl/ a. minute. ● n.f. (lettre) ~, small letter.

minut|e /minyt/ n.f. minute. **~er** v.t. time (to the minute).

minuterie /minytri/ n.f. time-switch.

minutie /minysi/ n.f. meticulousness.

minutieu|x, ~se /minysjø, -z/ a. meticulous. **~sement** adv. meticulously.

mioche /mjɔʃ/ n.m., f. (fam.) youngster, kid.

mirabelle /mirabɛl/ n.f. (mirabelle) plum.

miracle /mirakl/ n.m. miracle.

miraculeu|x, ~se /mirakylø, -z/ a. miraculous. **~sement** adv. miraculously.

mirage /miraʒ/ n.m. mirage.

mire /mir/ n.f. (fig.) centre of attraction; (TV) test card.

miro /miro/ a. invar. (fam.) short-sighted.

mirobolant, ~e /mirɔbɔlɑ̃, -t/ a. (fam.) marvellous.

miroir /mirwar/ n.m. mirror.

miroiter /mirwate/ v.i. gleam, shimmer.

mis, ~e¹ /mi, miz/ voir **mettre**. ● a. **bien ~**, well-dressed.

misanthrope /mizɑ̃trɔp/ n.m. misanthropist. ● a. misanthropic.

mise² /miz/ n.f. (argent) stake; (tenue) attire. **~ à feu**, blast-off. **~ au point**, adjustment; (fig.) clarification. **~ de fonds**, capital outlay. **~ en garde**, warning. **~ en scène**, (théâtre) production; (cinéma) direction.

miser /mize/ v.t. (argent) bet, stake (sur, on). ~ **sur,** (compter sur: fam.) bank on.

misérable /mizerabl/ a. miserable, wretched; (indigent) poverty-stricken; (minable) seedy. ● n.m./f. wretch.

mis|ère /mizɛr/ n.f. (grinding poverty; (malheur) misery. ~**éreux,** ~**éreuse** n.m., f. pauper.

miséricorde /mizerikɔrd/ n.f. mercy.

missel /misɛl/ n.m. missal.

missile /misil/ n.m. missile.

mission /misjɔ̃/ n.m. mission. ~**naire** /-jɔnɛr/ n.m./f. missionary.

missive /misiv/ n.f. missive.

mistral /mistral/ n.m. invar. (vent) mistral.

mitaine /mitɛn/ n.f. mitten.

mit|e /mit/ n.f. (clothes-)moth. ~**é** a. moth-eaten.

mi-temps /mitɑ̃/ n.f. invar. (repos: sport) half-time; (période: sport) half. **à** ~, part time.

miteu|x, ~se /mitø, -z/ a. shabby.

mitigé /mitiʒe/ a. (modéré) lukewarm.

mitonner /mitɔne/ v.t. cook slowly with care; (fig.) cook up.

mitoyen, ~ne /mitwajɛ̃, -ɛn/ a. **mur** ~, party wall.

mitrailler /mitraje/ v.t. machine-gun; (fig.) bombard.

mitraill|ette /mitrajɛt/ n.f. submachine-gun. ~**euse** n.f. machine-gun.

mi-voix (à) /(a)mivwa/ adv. in an undertone.

mixeur /miksœr/ n.m. liquidizer, blender.

mixte /mikst/ a. mixed; (usage) dual; (tribunal) joint; (école) co-educational.

mixture /mikstyr/ n.f. (péj.) mixture.

mobile¹ /mɔbil/ a. mobile; (pièce) moving; (feuillet) loose. ● n.m. (art) mobile.

mobile² /mɔbil/ n.m. (raison) motive.

mobilier /mɔbilje/ n.m. furniture.

mobilis|er /mɔbilize/ v.t. mobilize. ~**ation** n.f. mobilization.

mobilité /mɔbilite/ n.f. mobility.

mobylette /mɔbilɛt/ n.f. (P.) moped.

mocassin /mɔkasɛ̃/ n.m. moccasin.

moche /mɔʃ/ a. (laid: fam.) ugly; (mauvais: fam.) lousy.

modalité /mɔdalite/ n.f. mode.

mode¹ /mɔd/ n.f. fashion; (coutume) custom. **à la** ~, fashionable.

mode² /mɔd/ n.m. method, mode; (genre) way. ~ **d'emploi,** directions (for use).

modèle /mɔdɛl/ n.m. & a. model. ~ **réduit,** (small-scale) model.

modeler /mɔdle/ v.t. model (sur, on). se ~ **sur,** model o.s. on.

modem /mɔdɛm/ n.m. modem.

modéré, ~e /mɔdere/ a. & n.m., f. moderate. ~**ment** adv. moderately.

modér|er /mɔdere/ v.t. moderate. se ~**er** v. pr. restrain o.s. ~**ateur, ~atrice** a. moderating. ~**ation** n.f. moderation.

modern|e /mɔdɛrn/ a. modern. ● n.m. modern style. ~**iser** v.t. modernize.

modest|e /mɔdɛst/ a. modest. ~**ement** adv. modestly. ~**ie** n.f. modesty.

modifi|er /mɔdifje/ v.t. modify. se ~**ier** v. pr. alter. ~**ication** n.f. modification.

modique /mɔdik/ a. low.

modiste /mɔdist/ n.f. milliner.

module /mɔdyl/ n.m. module.

modul|er /mɔdyle/ v.t./i. modulate. ~**ation** n.f. modulation.

moelle /mwal/ n.f. marrow. ~ **épinière,** spinal cord.

moelleu|x, ~se /mwalø, -z/ a. soft; (onctueux) smooth.

mœurs /mœr(s)/ n.f. pl. (morale) morals; (habitudes) customs; (manières) ways.

moi /mwa/ pron. me; (indirect) (to) me; (sujet) I. ● n.m. self. ~-**même** pron. myself.

moignon /mwaɲɔ̃/ n.m. stump.

moindre /mwɛ̃dr/ a. (moins grand) less(er). **le** ou **la** ~, **les** ~**s,** the slightest, the least.

moine /mwan/ n.m. monk.

moineau (pl. ~**x**) /mwano/ n.m. sparrow.

moins /mwɛ̃/ adv. less (que, than). ● prép. (soustraction) minus. ~ **de,** (quantité) less, not so much (que, as); (objets, personnes) fewer, not so many (que, as). ~ **de dix francs/ d'une livre/etc.,** less than ten francs/one pound/etc. **le** ou **la** ou **les** ~, the least. **le** ~ **grand/haut,** the smallest/lowest. **au** ~, **du** ~, at least. **de** ~, less. **en** ~, less; (manquant) missing. **une heure** ~ **dix,** ten to one. **à** ~ **que,** unless. **de** ~ **en moins,** less and less.

mois /mwa/ n.m. month.

moïse /mɔiz/ *n.m.* moses basket.

mois|i /mwazi/ *a.* mouldy. ● *n.m.* mould. de ~i, (*odeur, goût*) musty. ~ir *v.i.* go mouldy. ~issure *n.f.* mould.

moisson /mwasɔ̃/ *n.f.* harvest.

moissonn|er /mwasɔne/ *v.t.* harvest, reap. ~eur, ~euse *n.m., f.* harvester. ~euse-batteuse (*pl.* ~euses-batteuses) *n.f.* combine harvester.

moit|e /mwat/ *a.* sticky, clammy. ~eur *n.f.* stickiness.

moitié /mwatje/ *n.f.* half; (*milieu*) half-way mark. à ~, half-way. à ~ vide/fermé/*etc.*, half empty/closed/ *etc.* à ~ prix, (at) half-price. la ~ de, half (of). ~ moitié, half-and-half.

moka /mɔka/ *n.m.* (*gâteau*) coffee cream cake.

mol /mɔl/ *voir* mou.

molaire /mɔlɛr/ *n.f.* molar.

molécule /mɔlekyl/ *n.f.* molecule.

molester /mɔlɛste/ *v.t.* manhandle, rough up.

molle /mɔl/ *voir* mou.

moll|ement /mɔlmɑ̃/ *adv.* softly; (*faiblement*) feebly. ~esse *n.f.* softness; (*faiblesse, indolence*) feebleness.

mollet /mɔlɛ/ *n.m.* (*de jambe*) calf.

molletonné /mɔltɔne/ *a.* (fleece-) lined.

mollir /mɔlir/ *v.i.* soften; (*céder*) yield.

mollusque /mɔlysk/ *n.m.* mollusc.

môme /mom/ *n.m./f.* (*fam.*) kid.

moment /mɔmɑ̃/ *n.m.* moment; (*période*) time. (**petit**) ~, short while. au ~ où, when. par ~s, now and then. du ~ où *ou* que, seeing that. en ce ~, at the moment.

momentané /mɔmɑ̃tane/ *a.* momentary. ~ment *adv.* momentarily; (*en ce moment*) at present.

momie /mɔmi/ *n.f.* mummy.

mon, ma *ou* **mon*** (*pl.* **mes**) /mɔ̃, ma, mɔ̃, me/ *a.* my.

Monaco /mɔnako/ *n.f.* Monaco.

monarchie /mɔnarʃi/ *n.f.* monarchy.

monarque /mɔnark/ *n.m.* monarque.

monastère /mɔnastɛr/ *n.m.* monastery.

monceau (*pl.* ~x) /mɔ̃so/ *n.m.* heap, pile.

mondain, ~e /mɔ̃dɛ̃, -ɛn/ *a.* society, social.

monde /mɔ̃d/ *n.m.* world. du ~, (a lot of) people; (*quelqu'un*) somebody. le (**grand**) ~, (high) society. se faire

un ~ de qch., make a great deal of fuss about sth.

mond|ial (*m. pl.* ~iaux) /mɔ̃djal, -jo/ *a.* world; (*influence*) worldwide. ~ialement *adv.* the world over.

monégasque /mɔnegask/ *a.* & *n.m./ f.* Monegasque.

monétaire /mɔnetɛr/ *a.* monetary.

moni|teur, ~trice /mɔnitœr, -tris/ *n.m., f.* instructor, instructress; (*de colonie de vacances*) supervisor; (*Amer.*) (camp) counselor.

monnaie /mɔnɛ/ *n.f.* currency; (*pièce*) coin; (*appoint*) change. **faire la ~ de**, get change for. **faire à qn. la ~ de**, give s.o. change for. **menue** *ou* **petite ~**, small change.

monnayer /mɔneje/ *v.t.* convert into cash.

mono /mɔno/ *a. invar.* mono.

monocle /mɔnɔkl/ *n.m.* monocle.

monocorde /mɔnɔkɔrd/ *a.* monotonous.

monogramme /mɔnɔgram/ *n.m.* monogram.

monologue /mɔnɔlɔg/ *n.m.* monologue.

monopol|e /mɔnɔpɔl/ *n.m.* monopoly. ~iser *v.t.* monopolize.

monosyllabe /mɔnɔsilab/ *n.m.* monosyllable.

monoton|e /mɔnɔtɔn/ *a.* monotonous. ~ie *n.f.* monotony.

monseigneur /mɔ̃sɛɲœr/ *n.m.* Your *ou* His Grace.

monsieur (*pl.* **messieurs**) /məsjø, mesjø/ *n.m.* gentleman. **M~** *ou* **M. Dupont**, Mr Dupont. **Messieurs** *ou* **MM. Dupont**, Messrs Dupont. **oui ~**, yes; (*avec déférence*) yes, sir.

monstre /mɔ̃str/ *n.m.* monster. ● *a.* (*fam.*) colossal.

monstr|ueux, ~ueuse /mɔ̃stryø, -z/ *a.* monstrous. ~uosité *n.f.* monstrosity.

mont /mɔ̃/ *n.m.* mount. **par ~s et par vaux**, up hill and down dale.

montage /mɔ̃taʒ/ *n.m.* (*assemblage*) assembly; (*cinéma*) editing.

montagn|e /mɔ̃taɲ/ *n.f.* mountain; (*région*) mountains. ~es russes, roller-coaster. ~ard, ~arde *n.m., f.* mountain dweller. ~eux, ~euse *a.* mountainous.

montant¹, ~e /mɔ̃tɑ̃, -t/ *a.* rising; (*col*) high-necked.

montant² /mɔ̃tɑ̃/ *n.m.* amount; (*pièce de bois*) upright.

mont-de-piété (*pl.* **monts-de-piété**) /mõdpjete/ *n.m.* pawnshop.

monte-charge /mõtʃarʒ/ *n.m. invar.* service lift; (*Amer.*) dumb waiter.

montée /mõte/ *n.f.* ascent, climb; (*de prix*) rise; (*côte*) hill. **au milieu de la ~**, halfway up. **à la ~ de lait**, when the milk comes.

monter /mõte/ *v.i.* (*aux. être*) go *ou* come up; (*grimper*) climb; (*prix, mer*) rise. **~ à**, (*cheval*) mount. **~ dans**, (*train, avion*) get on to; (*voiture*) get into. **~ sur**, (*colline*) climb up; (*trône*) ascend. ● *v.t.* (*aux. avoir*) go *ou* come up; (*objet*) take *ou* bring up; (*cheval, garde*) mount; (*société*) start up. **~ à cheval**, (*sport*) ride. **~ en flèche**, soar. **en graine**, go to seed.

monteu|r, ~se /mõtœr, -øz/ *n.m., f.* (*techn.*) fitter; (*cinéma*) editor.

monticule /mõtikyl/ *n.m.* mound.

montre /mõtr/ *n.f.* watch. **~-bracelet** (*pl.* **~s-bracelets**) *n.f.* wristwatch. **faire ~ de**, show.

montrer /mõtre/ *v.t.* show (à, to). **se ~** *v. pr.* show o.s.; (*être*) be; (*s'avérer*) prove to be. **~ du doigt**, point to.

monture /mõtyr/ *n.f.* (*cheval*) mount; (*de lunettes*) frame; (*de bijou*) setting.

monument /mɔnymã/ *n.m.* monument. **~ aux morts**, war memorial. **~al** (*m. pl.* **~aux**) /-tal, -to/ *a.* monumental.

moqu|er (se) /(sə)mɔke/ *v. pr.* **se ~er de**, make fun of. **je m'en ~e**, (*fam.*) I couldn't care less. **~erie** *n.f.* mockery. **~eur, ~euse** *a.* mocking.

moquette /mɔkɛt/ *n.f.* fitted carpet; (*Amer.*) wall-to-wall carpeting.

mor|al, ~ale (*m. pl.* **~aux**) /mɔral, -o/ *a.* moral. ● *n.m.* (*pl.* **~aux**) morale. ● *n.f.* moral code; (*mœurs*) morals; (*de fable*) moral. **avoir le ~al**, be on form. **ça m'a remonté le ~al**, it gave me a boost. **faire la ~ale à**, lecture. **~alement** *adv.* morally. **~alité** *n.f.* morality; (*de fable*) moral.

moralisa|teur, ~trice /mɔralizatœr, -tris/ *a.* moralizing.

morbide /mɔrbid/ *a.* morbid.

morceau (*pl.* **~x**) /mɔrso/ *n.m.* piece, bit; (*de sucre*) lump; (*de viande*) cut; (*passage*) passage. **manger un ~**, have a bite to eat. **mettre en ~x**, smash *ou* tear *etc.* to bits.

morceler /mɔrsəle/ *v.t.* fragment.

mordant, ~e /mɔrdã, -t/ *a.* scathing; (*froid*) biting. ● *n.m.* (*énergie*) vigour, punch.

mordiller /mɔrdije/ *v.t.* nibble at.

mor|dre /mɔrdr/ *v.t./i.* bite. **~re sur**, overlap into. **~re à l'hameçon**, bite. **~u, ~ue** *n.m., f.* (*fam.*) fan; *a.* bitten. **~u de**, (*fam.*) crazy about.

morfondre (se) /(sə)mɔrfõdr/ *v. pr.* mope, wait anxiously.

morgue[1] /mɔrg/ *n.f.* morgue, mortuary.

morgue[2] /mɔrg/ *n.f.* (*attitude*) haughtiness.

moribond, ~e /mɔribõ, -d/ *a.* dying.

morne /mɔrn/ *a.* dull.

morose /mɔroz/ *a.* morose.

morphine /mɔrfin/ *n.f.* morphine.

mors /mɔr/ *n.m.* (*de cheval*) bit.

morse[1] /mɔrs/ *n.m.* walrus.

morse[2] /mɔrs/ *n.m.* (*code*) Morse code.

morsure /mɔrsyr/ *n.f.* bite.

mort[1] /mɔr/ *n.f.* death.

mort[2], **~e** /mɔr, -t/ *a.* dead. ● *n.m., f.* dead man, dead woman. **les ~s**, the dead. **~ de fatigue**, dead tired. **~-né** *a.* stillborn.

mortadelle /mɔrtadɛl/ *n.f.* mortadella.

mortalité /mɔrtalite/ *n.f.* death rate.

mortel, ~le /mɔrtɛl/ *a.* mortal; (*accident*) fatal; (*poison, silence*) deadly. ● *n.m., f.* mortal. **~lement** *adv.* mortally.

mortier /mɔrtje/ *n.m.* mortar.

mortifier /mɔrtifje/ *v.t.* mortified.

mortuaire /mɔrtɥɛr/ *a.* (*cérémonie*) funeral; (*avis*) death.

morue /mɔry/ *n.f.* cod.

mosaïque /mɔzaik/ *n.f.* mosaic.

Moscou /mɔsku/ *n.m./f.* Moscow.

mosquée /mɔske/ *n.f.* mosque.

mot /mo/ *n.m.* word; (*lettre, message*) line, note. **~ d'ordre**, watchword. **~ de passe**, password. **~s croisés**, crossword (puzzle).

motard /mɔtar/ *n.m.* biker; (*policier*) police motorcyclist.

motel /mɔtɛl/ *n.m.* motel.

moteur[1] /mɔtœr/ *n.m.* engine, motor. **barque à ~**, motor launch.

mo|teur[2], **~trice** /mɔtœr, -tris/ *a.* (*nerf*) motor; (*force*) driving. **à 4 roues motrices**, 4-wheel drive.

motif /mɔtif/ *n.m.* reason; (*jurid.*) motive; (*dessin*) pattern.

motion /mɔsjõ/ *n.f.* motion.

motiv|er /mɔtive/ v.t. motivate; (*justifier*) justify. **~ation** n.f. motivation.

moto /mɔto/ n.f. motor cycle. **~cycliste** n.m./f. motorcyclist.

motorisé /mɔtɔrize/ a. motorized.

motrice /mɔtris/ voir **moteur²**.

motte /mɔt/ n.f. lump; (*de beurre*) slab; (*de terre*) clod. **~ de gazon,** turf.

mou *ou* **mol***, **molle** /mu, mɔl/ a. soft; (*péj.*) flabby; (*faible, indolent*) feeble. ● n.m. **du ~,** slack. **avoir du ~,** be slack.

mouchard, **~e** /muʃar, -d/ n.m., f. informer; (*scol.*) sneak. **~er** /-de/ v.t. (*fam.*) inform on.

mouche /muʃ/ n.f. fly.

moucher (se) /(sə)muʃe/ v. pr. blow one's nose.

moucheron /muʃrɔ̃/ n.m. midge.

moucheté /muʃte/ a. speckled.

mouchoir /muʃwar/ n.m. hanky; (*en papier*) tissue.

moudre /mudr/ v.t. grind.

moue /mu/ n.f. long face. **faire la ~,** pull a long face.

mouette /mwɛt/ n.f. (sea)gull.

moufle /mufl/ n.f. (*gant*) mitten.

mouill|er /muje/ v.t. wet, make wet. **se ~er** v. pr. get (o.s.) wet. **~er (l'ancre),** anchor. **~é** a. wet.

moulage /mulaʒ/ n.m. cast.

moul|e¹ /mul/ n.m. mould. **~er** v.t. mould; (*statue*) cast. **~e à gâteau,** cake tin. **~e à tarte,** flan dish.

moule² /mul/ n.f. (*coquillage*) mussel.

moulin /mulɛ̃/ n.m. mill; (*moteur: fam.*) engine. **~ à vent,** windmill.

moulinet /mulinɛ/ n.m. (*de canne à pêche*) reel. **faire des ~s avec qch.,** twirl sth. around.

moulinette /mulinɛt/ n.f. (P.) purée maker.

moulu /muly/ a. ground; (*fatigué: fam.*) dead beat.

moulure /mulyr/ n.f. moulding.

mourant, **~e** /murɑ̃, -t/ a. dying. ● n.m., f. dying person.

mourir† /murir/ v.i. (*aux. être*) die. **~ d'envie de,** be dying to. **~ de faim,** be starving. **~ d'ennui,** be dead bored.

mousquetaire /muskətɛr/ n.m. musketeer.

mousse¹ /mus/ n.f. moss; (*écume*) froth, foam; (*de savon*) lather; (*des-*

sert) mousse. **~ à raser,** shaving cream.

mousse² /mus/ n.m. ship's boy.

mousseline /muslin/ n.f. muslin; (*de soie*) chiffon.

mousser /muse/ v.i. froth, foam; (*savon*) lather.

mousseu|x, **~se** /musø, -z/ a. frothy. ● n.m. sparkling wine.

mousson /musɔ̃/ n.f. monsoon.

moustach|e /mustaʃ/ n.f. moustache. **~es,** (*d'animal*) whiskers. **~u** a. wearing a moustache.

moustiquaire /mustikɛr/ n.f. mosquito-net.

moustique /mustik/ n.m. mosquito.

moutarde /mutard/ n.f. mustard.

mouton /mutɔ̃/ n.m. sheep; (*peau*) sheepskin; (*viande*) mutton.

mouvant, **~e** /muvɑ̃, -t/ a. changing; (*terrain*) shifting.

mouvement /muvmɑ̃/ n.m. movement; (*agitation*) bustle; (*en gymnastique*) exercise; (*impulsion*) impulse; (*tendance*) tendency. **en ~,** in motion.

mouvementé /muvmɑ̃te/ a. eventful.

mouvoir† /muvwar/ v.t. (*membre*) move. **se ~** v. pr. move.

moyen¹, **~ne** /mwajɛ̃, -jɛn/ a. average; (*médiocre*) poor. ● n.f. average; (*scol.*) pass-mark. **de taille ~ne,** medium-sized. **~ âge,** Middle Ages. **~ne d'âge,** average age. **M~Orient** n.m. Middle East. **~nement** /-jɛnmɑ̃/ adv. moderately.

moyen² /mwajɛ̃/ n.m. means, way. **~s,** means; (*dons*) abilities. **au ~ de,** by means of. **il n'y a pas ~ de,** it is not possible to.

moyennant /mwajɛnɑ̃/ prép. (*pour*) for; (*grâce à*) with.

moyeu (*pl.* **~x**) /mwajø/ n.m. hub.

mû, **mue¹** /my/ a. driven (**par,** by).

mucoviscidose /mykɔvisidoz/ n.f. cystic fibrosis.

mue² /my/ n.f. moulting; (*de voix*) breaking of the voice.

muer /mɥe/ v.i. moult; (*voix*) break. **se ~ en,** change into.

muesli /mysli/ n.m. muesli.

muet, **~te** /mɥɛ, -t/ a. (*personne*) dumb; (*fig.*) speechless (**de,** with); (*silencieux*) silent. ● n.m., f. dumb person.

mufle /myfl/ n.m. nose, muzzle; (*personne: fam.*) boor, lout.

mugir /myʒir/ *v.i.* (*vache*) moo; (*bœuf*) bellow; (*fig.*) howl.

muguet /mygɛ/ *n.m.* lily of the valley.

mule /myl/ *n.f.* (she-)mule; (*pantoufle*) mule.

mulet /mylɛ/ *n.m.* (he-)mule.

multi- /mylti/ *préf.* multi-.

multicolore /myltikɔlɔr/ *a.* multicoloured.

multinational, ~ale (*m. pl.* ~**aux**) /myltinasjɔnal, -o/ *a.* & *n.f.* multinational.

multiple /myltipl/ *a.* & *n.m.* multiple.

multiplicité /myltiplisite/ *n.f.* multiplicity, abundance.

multipli|ier /myltiplije/ *v.t.*, **se ~ier** *v. pr.* multiply. ~**ication** *n.f.* multiplication.

multitude /myltityd/ *n.f.* multitude, mass.

municip|al (*m. pl.* ~**aux**) /mynisipal, -o/ *a.* municipal; (*conseil*) town. ~**alité** *n.f.* (*ville*) municipality; (*conseil*) town council.

munir /mynir/ *v.t.* ~ **de**, provide with. **se ~ de**, provide o.s. with.

munitions /mynisjɔ̃/ *n.f. pl.* ammunition.

mur /myr/ *n.m.* wall. ~ **du son**, sound barrier.

mûr /myr/ *a.* ripe; (*personne*) mature.

muraille /myrɑj/ *n.f.* (high) wall.

mur|al (*m. pl.* ~**aux**) /myral, -o/ *a.* wall; (*tableau*) mural.

mûre /myr/ *n.f.* blackberry.

muret /myrɛ/ *n.m.* low wall.

mûrir /myrir/ *v.t./i.* ripen; (*abcès*) come to a head; (*personne, projet*) mature.

murmur|e /myrmyr/ *n.m.* murmur. ~**er** *v.t./i.* murmur.

musc /mysk/ *n.m.* musk.

muscade /myskad/ *n.f.* **noix (de) ~**, nutmeg.

muscl|e /myskl/ *n.m.* muscle. ~**é** *a.* muscular, brawny.

muscul|aire /myskylɛr/ *a.* muscular. ~**ature** *n.f.* muscles.

museau (*pl.* ~**x**) /myzo/ *n.m.* muzzle; (*de porc*) snout.

musée /myze/ *n.m.* museum; (*de peinture*) art gallery.

museler /myzle/ *v.t.* muzzle.

muselière /myzəljɛr/ *n.f.* muzzle.

musette /myzɛt/ *n.f.* haversack.

muséum /myzeɔm/ *n.m.* (natural history) museum.

music|al (*m. pl.* ~**aux**) /myzikal, -o/ *a.* musical.

music-hall /myzikɔl/ *n.m.* variety theatre.

musicien, ~ne /myzisjɛ̃, -jɛn/ *a.* musical. ● *n.m., f.* musician.

musique /myzik/ *n.f.* music; (*orchestre*) band.

musulman, ~e /myzylmɑ̃, -an/ *a.* & *n.m., f.* Muslim.

mutation /mytɑsjɔ̃/ *n.f.* change; (*biologique*) mutation.

muter /myte/ *v.t.* transfer.

mutil|er /mytile/ *v.t.* mutilate. ~**ation** *n.f.* mutilation. ~**é, ée** *a.* & *n.m., f.* disabled (person).

mutin, ~e /mytɛ̃, -in/ *a.* saucy. ● *n.m., f.* rebel.

mutin|er (se) /(sə)mytine/ *v. pr.* mutiny. ~**é** *a.* mutinous. ~**erie** *n.f.* mutiny.

mutisme /mytism/ *n.m.* silence.

mutuel, ~le /mytɥɛl/ *a.* mutual. ● *n.f.* Friendly Society; (*Amer.*) benefit society. ~**lement** *adv.* mutually; (*l'un l'autre*) each other.

myope /mjɔp/ *a.* short-sighted. ~**ie** *n.f.* short-sightedness.

myosotis /mjozɔtis/ *n.m.* forget-me-not.

myriade /mirjad/ *n.f.* myriad.

myrtille /mirtij/ *n.f.* bilberry; (*Amer.*) blueberry.

mystère /mistɛr/ *n.m.* mystery.

mystérieu|x, ~se /misterjø, -z/ *a.* mysterious.

mystif|ier /mistifje/ *v.t.* deceive, hoax. ~**ication** *n.f.* hoax.

mysti|que /mistik/ *a.* mystic(al). ● *n.m./f.* mystic. ● *n.f.* (*puissance*) mystique. ~**cisme** *n.m.* mysticism.

myth|e /mit/ *n.m.* myth. ~**ique** *a.* mythical.

mytholog|ie /mitɔlɔʒi/ *n.f.* mythology. ~**ique** *a.* mythological.

mythomane /mitɔman/ *n.m./f.* compulsive liar (and fantasizer).

N

n' /n/ *voir* ne.

nacr|e /nakr/ *n.f.* mother-of-pearl. ~**é** *a.* pearly.

nage /naʒ/ *n.f.* swimming; (*manière*) (swimming) stroke. **à la ~**, by swimming. **traverser à la ~,** swim across. **en ~,** sweating.

nageoire /naʒwar/ *n.f.* fin.

nag|er /naʒe/ *v.t./i.* swim. **~eur, ~euse** *n.m., f.* swimmer.

naguère /nagɛr/ *adv.* some time ago.

naï|f, ~ve /naif, -v/ *a.* naïve.

nain, ~e /nɛ̃, nɛn/ *n.m., f. & a.* dwarf.

naissance /nɛsɑ̃s/ *n.f.* birth. **donner ~ à,** give birth to, (*fig.*) give rise to.

naître† /nɛtr/ *v.i.* be born; (*résulter*) arise (**de,** from). **faire ~,** (*susciter*) give rise to.

naïveté /naivte/ *n.f.* naïvety.

nana /nana/ *n.f.* (*fam.*) girl.

nanti /nɑ̃ti/ *n.m.* **les ~s,** the affluent.

nantir /nɑ̃tir/ *v.t.* **~ de,** provide with.

naphtaline /naftalin/ *n.f.* mothballs.

nappe /nap/ *n.f.* table-cloth; (*de pétrole, gaz*) layer. **~ phréatique,** ground water.

napperon /naprɔ̃/ *n.m.* (cloth) table-mat.

narcotique /narkɔtik/ *a. & n.m.* narcotic.

narguer /narge/ *v.t.* mock.

narine /narin/ *n.f.* nostril.

narquois, ~e /narkwa, -z/ *a.* derisive.

narr|er /nare/ *v.t.* narrate. **~ateur, ~atrice** *n.m., f.* narrator. **~ation** *n.f.* narrative; (*action*) narration; (*scol.*) composition.

nas|al (*m. pl.* **~aux**) /nazal, -o/ *a.* nasal.

naseau (*pl.* **~x**) /nazo/ *n.m.* nostril.

nasiller /nazije/ *v.i.* have a nasal twang.

nat|al (*m. pl.* **~als**) /natal/ *a.* native.

natalité /natalite/ *n.f.* birth rate.

natation /natasjɔ̃/ *n.f.* swimming.

nati|f, ~ve /natif, -v/ *a.* native.

nation /nasjɔ̃/ *n.f.* nation.

nation|al, ~ale (*m. pl.* **~aux**) /nasjɔnal, -o/ *a.* national. ● *n.f.* A road; (*Amer.*) highway. **~aliser** *v.t.* nationalize. **~alisme** *n.m.* nationalism.

nationalité /nasjɔnalite/ *n.f.* nationality.

Nativité /nativite/ *n.f.* **la ~,** the Nativity.

natte /nat/ *n.f.* (*de cheveux*) plait; (*tapis de paille*) mat.

naturaliser /natyralize/ *v.t.* naturalize.

nature /natyr/ *n.f.* nature. ● *a. invar.* (*eau, omelette, etc.*) plain. **de ~**

à, likely to. **payer en ~,** pay in kind. **~ morte,** still life.

naturel, ~le /natyrɛl/ *a.* natural. ● *n.m.* nature; (*simplicité*) naturalness. **~lement** *adv.* naturally.

naufrag|e /nofraʒ/ *n.m.* (ship-)wreck. **faire ~e,** be shipwrecked; (*bateau*) be wrecked. **~é, ~ée** *a. & n.m., f.* shipwrecked (person).

nauséabond, ~e /nozeabɔ̃, -d/ *a.* nauseating.

nausée /noze/ *n.f.* nausea.

nautique /notik/ *a.* nautical; (*sports*) aquatic.

naval (*m. pl.* **~s**) /naval/ *a.* naval.

navet /navɛ/ *n.m.* turnip; (*film, tableau*) dud.

navette /navɛt/ *n.f.* shuttle (service). **faire la ~,** shuttle back and forth.

navigable /navigabl/ *a.* navigable.

navig|uer /navige/ *v.i.* sail; (*piloter*) navigate. **~ateur** *n.m.* seafarer; (*d'avion*) navigator. **~ation** *n.f.* navigation; (*trafic*) shipping.

navire /navir/ *n.m.* ship.

navré /navre/ *a.* sorry (**de,** to).

navrer /navre/ *v.t.* upset.

ne, n' * /nə, n/ *adv.* **ne pas,** not. **ne jamais,** never. **ne plus,** (*temps*) no longer, not any more. **ne que,** only. **je crains qu'il ne parte,** (*sans valeur négative*) I am afraid he will leave.

né, née /ne/ *voir* naître. ● *a. & n.m., f.* born. **il est né,** he was born. **premier-/dernier-né,** first-/last-born. **née Martin,** née Martin.

néanmoins /neɑ̃mwɛ̃/ *adv.* nevertheless.

néant /neɑ̃/ *n.m.* nothingness; (*aucun*) none.

nébuleu|x, ~se /nebylø, -z/ *a.* nebulous.

nécessaire /nesesɛr/ *a.* necessary. ● *n.m.* (*sac*) bag; (*trousse*) kit. **le ~,** (*l'indispensable*) the necessities. **faire le ~,** do what is necessary. **~ment** *adv.* necessarily.

nécessité /nesesite/ *n.f.* necessity.

nécessiter /nesesite/ *v.t.* necessitate.

nécrologie /nekrɔlɔʒi/ *n.f.* obituary.

néerlandais, ~e /neɛrlɑ̃dɛ, -z/ *a.* Dutch. ● *n.m., f.* Dutchman, Dutchwoman. ● *n.m.* (*lang.*) Dutch.

nef /nɛf/ *n.f.* nave.

néfaste /nefast/ *a.* harmful (**à,** to); (*funeste*) ill-fated.

négati|f, **~ve** /negatif, -v/ a. & n.m., f. negative.

négation /negasjɔ̃/ n.f. negation.

négligé /negliʒe/ a. (tenue, travail) slovenly. ● n.m. (tenue) négligé.

négligeable /negliʒablə/ a. negligible, insignificant.

négligen|t, **~te** /negliʒã, -t/ a. careless, negligent. **~ce** n.f. carelessness, negligence; (erreur) omission.

négliger /negliʒe/ v.t. neglect; (ne pas tenir compte de) disregard. **se ~** v. pr. neglect o.s.

négoc|e /negɔs/ n.m. business. **~iant**, **~iante** n.m., f. merchant.

négoc|ier /negɔsje/ v.t./i. negotiate. **~iable** a. negotiable. **~iateur**, **~iatrice** n.m., f. negotiator. **~iation** n.f. negotiation.

nègre[1] /nɛgr/ a. (musique etc.) Negro.

nègre[2] /nɛgr/ n.m. (écrivain) ghost writer.

neig|e /nɛʒ/ n.f. snow. **~eux**, **~euse** a. snowy.

neiger /neʒe/ v.i. snow.

nénuphar /nenyfar/ n.m. waterlily.

néologisme /neɔlɔʒism/ n.m. neologism.

néon /neɔ̃/ n.m. neon.

néo-zélandais, **~e** /neɔzelɑ̃dɛ, -z/ a. New Zealand. ● n.m., f. New Zealander.

nerf /nɛr/ n.m. nerve; (vigueur: fam.) stamina.

nerv|eux, **~euse** /nɛrvø, -z/ a. nervous; (irritable) nervy; (centre, cellule) nerve-; (voiture) responsive. **~eusement** adv. nervously. **~osité** n.f. nervousness; (irritabilité) touchiness.

nervure /nɛrvyr/ n.f. (bot.) vein.

net, **~te** /nɛt/ a. (clair, distinct) clear; (propre) clean; (soigné) neat; (prix, poids) net. ● adv. (s'arrêter) dead; (refuser) flatly; (parler) plainly; (se casser) clean. **~tement** adv. clearly; (certainement) definitely.

netteté /nɛtte/ n.f. clearness.

nettoy|er /nɛtwaje/ v.t. clean. **~age** n.m. cleaning. **~age à sec**, dry-cleaning.

neuf[1] /nœf/ (/nœv/ before heures, ans) a. & n.m. nine.

neu|f[2], **~ve** /nœf, -v/ a. & n.m. new. **remettre à ~f**, brighten up. **du ~f**, (fait nouveau) some new development.

neutr|e /nøtr/ a. neutral; (gram.) neuter. ● n.m. (gram.) neuter. **~alité** n.f. neutrality.

neutron /nøtrɔ̃/ n.m. neutron.

neuve /nœv/ voir neuf[2].

neuvième /nœvjɛm/ a. & n.m./f. ninth.

neveu (pl. **~x**) /nəvø/ n.m. nephew.

névros|e /nevroz/ n.f. neurosis. **~é**, **~ée** a. & n.m., f. neurotic.

nez /ne/ n.m. nose. **~ à nez**, face to face. **~ épaté**, flat nose. **~ retroussé**, turned-up nose. **avoir du ~**, have flair.

ni /ni/ conj. neither, nor. **ni grand ni petit**, neither big nor small. **ni l'un ni l'autre ne fument**, neither (one nor the other) smokes.

niais, **~e** /njɛ, -z/ a. silly. ● n.m., f. simpleton. **~erie** /-zri/ n.f. silliness.

niche /niʃ/ n.f. (de chien) kennel; (cavité) niche; (farce) trick.

nichée /niʃe/ n.f. brood.

nicher /niʃe/ v.i. nest. **se ~** v. pr. nest; (se cacher) hide.

nickel /nikɛl/ n.m. nickel. **c'est ~!**, (fam.) it's spotless.

nicotine /nikɔtin/ n.f. nicotine.

nid /ni/ n.m. nest. **~ de poule**, pot-hole.

nièce /njɛs/ n.f. niece.

nier /nje/ v.t. deny.

nigaud, **~e** /nigo, -d/ a. silly. ● n.m., f. silly idiot.

nippon, **~e** /nipɔ̃, -ɔn/ a. & n.m., f. Japanese.

niveau (pl. **~x**) /nivo/ n.m. level; (compétence) standard. **au ~**, up to standard. **~ à bulle**, spirit-level. **~ de vie**, standard of living.

nivel|er /nivle/ v.t. level. **~lement** /-ɛlmã/ n.m. levelling.

noble /nɔbl/ a. noble. ● n.m./f. nobleman, noblewoman.

noblesse /nɔblɛs/ n.f. nobility.

noce /nɔs/ n.f. wedding; (personnes) wedding guests. **~s**, wedding. **faire la ~**, (fam.) make merry.

noci|f, **~ve** /nɔsif, -v/ a. harmful.

noctambule /nɔktɑ̃byl/ n.m./f. night-owl, late-night reveller.

nocturne /nɔktyrn/ a. nocturnal.

Noël /nɔɛl/ n.m. Christmas.

nœud[1] /nø/ n.m. knot; (ornemental) bow. **~s**, (fig.) ties. **~ coulant**, noose. **~ papillon**, bow-tie.

nœud[2] /nø/ n.m. (naut.) knot.

noir, **~e** /nwar/ a. black; (obscur, sombre) dark; (triste) gloomy.

● *n.m.* black; (*obscurité*) dark. **travail au ~,** moonlighting. ● *n.m., f.* (*personne*) Black. ● *n.f.* (*mus.*) crotchet. **~ceur** *n.f.* blackness; (*indignité*) vileness.

noircir /nwarsir/ *v.t./i.,* **se ~** *v. pr.* blacken.

nois|ette /nwazɛt/ *n.f.* hazel-nut; (*de beurre*) knob. **~etier** *n.m.* hazel tree.

noix /nwa/ *n.f.* nut; (*du noyer*) walnut; (*de beurre*) knob. **~ de cajou,** cashew nut. **~ de coco,** coconut. **à la ~,** (*fam.*) useless.

nom /nɔ̃/ *n.m.* name; (*gram.*) noun. **au ~ de,** on behalf of. **~ de famille,** surname. **~ de jeune fille,** maiden name. **~ propre,** proper noun.

nomade /nɔmad/ *a.* nomadic. ● *n.m./f.* nomad.

no man's land /nomanslɑ̃d/ *n.m. invar.* no man's land.

nombre /nɔ̃br/ *n.m.* number. **au ~ de,** (*parmi*) among; (*l'un de*) one of. **en (grand) ~,** in large numbers.

nombreu|x, ~se /nɔ̃brø, -z/ *a.* numerous; (*important*) large.

nombril /nɔ̃bri/ *n.m.* navel.

nomin|al (*m. pl.* **~aux**) /nɔminal, -o/ *a.* nominal.

nomination /nɔminasjɔ̃/ *n.f.* appointment.

nommément /nɔmemɑ̃/ *adv.* by name.

nommer /nɔme/ *v.t.* name; (*élire*) appoint. **se ~** *v. pr.* (*s'appeler*) be called.

non /nɔ̃/ *adv.* no; (*pas*) not. ● *n.m. invar.* no. **~ (pas) que,** not that. **il vient, ~?,** he is coming, isn't he? **moi ~ plus,** neither am, do, can, *etc.* I.

non- /nɔ̃/ *préf.* non-. **~-fumeur,** non-smoker.

nonante /nɔnɑ̃t/ *a. & n.m.* ninety.

nonchalance /nɔ̃ʃalɑ̃s/ *n.f.* nonchalance.

non-sens /nɔ̃sɑ̃s/ *n.m.* absurdity.

non-stop /nɔnstɔp/ *a. invar.* non-stop.

nord /nɔr/ *n.m.* north. ● *a. invar.* north; (*partie*) northern; (*direction*) northerly. **au ~ de,** to the north of. **~-africain, ~-africaine** *a. & n.m., f.* North African. **~-est** *n.m.* north-east. **~-ouest** *n.m.* north-west.

nordique /nɔrdik/ *a. & n.m./f.* Scandinavian.

norm|al, ~ale (*m. pl.* **~aux**) /nɔrmal, -o/ *a.* normal. ● *n.f.* normality; (*norme*) norm; (*moyenne*) average. **~alement** *adv.* normally.

normand, ~e /nɔrmɑ̃, -d/ *a. & n.m., f.* Norman.

Normandie /nɔrmɑ̃di/ *n.f.* Normandy.

norme /nɔrm/ *n.f.* norm; (*de production*) standard.

Norvège /nɔrvɛʒ/ *n.f.* Norway.

norvégien, ~ne /nɔrveʒjɛ̃, -jɛn/ *a. & n.m., f.* Norwegian.

nos /no/ *voir* notre.

nostalg|ie /nɔstalʒi/ *n.f.* nostalgia. **~ique** *a.* nostalgic.

notable /nɔtabl/ *a. & n.m.* notable.

notaire /nɔtɛr/ *n.m.* notary.

notamment /nɔtamɑ̃/ *adv.* notably.

notation /nɔtasjɔ̃/ *n.f.* notation; (*remarque*) remark.

note /nɔt/ *n.f.* note; (*chiffrée*)·mark; (*facture*) bill; (*mus.*) note. **~ (de service),** memorandum. **prendre ~ de,** take note of.

not|er /nɔte/ *v.t.* note, notice; (*écrire*) note (down); (*devoir*) mark. **bien/mal ~é,** (*employé etc.*) highly/poorly rated.

notice /nɔtis/ *n.f.* note; (*mode d'emploi*) directions.

notif|ier /nɔtifje/ *v.t.* notify (à, to). **~ication** *n.f.* notification.

notion /nɔsjɔ̃/ *n.f.* notion.

notoire /nɔtwar/ *a.* well-known; (*criminel*) notorious.

notre (*pl.* **nos**) /nɔtr, no/ *a.* our.

nôtre /nɔtr/ *pron.* **le** *ou* **la ~, les ~s,** ours.

nouer /nwe/ *v.t.* tie, knot; (*relations*) strike up.

noueu|x, ~se /nwø, -z/ *a.* gnarled.

nougat /nuga/ *n.m.* nougat.

nouille /nuj/ *n.f.* (*idiot. fam.*) idiot.

nouilles /nuj/ *n.f. pl.* noodles.

nounours /nunurs/ *n.m.* teddy bear.

nourri /nuri/ *a.* (*fig.*) intense. **logé ~,** bed and board. **~ au sein,** breastfed.

nourrice /nuris/ *n.f.* child-minder; (*qui allaite*) wet-nurse.

nourr|ir /nurir/ *v.t.* feed; (*faire vivre*) feed, provide for; (*sentiment: fig.*) nourish. ● *v.i.* be nourishing. **se ~ir** *v. pr.* eat. **se ~ir de,** feed on. **~issant, ~issante** *a.* nourishing.

nourrisson /nurisɔ̃/ *n.m.* infant.

nourriture /nurityr/ *n.f.* food.

nous /nu/ *pron.* we; (*complément*) us; (*indirect*) (to) us; (*réfléchi*) ourselves; (*l'un l'autre*) each other. **~-mêmes** *pron.* ourselves.

nouveau *ou* **nouvel***, **nouvelle**¹ (*m. pl.* **~x**) /nuvo, nuvɛl/ *a. & n.m.* new. ● *n.m., f.* (*élève*) new girl. **de ~**, **à ~**, again. **du ~**, (*fait nouveau*) some new development. **nouvel an**, new year. **~x mariés**, newly-weds. **~-né**, **~-née** *a.* newborn; *n.m., f.* newborn baby. **~venu, nouvelle venue**, newcomer. **Nouvelle Zélande**, New Zealand.

nouveauté /nuvote/ *n.f.* novelty; (*chose*) new thing.

nouvelle² /nuvɛl/ *n.f.* (piece of) news; (*récit*) short story. **~s**, news.

nouvellement /nuvɛlmɑ̃/ *adv.* newly, recently.

novembre /novɑ̃br/ *n.m.* November.

novice /novis/ *a.* inexperienced. ● *n.m./f.* novice.

noyade /nwajad/ *n.f.* drowning.

noyau (*pl.* **~x**) /nwajo/ *n.m.* (*de fruit*) stone; (*de cellule*) nucleus; (*groupe*) group; (*centre: fig.*) core.

noyauter /nwajote/ *v.t.* (*organisation*) infiltrate.

noyer¹ /nwaje/ *v.t.* drown; (*inonder*) flood. **se ~er** *v. pr.* drown; (*volontairement*) drown o.s. **se ~er dans un verre d'eau**, make a mountain out of a molehill. **~é, ~ée** *n.m., f.* drowning person; (*mort*) drowned person.

noyer² /nwaje/ *n.m.* (*arbre*) walnut-tree.

nu /ny/ *a.* naked; (*mains, mur, fil*) bare. ● *n.m.* nude. **se mettre à nu**, (*fig.*) bare one's heart. **mettre à nu**, lay bare. **nu-pieds** *adv.* barefoot; *n.m. pl.* beach shoes. **nu-tête** *adv.* bareheaded. **à l'œil nu**, to the naked eye.

nuage /nyaʒ/ *n.m.* cloud. **~eux, ~euse** *a.* cloudy.

nuance /nyɑ̃s/ *n.f.* shade; (*de sens*) nuance; (*différence*) difference.

nuancer /nyɑ̃se/ *v.t.* (*opinion*) qualify.

nucléaire /nykleɛr/ *a.* nuclear.

nudis|te /nydist/ *n.m./f.* nudist. **~me** *n.m.* nudism.

nudité /nydite/ *n.f.* (*de personne*) nudity; (*de chambre etc.*) bareness.

nuée /nye/ *n.f.* (*foule*) host.

nues /ny/ *n.f. pl.* **tomber des ~**, be amazed. **porter aux ~**, extol.

nuire† /nɥir/ *v.i.* **~ à**, harm.

nuisible /nɥizibl/ *a.* harmful.

nuit /nɥi/ *n.f.* night. **cette ~**, tonight; (*hier*) last night. **il fait ~**, it is dark. **~ blanche**, sleepless night. **la ~, de ~**, at night. **~ de noces**, wedding night.

nul, **~le** /nyl/ *a.* (*aucun*) no; (*zéro*) nil; (*qui ne vaut rien*) useless; (*non valable*) null. **match ~**, draw. **~ en**, no good at. ● *pron.* no one. **~ autre**, no one else. **~le part**, nowhere. **~lement** *adv.* not at all. **~lité** *n.f.* uselessness; (*personne*) useless person.

numéraire /nymerɛr/ *n.m.* cash.

numér|al (*pl.* **~aux**) /nymeral, -o/ *n.m.* numeral.

numérique /nymerik/ *a.* numerical; (*montre, horloge*) digital.

numéro /nymero/ *n.m.* number; (*de journal*) issue; (*spectacle*) act. **~ter** /-ɔte/ *v.t.* number.

nuque /nyk/ *n.f.* nape (of the neck).

nurse /nœrs/ *n.f.* (children's) nurse.

nutriti|f, **~ve** /nytritif, -v/ *a.* nutritious; (*valeur*) nutritional.

nutrition /nytrisjɔ̃/ *n.f.* nutrition.

nylon /nilɔ̃/ *n.m.* nylon.

nymphe /nɛ̃f/ *n.f.* nymph.

O

oasis /ɔazis/ *n.f.* oasis.

obéir /ɔbeir/ *v.i.* obey. **~ à**, obey. **être obéi**, be obeyed.

obéissan|t, **~te** /ɔbeisɑ̃, -t/ *a.* obedient. **~ce** *n.f.* obedience.

obèse /ɔbɛz/ *a.* obese.

obésité /ɔbezite/ *n.f.* obesity.

object|er /ɔbʒɛkte/ *v.t.* put forward (as an excuse). **~er que**, object that. **~ion** /-ksjɔ̃/ *n.f.* objection.

objecteur /ɔbʒɛktœr/ *n.m.* **~ de conscience**, conscientious objector.

objecti|f, **~ve** /ɔbʒɛktif, -v/ *a.* objective. ● *n.m.* objective; (*photo.*) lens. **~vement** *adv.* objectively. **~vité** *n.f.* objectivity.

objet /ɔbʒɛ/ *n.m.* object; (*sujet*) subject. **être** *ou* **faire l'~ de**, be the subject of; (*recevoir*) receive. **~ d'art**, objet d'art. **~s de toilette**, toilet requisites. **~s trouvés**, lost property; (*Amer.*) lost and found.

obligation /ɔbligasjɔ̃/ *n.f.* obligation; (*comm.*) bond. **être dans l'~ de**, be under obligation to.

obligatoire /ɔbligatwar/ *a.* compulsory. **~ment** *adv.* of necessity; (*fam.*) inevitably.

obligean|t, ~te /ɔbliʒɑ̃, -t/ *a.* obliging, kind. **~ce** *n.f.* kindness.

oblig|er /ɔbliʒe/ *v.t.* compel, oblige (**à faire**, to do); (*aider*) oblige. **être ~é de**, have to. **~é à qn.**, obliged to s.o. (**de**, for).

oblique /ɔblik/ *a.* oblique. **regard ~**, sidelong glance. **en ~**, at an angle.

obliquer /ɔblike/ *v.i.* turn off (**vers**, towards).

oblitérer /ɔblitere/ *v.t.* (*timbre*) cancel.

oblong, ~ue /ɔblɔ̃, -g/ *a.* oblong.

obnubilé, ~e /ɔbnybile/ *a.* obsessed.

obsc|ène /ɔpsɛn/ *a.* obscene. **~énité** *n.f.* obscenity.

obscur /ɔpskyr/ *a.* dark; (*confus*, *humble*) obscure.

obscurantisme /ɔpskyrɑ̃tism/ *n.m.* obscurantism.

obscurcir /ɔpskyrsir/ *v.t.* darken; (*fig.*) obscure. **s'~** *v. pr.* (*ciel etc.*) darken.

obscurité /ɔpskyrite/ *n.f.* dark(-ness); (*passage*, *situation*) obscurity.

obséd|er /ɔpsede/ *v.t.* obsess. **~ant, ~ante** *a.* obsessive. **~é, ~ée** *n.m.*, *f.* maniac.

obsèques /ɔpsɛk/ *n.f. pl.* funeral.

observation /ɔpsɛrvasjɔ̃/ *n.f.* observation; (*reproche*) criticism; (*obéissance*) observance. **en ~**, under observation.

observatoire /ɔpsɛrvatwar/ *n.m.* observatory; (*mil.*) observation post.

observ|er /ɔpsɛrve/ *v.t.* observe; (*surveiller*) watch, observe. **faire ~ qch.**, point sth. out (**à**, to). **~ateur, ~atrice** *a.* observant; *n.m.*, *f.* observer.

obsession /ɔpsesjɔ̃/ *n.f.* obsession.

obstacle /ɔpstakl/ *n.m.* obstacle; (*cheval*) jump; (*athlète*) hurdle. **faire ~ à**, stand in the way of.

obstétrique /ɔpstetrik/ *n.f.* obstetrics.

obstin|é /ɔpstine/ *a.* obstinate. **~ation** *n.f.* obstinacy.

obstiner (s') /(s)ɔpstine/ *v. pr.* persist (**à**, in).

obstruction /ɔpstryksjɔ̃/ *n.f.* obstruction. **faire de l'~**, obstruct.

obstruer /ɔpstrye/ *v.t.* obstruct.

obten|ir† /ɔptənir/ *v.t.* get, obtain. **~tion** /-ɑ̃sjɔ̃/ *n.f.* obtaining.

obturateur /ɔptyratœr/ *n.m.* (*photo.*) shutter.

obtus, ~e /ɔpty, -z/ *a.* obtuse.

obus /ɔby/ *n.m.* shell.

occasion /ɔkazjɔ̃/ *n.f.* opportunity (**de faire**, of doing); (*circonstance*) occasion; (*achat*) bargain; (*article non neuf*) second-hand buy. **à l'~**, sometimes. **d'~**, second-hand. **~nel, ~nelle** /-jɔnɛl/ *a.* occasional.

occasionner /ɔkazjɔne/ *v.t.* cause.

occident /ɔksidɑ̃/ *n.m.* west. **~al, ~ale** (*m. pl.* **~aux**) /-tal, -to/ *a.* western. ● *n.m.*, *f.* westerner.

occulte /ɔkylt/ *a.* occult.

occupant, ~e /ɔkypɑ̃, -t/ *n.m.*, *f.* occupant. ● *n.m.* (*mil.*) forces of occupation.

occupation /ɔkypasjɔ̃/ *n.f.* occupation.

occupé /ɔkype/ *a.* busy; (*place*, *pays*) occupied; (*téléphone*) engaged; (*Amer.*) busy.

occuper /ɔkype/ *v.t.* occupy; (*poste*) hold. **s'~** *v. pr.* (*s'affairer*) keep busy (**à faire**, doing). **s'~ de**, (*personne*, *problème*) take care of; (*bureau*, *firme*) be in charge of.

occurrence (en l') /(ɑ̃l)ɔkyrɑ̃s/ *adv.* in this case.

océan /ɔseɑ̃/ *n.m.* ocean.

ocre /ɔkr/ *a. invar.* ochre.

octane /ɔktan/ *n.m.* octane.

octante /ɔktɑ̃t/ *a.* (*régional*) eighty.

octave /ɔktav/ *n.f.* (*mus.*) octave.

octet /ɔktɛ/ *n.m.* byte.

octobre /ɔktɔbr/ *n.m.* October.

octogone /ɔktɔgɔn/ *n.m.* octagon.

octroyer /ɔktrwaje/ *v.t.* grant.

oculaire /ɔkylɛr/ *a.* ocular.

oculiste /ɔkylist/ *n.m./f.* eye-specialist.

ode /ɔd/ *n.f.* ode.

odeur /ɔdœr/ *n.f.* smell.

odieu|x, ~se /ɔdjø, -z/ *a.* odious.

odorant, ~e /ɔdɔrɑ̃, -t/ *a.* sweet-smelling.

odorat /ɔdɔra/ *n.m.* (sense of) smell.

œcuménique /ekymenik/ *a.* ecumenical.

œil (*pl.* **yeux**) /œj, jø/ *n.m.* eye. **à l'~**, (*fam.*) free. **à mes yeux**, in my view. **faire de l'~ à**, make eyes at. **faire les gros yeux à**, scowl at. **ouvrir l'~**, keep one's eye open. **fermer l'~**, shut one's eyes. **~ poché**, black eye. **yeux bridés**, slit eyes.

œillade /œjad/ n.f. wink.

œillères /œjɛr/ n.f. pl. blinkers.

œillet /œjɛ/ n.m. (*plante*) carnation; (*trou*) eyelet.

œuf (*pl.* ~s) /œf, ø/ n.m. egg. ~ à la coque/dur/sur le plat, boiled/hard-boiled/fried egg.

œuvre /œvr/ n.f. (*ouvrage, travail*) work. ~ d'art, work of art. ~ (de bienfaisance), charity. être à l'~, be at work. mettre en ~, (*moyens*) implement.

œuvrer /œvre/ v.i. work.

off /ɔf/ a. invar. voix ~, voice off.

offense /ɔfɑ̃s/ n.f. insult; (*péché*) offence.

offens|er /ɔfɑ̃se/ v.t. offend. s'~er de, take offence at. ~ant, ~ante a. offensive.

offensi|f, ~ve /ɔfɑ̃sif, -v/ a. & n.f. offensive.

offert, ~e /ɔfɛr, -t/ *voir* offrir.

office /ɔfis/ n.m. office; (*relig.*) service; (*de cuisine*) pantry. d'~, automatically.

officiel, ~le /ɔfisjɛl/ a. & n.m., f. official. ~lement adv. officially.

officier¹ /ɔfisje/ n.m. officer.

officier² /ɔfisje/ v.i. (*relig.*) officiate.

officieu|x, ~se /ɔfisjø, -z/ a. unofficial. ~sement adv. unofficially.

offrande /ɔfrɑ̃d/ n.f. offering.

offrant /ɔfrɑ̃/ n.m. au plus ~, to the highest bidder.

offre /ɔfr/ n.f. offer; (*aux enchères*) bid. l'~ et la demande, supply and demand. ~s d'emploi, jobs advertised, (*rubrique*) situations vacant.

offrir† /ɔfrir/ v.t. offer (de faire, to do); (*cadeau*) give; (*acheter*) buy. s'~ v. pr. offer o.s. (comme, as); (*spectacle*) present itself; (*s'acheter*) treat o.s. to. ~ à boire à, (*chez soi*) give a drink to; (*au café*) buy a drink for.

offusquer /ɔfyske/ v.t. offend.

ogive /ɔʒiv/ n.f. (*atomique etc.*) warhead.

ogre /ɔgr/ n.m. ogre.

oh /o/ int. oh.

oie /wa/ n.f. goose.

oignon /ɔɲɔ̃/ n.m. (*légume*) onion; (*de tulipe etc.*) bulb.

oiseau (*pl.* ~x) /wazo/ n.m. bird.

oisi|f, ~ve /wazif, -v/ a. idle. ~veté n.f. idleness.

O.K. /ɔke/ int. O.K.

oléoduc /ɔleɔdyk/ n.m. oil pipeline.

olive /ɔliv/ n.f. & a. invar. olive. ~ier n.m. olive-tree.

olympique /ɔlɛ̃pik/ a. Olympic.

ombrag|e /ɔ̃braʒ/ n.m. shade. prendre ~e de, take offence at. ~é a. shady. ~eux, ~euse a. easily offended.

ombre /ɔ̃br/ n.f. (*pénombre*) shade; (*contour*) shadow; (*soupçon: fig.*) hint, shadow. dans l'~, (*secret*) in the dark. faire de l'~ à qn., be in s.o.'s light.

ombrelle /ɔ̃brɛl/ n.f. parasol.

omelette /ɔmlɛt/ n.f. omelette.

omettre† /ɔmɛtr/ v.t. omit.

omission /ɔmisjɔ̃/ n.f. omission.

omnibus /ɔmnibys/ n.m. stopping train.

omoplate /ɔmɔplat/ n.f. shoulder-blade.

on /ɔ̃/ pron. we, you, one; (*les gens*) people, they; (*quelqu'un*) someone. on dit, people say, they say, it is said (que, that).

once /ɔ̃s/ n.f. ounce.

oncle /ɔ̃kl/ n.m. uncle.

onctueu|x, ~se /ɔktɥø, -z/ a. smooth.

onde /ɔ̃d/ n.f. wave. ~s courtes/longues, short/long wave. sur les ~s, on the radio.

ondée /ɔ̃de/ n.f. shower.

on-dit /ɔ̃di/ n.m. invar. les ~, rumour.

ondul|er /ɔ̃dyle/ v.i. undulate; (*cheveux*) be wavy. ~ation n.f. wave, undulation. ~é a. (*chevelure*) wavy.

onéreu|x, ~se /ɔnerø, -z/ a. costly.

ongle /ɔ̃gl/ n.m. (finger-)nail. se faire les ~s, do one's nails.

ont /ɔ̃/ *voir* avoir.

ONU /ɔny/ abrév. (*Organisation des nations unies*) UN.

onyx /ɔniks/ n.m. onyx.

onz|e /ɔ̃z/ a. & n.m. eleven. ~ième a. & n.m./f. eleventh.

opale /ɔpal/ n.f. opal.

opa|que /ɔpak/ a. opaque. ~cité n.f. opaqueness.

open /ɔpɛn/ n.m. open (championship).

opéra /ɔpera/ n.m. opera; (*édifice*) opera-house. ~-comique (*pl.* ~s-comiques) n.m. light opera.

opérateur /ɔperatœr/ n.m. (*caméraman*) cameraman.

opération /ɔperasjɔ̃/ n.f. operation; (*comm.*) deal.

opérationnel, **~le** /operasjɔnɛl/ a. operational.

opératoire /operatwar/ a. (méd.) surgical. **bloc ~**, operating suite.

opérer /opere/ v.t. (personne) operate on; (kyste etc.) remove; (exécuter) carry out, make. **se faire ~**, have an operation. ● v.i. (méd.) operate; (faire effet) work. **s'~** v. pr. (se produire) occur.

opérette /operɛt/ n.f. operetta.

opiner /opine/ v.i. nod.

opiniâtre /opinjɑtr/ a. obstinate.

opinion /opinjɔ̃/ n.f. opinion.

opium /opjɔm/ n.m. opium.

opportun, **~e** /opɔrtœ̃, -yn/ a. opportune. **~ité** /-ynite/ n.f. opportuneness.

opposant, **~e** /opozɑ̃, -t/ n.m., f. opponent.

opposé /opoze/ a. (sens, angle, etc.) opposite; (factions) opposing; (intérêts) conflicting. ● n.m. opposite. **à l'~**, (opinion etc.) contrary (**de**, to). **être ~ à**, be opposed to.

opposer /opoze/ v.t. (objets) place opposite each other; (personnes) oppose; (contraster) contrast; (résistance, argument) put up. **s'~** v. pr. (personnes) confront each other; (styles) contrast. **s'~ à**, oppose.

opposition /opozisjɔ̃/ n.f. opposition. **par ~ à**, in contrast with. **entrer en ~ avec**, come into conflict with. **faire ~ à un chèque**, stop a cheque.

oppress|**er** /oprese/ v.t. oppress. **~ant**, **~ante** a. oppressive. **~eur** n.m. oppressor. **~ion** n.f. oppression.

opprimer /oprime/ v.t. oppress.

opter /opte/ v.i. **~ pour**, opt for.

opticien, **~ne** /optisjɛ̃, -jɛn/ n.m., f. optician.

optimis|**te** /optimist/ n.m./f. optimist. ● a. optimistic. **~me** n.m. optimism.

optimum /optimom/ a. & n.m. optimum.

option /opsjɔ̃/ n.f. option.

optique /optik/ a. (verre) optical. ● n.f. (perspective) perspective.

opulen|**t**, **~te** /opylɑ̃, -t/ a. opulent. **~ce** n.f. opulence.

or [1] /ɔr/ n.m. gold. **d'~**, gold. **en ~**, gold; (occasion) golden.

or [2] /ɔr/ conj. now, well.

oracle /orɑkl/ n.m. oracle.

orag|**e** /oraʒ/ n.m. (thunder)storm. **~eux**, **~euse** a. stormy.

oraison /orɛzɔ̃/ n.f. prayer.

or|**al** (m. pl. **~aux**) /oral, -o/ a. oral. ● n.m. (pl. **~aux**) oral.

orang|**e** /orɑ̃ʒ/ n.f. & a. invar. orange. **~é** a. orange-coloured. **~er** n.m. orange-tree.

orangeade /orɑ̃ʒad/ n.f. orangeade.

orateur /oratœr/ n.m. speaker.

oratorio /oratorjo/ n.m. oratorio.

orbite /orbit/ n.f. orbit; (d'œil) socket.

orchestr|**e** /orkɛstr/ n.m. orchestra; (de jazz) band; (parterre) stalls. **~er** v.t. orchestrate.

orchidée /orkide/ n.f. orchid.

ordinaire /ordinɛr/ a. ordinary; (habituel) usual; (qualité) standard. ● n.m. l'**~**, the ordinary; (nourriture) the standard fare. **d'~**, **à l'~**, usually. **~ment** adv. usually.

ordinateur /ordinatœr/ n.m. computer.

ordination /ordinasjɔ̃/ n.f. (relig.) ordination.

ordonnance /ordonɑ̃s/ n.f. (ordre, décret) order; (de médecin) prescription; (soldat) orderly.

ordonné /ordone/ a. tidy.

ordonner /ordone/ v.t. order (**à qn. de**, s.o. to); (agencer) arrange; (méd.) prescribe; (prêtre) ordain.

ordre /ordr/ n.m. order; (propreté) tidiness. **aux ~s de qn.**, at s.o.'s disposal. **avoir de l'~**, be tidy. **de premier ~**, first-rate. **l'~ du jour**, (programme) agenda. **mettre en ~**, tidy (up). **de premier ~**, first rate. **jusqu'à nouvel ~**, until further notice. **un ~ de grandeur**, an approximate idea.

ordure /ordyr/ n.f. filth. **~s**, (détritus) rubbish; (Amer.) garbage. **~s ménagères**, household refuse.

oreille /orɛj/ n.f. ear.

oreiller /oreje/ n.m. pillow.

oreillons /orejɔ̃/ n.m. pl. mumps.

orfèvr|**e** /orfɛvr/ n.m. goldsmith, silversmith. **~erie** n.f. goldsmith's ou silversmith's trade.

organe /organ/ n.m. organ; (porteparole) mouthpiece.

organigramme /organigram/ n.m. flow chart.

organique /organik/ a. organic.

organisation /organizasjɔ̃/ n.f. organization.

organis|er /ɔrganize/ v.t. organize. **s'~er** v. pr. organize o.s. **~ateur, ~atrice** n.m., f. organizer.
organisme /ɔrganism/ n.m. body, organism.
organiste /ɔrganist/ n.m./f. organist.
orgasme /ɔrgasm/ n.m. orgasm.
orge /ɔrʒ/ n.f. barley.
orgelet /ɔrʒəlɛ/ n.m. (furoncle) sty.
orgie /ɔrʒi/ n.f. orgy.
orgue /ɔrg/ n.m. organ. **~s** n.f. pl. organ. **~ de Barbarie,** barrel-organ.
orgueil /ɔrgœj/ n.m. pride.
orgueilleu|x, ~se /ɔrgœjø, -z/ a. proud.
Orient /ɔrjɑ̃/ n.m. l'**~,** the Orient.
orientable /ɔrjɑ̃tabl/ a. adjustable.
orient|al, ~ale (m. pl. **~aux**) /ɔrjɑ̃tal, -o/ a. eastern; (de l'Orient) oriental. ● n.m., f. Oriental.
orientation /ɔrjɑ̃tasjɔ̃/ n.f. direction; (d'une politique) course; (de maison) aspect. **~ professionnelle,** careers advisory service.
orienté /ɔrjɑ̃te/ a. (partial) slanted, tendentious.
orienter /ɔrjɑ̃te/ v.t. position; (personne) direct. **s'~** v. pr. (se repérer) find one's bearings. **s'~ vers,** turn towards.
orifice /ɔrifis/ n.m. orifice.
origan /ɔrigɑ̃/ n.m. oregano.
originaire /ɔriʒinɛr/ a. être **~ de,** be a native of.
origin|al, ~ale (m. pl. **~aux**) /ɔriʒinal, -o/ a. original; (curieux) eccentric. ● n.m. original. ● n.m., f. eccentric. **~alité** n.f. originality; eccentricity.
origine /ɔriʒin/ n.f. origin. à l'**~,** originally. **d'~,** (pièce, pneu) original.
originel, ~le /ɔriʒinɛl/ a. original.
orme /ɔrm/ n.m. elm.
ornement /ɔrnəmɑ̃/ n.m. ornament. **~al** (m. pl. **~aux**) /-tal, -to/ a. ornamental.
orner /ɔrne/ v.t. decorate.
ornière /ɔrnjɛr/ n.f. rut.
ornithologie /ɔrnitɔlɔʒi/ n.f. ornithology.
orphelin, ~e /ɔrfəlɛ̃, -in/ n.m., f. orphan. ● a. orphaned. **~at** /-ina/ n.m. orphanage.
orteil /ɔrtɛj/ n.m. toe.
orthodox|e /ɔrtɔdɔks/ a. orthodox. **~ie** n.f. orthodoxy.
orthographe /ɔrtɔgraf/ n.f. spelling. **~ier** v.t. spell.

orthopédique /ɔrtɔpedik/ a. orthopaedic.
ortie /ɔrti/ n.f. nettle.
os (pl. **os**) /ɔs, o/ n.m. bone.
OS abrév. voir ouvrier spécialisé.
oscar /ɔskar/ n.m. award; (au cinéma) oscar.
oscill|er /ɔsile/ v.i. sway; (techn.) oscillate; (hésiter) waver, fluctuate. **~ation** n.f. (techn.) oscillation; (variation) fluctuation.
oseille /ozɛj/ n.f. (plante) sorrel.
os|er /oze/ v.t./i. dare. **~é** a. daring.
osier /ozje/ n.m. wicker.
ossature /ɔsatyr/ n.f. frame.
ossements /ɔsmɑ̃/ n.m. pl. bones.
osseu|x, ~se /ɔsø, -z/ a. bony; (tissu) bone.
ostensible /ɔstɑ̃sibl/ a. conspicuous, obvious.
ostentation /ɔstɑ̃tasjɔ̃/ n.f. ostentation.
ostéopathe /ɔsteɔpat/ n.m./f. osteopath.
otage /ɔtaʒ/ n.m. hostage.
otarie /ɔtari/ n.f. sea-lion.
ôter /ote/ v.t. remove (à qn., from s.o.); (déduire) take away.
otite /ɔtit/ n.f. ear infection.
ou /u/ conj. or. **ou bien,** or else. **vous ou moi,** either you or me.
où /u/ adv. & pron. where; (dans lequel) in which; (sur lequel) on which; (auquel) at which. **d'où,** from which; (pour cette raison) hence. **d'où?,** from where? **par où,** through which. **par où?,** which way? **où qu'il soit,** wherever he may be. **au prix où c'est,** at those prices. **le jour où,** the day when.
ouate /wat/ n.f. cotton wool; (Amer.) absorbent cotton.
oubli /ubli/ n.m. forgetfulness; (trou de mémoire) lapse of memory; (négligence) oversight. l'**~,** (tomber dans, sauver de) oblivion.
oublier /ublije/ v.t. forget. **s'~** v. pr. forget o.s.; (chose) be forgotten.
oublieu|x, ~se /ublijø, -z/ a. forgetful (de, of).
ouest /wɛst/ n.m. west. ● a. invar. west; (partie) western; (direction) westerly.
ouf /uf/ int. phew.
oui /wi/ adv. yes.
ouï-dire (par) /(par)widir/ adv. by hearsay.
ouïe /wi/ n.f. hearing.
ouïes /wi/ n.f. pl. gills.

ouille /uj/ *int.* ouch.

ouïr /wir/ *v.t.* hear.

ouragan /uragɑ̃/ *n.m.* hurricane.

ourler /urle/ *v.t.* hem.

ourlet /urlɛ/ *n.m.* hem.

ours /urs/ *n.m.* bear. **~ blanc,** polar bear. **~ en peluche,** teddy bear. **~ mal léché,** boor.

ouste /ust/ *int.* (*fam.*) scram.

outil /uti/ *n.m.* tool.

outillage /utijaʒ/ *n.m.* tools; (*d'une usine*) equipment.

outiller /utije/ *v.t.* equip.

outrage /utraʒ/ *n.m.* (grave) insult.

outrag|er /utraʒe/ *v.t.* offend. **~eant, ~eante** *a.* offensive.

outranc|e /utrɑ̃s/ *n.f.* excess. **à ~e,** to excess; (*guerre*) all-out. **~ier, ~ière** *a.* excessive.

outre /utr/ *prép.* besides. **en ~,** besides. **~-mer** *adv.* overseas. **~ mesure,** excessively.

outrepasser /utrəpase/ *v.t.* exceed.

outrer /utre/ *v.t.* exaggerate; (*indigner*) incense.

outsider /utsajdœr/ *n.m.* outsider.

ouvert, ~e /uver, -t/ *voir* ouvrir.
  ● *a.* open; (*gaz, radio, etc.*) on. **~ement** /-təmɑ̃/ *adv.* openly.

ouverture /uvertyr/ *n.f.* opening; (*mus.*) overture; (*photo.*) aperture. **~s,** (*offres*) overtures. **~ d'esprit,** open-mindedness.

ouvrable /uvrabl/ *a.* working. **jour ~,** working day.

ouvrag|e /uvraʒ/ *n.m.* (*travail, livre*) work; (*couture*) needlework. **~é** *a.* finely worked.

ouvreuse /uvrøz/ *n.f.* usherette.

ouvr|ier, ~ière /uvrije, -jer/ *n.m., f.* worker. ● *a.* working-class; (*conflit*) industrial; (*syndicat*) workers'. **~ier qualifié/spécialisé,** skilled/unskilled worker.

**ouvr|ir† /uvrir/ *v.t.* open (up); (*gaz, robinet, etc.*) turn *ou* switch on.
  ● *v.i.* open (up). **s'~ir** *v. pr.* open (up). **s'~ir à qn.,** open one's heart to s.o. **~e-boîte(s)** *n.m.* tin-opener. **~e-bouteille(s)** *n.m.* bottle-opener.

ovaire /over/ *n.m.* ovary.

ovale /ɔval/ *a. & n.m.* oval.

ovation /ɔvasjɔ̃/ *n.f.* ovation.

overdose /ɔverdoz/ *n.f.* overdose.

ovni /ɔvni/ *n.m.* (*abrév.*) UFO.

ovule /ɔvyl/ *n.m.* (*à féconder*) egg; (*gynécologique*) pessary.

oxyder (s') /(s)ɔkside/ *v. pr.* become oxidized.

oxygène /ɔksiʒen/ *n.m.* oxygen.

oxygéner (s') /(s)ɔksiʒene/ *v. pr.* (*fam.*) get some fresh air.

ozone /ozon/ *n.f.* ozone. **la couche d'~,** the ozone layer.

P

pacemaker /pesmekœr/ *n.m.* pacemaker.

pachyderme /paʃiderm/ *n.m.* elephant.

pacifier /pasifje/ *v.t.* pacify.

pacifique /pasifik/ *a.* peaceful; (*personne*) peaceable; (*géog.*) Pacific. ● *n.m.* **P~,** Pacific (Ocean).

pacifiste /pasifist/ *n.m./f.* pacifist.

pacotille /pakɔtij/ *n.f.* trash.

pacte /pakt/ *n.m.* pact.

pactiser /paktize/ *v.i.* **~ avec,** be in league *ou* agreement with.

paddock /padɔk/ *n.m.* paddock.

pag|aie /page/ *n.f.* paddle. **~ayer** *v.i.* paddle.

pagaille /pagaj/ *n.f.* mess, shambles.

page /paʒ/ *n.f.* page. **être à la ~,** be up to date.

pagode /pagɔd/ *n.f.* pagoda.

paie /pe/ *n.f.* pay.

paiement /pɛmɑ̃/ *n.m.* payment.

païen, ~ne /pajɛ̃, -jɛn/ *a. & n.m., f.* pagan.

paillasse /pajas/ *n.f.* straw mattress; (*dans un laboratoire*) draining-board.

paillasson /pajasɔ̃/ *n.m.* doormat.

paille /paj/ *n.f.* straw; (*défaut*) flaw.

paillette /pajet/ *n.f.* (*sur robe*) sequin; (*de savon*) flake. **~s d'or,** gold-dust.

pain /pɛ̃/ *n.m.* bread: (*unité*) loaf (of bread); (*de savon etc.*) bar. **~ d'épice,** gingerbread. **~ grillé,** toast.

pair ¹ /per/ *a.* (*nombre*) even.

pair ² /per/ *n.m.* (*personne*) peer. **au ~,** (*jeune fille etc.*) au pair. **aller de ~,** go together (**avec,** with).

paire /per/ *n.f.* pair.

paisible /pezibl/ *a.* peaceful.

paître /pɛtr/ *v.i.* (*brouter*) graze.

paix /pe/ *n.f.* peace; (*traité*) peace treaty.

Pakistan /pakistɑ̃/ *n.m.* Pakistan.

pakistanais, ~e /pakistane, -z/ *a. & n.m., f.* Pakistani.

palace /palas/ *n.m.* luxury hotel.

palais[1] /palɛ/ *n.m.* palace. **P~ de Justice,** Law Courts. **~ des sports,** sports stadium.

palais[2] /palɛ/ *n.m.* (*anat.*) palate.

palan /palɑ̃/ *n.m.* hoist.

pâle /pɑl/ *a.* pale.

Palestine /palɛstin/ *n.f.* Palestine.

palestinien, ~ne /palɛstinjɛ̃, -jɛn/ *a. & n.m., f.* Palestinian.

palet /palɛ/ *n.m.* (*hockey*) puck.

paletot /palto/ *n.m.* thick jacket.

palette /palɛt/ *n.f.* palette.

pâleur /pɑlœr/ *n.f.* paleness.

palier /palje/ *n.m.* (*d'escalier*) landing; (*étape*) stage; (*de route*) level stretch.

pâlir /pɑlir/ *v.t./i.* (turn) pale.

palissade /palisad/ *n.f.* fence.

pallier /palje/ *v.t.* alleviate.

palmarès /palmarɛs/ *n.m.* list of prize-winners.

palm|e /palm/ *n.f.* palm leaf; (*symbole*) palm; (*de nageur*) flipper. **~ier** *n.m.* palm(-tree).

palmé /palme/ *a.* (*patte*) webbed.

pâlot, ~te /palo, -ɔt/ *a.* pale.

palourde /palurd/ *n.f.* clam.

palper /palpe/ *v.t.* feel.

palpit|er /palpite/ *v.i.* (*battre*) pound, palpitate; (*frémir*) quiver. **~ations** *n.f. pl.* palpitations. **~ant, ~ante** *a.* thrilling.

paludisme /palydism/ *n.m.* malaria.

pâmer (se) /(sə)pame/ *v. pr.* swoon.

pamphlet /pɑ̃flɛ/ *n.m.* satirical pamphlet.

pamplemousse /pɑ̃pləmus/ *n.m.* grapefruit.

pan[1] /pɑ̃/ *n.m.* piece; (*de chemise*) tail.

pan[2] /pɑ̃/ *int.* bang.

panacée /panase/ *n.f.* panacea.

panache /panaʃ/ *n.m.* plume; (*bravoure*) gallantry; (*allure*) panache.

panaché /panaʃe/ *a.* (*bariolé, mélangé*) motley. **glace ~e,** mixed-flavour ice cream. ● *n.m.* shandy. **bière ~e, demi ~,** shandy.

pancarte /pɑ̃kart/ *n.f.* sign; (*de manifestant*) placard.

pancréas /pɑ̃kreas/ *n.m.* pancreas.

pané /pane/ *a.* breaded.

panier /panje/ *n.m.* basket. **~ à provisions,** shopping basket. **~ à salade,** (*fam.*) police van.

paniqu|e /panik/ *n.f.* panic. (*fam.*) **~er** *v.i.* panic.

panne /pan/ *n.f.* breakdown. **être en ~,** have broken down. **être en ~ sèche,** have run out of petrol *ou* gas (*Amer.*). **~ d'électricité** *ou* **de courant,** power failure.

panneau (*pl.* **~x**) /pano/ *n.m.* sign; (*publicitaire*) hoarding; (*de porte etc.*) panel. **~ (d'affichage),** notice-board. **~ (de signalisation),** road sign.

panoplie /panɔpli/ *n.f.* (*jouet*) outfit; (*gamme*) range.

panoram|a /panɔrama/ *n.m.* panorama. **~ique** *a.* panoramic.

panse /pɑ̃s/ *n.f.* paunch.

pans|er /pɑ̃se/ *v.t.* (*plaie*) dress; (*personne*) dress the wound(s) of; (*cheval*) groom. **~ement** *n.m.* dressing. **~ement adhésif,** sticking-plaster.

pantalon /pɑ̃talɔ̃/ *n.m.* (pair of) trousers. **~s,** trousers.

panthère /pɑ̃tɛr/ *n.f.* panther.

pantin /pɑ̃tɛ̃/ *n.m.* puppet.

pantomime /pɑ̃tomim/ *n.f.* mime; (*spectacle*) mime show.

pantoufle /pɑ̃tufl/ *n.f.* slipper.

paon /pɑ̃/ *n.m.* peacock.

papa /papa/ *n.m.* dad(dy). **de ~,** (*fam.*) old-time.

papauté /papote/ *n.f.* papacy.

pape /pap/ *n.m.* pope.

paperass|e /papras/ *n.f.* **~e(s),** (*péj.*) papers. **~erie** *n.f.* (*péj.*) papers; (*tracasserie*) red tape.

papet|ier, ~ière /paptje, -jɛr/ *n.m., f.* stationer. **~erie** /papetri/ *n.f.* (*magasin*) stationer's shop.

papier /papje/ *n.m.* paper; (*formulaire*) form. **~s (d'identité),** (identity) papers. **~ à lettres,** writing-paper. **~ aluminium,** tin foil. **~ buvard,** blotting-paper. **~ calque,** tracing-paper. **~ carbone,** carbon paper. **~ collant,** sticky paper. **~ de verre,** sandpaper. **~ hygiénique,** toilet-paper. **~ journal,** newspaper. **~ mâché,** papier mâché. **~ peint,** wallpaper.

papillon /papijɔ̃/ *n.m.* butterfly; (*contravention*) parking-ticket. **~ (de nuit),** moth.

papot|er /papote/ *v.i.* prattle. **~age** *n.m.* prattle.

paprika /paprika/ *n.m.* paprika.

Pâque /pɑk/ *n.f.* Passover.

paquebot /pakbo/ *n.m.* liner.

pâquerette /pakrɛt/ *n.f.* daisy.

Pâques /pɑk/ *n.f. pl. & n.m.* Easter.

paquet /pakɛ/ *n.m.* packet; (*de cartes*) pack; (*colis*) parcel. **un ~ de,** (*tas*) a mass of.

par /par/ *prép.* by; (*à travers*) through; (*motif*) out of, from; (*provenance*) from. **commencer/finir ~ qch.,** begin/end with sth. **commencer/finir ~ faire,** begin by/end up (by) doing. **~ an/mois/etc.,** a *ou* per year/month/etc. **~ avion,** (*lettre*) (by) airmail. **~-ci, par-là,** here and there. **~ contre,** on the other hand. **~ hasard,** by chance. **~ ici/là,** this/that way. **~ inadvertance,** inadvertently. **~ intermittence,** intermittently. **~ l'intermédiaire de,** through. **~ jour,** a day. **~ malheur** *ou* **malchance,** unfortunately. **~ miracle,** miraculously. **~ moments,** at times. **~ opposition à,** as opposed to. **~ personne,** each, per person.

parabole /parabɔl/ *n.f.* (*relig.*) parable; (*maths*) parabola.

paracétamol /parasetamɔl/ *n.m.* paracetamol.

parachever /paraʃve/ *v.t.* perfect.

parachut|e /paraʃyt/ *n.m.* parachute. **~er** *v.t.* parachute. **~iste** *n.m./f.* parachutist; (*mil.*) paratrooper.

parad|e /parad/ *n.f.* parade; (*sport*) parry; (*réplique*) reply. **~er** *v.i.* show off.

paradis /paradi/ *n.m.* paradise. **~ fiscal,** tax haven.

paradox|e /paradɔks/ *n.m.* paradox. **~al** (*m. pl.* **~aux**) *a.* paradoxical.

paraffine /parafin/ *n.f.* paraffin wax.

parages /paraʒ/ *n.m. pl.* area, vicinity.

paragraphe /paragraf/ *n.m.* paragraph.

paraître† /parɛtr/ *v.i.* appear; (*sembler*) seem, appear; (*ouvrage*) be published, come out. **faire ~,** (*ouvrage*) bring out.

parallèle /paralɛl/ *a.* parallel; (*illégal*) unofficial. ● *n.m.* parallel. **faire un ~ entre,** draw a parallel between. **faire le ~,** make a connection. ● *n.f.* parallel (line). **~ment** *adv.* parallel (à, to).

paraly|ser /paralize/ *v.t.* paralyse. **~sie** *n.f.* paralysis. **~tique** *a.* & *n.m./f.* paralytic.

paramètre /paramɛtr/ *n.m.* parameter.

paranoïa /paranɔja/ *n.f.* paranoia.

parapet /parapɛ/ *n.m.* parapet.

paraphe /paraf/ *n.m.* signature.

paraphrase /parafraz/ *n.f.* paraphrase.

parapluie /paraplɥi/ *n.m.* umbrella.

parasite /parazit/ *n.m.* parasite. **~s,** (*radio*) interference.

parasol /parasɔl/ *n.m.* sunshade.

paratonnerre /paratɔnɛr/ *n.m.* lightning-conductor *ou* -rod.

paravent /paravã/ *n.m.* screen.

parc /park/ *n.m.* park; (*de bétail*) pen; (*de bébé*) play-pen; (*entrepôt*) depot. **~ de stationnement,** car- park.

parcelle /parsɛl/ *n.f.* fragment; (*de terre*) plot.

parce que /parsk(ə)/ *conj.* because.

parchemin /parʃəmɛ̃/ *n.m.* parchment.

parcimon|ie /parsimɔni/ *n.f.* **avec ~ie,** parsimoniously. **~ieux, ~ieuse** *a.* parsimonious.

parcmètre /parkmɛtr/ *n.m.* parking-meter.

parcourir† /parkurir/ *v.t.* travel *ou* go through; (*distance*) travel; (*des yeux*) glance at *ou* over.

parcours /parkur/ *n.m.* route; (*voyage*) journey.

par-delà /pardəla/ *prép. & adv.* beyond.

par-derrière /pardɛrjɛr/ *prép. & adv.* behind, at the back *ou* rear (of).

par-dessous /pardsu/ *prép. & adv.* under(neath).

pardessus /pardəsy/ *n.m.* overcoat.

par-dessus /pardsy/ *prép. & adv.* over. **~ bord,** overboard. **~ le marché,** into the bargain. **~ tout,** above all.

par-devant /pardəvã/ *adv.* at *ou* from the front, in front.

pardon /pardɔ̃/ *n.m.* forgiveness. **(je vous demande) ~!,** (I am) sorry!; (*pour demander qch.*) excuse me!

pardonn|er /pardɔne/ *v.t.* forgive. **~er qch. à qn.,** forgive s.o. for sth. **~able** *a.* forgivable.

paré /pare/ *a.* ready.

pare-balles /parbal/ *a. invar.* bullet-proof.

pare-brise /parbriz/ *n.m. invar.* windscreen; (*Amer.*) windshield.

pare-chocs /parʃɔk/ *n.m. invar.* bumper.

pareil, ~le /parɛj/ *a.* similar (à to); (*tel*) such a. **~ a,** like, equal. ● *adv.* (*fam.*) the same. **c'est ~,** it is the same. **vos ~s,** (*péj.*) those of

your type, those like you. **~lement**
adv. the same.

parement /parmɑ̃/ n.m. facing.

parent, ~e /parɑ̃, -t/ a. related (**de,**
to). ● n.m., f. relative, relation. **~s**
(*père et mère*) n.m. pl. parents. **~**
seul, single parent.

parenté /parɑ̃te/ n.f. relationship.

parenthèse /parɑ̃tɛz/ n.f. bracket,
parenthesis; (*fig.*) digression.

parer[1] /pare/ v.t. (*coup*) parry. ● v.i.
~ à, deal with. **~ au plus pressé,**
tackle the most urgent things first.

parer[2] /pare/ v.t. (*orner*) adorn.

paresse /parɛs/ n.f. laziness. **~er**
/-ese/ v.i. laze (about). **~eux, ~euse**
a. lazy; n.m., f. lazybones.

parfaire /parfɛr/ v.t. perfect.

parfait, ~e /parfɛ, -t/ a. perfect.
~ement /-tmɑ̃/ adv. perfectly; (*bien*
sûr) certainly.

parfois /parfwa/ adv. sometimes.

parfum /parfœ̃/ n.m. scent; (*substance*) perfume, scent; (*goût*) flavour.

parfum|er /parfyme/ v.t. perfume;
(*gâteau*) flavour. **se ~er** v. pr. put
on one's perfume. **~é** a. fragrant;
(*savon*) scented. **~erie** n.f. (*produits*) perfumes; (*boutique*) perfume
shop.

pari /pari/ n.m. bet.

par|ier /parje/ v.t. bet. **~ieur, ~ieuse**
n.m., f. punter, better.

Paris /pari/ n.m./f. Paris.

parisien, ~ne /parizjɛ̃, -jɛn/ a. Paris,
Parisian. ● n.m., f. Parisian.

parit|é /parite/ n.f. parity. **~aire** a.
(*commission*) joint.

parjur|e /parʒyr/ n.m. perjury.
● n.m./f. perjurer. **se ~er** v. pr.
perjure o.s.

parking /parkiŋ/ n.m. car-park;
(*Amer.*) parking-lot; (*stationnement*)
parking.

parlement /parləmɑ̃/ n.m. parliament. **~aire** /-tɛr/ a. parliamen-
tary; n.m./f. Member of Parliament;
(*fig.*) negotiator. **~er** /-te/ v.i. ne-
gotiate.

parl|er /parle/ v.i. talk, speak (**à,** to).
● v.t. (*langue*) speak; (*politique,*
affaires, etc.) talk. **se ~er** v. pr.
(*langue*) be spoken. ● n.m. speech;
(*dialecte*) dialect. **~ant, ~ante** a.
(*film*) talking; (*fig.*) eloquent. **~eur,
~euse** n.m., f. talker.

parloir /parlwar/ n.m. visiting room.

parmi /parmi/ prép. among(st).

parod|ie /parɔdi/ n.f. parody. **~ier**
v.t. parody.

paroi /parwa/ n.f. wall; (*cloison*)
partition (wall). **~ rocheuse,** rock
face.

paroiss|e /parwas/ n.f. parish. **~ial**
(m. pl. **~iaux**) a. parish. **~ien,
~ienne** n.m., f. parishioner.

parole /parɔl/ n.f. (*mot, promesse*)
word; (*langage*) speech. **demander
la ~,** ask to speak. **prendre la ~,**
(begin to) speak. **tenir ~,** keep one's
word. **croire qn. sur ~,** take s.o.'s
word for it.

paroxysme /parɔksism/ n.m. height,
highest point.

parquer /parke/ v.t., **se ~** v. pr.
(*auto.*) park. **~ des réfugiés,** pen
up refugees.

parquet /parke/ n.m. floor; (*jurid.*)
public prosecutor's department.

parrain /parɛ̃/ n.m. godfather; (*fig.*)
sponsor. **~er** /-ene/ v.t. sponsor.

pars, part[1] /par/ voir **partir.**

parsemer /parsəme/ v.t. strew (**de,**
with).

part[2] /par/ n.f. share, part. **à ~,** (*de
côté*) aside; (*séparément*) apart; (*excepté*) apart from. **d'autre ~,** on the
other hand; (*de plus*) moreover. **de
la ~ de,** from. **de toutes ~s,** from
all sides. **de ~ et d'autre,** on both
sides. **d'une ~,** on the one hand.
faire ~ à qn., inform s.o. (**de,** of).
faire la ~ des choses, make
allowances. **prendre ~ à,** take part
in; (*joie, douleur*) share. **pour ma ~,**
as for me.

partag|e /partaʒ/ n.m. dividing; shar-
ing out; (*part*) share. **~er** v.t. divide;
(*distribuer*) share out; (*avoir en
commun*) share. **se ~er qch.,** share
sth.

partance (en) /(ɑ̃)partɑ̃s/ adv. about
to depart.

partant /partɑ̃/ n.m. (*sport*) starter.

partenaire /partənɛr/ n.m./f. partner.

parterre /partɛr/ n.m. flower-bed;
(*théâtre*) stalls.

parti /parti/ n.m. (*pol.*) party; (*en
mariage*) match; (*décision*) decision.
~ pris, prejudice. **prendre ~ pour,**
side with. **j'en prends mon ~,** I've
come to terms with that.

part|ial (m. pl. **~iaux**) /parsjal, -jo/ a.
biased. **~ialité** n.f. bias.

participe /partisip/ n.m. (*gram.*)
participle.

particip|er /partisipe/ v.i. ~**er à**, take part in, participate in; (profits, frais) share; (spectacle) appear in. ~**ant**, ~**ante** n.m., f. participant (à, in); (à un concours) entrant. ~**ation** n.f. participation; sharing; (comm.) interest. (d'un artiste) appearance.

particularité /partikylarite/ n.f. particularity.

particule /partikyl/ n.f. particle.

particul|ier, ~**ière** /partikylje, -jɛr/ a. (spécifique) particular; (bizarre) peculiar; (privé) private. ● n.m. private individual. **en** ~**ier**, in particular; (en privé) in private. ~**ier à**, peculiar to. ~**ièrement** adv. particularly.

partie /parti/ n.f. part; (cartes, sport) game; (jurid.) party; (sortie) outing, party. **une** ~ **de pêche**, a fishing trip. **en** ~, partly. **faire** ~ **de**, be part of; (adhérer à) belong to. **en grande** ~, largely. ~ **intégrante**, integral part.

partiel, ~**le** /parsjɛl/ a. partial. ● n.m. (univ.) class examination. ~**lement** adv. partially, partly.

partir† /partir/ v.i. (aux. être) go; (quitter un lieu) leave, go; (tache) come out; (bouton) come off; (coup de feu) go off; (commencer) start. **à** ~ **de**, from.

partisan, ~**e** /partizã, -an/ n.m., f. supporter. ● n.m. (mil.) partisan. **être** ~ **de**, be in favour of.

partition /partisjɔ̃/ n.f. (mus.) score.

partout /partu/ adv. everywhere. ~ **où**, wherever.

paru /pary/ voir **paraître**.

parure /paryr/ n.f. adornment; (bijoux) jewellery; (de draps) set.

parution /parysjɔ̃/ n.f. publication.

parvenir† /parvənir/ v.i. (aux. être) ~ **à**, reach; (résultat) achieve. ~ **à faire**, manage to do. **faire** ~, send.

parvenu, ~**e** /parvəny/ n.m., f. upstart.

parvis /parvi/ n.m. (place) square.

pas¹ /pɑ/ adv. not. **(ne)** ~, not. **je ne sais** ~, I do not know. ~ **de sucre/livres/etc.**, no sugar/books/etc. **du tout**, not at all. ~ **encore**, not yet. ~ **mal**, not bad; (beaucoup) quite a lot (**de**, of). ~ **vrai?**, (fam.) isn't that so?

pas² /pɑ/ n.m. step; (bruit) footstep; (trace) footprint; (vitesse) pace; (de vis) thread. **à deux** ~ **(de)**, close by.

au ~, at a walking pace; (véhicule) very slowly. **au** ~ **(cadencé)**, in step. **à** ~ **de loup**, stealthily. **faire les cent** ~, walk up and down. **faire les premiers** ~, take the first steps. **sur le** ~ **de la porte**, on the doorstep.

passable /pɑsabl/ a. tolerable. **mention** ~, pass mark.

passage /pɑsaʒ/ n.m. passing, passage; (traversée) crossing; (visite) visit; (chemin) way, passage; (d'une œuvre) passage. **de** ~, (voyageur) visiting; (amant) casual. ~ **à niveau**, level crossing. ~ **clouté**, pedestrian crossing. ~ **interdit**, (panneau) no thoroughfare. ~ **souterrain**, subway; (Amer.) underpass.

passag|er, ~**ère** /pɑsaʒe, -ɛr/ a. temporary. ● n.m., f. passenger. ~**er clandestin**, stowaway.

passant, ~**e** /pɑsɑ̃, -t/ a. (rue) busy. ● n.m., f. passer-by. ● n.m. (anneau) loop.

passe /pɑs/ n.f. pass. **bonne/mauvaise** ~, good/bad patch. **en** ~ **de**, on the road to. ~**-droit**, n.m. special privilege. ~**-montagne** n.m. Balaclava. ~**-partout** n.m. invar. master-key; a. invar. for all occasions. ~**-temps** n.m. invar. pastime.

passé /pɑse/ a. (révolu) past; (dernier) last; (fini) over; (fané) faded. ● prép. after. ● n.m. past. ~ **de mode**, out of fashion.

passeport /pɑspɔr/ n.m. passport.

passer /pɑse/ v.i. (aux. être ou avoir) pass; (aller) go; (venir) come; (temps) pass (by), go by; (film) be shown; (couleur) fade. ● v.t. (aux. avoir) pass, cross; (donner) pass, hand; (mettre) put; (oublier) overlook; (enfiler) slip on; (dépasser) go beyond; (temps) spend, pass; (film) show; (examen) take; (commande) place; (soupe) strain. **se** ~ v. pr. happen, take place. **laisser** ~, let through; (occasion) miss. ~ **à tabac**, (fam.) beat up. ~ **devant**, (édifice) go past. ~ **en fraude**, smuggle. ~ **outre**, take no notice (**à**, of). ~ **par**, go through to be. ~ **pour**, (riche etc.) be taken to be. ~ **sur**, (détail) pass over. ~ **l'aspirateur**, hoover, vacuum. ~ **un coup de fil à qn.**, give s.o. a ring. **je vous passe Mme X**, (par le standard) I'm putting you through to Mrs X; (en donnant *l'appareil*) I'll hand you over to Mrs X. **se ~ de**, go *ou* do without.

passerelle /pɑsʀɛl/ *n.f.* footbridge; (*pour accéder à un avion, à un navire*) gangway.

pass|eur, **~euse** /pɑsœr, øz/ *n.m.*, *f.* smuggler.

passible /pasibl/ *a.* **~ de**, liable to.

passi|f, **~ve** /pasif, -v/ *a.* passive. ● *n.m.* (*comm.*) liabilities. **~vité** *n.f.* passiveness.

passion /pɑsjɔ̃/ *n.f.* passion.

passionn|er /pɑsjɔne/ *v.t.* fascinate. **se ~er pour**, have a passion for. **~é** *a.* passionate. **être ~é de**, have a passion for. **~ément** *adv.* passionately.

passoire /pɑswar/ *n.f.* (*à thé*) strainer; (*à légumes*) colander.

pastel /pastɛl/ *n.m. & a. invar.* pastel.

pastèque /pastɛk/ *n.f.* watermelon.

pasteur /pastœr/ *n.m.* (*relig.*) minister.

pasteurisé /pastœrize/ *a.* pasteurized.

pastiche /pastiʃ/ *n.m.* pastiche.

pastille /pastij/ *n.f.* (*bonbon*) pastille, lozenge.

pastis /pastis/ *n.m.* aniseed liqueur.

patate /patat/ *n.f.* (*fam.*) potato. **~ (douce)**, sweet potato.

patauger /patoʒe/ *v.i.* splash about.

pâte /pɑt/ *n.f.* paste; (*farine*) dough; (*à tarte*) pastry; (*à frire*) batter. **~s (alimentaires)**, pasta. **~ à modeler**, Plasticine (P.). **~ dentifrice**, toothpaste.

pâté /pɑte/ *n.m.* (*culin.*) pâté; (*d'encre*) ink-blot. **~ de maisons**, block of houses; (*de sable*) sand-pie. **~ en croûte**, meat pie.

pâtée /pɑte/ *n.f.* feed, mash.

patelin /patlɛ̃/ *n.m.* (*fam.*) village.

patent, **~e** /patɑ̃, -t/ *a.* patent.

patent|e /patɑ̃t/ *n.f.* trade licence. **~é** *a.* licensed.

patère /patɛr/ *n.f.* (coat) peg.

patern|el, **~elle** /patɛrnɛl/ *a.* paternal. **~ité** *n.f.* paternity.

pâteu|x, **~se** /pɑtø, -z/ *a.* pasty; (*langue*) coated.

pathétique /patetik/ *a.* moving. ● *n.m.* pathos.

patholog|ie /patɔlɔʒi/ *n.f.* pathology. **~ique** *a.* pathological.

pat|ient, **~iente** /pasjɑ̃, -t/ *a. & n.m.*, *f.* patient. **~iemment** /-jamɑ̃/ *adv.* patiently. **~ience** *n.f.* patience.

patienter /pasjɑ̃te/ *v.i.* wait.

patin /patɛ̃/ *n.m.* skate. **~ à roulettes**, roller-skate.

patin|er /patine/ *v.i.* skate; (*voiture*) spin. **~age** *n.m.* skating. **~eur**, **~euse** *n.m.*, *f.* skater.

patinoire /patinwar/ *n.f.* skating-rink.

pâtir /pɑtir/ *v.i.* suffer (**de**, from).

pâtiss|ier, **~ière** /pɑtisje, -jɛr/ *n.m.*, *f.* pastry-cook, cake shop owner. **~erie** *n.f.* cake shop; (*gâteau*) pastry; (*art*) cake making.

patois /patwa/ *n.m.* patois.

patraque /patrak/ *a.* (*fam.*) peaky, out of sorts.

patrie /patri/ *n.f.* homeland.

patrimoine /patrimwan/ *n.m.* heritage.

patriot|e /patrijɔt/ *a.* patriotic. ● *n.m./f.* patriot. **~ique** *a.* patriotic. **~isme** *n.m.* patriotism.

patron[1], **~ne** /patrɔ̃, -ɔn/ *n.m.*, *f.* employer, boss; (*propriétaire*) owner, boss; (*saint*) patron saint. **~al** (*m. pl.* **~aux**) /-ɔnal, -o/ *a.* employers'. **~at** /-ɔna/ *n.m.* employers.

patron[2] /patrɔ̃/ *n.m.* (*couture*) pattern.

patronage /patrɔnaʒ/ *n.m.* patronage; (*foyer*) youth club.

patronner /patrɔne/ *v.t.* support.

patrouill|e /patruj/ *n.f.* patrol. **~er** *v.i.* patrol.

patte /pat/ *n.f.* leg; (*pied*) foot; (*de chat*) paw. **~s**, (*favoris*) sideburns.

pâturage /pɑtyraʒ/ *n.m.* pasture.

pâture /pɑtyr/ *n.f.* food.

paume /pom/ *n.f.* (*de main*) palm.

paumé, **~e** /pome/ *n.m.*, *f.* (*fam.*) wretch, loser.

paumer /pome/ *v.t.* (*fam.*) lose.

paupière /popjɛr/ *n.f.* eyelid.

pause /poz/ *n.f.* pause; (*halte*) break.

pauvre /povr/ *a.* poor. ● *n.m./f.* poor man, poor woman. **~ment** /-əmɑ̃/ *adv.* poorly. **~té** /-əte/ *n.f.* poverty.

pavaner (se) /(sə)pavane/ *v. pr.* strut.

pav|er /pave/ *v.t.* pave; (*chaussée*) cobble. **~é** *n.m.* paving-stone; cobble(-stone).

pavillon[1] /pavijɔ̃/ *n.m.* house; (*de gardien*) lodge.

pavillon[2] /pavijɔ̃/ *n.m.* (*drapeau*) flag.

pavoiser /pavwaze/ *v.t.* deck with flags. ● *v.i.* put out the flags.

pavot /pavo/ *n.m.* poppy.

payant, ~e /pɛjɑ̃, -t/ a. (billet) for which a charge is made; (spectateur) (fee-)paying; (rentable) profitable.

payer /peje/ v.t./i. pay; (service, travail, etc.) pay for; (acheter) buy (à, for). **se ~** v. pr. (s'acheter) buy o.s. **~ à qn.** (cent francs etc.) charge s.o. (pour, for). **se ~ la tête de,** make fun of. **il me le paiera!,** he'll pay for this.

pays /pei/ n.m. country; (région) region; (village) village. **du ~,** local. **les P~-Bas,** the Netherlands. **le ~ de Galles,** Wales.

paysage /peizaʒ/ n.m. landscape.

paysan, ~ne /peizɑ̃, -an/ n.m., f. farmer, country person; (péj.) peasant. ● a. (agricole) farming; (rural) country.

PCV (en) /(ɑ̃)peseve/ adv. **appeler** ou **téléphoner en ~,** reverse the charges; (village) (Amer.) call collect.

PDG abrév. voir président directeur général.

péage /peaʒ/ n.m. toll; (lieu) toll-gate.

peau (pl. ~x) /po/ n.f. skin; (cuir) hide. **~ de chamois,** chamois (-leather). **~ de mouton,** sheepskin. **être bien/mal dans sa ~,** be/not be at ease with oneself.

pêche¹ /pɛʃ/ n.f. peach.

pêche² /pɛʃ/ n.f. (activité) fishing; (poissons) catch. **~ à la ligne,** angling.

péché /peʃe/ n.m. sin.

péch|er /peʃe/ v.i. sin. **~er par timidité/**etc., be too timid/etc. **~eur, ~eresse** n.m., f. sinner.

pêch|er /peʃe/ v.t. (poisson) catch; (dénicher: fam.) dig up. ● v.i. fish. **~eur** n.m. fisherman; (à la ligne) angler.

pécule /pekyl/ n.m. (économies) savings.

pécuniaire /pekynjɛr/ a. financial.

pédago|gie /pedagɔʒi/ n.f. education. **~gique** a. educational. **~gue** n.m./f. teacher.

pédal|e /pedal/ n.f. pedal. **~er** v.i. pedal.

pédalo /pedalo/ n.m. pedal boat.

pédant, ~e /pedɑ̃, -t/ a. pedantic.

pédé /pede/ n.m. (argot) queer, fag (Amer.).

pédestre /pedɛstr/ a. **faire de la randonnée ~,** go walking ou hiking.

pédiatre /pedjatr/ n.m./f. paediatrician.

pédicure /pedikyr/ n.m./f. chiropodist.

pedigree /pedigre/ n.m. pedigree.

pègre /pɛgr/ n.f. underworld.

peign|e /pɛɲ/ n.m. comb. **~er** /peɲe/ v.t. comb; (personne) comb the hair of. **se ~er** v. pr. comb one's hair.

peignoir /pɛɲwar/ n.m. dressing-gown.

peindre† /pɛ̃dr/ v.t. paint.

peine /pɛn/ n.f. sadness, sorrow; (effort, difficulté) trouble; (punition) punishment; (jurid.) sentence. **avoir de la ~,** feel sad. **faire de la ~ à,** hurt. **ce n'est pas la ~ de faire,** it is not worth (while) doing. **se donner** ou **prendre la ~ de faire,** go to the trouble of doing. **~ de mort** death penalty.

peine (à) /(a)pɛn/ adv. hardly.

peiner /pene/ v.i. struggle. ● v.t. sadden.

peintre /pɛ̃tr/ n.m. painter. **~ en bâtiment,** house painter.

peinture /pɛ̃tyr/ n.f. painting; (matière) paint. **~ à l'huile,** oil-painting.

péjorati|f, ~ve /peʒɔratif, -v/ a. pejorative.

pelage /pəlaʒ/ n.m. coat, fur.

pêle-mêle /pɛlmɛl/ adv. in a jumble.

peler /pəle/ v.t./i. peel.

pèlerin /pɛlrɛ̃/ n.m. pilgrim. **~age** /-inaʒ/ n.m. pilgrimage.

pèlerine /pɛlrin/ n.f. cape.

pélican /pelikɑ̃/ n.m. pelican.

pelle /pɛl/ n.f. shovel; (d'enfant) spade. **~tée** n.f. shovelful.

pellicule /pelikyl/ n.f. film. **~s,** (cheveux) dandruff.

pelote /pəlɔt/ n.f. ball; (d'épingles) pincushion.

peloton /plɔtɔ̃/ n.m. troop, squad; (sport) pack. **~ d'exécution,** firing-squad.

pelotonner (se) /(sə)plɔtɔne/ v. pr. curl up.

pelouse /pluz/ n.f. lawn.

peluche /plyʃ/ n.f. (tissu) plush; (jouet) cuddly toy. **en ~,** (lapin, chien) fluffy, furry.

pelure /plyr/ n.f. peeling.

pén|al (m. pl. ~aux) /penal, -o/ a. penal. **~aliser** v.t. penalize. **~alité** n.f. penalty.

penalt|y (pl. ~ies) /penalti/ n.m. penalty (kick).

penaud, ~e /pəno, -d/ a. sheepish.

penchant /pɑ̃ʃɑ̃/ *n.m.* inclination; (*goût*) liking (**pour**, for).

pench|er /pɑ̃ʃe/ *v.t.* tilt. ● *v.i.* lean (over), tilt. **se ~er** *v. pr.* lean (forward). **~er pour**, favour. **se ~er sur**, (*problème etc.*) examine.

pendaison /pɑ̃dɛzɔ̃/ *n.f.* hanging.

pendant [1] /pɑ̃dɑ̃/ *prép.* (*au cours de*) during; (*durée*) for. **~ que**, while.

pendant [2], **~e** /pɑ̃dɑ̃, -t/ *a.* hanging; (*question etc.*) pending. ● *n.m.* (*contrepartie*) matching piece (**de**, to). **faire ~ à**, match. **~ d'oreille**, drop ear-ring.

pendentif /pɑ̃dɑ̃tif/ *n.m.* pendant.

penderie /pɑ̃dri/ *n.f.* wardrobe.

pend|re /pɑ̃dr/ *v.t./i.* hang. **se ~re** *v. pr.* hang (**à**, from); (*se tuer*) hang o.s. **~re la crémaillère**, have a house-warming. **~u**, **~ue** *a.* hanging (**à**, from); *n.m.*, *f.* hanged man, hanged woman.

pendul|e /pɑ̃dyl/ *n.f.* clock. ● *n.m.* pendulum. **~ette** *n.f.* (travelling) clock.

pénétr|er /penetre/ *v.i.* **~er (dans)**, enter. ● *v.t.* penetrate. **se ~er de**, become convinced of. **~ant**, **~ante** *a.* penetrating.

pénible /penibl/ *a.* difficult; (*douloureux*) painful; (*fatigant*) tiresome. **~ment** /-əmɑ̃/ *adv.* with difficulty; (*cruellement*) painfully.

péniche /peniʃ/ *n.f.* barge.

pénicilline /penisilin/ *n.f.* penicillin.

péninsule /penɛ̃syl/ *n.f.* peninsula.

pénis /penis/ *n.m.* penis.

pénitence /penitɑ̃s/ *n.f.* (*peine*) penance; (*regret*) penitence; (*fig.*) punishment. **faire ~**, repent.

péniten|cier /penitɑ̃sje/ *n.m.* penitentiary. **~tiaire** /-sjɛr/ *a.* prison.

pénombre /penɔ̃br/ *n.f.* half-light.

pensée [1] /pɑ̃se/ *n.f.* thought.

pensée [2] /pɑ̃se/ *n.f.* (*fleur*) pansy.

pens|er /pɑ̃se/ *v.t./i.* think. **~er à**, (*réfléchir à*) think about; (*se souvenir de*, *prévoir*) think of. **~er faire**, think of doing. **faire ~er à**, remind one of. **~eur** *n.m.* thinker.

pensi|f, **~ve** /pɑ̃sif, -v/ *a.* pensive.

pension /pɑ̃sjɔ̃/ *n.f.* (*scol.*) boarding-school; (*repas*, *somme*) board; (*allocation*) pension. **~ (de famille)**, guest-house. **~ alimentaire**, (*jurid.*) alimony. **~naire** /-jɔnɛr/ *n.m./f.* boarder; (*d'hôtel*) guest. **~nat** /-jɔna/ *n.m.* boarding-school.

pente /pɑ̃t/ *n.f.* slope. **en ~**, sloping.

Pentecôte /pɑ̃tkot/ *n.f.* **la ~**, Whit-sun.

pénurie /penyri/ *n.f.* shortage.

pépé /pepe/ *n.m.* (*fam.*) grandad.

pépier /pepje/ *v.i.* chirp.

pépin /pepɛ̃/ *n.m.* (*graine*) pip; (*ennui*: *fam.*) hitch; (*parapluie*: *fam.*) brolly.

pépinière /pepinjɛr/ *n.f.* (tree) nursery.

perçant, **~e** /pɛrsɑ̃, -t/ *a.* (*froid*) piercing; (*regard*) keen.

percée /pɛrse/ *n.f.* opening; (*attaque*) breakthrough.

perce-neige /pɛrsənɛʒ/ *n.m./f. invar.* snowdrop.

percepteur /pɛrsɛptœr/ *n.m.* tax-collector.

perceptible /pɛrsɛptibl/ *a.* perceptible.

perception /pɛrsɛpsjɔ̃/ *n.f.* perception; (*d'impôts*) collection.

percer /pɛrse/ *v.t.* pierce; (*avec perceuse*) drill; (*mystère*) penetrate. ● *v.i.* break through; (*dent*) come through.

perceuse /pɛrsøz/ *n.f.* drill.

percevoir† /pɛrsəvwar/ *v.t.* perceive; (*impôt*) collect.

perche /pɛrʃ/ *n.f.* (*bâton*) pole.

perch|er /pɛrʃe/ *v.t.i.*, **se ~er** *v. pr.* perch. **~oir** *n.m.* perch.

percolateur /pɛrkɔlatœr/ *n.m.* percolator.

percussion /pɛrkysjɔ̃/ *n.f.* percussion.

percuter /pɛrkyte/ *v.t.* strike; (*véhicule*) crash into.

perd|re /pɛrdr/ *v.t./i.* lose; (*gaspiller*) waste; (*ruiner*) ruin. **se ~re** *v. pr.* get lost; (*rester inutilisé*) go to waste. **~ant**, **~ante** *a.* losing; *n.m.*, *f.* loser. **~u** *a.* (*endroit*) isolated; (*moments*) spare; (*malade*) finished.

perdreau (*pl.* **~x**) /pɛrdro/ *n.m.* (young) partridge.

perdrix /pɛrdri/ *n.f.* partridge.

père /pɛr/ *n.m.* father. **~ de famille**, father, family man. **~ spirituel**, father figure. **le ~ Noël**, Father Christmas, Santa Claus.

péremptoire /perɑ̃ptwar/ *a.* peremptory.

perfection /pɛrfɛksjɔ̃/ *n.f.* perfection.

perfectionn|er /pɛrfɛksjɔne/ *v.t.* improve. **se ~er en anglais**/*etc.*, improve one's English/*etc.* **~é** *a.*

sophisticated. **~ement** *n.m.* improvement.

perfectionniste /pɛrfɛksjɔnist/ *n.m./f.* perfectionist.

perfid|e /pɛrfid/ *a.* perfidious, treacherous. **~ie** *n.f.* perfidy.

perfor|er /pɛrfɔre/ *v.t.* perforate; (*billet, bande*) punch. **~ateur** *n.m.* (*appareil*) punch. **~ation** *n.f.* perforation; (*trou*) hole.

performan|ce /pɛrfɔrmɑ̃s/ *n.f.* performance. **~t, ~te** *a.* high-performance, successful.

perfusion /pɛrfyzjɔ̃/ *n.f.* drip. **mettre qn. sous ~,** put s.o. on a drip.

péricliter /periklite/ *v.i.* decline, be in rapid decline.

péridural /peridyral/ *a.* (**anesthésie**) **~e,** epidural.

péril /peril/ *n.m.* peril.

périlleu|x, ~se /perijø, -z/ *a.* perilous.

périmé /perime/ *a.* expired; (*désuet*) outdated.

périmètre /perimɛtr/ *n.m.* perimeter.

périod|e /perjɔd/ *n.f.* period. **~ique** *a.* periodic(al); *n.m.* (*journal*) periodical.

péripétie /peripesi/ *n.f.* (unexpected) event, adventure.

périphér|ie /periferi/ *n.f.* periphery; (*banlieue*) outskirts. **~ique** *a.* peripheral; *n.m.* (*boulevard*) **~ique,** ring road.

périple /peripl/ *n.m.* journey.

pér|ir /perir/ *v.i.* perish, die. **~issable** *a.* perishable.

périscope /periskɔp/ *n.m.* periscope.

perle /pɛrl/ *n.f.* (*bijou*) pearl; (*boule, de sueur*) bead.

permanence /pɛrmanɑ̃s/ *n.f.* permanence; (*bureau*) duty office; (*scol.*) study room. **de ~,** on duty. **en ~,** permanently. **assurer une ~,** keep the office open.

permanent, ~e /pɛrmanɑ̃, -t/ *a.* permanent; (*spectacle*) continuous; (*comité*) standing. ● *n.f.* (*coiffure*) perm.

perméable /pɛrmeabl/ *a.* permeable; (*personne*) susceptible (**à,** to).

permettre† /pɛrmɛtr/ *v.t.* allow, permit. **~ à qn. de,** allow *ou* permit s.o. to. **se ~ de,** take the liberty to.

permis, ~e /pɛrmi, -z/ *a.* allowed. ● *n.m.* licence, permit. **~ (de conduire),** driving-licence.

permission /pɛrmisjɔ̃/ *n.f.* permission. **en ~,** (*mil.*) on leave.

permut|er /pɛrmyte/ *v.t.* change round. **~ation** *n.f.* permutation.

pernicieu|x, ~se /pɛrnisjø, -z/ *a.* pernicious.

Pérou /peru/ *n.m.* Peru.

perpendiculaire /pɛrpɑ̃dikylɛr/ *a.* & *n.f.* perpendicular.

perpétrer /pɛrpetre/ *v.t.* perpetrate.

perpétu|el, ~le /pɛrpetɥɛl/ *a.* perpetual.

perpétuer /pɛrpetɥe/ *v.t.* perpetuate.

perpétuité (à) /(a)pɛrpetɥite/ *adv.* for life.

perplex|e /pɛrplɛks/ *a.* perplexed. **~ité** *n.f.* perplexity.

perquisition /pɛrkizisjɔ̃/ *n.f.* (police) search. **~ner** /-jɔne/ *v.t./i.* search.

perron /pɛrɔ̃/ *n.m.* (front) steps.

perroquet /pɛrɔkɛ/ *n.m.* parrot.

perruche /pɛryʃ/ *n.f.* budgerigar.

perruque /pɛryk/ *n.f.* wig.

persan, ~e /pɛrsɑ̃, -an/ *a.* & *n.m.* (*lang.*) Persian.

persécut|er /pɛrsekyte/ *v.t.* persecute. **~ion** /-ysjɔ̃/ *n.f.* persecution.

persévér|er /pɛrsevere/ *v.i.* persevere. **~ance** *n.f.* perseverance.

persienne /pɛrsjɛn/ *n.f.* (outside) shutter.

persil /pɛrsi/ *n.m.* parsley.

persistan|t, ~te /pɛrsistɑ̃, -t/ *a.* persistent; (*feuillage*) evergreen. **~ce** *n.f.* persistence.

persister /pɛrsiste/ *v.i.* persist (**à faire,** in doing).

personnage /pɛrsɔnaʒ/ *n.m.* character; (*important*) personality.

personnalité /pɛrsɔnalite/ *n.f.* personality.

personne /pɛrsɔn/ *n.f.* person. **~s,** people. ● *pron.* (*quelqu'un*) anybody. **(ne) ~,** nobody.

personnel, ~le /pɛrsɔnɛl/ *a.* personal; (*égoïste*) selfish. ● *n.m.* staff. **~lement** *adv.* personally.

personnifier /pɛrsɔnifje/ *v.t.* personify.

perspective /pɛrspɛktiv/ *n.f.* (*art*) perspective; (*vue*) view; (*possibilité*) prospect; (*point de vue*) viewpoint, perspective.

perspicac|e /pɛrspikas/ *a.* shrewd. **~ité** *n.f.* shrewdness.

persua|der /pɛrsɥade/ *v.t.* persuade (**de faire,** to do). **~sion** /-ɥazjɔ̃/ *n.f.* persuasion.

persuasi|f, **~ve** /pɛrsɥazif, -v/ a. persuasive.

perte /pɛrt/ n.f. loss; (*ruine*) ruin. **à ~ de vue**, as far as the eye can see. **~ de**, (*temps, argent*) waste of. **~ sèche**, total loss. **~s**, (*méd.*) discharge.

pertinen|t, **~te** /pɛrtinɑ̃, -t/ a. pertinent; (*esprit*) judicious. **~ce** n.f. pertinence.

perturb|er /pɛrtyrbe/ v.t. disrupt; (*personne*) perturb. **~ateur**, **~atrice** a. disruptive; n.m., f. disruptive element. **~ation** n.f. disruption.

pervenche /pɛrvɑ̃ʃ/ n.f. periwinkle; (*fam.*) traffic warden.

pervers, **~e** /pɛrvɛr, -s/ a. perverse; (*dépravé*) perverted. **~ion** /-sjɔ̃/ n.f. perversion.

pervert|ir /pɛrvɛrtir/ v.t. pervert. **~i**, **~ie** n.m., f. pervert.

pes|ant, **~ante** /pəzɑ̃, -t/ a. heavy. **~amment** adv. heavily. **~anteur** n.f. heaviness. **la ~anteur**, (*force*) gravity.

pèse-personne /pɛzpɛrsɔn/ n.m. (bathroom) scales.

pes|er /pəze/ v.t./i. weigh. **~er sur**, bear upon. **~ée** n.f. weighing; (*effort*) pressure.

peseta /pezeta/ n.f. peseta.

pessimis|te /pesimist/ a. pessimistic. ● n.m. pessimist. **~me** n.m. pessimism.

peste /pɛst/ n.f. plague; (*personne*) pest.

pester /pɛste/ v.i. **~ (contre)**, curse.

pestilentiel, **~le** /pɛstilɑ̃sjɛl/ a. fetid, stinking.

pet /pɛ/ n.m. fart.

pétale /petal/ n.m. petal.

pétanque /petɑ̃k/ n.f. bowls.

pétarader /petarade/ v.i. backfire.

pétard /petar/ n.m. banger.

péter /pete/ v.i. fart; (*fam.*) go bang; (*casser: fam.*) snap.

pétill|er /petije/ v.i. (*feu*) crackle; (*champagne, yeux*) sparkle. **~er d'intelligence**, sparkle with intelligence. **~ant**, **~ante** a. (*gazeux*) fizzy.

petit, **~e** /pti, -t/ a. small; (*avec nuance affective*) little; (*jeune*) young, small; (*faible*) slight; (*mesquin*) petty. ● n.m., f. little child; (*scol.*) junior. **~s**, (*de chat*) kittens; (*de chien*) pups. **en ~**, in miniature. **~ ami**, boy-friend. **~e amie**, girl-friend. **~ à petit**, little by little. **~es annonces**, small ads. **~e cuiller**, teaspoon. **~ déjeuner**, breakfast. **le ~ écran**, the small screen, television. **~-enfant** (pl. **~s-enfants**) n.m. grandchild. **~e-fille** (pl. **~es-filles**) n.f. granddaughter. **~-fils** (pl. **~s-fils**) n.m. grandson. **~ pain**, roll. **~-pois** (pl. **~s-pois**) n.m. garden pea.

petitesse /ptitɛs/ n.f. smallness; (*péj.*) meanness.

pétition /petisjɔ̃/ n.f. petition.

pétrifier /petrifje/ v.t. petrify.

pétrin /petrɛ̃/ n.m. (*situation: fam.*) **dans le ~**, in a fix.

pétrir /petrir/ v.t. knead.

pétrol|e /petrol/ n.m. (*brut*) oil; (*pour lampe etc.*) paraffin. **lampe à ~e**, oil lamp. **~ier**, **~ière** a. oil; n.m. (*navire*) oil-tanker.

pétulant, **~e** /petylɑ̃, -t/ a. exuberant, full of high spirits.

peu /pø/ adv. **~ (de)**, (*quantité*) little, not much; (*nombre*) few, not many. **~ intéressant**/etc., not very interesting/etc. ● pron. few. **un ~ (de)**, a little. **à ~ près**, more or less. **de ~**, only just. **~ à peu**, gradually. **~ après/avant**, shortly after/before. **~ de chose**, not much. **~ nombreux**, few. **~ souvent**, seldom. **pour ~ que**, as long as.

peuplade /pœplad/ n.f. tribe.

peuple /pœpl/ n.m. people.

peupler /pœple/ v.t. populate.

peuplier /pøplije/ n.m. poplar.

peur /pœr/ n.f. fear. **avoir ~**, be afraid (**de**, of). **de ~ de**, for fear of. **faire ~ à**, frighten. **~eux**, **~euse** a. fearful, timid.

peut /pø/ voir **pouvoir** [1].

peut-être /pøtɛtr/ adv. perhaps, maybe. **~ que**, perhaps, maybe.

peux /pø/ voir **pouvoir** [1].

pèze /pɛz/ n.m. (*fam.*) **du ~**, money, dough.

phallique /falik/ a. phallic.

phantasme /fɑ̃tasm/ n.m. fantasy.

phare /far/ n.m. (*tour*) lighthouse; (*de véhicule*) headlight. **~ antibrouillard**, fog lamp.

pharmaceutique /farmasøtik/ a. pharmaceutical.

pharmac|ie /farmasi/ n.f. (*magasin*) chemist's (shop); (*Amer.*) pharmacy; (*science*) pharmacy; (*armoire*) medicine cabinet. **~ien**, **~ienne** n.m., f. chemist, pharmacist.

pharyngite /faʀɛ̃ʒit/ *n.f.* pharyngitis.

phase /fɑz/ *n.f.* phase.

phénomène /fenɔmɛn/ *n.m.* phenomenon; (*original*: *fam.*) eccentric.

philanthrop|e /filɑ̃tʀɔp/ *n.m./f.* philanthropist. ~**ique** *a.* philanthropic.

philatél|ie /filateli/ *n.f.* philately. ~**iste** *n.m./f.* philatelist.

philharmonique /filaʀmɔnik/ *a.* philharmonic.

Philippines /filipin/ *n.f. pl.* **les ~**, the Philippines.

philosoph|e /filozɔf/ *n.m./f.* philosopher. ● *a.* philosophical. ~**ie** *n.f.* philosophy. ~**ique** *a.* philosophical.

phobie /fɔbi/ *n.f.* phobia.

phonétique /fɔnetik/ *a.* phonetic.

phoque /fɔk/ *n.m.* (*animal*) seal.

phosphate /fɔsfat/ *n.m.* phosphate.

phosphore /fɔsfɔʀ/ *n.m.* phosphorus.

photo /fɔto/ *n.f.* photo; (*art*) photography. **prendre en ~**, take a photo of. ~ **d'identité**, passport photograph.

photocop|ie /fɔtokɔpi/ *n.f.* photocopy. ~**ier** *v.t.* photocopy. ~**ieuse** *n.f.* photocopier.

photogénique /fɔtɔʒenik/ *a.* photogenic.

photograph|e /fɔtɔgʀaf/ *n.m./f.* photographer. ~**ie** *n.f.* photograph; (*art*) photography. ~**ier** *v.t.* take a photo of. ~**ique** *a.* photographic.

phrase /fʀɑz/ *n.f.* sentence.

physicien, ~ne /fizisjɛ̃, -jɛn/ *n.m.*, *f.* physicist.

physiologie /fizjɔlɔʒi/ *n.f.* physiology.

physionomie /fizjɔnɔmi/ *n.f.* face.

physique¹ /fizik/ *a.* physical. ● *n.m.* physique. **au ~**, physically. ~**ment** *adv.* physically.

physique² /fizik/ *n.f.* physics.

piailler /pjɑje/ *v.i.* squeal, squawk.

pian|o /pjano/ *n.m.* piano. ~**iste** *n.m./f.* pianist.

pianoter /pjanɔte/ *v.t.* (*air*) tap out. ● *v.i.* (**sur**, on) (*ordinateur*) tap away; (*table*) tap one's fingers.

pic /pik/ *n.m.* (*outil*) pickaxe; (*sommet*) peak; (*oiseau*) woodpecker. **à ~**, (*verticalement*) sheer; (*couler*) straight to the bottom; (*arriver*) just at the right time.

pichenette /piʃnɛt/ *n.f.* flick.

pichet /piʃɛ/ *n.m.* jug.

pickpocket /pikpɔkɛt/ *n.m.* pickpocket.

pick-up /pikœp/ *n.m. invar.* record-player.

picorer /pikɔʀe/ *v.t./i.* peck.

picot|er /pikɔte/ *v.t.* prick; (*yeux*) make smart. ~**ement** *n.m.* pricking; smarting.

pie /pi/ *n.f.* magpie.

pièce /pjɛs/ *n.f.* piece; (*chambre*) room; (*pour raccommoder*) patch; (*écrit*) document. ~ **(de monnaie)**, coin. ~ **(de théâtre)**, play. **dix francs/etc. (la)** ~, ten francs/etc. each. ~ **de rechange**, spare part. ~ **détachée**, part. ~ **d'identité**, identity paper. ~ **montée**, tiered cake. ~**s justificatives**, supporting documents. **deux/trois etc.** ~**s**, two-/three-/etc. room flat *ou* apartment (*Amer.*).

pied /pje/ *n.m.* foot; (*de meuble*) leg; (*de lampe*) base; (*de salade*) plant. **à ~**, on foot. **au ~ de la lettre**, literally. **avoir ~**, have a footing. **avoir les ~s plats**, have flat feet. **comme un ~**, (*fam.*) terribly. **mettre sur ~**, set up. ~ **bot**, club-foot. **sur un ~ d'égalité**, on an equal footing. **mettre les ~s dans le plat**, put one's foot in it. **c'est le ~!**, (*fam.*) it's great!

piédest|al (*pl.* ~**aux**) /pjedɛstal, -o/ *n.m.* pedestal.

piège /pjɛʒ/ *n.m.* trap.

piég|er /pjeʒe/ *v.t.* trap; (*avec explosifs*) booby-trap. **lettre/voiture** ~**ée**, letter-/car-bomb.

pierr|e /pjɛʀ/ *n.f.* stone. ~**e d'achoppement**, stumbling-block. ~**e de touche**, touchstone. ~**e précieuse**, precious stone. ~**e tombale**, tombstone. ~**eux, ~euse** *a.* stony.

piété /pjete/ *n.f.* piety.

piétiner /pjetine/ *v.i.* stamp one's feet; (*ne pas avancer*: *fig.*) mark time. ● *v.t.* trample (on).

piéton /pjetɔ̃/ *n.m.* pedestrian. ~**nier**, ~**nière** /-ɔnje, -jɛʀ/ *a.* pedestrian.

piètre /pjɛtʀ/ *a.* wretched.

pieu (*pl.* ~**x**) /pjø/ *n.m.* post, stake.

pieuvre /pjœvʀ/ *n.f.* octopus.

pieu|x, ~se /pjø, -z/ *a.* pious.

pif /pif/ *n.m.* (*fam.*) nose.

pigeon /piʒɔ̃/ *n.m.* pigeon.

piger /piʒe/ *v.t./i.* (*fam.*) understand, get (it).

pigment /pigmã/ *n.m.* pigment.

pignon /piɲõ/ *n.m.* (*de maison*) gable.

pile /pil/ *n.f.* (*tas, pilier*) pile; (*électr.*) battery; (*atomique*) pile. ● *adv.* (*s'arrêter: fam.*) dead. **à dix heures ~,** (*fam.*) at ten on the dot. **~ ou face?,** heads or tails?

piler /pile/ *v.t.* pound.

pilier /pilje/ *n.m.* pillar.

pill|er /pije/ *v.t.* loot. **~age** *n.m.* looting. **~ard, ~arde** *n.m., f.* looter.

pilonner /pilɔne/ *v.t.* pound.

pilori /pilɔri/ *n.m.* **mettre** *ou* **clouer au ~,** pillory.

pilot|e /pilɔt/ *n.m.* pilot; (*auto.*) driver. ● *a.* pilot. **~er** *v.t.* (*aviat., naut.*) pilot; (*auto.*) drive; (*fig.*) guide.

pilule /pilyl/ *n.f.* pill. **la ~,** the pill.

piment /pimã/ *n.m.* pepper, pimento; (*fig.*) spice. **~é** /-te/ *a.* spicy.

pimpant, ~e /pẽpã, -t/ *a.* spruce.

pin /pẽ/ *n.m.* pine.

pinard /pinar/ *n.m.* (*vin: fam.*) plonk, cheap wine.

pince /pẽs/ *n.f.* (*outil*) pliers; (*levier*) crowbar; (*de crabe*) pincer; (*à sucre*) tongs. **~ (à épiler),** tweezers. **~ (à linge),** (clothes-)peg.

pinceau (*pl.* **~x**) /pẽso/ *n.m.* paint-brush.

pinc|er /pẽse/ *v.t.* pinch; (*arrêter: fam.*) pinch. **se ~er le doigt,** catch one's finger. **~é** *a.* (*ton, air*) stiff. **~ée** *n.f.* pinch (**de,** of).

pince-sans-rire /pẽsãrir/ *a. invar.* po-faced. **c'est un ~,** he's po-faced.

pincettes /pẽset/ *n.f. pl.* (fire) tongs.

pinède /pined/ *n.f.* pine forest.

pingouin /pẽgwẽ/ *n.m.* penguin.

ping-pong /piɲpõg/ *n.m.* table tennis, ping-pong.

pingre /pẽgr/ *a.* miserly.

pinson /pẽsõ/ *n.m.* chaffinch.

pintade /pẽtad/ *n.f.* guinea-fowl.

pioch|e /pjɔʃ/ *n.f.* pick(axe). **~er** *v.t./ i.* dig; (*étudier: fam.*) study hard, slog away (at).

pion /pjõ/ *n.m.* (*de jeu*) piece; (*échecs*) pawn; (*scol., fam.*) supervisor.

pionnier /pjɔnje/ *n.m.* pioneer.

pipe /pip/ *n.f.* pipe. **fumer la ~,** smoke a pipe.

pipe-line /piplin/ *n.m.* pipeline.

piquant, ~e /pikã, -t/ *a.* (*barbe etc.*) prickly; (*goût*) pungent; (*détail etc.*) spicy. ● *n.m.* prickle; (*de hérisson*) spine, prickle; (*fig.*) piquancy.

pique[1] /pik/ *n.f.* (*arme*) pike.

pique[2] /pik/ *n.m.* (*cartes*) spades.

pique-niqu|e /piknik/ *n.m.* picnic. **~er** *v.i.* picnic.

piquer /pike/ *v.t.* prick; (*langue*) burn, sting; (*abeille etc.*) sting; (*serpent etc.*) bite; (*enfoncer*) stick; (*coudre*) (machine-)stitch; (*curiosité*) excite; (*crise*) have; (*voler: fam.*) pinch. ● *v.i.* (*avion*) dive; (*goût*) be hot. **~ une tête,** plunge headlong. **se ~ de,** pride o.s. on.

piquet /pikε/ *n.m.* stake; (*de tente*) peg. **au ~,** (*scol.*) in the corner. **~ de grève,** (strike) picket.

piqûre /pikyr/ *n.f.* prick; (*d'abeille etc.*) sting; (*de serpent etc.*) bite; (*point*) stitch; (*méd.*) injection, shot (*Amer.*). **faire une ~ à qn.,** give s.o. an injection.

pirate /pirat/ *n.m.* pirate. **~ de l'air,** hijacker. **~rie** *n.f.* piracy.

pire /pir/ *a.* worse (**que,** than). **le ~ livre**/*etc.*, the worst book/*etc.* ● *n.m.* **le ~,** the worst (thing). **au ~,** at worst.

pirogue /pirɔg/ *n.f.* canoe, dug-out.

pirouette /pirwet/ *n.f.* pirouette.

pis[1] /pi/ *n.m.* (*de vache*) udder.

pis[2] /pi/ *a. invar. & adv.* worse. **aller de mal en ~,** go from bad to worse.

pis-aller /pizale/ *n.m. invar.* stopgap, temporary expedient.

piscine /pisin/ *n.f.* swimming-pool. **~ couverte,** indoor swimming-pool.

pissenlit /pisãli/ *n.m.* dandelion.

pistache /pistaʃ/ *n.f.* pistachio.

piste /pist/ *n.f.* track; (*de personne, d'animal*) track, trail; (*aviat.*) runway; (*de cirque*) ring; (*de ski*) run; (*de patinage*) rink; (*de danse*) floor; (*sport*) race-track. **~ cyclable,** cycle-track; (*Amer.*) bicycle path.

pistolet /pistɔlε/ *n.m.* gun, pistol; (*de peintre*) spray-gun.

piston /pistõ/ *n.m.* (*techn.*) piston. **il a un ~,** (*fam.*) somebody is pulling strings for him.

pistonner /pistɔne/ *v.t.* (*fam.*) recommend, pull strings for.

piteu|x, ~se /pitø, -z/ *a.* pitiful.

pitié /pitje/ *n.f.* pity. **il me fait ~, j'ai ~ de lui,** I pity him.

piton /pitõ/ *n.m.* (*à crochet*) hook; (*sommet pointu*) peak.

pitoyable /pitwajabl/ *a.* pitiful.

pitre /pitr/ *n.m.* clown. **faire le ~,** clown around.

pittoresque /pitɔrɛsk/ *a.* picturesque.

pivot /pivo/ *n.m.* pivot. **~er** /-ɔte/ *v.i.* revolve; (*personne*) swing round.

pizza /pidza/ *n.f.* pizza.

placage /plakaʒ/ *n.m.* (*en bois*) veneer; (*sur un mur*) facing.

placard /plakar/ *n.m.* cupboard; (*affiche*) poster. **~er** /-de/ *v.t.* (*affiche*) post up; (*mur*) cover with posters.

place /plas/ *n.f.* place; (*espace libre*) room, space; (*siège*) seat, place; (*prix d'un trajet*) fare; (*esplanade*) square; (*emploi*) position; (*de parking*) space. **à la ~ de**, instead of. **en ~, à sa ~**, in its place. **faire ~ à**, give way to. **sur ~**, on the spot. **remettre qn. à sa ~**, put s.o. in his place. **ça prend de la ~**, it takes up a lot of room. **se mettre à la ~ de qn.** put oneself in s.o.'s shoes *ou* place.

placebo /plasebo/ *n.m.* placebo.

placenta /plasɛ̃ta/ *n.m.* placenta.

plac|er /plase/ *v.t.* place; (*invité, spectateur*) seat; (*argent*) invest. **se ~er** *v. pr.* (*personne*) take up a position; (*troisième etc.: sport*) come (in); (*à un endroit*) to go and stand (à, in). **~é a.** (*sport*) placed. **bien ~é pour**, in a position to. **~ement** *n.m.* (*d'argent*) investment.

placide /plasid/ *a.* placid.

plafond /plafɔ̃/ *n.m.* ceiling.

plage /plaʒ/ *n.f.* beach; (*station*) (seaside) resort; (*aire*) area.

plagiat /plaʒja/ *n.m.* plagiarism.

plaid /plɛd/ *n.m.* travelling-rug.

plaider /plede/ *v.t./i.* plead.

plaid|oirie /plɛdwari/ *n.f.* (defence) speech. **~oyer** *n.m.* plea.

plaie /plɛ/ *n.f.* wound; (*personne: fam.*) nuisance.

plaignant, ~e /plɛɲɑ̃, -t/ *n.m., f.* plaintiff.

plaindre† /plɛ̃dr/ *v.t.* pity. **se ~** *v. pr.* complain (**de**, about). **se ~ de**, (*souffrir de*) complain of.

plaine /plɛn/ *n.f.* plain.

plaint|e /plɛ̃t/ *n.f.* complaint; (*gémissement*) groan. **~if, ~ive** *a.* plaintive.

plaire† /plɛr/ *v.i.* **~ à**, please. **ça lui plaît**, he likes it. **elle lui plaît**, he likes her. **ça me plaît de faire**, I like *ou* enjoy doing. **s'il vous plaît**, please. **se ~** *v. pr.* (*à Londres etc.*) like *ou* enjoy it.

plaisance /plɛzɑ̃s/ *n.f.* **la (navigation de) ~**, yachting.

plaisant, ~e /plɛzɑ̃, -t/ *a.* pleasant; (*drôle*) amusing.

plaisant|er /plɛzɑ̃te/ *v.i.* joke. **~erie** *n.f.* joke. **~in** *n.m.* joker.

plaisir /plezir/ *n.m.* pleasure. **faire ~ à**, please. **pour le ~**, for fun *ou* pleasure.

plan¹ /plɑ̃/ *n.m.* plan; (*de ville*) map; (*surface, niveau*) plane. **~ d'eau**, expanse of water. **premier ~**, foreground. **dernier ~**, background.

plan², ~e /plɑ̃, -an/ *a.* flat.

planche /plɑ̃ʃ/ *n.f.* board, plank; (*gravure*) plate; (*de potager*) bed. **~ à repasser**, ironing-board. **~ à voile**, sailboard; (*sport*) windsurfing.

plancher /plɑ̃ʃe/ *n.m.* floor.

plancton /plɑ̃ktɔ̃/ *n.m.* plankton.

plan|er /plane/ *v.i.* glide. **~er sur**, (*mystère, danger*) hang over. **~eur** *n.m.* (*avion*) glider.

planète /planɛt/ *n.f.* planet.

planif|ier /planifje/ *v.t.* plan. **~ication** *n.f.* planning.

planqu|e /plɑ̃k/ *n.f.* (*fam.*) hideout; (*emploi: fam.*) cushy job. **~er** *v.t.*, **se ~er** *v. pr.* hide.

plant /plɑ̃/ *n.m.* seedling; (*de légumes*) bed.

plante /plɑ̃t/ *n.f.* plant. **~ des pieds**, sole (of the foot).

plant|er /plɑ̃te/ *v.t.* (*plante etc.*) plant; (*enfoncer*) drive in; (*installer*) put up; (*mettre*) put. **rester ~é**, stand still, remain standing. **~ation** *n.f.* planting; (*de tabac etc.*) plantation.

plantureu|x, ~se /plɑ̃tyrø, -z/ *a.* abundant; (*femme*) buxom.

plaque /plak/ *n.f.* plate; (*de marbre*) slab; (*insigne*) badge; (*commémorative*) plaque. **~ chauffante**, hotplate. **~ minéralogique**, numberplate.

plaqu|er /plake/ *v.t.* (*bois*) veneer; (*aplatir*) flatten; (*rugby*) tackle; (*abandonner: fam.*) ditch. **~er qch. sur** *ou* **contre**, make sth. stick to. **~age** *n.m.* (*rugby*) tackle.

plasma /plasma/ *n.m.* plasma.

plastic /plastik/ *n.m.* plastic explosive.

plastique /plastik/ *a. & n.m.* plastic. **en ~**, plastic.

plastiquer /plastike/ *v.t.* blow up.

plat[1], ~**e** /pla, -t/ a. flat. ● n.m. (de la main) flat. **à** ~ adv. (poser) flat; a. (batterie, pneu) flat. **à** ~ **ventre**, flat on one's face.

plat[2] /pla/ n.m. (culin.) dish; (partie de repas) course.

platane /platan/ n.m. plane(-tree).

plateau (pl. ~**x**) /plato/ n.m. tray; (d'électrophone) turntable, deck; (de balance) pan; (géog.) plateau. ~ **de fromages**, cheeseboard.

plateau-repas (pl. **plateaux-repas**) n.m. tray meal.

plate-bande (pl. **plates-bandes**) /platbɑ̃d/ n.f. flower-bed.

plate-forme (pl. **plates-formes**) /platfɔrm/ n.f. platform.

platine[1] /platin/ n.m. platinum.

platine[2] /platin/ n.f. (de tourne-disque) turntable.

platitude /platityd/ n.f. platitude.

platonique /platɔnik/ a. platonic.

plâtr|e /plɑtr/ n.m. plaster; (méd.) (plaster) cast. ~**er** v.t. plaster; (membre) put in plaster.

plausible /plozibl/ a. plausible.

plébiscite /plebisit/ n.m. plebiscite.

plein, ~**e** /plɛ̃, plɛn/ a. full (**de**, of); (total) complete. ● n.m. **faire le** ~ (**d'essence**), fill up (the tank). **à** ~, to the full. **à** ~ **temps**, full-time. **en** ~ **air**, in the open air. **en** ~ **milieu/visage**, right in the middle/the face. **en** ~**e nuit**/etc., in the middle of the night/etc. ~ **les mains**, all over one's hands.

pleinement /plɛnmɑ̃/ adv. fully.

pléthore /pletɔr/ n.f. over-abundance, plethora.

pleurer /plœre/ v.i. cry, weep (**sur**, over); (yeux) water. ● v.t. mourn.

pleurésie /plœrezi/ n.f. pleurisy.

pleurnicher /plœrniʃe/ v.i. (fam.) snivel.

pleurs (en) /(ɑ̃)plœr/ adv. in tears.

pleuvoir† /pløvwar/ v.i. rain; (fig.) rain ou shower down. **il pleut**, it is raining. **il pleut à verse** ou **à torrents**, it is pouring.

pli /pli/ n.m. fold; (de jupe) pleat; (de pantalon) crease; (enveloppe) cover; (habitude) habit. (**faux**) ~, crease.

pliant, ~**e** /plijɑ̃, -t/ a. folding; (parapluie) telescopic. ● n.m. folding stool, camp-stool.

plier /plije/ v.t. fold; (courber) bend; (personne) submit (**à**, to). ● v.i. bend; (personne) submit. **se** ~ v. pr. fold. **se** ~ **à**, to submit to.

plinthe /plɛ̃t/ n.f. skirting-board; (Amer.) baseboard.

plisser /plise/ v.t. crease; (yeux) screw up; (jupe) pleat.

plomb /plɔ̃/ n.m. lead; (fusible) fuse. ~**s**, (de chasse) lead shot. **de** ou **en** ~, lead. **de** ~, (ciel) leaden.

plomb|er /plɔ̃be/ v.t. (dent) fill. ~**age** n.m. filling.

plomb|ier /plɔ̃bje/ n.m. plumber. ~**erie** n.f. plumbing.

plongeant, ~**e** /plɔ̃ʒɑ̃, -t/ a. (vue) from above; (décolleté) plunging.

plongeoir /plɔ̃ʒwar/ n.m. diving-board.

plongeon /plɔ̃ʒɔ̃/ n.m. dive.

plong|er /plɔ̃ʒe/ v.i. dive; (route) plunge. ● v.t. plunge. **se** ~**er** v. pr. plunge (**dans**, into). ~**é dans**, (lecture) immersed in. ~**ée** n.f. diving. **en** ~**ée** (sous-marin) submerged. ~**eur**, ~**euse** n., f. diver; (employé) dishwasher.

plouf /pluf/ n.m. & int. splash.

ployer /plwaje/ v.t./i. bend.

plu /ply/ voir **plaire, pleuvoir**.

pluie /plɥi/ n.f. rain; (averse) shower. ~ **battante/diluvienne**, driving/torrential rain.

plumage /plymaʒ/ n.m. plumage.

plume /plym/ n.f. feather; (stylo) pen; (pointe) nib.

plumeau (pl. ~**x**) /plymo/ n.m. feather duster.

plumer /plyme/ v.t. pluck.

plumier /plymje/ n.m. pencil box.

plupart /plypar/ n.f. most. **la** ~ **des**, (gens, cas, etc.) most. **la** ~ **du temps**, most of the time. **pour la** ~, for the most part.

pluriel, ~**le** /plyrjɛl/ a. & n.m. plural. **au** ~, (nom) plural.

plus[1] /ply/ adv. de négation. (**ne**) ~, (temps) no longer, not any more. (**ne**) ~ **de**, (quantité) no more. **je n'y vais** ~, I do not go there any longer ou any more. (**il n'y a**) ~ **de pain**, (there is) no more bread.

plus[2] /ply/ (/plyz/ before vowel, /plys/ in final position) adv. more (**que**, than). ~ **âgé/tard**/etc., older/later/etc. ~ **beau**/etc., more beautiful/etc. **le** ~, the most. **le** ~ **beau**/etc., the most beautiful; (de deux) the more beautiful. **le** ~ **de**, (gens etc.) most. ~ **de**, (pain etc.) more. ~ **de**, (dix jours etc.) more than. **il est** ~ **de huit heures**/etc. it is after eight/etc. o'clock. **de** ~, more (**que**, than);

(*en outre*) moreover. (*âgés*) de ~ de (*huit ans etc.*) over, more than. de ~ en plus, more and more. en ~, extra. en ~ de, in addition to. ~ ou moins, more or less.

plus³ /plys/ *conj.* plus.

plusieurs /plyzjœr/ *a. & pron.* several.

plus-value /plyvaly/ *n.f.* (*bénéfice*) profit.

plutôt /plyto/ *adv.* rather (**que**, than).

pluvieu|x, **~se** /plyvjø, -z/ *a.* rainy.

pneu (*pl.* ~s) /pnø/ *n.m.* tyre; (*lettre*) express letter. **~matique** *a.* inflatable.

pneumonie /pnømɔni/ *n.f.* pneumonia.

poche /pɔʃ/ *n.f.* pocket; (*sac*) bag. ~s, (*sous les yeux*) bags.

pocher /pɔʃe/ *v.t.* (*œuf*) poach.

pochette /pɔʃɛt/ *n.f.* pack(et), envelope; (*sac*) bag, pouch; (*d'allumettes*) book; (*de disque*) sleeve; (*mouchoir*) pocket handkerchief. ~ surprise, lucky bag.

podium /pɔdjɔm/ *n.m.* rostrum.

poêle¹ /pwal/ *n.f.* ~ (à frire), frying-pan.

poêle² /pwal/ *n.m.* stove.

poème /pɔɛm/ *n.m.* poem.

poésie /pɔezi/ *n.f.* poetry; (*poème*) poem.

poète /pɔɛt/ *n.m.* poet.

poétique /pɔetik/ *a.* poetic.

poids /pwa/ *n.m.* weight. ~ coq/lourd/plume, bantam weight/heavyweight/featherweight. ~ lourd, (*camion*) lorry, juggernaut; (*Amer.*) truck.

poignant, **~e** /pwaɲɑ̃, -t/ *a.* poignant.

poignard /pwaɲar/ *n.m.* dagger. ~er /-de/ *v.t.* stab.

poigne /pwaɲ/ *n.f.* grip. avoir de la ~, have an iron fist.

poignée /pwaɲe/ *n.f.* handle; (*quantité*) handful. ~ de main, handshake.

poignet /pwaɲɛ/ *n.m.* wrist; (*de chemise*) cuff.

poil /pwal/ *n.m.* hair; (*pelage*) fur; (*de brosse*) bristle. ~s, (*de tapis*) pile. à ~, (*fam.*) naked. ~u *a.* hairy.

poinçon /pwɛ̃sɔ̃/ *n.m.* awl; (*marque*) hallmark. ~ner /-ɔne/ *v.t.* (*billet*) punch. ~neuse /-ɔnøz/ *n.f.* punch.

poing /pwɛ̃/ *n.m.* fist.

point¹ /pwɛ̃/ *n.m.* point; (*note: scol.*) mark; (*tache*) spot, dot; (*de couture*) stitch. ~ (final), full stop, period. à ~, (*culin.*) medium; (*arriver*) at the right time. faire le ~, take stock. mettre au ~, (*photo.*) focus; (*technique*) perfect; (*fig.*) clear up. deux ~s, colon. ~ culminant, peak. ~ de repère, landmark. ~s de suspension, suspension points. ~ de suture, (*méd.*) stitch. ~ de vente, retail outlet. ~ de vue, point of view. ~ d'interrogation/d'exclamation, question/exclamation mark. ~ du jour, daybreak. ~ mort, (*auto.*) neutral. ~ virgule, semicolon. sur le ~ de, about to.

point² /pwɛ̃/ *adv.* (ne) ~, not.

pointe /pwɛ̃t/ *n.f.* point, tip; (*clou*) tack; (*de grille*) spike; (*fig.*) touch (de, of). de ~, (*industrie*) highly advanced. en ~, pointed. heure de ~, peak hour. sur la ~ des pieds, on tiptoe.

pointer¹ /pwɛ̃te/ *v.t.* (*cocher*) tick off. ● *v.i.* (*employé*) clock in ou out. se ~ *v. pr.* (*fam.*) turn up.

pointer² /pwɛ̃te/ *v.t.* (*diriger*) point, aim.

pointillé /pwɛ̃tije/ *n.m.* dotted line. ● *a.* dotted.

pointilleu|x, **~se** /pwɛ̃tijø, -z/ *a.* fastidious, particular.

pointu /pwɛ̃ty/ *a.* pointed; (*aiguisé*) sharp.

pointure /pwɛ̃tyr/ *n.f.* size.

poire /pwar/ *n.f.* pear.

poireau (*pl.* ~x) /pwaro/ *n.m.* leek.

poireauter /pwarote/ *v.i.* (*fam.*) hang about.

poirier /pwarje/ *n.m.* pear-tree.

pois /pwa/ *n.m.* pea; (*dessin*) dot.

poison /pwazɔ̃/ *n.m.* poison.

poisseu|x, **~se** /pwasø, -z/ *a.* sticky.

poisson /pwasɔ̃/ *n.m.* fish. ~ rouge, goldfish. ~ d'avril, April fool. les P~s, Pisces.

poissonn|ier, **~ière** /pwasɔnje, -jɛr/ *n.m.*, *f.* fishmonger. ~erie *n.f.* fish shop.

poitrail /pwatraj/ *n.m.* breast.

poitrine /pwatrin/ *n.f.* chest; (*seins*) bosom; (*culin.*) breast.

poivr|e /pwavr/ *n.m.* pepper. ~é *a.* peppery. ~ière *n.f.* pepper-pot.

poivron /pwavrɔ̃/ *n.m.* pepper, capsicum.

poivrot, ~**e** /pwavro, -ɔt/ *n.m.*, *f.*
(*fam.*) drunkard.

poker /pɔkɛr/ *n.m.* poker.

polaire /pɔlɛr/ *a.* polar.

polariser /pɔlarize/ *v.t.* polarize.

polaroïd /pɔlarɔid/ *n.m.* (P.) Polaroid
(P.).

pôle /pol/ *n.m.* pole.

polémique /pɔlemik/ *n.f.* argument.
● *a.* controversial.

poli /pɔli/ *a.* (*personne*) polite.
~**ment** *adv.* politely.

polic|e [1] /pɔlis/ *n.f.* police; (*disci-
pline*) (law and) order. ~**ier,** ~**ière**
a. police; (*roman*) detective; *n.m.*
policeman.

police [2] /pɔlis/ *n.f.* (*d'assurance*) policy.

polio(myélite) /pɔljɔ(mjelit)/ *n.f.* po-
lio(myelitis).

polir /pɔlir/ *v.t.* polish.

polisson, ~**ne** /pɔlisɔ̃, -ɔn/ *a.*
naughty. ● *n.m.*, *f.* rascal.

politesse /pɔlitɛs/ *n.f.* politeness;
(*parole*) polite remark.

politicien, ~**ne** /pɔlitisjɛ̃, -jɛn/ *n.m.*,
f. (*péj.*) politician.

politi|que /pɔlitik/ *a.* political. ● *n.f.*
politics; (*ligne de conduite*) policy.
~**ser** *v.t.* politicize.

pollen /pɔlɛn/ *n.m.* pollen.

polluant, ~**e** /pɔlɥɑ̃, -t/ *a.* polluting.
● *n.m.* pollutant.

poll|uer /pɔlɥe/ *v.t.* pollute. ~**ution**
n.f. pollution.

polo /pɔlo/ *n.m.* polo; (*vêtement*)
sports shirt, tennis shirt.

Pologne /pɔlɔɲ/ *n.f.* Poland.

polonais, ~**e** /pɔlɔnɛ, -z/ *a.* Polish.
● *n.m.*, *f.* Pole. ● *n.m.* (*lang.*) Polish.

poltron, ~**ne** /pɔltrɔ̃, -ɔn/ *a.*
cowardly. ● *n.m.*, *f.* coward.

polycopier /pɔlikɔpje/ *v.t.* duplicate,
stencil.

polygamie /pɔligami/ *n.f.* polygamy.

polyglotte /pɔliglɔt/ *n.m./f.* polyglot.

polyvalent, ~**e** /pɔlivalɑ̃, -t/ *a.* var-
ied; (*personne*) versatile.

pommade /pɔmad/ *n.f.* ointment.

pomme /pɔm/ *n.f.* apple; (*d'arrosoir*)
rose. ~ **d'Adam,** Adam's apple. ~
de pin, pine cone. ~ **de terre,**
potato. ~**s frites,** chips; (*Amer.*)
French fries. **tomber dans les** ~**s,**
(*fam.*) pass out.

pommeau (*pl.* ~**x**) /pɔmo/ *n.m.* (*de
canne*) knob.

pommette /pɔmɛt/ *n.f.* cheek-bone.

pommier /pɔmje/ *n.m.* apple-tree.

pompe /pɔ̃p/ *n.f.* pump; (*splendeur*)
pomp. ~ **à incendie,** fire-engine. ~**s
funèbres,** undertaker's.

pomper /pɔ̃pe/ *v.t.* pump; (*copier*)
(*fam.*) copy, crib. ~ **l'air à qn.,**
(*fam.*) get on s.o.'s nerves.

pompeu|x, ~**se** /pɔ̃pø, -z/ *a.* pom-
pous.

pompier /pɔ̃pje/ *n.m.* fireman.

pompiste /pɔ̃pist/ *n.m./f.* petrol
pump attendant; (*Amer.*) gas station
attendant.

pompon /pɔ̃pɔ̃/ *n.m.* pompon.

pomponner /pɔ̃pɔne/ *v.t.* deck out.

poncer /pɔ̃se/ *v.t.* rub down.

ponctuation /pɔ̃ktɥasjɔ̃/ *n.f.* punc-
tuation.

ponct|uel, ~**uelle** /pɔ̃ktɥɛl/ *a.*
punctual. ~**ualité** *n.f.* punctuality.

ponctuer /pɔ̃ktɥe/ *v.t.* punctuate.

pondéré /pɔ̃dere/ *a.* level-headed.

pondre /pɔ̃dr/ *v.t./i.* lay.

poney /pɔnɛ/ *n.m.* pony.

pont /pɔ̃/ *n.m.* bridge; (*de navire*)
deck; (*de graissage*) ramp. **faire le**
~, take the extra day(s) off (*between
holidays*). ~ **aérien,** airlift. ~**-levis**
(*pl.* ~**s-levis**) *n.m.* drawbridge.

ponte /pɔ̃t/ *n.f.* laying (of eggs).

pontife /pɔ̃tif/ *n.m.* **(souverain)** ~,
pope.

pontific|al (*m. pl.* ~**aux**) /pɔ̃tifikal,
-o/ *a.* papal.

pop /pɔp/ *n.m. & a. invar.* (*mus.*) pop.

popote /pɔpɔt/ *n.f.* (*fam.*) cooking.

populace /pɔpylas/ *n.f.* (*péj.*) rabble.

popul|aire /pɔpylɛr/ *a.* popular; (*ex-
pression*) colloquial; (*quartier, origine*) working-class. ~**arité** *n.f.*
popularity.

population /pɔpylasjɔ̃/ *n.f.* population.

populeu|x, ~**se** /pɔpylø, -z/ *a.* popu-
lous.

porc /pɔr/ *n.m.* pig; (*viande*) pork.

porcelaine /pɔrsəlɛn/ *n.f.* china, porcelain.

porc-épic (*pl.* **porcs-épics**) /pɔrk-
epik/ *n.m.* porcupine.

porche /pɔrʃ/ *n.m.* porch.

porcherie /pɔrʃəri/ *n.f.* pigsty.

por|e /pɔr/ *n.m.* pore. ~**eux,** ~**euse**
a. porous.

pornograph|ie /pɔrnɔgrafi/ *n.f.*
pornography. ~**ique** *a.* porno-
graphic.

port [1] /pɔr/ *n.m.* port, harbour. **à bon**
~, safely. ~ **maritime,** seaport.

port[2] /pɔr/ *n.m.* (*transport*) carriage; (*d'armes*) carrying; (*de barbe*) wearing.

portail /pɔrtaj/ *n.m.* portal.

portant, **~e** /pɔrtɑ̃, -t/ *a.* **bien/mal ~**, in good/bad health.

portati|f, **~ve** /pɔrtatif, -v/ *a.* portable.

porte /pɔrt/ *n.f.* door; (*passage*) doorway; (*de jardin, d'embarquement*) gate. **mettre à la ~**, throw out. **~ d'entrée**, front door. **~- fenêtre** (*pl.* **~s-fenêtres**) *n.f.* French window.

porté /pɔrte/ *a.* **~ à**, inclined to. **~ sur**, fond of.

portée /pɔrte/ *n.f.* (*d'une arme*) range; (*de voûte*) span; (*d'animaux*) litter; (*impact*) significance; (*mus.*) stave. **à ~ de**, within reach of. **à ~ de (la) main**, within (arm's) reach. **hors de ~ (de)**, out of reach (of). **à la ~ de qn.** at s.o.'s level.

portefeuille /pɔrtafœj/ *n.m.* wallet; (*de ministre*) portfolio.

portemanteau (*pl.* **~x**) /pɔrtmɑ̃to/ *n.m.* coat *ou* hat stand.

port|er /pɔrte/ *v.t.* carry; (*vêtement, bague*) wear; (*fruits, responsabilité, nom*) bear; (*coup*) strike; (*amener*) bring; (*inscrire*) enter. ● *v.i.* (*bruit*) carry; (*coup*) hit home. **~er sur**, rest on; (*concerner*) bear on. **se ~er bien**, be *ou* feel well. **se ~er candidat**, stand as a candidate. **~er aux nues**, praise to the skies. **~e-avions** *n.m. invar.* aircraft-carrier. **~e-bagages** *n.m. invar.* luggage rack. **~e-bonheur** *n.m. invar.* (*objet*) charm. **~e-clefs** *n.m. invar.* keyring. **~e-documents** *n.m. invar.* attaché case, document wallet. **~e-monnaie** *n.m. invar.* purse. **~e-parole** *n.m. invar.* spokesman. **~e-voix** *n.m. invar.* megaphone.

porteu|r, **~se** /pɔrtœr, -øz/ *n.m., f.* (*de nouvelles*) bearer; (*méd.*) carrier. ● *n.m.* (*rail.*) porter.

portier /pɔrtje/ *n.m.* door-man.

portière /pɔrtjɛr/ *n.f.* door.

portillon /pɔrtijɔ̃/ *n.m.* gate.

portion /pɔrsjɔ̃/ *n.f.* portion.

portique /pɔrtik/ *n.m.* portico; (*sport*) crossbar.

porto /pɔrto/ *n.m.* port (wine).

portrait /pɔrtrɛ/ *n.m.* portrait. **~-robot** (*pl.* **~s-robots**) *n.m.* identikit, photofit.

portuaire /pɔrtɥɛr/ *a.* port.

portugais, **~e** /pɔrtygɛ, -z/ *a. & n.m., f.* Portuguese. ● *n.m.* (*lang.*) Portuguese.

Portugal /pɔrtygal/ *n.m.* Portugal.

pose /poz/ *n.f.* installation; (*attitude*) pose; (*photo.*) exposure.

posé /poze/ *a.* calm, serious.

poser /poze/ *v.t.* put (down); (*installer*) install, put in; (*fondations*) lay; (*question*) ask; (*problème*) pose. ● *v.i.* (*modèle*) pose. **se ~** *v. pr.* (*avion, oiseau*) land; (*regard*) alight; (*se présenter*) arise. **~ sa candidature**, apply (à, for).

positi|f, **~ve** /pozitif, -v/ *a.* positive.

position /pozisjɔ̃/ *n.f.* position; (*banque*) balance (of account). **prendre ~**, take a stand.

posologie /pozɔlɔʒi/ *n.f.* directions for use.

poss|éder /pɔsede/ *v.t.* possess; (*propriété*) own, possess. **~esseur** *n.m.* possessor; owner.

possessi|f, **~ve** /pɔsesif, -v/ *a.* possessive.

possession /pɔsesjɔ̃/ *n.f.* possession. **prendre ~ de**, take possession of.

possibilité /pɔsibilite/ *n.f.* possibility.

possible /pɔsibl/ *a.* possible. ● *n.m.* **le ~**, what is possible. **dès que ~**, as soon as possible. **faire son ~**, do one's utmost. **le plus tard/etc. ~**, as late/etc. as possible. **pas ~**, impossible! (*int.*) really!

post- /pɔst/ *préf.* post- .

post|al (*m. pl.* **~aux**) /pɔstal, -o/ *a.* postal.

poste[1] /pɔst/ *n.f.* (*service*) post; (*bureau*) post office. **~ aérienne**, airmail. **mettre à la ~**, post. **~ restante**, poste restante.

poste[2] /pɔst/ *n.m.* (*lieu, emploi*) post; (*de radio, télévision*) set; (*téléphone*) extension (number). **~ d'essence**, petrol *ou* gas (*Amer.*) station. **~ d'incendie**, fire point. **~ de pilotage**, cockpit. **~ de police**, police station. **~ de secours**, first-aid post.

poster[1] /pɔste/ *v.t.* (*lettre, personne*) post.

poster[2] /pɔstɛr/ *n.m.* poster.

postérieur /pɔsterjœr/ *a.* later; (*partie*) back. **~ à**, after. ● *n.m.* (*fam.*) posterior.

postérité /pɔsterite/ *n.f.* posterity.

posthume /pɔstym/ *a.* posthumous.

postiche /pɔstiʃ/ *a.* false.

post|ier, **~ière** /postje, -jɛr/ *n.m.*, *f.* postal worker.

post-scriptum /postskriptom/ *n.m. invar.* postscript.

postul|er /postyle/ *v.t./i.* apply (à ou pour, for); (*principe*) postulate. **~ant**, **~ante** *n.m.*, *f.* applicant.

posture /postyr/ *n.f.* posture.

pot /po/ *n.m.* pot; (*en carton*) carton; (*en verre*) jar; (*chance: fam.*) luck; (*boisson: fam.*) drink. **~-au-feu** /potofø/ *n.m. invar.* (*plat*) stew. **~ d'échappement**, exhaust-pipe. **~-de-vin** (*pl.* **~s-de-vin**) *n.m.* bribe. **~-pourri**, (*pl.* **~s-pourris**) *n.m.* pot pourri.

potable /potabl/ *a.* drinkable. **eau ~**, drinking water.

potage /potaʒ/ *n.m.* soup.

potag|er, **~ère** /potaʒe, -ɛr/ *a.* vegetable. ● *n.m.* vegetable garden.

pote /pot/ *n.m.* (*fam.*) chum.

poteau (*pl.* **~x**) /poto/ *n.m.* post; (*télégraphique*) pole. **~ indicateur**, signpost.

potelé /potle/ *a.* plump.

potence /potɑ̃s/ *n.f.* gallows.

potentiel, **~le** /potɑ̃sjɛl/ *a.* & *n.m.* potential.

pot|erie /potri/ *n.f.* pottery; (*objet*) piece of pottery. **~ier** *n.m.* potter.

potins /potɛ̃/ *n.m. pl.* gossip.

potion /posjɔ̃/ *n.f.* potion.

potiron /potirɔ̃/ *n.m.* pumpkin.

pou (*pl.* **~x**) /pu/ *n.m.* louse.

poubelle /pubɛl/ *n.f.* dustbin; (*Amer.*) garbage can.

pouce /pus/ *n.m.* thumb; (*de pied*) big toe; (*mesure*) inch.

poudr|e /pudr/ *n.f.* powder. **~e (à canon**), gunpowder. **en ~e**, (*lait*) powdered; (*chocolat*) drinking. **~er** *v.t.* powder. **~eux**, **~euse** *a.* powdery.

poudrier /pudrije/ *n.m.* (powder) compact.

poudrière /pudrijɛr/ *n.f.* (*région: fig.*) powder-keg.

pouf /puf/ *n.m.* pouffe.

pouffer /pufe/ *v.i.* guffaw.

pouilleu|x, **~se** /pujø, -z/ *a.* filthy.

poulailler /pulaje/ *n.m.* (hen-)coop.

poulain /pulɛ̃/ *n.m.* foal; (*protégé*) protégé.

poule /pul/ *n.f.* hen; (*culin.*) fowl; (*femme: fam.*) tart; (*rugby*) group.

poulet /pulɛ/ *n.m.* chicken.

pouliche /puliʃ/ *n.f.* filly.

poulie /puli/ *n.f.* pulley.

pouls /pu/ *n.m.* pulse.

poumon /pumɔ̃/ *n.m.* lung.

poupe /pup/ *n.f.* stern.

poupée /pupe/ *n.f.* doll.

poupon /pupɔ̃/ *n.m.* baby. **~nière** /-ɔnjɛr/ *n.f.* crèche, day nursery.

pour /pur/ *prép.* for; (*envers*) to; (*à la place de*) on behalf of; (*comme*) as. **~ cela**, for that reason. **~ cent**, per cent. **~ de bon**, for good. **~ faire**, (in order) to do. **~ que**, so that. **~ moi**, as for me. **~ petit/etc. qu'il soit**, however small/*etc.* he may be. **trop poli/etc. ~**, too polite/*etc.* to. **le ~ et le contre**, the pros and cons. **~ ce qui est de**, as for.

pourboire /purbwar/ *n.m.* tip.

pourcentage /pursɑ̃taʒ/ *n.m.* percentage.

pourchasser /purʃase/ *v.t.* pursue.

pourparlers /purparle/ *n.m. pl.* talks.

pourpre /purpr/ *a.* & *n.m.* crimson; (*violet*) purple.

pourquoi /purkwa/ *conj.* & *adv.* why. ● *n.m. invar.* reason.

pourra, **pourrait** /pura, purɛ/ *voir* pouvoir¹.

pourr|ir /purir/ *v.t./i.* rot. **~i** *a.* rotten. **~iture** *n.f.* rot.

poursuite /pursɥit/ *n.f.* pursuit (de, of). **~s**, (*jurid.*) legal action.

poursuiv|re† /pursɥivr/ *v.t.* pursue; (*continuer*) continue (with). **~re (en justice**), (*au criminel*) prosecute; (*au civil*) sue. ● *v.i.*, se **~re** *v. pr.* continue. **~ant**, **~ante** *n.m.*, *f.* pursuer.

pourtant /purtɑ̃/ *adv.* yet.

pourtour /purtur/ *n.m.* perimeter.

pourv|oir† /purvwar/ *v.t.* **~oir de**, provide with. ● *v.i.* **~oir à**, provide for. **~u de**, supplied with. ● *v. pr.* se **~oir de** (*argent*) provide o.s. with. **~oyeur**, **~oyeuse** *n.m.*, *f.* supplier.

pourvu que /purvyk(ə)/ *conj.* (*condition*) provided (that); (*souhait*) let us hope (that). **pourvu qu'il ne soit rien arrivé**, I hope nothing's happened.

pousse /pus/ *n.f.* growth; (*bourgeon*) shoot.

poussé /puse/ *a.* (*études*) advanced.

poussée /puse/ *n.f.* pressure; (*coup*) push; (*de prix*) upsurge; (*méd.*) outbreak.

pousser /puse/ *v.t.* push; (*du coude*) nudge; (*cri*) let out; (*soupir*) heave; (*continuer*) continue; (*exhorter*) urge (**à**, to); (*forcer*) drive (**à**, to); (*amener*) bring (**à**, to). ● *v.i.* push; (*grandir*) grow. **faire ~** (*cheveux*) let grow; (*plante*) grow. **se ~** *v. pr.* move over *ou* up.

poussette /puset/ *n.f.* push-chair; (*Amer.*) (baby) stroller.

poussière /pusjɛr/ *n.f.* dust. **~iéreux, ~iéreuse** *a.* dusty.

poussif, ~ve /pusif, -v/ *a.* short-winded, wheezing.

poussin /pusɛ̃/ *n.m.* chick.

poutre /putr/ *n.f.* beam: (*en métal*) girder.

pouvoir [1]† /puvwar/ *v. aux.* (*possibilité*) can, be able; (*permission, éventualité*) may, can. **il peut/pouvait/pourrait venir,** he can/could/might come. **je n'ai pas pu,** I could not. **j'ai pu faire,** (*réussi à*) I managed to do. **je n'en peux plus,** I am exhausted. **il se peut que,** it may be that.

pouvoir [2] /puvwar/ *n.m.* power; (*gouvernement*) government. **au ~,** in power. **~s publics,** authorities.

prairie /preri/ *n.f.* meadow.

praline /pralin/ *n.f.* sugared almond.

praticable /pratikabl/ *a.* practicable.

praticien, ~ne /pratisjɛ̃, -jɛn/ *n.m., f.* practitioner.

pratiquant, ~e /pratikɑ̃, -t/ *a.* practising. ● *n.m., f.* churchgoer.

pratique /pratik/ *a.* practical. ● *n.f.* practice; (*expérience*) experience. **la ~ du golf/du cheval,** golfing/riding. **~ment** *adv.* in practice; (*presque*) practically.

pratiquer /pratike/ *v.t./i.* practise; (*sport*) play; (*faire*) make.

pré /pre/ *n.m.* meadow.

pré- /pre/ *préf.* pre-.

préalable /prealabl/ *a.* preliminary, prior. ● *n.m.* precondition. **au ~,** first.

préambule /preɑ̃byl/ *n.m.* preamble.

préau (*pl.* **~x**) /preo/ *n.m.* (*scol.*) playground shelter.

préavis /preavi/ *n.m.* (advance) notice.

précaire /prekɛr/ *a.* precarious.

précaution /prekosjɔ̃/ *n.f.* (*mesure*) precaution; (*prudence*) caution.

précédent, ~ente /presedɑ̃, -t/ *a.* previous. ● *n.m.* precedent. **~emment** /-amɑ̃/ *adv.* previously.

précéder /presede/ *v.t./i.* precede.

précepte /presɛpt/ *n.m.* precept.

précepteur, ~trice /preseptœr, -tris/ *n.m., f.* tutor.

prêcher /preʃe/ *v.t./i.* preach.

précieux, ~se /presjø, -z/ *a.* precious.

précipice /presipis/ *n.m.* abyss, chasm.

précipité /presipite/ *a.* hasty. **~amment** *adv.* hastily. **~ation** *n.f.* haste.

précipiter /presipite/ *v.t.* throw, precipitate; (*hâter*) hasten. **se ~** *v. pr.* rush (**sur,** at, on to); (*se jeter*) throw o.s; (*s'accélérer*) speed up.

précis, ~e /presi, -z/ *a.* precise; (*mécanisme*) accurate. ● *n.m.* summary. **dix heures/etc. ~es,** ten o'clock/etc. sharp. **~ément** /-zemɑ̃/ *adv.* precisely.

préciser /presize/ *v.t./i.* specify; (*pensée*) be more specific about. **se ~** *v. pr.* become clear(er).

précision /presizjɔ̃/ *n.f.* precision; (*détail*) detail.

précoce /prekɔs/ *a.* early; (*enfant*) precocious. **~ité** *n.f.* earliness; precociousness.

préconçu /prekɔ̃sy/ *a.* preconceived.

préconiser /prekɔnize/ *v.t.* advocate.

précurseur /prekyrsœr/ *n.m.* forerunner.

prédécesseur /predesesœr/ *n.m.* predecessor.

prédicateur /predikatœr/ *n.m.* preacher.

prédilection /predilɛksjɔ̃/ *n.f.* preference.

prédire† /predir/ *v.t.* predict. **~iction** *n.f.* prediction.

prédisposer /predispoze/ *v.t.* predispose.

prédominant, ~e /predɔminɑ̃, -t/ *a.* predominant.

prédominer /predɔmine/ *v.i.* predominate.

préfabriqué /prefabrike/ *a.* prefabricated.

préface /prefas/ *n.f.* preface.

préfecture /prefɛktyr/ *n.f.* prefecture. **~ de police,** police headquarters.

préférence /preferɑ̃s/ *n.f.* preference. **de ~,** preferably. **de ~ à,** in preference to.

préférentiel, ~le /preferɑ̃sjɛl/ *a.* preferential.

préférer /prefere/ *v.t.* prefer (**à,** to). **je ne préfère pas,** I'd rather not. **~er faire,** prefer to do. **~able** *a.* preferable. **~é, ~ée** *a. & n.m., f.* favourite.

préfet /prefε/ *n.m.* prefect. ~ **de police**, prefect *ou* chief of police.

préfixe /prefiks/ *n.m.* prefix.

préhistorique /preistɔrik/ *a.* prehistoric.

préjudic|e /preʒydis/ *n.m.* harm, prejudice. **porter** ~ **e à**, harm. ~**iable** *a.* harmful.

préjugé /preʒyʒe/ *n.m.* prejudice. **avoir un** ~ **contre**, be prejudiced against. **sans** ~**s**, without prejudices.

préjuger /preʒyʒe/ *v.i.* ~ **de**, prejudge.

prélasser (se) /(sə)prelɑse/ *v. pr.* loll (about).

prél|ever /prelve/ *v.t.* deduct (**sur**, from); (*sang*) take. ~**èvement** *n.m.* deduction. ~**èvement de sang**, blood sample.

préliminaire /preliminεr/ *a. & n.m.* preliminary. ~**s**, (*sexuels*) foreplay.

prélude /prelyd/ *n.m.* prelude.

prématuré /prematyre/ *a.* premature. ● *n.m.* premature baby.

prémédit|er /premedite/ *v.t.* premeditate. ~**ation** *n.f.* premeditation.

prem|ier, ~**ière** /prəmje, -jεr/ *a.* first; (*rang*) front, first; (*enfance*) early; (*nécessité, souci*) prime; (*qualité*) top, prime; (*état*) original. ● *n.m.*, *f.* first (one). ● *n.m.* (*date*) first; (*étage*) first floor. ● *n.f.* (*rail.*) first class; (*exploit jamais vu*) first; (*cinéma, théâtre*) première. **de** ~**ier ordre**, first-rate. **en** ~**ier**, first. ~**ier jet**, first draft. ~**ier ministre**, Prime Minister.

premièrement /prəmjεrmɑ̃/ *adv.* firstly.

prémisse /premis/ *n.f.* premiss.

prémonition /premɔnisjɔ̃/ *n.f.* premonition.

prémunir /premynir/ *v.t.* protect (**contre**, against).

prenant, ~**e** /prənɑ̃, -t/ *a.* (*activité*) engrossing; (*enfant*) demanding.

prénatal (*m. pl.* ~**s**) /prenatal/ *a.* antenatal; (*Amer.*) prenatal.

prendre† /prɑ̃dr/ *v.t.* take; (*attraper*) catch, get; (*acheter*) get; (*repas*) have; (*engager, adopter*) take on; (*poids*) put on; (*chercher*) pick up; (*panique, colère*) take hold of. ● *v.i.* (*liquide*) set; (*feu*) catch; (*vaccin*) take. **se** ~ **pour**, think one is. **s'en** ~ **à**, attack; (*rendre responsable*) blame. **s'y** ~, set about (it).

preneu|r, ~**se** /prənœr, -øz/ *n.m.*, *f.* buyer. **être** ~**r**, be willing to buy. **trouver** ~**r**, find a buyer.

prénom /prenɔ̃/ *n.m.* first name. ~**mer** /-ɔme/ *v.t.* call. **se** ~**mer** *v. pr.* be called.

préoccup|er /preɔkype/ *v.t.* worry; (*absorber*) preoccupy. **se** ~**er de**, be worried about; be preoccupied about. ~**ation** *n.f.* worry; (*idée fixe*) preoccupation.

préparatifs /preparatif/ *n.m. pl.* preparations.

préparatoire /preparatwar/ *a.* preparatory.

prépar|er /prepare/ *v.t.* prepare; (*repas, café*) make. **se** ~**er** *v. pr.* prepare o.s.; (*être proche*) be brewing. ~**er à qn.**, (*surprise*) have (got) in store for s.o. ~**ation** *n.f.* preparation.

prépondéran|t, ~**te** /prepɔ̃derɑ̃, -t/ *a.* dominant. ~**ce** *n.f.* dominance.

prépos|er /prepoze/ *v.t.* put in charge (**à**, of). ~**é**, ~**ée** *n.m.*, *f.* employee; (*des postes*) postman, postwoman.

préposition /prepozisjɔ̃/ *n.f.* preposition.

préretraite /prerətrεt/ *n.f.* early retirement.

prérogative /prerɔgativ/ *n.f.* prerogative.

près /prε/ *adv.* near, close. ~ **de**, near (to), close to; (*presque*) nearly. **à cela** ~, apart from that. **de** ~, closely.

présag|e /prezaʒ/ *n.m.* foreboding, omen. ~**er** *v.t.* forebode.

presbyte /presbit/ *a.* long-sighted, far-sighted.

presbytère /presbitεr/ *n.m.* presbytery.

prescr|ire† /preskrir/ *v.t.* introduce. ~**iption** *n.f.* prescription.

préséance /preseɑ̃s/ *n.f.* precedence.

présence /prezɑ̃s/ *n.f.* presence; (*scol.*) attendance.

présent, ~**e** /prezɑ̃, -t/ *a.* present. ● *n.m.* (*temps, cadeau*) present. **à** ~, now.

présent|er /prezɑ̃te/ *v.t.* present; (*personne*) introduce (**à**, to); (*montrer*) show. **se** ~**er** *v. pr.* introduce o.s. (**à**, to); (*aller*) go; (*apparaître*) appear; (*candidat*) come forward; (*occasion etc.*) arise. ~**er bien**, have a pleasing appearance. **se** ~**er à**, (*examen*) sit for; (*élection*) stand for. **se** ~**er bien**, look good. ~**able** *a.* presentable. ~**ateur**, ~**atrice** *n.m.*,

f. presenter. **~ation** *n.f.* presentation; introduction.
préservatif /prezɛrvatif/ *n.m.* condom.
préserv|er /prezɛrve/ *v.t.* protect. **~ation** *n.f.* protection, preservation.
présiden|t, ~te /prezidɑ̃, -t/ *n.m., f.* president; (*de firme, comité*) chairman, chairwoman. **~t directeur général,** managing director. **~ce** *n.f.* presidency; chairmanship.
présidentiel, ~le /prezidɑ̃sjɛl/ *a.* presidential.
présider /prezide/ *v.t.* preside over. ● *v.i.* preside.
présomption /prezɔ̃psjɔ̃/ *n.f.* presumption.
présomptueu|x, ~se /prezɔ̃ptɥø, -z/ *a.* presumptuous.
presque /prɛsk(ə)/ *adv.* almost, nearly. **~ jamais,** hardly ever. **~ rien,** hardly anything. **~ pas (de),** hardly any.
presqu'île /prɛskil/ *n.f.* peninsula.
pressant, ~e /presɑ̃, -t/ *a.* pressing, urgent.
presse /prɛs/ *n.f.* (*journaux, appareil*) press.
pressent|ir /presɑ̃tir/ *v.t.* sense. **~iment** *n.m.* presentiment.
press|er /prese/ *v.t.* squeeze, press; (*appuyer sur, harceler*) press; (*hâter*) hasten; (*inciter*) urge (**de,** to). ● *v.i.* (*temps*) press; (*affaire*) be pressing. **se ~er** *v. pr.* (*se hâter*) hurry; (*se grouper*) crowd. **~é a.** in a hurry; (*orange, citron*) freshly squeezed. **~e-papiers** *n.m. invar.* paperweight.
pressing /presiŋ/ *n.m.* (*magasin*) dry-cleaner's.
pression /presjɔ̃/ *n.f.* pressure. ● *n.m./f.* (*bouton*) press-stud; (*Amer.*) snap.
pressoir /preswar/ *n.m.* press.
pressuriser /presyrize/ *v.t.* pressurize.
prestance /prɛstɑ̃s/ *n.f.* (imposing) presence.
prestation /prɛstasjɔ̃/ *n.f.* allowance; (*d'artiste etc.*) performance.
prestidigita|teur, ~trice /prɛstidiʒitatœr, -tris/ *n.m., f.* conjuror. **~tion** /-asjɔ̃/ *n.f.* conjuring.
prestig|e /prɛstiʒ/ *n.m.* prestige. **~ieux, ~ieuse** *a.* prestigious.
présumer /prezyme/ *v.t.* presume. **~ que,** assume that. **~ de,** overrate.

prêt¹, ~e /prɛ, -t/ *a.* ready (**à qch.,** for sth., **à faire,** to do). **~-à-porter** /prɛ(t)aporte/ *n.m. invar.* ready-to-wear clothes.
prêt² /prɛ/ *n.m.* loan.
prétendant /pretɑ̃dɑ̃/ *n.m.* (*amoureux*) suitor.
prétend|re /pretɑ̃dr/ *v.t.* claim (**que,** that); (*vouloir*) intend. **~re qn. riche/etc.,** claim that s.o. is rich/*etc.* **~u a.** so-called. **~ument** *adv.* supposedly, allegedly.
prétent|ieux, ~ieuse /pretɑ̃sjø, -z/ *a.* pretentious. **~ion** *n.f.* pretentiousness; (*exigence*) claim.
prêt|er /prete/ *v.t.* lend (**à,** to); (*attribuer*) attribute. ● *v.i.* **~er à,** lead to. **~er attention,** pay attention. **~er serment,** take an oath. **~eur, ~euse** /pretœr, -øz/ *n.m., f.* (money-)lender. **~eur sur gages,** pawnbroker.
prétext|e /pretɛkst/ *n.m.* pretext, excuse. **~er** *v.t.* plead.
prêtre /prɛtr/ *n.m.* priest.
prêtrise /pretriz/ *n.f.* priesthood.
preuve /prœv/ *n.f.* proof. **faire ~ de,** show. **faire ses ~s,** prove one's *ou* its worth.
prévaloir /prevalwar/ *v.i.* prevail.
prévenan|t, ~te /prevnɑ̃, -t/ *a.* thoughtful. **~ce(s)** *n.f. (pl.)* thoughtfulness.
prévenir† /prevnir/ *v.t.* (*menacer*) warn; (*informer*) tell; (*éviter, anticiper*) forestall.
préventi|f, ~ve /prevɑ̃tif, -v/ *a.* preventive.
prévention /prevɑ̃sjɔ̃/ *n.f.* prevention; (*préjuge*) prejudice. **~ routière,** road safety.
prévenu, ~e /prevny/ *n.m., f.* defendant.
prév|oir† /prevwar/ *v.t.* foresee; (*temps*) forecast; (*organiser*) plan (for), provide for; (*envisager*) allow (for). **~u pour,** (*jouet etc.*) designed for. **~isible** *a.* foreseeable. **~ision** *n.f.* prediction; (*météorologique*) forecast.
prévoyan|t, ~te /prevwajɑ̃, -t/ *a.* showing foresight. **~ce** *n.f.* foresight.
prier /prije/ *v.i.* pray. ● *v.t.* pray to; (*implorer*) beg (**de,** to); (*demander à*) ask (**de,** to). **je vous en prie,**

please; (*il n'y a pas de quoi*) don't mention it.

prière /prijɛr/ *n.f.* prayer; (*demande*) request. **~ de**, (*vous êtes prié de*) will you please.

primaire /primɛr/ *a.* primary.

primauté /primote/ *n.f.* primacy.

prime /prim/ *n.f.* free gift; (*d'employé*) bonus; (*subvention*) subsidy; (*d'assurance*) premium.

primé /prime/ *a.* prize-winning.

primer /prime/ *v.t./i.* excel.

primeurs /primœr/ *n.f. pl.* early fruit and vegetables.

primevère /primvɛr/ *n.f.* primrose.

primiti|f, **~ve** /primitif, -v/ *a.* primitive; (*originel*) original. ● *n.m.*, *f.* primitive.

primord|ial (*m. pl.* **~iaux**) /primɔrdjal, -jo/ *a.* essential.

princ|e /prɛ̃s/ *n.m.* prince. **~esse** *n.f.* princess. **~ier**, **~ière** *a.* princely.

princip|al (*m. pl.* **~aux**) /prɛ̃sipal, -o/ *a.* main, principal. ● *n.m.* (*pl.* **~aux**) headmaster; (*chose*) main thing. **~alement** *adv.* mainly.

principauté /prɛ̃sipote/ *n.f.* principality.

principe /prɛ̃sip/ *n.m.* principle. **en ~**, theoretically; (*d'habitude*) as a rule.

printan|ier, **~ière** /prɛ̃tanje, -jɛr/ *a.* spring(-like).

printemps /prɛ̃tɑ̃/ *n.m.* spring.

priorit|é /prijɔrite/ *n.f.* priority; (*auto.*) right of way. **~aire** *a.* priority. **être ~aire**, have priority.

pris, **~e**[1] /pri, -z/ *voir* prendre. ● *a.* (*place*) taken; (*personne*, *journée*) busy; (*gorge*) infected. **~ de**, (*peur*, *fièvre*, *etc.*) stricken with. **~ de panique**, panic-stricken.

prise /priz/ *n.f.* hold, grip; (*animal etc. attrapé*) catch; (*mil.*) capture. **~ (de courant)**, (*mâle*) plug; (*femelle*) socket. **aux ~s avec**, at grips with. **~ de conscience**, awareness. **~ de contact**, first contact; initial meeting. **~ de position**, stand. **~ de sang**, blood test.

priser /prize/ *v.t.* (*estimer*) prize.

prisme /prism/ *n.m.* prism.

prison /prizɔ̃/ *n.f.* prison, gaol, jail; (*réclusion*) imprisonment. **~nier**, **~nière** /-ɔnje, -jɛr/ *n.m.*, *f.* prisoner.

privé /prive/ *a.* private. ● *n.m.* (*comm.*) private sector. **en ~**, **dans le ~**, in private.

priv|er /prive/ *v.t.* **~er de**, deprive of. **se ~er de**, go without. **~ation** *n.f.* deprivation; (*sacrifice*) hardship.

privil|ège /privilɛʒ/ *n.m.* privilege. **~égié**, **~égiée** *a.* & *n.m.*, *f.* privileged (person).

prix /pri/ *n.m.* price; (*récompense*) prize. **à tout ~**, at all costs. **au ~ de**, (*fig.*) at the expense of. **~ coûtant**, **~ de revient**, cost price. **à ~ fixe**, set price.

pro- /prɔ/ *préf.* pro-.

probab|le /prɔbabl/ *a.* probable, likely. **~ilité** *n.f.* probability. **~lement** *adv.* probably.

probant, **~e** /prɔbɑ̃, -t/ *a.* convincing, conclusive.

probité /prɔbite/ *n.f.* integrity.

problème /prɔblɛm/ *n.m.* problem.

procéd|er /prɔsede/ *v.i.* proceed. **~er à**, carry out. **~é** *n.m.* process; (*conduite*) behaviour.

procédure /prɔsedyr/ *n.f.* procedure.

procès /prɔsɛ/ *n.m.* (*criminel*) trial; (*civil*) lawsuit, proceedings. **~-verbal** (*pl.* **~-verbaux**) *n.m.* report; (*contravention*) ticket.

procession /prɔsesjɔ̃/ *n.f.* procession.

processus /prɔsesys/ *n.m.* process.

prochain, **~e** /prɔʃɛ̃, -ɛn/ *a.* (*suivant*) next; (*proche*) imminent; (*avenir*) near. **je descends à la ~e**, I'm getting off at the next stop. ● *n.m.* fellow. **~ement** /-ɛnmɑ̃/ *adv.* soon.

proche /prɔʃ/ *a.* near, close; (*avoisinant*) neighbouring; (*parent*, *ami*) close. **~ de**, close *ou* near to. **de ~ en proche**, gradually. **dans un ~ avenir**, in the near future. **être ~**, (*imminent*) be approaching. **~s** *n.m. pl.* close relations. **P~-Orient** *n.m.* Near East.

proclam|er /prɔklame/ *v.t.* declare, proclaim. **~ation** *n.f.* declaration, proclamation.

procréation /prɔkreasjɔ̃/ *n.f.* procreation.

procuration /prɔkyrasjɔ̃/ *n.f.* proxy.

procurer /prɔkyre/ *v.t.* bring (à, to). **se ~** *v. pr.* obtain.

procureur /prɔkyrœr/ *n.m.* public prosecutor.

prodig|e /prɔdiʒ/ *n.m.* marvel; (*personne*) prodigy. **enfant/musicien ~e**, child/musical prodigy. **~ieux**, **~ieuse** *a.* tremendous, prodigious.

prodigu|e /prɔdig/ *a.* wasteful. **fils ~e**, prodigal son. **~er** *v.t.* **~er à**, lavish on.

producti|f, **~ve** /prɔdyktif, -v/ *a.*
productive. **~vité** *n.f.* productivity.

prod|uire† /prɔdɥir/ *v.t.* produce. **se
~uire** *v. pr.* (*survenir*) happen;
(*acteur*) perform. **~ucteur,
~uctrice** *a.* producing; *n.m., f.*
producer. **~uction** *n.f.* production;
(*produit*) product.

produit /prɔdɥi/ *n.m.* product. **~s,**
(*de la terre*) produce. **~ chimique,**
chemical. **~s alimentaires,** foodstuffs. **~ de consommation,** consumer goods. **~ national brut,** gross
national product.

proéminent, **~e** /prɔeminã, -t/ *a.*
prominent.

prof /prɔf/ *n.m.* (*fam.*) teacher.

profane /prɔfan/ *a.* secular. ● *n.m./
f.* lay person.

profaner /prɔfane/ *v.t.* desecrate.

proférer /prɔfere/ *v.t.* utter.

professer[1] /prɔfese/ *v.t.* (*déclarer*)
profess.

professer[2] /prɔfese/ *v.t./i.* (*enseigner*) teach.

professeur /prɔfesœr/ *n.m.* teacher;
(*univ.*) lecturer; (*avec chaire*) professor.

profession /prɔfesjɔ̃/ *n.f.* occupation;
(*intellectuelle*) profession. **~nel,
~nelle** /-jɔnɛl/ *a.* professional;
(*école*) vocational; *n.m., f.* professional.

professorat /prɔfesɔra/ *n.m.* teaching.

profil /prɔfil/ *n.m.* profile.

profiler (se) /(sə)prɔfile/ *v. pr.* be
outlined.

profit /prɔfi/ *n.m.* profit. **au ~ de,** in
aid of. **~able** /-tabl/ *a.* profitable.

profiter /prɔfite/ *v.i.* **~ à,** benefit. **~
de,** take advantage of.

profond, **~e** /prɔfɔ̃, -d/ *a.* deep;
(*sentiment, intérêt*) profound;
(*causes*) underlying. **au plus ~ de,**
in the depths of. **~ément** /-demã/
adv. deeply; (*différent, triste*) pro-
foundly; (*dormir*) soundly. **~eur**
/-dœr/ *n.f.* depth.

profusion /prɔfyzjɔ̃/ *n.f.* profusion.

progéniture /prɔʒenityr/ *n.f.* offspring.

programmation /prɔgramɑsjɔ̃/ *n.f.*
programming.

programm|e /prɔgram/ *n.m.* pro-
gramme; (*matières: scol.*) syllabus;
(*informatique*) program;
(d'études), curriculum. **~er** *v.t.*
(*ordinateur, appareil*) program;

(*émission*) schedule. **~eur, ~euse**
n.m., f. computer programmer.

progrès /prɔgrɛ/ *n.m. & n.m. pl.*
progress. **faire des ~,** make progress.

progress|er /prɔgrese/ *v.i.* progress.
~ion /-ɛsjɔ̃/ *n.f.* progression.

progressi|f, **~ve** /prɔgresif, -v/ *a.*
progressive. **~vement** *adv.* progressively.

progressiste /prɔgresist/ *a.* progressive.

prohib|er /prɔibe/ *v.t.* prohibit.
~ition *n.f.* prohibition.

prohibiti|f, **~ve** /prɔibitif, -v/ *a.*
prohibitive.

proie /prwa/ *n.f.* prey. **en ~ à,**
tormented by.

projecteur /prɔʒɛktœr/ *n.m.* floodlight; (*mil.*) searchlight; (*cinéma*)
projector.

projectile /prɔʒɛktil/ *n.m.* missile.

projection /prɔʒɛksjɔ̃/ *n.f.* projection; (*séance*) show.

projet /prɔʒɛ/ *n.m.* plan; (*ébauche*)
draft. **~ de loi,** bill.

projeter /prɔʒte/ *v.t.* plan (**de,** to);
(*film*) project, show; (*jeter*) hurl,
project.

prolét|aire /prɔletɛr/ *n.m./f.* pro-
letarian. **~ariat** *n.m.* proletariat.
~arien, ~arienne *a.* proletarian.

prolifér|er /prɔlifere/ *v.i.* proliferate.
~ation *n.f.* proliferation.

prolifique /prɔlifik/ *a.* prolific.

prologue /prɔlɔg/ *n.m.* prologue.

prolongation /prɔlɔ̃gɑsjɔ̃/ *n.f.*
extension. **~s,** (*football*) extra time.

prolong|er /prɔlɔ̃ʒe/ *v.t.* prolong. **se
~er** *v. pr.* continue, extend. **~é** *a.*
prolonged. **~ement** *n.m.* extension.

promenade /prɔmnad/ *n.f.* walk; (*à
bicyclette, à cheval*) ride; (*en auto*)
drive, ride. **faire une ~,** go for a
walk.

promen|er /prɔmne/ *v.t.* take for a
walk. **~er sur qch.,** (*main, regard*)
run over sth. **se ~er** *v. pr.* walk.
(**aller) se ~er,** go for a walk. **~eur,
~euse** *n.m., f.* walker.

promesse /prɔmɛs/ *n.f.* promise.

prome|ttre† /prɔmɛtr/ *v.t./i.* prom-
ise. **~re (beaucoup),** be promising.
se ~re de, resolve to. **~eur, ~euse**
a. promising.

promontoire /prɔmɔ̃twar/ *n.m.*
headland.

promoteur /prɔmɔtœr/ *n.m.* (*immobilier*) property developer.

prom|ouvoir /prɔmuvwar/ *v.t.* promote. **être ~u,** be promoted. **~otion** *n.f.* promotion; (*univ.*) year; (*comm.*) special offer.

prompt, ~e /prɔ̃, -t/ *a.* swift.

prôner /prone/ *v.t.* extol; (*préconiser*) preach, advocate.

pronom /prɔnɔ̃/ *n.m.* pronoun. **~inal** (*m. pl.* **~inaux**) /-ɔminal, -o/ *a.* pronominal.

prononc|er /prɔnɔ̃se/ *v.t.* pronounce; (*discours*) make. **se ~er** *v. pr.* (*mot*) be pronounced; (*personne*) make a decision (**pour,** in favour of). **~é** *a.* pronounced. **~iation** *n.f.* pronunciation.

pronosti|c /prɔnɔstik/ *n.m.* forecast; (*méd.*) prognosis. **~quer** *v.t.* forecast.

propagande /prɔpagɑ̃d/ *n.f.* propaganda.

propag|er /prɔpaʒe/ *v.t.,* **se ~er** *v. pr.* spread. **~ation** /-gasjɔ̃/ *n.f.* spread (-ing).

proph|ète /prɔfɛt/ *n.m.* prophet. **~étie** /-esi/ *n.f.* prophecy. **~étique** *a.* prophetic. **~étiser** *v.t./i.* prophesy.

propice /prɔpis/ *a.* favourable.

proportion /prɔpɔrsjɔ̃/ *n.f.* proportion; (*en mathématiques*) ratio. **toutes ~s gardées,** making appropriate allowances. **~né** /-jɔne/ *a.* proportionate (**à,** to). **~nel, ~nelle** /-jɔnɛl/ *a.* proportional. **~ner** /-jɔne/ *v.t.* proportion.

propos /prɔpo/ *n.m.* intention; (*sujet*) subject. ● *n.m. pl.* (*paroles*) remarks. **à ~,** at the right time; (*dans un dialogue*) by the way. **à ~ de,** about. **à tout ~,** at every possible occasion.

propos|er /prɔpoze/ *v.t.* propose; (*offrir*) offer. **se ~er** *v. pr.* volunteer (**pour,** to); (*but*) set o.s. **se ~er de faire,** propose to do. **~ition** *n.f.* proposal; (*affirmation*) proposition; (*gram.*) clause.

propre[1] /prɔpr/ *a.* clean; (*soigné*) neat; (*honnête*) decent. **mettre au ~,** write out again neatly. **c'est du ~!** (*ironique*) well done! **~ment**[1] /-əmɑ̃/ *adv.* cleanly; neatly; decently.

propre[2] /prɔpr/ *a.* (*à soi*) own; (*sens*) literal. **~ à,** (*qui convient*) peculiar to; (*spécifique*) peculiar to. **~-à-rien** *n.m./f.* good-for-nothing. **~ment**[2] /-əmɑ̃/ *adv.* strictly. **le bureau/*etc.* ~ment dit,** the office/*etc.* itself.

propreté /prɔprəte/ *n.f.* cleanliness; (*netteté*) neatness.

propriétaire /prɔprijetɛr/ *n.m./f.* owner; (*comm.*) proprietor; (*qui loue*) landlord, landlady.

propriété /prɔprijete/ *n.f.* property; (*droit*) ownership.

propuls|er /prɔpylse/ *v.t.* propel. **~ion** *n.f.* propulsion.

prorata /prɔrata/ *n.m. invar.* **au ~ de,** in proportion to.

proroger /prɔrɔʒe/ *v.t.* (*contrat*) defer; (*passeport*) extend.

prosaïque /prozaik/ *a.* prosaic.

proscr|ire /prɔskrir/ *v.t.* proscribe. **~it, ~ite** *a.* proscribed; *n.m., f.* (*exilé*) exile.

prose /proz/ *n.f.* prose.

prospec|ter /prɔspɛkte/ *v.t.* prospect. **~teur, ~trice** *n.m., f.* prospector. **~tion** /-ksjɔ̃/ *n.f.* prospecting.

prospectus /prɔspɛktys/ *n.m.* leaflet.

prosp|ère /prɔspɛr/ *a.* flourishing, thriving. **~érer** *v.i.* thrive, prosper. **~érité** *n.f.* prosperity.

prostern|er (se) /(sə)prɔstɛrne/ *v. pr.* bow down. **~é** *a.* prostrate.

prostit|uée /prɔstitɥe/ *n.f.* prostitute. **~ution** *n.f.* prostitution.

prostré /prɔstre/ *a.* prostrate.

protagoniste /prɔtagɔnist/ *n.m.* protagonist.

protec|teur, ~trice /prɔtɛktœr, -tris/ *n.m., f.* protector. ● *a.* protective.

protection /prɔtɛksjɔ̃/ *n.f.* protection; (*fig.*) patronage.

protég|er /prɔteʒe/ *v.t.* protect; (*fig.*) patronize. **se ~er** *v. pr.* protect o.s. **~é** *n.m.* protégé. **~ée** *n.f.* protégée.

protéine /prɔtein/ *n.f.* protein.

protestant, ~e /prɔtɛstɑ̃, -t/ *a. & n.m., f.* Protestant.

protest|er /prɔtɛste/ *v.t./i.* protest. **~ation** *n.f.* protest.

protocole /prɔtɔkɔl/ *n.m.* protocol.

prototype /prɔtɔtip/ *n.m.* prototype.

protubéran|t, ~te /prɔtyberɑ̃, -t/ *a.* bulging. **~ce,** *n.f.* protuberance.

proue /pru/ *n.f.* bow, prow.

prouesse /prues/ *n.f.* feat, exploit.

prouver /pruve/ *v.t.* prove.

provenance /prɔvnɑ̃s/ *n.f.* origin. **en ~ de,** from.

provenç|al, ~ale (*m. pl.* **~aux**) /prɔvɑ̃sal, -o/ *a. & n.m., f.* Provençal.

Provence /prɔvɑ̃s/ *n.f.* Provence.

provenir† /prɔvnir/ v.i. ~ **de**, come from.

proverb|e /prɔvɛrb/ n.m. proverb. ~**ial** (m. pl. ~**iaux**) a. proverbial.

providence /prɔvidɑ̃s/ n.f. providence.

provinc|e /prɔvɛ̃s/ n.f. province. **de** ~**e**, provincial. **la** ~**e**, the provinces. ~**ial**, ~**iale** (m. pl. ~**iaux**) a. & n.m., f. provincial.

proviseur /prɔvizœr/ n.m. headmaster, principal.

provision /prɔvizjɔ̃/ n.f. supply, store; (dans un compte) funds; (acompte) deposit. ~**s**, (vivres) provisions. **panier à** ~**s**, shopping basket.

provisoire /prɔvizwar/ a. temporary. ~**ment** adv. temporarily.

provo|quer /prɔvɔke/ v.t. cause; (exciter) arouse; (défier) provoke. ~**cant**, ~**cante** a. provocative. ~**cation** n.f. provocation.

proximité /prɔksimite/ n.f. proximity. **à** ~ **de**, close to.

prude /pryd/ a. prudish. ● n.f. prude.

prud|ent, ~**ente** /prydɑ̃, -t/ a. cautious; (sage) wise. **soyez** ~**ent**, be careful. ~**emment** /-amɑ̃/ adv. cautiously; wisely. ~**ence** n.f. caution; wisdom.

prune /pryn/ n.f. plum.

pruneau (pl. ~**x**) /pryno/ n.m. prune.

prunelle[1] /prynɛl/ n.f. (pupille) pupil.

prunelle[2] /prynɛl/ n.f. (fruit) sloe.

psaume /psom/ n.m. psalm.

pseudo- /psødɔ/ préf. pseudo-.

pseudonyme /psødɔnim/ n.m. pseudonym.

psychanalys|e /psikanaliz/ n.f. psychoanalysis. ~**er** v.t. psychoanalyse. ~**te** /-st/ n.m./f. psychoanalyst.

psychiatr|e /psikjatr/ n.m./f. psychiatrist. ~**ie** n.f. psychiatry. ~**ique** a. psychiatric.

psychique /psiʃik/ a. mental, psychological.

psycholo|gie /psikɔlɔʒi/ n.f. psychology. ~**gique** a. psychological. ~**gue** n.m./f. psychologist.

psychosomatique /psikɔsɔmatik/ a. psychosomatic.

psychothérapie /psikɔterapi/ n.f. psychotherapy.

PTT abrév. (Postes, Télécommunications et Télédiffusion) Post Office.

pu /py/ voir **pouvoir**[1].

puant, ~**e** /pɥɑ̃, -t/ a. stinking. ~**eur** /-tœr/ n.f. stink.

pub /pyb/ n.f. **la** ~, advertising. **une** ~, an advert.

puberté /pybɛrte/ n.f. puberty.

publi|c, ~**que** /pyblik/ a. public. ● n.m. public; (assistance) audience. **en** ~**c**, in public.

publicit|é /pyblisite/ n.f. publicity, advertising; (annonce) advertisement. ~**aire** a. publicity.

publ|ier /pyblije/ v.t. publish. ~**ication** n.f. publication.

publiquement /pyblikmɑ̃/ adv. publicly.

puce[1] /pys/ n.f. flea. **marché aux** ~**s**, flea market.

puce[2] /pys/ n.f. (électronique) chip.

pud|eur /pydœr/ n.f. modesty. ~**ique** a. modest.

pudibond, ~**e** /pydibɔ̃, -d/ a. prudish.

puer /pɥe/ v.i. stink. ● v.t. stink of.

puéricultrice /pɥerikyltris/ n.f. children's nurse.

puéril /pɥeril/ a. puerile.

pugilat /pyʒila/ n.m. fight.

puis /pɥi/ adv. then.

puiser /pɥize/ v.t. draw (**qch. dans**, sth. from). ● v.i. ~ **dans qch.**, dip into sth.

puisque /pɥisk(ə)/ conj. since, as.

puissance /pɥisɑ̃s/ n.f. power. **en** ~ a. potential; adv. potentially.

puiss|ant, ~**ante** /pɥisɑ̃, -t/ a. powerful. ~**amment** adv. powerfully.

puits /pɥi/ n.m. well; (de mine) shaft.

pull(-over) /pyl(ɔvɛr)/ n.m. pullover, jumper.

pulpe /pylp/ n.f. pulp.

pulsation /pylsasjɔ̃/ n.f. (heart-)beat.

pulvéris|er /pylverize/ v.t. pulverize; (liquide) spray. ~**ateur** n.m. spray.

punaise /pynɛz/ n.f. (insecte) bug; (clou) drawing-pin; (Amer.) thumbtack.

punch[1] /pɔ̃ʃ/ n.m. punch.

punch[2] /pœnʃ/ n.m. **avoir du** ~, have drive.

pun|ir /pynir/ v.t. punish. ~**ition** n.f. punishment.

punk /pœnk/ a. invar. punk.

pupille[1] /pypij/ n.f. (de l'œil) pupil.

pupille[2] /pypij/ n.m./f. (enfant) ward.

pupitre /pypitr/ *n.m.* (*scol.*) desk. ~ à musique, music stand.

pur /pyr/ *a.* pure; (*whisky*) neat. ~**ement** *adv.* purely. ~**eté** *n.f.* purity. ~**-sang** *n.m. invar.* (*cheval*) thoroughbred.

purée /pyre/ *n.f.* purée; (*de pommes de terre*) mashed potatoes.

purgatoire /pyrgatwar/ *n.m.* purgatory.

purg|e /pyrʒ/ *n.f.* purge. ~**er** *v.t.* (*pol., méd.*) purge; (*peine: jurid.*) serve.

purif|ier /pyrifje/ *v.t.* purify. ~**ication** *n.f.* purification.

purin /pyrɛ̃/ *n.m.* (liquid) manure.

puritain, ~e /pyritɛ̃, -ɛn/ *n.m., f.* puritan. ● *a.* puritanical.

pus /py/ *n.m.* pus.

pustule /pystyl/ *n.f.* pimple.

putain /pytɛ̃/ *n.f.* (*fam.*) whore.

putréfier (se) /(sə)pytrefje/ *v. pr.* putrefy.

putsch /putʃ/ *n.m.* putsch.

puzzle /pœzl/ *n.m.* jigsaw (puzzle).

P-V *abrév.* (*procès-verbal*) ticket, traffic fine.

pygmée /pigme/ *n.m.* pygmy.

pyjama /piʒama/ *n.m.* pyjamas. **un ~**, a pair of pyjamas.

pylône /pilon/ *n.m.* pylon.

pyramide /piramid/ *n.f.* pyramid.

Pyrénées /pirene/ *n.f. pl.* **les ~**, the Pyrenees.

pyromane /piromane/ *n.m./f.* arsonist.

Q

QG *abrév.* (*quartier général*) HQ.

QI *abrév.* (*quotient intellectuel*) IQ.

qu' /k/ *voir* que.

quadrill|er /kadrije/ *v.t.* (*zone*) comb, control. ~**age** *n.m.* (*mil.*) control. ~**é** *a.* (*papier*) squared.

quadrupède /kadrypɛd/ *n.m.* quadruped.

quadrupl|e /kadrypl/ *a. & n.m.* quadruple. ~**er** *v.t./i.* quadruple. ~**és, ~ées** *n.m., f. pl.* quadruplets.

quai /ke/ *n.m.* (*de gare*) platform; (*de port*) quay; (*de rivière*) embankment.

qualificatif /kalifikatif/ *n.m.* (*épithète*) term.

qualif|ier /kalifje/ *v.t.* qualify; (*décrire*) describe (de, as). **se ~ier** *v. pr.* qualify (**pour**, for). ~**ication** *n.f.* qualification; description. ~**ié** *a.* qualified; (*main d'œuvre*) skilled.

qualit|é /kalite/ *n.f.* quality; (*titre*) occupation. **en ~é de**, as. ~**atif, ~ative** *a.* qualitative.

quand /kɑ̃/ *conj. & adv.* when. ~ **même**, all the same. ~ **(bien) même**, even if.

quant (à) /kɑ̃t(a)/ *prép.* as for.

quant-à-soi /kɑ̃taswa/ *n.m.* **rester sur son ~**, stand aloof.

quantit|é /kɑ̃tite/ *n.f.* quantity. **une ~é de**, a lot of. **des ~és**, masses. ~**atif, ~ative** *a.* quantitative.

quarantaine /karɑ̃tɛn/ *n.f.* (*méd.*) quarantine. **une ~ (de)**, about forty.

quarant|e /karɑ̃t/ *a. & n.m.* forty. ~**ième** *a. & n.m./f.* fortieth.

quart /kar/ *n.m.* quarter; (*naut.*) watch. ~ **(de litre)**, quarter litre. ~ **de finale**, quarter-final. ~ **d'heure**, quarter of an hour.

quartier /kartje/ *n.m.* neighbourhood, district; (*de lune, bœuf*) quarter; (*de fruit*) segment. ~**s**, (*mil.*) quarters. **de ~, du ~**, local. ~ **général**, headquarters. **avoir ~ libre**, be free.

quartz /kwarts/ *n.m.* quartz.

quasi- /kazi/ *préf.* quasi-.

quasiment /kazimɑ̃/ *adv.* almost.

quatorz|e /katorz/ *a. & n.m.* fourteen. ~**ième** *a. & n.m./f.* fourteenth.

quatre /katr(ə)/ *a. & n.m.* four. ~**-vingt(s)** *a. & n.m.* eighty. ~**-vingt-dix** *a. & n.m.* ninety.

quatrième /katrijɛm/ *a. & n.m./f.* fourth. ~**ment** *adv.* fourthly.

quatuor /kwatɥɔr/ *n.m.* quartet.

que, qu' */kə, k/ *conj.* that; (*comparaison*) than. **qu'il vienne**, let him come. **qu'il vienne ou non**, whether he comes or not. **ne faire ~ demander**/*etc.*, only ask/*etc.* ● *adv.* (ce) ~ **tu es bête, qu'est-ce ~ tu es bête**, how silly you are. ~ **de**, what a lot of. ● *pron. rel.* (*personne*) that, whom; (*chose*) that, which; (*temps, moment*) when; (*interrogatif*) what. **un jour**/*etc.* ~, one day/*etc.* when. ~ **faites-vous?, qu'est-ce ~ vous faites?**, what are you doing?

Québec /kebɛk/ *n.m.* Quebec.

quel, ~le /kɛl/ *a.* what; (*interrogatif*) which, what; (*qui*) who. ● *pron.*

which. **~ dommage,** what a pity. **~ qu'il soit,** (*chose*) whatever ou whichever it may be; (*personne*) whoever he may be.

quelconque /kɛlkɔ̃k/ a. any, some; (*banal*) ordinary; (*médiocre*) poor.

quelque /kɛlkə/ a. **~s,** a few, some. ● adv. (*environ*) some. **et ~,** (*fam.*) and a bit. **~ chose,** something; (*interrogation*) anything. **~ part,** somewhere. **~ peu,** somewhat.

quelquefois /kɛlkəfwa/ adv. sometimes.

quelques|-uns, ~-unes /kɛlkəzœ̃, -yn/ pron. some, a few.

quelqu'un /kɛlkœ̃/ pron. someone, somebody; (*interrogation*) anyone, anybody.

quémander /kemɑ̃de/ v.t. beg for.

qu'en-dira-t-on /kɑ̃diratɔ̃/ n.m. invar. **le ~,** gossip.

querell|e /kərɛl/ n.f. quarrel. **~eur, ~euse** a. quarrelsome.

quereller (se) /(sə)kərele/ v. pr. quarrel.

question /kɛstjɔ̃/ n.f. question; (*affaire*) matter, question. **en ~,** in question; (*en jeu*) at stake. **il est ~ de,** (*cela concerne*) it is about; (*on parle de*) there is talk of. **il n'en est pas ~,** it is out of the question. **~ner** /-jɔne/ v.t. question.

questionnaire /kɛstjɔnɛr/ n.m. questionnaire.

quêt|e /kɛt/ n.f. (*relig.*) collection. **en ~e de,** in search of. **~er** /kete/ v.i. collect money; v.t. seek.

quetsche /kwɛtʃ/ n.f. (sort of dark red) plum.

queue /kø/ n.f. tail; (*de poêle*) handle; (*de fruit*) stalk; (*de fleur*) stem; (*file*) queue; (*file: Amer.*) line; (*de train*) rear. **faire la ~,** queue (up); (*Amer.*) line up. **~ de cheval,** pony-tail.

qui /ki/ pron. rel. (*personne*) who; (*chose*) which, that; (*interrogatif*) who; (*après prép.*) whom; (*quiconque*) whoever. **à ~ est ce stylo/etc.?,** whose pen/etc. is this? **qu'est-ce ~,** what? **~ est-ce qui?,** who? **~ que ce soit,** anyone.

quiche /kiʃ/ n.f. quiche.

quiconque /kikɔ̃k/ pron. whoever; (*n'importe qui*) anyone.

quiétude /kjetyd/ n.f. quiet.

quignon /kiɲɔ̃/ n.m. **~ de pain,** chunk of bread.

quille[1] /kij/ n.f. (*de bateau*) keel.

quille[2] /kij/ n.f. (*jouet*) skittle.

quincaill|ier, ~ière /kɛ̃kaje, -jɛr/ n.m., f. hardware dealer. **~erie** n.f. hardware; (*magasin*) hardware shop.

quinine /kinin/ n.f. quinine.

quinquenn|al (*m. pl.* **~aux**) /kɛ̃kenal, -o/ a. five-year.

quint|al (*pl.* **~aux**) /kɛ̃tal, -o/ n.m. quintal (= 100 kg.).

quinte /kɛ̃t/ n.f. **~ de toux,** coughing fit.

quintette /kɛ̃tɛt/ n.m. quintet.

quintupl|e /kɛ̃typl/ a. fivefold. ● n.m. quintuple. **~er** v.t./i. increase fivefold. **~és, ~ées,** n.m., f. pl. quintuplets.

quinzaine /kɛ̃zɛn/ n.f. **une ~ (de),** about fifteen.

quinz|e /kɛ̃z/ a. & n.m. fifteen. **~e jours,** two weeks. **~ième** a. & n.m./ f. fifteenth.

quiproquo /kiprɔko/ n.m. misunderstanding.

quittance /kitɑ̃s/ n.f. receipt.

quitte /kit/ a. quits (envers, with). **~ à faire,** even if it means doing.

quitter /kite/ v.t. leave; (*vêtement*) take off. **se ~** v. pr. part.

quoi /kwa/ pron. what; (*après prép.*) which. **de ~ vivre/manger/etc.,** (*assez*) enough to live on/to eat/etc. **de ~ écrire,** sth. to write with, what is necessary to write with. **~ que,** whatever. **~ que ce soit,** anything.

quoique /kwak(ə)/ conj. (al)though.

quolibet /kɔlibɛ/ n.m. gibe.

quorum /kɔrɔm/ n.m. quorum.

quota /kɔta/ n.m. quota.

quote-part (*pl.* **quotes-parts**) /kɔtpar/ n.f. share.

quotidien, ~ne /kɔtidjɛ̃, -jɛn/ a. daily; (*banal*) everyday. ● n.m. daily (paper). **~nement** /-jɛnmɑ̃/ adv. daily.

quotient /kɔsjɑ̃/ n.m. quotient.

R

rab /rab/ n.m. (*fam.*) extra. **il y en a en ~,** there's some over.

rabâcher /rabaʃe/ v.t. keep repeating.

rabais /rabɛ/ n.m. (price) reduction.

rabaisser /rabese/ v.t. (*déprécier*) belittle; (*réduire*) reduce.

rabat /raba/ *n.m.* flap. **~-joie** *n.m. invar.* killjoy.

rabattre /rabatr/ *v.t.* pull *ou* put down; (*diminuer*) reduce; (*déduire*) take off. **se ~** *v. pr.* (*se refermer*) close; (*véhicule*) cut in, turn sharply. **se ~ sur**, fall back on.

rabbin /rabɛ̃/ *n.m.* rabbi.

rabibocher /rabibɔʃe/ *v.t.* (*fam.*) reconcile.

rabiot /rabjo/ *n.m.* (*fam.*) = **rab**.

râblé /rɑble/ *a.* stocky, sturdy.

rabot /rabo/ *n.m.* plane. **~er** /-ɔte/ *v.t.* plane.

raboteu|x, ~se /rabotø, -z/ *a.* uneven.

rabougri /rabugri/ *a.* stunted.

rabrouer /rabrue/ *v.t.* snub.

racaille /rakɑj/ *n.f.* rabble.

raccommoder /rakɔmɔde/ *v.t.* mend; (*personnes: fam.*) reconcile.

raccompagner /rakɔ̃paɲe/ *v.t.* see *ou* take back (home).

raccord /rakɔr/ *n.m.* link; (*de papier peint*) join. **~ (de peinture)**, touch-up.

raccord|er /rakɔrde/ *v.t.* connect, join. **~ement** *n.m.* connection.

raccourci /rakursi/ *n.m.* short cut. **en ~**, in brief.

raccourcir /rakursir/ *v.t.* shorten. **●** *v.i.* get shorter.

raccrocher /rakrɔʃe/ *v.t.* hang back up; (*personne*) grab hold of; (*relier*) connect. **~ (le récepteur)**, hang up. **se ~ à**, cling to; (*se relier à*) be connected to *ou* with.

rac|e /ras/ *n.f.* race; (*animale*) breed. **de ~e**, pure-bred. **~ial** (*m. pl. ~iaux*) *a.* racial.

rachat /raʃa/ *n.m.* buying (back); (*de pécheur*) redemption.

racheter /raʃte/ *v.t.* buy (back); (*davantage*) buy more; (*nouvel objet*) buy another; (*pécheur*) redeem. **se ~** *v. pr.* make amends.

racine /rasin/ *n.f.* root. **~ carrée/ cubique**, square/cube root.

racis|te /rasist/ *a.* & *n.m./f.* racist. **~me** *n.m.* racism.

racket /raket/ *n.m.* racketeering.

raclée /rɑkle/ *n.f.* (*fam.*) thrashing.

racler /rɑkle/ *v.t.* scrape. **se ~ la gorge**, clear one's throat.

racol|er /rakɔle/ *v.t.* solicit; (*marchand, parti*) drum up. **~age** *n.m.* soliciting.

racontars /rakɔ̃tar/ *n.m. pl.* (*fam.*) gossip, stories.

raconter /rakɔ̃te/ *v.t.* (*histoire*) tell, relate; (*vacances etc.*) tell about. **~ à qn. que**, tell s.o. that, say to s.o. that.

racorni /rakɔrni/ *a.* hard(ened).

radar /radar/ *n.m.* radar.

rade /rad/ *n.f.* harbour. **en ~**, (*personne: fam.*) stranded, behind.

radeau (*pl. ~x*) /rado/ *n.m.* raft.

radiateur /radjatœr/ *n.m.* radiator; (*électrique*) heater.

radiation /radjasjɔ̃/ *n.f.* (*énergie*) radiation.

radic|al (*m. pl. ~aux*) /radikal, -o/ *a.* radical. **●** *n.m.* (*pl. ~aux*) radical.

radier /radje/ *v.t.* cross off.

radieu|x, ~se /radjø, -z/ *a.* radiant.

radin, ~e /radɛ̃, -in/ *a.* (*fam.*) stingy.

radio /radjo/ *n.f.* radio; (*radiographie*) X-ray.

radioacti|f, ~ve /radjoaktif, -v/ *a.* radioactive. **~vité** *n.f.* radioactivity.

radiocassette /radjokaset/ *n.f.* radio-cassette-player.

radiodiffus|er /radjodifyze/ *v.t.* broadcast. **~ion** *n.f.* broadcasting.

radiograph|ie /radjografi/ *n.f.* (*photographie*) X-ray. **~ier** *v.t.* X-ray. **~ique** *a.* X-ray.

radiologue /radjolog/ *n.m./f.* radiographer.

radiophonique /radjofɔnik/ *a.* radio.

radis /radi/ *n.m.* radish. **ne pas avoir un ~**, be broke.

radoter /radote/ *v.i.* (*fam.*) talk drivel.

radoucir (se) /(sə)radusir/ *v. pr.* calm down; (*temps*) become milder.

rafale /rafal/ *n.f.* (*de vent*) gust; (*tir*) burst of gunfire.

raffermir /rafɛrmir/ *v.t.* strengthen. **se ~** *v. pr.* become stronger.

raffin|é /rafine/ *a.* refined. **~ement** *n.m.* refinement.

raffin|er /rafine/ *v.t.* refine. **~age** *n.m.* refining. **~erie** *n.f.* refinery.

raffoler /rafole/ *v.i.* **~ de**, be extremely fond of.

raffut /rafy/ *n.m.* (*fam.*) din.

rafiot /rafjo/ *n.m.* (*fam.*) boat.

rafistoler /rafistole/ *v.t.* (*fam.*) patch up.

rafle /rɑfl/ *n.f.* (*police*) raid.

rafler /rɑfle/ *v.t.* grab, swipe.

rafraîch|ir /rafreʃir/ *v.t.* cool (down); (*raviver*) brighten up; (*personne, mémoire*) refresh. **se ~ir** *v. pr.* (*se laver*) freshen up; (*boire*) refresh o.s.; (*temps*) get cooler. **~issant**, **~issante** *a.* refreshing.

rafraîchissement /rafreʃismã/ *n.m.* (*boisson*) cold drink. **~s**, (*fruits etc.*) refreshments.

ragaillardir /ragajardir/ *v.t.* (*fam.*) buck up. **se ~** *v. pr.* buck up.

rag|e /raʒ/ *n.f.* rage; (*maladie*) rabies. **faire ~e**, rage. **~e de dents**, raging toothache. **~er** *v.i.* rage. **~eur**, **~euse** *a.* ill-tempered. **~eant**, **~eante** *a.* maddening.

ragot(s) /rago/ *n.m.* (*pl.*) (*fam.*) gossip.

ragoût /ragu/ *n.m.* stew.

raid /rɛd/ *n.m.* (*mil.*) raid; (*sport*) rally.

raid|e /rɛd/ *a.* stiff; (*côte*) steep; (*corde*) tight; (*cheveux*) straight. ● *adv.* (*en pente*) steeply. **~eur** *n.f.* stiffness; steepness.

raidir /redir/ *v.t.*, **se ~** *v. pr.* stiffen; (*position*) harden; (*corde*) tighten.

raie¹ /rɛ/ *n.f.* line; (*bande*) strip; (*de cheveux*) parting.

raie² /rɛ/ *n.f.* (*poisson*) skate.

raifort /refɔr/ *n.m.* horse-radish.

rail /raj/ *n.m.* (*barre*) rail. **le ~**, (*transport*) rail.

raill|er /raje/ *v.t.* mock (at). **~erie** *n.f.* mocking remark. **~eur**, **~euse** *a.* mocking.

rainure /renyr/ *n.f.* groove.

raisin /rezɛ̃/ *n.m.* **~(s)**, grapes. **~ sec**, raisin.

raison /rezõ/ *n.f.* reason. **à ~ de**, at the rate of. **avec ~**, rightly. **avoir ~**, be right (**de faire**, to do). **avoir ~ de qn.**, get the better of s.o. **donner ~ à**, prove right. **en ~ de**, (*cause*) because of. **~ de plus**, all the more reason. **perdre la ~**, lose one's mind.

raisonnable /rezɔnabl/ *a.* reasonable, sensible.

raisonn|er /rezɔne/ *v.i.* reason. ● *v.t.* (*personne*) reason with. **~ement** *n.m.* reasoning; (*propositions*) argument.

rajeunir /raʒœnir/ *v.t.* make (look) younger; (*moderniser*) modernize; (*méd.*) rejuvenate. ● *v.i.* look younger.

rajout /raʒu/ *n.m.* addition. **~er** /-te/ *v.t.* add.

rajust|er /raʒyste/ *v.t.* straighten; (*salaires*) (re)adjust. **~ement** *n.m.* (re)adjustment.

râl|e /rɑl/ *n.m.* (*de blessé*) groan. **~er** *v.i.* groan; (*protester*: *fam.*) moan.

ralent|ir /ralɑ̃tir/ *v.t./i.*, **se ~ir** *v. pr.* slow down. **~i** *a.* slow; *n.m.* (*cinéma*) slow motion. **être** *ou* **tourner au ~i**, tick over, idle.

rall|ier /ralje/ *v.t.* rally; (*rejoindre*) rejoin. **se ~ier** *v. pr.* rally. **se ~ier à**, (*avis*) come over to. **~iement** *n.m.* rallying.

rallonge /ralõʒ/ *n.f.* (*de table*) extension. **~ de**, (*supplément de*) extra.

rallonger /ralõʒe/ *v.t.* lengthen.

rallumer /ralyme/ *v.t.* light (up) again; (*lampe*) switch on again; (*ranimer*: *fig.*) revive.

rallye /rali/ *n.m.* rally.

ramadan /ramadã/ *n.m.* Ramadan.

ramassé /ramase/ *a.* squat; (*concis*) concise.

ramass|er /ramase/ *v.t.* pick up; (*récolter*) gather; (*recueillir*) collect. **se ~er** *v. pr.* draw o.s. together, curl up. **~age** *n.m.* (*cueillette*) gathering. **~age scolaire**, school bus service.

rambarde /rãbard/ *n.f.* guardrail.

rame /ram/ *n.f.* (*aviron*) oar; (*train*) train; (*perche*) stake.

rameau (*pl.* **~x**) /ramo/ *n.m.* branch.

ramener /ramne/ *v.t.* bring back. **~ à**, (*réduire à*) reduce to. **se ~** *v. pr.* (*fam.*) turn up. **se ~ à**, (*problème*) come down to.

ram|er /rame/ *v.i.* row. **~eur**, **~euse** *n.m.*, *f.* rower.

ramif|ier (se) /(sə)ramifje/ *v. pr.* ramify. **~ication** *n.f.* ramification.

ramollir /ramɔlir/ *v.t.*, **se ~** *v. pr.* soften.

ramon|er /ramɔne/ *v.t.* sweep. **~eur** *n.m.* (chimney-)sweep.

rampe /rɑ̃p/ *n.f.* banisters; (*pente*) ramp. **~ de lancement**, launching pad.

ramper /rɑ̃pe/ *v.i.* crawl.

rancard /rɑ̃kar/ *n.m.* (*fam.*) appointment.

rancart /rɑ̃kar/ *n.m.* **mettre** *ou* **jeter au ~**, (*fam.*) scrap.

ranc|e /rɑ̃s/ *a.* rancid. **~ir** *v.i.* go *ou* turn rancid.

rancœur /rɑ̃kœr/ *n.f.* resentment.

rançon /rɑ̃sõ/ *n.f.* ransom. **~ner** /-ɔne/ *v.t.* hold to ransom.

rancun|e /rɑ̃kyn/ *n.f.* grudge. **sans ~!**, no hard feelings. **~ier**, **~ière** *a.* vindictive.

randonnée /rɑ̃dɔne/ n.f. walk; (en auto, vélo) ride.

rang /rɑ̃/ n.m. row; (hiérarchie, condition) rank. **se mettre en ~,** line up. **au premier ~,** in the first row; (fig.) at the forefront. **de second ~,** (péj.) second-rate.

rangée /rɑ̃ʒe/ n.f. row.

rang|er /rɑ̃ʒe/ v.t. put away; (chambre etc.) tidy (up); (disposer) place; (véhicule) park. **se ~er** v. pr. (véhicule) park; (s'écarter) stand aside; (s'assagir) settle down. **se ~er à,** (avis) accept. **~ement** n.m. (de chambre) tidying (up); (espace) storage space.

ranimer /ranime/ v.t., **se ~** v. pr. revive.

rapace¹ /rapas/ n.m. bird of prey.

rapace² /rapas/ a. grasping.

rapatr|ier /rapatrije/ v.t. repatriate. **~iement** n.m. repatriation.

râp|e /rɑp/ n.f. (culin.) grater; (lime) rasp. **~er** v.t. grate; (bois) rasp.

râpé /rɑpe/ a. threadbare. **c'est ~!,** (fam.) that's right out!

rapetisser /raptise/ v.t. make smaller. • v.i. get smaller.

râpeu|x, ~se /rɑpø, -z/ a. rough.

rapid|e /rapid/ a. fast, rapid. • n.m. (train) express (train); (cours d'eau) rapids pl. **~ement** adv. fast, rapidly. **~ité** n.f. speed.

rapiécer /rapjese/ v.t. patch.

rappel /rapɛl/ n.m. recall; (deuxième avis) reminder; (de salaire) back pay; (méd.) booster.

rappeler /raple/ v.t. call back; (diplomate, réserviste) recall; (évoquer) remind, recall. **~ qch. à qn.,** (redire) remind s.o. of sth. **se ~** v. pr. remember, recall.

rapport /rapɔr/ n.m. connection; (compte rendu) report; (profit) yield. **~s,** (relations) relations. **en ~ avec,** (accord) in keeping with. **mettre/se mettre en ~ avec,** put/ get in touch with. **par ~ à,** in relation to. **~s (sexuels),** intercourse.

rapport|er /rapɔrte/ v.t. bring back; (profit) bring in; (dire, répéter) report. • v.i. (comm.) bring in a good return; (mouchard: fam.) tell. **se ~er à,** relate to. **s'en ~er à,** rely on. **~eur, ~euse** n.m., f. (mouchard) tell-tale; n.m. (instrument) protractor.

rapproch|er /raprɔʃe/ v.t. bring closer (de, to); (réconcilier) bring together; (comparer) compare. **se ~er** v. pr. get ou come closer (de, to); (personnes, pays) come together; (s'apparenter) be close (de, to). **~é** a. close. **~ement** n.m. reconciliation; (rapport) connection; (comparaison) parallel.

rapt /rapt/ n.m. abduction.

raquette /rakɛt/ n.f. (de tennis) racket; (de ping-pong) bat.

rare /rar/ a. rare; (insuffisant) scarce. **~ment** adv. rarely, seldom. **~té** n.f. rarity; scarcity; (objet) rarity.

raréfier (se) /(sə)rarefje/ v. pr. (nourriture etc.) become scarce.

ras, ~e /rɑ, rɑz/ a. (herbe, poil) short. **à ~ de,** very close to. **en avoir ~ le bol,** (fam.) be really fed up. **~e campagne,** open country. **coupé à ~,** cut short. **à ~ bord,** to the brim. **pull ~ du cou,** round-neck pull-over. **~-le-bol** n.m. (fam.) anger.

ras|er /rɑze/ v.t. shave; (cheveux, barbe) shave off; (frôler) skim; (abattre) raze; (ennuyer: fam.) bore. **se ~er** v. pr. shave. **~age** n.m. shaving. **~eur, ~euse** n.m., f. (fam.) bore.

rasoir /rɑzwar/ n.m. razor.

rassas|ier /rasazje/ v.t. satisfy. **être ~ié de,** have had enough of.

rassembl|er /rasɑ̃ble/ v.t. gather; (courage) muster. **se ~er** v. pr. gather. **~ement** n.m. gathering.

rasseoir (se) /(sə)raswar/ v. pr. sit down again.

rass|is, ~ise ou **~ie** /rasi, -z/ a. (pain) stale.

rassurer /rasyre/ v.t. reassure.

rat /ra/ n.m. rat.

ratatiner (se) /(sə)ratatine/ v. pr. shrivel up.

rate /rat/ n.f. spleen.

râteau (pl. **~x**) /rɑto/ n.m. rake.

râtelier /rɑtəlje/ n.m. (stable-)rack; (fam.) dentures.

rat|er /rate/ v.t./i. miss; (gâcher) spoil; (échouer) fail. **c'est ~é,** that's right out. **~é, ~ée** n.m., f. (personne) failure. **avoir des ~és,** (auto.) backfire.

ratif|ier /ratifje/ v.t. ratify. **~ication** n.f. ratification.

ratio /rasjo/ n.m. ratio.

ration /rasjɔ̃/ n.f. ration.

rationaliser /rasjɔnalize/ v.t. rationalize.

rationnel, ∼le /rasjɔnɛl/ a. rational.

rationn|er /rasjɔne/ v.t. ration. **∼ement** n.m. rationing.

ratisser /ratise/ v.t. rake; (fouiller) comb.

rattacher /rataʃe/ v.t. tie up again; (relier) link; (incorporer) join.

rattrapage /ratrapaʒ/ n.m. ∼ scolaire, remedial classes.

rattraper /ratrape/ v.t. catch; (rejoindre) catch up with; (retard, erreur) make up for. **se ∼** v. pr. catch up; (se dédommager) make up for it. **se ∼ à**, catch hold of.

ratur|e /ratyr/ n.f. deletion. **∼er** v.t. delete.

rauque /rok/ a. raucous, harsh.

ravager /ravaʒe/ v.t. devastate, ravage.

ravages /ravaʒ/ n.m. pl. **faire des ∼**, wreak havoc.

raval|er /ravale/ v.t. (façade etc.) clean; (humilier) lower (à, down to). **∼ement** n.m. cleaning.

ravi /ravi/ a. delighted (que, that).

ravier /ravje/ n.m. hors-d'œuvre dish.

ravigoter /ravigɔte/ v.t. (fam.) buck up.

ravin /ravɛ̃/ n.m. ravine.

ravioli /ravjoli/ n.m. pl. ravioli.

ravir /ravir/ v.t. delight. **∼ à qn.**, (enlever) rob s.o. of.

raviser (se) /(sə)ravize/ v. pr. change one's mind.

ravissant, ∼e /ravisɑ̃, -t/ a. beautiful.

ravisseu|r, ∼se /raviscer, -øz/ n.m., f. kidnapper.

ravitaill|er /ravitɑje/ v.t. provide with supplies; (avion) refuel. **se ∼er** v. pr. stock up. **∼ement** n.m. provision of supplies (de, to), refuelling; (denrées) supplies.

raviver /ravive/ v.t. revive.

rayé /reje/ a. striped.

rayer /reje/ v.t. scratch; (biffer) cross out.

rayon /rejɔ̃/ n.m. ray; (planche) shelf; (de magasin) department; (de roue) spoke; (de cercle) radius. **∼ d'action**, range. **∼ de miel**, honeycomb. **∼ X**, X-ray. **en connaître un ∼**, (fam.) know one's stuff.

rayonn|er /rejɔne/ v.i. radiate; (de joie) beam; (se déplacer) tour around (from a central point). **∼ement** n.m. (éclat) radiance; (influence) influence; (radiations) radiation.

rayure /rejyr/ n.f. scratch; (dessin) stripe. **à ∼s**, striped.

raz-de-marée /rɑdmare/ n.m. invar. tidal wave. **∼ électoral**, landslide.

re- /rə/ préf. re-.

ré- /re/ préf. re-.

réacteur /reaktœr/ n.m. jet engine; (nucléaire) reactor.

réaction /reaksjɔ̃/ n.f. reaction. **∼ en chaîne**, chain reaction. **∼naire** /-jɔnɛr/ a. & n.m./f. reactionary.

réadapter /readapte/ v.t., **se ∼** v. pr. readjust (à, to).

réaffirmer /reafirme/ v.t. reaffirm.

réagir /reaʒir/ v.i. react.

réalis|er /realize/ v.t. carry out; (effort, bénéfice, achat) make; (rêve) fulfil; (film) produce, direct; (capital) realize; (se rendre compte de) realize. **se ∼er** v. pr. materialize. **∼ateur, ∼atrice** n.m., f. (cinéma) director; (TV) producer. **∼ation** n.f. realization; (œuvre) achievement.

réalis|te /realist/ a. realistic. ● n.m./f. realist. **∼me** n.m. realism.

réalité /realite/ n.f. reality.

réanim|er /reanime/ v.t. resuscitate. **∼ation** n.f. resuscitation. **service de ∼ation**, intensive care.

réapparaître /reaparɛtr/ v.i. reappear.

réarm|er (se) /(sə)rearme/ v. pr. rearm. **∼ement** n.m. rearmament.

rébarbati|f, ∼ve /rebarbatif, -v/ a. forbidding, off-putting.

rebâtir /rəbɑtir/ v.t. rebuild.

rebelle /rəbɛl/ a. rebellious; (soldat) rebel. ● n.m./f. rebel.

rebeller (se) /(sə)rəbele/ v. pr. rebel, hit back defiantly.

rébellion /rebeljɔ̃/ n.f. rebellion.

rebiffer (se) /(sə)rəbife/ v. pr. (fam.) rebel.

rebond /rəbɔ̃/ n.m. bounce; (par ricochet) rebound. **∼ir** /-dir/ v.i. bounce; rebound.

rebondi /rəbɔ̃di/ a. chubby.

rebondissement /rəbɔ̃dismɑ̃/ n.m. (new) development.

rebord /rəbɔr/ n.m. edge. **∼ de la fenêtre**, window-ledge.

rebours (à) /(a)rəbur/ adv. the wrong way.

rebrousse-poil (à) /(a)rəbruspwal/ adv. (fig.) **prendre qn. ∼**, rub s.o. up the wrong way.

rebrousser /rəbruse/ v.t. ~ chemin, turn back.

rebuffade /rəbyfad/ n.f. rebuff.

rébus /rebys/ n.m. rebus.

rebut /rəby/ n.m. mettre ou jeter au ~, scrap.

rebut|er /rəbyte/ v.t. put off. ~ant, ~ante a. off-putting.

récalcitrant, ~e /rekalsitrɑ̃, -t/ a. stubborn.

recal|er /rəkale/ v.t. (fam.) fail. se faire ~ ou être ~é, fail.

récapitul|er /rekapityle/ v.t./i. recapitulate. ~ation n.f. recapitulation.

recel /rəsɛl/ n.m. receiving. ~er /rəs(ə)le/ v.t. (objet volé) receive; (cacher) conceal.

récemment /resamɑ̃/ adv. recently.

recens|er /rəsɑ̃se/ v.t. (population) take a census of; (objets) list. ~ement n.m. census; list.

récent, ~e /resɑ̃, -t/ a. recent.

récépissé /resepise/ n.m. receipt.

récepteur /reseptœr/ n.m. receiver.

récepti|f, ~ve /reseptif, -v/ a. receptive.

réception /resɛpsjɔ̃/ n.f. reception. ~ de, (lettre etc.) receipt of. ~niste /-jɔnist/ n.m./f. receptionist.

récession /resesjɔ̃/ n.f. recession.

recette /rəsɛt/ n.f. (culin.) recipe; (argent) takings. ~s, (comm.) receipts.

receveu|r, ~se /rəsvœr, -øz/ n.m., f. (des impôts) tax collector.

recevoir† /rəsəvwar/ v.t. receive; (client, malade) see; (obtenir) get, receive. être reçu (à), pass. ● v.i. (médecin) receive patients. se ~ v. pr. (tomber) land.

rechange (de) /(də)rəʃɑ̃ʒ/ a. (roue, vêtements, etc.) spare; (solution etc.) alternative.

réchapper /reʃape/ v.i. ~ de ou à, come through, survive.

recharg|e /rəʃarʒ/ n.f. (de stylo) refill. ~er v.t. refill; (batterie) recharge.

réchaud /reʃo/ n.m. stove.

réchauff|er /reʃofe/ v.t. warm up. se ~er v. pr. warm o.s. up; (temps) get warmer. ~ement n.m. (de température) rise (de, in).

rêche /rɛʃ/ a. rough.

recherche /rəʃɛrʃ/ n.f. search (de, for); (raffinement) elegance. ~(s), (univ.) research. ~s, (enquête) investigations.

recherch|er /rəʃɛrʃe/ v.t. search for. ~é a. in great demand; (élégant) elegant. ~é pour meurtre, wanted for murder.

rechigner /rəʃiɲe/ v.i. ~ à, balk at.

rechut|e /rəʃyt/ n.f. (méd.) relapse. ~er v.i. relapse.

récidiv|e /residiv/ n.f. second offence. ~er v.i. commit a second offence.

récif /resif/ n.m. reef.

récipient /resipjɑ̃/ n.m. container.

réciproque /resiprɔk/ a. mutual, reciprocal. ~ment adv. each other; (inversement) conversely.

récit /resi/ n.m. (compte rendu) account, story; (histoire) story.

récital (pl. ~s) /resital/ n.m. recital.

récit|er /resite/ v.t. recite. ~ation n.f. recitation.

réclame /reklam/ n.f. faire de la ~, advertise. en ~, on offer.

réclam|er /reklame/ v.t. call for, demand; (revendiquer) claim. ● v.i. complain. ~ation n.f. complaint.

reclus, ~e /rəkly, -z/ n.m., f. recluse. ● a. cloistered.

réclusion /reklyzjɔ̃/ n.f. imprisonment.

recoin /rəkwɛ̃/ n.m. nook.

récolt|e /rekɔlt/ n.f. (action) harvest; (produits) crop, harvest; (fig.) crop. ~er v.t. harvest, gather; (fig.) collect.

recommand|er /rəkɔmɑ̃de/ v.t. recommend; (lettre) register. envoyer en ~é, send registered. ~ation n.f. recommendation.

recommencer /rəkɔmɑ̃se/ v.t./i. (reprendre) begin ou start again; (refaire) repeat. ne recommence pas, don't do it again.

récompens|e /rekɔ̃pɑ̃s/ n.f. reward; (prix) award. ~er v.t. reward (de, for).

réconcil|ier /rekɔ̃silje/ v.t. reconcile. se ~ier v. pr. become reconciled (avec, with). ~iation n.f. reconciliation.

reconduire† /rəkɔ̃dɥir/ v.t. see home; (à la porte) show out; (renouveler) renew.

réconfort /rekɔ̃fɔr/ n.m. comfort. ~er /-te/ v.t. comfort.

reconnaissable /rəkɔnɛsabl/ a. recognizable.

reconnaissan|t, ~te /rəkɔnɛsɑ̃, -t/ a. grateful (de, for). ~ce n.f. gratitude; (fait de reconnaître) recognition; (mil.) reconnaissance.

reconnaître† /rəkɔnɛtr/ v.t. recognize; (*admettre*) admit (**que**, that); (*mil.*) reconnoitre; (*enfant, tort*) acknowledge.

reconstituant /rəkɔ̃stitɥɑ̃/ n.m. tonic.

reconstituer /rəkɔ̃stitɥe/ v.t. reconstitute; (*crime*) reconstruct.

reconstr|uire† /rəkɔ̃strɥir/ v.t. rebuild. **~uction** n.f. rebuilding.

reconversion /rəkɔ̃vɛrsjɔ̃/ n.f. (*de main-d'œuvre*) redeployment.

recopier /rəkɔpje/ v.t. copy out.

record /rəkɔr/ n.m. & a. invar. record.

recoupe|r /rəkupe/ v.t. confirm. **se ~** v. pr. check, tally, match up. **par ~ment**, by making connections.

recourbé /rəkurbe/ a. curved; (*nez*) hooked.

recourir /rəkurir/ v.i. **~ à**, resort to.

recours /rəkur/ n.m. resort. **avoir ~ à**, have recourse to, resort to.

recouvrer /rəkuvre/ v.t. recover.

recouvrir† /rəkuvrir/ v.t. cover.

récréation /rekreasjɔ̃/ n.f. recreation; (*scol.*) playtime.

récrier (se) /(sə)rekrije/ v. pr. cry out.

récrimination /rekriminɑsjɔ̃/ n.f. recrimination.

recroqueviller (se) /(sə)rəkrɔkvije/ v. pr. curl up.

recrudescence /rəkrydesɑ̃s/ n.f. new outbreak.

recrue /rəkry/ n.f. recruit.

recrut|er /rəkryte/ v.t. recruit. **~ement** n.m. recruitment.

rectang|le /rɛktɑ̃gl/ n.m. rectangle. **~ulaire** a. rectangular.

rectif|ier /rɛktifje/ v.t. correct, rectify. **~ication** n.f. correction.

recto /rɛkto/ n.m. front of the page.

reçu /rəsy/ voir **recevoir**. ● n.m. receipt. ● a. accepted; (*candidat*) successful.

recueil /rəkœj/ n.m. collection.

recueill|ir† /rəkœjir/ v.t. collect; (*prendre chez soi*) take in. **se ~ir** v. pr. meditate. **~ement** n.m. meditation. **~i** a. meditative.

recul /rəkyl/ n.m. retreat; (*éloignement*) distance; (*déclin*) decline. (**mouvement de**) **~**, backward movement. **~ade** n.f. retreat.

reculé /rəkyle/ a. (*région*) remote.

reculer /rəkyle/ v.t./i. reverse; (*véhicule*) reverse; (*armée*) retreat; (*diminuer*) decline; (*différer*) postpone. **~ devant**, (*fig.*) shrink from.

reculons (à) /(a)rəkylɔ̃/ adv. backwards.

récupér|er /rekypere/ v.t./i. recover; (*vieux objets*) salvage. **~ation** n.f. recovery; salvage.

récurer /rekyre/ v.t. scour. **poudre à ~**, scouring powder.

récuser /rekyze/ v.t. challenge. **se ~** v. pr. state that one is not qualified to judge.

recycl|er /rəsikle/ v.t. (*personne*) retrain; (*chose*) recycle. **se ~er** v. pr. retrain. **~age** n.m. retraining; recycling.

rédac|teur, ~trice /redaktœr, -tris/ n.m., f. writer, editor. **le ~teur en chef**, the editor (in chief).

rédaction /redaksjɔ̃/ n.f. writing; (*scol.*) composition; (*personnel*) editorial staff.

reddition /redisjɔ̃/ n.f. surrender.

redemander /rədmɑ̃de/ v.t. ask again for; ask for more of.

redevable /rədvabl/ a. **être ~ à qn. de**, (*argent*) owe sb; (*fig.*) be indebted to s.o. for.

redevance /rədvɑ̃s/ n.f. (*de télévision*) licence fee.

rédiger /rediʒe/ v.t. write; (*contrat*) draw up.

redire† /rədir/ v.t. repeat. **avoir ou trouver à ~ à**, find fault with.

redondant, ~e /rədɔ̃dɑ̃, -t/ a. superfluous.

redonner /rədɔne/ v.t. give back; (*davantage*) give more.

redoubl|er /rəduble/ v.t./i. increase; (*classe: scol.*) repeat. **~er de prudence/etc.**, be more careful/etc. **~ement** n.m. (*accroissement*) increase (**de**, in).

redout|er /rədute/ v.t. dread. **~able** a. formidable.

redoux /rədu/ n.m. milder weather.

redress|er /rədrese/ v.t. straighten (out ou up); (*situation*) right, redress. **se ~er** v. pr. (*personne*) straighten (o.s.) up; (*se remettre debout*) stand up; (*pays, économie*) recover. **~ement** /rədrɛsmɑ̃/ n.m. (*relèvement*) recovery.

réduction /redyksjɔ̃/ n.f. reduction.

réduire† /redɥir/ v.t. reduce (**à**, to). **se ~ à**, (*revenir à*) come down to.

réduit¹, ~e /redɥi, -t/ a. (*objet*) small-scale; (*limité*) limited.

réduit² /redɥi/ n.m. recess.

rééduquer /reedyke/ v.t. (personne) rehabilitate; (membre) re-educate. ~cation n.f. rehabilitation; re-education.

réel, ~le /reɛl/ a. real. ● n.m. reality. ~lement adv. really.

réexpédier /reɛkspedje/ v.t. forward; (retourner) send back.

refaire† /rəfɛr/ v.t. do again; (erreur, voyage) make again; (réparer) do up, redo.

réfection /refɛksjɔ̃/ n.f. repair.

réfectoire /refɛktwar/ n.m. refectory.

référence /referɑ̃s/ n.f. reference.

référendum /referɛ̃dɔm/ n.m. referendum.

référer /refere/ v.i. en ~ à, refer the matter to. se ~ à, refer to.

refermer /rəfɛrme/ v.t., se ~, v. pr. close (again).

refiler /rəfile/ v.t. (fam.) palm off (à, on).

réfléchir /refleʃir/ v.i. think (à, about). ● v.t. reflect. se ~ir v. pr. be reflected. ~i a. (personne) thoughtful; (verbe) reflexive.

reflet /rəflɛ/ n.m. reflection; (lumière) ~éter /-ete/ v.t. reflect. se ~éter v. pr. be reflected.

réflexe /reflɛks/ a. & n.m. reflex.

réflexion /reflɛksjɔ̃/ n.f. reflection; (pensée) thought, reflection. à la ~, on second thoughts.

refluer /rəflye/ v.i. flow back; (foule) retreat.

reflux /rəfly/ n.m. (de marée) ebb.

refondre /rəfɔ̃dr/ v.t. recast.

réforme /reform/ n.f. reform. ~ateur, ~atrice n.m., f. reformer. ~er v.t. reform; (soldat) invalid (out of the army).

refouler /rəfule/ v.t. (larmes) force back; (désir) repress. ~é a. repressed. ~ement n.m. repression.

réfractaire /refraktɛr/ a. être ~ à, resist.

refrain /rəfrɛ̃/ n.m. chorus. le même ~, the same old story.

réfréner /refrene/ v.t. curb, check.

réfrigérer /refriʒere/ v.t. refrigerate. ~ateur n.m. refrigerator.

refroidir /rəfrwadir/ v.t./i. cool (down). se ~ir v. pr. (personne, temps) get cold; (ardeur) cool (off). ~issement n.m. cooling; (rhume) chill.

refuge /rəfyʒ/ n.m. refuge; (chalet) mountain hut.

réfugier (se) /(sə)refyʒje/ v. pr. take refuge. ~ié, ~iée n.m., f. refugee.

refus /rəfy/ n.m. refusal. ce n'est pas de ~, I wouldn't say no. ~er /-ze/ v.t. refuse (de, to); (recaler) fail. se ~er à, (évidence etc.) reject.

réfuter /refyte/ v.t. refute.

regagner /rəgɑɲe/ v.t. regain; (revenir à) get back to.

regain /rəgɛ̃/ n.m. ~ de, renewal of.

régal (pl. ~s) /regal/ n.m. treat. ~er v.t. treat (de, to). se ~er v. pr. treat o.s. (de, to).

regard /rəgar/ n.m. (expression, coup d'œil) look; (fixe) stare; (vue, œil) eye. au ~ de, in regard to. en ~ de, compared with.

regardant, ~e /rəgardɑ̃, -t/ a. careful (with money). peu ~ (sur), not fussy (about).

regarder /rəgarde/ v.t. look at; (observer) watch; (considérer) consider; (concerner) concern. ~ (fixement), stare at. ● v.i. look. ~ à, (qualité etc.) pay attention to. ~ vers, (maison) face. se ~ v. pr. (personnes) look at each other.

régates /regat/ n.f. pl. regatta.

régénérer /reʒenere/ v.t. regenerate.

régent, ~te /reʒɑ̃, -t/ n.m., f. regent. ~ce n.f. regency.

régenter /reʒɑ̃te/ v.t. rule.

reggae /rege/ n.m. reggae.

régie /reʒi/ n.f. (entreprise) public corporation; (radio, TV) control room; (cinéma, théâtre) production.

regimber /rəʒɛ̃be/ v.i. balk.

régime /reʒim/ n.m. (organisation) system; (pol.) regime; (méd.) diet; (de moteur) speed; (de bananes) bunch. se mettre au ~, go on a diet.

régiment /reʒimɑ̃/ n.m. regiment.

région /reʒjɔ̃/ n.f. region. ~al (m. pl. ~aux) /-jɔnal, -o/ a. regional.

régir /reʒir/ v.t. govern.

régisseur /reʒisœr/ n.m. (théâtre) stage-manager; (cinéma, TV) assistant director.

registre /rəʒistr/ n.m. register.

réglage /reglaʒ/ n.m. adjustment.

règle /rɛgl/ n.f. rule; (instrument) ruler. ~s, (de femme) period. en ~, in order. ~ à calculer, slide-rule.

réglé /regle/ a. (vie) ordered; (arrangé) settled.

règlement /rɛgləmɑ̃/ n.m. regulation; (règles) regulations; (solution, paiement) settlement. ~aire /-tɛr/ a. (uniforme) regulation.

réglement|er /rɛgləmɑ̃te/ v.t. regulate. **~ation** n.f. regulation.

régler /regle/ v.t. settle; (machine) adjust; (programmer) set; (facture) settle; (personne) settle up with; (papier) rule. **~ son compte à**, settle a score with.

réglisse /reglis/ n.f. liquorice.

règne /rɛɲ/ n.m. reign; (végétal, animal, minéral) kingdom.

régner /reɲe/ v.i. reign.

regorger /rəgɔrʒe/ v.i. **~ de**, be overflowing with.

regret /rəgrɛ/ n.m. regret. **à ~**, with regret.

regrett|er /rəgrete/ v.t. regret; (personne) miss. **~able** a. regrettable.

regrouper /rəgrupe/ v.t., group together. **se ~** v. pr. gather (together).

régulariser /regylarize/ v.t. regularize.

régulation /regylasjɔ̃/ n.f. regulation.

régul|ier, ~ière /regylje, -jɛr/ a. regular; (qualité, vitesse) steady, even; (ligne, paysage) even; (légal) legal; (honnête) honest. **~arité** n.f. regularity; steadiness; evenness. **~ièrement** adv. regularly; (d'ordinaire) normally.

réhabilit|er /reabilite/ v.t. rehabilitate. **~ation** n.f. rehabilitation.

rehausser /rəose/ v.t. raise; (faire valoir) enhance.

rein /rɛ̃/ n.m. kidney. **~s**, (dos) back.

réincarnation /reɛ̃karnasjɔ̃/ n.f. reincarnation.

reine /rɛn/ n.f. queen. **~-claude** n.f. greengage.

réinsertion /reɛ̃sɛrsjɔ̃/ n.f. reintegration, rehabilitation.

réintégrer /reɛ̃tegre/ v.t. (lieu) return to; (jurid.) reinstate.

réitérer /reitere/ v.t. repeat.

rejaillir /rəʒajir/ v.i. **~ sur**, rebound on.

rejet /rəʒɛ/ n.m. rejection.

rejeter /rəʒte/ v.t. throw back; (refuser) reject; (vomir) bring up; (déverser) discharge. **~ une faute/etc. sur qn.**, shift the blame for a mistake/etc. on to s.o.

rejeton(s) /rəʒtɔ̃/ n.m. (pl.) (fam.) offspring.

rejoindre /rəʒwɛ̃dr/ v.t. go back to, rejoin; (rattraper) catch up with; (rencontrer) join, meet. **se ~** v. pr.

(personnes) meet; (routes) join, meet.

réjoui /reʒwi/ a. joyful.

réjou|ir /reʒwir/ v.t. delight. **se ~** ir v. pr. be delighted (de qch., at sth.). **~issances** n.f. pl. festivities. **~issant, ~issante** a. cheering.

relâche /rəlɑʃ/ n.m. (repos) respite. **faire ~**, (théâtre) close.

relâché /rəlɑʃe/ a. lax.

relâch|er /rəlɑʃe/ v.t. slacken; (personne) release; (discipline) relax. **se ~er** v. pr. slacken. **~ement** n.m. slackening.

relais /rəlɛ/ n.m. relay. **~ (routier)**, roadside café.

relanc|e /rəlɑ̃s/ n.f. boost. **~er** v.t. boost, revive; (renvoyer) throw back.

relati|f, ~ve /rəlatif, -v/ a. relative.

relation /rəlasjɔ̃/ n.f. relation(ship); (ami) acquaintance; (récit) account. **~s**, relation. **en ~ avec qn.**, in touch with s.o.

relativement /rəlativmɑ̃/ adv. relatively. **~ à**, in relation to.

relativité /rəlativite/ n.f. relativity.

relax|er (se) /(sə)rəlakse/ v. pr. relax. **~ation** n.f. relaxation. **~e** a. (fam.) laid-back.

relayer /rəleje/ v.t. relieve; (émission) relay. **se ~** v. pr. take over from one another.

reléguer /rəlege/ v.t. relegate.

relent /rəlɑ̃/ n.m. stink.

relève /rəlɛv/ n.f. relief. **prendre ou assurer la ~**, take over (de, from).

relevé /rəlve/ n.m. list; (de compte) statement; (de compteur) reading. ● a. spicy.

relever /rəlve/ v.t. pick up; (personne tombée) help up; (remonter) raise; (col) turn up; (manches) roll up; (sauce) season; (goût) bring out; (compteur) read; (défi) accept; (relayer) relieve; (remarquer, noter) note; (rebâtir) rebuild. ● v.i. **~ de**, (dépendre de) be the concern of; (méd.) recover from. **se ~** v. pr. (personne) get up (again); (pays, économie) recover.

relief /rəljɛf/ n.m. relief. **mettre en ~**, highlight.

relier /rəlje/ v.t. link (à, to); (ensemble) link together; (livre) bind.

religieu|x, ~se /rəliʒjø, -z/ a. religious. ● n.m. monk. ● n.f. nun; (culin.) choux bun.

religion /rəliʒjɔ̃/ n.f. religion.

reliquat /rəlika/ *n.m.* residue.

relique /rəlik/ *n.f.* relic.

reliure /rəljyr/ *n.f.* binding.

reluire /rəlɥir/ *v.i.* shine. **faire ~,** shine.

reluisant, ~e /rəlɥizã, -t/ *a.* **peu** *ou* **pas ~,** not brilliant.

reman|ier /rəmanje/ *v.t.* revise; (*ministère*) reshuffle. **~iement** *n.m.* revision; reshuffle.

remarier (se) /(sə)rəmarje/ *v. pr.* remarry.

remarquable /rəmarkabl/ *a.* remarkable.

remarque /rəmark/ *n.f.* remark; (*par écrit*) note.

remarquer /rəmarke/ *v.t.* notice; (*dire*) say. **faire ~,** point out (**à,** to). **se faire ~,** attract attention. **remarque(z),** mind you.

remblai /rãblɛ/ *n.m.* embankment.

rembourrer /rãbure/ *v.t.* pad.

rembours|er /rãburse/ *v.t.* repay; (*billet, frais*) refund. **~ement** *n.m.* repayment; refund.

remède /rəmɛd/ *n.m.* remedy; (*médicament*) medicine.

remédier /rəmedje/ *v.i.* **~ à,** remedy.

remémorer (se) /(sə)rəmemɔre/ *v. pr.* recall.

remerc|ier /rəmɛrsje/ *v.t.* thank (**de,** for); (*licencier*) dismiss. **~iements** *n.m. pl.* thanks.

remettre† /rəmɛtr/ *v.t.* put back; (*vêtement*) put back on; (*donner*) hand (over); (*devoir, démission*) hand in; (*restituer*) give back; (*différer*) put off; (*ajouter*) add; (*se rappeler*) remember; (*peine*) remit. **se ~** *v. pr.* (*guérir*) recover. **se ~ à,** go back to. **se ~ à faire,** start doing again. **s'en ~ à,** leave it to. **~ en cause** *ou* **en question,** call into question.

réminiscence /reminisãs/ *n.f.* reminiscence.

remise [1] /rəmiz/ *n.f.* (*abri*) shed.

remise [2] /rəmiz/ *n.f.* (*rabais*) discount; (*livraison*) delivery; (*ajournement*) postponement. **~ en cause** *ou* **en question,** calling into question.

remiser /rəmize/ *v.t.* put away.

rémission /remisjɔ̃/ *n.f.* remission.

remontant /rəmɔ̃tã/ *n.m.* tonic.

remontée /rəmɔ̃te/ *n.f.* ascent; (*d'eau, de prix*) rise. **~ mécanique,** ski-lift.

remont|er /rəmɔ̃te/ *v.i.* go *ou* come (back) up; (*prix, niveau*) rise (again); (*revenir*) go back. ● *v.t.* (*rue etc.*) go *ou* come (back) up; (*relever*) raise; (*montre*) wind up; (*objet démonté*) put together again; (*personne*) buck up. **~e-pente** *n.m.* ski-lift.

remontoir /rəmɔ̃twar/ *n.m.* winder.

remontrer /rəmɔ̃tre/ *v.t.* show again. **en ~ à qn.,** go one up on s.o.

remords /rəmɔr/ *n.m.* remorse. **avoir un** *ou* **des ~,** feel remorse.

remorqu|e /rəmɔrk/ *n.f.* (*véhicule*) trailer. **en ~e,** on tow. **~er** *v.t.* tow.

remorqueur /rəmɔrkœr/ *n.m.* tug.

remous /rəmu/ *n.m.* eddy; (*de bateau*) backwash; (*fig.*) turmoil.

rempart /rãpar/ *n.m.* rampart.

remplaçant, ~e /rãplasã, -t/ *n.m., f.* replacement; (*joueur*) reserve.

remplac|er /rãplase/ *v.t.* replace. **~ement** *n.m.* replacement.

rempli /rãpli/ *a.* full (**de,** of).

rempl|ir /rãplir/ *v.t.* fill (up); (*formulaire*) fill (in *ou* out); (*tâche, condition*) fulfil. **se ~ir** *v. pr.* fill (up). **~issage** *n.m.* filling; (*de texte*) padding.

remporter /rãpɔrte/ *v.t.* take back; (*victoire*) win.

remuant, ~e /rəmɥã, -t/ *a.* restless.

remue-ménage /rəmymenaʒ/ *n.m. invar.* commotion, bustle.

remuer /rəmɥe/ *v.t./i.* move; (*thé, café*) stir; (*gigoter*) fidget. **se ~** *v. pr.* move.

rémunér|er /remynere/ *v.t.* pay. **~ation** *n.f.* payment.

renâcler /rənakle/ *v.i.* snort. **~ à,** balk at, jib at.

ren|aître /rənɛtr/ *v.i.* be reborn; (*sentiment*) be revived. **~aissance** *n.f.* rebirth.

renard /rənar/ *n.m.* fox.

renchérir /rãʃerir/ *v.i.* become dearer. **~ sur,** go one better than.

rencontr|e /rãkɔ̃tr/ *n.f.* meeting; (*de routes*) junction; (*mil.*) encounter; (*match*) match; (*Amer.*) game. **~er** *v.t.* meet; (*heurter*) strike; (*trouver*) find. **se ~er** *v. pr.* meet.

rendement /rãdmã/ *n.m.* yield; (*travail*) output.

rendez-vous /rãdevu/ *n.m.* appointment; (*d'amoureux*) date; (*lieu*) meeting-place. **prendre ~ (avec),** make an appointment (with).

rendormir (se) /(sə)rãdɔrmir/ *v. pr.* go back to sleep.

rendre /rɑ̃dr/ *v.t.* give back, return; (*donner en retour*) return; (*monnaie*) give; (*hommage*) pay; (*justice*) dispense; (*jugement*) pronounce. **~ heureux/possible**/*etc.*, make happy/possible/ *etc.* ● *v.i.* (*terres*) yield; (*vomir*) vomit. **se ~** *v. pr.* (*capituler*) surrender; (*aller*) go (**à**, to); (*ridicule, utile, etc.*) make o.s. **~ compte de**, report on. **~ des comptes à**, be accountable to. **~ justice à qn.**, do so. justice. **~ service (à)**, help. **~ visite à**, visit. **se ~ compte de**, realize.

rendu /rɑ̃dy/ *a.* **être ~**, (*arrivé*) have arrived.

rêne /rɛn/ *n.f.* rein.

renégat, ~e /rənega, -t/ *n.m., f.* renegade.

renfermé /rɑ̃fɛrme/ *n.m.* stale smell. **sentir le ~**, smell stale. ● *a.* withdrawn.

renfermer /rɑ̃fɛrme/ *v.t.* contain. **se ~ (en soi-même)**, withdraw (into o.s.)

renflé /rɑ̃fle/ *a.* bulging. **~ement** *n.m.* bulge.

renflouer /rɑ̃flue/ *v.t.* refloat.

renfoncement /rɑ̃fɔ̃smɑ̃/ *n.m.* recess.

renforcer /rɑ̃fɔrse/ *v.t.* reinforce.

renfort /rɑ̃fɔr/ *n.m.* reinforcement. **de ~**, (*armée, personnel*) back-up. **à grand ~ de**, with a great deal of.

renfrogn|er (se) /(sə)rɑ̃frɔɲe/ *v. pr.* scowl. **~é** *a.* surly, sullen.

rengaine /rɑ̃gɛn/ *n.f.* (*péj.*) **la même ~**, the same old story.

renier /rənje/ *v.t.* (*personne, pays*) disown, deny; (*foi*) renounce.

renifler /rənifle/ *v.t./i.* sniff.

renne /rɛn/ *n.m.* reindeer.

renom /rənɔ̃/ *n.m.* renown; (*réputation*) reputation. **~mé** /-ɔme/ *a.* famous. **~mée** /-ɔme/ *n.f.* fame; reputation.

renonc|er /rənɔ̃se/ *v.i.* **~er à**, (*habitude, ami, etc.*) give up, renounce. **~er à faire**, give up (all thought of) doing. **~ement** *n.m.*, **~iation** *n.f.* renunciation.

renouer /rənwe/ *v.t.* tie up (again); (*reprendre*) renew. ● *v.i.* **~ avec**, start up again with.

renouveau (*pl.* **~x**) /rənuvo/ *n.m.* revival.

renouvel|er /rənuvle/ *v.t.* renew; (*réitérer*) repeat. **se ~er** *v. pr.* be renewed; be repeated. **~lement** /-ɛlmɑ̃/ *n.m.* renewal.

rénov|er /renɔve/ *v.t.* (*édifice*) renovate; (*institution*) reform. **~ation** *n.f.* renovation; reform.

renseignement /rɑ̃sɛɲmɑ̃/ *n.m.* **~(s)**, information. **(bureau des) ~s**, information desk.

renseigner /rɑ̃sɛɲe/ *v.t.* inform, give information to. **se ~** *v. pr.* enquire, make enquiries, find out.

rentab|le /rɑ̃tabl/ *a.* profitable. **~ilité** *n.f.* profitability.

rent|e /rɑ̃t/ *n.f.* (*private*) income; (*pension*) pension, annuity. **~ier, ~ière** *n.m., f.* person of private means.

rentrée /rɑ̃tre/ *n.f.* return; **la ~ parlementaire**, the reopening of Parliament; (*scol.*) start of the new year.

rentrer /rɑ̃tre/ (*aux. être*) *v.i.* go ou come back home, return home; (*entrer*) go ou come in; (*entrer à nouveau*) go ou come back in; (*revenu*) come in; (*élèves*) go back. **~ dans**, (*heurter*) smash into. ● *v.t.* (*aux. avoir*) bring in; (*griffes*) draw in; (*vêtement*) tuck in. **~ dans l'ordre**, be back to normal. **~ dans ses frais**, break even.

renverse (à la) /(ala)rɑ̃vɛrs/ *adv.* backwards.

renvers|er /rɑ̃vɛrse/ *v.t.* knock over ou down; (*piéton*) knock down; (*liquide*) upset, spill; (*mettre à l'envers*) turn upside down; (*gouvernement*) overturn; (*inverser*) reverse. **se ~er** *v. pr.* (*véhicule*) overturn; (*verre, vase*) fall over. **~ement** *n.m.* (*pol.*) overthrow.

renv|oi /rɑ̃vwa/ *n.m.* return; dismissal; expulsion; postponement; reference; (*rot*) belch. **~oyer†** *v.t.* send back, return; (*employé*) dismiss; (*élève*) expel; (*ajourner*) 1postpone; (*référer*) refer; (*réfléchir*) reflect.

réorganiser /reɔrganize/ *v.t.* reorganize.

réouverture /reuvɛrtyr/ *n.f.* reopening.

repaire /rəpɛr/ *n.m.* den.

répandre /repɑ̃dr/ *v.t.* (*liquide*) spill; (*étendre, diffuser*) spread; (*lumière, sang*) shed; (*odeur*) give off. **se ~** *v. pr.* spread; (*liquide*) spill. **se ~ en**, (*injures etc.*) pour forth, launch forth into.

répandu /repɑ̃dy/ a. (*courant*) widespread.

répar|er /repare/ v.t. repair, mend; (*faute*) make amends for; (*remédier à*) put right. **~ateur** n.m. repairer. **~ation** n.f. repair; (*compensation*) compensation.

repartie /rəparti/ n.f. retort. **avoir (le sens) de la ~,** be good at repartee.

repartir† /rəpartir/ v.i. start (up) again; (*voyageur*) set off again; (*s'en retourner*) go back.

répart|ir /repartir/ v.t. distribute; (*partager*) share out; (*étaler*) spread. **~ition** n.f. distribution.

repas /rəpɑ/ n.m. meal.

repass|er /rəpɑse/ v.i. come *ou* go back. ● v.t. (*linge*) iron; (*leçon*) go over; (*examen*) retake, (*film*) show again. **~age** n.m. ironing.

repêcher /rəpeʃe/ v.t. fish out; (*candidat*) allow to pass.

repentir† /rəpɑ̃tir/ n.m. repentance. **se ~** v. pr. (*relig.*) repent (**de,** of). **se ~ de,** (*regretter*) regret.

répercu|ter /repɛrkyte/ v.t. (*bruit*) echo. **se ~ter** v. pr. echo. **se ~ter sur,** have repercussions on. **~ssion** n.f. repercussion.

repère /rəpɛr/ n.m. mark; (*jalon*) marker; (*fig.*) landmark.

repérer /rəpere/ v.t. locate, spot. **se ~** v. pr. find one's bearings.

répert|oire /repertwar/ n.m. index; (*artistique*) repertoire. **~orier** v.t. index.

répéter /repete/ v.t. repeat. ● v.t./i. (*théâtre*) rehearse. **se ~** v. pr. be repeated; (*personne*) repeat o.s.

répétition /repetisjɔ̃/ n.f. repetition; (*théâtre*) rehearsal.

repiquer /rəpike/ v.t. (*plante*) plant out.

répit /repi/ n.m. rest, respite.

replacer /rəplase/ v.t. replace.

repl|i /rəpli/ n.m. fold; (*retrait*) withdrawal. **~ier** v.t. fold (up); (*ailes, jambes*) tuck in. **se ~ier** v. pr. withdraw (**sur soi-même,** into o.s.).

répliqu|e /replik/ n.f. reply; (*riposte*) retort; (*discussion*) objection; (*théâtre*) line(s); (*copie*) replica. **~er** v.t./i. reply; (*riposter*) retort; (*objecter*) answer back.

répondant, ~e /repɔ̃dɑ̃, -t/ n.m., f. guarantor. **avoir du ~,** have money behind one.

répondeur /repɔ̃dœr/ n.m. answering machine.

répondre /repɔ̃dr/ v.t. (*remarque etc.*) reply with. ● v.i. answer, reply; (*être insolent*) answer back; (*réagir*) respond (**à,** to). **~ à,** answer. **~ de,** answer for.

réponse /repɔ̃s/ n.f. answer, reply; (*fig.*) response.

report /rəpɔr/ n.m. (*transcription*) transfer; (*renvoi*) postponement.

reportage /rəpɔrtaʒ/ n.m. report; (*en direct*) commentary, (*par écrit*) article.

reporter¹ /rəpɔrte/ v.t. take back; (*ajourner*) put off; (*transcrire*) transfer. **se ~ à,** refer to.

reporter² /rəpɔrtɛr/ n.m. reporter.

repos /rəpo/ n.m. rest; (*paix*) peace; (*tranquillité*) peace and quiet; (*moral*) peace of mind.

repos|er /rəpoze/ v.t. put down again; (*délasser*) rest. ● v.i. rest (**sur,** on). **se ~er** v. pr. rest. **se ~er sur,** rely on. **~ant, ~ante** a. restful. **laisser ~er,** (*pâte*) leave to stand.

repoussant, ~e /rəpusɑ̃, -t/ a. repulsive.

repousser /rəpuse/ v.t. push back; (*écarter*) push away; (*dégoûter*) repel; (*décliner*) reject; (*ajourner*) put back. ● v.i. grow again.

répréhensible /repreɑ̃sibl/ a. blameworthy.

reprendre† /rəprɑ̃dr/ v.t. take back; (*retrouver*) regain; (*souffle*) get back; (*évadé*) recapture; (*recommencer*) resume; (*redire*) repeat; (*modifier*) alter; (*blâmer*) reprimand. **~ du pain/etc.,** take some more bread/ etc. ● v.i. (*recommencer*) resume; (*affaires*) pick up. **se ~** v. pr. (*se ressaisir*) pull o.s. together; (*se corriger*) correct o.s. **on ne m'y reprendra pas,** I won't be caught out again.

représailles /rəprezaj/ n.f. pl. reprisals.

représentati|f, ~ve /rəprezɑ̃tatif, -v/ a. representative.

représent|er /rəprezɑ̃te/ v.t. represent; (*théâtre*) perform. **se ~er** v. pr. (*s'imaginer*) imagine. **~ant, ~ante** n.m., f. representative. **~ation** n.f. representation; (*théâtre*) performance.

réprimand|e /reprimɑ̃d/ n.f. reprimand. **~er** v.t. reprimand.

répr|imer /reprime/ *v.t.* (*peuple*) repress; (*sentiment*) suppress. **~ession** *n.f.* repression.

repris /rapri/ *n.m.* **~ de justice,** ex-convict.

reprise /rapriz/ *n.f.* resumption; (*théâtre*) revival; (*télévision*) repeat; (*de tissu*) darn, mend; (*essor*) recovery; (*comm.*) part-exchange, trade-in. **à plusieurs ~s,** on several occasions.

repriser /raprize/ *v.t.* darn, mend.

réprobation /reprɔbasjɔ̃/ *n.f.* condemnation.

reproch|e /raprɔʃ/ *n.m.* reproach, blame. **~er** *v.t.* **~er qch. à qn.,** reproach *ou* blame s.o. for sth.

reprod|uire† /raprɔdɥir/ *v.t.* reproduce. **se ~uire** *v. pr.* reproduce; (*arriver*) recur. **~ucteur, ~uctrice** *a.* reproductive. **~uction** *n.f.* reproduction.

réprouver /repruve/ *v.t.* condemn.

reptile /rɛptil/ *n.m.* reptile.

repu /rapy/ *a.* satiated.

républi|que /repyblik/ *n.f.* republic. **~que populaire,** people's republic. **~cain, ~caine** *a.* & *n.m.*, *f.* republican.

répudier /repydje/ *v.t.* repudiate.

répugnance /repyɲɑ̃s/ *n.f.* repugnance; (*hésitation*) reluctance.

répugn|er /repyɲe/ *v.i.* **~er à,** be repugnant to. **~er à faire,** be reluctant to do. **~ant, ~ante** *a.* repulsive.

répulsion /repylsjɔ̃/ *n.f.* repulsion.

réputation /repytasjɔ̃/ *n.f.* reputation.

réputé /repyte/ *a.* renowned (**pour,** for). **~ pour être,** reputed to be.

requérir /rakerir/ *v.t.* require, demand.

requête /rakɛt/ *n.f.* request; (*jurid.*) petition.

requiem /rekɥijɛm/ *n.m. invar.* requiem.

requin /rakɛ̃/ *n.m.* shark.

requis, ~e /raki, -z/ *a.* required.

réquisition /rekizisjɔ̃/ *n.f.* requisition. **~ner** /-jɔne/ *v.t.* requisition.

rescapé, ~e /rɛskape/ *n.m.*, *f.* survivor. ● *a.* surviving.

rescousse /rɛskus/ *n.f.* **à la ~,** to the rescue.

réseau (*pl.* **~x**) /rezo/ *n.m.* network.

réservation /rezɛrvasjɔ̃/ *n.f.* reservation. **bureau de ~,** booking office.

réserve /rezɛrv/ *n.f.* reserve; (*restriction*) reservation, reserve; (*indienne*) reservation; (*entrepôt*) store-room. **en ~,** in reserve. **les ~s,** (*mil.*) the reserves.

réserv|er /rezɛrve/ *v.t.* reserve; (*place*) book, reserve. **se ~er le droit de,** reserve the right to. **~é** *a.* (*personne, place*) reserved.

réserviste /rezɛrvist/ *n.m.* reservist.

réservoir /rezɛrvwar/ *n.m.* tank; (*lac*) reservoir.

résidence /rezidɑ̃s/ *n.f.* residence.

résident, ~e /rezidɑ̃, -t/ *n.m.*, *f.* resident foreigner. **~iel, ~ielle** /-sjɛl/ *a.* residential.

résider /rezide/ *v.i.* reside.

résidu /rezidy/ *n.m.* residue.

résign|er (se) /(sa)reziɲe/ *v. pr.* **se ~er à faire,** resign o.s. to doing. **~ation** *n.f.* resignation.

résilier /rezilje/ *v.t.* terminate.•

résille /rezij/ *n.f.* (hair-)net.

résine /rezin/ *n.f.* resin.

résistance /rezistɑ̃s/ *n.f.* resistance; (*fil électrique*) element.

résistant, ~e /rezistɑ̃, -t/ *a.* tough.

résister /reziste/ *v.i.* resist. **~ à,** resist; (*examen, chaleur*) stand up to.

résolu /rezɔly/ *voir* **résoudre.** ● *a.* resolute. **~ à,** resolved to. **~ment** *adv.* resolutely.

résolution /rezɔlysjɔ̃/ *n.f.* (*fermeté*) resolution; (*d'un problème*) solving.

résonance /rezɔnɑ̃s/ *n.f.* resonance.

résonner /rezɔne/ *v.i.* resound.

résor|ber /rezɔrbe/ *v.t.* reduce. **se ~ber** *v. pr.* be reduced. **~ption** *n.f.* reduction.

résoudre† /rezudr/ *v.t.* solve; (*décider*) decide on. **se ~ à,** resolve to.

respect /rɛspɛ/ *n.m.* respect.

respectab|le /rɛspɛktabl/ *a.* respectable. **~ilité** *n.f.* respectability.

respecter /rɛspɛkte/ *v.t.* respect. **faire ~,** (*loi, décision*) enforce.

respecti|f, ~ve /rɛspɛktif, -v/ *a.* respective. **~vement** *adv.* respectively.

respectueu|x, ~se /rɛspɛktɥø, -z/ *a.* respectful.

respir|er /rɛspire/ *v.i.* breathe; (*se reposer*) get one's breath. ● *v.t.* breathe; (*exprimer*) radiate.

~ation *n.f.* breathing; (*haleine*) breath. ~atoire *a.* breathing.

resplend|ir /rɛsplɑ̃dir/ *v.i.* shine (**de**, with). ~issant, ~issante *a.* radiant.

responsabilité /rɛspɔ̃sabilite/ *n.f.* responsibility; (*légale*) liability.

responsable /rɛspɔ̃sabl/ *a.* responsible (**de**, for). ● ~ **de**, (*chargé de*) in charge of. ● *n.m./f.* person in charge; (*coupable*) person responsible.

resquiller /rɛskije/ *v.i.* (*fam.*) get in without paying; (*dans la queue*) jump the queue.

ressaisir (se) /(sə)rəsezir/ *v. pr.* pull o.s. together.

ressasser /rəsase/ *v.t.* keep going over.

ressembl|er /rəsɑ̃ble/ *v.i.* ~er à, resemble, look like. se ~er *v. pr.* look alike. ~ance *n.f.* resemblance. ~ant, ~ante *a.* (*portrait*) true to life; (*pareil*) alike.

ressemeler /rəsəmle/ *v.t.* sole.

ressentiment /rəsɑ̃timɑ̃/ *n.m.* resentment.

ressentir /rəsɑ̃tir/ *v.t.* feel. se ~ **de**, feel the effects of.

resserre /rəsɛr/ *n.f.* shed.

resserrer /rəsere/ *v.t.* tighten; (*contracter*) contract. se ~ *v. pr.* tighten; contract; (*route etc.*) narrow.

resservir /rəsɛrvir/ *v.i.* come in useful (again).

ressort /rəsɔr/ *n.m.* (*objet*) spring; (*fig.*) energy. du ~ **de**, within the jurisdiction *ou* scope of. en dernier ~, in the last resort.

ressortir /rəsɔrtir/ *v.i.* go *ou* come back out; (*se voir*) stand out. faire ~, bring out. ~ **de**, (*résulter*) result *ou* emerge from.

ressortissant, ~e /rəsɔrtisɑ̃, -t/ *n.m.*, *f.* national.

ressource /rəsurs/ *n.f.* resource. ~s, resources.

ressusciter /resysite/ *v.i.* come back to life.

restant, ~e /rɛstɑ̃, -t/ *a.* remaining. ● *n.m.* remainder.

restaur|ant /rɛstɔrɑ̃/ *n.m.* restaurant. ~ateur, ~atrice *n.m.*, *f.* restaurant owner.

restaur|er /rɛstɔre/ *v.t.* restore. se ~er *v. pr.* eat. ~ation *n.f.* restoration; (*hôtellerie*) catering.

reste /rɛst/ *n.m.* rest; (*d'une soustraction*) remainder. ~s, remains (**de**, of); (*nourriture*) leftovers. un ~ **de**

pain/*etc.*, some left-over bread/*etc.* au ~, du ~, moreover, besides.

rest|er /rɛste/ *v.i.* (aux. être) stay, remain; (*subsister*) be left, remain. **il ~e du pain**/*etc.*, there is some bread/*etc.* left (over). **il me ~e du pain,** I have some bread left (over). **il me ~e à,** it remains for me to. **en ~er à,** go no further than. **en ~er là,** stop there.

restit|uer /rɛstitɥe/ *v.t.* (*rendre*) return, restore; (*son*) reproduce. ~ution *n.f.* return.

restreindre† /rɛstrɛ̃dr/ *v.t.* restrict. se ~ *v. pr.* (*dans les dépenses*) cut down.

restricti|f, ~ve /rɛstriktif, -v/ *a.* restrictive.

restriction /rɛstriksjɔ̃/ *n.f.* restriction.

résultat /rezylta/ *n.m.* result.

résulter /rezylte/ *v.i.* ~ **de**, result from.

résum|er /rezyme/ *v.t.*, se ~er *v. pr.* summarize. ~é *n.m.* summary. en ~é, in short.

résurrection /rezyrɛksjɔ̃/ *n.f.* resurrection; (*renouveau*) revival.

rétabl|ir /retablir/ *v.t.* restore; (*personne*) restore to health. se ~ir *v. pr.* be restored; (*guérir*) recover. ~issement *n.m.* restoring; (*méd.*) recovery.

retaper /rətape/ *v.t.* (*maison etc.*) do up. se ~ *v. pr.* (*guérir*) get back on one's feet.

retard /rətar/ *n.m.* lateness; (*sur un programme*) delay; (*infériorité*) backwardness. avoir du ~, be late; (*montre*) be slow. en ~, late; (*retardé*) backward. en ~ **sur**, behind. rattraper *ou* combler son ~, catch up.

retardataire /rətardatɛr/ *n.m./f.* latecomer. ● *a.* (*arrivant*) late.

retardé /rətarde/ *a.* backward.

retardement (à) /(a)rətardəmɑ̃/ *a.* (*bombe etc.*) delayed-action.

retarder /rətarde/ *v.t.* delay; (*sur un programme*) set back; (*montre*) put back. ● *v.i.* (*montre*) be slow; (*fam.*) be out of touch.

retenir† /rətnir/ *v.t.* hold back; (*souffle, attention, prisonnier*) hold; (*eau, chaleur*) retain, hold; (*larmes*) hold back; (*garder*) keep; (*retarder*) detain; (*réserver*) book; (*se rappeler*) remember; (*déduire*) deduct; (*accepter*) accept. se ~ *v. pr.* (*se contenir*) restrain o.s. **se ~ à**, hold on to. **se ~ de**, stop o.s. from.

rétention /retɑ̃sjɔ̃/ *n.f.* retention.

retent|ir /rətɑ̃tir/ *v.i.* ring out (**de**, with). **~issant, ~issante** *a.* resounding. **~issement** *n.m.* (*effet, répercussion*) effect.

retenue /rətny/ *n.f.* restraint; (*somme*) deduction; (*scol.*) detention.

réticen|t, ~te /retisɑ̃, -t/ *a.* (*hésitant*) reluctant; (*réservé*) reticent. **~ce** *n.f.* reluctance; reticence.

rétif, ~ve /retif, -v/ *a.* restive, recalcitrant.

rétine /retin/ *n.f.* retina.

retiré /rətire/ *a.* (*vie*) secluded; (*lieu*) remote.

retirer /rətire/ *v.t.* (*sortir*) take out; (*ôter*) take off; (*argent, candidature*) withdraw; (*avantage*) derive. **~ à qn.**, take away from s.o. **se ~ *v. pr.* withdraw, retire.

retombées /rətɔ̃be/ *n.f. pl.* fall-out.

retomber /rətɔ̃be/ *v.i.* fall; (*à nouveau*) fall again. **~ dans**, (*erreur etc.*) fall back into.

rétorquer /retɔrke/ *v.t.* retort.

rétorsion /retɔrsjɔ̃/ *n.f.* **mesures de ~**, retaliation.

retouch|e /rətuʃ/ *n.f.* touch-up; alteration. **~er** *v.t.* touch up; (*vêtement*) alter.

retour /rətur/ *n.m.* return. **être de ~**, be back (**de**, from). **~ en arrière**, flashback. **par ~ du courrier**, by return of post. **en ~**, in return.

retourner /rəturne/ *v.t.* (*aux. avoir*) turn over; (*vêtement*) turn inside out; (*lettre, compliment*) return; (*émouvoir: fam.*) upset. ● *v.i.* (*aux. être*) go back, return. **se ~ *v. pr.* turn round; (*dans son lit*) twist and turn. **s'en ~**, go back. **se ~ contre**, turn against.

retracer /rətrase/ *v.t.* retrace.

rétracter /retrakte/ *v.t., se ~ *v. pr.* retract.

retrait /rətrɛ/ *n.m.* withdrawal; (*des eaux*) ebb, receding. **être (situé) en ~**, be set back.

retraite /rətrɛt/ *n.f.* retirement; (*pension*) (retirement) pension; (*fuite, refuge*) retreat. **mettre à la ~**, pension off. **prendre sa ~**, retire.

retraité, ~e /rətrete/ *a.* retired. ● *n.m., f.* (old-age) pensioner, senior citizen.

retrancher /rətrɑ̃ʃe/ *v.t.* remove; (*soustraire*) deduct. **se ~ *v. pr.* (*mil.*) entrench o.s. **se ~ derrière/ dans**, take refuge behind/in.

retransm|ettre /rətrɑ̃smɛtr/ *v.t.* broadcast. **~ission** *n.f.* broadcast.

rétrécir /retresir/ *v.t.* narrow; (*vêtement*) take in. ● *v.i.* (*tissu*) shrink. **se ~**, (*rue*) narrow.

rétrib|uer /retribɥe/ *v.t.* pay. **~ution** *n.f.* payment.

rétroacti|f, ~ve /retrɔaktif, -v/ *a.* retrospective. **augmentation à effet ~f**, backdated pay rise.

rétrograd|e /retrɔgrad/ *a.* retrograde. **~er** *v.i.* (*reculer*) fall back, recede; *v.t.* demote.

rétrospectivement /retrɔspɛktivmɑ̃/ *adv.* in retrospect.

retrousser /rətruse/ *v.t.* pull up.

retrouvailles /rətruvaj/ *n.f. pl.* reunion.

retrouver /rətruve/ *v.t.* find (again); (*rejoindre*) meet (again); (*forces, calme*) regain; (*se rappeler*) remember. **se ~ *v. pr.* find (back); (*se réunir*) meet (again). **s'y ~**, (*s'orienter, comprendre*) find one's way; (*rentrer dans ses frais*) break even.

rétroviseur /retrɔvizœr/ *n.m.* (*auto.*) (rear-view) mirror.

réunion /reynjɔ̃/ *n.f.* meeting; (*d'objets*) collection.

réunir /reynir/ *v.t.* gather, collect; (*rapprocher*) bring together; (*convoquer*) call together; (*raccorder*) join; (*qualités*) combine. **se ~ *v. pr.* meet.

réussi /reysi/ *a.* successful.

réussir /reysir/ *v.i.* succeed, be successful (**à faire**, in doing). **~ à qn.**, work well for s.o.; (*climat etc.*) agree with s.o. ● *v.t.* make a success of.

réussite /reysit/ *n.f.* success; (*jeu*) patience.

revaloir /rəvalwar/ *v.t.* **je vous revaudrai cela**, (*en mal*) I'll pay you back for this; (*en bien*) I'll repay you some day.

revaloriser /rəvalɔrize/ *v.t.* (*monnaie*) revalue; (*salaires*) raise.

revanche /rəvɑ̃ʃ/ *n.f.* revenge; (*sport*) return *ou* revenge match. **en ~**, on the other hand.

rêvasser /rɛvase/ *v.i.* day-dream.

rêve /rɛv/ *n.m.* dream. **faire un ~**, have a dream.

revêche /rəvɛʃ/ *a.* ill-tempered.

réveil /revɛj/ *n.m.* waking up, (*fig.*) awakening; (*pendule*) alarm-clock.

réveill|er /reveje/ *v.t.*, se ~er *v. pr.* wake (up); (*fig.*) awaken. ~é *a.* awake. ~e-matin *n.m. invar.* alarm-clock.

réveillon /revɛjɔ̃/ *n.m.* (*Noël*) Christmas Eve; (*nouvel an*) New Year's Eve. ~ner /-jɔne/ *v.i.* celebrate the *réveillon*.

révél|er /revele/ *v.t.* reveal. se ~er *v. pr.* be revealed. se ~er *facile/etc.*, prove easy/*etc.* ~ateur, ~atrice *a.* revealing. ● *n.m.* (*photo*) developer. ~ation *n.f.* revelation.

revenant /rəvnɑ̃/ *n.m.* ghost.

revendi|quer /rəvɑ̃dike/ *v.t.* claim. ~catif, ~cative *a.* (*mouvement etc.*) in support of one's claims. ~cation *n.f.* claim; (*action*) claiming.

revend|re /rəvɑ̃dr/ *v.t.* sell (again). ~eur, ~euse *n.m.*, *f.* dealer.

revenir† /rəvnir/ *v.i.* (*aux. être*) come back, return (à, to). ~ à, (*activité*) go back to; (*se résumer à*) come down to; (*échoir à*) fall to; (*coûter à*) cost. ~ de, (*maladie, surprise*) get over. ~ sur ses pas, retrace one's steps. faire ~, (*culin.*) brown. ça me revient, it comes back to me.

revente /rəvɑ̃t/ *n.f.* resale.

revenu /rəvny/ *n.m.* income; (*d'un état*) revenue.

rêver /reve/ *v.t./i.* dream (à *ou* de, of).

réverbération /reverberasjɔ̃/ *n.f.* reflection, reverberation.

réverbère /reverber/ *n.m.* street lamp.

révérenc|e /reverɑ̃s/ *n.f.* reverence; (*salut d'homme*) bow; (*salut de femme*) curtsy. ~ieux, ~ieuse *a.* reverent.

révérend, ~e /reverɑ̃, -d/ *a.* & *n.m.* reverend.

rêverie /revri/ *n.f.* day-dream; (*activité*) day-dreaming.

revers /rəver/ *n.m.* reverse; (*de main*) back; (*d'étoffe*) wrong side; (*de veste*) lapel; (*tennis*) backhand; (*fig.*) set-back.

réversible /reversibl/ *a.* reversible.

revêt|ir /rəvetir/ *v.t.* cover; (*habit*) put on; (*prendre, avoir*) assume. ~ement /-vɛtmɑ̃/ *n.m.* covering; (*de route*) surface.

rêveu|r, ~se /revœr, -øz/ *a.* dreamy. ● *n.m.*, *f.* dreamer.

revigorer /rəvigore/ *v.t.* revive.

revirement /rəvirmɑ̃/ *n.m.* sudden change.

révis|er /revize/ *v.t.* revise; (*véhicule*) overhaul. ~ion *n.f.* revision; overhaul.

revivre† /rəvivr/ *v.i.* live again. ● *v.t.* relive. faire ~, revive.

révocation /revɔkasjɔ̃/ *n.f.* repeal; (*d'un fonctionnaire*) dismissal.

revoir† /rəvwar/ *v.t.* see (again); (*réviser*) revise. au ~, goodbye.

révolte /revɔlt/ *n.f.* revolt.

révolt|er /revɔlte/ *v.t.*, se ~er *v. pr.* revolt. ~ant, ~ante *a.* revolting. ~é, ~ée *n.m.*, *f.* rebel.

révolu /revɔly/ *a.* past.

révolution /revɔlysjɔ̃/ *n.f.* revolution. ~naire /-jɔner/ *a.* & *n.m./f.* revolutionary. ~ner /- jɔne/ *v.t.* revolutionize.

revolver /revɔlver/ *n.m.* revolver, gun.

révoquer /revɔke/ *v.t.* repeal; (*fonctionnaire*) dismiss.

revue /rəvy/ *n.f.* (*examen, défilé*) review; (*magazine*) magazine; (*spectacle*) variety show.

rez-de-chaussée /redʃose/ *n.m. invar.* ground floor; (*Amer.*) first floor.

RF *abrév.* (*République Française*) French Republic.

rhabiller (se) /(sə)rabije/ *v. pr.* get dressed (again), dress (again).

rhapsodie /rapsɔdi/ *n.f.* rhapsody.

rhétorique /retɔrik/ *n.f.* rhetoric. ● *a.* rhetorical.

rhinocéros /rinɔserɔs/ *n.m.* rhinoceros.

rhubarbe /rybarb/ *n.f.* rhubarb.

rhum /rɔm/ *n.m.* rum.

rhumatis|me /rymatism/ *n.m.* rheumatism. ~ant, ~ante /-zɑ̃, -t/ *a.* rheumatic.

rhume /rym/ *n.m.* cold. ~ des foins, hay fever.

ri /ri/ *voir* **rire**.

riant, ~e /rjɑ̃, -t/ *a.* cheerful.

ricaner /rikane/ *v.i.* snigger, giggle.

riche /riʃ/ *a.* rich (en, in). ● *n.m./f.* rich person. ~ment *adv.* richly.

richesse /riʃes/ *n.f.* wealth; (*de sol, décor*) richness. ~s, wealth.

ricoch|er /rikɔʃe/ *v.i.* rebound, ricochet. ~et *n.m.* rebound, ricochet. par ~er, indirectly.

rictus /riktys/ *n.m.* grin, grimace.

rid|e /rid/ *n.f.* wrinkle; (*sur l'eau*) ripple. ~er *v.t.* wrinkle; (*eau*) ripple.

rideau /pl. ~x/ /rido/ n.m. curtain; (*métallique*) shutter; (*fig.*) screen. ~ **de fer**, (*pol.*) Iron Curtain.

ridicul|**e** /ridikyl/ a. ridiculous. ● n.m. absurdity. **le ~e**, ridicule. ~**iser** v.t. ridicule.

rien /rjɛ̃/ pron. **(ne) ~**, nothing. ● n.m. trifle. **de ~!**, don't mention it! **d'autre/de plus**, nothing else/more. **~ du tout**, nothing at all. **~ que**, just, only. **trois fois ~**, next to nothing. **il n'y est pour ~**, he has nothing to do with it. **en un ~ de temps**, in next to no time. **~ à faire**, it's no good!

rieu|**r**, ~**se** /rijœr, rijøz/ a. merry.

rigid|**e** /riʒid/ a. rigid; (*muscle*) stiff. ~**ité** n.f. rigidity; stiffness.

rigole /rigɔl/ n.f. channel.

rigol|**er** /rigɔle/ v.i. laugh; (*s'amuser*) have some fun; (*plaisanter*) joke. ~**ade** n.f. fun.

rigolo, ~**te** /rigolo, -ɔt/ a. (*fam.*) funny. ● n.m., f. (*fam.*) joker.

rigoureu|**x**, ~**se** /riguro, -z/ a. rigorous; (*hiver*) harsh. ~**sement** adv. rigorously.

rigueur /rigœr/ n.f. rigour. **à la ~**, at a pinch. **être de ~**, be the rule. **tenir ~ à qn. de qch.**, hold sth. against s.o.

rim|**e** /rim/ n.f. rhyme. ~**er** v.i. rhyme (**avec**, with). **cela ne ~e à rien**, it makes no sense.

rin|**cer** /rɛ̃se/ v.t. rinse. ~**çage** n.m. rinse; (*action*) rinsing. ~**ce-doigts** n.m. invar. finger-bowl.

ring /riŋ/ n.m. boxing ring.

ripost|**e** /ripɔst/ n.f. retort; (*mil.*) reprisal. ~**er** v.i. retaliate; v.t. retort (**que**, that). ~**er à**, (*attaque*) counter; (*insulte etc.*) reply to.

rire† /rir/ v.i. laugh (**de**, at); (*plaisanter*) joke; (*s'amuser*) have fun. **c'était pour ~**, it was a joke. ● n.m. laugh. ~**s, le ~** laughter.

risée /rize/ n.f. **la ~ de**, the laughing-stock of.

risible /rizibl/ a. laughable.

risqu|**e** /risk/ n.m. risk. ~**é** a. risky; (*osé*) daring. ~**er** v.t. risk. ~**er de faire**, stand a good chance of doing. **se ~er à/dans**, venture to/into.

rissoler /risɔle/ v.t./i. brown. **(faire) ~**, brown.

ristourne /risturn/ n.f. discount.

rite /rit/ n.m. rite; (*habitude*) ritual.

rituel, ~**le** /rituɛl/ a. & n.m. ritual.

rivage /rivaʒ/ n.m. shore.

riv|**al**, ~**ale** (m. pl. ~**aux**) /rival, -o/ n.m., f. rival. ● a. rival. ~**aliser** v.i. compete (**avec**, with). ~**alité** n.f. rivalry.

rive /riv/ n.f. (*de fleuve*) bank; (*de lac*) shore.

riv|**er** /rive/ v.t. rivet. ~**er son clou à qn.**, shut s.o. up. ~**et** n.m. rivet.

riverain, ~**e** /rivrɛ̃, -ɛn/ a. riverside. ● n.m., f. riverside resident; (*d'une rue*) resident.

rivière /rivjɛr/ n.f. river.

rixe /riks/ n.f. brawl.

riz /ri/ n.m. rice. ~**ière** /rizjɛr/ n.f. paddy(-field); rice field.

robe /rɔb/ n.f. (*de femme*) dress; (*de juge*) robe; (*de cheval*) coat. **~ de chambre**, dressing-gown.

robinet /rɔbinɛ/ n.m. tap; (*Amer.*) faucet.

robot /rɔbo/ n.m. robot.

robuste /rɔbyst/ a. robust. ~**sse** /-ɛs/ n.f. robustness.

roc /rɔk/ n.m. rock.

rocaill|**e** /rɔkɑj/ n.f. rocky ground; (*de jardin*) rockery. ~**eux**, ~**euse** a. (*terrain*) rocky.

roch|**e** /rɔʃ/ n.f. rock. ~**eux**, ~**euse** a. rocky.

rocher /rɔʃe/ n.m. rock.

rock /rɔk/ n.m. (*mus.*) rock.

rod|**er** /rɔde/ v.t. (*auto.*) run in; (*auto., Amer.*) break in. **être ~é**, (*personne*) be broken in. ~**age** n.m. running in; breaking in.

rôd|**er** /rode/ v.i. roam; (*suspect*) prowl. ~**eur**, ~**euse** n.m., f. prowler.

rogne /rɔɲ/ n.f. (*fam.*) anger.

rogner /rɔɲe/ v.t. trim; (*réduire*) cut. **~ sur**, cut down on.

rognon /rɔɲɔ̃/ n.m. (*culin.*) kidney.

rognures /rɔɲyr/ n.f. pl. scraps.

roi /rwa/ n.m. king. **les Rois mages**, the Magi. **la fête des Rois**, Twelfth Night.

roitelet /rwatlɛ/ n.m. wren.

rôle /rol/ n.m. role, part.

romain, ~**e** /rɔmɛ̃, -ɛn/ a. & n.m., f. Roman. ● n.f. (*laitue*) cos.

roman /rɔmɑ̃/ n.m. novel; (*fig.*) story; (*genre*) fiction.

romance /rɔmɑ̃s/ n.f. sentimental ballad.

romanc|**ier**, ~**ière** /rɔmɑ̃sje, -jɛr/ n.m., f. novelist.

romanesque /rɔmanɛsk/ a. romantic; (*fantastique*) fantastic. **œuvres ~s**, novels, fiction.

romanichel, **~le** /rɔmaniʃɛl/ *n.m.*, *f.* gypsy.

romanti|que /rɔmɑ̃tik/ *a.* & *n.m./f.* romantic. **~sme** *n.m.* romanticism.

rompre† /rɔ̃pr/ *v.t./i.* break; (*relations*) break off; (*fiancés*) break it off. **se ~** *v. pr.* break.

rompu /rɔ̃py/ *a.* (*exténué*) exhausted.

ronces /rɔ̃s/ *n.f. pl.* brambles.

ronchonner /rɔ̃ʃɔne/ *v.i.* (*fam.*) grumble.

rond, **~e** [1] /rɔ̃, rɔ̃d/ *a.* round; (*gras*) plump; (*ivre: fam.*) tight. ● *n.m.* (*cercle*) ring; (*tranche*) slice. **il n'a pas un ~**, (*fam.*) he hasn't got a penny. **en ~**, in a circle. **~ement** /rɔ̃dmɑ̃/ *adv.* briskly; (*franchement*) straight. **~eur** /rɔ̃dœr/ *n.f.* roundness; (*franchise*) frankness; (*embonpoint*) plumpness. **~-point** (*pl.* **~s-points**) *n.m.* roundabout; (*Amer.*) traffic circle.

ronde [2] /rɔ̃d/ *n.f.* round(s); (*de policier*) beat; (*mus.*) semibreve.

rondelet, **~te** /rɔ̃dlɛ, -t/ *a.* chubby.

rondelle /rɔ̃dɛl/ *n.f.* (*techn.*) washer; (*tranche*) slice.

rondin /rɔ̃dɛ̃/ *n.m.* log.

ronfl|er /rɔ̃fle/ *v.i.* snore; (*moteur*) hum. **~ement(s)** *n.m.* (*pl.*) snoring; humming.

rong|er /rɔ̃ʒe/ *v.t.* gnaw (at); (*vers, acide*) eat into; (*personne: fig.*) consume. **se ~er les ongles**, bite one's nails. **~eur** *n.m.* rodent.

ronronn|er /rɔ̃rɔne/ *v.i.* purr. **~ement** *n.m.* purr(ing).

roquette /rɔkɛt/ *n.f.* rocket.

rosace /rɔzas/ *n.f.* (*d'église*) rose window.

rosaire /rɔzɛr/ *n.m.* rosary.

rosbif /rɔsbif/ *n.m.* roast beef.

rose /roz/ *n.f.* rose. ● *a.* pink; (*situation, teint*) rosy. ● *n.m.* pink.

rosé /roze/ *a.* pinkish; (*vin*) rosé. ● *n.m.* rosé.

roseau (*pl.* **~x**) /rozo/ *n.m.* reed.

rosée /roze/ *n.f.* dew.

roseraie /rozrɛ/ *n.f.* rose garden.

rosette /rozɛt/ *n.f.* rosette.

rosier /rozje/ *n.m.* rose-bush, rose tree.

rosse /rɔs/ *a.* (*fam.*) nasty.

rosser /rɔse/ *v.t.* thrash.

rossignol /rɔsiɲɔl/ *n.m.* nightingale.

rot /ro/ *n.m.* (*fam.*) burp.

rotati|f, **~ve** /rɔtatif, -v/ *a.* rotary.

rotation /rɔtasjɔ̃/ *n.f.* rotation.

roter /rɔte/ *v.i.* (*fam.*) burp.

rotin /rɔtɛ̃/ *n.m.* (rattan) cane.

rôt|ir /rotir/ *v.t./i.*, **se ~ir** *v. pr.* roast. **~i** *n.m.* roasting meat; (*cuit*) roast. **~i de porc**, roast pork.

rôtisserie /rotisri/ *n.f.* grill-room.

rôtissoire /rotiswar/ *n.f.* (roasting) spit.

rotule /rɔtyl/ *n.f.* kneecap.

roturi|er, **ère** /rɔtyrje, -ɛr/ *n.m.*, *f.* commoner.

rouage /rwaʒ/ *n.m.* (*techn.*) (working) part. **~s**, (*d'une organisation: fig.*) wheels.

roucouler /rukule/ *v.i.* coo.

roue /ru/ *n.f.* wheel. **~ (dentée)**, cog(-wheel). **~ de secours**, spare wheel.

roué /rwe/ *a.* wily, calculating.

rouer /rwe/ *v.t.* **~ de coups**, thrash.

rouet /rwe/ *n.m.* spinning-wheel.

rouge /ruʒ/ *a.* red; (*fer*) red-hot. ● *n.m.* red; (*vin*) red wine; (*fard*) rouge. **~ (à lèvres)**, lipstick. ● *n.m./f.* (*pol.*) red. **~-gorge** (*pl.* **~s-gorges**) *n.m.* robin.

rougeole /ruʒɔl/ *n.f.* measles.

rougeoyer /ruʒwaje/ *v.i.* glow (red).

rouget /ruʒɛ/ *n.m.* red mullet.

rougeur /ruʒœr/ *n.f.* redness; (*tache*) red blotch; (*gêne, honte*) red face.

rougir /ruʒir/ *v.t./i.* turn red; (*de honte*) blush.

rouill|e /ruj/ *n.f.* rust. **~é** *a.* rusty. **~er** *v.i.*, **se ~er** *v. pr.* get rusty, rust.

roulant, **~e** /rulɑ̃, -t/ *a.* (*meuble*) on wheels; (*escalier*) moving.

rouleau (*pl.* **~x**) /rulo/ *n.m.* roll; (*outil, vague*) roller. **~ à pâtisserie**, rolling-pin. **~ compresseur**, steam-roller.

roulement /rulmɑ̃/ *n.m.* rotation; (*bruit*) rumble; (*succession de personnes*) turnover; (*de tambour*) roll. **~ à billes**, ball-bearing. **par ~**, in rotation.

rouler /rule/ *v.t./i.* roll; (*ficelle, manches*) roll up; (*duper: fam.*) cheat; (*véhicule, train*) go, travel; (*conducteur*) drive. **se ~ dans** *v. pr.* roll (over) in.

roulette /rulɛt/ *n.f.* (*de meuble*) castor; (*de dentiste*) drill; (*jeu*) roulette. **comme sur des ~s**, very smoothly.

roulis /ruli/ *n.m.* rolling.

roulotte /rulɔt/ *n.f.* caravan.

roumain, **~e** /rumɛ̃, -ɛn/ *a.* & *n.m.*, *f.* Romanian.

Roumanie /rumani/ *n.f.* Romania.

roupiller /rupije/ *v.i.* (*fam.*) sleep.

rouquin, ~e /rukɛ̃, -in/ a. (fam.) red-haired. ● n.m., f. (fam.) redhead.

rouspéter /ruspete/ v.i. (fam.) grumble, moan, complain.

rousse /rus/ voir roux.

roussir /rusir/ v.t. scorch. ● v.i. turn brown.

route /rut/ n.f. road; (naut., aviat.) route; (direction) way; (voyage) journey; (chemin: fig.) path. **en ~**, on the way. **en ~!**, let's go! **mettre en ~**, start. **~ nationale**, trunk road, main road. **se mettre en ~**, set out.

rout|ier, ~ière /rutje, -jɛr/ a. road. ● n.m. long-distance lorry driver ou truck driver (Amer.); (restaurant) roadside café.

routine /rutin/ n.f. routine.

rouvrir /ruvrir/ v.t., **se ~ir** v. pr. reopen, open again.

rou|x, ~sse /ru, rus/ a. red, reddish-brown; (personne) red-haired. ● n.m., f. redhead.

roy|al (m. pl. ~aux) /rwajal, -jo/ a. royal; (total: fam.) thorough. **~alement** adv. royally.

royaume /rwajom/ n.m. kingdom. **R~-Uni** n.m. United Kingdom.

royauté /rwajote/ n.f. royalty.

ruade /ryad, ryad/ n.f. kick.

ruban /rybã/ n.m. ribbon; (de magnétophone) tape; (de chapeau) band. **~ adhésif**, sticky tape.

rubéole /rybeɔl/ n.f. German measles.

rubis /rybi/ n.m. ruby; (de montre) jewel.

rubrique /rybrik/ n.f. heading; (article) column.

ruche /ryʃ/ n.f. beehive.

rude /ryd/ a. rough; (pénible) tough; (grossier) crude; (fameux: fam.) tremendous. **~ment** adv. (frapper etc.) hard; (traiter) harshly; (très: fam.) awfully.

rudiment|s /rydimã/ n.m. pl. rudiments. **~aire** /-tɛr/ a. rudimentary.

rudoyer /rydwaje/ v.t. treat harshly.

rue /ry/ n.f. street.

ruée /rye/ n.f. rush.

ruelle /rɥɛl/ n.f. alley.

ruer /rɥe/ v.i. (cheval) kick. **se ~ dans/vers**, rush into/towards. **se ~ sur**, pounce on.

rugby /rygbi/ n.m. Rugby.

rugby|man (pl. ~men) /rygbiman, -mɛn/ n.m. Rugby player.

rug|ir /ryʒir/ v.i. roar. **~issement** n.m. roar.

rugueu|x, ~se /rygø, -z/ a. rough.

ruin|e /rɥin/ n.f. ruin. **en ~e(s)**, in ruins. **~er** v.t. ruin.

ruineu|x, ~se /rɥinø, -z/ a. ruinous.

ruisseau (pl. ~x) /rɥiso/ n.m. stream; (rigole) gutter.

ruisseler /rɥisle/ v.i. stream.

rumeur /rymœr/ n.f. (nouvelle) rumour; (son) murmur, hum; (protestation) rumblings.

ruminer /rymine/ v.t./i. (herbe) ruminate; (méditer) meditate.

rupture /ryptyr/ n.f. break; (action) breaking; (de contrat) breach; (de pourparlers) breakdown.

rur|al (m. pl. ~aux) /ryral, -o/ a. rural.

rus|e /ryz/ n.f. cunning; (perfidie) trickery. **une ~e**, a trick, a ruse. **~é** a. cunning.

russe /rys/ a. & n.m./f. Russian. ● n.m. (lang.) Russian.

Russie /rysi/ n.f. Russia.

rustique /rystik/ a. rustic.

rustre /rystr/ n.m. lout, boor.

rutilant, ~e /rytilã, -t/ a. sparkling, gleaming.

rythm|e /ritm/ n.m. rhythm; (vitesse) rate; (de la vie) pace. **~é, ~ique** adjs. rhythmical.

S

s' /s/ voir se.

sa /sa/ voir son [1].

SA abrév. (société anonyme) PLC.

sabbat /saba/ n.m. sabbath. **~ique** a. **année ~ique**, sabbatical year.

sabl|e /sabl/ n.m. sand. **~es mouvants**, quicksands. **~er** v.t. sand. **~er le champagne**, drink champagne. **~eux, ~euse, ~onneux, ~onneuse** adjs. sandy.

sablier /sablije/ n.m. (culin.) eggtimer.

saborder /saborde/ v.t. (navire, projet) scuttle.

sabot /sabo/ n.m. (de cheval etc.) hoof; (chaussure) clog; (de frein) shoe. **~ de Denver**, (wheel) clamp.

sabot|er /sabote/ v.t. sabotage; (bâcler) botch. **~age** n.m. sabotage; (acte) act of sabotage. **~eur, ~euse** n.m., f. saboteur.

sabre /sɑbr/ n.m. sabre.

sac /sak/ n.m. bag; (*grand, en toile*) sack. **mettre à ~,** (*maison*) ransack; (*ville*) sack. **~ à dos,** rucksack. **~ à main,** handbag. **~ de couchage,** sleeping-bag. **mettre dans le même ~,** lump together.

saccad|e /sakad/ n.f. jerk. **~é** a. jerky.

saccager /sakaʒe/ v.t. (*ville, pays*) sack; (*maison*) ransack; (*ravager*) wreck.

saccharine /sakarin/ n.f. saccharin.

sacerdoce /sasɛrdɔs/ n.m. priesthood; (*fig.*) vocation.

sachet /saʃɛ/ n.m. (small) bag; (*de médicament etc.*) sachet. **~ de thé,** tea-bag.

sacoche /sakɔʃ/ n.f. bag; (*d'élève*) satchel; (*de moto*) saddle-bag.

sacquer /sake/ v.t. (*fam.*) sack. **je ne peux pas le ~,** I can't stand him.

sacr|e /sakr/ n.m. (*de roi*) coronation; (*d'évêque*) consecration. **~er** v.t. crown; consecrate.

sacré /sakre/ a. sacred; (*maudit: fam.*) damned.

sacrement /sakrəmɑ̃/ n.m. sacrament.

sacrifice /sakrifis/ n.m. sacrifice.

sacrifier /sakrifje/ v.t. sacrifice. **~ à,** conform to. **se ~** v. pr. sacrifice o.s.

sacrilège /sakrilɛʒ/ n.m. sacrilege. ● a. sacrilegious.

sacristain /sakristɛ̃/ n.m. sexton.

sacristie /sakristi/ n.f. (*protestante*) vestry; (*catholique*) sacristy.

sacro-saint, ~e /sakrosɛ̃, -t/ a. sacrosanct.

sadi|que /sadik/ a. sadistic. ● n.m./f. sadist. **~sme** n.m. sadism.

safari /safari/ n.m. safari.

sagace /sagas/ a. shrewd.

sage /saʒ/ a. wise; (*docile*) good. ● n.m. wise man. **~-femme** (*pl.* **~s-femmes**) n.f. midwife. **~ment** adv. wisely; (*docilement*) quietly. **~sse** /-ɛs/ n.f. wisdom.

Sagittaire /saʒitɛr/ n.m. le **~,** Sagittarius.

Sahara /saara/ n.m. le **~,** the Sahara (desert).

saignant, ~e /sɛɲɑ̃, -t/ a. (*culin.*) rare.

saign|er /seɲe/ v.t./i. bleed. **~er du nez,** have a nosebleed. **~ée** n.f. bleeding. **~ement** n.m. bleeding. **~ement de nez,** nosebleed.

saill|ie /saji/ n.f. projection. **faire ~ie,** project. **~ant, ~ante** a. projecting; (*remarquable*) salient.

sain, ~e /sɛ̃, sɛn/ a. healthy; (*moralement*) sane. **~ et sauf,** safe and sound. **~ement** /sɛnmɑ̃/ adv. healthily; (*juger*) sanely.

saindoux /sɛ̃du/ n.m. lard.

saint, ~e /sɛ̃, sɛ̃t/ a. holy; (*bon, juste*) saintly. ● n.m., f. saint. **S~-Esprit** n.m. Holy Spirit. **S~-Siège** n.m. Holy See. **S~-Sylvestre** n.f. New Year's Eve. **S~e Vierge,** Blessed Virgin.

sainteté /sɛ̃tte/ n.f. holiness; (*d'un lieu*) sanctity.

sais /sɛ/ *voir* savoir.

saisie /sezi/ n.f. (*jurid.*) seizure; (*comput.*) keyboarding. **~ de données,** data capture.

sais|ir /sezir/ v.t. grab (hold of), seize; (*occasion, biens*) seize; (*comprendre*) grasp; (*frapper*) strike; (*comput.*) keyboard, capture. **~i de,** (*peur*) stricken by, overcome by. **se ~ir de,** seize. **~issant, ~issante** a. (*spectacle*) gripping.

saison /sezɔ̃/ n.f. season. **la morte ~,** the off season. **~nier, ~nière** /-ɔnje, -jɛr/ a. seasonal.

sait /sɛ/ *voir* savoir.

salad|e /salad/ n.f. salad; (*laitue*) lettuce; (*désordre: fam.*) mess. **~ier** n.m. salad bowl.

salaire /salɛr/ n.m. wages, salary.

salami /salami/ n.m. salami.

salari|é, ~e /salarje/ a. wage-earning. ● n.m., f. wage-earner.

salaud /salo/ n.m. (*argot*) bastard.

sale /sal/ a. dirty, filthy; (*mauvais*) nasty.

sal|er /sale/ v.t. salt. **~é a.** (*goût*) salty; (*plat*) salted; (*viande, poisson*) salt; (*grivois: fam.*) spicy; (*excessif: fam.*) steep.

saleté /salte/ n.f. dirtiness; (*crasse*) dirt; (*action*) dirty trick; (*obscénité*) obscenity. **~(s),** (*camelote*) rubbish. **~s,** (*détritus*) mess.

salière /saljɛr/ n.f. salt-cellar.

salin, ~e /salɛ̃, -in/ a. saline.

sal|ir /salir/ v.t. (make) dirty; (*réputation*) tarnish. **se ~ir** v. pr. get dirty. **~issant, ~issante** a. dirty; (*étoffe*) easily dirtied.

salive /saliv/ n.f. saliva.

salle /sal/ n.f. room; (*grande, publique*) hall; (*d'hôpital*) ward; (*théâtre, cinéma*) auditorium. **~ à manger,**

dining-room. **~ d'attente,** waiting-room. **~ de bains,** bathroom. **~ de séjour,** living-room. **~ de classe,** classroom. **~ d'embarquement,** departure lounge. **~ d'opération,** operating theatre. **~ des ventes,** saleroom.

salon /salɔ̃/ n.m. lounge; (de coiffure, beauté) salon; (exposition) show. **~ de thé,** tea-room.

salope /salɔp/ n.f. (argot) bitch.

saloperie /salɔpri/ n.f. (fam.) (action) dirty trick; (chose de mauvaise qualité) rubbish.

salopette /salɔpɛt/ n.f. dungarees; (d'ouvrier) overalls.

salsifis /salsifi/ n.m. salsify.

saltimbanque /saltɛ̃bɑ̃k/ n.m./f. (street ou fairground) acrobat.

salubre /salybr/ a. healthy.

saluer /salɥe/ v.t. greet; (en partant) take one's leave of; (de la tête) nod to; (de la main) wave to; (mil.) salute.

salut /saly/ n.m. greeting; (de la tête) nod; (de la main) wave; (mil.) salute; (sauvegarde, rachat) salvation. ● int. (bonjour: fam.) hallo; (au revoir: fam.) bye-bye.

salutaire /salytɛr/ a. salutary.

salutation /salytɑsjɔ̃/ n.f. greeting. **veuillez agréer, Monsieur, mes ~s distingués,** yours faithfully.

salve /salv/ n.f. salvo.

samedi /samdi/ n.m. Saturday.

sanatorium /sanatɔrjɔm/ n.m. sanatorium.

sanctifier /sɑ̃ktifje/ v.t. sanctify.

sanction /sɑ̃ksjɔ̃/ n.f. sanction. **~ner** /-jɔne/ v.t. sanction; (punir) punish.

sanctuaire /sɑ̃ktɥɛr/ n.m. sanctuary.

sandale /sɑ̃dal/ n.f. sandal.

sandwich /sɑ̃dwitʃ/ n.m. sandwich.

sang /sɑ̃/ n.m. blood. **~-froid** n.m. invar. calm, self-control. **se faire du mauvais ~ ou un ~ d'encre** be worried stiff.

sanglant, ~e /sɑ̃glɑ̃, -t/ a. bloody.

sangl|e /sɑ̃gl/ n.f. strap. **~er** v.t. strap.

sanglier /sɑ̃glije/ n.m. wild boar.

sanglot /sɑ̃glo/ n.m. sob. **~er** /-ɔte/ v.i. sob.

sangsue /sɑ̃sy/ n.f. leech.

sanguin, ~e /sɑ̃gɛ̃, -in/ a. (groupe etc.) blood; (caractère) fiery.

sanguinaire /sɑ̃ginɛr/ a. blood-thirsty.

sanitaire /sanitɛr/ a. health; (conditions) sanitary; (appareils, installations) bathroom, sanitary. **~s** n.m. pl. bathroom.

sans /sɑ̃/ prép. without. **~ que vous le sachiez,** without your knowing. **~-abri** /sɑ̃zabri/ n.m./f. invar. homeless person. **~ ça, ~ quoi,** otherwise. **~ arrêt,** nonstop. **~ encombre/faute/ tarder,** without incident/fail/delay. **~ fin/goût/ limite,** endless/tasteless/limitless. **~-gêne** a. invar. inconsiderate, thoughtless; **~** n.m. invar. thoughtlessness. **~ importance/pareil/ précédent/travail,** unimportant/ unparalleled/unprecedented/ unemployed. **~ plus,** but no more than that, but nothing more.

santé /sɑ̃te/ n.f. health. **à ta ou votre santé,** cheers!

saoul, ~e /su, sul/ voir soûl.

saper /sape/ v.t. undermine.

sapeur /sapœr/ n.m. (mil.) sapper. **~-pompier** (pl. **~s-pompiers**) n.m. fireman.

saphir /safir/ n.m. sapphire.

sapin /sapɛ̃/ n.m. fir(-tree). **~ de Noël,** Christmas tree.

sarbacane /sarbakan/ n.f. (jouet) pea-shooter.

sarcas|me /sarkasm/ n.m. sarcasm. **~tique** a. sarcastic.

sarcler /sarkle/ v.t. weed.

sardine /sardin/ n.f. sardine.

sardonique /sardɔnik/ a. sardonic.

sarment /sarmɑ̃/ n.m. vine shoot.

sas /sɑs/ n.m. (naut., aviat.) airlock.

satané /satane/ a. (fam.) blasted.

satanique /satanik/ a. satanic.

satellite /satelit/ n.m. satellite.

satin /satɛ̃/ n.m. satin.

satir|e /satir/ n.f. satire. **~ique** a. satirical.

satisfaction /satisfaksjɔ̃/ n.f. satisfaction.

satis|faire† /satisfɛr/ v.t. satisfy. ● v.i. **~faire à,** satisfy. **~faisant, ~faisante** a. (acceptable) satisfactory. **~fait, ~faite** a. satisfied (**de,** with).

satur|er /satyre/ v.t. saturate. **~ation** n.f. saturation.

sauc|e /sos/ n.f. sauce; (jus de viande) gravy. **~er** v.t. (plat) wipe. **se faire ~er** (fam.) get soaked. **~e tartare,** tartar sauce. **~ière** n.f. sauce-boat.

saucisse /sosis/ n.f. sausage.

saucisson /sosisõ/ *n.m.* (slicing) sausage.

sauf[1] /sof/ *prép.* except. ~ **erreur/ imprévu**, barring error/the unforeseen. ~ **avis contraire**, unless you hear otherwise.

sauf[2], ~**ve** /sof, sov/ *a.* safe, unharmed. ~**f-conduit** *n.m.* safe conduct.

sauge /soʒ/ *n.f.* (*culin.*) sage.

saugrenu /sogrəny/ *a.* preposterous, ludicrous.

saule /sol/ *n.m.* willow. ~ **pleureur**, weeping willow.

saumon /somõ/ *n.m.* salmon. ● *a. invar.* salmon-pink.

saumure /somyr/ *n.f.* brine.

sauna /sona/ *n.m.* sauna.

saupoudrer /sopudre/ *v.t.* sprinkle (**de**, with).

saut /so/ *n.m.* jump, leap. **faire un ~ chez s.o.**, pop round to s.o.'s (place). **le ~**, (*sport*) jumping. ~ **en hauteur/longueur**, high/long jump. ~ **périlleux**, somersault. **au ~ du lit**, on getting up.

sauté /sote/ *a. & n.m.* (*culin.*) sauté.

saut|er /sote/ *v.i.* jump, leap; (*exploser*) blow up; (*fusible*) blow; (*se détacher*) come off. ● *v.t.* jump (over); (*page, classe*) skip. **faire ~er**, (*détruire*) blow up; (*fusible*) blow; (*casser*) break; (*culin.*) sauté; (*renvoyer: fam.*) kick out. ~**er à la corde**, skip. ~**er aux yeux**, obvious. ~**e-mouton** *n.m.* leapfrog. ~**er au cou de qn.**, fling one's arms round s.o. ~**er sur une occasion**, jump at an opportunity.

sauterelle /sotrɛl/ *n.f.* grasshopper.

sautiller /sotije/ *v.i.* hop.

sauvage /sovaʒ/ *a.* wild; (*primitif, cruel*) savage; (*farouche*) unsociable; (*illégal*) unauthorized. ● *n.m./f.* unsociable person; (*brute*) savage. ~**rie** *n.f.* savagery.

sauve /sov/ *voir* **sauf**[2].

sauvegard|e /sovgard/ *n.f.* safeguard; (*comput.*) backup. ~**er** *v.t.* safeguard; (*comput.*) save.

sauv|er /sove/ *v.t.* save; (*d'un danger*) rescue, save; (*matériel*) salvage. **se ~er** *v. pr.* (*fuir*) run away; (*partir: fam.*) be off. ~**e-qui-peut** *n.m. invar.* stampede. ~**etage** *n.m.* rescue; salvage. ~**eteur** *n.m.* rescuer. ~**eur** *n.m.* saviour.

sauvette (à la) /(ala)sovɛt/ *adv.* hastily; (*vendre*) illicitly.

savamment /savamã/ *adv.* learnedly; (*avec habileté*) skilfully.

savan|t, ~e /savã, -t/ *a.* learned; (*habile*) skilful. ● *n.m.* scientist.

saveur /savœr/ *n.f.* flavour; (*fig.*) savour.

savoir† /savwar/ *v.t.* know; (*apprendre*) hear. **elle sait conduire/ nager**, she can drive/swim. ● *n.m.* learning. **à ~**, namely. **faire ~ à qn. que**, inform s.o. that. **je ne saurais pas**, I could not, I cannot. **(pas) que je sache**, (not) as far as I know.

savon /savõ/ *n.m.* soap. **passer un ~ à qn.**, (*fam.*) give s.o. a dressing down. ~**ner** /-ɔne/ *v.t.* soap. ~**nette** /-ɔnɛt/ *n.f.* bar of soap. ~**neux, ~neuse** /-ɔnø, -z/ *a.* soapy.

savour|er /savure/ *v.t.* savour. ~**eux, ~euse** *a.* tasty; (*fig.*) spicy.

saxo(phone) /saksɔ(fɔn)/ *n.m.* sax(o-phone).

scabreu|x, ~se /skabrø, -z/ *a.* risky; (*indécent*) obscene.

scandal|e /skãdal/ *n.m.* scandal; (*tapage*) uproar; (*en public*) noisy scene. **faire ~e**, shock people. **faire un ~e**, make a scene. ~**eux, ~euse** *a.* scandalous. ~**iser** *v.t.* scandalize, shock.

scander /skãde/ *v.t.* (*vers*) scan; (*slogan*) chant.

scandinave /skãdinav/ *a. & n.m./f.* Scandinavian.

Scandinavie /skãdinavi/ *n.f.* Scandinavia.

scarabée /skarabe/ *n.m.* beetle.

scarlatine /skarlatin/ *n.f.* scarlet fever.

scarole /skarɔl/ *n.f.* endive.

sceau (*pl.* ~**x**) /so/ *n.m.* seal.

scélérat /selera/ *n.m.* scoundrel.

scell|er /sele/ *v.t.* seal; (*fixer*) cement. ~**és** *n.m. pl.* seals.

scénario /senarjo/ *n.m.* scenario.

scène /sɛn/ *n.f.* scene; (*estrade, art dramatique*) stage. **mettre en ~**, (*pièce*) stage. ~ **de ménage**, domestic scene.

sceptique /sɛptik/ *a.* sceptical. ● *n.m./f.* sceptic. ~**cisme** *n.m.* scepticism.

sceptre /sɛptr/ *n.m.* sceptre.

schéma /ʃema/ *n.m.* diagram. ~**tique** *a.* diagrammatic; (*sommaire*) sketchy.

schisme /ʃism/ *n.m.* schism.

schizophrène /skizɔfrɛn/ *a. & n.m./f.* schizophrenic.

sciatique /sjatik/ *n.f.* sciatica.

scie /si/ *n.f.* saw.

sciemment /sjamɑ̃/ *adv.* knowingly.

scien|ce /sjɑ̃s/ *n.f.* science; (*savoir*) knowledge. **~ce-fiction** *n.f.* science fiction. **~tifique** *a.* scientific; *n.m./f.* scientist.

scier /sje/ *v.t.* saw.

scinder /sɛ̃de/ *v.t.*, **se ~** *v. pr.* split.

scintill|er /sɛ̃tije/ *v.i.* glitter; (*étoile*) twinkle. **~ement** *n.m.* glittering; twinkling.

scission /sisjɔ̃/ *n.f.* split.

sciure /sjyr/ *n.f.* sawdust.

sclérose /skleroz/ *n.f.* sclerosis. **~ en plaques,** multiple sclerosis.

scol|aire /skɔlɛr/ *a.* school. **~arisation** *n.f.*, **~arité** *n.f.* schooling. **~arisé** *a.* provided with schooling.

scorbut /skɔrbyt/ *n.m.* scurvy.

score /skɔr/ *n.m.* score.

scories /skɔri/ *n.f. pl.* slag.

scorpion /skɔrpjɔ̃/ *n.m.* scorpion. **le S~,** Scorpio.

scotch[1] /skɔtʃ/ *n.m.* (*boisson*) Scotch (whisky).

scotch[2] /skɔtʃ/ *n.m.* (P.) Sellotape (P.); (*Amer.*) Scotch (tape) (P.).

scout, ~e /skut/ *n.m. & a.* scout.

script /skript/ *n.m.* (*cinéma*) script; (*écriture*) printing. **~-girl,** continuity girl.

scrupul|e /skrypyl/ *n.m.* scruple. **~eusement** *adv.* scrupulously. **~eux, ~euse** *a.* scrupulous.

scruter /skryte/ *v.t.* examine, scrutinize.

scrutin /skrytɛ̃/ *n.m.* (*vote*) ballot; (*opération électorale*) poll.

sculpt|er /skylte/ *v.t.* sculpture; (*bois*) carve (**dans,** out of). **~eur** *n.m.* sculptor. **~ure** *n.f.* sculpture.

se, s' * /sə, s/ *pron.* himself; (*femelle*) herself; (*indéfini*) oneself; (*non humain*) itself; (*pl.*) themselves; (*réciproque*) each other, one another. **se parler,** (*à soi-même*) talk to o.s.; (*réciproque*) talk to each other. **se faire,** (*passif*) be done. **se laver les mains,** (*possessif*) wash one's hands.

séance /seɑ̃s/ *n.f.* session; (*cinéma, théâtre*) show. **~ de pose,** sitting. **~ tenante,** forthwith.

seau (*pl.* **~x**) /so/ *n.m.* bucket, pail.

sec, sèche /sɛk, sɛʃ/ *a.* dry; (*fruits*) dried; (*coup, bruit*) sharp; (*cœur*) hard; (*whisky*) neat; (*Amer.*) straight. ● *n.m.* **à ~,** (*sans eau*) dry; (*sans argent*) broke. **au ~,** in a dry place. ● *n.f.* (*fam.*) (*cigarette*) fag.

sécateur /sekatœr/ *n.m.* (*pour les haies*) shears; (*petit*) secateurs.

sécession /sesesjɔ̃/ *n.f.* secession. **faire ~,** secede.

sèche /sɛʃ/ *voir* **sec. ~ment** *adv.* drily.

sèche-cheveux /sɛʃʃəvø/ *n.m. invar.* hair-drier.

sécher /seʃe/ *v.t./i.* dry; (*cours: fam.*) skip; (*ne pas savoir: fam.*) be stumped. **se ~** *v. pr.* dry o.s.

sécheresse /seʃrɛs/ *n.f.* dryness; (*temps sec*) drought.

séchoir /seʃwar/ *n.m.* drier.

second, ~e[1] /sgɔ̃, -d/ *a. & n.m., f.* second. ● *n.m.* (*adjoint*) second in command; (*étage*) second floor, (*Amer.*) third floor. ● *n.f.* (*transport*) second class.

secondaire /sgɔ̃dɛr/ *a.* secondary.

seconde[2] /sgɔ̃d/ *n.f.* (*instant*) second.

seconder /sgɔ̃de/ *v.t.* assist.

secouer /skwe/ *v.t.* shake; (*poussière, torpeur*) shake off. **se ~,** (*fam.*) (*se dépêcher*) get a move on; (*réagir*) shake o.s. up.

secour|ir /skurir/ *v.t.* assist, help. **~able** *a.* helpful. **~iste** *n.m./f.* first-aid worker.

secours /skur/ *n.m.* assistance, help. ● *n.m. pl.* (*méd.*) first aid. **au ~!,** help! **de ~,** emergency; (*équipe, opération*) rescue.

secousse /skus/ *n.f.* jolt, jerk; (*électrique*) shock; (*séisme*) tremor.

secr|et, ~ète /səkrɛ, -t/ *a.* secret. ● *n.m.* secret; (*discrétion*) secrecy. **le ~et professionnel,** professional secrecy. **~et de Polichinelle,** open secret. **en ~et,** in secret, secretly.

secrétaire /skretɛr/ *n.m./f.* secretary. **~ de direction,** executive secretary. ● *n.m.* (*meuble*) writing-desk. **~ d'État,** junior minister.

secrétariat /skretarja/ *n.m.* secretarial work; (*bureau*) secretary's office; (*d'un organisme*) secretariat.

sécrét|er /sekrete/ *v.t.* secrete. **~ion** /-sjɔ̃/ *n.f.* secretion.

sect|e /sɛkt/ *n.f.* sect. **~aire** *a.* sectarian.

secteur /sɛktœr/ *n.m.* area; (*mil., comm.*) sector; (*circuit: électr.*) mains. **~ primaire/secondaire/ter-**

tiaire, primary/secondary/tertiary industry.

section /sɛksjɔ̃/ *n.f.* section; (*transports publics*) fare stage; (*mil.*) platoon. **~ner** /-jɔne/ *v.t.* sever.

sécu /seky/ *n.f.* (*fam.*) **la ~,** the social security services.

séculaire /sekylɛr/ *a.* age-old.

sécu|lier, **~ière** /sekylje, -jɛr/ *a.* secular.

sécuriser /sekyrize/ *v.t.* reassure.

sécurité /sekyrite/ *n.f.* security; (*absence de danger*) safety. **en ~,** safe, secure. **S~ sociale,** social services, social security services.

sédatif /sedatif/ *n.m.* sedative.

sédentaire /sedɑ̃tɛr/ *a.* sedentary.

sédiment /sedimɑ̃/ *n.m.* sediment.

séditieu|x, **~se** /sedisjø, -z/ *a.* seditious.

sédition /sedisjɔ̃/ *n.f.* sedition.

séd|uire† /sedɥir/ *v.t.* charm; (*plaire à*) appeal to; (*abuser de*) seduce. **~ucteur,** **~uctrice** *a.* seductive; *n.m.,* *f.* seducer. **~uction** *n.f.* seduction; (*charme*) charm. **~uisant,** **~uisante** *a.* attractive.

segment /sɛgmɑ̃/ *n.m.* segment.

ségrégation /segregɑsjɔ̃/ *n.f.* segregation.

seigle /sɛgl/ *n.m.* rye.

seigneur /sɛɲœr/ *n.m.* lord. **le S~,** the Lord.

sein /sɛ̃/ *n.m.* breast; (*fig.*) bosom. **au ~ de,** in the midst of.

Seine /sɛn/ *n.f.* Seine.

séisme /seism/ *n.m.* earthquake.

seiz|e /sɛz/ *a. & n.m.* sixteen. **~ième** *a. & n.m./f.* sixteenth.

séjour /seʒur/ *n.m.* stay; (*pièce*) living-room. **~ner** *v.i.* stay.

sel /sɛl/ *n.m.* salt; (*piquant*) spice.

sélect /selɛkt/ *a.* select.

sélecti|f, **~ve** /selɛktif, -v/ *a.* selective.

sélection /selɛksjɔ̃/ *n.f.* selection. **~ner** /-jɔne/ *v.t.* select.

self(-service) /sɛlf(sɛrvis)/ *n.m.* self-service.

selle /sɛl/ *n.f.* saddle.

seller /sele/ *v.t.* saddle.

sellette /selɛt/ *n.f.* **sur la ~,** (*question*) under examination; (*personne*) in the hot seat.

selon /slɔ̃/ *prép.* according to (**que,** whether).

semaine /smɛn/ *n.f.* week. **en ~,** in the week.

sémantique /semɑ̃tik/ *a.* semantic. ● *n.f.* semantics.

sémaphore /semafɔr/ *n.m.* (*appareil*) semaphore.

semblable /sɑ̃blabl/ *a.* similar (**à,** to). **de ~s propos/***etc.,* (*tels*) such remarks/*etc.* ● *n.m.* fellow (creature).

semblant /sɑ̃blɑ̃/ *n.m.* **faire ~ de,** pretend to. **un ~ de,** a semblance of.

sembl|er /sɑ̃ble/ *v.i.* seem (**à,** to; that). **il me ~e que,** it seems to me that.

semelle /smɛl/ *n.f.* sole.

semence /smɑ̃s/ *n.f.* seed; (*clou*) tack. **~s,** (*graines*) seed.

sem|er /sme/ *v.t.* sow; (*jeter, parsemer*) strew; (*répandre*) spread; (*personne:* *fam.*) lose. **~eur,** **~euse** *n.m.,* *f.* sower.

semestr|e /smɛstr/ *n.m.* half-year; (*univ.*) semester. **~iel,** **~ielle** *a.* half-yearly.

semi- /səmi/ *préf.* semi-.

séminaire /seminɛr/ *n.m.* (*relig.*) seminary; (*univ.*) seminar.

semi-remorque /səmirəmɔrk/ *n.m.* articulated lorry; (*Amer.*) semi(-trailer).

semis /smi/ *n.m.* (*terrain*) seed-bed; (*plant*) seedling.

sémit|e /semit/ *a.* Semitic. ● *n.m./f.* Semite. **~ique** *a.* Semitic.

semonce /səmɔ̃s/ *n.f.* reprimand. **coup de ~,** warning shot.

semoule /smul/ *n.f.* semolina.

sénat /sena/ *n.m.* senate. **~eur** /-tœr/ *n.m.* senator.

sénil|e /senil/ *a.* senile. **~ité** *n.f.* senility.

sens /sɑ̃s/ *n.m.* sense; (*signification*) meaning, sense; (*direction*) direction. **à mon ~,** to my mind. **à ~ unique,** (*rue etc.*) one-way. **ça n'a pas de ~,** that does not make sense. **~ commun,** common sense. **~ giratoire,** roundabout; (*Amer.*) rotary. **~ interdit,** no entry; (*rue*) one-way street. **dans le ~ des aiguilles d'une montre,** clockwise. **~ dessus dessous,** upside down.

sensation /sɑ̃sɑsjɔ̃/ *n.f.* feeling, sensation. **faire ~,** create a sensation. **~nel,** **~nelle** /-jɔnɛl/ *a.* sensational.

sensé /sɑ̃se/ *a.* sensible.

sensibiliser /sɑ̃sibilize/ *v.t.* **~ à,** make sensitive to.

sensib|le /sɑ̃sibl/ *a.* sensitive (**à,** to); (*appréciable*) noticeable. **~ilité** *n.f.*

sensitivity. **~lement** *adv.* noticeably; (*à peu près*) more or less.

sensoriel, **~le** /sɑ̃sɔrjɛl/ *a.* sensory.

sens|uel, **~uelle** /sɑ̃sɥɛl/ *a.* sensuous; (*sexuel*) sensual. **~ualité** *n.f.* sensuousness; sensuality.

sentenc|e /sɑ̃tɑ̃s/ *n.f.* sentence. **~ieux**, **~ieuse** *a.* sententious.

senteur /sɑ̃tœr/ *n.f.* scent.

sentier /sɑ̃tje/ *n.m.* path.

sentiment /sɑ̃timɑ̃/ *n.m.* feeling. **avoir le ~ de**, be aware of.

sentiment|al (*m. pl.* **~aux**) /sɑ̃timɑ̃tal, -o/ *a.* sentimental. **~alité** *n.f.* sentimentality.

sentinelle /sɑ̃tinɛl/ *n.f.* sentry.

sentir† /sɑ̃tir/ *v.t.* feel; (*odeur*) smell; (*goût*) taste; (*pressentir*) sense. **~ la lavande**/*etc.*, smell of lavender/*etc.* ● *v.i.* smell. **je ne peux pas le ~,** (*fam.*) I can't stand him. **se ~ fier/ mieux**/*etc.*, feel proud/better/*etc.*

séparatiste /separatist/ *a. & n.m./f.* separatist.

séparé /separe/ *a.* separate; (*conjoints*) separated. **~ment** *adv.* separately.

sépar|er /separe/ *v.t.* separate; (*en deux*) split. **se ~er** *v. pr.* separate, part (**de**, from); (*se détacher*) split. **se ~er de**, (*se défaire de*) part with. **~ation** *n.f.* separation.

sept /sɛt/ *a. & n.m.* seven.

septante /sɛptɑ̃t/ *a. & n.m.* (*en Belgique, Suisse*) seventy.

septembre /sɛptɑ̃br/ *n.m.* September.

septentrion|al (*m. pl.* **~aux**) /sɛptɑ̃trijɔnal, -o/ *a.* northern.

septième /sɛtjɛm/ *a. & n.m./f.* seventh.

sépulcre /sepylkr/ *n.m.* (*relig.*) sepulchre.

sépulture /sepyltyr/ *n.f.* burial; (*lieu*) burial place.

séquelles /sekɛl/ *n.f. pl.* (*maladie*) after-effects; (*fig.*) aftermath.

séquence /sekɑ̃s/ *n.f.* sequence.

séquestrer /sekɛstre/ *v.t.* confine (illegally); (*biens*) impound.

sera, serait /sra, srɛ/ *voir* être.

serein, **~e** /sarɛ̃, -ɛn/ *a.* serene.

sérénade /serenad/ *n.f.* serenade.

sérénité /serenite/ *n.f.* serenity.

sergent /sɛrʒɑ̃/ *n.m.* sergeant.

série /seri/ *n.f.* series; (*d'objets*) set. **de ~**, (*véhicule etc.*) standard. **fabrication** *ou* **production en ~,** mass production.

sérieu|x, **~se** /serjø, -z/ *a.* serious; (*digne de foi*) reliable; (*chances, raison*) good. ● *n.m.* seriousness. **garder/perdre son ~x,** keep/be unable to keep a straight face. **prendre au ~x,** take seriously. **~sement** *adv.* seriously.

serin /srɛ̃/ *n.m.* canary.

seringue /srɛ̃g/ *n.f.* syringe.

serment /sɛrmɑ̃/ *n.m.* oath; (*promesse*) pledge.

sermon /sɛrmɔ̃/ *n.m.* sermon. **~ner** /-ɔne/ *v.t.* (*fam.*) lecture.

séropositi|f, **~ve** /seropozitif, -v/ *a.* HIV-positive.

serpe /sɛrp/ *n.f.* bill(hook).

serpent /sɛrpɑ̃/ *n.m.* snake. **~ à sonnettes**, rattlesnake.

serpenter /sɛrpɑ̃te/ *v.i.* meander.

serpentin /sɛrpɑ̃tɛ̃/ *n.m.* streamer.

serpillière /sɛrpijɛr/ *n.f.* floor-cloth.

serre¹ /sɛr/ *n.f.* (*local*) greenhouse.

serre² /sɛr/ *n.f.* (*griffe*) claw.

serré /sere/ *a.* (*habit, nœud, programme*) tight; (*personnes*) packed, crowded; (*lutte, mailles*) close; (*cœur*) heavy.

serrer /sere/ *v.t.* (*saisir*) grip; (*presser*) squeeze; (*vis, corde, ceinture*) tighten; (*poing, dents*) clench; (*pieds*) pinch. **~ qn. dans ses bras,** hug. **~ les rangs**, close ranks. **~ qn.**, (*vêtement*) be tight on s.o. ● *v.i.* **~ à droite**, keep over to the right. **se ~** *v. pr.* (*se rapprocher*) squeeze (up) (**contre**, against). **~ de près**, follow closely. **~ la main à**, shake hands with.

serrur|e /seryr/ *n.f.* lock. **~ier** *n.m.* locksmith.

sertir /sɛrtir/ *v.t.* (*bijou*) set.

sérum /serɔm/ *n.m.* serum.

servante /sɛrvɑ̃t/ *n.f.* (maid)servant.

serve|ur, **~se** /sɛrvœr, -øz/ *n.m., f.* waiter, waitress; (*au bar*) barman, barmaid.

serviable /sɛrvjabl/ *a.* helpful.

service /sɛrvis/ *n.m.* service; (*fonction, temps de travail*) duty; (*pourboire*) service (charge). **~ (non) compris**, service (not) included. **être de ~**, be on duty. **pendant le ~**, (when) on duty. **rendre un ~/mauvais ~ à** qn., do s.o. a favour/disservice. **~ d'ordre**, (*policiers*) police. **~ après-vente**, after-sales service. **~ militaire**, military service.

serviette /sɛrvjɛt/ *n.f.* (*de toilette*) towel; (*sac*) briefcase. ~ **(de table)**, serviette; (*Amer.*) napkin. ~ **hygiénique**, sanitary towel.

servile /sɛrvil/ *a.* servile.

servir† /sɛrvir/ *v.t./i.* serve; (*être utile*) be of use, serve. ~ **qn.** (**à table**), wait on s.o. **ça sert à**, (*outil, récipient, etc.*) it is used for. **ça me sert à/de**, I use it for/as. ~ **de**, serve as, be used as. ~ **à qn. de guide**/*etc.*, act as a guide/*etc.* for s.o. **se** ~ *v. pr.* (*à table*) help o.s. **(de, to). se** ~ **de**, use.

serviteur /sɛrvitœr/ *n.m.* servant.

servitude /sɛrvityd/ *n.f.* servitude.

ses /se/ *voir* **son**¹.

session /sesjɔ̃/ *n.f.* session.

seuil /sœj/ *n.m.* doorstep; (*entrée*) doorway; (*fig.*) threshold.

seul, ~e /sœl/ *a.* alone, on one's own; (*unique*) only. **un ~ travail**/*etc.*, only one job/*etc.* **pas un ~ ami**/*etc.*, not a single friend/*etc.* **parler tout** ~, talk to o.s. **faire qch. tout** ~, do sth. on one's own. ● *n.m., f.* **le** ~, **la** ~**e**, the only one. **un** ~, **une** ~**e**, only one. **pas un** ~, not (a single) one.

seulement /sœlmɑ̃/ *adv.* only.

sève /sɛv/ *n.f.* sap.

sév|ère /sevɛr/ *a.* severe. **~èrement** *adv.* severely. **~érité** /-erite/ *n.f.* severity.

sévices /sevis/ *n.m. pl.* cruelty.

sévir /sevir/ *v.i.* (*fléau*) rage. ~ **contre**, punish.

sevrer /səvre/ *v.t.* wean.

sex|e /sɛks/ *n.m.* sex; (*organes*) sex organs. **~isme** *n.m.* sexism. **~iste** *a.* sexist.

sex|uel, ~uelle /sɛksɥɛl/ *a.* sexual. **~ualité** *n.f.* sexuality.

seyant, ~e /sejɑ̃, -t/ *a.* becoming.

shampooing /ʃɑ̃pwɛ̃/ *n.m.* shampoo.

shérif /ʃerif/ *n.m.* sheriff.

short /ʃɔrt/ *n.m.* (pair of) shorts.

si¹ (**s'** *before il, ils*) /si, s/ *conj.* if; (*interrogation indirecte*) if, whether. **si on partait?**, (*suggestion*) what about going? **s'il vous ou te plaît**, please. **si oui**, if so. **si seulement**, if only.

si² /si/ *adv.* (*tellement*) so; (*oui*) yes. **un si bon repas**, such a good meal. **pas si riche que**, not as rich as. **si habile qu'il soit**, however skilful he may be. **si bien que**, with the result that.

siamois, ~e /sjamwa, -z/ *a.* Siamese.

Sicile /sisil/ *n.f.* Sicily.

sida /sida/ *n.m.* (*méd.*) AIDS.

sidéré /sidere/ *a.* staggered.

sidérurgie /sideryrʒi/ *n.f.* iron and steel industry.

siècle /sjɛkl/ *n.m.* century; (*époque*) age.

siège /sjɛʒ/ *n.m.* seat; (*mil.*) siege. ~ **éjectable**, ejector seat. ~ **social**, head office, headquarters.

siéger /sjeʒe/ *v.i.* (*assemblée*) sit.

sien, ~ne /sjɛ̃, sjɛn/ *pron.* **le** ~, **la** ~**ne, les** ~(**ne**)**s**, his; (*femme*) hers; (*chose*) its. **les** ~**s**, (*famille*) one's family.

sieste /sjɛst/ *n.f.* nap; (*en Espagne*) siesta. **faire la** ~, have an afternoon nap.

siffl|er /sifle/ *v.i.* whistle; (*avec un sifflet*) blow one's whistle; (*serpent, gaz*) hiss. ● *v.t.* (*air*) whistle; (*chien*) whistle to ou for; (*acteur*) hiss; (*signaler*) blow one's whistle for. **~ement** *n.m.* whistling. **un ~ement**, a whistle.

sifflet /siflɛ/ *n.m.* whistle. **~s**, (*huées*) boos.

siffloter /siflɔte/ *v.t./i.* whistle.

sigle /sigl/ *n.m.* abbreviation, acronym.

sign|al (*pl.* **~aux**) /siɲal, -o/ *n.m.* signal. **~aux lumineux**, (*auto.*) traffic signals.

signal|er /siɲale/ *v.t.* indicate; (*par une sonnerie, un écriteau*) signal; (*dénoncer, mentionner*) report; (*faire remarquer*) point out. **se ~er par**, distinguish o.s. by. **~ement** *n.m.* description.

signalisation /siɲalizasjɔ̃/ *n.f.* signalling, signposting; (*signaux*) signals.

signataire /siɲatɛr/ *n.m./f.* signatory.

signature /siɲatyr/ *n.f.* signature; (*action*) signing.

signe /siɲ/ *n.m.* sign; (*de ponctuation*) mark. **faire** ~ **à**, beckon (**de**, to); (*contacter*) contact. **faire** ~ **que non**, shake one's head. **faire** ~ **que oui**, nod.

signer /siɲe/ *v.t.* sign. **se** ~ *v. pr.* (*relig.*) cross o.s.

signet /siɲɛ/ *m.* bookmark.

significati|f, ~ve /siɲifikatif, -v/ *a.* significant.

signification /siɲifikasjɔ̃/ *n.f.* meaning.

signifier /siɲifje/ v.t. mean, signify; (*faire connaître*) make known (**à**, to).

silenc|e /silɑ̃s/ n.m. silence; (*mus.*) rest. **garder le ~e**, keep silent. **~ieux, ~ieuse** a. silent; n.m. (*auto.*) silencer; (*auto.*, *Amer.*) muffler.

silex /silɛks/ n.m. flint.

silhouette /silwɛt/ n.f. outline, silhouette.

silicium /silisjɔm/ n.m. silicon.

sillage /sijaʒ/ n.m. (*trace d'eau*) wake.

sillon /sijɔ̃/ n.m. furrow; (*de disque*) groove.

sillonner /sijɔne/ v.t. criss-cross.

silo /silo/ n.m. silo.

simagrées /simagre/ n.f. pl. fuss, pretence.

simil|aire /similɛr/ a. similar. **~itude** n.f. similarity.

simple /sɛ̃pl/ a. simple; (*non double*) single. ● n.m. (*tennis*) singles. **~ d'esprit** n.m./f. simpleton. **~ soldat**, private. **~ment** /-əmɑ̃/ adv. simply.

simplicité /sɛ̃plisite/ n.f. simplicity; (*naïveté*) simpleness.

simplif|ier /sɛ̃plifje/ v.t. simplify. **~ication** n.f. simplification.

simpliste /sɛ̃plist/ a. simplistic.

simulacre /simylakr/ n.m. pretence, sham.

simul|er /simyle/ v.t. simulate. **~ateur** m. (*appareil*) simulator. **~ation** n.f. simulation.

simultané /simyltane/ a. simultaneous. **~ment** adv. simultaneously.

sinc|ère /sɛ̃sɛr/ a. sincere. **~èrement** adv. sincerely. **~érité** n.f. sincerity.

singe /sɛ̃ʒ/ n.m. monkey, ape.

singer /sɛ̃ʒe/ v.t. mimic, ape.

singeries /sɛ̃ʒri/ n.f. pl. antics.

singulariser (se) /(sə)sɛ̃gylarize/ v. pr. make o.s. conspicuous.

singul|ier, ~ière /sɛ̃gylje, -jɛr/ a. peculiar, remarkable; (*gram.*) singular. ● n.m. (*gram.*) singular. **~arité** n.f. peculiarity. **~ièrement** adv. peculiarly; (*beaucoup*) remarkably.

sinistre ¹ /sinistr/ a. sinister.

sinistr|e ² /sinistr/ n.m. disaster; (*incendie*) blaze; (*dommages*) damage. **~é** a. disaster-stricken; n.m., f. disaster victim.

sinon /sinɔ̃/ conj. (*autrement*) otherwise; (*sauf*) except (**que**, that); (*si ce n'est*) if not.

sinueu|x, ~se /sinɥø, -z/ a. winding; (*fig.*) tortuous.

sinus /sinys/ n.m. (*anat.*) sinus.

sionisme /sjɔnism/ n.m. Zionism.

siphon /sifɔ̃/ n.m. siphon; (*de WC*) U-bend.

sirène ¹ /sirɛn/ n.f. (*appareil*) siren.

sirène ² /sirɛn/ n.f. (*femme*) mermaid.

sirop /siro/ n.m. syrup; (*boisson*) cordial.

siroter /sirɔte/ v.t. sip.

sirupeu|x, ~se /sirypø, -z/ a. syrupy.

sis, ~e /si, siz/ a. situated.

sismique /sismik/ a. seismic.

site /sit/ n.m. setting; (*pittoresque*) beauty spot; (*emplacement*) site; (*monument etc.*) place of interest.

sitôt /sito/ adv. **~ entré** /etc.*, immediately after coming in/etc.* **~ que**, as soon as. **pas de ~**, not for a while.

situation /sitɥasjɔ̃/ n.f. situation, position. **~ de famille**, marital status.

situ|er /sitɥe/ v.t. situate, locate. **se ~er** v. pr. (*se trouver*) be situated. **~é** a. situated.

six /sis/ (/si/ *before consonant*, /siz/ *before vowel*) a. & n.m. six. **~ième** /sizjɛm/ a. & n.m./f. sixth.

sketch (pl. **~es**) /skɛtʃ/ n.m. (*théâtre*) sketch.

ski /ski/ n.m. (*patin*) ski; (*sport*) skiing. **faire du ~**, ski. **~ de fond**, cross-country skiing. **~ nautique**, water-skiing.

sk|ier /skje/ v.i. ski. **~ieur, ~ieuse** n.m., f. skier.

slalom /slalɔm/ n.m. slalom.

slave /slav/ a. Slav; (*lang.*) Slavonic. ● n.m./f. Slav.

slip /slip/ n.m. (*d'homme*) (under-)pants; (*de femme*) knickers; (*Amer.*) panties. **~ de bain**, (swimming) trunks; (*du bikini*) briefs.

slogan /slɔgɑ̃/ n.m. slogan.

smoking /smɔkiŋ/ n.m. evening *ou* dinner suit, dinner-jacket.

snack(-bar) /snak(bar)/ n.m. snack-bar.

snob /snɔb/ n.m./f. snob. ● a. snobbish. **~isme** n.m. snobbery.

sobr|e /sɔbr/ a. sober. **~iété** n.f. sobriety.

sobriquet /sɔbrikɛ/ n.m. nickname.

sociable /sɔsjabl/ a. sociable.

soc|ial (*m. pl.* ~**iaux**) /sɔsjal, -jo/ *a.* social.

socialis|te /sɔsjalist/ *n.m./f.* socialist. ~**me** *n.m.* socialism.

société /sɔsjete/ *n.f.* society; (*compagnie, firme*) company.

sociolo|gie /sɔsjɔlɔʒi/ *n.f.* sociology. ~**gique** *a.* sociological. ~**gue** *n.m./f.* sociologist.

socle /sɔkl/ *n.m.* (*de colonne, statue*) plinth; (*de lampe*) base.

socquette /sɔket/ *n.f.* ankle sock.

soda /sɔda/ *n.m.* (fizzy) drink.

sodium /sɔdjɔm/ *n.m.* sodium.

sœur /sœr/ *n.f.* sister.

sofa /sɔfa/ *n.m.* sofa.

soi /swa/ *pron.* oneself. **en ~,** in itself. **~-disant** *a. invar.* so-called; (*qui se veut tel*) self-styled; *adv.* supposedly.

soie /swa/ *n.f.* silk.

soif /swaf/ *n.f.* thirst. **avoir ~,** be thirsty. **donner ~ à,** make thirsty.

soigné /swaɲe/ *a.* tidy, neat; (*bien fait*) careful.

soigner /swaɲe/ *v.t.* look after, take care of; (*tenue, style*) take care over; (*maladie*) treat. **se ~** *v. pr.* look after o.s.

soigneu|x, ~**se** /swaɲø, -z/ *a.* careful (**de,** about); (*ordonné*) tidy. ~**se-ment** *adv.* carefully.

soi-même /swamɛm/ *pron.* oneself.

soin /swɛ̃/ *n.m.* care; (*ordre*) tidiness. ~**s,** care; (*méd.*) treatment. **avoir** *ou* **prendre ~ de qn./de faire,** take care of s.o./to do. **premiers ~s,** first aid.

soir /swar/ *n.m.* evening.

soirée /sware/ *n.f.* evening; (*récep-tion*) party. **~ dansante,** dance.

soit /swa/ *voir* **être.** ● *conj.* (*à savoir*) that is to say. **~ . . . soit,** either . . . or.

soixantaine /swasɑ̃tɛn/ *n.f.* **une ~ (de),** about sixty.

soixant|e /swasɑ̃t/ *a. & n.m.* sixty. ~**e-dix** *a. & n.m.* seventy. ~**e-dixième** *a. & n.m./f.* seventieth. ~**ième** *a. & n.m./f.* sixtieth.

soja /sɔʒa/ *n.m.* (*graines*) soya beans; (*plante*) soya.

sol /sɔl/ *n.m.* ground; (*de maison*) floor; (*terrain agricole*) soil.

solaire /sɔlɛr/ *a.* solar; (*huile, filtre*) sun. **les rayons ~s,** the sun's rays.

soldat /sɔlda/ *n.m.* soldier.

solde[1] /sɔld/ *n.f.* (*salaire*) pay.

solde[2] /sɔld/ *n.m.* (*comm.*) balance. ~**s,** (*articles*) sale goods. **en ~,** (*acheter etc.*) at sale price. **les ~s,** the sales.

solder /sɔlde/ *v.t.* reduce; (*liquider*) sell off at sale price; (*compte*) settle. **se ~ par,** (*aboutir à*) end in.

sole /sɔl/ *n.f.* (*poisson*) sole.

soleil /sɔlɛj/ *n.m.* sun; (*chaleur*) sun-shine; (*fleur*) sunflower. **il y a du ~,** it is sunny.

solennel, ~**le** /sɔlanɛl/ *a.* solemn.

solennité /sɔlanite/ *n.f.* solemnity.

solex /sɔlɛks/ *n.m.* (P.) moped.

solfège /sɔlfɛʒ/ *n.m.* elementary mu-sical theory.

solid|aire /sɔlidɛr/ *a.* (*mécanismes*) interdependent; (*couple*) (mutually) supportive; (*ouvriers*) who show solidarity. ~**arité** *n.f.* solidarity.

solidariser (se) /(sə)sɔlidarize/ *v. pr.* show solidarity (**avec,** with).

solid|e /sɔlid/ *a.* solid. ● *n.m.* (*objet*) solid; (*corps*) sturdy. ~**ement** *adv.* solidly. ~**ité** *n.f.* solidity.

solidifier /sɔlidifje/ *v.t.,* **se ~** *v. pr.* solidify.

soliste /sɔlist/ *n.m./f.* soloist.

solitaire /sɔlitɛr/ *a.* solitary. ● *n.m./f.* (*ermite*) hermit; (*personne inso-ciable*) loner.

solitude /sɔlityd/ *n.f.* solitude.

solive /sɔliv/ *n.f.* joist.

sollicit|er /sɔlisite/ *v.t.* request; (*attirer, pousser*) prompt; (*tenter*) tempt; (*faire travailler*) make de-mands on. ~**ation** *n.f.* earnest re-quest.

sollicitude /sɔlisityd/ *n.f.* concern.

solo /sɔlo/ *n.m. & a. invar.* (*mus.*) solo.

solstice /sɔlstis/ *n.m.* solstice.

soluble /sɔlybl/ *a.* soluble.

solution /sɔlysjɔ̃/ *n.f.* solution.

solvable /sɔlvabl/ *a.* solvent.

solvant /sɔlvɑ̃/ *n.m.* solvent.

sombre /sɔ̃br/ *a.* dark; (*triste*) som-bre.

sombrer /sɔ̃bre/ *v.i.* sink (**dans,** into).

sommaire /sɔmɛr/ *a.* summary; (*tenue, repas*) scant. ● *n.m.* sum-mary.

sommation /sɔmasjɔ̃/ *n.f.* (*mil.*) warning; (*jurid.*) summons.

somme[1] /sɔm/ *n.f.* sum. **en ~, ~ toute,** in short. **faire la ~ de,** add (up), total (up).

somme[2] /sɔm/ *n.m.* (*sommeil*) nap.

sommeil /sɔmɛj/ *n.m.* sleep; (*besoin de dormir*) drowsiness. **avoir ~,** be *ou* feel sleepy. **~ler** /-meje/ *v.i.* doze; (*fig.*) lie dormant.

sommelier /sɔmǝlje/ *n.m.* wine waiter.

sommer /sɔme/ *v.t.* summon.

sommes /sɔm/ *voir* être.

sommet /sɔmɛ/ *n.m.* top; (*de montagne*) summit; (*de triangle*) apex; (*gloire*) height.

sommier /sɔmje/ *n.m.* base (of bed).

somnambule /sɔmnɑ̃byl/ *n.m.* sleepwalker.

somnifère /sɔmnifɛr/ *n.m.* sleeping-pill.

somnolen|t, **~te** /sɔmnɔlɑ̃, -t/ *a.* drowsy. **~ce** *n.f.* drowsiness.

somnoler /sɔmnɔle/ *v.i.* doze.

sompt|ueux, **~ueuse** /sɔ̃ptɥø, -z/ *a.* sumptuous. **~uosité** *n.f.* sumptuousness.

son [1], **sa** *ou* **son*** (*pl.* **ses**) /sɔ̃, sa, sɔ̃, se/ *a.* his; (*femme*) her; (*chose*) its; (*indéfini*) one's.

son [2] /sɔ̃/ *n.m.* (*bruit*) sound.

son [3] /sɔ̃/ *n.m.* (*de blé*) bran.

sonar /sɔnar/ *n.m.* Sonar.

sonate /sɔnat/ *n.f.* sonata.

sonde /sɔ̃d/ *n.f.* (*pour les forages*) drill; (*méd.*) probe.

sond|er /sɔ̃de/ *v.t.* sound; (*terrain*) drill; (*personne*) sound out. **~age** *n.m.* sounding; drilling. **~age** (**d'opinion**), (opinion) poll.

song|e /sɔ̃ʒ/ *n.m.* dream. **~er** *v.i.* dream; *v.t.* **~er que**, think that. **~er à**, think about. **~eur**, **~euse** *a.* pensive.

sonnantes /sɔnɑ̃t/ *a.f. pl.* **à six**/*etc.* **heures ~**, on the stroke of six/*etc.*

sonné /sɔne/ *a.* (*fam.*) crazy; (*fatigué*) knocked out.

sonn|er /sɔne/ *v.t./i.* ring; (*clairon, glas*) sound; (*heure*) strike; (*domestique*) ring for. **midi ~é**, well past noon. **~er de**, (*clairon etc.*) sound, blow.

sonnerie /sɔnri/ *n.f.* ringing; (*de clairon*) sound; (*mécanisme*) bell.

sonnet /sɔnɛ/ *n.m.* sonnet.

sonnette /sɔnɛt/ *n.f.* bell.

sonor|e /sɔnɔr/ *a.* resonant; (*onde, effets, etc.*) sound. **~ité** *n.f.* resonance; (*d'un instrument*) tone.

sonoris|er /sɔnɔrize/ *v.t.* (*salle*) wire for sound. **~ation** *n.f.* (*matériel*) sound equipment.

sont /sɔ̃/ *voir* être.

sophistiqué /sɔfistike/ *a.* sophisticated.

soporifique /sɔpɔrifik/ *a.* soporific.

sorbet /sɔrbɛ/ *n.m.* sorbet.

sorcellerie /sɔrsɛlri/ *n.f.* witchcraft.

sorc|ier /sɔrsje/ *n.m.* sorcerer. **~ière** *n.f.* witch.

sordide /sɔrdid/ *a.* sordid; (*lieu*) squalid.

sort /sɔr/ *n.m.* (*destin, hasard*) fate; (*condition*) lot; (*maléfice*) spell. **tirer** (**qch.**) **au ~**, draw lots (for sth.).

sortant, **~e** /sɔrtɑ̃, -t/ *a.* (*président etc.*) outgoing.

sorte /sɔrt/ *n.f.* sort, kind. **de ~ que**, so that. **en quelque ~**, in a way. **faire en ~ que**, see to it that.

sortie /sɔrti/ *n.f.* departure, exit; (*porte*) exit; (*promenade, dîner*) outing; (*invective*) outburst; (*parution*) appearance; (*de disque, gaz*) release; (*d'un ordinateur*) output. **~s**, (*argent*) outgoings.

sortilège /sɔrtilɛʒ/ *n.m.* (magic) spell.

sortir† /sɔrtir/ *v.i.* (*aux.* être) go out, leave; (*venir*) come out; (*aller au spectacle etc.*) go out; (*livre, film*) come out; (*plante*) come up. **~ de**, (*pièce*) leave; (*milieu social*) come from; (*limites*) go beyond. ● *v.t.* (*aux.* avoir) take out; (*livre, modèle*) bring out; (*dire*: *fam.*) come out with. **~ d'affaire**, (**s'**)**en**, get out of an awkward situation. **~ du commun** *ou* **de l'ordinaire**, be out of the ordinary.

sosie /sɔzi/ *n.m.* double.

sot, **~te** /so, sɔt/ *a.* foolish.

sottise /sɔtiz/ *n.f.* foolishness; (*action, remarque*) foolish thing.

sou /su/ *n.m.* **~s**, money. **pas un ~**, not a penny. **sans le ~**, without a penny. **près de ses ~s**, tight-fisted.

soubresaut /subrǝso/ *n.m.* (sudden) start.

souche /suʃ/ *n.f.* (*d'arbre*) stump; (*de famille, vigne*) stock; (*de carnet*) counterfoil. **planté comme une ~**, standing like an idiot.

souci [1] /susi/ *n.m.* (*inquiétude*) worry; (*préoccupation*) concern. **se faire du ~**, worry.

souci [2] /susi/ *n.m.* (*plante*) marigold.

soucier (**se**) /(sǝ)susje/ *v. pr.* **se ~ de**, be concerned about.

soucieu|x, **~se** /susjø, -z/ *a.* concerned (**de**, about).

soucoupe /sukup/ *n.f.* saucer. **~ volante**, flying saucer.

soudain, **~e** /sudɛ̃, -ɛn/ *a.* sudden. ● *adv.* suddenly. **~ement** /-ɛnmɑ̃/

adv. suddenly. **~eté** /-ɛnte/ *n.f.* suddenness.

soude /sud/ *n.f.* soda.

soud|er /sude/ *v.t.* solder, (*à la flamme*) weld. **se ~er** *v. pr.* (*os*) knit (together). **~ure** *n.f.* soldering, welding; (*substance*) solder.

soudoyer /sudwaje/ *v.t.* bribe.

souffle /sufl/ *n.m.* blow, puff; (*haleine*) breath; (*respiration*) breathing; (*explosion*) blast; (*vent*) breath of air.

soufflé /sufle/ *n.m.* (*culin.*) soufflé.

souffl|er /sufle/ *v.i.* blow; (*haleter*) puff. ● *v.t.* (*bougie*) blow out; (*poussière, fumée*) blow; (*par explosion*) destroy; (*chuchoter*) whisper. **~er son rôle à**, prompt. **~eur, ~euse** *n.m., f.* (*théâtre*) prompter.

soufflet /suflɛ/ *n.m.* (*instrument*) bellows.

souffrance /sufrɑ̃s/ *n.f.* suffering. **en ~**, (*affaire*) pending.

souffr|ir† /sufrir/ *v.i.* suffer (**de**, from). ● *v.t.* (*endurer*) suffer; (*admettre*) admit of. **il ne peut pas le ~ir**, he cannot stand *ou* bear him. **~ant, ~ante** *a.* unwell.

soufre /sufr/ *n.m.* sulphur.

souhait /swɛ/ *n.m.* wish. **nos ~s de**, (*vœux*) good wishes for. **à vos ~s!**, bless you!

souhait|er /swete/ *v.t.* (*bonheur etc.*) wish for. **~er qch. à qn.**, wish s.o. sth. **~er que/faire**, hope that/to do. **~able** /swetabl/ *a.* desirable.

souiller /suje/ *v.t.* soil.

soûl, ~e /su, sul/ *a.* drunk. ● *n.m.* **tout son ~**, as much as one can.

soulag|er /sulaʒe/ *v.t.* relieve. **~ement** *n.m.* relief.

soûler /sule/ *v.t.* make drunk. **se ~** *v. pr.* get drunk.

soulèvement /sulɛvmɑ̃/ *n.m.* uprising.

soulever /sulve/ *v.t.* lift, raise; (*exciter*) stir; (*question, poussière*) raise. **se ~** *v. pr.* lift *ou* raise o.s. up; (*se révolter*) rise up.

soulier /sulje/ *n.m.* shoe.

souligner /suliɲe/ *v.t.* underline; (*taille, yeux*) emphasize.

soum|ettre† /sumɛtr/ *v.t.* (*dompter, assujettir*) subject (**à**, to); (*présenter*) submit (**à**, to). **se ~ettre** *v. pr.* submit (**à**, to). **~is, ~ise** *a.* submissive. **~ission** *n.f.* submission.

soupape /supap/ *n.f.* valve.

soupçon /supsɔ̃/ *n.m.* suspicion. **un ~ de**, (*fig.*) a touch of. **~ner** /-ɔne/ *v.t.* suspect. **~neux, ~neuse** /-ɔnø, -ɔnøz/ *a.* suspicious.

soupe /sup/ *n.f.* soup.

souper /supe/ *n.m.* supper. ● *v.i.* have supper.

soupeser /supəze/ *v.t.* judge the weight of; (*fig.*) weigh up.

soupière /supjɛr/ *n.f.* (soup) tureen.

soupir /supir/ *n.m.* sigh. **pousser un ~**, heave a sigh. **~er** *v.i.* sigh.

soupir|ail (*pl.* **~aux**) /supiraj, -o/ *n.m.* small basement window.

soupirant /supirɑ̃/ *n.m.* suitor.

souple /supl/ *a.* supple; (*règlement, caractère*) flexible. **~sse** /-ɛs/ *n.f.* suppleness; flexibility.

source /surs/ *n.f.* source; (*eau*) spring. **de ~ sûre**, from a reliable source. **~ thermale**, hot springs.

sourcil /sursi/ *n.m.* eyebrow.

sourciller /sursije/ *v.i.* **sans ~**, without batting an eyelid.

sourd, ~e /sur, -d/ *a.* deaf; (*bruit, douleur*) dull; (*inquiétude, conflit*) silent, hidden. ● *n.m.,* f. deaf person. **faire la ~e oreille**, turn a deaf ear. **~-muet** (*pl.* **~s-muets**), **~e-muette** (*pl.* **~es-muettes**) *a.* deaf and dumb; *n.m., f.* deaf mute.

sourdine /surdin/ *n.f.* (*mus.*) mute. **en ~**, quietly.

souricière /surisjɛr/ *n.f.* mousetrap; (*fig.*) trap.

sourire /surir/ *n.m.* smile. **garder le ~**, keep smiling. ● *v.i.* smile (**à**, at). **~ à**, (*fortune*) smile on.

souris /suri/ *n.f.* mouse.

sournois, ~e /surnwa, -z/ *a.* sly, underhand. **~ement** /-zmɑ̃/ *adv.* slyly.

sous /su/ *prép.* under, beneath. **~ la main**, handy. **~ la pluie**, in the rain. **~ peu**, shortly. **~ terre**, underground.

sous- /su/ *préf.* (*subordination*) sub-; (*insuffisance*) under-.

sous-alimenté /suzalimɑ̃te/ *a.* undernourished.

sous-bois /subwa/ *n.m. invar.* undergrowth.

souscr|ire /suskrir/ *v.i.* **~ire à**, subscribe to. **~iption** /-ipsjɔ̃/ *n.f.* subscription.

sous-directeur, ~rice /sudirɛktœr, -ris/ *n.m., f.* assistant manager.

sous-entend|re /suzɑ̃tɑ̃dr/ *v.t.* imply. **~u** *n.m.* insinuation.

sous-estimer /suzɛstime/ v.t. under-estimate.

sous-jacent, ~e /suʒasã, -t/ a. underlying.

sous-marin, ~e /sumarɛ̃, -in/ a. underwater. ● n.m. submarine.

sous-officier /suzɔfisje/ n.m. non-commissioned officer.

sous-préfecture /suprefɛktyr/ n.f. sub-prefecture.

sous-produit /suprɔdɥi/ n.m. by-product.

sous-programme /suprɔgram/ n.m. subroutine.

soussigné, ~e /susiɲe/ a. & n.m., f. undersigned.

sous-sol /susɔl/ n.m. (cave) basement.

sous-titr|e /sutitr/ n.m. subtitle. **~er** v.t. subtitle.

soustr|aire† /sustrɛr/ v.t. remove; (déduire) subtract. **se ~aire à**, escape from. **~action** n.f. (déduction) subtraction.

sous-trait|er /sutrete/ v.t. subcontract. **~ant** n.m. subcontractor.

sous-verre /suvɛr/ n.m. invar. picture frame, glass mount.

sous-vêt|ement /suvɛtmã/ n.m. undergarment. **~s**, underwear.

soutane /sutan/ n.f. cassock.

soute /sut/ n.f. (de bateau) hold. **~ à charbon**, coal-bunker.

soutenir† /sutnir/ v.t. support; (fortifier, faire durer) sustain; (résister à) withstand. **~ que**, maintain that. **se ~** v. pr. (se tenir debout) support o.s.

soutenu /sutny/ a. (constant) sustained; (style) lofty.

souterrain, ~e /sutɛrɛ̃, -ɛn/ a. underground. ● n.m. underground passage, subway.

soutien /sutjɛ̃/ n.m. support. **~-gorge** (pl. **~s-gorge**) n.m. bra.

soutirer /sutire/ v.t. **~ à qn.**, extract from s.o.

souvenir[1] /suvnir/ n.m. memory, recollection; (objet) memento; (cadeau) souvenir. **en ~ de**, in memory of.

souvenir[2]† **(se)** /(sə)suvnir/ v. pr. **se ~ de**, remember. **se ~ que**, remember that.

souvent /suvã/ adv. often.

souverain, ~e /suvrɛ̃, -ɛn/ a. sovereign; (extrême: péj.) supreme.

● n.m., f. sovereign. **~eté** /-ɛnte/ n.f. sovereignty.

soviétique /sɔvjetik/ a. Soviet. ● n.m./f. Soviet citizen.

soyeu|x, ~se /swajø, -z/ a. silky.

spacieu|x, ~se /spasjø, -z/ a. spacious.

spaghetti /spageti/ n.m. pl. spaghetti.

sparadrap /sparadra/ n.m. sticking-plaster; (Amer.) adhesive tape ou bandage.

spasm|e /spasm/ n.m. spasm. **~odique** a. spasmodic.

spat|ial (m. pl. **~iaux**) /spasjal, -jo/ a. space.

spatule /spatyl/ n.f. spatula.

speaker, ~ine /spikœr, -rin/ n.m., f. announcer.

spéc|ial (m. pl. **~iaux**) /spesjal, -jo/ a. special; (singulier) peculiar. **~ialement** adv. especially; (exprès) specially.

spécialis|er (se) /(sə)spesjalize/ v. pr. specialize (dans, in). **~ation** n.f. specialization.

spécialiste /spesjalist/ n.m./f. specialist.

spécialité /spesjalite/ n.f. speciality; (Amer.) specialty.

spécif|ier /spesifje/ v.t. specify. **~ication** n.f. specification.

spécifique /spesifik/ a. specific.

spécimen /spesimɛn/ n.m. specimen.

spectacle /spɛktakl/ n.m. sight, spectacle; (représentation) show.

spectaculaire /spɛktakylɛr/ a. spectacular.

specta|teur, ~trice /spɛktatœr, -tris/ n.m., f. onlooker; (sport) spectator. **les ~teurs**, (théâtre) the audience.

spectre /spɛktr/ n.m. (revenant) spectre; (images) spectrum.

spécul|er /spekyle/ v.i. speculate. **~ateur, ~atrice** n.m., f. speculator. **~ation** n.f. speculation.

spéléologie /speleɔlɔʒi/ n.f. cave exploration, pot-holing; (Amer.) spelunking.

sperme /spɛrm/ n.m. sperm.

sph|ère /sfɛr/ n.f. sphere. **~érique** a. spherical.

sphinx /sfɛ̃ks/ n.m. sphinx.

spirale /spiral/ n.f. spiral.

spirite /spirit/ n.m./f. spiritualist.

spirituel, ~le /spiritɥɛl/ a. spiritual; (amusant) witty.

spiritueux /spirituø/ *n.m.* (*alcool*) spirit.

splend|ide /splɑ̃did/ *a.* splendid. **~eur** *n.f.* splendour.

spongieu|x, **~se** /spɔ̃ʒjø, -z/ *a.* spongy.

sponsor /spɔ̃sɔr/ *n.m.* sponsor. **~iser** *v.t.* sponsor.

spontané /spɔ̃tane/ *a.* spontaneous. **~ité** *n.f.* spontaneity. **~ment** *adv.* spontaneously.

sporadique /spɔradik/ *a.* sporadic.

sport /spɔr/ *n.m.* sport. ● *a. invar.* (*vêtements*) casual. **veste/voiture de ~**, sports jacket/car.

sporti|f, **~ve** /spɔrtif, -v/ *a.* sporting. (*physique*) athletic; (*résultats*) sports. ● *n.m.* sportsman. ● *n.f.* sportswoman.

spot /spɔt/ *n.m.* spotlight; (*publicitaire*) ad.

spray /sprɛ/ *n.m.* spray; (*méd.*) inhaler.

sprint /sprint/ *n.m.* sprint. **~er** *v.i.* sprint; *n.m.* /-œr/ sprinter.

square /skwar/ *n.m.* (public) garden.

squash /skwaʃ/ *n.m.* squash.

squatter /skwatœr/ *n.m.* squatter. **~iser** *v.t.* squat in.

squelett|e /skəlɛt/ *n.m.* skeleton. **~ique** /-etik/ *a.* skeletal; (*maigre*) all skin and bone.

stabiliser /stabilize/ *v.t.* stabilize.

stab|le /stabl/ *a.* stable. **~ilité** *n.f.* stability.

stade¹ /stad/ *n.m.* (*sport*) stadium.

stade² /stad/ *n.m.* (*phase*) stage.

stag|e /staʒ/ *n.m.* course. **~iaire** *a.* & *n.m./f.* course member; (*apprenti*) trainee.

stagn|er /stagne/ *v.i.* stagnate. **~ante** *a.* stagnant. **~ation** *n.f.* stagnation.

stand /stɑ̃d/ *n.m.* stand, stall. **~ de tir,** (shooting-)range.

standard¹ /stɑ̃dar/ *n.m.* switchboard. **~iste** /-dist/ *n.m./f.* switchboard operator.

standard² /stɑ̃dar/ *a. invar.* standard. **~iser** /-dize/ *v.t.* standardize.

standing /stɑ̃diŋ/ *n.m.* status, standing. **de ~**, (*hôtel etc.*) luxury.

star /star/ *n.f.* (*actrice*) star.

starter /startɛr/ *n.m.* (*auto.*) choke.

station /stasjɔ̃/ *n.f.* station; (*halte*) stop. **~ balnéaire,** seaside resort. **~ debout,** standing position. **~ de taxis,** taxi rank; (*Amer.*) taxi stand.

~-service (*pl.* **~s-service**) *n.f.* service station. **~ thermale,** spa.

stationnaire /stasjɔnɛr/ *a.* stationary.

stationn|er /stasjɔne/ *v.i.* park. **~ement** *n.m.* parking.

statique /statik/ *a.* static.

statistique /statistik/ *n.f.* statistic; (*science*) statistics. ● *a.* statistical.

statue /staty/ *n.f.* statue.

statuer /statɥe/ *v.i.* **~ sur,** rule on.

statu quo /statykwo/ *n.m.* status quo.

stature /statyr/ *n.f.* stature.

statut /staty/ *n.m.* status. **~s,** (*règles*) statutes. **~aire** /-tɛr/ *a.* statutory.

steak /stɛk/ *n.m.* steak.

stencil /stɛnsil/ *n.m.* stencil.

sténo /steno/ *n.f.* (*personne*) stenographer; (*sténographie*) shorthand.

sténodactylo /stenɔdaktilo/ *n.f.* shorthand typist; (*Amer.*) stenographer.

sténographie /stenɔgrafi/ *n.f.* shorthand.

stéréo /stereo/ *n.f.* & *a. invar.* stereo. **~phonique** /-eɔfɔnik/ *a.* stereophonic.

stéréotyp|e /stereɔtip/ *n.m.* stereotype. **~é** *a.* stereotyped.

stéril|e /steril/ *a.* sterile. **~ité** *n.f.* sterility.

stérilet /sterilɛ/ *n.m.* coil, IUD.

stérilis|er /sterilize/ *v.t.* sterilize. **~ation** *n.f.* sterilization.

stéroïde /sterɔid/ *a.* & *n.m.* steroid.

stéthoscope /stetɔskɔp/ *n.m.* stethoscope.

stigmat|e /stigmat/ *n.m.* mark, stigma. **~iser** *v.t.* stigmatize.

stimul|er /stimyle/ *v.t.* stimulate. **~ant** *n.m.* stimulus; (*médicament*) stimulant. **~ateur cardiaque,** pacemaker. **~ation** *n.f.* stimulation.

stipul|er /stipyle/ *v.t.* stipulate. **~ation** *n.f.* stipulation.

stock /stɔk/ *n.m.* stock. **~er** *v.t.* stock. **~iste** *n.m.* stockist; (*Amer.*) dealer.

stoïque /stɔik/ *a.* stoical. ● *n.m./f.* stoic.

stop /stɔp/ *int.* stop. ● *n.m.* stop sign; (*feu arrière*) brake light. **faire du ~,** (*fam.*) hitch-hike.

stopper /stɔpe/ *v.t./i.* stop; (*vêtement*) mend, reweave.

store /stɔr/ *n.m.* blind; (*Amer.*) shade; (*de magasin*) awning.

strabisme /strabism/ *n.m.* squint.

strapontin /strapɔ̃tɛ̃/ *n.m.* folding seat, jump seat.

stratagème /strataʒɛm/ *n.m.* stratagem.

stratég|ie /strateʒi/ *n.f.* strategy. **~ique** *a.* strategic.

stress /strɛs/ *n.* stress. **~ant** *a.* stressful. **~er** *v.t.* put under stress.

strict /strikt/ *a.* strict; (*tenue, vérité*) plain. **le ~ minimum**, the absolute minimum. **~ement** *adv.* strictly.

strident, ~e /stridɑ̃, -t/ *a.* shrill.

str|ie /stri/ *n.f.* streak. **~ier** *v.t.* streak.

strip-tease /striptiz/ *n.m.* strip-tease.

strophe /strɔf/ *n.f.* stanza, verse.

structur|e /stryktyr/ *n.f.* structure. **~al** (*m. pl.* **~aux**) *a.* structural. **~er** *v.t.* structure.

studieu|x, ~se /stydjø, -z/ *a.* studious; (*période*) devoted to study.

studio /stydjo/ *n.m.* (*d'artiste, de télévision, etc.*) studio; (*logement*) studio flat, bed-sitter.

stupéf|ait, ~aite /stypefɛ, -t/ *a.* amazed. **~action** *n.f.* amazement.

stupéf|ier /stypefje/ *v.t.* amaze. **~iant, ~iante** *a.* amazing; *n.m.* drug, narcotic.

stupeur /stypœr/ *n.f.* amazement; (*méd.*) stupor.

stupid|e /stypid/ *a.* stupid. **~ité** *n.f.* stupidity.

styl|e /stil/ *n.m.* style. **~isé** *a.* stylized.

stylé /stile/ *a.* well-trained.

styliste /stilist/ *n.m./f.* fashion designer.

stylo /stilo/ *n.m.* pen. **~ (à) bille**, ball-point pen. **~ (à) encre**, fountain-pen.

su /sy/ *voir* savoir.

suave /sɥav/ *a.* sweet.

subalterne /sybaltɛrn/ *a. & n.m./f.* subordinate.

subconscient, ~e /sypkɔ̃sjɑ̃, -t/ *a. & n.m.* subconscious.

subdiviser /sybdivize/ *v.t.* subdivide.

subir /sybir/ *v.t.* suffer; (*traitement, expériences*) undergo.

subit, ~e /sybi, -t/ *a.* sudden. **~ement** /-tmɑ̃/ *adv.* suddenly.

subjecti|f, ~ve /sybʒɛktif, -v/ *a.* subjective. **~vité** *n.f.* subjectivity.

subjonctif /sybʒɔ̃ktif/ *a. & n.m.* subjunctive.

subjuguer /sybʒyge/ *v.t.* (*charmer*) captivate.

sublime /syblim/ *a.* sublime.

submer|ger /sybmɛrʒe/ *v.t.* submerge; (*fig.*) overwhelm. **~sion** *n.f.* submersion.

subordonné, ~e /sybɔrdɔne/ *a. & n.m., f.* subordinate.

subord|onner /sybɔrdɔne/ *v.t.* subordinate (**à**, to). **~ination** *n.f.* subordination.

subreptice /sybrɛptis/ *a.* surreptitious.

subside /sybzid/ *n.m.* grant.

subsidiare /sypsidjɛr/ *a.* subsidiary.

subsist|er /sybziste/ *v.i.* subsist; (*durer, persister*) exist. **~ance** *n.f.* subsistence.

substance /sypstɑ̃s/ *n.f.* substance.

substantiel, ~le /sypstɑ̃sjɛl/ *a.* substantial.

substantif /sypstɑ̃tif/ *n.m.* noun.

substit|uer /sypstitɥe/ *v.t.* substitute (**à**, for). **se ~uer à**, (*remplacer*) substitute for; (*évincer*) take over from. **~ut** *n.m.* substitute; (*jurid.*) deputy public prosecutor. **~ution** *n.f.* substitution.

subterfuge /syptɛrfyʒ/ *n.m.* subterfuge.

subtil /syptil/ *a.* subtle. **~ité** *n.f.* subtlety.

subtiliser /syptilize/ *v.t.* **~ qch. (à qn.)**, spirit sth. away (from s.o.).

subvenir /sybvənir/ *v.i.* **~ à**, provide for.

subvention /sybvɑ̃sjɔ̃/ *n.f.* subsidy. **~ner** /-jɔne/ *v.t.* subsidize.

subversi|f, ~ve /sybvɛrsif, -v/ *a.* subversive.

subversion /sybvɛrsjɔ̃/ *n.f.* subversion.

suc /syk/ *n.m.* juice.

succédané /syksedane/ *n.m.* substitute (**de**, for).

succéder /syksede/ *v.i.* **~ à**, succeed. **se ~** *v. pr.* succeed one another.

succès /syksɛ/ *n.m.* success. **à ~**, (*film, livre, etc.*) successful. **avoir du ~**, be a success.

successeur /syksesœr/ *n.m.* successor.

successi|f, ~ve /syksesif, -v/ *a.* successive. **~vement** *adv.* successively.

succession /syksesjɔ̃/ *n.f.* succession; (*jurid.*) inheritance.

succinct, ~e /syksɛ̃, -t/ *a.* succinct.

succomber /sykɔ̃be/ *v.i.* die. **~ à**, succumb to.

succulent, ~e /sykylɑ̃, -t/ *a.* succulent.

succursale /sykyrsal/ *n.f.* (*comm.*) branch.

sucer /syse/ *v.t.* suck.

sucette /syset/ *n.f.* (*bonbon*) lollipop; (*tétine*) dummy; (*Amer.*) pacifier.

sucr|e /sykr/ *n.m.* sugar. ~**e en poudre**, barley sugar. ~**e en poudre**, caster sugar; (*Amer.*) finely ground sugar. ~**e glace**, icing sugar. ~**e roux**, brown sugar. ~**ier**, ~**ière** *a.* sugar; *n.m.* (*récipient*) sugar-bowl.

sucr|er /sykre/ *v.t.* sugar, sweeten. ~**é** *a.* sweet; (*additionné de sucre*) sweetened.

sucreries /sykrəri/ *n.f. pl.* sweets.

sud /syd/ *n.m.* south. ● *a. invar.* south; (*partie*) southern; (*direction*) southerly. ~**-africain**, ~**-africaine** *a. & n.m., f.* South African. ~**-est** *n.m.* south-east. ~**-ouest** *n.m.* south-west.

Suède /sɥɛd/ *n.f.* Sweden.

suédois, ~**e** /sɥedwa, -z/ *a.* Swedish. ● *n.m., f.* Swede. ● *n.m.* (*lang.*) Swedish.

suer /sɥe/ *v.t./i.* sweat. **faire ~ qn.**, (*fam.*) get on s.o.'s nerves.

sueur /sɥœr/ *n.f.* sweat. **en ~**, sweating.

suff|ire† /syfir/ *v.i.* be enough (**à qn.**, for s.o.). **il ~it de faire**, one only has to do. **il ~it d'une goutte pour**, a drop is enough to. ~**ire à**, (*besoin*) satisfy. **se ~ire à soi-même**, be self-sufficient.

suffis|ant, ~**ante** /syfizã, -t/ *a.* sufficient; (*vaniteux*) conceited. ~**amment** *adv.* sufficiently. ~**amment de**, sufficient. ~**ance** *n.f.* (*vanité*) conceit.

suffixe /syfiks/ *n.m.* suffix.

suffoquer /syfoke/ *v.t./i.* choke, suffocate.

suffrage /syfraʒ/ *n.m.* (*voix; pol.*) vote; (*modalité*) suffrage.

sugg|érer† /sygʒere/ *v.t.* suggest. ~**estion** /-ʒɛstjɔ̃/ *n.f.* suggestion.

suggesti|f, ~**ve** /sygʒɛstif, -v/ *a.* suggestive.

suicid|e /sɥisid/ *n.m.* suicide. ~**aire** *a.* suicidal.

suicid|er (se) /(sə)sɥiside/ *v. pr.* commit suicide. ~**é**, ~**ée** *n.m., f.* suicide.

suie /sɥi/ *n.f.* soot.

suint|er /sɥɛ̃te/ *v.i.* ooze. ~**ement** *n.m.* oozing.

suis /sɥi/ *voir* être, suivre.

Suisse /sɥis/ *n.f.* Switzerland.

suisse /sɥis/ *a. & n.m.* Swiss. ~**sse** /-ɛs/ *n.f.* Swiss (woman).

suite /sɥit/ *n.f.* continuation, rest; (*d'un film*) sequel; (*série*) series; (*appartement, escorte*) suite; (*résultat*) consequence; (*cohérence*) order. ~**s**, (*de maladie*) after-effects. **à la ~, de ~**, (*successivement*) in succession. **à la ~ de**, (*derrière*) behind. **à la ~ de, par ~ de**, as a result of. **faire ~ (à)**, follow. **par la ~**, afterwards. ~ **à votre lettre du**, further to your letter of the.

suivant[1], ~**e** /sɥivã, -t/ *a.* following, next. ● *n.m., f.* following *ou* next person.

suivant[2] /sɥivã/ *prép.* (*selon*) according to.

suivi /sɥivi/ *a.* steady, sustained; (*cohérent*) consistent. **peu/très ~**, (*cours*) poorly-/well-attended.

suivre† /sɥivr/ *v.t./i.* follow; (*comprendre*) keep up (with), follow. **se ~** *v. pr.* follow each other. **faire ~**, (*courrier etc.*) forward.

sujet[1], ~**te** /syʒɛ, -t/ *a.* ~ **à**, liable *ou* subject to. ● *n.m., f.* (*gouverné*) subject.

sujet[2] /syʒɛ/ *n.m.* (*matière, individu*) subject; (*motif*) cause; (*gram.*) subject. **au ~ de**, about.

sulfurique /sylfyrik/ *a.* sulphuric.

sultan /syltã/ *n.m.* sultan.

summum /somɔm/ *n.m.* height.

super /syper/ *n.m.* (*essence*) four-star, premium (*Amer.*). ● *a. invar.* (*fam.*) great. ● *adv.* (*fam.*) ultra, fantastically.

superbe /sypɛrb/ *a.* superb.

supercherie /sypɛrʃəri/ *n.f.* trickery.

supérette /syperet/ *n.f.* minimarket.

superficie /sypɛrfisi/ *n.f.* area.

superficiel, ~**le** /sypɛrfisjɛl/ *a.* superficial.

superflu /sypɛrfly/ *a.* superfluous. ● *n.m.* (*excédent*) surplus.

supérieur, ~**e** /syperjœr/ *a.* (*plus haut*) upper; (*quantité, nombre*) greater (**à**, than); (*études, principe*) higher (**à**, than); (*meilleur, hautain*) superior (**à**, to). ● *n.m., f.* superior.

supériorité /syperjorite/ *n.f.* superiority.

superlati|f, ~**ve** /sypɛrlatif, -v/ *a. & n.m.* superlative.

supermarché /sypɛrmarʃe/ *n.m.* supermarket.

superposer /sypɛrpoze/ *v.t.* super-impose.

superproduction /sypɛrprɔdyksjɔ̃/ *n.f.* (*film*) spectacular.

superpuissance /sypɛrpɥisɑ̃s/ *n.f.* superpower.

supersonique /sypɛrsɔnik/ *a.* super-sonic.

superstit|ion /sypɛrstisjɔ̃/ *n.f.* su-perstition. **~ieux, ~ieuse** *a.* su-perstitious.

superviser /sypɛrvize/ *v.t.* supervise.

supplanter /syplɑ̃te/ *v.t.* supplant.

suppléan|t, ~te /sypleɑ̃, -t/ *n.m., f. & a.* (**professeur**) **~t,** supply tea-cher; (**juge**) **~t,** deputy (judge). **~ce** *n.f.* (*fonction*) temporary appoint-ment.

suppléer /syplee/ *v.t.* (*remplacer*) replace; (*ajouter*) supply. ● *v.i.* **~ à,** (*compenser*) make up for.

supplément /syplemɑ̃/ *n.m.* (*argent*) extra charge; (*de frites, légumes*) extra portion. **en ~,** extra. **un ~ de,** (*travail etc.*) extra. **payer pour un ~ de bagages,** pay extra for excess luggage. **~aire** /-tɛr/ *a.* extra, additional.

supplic|e /syplis/ *n.m.* torture. **~ier** *v.t.* torture.

supplier /syplije/ *v.t.* beg, beseech (**de,** to).

support /sypɔr/ *n.m.* support; (*publicitaire*: *fig.*) medium.

support|er[1] /sypɔrte/ *v.t.* (*endurer*) bear; (*subir*) suffer; (*soutenir*) sup-port; (*résister à*) withstand. **~able** *a.* bearable.

supporter[2] /sypɔrtɛr/ *n.m.* (*sport*) supporter.

suppos|er /sypoze/ *v.t.* suppose; (*im-pliquer*) imply. **à ~er que,** suppos-ing that. **~ition** *n.f.* supposition.

suppositoire /sypozitwar/ *n.m.* sup-pository.

suppr|imer /syprime/ *v.t.* get rid of, remove; (*annuler*) cancel; (*mot*) delete. **~imer à qn.,** (*enlever*) take away from s.o. **~ession** *n.f.* re-moval; cancellation; deletion.

suprématie /sypremasi/ *n.f.* supre-macy.

suprême /syprɛm/ *a.* supreme.

sur /syr/ *prép.* on, upon; (*par-dessus*) over; (*au sujet de*) about, on; (*pro-portion*) out of; (*mesure*) by. **al-ler/tourner/etc.** **~,** go/turn/etc. towards. **mettre/jeter/etc.** **~,** put/ throw/etc. on to. **~-le-champ** *adv.*

immediately. **~ le qui-vive,** on the alert. **~ mesure,** made to measure. **~ place,** on the spot. **~ ce,** here-upon.

sur- /syr/ *préf.* over-.

sûr /syr/ *a.* certain, sure; (*sans dan-ger*) safe; (*digne de confiance*) reli-able; (*main*) steady; (*jugement*) sound.

surabondance /syrabɔ̃dɑ̃s/ *n.f.* superabundance.

suranné /syrane/ *a.* outmoded.

surcharg|e /syrʃarʒ/ *n.f.* overloading; (*poids*) extra load. **~er** *v.t.* overload; (*texte*) alter.

surchauffer /syrʃofe/ *v.t.* overheat.

surchoix /syrʃwa/ *a. invar.* of finest quality.

surclasser /syrklase/ *v.t.* outclass.

surcroît /syrkrwa/ *n.m.* increase (**de,** in), additional amount (**de,** of). **de ~,** in addition.

surdité /syrdite/ *n.f.* deafness.

sureau (*pl.* **~x**) /syro/ *n.m.* (*arbre*) elder.

surélever /syrelve/ *v.t.* raise.

sûrement /syrmɑ̃/ *adv.* certainly; (*sans danger*) safely.

surench|ère /syrɑ̃ʃɛr/ *n.f.* higher bid. **~érir** *v.i.* bid higher (**sur,** than).

surestimer /syrɛstime/ *v.t.* overesti-mate.

sûreté /syrte/ *n.f.* safety; (*garantie*) surety; (*d'un geste*) steadiness. **être en ~,** be safe. **S~ (nationale),** divi-sion of French Ministère de l'Intérieur in charge of police.

surexcité /syrɛksite/ *a.* very excited.

surf /syrf/ *n.m.* surfing.

surface /syrfas/ *n.f.* surface. **faire ~,** (*sous-marin etc.*) surface. **en ~,** (*fig.*) superficially.

surfait, ~e /syrfɛ, -t/ *a.* overrated.

surgelé /syrʒəle/ *a.* (deep-)frozen. (**aliments**) **~s,** frozen food.

surgir /syrʒir/ *v.i.* appear (suddenly); (*difficulté*) arise.

surhomme /syrɔm/ *n.m.* superman.

surhumain, ~e /syrymɛ̃, -ɛn/ *a.* superhuman.

surlendemain /syrlɑ̃dmɛ̃/ *n.m.* **le ~,** two days later. **le ~ de,** two days after.

surligneur /syrliɲœr/ *n.m.* highlight-er (pen).

surmen|er /syrməne/ *v.t., se ~er v. pr.* overwork. **~age** *n.m.* overwork-ing; (*méd.*) overwork.

surmonter /syrmɔ̃te/ *v.t.* (*vaincre*) overcome, surmount; (*être au-dessus de*) surmount, top.

surnager /syrnaʒe/ *v.i.* float.

surnaturel, **~le** /syrnatyrɛl/ *a.* supernatural.

surnom /syrnɔ̃/ *n.m.* nickname. **~mer** /-ɔme/ *v.t.* nickname.

surnombre (en) /(ɑ̃)syrnɔ̃br/ *adv.* too many. **il est en ~**, he is one too many.

surpasser /syrpase/ *v.t.* surpass.

surpeuplé /syrpœple/ *a.* overpopulated.

surplomb /syrplɔ̃/ *n.m.* **en ~**, overhanging. **~er** /-be/ *v.t./i.* overhang.

surplus /syrply/ *n.m.* surplus.

surpr|endre† /syrprɑ̃dr/ *v.t.* (*étonner*) surprise; (*prendre au dépourvu*) catch, surprise; (*entendre*) overhear. **~enant**, **~enante** *a.* surprising. **~is**, **~ise** *a.* surprised (**de**, at).

surprise /syrpriz/ *n.f.* surprise. **~-partie** (*pl.* **~s-parties**) *n.f.* party.

surréalisme /syrrealism/ *n.m.* surrealism.

sursaut /syrso/ *n.m.* start, jump. **en ~**, with a start. **~ de**, (*regain*) burst of. **~er** /-te/ *v.i.* start, jump.

sursis /syrsi/ *n.m.* reprieve; (*mil.*) deferment. **deux ans de prison avec ~**, a two-year suspended sentence.

surtaxe /syrtaks/ *n.f.* surcharge.

surtout /syrtu/ *adv.* especially, mainly; (*avant tout*) above all. **~ pas**, certainly not.

surveillant, **~e** /syrvɛjɑ̃, -t/ *n.m.,f.* (*de prison*) warder; (*au lycée*) supervisor (in charge of discipline).

surveill|er /syrveje/ *v.t.* watch; (*travaux, élèves*) supervise. **~ance** *n.f.* watch; supervision; (*de la police*) surveillance.

survenir /syrvənir/ *v.i.* occur, come about; (*personne*) turn up; (*événement*) take place.

survêtement /syrvɛtmɑ̃/ *n.m.* (*sport*) track suit.

survie /syrvi/ *n.f.* survival.

survivance /syrvivɑ̃s/ *n.f.* survival.

surviv|re† /syrvivr/ *v.i.* survive. **~re à**, (*conflit etc.*) survive; (*personne*) outlive. **~ant**, **~ante** *a.* surviving; *n.m.,f.* survivor.

survol /syrvɔl/ *n.m.* **le ~ de**, flying over. **~er** *v.t.* fly over; (*livre*) skim through.

survolté /syrvɔlte/ *a.* (*surexcité*) worked up.

susceptib|le /sysɛptibl/ *a.* touchy. **~le de faire**, (*possibilité*) liable to do; (*capacité*) able to do. **~lité** *n.f.* susceptibility.

susciter /sysite/ *v.t.* (*éveiller*) arouse; (*occasionner*) create.

suspect, **~e** /syspɛ, -ɛkt/ *a.* (*témoignage*) suspect; (*individu*) suspicious. **~ de**, suspected of. ● *n.m., f.* suspect. **~er** /-ɛkte/ *v.t.* suspect.

suspend|re /syspɑ̃dr/ *v.t.* (*arrêter, différer, destituer*) suspend; (*accrocher*) hang (up). **se ~re à**, hang from. **~u à**, hanging from.

suspens (en) /(ɑ̃)syspɑ̃/ *adv.* (*affaire*) in abeyance; (*dans l'indécision*) in suspense.

suspense /syspɛns/ *n.m.* suspense.

suspension /syspɑ̃sjɔ̃/ *n.f.* suspension; (*lustre*) chandelier.

suspicion /syspisjɔ̃/ *n.f.* suspicion.

susurrer /sysyre/ *v.t./i.* murmur.

suture /sytyr/ *n.f.* **point de ~**, stitch.

svelte /svɛlt/ *a.* slender.

S.V.P. *abrév. voir* s'il vous plaît.

sweat-shirt /switʃœrt/ *n.m.* sweatshirt.

syllabe /silab/ *n.f.* syllable.

symbol|e /sɛ̃bɔl/ *n.m.* symbol. **~ique** *a.* symbolic(al). **~iser** *v.t.* symbolize.

symétr|ie /simetri/ *n.f.* symmetry. **~ique** *a.* symmetrical.

sympa /sɛ̃pa/ *a. invar.* (*fam.*) nice. **sois ~**, be a pal.

sympath|ie /sɛ̃pati/ *n.f.* (*goût*) liking; (*affinité*) affinity; (*condoléances*) sympathy. **~ique** *a.* nice, pleasant.

sympathis|er /sɛ̃patize/ *v.i.* get on well (**avec**, with). **~ant**, **~ante** *n.m., f.* sympathizer.

symphon|ie /sɛ̃fɔni/ *n.f.* symphony. **~ique** *a.* symphonic; (*orchestre*) symphony.

symposium /sɛ̃pozjɔm/ *n.m.* symposium.

sympt|ôme /sɛ̃ptom/ *n.m.* symptom. **~omatique** /-ɔmatik/ *a.* symptomatic.

synagogue /sinagɔg/ *n.f.* synagogue.

synchroniser /sɛ̃krɔnize/ *v.t.* synchronize.

syncope /sɛ̃kɔp/ *n.f.* (*méd.*) black-out.

syncoper /sɛ̃kɔpe/ *v.t.* syncopate.

syndic /sɛ̃dik/ *n.m.* ~ (**d'immeuble**), managing agent.

syndic|at /sɛ̃dika/ *n.m.* (trade) union. **~at d'initiative**, tourist office. **~al** (*m. pl.* **~aux**) *a.* (trade-)union. **~aliste** *n.m./f.* trade-unionist; *a.* (trade-)union.

syndiqué, **~e** /sɛ̃dike/ *n.m.*, *f.* (trade-)union member.

syndrome /sɛ̃drom/ *n.m.* syndrome.

synonyme /sinɔnim/ *a.* synonymous. ● *n.m.* synonym.

syntaxe /sɛ̃taks/ *n.f.* syntax.

synthèse /sɛ̃tɛz/ *n.f.* synthesis.

synthétique /sɛ̃tetik/ *a.* synthetic.

synthé(tiseur) /sɛ̃te(tizœr)/ *n.m.* synthesizer.

syphilis /sifilis/ *n.f.* syphilis.

Syrie /siri/ *n.f.* Syria.

syrien, **~ne** /sirjɛ̃, -jɛn/ *a. & n.m.*, *f.* Syrian.

systématique /sistematik/ *a.* systematic. **~ment** *adv.* systematically.

système /sistɛm/ *n.m.* system. **le ~ D**, coping with problems.

T

t' /t/ *voir* te.

ta /ta/ *voir* ton¹.

tabac /taba/ *n.m.* tobacco; (*magasin*) tobacconist's shop. ● *a. invar.* buff. **~ à priser**, snuff.

tabasser /tabase/ *v.t.* (*fam.*) beat up.

table /tabl/ *n.f.* table. **à ~!**, come and eat! **faire ~ rase**, make a clean sweep (**de**, of). **~ de nuit**, bedside table. **~ des matières**, table of contents. **~ roulante**, (tea-)trolley; (*Amer.*) (serving) cart.

tableau (*pl.* **~x**) /tablo/ *n.m.* picture; (*peinture*) painting; (*panneau*) board; (*graphique*) chart; (*liste*) list. **~ (noir)**, blackboard. **~ d'affichage**, notice-board. **~ de bord**, dashboard.

tabler /table/ *v.i.* **~ sur**, count on.

tablette /tablɛt/ *n.f.* shelf. **~ de chocolat**, bar of chocolate.

tablier /tablije/ *n.m.* apron; (*de pont*) platform; (*de magasin*) shutter.

tabloïd(e) /tabloid/ *a. & n.m.* tabloïd.

tabou /tabu/ *n.m. & a.* taboo.

tabouret /taburɛ/ *n.m.* stool.

tabulateur /tabylatœr/ *n.m.* tabulator.

tac /tak/ *n.m.* **du ~ au tac**, tit for tat.

tache /taʃ/ *n.f.* mark, spot; (*salissure*) stain. **faire ~ d'huile**, spread. **~ de rousseur**, freckle.

tâche /taʃ/ *n.f.* task, job.

tacher /taʃe/ *v.t.* stain. **se ~** *v. pr.* (*personne*) get stains on one's clothes.

tâcher /taʃe/ *v.i.* **~ de faire**, try to do.

tacheté /taʃte/ *a.* spotted.

tacite /tasit/ *a.* tacit.

taciturne /tasityrn/ *a.* taciturn.

tact /takt/ *n.m.* tact.

tactile /taktil/ *a.* tactile.

tactique /taktik/ *a.* tactical. ● *n.f.* tactics. **une ~**, a tactic.

taie /tɛ/ *n.f.* **~ d'oreiller**, pillowcase.

taillader /tɑjade/ *v.t.* gash, slash.

taille¹ /tɑj/ *n.f.* (*milieu du corps*) waist; (*hauteur*) height; (*grandeur*) size. **de ~**, sizeable. **être de ~ à faire**, be up to doing.

taill|e² /tɑj/ *n.f.* cutting; pruning; (*forme*) cut. **~er** *v.t.* cut; (*arbre*) prune; (*crayon*) sharpen; (*vêtement*) cut out. **se ~er** *v. pr.* (*argot*) clear off. **~e-crayon(s)** *n.m. invar.* pencil-sharpener.

tailleur /tɑjœr/ *n.m.* tailor; (*costume*) lady's suit. **en ~**, cross-legged.

taillis /tɑji/ *n.m.* copse.

taire† /tɛr/ *v.t.* say nothing about. **se ~** *v. pr.* be silent *ou* quiet; (*devenir silencieux*) fall silent. **faire ~**, silence.

talc /talk/ *n.m.* talcum powder.

talent /talɑ̃/ *n.m.* talent. **~ueux**, **~ueuse** -tɥø, -z/ *a.* talented.

taloche /talɔʃ/ *n.f.* (*fam.*) slap.

talon /talɔ̃/ *n.m.* heel; (*de chèque*) stub.

talonner /talɔne/ *v.t.* follow hard on the heels of.

talus /taly/ *n.m.* embankment.

tambour /tɑ̃bur/ *n.m.* drum; (*personne*) drummer; (*porte*) revolving door.

tambourin /tɑ̃burɛ̃/ *n.m.* tambourine.

tambouriner /tɑ̃burine/ *v.t./i.* drum (**sur**, on).

tamis /tami/ *n.m.* sieve. **~er** /-ze/ *v.t.* sieve.

Tamise /tamiz/ *n.f.* Thames.

tamisé /tamize/ *a.* (*lumière*) subdued.

tampon /tãpɔ̃/ *n.m.* (*pour boucher*) plug; (*ouate*) wad, pad; (*timbre*) stamp; (*de train*) buffer. ~ **(hygiénique)**, tampon.

tamponner /tãpɔne/ *v.t.* crash into; (*timbrer*) stamp; (*plaie*) dab; (*mur*) plug. **se** ~ *v. pr.* (*véhicules*) crash into each other.

tandem /tãdɛm/ *n.m.* (*bicyclette*) tandem; (*personnes: fig.*) duo.

tandis que /tãdi(s)ə/ *conj.* while.

tangage /tãgaʒ/ *n.m.* pitching.

tangente /tãʒãt/ *n.f.* tangent.

tangible /tãʒibl/ *a.* tangible.

tango /tãgo/ *n.m.* tango.

tanguer /tãge/ *v.i.* pitch.

tanière /tanjɛr/ *n.f.* den.

tank /tãk/ *n.m.* tank.

tann|er /tane/ *v.t.* tan. ~**é** *a.* (*visage*) tanned, weather-beaten.

tant /tã/ *adv.* (*travailler, manger, etc.*) so much. ~ **(de)**, (*quantité*) so much; (*nombre*) so many. ~ **que**, as long as; (*autant que*) as much as. **en** ~ **que**, (*comme*) as. ~ **mieux!**, fine!, all the better! ~ **pis!**, too bad!

tante /tãt/ *n.f.* aunt.

tantôt /tãto/ *adv.* sometimes; (*cet après-midi*) this afternoon.

tapag|e /tapaʒ/ *n.m.* din. ~**eur**, ~**euse** *a.* rowdy; (*tape-à-l'œil*) flashy.

tapant, ~e /tapã, -t/ *a.* **à deux/trois/** *etc.* **heures ~es** at exactly two/three/*etc.* o'clock.

tape /tap/ *n.f.* slap. ~**-à-l'œil** *a. invar.* flashy, tawdry.

taper /tape/ *v.t.* bang; (*enfant*) slap; (*emprunter: fam.*) touch for money. ~ **(à la machine)**, type. ● *v.i.* (*cogner*) bang; (*soleil*) beat down. ~ **dans**, (*puiser dans*) dig into. ~ **sur**, thump; (*critiquer: fam.*) knock. **se** ~ *v. pr.* (*repas: fam.*) put away; (*corvée: fam.*) do.

tap|ir (se) /(sə)tapir/ *v. pr.* crouch. ~**i** *a.* crouching.

tapis /tapi/ *n.m.* carpet; (*petit*) rug; (*aux cartes*) baize. ~ **de bain**, bath mat. ~**-brosse** *n.m.* doormat. ~ **de sol**, groundsheet. ~ **roulant**, (*pour objets*) conveyor belt.

tapiss|er /tapise/ *v.t.* (*wall*)paper; (*fig.*) cover (**de**, with). ~**erie** *n.f.* tapestry; (*papier peint*) wallpaper. ~**ier**, ~**ière** *n.m., f.* (*décorateur*) interior decorator; (*qui recouvre un siège*) upholsterer.

tapoter /tapote/ *v.t.* tap, pat.

taquin, ~e /takɛ̃, -in/ *a.* fond of teasing. ● *n.m., f.* tease(r). ~**er** /-ine/ *v.t.* tease. ~**erie(s)** /-inri/ *n.f.* (*pl.*) teasing.

tarabiscoté /tarabiskote/ *a.* overelaborate.

tard /tar/ *adv.* late. **au plus** ~, at the latest. **plus** ~, later. **sur le** ~, late in life.

tard|er /tarde/ *v.i.* (*être lent à venir*) be a long time coming. ~**er (à faire)**, take a long time (doing, to do (doing). **sans (plus)** ~**er**, without (further) delay. **il me tarde de**, I long to.

tardi|f, ~ve /tardif, -v/ *a.* late; (*regrets*) belated.

tare /tar/ *n.f.* (*défaut*) defect.

taré /tare/ *a.* cretin.

targette /tarʒɛt/ *n.f.* bolt.

targuer (se) /(sə)targe/ *v. pr.* **se** ~ **de**, boast about.

tarif /tarif/ *n.m.* tariff; (*de train, taxi*) fare. ~**s postaux**, postage *ou* postal rates. ~**aire** *a.* tariff.

tarir /tarir/ *v.t./i.*, **se** ~ *v. pr.* dry up.

tartare /tartar/ *a.* (*culin.*) tartar.

tarte /tart/ *n.f.* tart; (*Amer.*) (open) pie. ● *a. invar.* (*sot: fam.*) stupid; (*laid: fam.*) ugly.

tartin|e /tartin/ *n.f.* slice of bread. ~**e beurrée**, slice of bread and butter. ~**er** *v.t.* spread.

tartre /tartr/ *n.m.* (*bouilloire*) fur, calcium deposit; (*dents*) tartar.

tas /tɑ/ *n.m.* pile, heap. **un** *ou* **des** ~ **de**, (*fam.*) lots of.

tasse /tɑs/ *n.f.* cup. ~ **à thé**, teacup.

tasser /tɑse/ *v.t.* pack, squeeze; (*terre*) pack (down). **se** ~ *v. pr.* (*terrain*) sink; (*se serrer*) squeeze up.

tâter /tɑte/ *v.t.* feel; (*fig.*) sound out. ● *v.i.* ~ **de**, try out.

tatillon, ~ne /tatijɔ̃, -jɔn/ *a.* finicky.

tâtonn|er /tɑtone/ *v.i.* grope about. ~**ements** *n.m. pl.* (*essais*) trial and error.

tâtons (à) /(a)tɑtɔ̃/ *adv.* **avancer** *ou* **marcher à** ~, grope one's way along.

tatou|er /tatwe/ *v.t.* tattoo. ~**age** *n.m.* (*dessin*) tattoo.

taudis /todi/ *n.m.* hovel.

taule /tol/ *n.f.* (*fam.*) prison.

taup|e /top/ *n.f.* mole. ~**inière** *n.f.* molehill.

taureau (pl. ~x) /tɔro/ n.m. bull. **le T~,** Taurus.

taux /to/ n.m. rate.

taverne /tavɛrn/ n.f. tavern.

tax|e /taks/ n.f. tax. **~e sur la valeur ajoutée,** value added tax. **~er** v.t. tax; (produit) fix the price of. **~er qn. de,** accuse s.o. of.

taxi /taksi/ n.m. taxi(-cab); (personne: fam.) taxi-driver.

taxiphone /taksifɔn/ n.m. pay phone.

Tchécoslovaquie /tʃekɔslɔvaki/ n.f. Czechoslovakia.

tchèque /tʃɛk/ a. & n.m./f. Czech.

te, t'* /tə, t/ pron. you; (indirect) (to) you; (réfléchi) yourself.

technicien, ~ne /tɛknisjɛ̃, -jɛn/ n.m., f. technician.

technique /tɛknik/ a. technical. ● n.f. technique. **~ment** adv. technically.

technolog|ie /tɛknɔlɔʒi/ n.f. technology. **~ique** a. technological.

teck /tɛk/ n.m. teak.

tee-shirt /tiʃœrt/ n.m. tee-shirt.

teindre† /tɛ̃dr/ v.t. dye. **se ~ les cheveux** v. pr. dye one's hair.

teint /tɛ̃/ n.m. complexion.

teint|e /tɛ̃t/ n.f. shade, tint. **une ~e de,** (fig.) a tinge of. **~er** v.t. (papier, verre, etc.) tint; (bois) stain.

teintur|e /tɛ̃tyr/ n.f. dyeing; (produit) dye. **~erie** (boutique) dry-cleaner's. **~ier, ~ière** n.m., f. dry-cleaner.

tel, ~le /tɛl/ a. such. **un ~ livre**/etc., such a book/etc. **un ~ chagrin**/etc., such sorrow/etc. **~ que,** such as, like; (ainsi que) (just) as. **~ ou tel,** such-and-such. **~ quel,** (just) as it is.

télé /tele/ n.f. (fam.) TV.

télécommande /telekɔmɑ̃d/ n.f. remote control.

télécommunications /telekɔmynikasjɔ̃/ n.f. pl. telecommunications.

télécopi|e /telekɔpi/ n.f. tele(fax). **~eur** n.m. fax machine.

téléfilm /telefilm/ n.m. (tele)film.

télégramme /telegram/ n.m. telegram.

télégraph|e /telegraf/ n.m. telegraph. **~ier** v.t./i. **~ier (à),** cable. **~ique** a. telegraphic; (fil, poteau) telegraph.

téléguid|er /telegide/ v.t. control by radio. **~é** a. radio-controlled.

télématique /telematik/ n.f. computer communications.

télépathe /telepat/ a. & n.m., f. psychic.

télépathie /telepati/ n.f. telepathy.

téléphérique /teleferik/ n.m. cable-car.

téléphon|e /telefɔn/ n.m. (tele)phone. **~e rouge,** (pol.) hot line. **~er** v.t./i. **~er (à),** (tele)phone. **~ique** a. (tele)phone. **~iste** n.m./f. operator.

télescop|e /telɛskɔp/ n.m. telescope. **~ique** a. telescopic.

télescoper /telɛskɔpe/ v.t. smash into. **se ~** v. pr. (véhicules) smash into each other.

télésiège /telesjɛʒ/ n.m. chair-lift.

téléski /teleski/ n.m. ski tow.

téléspecta|teur, ~trice /telespɛktatœr, -tris/ n.m., f. (television) viewer.

télévente /televɑ̃t/ n.f. telesales.

télévis|é /televize/ a. **émission ~ée,** television programme. **~eur** n.m. television set.

télévision /televizjɔ̃/ n.f. television.

télex /telɛks/ n.m. telex.

télexer /telɛkse/ v.t. telex.

telle /tɛl/ voir tel.

tellement /tɛlmɑ̃/ adv. (tant) so much; (si) so. **~ de,** (quantité) so much; (nombre) so many.

témér|aire /temerɛr/ a. rash. **~ité** n.f. rashness.

témoignage /temwaɲaʒ/ n.m. testimony, evidence; (récit) account. **~ de,** (sentiment) token of.

témoigner /temwaɲe/ v.i. testify (de, to). ● v.t. show. **~ que,** testify that.

témoin /temwɛ̃/ n.m. witness; (sport) baton. **être ~ de,** witness. **~ oculaire,** eyewitness.

tempe /tɑ̃p/ n.f. (anat.) temple.

tempérament /tɑ̃peramɑ̃/ n.m. temperament; (physique) constitution. **à ~,** (acheter) on hire-purchase; (Amer.) on the instalment plan.

température /tɑ̃peratyr/ n.f. temperature.

tempér|er /tɑ̃pere/ v.t. temper. **~é** a. (climat) temperate.

tempête /tɑ̃pɛt/ n.f. storm. **~ de neige,** snowstorm.

tempêter /tɑ̃pɛte/ v.i. (crier) rage.

temple /tɑ̃pl/ n.m. temple; (protestant) church.

temporaire /tɑ̃pɔrɛr/ a. temporary. **~ment** adv. temporarily.

temporel, ~le /tɑ̃pɔrɛl/ a. temporal.

temporiser /tɑ̃pɔrize/ *v.i.* play for time.

temps[1] /tɑ̃/ *n.m.* time; (*gram.*) tense; (*étape*) stage. **à ~ partiel/plein**, part-/full-time. **ces derniers ~**, lately. **dans le ~**, at one time. **dans quelque ~**, in a while. **de ~ en temps**, from time to time. **~ d'arrêt**, pause. **avoir tout son ~**, have plenty of time.

temps[2] /tɑ̃/ *n.m.* (*atmosphère*) weather. **~ de chien**, filthy weather. **quel ~ fait-il?**, what's the weather like?

tenace /tənas/ *a.* stubborn.

ténacité /tenasite/ *n.f.* stubbornness.

tenaille(s) /tənɑj/ *n.f.* (*pl.*) pincers.

tenanc|ier, ~ière /tənɑ̃sje, -jɛr/ *n.m., f.* keeper (**de**, of).

tenant /tənɑ̃/ *n.m.* (*partisan*) supporter; (*d'un titre*) holder.

tendance /tɑ̃dɑ̃s/ *n.f.* tendency; (*opinions*) leanings; (*évolution*) trend. **avoir ~ à**, have a tendency to, tend to.

tendon /tɑ̃dɔ̃/ *n.m.* tendon.

tendre[1] /tɑ̃dr/ *v.t.* stretch; (*piège*) set; (*bras*) stretch out; (*main*) hold out; (*cou*) crane; (*tapisserie*) hang. **~ à qn.**, hold out to s.o. ● *v.i.* **~ à**, tend to. **~ l'oreille**, prick up one's ears.

tendre[2] /tɑ̃dr/ *a.* tender; (*couleur, bois*) soft. **~ment** /-əmɑ̃/ *adv.* tenderly. **~sse** /-ɛs/ *n.f.* tenderness.

tendu /tɑ̃dy/ *a.* (*corde*) tight; (*personne, situation*) tense; (*main*) outstretched.

tén|èbres /tenɛbr/ *n.f. pl.* darkness. **~ébreux, ~ébreuse** *a.* dark.

teneur /tənœr/ *n.f.* content.

tenir† /tənir/ *v.t.* hold; (*pari, promesse, hôtel*) keep; (*place*) take up; (*propos*) utter; (*rôle*) play. **~ de**, (*avoir reçu de*) have got from. **~ pour**, regard as. **~ propre/chaud/** *etc.*, keep clean/warm/*etc.* ● *v.i.* hold. **~ à**, be attached to. **~ à faire**, be anxious to do. **~ dans**, fit into. **~ de qn.**, take after s.o. **se ~** *v. pr.* (*rester*) remain; (*debout*) stand; (*avoir lieu*) be held. **se ~ bien**, behave o.s. **s'en ~ à**, (*se limiter à*) confine o.s. to. **~ bon**, stand firm. **~ compte de**, take into account. **~ le coup**, hold out. **~ tête à**, stand up to. **tiens!**, (*surprise*) hey!

tennis /tenis/ *n.m.* tennis; (*terrain*) tennis-court. ● *n.m. pl.* (*chaussures*) sneakers. **~ de table**, table tennis.

ténor /tenɔr/ *n.m.* tenor.

tension /tɑ̃sjɔ̃/ *n.f.* tension. **avoir de la ~**, have high blood-pressure.

tentacule /tɑ̃takyl/ *n.m.* tentacle.

tentative /tɑ̃tativ/ *n.f.* attempt.

tente /tɑ̃t/ *n.f.* tent.

tenter[1] /tɑ̃te/ *v.t.* try (**de faire**, to do).

tent|er[2] /tɑ̃te/ *v.t.* (*allécher*) tempt. **~é de**, tempted to. **~ation** *n.f.* temptation.

tenture /tɑ̃tyr/ *n.f.* (wall) hanging. **~s**, drapery.

tenu /təny/ *voir* **tenir**. ● *a.* **bien ~**, well-kept. **~ de**, obliged to.

ténu /teny/ *a.* (*fil etc.*) fine; (*cause, nuance*) tenuous.

tenue /təny/ *n.f.* (*habillement*) dress; (*de sport*) clothes; (*de maison*) upkeep; (*conduite*) (good) behaviour; (*maintien*) posture. **~ de soirée**, evening dress.

ter /tɛr/ *a. invar.* (*numéro*) B, b.

térébenthine /terebɑ̃tin/ *n.f.* turpentine.

tergiverser /tɛrʒivɛrse/ *v.i.* procrastinate.

terme /tɛrm/ *n.m.* (*mot*) term; (*date limite*) time-limit; (*fin*) end; (*date de loyer*) term. **à long/court ~**, long-/short-term. **en bons ~s**, on good terms (**avec**, with).

termin|al, ~ale (*m. pl.* **~aux**) /tɛrminal, -o/ *a.* terminal. (**classe**) **~ale**, sixth form; (*Amer.*) twelfth grade. ● *n.m.* (*pl.* **~aux**) terminal.

termin|er /tɛrmine/ *v.t./i.* finish; (*soirée, débat*) end, finish. **se ~er** *v. pr.* end (**par**, with). **~aison** *n.f.* (*gram.*) ending.

terminologie /tɛrminɔlɔʒi/ *n.f.* terminology.

terminus /tɛrminys/ *n.m.* terminus.

terne /tɛrn/ *a.* dull, drab.

ternir /tɛrnir/ *v.t./i.*, **se ~** *v. pr.* tarnish.

terrain /tɛrɛ̃/ *n.m.* ground; (*parcelle*) piece of land; (*à bâtir*) plot. **~ d'aviation**, airfield. **~ de camping**, campsite. **~ de golf**, golf-course. **~ de jeu**, playground. **~ vague**, waste ground; (*Amer.*) vacant lot.

terrasse /tɛras/ *n.f.* terrace; (*de café*) pavement area.

terrassement /tɛrasmɑ̃/ *n.m.* excavation.

terrasser /tɛrase/ v.t. (*adversaire*) floor; (*maladie*) strike down.

terrassier /tɛrasje/ n.m. navvy, labourer, ditch-digger.

terre /tɛr/ n.f. (*planète, matière*) earth; (*étendue, pays*) land; (*sol*) ground; (*domaine*) estate. **à ~,** (*naut.*) ashore. **par ~,** (*tomber, jeter*) to the ground; (*s'asseoir, poser*) on the ground. **~ (cuite),** terracotta. **~-à-terre** a. invar. matter-of-fact, down-to-earth. **~-plein** n.m. platform, (*auto.*) central reservation. **la ~ ferme,** dry land. **~ glaise,** clay.

terreau (*m. pl. ~x*) /tɛro/ n.m. compost.

terrer (se) /(sə)tɛre/ v. pr. hide o.s., dig o.s. in.

terrestre /tɛrɛstr/ a. terrible; (*de notre planète*) earth's; (*fig.*) earthly.

terreur /tɛrœr/ n.f. terror.

terreu|x, ~se /tɛrø, -z/ a. earthy; (*sale*) grubby.

terrible /tɛribl/ a. terrible; (*formidable: fam.*) terrific.

terrien, ~ne /tɛrjɛ̃, -jɛn/ n.m., f. earth-dweller.

terrier /tɛrje/ n.m. (*trou de lapin etc.*) burrow; (*chien*) terrier.

terrifier /tɛrifje/ v.t. terrify.

terrine /tɛrin/ n.f. (*culin.*) terrine.

territ|oire /tɛritwar/ n.m. territory. **~orial** (*m. pl. ~oriaux*) a. territorial.

terroir /tɛrwar/ n.m. (*sol*) soil; (*région*) region. **du ~,** country.

terroriser /tɛrorize/ v.t. terrorize.

terroris|te /tɛrorist/ n.m./f. terrorist. **~me** n.m. terrorism.

tertre /tɛrtr/ n.m. mound.

tes /te/ voir **ton**[1].

tesson /tɛsɔ̃/ n.m. **~ de bouteille,** piece of broken bottle.

test /tɛst/ n.m. test. **~er** v.t. test.

testament /tɛstamɑ̃/ n.m. (*jurid.*) will; (*politique, artistique*) testament. **Ancien/Nouveau T~,** Old/New Testament.

testicule /tɛstikyl/ n.m. testicle.

tétanos /tetanos/ n.m. tetanus.

têtard /tɛtar/ n.m. tadpole.

tête /tɛt/ n.f. head; (*figure*) face; (*cheveux*) hair; (*cerveau*) brain. **à la ~ de,** at the head of. **à ~ reposée,** in a leisurely moment. **de ~,** (*calculer*) in one's head. **en ~,** (*sport*) in the lead. **faire la ~,** sulk. **faire une ~,** (*football*) head the ball. **tenir ~ à qn.,** stand up to s.o. **une forte ~,** a

rebel. **la ~ la première,** head first. **il n'en fait qu'à sa ~,** he does just as he pleases. **de la ~ aux pieds,** from head to toe. **~-à-queue** n.m. invar. (*auto.*) spin. **~-à-tête** n.m. invar. tête-à-tête. **en ~-à-tête,** in private.

têtée /tete/ n.f. feed.

téter /tete/ v.t./i. suck.

tétine /tetin/ n.f. (*de biberon*) teat; (*sucette*) dummy; (*Amer.*) pacifier.

têtu /tety/ a. stubborn.

texte /tɛkst/ n.m. text; (*de leçon*) subject; (*morceau choisi*) passage.

textile /tɛkstil/ n.m. & a. textile.

textuel, ~le /tɛkstɥɛl/ a. literal.

texture /tɛkstyr/ n.f. texture.

thaïlandais, ~e /tailɑ̃dɛ, -z/ a. & n.m., f. Thai.

Thaïlande /tailɑ̃d/ n.f. Thailand.

thé /te/ n.m. tea.

théâtr|al (*m. pl. ~aux*) /teatral, -o/ a. theatrical.

théâtre /teatr/ n.m. theatre; (*jeu forcé*) play-acting; (*d'un crime*) scene. **faire du ~,** act.

théière /tejɛr/ n.f. teapot.

thème /tɛm/ n.m. theme; (*traduction: scol.*) prose.

théolog|ie /teolɔʒi/ n.f. theology. **~ien** n.m. theologian. **~ique** a. theological.

théorème /teorɛm/ n.m. theorem.

théor|ie /teori/ n.f. theory. **~icien, ~icienne** n.m., f. theorist. **~ique** a. theoretical. **~iquement,** adv. theoretically.

thérap|ie /terapi/ n.f. therapy. **~eutique** a. therapeutic.

thermique /tɛrmik/ a. thermal.

thermomètre /tɛrmomɛtr/ n.m. thermometer.

thermonucléaire /tɛrmonykleɛr/ a. thermonuclear.

thermos /tɛrmos/ n.m./f. (P.) Thermos (P.) (flask).

thermostat /tɛrmosta/ n.m. thermostat.

thésauriser /tezorize/ v.t./i. hoard.

thèse /tɛz/ n.f. thesis.

thon /tɔ̃/ n.m. (*poisson*) tuna.

thrombose /trɔ̃boz/ n.f. thrombosis.

thym /tɛ̃/ n.m. thyme.

thyroïde /tiroid/ n.f. thyroid.

tibia /tibja/ n.m. shin-bone.

tic /tik/ n.m. (*contraction*) twitch; (*manie*) mannerism.

ticket /tikɛ/ n.m. ticket.

tic-tac /tiktak/ n.m. invar. (*de pendule*) ticking. **faire ~,** go tick tock.

tiède /tjɛd/ a. lukewarm; (atmosphère) mild. **tiédeur** /tjedœr/ n.f. lukewarmness; mildness.

tiédir /tjedir/ v.t./i. (faire) ~, warm slightly.

tien, ~ne /tjɛ̃, tjɛn/ pron. le ~, la ~ne, les ~(ne)s, yours. à la ~ ne!, cheers!

tiens, tient /tjɛ̃/ voir tenir.

tiercé /tjɛrse/ n.m. place-betting.

tier|s, ~ce /tjɛr, -s/ a. third. ● n.m. (fraction) third; (personne) third party. **T~s-Monde** n.m. Third World.

tifs /tif/ n.m. pl. (fam.) hair.

tige /tiʒ/ n.f. (bot.) stem, stalk; (en métal) shaft.

tignasse /tiɲas/ n.f. mop of hair.

tigre /tigr/ n.m. tiger. ~sse /-ɛs/ n.f. tigress.

tigré /tigre/ a. (rayé) striped; (chat) tabby.

tilleul /tijœl/ n.m. lime(-tree), linden (-tree); (infusion) lime tea.

timbale /tɛ̃bal/ n.f. (gobelet) (metal) tumbler.

timbr|e /tɛ̃br/ n.m. stamp; (sonnette) bell; (de voix) tone. ~e-poste (pl. ~es-poste) n.m. postage stamp. ~er v.t. stamp.

timbré /tɛ̃bre/ a. (fam.) crazy.

timid|e /timid/ a. timid. ~ité n.f. timidity.

timoré /timɔre/ a. timorous.

tintamarre /tɛ̃tamar/ n.m. din.

tint|er /tɛ̃te/ v.i. ring; (clefs) jingle. ~ement n.m. ringing; jingling.

tique /tik/ n.f. (insecte) tick.

tir /tir/ n.m. (sport) shooting; (action de tirer) firing; (feu, rafale) fire. ~ à l'arc, archery. ~ forain, shooting-gallery.

tirade /tirad/ n.f. soliloquy.

tirage /tiraʒ/ n.m. (de photo) printing; (de journal) circulation; (de livre) edition; (de loterie) draw; (de cheminée) draught. ~ au sort, drawing lots.

tiraill|er /tiraje/ v.t. pull (away) at; (harceler) plague. ~é entre, (possibilités etc.) torn between. ~ement n.m. (douleur) gnawing pain; (conflit) conflict.

tiré /tire/ a. (traits) drawn.

tire-bouchon /tirbuʃɔ̃/ n.m. corkscrew.

tire-lait /tirlɛ/ n.m. breastpump.

tirelire /tirlir/ n.f. money-box; (Amer.) coin-bank.

tirer /tire/ v.t. pull; (navire) tow, tug; (langue) stick out; (conclusion, trait, rideaux) draw; (coup de feu) fire; (gibier) shoot; (photo) print. ~ de, (sortir) take ou get out of; (extraire) extract from; (plaisir, nom) derive from. ● v.i. shoot, fire (sur, at). ~ sur, (couleur) verge on; (corde) pull at. se ~ v. pr. (fam.) clear off. se ~ de, get out of. s'en ~, (en réchapper) pull through; (réussir: fam.) cope. ~ à sa fin, be drawing to a close. ~ au clair, clarify. ~ au sort, draw lots (for). ~ parti de, take advantage of. ~ profit de, profit from.

tiret /tire/ n.m. dash.

tireur /tirœr/ n.m. gunman. ~ d'élite, marksman. ~ isolé, sniper.

tiroir /tirwar/ n.m. drawer. ~-caisse (pl. ~s-caisses) n.m. till.

tisane /tizan/ n.f. herb-tea.

tison /tizɔ̃/ n.m. ember.

tisonnier /tizɔnje/ n.m. poker.

tiss|er /tise/ v.t. weave. ~age n.m. weaving. ~erand /tisrɑ̃/ n.m. weaver.

tissu /tisy/ n.m. fabric, material; (biologique) tissue. un ~ de, (fig.) a web of. ~-éponge (pl. ~s-éponge) n.m. towelling.

titre /titr/ n.m. title; (diplôme) qualification; (comm.) bond. ~s, (droits) claims. **(gros)** ~s, headlines. à ce ~, (pour cette qualité) as such. à ~ d'exemple, as an example. à juste ~, rightly. à ~ privé, in a private capacity. ~ de propriété, title-deed.

titré /titre/ a. titled.

titrer /titre/ v.t. (journal) give as a headline.

tituber /titybe/ v.i. stagger.

titul|aire /titylɛr/ a. être ~aire, have tenure. être ~aire de, hold. ● n.m./f. (de permis etc.) holder. ~ariser v.t. give tenure to.

toast /tost/ n.m. piece of toast; (allocution) toast.

toboggan /tɔbɔgɑ̃/ n.m. (traîneau) toboggan; (glissière) slide; (auto.) flyover; (auto., Amer.) overpass.

toc /tɔk/ int. ~ toc! knock knock!

tocsin /tɔksɛ̃/ n.m. alarm (bell).

toge /tɔʒ/ n.f. (de juge etc.) gown.

tohu-bohu /tɔyboy/ n.m. hubbub.

toi /twa/ pron. you; (réfléchi) yourself. lève-~, stand up.

toile /twal/ n.f. cloth; (sac, tableau) canvas; (coton) cotton. ~ d'arai-

gnée, (spider's) web; (*délabrée*) cobweb. **~ de fond,** backdrop, backcloth.

toilette /twalɛt/ *n.f.* washing; (*habillement*) clothes, dress. **~s,** (*cabinets*) toilet(s). **de ~,** (*articles, savon, etc.*) toilet. **faire sa ~,** wash (and get ready).

toi-même /twamɛm/ *pron.* yourself.

toiser /twaze/ *v.t.* **~ qn.,** look s.o. up and down.

toison /twazɔ̃/ *n.f.* (*laine*) fleece.

toit /twa/ *n.m.* roof. **~ ouvrant,** (*auto.*) sun-roof.

toiture /twatyr/ *n.f.* roof.

tôle /tol/ *n.f.* (*plaque*) iron sheet. **~ ondulée,** corrugated iron.

tolérable /tolerabl/ *a.* tolerable.

tolérant, **~te** /tolerɑ̃, -t/ *a.* tolerant. **~ce** *n.f.* tolerance; (*importations: comm.*) allowance.

tolérer /tolere/ *v.t.* tolerate; (*importations: comm.*) allow.

tollé /tole/ *n.m.* hue and cry.

tomate /tomat/ *n.f.* tomato.

tombe /tɔ̃b/ *n.f.* grave; (*avec monument*) tomb.

tombeau (*pl.* **~x**) /tɔ̃bo/ *n.m.* tomb.

tombée /tɔ̃be/ *n.f.* **~ de la nuit,** nightfall.

tomber /tɔ̃be/ *v.i.* (*aux. être*) fall; (*fièvre, vent*) drop; (*enthousiasme*) die down. **faire ~,** knock over; (*gouvernement*) bring down. **laisser ~,** drop; (*abandonner*) let down. **laisse ~!,** forget it! **~ à l'eau,** (*projet*) fall through. **~ bien** *ou* **à point,** come at the right time. **~ en panne,** break down. **~ en syncope,** faint. **~ sur,** (*trouver*) run across.

tombola /tɔ̃bola/ *n.f.* tombola; (*Amer.*) lottery.

tome /tom/ *n.m.* volume.

ton[1]**, ta** *ou* **ton*** (*pl.* **tes**) /tɔ̃, ta, tɔ̃, te/ *a.* your.

ton[2] /tɔ̃/ *n.m.* tone; (*gamme: mus.*) key; (*hauteur de la voix*) pitch. **de bon ~,** in good taste.

tonalité /tonalite/ *n.f.* tone; (*téléphone*) dialling tone; (*téléphone: Amer.*) dial tone.

tond|re /tɔ̃dr/ *v.t.* (*herbe*) mow; (*mouton*) shear; (*cheveux*) clip. **~euse** *n.f.* shears; clippers. **~euse (à gazon),** (lawn-)mower.

tongs /tɔ̃g/ *n.f. pl.* flip-flops.

tonifier /tonifje/ *v.t.* tone up.

tonique /tonik/ *a. & n.m.* tonic.

tonne /tɔn/ *n.f.* ton(ne).

tonneau (*pl.* **~x**) /tɔno/ *n.m.* (*récipient*) barrel; (*naut.*) ton; (*culbute*) somersault.

tonnelle /tɔnɛl/ *n.f.* bower.

tonner /tone/ *v.i.* thunder.

tonnerre /tɔnɛr/ *n.m.* thunder.

tonte /tɔ̃t/ *n.f.* (*de gazon*) mowing; (*de moutons*) shearing.

tonton /tɔ̃tɔ̃/ *n.m.* (*fam.*) uncle.

tonus /tonys/ *n.m.* energy.

top /tɔp/ *n.m.* (*signal pour marquer un instant précis*) stroke.

topo /topo/ *n.m.* (*fam.*) talk, oral report.

toquade /tokad/ *n.f.* craze; (*pour une personne*) infatuation.

toque /tok/ *n.f.* (fur) hat; (*de jockey*) cap; (*de cuisinier*) hat.

toqué /toke/ *a.* (*fam.*) crazy.

torche /tɔrʃ/ *n.f.* torch.

torcher /tɔrʃe/ *v.t.* (*fam.*) wipe.

torchon /tɔrʃɔ̃/ *n.m.* cloth, duster; (*pour la vaisselle*) tea-towel; (*Amer.*) dish-towel.

tord|re /tɔrdr/ *v.t.* twist; (*linge*) wring. **se ~** *v. pr.* twist, bend; (*de douleur*) writhe. **se ~ (de rire),** split one's sides.

tordu /tɔrdy/ *a.* twisted, bent; (*esprit*) warped.

tornade /tɔrnad/ *n.f.* tornado.

torpeur /tɔrpœr/ *n.f.* lethargy.

torpill|e /tɔrpij/ *n.f.* torpedo. **~er** *v.t.* torpedo.

torréfier /tɔrefje/ *v.t.* roast.

torrent /tɔrɑ̃/ *n.m.* torrent. **~iel,** **~ielle** /-sjɛl/ *a.* torrential.

torride /tɔrid/ *a.* torrid.

torsade /tɔrsad/ *n.f.* twist.

torse /tɔrs/ *n.m.* chest; (*sculpture*) torso.

tort /tɔr/ *n.m.* wrong. **à ~,** wrongly. **à ~ et à travers,** without thinking. **avoir ~,** be wrong (**de faire,** to do). **donner ~ à,** prove wrong. **être dans son ~,** be in the wrong. **faire (du) ~ à,** harm.

torticolis /tɔrtikoli/ *n.m.* stiff neck.

tortiller /tɔrtije/ *v.t.* twist, twirl. **se ~** *v. pr.* wriggle, wiggle.

tortionnaire /tɔrsjoner/ *n.m.* torturer.

tortue /tɔrty/ *n.f.* tortoise; (*de mer*) turtle.

tortueu|x, **~se** /tɔrtɥø, -z/ *a.* (*explication*) tortuous; (*chemin*) twisting.

tortur|e(s) /tɔrtyr/ *n.f.* (*pl.*) torture. **~er** *v.t.* torture.

tôt /to/ *adv.* early. **plus ~**, earlier. **au plus ~**, at the earliest. **le plus ~ possible**, as soon as possible. **~ ou tard**, sooner or later.

tot|al (*m. pl.* **~aux**) /total, -o/ *a.* total. ● *n.m.* (*pl.* **~aux**) total. ● *adv.* (*fam.*) to conclude, in short. **au ~al**, all in all. **~alement** *adv.* totally. **~aliser** *v.t.* total.

totalitaire /tɔtalitɛr/ *a.* totalitarian.

totalité /tɔtalite/ *n.f.* entirety. **la ~ de**, all of.

toubib /tubib/ *n.m.* (*fam.*) doctor.

touchant, ~e /tuʃɑ̃, -t/ *a.* (*émouvant*) touching.

touche /tuʃ/ *n.f.* (*de piano*) key; (*de peintre*) touch. (**ligne de**) **~**, touchline. **une ~ de**, a touch of.

toucher[1] /tuʃe/ *v.t.* touch; (*émouvoir*) move, touch; (*contacter*) get in touch with; (*cible*) hit; (*argent*) draw; (*chèque*) cash; (*concerner*) affect. ● *v.i.* **~ à**, touch; (*question*) touch on; (*fin, but*) approach. **je vais lui en ~ un mot**, I'll talk to him about it. **se ~** *v. pr.* (*lignes*) touch.

toucher[2] /tuʃe/ *n.m.* (*sens*) touch.

touffe /tuf/ *n.f.* (*de poils, d'herbe*) tuft; (*de plantes*) clump.

touffu /tufy/ *a.* thick, bushy; (*fig.*) complex.

toujours /tuʒur/ *adv.* always; (*encore*) still; (*en tout cas*) anyhow. **pour ~**, for ever.

toupet /tupɛ/ *n.m.* (*culot: fam.*) cheek, nerve.

toupie /tupi/ *n.f.* (*jouet*) top.

tour[1] /tur/ *n.f.* tower; (*immeuble*) tower block; (*échecs*) rook. **~ de contrôle**, control tower.

tour[2] /tur/ *n.m.* (*mouvement, succession, tournure*) turn; (*excursion*) trip; (*à pied*) walk; (*en auto*) drive; (*artifice*) trick; (*circonférence*) circumference; (*techn.*) lathe. **~ (de piste)**, lap. **à ~ de rôle**, in turn. **à mon/etc. ~**, when it is my/etc. turn. **c'est mon/etc. ~ de**, it is my/etc. turn to. **faire le ~ de**, go round; (*question*) survey. **~ d'horizon**, survey. **~ de passe-passe**, sleight of hand. **~ de taille**, waist measurement; (*ligne*) waistline.

tourbe /turb/ *n.f.* peat.

tourbillon /turbijɔ̃/ *n.m.* whirlwind; (*d'eau*) whirlpool; (*fig.*) whirl, swirl. **~ner** /-jɔne/ *v.i.* whirl, swirl.

tourelle /turɛl/ *n.f.* turret.

tourisme /turism/ *n.m.* tourism. **faire du ~**, do some sightseeing.

tourist|e /turist/ *n.m./f.* tourist. **~ique** *a.* tourist; (*route*) scenic.

tourment /turmɑ̃/ *n.m.* torment. **~er** /-te/ *v.t.* torment. **se ~er** *v. pr.* worry.

tournage /turnaʒ/ *n.m.* (*cinéma*) shooting.

tournant[1], **~e** /turnɑ̃, -t/ *a.* (*qui pivote*) revolving.

tournant[2] /turnɑ̃/ *n.m.* bend; (*fig.*) turning-point.

tourne-disque /turnədisk/ *n.m.* record-player.

tournée /turne/ *n.f.* (*voyage, consommations*) round; (*théâtre*) tour. **faire la ~**, make the rounds (**de**, of). **je paye** *ou* **j'offre la ~**, I'll buy this round.

tourner /turne/ *v.t.* turn; (*film*) shoot, make. ● *v.i.* turn; (*toupie, tête*) spin; (*moteur, usine*) run. **se ~** *v. pr.* turn. **~ au froid**, turn cold. **~ autour de**, go round; (*personne, maison*) hang around; (*terre*) revolve round; (*question*) centre on. **~ de l'œil**, (*fam.*) faint. **~ en dérision**, mock. **~ en ridicule**, ridicule. **~ le dos à**, turn one's back on. **~ mal**, turn out badly.

tournesol /turnəsɔl/ *n.m.* sunflower.

tournevis /turnəvis/ *n.m.* screwdriver.

tourniquet /turnikɛ/ *n.m.* (*barrière*) turnstile.

tournoi /turnwa/ *n.m.* tournament.

tournoyer /turnwaje/ *v.i.* whirl.

tournure /turnyr/ *n.f.* turn; (*locution*) turn of phrase.

tourte /turt/ *n.f.* pie.

tourterelle /turtərɛl/ *n.f.* turtle-dove.

Toussaint /tusɛ̃/ *n.f.* **la ~**, All Saints' Day.

tousser /tuse/ *v.i.* cough.

tout[1], **~e** (*pl.* **tous, toutes** /tu, tut/) *a.* all; (*n'importe quel*) any; (*tout à fait*) entirely. **~ le pays/etc.**, the whole country/etc., all the country/etc. **~e la nuit/journée**, the whole night/day. **~ un paquet**, a whole pack. **tous les jours/mois/etc.**, every day/month/etc. ● *pron.* everything, all. **tous** /tus/, **toutes**, all. **prendre ~**, take everything, take it all. **~ ce que**, all that. **~ le monde**, everyone. **tous les deux, toutes les deux**, both of them. **tous les trois**, all three (of them). ● *adv.*

(*très*) very; (*tout à fait*) quite. ~ **au bout/début**/*etc.*, right at the end/ beginning/*etc.* **le ~ premier**, the very first. ~ **en chantant/marchant**/*etc.*, while singing/walking/ *etc.* ~ **à coup**, all of a sudden. ~ **à fait**, quite, completely. ~ **à l'heure**, in a moment; (*passé*) a moment ago. ~ **au** *ou* **le long de**, throughout. ~ **au plus/moins**, at most/least. ~ **de même**, all the same. ~ **de suite**, straight away. ~ **entier**, whole. ~ **le contraire**, quite the opposite. ~ **neuf**, brand-new. ~ **nu**, stark naked. ~ **près**, nearby. ~-**puissant**, ~**e-puissante** *a.* omnipotent. ~ **seul**, alone. ~ **terrain** *a. invar.* all terrain.

tout [2] /tu/ *n.m.* (*ensemble*) whole. **en** ~, in all. **pas du** ~! not at all!

tout-à-l'égout /tutalegu/ *n.m.* main drainage.

toutefois /tutfwa/ *adv.* however.

toux /tu/ *n.f.* cough.

toxicomane /tɔksikɔman/ *n.m./f.* drug addict.

toxine /tɔksin/ *n.f.* toxin.

toxique /tɔksik/ *a.* toxic.

trac /trak/ *n.m.* **le** ~, nerves; (*théâtre*) stage fright.

tracas /traka/ *n.m.* worry. ~**ser** /-se/ *v.t.*, **se** ~**ser** *v. pr.* worry.

trace /tras/ *n.f.* trace, mark; (*d'animal, de pneu*) tracks; (*vestige*) trace. **sur la** ~ **de**, on the track of. ~**s de pas**, footprints.

tracé /trase/ *n.m.* (*ligne*) line; (*plan*) layout.

tracer /trase/ *v.t.* draw, trace; (*écrire*) write; (*route*) mark out.

trachée(-artère) /traʃe(artɛr)/ *n.f.* windpipe.

tract /trakt/ *n.m.* leaflet.

tractations /traktasjɔ̃/ *n.f. pl.* dealings.

tracteur /traktœr/ *n.m.* tractor.

traction /traksjɔ̃/ *n.f.* (*sport*) press-up, push-up.

tradition /tradisjɔ̃/ *n.f.* tradition. ~**nel**, ~**nelle** /-jɔnɛl/ *a.* traditional.

trad|uire† /tradɥir/ *v.t.* translate; (*sentiment*) express. ~**uire en justice**, take to court. ~**ucteur**, ~**uctrice** *n.m.*, *f.* translator. ~**uction** *n.f.* translation.

trafic /trafik/ *n.m.* (*commerce, circulation*) traffic.

trafiqu|er /trafike/ *v.i.* traffic. ● *v.t.* (*fam.*) (*vin*) doctor; (*moteur*) fiddle

with. ~**ant**, ~**ante** *n.m.*, *f.* trafficker; (*d'armes, de drogues*) dealer.

tragédie /traʒedi/ *n.f.* tragedy.

tragique /traʒik/ *a.* tragic. ~**ment** *adv.* tragically.

trah|ir /trair/ *v.t.* betray. ~**ison** *n.f.* betrayal; (*crime*) treason.

train /trɛ̃/ *n.m.* (*rail.*) train; (*allure*) pace. **en** ~, (*en forme*) in shape. **en** ~ **de faire**, (busy) doing. **mettre en** ~, start up. ~ **d'atterrissage**, undercarriage. ~ **électrique**, (*jouet*) electric train set. ~ **de vie**, lifestyle.

traînard, ~**e** /trɛnar, -d/ *n.m.*, *f.* slowcoach; (*Amer.*) slowpoke; (*en marchant*) straggler.

traîne /trɛn/ *n.f.* (*de robe*) train. **à la** ~, lagging behind; (*en remorque*) in tow.

traîneau (*pl.* ~**x**) /trɛno/ *n.m.* sledge.

traînée /trɛne/ *n.f.* (*trace*) trail; (*bande*) streak; (*femme: péj.*) slut.

traîner /trɛne/ *v.t.* drag (along); (*véhicule*) pull. ● *v.i.* (*pendre*) trail; (*rester en arrière*) trail behind; (*flâner*) hang about; (*papiers, affaires*) lie around. ~ **(en longueur)**, drag on. **se** ~ *v. pr.* (*par terre*) crawl. **(faire)** ~ **en longueur**, drag out. ~ **les pieds**, drag one's feet. **ça n'a pas traîné!**, that didn't take long.

train-train /trɛ̃trɛ̃/ *n.m.* routine.

traire† /trɛr/ *v.t.* milk.

trait /trɛ/ *n.m.* line; (*en dessinant*) stroke; (*caractéristique*) feature, trait; (*acte*) act. ~**s**, (*du visage*) features. **avoir** ~ **à**, relate to. **d'un** ~, (*boire*) in one gulp. ~ **d'union**, hyphen; (*fig.*) link.

traite /trɛt/ *n.f.* (*de vache*) milking; (*comm.*) draft. **d'une (seule)** ~, in one go, at a stretch.

traité /trete/ *n.m.* (*pacte*) treaty; (*ouvrage*) treatise.

traitement /trɛtmɑ̃/ *n.m.* treatment; (*salaire*) salary. ~ **de données**, data processing. ~ **de texte**, word processing.

traiter /trete/ *v.t.* treat; (*affaire*) deal with; (*données, produit*) process. ~ **qn. de lâche**/*etc.*, call s.o. a coward/ *etc.* ● *v.i.* deal (**avec**, with). ~ **de**, (*sujet*) deal with.

traiteur /trɛtœr/ *n.m.* caterer; (*boutique*) delicatessen.

traître, ~**sse** /trɛtr, -ɛs/ *a.* treacherous. ● *n.m./f.* traitor.

trajectoire /traʒɛktwar/ *n.f.* path.

trajet /traʒɛ/ *n.m.* (*à parcourir*) distance; (*voyage*) journey; (*itinéraire*) route.

trame /tram/ *n.f.* (*de tissu*) weft; (*de récit etc.*) framework. **usé jusqu'à la ~,** threadbare.

tramer /trame/ *v.t.* plot; (*complot*) hatch. **qu'est-ce qui se trame?,** what's brewing?

tramway /tramwɛ/ *n.m.* tram; (*Amer.*) streetcar.

tranchant, ~e /trɑ̃ʃɑ̃, -t/ *a.* sharp; (*fig.*) cutting. ● *n.m.* cutting edge. **à double ~,** two-edged.

tranche /trɑ̃ʃ/ *n.f.* (*rondelle*) slice; (*bord*) edge; (*partie*) portion.

tranchée /trɑ̃ʃe/ *n.f.* trench.

tranch|er[1] /trɑ̃ʃe/ *v.t.* cut; (*question*) decide. ● *v.i.* (*décider*) decide. **~é a.** (*net*) clear-cut.

trancher[2] /trɑ̃ʃe/ *v.i.* (*contraster*) contrast (**sur,** with).

tranquill|e /trɑ̃kil/ *a.* quiet; (*esprit*) at rest; (*conscience*) clear. **être/laisser ~e,** be/leave in peace. **~ement** *adv.* quietly. **~ité** *n.f.* (*peace and*) quiet; (*d'esprit*) peace of mind.

tranquillisant /trɑ̃kilizɑ̃/ *n.m.* tranquillizer.

tranquilliser /trɑ̃kilize/ *v.t.* reassure.

transaction /trɑ̃zaksjɔ̃/ *n.f.* transaction.

transat /trɑ̃zat/ *n.m.* (*fam.*) deckchair.

transatlantique /trɑ̃zatlɑ̃tik/ *n.m.* transatlantic liner. ● *a.* transatlantic.

transborder /trɑ̃sbɔrde/ *v.t.* transfer, tranship.

transcend|er /trɑ̃sɑ̃de/ *v.t.* transcend. **~ant, ~ante** *a.* transcendent.

transcr|ire /trɑ̃skrir/ *v.t.* transcribe. **~iption** *n.f.* transcription; (*copie*) transcript.

transe /trɑ̃s/ *n.f.* **en ~,** in a trance; (*fig.*) very excited.

transférer /trɑ̃sfere/ *v.t.* transfer.

transfert /trɑ̃sfɛr/ *n.m.* transfer.

transform|er /trɑ̃sfɔrme/ *v.t.* change; (*radicalement*) transform; (*vêtement*) alter. **se ~er** *v. pr.* change; be transformed. **(se) ~er en,** turn into. **~ateur** *n.m.* transformer. **~ation** *n.f.* change; transformation.

transfuge /trɑ̃sfyʒ/ *n.m.* renegade.

transfusion /trɑ̃sfyzjɔ̃/ *n.f.* transfusion.

transgresser /trɑ̃sgrese/ *v.t.* disobey.

transiger /trɑ̃ziʒe/ *v.i.* compromise. **ne pas ~ sur,** not compromise on.

transi /trɑ̃zi/ *a.* chilled to the bone.

transistor /trɑ̃zistɔr/ *n.m.* (*dispositif, poste de radio*) transistor.

transit /trɑ̃zit/ *n.m.* transit. **~er** *v.t./i.* pass in transit.

transiti|f, ~ve /trɑ̃zitif, -v/ *a.* transitive.

transi|tion /trɑ̃zisjɔ̃/ *n.f.* transition. **~toire** *a.* (*provisoire*) transitional.

translucide /trɑ̃slysid/ *a.* translucent.

transm|ettre† /trɑ̃smɛtr/ *v.t.* pass on; (*techn.*) transmit; (*radio*) broadcast. **~ission** *n.f.* transmission; (*radio*) broadcasting.

transparaître /trɑ̃sparɛtr/ *v.i.* show (through).

transparen|t, ~te /trɑ̃sparɑ̃, -t/ *a.* transparent. **~ce** *n.f.* transparency.

transpercer /trɑ̃sperse/ *v.t.* pierce.

transpir|er /trɑ̃spire/ *v.i.* perspire. **~ation** *n.f.* perspiration.

transplant|er /trɑ̃splɑ̃te/ *v.t.* (*bot., méd.*) transplant. **~ation** *n.f.* (*bot.*) transplantation; (*méd.*) transplant.

transport /trɑ̃spɔr/ *n.m.* transport(ation); (*sentiment*) rapture. **les ~s,** transport. **les ~s en commun,** public transport.

transport|er /trɑ̃spɔrte/ *v.t.* transport; (*à la main*) carry. **se ~er** *v. pr.* take o.s. (**à,** to). **~eur** *n.m.* haulier; (*Amer.*) trucker.

transposer /trɑ̃spoze/ *v.t.* transpose.

transvaser /trɑ̃svaze/ *v.t.* decant.

transvers|al (*m. pl. ~aux*) /trɑ̃sversal, -o/ *a.* cross, transverse.

trap|èze /trapɛz/ *n.m.* (*sport*) trapeze. **~éziste** /-ezist/ *n.m./f.* trapeze artist.

trappe /trap/ *n.f.* trapdoor.

trappeur /trapœr/ *n.m.* trapper.

trapu /trapy/ *a.* stocky.

traquenard /traknar/ *n.m.* trap.

traquer /trake/ *v.t.* track down.

traumatis|me /tromatism/ *n.m.* trauma. **~ant, ~ante** /-zɑ̃, -t/ *a.* traumatic. **~er** /-ze/ *v.t.* traumatize.

trav|ail (*pl. ~aux*) /travaj, -o/ *n.m.* work; (*emploi, poste*) job; (*façonnage*) working. **~aux,** work. **en ~ail,** (*femme*) in labour. **~ail à la chaîne,** production line work. **~ail à la pièce** *ou* **à la tâche,** piece-work. **~ail au noir,** (*fam.*) moonlighting. **~aux forcés,** hard labour. **~aux**

manuels, handicrafts. **~aux ména-gers,** housework.

travaill|er /travaje/ *v.i.* work; (*se déformer*) warp. **~er à,** (*livre etc.*) work on. ● *v.t.* (*façonner*) work; (*étudier*) work at *ou* on; (*tourmenter*) worry. **~eur, ~euse** *n.m., f.* worker; *a.* hardworking.

travailliste /travajist/ *a.* Labour. ● *n.m./f.* Labour party member.

travers /travɛr/ *n.m.* (*défaut*) failing. **à ~,** through. **au ~ (de),** through. **de ~,** (*chapeau, nez*) crooked; (*mal*) badly, the wrong way; (*regarder*) askance. **en ~ (de),** across.

traverse /travɛrs/ *n.f.* (*rail.*) sleeper; (*rail., Amer.*) tie.

traversée /travɛrse/ *n.f.* crossing.

traverser /travɛrse/ *v.t.* cross; (*transpercer*) go (right) through; (*période, forêt*) go *ou* pass through.

traversin /travɛrsɛ̃/ *n.m.* bolster.

travesti /travɛsti/ *n.m.* transvestite.

travestir /travɛstir/ *v.t.* disguise; (*vérité*) misrepresent.

trébucher /trebyʃe/ *v.i.* stumble, trip (over). **faire ~,** trip (up).

trèfle /trɛfl/ *n.m.* (*plante*) clover; (*cartes*) clubs.

treillage /trɛjaʒ/ *n.m.* trellis.

treillis[1] /trɛji/ *n.m.* trellis; (*en métal*) wire mesh.

treillis[2] /trɛji/ *n.m.* (*tenue militaire*) combat uniform.

treiz|e /trɛz/ *a. & n.m.* thirteen. **~ième** *a. & n.m./f.* thirteenth.

tréma /trema/ *n.m.* diaeresis.

trembl|er /trɑ̃ble/ *v.i.* shake, tremble; (*lumière, voix*) quiver. **~ement** *n.m.* shaking; (*frisson*) shiver. **~ement de terre,** earthquake.

trembloter /trɑ̃blɔte/ *v.i.* quiver.

trémousser (se) /(sə)tremuse/ *v. pr.* wriggle, wiggle.

trempe /trɑ̃p/ *n.f.* (*caractère*) calibre.

tremper /trɑ̃pe/ *v.t./i.* soak; (*plonger*) dip; (*acier*) temper. **mettre à ~ ou faire ~,** soak. **~ dans,** (*fig.*) be involved in. **se ~** *v. pr.* (*se baigner*) have a dip.

trempette /trɑ̃pɛt/ *n.f.* **faire ~,** have a little dip.

tremplin /trɑ̃plɛ̃/ *n.m.* springboard.

trentaine /trɑ̃tɛn/ *n.f.* **une ~ (de),** about thirty. **il a la ~,** he's about thirty.

trent|e /trɑ̃t/ *a. & n.m.* thirty. **~ième** *a. & n.m./f.* thirtieth. **se mettre sur son ~e et un,** put on one's Sunday best. **tous les ~e-six du mois,** once in a blue moon.

trépider /trepide/ *v.i.* vibrate.

trépied /trepje/ *n.m.* tripod.

trépigner /trepiɲe/ *v.i.* stamp one's feet.

très /trɛ/ (/trɛz/ *before vowel*) *adv.* very. **~ aimé/estimé,** much liked/ esteemed.

trésor /trezɔr/ *n.m.* treasure; (*ressources: comm.*) finances. **le T~,** the revenue department.

trésorerie /trezɔrri/ *n.f.* (*bureaux*) accounts department; (*du Trésor*) revenue office; (*argent*) finances; (*gestion*) accounts.

trésor|ier, ~ière /trezɔrje, -jɛr/ *n.m., f.* treasurer.

tressaill|ir /tresajir/ *v.i.* shake, quiver; (*sursauter*) start. **~ement** *n.m.* quiver; start.

tressauter /tresote/ *v.i.* (*sursauter*) start, jump.

tresse /trɛs/ *n.f.* braid, plait.

tresser /trese/ *v.t.* braid, plait.

tréteau (*pl.* **~x**) /treto/ *n.m.* trestle. **~x,** (*théâtre*) stage.

treuil /trœj/ *n.m.* winch.

trêve /trɛv/ *n.f.* truce; (*fig.*) respite. **~ de plaisanteries,** enough of this joking.

tri /tri/ *n.m.* (*classement*) sorting; (*sélection*) selection. **faire le ~ de,** sort; select. **~age** /-jaʒ/ *n.m.* sorting.

triang|le /trijɑ̃gl/ *n.m.* triangle. **~ulaire** *a.* triangular.

trib|al (*m. pl.* **~aux**) /tribal, -o/ *a.* tribal.

tribord /tribɔr/ *n.m.* starboard.

tribu /triby/ *n.f.* tribe.

tribulations /tribylasjɔ̃/ *n.f. pl.* tribulations.

tribun|al (*m. pl.* **~aux**) /tribynal, -o/ *n.m.* court. **~al d'instance,** magistrates' court.

tribune /tribyn/ *n.f.* (*public*) gallery; (*dans un stade*) grandstand; (*d'orateur*) rostrum; (*débat*) forum.

tribut /triby/ *n.m.* tribute.

tributaire /tribytɛr/ *a.* **~ de,** dependent on.

trich|er /triʃe/ *v.i.* cheat. **~erie** *n.f.* cheating. **une ~erie,** piece of trickery. **~eur, ~euse** *n.m., f.* cheat.

tricolore /trikɔlɔr/ *a.* three-coloured; (*français*) red, white and blue; (*français: fig.*) French.

tricot /triko/ *n.m.* knitting; (*pull*) sweater. **en ~,** knitted. **de corps,**

vest; (*Amer.*) undershirt. ~**er** /-ɔte/ *v.t./i.* knit.

trictrac /triktrak/ *n.m.* backgammon.

tricycle /trisikl/ *n.m.* tricycle.

trier /trije/ *v.t.* (*classer*) sort; (*choisir*) select.

trilogie /trilɔʒi/ *n.f.* trilogy.

trimbaler /trɛ̃bale/ *v.t.*, **se ~** *v. pr.* (*fam.*) trail around.

trimer /trime/ *v.i.* (*fam.*) slave.

trimestr|**e** /trimɛstr/ *n.m.* quarter; (*scol.*) term. ~**iel**, ~**ielle** *a.* quarterly; (*bulletin*) end-of-term.

tringle /trɛ̃gl/ *n.f.* rod.

Trinité /trinite/ *n.f.* **la ~**, (*dogme*) the Trinity; (*fête*) Trinity.

trinquer /trɛ̃ke/ *v.i.* clink glasses.

trio /trijo/ *n.m.* trio.

triomph|**e** /trijɔ̃f/ *n.m.* triumph. ~**al** (*m. pl.* ~**aux**) *a.* triumphant.

triomph|**er** /trijɔ̃fe/ *v.i.* triumph (**de**, over); (*jubiler*) be triumphant. ~**ant**, ~**ante** *a.* triumphant.

trip|**es** /trip/ *n.f. pl.* (*mets*) tripe; (*entrailles: fam.*) guts.

triple /tripl/ *a.* triple, treble. ● *n.m.* **le ~**, three times as much (**de**, as). ~**ment** /-əmɑ̃/ *adv.* trebly.

tripl|**er** /triple/ *v.t./i.* triple, treble. ~**és**, ~**ées** *n.m., f. pl.* triplets.

tripot /tripo/ *n.m.* gambling den.

tripoter /tripɔte/ *v.t.* (*fam.*) fiddle with. ● *v.i.* (*fam.*) fiddle about.

trique /trik/ *n.f.* cudgel.

trisomique /trizɔmik/ *a.* **enfant ~**, Down's (syndrome) child.

triste /trist/ *a.* sad; (*rue, temps, couleur*) gloomy; (*lamentable*) wretched, dreadful. ~**ment** /-əmɑ̃/ *adv.* sadly. ~**sse** /-ɛs/ *n.f.* sadness; gloominess.

triv|**ial** (*m. pl.* ~**iaux**) /trivjal, -jo/ *a.* coarse. ~**ialité** *n.f.* coarseness.

troc /trɔk/ *n.m.* exchange; (*comm.*) barter.

troène /trɔɛn/ *n.m.* (*bot.*) privet.

trognon /trɔɲɔ̃/ *n.m.* (*de pomme*) core.

trois /trwa/ *a. & n.m.* three. **hôtel ~-étoiles**, three-star hotel. ~**ième** /-zjɛm/ *a. & n.m./f.* third. ~**ièmement** /-zjɛmmɑ̃/ *adv.* thirdly.

trombe /trɔ̃b/ *n.f.* **~ d'eau**, downpour.

trombone /trɔ̃bɔn/ *n.m.* (*mus.*) trombone; (*agrafe*) paper-clip.

trompe /trɔ̃p/ *n.f.* (*d'éléphant*) trunk; (*mus.*) horn.

tromp|**er** /trɔ̃pe/ *v.t.* deceive, mislead; (*déjouer*) elude. **se ~er** *v. pr.* be mistaken. **se ~er de route/train/***etc.*, take the wrong road/train/*etc.* ~**erie** *n.f.* deception. ~**eur**, ~**euse** *a.* (*personne*) deceitful; (*chose*) deceptive.

trompette /trɔ̃pɛt/ *n.f.* trumpet.

tronc /trɔ̃/ *n.m.* trunk; (*boîte*) collection box.

tronçon /trɔ̃sɔ̃/ *n.m.* section. ~**ner** /-ɔne/ *v.t.* cut into sections.

trôn|**e** /tron/ *n.m.* throne. ~**er** *v.i.* occupy the place of honour.

tronquer /trɔ̃ke/ *v.t.* truncate.

trop /tro/ *adv.* (*grand, loin, etc.*) too; (*boire, marcher, etc.*) too much. **~ (de)**, (*quantité*) too much; (*nombre*) too many. **c'est ~ chauffé**, it's overheated. **de ~**, **en ~**, too much; too many. **il a bu un verre de ~**, he's had one too many. **de ~**, (*intrus*) in the way. ~**-plein** *n.m.* excess; (*dispositif*) overflow.

trophée /trɔfe/ *n.m.* trophy.

tropic|**al** (*m. pl.* ~**aux**) /trɔpikal, -o/ *a.* tropical.

tropique /trɔpik/ *n.m.* tropic. ~**s**, tropics.

troquer /trɔke/ *v.t.* exchange; (*comm.*) barter (**contre**, for).

trot /tro/ *n.m.* trot. **aller au ~**, trot. **au ~**, (*fam.*) on the double.

trotter /trɔte/ *v.i.* trot.

trotteuse /trɔtøz/ *n.f.* (*aiguille de montre*) second hand.

trottiner /trɔtine/ *v.i.* patter along.

trottinette /trɔtinɛt/ *n.f.* (*jouet*) scooter.

trottoir /trɔtwar/ *n.m.* pavement; (*Amer.*) sidewalk. **~ roulant**, moving walkway.

trou /tru/ *n.m.* hole; (*moment*) gap; (*lieu: péj.*) dump. **~ (de mémoire)**, lapse (of memory). **~ de la serrure**, keyhole. **faire son ~**, carve one's niche.

trouble /trubl/ *a.* (*eau, image*) unclear; (*louche*) shady. ● *n.m.* agitation. ~**s**, (*pol.*) disturbances; (*méd.*) trouble.

troubl|**er** /truble/ *v.t.* disturb; (*eau*) make cloudy; (*inquiéter*) trouble. ~**ant**, ~**ante** *a.* disturbing. **se ~er** *v. pr.* (*personne*) become flustered. ~**e-fête** *n.m./f. invar.* killjoy.

trouée /true/ *n.f.* gap, open space; (*mil.*) breach (**dans**, in).

trouer /true/ *v.t.* make a hole *ou* holes in. **mes chaussures se sont trouées,** my shoes have got holes in them.

trouille /truj/ *n.f.* **avoir la ~,** *(fam.)* be scared.

troupe /trup/ *n.f.* troop; *(d'acteurs)* troupe. **~s,** *(mil.)* troops.

troupeau *(pl. ~x)* /trupo/ *n.m.* herd; *(de moutons)* flock.

trousse /trus/ *n.f.* case, bag; *(de réparations)* kit. **aux ~s de,** on the tail of. **~ de toilette,** toilet bag.

trousseau *(pl. ~x)* /truso/ *n.m. (de clefs)* bunch; *(de mariée)* trousseau.

trouvaille /truvɑj/ *n.f.* find.

trouver /truve/ *v.t.* find; *(penser)* think. **aller/venir ~,** *(rendre visite à)* go/come and see. **se ~** *v. pr.* find o.s.; *(être)* be; *(se sentir)* feel. **il se trouve que,** it happens that. **se ~ mal,** faint.

truand /tryɑ̃/ *n.m.* gangster.

truc /tryk/ *n.m. (moyen)* way; *(artifice)* trick; *(chose: fam.)* thing. **~age** *n.m.* = **truquage.**

truchement /tryʃmɑ̃/ *n.m.* **par le ~ de,** through.

truculent, ~e /trykylɑ̃, -t/ *a.* colourful.

truelle /tryɛl/ *n.f.* trowel.

truffe /tryf/ *n.f. (champignon, chocolat)* truffle; *(nez)* nose.

truffer /tryfe/ *v.t. (fam.)* fill, pack *(de,* with).

truie /trɥi/ *n.f. (animal)* sow.

truite /trɥit/ *n.f.* trout.

truquer /tryke/ *v.t.* fix, rig; *(photo, texte)* fake. **~age** *n.m.* fixing; faking; *(cinéma)* special effect.

trust /trœst/ *n.m. (comm.)* trust.

tsar /tsar/ *n.m.* tsar, czar.

tsigane /tsigan/ *a. & n.m./f.* (Hungarian) gypsy.

tu [1] /ty/ *pron. (parent, ami, enfant, etc.)* you.

tu [2] /ty/ *voir* taire.

tuba /tyba/ *n.m. (mus.)* tuba; *(sport)* snorkel.

tube /tyb/ *n.m.* tube.

tubercul|eux, ~euse /tybɛrkylø, -z/ *a.* être **~eux,** have tuberculosis. **~ose** *n.f.* tuberculosis.

tubulaire /tybylɛr/ *a.* tubular.

tubulure /tybylyr/ *n.f.* tubing.

tu|er /tɥe/ *v.t.* kill; *(d'une balle)* shoot, kill; *(épuiser)* exhaust. **se ~er** *v. pr.* kill o.s.; *(accident)* be killed. **~ant, ~ante,** *a.* exhausting.

~é, ~ée *n.m., f.* person killed.

~eur, ~euse *n.m., f.* killer.

tuerie /tyri/ *n.f.* slaughter.

tue-tête (à) /(a)tytɛt/ *adv.* at the top of one's voice.

tuile /tɥil/ *n.f.* tile; *(malchance: fam.)* (stroke of) bad luck.

tulipe /tylip/ *n.f.* tulip.

tuméfié /tymefje/ *a.* swollen.

tumeur /tymœr/ *n.f.* tumour.

tumult|e /tymylt/ *n.m.* commotion; *(désordre)* turmoil. **~ueux, ~ueuse** *a.* turbulent.

tunique /tynik/ *n.f.* tunic.

Tunisie /tynizi/ *n.f.* Tunisia.

tunisien, ~ne /tynizjɛ̃, -jɛn/ *a. & n.m., f.* Tunisian.

tunnel /tynɛl/ *n.m.* tunnel.

turban /tyrbɑ̃/ *n.m.* turban.

turbine /tyrbin/ *n.f.* turbine.

turbo /tyrbo/ *a.* turbo. *n.f. (voiture)* turbo.

turbulen|t, ~te /tyrbylɑ̃, -t/ *a.* boisterous, turbulent. **~ce** *n.f.* turbulence.

tur|c, ~que /tyrk/ *a.* Turkish. ● *n.m., f.* Turk. ● *n.m. (lang.)* Turkish.

turf /tyrf/ *n.m.* **le ~,** the turf. **~iste** *n.m./f.* racegoer.

Turquie /tyrki/ *n.f.* Turkey.

turquoise /tyrkwaz/ *a. invar.* turquoise.

tutelle /tytɛl/ *n.f. (jurid.)* guardianship; *(fig.)* protection.

tu|teur, ~trice /tytœr, -tris/ *n.m., f. (jurid.)* guardian. ● *n.m. (bâton)* stake.

tut|oyer /tytwaje/ *v.t.* address familiarly (using *tu).* **~oiement** *n.m.* use of (familiar) *tu.*

tuyau *(pl. ~x)* /tɥijo/ *n.m.* pipe; *(conseil: fam.)* tip. **~ d'arrosage,** hose-pipe. **~ter** *v.t. (fam.)* give a tip to. **~terie** *n.f.* piping.

TVA *abrév. (taxe sur la valeur ajoutée)* VAT.

tympan /tɛ̃pɑ̃/ *n.m.* ear-drum.

type /tip/ *n.m. (modèle)* type; *(traits)* features; *(individu: fam.)* bloke, guy. ● *a. invar.* typical. **le ~ même de,** a classic example of.

typhoïde /tifoid/ *n.f.* typhoid (fever).

typhon /tifɔ̃/ *n.m.* typhoon.

typhus /tifys/ *n.m.* typhus.

typique /tipik/ *a.* typical. **~ment** *adv.* typically.

tyran /tirɑ̃/ *n.m.* tyrant.

tyrann|ie /tirani/ *n.f.* tyranny. **~ique** *a.* tyrannical. **~iser** *v.t.* oppress, tyrannize.

U

ulcère /ylsɛr/ *n.m.* ulcer.

ulcérer /ylsere/ *v.t.* (*vexer*) embitter, gall.

ULM *abrév. m.* (*ultraléger motorisé*) microlight.

ultérieur /ylterjœr/ *a.*, **~ement** *adv.* later.

ultimatum /yltimatɔm/ *n.m.* ultimatum.

ultime /yltim/ *a.* final.

ultra /yltra/ *n.m./f.* hardliner.

ultra- /yltra/ *préf.* ultra-.

un, une /œ̃, yn/ *a.* one; (*indéfini*) a, an. **un enfant**, /œ̃nɑ̃fɑ̃/ a child. ● *pron. & n.m., f.* one. **l'un, une. les uns**, some. **l'un et l'autre**, both. **l'un l'autre, les uns les autres**, each other. **l'un ou l'autre**, either. **la une**, (*de journal*) front page. **un autre**, another. **un par un**, one by one.

unanim|e /ynanim/ *a.* unanimous. **~ité** *n.f.* unanimity. **à l'~ité**, unanimously.

uni /yni/ *a.* united; (*couple*) close; (*surface*) smooth; (*sans dessins*) plain.

unième /ynjɛm/ *a.* -first. **vingt et ~**, twenty-first. **cent ~**, one hundred and first.

unif|ier /ynifje/ *v.t.* unify. **~ication** *n.f.* unification.

uniform|e /ynifɔrm/ *n.m.* uniform. ● *a.* uniform. **~ément** *adv.* uniformly. **~iser** *v.t.* standardize. **~ité** *n.f.* uniformity.

unilatér|al (*m. pl.* **~aux**) /ynilateral, -o/ *a.* unilateral.

union /ynjɔ̃/ *n.f.* union. **l'U~ soviétique**, the Soviet Union.

unique /ynik/ *a.* (*seul*) only; (*prix, voie*) one; (*incomparable*) unique. **enfant ~**, only child. **sens ~**, one-way street. **~ment** *adv.* only, solely.

unir /ynir/ *v.t.*, **s'~** *v. pr.* unite, join.

unisson (à l') /(al)ynisɔ̃/ *adv.* in unison.

unité /ynite/ *n.f.* unit; (*harmonie*) unity.

univers /univɛr/ *n.m.* universe.

universel, ~le /ynivɛrsɛl/ *a.* universal.

universit|é /ynivɛrsite/ *n.f.* university. **~aire** *a.* university; *n.m./f.* academic.

uranium /yranjɔm/ *n.m.* uranium.

urbain, ~e /yrbɛ̃, -ɛn/ *a.* urban.

urbanisme /yrbanism/ *n.m.* town planning; (*Amer.*) city planning.

urgence /yrʒɑ̃s/ *n.f.* (*cas*) emergency; (*de situation, tâche, etc.*) urgency. **d'~** *a.* emergency; *adv.* urgently.

urgent, ~e /yrʒɑ̃, -t/ *a.* urgent.

urger /yrʒe/ *v.i.* **ça urge!**, (*fam.*) it's getting urgent.

urin|e /yrin/ *n.f.* urine. **~er** *v.i.* urinate.

urinoir /yrinwar/ *n.m.* urinal.

urne /yrn/ *n.f.* (*électorale*) ballot-box; (*vase*) urn. **aller aux ~s**, go to the polls.

URSS *abrév.* (*Union des Républiques Socialistes Soviétiques*) USSR.

urticaire /yrtikɛr/ *n.f.* **une crise d' ~**, nettle rash.

us /ys/ *n.m. pl.* **les us et coutumes**, habits and customs.

usage /yzaʒ/ *n.m.* use; (*coutume*) custom; (*de langage*) usage. **à l'~ de**, for. **d'~**, (*habituel*) customary. **faire ~ de**, make use of.

usagé /yzaʒe/ *a.* worn.

usager /yzaʒe/ *n.m.* user.

usé /yze/ *a.* worn (out); (*banal*) trite.

user /yze/ *v.t.* wear (out); (*consommer*) use (up). ● *v.i.* **~ de**, use. **s'~** *v. pr.* (*tissu etc.*) wear (out).

usine /yzin/ *n.f.* factory; (*de métallurgie*) works.

usité /yzite/ *a.* common.

ustensile /ystɑ̃sil/ *n.m.* utensil.

usuel, ~le /yzɥɛl/ *a.* ordinary, everyday.

usufruit /yzyfrɥi/ *n.m.* usufruct.

usure /yzyr/ *n.f.* (*détérioration*) wear (and tear).

usurper /yzyrpe/ *v.t.* usurp.

utérus /yterys/ *n.m.* womb, uterus.

utile /ytil/ *a.* useful. **~ment** *adv.* usefully.

utilis|er /ytilize/ *v.t.* use. **~able** *a.* usable. **~ation** *n.f.* use.

utilitaire /ytiliter/ *a.* utilitarian.

utilité /ytilite/ *n.f.* use(fulness).

utop|ie /ytɔpi/ *n.f.* Utopia; (*idée*) Utopian idea. **~ique** *a.* Utopian.

UV *abrév. f.* (*unité de valeur*) (*scol.*) credit.

V

va /va/ *voir* aller[1].

vacanc|e /vakɑ̃s/ *n.f.* (*poste*) vacancy. **~es,** holiday(s); (*Amer.*) vacation. **en ~es,** on holiday. **~ier, ~ière** *n.m.,* *f.* holiday-maker; (*Amer.*) vacationer.

vacant, ~e /vakɑ̃, -t/ *a.* vacant.

vacarme /vakarm/ *n.m.* uproar.

vaccin /vaksɛ̃/ *n.m.* vaccine; (*inoculation*) vaccination.

vaccin|er /vaksine/ *v.t.* vaccinate. **~ation** *n.f.* vaccination.

vache /vaʃ/ *n.f.* cow. ● *a.* (*méchant: fam.*) nasty. **~ment** *adv.* (*très: fam.*) damned; (*pleuvoir, manger, etc.: fam.*) a hell of a lot. **~rie** *n.f.* (*fam.*) nastiness; (*chose: fam.*) nasty thing.

vacill|er /vasije/ *v.i.* sway, wobble; (*lumière*) flicker; (*fig.*) falter. **~ant, ~ante** *a.* (*mémoire, démarche*) shaky.

vadrouiller /vadruje/ *v.i.* (*fam.*) wander about.

va-et-vient /vaevjɛ̃/ *n.m. invar.* to and fro (motion); (*de personnes*) comings and goings.

vagabond, ~e /vagabɔ̃, -d/ *n.m., f.* (*péj.*) vagrant, vagabond. **~er** /-de/ *v.i.* wander.

vagin /vaʒɛ̃/ *n.m.* vagina.

vagir /vaʒir/ *v.i.* cry.

vague[1] /vag/ *a.* vague. ● *n.m.* vagueness. **il est resté dans le ~,** he was vague about it. **~ment** *adv.* vaguely.

vague[2] /vag/ *n.f.* wave. **~ de fond,** ground swell. **~ de froid,** cold spell. **~ de chaleur,** hot spell.

vaill|ant, ~ante /vajɑ̃, -t/ *a.* brave; (*vigoureux*) healthy. **~amment** /-amɑ̃/ *adv.* bravely.

vaille /vaj/ *voir* valoir.

vain, ~e /vɛ̃, vɛn/ *a.* vain. **en ~,** in vain. **~ement** /vɛnmɑ̃/ *adv.* vainly.

vain|cre† /vɛ̃kr/ *v.t.* defeat; (*surmonter*) overcome. **~cu, ~cue** *n.m., f.* (*sport*) loser. **~queur** *n.m.* victor; (*sport*) winner.

vais /vɛ/ *voir* aller[1].

vaisseau (*pl.* **~x**) /vɛso/ *n.m.* ship; (*veine*) vessel. **~ spatial,** space-ship.

vaisselle /vɛsɛl/ *n.f.* crockery; (*à laver*) dishes. **faire la ~,** do the

washing-up, wash the dishes. **produit pour la ~,** washing-up liquid.

val (*pl.* **~s** *ou* **vaux**) /val, vo/ *n.m.* valley.

valable /valabl/ *a.* valid; (*de qualité*) worthwhile.

valet /valɛ/ *n.m.* (*cartes*) jack. **~ (de chambre),** manservant. **~ de ferme,** farm-hand.

valeur /valœr/ *n.f.* value; (*mérite*) worth, value. **~s,** (*comm.*) stocks and shares. **avoir de la ~,** be valuable.

valid|e /valid/ *a.* (*personne*) fit; (*billet*) valid. **~er** *v.t.* validate. **~ité** *n.f.* validity.

valise /valiz/ *n.f.* (suit)case. **faire ses ~s,** pack (one's bags).

vallée /vale/ *n.f.* valley.

vallon /valɔ̃/ *n.m.* (small) valley. **~né** /-ɔne/ *a.* undulating.

valoir† /valwar/ *v.i.* be worth; (*s'appliquer*) apply. **~ qch.,** be worth sth.; (*être aussi bon que*) be as good as sth. ● *v.t.* **~ qch. à qn.,** bring s.o. sth. **se ~** *v. pr.* (*être équivalents*) be as good as each other. **faire ~,** put forward to advantage; (*droit*) assert. **~ la peine, le coup,** be worth it. **ça ne vaut rien,** it is no good. **il vaudrait mieux faire,** we'd better do. **ça ne me dit rien qui vaille,** I don't think much of it.

valoriser /valɔrize/ *v.t.* add value to. **se sentir valorisé,** feel valued.

vals|e /vals/ *n.f.* waltz. **~er** *v.i.* waltz.

valve /valv/ *n.f.* valve.

vampire /vɑ̃pir/ *n.m.* vampire.

van /vɑ̃/ *n.m.* van.

vandal|e /vɑ̃dal/ *n.m./f.* vandal. **~isme** *n.m.* vandalism.

vanille /vanij/ *n.f.* vanilla.

vanit|é /vanite/ *n.f.* vanity. **~eux, ~euse** *a.* vain, conceited.

vanne /van/ *n.f.* (*d'écluse*) sluice (-gate); (*fam.*) joke.

vant|ail (*pl.* **~aux**) /vɑ̃taj, -o/ *n.m.* door, flap.

vantard, ~e /vɑ̃tar, -d/ *a.* boastful; *n.m., f.* boaster. **~ise** /-diz/ *n.f.* boastfulness; (*acte*) boast.

vanter /vɑ̃te/ *v.t.* praise. **se ~** *v. pr.* boast (**de,** about).

va-nu-pieds /vanypje/ *n.m./f. invar.* vagabond, beggar.

vapeur[1] /vapœr/ *n.f.* (*eau*) steam; (*brume, émanation*) vapour.

vapeur[2] /vapœr/ *n.m.* (*bateau*) steamer.

vaporeu|x, **~se** /vapɔrø, -z/ a. hazy; (*léger*) filmy, flimsy.

vaporis|er /vapɔrize/ v.t. spray. **~ateur** n.m. spray.

vaquer /vake/ v.i. **~ à**, attend to.

varappe /varap/ n.f. rock climbing.

vareuse /varøz/ n.f. (*d'uniforme*) tunic.

variable /varjabl/ a. variable; (*temps*) changeable.

variante /varjɑ̃t/ n.f. variant.

varicelle /varisɛl/ n.f. chicken-pox.

varices /varis/ n.f. pl. varicose veins.

var|ier /varje/ v.t./i. vary. **~iation** n.f. variation. **~ié** a. (*non monotone, étendu*) varied; (*divers*) various.

variété /varjete/ n.f. variety. **~s**, (*spectacle*) variety.

variole /varjɔl/ n.f. smallpox.

vase 1 /vɑz/ n.m. vase.

vase 2 /vɑz/ n.f. (*boue*) silt, mud.

vaseu|x, **~se** /vazø, -z/ a. (*confus: fam.*) woolly, hazy.

vasistas /vazistas/ n.m. fanlight, hinged panel (*in door or window*).

vaste /vast/ a. vast, huge.

vaudeville /vodvil/ n.m. vaudeville, light comedy.

vau-l'eau (à) /(a)volo/ adv. downhill.

vaurien, **~ne** /vorjɛ̃, -jɛn/ n.m., f. good-for-nothing.

vautour /votur/ n.m. vulture.

vautrer (se) /(sə)votre/ v. pr. sprawl. **se ~ dans**, (*vice, boue*) wallow in.

va-vite (à la) /(ala)vavit/ adv. (*fam.*) in a hurry.

veau (pl. **~x**) /vo/ n.m. calf; (*viande*) veal; (*cuir*) calfskin.

vécu /veky/ voir **vivre**. ● a. (*réel*) true, real.

vedette 1 /vədɛt/ n.f. (*artiste*) star. **en ~**, (*objet*) in a prominent position; (*personne*) in the limelight.

vedette 2 /vədɛt/ n.f. (*bateau*) launch.

végét|al (m. pl. **~aux**) /veʒetal, -o/ a. plant. ● n.m. (pl. **~aux**) plant.

végétalien, **~ne** /veʒetaljɛ̃, -jɛn/ a. & n.m., f. vegan.

végétarien, **~ne** /veʒetarjɛ̃, -jɛn/ a. & n.m., f. vegetarian.

végétation /veʒetasjɔ̃/ n.f. vegetation. **~s**, (*méd.*) adenoids.

végéter /veʒete/ v.i. vegetate.

véhémen|t, **~te** /veemɑ̃, -t/ a. vehement. **~ce** n.f. vehemence.

véhicul|e /veikyl/ n.m. vehicle. **~er** v.t. convey.

veille 1 /vɛj/ n.f. **la ~ (de)**, the day before. **la ~ de Noël**, Christmas Eve. **à la ~ de**, on the eve of.

veille 2 /vɛj/ n.f. (*état*) wakefulness.

veillée /veje/ n.f. evening (gathering); (*mortuaire*) vigil, wake.

veiller /veje/ v.i. stay up ou awake. **~ à**, attend to. **~ sur**, watch over. ● v.t. (*malade*) watch over.

veilleur /vɛjœr/ n.m. **~ de nuit**, night-watchman.

veilleuse /vɛjøz/ n.f. night-light; (*de véhicule*) sidelight; (*de réchaud*) pilot-light. **mettre qch. en ~**, put sth. on the back burner.

veinard, **~e** /vɛnar, -d/ n.m., f. (*fam.*) lucky devil.

veine 1 /vɛn/ n.f. (*anat.*) vein; (*nervure, filon*) vein.

veine 2 /vɛn/ n.f. (*chance: fam.*) luck. **avoir de la ~**, (*fam.*) be lucky.

velcro /vɛlkrɔ/ n.m. (P.) velcro.

véliplanchiste /veliplɑ̃ʃist/ n.m./f. windsurfer.

vélo /velo/ n.m. bicycle, bike; (*activité*) cycling.

vélodrome /velodrom/ n.m. velodrome, cycle-racing track.

vélomoteur /velomotœr/ n.m. moped.

velours /vlur/ n.m. velvet. **~ côtelé**, **~ à côtes**, corduroy.

velouté /velute/ a. smooth. ● n.m. smoothness.

velu /vəly/ a. hairy.

venaison /vənɛzɔ̃/ n.f. venison.

vendang|es /vɑ̃dɑ̃ʒ/ n.f. pl. grape harvest. **~er** v.i. pick the grapes. **~eur**, **~euse** n.m., f. grape-picker.

vendetta /vɑ̃deta/ n.f. vendetta.

vendeu|r, **~se** /vɑ̃dœr, -øz/ n.m., f. shop assistant; (*marchand*) salesman, saleswoman; (*jurid.*) vendor, seller.

vendre /vɑ̃dr/ v.t. sell. **se ~** v. pr. sell. **à ~**, for sale.

vendredi /vɑ̃drədi/ n.m. Friday. **V~ saint**, Good Friday.

vénéneu|x, **~se** /venenø, -z/ a. poisonous.

vénérable /venerabl/ a. venerable.

vénérer /venere/ v.t. revere.

vénérien, **~ne** /venerjɛ̃, -jɛn/ a. venereal.

vengeance /vɑ̃ʒɑ̃s/ n.f. revenge, vengeance.

veng|er /vɑ̃ʒe/ v.t. avenge. **se ~er** v. pr. take (one's) revenge (**de**, for).

~eur, ~eresse *a.* vengeful; *n.m., f.* avenger.

ven|in /vənɛ̃/ *n.m.* venom. **~imeux, ~imeuse** *a.* poisonous, venomous.

venir† /vənir/ *v.i.* (*aux. être*) come (**de,** from). **~ faire,** come to do. **venez faire,** come and do. **~ de faire,** to have just done. **il vient/ venait d'arriver,** he has/had just arrived. **en ~ à,** (*question, conclusion, etc.*) come to. **en ~ aux mains,** come to blows. **faire ~,** send for. **il m'est venu à l'esprit** *ou* **à l'idée que,** it occurred to me that.

vent /vɑ̃/ *n.m.* wind. **être dans le ~,** (*fam.*) be with it. **il fait du ~,** it is windy.

vente /vɑ̃t/ *n.f.* sale. **~ (aux enchères),** auction. **en ~,** on *ou* for sale. **~ de charité,** (charity) bazaar.

ventil|er /vɑ̃tile/ *v.t.* ventilate. **~ateur** *n.m.* fan, ventilator. **~ation** *n.f.* ventilation.

ventouse /vɑ̃tuz/ *n.f.* (*dispositif*) suction pad; (*pour déboucher l'évier etc.*) plunger.

ventre /vɑ̃tr/ *n.m.* belly, stomach; (*utérus*) womb. **avoir/prendre du ~,** have/develop a paunch.

ventriloque /vɑ̃trilɔk/ *n.m./f.* ventriloquist.

ventru /vɑ̃try/ *a.* pot-bellied.

venu /vəny/ *voir* venir. ● *a.* **bien ~,** (*à propos*) timely. **mal ~,** untimely. **être mal ~ de faire,** have no grounds for doing.

venue /vəny/ *n.f.* coming.

vêpres /vɛpr/ *n.f. pl.* vespers.

ver /vɛr/ *n.m.* worm; (*des fruits, de la viande*) maggot; (*du bois*) woodworm. **~ luisant,** glow-worm. **~ à soie,** silkworm. **~ solitaire,** tapeworm. **~ de terre,** earthworm.

véranda /verɑ̃da/ *n.f.* veranda.

verb|e /vɛrb/ *n.m.* (*gram.*) verb. **~al** (*m. pl.* **~aux**) *a.* verbal.

verdâtre /vɛrdɑtr/ *a.* greenish.

verdict /vɛrdikt/ *n.m.* verdict.

verdir /vɛrdir/ *v.i.* turn green.

verdoyant, ~e /vɛrdwajɑ̃, -t/ *a.* green, verdant.

verdure /vɛrdyr/ *n.f.* greenery.

véreu|x, ~se /verø, -z/ *a.* maggoty, wormy; (*malhonnête: fig.*) shady.

verger /vɛrʒe/ *n.m.* orchard.

vergla|s /vɛrgla/ *n.m.* (black) ice; (*Amer.*) sleet. **~cé** *a.* icy.

vergogne (sans) /(sɑ̃)vɛrgɔɲ/ *a.* shameless. ● *adv.* shamelessly.

véridique /veridik/ *a.* truthful.

vérif|ier /verifje/ *v.t.* check, verify; (*compte*) audit; (*confirmer*) confirm. **~ication** *n.f.* check(ing), verification.

véritable /veritabl/ *a.* true, real; (*authentique*) real. **~ment** /- əmɑ̃/ *adv.* really.

vérité /verite/ *n.f.* truth; (*de tableau, roman*) trueness to life. **en ~,** in fact.

vermeil, ~le /vɛrmɛj/ *a.* bright red.

vermicelle(s) /vɛrmisɛl/ *n.m.* (*pl.*) vermicelli.

vermine /vɛrmin/ *n.f.* vermin.

vermoulu /vɛrmuly/ *a.* wormeaten.

vermouth /vɛrmut/ *n.m.* (*apéritif*) vermouth.

verni /vɛrni/ *a.* (*fam.*) lucky. **chaussures ~es,** patent (leather) shoes.

vernir /vɛrnir/ *v.t.* varnish.

vernis /vɛrni/ *n.m.* varnish; (*de poterie*) glaze. **~ à ongles,** nail polish *ou* varnish.

vernissage /vɛrnisaʒ/ *n.m.* (*exposition*) preview.

vernisser /vɛrnise/ *v.t.* glaze.

verra, verrait /vɛra, vɛrɛ/ *voir* voir.

verre /vɛr/ *n.m.* glass. **prendre** *ou* **boire un ~,** have a drink. **~ de contact,** contact lens. **~ dépoli/ grossissant,** frosted/magnifying glass. **~rie** *n.f.* (*objets*) glassware.

verrière /vɛrjɛr/ *n.f.* (*toit*) glass roof; (*paroi*) glass wall.

verrou /vɛru/ *n.m.* bolt. **sous les ~s,** behind bars.

verrouiller /vɛruje/ *v.t.* bolt.

verrue /vɛry/ *n.f.* wart.

vers¹ /vɛr/ *prép.* towards; (*temps*) about.

vers² /vɛr/ *n.m.* (*ligne*) line. **les ~,** (*poésie*) verse.

versant /vɛrsɑ̃/ *n.m.* slope, side.

versatile /vɛrsatil/ *a.* fickle.

verse (à) /(a)vɛrs/ *adv.* in torrents.

versé /vɛrse/ *a.* **~ dans,** versed in.

Verseau /vɛrso/ *n.m.* **le ~,** Aquarius.

vers|er /vɛrse/ *v.t./i.* pour; (*larmes, sang*) shed; (*basculer*) overturn; (*payer*) pay. **~ement** *n.m.* payment.

verset /vɛrse/ *n.m.* (*relig.*) verse.

version /vɛrsjɔ̃/ *n.f.* version; (*traduction*) translation.

verso /vɛrso/ *n.m.* back (of the page).

vert, ~e /vɛr, -t/ *a.* green; (*vieillard*) sprightly. ● *n.m.* green.

vertèbre /vɛrtɛbr/ *n.f.* vertebra.

vertement /vɛrtəmã/ adv. sharply.

vertic|al, **~ale** (m. pl. **~aux**) /vɛrtikal, -o/ a. & n.f. vertical. **à la ~ale**, **~alement** adv. vertically.

vertig|e /vɛrtiʒ/ n.m. dizziness. **~es**, dizzy spells. **avoir le** ou **un ~e**, feel dizzy. **~ineux**, **~ineuse** a. dizzy; (très grand) staggering.

vertu /vɛrty/ n.f. virtue. **en ~ de**, by virtue of. **~eux**, **~euse** -tɥø, -z/ a. virtuous.

verve /vɛrv/ n.f. spirit, wit.

verveine /vɛrvɛn/ n.f. verbena.

vésicule /vezikyl/ n.f. **~ biliaire**, gall-bladder.

vessie /vesi/ n.f. bladder.

veste /vɛst/ n.f. jacket.

vestiaire /vɛstjɛr/ n.m. cloakroom; (sport) changing-room.

vestibule /vɛstibyl/ n.m. hall.

vestige /vɛstiʒ/ n.m. (objet) relic; (trace) vestige.

veston /vɛstɔ̃/ n.m. jacket.

vêtement /vɛtmã/ n.m. article of clothing. **~s**, clothes.

vétéran /veterã/ n.m. veteran.

vétérinaire /veterinɛr/ n.m./f. vet, veterinary surgeon, (Amer.) veterinarian.

vétille /vetij/ n.f. trifle.

vêt|ir /vetir/ v.t., **se ~ir** v.pr. dress. **~u** a. dressed (de, in).

veto /veto/ n.m. invar. veto.

vétuste /vetyst/ a. dilapidated.

veu|f, **~ve** /vœf, -v/ a. widowed. ● n.m. widower. ● n.f. widow.

veuille /vœj/ voir **vouloir**.

veule /vøl/ a. feeble.

veut, **veux** /vø/ voir **vouloir**.

vexation /vɛksasjɔ̃/ n.f. humiliation.

vex|er /vɛkse/ v.t. upset, hurt. **se ~er** v.pr. be upset, be hurt. **~ant**, **~ante** a. upsetting.

via /vja/ prép. via.

viable /vjabl/ a. viable.

viaduc /vjadyk/ n.m. viaduct.

viande /vjɑ̃d/ n.f. meat.

vibr|er /vibre/ v.i. vibrate; (être ému) thrill. **~ant**, **~ante** a. (émouvant) vibrant. **~ation** n.f. vibration.

vicaire /vikɛr/ n.m. curate.

vice /vis/ n.m. (moral) vice; (défectuosité) defect.

vice- /vis/ préf. vice-.

vice versa /vis(e)vɛrsa/ adv. vice versa.

vicier /visje/ v.t. taint.

vicieu|x, **~se** /visjø, -z/ a. depraved. ● n.m., f. pervert.

vicin|al (pl. **~aux**) /visinal, -o/ a.m. **chemin ~al**, by-road, minor road.

vicomte /vikɔ̃t/ n.m. viscount.

victime /viktim/ n.f. victim; (d'un accident) casualty.

vict|oire /viktwar/ n.f. victory; (sport) win. **~orieux**, **~orieuse** a. victorious; (équipe) winning.

victuailles /viktɥaj/ n.f. pl. provisions.

vidang|e /vidãʒ/ n.f. emptying; (auto.) oil change; (dispositif) waste pipe. **~er** v.t. empty.

vide /vid/ a. empty. ● n.m. emptiness, void; (trou, manque) gap; (espace sans air) vacuum. **à ~**, empty.

vidéo /video/ a. invar. video. **jeu ~**, video game. **~cassette** n.f. video(tape). **~thèque** n.f. video library.

vide-ordures /vidɔrdyr/ n.m. invar. (rubbish) chute.

vider /vide/ v.t. empty; (poisson) gut; (expulser: fam.) throw out. **~ les lieux**, vacate the premises. **se ~** v. pr. empty.

videur /vidœr/ n.m. bouncer.

vie /vi/ n.f. life; (durée) lifetime. **à ~**, **pour la ~**, for life. **donner le ~ à**, give birth to. **en ~**, alive. **~ chère**, high cost of living.

vieil /vjɛj/ voir **vieux**.

vieillard /vjɛjar/ n.m. old man.

vieille /vjɛj/ voir **vieux**.

vieillesse /vjɛjɛs/ n.f. old age.

vieill|ir /vjejir/ v.i. grow old, age; (mot, idée) become old-fashioned. ● v.t. age. **~issement** n.m. ageing.

viens, **vient** /vjɛ̃/ voir **venir**.

vierge /vjɛrʒ/ n.f. virgin. **la V~**, Virgo. ● a. virgin; (feuille, film) blank.

vieux ou **vieil***, **vieille** (m. pl. **vieux**) /vjø, vjɛj/ a. old. ● n.m. old man. ● n.f. old woman. **les ~**, old people. **mon ~**, (fam.) old man ou boy. **ma vieille**, (fam.) old girl, dear. **vieille fille**, (péj.) spinster. **~ garçon**, bachelor. **~ jeu** a. invar. old-fashioned.

vif, **vive** /vif, viv/ a. lively; (émotion, vent) keen; (froid) biting; (lumière) bright; (douleur, parole) sharp; (souvenir, style, teint) vivid; (succès, impatience) great. **brûler/enterrer ~**, burn/bury alive. **de vive voix**, personally. **avoir les nerfs à ~,** be on edge.

vigie /viʒi/ *n.f.* look-out.

vigilan|t, ~te /viʒilɑ̃, -t/ *a.* vigilant. **~ce** *n.f.* vigilance.

vigne /viɲ/ *n.f.* (*plante*) vine; (*vignoble*) vineyard.

vigneron, ~ne /viɲrɔ̃, -ɔn/ *n.m.*, *f.* wine-grower.

vignette /viɲɛt/ *n.f.* (*étiquette*) label; (*auto.*) road tax sticker.

vignoble /viɲɔbl/ *n.m.* vineyard.

vigoureu|x, ~se /viguʁø, -z/ *a.* vigorous, sturdy.

vigueur /vigœʁ/ *n.f.* vigour. **être/ entrer en ~,** (*loi*) be/come into force. **en ~,** (*terme*) in use.

VIH *abrév.* (*virus d'immunodéficience humaine*) HIV.

vil /vil/ *a.* vile, base.

vilain, ~e /vilɛ̃, -ɛn/ *a.* (*mauvais*) nasty; (*laid*) ugly.

villa /villa/ *n.f.* (detached) house.

village /vilaʒ/ *n.m.* village.

villageois, ~e /vilaʒwa, -z/ *a.* village. ● *n.m.*, *f.* villager.

ville /vil/ *n.f.* town; (*importante*) city. **~ d'eaux,** spa.

vin /vɛ̃/ *n.m.* wine. **~ d'honneur,** reception. **~ ordinaire,** table wine.

vinaigre /vinɛgʁ/ *n.m.* vinegar.

vinaigrette /vinɛgʁɛt/ *n.f.* oil and vinegar dressing, vinaigrette.

vindicati|f, ~ve /vɛ̃dikatif, -v/ *a.* vindictive.

vingt /vɛ̃/ (/vɛ̃t/ before vowel and in numbers 22-29) *a.* & *n.m.* twenty. **~ième** *a.* & *n.m./f.* twentieth.

vingtaine /vɛ̃tɛn/ *n.f.* **une ~ (de),** about twenty.

vinicole /vinikɔl/ *a.* wine(-growing).

vinyle /vinil/ *n.m.* vinyl.

viol /vjɔl/ *n.m.* (*de femme*) rape; (*de lieu, loi*) violation.

violacé /vjɔlase/ *a.* purplish.

viol|ent, ~ente /vjɔlɑ̃, -t/ *a.* violent. **~emment** /-amɑ̃/ *adv.* violently. **~ence** *n.f.* violence; (*acte*) act of violence.

viol|er /vjɔle/ *v.t.* rape; (*lieu, loi*) violate. **~ation** *n.f.* violation.

violet, ~te /vjɔlɛ, -t/ *a.* & *n.m.* purple. ● *n.f.* violet.

violon /vjɔlɔ̃/ *n.m.* violin. **~iste** /-ɔnist/ *n.m./f.* violinist. **~ d'Ingres,** hobby.

violoncelle /vjɔlɔ̃sɛl/ *n.m.* cello. **~iste** /-elist/ *n.m./f.* cellist.

vipère /vipɛʁ/ *n.f.* viper, adder.

virage /viʁaʒ/ *n.m.* bend; (*de véhicule*) turn; (*changement d'attitude: fig.*) change of course.

virée /viʁe/ *n.f.* (*fam.*) trip, outing.

vir|er /viʁe/ *v.i.* turn. **~er de bord,** tack. **~er au rouge/***etc.***,** turn red/ *etc.* ● *v.t.* (*argent*) transfer; (*expulser: fam.*) throw out. **~ement** *n.m.* (*comm.*) (credit) transfer.

virevolter /viʁvɔlte/ *v.i.* spin round, swing round.

virginité /viʁʒinite/ *n.f.* virginity.

virgule /viʁgyl/ *n.f.* comma; (*dans un nombre*) (decimal) point.

viril /viʁil/ *a.* manly, virile. **~ité** *n.f.* manliness, virility.

virtuel, ~le /viʁtɥɛl/ *a.* virtual. **~lement** *adv.* virtually.

virtuos|e /viʁtɥoz/ *n.m./f.* virtuoso. **~ité** *n.f.* virtuosity.

virulen|t, ~te /viʁylɑ̃, -t/ *a.* virulent. **~ce** *n.f.* virulence.

virus /viʁys/ *n.m.* virus.

vis¹ /vi/ *voir* vivre, voir.

vis² /vis/ *n.f.* screw.

visa /viza/ *n.m.* visa.

visage /vizaʒ/ *n.m.* face.

vis-à-vis /vizavi/ *adv.* face to face, opposite. **~ de,** opposite; (*à l'égard de*) with respect to. ● *n.m. invar.* (*personne*) person opposite.

viscères /visɛʁ/ *n.m. pl.* intestines.

visées /vize/ *n.f. pl.* aim. **avoir des ~ sur,** have designs on.

viser /vize/ *v.t.* aim at; (*concerner*) be aimed at; (*timbrer*) stamp. ● *v.i.* aim. **~ à,** aim at; (*mesure, propos*) be aimed at.

visib|le /vizibl/ *a.* visible. **~ilité** *n.f.* visibility. **~lement** *adv.* visibly.

visière /vizjɛʁ/ *n.f.* (*de casquette*) peak; (*de casque*) visor.

vision /vizjɔ̃/ *n.f.* vision.

visionnaire /vizjɔnɛʁ/ *a.* & *n.m./f.* visionary.

visionn|er /vizjɔne/ *v.t.* view. **~euse** *n.f.* (*appareil*) viewer.

visite /vizit/ *n.f.* visit; (*examen*) examination; (*personne*) visitor. **heures de ~,** visiting hours. **~ guidée,** guided tour. **rendre ~ à,** visit. **être en ~ (chez qn.),** be visiting (s.o.).

visit|er /vizite/ *v.t.* visit; (*examiner*) examine. **~eur, ~euse** *n.m.*, *f.* visitor.

vison /vizɔ̃/ *n.m.* mink.

visqueu|x, ~se /viskø, -z/ *a.* viscous.

visser /vise/ *v.t.* screw (on).

visuel, **~le** /vizɥɛl/ *a.* visual.

vit /vi/ *voir* vivre, voir.

vit|al (*m. pl.* **~aux**) /vital, -o/ *a.* vital. **~alité** *n.f.* vitality.

vitamine /vitamin/ *n.f.* vitamin.

vite /vit/ *adv.* fast, quickly; (*tôt*) soon. **~!**, quick! **faire ~**, be quick.

vitesse /vitɛs/ *n.f.* speed; (*régime: auto.*) gear. **à toute ~**, at top speed. **en ~**, in a hurry, quickly.

viti|cole /vitikɔl/ *a.* wine. **~ulteur** *n.m.* wine-grower. **~ulture** *n.f.* wine-growing.

vitrage /vitraʒ/ *n.m.* (*vitres*) windows. **double-~**, double glazing.

vitr|ail (*pl.* **~aux**) /vitraj, -o/ *n.m.* stained-glass window.

vitr|e /vitr/ *n.f.* (window) pane; (*de véhicule*) window. **~é** *a.* glass, glazed. **~er** *v.t.* glaze.

vitrine /vitrin/ *n.f.* (shop) window; (*meuble*) display cabinet.

vivable /vivabl/ *a.* **ce n'est pas ~**, it's unbearable.

vivace /vivas/ *a.* (*plante, sentiment*) perennial.

vivacité /vivasite/ *n.f.* liveliness; (*agilité*) quickness; (*d'émotion, de l'air*) keenness; (*de souvenir, style, teint*) vividness.

vivant, **~e** /vivã, -t/ *a.* (*doué de vie, en usage*) living; (*en vie*) alive, living; (*actif, vif*) lively. ● *n.m.* **un bon ~**, a bon viveur. **de son ~**, in one's lifetime. **les ~s**, the living.

vivats /viva/ *n.m. pl.* cheers.

vive [1] /viv/ *voir* vif.

vive [2] /viv/ *int.* **~ le roi/président/ etc.!**, long live the king/president/ etc.!

vivement /vivmã/ *adv.* (*vite, sèchement*) sharply; (*avec éclat*) vividly; (*beaucoup*) greatly. **~ la fin!**, roll on the end, I'll be glad when it's the end!

vivier /vivje/ *n.m.* fish-pond.

vivifier /vivifje/ *v.t.* invigorate.

vivisection /viviseksjɔ̃/ *n.f.* vivisection.

vivoter /vivɔte/ *v.i.* plod on, get by.

vivre† /vivr/ *v.i.* live. **~ de**, (*nourriture*) live on. ● *v.t.* (*vie*) live; (*période, aventure*) live through. **~s** *n.m. pl.* supplies. **faire ~**, (*famille etc.*) support. **~ encore**, be still alive.

vlan /vlã/ *int.* bang.

vocabulaire /vɔkabylɛr/ *n.m.* vocabulary.

voc|al (*m. pl.* **~aux**) /vɔkal, -o/ *a.* vocal.

vocalise /vɔkaliz/ *n.f.* voice exercise.

vocation /vɔkasjɔ̃/ *n.f.* vocation.

vociférer /vɔsifere/ *v.t./i.* scream.

vodka /vɔdka/ *n.f.* vodka.

vœu (*pl.* **~x**) /vø/ *n.m.* (*souhait*) wish; (*promesse*) vow.

vogue /vɔg/ *n.f.* fashion, vogue.

voguer /vɔge/ *v.i.* sail.

voici /vwasi/ *prép.* here is, this is; (*au pluriel*) here are, these are. **me ~**, here I am. **~ un an**, (*temps passé*) a year ago. **~ un an que**, it is a year since.

voie /vwa/ *n.f.* (*route*) road; (*chemin*) way; (*moyen*) means, way; (*partie de route*) lane; (*rails*) track; (*quai*) platform. **en ~ de**, in the process of. **en ~ de développement**, (*pays*) developing. **par la ~ des airs**, by air. **~ de dégagement**, slip-road. **~ ferrée**, railway; (*Amer.*) railroad. **~ lactée**, Milky Way. **~ navigable**, waterway. **~ publique**, public highway. **~ sans issue**, cul-de-sac, dead end. **sur la bonne ~**, (*fig.*) well under way. **mettre sur une ~ de garage**, (*fig.*) sideline.

voilà /vwala/ *prép.* there is, that is; (*au pluriel*) there are, those are; (*voici*) here is; here are. **le ~**, there he is. **~!**, right!; (*en offrant qch.*) there you are! **~ un an**, (*temps passé*) a year ago. **~ un an que**, it is a year since.

voilage /vwalaʒ/ *n.m.* net curtain.

voile [1] /vwal/ *n.f.* (*de bateau*) sail; (*sport*) sailing.

voile [2] /vwal/ *n.m.* veil; (*tissu léger et fin*) net.

voil|er [1] /vwale/ *v.t.* veil. **se ~er** *v. pr.* (*devenir flou*) become hazy. **~é** *a.* (*terme, femme*) veiled; (*flou*) hazy.

voiler [2] /vwale/ *v.t.*, **se ~** *v. pr.* (*roue etc.*) buckle.

voilier /vwalje/ *n.m.* sailing-ship.

voilure /vwalyr/ *n.f.* sails.

voir† /vwar/ *v.t./i.* see. **se ~** *v. pr.* (*être visible*) show; (*se produire*) be seen; (*se trouver*) find o.s.; (*se fréquenter*) see each other. **ça n'a rien à ~ avec**, that has nothing to do with. **faire ~**, **laisser ~**, show. **je ne peux pas le ~**, (*fam.*) I cannot stand him. **~ trouble**, have blurred vision. **voyons!**, (*irritation*) come on!

voire /vwar/ *adv.* indeed.

voirie /vwari/ *n.f.* (*service*) highway maintenance. **travaux de ~**, road-works.

voisin, ~e /vwazɛ̃, -in/ *a.* (*proche*) neighbouring; (*adjacent*) next (**de**, to); (*semblable*) similar (**de**, to). ● *n.m., f.* neighbour. **le ~**, the man next door.

voisinage /vwazinaʒ/ *n.m.* neighbourhood; (*proximité*) proximity.

voiture /vwatyr/ *n.f.* (motor) car; (*wagon*) coach, carriage. **en ~!**, all aboard! **à ~ cheval**, horse-drawn carriage. **~ de course**, racing-car. **~ d'enfant**, pram; (*Amer.*) baby carriage. **~ de tourisme**, private car.

voix /vwa/ *n.f.* voice; (*suffrage*) vote. **à ~ basse**, in a whisper.

vol[1] /vɔl/ *n.m.* (*d'avion, d'oiseau*) flight; (*groupe d'oiseaux etc.*) flock, flight. **à ~ d'oiseau**, as the crow flies. **~ libre**, hang-gliding. **~ plané**, gliding.

vol[2] /vɔl/ *n.m.* (*délit*) theft; (*hold-up*) robbery. **~ à la tire**, pickpocketing.

volage /vɔlaʒ/ *a.* fickle.

volaille /vɔlɑj/ *n.f.* **la ~**, (*poules etc.*) poultry. **une ~**, a fowl.

volant /vɔlɑ̃/ *n.m.* (steering-)wheel; (*de jupe*) flounce.

volcan /vɔlkɑ̃/ *n.m.* volcano. **~ique** /-anik/ *a.* volcanic.

volée /vɔle/ *n.f.* flight; (*oiseaux*) flight, flock; (*de coups, d'obus*) volley. **à toute ~**, with full force. **de ~, à la ~**, in flight.

voler[1] /vɔle/ *v.i.* (*oiseau etc.*) fly.

vol|er[2] /vɔle/ *v.t./i.* steal (**à**, from). **il ne l'a pas ~é**, he deserved it. **~er qn.**, rob s.o. **~eur, ~euse** *n.m., f.* thief; **a.** thieving.

volet /vɔlɛ/ *n.m.* (*de fenêtre*) shutter; (*de document*) (folded *ou* tear-off) section. **trié sur le ~**, hand-picked.

voleter /vɔlte/ *v.i.* flutter.

volière /vɔljɛr/ *n.f.* aviary.

volontaire /vɔlɔ̃tɛr/ *a.* voluntary; (*personne*) determined. ● *n.m./f.* volunteer. **~ment** *adv.* voluntarily; (*exprès*) intentionally.

volonté /vɔlɔ̃te/ *n.f.* (*faculté, intention*) will; (*souhait*) wish; (*énergie*) will-power. **à ~**, (*à son gré*) at will. **bonne ~**, goodwill. **mauvaise ~**, ill will. **faire ses quatre ~s**, do exactly as one pleases.

volontiers /vɔlɔ̃tje/ *adv.* (*de bon gré*) with pleasure, willingly, gladly; (*ordinairement*) readily.

volt /vɔlt/ *n.m.* volt. **~age** *n.m.* voltage.

volte-face /vɔltəfas/ *n.f. invar.* about-face. **faire ~**, turn round.

voltige /vɔltiʒ/ *n.f.* acrobatics.

voltiger /vɔltiʒe/ *v.i.* flutter.

volubile /vɔlybil/ *a.* voluble.

volume /vɔlym/ *n.m.* volume.

volumineu|x, ~se /vɔlyminø, -z/ *a.* bulky.

volupté /vɔlypte/ *n.f.* sensual pleasure. **~ueux, ~ueuse** *a.* voluptuous.

vom|ir /vɔmir/ *v.t./i.* vomit. **~i** *n.m.* vomit. **~issement(s)** *n.m.* (*pl.*) vomiting.

vont /vɔ̃/ *voir* aller[1].

vorace /vɔras/ *a.* voracious.

vos /vo/ *voir* votre.

vote /vɔt/ *n.m.* (*action*) voting; (*d'une loi*) passing; (*suffrage*) vote.

vot|er /vɔte/ *v.i.* vote. ● *v.t.* vote for; (*adopter*) pass; (*crédits*) vote. **~ant, ~ante** *n.m., f.* voter.

votre (*pl.* **vos**) /vɔtr, vo/ *a.* your.

vôtre /votr/ *pron.* **le** *ou* **la ~**, **les ~s**, yours.

vou|er /vwe/ *v.t.* dedicate (**à**, to); (*promettre*) vow. **~é à l'échec**, doomed to failure.

vouloir† /vulwar/ *v.t.* want (**faire**, to do). **ça ne veut pas bouger**/*etc.*, it will not move/*etc.* **je voudrais**/*etc.* I should *ou* **voudrais bien venir**/*etc.*, I should *ou* would like/really like to come/*etc.* **je veux bien venir**/*etc.*, I am happy to come/*etc.* **voulez-vous attendre**/*etc.*?, will you wait/*etc.*? **veuillez attendre**/*etc.*, kindly wait/*etc.* **en absolument faire**, insist on doing. **comme** *ou* **si vous voulez**, if you like *ou* wish. **en ~ à qn.**, have a grudge against s.o.; (*être en colère contre*) be annoyed with s.o. **qu'est-ce qu'il me veut?**, what does he want with me? **ne pas ~ de qch.**/**qn.**, not want sth./s.o. **~ dire**, mean. **~ du bien à**, wish well.

voulu /vuly/ *a.* (*délibéré*) intentional; (*requis*) required.

vous /vu/ *pron.* (*sujet, complément*) you; (*indirect*) (to) you; (*réfléchi*) yourself; (*pl.*) yourselves; (*l'un à l'autre*) each other. **~-même** *pron.* yourself. **~-mêmes** *pron.* yourselves.

voûte /vut/ *n.f.* (*plafond*) vault; (*porche*) archway.

voûté /vute/ *a.* bent, stooped. **il a le dos ~,** he's stooped.

vouv|oyer /vuvwaje/ *v.t.* address politely (using *vous*). **~oiement** *n.m.* use of (polite) *vous*.

voyage /vwajaʒ/ *n.m.* journey; trip; (*par mer*) voyage. **~(s),** (*action*) travelling. **~ d'affaires,** business trip. **~ de noces,** honeymoon. **~ organisé,** (package) tour.

voyag|er /vwajaʒe/ *v.i.* travel. **~eur, ~euse** *n.m.,f.* traveller.

voyant[1], **~e** /vwajɑ̃, -t/ *a.* gaudy. ● *n.f.* (*femme*) clairvoyant.

voyant[2] /vwajɑ̃/ *n.m.* (*signal*) (warning) light.

voyelle /vwajɛl/ *n.f.* vowel.

voyeur /vwajœr/ *n.m.* voyeur.

voyou /vwaju/ *n.m.* hooligan.

vrac (en) /(ɑ̃)vrak/ *adv.* in disorder; (*sans emballage, au poids*) loose, in bulk.

vrai /vrɛ/ *a.* true; (*réel*) real. ● *n.m.* truth. **à ~ dire,** to tell the truth.

vraiment /vrɛmɑ̃/ *adv.* really.

vraisembl|able /vrɛsɑ̃blabl/ *a.* likely. **~ablement** *adv.* very likely. **~ance** *n.f.* likelihood, plausibility.

vrille /vrij/ *n.f.* (*aviat.*) spin.

vromb|ir /vrɔ̃bir/ *v.i.* hum. **~issement** *n.m.* humming.

VRP *abrév. m.* (*voyageur représentant placier*) rep.

vu /vy/ *voir* voir. ● *a.* **bien/mal ~,** well/not well thought of. ● *prép.* in view of. **~ que,** seeing that.

vue /vy/ *n.f.* (*spectacle*) sight; (*sens*) (eye)sight; (*panorama, idée*) view. **avoir en ~,** have in mind. **à ~,** (*tirer, payable*) at sight. **de ~,** by sight. **perdre de ~,** lose sight of. **en ~,** (*proche*) in sight; (*célèbre*) in the public eye. **en ~ de faire,** with a view to doing.

vulg|aire /vylgɛr/ *a.* (*grossier*) vulgar; (*ordinaire*) common. **~arité** *n.f.* vulgarity.

vulgariser /vylgarize/ *v.t.* popularize.

vulnérab|le /vylnerabl/ *a.* vulnerable. **~ilité** *n.f.* vulnerability.

vulve /vylv/ *n.f.* vulva.

W

wagon /vagɔ̃/ *n.m.* (*de voyageurs*) carriage; (*Amer.*) car; (*de marchandises*) wagon; (*Amer.*) freight car. **~-lit** (*pl.* **~s-lits**) *n.m.* sleeping-car, sleeper. **~-restaurant** (*pl.* **~s-restaurants**) *n.m.* dining-car.

walkman /wokman/ *n.m.* (P.) walkman.

wallon, ~ne /walɔ̃, -ɔn/ *a. & n.m.,f.* Walloon.

waters /watɛr/ *n.m. pl.* toilet.

watt /wat/ *n.m.* watt.

w.-c. /(dubla)vese/ *n.m. pl.* toilet.

week-end /wikɛnd/ *n.m.* weekend.

western /wɛstɛrn/ *n.m.* western.

whisk|y (*pl.* **~ies**) /wiski/ *n.m.* whisky.

X

xénophob|e /ksenɔfɔb/ *a.* xenophobic. ● *n.m./f.* xenophobe. **~ie** *n.f.* xenophobia.

xérès /kseres/ *n.m.* sherry.

xylophone /ksilɔfɔn/ *n.m.* xylophone.

Y

y /i/ *adv. & pron.* there; (*dessus*) on it; (*pl.*) on them; (*dedans*) in it; (*pl.*) in them. **s'y habituer,** (*à cela*) get used to it. **s'y attendre,** expect it. **y penser,** think of it. **il y entra,** (*dans cela*) he entered it. **j'y vais,** I'm on my way. **ça y est,** that is it. **y être pour qch.,** have sth. to do with it.

yacht /jɔt/ *n.m.* yacht.

yaourt /jaur(t)/ *n.m.* yoghurt. **~ière** /-tjɛr/ *n.f.* yoghurt maker.

yeux /jø/ *voir* œil.

yiddish /(j)idiʃ/ *n.m.* Yiddish.

yoga /jɔga/ *n.m.* yoga.

yougoslave /jugɔslav/ *a. & n.m./f.* Yugoslav.

Yougoslavie /jugɔslavi/ *n.f.* Yugoslavia.

yo-yo /jojo/ *n.m. invar.* (P.) yo-yo (P.).

yuppie /jøpi/ *n.m./f.* yuppie.

Z

zèbre /zɛbr/ *n.m.* zebra.
zébré /zebre/ *a.* striped.
zèle /zɛl/ *n.m.* zeal.
zélé /zele/ *a.* zealous.
zénith /zenit/ *n.m.* zenith.
zéro /zero/ *n.m.* nought, zero; (*température*) zero; (*dans un numéro*) 0; (*football*) nil; (*football: Amer.*) zero; (*personne*) nonentity. **(re)partir de ~**, start from scratch.
zeste /zɛst/ *n.m.* peel. **un ~ de**, (*fig.*) a pinch of.
zézayer /zezeje/ *v.i.* lisp.
zigzag /zigzag/ *n.m.* zigzag. **en ~**, zigzag. **~uer** /-e/ *v.i.* zigzag.
zinc /zɛ̃g/ *n.m.* (*métal*) zinc; (*comptoir: fam.*) bar.
zizanie /zizani/ *n.f.* **semer la ~**, put the cat among the pigeons.
zizi /zizi/ *n.m.* (*fam.*) willy.
zodiaque /zɔdjak/ *n.m.* zodiac.
zona /zona/ *n.m.* (*méd.*) shingles.
zone /zon/ *n.f.* zone, area; (*faubourgs*) shanty town. **~ bleue**, restricted parking zone.
zoo /zo(o)/ *n.m.* zoo.
zoolog|ie /zɔɔlɔʒi/ *n.f.* zoology. **~ique** *a.* zoological. **~iste** *n.m./f.* zoologist.
zoom /zum/ *n.m.* zoom lens.
zut /zyt/ *int.* blast (it), (oh) hell.

TEST YOURSELF WITH WORD GAMES

This section contains a number of word games which will help you to use your dictionary more effectively and to build up your knowledge of French vocabulary and usage in a fun and entertaining way. You will find answers to all puzzles and games at the end of the section.

1. Madame Irma

Madame Irma is very good at predicting the future, but she is not very good at conjugating French verbs in the future tense. Help her to replace all the verbs in brackets with the correct future form.

Lion 23 juillet-22 août

Cette semaine, les Lions (être) à la fête. **Travail**: Il ne (falloir) pas vous laisser démoraliser par les problèmes et les discussions qui (pouvoir) surgir en début de semaine. Les 19 et 20 avril vous (offrir) la possibilité d'un changement radical dans votre carrière. Pourquoi ne pas saisir votre chance? **Santé**: Le stress ne vous (épargner) pas, surtout le 18. Attention! Pour décompresser, faites un peu de sport et tout (aller) bien. **Amitié**: Vous êtes très sociable et cette semaine, vous vous (faire) encore de nouveaux amis. **Côté cœur**: Vénus (veiller) sur vous. Une nouvelle rencontre (survenir) peut-être. Si vous avez un partenaire, votre relation (être) au beau fixe.

2 Power cut

Unfortunately, there was a power cut while Jean was writing a computer manual for his office staff. He had just began to label his diagram of a computer. Can you help Jean unscramble the letters and get on with his labelling.

TURANIDORE

VARICLE

ROUSSI

QUITTEDES

NARCE

RUCRUSE

MOCR-D

3 From one word to the other

By changing only one letter on each line, you can get from the first word to the last one. Try it!

C	A	R
B	I	S

B	A	I	N
S	A	N	G

4 The odd meaning out

Watch out: one word can have different meanings. In the following exercise, only two of the suggested translations are correct. Use the dictionary to spot the odd one out, then find the correct French translation for it.

example:
blindé
- ❑ armoured
- ☑ blind
- ❑ immune

blind = aveugle

lentille
- ❑ lentil
- ❑ lense
- ❑ lent

porte
- ❑ door
- ❑ carry
- ❑ port

gauche
- ❑ left
- ❑ gauge
- ❑ awkward

broche
- ❑ broach
- ❑ brooch
- ❑ spit

duvet
- ❑ duvet
- ❑ down
- ❑ sleeping-bag

livret
- ❑ book
- ❑ liver
- ❑ libretto

5 Word magnets

Antoine's brother took all his magnets off the fridge door to wipe it clean. He put them back the wrong way round. Can you help Antoine rewrite the correct sentences?

| heure | hier | suis | me | levé | bonne | de | je |

| dit | pourtant | je | fois | lui | plusieurs | ai | le |

| sur | sortant | table | les | prends | clés | en | la |

| ira | Portugal | elle | prochaine | au | vacances | l'année | en |

| film | voir | un | allés | cinéma | sommes | nous | au |

| voisine | de | là | frère | pas | le | la | n'est |

---

6 What are they like?

Here are two lists of adjectives you can use to describe people's characteristics. Each word in the second column is the opposite of one of the adjectives in the first column. Can you link them?

1. grand		A. intelligent
2. blond		B. méchant
3. bête		C. gros
4. énervé		D. petit
5. gentil		E. sympathique
6. timide		F. brun
7. patient		G. calme
8. désagréable		H. extraverti
9. poli		I. impatient
10. maigre		J. malpoli

example: 1.D. *grand* est le contraire de *petit*.

7 Crossword

```
    A  B  C  D  E  F  G  H  I  J
1  ☐  ☐  ☐  ☐  ☐  ☐  ☐  ☐  ☐  ■
2  ☐  ■  ☐  ■  ☐  ☐  ☐  ■  ☐  ☐
3  ■  ☐  ☐  ☐  ☐  ☐  ☐  ☐  ☐  ☐
4  ☐  ☐  ☐  ☐  ☐  ■  ☐  ■  ☐  ☐
5  ☐  ☐  ☐  ☐  ■  ☐  ☐  ☐  ☐  ☐
6  ☐  ☐  ☐  ☐  ☐  ☐  ☐  ☐  ☐  ■
7  A  N  T  A  N  ■  ☐  ☐  ☐  ☐
8  ☐  ■  ☐  ☐  ■  ☐  ■  ☐  ☐  ☐
9  ☐  ☐  ☐  ☐  ■  ☐  ☐  ■  ☐  ☐
```

Across

1. the following day = le . . .
2. (a) a noun starting with the same three letters as 'émotion'
   (b) a yew
3. a day
4. toys
5. harmful
6. (a) my
   (b) a girl's name which sounds like the word Christmas in French
eg. 7. (a) (of) long ago = (d')ANTAN
   (b) an egg = un . . .
8. (a) (c) past participle of the verb meaning "to laugh"
   (b) and
9. (a) past participle of the verb meaning 'to grab'
   (b) present form of the verb meaning 'to be' = il . . .

down

A. (a) masculine article meaning 'the'
   (b) never
B. (a) short for knock-out (both in English and in French)
   (b) a year = un . . .
C. (a) masculine article meaning 'a'
   (b) the noun corresponding to the verb 'trier'
D. the verb meaning 'to have lunch' in the imperfect = je . . .
E. an emotion = une . . .
F. lather = la . . .
G. (a) a tune = un . . .
   (b) a small island (starting with the same two letters as 'île')
H. a nobleman = un . . .
 I. (a) the present form of the verb meaning 'to deny' = je . . .
   (b) a possessive adjective. Ces livres sont à mes parents. Ce
   sont . . . livres.
 J. (a) a broad bean = une . . .
   (b) perfect form of the verb meaning 'to do' = il . . .

8. The odd one out

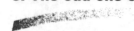

In each of the following series, all the words but one are related.
Find the odd one out and explain why. If there are words you don't
know, use your dictionary to find out what they mean.

example: stylo, agenda, livre, carnet scolaire, brosse à dents

The odd one out is 'brosse à dents', because you wouldn't find it in a
schoolbag.

1. voiture, avion, moteur, train, autocar

2. casserole, poêle, cafetière, cendrier, saladier

3. télévision, cassette, chaîne-hifi, magnétoscope, baladeur

4. ski nautique, natation, plongée, varappe, planche à voile

5. redoubler, courir, sauter, glisser, descendre, monter

6. chou, sou, caillou, genou, hibou, bijou

9 The shopping list

Paul has prepared a shopping list. When his friend sees the list, he realises that he needs exactly the same things. He asks Paul whether he would mind buying two of everything. Help Paul rewrite his list. Watch out: the plurals of compound nouns are irregular. If in doubt, look them up in your dictionary.

Acheter:	Acheter:
un taille-crayons	deux taille-crayons
un bloc-notes	....
un timbre-poste	....
un abat-jour	....
un couvre-lit	....
un cache-pot	....
un tire-bouchon	....
un ouvre-boîte	....
un réveille-matin	....
un chou-fleur	....

10 The vocabulary tree

Once you have found the correct translations for the following words, write them down on the tree. Some of the letters will be used for more than one word.

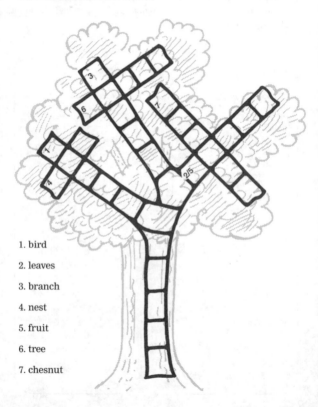

1. bird

2. leaves

3. branch

4. nest

5. fruit

6. tree

7. chesnut

11 The mystery word

To fill in the grid, find the French words for all the musical instruments illustrated below. Once you have completed the grid, you'll discover the name of a famous classical musician.

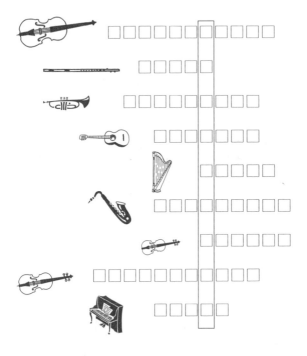

The musician is _ _ _ _ _ _ _ _ _ .

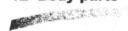

12 Body parts

Can you put the right number in the boxes next to the French words in the list?

	la bouche
☐	la bouche
☐	le bras
☐	la cheville
☐	le cou
☐	le coude
☐	la cuisse
☐	le doigt
☐	l'épaule
☐	le front
☐	le genou
☐	la hanche
☐	la jambe
☐	la joue
☐	la main
☐	le menton
☐	le mollet
☐	le nez
☐	le nombril
☐	l'œil
☐	l'oreille
☐	l'orteil
☐	le pied
☐	le poignet
☐	la tête

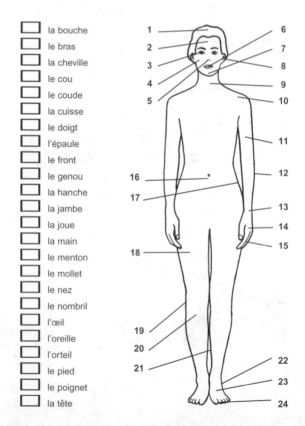

13 Liar liar!

Today, Sabine had a day-off. She tells her mother what she has been up to:

" *Ce matin, je me suis levée juste après ton départ. J'ai bu du café au lait et j'ai mangé des tartines. Après avoir fait ma toilette et m'être habillée, je suis allée au parc. Il faisait très beau et j'avais envie de me promener. Je suis revenue à la maison pour chercher mon maillot de bain et je suis allée à la piscine découverte. J'y suis restée pendant deux heures. En sortant, j'avais très faim, alors je me suis installée dans un café. J'ai commandé un sandwich. Après ça, je suis allée au cinéma. Le film était super! Je suis rentrée à la maison un peu avant que tu arrives.* "

What she doesn't say is that her little brother, Adrien, skipped school to spend the day with her. Rewrite her statement.

" *Ce matin, nous nous sommes levés juste après ton départ...* "

Answers

1

seront	ira
faudra	ferez
pourront	veillera
offriront	surviendra
épargnera	sera

2

ordinateur	écran
clavier	curseur
souris	cd-rom
disquette	

3

C	A	R		B	A	I	N
B	A	R		M	A	I	N
B	A	S		S	A	I	N
B	U	S		S	A	I	S
B	I	S		S	A	N	S
				S	A	N	G

4

lent = prêté	broach = entamer
port = porto	duvet = couette
gauge = jauge	liver = foie

5

Hier, je me suis levé de bonne heure.
Pourtant, je le lui ai dit plusieurs fois.
Prends les clés sur la table en sortant.
L'année prochaine, elle ira en vacances au Portugal.
Nous sommes allés voir un film au cinéma.
Le frère de la voisine n'est pas là.

6

1.D. *grand* est le contraire de *petit*.
2.F. *blond* est le contraire de *brun*.
3.A. *bête* est le contraire d'*intelligent*.

4.G. *énervé* est le contraire de *calme*.
5.B. *gentil* est le contraire de *méchant*.
6.H. *timide* est le contraire d'*extraverti*.
7.I. *patient* est le contraire d'*impatient*.
8.E. *désagréable* est le contraire de *sympathique*.
9.J. *poli* est le contraire de *malpoli*.
10.C. *maigre* est le contraire de *gros*.

7

8
1. moteur - because it isn't a vehicle
2. cendrier - because it is not used for cooking
3. cassette - because it isn't an electrical device
4. varappe - because it is the only sport in the list which isn't a water-sport
5. redoubler - because it is the only verb in the list which doesn't describe a movement
6. sou - because it ends in "-s" in the plural, not in "-x" like the other five

9

deux taille-crayons	deux cache-pots
deux blocs-notes	deux tire-bouchons
deux timbres-poste	deux ouvre-boîtes
deux abat-jour	deux réveille-matin
deux couvre-lits	deux choux-fleurs

10

1. oiseau
2. feuilles
3. branche
4. nid

5. fruit
6. arbre
7. marron

11

```
      C  O    N    T    R    E    B    A    S    S    E
            F    L    U    T    E
      T    R  O    M    P    E    T    T    E
            G    U    I    T    A    R    E
                      H    A    R    P    E
            S    A    X    O    P    H    O    N    E
                      V    I    O    L    O    N
V  I  O  L    O    N    C    E    L    L    E
            P    I    A    N    O
```

12

6.	la bouche	4.	la joue
11.	le bras	14.	la main
22.	la cheville	7.	le menton
9.	le cou	21.	le mollet
12.	le coude	5.	le nez
18.	la cuisse	16.	le nombril
15.	le doigt	3.	l'œil
10.	l'épaule	8.	l'oreille
2.	le front	24.	l'orteil
20.	le genou	23.	le pied
17.	la hanche	13.	le poignet
19.	la jambe	1.	la tête

13

"Ce matin, nous nous sommes levés juste après ton départ. Nous avons bu du café au lait et nous avons mangé des tartines. Après avoir fait notre toilette et nous être habillés, nous sommes allés au parc. Il faisait très beau et nous avions envie de nous promener. Nous sommes revenus à la maison pour chercher nos maillots de bain et nous sommes allés à la piscine découverte. Nous y sommes restés pendant deux heures. En sortant, nous avions très faim, alors nous nous sommes installés dans un café. Nous avons commandé des sandwichs. Après ça, nous sommes allés au cinéma. Le film était super! Nous sommes rentrés à la maison un peu avant que tu arrives."

Anglais-Français
English-French

A

a /eɪ, *unstressed* ə/ a. (*before vowel* **an** /æn, ən/) un(e). **I'm a painter,** je suis peintre. **ten pence a kilo,** dix pence le kilo. **once a year,** une fois par an.

aback /ə'bæk/ adv. **taken ~,** déconcerté, interdit.

abandon /ə'bændən/ v.t. abandonner. ● n. désinvolture f. **~ed** a. (*behaviour*) débauché. **~ment** n. abandon m.

abashed /ə'bæʃt/ a. confus.

abate /ə'beɪt/ v.i. se calmer. ● v.t. diminuer. **~ment** n. diminution f.

abattoir /'æbətwɑː(r)/ n. abattoir m.

abbey /'æbɪ/ n. abbaye f.

abb|ot /'æbət/ n. abbé m. **~ess** n. abbesse f.

abbreviat|e /ə'briːvɪeɪt/ v.t. abréger. **~ion** /-'eɪʃn/ n. abréviation f.

abdicat|e /'æbdɪkeɪt/ v.t./i. abdiquer. **~ion** /-'keɪʃn/ n. abdication f.

abdom|en /'æbdəmən/ n. abdomen m. **~inal** /-'dɒmɪnl/ a. abdominal.

abduct /æb'dʌkt/ v.t. enlever. **~ion** /-kʃn/ n. rapt m. **~or** n. ravisseu|r, -se m., f.

aberration /æbə'reɪʃn/ n. aberration f.

abet /ə'bet/ v.t. (*p.t.* **abetted**) (*jurid.*) encourager.

abeyance /ə'beɪəns/ n. **in ~,** (*matter*) en suspens; (*custom*) en désuétude.

abhor /əb'hɔː(r)/ v.t. (*p.t.* **abhorred**) exécrer. **~rence** /-'hɒrəns/ n. horreur f. **~rent** /-'hɒrənt/ a. exécrable.

abide /ə'baɪd/ v.t. supporter. **~ by,** respecter.

abiding /ə'baɪdɪŋ/ a. éternel.

ability /ə'bɪlətɪ/ n. aptitude f. (**to do,** à faire); (*talent*) talent m.

abject /'æbdʒekt/ a. abject.

ablaze /ə'bleɪz/ a. en feu. **~ with,** (*anger etc.: fig.*) enflammé de.

abl|e /'eɪbl/ a. (**-er, -est**) capable (**to,** de). **be ~e,** pouvoir; (*know how to*) savoir. **~y** adv. habilement.

ablutions /ə'bluːʃnz/ n. pl. ablutions f. pl.

abnormal /æb'nɔːml/ a. anormal. **~ity** /-'mælətɪ/ n. anomalie f. **~ly** adv. (*unusually*) exceptionnellement.

aboard /ə'bɔːd/ adv. à bord. ● prep. à bord de.

abode /ə'bəʊd/ n. (*old use*) demeure f. **of no fixed ~,** sans domicile fixe.

aboli|sh /ə'bɒlɪʃ/ v.t. supprimer, abolir. **~tion** /æbə'lɪʃn/ n. suppression f., abolition f.

abominable /ə'bɒmɪnəbl/ a. abominable.

abominat|e /ə'bɒmɪneɪt/ v.t. exécrer. **~ion** /-'neɪʃn/ n. abomination f.

aboriginal /æbə'rɪdʒənl/ a. & n. aborigène (m.).

aborigines /æbə'rɪdʒɪniːz/ n. pl. aborigènes m. pl.

abort /ə'bɔːt/ v.t. faire avorter. ● v.i. avorter. **~ive** a. (*attempt etc.*) manqué.

abortion /ə'bɔːʃn/ n. avortement m. **have an ~,** se faire avorter.

abound /ə'baʊnd/ v.i. abonder (**in,** en).

about /ə'baʊt/ adv. (*approximately*) environ; (*here and there*) çà et là; (*all round*) partout, autour; (*nearby*) dans les parages; (*of rumour*) en circulation. ● prep. au sujet de; (*round*) autour de; (*somewhere in*) dans. **~-face, ~-turn** ns. (*fig.*) volteface f. *invar.* **~ here,** par ici. **be ~ to do,** être sur le point de faire. **how *or* what ~ leaving,** si on partait. **what's the film ~?,** quel est le sujet du film? **talk ~,** parler de.

above /ə'bʌv/ adv. au-dessus; (*on page*) ci-dessus. ● prep. au-dessus de. **he is not ~ lying,** il n'est pas incapable de mentir. **~ all,** par-dessus tout. **~-board** a. honnête. **~-mentioned** a. mentionné ci-dessus.

abrasion /əˈbreɪʒn/ n. frottement m.; (*injury*) écorchure f.

abrasive /əˈbreɪsɪv/ a. abrasif; (*manner*) brusque. ● n. abrasif m.

abreast /əˈbrest/ adv. de front. **keep ~ of**, se tenir au courant de.

abridge /əˈbrɪdʒ/ v.t. abréger. **~ment** n. abrégement m., réduction f.; (*abridged text*) abrégé m.

abroad /əˈbrɔːd/ adv. à l'étranger; (*far and wide*) de tous côtés.

abrupt /əˈbrʌpt/ a. (*sudden, curt*) brusque; (*steep*) abrupt. **~ly** adv. (*suddenly*) brusquement; (*curtly, rudely*) avec brusquerie. **~ness** n. brusquerie f.

abscess /ˈæbses/ n. abcès m.

abscond /əbˈskɒnd/ v.i. s'enfuir.

abseil /ˈæbseɪl/ v.i. descendre en rappel.

absen|t [1] /ˈæbsənt/ a. absent; (*look etc.*) distrait. **~ce** n. absence f.; (*lack*) manque m. **in the ~ce of**, à défaut de. **~tly** adv. distraitement. **~t-minded** a. distrait. **~t-mindedness** n. distraction f.

absent [2] /əbˈsent/ v. pr. **~ o.s.**, s'absenter.

absentee /æbsənˈtiː/ n. absent(e) m. (f.). **~ism** n. absentéisme m.

absolute /ˈæbsəluːt/ a. absolu; (*coward etc.: fam.*) véritable. **~ly** adv. absolument.

absolution /æbsəˈluːʃn/ n. absolution f.

absolve /əbˈzɒlv/ v.t. (*from sin*) absoudre (**from**, de); (*from vow etc.*) délier (**from**, de).

absor|b /əbˈsɔːb/ v.t. absorber. **~ption** n. absorption f.

absorbent /əbˈsɔːbənt/ a. absorbant. **~ cotton**, (*Amer.*) coton hydrophile m.

abst|ain /əbˈsteɪn/ v.i. s'abstenir (**from**, de). **~ention** /-ˈstenʃn/ n. abstention f.; (*from drink*) abstinence f.

abstemious /əbˈstiːmɪəs/ a. sobre.

abstinen|ce /ˈæbstɪnəns/ n. abstinence f. **~t** a. sobre.

abstract [1] /ˈæbstrækt/ a. abstrait. ● n. (*quality*) abstrait m.; (*summary*) résumé m.

abstract [2] /əbˈstrækt/ v.t. retirer, extraire. **~ion** /-kʃn/ n. extraction f.; (*idea*) abstraction f.

abstruse /əbˈstruːs/ a. obscur.

absurd /əbˈsɜːd/ a. absurde. **~ity** n. absurdité f.

abundan|t /əˈbʌndənt/ a. abondant. **~ce** n. abondance f. **~tly** adv. (*entirely*) tout à fait.

abuse [1] /əˈbjuːz/ v.t. (*misuse*) abuser de; (*ill-treat*) maltraiter; (*insult*) injurier.

abus|e [2] /əˈbjuːs/ n. (*misuse*) abus m. (**of**, de); (*insults*) injures f. pl. **~ive** a. injurieux. **get ~ive**, devenir grossier.

abut /əˈbʌt/ v.i. (*p.t.* **abutted**) être contigu (**on**, à).

abysmal /əˈbɪzməl/ a. (*great*) profond; (*bad: fam.*) exécrable.

abyss /əˈbɪs/ n. abîme m.

academic /ækəˈdemɪk/ a. universitaire; (*scholarly*) intellectuel; (*pej.*) théorique. ● n. universitaire m./f. **~ally** /-lɪ/ adv. intellectuellement.

academ|y /əˈkædəmɪ/ n. (*school*) école f. **A~y**, (*society*) Académie f. **~ician** /-ˈmɪʃn/ n. académicien(ne) m. (f.).

accede /əkˈsiːd/ v.i. **~ to**, (*request, post, throne*) accéder à.

accelerat|e /əkˈseləreɪt/ v.t. accélérer. ● v.i. (*speed up*) s'accélérer; (*auto.*) accélérer. **~ion** /-ˈreɪʃn/ n. accélération f.

accelerator /əkˈseləreɪtə(r)/ n. (*auto.*) accélérateur m.

accent [1] /ˈæksənt/ n. accent m.

accent [2] /ækˈsent/ v.t. accentuer.

accentuat|e /əkˈsentʃʊeɪt/ v.t. accentuer. **~ion** /-ˈeɪʃn/ n. accentuation f.

accept /əkˈsept/ v.t. accepter. **~able** a. acceptable. **~ance** n. acceptation f.; (*approval, favour*) approbation f.

access /ˈækses/ n. accès m. (**to sth.**, à qch.; **to s.o.**, auprès de qn.). **~ible** /əkˈsesəbl/ a. accessible. **~ road**, route d'accès f.

accession /ækˈseʃn/ n. accession f.; (*thing added*) nouvelle acquisition f.

accessory /əkˈsesərɪ/ a. accessoire. ● n. accessoire m.; (*person: jurid.*) complice m./f.

accident /ˈæksɪdənt/ n. accident m.; (*chance*) hasard m. **~al** /-ˈdentl/ a. accidentel, fortuit. **~ally** /-ˈdentəlɪ/ adv. involontairement. **~-prone** a. qui attire les accidents.

acclaim /əˈkleɪm/ v.t. acclamer. ● n. acclamation(s) f. (pl.).

acclimat|e /ˈæklɪmeɪt/ v.t./i. (*Amer.*) (s')acclimater. **~ion** /-ˈmeɪʃn/ n. (*Amer.*) acclimatation f.

acclimatiz|e /əˈklaɪmətaɪz/ *v.t./i.* (s')acclimater. **~ation** /-ˈzeɪʃn/ *n.* acclimatation *f.*

accommodat|e /əˈkɒmədeɪt/ *v.t.* loger, avoir de la place pour; (*adapt*) adapter; (*supply*) fournir; (*oblige*) obliger. **~ing** *a.* obligeant. **~ion** /-ˈdeɪʃn/ *n.* (*living premises*) logement *m.*; (*rented rooms*) chambres *f. pl.*

accompan|y /əˈkʌmpənɪ/ *v.t.* accompagner. **~iment** *n.* accompagnement *m.* **~ist** *n.* accompagnateur, -trice *m., f.*

accomplice /əˈkʌmplɪs/ *n.* complice *m./f.*

accomplish /əˈkʌmplɪʃ/ *v.t.* (*perform*) accomplir; (*achieve*) réaliser. **~ed** *a.* accompli. **~ment** *n.* accomplissement *m.* **~ments** *n. pl.* (*abilities*) talents *m. pl.*

accord /əˈkɔːd/ *v.i.* concorder. ● *v.t.* accorder. ● *n.* accord *m.* **of one's own ~,** de sa propre initiative. **~ance** *n.* **in ~ance with,** conformément à.

according /əˈkɔːdɪŋ/ *adv.* **~ to,** selon, suivant. **~ly** *adv.* en conséquence.

accordion /əˈkɔːdɪən/ *n.* accordéon *m.*

accost /əˈkɒst/ *v.t.* aborder.

account /əˈkaʊnt/ *n.* (*comm.*) compte *m.*; (*description*) compte rendu *m.*; (*importance*) importance *f.* ● *v.t.* considérer. **~ for,** rendre compte de, expliquer. **on ~ of,** à cause de. **on no ~,** en aucun cas. **take into ~,** tenir compte de. **~able** *a.* responsable (**for,** de; **to,** envers). **~ability** /-əˈbɪlətɪ/ *n.* responsabilité *f.*

accountan|t /əˈkaʊntənt/ *n.* comptable *m./f.*, expert-comptable *m.* **~cy** *n.* comptabilité *f.*

accredited /əˈkredɪtɪd/ *a.* accrédité.

accrue /əˈkruː/ *v.i.* s'accumuler. **~ to,** (*come to*) revenir à.

accumulat|e /əˈkjuːmjʊleɪt/ *v.t./i.* (s')accumuler. **~ion** /-ˈleɪʃn/ *n.* accumulation *f.*

accumulator /əˈkjuːmjʊleɪtə(r)/ *n.* (*battery*) accumulateur *m.*

accura|te /ˈækjərət/ *a.* exact, précis. **~cy** *n.* exactitude *f.*, précision *f.* **~tely** *adv.* exactement, avec précision.

accus|e /əˈkjuːz/ *v.t.* accuser. **the ~ed,** l'accusé(e) *m.(f.).* **~ation** /ækjuːˈzeɪʃn/ *n.* accusation *f.*

accustom /əˈkʌstəm/ *v.t.* accoutumer. **~ed** *a.* accoutumé. **become ~ed to,** s'accoutumer à.

ace /eɪs/ *n.* (*card, person*) as *m.*

ache /eɪk/ *n.* douleur *f.*, mal *m.* ● *v.i.* faire mal. **my leg ~s,** ma jambe me fait mal, j'ai mal à la jambe.

achieve /əˈtʃiːv/ *v.t.* réaliser, accomplir; (*success*) obtenir. **~ment** *n.* réalisation *f.* (**of,** de); (*feat*) exploit *m.*, réussite *f.*

acid /ˈæsɪd/ *a. & n.* acide (*m.*). **~ity** /əˈsɪdətɪ/ *n.* acidité *f.* **~ rain,** pluies acides *f. pl.*

acknowledge /əkˈnɒlɪdʒ/ *v.t.* reconnaître. **~ (receipt of),** accuser réception de. **~ment** *n.* reconnaissance *f.*; accusé de réception *m.*

acme /ˈækmɪ/ *n.* sommet *m.*

acne /ˈæknɪ/ *n.* acné *f.*

acorn /ˈeɪkɔːn/ *n.* (*bot.*) gland *m.*

acoustic /əˈkuːstɪk/ *a.* acoustique. **~s** *n. pl.* acoustique *f.*

acquaint /əˈkweɪnt/ *v.t.* **~ s.o. with sth.,** mettre qn. au courant de qch. **be ~ed with,** (*person*) connaître; (*fact*) savoir. **~ance** *n.* (*knowledge, person*) connaissance *f.*

acquiesce /ækwɪˈes/ *v.i.* consentir. **~nce** *n.* consentement *m.*

acqui|re /əˈkwaɪə(r)/ *v.t.* acquérir; (*habit*) prendre. **~sition** /ækwɪˈzɪʃn/ *n.* acquisition *f.* **~sitive** /əˈkwɪzətɪv/ *a.* avide, âpre au gain.

acquit /əˈkwɪt/ *v.t.* (*p.t.* **acquitted**) acquitter. **~ o.s. well,** bien s'en tirer. **~tal** *n.* acquittement *m.*

acre /ˈeɪkə(r)/ *n.* (*approx.*) demi-hectare *m.* **~age** *n.* superficie *f.*

acrid /ˈækrɪd/ *a.* âcre.

acrimon|ious /ækrɪˈməʊnɪəs/ *a.* acerbe, acrimonieux. **~y** /ˈækrɪmənɪ/ *n.* acrimonie *f.*

acrobat /ˈækrəbæt/ *n.* acrobate *m./f.* **~ic** /-ˈbætɪk/ *a.* acrobatique. **~ics** /-ˈbætɪks/ *n. pl.* acrobatie *f.*

acronym /ˈækrənɪm/ *n.* sigle *m.*

across /əˈkrɒs/ *adv. & prep.* (*side to side*) d'un côté à l'autre (de); (*on other side*) de l'autre côté (**from,** de); (*crosswise*) en travers (de), à travers. **go or walk ~,** traverser.

acrylic /əˈkrɪlɪk/ *a. & n.* acrylique (*m.*).

act /ækt/ *n.* (*deed, theatre*) acte *m.*; (*in variety show*) numéro *m.*; (*decree*) loi *f.* ● *v.i.* agir; (*theatre*) jouer; (*function*) marcher; (*pretend*) jouer la comédie. ● *v.t.* (*part, role*) jouer. **~ as,** servir de. **~ing** *a.* (*temporary*) intérimaire; *n.* (*theatre*) jeu *m.*

action /'ækʃn/ *n.* action *f.*; (*mil.*) combat *m.* **out of ~,** hors service. **take ~,** agir.

activate /'æktɪveɪt/ *v.t.* (*machine*) actionner; (*reaction*) activer.

activ|e /'æktɪv/ *a.* actif; (*interest*) vif; (*volcano*) en activité. **~ism** *n.* activisme *m.* **~ist** *n.* activiste *m./f.* **~ity** /-'tɪvətɪ/ *n.* activité *f.*

ac|tor /'ækta(r)/ *n.* acteur *m.* **~tress** *n.* actrice *f.*

actual /'æktʃʊəl/ *a.* réel; (*example*) concret. **the ~ pen which,** le stylo même que. **in the ~ house,** (*the house itself*) dans la maison elle-même. **no ~ promise,** pas de promesse en tant que telle. **~ity** /-'æləti/ *n.* réalité *f.* **~ly** *adv.* (*in fact*) en réalité, réellement.

actuary /'æktʃʊərɪ/ *n.* actuaire *m./f.*

acumen /'ækjʊmen, *Amer.* ə'kju:mən/ *n.* perspicacité *f.*

acupunctur|e /'ækjʊpʌŋktʃə(r)/ *n.* acupuncture *f.* **~ist** *n.* acupuncteur *m.*

acute /ə'kju:t/ *a.* aigu; (*mind*) pénétrant; (*emotion*) intense, vif; (*shortage*) grave. **~ly** *adv.* vivement. **~ness** *n.* intensité *f.*

ad /æd/ *n.* (*fam.*) annonce *f.*

AD *abbr.* après J.-C.

adamant /'ædəmənt/ *a.* inflexible.

Adam's apple /'ædəmz'æpl/ *n.* pomme d'Adam *f.*

adapt /ə'dæpt/ *v.t./i.* (s')adapter. **~ation** /-'teɪʃn/ *n.* adaptation *f.* **~or** *n.* (*electr.*) adaptateur *m.*; (*for two plugs*) prise multiple *f.*

adaptab|le /ə'dæptəbl/ *a.* souple; (*techn.*) adaptable. **~ility** /-'bɪlətɪ/ *n.* souplesse *f.*

add /æd/ *v.t./i.* ajouter. **~ (up),** (*total*) additionner. **~ up to,** (*total*) s'élever à. **~ing machine,** machine à calculer *f.*

adder /'ædə(r)/ *n.* vipère *f.*

addict /'ædɪkt/ *n.* intoxiqué(e) *m.* (*f.*); (*fig.*) fanatique *m./f.*

addict|ed /ə'dɪktɪd/ *a.* **~ed to,** (*drink*) adonné à. **be ~ed to,** (*fig.*) être un fanatique de. **~ion** /-kʃn/ *n.* (*med.*) dépendance *f.*; (*fig.*) manie *f.* **~ive** *a.* (*drug etc.*) qui crée une dépendance.

addition /ə'dɪʃn/ *n.* addition *f.* **in ~,** en outre. **~al** /-ʃənl/ *a.* supplémentaire.

additive /'ædɪtɪv/ *n.* additif *m.*

address /ə'dres/ *n.* adresse *f.*; (*speech*) allocution *f.* ● *v.t.* adresser; (*speak to*) s'adresser à. **~ee** /ædre'siː/ *n.* destinataire *m./f.*

adenoids /'ædɪnɔɪdz/ *n. pl.* végétations (adénoïdes) *f. pl.*

adept /'ædept, *Amer.* ə'dept/ *a. & n.* expert (**at,** en) (*m.*).

adequa|te /'ædɪkwət/ *a.* suffisant; (*satisfactory*) satisfaisant. **~cy** *n.* quantité suffisante *f.*; (*of person*) compétence *f.* **~tely** *adv.* suffisamment.

adhere /əd'hɪə(r)/ *v.i.* adhérer (**to,** à). **~ to,** (*fig.*) respecter. **~nce** /-rəns/ *n.* adhésion *f.*

adhesion /əd'hiːʒn/ *n.* (*grip*) adhérence *f.*; (*support: fig.*) adhésion *f.*

adhesive /əd'hiːsɪv/ *a. & n.* adhésif (*m.*).

ad infinitum /ædɪnfɪ'naɪtəm/ *adv.* à l'infini.

adjacent /ə'dʒeɪsnt/ *a.* contigu (**to,** à).

adjective /'ædʒɪktɪv/ *n.* adjectif *m.*

adjoin /ə'dʒɔɪn/ *v.t.* être contigu à.

adjourn /ə'dʒɜːn/ *v.t.* ajourner. ● *v.t./i.* **~ (the meeting),** suspendre la séance. **~ to,** (*go*) se retirer à.

adjudicate /ə'dʒuːdɪkeɪt/ *v.t./i.* juger.

adjust /ə'dʒʌst/ *v.t.* (*machine*) régler; (*prices*) (r)ajuster; (*arrange*) rajuster, arranger. ● *v.t./i.* **~ (o.s.) to,** s'adapter à. **~able** *a.* réglable. **~ment** *n.* (*techn.*) réglage *m.*; (*of person*) adaptation *f.*

ad lib /æd'lɪb/ *v.i.* (*p.t.* **ad libbed**) (*fam.*) improviser.

administer /əd'mɪnɪstə(r)/ *v.t.* administrer.

administration /ədmɪnɪ'streɪʃn/ *n.* administration *f.*

administrative /əd'mɪnɪstrətɪv/ *a.* administratif.

administrator /əd'mɪnɪstreɪtə(r)/ *n.* administra|teur, -trice *m.*, *f.*

admirable /'ædmərəbl/ *a.* admirable.

admiral /'ædmərəl/ *n.* amiral *m.*

admir|e /əd'maɪə(r)/ *v.t.* admirer. **~ation** /ædmə'reɪʃn/ *n.* admiration *f.* **~er** *n.* admira|teur, -trice *m.*, *f.*

admissible /əd'mɪsəbl/ *a.* admissible.

admission /əd'mɪʃn/ *n.* admission *f.*; (*to museum, theatre, etc.*) entrée *f.*; (*confession*) aveu *m.*

admit /əd'mɪt/ v.t. (p.t. **admitted**) laisser entrer; (acknowledge) reconnaître, admettre. **~ to**, avouer. **~tance** n. entrée f. **~tedly** adv. il est vrai (que).

admonish /əd'mɒnɪʃ/ v.t. réprimander.

ado /ə'duː/ n. without more **~**, sans plus de cérémonies.

adolescen|t /ædə'lesnt/ n. & a. adolescent(e) (m. (f.)). **~ce** n. adolescence f.

adopt /ə'dɒpt/ v.t. adopter. **~ed** a. (child) adoptif. **~ion** /-pʃn/ n. adoption f.

adoptive /ə'dɒptɪv/ a. adoptif.

ador|e /ə'dɔː(r)/ v.t. adorer. **~able** a. adorable. **~ation** /ædə'reɪʃn/ n. adoration f.

adorn /ə'dɔːn/ v.t. orner. **~ment** n. ornement m.

adrift /ə'drɪft/ a. & adv. à la dérive.

adroit /ə'drɔɪt/ a. adroit.

adulation /ædjʊ'leɪʃn/ n. adulation f.

adult /'ædʌlt/ a. & n. adulte (m./f.). **~hood** n. condition d'adulte f.

adulterate /ə'dʌltəreɪt/ v.t. falsifier, frelater, altérer.

adulter|y /ə'dʌltərɪ/ n. adultère m. **~er**, **~ess** ns. épou|x, -se adultère m., f. **~ous** a. adultère.

advance /əd'vɑːns/ v.t. avancer. ● v.i. (s')avancer; (progress) avancer. ● n. avance f. ● a. (payment) anticipé. **in ~**, à l'avance. **~d** a. avancé; (studies) supérieur. **~ment** n. avancement m.

advantage /əd'vɑːntɪdʒ/ n. avantage m. **take ~ of**, profiter de; (person) exploiter. **~ous** /ædvən'teɪdʒəs/ a. avantageux.

advent /'ædvənt/ n. arrivée f.

Advent /'ædvənt/ n. Avent m.

adventur|e /əd'ventʃə(r)/ n. aventure f. **~er** n. explora|teur, -trice m., f.; (pej.) aventur|ier, -ière m., f. **~ous** a. aventureux.

adverb /'ædvɜːb/ n. adverbe m.

adversary /'ædvəsərɪ/ n. adversaire m./f.

advers|e /'ædvɜːs/ a. défavorable. **~ity** /əd'vɜːsətɪ/ n. adversité f.

advert /'ædvɜːt/ n. (fam.) annonce f.; (TV) pub f., publicité f. **~isement** /əd'vɜːtɪsmənt/ n. publicité f.; (in paper etc.) annonce f.

advertis|e /'ædvətaɪz/ v.t./i. faire de la publicité (pour); (sell) mettre une annonce (pour vendre). **~ for**, (seek) chercher (par voie d'annonce). **~ing** n. publicité f. **~er** /-ə(r)/ n. annonceur m.

advice /əd'vaɪs/ n. conseil(s) m. (pl.); (comm.) avis m. **some ~, a piece of ~,** un conseil.

advis|e /əd'vaɪz/ v.t. conseiller; (inform) aviser. **~e against**, déconseiller. **~able** a. conseillé, prudent (**to**, de). **~er** n. conseill|er, -ère m., f. **~ory** a. consultatif.

advocate[1] /'ædvəkət/ n. (jurid.) avocat m. **~s of**, les défenseurs de.

advocate[2] /'ædvəkeɪt/ v.t. recommander.

aegis /'iːdʒɪs/ n. **under the ~ of**, sous l'égide de f.

aeon /'iːən/ n. éternité f.

aerial /'eərɪəl/ a. aérien. ● n. antenne f.

aerobatics /eərə'bætɪks/ n. pl. acrobatie aérienne f.

aerobics /eə'rəʊbɪks/ n. aérobic m.

aerodrome /'eərədrəʊm/ n. aérodrome m.

aerodynamic /eərəʊdaɪ'næmɪk/ a. aérodynamique.

aeroplane /'eərəpleɪn/ n. avion m.

aerosol /'eərəsɒl/ n. atomiseur m.

aesthetic /iːs'θetɪk, Amer. es'θetɪk/ a. esthétique.

afar /ə'fɑː(r)/ adv. **from ~**, de loin.

affable /'æfəbl/ a. affable.

affair /ə'feə(r)/ n. (matter) affaire f.; (romance) liaison f.

affect /ə'fekt/ v.t. affecter. **~ation** /æfek'teɪʃn/ n. affectation f. **~ed** a. affecté.

affection /ə'fekʃn/ n. affection f.

affectionate /ə'fekʃənət/ a. affectueux.

affiliat|e /ə'fɪlɪeɪt/ v.t. affilier. **~ed company**, filiale f. **~ion** /-'eɪʃn/ n. affiliation f.

affinity /ə'fɪnətɪ/ n. affinité f.

affirm /ə'fɜːm/ v.t. affirmer. **~ation** /æfə'meɪʃn/ n. affirmation f.

affirmative /ə'fɜːmətɪv/ a. affirmatif. ● n. affirmative f.

affix /ə'fɪks/ v.t. apposer.

afflict /ə'flɪkt/ v.t. affliger. **~ion** /-kʃn/ n. affliction f., détresse f.

affluen|t /'æfluənt/ a. riche. **~ce** n. richesse f.

afford /ə'fɔːd/ v.t. avoir les moyens d'acheter; (provide) fournir. **~ to do**, avoir les moyens de faire; (be able) se permettre de faire. **can you ~ the time?**, avez-vous le temps?

affray /ə'freɪ/ n. rixe f.

affront /ə'frʌnt/ n. affront m. ● v.t. insulter.

afield /ə'fiːld/ adv. **far ~**, loin.

afloat /ə'fləʊt/ adv. à flot.

afoot /ə'fʊt/ adv. **sth. is ~**, il se trame or se prépare qch.

aforesaid /ə'fɔːsed/ a. susdit.

afraid /ə'freɪd/ a. **be ~**, avoir peur (**of, to, de; that, que**); (**be sorry**) regretter. **I am ~ that**, (**regret to say**) je regrette de dire que.

afresh /ə'freʃ/ adv. de nouveau.

Africa /'æfrɪkə/ n. Afrique f. **~n** a. & n. africain(e) (m. (f.)).

after /'ɑːftə(r)/ adv. & prep. après. ● conj. après que. **~ doing**, après avoir fait. **~ all** après tout. **~-effect** n. suite f. **~-sales service**, service après-vente m. **~ the manner of**, d'après. **be ~**, (**seek**) chercher.

aftermath /'ɑːftəmæθ/ n. suites f. pl.

afternoon /ɑːftə'nuːn/ n. après-midi m./f. invar.

afters /'ɑːftəz/ n. pl. (**fam.**) dessert m.

aftershave /'ɑːftəʃeɪv/ n. lotion après-rasage f.

afterthought /'ɑːftəθɔːt/ n. réflexion après coup f. **as an ~**, en y repensant.

afterwards /'ɑːftəwədz/ adv. après, par la suite.

again /ə'gen/ adv. de nouveau, encore une fois; (**besides**) en outre. **do ~**, **see ~/etc.**, refaire, revoir/etc.

against /ə'genst/ prep. contre. **~ the law**, illégal.

age /eɪdʒ/ n. âge m. ● v.t./i. (**pres. p. ageing**) vieillir. **~ group**, tranche d'âge f. **~ limit**, limite d'âge. **for ~s**, (**fam.**) une éternité. **of ~**, (**jurid.**) majeur. **ten years of ~**, âgé de dix ans. **~less** a. toujours jeune.

aged[1] /eɪdʒd/ a. **~ six**, âgé de six ans.

aged[2] /'eɪdʒɪd/ a. âgé, vieux.

agen|cy /'eɪdʒənsɪ/ n. agence f.; (**means**) entremise f. **~t** n. agent m.

agenda /ə'dʒendə/ n. ordre du jour m.

agglomeration /əglɒmə'reɪʃn/ n. agglomération f.

aggravat|e /'ægrəveɪt/ v.t. (**make worse**) aggraver; (**annoy: fam.**) exaspérer. **~ion** /-'veɪʃn/ n. aggravation f.; exaspération f.; (**trouble: fam.**) ennuis m. pl.

aggregate /'ægrɪgət/ a. & n. total (m.).

aggress|ive /ə'gresɪv/ a. agressif. **~ion** /-ʃn/ n. agression f. **~iveness** n. agressivité f. **~or** n. agresseur m.

aggrieved /ə'griːvd/ a. peiné.

aghast /ə'gɑːst/ a. horrifié.

agil|e /'ædʒaɪl, Amer. 'ædʒl/ a. agile. **~ity** /ə'dʒɪlətɪ/ n. agilité f.

agitat|e /'ædʒɪteɪt/ v.t. agiter. **~ion** /-'teɪʃn/ n. agitation f. **~or** n. agita|teur, -trice m., f.

agnostic /æg'nɒstɪk/ a. & n. agnostique (m./f.).

ago /ə'gəʊ/ adv. il y a. **a month ~**, il y a un mois. **long ~**, il y a longtemps. **how long ~?**, il y a combien de temps?

agog /ə'gɒg/ a. impatient, en émoi.

agon|y /'ægənɪ/ n. grande souffrance f.; (**mental**) angoisse f. **~ize** v.i. souffrir. **~ize over**, se torturer l'esprit pour. **~ized** a. angoissé. **~izing** a. angoissant.

agree /ə'griː/ v.i. être or se mettre d'accord (**on, sur**); (**of figures**) concorder. ● v.t. (**date**) convenir de. **~ that**, reconnaître que. **~ to do**, accepter de faire. **~ to sth.**, accepter qch. **onions don't ~ with me**, je ne digère pas les oignons. **~d** a. (**time, place**) convenu. **be ~d**, être d'accord.

agreeable /ə'griːəbl/ a. agréable. **be ~**, (**willing**) être d'accord.

agreement /ə'griːmənt/ n. accord m. **in ~**, d'accord.

agricultur|e /'ægrɪkʌltʃə(r)/ n. agriculture f. **~al** /-'kʌltʃərəl/ a. agricole.

aground /ə'graʊnd/ adv. **run ~**, (**of ship**) (s')échouer.

ahead /ə'hed/ adv. (**in front**) en avant, devant; (**in advance**) à l'avance. **~ of s.o.**, devant qn.; en avance sur qn. **~ of time**, en avance. **straight ~**, tout droit.

aid /eɪd/ v.t. aider. ● n. aide f. **in ~ of**, au profit de.

aide /eɪd/ n. aide m./f.

AIDS /eɪdz/ n. (**med.**) sida m.

ail /eɪl/ v.t. **what ~s you?**, qu'avez-vous? **~ing** a. souffrant. **~ment** n. maladie f.

aim /eɪm/ v.t. diriger; (**gun**) braquer (**at, sur**); (**remark**) destiner. ● v.i. viser. ● n. but m. **~ at**, viser. **~ to**, avoir l'intention de. **take ~**, viser. **~less** a., **~lessly** adv. sans but.

air /eə(r)/ n. air m. ● v.t. aérer; (**views**) exposer librement. ● a.

(*base etc.*) aérien. ~**-bed** *n.* matelas pneumatique *m.* ~**-conditioned** *a.* climatisé. ~**-conditioning** *n.* climatisation *f.* ~ **force/hostess,** armée/ hôtesse de l'air *f.* ~ **letter,** aérogramme *m.* ~**mail,** poste aérienne *f.* **by ~mail,** par avion. ~ **raid,** attaque aérienne *f.* ~ **terminal,** aérogare *f.* ~ **traffic controller,** aiguilleur du ciel *m.* **by ~,** par avion. **in the ~,** (*rumour*) répandu; (*plan*) incertain. **on the ~,** à l'antenne.

airborne /ˈɛəbɔːn/ *a.* (en cours de) vol; (*troops*) aéroporté.

aircraft /ˈɛəkrɑːft/ *n. invar.* avion *m.* ~**-carrier** *n.* porte-avions *m. invar.*

airfield /ˈɛəfiːld/ *n.* terrain d'aviation *m.*

airgun /ˈɛəɡʌn/ *n.* carabine à air comprimé *f.*

airlift /ˈɛəlɪft/ *n.* pont aérien *m.* ● *v.t.* transporter par pont aérien.

airline /ˈɛəlaɪn/ *n.* ligne aérienne *f.* ~**r** /-ə(r)/ *n.* avion de ligne *m.*

airlock /ˈɛəlɒk/ *n.* (*in pipe*) bulle d'air *f.*; (*chamber: techn.*) sas *m.*

airman /ˈɛəmən/ *n.* (*pl.* **-men**) aviateur *m.*

airplane /ˈɛəpleɪn/ *n.* (*Amer.*) avion *m.*

airport /ˈɛəpɔːt/ *n.* aéroport *m.*

airsickness /ˈɛəsɪknɪs/ *n.* mal de l'air *m.*

airtight /ˈɛətaɪt/ *a.* hermétique.

airways /ˈɛəweɪz/ *n. pl.* compagnie d'aviation *f.*

airworthy /ˈɛəwɜːðɪ/ *a.* en état de navigation.

airy /ˈɛərɪ/ *a.* (**-ier, -iest**) bien aéré; (*manner*) désinvolte.

aisle /aɪl/ *n.* (*of church*) nef latérale *f.*; (*gangway*) couloir *m.*

ajar /əˈdʒɑː(r)/ *adv. & a.* entrouvert.

akin /əˈkɪn/ *a.* ~ **to,** apparenté à.

alabaster /ˈæləbɑːstə(r)/ *n.* albâtre *m.*

à la carte /ɑːlɑːˈkɑːt/ *adv. & a.* (*culin.*) à la carte.

alacrity /əˈlækrətɪ/ *n.* empressement *m.*

alarm /əˈlɑːm/ *n.* alarme *f.*; (*clock*) réveil *m.* ● *v.t.* alarmer. ~**-clock** *n.* réveil *m.*, réveille-matin *m. invar.* ~**ist** *n.* alarmiste *m./f.*

alas /əˈlæs/ *int.* hélas.

albatross /ˈælbətrɒs/ *n.* albatros *m.*

album /ˈælbəm/ *n.* album *m.*

alcohol /ˈælkəhɒl/ *n.* alcool *m.* ~**ic** /-ˈhɒlɪk/ *a.* alcoolique; (*drink*) alcoo-

lisé; *n.* alcoolique *m./f.* ~**ism** *n.* alcoolisme *m.*

alcove /ˈælkəʊv/ *n.* alcôve *f.*

ale /eɪl/ *n.* bière *f.*

alert /əˈlɜːt/ *a.* (*lively*) vif; (*watchful*) vigilant. ● *n.* alerte *f.* ● *v.t.* alerter. ~ **s.o. to,** prévenir qn. de. **on the ~,** sur le qui-vive. ~**ness** *n.* vivacité *f.*; vigilance *f.*

A-level /ˈeɪlevl/ *n.* baccalauréat *m.*

algebra /ˈældʒɪbrə/ *n.* algèbre *f.* ~**ic** /-ˈbreɪk/ *a.* algébrique.

Algeria /ælˈdʒɪərɪə/ *n.* Algérie *f.* ~**n** *a. & n.* algérien(ne) (*m.* (*f.*)).

algorithm /ˈælɡərɪðm/ *n.* algorithme *m.*

alias /ˈeɪlɪəs/ *n.* (*pl.* **-ases**) faux nom *m.* ● *adv.* alias.

alibi /ˈælɪbaɪ/ *n.* (*pl.* **-is**) alibi *m.*

alien /ˈeɪlɪən/ *n. & a.* étrang|er, -ère (*m., f.*) (**to,** à).

alienat|e /ˈeɪlɪəneɪt/ *v.t.* aliéner. ~**e one's friends/etc.,** s'aliéner ses amis/*etc.* ~**ion** /-ˈneɪʃn/ *n.* aliénation *f.*

alight [1] /əˈlaɪt/ *v.i.* (*person*) descendre; (*bird*) se poser.

alight [2] /əˈlaɪt/ *a.* en feu, allumé.

align /əˈlaɪn/ *v.t.* aligner. ~**ment** *n.* alignement *m.*

alike /əˈlaɪk/ *a.* semblable. ● *adv.* de la même façon. **look** *or* **be ~,** se ressembler.

alimony /ˈælɪmənɪ, *Amer.* -məʊnɪ/ *n.* pension alimentaire *f.*

alive /əˈlaɪv/ *a.* vivant. ~ **to,** sensible à, sensibilisé à. ~ **with,** grouillant de.

alkali /ˈælkəlaɪ/ *n.* (*pl.* **-is**) alcali *m.*

all /ɔːl/ *a.* tout(e), tous, toutes. ● *pron.* tous, toutes; (*everything*) tout. ● *adv.* tout. ~ **(the) men,** tous les hommes. ~ **of it,** (le) tout. ~ **of us,** nous tous. ~ **but,** presque. ~ **for sth.,** à fond pour qch. ~ **in,** (*exhausted*) épuisé. ~**-in** *a.* tout compris. ~**-in wrestling,** catch *m.* ~ **out,** à fond. ~**-out** *a.* (*effort*) maximum; (*finished*) fini. ~ **over,** partout (sur *or* dans); (*finished*) fini. ~ **right,** bien; (*agreeing*) bon! ~ **round,** dans tous les domaines; (*for all*) pour tous. ~**-round** *a.* général. ~ **there,** (*alert*) éveillé. ~ **the better,** tant mieux. ~ **the same,** tout de même. **the best of ~,** le meilleur.

allay /əˈleɪ/ *v.t.* calmer.

allegation /ælɪˈɡeɪʃn/ *n.* allégation *f.*

allege /əˈledʒ/ v.t. prétendre. ~**dly** /-ɪdlɪ/ adv. d'après ce qu'on dit.

allegiance /əˈliːdʒəns/ n. fidélité f.

allerg|**y** /ˈælədʒɪ/ n. allergie f. ~**ic** /əˈlɜːdʒɪk/ a. allergique (**to**, à).

alleviate /əˈliːvɪeɪt/ v.t. alléger.

alley /ˈælɪ/ n. (street) ruelle f.

alliance /əˈlaɪəns/ n. alliance f.

allied /ˈælaɪd/ a. allié.

alligator /ˈælɪɡeɪtə(r)/ n. alligator m.

allocat|**e** /ˈæləkeɪt/ v.t. (assign) attribuer; (share out) distribuer. ~**ion** /-ˈkeɪʃn/ n. allocation f.

allot /əˈlɒt/ v.t. (p.t. **allotted**) attribuer. ~**ment** n. attribution f.; (share) partage m.; (land) parcelle de terre f. (louée pour la culture).

allow /əˈlaʊ/ v.t. permettre; (grant) accorder; (reckon on) prévoir; (agree) reconnaître. ~ **s.o. to**, permettre à qn. de. ~ **for**, tenir compte de.

allowance /əˈlaʊəns/ n. allocation f., indemnité f. **make** ~**s for**, être indulgent envers; (take into account) tenir compte de.

alloy /ˈælɔɪ/ n. alliage m.

allude /əˈluːd/ v.i. ~ **to**, faire allusion à.

allure /əˈlʊə(r)/ v.t. attirer.

allusion /əˈluːʒn/ n. allusion f.

ally[1] /ˈælaɪ/ n. allié(e) m. (f.).

ally[2] /əˈlaɪ/ v.t. allier. ~ **o.s. with**, s'allier à or avec.

almanac /ˈɔːlmənæk/ n. almanach m.

almighty /ɔːlˈmaɪtɪ/ a. tout-puissant; (very great: fam.) sacré, formidable.

almond /ˈɑːmənd/ n. amande f.

almost /ˈɔːlməʊst/ adv. presque.

alms /ɑːmz/ n. aumône f.

alone /əˈləʊn/ a. & adv. seul.

along /əˈlɒŋ/ prep. le long de. ● adv. **come** ~, venir. **go** or **walk** ~, passer. **all** ~, (time) tout le temps, depuis le début. ~ **with**, avec.

alongside /əlɒŋˈsaɪd/ adv. (naut.) bord à bord. **come** ~, accoster. ● prep. le long de.

aloof /əˈluːf/ adv. à l'écart. ● a. distant. ~**ness** n. réserve f.

aloud /əˈlaʊd/ adv. à haute voix.

alphabet /ˈælfəbet/ n. alphabet m. ~**ical** /-ˈbetɪkl/ a. alphabétique.

alpine /ˈælpaɪn/ a. (landscape) alpestre; (climate) alpin.

Alpine /ˈælpaɪn/ a. des Alpes.

Alps /ælps/ n. pl. **the** ~, les Alpes f. pl.

already /ɔːlˈredɪ/ adv. déjà.

alright /ɔːlˈraɪt/ a. & adv. = **all right**.

Alsatian /ælˈseɪʃn/ n. (dog) berger allemand m.

also /ˈɔːlsəʊ/ adv. aussi.

altar /ˈɔːltə(r)/ n. autel m.

alter /ˈɔːltə(r)/ v.t./i. changer. ~**ation** /-ˈreɪʃn/ n. changement m.; (to garment) retouche f.

alternate[1] /ɔːlˈtɜːnət/ a. alterné, alternatif; (Amer.) = **alternative**. **on** ~ **days**/etc., (first one then the other) tous les deux jours/etc. ~**ly** adv. tour à tour.

alternate[2] /ˈɔːltəneɪt/ v.i. alterner. ● v.t. faire alterner.

alternative /ɔːlˈtɜːnətɪv/ a. autre; (policy) de rechange. ● n. alternative f., choix m. ~**ly** adv. comme alternative. **or** ~**ly**, ou alors.

alternator /ˈɔːltəneɪtə(r)/ n. alternateur m.

although /ɔːlˈðəʊ/ conj. bien que.

altitude /ˈæltɪtjuːd/ n. altitude f.

altogether /ɔːltəˈɡeðə(r)/ adv. (completely) tout à fait; (on the whole) à tout prendre.

alumini|**um** /æljʊˈmɪnɪəm/ (Amer. **aluminum** /əˈluːmɪnəm/) n. aluminium m.

always /ˈɔːlweɪz/ adv. toujours.

am /æm/ see **be**.

a.m. /ˈeɪˈem/ adv. du matin.

amalgamate /əˈmælɡəmeɪt/ v.t./i. (s')amalgamer; (comm.) fusionner.

amass /əˈmæs/ v.t. amasser.

amateur /ˈæmətə(r)/ n. amateur m. ● a. (musician etc.) amateur invar. ~**ish** a. (pej.) d'amateur. ~**ishly** adv. en amateur.

amaz|**e** /əˈmeɪz/ v.t. étonner. ~**ed** a. étonné. ~**ement** n. étonnement m. ~**ingly** adv. étonnamment.

ambassador /æmˈbæsədə(r)/ n. ambassadeur m.

amber /ˈæmbə(r)/ n. ambre m.; (auto.) feu orange m.

ambigu|**ous** /æmˈbɪɡjʊəs/ a. ambigu. ~**ity** /-ˈgjuːətɪ/ n. ambiguïté f.

ambiti|**on** /æmˈbɪʃn/ n. ambition f. ~**ous** a. ambitieux.

ambivalent /æmˈbɪvələnt/ a. ambigu, ambivalent.

amble /ˈæmbl/ v.i. marcher sans se presser, s'avancer lentement.

ambulance /ˈæmbjʊləns/ n. ambulance f.

ambush /ˈæmbʊʃ/ n. embuscade f. ● v.t. tendre une embuscade à.

amenable /ə'mi:nəbl/ a. obligeant. ~ **to**, (*responsive*) sensible à.

amend /ə'mend/ v.t. modifier, corriger. ~**ment** n. (*to rule*) amendement m.

amends /ə'mendz/ n. pl. **make ~**, réparer son erreur.

amenities /ə'mi:nətɪz/ n. pl. (*pleasant features*) attraits m. pl.; (*facilities*) aménagements m. pl

America /ə'merɪkə/ n. Amérique f. ~**n** a. & n. américain(e) (m. (f.)).

amiable /'eɪmɪəbl/ a. aimable.

amicable /'æmɪkəbl/ a. amical.

amid(st) /ə'mɪd(st)/ prep. au milieu de.

amiss /ə'mɪs/ a. & adv. mal. **sth. ~**, qch. qui ne va pas. **take sth. ~**, être offensé par qch.

ammonia /ə'məʊnɪə/ n. (*gas*) ammoniac m.; (*water*) ammoniaque m.

ammunition /æmjʊ'nɪʃn/ n. munitions f. pl.

amnesia /æm'ni:zɪə/ n. amnésie f.

amnesty /'æmnəstɪ/ n. amnistie f.

amok /ə'mɒk/ adv. **run ~**, devenir fou furieux; (*crowd*) se déchaîner.

among(st) /ə'mʌŋ(st)/ prep. parmi, entre. ~ **the crowd**, (*in the middle of*) parmi la foule. ~ **the English**/etc., (*race, group*) chez les Anglais/etc. ~ **ourselves**/etc., entre nous/etc.

amoral /eɪ'mɒrəl/ a. amoral.

amorous /'æmərəs/ a. amoureux.

amorphous /ə'mɔ:fəs/ a. amorphe.

amount /ə'maʊnt/ n. quantité f.; (*total*) montant m.; (*sum of money*) somme f. ● v.i. ~ **to**, (*add up to*) s'élever à; (*be equivalent to*) revenir à.

amp /æmp/ n. (*fam.*) ampère m.

ampere /'æmpeə(r)/ n. ampère m.

amphibian /æm'fɪbɪən/ n. amphibie m. ~**ous** a. amphibie.

ample /'æmpl/ a. (**-er, -est**) (*enough*) (bien) assez de; (*large, roomy*) ample. ~**y** adv. amplement.

amplify /'æmplɪfaɪ/ v.t. amplifier. ~**ier** n. amplificateur m.

amputate /'æmpjʊteɪt/ v.t. amputer. ~**ion** /-'teɪʃn/ n. amputation f.

amuck /ə'mʌk/ see amok.

amuse /ə'mju:z/ v.t. amuser. ~**ment** n. amusement m., divertissement m. ~**ment arcade**, salle de jeux f.

an /æn, unstressed ən/ see a.

anachronism /ə'nækrənɪzəm/ n. anachronisme m.

anaemia /ə'ni:mɪə/ n. anémie f. ~**ic** a. anémique.

anaesthetic /ænɪs'θetɪk/ n. anesthésique m. **give an ~**, faire une anesthésie (**to**, à).

analogue, analog /'ænəlɒg/ a. analogique.

analogy /ə'nælədʒɪ/ n. analogie f.

analyse (*Amer.* **analyze**) /'ænəlaɪz/ v.t. analyser. ~**t** /-ɪst/ n. analyste m./f.

analysis /ə'næləsɪs/ n. (pl. **-yses** /-əsi:z/) analyse f.

analytic(al) /ænə'lɪtɪk(l)/ a. analytique.

anarchy /'ænəkɪ/ n. anarchie f. ~**ist** n. anarchiste m./f.

anathema /ə'næθəmə/ n. **that is ~ to me**, j'ai cela en abomination.

anatomy /ə'nætəmɪ/ n. anatomie f. ~**ical** /ænə'tɒmɪkl/ a. anatomique.

ancestor /'ænsestə(r)/ n. ancêtre m. ~**ral** /-'sestrəl/ a. ancestral.

anchor /'æŋkə(r)/ n. ancre f. ● v.t. mettre à l'ancre. ● v.i. jeter l'ancre.

anchovy /'æntʃəvɪ/ n. anchois m.

ancient /'eɪnʃənt/ a. ancien.

ancillary /æn'sɪlərɪ/ a. auxiliaire.

and /ænd, unstressed ən(d)/ conj. et. **go ~ see him**, allez le voir. **richer ~ richer**, de plus en plus riche.

anecdote /'ænɪkdəʊt/ n. anecdote f.

anemia /ə'ni:mɪə/ n. (*Amer.*) = **anaemia**.

anesthetic /ænɪs'θetɪk/ (*Amer.*) = **anaesthetic**.

anew /ə'nju:/ adv. de or à nouveau.

angel /'eɪndʒl/ n. ange m. ~**ic** /æn'dʒelɪk/ a. angélique.

anger /'æŋgə(r)/ n. colère f. ● v.t. mettre en colère, fâcher.

angle¹ /'æŋgl/ n. angle m.

angle² /'æŋgl/ v.i. pêcher (à la ligne). ~ **for**, (*fig.*) quêter. ~**r** /-ə(r)/ n. pêcheur/-se m., f.

Anglican /'æŋglɪkən/ a. & n. anglican(e) (m. (f.)).

Anglo- /'æŋgləʊ/ pref. anglo-.

Anglo-Saxon /'æŋgləʊ'sæksn/ a. & n. anglo-saxon(ne) (m. (f.)).

angry /'æŋgrɪ/ a. (**-ier, -iest**) fâché, en colère. **get ~y**, se fâcher, se mettre en colère (**with**, contre). **make s.o. ~y**, mettre qn. en colère. ~**ily** adv. en colère.

anguish /'æŋgwɪʃ/ n. angoisse f.

angular /'æŋgjʊlə(r)/ a. (*features*) anguleux.

animal /'ænɪml/ n. & a. animal (m.).

animate¹ /'ænɪmət/ a. animé.

animat|e² /'ænɪmeɪt/ v.t. animer. **~ion** /-'meɪʃn/ n. animation f.

animosity /ænɪ'mɒsətɪ/ n. animosité f.

aniseed /'ænɪsiːd/ n. anis m.

ankle /'æŋkl/ n. cheville f. **~ sock**, socquette f.

annex /ə'neks/ v.t. annexer. **~ation** /ænek'seɪʃn/ n. annexion f.

annexe /'æneks/ n. annexe f.

annihilate /ə'naɪəleɪt/ v.t. anéantir.

anniversary /ænɪ'vɜːsərɪ/ n. anniversaire m.

announce /ə'naʊns/ v.t. annoncer. **~ment** n. annonce f. **~r** /-ə(r)/ n. (radio, TV) speaker(ine) m. (f.).

annoy /ə'nɔɪ/ v.t. agacer, ennuyer. **~ance** n. contrariété f. **~ed** a. fâché (with, contre). **get ~ed**, se fâcher. **~ing** a. ennuyeux.

annual /'ænjʊəl/ a. annuel. ● n. publication annuelle f. **~ly** adv. annuellement.

annuity /ə'njuːətɪ/ n. rente (viagère) f.

annul /ə'nʌl/ v.t. (p.t. **annulled**) annuler. **~ment** n. annulation f.

anomal|y /ə'nɒməlɪ/ n. anomalie f. **~ous** a. anormal.

anonym|ous /ə'nɒnɪməs/ a. anonyme. **~ity** /ænə'nɪmətɪ/ n. anonymat m.

anorak /'ænəræk/ n. anorak m.

another /ə'nʌðə(r)/ a. & pron. un(e) autre. **~ coffee**, (one more) encore un café. **~ ten minutes**, dix minutes de plus.

answer /'ɑːnsə(r)/ n. réponse f.; (solution) solution f. ● v.t. répondre à; (prayer) exaucer. ● v.i. répondre. **~ the door**, ouvrir la porte. **~ back**, répondre. **~ for**, répondre de. **~ to**, (superior) dépendre de; (description) répondre à. **~able** a. responsable (for, de; to, devant). **~ing machine**, répondeur m.

ant /ænt/ n. fourmi f.

antagonis|m /æn'tægənɪzəm/ n. antagonisme m. **~tic** /-'nɪstɪk/ a. antagoniste.

antagonize /æn'tægənaɪz/ v.t. provoquer l'hostilité de.

Antarctic /æn'tɑːktɪk/ a. & n. antarctique (m.).

ante- /'æntɪ/ pref. anti-, anté-.

antelope /'æntɪləʊp/ n. antilope f.

antenatal /'æntɪneɪtl/ a. prénatal.

antenna /æn'tenə/ n. (pl. **-ae** /-iː/) (of insect) antenne f.; (pl. **-as**; aerial: Amer.) antenne f.

anthem /'ænθəm/ n. (relig.) motet m.; (of country) hymne national m.

anthology /æn'θɒlədʒɪ/ n. anthologie f.

anthropolog|y /ænθrə'pɒlədʒɪ/ n. anthropologie f. **~ist** n. anthropologue m./f.

anti- /'æntɪ/ pref. anti-. **~-aircraft** a. antiaérien.

antibiotic /æntɪbaɪ'ɒtɪk/ n. antibiotique m.

antibody /'æntɪbɒdɪ/ n. anticorps m.

antic /'æntɪk/ n. bouffonnerie f.

anticipat|e /æn'tɪsɪpeɪt/ v.t. (foresee, expect) prévoir, s'attendre à; (forestall) devancer. **~ion** /-'peɪʃn/ n. attente f. **in ~ion of**, en prévision or attente de.

anticlimax /æntɪ'klaɪmæks/ n. (letdown) déception f. **it was an ~**, ça n'a pas répondu à l'attente.

anticlockwise /æntɪ'klɒkwaɪz/ adv. & a. dans le sens inverse des aiguilles d'une montre.

anticyclone /æntɪ'saɪkləʊn/ n. anticyclone m.

antidote /'æntɪdəʊt/ n. antidote m.

antifreeze /'æntɪfriːz/ n. antigel m.

antihistamine /æntɪ'hɪstəmiːn/ n. antihistaminique m.

antipathy /æn'tɪpəθɪ/ n. antipathie f.

antiquated /'æntɪkweɪtɪd/ a. vieillot, suranné.

antique /æn'tiːk/ a. (old) ancien; (from antiquity) antique. ● n. objet ancien m., antiquité f. **~ dealer**, antiquaire m./f. **~ shop**, magasin d'antiquités m.

antiquity /æn'tɪkwətɪ/ n. antiquité f.

anti-Semiti|c /æntɪsɪ'mɪtɪk/ a. antisémite. **~sm** /-'semɪtɪzəm/ n. antisémitisme m.

antiseptic /æntɪ'septɪk/ a. & n. antiseptique (m.).

antisocial /æntɪ'səʊʃl/ a. asocial, antisocial; (unsociable) insociable.

antithesis /æn'tɪθəsɪs/ n. (pl. **-eses** /-əsiːz/) antithèse f.

antlers /'æntləz/ n. pl. bois m. pl.

anus /'eɪnəs/ n. anus m.

anvil /'ænvɪl/ n. enclume f.

anxiety /æŋ'zaɪətɪ/ n. (worry) anxiété f.; (eagerness) impatience f.

anxious /'æŋkʃəs/ a. (troubled) anxieux; (eager) impatient (to, de).

~ly adv. anxieusement; impatiemment.

any /'enɪ/ a. (some) du, de l', de la, des; (after negative) de, d'; (every) tout; (no matter which) n'importe quel. **at ~ moment**, à tout moment. **have you ~ water?**, avez-vous de l'eau? ● pron. (no matter which one) n'importe lequel; (someone) quelqu'un; (any amount of it or them) en. **I do not have ~**, je n'en ai pas. **did you see ~ of them?**, en avez-vous vu? ● adv. (a little) un peu. **do you have ~ more?**, en avez-vous encore? **do you have ~ more tea?**, avez-vous encore du thé? **not ~**, nullement. **I don't do it ~ more**, je ne le fais plus.

anybody /'enɪbɒdɪ/ pron. n'importe qui; (somebody) quelqu'un; (after negative) personne. **he did not see ~**, il n'a vu personne.

anyhow /'enɪhaʊ/ adv. de toute façon; (badly) n'importe comment.

anyone /'enɪwʌn/ pron. = **anybody**.

anything /'enɪθɪŋ/ pron. n'importe quoi; (something) quelque chose; (after negative) rien. **he did not see ~**, il n'a rien vu. **~ but**, (cheap etc.) nullement. **~ you do**, tout ce que tu fais.

anyway /'enɪweɪ/ adv. de toute façon.

anywhere /'enɪweə(r)/ adv. n'importe où; (somewhere) quelque part; (after negative) nulle part. **he does not go ~**, il ne va nulle part. **~ you go**, partout où tu vas, où que tu ailles. **~ else**, partout ailleurs.

apart /ə'pɑːt/ adv. (on or to one side) à part; (separated) séparé; (into pieces) en pièces. **~ from**, à part, excepté. **ten metres ~**, (distant) à dix mètres l'un de l'autre. **come ~**, (break) tomber en morceaux; (machine) se démonter. **legs ~**, les jambes écartées. **keep ~**, séparer. **take ~**, démonter.

apartment /ə'pɑːtmənt/ n. (Amer.) appartement m. **~s**, logement m.

apath|y /'æpəθɪ/ n. apathie f. **~etic** /-'θetɪk/ a. apathique.

ape /eɪp/ n. singe m. ● v.t. singer.

aperitif /ə'perətɪf/ n. apéritif m.

aperture /'æpətʃə(r)/ n. ouverture f.

apex /'eɪpeks/ n. sommet m.

apiece /ə'piːs/ adv. chacun.

apologetic /əpɒlə'dʒetɪk/ a. (tone etc.) d'excuse. **be ~**, s'excuser. **~ally** /-lɪ/ adv. en s'excusant.

apologize /ə'pɒlədʒaɪz/ v.i. s'excuser (for, de; to, auprès de).

apology /ə'pɒlədʒɪ/ n. excuses f. pl.; (defence of belief) apologie f.

Apostle /ə'pɒsl/ n. apôtre m.

apostrophe /ə'pɒstrəfɪ/ n. apostrophe f.

appal /ə'pɔːl/ v.t. (p.t. **appalled**) épouvanter. **~ling** a. épouvantable.

apparatus /æpə'reɪtəs/ n. (machine & anat.) appareil m.

apparel /ə'pærəl/ n. habillement m.

apparent /ə'pærənt/ a. apparent. **~ly** adv. apparemment.

appeal /ə'piːl/ n. appel m.; (attractiveness) attrait m., charme m. ● v.i. (jurid.) faire appel. **~ to s.o.**, (beg) faire appel à qn.; (attract) plaire à qn. **~ to s.o. for sth.**, demander qch. à qn. **~ing** a. (attractive) attirant.

appear /ə'pɪə(r)/ v.i. apparaître; (arrive) se présenter; (seem, be published) paraître; (theatre) jouer. **~ on TV**, passer à la télé. **~ance** n. apparition f.; (aspect) apparence f.

appease /ə'piːz/ v.t. apaiser.

appendicitis /əpendɪ'saɪtɪs/ n. appendicite f.

appendix /ə'pendɪks/ n. (pl. **-ices** /-ɪsiːz/) appendice m.

appetite /'æpɪtaɪt/ n. appétit m.

appetizer /'æpɪtaɪzə(r)/ n. (snack) amuse-gueule m. invar.; (drink) apéritif m.

appetizing /'æpɪtaɪzɪŋ/ a. appétissant.

applau|d /ə'plɔːd/ v.t./i. applaudir; (decision) applaudir à. **~se** n. applaudissements m. pl.

apple /'æpl/ n. pomme f. **~-tree** n. pommier m.

appliance /ə'plaɪəns/ n. appareil m.

applicable /'æplɪkəbl/ a. applicable.

applicant /'æplɪkənt/ n. candidat(e) m. (f.) (for, à).

application /æplɪ'keɪʃn/ n. application f.; (request, form) demande f.; (for job) candidature f.

apply /ə'plaɪ/ v.t. appliquer. ● v.i. **~ to**, (refer) s'appliquer à; (ask) s'adresser à. **~ for**, (job) postuler pour; (grant) demander. **~ o.s. to**, s'appliquer à. **applied** a. appliqué.

appoint /ə'pɔɪnt/ v.t. (to post) nommer; (fix) désigner. **well-~ed** a. bien équipé. **~ment** n. nomination f.; (meeting) rendez-vous m. invar.;

(*job*) poste *m*. **make an ~ment**, prendre rendez-vous (**with**, avec).

apportion /ə'pɔːʃn/ *v.t.* répartir.

apprais|e /ə'preɪz/ *v.t.* évaluer. **~al** *n*. évaluation *f*.

appreciable /ə'priːʃəbl/ *a*. appréciable.

appreciat|e /ə'priːʃɪeɪt/ *v.t.* (*like*) apprécier; (*understand*) comprendre; (*be grateful for*) être reconnaissant de. ● *v.i.* prendre de la valeur. **~ion** /-'eɪʃn/ *n*. appréciation *f*.; (*gratitude*) reconnaissance *f*.; (*rise*) augmentation *f*. **~ive** /ə'priːʃɪətɪv/ *a*. reconnaissant; (*audience*) enthousiaste.

apprehend /æprɪ'hend/ *v.t.* (*arrest, fear*) appréhender; (*understand*) comprendre. **~sion** *n*. appréhension *f*.

apprehensive /æprɪ'hensɪv/ *a*. inquiet. **be ~ of**, craindre.

apprentice /ə'prentɪs/ *n*. apprenti *m*. ● *v.t.* mettre en apprentissage. **~ship** *n*. apprentissage *m*.

approach /ə'prəʊtʃ/ *v.t.* (s')approcher de; (*accost*) aborder; (*with request*) s'adresser à. ● *v.i.* (s')approcher. ● *n*. approche *f*. **an ~ to**, (*problem*) une façon d'aborder; (*person*) une démarche auprès de. **~able** *a*. accessible; (*person*) abordable.

appropriate [1] /ə'prəʊprɪət/ *a*. approprié, propre. **~ly** *adv*. à propos.

appropriate [2] /ə'prəʊprɪeɪt/ *v.t.* s'approprier.

approval /ə'pruːvl/ *n*. approbation *f*. **on ~**, à *or* sous condition.

approv|e /ə'pruːv/ *v.t./i.* approuver. **~e of**, approuver. **~ingly** *adv*. d'un air *or* d'un ton approbateur.

approximate [1] /ə'prɒksɪmət/ *a*. approximatif. **~ly** *adv*. approximativement.

approximat|e [2] /ə'prɒksɪmeɪt/ *v.i.* **~e to**, se rapprocher de. **~ion** /-'meɪʃn/ *n*. approximation *f*.

apricot /'eɪprɪkɒt/ *n*. abricot *m*.

April /'eɪprəl/ *n*. avril *m*. **make an ~ fool of**, faire un poisson d'avril à.

apron /'eɪprən/ *n*. tablier *m*.

apse /æps/ *n*. (*of church*) abside *f*.

apt /æpt/ *a*. (*suitable*) approprié; (*pupil*) doué. **be ~ to**, avoir tendance à. **~ly** *adv*. à propos.

aptitude /'æptɪtjuːd/ *n*. aptitude *f*.

aqualung /'ækwəlʌŋ/ *n*. scaphandre autonome *m*.

aquarium /ə'kweərɪəm/ *n*. (*pl.* **-ums**) aquarium *m*.

Aquarius /ə'kweərɪəs/ *n*. le Verseau.

aquatic /ə'kwætɪk/ *a*. aquatique; (*sport*) nautique.

aqueduct /'ækwɪdʌkt/ *n*. aqueduc *m*.

Arab /'ærəb/ *n*. & *a*. arabe (*m./f.*). **~ic** *a*. & *n*. (*lang.*) arabe (*m.*). **~ic numerals**, chiffres arabes *m. pl.*

Arabian /ə'reɪbɪən/ *a*. arabe.

arable /'ærəbl/ *a*. arable.

arbiter /'ɑːbɪtə(r)/ *n*. arbitre *m*.

arbitrary /'ɑːbɪtrərɪ/ *a*. arbitraire.

arbitrat|e /'ɑːbɪtreɪt/ *v.i.* arbitrer. **~ion** /-'treɪʃn/ *n*. arbitrage *m*. **~or** *n*. arbitre *m*.

arc /ɑːk/ *n*. arc *m*.

arcade /ɑː'keɪd/ *n*. (*shops*) galerie *f*.; (*arches*) arcades *f. pl*.

arch [1] /ɑːtʃ/ *n*. arche *f*.; (*in church etc.*) arc *m*.; (*of foot*) voûte plantaire *f*. ● *v.t./i.* (s')arquer.

arch [2] /ɑːtʃ/ *a*. (*playful*) malicieux.

arch- /ɑːtʃ/ *pref*. (*hypocrite etc.*) grand, achevé.

archaeolog|y /ɑːkɪ'ɒlədʒɪ/ *n*. archéologie *f*. **~ical** /-ə'lɒdʒɪkl/ *a*. archéologique. **~ist** *n*. archéologue *m./f*.

archaic /ɑː'keɪɪk/ *a*. archaïque.

archbishop /ɑːtʃ'bɪʃəp/ *n*. archevêque *m*.

archeology /ɑːkɪ'ɒlədʒɪ/ *n*. (*Amer.*) = **archaeology**.

archer /'ɑːtʃə(r)/ *n*. archer *m*. **~y** *n*. tir à l'arc *m*.

archetype /'ɑːkɪtaɪp/ *n*. archétype *m*., modèle *m*.

archipelago /ɑːkɪ'peləgəʊ/ *n*. (*pl.* **-os**) archipel *m*.

architect /'ɑːkɪtekt/ *n*. architecte *m*.

architectur|e /'ɑːkɪtektʃə(r)/ *n*. architecture *f*. **~al** /-'tektʃərəl/ *a*. architectural.

archiv|es /'ɑːkaɪvz/ *n. pl*. archives *f. pl*. **~ist** /-ɪvɪst/ *n*. archiviste *m./f*.

archway /'ɑːtʃweɪ/ *n*. voûte *f*.

Arctic /'ɑːktɪk/ *a*. & *n*. arctique (*m.*). **arctic** *a*. glacial.

ardent /'ɑːdnt/ *a*. ardent. **~ly** *adv*. ardemment.

ardour /'ɑːdə(r)/ *n*. ardeur *f*.

arduous /'ɑːdjʊəs/ *a*. ardu.

are /ɑː(r)/ *see* **be**.

area /'eərɪə/ *n*. (*surface*) superficie *f*.; (*region*) région *f*.; (*district*) quartier *m*.; (*fig.*) domaine *m*. **parking/picnic ~**, aire de parking/de pique-nique *f*.

arena /ə'riːnə/ *n*. arène *f*.

aren't /ɑːnt/ = are not.

Argentin|a /ɑːdʒən'tiːnə/ n. Argentine f. **~e** /'ɑːdʒəntain/, **~ian** /-'tɪnɪən/ a. & n. argentin(e) (m. (f.)).

argu|e /'ɑːgjuː/ v.i. (quarrel) se disputer; (reason) argumenter. ● v.t. (debate) discuter. **~e that**, alléguer que. **~able** /-'vəbl/ a. le cas selon certains. **~ably** adv. selon certains.

argument /'ɑːgjʊmənt/ n. dispute f.; (reasoning) argument m.; (discussion) débat m. **~ative** /-'mentətɪv/ a. raisonneur, contrariant.

arid /'ærɪd/ a. aride.

Aries /'eəriːz/ n. le Bélier.

arise /ə'raɪz/ v.i. (p.t. **arose**, p.p. **arisen**) se présenter; (old use) se lever. **~ from**, résulter de.

aristocracy /ærɪ'stɒkrəsɪ/ n. aristocratie f.

aristocrat /'ærɪstəkræt/, Amer. ə'rɪstəkræt/ n. aristocrate m./f. **~ic** /-'krætɪk/ a. aristocratique.

arithmetic /ə'rɪθmətɪk/ n. arithmétique f.

ark /ɑːk/ n. (relig.) arche f.

arm [1] /ɑːm/ n. bras m. **~ in arm**, bras dessus bras dessous. **~-band** n. brassard m.

arm [2] /ɑːm/ v.t. armer. **~ed robbery**, vol à main armée m.

armament /'ɑːməmənt/ n. armement m.

armchair /'ɑːmtʃeə(r)/ n. fauteuil m.

armistice /'ɑːmɪstɪs/ n. armistice m.

armour /'ɑːmə(r)/ n. armure f.; (on tanks etc.) blindage m. **~-clad**, **~ed** adjs. blindé.

armoury /'ɑːmərɪ/ n. arsenal m.

armpit /'ɑːmpɪt/ n. aisselle f.

arms /ɑːmz/ n. pl. (weapons) armes f. pl. **~ dealer**, trafiquant d'armes m.

army /'ɑːmɪ/ n. armée f.

aroma /ə'rəʊmə/ n. arôme m. **~tic** /ærə'mætɪk/ a. aromatique.

arose /ə'rəʊz/ see arise.

around /ə'raʊnd/ adv. (tout) autour; (here and there) çà et là. ● prep. autour de. **~ here**, par ici.

arouse /ə'raʊz/ v.t. (awaken, cause) éveiller; (excite) exciter.

arrange /ə'reɪndʒ/ v.t. arranger; (time, date) fixer. **~ to**, s'arranger pour. **~ment** n. arrangement m. **make ~ments**, prendre des dispositions.

array /ə'reɪ/ v.t. (mil.) déployer; (dress) vêtir. ● n. **an ~ of**, (display) un étalage impressionnant de.

arrears /ə'rɪəz/ n. pl. arriéré m. **in ~**, (rent) arriéré. **he is in ~**, il a des paiements en retard.

arrest /ə'rest/ v.t. arrêter; (attention) retenir. ● n. arrestation f. **under ~**, en état d'arrestation.

arrival /ə'raɪvl/ n. arrivée f. **new ~**, nouveau venu m., nouvelle venue f.

arrive /ə'raɪv/ v.i. arriver.

arrogan|t /'ærəgənt/ a. arrogant. **~ce** n. arrogance f. **~tly** adv. avec arrogance.

arrow /'ærəʊ/ n. flèche f.

arse /ɑːs/ n. (sl.) cul m. (sl.)

arsenal /'ɑːsənl/ n. arsenal m.

arsenic /'ɑːsnɪk/ n. arsenic m.

arson /'ɑːsn/ n. incendie criminel m. **~ist** n. incendiaire m./f.

art /ɑːt/ n. art m.; (fine arts) beaux-arts m. pl. **~s**, (univ.) lettres f. pl. **~ gallery**, (public) musée (d'art) m.; (private) galerie (d'art) f. **~ school**, école des beaux-arts f.

artefact /'ɑːtɪfækt/ n. objet fabriqué m.

arter|y /'ɑːtərɪ/ n. artère f. **~ial** /-'tɪərɪəl/ a. artériel. **~ial road**, route principale f.

artful /'ɑːtfl/ a. astucieux, rusé. **~ness** n. astuce f.

arthriti|s /ɑː'θraɪtɪs/ n. arthrite f. **~c** /-ɪtɪk/ a. arthritique.

artichoke /'ɑːtɪtʃəʊk/ n. artichaut m.

article /'ɑːtɪkl/ n. article m. **~ of clothing**, vêtement m. **~d** a. (jurid.) en stage.

articulate [1] /ɑː'tɪkjʊlət/ a. (person) capable de s'exprimer clairement; (speech) distinct.

articulat|e [2] /ɑː'tɪkjʊleɪt/ v.t./i. articuler. **~ed lorry**, semi-remorque m. **~ion** /-'leɪʃn/ n. articulation f.

artifice /'ɑːtɪfɪs/ n. artifice m.

artificial /ɑːtɪ'fɪʃl/ a. artificiel. **~ity** /-fɪ'ælətɪ/ n. manque de naturel m.

artillery /ɑː'tɪlərɪ/ n. artillerie f.

artisan /ɑːtɪ'zæn/ n. artisan m.

artist /'ɑːtɪst/ n. artiste m./f. **~ic** /-'tɪstɪk/ a. artistique. **~ry** n. art m.

artiste /ɑː'tiːst/ n. (entertainer) artiste m./f.

artless /'ɑːtlɪs/ a. ingénu, naïf.

artwork /'ɑːtwɜːk/ n. (of book) illustrations f. pl.

as /æz, unstressed əz/ adv. & conj. comme; (while) pendant que. **as you get older**, en vieillissant. **as she came in**, en entrant. **as a mother**, en tant que mère. **as a gift**, en cadeau.

as from Monday, à partir de lundi. **as tall as**, aussi grand que. **~ for, as to**, quant à. **~ if**, comme si. **you look as if you're tired**, vous avez l'air (d'être) fatigué. **as much, as many**, autant (**as**, que). **as soon as**, aussitôt que. **as well**, aussi (**as**, bien que). **as wide as possible**, aussi large que possible.

asbestos /æz'bestɒs/ *n.* amiante *f.*

ascend /ə'send/ *v.t.* gravir; (*throne*) monter sur. ● *v.i.* monter. **~ant** *n.* **be in the ~ant**, monter.

ascent /ə'sent/ *n.* (*climbing*) ascension *f.*; (*slope*) côte *f.*

ascertain /æsə'tem/ *v.t.* s'assurer de. **~ that**, s'assurer que.

ascetic /ə'setik/ *a.* ascétique. ● *n.* ascète *m./f.*

ascribe /ə'skraib/ *v.t.* attribuer.

ash [1] /æʃ/ *n.* **~(-tree)**, frêne *m.*

ash [2] /æʃ/ *n.* cendre *f.* **Ash Wednesday**, Mercredi des Cendres *m.* **~en** *a.* cendreux.

ashamed /ə'ʃeimd/ *a.* **be ~**, avoir honte (**of**, de).

ashore /ə'ʃɔː(r)/ *adv.* à terre.

ashtray /'æʃtrei/ *n.* cendrier *m.*

Asia /'eiʃə, *Amer.* 'eiʒə/ *n.* Asie *f.* **~n** *a.* & *n.* asiatique (*m./f.*). **the ~n community**, la communauté indo-pakistanaise. **~tic** /-r'ætik/ *a.* asiatique.

aside /ə'said/ *adv.* de côté. ● *n.* aparté *m.* **~ from**, à part.

ask /ɑːsk/ *v.t./i.* demander; (*a question*) poser; (*invite*) inviter. **~ s.o. sth.**, demander qch. à qn. **~ s.o. to do**, demander à qn. de faire. **~ about**, (*thing*) se renseigner sur; (*person*) demander des nouvelles de. **~ for**, demander.

askance /ə'skæns/ *adv.* **look ~ at**, regarder avec méfiance.

askew /ə'skjuː/ *adv.* & *a.* de travers.

asleep /ə'sliːp/ *a.* endormi; (*numb*) engourdi. ● *adv.* **fall ~**, s'endormir.

asparagus /ə'spærəgəs/ *n.* (*plant*) asperge *f.*; (*culin.*) asperges *f. pl.*

aspect /'æspekt/ *n.* aspect *m.*; (*direction*) orientation *f.*

aspersions /ə'spɜːʃnz/ *n. pl.* **cast ~ on**, calomnier.

asphalt /'æsfælt, *Amer.* 'æsfɔːlt/ *n.* asphalte *m.* ● *v.t.* asphalter.

asphyxiate /əs'fiksieit/ *v.t./i.* (s')asphyxier. **~ion** /-'eiʃn/ *n.* asphyxie *f.*

aspir|e /əs'paiə(r)/ *v.i.* **~e to**, aspirer à. **~ation** /æspə'reiʃn/ *n.* aspiration *f.*

aspirin /'æsprin/ *n.* aspirine *f.*

ass /æs/ *n.* âne *m.*; (*person: fam.*) idiot(e) *m.* (*f.*).

assail /ə'seil/ *v.t.* assaillir. **~ant** *n.* agresseur *m.*

assassin /ə'sæsin/ *n.* assassin *m.*

assassinat|e /ə'sæsineit/ *v.t.* assassiner. **~ion** /-'neiʃn/ *n.* assassinat *m.*

assault /ə'sɔːlt/ *n.* (*mil.*) assaut *m.*; (*jurid.*) agression *f.* ● *v.t.* (*person: jurid.*) agresser.

assembl|e /ə'sembl/ *v.t.* (*things*) assembler; (*people*) rassembler. ● *v.i.* s'assembler, se rassembler. **~age** *n.* assemblage *m.*

assembly /ə'sembli/ *n.* assemblée *f.* **~ line**, chaîne de montage *f.*

assent /ə'sent/ *n.* assentiment *m.* ● *v.i.* consentir.

assert /ə'sɜːt/ *v.t.* affirmer; (*one's rights*) revendiquer. **~ion** /-ʃn/ *n.* affirmation *f.* **~ive** *a.* affirmatif, péremptoire.

assess /ə'ses/ *v.t.* évaluer; (*payment*) déterminer le montant de. **~ment** *n.* évaluation *f.* **~or** *n.* (*valuer*) expert *m.*

asset /'æset/ *n.* (*advantage*) atout *m.* **~s**, (*comm.*) actif *m.*

assiduous /ə'sidjʊəs/ *a.* assidu.

assign /ə'sain/ *v.t.* (*allot*) assigner. **~ s.o. to**, (*appoint*) affecter qn. à.

assignment /ə'sainmənt/ *n.* (*task*) mission *f.*, tâche *f.*; (*schol.*) rapport *m.*

assimilat|e /ə'simileit/ *v.t./i.* (s')assimiler. **~ion** /-'leiʃn/ *n.* assimilation *f.*

assist /ə'sist/ *v.t./i.* aider. **~ance** *n.* aide *f.*

assistant /ə'sistənt/ *n.* aide *m./f.*; (*in shop*) vendeu|r, -se *m., f.* ● *a.* (*manager etc.*) adjoint.

associate [1] /ə'səʊʃieit/ *v.t.* associer. ● *v.i.* **~e with**, fréquenter. **~ion** /-'eiʃn/ *n.* association *f.*

associate [2] /ə'səʊʃiət/ *n.* & *a.* associé(e) (*m.* (*f.*)).

assorted /ə'sɔːtid/ *a.* divers; (*foods*) assortis. **~ment** *n.* assortiment *m.* **an ~ment of guests/etc.**, des invités/etc. divers.

assume /ə'sjuːm/ *v.t.* supposer, présumer; (*power, attitude*) prendre; (*role, burden*) assumer.

assumption /əˈsʌmpʃn/ n. (sth. supposed) supposition f.

assurance /əˈʃʊərəns/ n. assurance f.

assure /əˈʃʊə(r)/ v.t. assurer. **~dly** /-rɪdlɪ/ adv. assurément.

asterisk /ˈæstərɪsk/ n. astérisque m.

astern /əˈstɜːn/ adv. à l'arrière.

asthma /ˈæsmə/ n. asthme m. **~tic** /-ˈmætɪk/ a. & n. asthmatique (m./f.).

astonish /əˈstɒnɪʃ/ v.t. étonner. **~ingly** adv. étonnamment. **~ment** n. étonnement m.

astound /əˈstaʊnd/ v.t. stupéfier.

astray /əˈstreɪ/ adv. & a. go **~**, s'égarer. **lead ~**, égarer.

astride /əˈstraɪd/ adv. & prep. à califourchon (sur).

astrolog|y /əˈstrɒlədʒɪ/ n. astrologie f. **~er** n. astrologue m.

astronaut /ˈæstrənɔːt/ n. astronaute m./f.

astronom|y /əˈstrɒnəmɪ/ n. astronomie f. **~er** n. astronome m. **~ical** /æstrəˈnɒmɪkl/ a. astronomique.

astute /əˈstjuːt/ a. astucieux. **~ness** n. astuce f.

asylum /əˈsaɪləm/ n. asile m.

at /æt, unstressed ət/ prep. à. **at the doctor's**/etc., chez le médecin/etc. **surprised at**, (cause) étonné de. **angry at**, fâché contre. **not at all**, pas du tout. **no wind**/etc. **at all**, (of any kind) pas le moindre vent/etc. **at night**, la nuit. **at once**, tout de suite; (simultaneously) à la fois. **~ sea**, en mer. **at times**, parfois.

ate /et/ see eat.

atheis|t /ˈeɪθɪɪst/ n. athée m./f. **~m** /-zəm/ n. athéisme m.

athlet|e /ˈæθliːt/ n. athlète m./f. **~ic** /-ˈletɪk/ a. athlétique. **~ics** /-ˈletɪks/ n. pl. athlétisme m.

Atlantic /ətˈlæntɪk/ a. atlantique. ● n. **~ (Ocean)**, Atlantique m.

atlas /ˈætləs/ n. atlas m.

atmospher|e /ˈætməsfɪə(r)/ n. atmosphère f. **~ic** /-ˈferɪk/ a. atmosphérique.

atoll /ˈætɒl/ n. atoll m.

atom /ˈætəm/ n. atome m. **~ic** /əˈtɒmɪk/ a. atomique. **~(ic) bomb**, bombe atomique f.

atomize /ˈætəmaɪz/ v.t. atomiser. **~r** /-ə(r)/ n. atomiseur m.

atone /əˈtəʊn/ v.i. **~ for**, expier. **~ment** n. expiation f.

atrocious /əˈtrəʊʃəs/ a. atroce.

atrocity /əˈtrɒsətɪ/ n. atrocité f.

atroph|y /ˈætrəfɪ/ n. atrophie f. ● v.t./i. (s')atrophier.

attach /əˈtætʃ/ v.t./i. (s')attacher; (letter) joindre (**to**, à). **~ed** a. **be ~ed to**, (like) être attaché à. **the ~ed letter**, la lettre ci-jointe. **~ment** n. (accessory) accessoire m.; (affection) attachement m.

attaché /əˈtæʃeɪ/ n. (pol.) attaché(e) m. (f.). **~ case**, mallette f.

attack /əˈtæk/ n. attaque f.; (med.) crise f. ● v.t. attaquer. **~er** n. agresseur m., attaquant(e) m. (f.).

attain /əˈteɪn/ v.t. atteindre (à); (gain) acquérir. **~able** a. accessible. **~ment** n. acquisition f. (of, de). **~ments**, réussites f. pl.

attempt /əˈtempt/ v.t. tenter. ● n. tentative f. **an ~ on s.o.'s life**, un attentat contre qn.

attend /əˈtend/ v.t. assister à; (class) suivre; (school, church) aller à; (escort) accompagner. ● v.i. assister. **~ (to)**, (look after) s'occuper de. **~ance** n. présence f.; (people) assistance f.

attendant /əˈtendənt/ n. employé(e) m. (f.); (servant) serviteur m. ● a. concomitant.

attention /əˈtenʃn/ n. attention f.; **~!**, (mil.) garde-à-vous! **pay ~**, faire or prêter attention (**to**, à).

attentive /əˈtentɪv/ a. attentif; (considerate) attentionné. **~ly** adv. attentivement. **~ness** n. attention f.

attenuate /əˈtenjʊeɪt/ v.t. atténuer.

attest /əˈtest/ v.t./i. **~ (to)**, attester. **~ation** /æteˈsteɪʃn/ n. attestation f.

attic /ˈætɪk/ n. grenier m.

attitude /ˈætɪtjuːd/ n. attitude f.

attorney /əˈtɜːnɪ/ n. mandataire m.; (Amer.) avocat m.

attract /əˈtrækt/ v.t. attirer. **~ion** /-kʃn/ n. attraction f.; (charm) attrait m.

attractive /əˈtræktɪv/ a. attrayant, séduisant. **~ly** adv. agréablement. **~ness** n. attrait m., beauté f.

attribute[1] /əˈtrɪbjuːt/ v.t. **~ to**, attribuer à.

attribute[2] /ˈætrɪbjuːt/ n. attribut m.

attrition /əˈtrɪʃn/ n. **war of ~**, guerre d'usure f.

aubergine /ˈəʊbəʒiːn/ n. aubergine f.

auburn /ˈɔːbən/ a. châtain roux invar.

auction /ˈɔːkʃn/ n. vente aux enchères f. ● v.t. vendre aux enchères. **~eer** /-ə'nɪə(r)/ n. commissaire-priseur m.

audaci|ous /ɔː'deɪʃəs/ a. audacieux. **~ty** /-æsəti/ n. audace f.

audible /'ɔːdəbl/ a. audible.

audience /'ɔːdɪəns/ n. auditoire m.; (theatre, radio) public m.; (interview) audience f.

audio typist /'ɔːdɪəʊ'taɪpɪst/ n. audio-typiste m./f.

audio-visual /ɔːdɪəʊ'vɪʒʊəl/ a. audio-visuel.

audit /'ɔːdɪt/ n. vérification des comptes f. ● v.t. vérifier.

audition /ɔː'dɪʃn/ n. audition f. ● v.t./i. auditionner.

auditor /'ɔːdɪtə(r)/ n. commissaire aux comptes m.

auditorium /ɔːdɪ'tɔːrɪəm/ n. (of theatre etc.) salle f.

augur /'ɔːgə(r)/ v.i. ~ well/ill, être de bon/mauvais augure.

August /'ɔːgəst/ n. août m.

aunt /ɑːnt/ n. tante f.

au pair /əʊ'peə(r)/ n. jeune fille au pair f.

aura /'ɔːrə/ n. atmosphère f.

auspices /'ɔːspɪsɪz/ n. pl. auspices m. pl., égide f.

auspicious /ɔː'spɪʃəs/ a. favorable.

auster|e /ɔː'stɪə(r)/ a. austère. **~ity** /-erəti/ n. austérité f.

Australia /ɒ'streɪlɪə/ n. Australie f. **~n** a. & n. australien(ne) (m. (f.)).

Austria /'ɒstrɪə/ n. Autriche f. **~n** a. & n. autrichien(ne) (m. (f.)).

authentic /ɔː'θentɪk/ a. authentique. **~ity** /-ən'tɪsətɪ/ n. authenticité f.

authenticate /ɔː'θentɪkeɪt/ v.t. authentifier.

author /'ɔːθə(r)/ n. auteur m. **~ship** n. (origin) paternité f.

authoritarian /ɔː'θɒrɪ'teərɪən/ a. autoritaire.

authorit|y /ɔː'θɒrətɪ/ n. autorité f.; (permission) autorisation f. **~ative** /-ɪtətɪv/ a. (credible) qui fait autorité; (trusted) autorisé; (manner) autoritaire.

authoriz|e /'ɔːθəraɪz/ v.t. autoriser. **~ation** /-'zeɪʃn/ n. autorisation f.

autistic /ɔː'tɪstɪk/ a. autistique.

autobiography /ɔːtəbaɪ'ɒgrəfɪ/ n. autobiographie f.

autocrat /'ɔːtəkræt/ n. autocrate m. **~ic** /-'krætɪk/ a. autocratique.

autograph /'ɔːtəgrɑːf/ n. autographe m. ● v.t. signer, dédicacer.

auto-immune /ɔːtəʊ'mjuːn/ a. auto-immune.

automat|e /'ɔːtəmeɪt/ v.t. automatiser. **~ion** /-'meɪʃn/ n. automatisation f.

automatic /ɔːtə'mætɪk/ a. automatique. ● n. (auto.) voiture automatique. f. **~ally** /-klɪ/ adv. automatiquement.

automobile /'ɔːtəməbiːl/ n. (Amer.) auto(mobile) f.

autonom|y /ɔː'tɒnəmɪ/ n. autonomie f. **~ous** a. autonome.

autopsy /'ɔːtɒpsɪ/ n. autopsie f.

autumn /'ɔːtəm/ n. automne m. **~al** /-'tʌmnəl/ a. automnal.

auxiliary /ɔːg'zɪlɪərɪ/ a. & n. auxiliaire (m./f.) **~ (verb)**, auxiliaire m.

avail /ə'veɪl/ v.t. ~ o.s. of, profiter de. ● n. of no ~, inutile. to no ~, sans résultat.

availab|le /ə'veɪləbl/ a. disponible. **~ility** /-'bɪlətɪ/ n. disponibilité f.

avalanche /'ævəlɑːnʃ/ n. avalanche f.

avant-garde /ævɑ̃'gɑːd/ a. d'avant-garde.

avaric|e /'ævərɪs/ n. avarice f. **~ious** /-'rɪʃəs/ a. avare.

avenge /ə'vendʒ/ v.t. venger. ~ o.s., se venger (on, de).

avenue /'ævənjuː/ n. avenue f.; (line of approach: fig.) voie f.

average /'ævərɪdʒ/ n. moyenne f. ● a. moyen. ● v.t./i. faire la moyenne de; (produce, do) faire en moyenne. on ~, en moyenne.

avers|e /ə'vɜːs/ a. be ~e to, répugner à. **~ion** /-ʃn/ n. aversion f.

avert /ə'vɜːt/ v.t. (turn away) détourner; (ward off) éviter.

aviary /'eɪvɪərɪ/ n. volière f.

aviation /eɪvɪ'eɪʃn/ n. aviation f.

avid /'ævɪd/ a. avide.

avocado /ævə'kɑːdəʊ/ n. (pl. -os) avocat m.

avoid /ə'vɔɪd/ v.t. éviter. **~able** a. évitable. **~ance** n. the **~ance of s.o./sth. is . . .**, éviter qn./qch., c'est . . .

await /ə'weɪt/ v.t. attendre.

awake /ə'weɪk/ v.t./i. (p.t. awoke, p.p. awoken) (s')éveiller. ● a. be ~, ne pas dormir, être (r)éveillé.

awaken /ə'weɪkən/ v.t./i. (s')éveiller.

award /ə'wɔːd/ v.t. attribuer. ● n. récompense f., prix m.; (scholarship) bourse f. **pay ~**, augmentation (de salaire) f.

aware /ə'weə(r)/ *a.* averti. **be ~ of**, (*danger*) être conscient de; (*fact*) savoir. **become ~ of**, prendre conscience de. **~ness** *n.* conscience *f.*

awash /ə'wɒʃ/ *a.* inondé (**with**, de).

away /ə'weɪ/ *adv.* (*far*) (au) loin; (*absent*) absent, parti; (*persistently*) sans arrêt; (*entirely*) complètement. **~ from**, loin de. **move ~**, s'écarter; (*to new home*) déménager. **six kilometres ~**, à six kilomètres (de distance). **take ~**, emporter. ● *a. & n.* **~ (match)**, match à l'extérieur *m.*

awe /ɔː/ *n.* crainte (révérencielle) *f.* **~-inspiring**, **~some** *adjs.* terrifiant; (*sight*) imposant. **~struck** *a.* terrifié.

awful /'ɔːfl/ *a.* affreux. **~ly** /'ɔːflɪ/ *adv.* (*badly*) affreusement; (*very: fam.*) rudement.

awhile /ə'waɪl/ *adv.* quelque temps.

awkward /'ɔːkwəd/ *a.* difficile; (*inconvenient*) inopportun; (*clumsy*) maladroit; (*embarrassing*) gênant; (*embarrassed*) gêné. **~ly** *adv.* maladroitement; avec gêne. **~ness** *n.* maladresse *f.*; (*discomfort*) gêne *f.*

awning /'ɔːnɪŋ/ *n.* auvent *m.*; (*of shop*) store *m.*

awoke, awoken /ə'wəʊk, ə'wəʊkən/ *see* awake.

awry /ə'raɪ/ *adv.* **go ~**, mal tourner. **sth. is ~**, qch. ne va pas.

axe (*Amer.*) **ax** /æks/ *n.* hache *f.* ● *v.t.* (*pres. p.* **axing**) réduire; (*eliminate*) supprimer; (*employee*) renvoyer.

axiom /'æksɪəm/ *n.* axiome *m.*

axis /'æksɪs/ *n.* (*pl.* **axes** /-siːz/) axe *m.*

axle /'æksl/ *n.* essieu *m.*

ay(e) /aɪ/ *adv. & n.* oui (*m. invar.*).

B

BA *abbr. see* Bachelor of Arts.

babble /'bæbl/ *v.i.* babiller; (*stream*) gazouiller. ● *n.* babillage *m.*

baboon /bə'buːn/ *n.* babouin *m.*

baby /'beɪbɪ/ *n.* bébé *m.* **~ carriage**, (*Amer.*) voiture d'enfant *f.* **~-sit** *v.i.* garder les enfants. **~-sitter** *n.* baby-sitter *m./f.*

babyish /'beɪbɪʃ/ *a.* enfantin.

bachelor /'bætʃələ(r)/ *n.* célibataire *m.* **B~ of Arts/Science**, licencié(e) ès lettres/sciences *m.* (*f.*).

back /bæk/ *n.* (*of person, hand, page, etc.*) dos *m.*; (*of house*) derrière *m.*; (*of vehicle*) arrière *m.*; (*of room*) fond *m.*; (*of chair*) dossier *m.*; (*football*) arrière *m.* ● *a.* de derrière, arrière *invar.*; (*taxes*) arriéré. ● *adv.* en arrière; (*returned*) de retour, rentré. ● *v.t.* (*support*) appuyer; (*bet on*) miser sur; (*vehicle*) faire reculer. ● *v.i.* (*of person, vehicle*) reculer. **at the ~ of beyond**, au diable. **at the ~ of the book**, à la fin du livre. **come ~**, revenir. **give ~**, rendre. **take ~**, reprendre. **I want it ~**, je veux le récupérer. **in ~ of**, (*Amer.*) derrière. **~-bencher** *n.* (*pol.*) membre sans portefeuille *m.* **~ down**, abandonner, se dégonfler. **~ number**, vieux numéro *m.* **~ out**, se dégager, se dégonfler; (*auto.*) sortir en reculant. **~-pedal** *v.i.* pédaler en arrière; (*fig.*) faire machine arrière (**on**, à propos de). **~ up**, (*support*) appuyer. **~-up** *n.* appui *m.*; (*Amer., fam.*) embouteillage *m.*; (*comput.*) sauvegarde *f.*; *a.* de réserve; (*comput.*) de sauvegarde.

backache /'bækeɪk/ *n.* mal de reins *m.*, mal aux reins *m.*

backbiting /'bækbaɪtɪŋ/ *n.* médisance *f.*

backbone /'bækbəʊn/ *n.* colonne vertébrale *f.*

backdate /bæk'deɪt/ *v.t.* antidater; (*arrangement*) rendre rétroactif.

backer /'bækə(r)/ *n.* partisan *m.*; (*comm.*) bailleur de fonds *m.*

backfire /bæk'faɪə(r)/ *v.i.* (*auto.*) pétarader; (*fig.*) mal tourner.

backgammon /bæk'gæmən/ *n.* trictrac *m.*

background /'bækgraʊnd/ *n.* fond *m.*, arrière-plan *m.*; (*context*) contexte *m.*; (*environment*) milieu *m.*; (*experience*) formation *f.* ● *a.* (*music, noise*) de fond.

backhand /'bækhænd/ *n.* revers *m.* **~ed** *a.* équivoque. **~ed stroke**, revers *m.* **~er** *n.* revers *m.*; (*bribe: sl.*) pot de vin *m.*

backing /'bækɪŋ/ *n.* appui *m.*

backlash /'bæklæʃ/ *n.* choc en retour *m.*, répercussions *f. pl.*

backlog /'bæklɒg/ *n.* accumulation (de travail) *f.*

backpack /'bækpæk/ *n.* sac à dos *m.*

backside /ˈbæksaɪd/ *n.* (*buttocks*: *fam.*) derrière *m.*

backstage /bækˈsteɪdʒ/ *a. & adv.* dans les coulisses.

backstroke /ˈbækstrəʊk/ *n.* dos crawlé *m.*

backtrack /ˈbæktræk/ *v.i.* rebrousser chemin; (*change one's opinion*) faire marche arrière.

backward /ˈbækwəd/ *a.* (*step etc.*) en arrière; (*retarded*) arriéré.

backwards /ˈbækwədz/ *adv.* en arrière; (*walk*) à reculons; (*read*) à l'envers; (*fall*) à la renverse. **go ~ and forwards**, aller et venir.

backwater /ˈbækwɔːtə(r)/ *n.* (*pej.*) trou perdu *m.*

bacon /ˈbeɪkən/ *n.* lard *m.*; (*in rashers*) bacon *m.*

bacteria /bækˈtɪərɪə/ *n. pl.* bactéries *f. pl.* **~l** *a.* bactérien.

bad /bæd/ *a.* (**worse, worst**) mauvais; (*wicked*) méchant; (*ill*) malade; (*accident*) grave; (*food*) gâté. **feel ~**, se sentir mal. **go ~**, se gâter. **~ language**, gros mots *m. pl.* **~-mannered** *a.* mal élevé. **~-tempered** *a.* grincheux. **~ly** *adv.* mal; (*hurt*) grièvement. **too ~!**, tant pis! (*I'm sorry*) dommage! **want ~ly**, avoir grande envie de.

badge /bædʒ/ *n.* insigne *m.*; (*of identity*) plaque *f.*

badger /ˈbædʒə(r)/ *n.* blaireau *m.* ● *v.t.* harceler.

badminton /ˈbædmɪntən/ *n.* badminton *m.*

baffle /ˈbæfl/ *v.t.* déconcerter.

bag /bæg/ *n.* sac *m.* **~s,** (*luggage*) bagages *m.pl.*; (*under eyes*) poches *f. pl.* ● *v.t.* (*p.t.* **bagged**) mettre en sac; (*take*: *fam.*) s'adjuger. **~s of,** (*fam.*) beaucoup de.

baggage /ˈbægɪdʒ/ *n.* bagages *m. pl.* **~ reclaim,** livraison des bagages *f.*

baggy /ˈbægɪ/ *a.* trop grand.

bagpipes /ˈbægpaɪps/ *n. pl.* cornemuse *f.*

Bahamas /bəˈhɑːməz/ *n. pl.* **the ~,** les Bahamas *f. pl.*

bail[1] /beɪl/ *n.* caution *f.* **on ~,** sous caution. ● *v.t.* mettre en liberté (provisoire) sous caution. **~ out,** (*fig.*) sortir d'affaire.

bail[2] /beɪl/ *n.* (*cricket*) bâtonnet *m.*

bail[3] /beɪl/ *v.t.* (*naut.*) écoper.

bailiff /ˈbeɪlɪf/ *n.* huissier *m.*

bait /beɪt/ *n.* appât *m.* ● *v.t.* appâter; (*fig.*) tourmenter.

bak|e /beɪk/ *v.t.* (faire) cuire (au four). ● *v.i.* cuire (au four); (*person*) faire du pain *or* des gâteaux. **~ed beans,** haricots blancs à la tomate *m.pl.* **~ed potato,** pomme de terre en robe des champs *f.* **~er** *n.* boulang|er, -ère *m.*, *f.* **~ing** *n.* cuisson *f.* **~ing-powder** *n.* levure *f.*

bakery /ˈbeɪkərɪ/ *n.* boulangerie *f.*

Balaclava /bæləˈklɑːvə/ *n.* **~ (helmet),** passe-montagne *m.*

balance /ˈbæləns/ *n.* équilibre *m.*; (*scales*) balance *f.*; (*outstanding sum*: *comm.*) solde *m.*; (*of payments, of trade*) balance *f.*; (*remainder*) reste *m.*; (*money in account*) position *f.* ● *v.t.* tenir en équilibre; (*weigh up & comm.*) balancer; (*budget*) équilibrer; (*to compensate*) contre-balancer. ● *v. i.* être en équilibre. **~d** *a.* équilibré.

balcony /ˈbælkənɪ/ *n.* balcon *m.*

bald /bɔːld/ *a.* (**-er, -est**) chauve; (*tyre*) lisse; (*fig.*) simple. **~ing** *a.* **be ~ing,** perdre ses cheveux. **~ness** *n.* calvitie *f.*

bale[1] /beɪl/ *n.* (*of cotton*) balle *f.*; (*of straw*) botte *f.*

bale[2] /beɪl/ *v.i.* **~ out,** sauter en parachute.

baleful /ˈbeɪlfʊl/ *a.* sinistre.

balk /bɔːk/ *v.t.* contrecarrer. ● *v.i.* **~ at,** reculer devant.

ball[1] /bɔːl/ *n.* (*golf, tennis, etc.*) balle *f.*; (*football*) ballon *m.*; (*croquet, billiards, etc.*) boule *f.*; (*of wool*) pelote *f.*; (*sphere*) boule *f.* **~-bearing** *n.* roulement à billes *m.* **~-cock** *n.* robinet à flotteur *m.* **~-point** *n.* stylo à bille *m.*

ball[2] /bɔːl/ *n.* (*dance*) bal *m.*

ballad /ˈbæləd/ *n.* ballade *f.*

ballast /ˈbæləst/ *n.* lest *m.*

ballerina /bæləˈriːnə/ *n.* ballerine *f.*

ballet /ˈbæleɪ/ *n.* ballet *m.*

ballistic /bəˈlɪstɪk/ *a.* **~ missile,** engin balistique *m.*

balloon /bəˈluːn/ *n.* ballon *m.*

ballot /ˈbælət/ *n.* scrutin *m.* **~(-paper),** bulletin de vote *m.* **~-box** *n.* urne *f.* ● *v.i.* (*p.t.* **balloted**) (*pol.*) voter. ● *v.t.* (*members*) consulter par voie de scrutin.

ballroom /ˈbɔːlrʊm/ *n.* salle de bal *f.*

ballyhoo /bælɪˈhuː/ *n.* (*publicity*) battage *m.*; (*uproar*) tapage *m.*

balm /bɑːm/ *n.* baume *m.* **~y** *a.* (*fragrant*) embaumé; (*mild*) doux; (*crazy*: *sl.*) dingue.

baloney /bə'ləʊnɪ/ *n.* (*sl.*) idioties *f. pl.*, calembredaines *f. pl.*

balustrade /ˌbælə'streɪd/ *n.* balustrade *f.*

bamboo /bæm'bu:/ *n.* bambou *m.*

ban /bæn/ *v.t.* (*p.t.* **banned**) interdire. **~ from**, exclure de. ● *n.* interdiction *f.*

banal /bə'nɑ:l, *Amer.* 'beml/ *a.* banal. **~ity** /-ælətɪ/ *n.* banalité *f.*

banana /bə'nɑ:nə/ *n.* banane *f.*

band /bænd/ *n.* (*strip, group of people*) bande *f.*; (*mus.*) orchestre *m.*; (*pop group*) groupe *m.* (*mil.*) fanfare *f.* ● *v.i.* **~ together**, liguer.

bandage /'bændɪdʒ/ *n.* pansement *m.* ● *v.t.* bander, panser.

bandit /'bændɪt/ *n.* bandit *m.*

bandstand /'bændstænd/ *n.* kiosque à musique *m.*

bandwagon /'bændwægən/ *n.* **climb on the ~**, prendre le train en marche.

bandy[1] /'bændɪ/ *v.t.* **~ about**, (*rumours, ideas, etc.*) faire circuler.

bandy[2] /'bændɪ/ *a.* (**-ier, -iest**) qui a les jambes arquées.

bang /bæŋ/ *n.* (*blow, noise*) coup (violent) *m.*; (*explosion*) détonation *f.*; (*of door*) claquement *m.* ● *v.t./i.* frapper; (*door*) claquer. ● *int.* vlan. ● *adv.* (*fam.*) exactement. **~ in the middle**, en plein milieu. **~ one's head**, se cogner la tête. **~s**, frange *f.*

banger /'bæŋə(r)/ *n.* (*firework*) pétard *m.*; (*culin., sl.*) saucisse *f.* (**old**) **~**, (*car: sl.*) guimbarde *f.*

bangle /'bæŋgl/ *n.* bracelet *m.*

banish /'bænɪʃ/ *v.t.* bannir.

banisters /'bænɪstəz/ *n. pl.* rampe (d'escalier) *f.*

banjo /'bændʒəʊ/ (*pl.* **-os**) banjo *m.*

bank[1] /bæŋk/ *n.* (*of river*) rive *f.*; (*of earth*) talus *m.*; (*of sand*) banc *m.* ● *v.t.* (*earth*) amonceler; (*fire*) couvrir. ● *v.i.* (*aviat.*) virer.

bank[2] /bæŋk/ *n.* banque *f.* ● *v.t.* mettre en banque. **~ with**, avoir un compte à. **~ account**, compte en banque *m.* **~ card**, carte bancaire *f.* **~ holiday**, jour férié *m.* **~ on**, compter sur. **~ statement**, relevé de compte *m.*

bank|ing /'bæŋkɪŋ/ *n.* opérations bancaires *f. pl.*; (*as career*) la banque. **~er** *n.* banquier *m.*

banknote /'bæŋknəʊt/ *n.* billet de banque *m.*

bankrupt /'bæŋkrʌpt/ *a.* **be ~**, être en faillite. **go ~**, faire faillite. ● *n.* failli(e) *m.* (*f.*). ● *v.t.* mettre en faillite. **~cy** *n.* faillite *f.*

banner /'bænə(r)/ *n.* bannière *f.*

banns /bænz/ *n. pl.* bans *m. pl.*

banquet /'bæŋkwɪt/ *n.* banquet *m.*

banter /'bæntə(r)/ *n.* plaisanterie *f.* ● *v.i.* plaisanter.

bap /bæp/ *n.* petit pain *m.*

baptism /'bæptɪzəm/ *n.* baptême *m.*

Baptist /'bæptɪst/ *n.* baptiste *m./f.*

baptize /bæp'taɪz/ *v.t.* baptiser.

bar /bɑ:(r)/ *n.* (*of metal*) barre *f.*; (*on window & jurid.*) barreau *m.*; (*of chocolate*) tablette *f.*; (*pub*) bar *m.*; (*counter*) comptoir *m.*, bar *m.*; (*division: mus.*) mesure *f.*; (*fig.*) obstacle *m.* ● *v.t.* (*p.t.* **barred**) (*obstruct*) barrer; (*prohibit*) interdire; (*exclude*) exclure. ● *prep.* sauf. **~ code**, code-barres *m. invar.* **~ of soap**, savonnette *f.*

Barbados /bɑ:'beɪdɒs/ *n.* Barbade *f.*

barbarian /bɑ:'beərɪən/ *n.* barbare *m./f.*

barbari|c /bɑ:'bærɪk/ *a.* barbare. **~ty** /-ətɪ/ *n.* barbarie *f.*

barbarous /'bɑ:bərəs/ *a.* barbare.

barbecue /'bɑ:bɪkju:/ *n.* barbecue *m.* ● *v.t.* griller, rôtir (au barbecue).

barbed /bɑ:bd/ *a.* **~ wire**, fil de fer barbelé *m.*

barber /bɑ:bə(r)/ *n.* coiffeur *m.* (*pour hommes*).

barbiturate /bɑ:'bɪtjʊərət/ *n.* barbiturique *m.*

bare /beə(r)/ *a.* (**-er, -est**) (*not covered or adorned*) nu; (*cupboard*) vide; (*mere*) simple. ● *v.t.* mettre à nu.

barefaced /'beəfeɪst/ *a.* éhonté.

barefoot /'beəfʊt/ *a.* nu-pieds *invar.*, pieds nus.

barely /'beəlɪ/ *adv.* à peine.

bargain /'bɑ:gɪn/ *n.* (*deal*) marché *m.*; (*cheap thing*) occasion *f.* ● *v.i.* négocier; (*haggle*) marchander. **not ~ for**, ne pas s'attendre à.

barge /bɑ:dʒ/ *n.* chaland *m.* ● *v.i.* **~ in**, interrompre; (*into room*) faire irruption.

baritone /'bærɪtəʊn/ *n.* baryton *m.*

bark[1] /bɑ:k/ *n.* (*of tree*) écorce *f.*

bark[2] /bɑ:k/ *n.* (*of dog*) aboiement *m.* ● *v.i.* aboyer.

barley /'bɑ:lɪ/ *n.* orge *f.* **~ sugar**, sucre d'orge *m.*

barmaid /'bɑːmeɪd/ *n.* serveuse *f.*

barman /'bɑːmən/ *n.* (*pl.* **-men**) barman *m.*

barmy /'bɑːmɪ/ *a.* (*sl.*) dingue.

barn /bɑːn/ *n.* grange *f.*

barometer /bə'rɒmɪtə(r)/ *n.* baromètre *m.*

baron /'bærən/ *n.* baron *m.* **~ess** *n.* baronne *f.*

baroque /bə'rɒk, *Amer.* bə'rəʊk/ *a.* & *n.* baroque (*m.*).

barracks /'bærəks/ *n. pl.* caserne *f.*

barrage /'bærɑːʒ, *Amer.* bə'rɑːʒ/ *n.* (*barrier*) barrage *m.*; (*mil.*) tir de barrage *m.*; (*of complaints*) série *f.*

barrel /'bærəl/ *n.* tonneau *m.*; (*of oil*) baril *m.*; (*of gun*) canon *m.* **~-organ** *n.* orgue de Barbarie *m.*

barren /'bærən/ *a.* stérile.

barricade /bærɪ'keɪd/ *n.* barricade *f.* ● *v.t.* barricader.

barrier /'bærɪə(r)/ *n.* barrière *f.*

barring /'bɑːrɪŋ/ *prep.* sauf.

barrister /'bærɪstə(r)/ *n.* avocat *m.*

barrow /'bærəʊ/ *n.* charrette à bras *f.*; (*wheelbarrow*) brouette *f.*

bartender /'bɑːtendə(r)/ *n.* (*Amer.*) barman *m.*

barter /'bɑːtə(r)/ *n.* troc *m.*, échange *m.* ● *v.t.* troquer, échanger (**for**, contre).

base /beɪs/ *n.* base *f.* ● *v.t.* baser (**on**, sur; **in**, à). ● *a.* bas, ignoble. **~less** *a.* sans fondement.

baseball /'beɪsbɔːl/ *n.* base-ball *m.*

baseboard /'beɪsbɔːd/ *n.* (*Amer.*) plinthe *f.*

basement /'beɪsmənt/ *n.* sous-sol *m.*

bash /bæʃ/ *v.t.* cogner. ● *n.* coup (violent) *m.* **have a ~ at**, (*sl.*) s'essayer à. **~ed in**, enfoncé.

bashful /'bæʃfl/ *a.* timide.

basic /'beɪsɪk/ *a.* fondamental, élémentaire. **the ~s**, les éléments de base *m. pl.* **~ally** /-klɪ/ *adv.* au fond.

basil /'bæzɪl, *Amer.* 'beɪzl/ *n.* basilic *m.*

basin /'beɪsn/ *n.* (*for liquids*) cuvette *f.*; (*for food*) bol *m.*; (*for washing*) lavabo *m.*; (*of river*) bassin *m.*

basis /'beɪsɪs/ *n.* (*pl.* **bases** /-siːz/) base *f.*

bask /bɑːsk/ *v.i.* se chauffer.

basket /'bɑːskɪt/ *n.* corbeille *f.*; (*with handle*) panier *m.*

basketball /'bɑːskɪtbɔːl/ *n.* basket (-ball) *m.*

Basque /bɑːsk/ *a.* & *n.* basque (*m./f.*).

bass [1] /beɪs/ *a.* (*mus.*) bas, grave. ● *n.* (*pl.* **basses**) basse *f.*

bass [2] /bæs/ *n. invar.* (*freshwater fish*) perche *f.*; (*sea*) bar *m.*

bassoon /bə'suːn/ *n.* basson *m.*

bastard /'bɑːstəd/ *n.* bâtard(e) *m.* (*f.*); (*sl.*) sal|aud, -ope *m., f.*

baste [1] /beɪst/ *v.t.* (*sew*) bâtir.

baste [2] /beɪst/ *v.t.* (*culin.*) arroser.

bastion /'bæstɪən/ *n.* bastion *m.*

bat [1] /bæt/ *n.* (*cricket etc.*) batte *f.*; (*table tennis*) raquette *f.* ● *v.t.* (*p.t.* **batted**) (*ball*) frapper. **not ~ an eyelid**, ne pas sourciller.

bat [2] /bæt/ *n.* (*animal*) chauve-souris *f.*

batch /bætʃ/ *n.* (*of people*) fournée *f.*; (*of papers*) paquet *m.*; (*of goods*) lot *m.*

bated /'beɪtɪd/ *a.* **with ~ breath**, en retenant son souffle.

bath /bɑːθ/ *n.* (*pl.* **-s** /bɑːðz/) bain *m.*; (*tub*) baignoire *f.* (**swimming**) **~s**, piscine *f.* ● *v.t.* donner un bain à ● *a.* de bain. **have a ~**, prendre un bain. **~ mat**, tapis de bain *m.*

bathe /beɪð/ *v.t.* baigner. ● *v.i.* se baigner; (*Amer.*) prendre un bain. ● *n.* bain (de mer) *m.* **~r** /-ə(r)/ *n.* baigneu|r, -se *m., f.*

bathing /'beɪðɪŋ/ *n.* baignade *f.* **~-costume** *n.* maillot de bain *m.*

bathrobe /'bæθrəʊb/ *m.* (*Amer.*) robe de chambre *f.*

bathroom /'bɑːθrʊm/ *n.* salle de bains *f.*

baton /'bætən/ *n.* (*mil.*) bâton *m.*; (*mus.*) baguette *f.*

battalion /bə'tælɪən/ *n.* bataillon *m.*

batter /'bætə(r)/ *v.t.* (*strike*) battre; (*ill-treat*) maltraiter. ● *n.* (*culin.*) pâte (à frire) *f.* **~ed** *a.* (*pan, car*) cabossé; (*face*) meurtri. **~ing** *n.* **take a ~ing**, subir des coups.

battery /'bætərɪ/ *n.* (*mil., auto.*) batterie *f.*; (*of torch, radio*) pile *f.*

battle /'bætl/ *n.* bataille *f.*; (*fig.*) lutte *f.* ● *v.i.* se battre.

battlefield /'bætlfiːld/ *n.* champ de bataille *m.*

battlements /'bætlmənts/ *n. pl.* (*crenellations*) créneaux *m. pl.*; (*wall*) remparts *m. pl.*

battleship /'bætlʃɪp/ *n.* cuirassé *m.*

baulk /bɔːk/ *v.t./i.* = **balk**.

bawdy /'bɔːdɪ/ *a.* (**-ier, -iest**) paillard. **~iness** *n.* paillardise *f.*

bawl /bɔːl/ *v.t./i.* brailler.

bay¹ /beɪ/ n. (bot.) laurier m. **~-leaf** n. feuille de laurier f.

bay² /beɪ/ n. (geog., archit.) baie f.; (area) aire f. **~ window,** fenêtre en saillie f.

bay³ /beɪ/ n. (bark) aboiement m. ● v.i. aboyer. **at ~,** aux abois. **keep** or **hold at ~,** tenir à distance.

bayonet /'beɪənɪt/ n. baïonnette f.

bazaar /bə'zɑː(r)/ n. (shop, market) bazar m.; (sale) vente f.

BC abbr. (before Christ) avant J.-C.

be /biː/ v.i. (present tense **am, are, is;** p.t. **was, were;** p.p. **been**) être. **be hot/right**/etc., avoir chaud/raison/ etc. **he is 30,** (age) il a 30 ans. **it is fine/cold**/etc., (weather) il fait beau/froid/etc. **I'm a painter** ● je suis peintre ● **how are you?,** (health) comment allez-vous? **he is to leave,** (must) il doit partir; (will) il va partir, il est prévu qu'il parte. **how much is it?,** (cost) ça fait or c'est combien? **be reading/walking**/etc., (aux.) lire/ marcher/etc. **the child was found,** l'enfant a été retrouvé, on a retrouvé l'enfant. **have been to,** avoir été à, être allé à.

beach /biːtʃ/ n. plage f.

beacon /'biːkən/ n. (lighthouse) phare m.; (marker) balise f.

bead /biːd/ n. perle f.

beak /biːk/ n. bec m.

beaker /'biːkə(r)/ n. gobelet m.

beam /biːm/ n. (timber) poutre f.; (of light) rayon m.; (of torch) faisceau m. ● v.i. (radiate) rayonner. ● v.t. (broadcast) diffuser. **~ing** a. radieux.

bean /biːn/ n. haricot m.; (of coffee) grain m.

bear¹ /beə(r)/ n. ours m.

bear² /beə(r)/ v.t. (p.t. **bore,** p.p. **borne**) (carry, show, feel) porter; (endure, sustain) supporter; (child) mettre au monde. ● v.i. **left**/etc., (go) prendre à gauche/etc. **~ in mind,** tenir compte de. **~ on,** se rapporter à. **~ out,** corroborer. **~ up!,** courage! **~able** a. supportable. **~er** n. porteu|r, -se m., f.

beard /bɪəd/ n. barbe f. **~ed** a. barbu.

bearing /'beərɪŋ/ n. (behaviour) maintien m.; (relevance) rapport m. **get one's ~s,** s'orienter.

beast /biːst/ n. bête f.; (person) brute f.

beastly /'biːstlɪ/ a. (**-ier, -iest**) (fam.) détestable.

beat /biːt/ v.t./i. (p.t. **beat,** p.p. **beaten**) battre. ● n. (of drum, heart) battement m.; (mus.) mesure f.; (of policeman) ronde f. **~ a retreat,** battre en retraite. **~ it!,** dégage! **~ s.o. down,** faire baisser son prix à qn. **~ off the competition,** éliminer la concurrence. **~ up,** tabasser. **it ~s me,** (fam.) ça me dépasse. **~er** n. batteur m. **~ing** n. raclée f.

beautician /bjuː'tɪʃn/ n. esthéticien(ne) m. (f.).

beautiful /'bjuːtɪfl/ a. beau. **~ly** /-flɪ/ adv. merveilleusement.

beautify /'bjuːtɪfaɪ/ v.t. embellir.

beauty /'bjuːtɪ/ n. beauté f. **~ parlour,** institut de beauté m. **~ spot,** grain de beauté m.; (fig.) site pittoresque m.

beaver /'biːvə(r)/ n. castor m.

became /bɪ'keɪm/ see become.

because /bɪ'kɒz/ conj. parce que. **~ of,** à cause de.

beck /bek/ n. **at the ~ and call of,** aux ordres de.

beckon /'bekən/ v.t./i. **~ (to),** faire signe à.

become /bɪ'kʌm/ v.t./i. (p.t. **became,** p.p. **become**) devenir; (befit) convenir à. **what has ~ of her?,** qu'est-elle devenue?

becoming /bɪ'kʌmɪŋ/ a. (seemly) bienséant; (clothes) seyant.

bed /bed/ n. lit m.; (layer) couche f.; (of sea) fond m.; (of flowers) parterre m. **go to ~,** (aller) se coucher. ● v.i. (p.t. **bedded**). **~ down,** se coucher. **~ding** n. literie f.

bedbug /'bedbʌg/ n. punaise f.

bedclothes /'bedkləʊðz/ n. pl. couvertures f. pl. et draps m. pl.

bedevil /bɪ'devl/ v.t. (p.t. **bedevilled**) (confuse) embrouiller; (plague) tourmenter.

bedlam /'bedləm/ n. chahut m.

bedraggled /bɪ'drægld/ a. (untidy) débraillé.

bedridden /'bedrɪdn/ a. cloué au lit.

bedroom /'bedrʊm/ n. chambre (à coucher) f.

bedside /'bedsaɪd/ n. chevet m. **~ book,** livre de chevet m.

bedsit, bedsitter /'bedsɪt, -'sɪtə(r)/ ns. (fam.) n. chambre meublée f., studio m.

bedspread /'bedspred/ n. dessus-delit m. invar.

bedtime /'bedtaɪm/ n. heure du coucher f.

bee /biː/ n. abeille f. **make a ~-line for,** aller tout droit vers.

beech /biːtʃ/ n. hêtre m.

beef /biːf/ n. bœuf m. ● v.i. (grumble: sl.) rouspéter.

beefburger /ˈbiːfbɜːgə(r)/ n. hamburger m.

beefeater /ˈbiːfiːtə(r)/ n. hallebardier m.

beefy /ˈbiːfɪ/ a. (-ier, -iest) musclé.

beehive /ˈbiːhaɪv/ n. ruche f.

been /biːn/ see be.

beer /bɪə(r)/ n. bière f.

beet /biːt/ n. (plant) betterave f.

beetle /ˈbiːtl/ n. scarabée m.

beetroot /ˈbiːtruːt/ n. invar. (culin.) betterave f.

befall /bɪˈfɔːl/ v.t. (p.t. befell, p.p. befallen) arriver à.

befit /bɪˈfɪt/ (v.t. (p.t. befitted) convenir à, seoir à.

before /bɪˈfɔː(r)/ prep. (time) avant; (place) devant. ● adv. avant; (already) déjà. ● conj. ~ leaving, avant de partir. ~ he leaves, avant qu'il (ne) parte. the day ~, la veille. two days ~, deux jours avant.

beforehand /bɪˈfɔːhænd/ adv. à l'avance, avant.

befriend /bɪˈfrend/ v.t. offrir son amitié à, aider.

beg /beg/ v.t. (p.t. begged) (entreat) supplier (to do, de faire). ~ (for), (money, food) mendier; (request) solliciter, demander. ● v.i. ~ (for alms), mendier. it is going ~ging, personne n'en veut.

began /bɪˈgæn/ see begin.

beggar /ˈbegə(r)/ n. mendiant(e) m. (f.); (sl.) individu m.

begin /bɪˈgɪn/ v.t./i. (p.t. began, p.p. begun, pres. p. beginning) commencer (to do, à faire). ~ner n. débutant(e) m. (f.). ~ning n. commencement m., début m.

begrudge /bɪˈgrʌdʒ/ v.t. (envy) envier; (give unwillingly) donner à contrecœur. ~ doing, faire à contrecœur.

beguile /bɪˈgaɪl/ v.t. tromper.

begun /bɪˈgʌn/ see begin.

behalf /bɪˈhɑːf/ n. on ~ of, pour; (as representative) au nom de, pour (le compte de).

behave /bɪˈheɪv/ v.i. se conduire. ~ (o.s.), se conduire bien.

behaviour, (Amer.) **behavior** /bɪˈheɪvjə(r)/ n. conduite f., comportement m.

behead /bɪˈhed/ v.t. décapiter.

behind /bɪˈhaɪnd/ prep. derrière; (in time) en retard sur. ● adv. derrière; (late) en retard. ● n. (buttocks) derrière m. **leave ~,** oublier.

behold /bɪˈhəʊld/ v.t. (p.t. beheld) (old use) voir.

beige /beɪʒ/ a. & n. beige (m.).

being /ˈbiːɪŋ/ n. (person) être m. **bring into ~,** créer. **come into ~,** prendre naissance.

belated /bɪˈleɪtɪd/ a. tardif.

belch /beltʃ/ v.i. faire un renvoi. ● v.t. ~ out, (smoke) vomir. ● n. renvoi m.

belfry /ˈbelfrɪ/ n. beffroi m.

Belgium /ˈbeldʒəm/ n. Belgique f. ~an a. & n. belge (m./f.).

belie /bɪˈlaɪ/ v.t. démentir.

belief /bɪˈliːf/ n. croyance f.; (trust) confiance f.; (faith: relig.) foi f.

believe /bɪˈliːv/ v.t./i. croire. ~e in, croire à; (deity) croire en. ~able a. croyable. ~er n. croyant(e) m. (f.).

belittle /bɪˈlɪtl/ v.t. déprécier.

bell /bel/ n. cloche f.; (small) clochette f.; (on door) sonnette f.; (of phone) sonnerie f.

belligerent /bɪˈlɪdʒərənt/ a. & n. belligérant(e) (m. (f.)).

bellow /ˈbeləʊ/ v.t./i. beugler.

bellows /ˈbeləʊz/ n. pl. soufflet m.

belly /ˈbelɪ/ n. ventre m. ~-ache n. mal au ventre m.

bellyful /ˈbelɪfʊl/ n. have a ~, en avoir plein le dos.

belong /bɪˈlɒŋ/ v.i. ~ to, appartenir à; (club) être membre de.

belongings /bɪˈlɒŋɪŋz/ n. pl. affaires f. pl.

beloved /bɪˈlʌvɪd/ a. & n. bien-aimé(e) (m. (f.)).

below /bɪˈləʊ/ prep. au-dessous de; (fig.) indigne de. ● adv. en dessous; (on page) ci-dessous.

belt /belt/ n. ceinture f.; (techn.) courroie f.; (fig.) région f. ● v.t. (hit: sl.) rosser. ● v.i. (rush: sl.) filer à toute allure.

beltway /ˈbeltweɪ/ n. (Amer.) périphérique m.

bemused /bɪˈmjuːzd/ a. (confused) stupéfié; (thoughtful) pensif.

bench /bentʃ/ n. banc m.; (working-table) établi m. **the ~,** (jurid.) la magistrature (assise). ~-mark n. repère m.

bend /bend/ v.t./i. (p.t. bent) (se) courber; (arm, leg) plier. ● n.

courbe *f*.; (*in road*) virage *m*.; (*of arm, knee*) pli *m*. ~ **down** *or* **over**, se pencher.

beneath /bɪˈniːθ/ *prep.* sous, au-dessous de; (*fig.*) indigne de. ● *adv.* (au-)dessous.

benefactor /ˈbenɪfæktə(r)/ *n.* bien-fai|teur, -trice *m., f.*

beneficial /benɪˈfɪʃl/ *a.* avantageux, favorable.

benefit /ˈbenɪfɪt/ *n.* avantage *m*.; (*allowance*) allocation *f*. ● *v.t.* (*p.t.* benefited, *pres. p.* benefiting) (*be useful to*) profiter à; (*do good to*) faire du bien à. ~ **from**, tirer profit de.

benevolen|t /bɪˈnevələnt/ *a.* bienveillant. ~**ce** *n.* bienveillance *f.*

benign /bɪˈnaɪn/ *a.* (*kindly*) bienveillant; (*med.*) bénin.

bent /bent/ *see* bend. ● *n.* (*talent*) aptitude *f*.; (*inclination*) penchant *m*. ● *a.* tordu; (*sl.*) corrompu. ~ **on doing**, décidé à faire.

bequeath /bɪˈkwiːð/ *v.t.* léguer.

bequest /bɪˈkwest/ *n.* legs *m.*

bereave|d /bɪˈriːvd/ *a.* the ~d **wife**/ *etc.*, la femme/*etc.* du disparu. ~**ment** *n.* deuil *m.*

beret /ˈbereɪ/ *n.* béret *m.*

Bermuda /bəˈmjuːdə/ *n.* Bermudes *f. pl.*

berry /ˈberɪ/ *n.* baie *f.*

berserk /bəˈsɜːk/ *a.* go ~, devenir fou furieux.

berth /bɜːθ/ *n.* (*in train, ship*) couchette *f*.; (*anchorage*) mouillage *m*. ● *v.i.* mouiller. give a wide ~ to, éviter.

beseech /bɪˈsiːtʃ/ *v.t.* (*p.t.* besought) implorer, supplier.

beset /bɪˈset/ *v.t.* (*p.t.* beset, *pres. p.* besetting) (*attack*) assaillir; (*surround*) entourer.

beside /bɪˈsaɪd/ *prep.* à côté de. ~ **o.s.**, hors de soi. ~ **the point**, sans rapport.

besides /bɪˈsaɪdz/ *prep.* en plus de; (*except*) excepté. ● *adv.* en plus.

besiege /bɪˈsiːdʒ/ *v.t.* assiéger.

best /best/ *a.* meilleur. the ~ **book**/ *etc.*, le meilleur livre/*etc.* ● *adv.* (the) ~, (*sing etc.*) le mieux. ● *n.* the ~ (one), le meilleur, la meilleure. ~ **man**, garçon d'hon-neur *m*. the ~ **part of**, la plus grande partie de. the ~ **thing is to** . . ., le mieux est de . . . **do one's** ~,

faire de son mieux. **make the** ~ **of**, s'accommoder de.

bestow /bɪˈstəʊ/ *v.t.* accorder.

best-seller /bestˈselə(r)/ *n.* best-seller *m*., succès de librairie *m.*

bet /bet/ *n.* pari *m*. ● *v.t./i.* (*p.t.* bet *or* betted, *pres. p.* betting) parier.

betray /bɪˈtreɪ/ *v.t.* trahir. ~**al** *n.* trahison *f.*

better /ˈbetə(r)/ *a.* meilleur. ● *adv.* mieux. ● *v.t.* (*improve*) améliorer; (*do better than*) surpasser. ● *n.* one's ~**s**, ses supérieurs *m. pl.* be ~ **off**, (*financially*) avoir plus d'argent. he's ~ **off at home**, il est mieux chez lui. I **had** ~ **go**, je ferais mieux de partir. the ~ **part of**, la plus grande partie de. **get** ~, s'amé-liorer; (*recover*) se remettre. **get the** ~ **of**, l'emporter sur. **so much the** ~, tant mieux.

betting-shop /ˈbetɪŋʃɒp/ *n.* bureau de P.M.U. *m.*

between /bɪˈtwiːn/ *prep.* entre. ● *adv.* in ~, au milieu.

beverage /ˈbevərɪdʒ/ *n.* boisson *f.*

bevy /ˈbevɪ/ *n.* essaim *m.*

beware /bɪˈweə(r)/ *v.i.* prendre garde (of, à).

bewilder /bɪˈwɪldə(r)/ *v.t.* désorien-ter, embarrasser. ~**ment** *n.* déso-rientation *f.*

bewitch /bɪˈwɪtʃ/ *v.t.* enchanter.

beyond /bɪˈjɒnd/ *prep.* au-delà de; (*doubt, reach*) hors de; (*besides*) excepté. ● *adv.* au-delà. it is ~ me, ça me dépasse.

bias /ˈbaɪəs/ *n.* (*inclination*) penchant *m*.; (*prejudice*) préjugé *m*. ● *v.t.* (*p.t.* biased) influencer. ~**ed** *a.* partial.

bib /bɪb/ *n.* bavoir *m.*

Bible /ˈbaɪbl/ *n.* Bible *f.*

biblical /ˈbɪblɪkl/ *a.* biblique.

bicarbonate /baɪˈkɑːbənət/ *n.* bicar-bonate *m.*

biceps /ˈbaɪseps/ *n.* biceps *m.*

bicker /ˈbɪkə(r)/ *v.i.* se chamailler.

bicycle /ˈbaɪsɪkl/ *n.* bicyclette *f*. ● *v.i.* faire de la bicyclette.

bid[1] /bɪd/ *n.* (*at auction*) offre *f*., enchère *f*.; (*attempt*) tentative *f*. ● *v.t./i.* (*p.t.* & *p.p.* bid, *pres. p.* bidding) (*offer*) faire une offre *or* une enchère (de). the highest ~**der**, le plus offrant.

bid[2] /bɪd/ *v.t.* (*p.t.* bade /bæd/, *p.p.* bidden *or* bid, *pres. p.* bidding) ordonner; (*say*) dire. ~**ding** *n.* ordre *m.*

bide /baɪd/ *v.t.* ~ **one's time,** attendre le bon moment.

biennial /baɪˈenɪəl/ *a.* biennal.

bifocals /baɪˈfəʊklz/ *n. pl.* lunettes bifocales *f. pl.*

big /bɪɡ/ *a.* (**bigger, biggest**) grand; (*in bulk*) gros; (*generous: sl.*) généreux. ● *adv.* (*fam.*) en grand; (*earn: fam.*) gros. ~ **business,** les grandes affaires. ~**-headed** *a.* prétentieux. ~ **shot,** (*sl.*) huile *f.* **think** ~, (*fam.*) voir grand.

bigam|**y** /ˈbɪɡəmɪ/ *n.* bigamie *f.* ~**ist** *n.* bigame *m./f.* ~**ous** *a.* bigame.

bigot /ˈbɪɡət/ *n.* fanatique *m./f.* ~**ed** *a.* fanatique. ~**ry** *n.* fanatisme *m.*

bike /baɪk/ *n.* (*fam.*) vélo *m.*

bikini /bɪˈkiːnɪ/ *n.* (*pl.* **-is**) bikini *m.*

bilberry /ˈbɪlbərɪ/ *n.* myrtille *f.*

bile /baɪl/ *n.* bile *f.*

bilingual /baɪˈlɪŋɡwəl/ *a.* bilingue.

bilious /ˈbɪlɪəs/ *a.* bilieux.

bill[1] /bɪl/ *n.* (*invoice*) facture *f.*; (*in hotel, for gas, etc.*) note *f.*; (*in restaurant*) addition *f.*; (*of sale*) acte *m.*; (*pol.*) projet de loi *m.*; (*banknote: Amer.*) billet de banque *m.* ● *v.t.* (*person: comm.*) envoyer la facture à. (*theatre*) **on the** ~, à l'affiche.

bill[2] /bɪl/ *n.* (*of bird*) bec *m.*

billboard /ˈbɪlbɔːd/ *n.* panneau d'affichage *m.*

billet /ˈbɪlɪt/ *n.* cantonnement *m.* ● *v.t.* (*p.t.* **billeted**) cantonner (**on,** chez).

billfold /ˈbɪlfəʊld/ *n.* (*Amer.*) portefeuille *m.*

billiards /ˈbɪljədz/ *n.* billard *m.*

billion /ˈbɪljən/ *n.* billion *m.*; (*Amer.*) milliard *m.*

billy-goat /ˈbɪlɪɡəʊt/ *n.* bouc *m.*

bin /bɪn/ *n.* (*for rubbish, litter*) boîte (à ordures) *f.*, poubelle *f.*; (*for bread*) huche *f.*, coffre *m.*

binary /ˈbaɪnərɪ/ *a.* binaire.

bind /baɪnd/ *v.t.* (*p.t.* **bound**) lier; (*book*) relier; (*jurid.*) obliger. ● *n.* (*bore: sl.*) plaie *f.* **be** ~**ing on,** être obligatoire pour.

binding /ˈbaɪndɪŋ/ *n.* reliure *f.*

binge /bɪndʒ/ *n.* **go on a** ~, (*spree: sl.*) faire la bringue.

bingo /ˈbɪŋɡəʊ/ *n.* loto *m.*

binoculars /bɪˈnɒkjʊləz/ *n. pl.* jumelles *f. pl.*

biochemistry /baɪəʊˈkemɪstrɪ/ *n.* biochimie *f.*

biodegradable /baɪəʊdɪˈɡreɪdəbl/ *a.* biodégradable.

biograph|**y** /baɪˈɒɡrəfɪ/ *n.* biographie *f.* ~**er** *n.* biographe *m./f.*

biolog|**y** /baɪˈɒlədʒɪ/ *n.* biologie *f.* ~**ical** /-əˈlɒdʒɪkl/ *a.* biologique. ~**ist** *n.* biologiste *m./f.*

biorhythm /ˈbaɪəʊrɪðəm/ *n.* biorythme *m.*

birch /bɜːtʃ/ *n.* (*tree*) bouleau *m.*; (*whip*) verge *f.*, fouet *m.*

bird /bɜːd/ *n.* oiseau *m.*; (*fam.*) individu *m.*; (*girl: sl.*) poule *f.*

Biro /ˈbaɪərəʊ/ *n.* (*pl.* **-os**) (P.) stylo à bille *m.*, Bic *m.* (P.).

birth /bɜːθ/ *n.* naissance *f.* **give** ~, accoucher. ~ **certificate,** acte de naissance *m.* ~**-control** *n.* contrôle des naissances *m.* ~**-rate** *n.* natalité *f.*

birthday /ˈbɜːθdeɪ/ *n.* anniversaire *m.*

birthmark /ˈbɜːθmɑːk/ *n.* tache de vin *f.*, envie *f.*

biscuit /ˈbɪskɪt/ *n.* biscuit *m.*; (*Amer.*) petit pain (au lait) *m.*

bisect /baɪˈsekt/ *v.t.* couper en deux.

bishop /ˈbɪʃəp/ *n.* évêque *m.*

bit[1] /bɪt/ *n.* morceau *m.*; (*of horse*) mors *m.*; (*of tool*) mèche *f.* **a** ~, (*a little*) un peu.

bit[2] /bɪt/ *see* **bite**.

bit[3] /bɪt/ *n.* (*comput.*) bit *m.*, élement binaire *m.*

bitch /bɪtʃ/ *n.* chienne *f.*; (*woman: fam.*) garce *f.* ● *v.i.* (*grumble: fam.*) râler. ~**y** *a.* (*fam.*) vache.

bite /baɪt/ *v.t./i.* (*p.t.* **bit**, *p.p.* **bitten**) mordre. ● *n.* morsure *f.*; (*by insect*) piqûre *f.*; (*mouthful*) bouchée *f.* ~ **one's nails,** se ronger les ongles. **have a** ~, manger un morceau.

biting /ˈbaɪtɪŋ/ *a.* mordant.

bitter /ˈbɪtə(r)/ *a.* amer; (*weather*) glacial, âpre. ● *n.* bière anglaise *f.* ~**ly** *adv.* amèrement. **it is** ~**ly cold,** il fait un temps glacial. ~**ness** *n.* amertume *f.*

bitty /ˈbɪtɪ/ *a.* décousu.

bizarre /bɪˈzɑː(r)/ *a.* bizarre.

blab /blæb/ *v.i.* (*p.t.* **blabbed**) jaser.

black /blæk/ *a.* (**-er, -est**) noir. ● *n.* (*colour*) noir *m.* **B~,** (*person*) Noir(e) *m.* (*f.*). ● *v.t.* noircir; (*goods*) boycotter. ~ **and blue,** couvert de bleus. ~ **eye,** œil poché *m.* ~ **ice,** verglas *m.* ~ **list,** liste noire *f.* ~ **market,** marché noir *m.* ~ **sheep,** brebis galeuse *f.* ~ **spot,** point noir *m.*

blackberry /'blækbərɪ/ *n.* mûre *f.*

blackbird /'blækbɜːd/ *n.* merle *m.*

blackboard /'blækbɔːd/ *n.* tableau noir *m.*

blackcurrant /'blækkʌrənt/ *n.* cassis *m.*

blacken /'blækən/ *v.t./i.* noircir.

blackhead /'blækhed/ *n.* point noir *m.*

blackleg /'blækleg/ *n.* jaune *m.*

blacklist /'blæklɪst/ *v.t.* mettre sur la liste noire *or* à l'index.

blackmail /'blækmeɪl/ *n.* chantage *m.* ● *v.t.* faire chanter. **~er** *n.* maître-chanteur *m.*

blackout /'blækaʊt/ *n.* panne d'électricité *f.*; (*med.*) syncope *f.*

blacksmith /'blæksmɪθ/ *n.* forgeron *m.*

bladder /'blædə(r)/ *n.* vessie *f.*

blade /bleɪd/ *n.* (*of knife etc.*) lame *f.*; (*of propeller, oar*) pale *f.* **~ of grass**, brin d'herbe *m.*

blame /bleɪm/ *v.t.* accuser. ● *n.* faute *f.* **~ s.o. for sth.**, reprocher qch. à qn. **he is to ~**, il est responsable (**for**, de). **~less** *a.* irréprochable.

bland /blænd/ *a.* (**-er, -est**) (*gentle*) doux; (*insipid*) fade.

blank /blæŋk/ *a.* blanc; (*look*) vide; (*cheque*) en blanc. ● *n.* blanc *m.* **~ (cartridge)**, cartouche à blanc *f.*

blanket /'blæŋkɪt/ *n.* couverture *f.*; (*layer: fig.*) couche *f.* ● *v.t.* (*p.t.* **blanketed**) recouvrir.

blare /bleə(r)/ *v.t./i.* beugler. ● *n.* vacarme *m.*, beuglement *m.*

blarney /'blɑːnɪ/ *n.* boniment *m.*

blasé /'blɑːzeɪ/ *a.* blasé.

blasphem|y /'blæsfəmɪ/ *n.* blasphème *m.* **~ous** *a.* blasphématoire; (*person*) blasphémateur.

blast /blɑːst/ *n.* explosion *f.*; (*wave of air*) souffle *m.*; (*of wind*) rafale *f.*; (*noise from siren etc.*) coup *m.* ● *v.t.* (*blow up*) faire sauter. **~ed** *a.* (*fam.*) maudit, fichu. **~-furnace** *n.* haut fourneau *m.* **~ off**, être mis à feu. **~-off** *n.* mise à feu *f.*

blatant /'bleɪtnt/ *a.* (*obvious*) flagrant; (*shameless*) éhonté.

blaze[1] /bleɪz/ *n.* flamme *f.*; (*conflagration*) incendie *m.*; (*fig.*) éclat *m.* ● *v.i.* (*fire*) flamber; (*sky, eyes, etc.*) flamboyer.

blaze[2] /bleɪz/ *v.t.* **~ a trail**, montrer *or* marquer la voie.

blazer /'bleɪzə(r)/ *n.* blazer *m.*

bleach /bliːtʃ/ *n.* décolorant *m.*; (*for domestic use*) eau de Javel *f.* ● *v.t./i.* blanchir; (*hair*) décolorer.

bleak /bliːk/ *a.* (**-er, -est**) morne.

bleary /'blɪərɪ/ *a.* (*eyes*) voilé.

bleat /bliːt/ *n.* bêlement *m.* ● *v.i.* bêler.

bleed /bliːd/ *v.t./i.* (*p.t.* **bled**) saigner.

bleep /bliːp/ *n.* bip *m.* **~er** *n.* bip *m.*

blemish /'blemɪʃ/ *n.* tare *f.*, défaut *m.*; (*on reputation*) tache *f.* ● *v.t.* entacher.

blend /blend/ *v.t./i.* (se) mélanger. ● *n.* mélange *m.* **~er** *n.* mixer *n.*

bless /bles/ *v.t.* bénir. **be ~ed with**, avoir le bonheur de posséder. **~ing** *n.* bénédiction *f.*; (*benefit*) avantage *m.*; (*stroke of luck*) chance *f.*

blessed /'blesɪd/ *a.* (*holy*) saint; (*damned: fam.*) sacré.

blew /bluː/ *see* blow[1].

blight /blaɪt/ *n.* (*disease: bot.*) rouille *f.*; (*fig.*) fléau *m.*

blind /blaɪnd/ *a.* aveugle. ● *v.t.* aveugler. ● *n.* (*on window*) store *m.*; (*deception*) feinte *f.* **be ~ to**, ne pas voir. **~ alley**, impasse *f.* **~ corner**, virage sans visibilité *m.* **~ man**, aveugle *m.* **~ spot**, (*auto.*) angle mort *m.* **~ers** *n. pl.* (*Amer.*) œillères *f. pl.* **~ly** *adv.* aveuglément. **~ness** *n.* cécité *f.*

blindfold /'blaɪndfəʊld/ *a. & adv.* les yeux bandés. ● *n.* bandeau *m.* ● *v.t.* bander les yeux à.

blink /blɪŋk/ *v.i.* cligner des yeux; (*of light*) clignoter.

blinkers /'blɪŋkəz/ *n. pl.* œillères *f. pl.*

bliss /blɪs/ *n.* félicité *f.* **~ful** *a.* bienheureux. **~fully** *adv.* joyeusement, merveilleusement.

blister /'blɪstə(r)/ *n.* ampoule *f.* (*on paint*) cloque *f.* ● *v.i.* se couvrir d'ampoules; cloquer.

blithe /blaɪð/ *a.* joyeux.

blitz /blɪts/ *n.* (*aviat.*) raid éclair *m.* ● *v.t.* bombarder.

blizzard /'blɪzəd/ *n.* tempête de neige *f.*

bloated /'bləʊtɪd/ *a.* gonflé.

bloater /'bləʊtə(r)/ *n.* hareng saur *m.*

blob /blɒb/ *n.* (*drop*) (grosse) goutte *f.*; (*stain*) tache *f.*

bloc /blɒk/ *n.* bloc *m.*

block /blɒk/ *n.* bloc *m.*; (*buildings*) pâté de maisons *m.*; (*in pipe*) obstruction *f.* **~ (of flats)**, immeuble *m.* ● *v.t.* bloquer. **~ letters**, majuscules *f. pl.* **~age** *n.* obstruction *f.* **~-buster** *n.* gros succès *m.*

blockade /blɒ'keɪd/ *n.* blocus *m.* ● *v.t.* bloquer.

bloke /bləʊk/ *n.* (*fam.*) type *m.*

blond /blɒnd/ *a. & n.* blond (*m.*).

blonde /blɒnd/ *a. & n.* blonde (*f.*).

blood /blʌd/ *n.* sang *m.* ● *a.* (*donor, bath, etc.*) de sang; (*bank, poisoning, etc.*) du sang; (*group, vessel*) sanguin. **~-curdling** *a.* à tourner le sang. **~less** *a.* (*fig.*) pacifique. **~pressure** *n.* tension artérielle *f.* **~test**, prise de sang *f.*

bloodhound /'blʌdhaʊnd/ *n.* limier *m.*

bloodshed /'blʌdʃed/ *n.* effusion de sang *f.*

bloodshot /'blʌdʃɒt/ *a.* injecté de sang.

bloodstream /'blʌdstriːm/ *n.* sang *m.*

bloodthirsty /'blʌdθɜːstɪ/ *a.* sanguinaire.

bloody /'blʌdɪ/ *a.* (**-ier, -iest**) sanglant; (*sl.*) sacré. ● *adv.* (*sl.*) vachement. **~-minded** *a.* (*fam.*) hargneux, obstiné.

bloom /bluːm/ *n.* fleur *f.* ● *v.i.* fleurir; (*fig.*) s'épanouir.

bloomer /'bluːmə(r)/ *n.* (*sl.*) gaffe *f.*

blossom /'blɒsəm/ *n.* fleur(s) *f.* (*pl.*). ● *v.i.* fleurir; (*person: fig.*) s'épanouir.

blot /blɒt/ *n.* tache *f.* ● *v.t.* (*p.t.* **blotted**) tacher; (*dry*) sécher. **~ out**, effacer. **~ter**, **~ting-paper** *ns.* buvard *m.*

blotch /blɒtʃ/ *n.* tache *f.* **~y** *a.* couvert de taches.

blouse /blaʊz/ *n.* chemisier *m.*

blow[1] /bləʊ/ *v.t./i.* (*p.t.* **blew**, *p.p.* **blown**) souffler; (*fuse*) (faire) sauter; (*squander: sl.*) claquer; (*opportunity*) rater. **~ one's nose**, se moucher. **~ a whistle**, siffler. **~ away** *or* **off**, emporter. **~ out**, (*candle*) souffler. **~-out** *n.* (*of tyre*) éclatement *m.* **~ over**, passer. **~ up**, (faire) sauter; (*tyre*) gonfler; (*photo.*) agrandir.

blow[2] /bləʊ/ *n.* coup *m.*

blowlamp /'bləʊlæmp/ *n.* chalumeau *m.*

blown /bləʊn/ *see* blow[1].

blowtorch /'bləʊtɔːtʃ/ *n.* (*Amer.*) chalumeau *m.*

blowy /'bləʊɪ/ *a.* **it is ~**, il y a du vent.

bludgeon /'blʌdʒən/ *n.* gourdin *m.* ● *v.t.* matraquer.

blue /bluː/ *a.* (**-er, -est**) bleu; (*film*) porno. ● *n.* bleu *m.* **come out of the ~**, être inattendu. **have the ~s**, avoir le cafard.

bluebell /'bluːbel/ *n.* jacinthe des bois *f.*

bluebottle /'bluːbɒtl/ *n.* mouche à viande *f.*

blueprint /'bluːprɪnt/ *n.* plan *m.*

bluff[1] /blʌf/ *v.t./i.* bluffer. ● *n.* bluff *m.* **call. s.o.'s ~**, dire chiche à qn.

bluff[2] /blʌf/ *a.* (*person*) brusque.

blunder /'blʌndə(r)/ *v.i.* faire une gaffe; (*move*) avancer à tâtons. ● *n.* gaffe *f.*

blunt /blʌnt/ *a.* (*knife*) émoussé; (*person*) brusque. ● *v.t.* émousser. **~ly** *adv.* carrément. **~ness** *n.* brusquerie *f.*

blur /blɜː(r)/ *n.* tache floue *f.* ● *v.t.* (*p.t.* **blurred**) rendre flou.

blurb /blɜːb/ *n.* résumé publicitaire *m.*

blurt /blɜːt/ *v.t.* **~ out**, lâcher, dire.

blush /blʌʃ/ *v.i.* rougir. ● *n.* rougeur *f.* **~er** *n.* blush *m.*

bluster /'blʌstə(r)/ *v.i.* (*wind*) faire rage; (*swagger*) fanfaronner. **~y** *a.* à bourrasques.

boar /bɔː(r)/ *n.* sanglier *m.*

board /bɔːd/ *n.* planche *f.*; (*for notices*) tableau *m.*; (*food*) pension *f.*; (*committee*) conseil *m.* ● *v.t./i.* (*bus, train*) monter dans; (*naut.*) monter à bord (de). **~ of directors**, conseil d'administration *m.* **go by the ~**, passer à l'as. **full ~**, pension complète *f.* **half ~**, demi-pension *f.* **on ~**, à bord. **~ up**, boucher. **~ with**, être en pension chez. **~er** *n.* pensionnaire *m./f.* **~ing-house** *n.* pension (de famille) *f.* **~ing-school** *n.* pensionnat *m.*, pension *f.*

boast /bəʊst/ *v.i.* se vanter (**about**, de). ● *v.t.* s'enorgueillir de. ● *n.* vantardise *f.* **~er** *n.* vantard(e) *m.* (*f.*). **~ful** *a.* vantard. **~fully** *adv.* en se vantant.

boat /bəʊt/ *n.* bateau *m.*; (*small*) canot *m.* **in the same ~**, logé à la même enseigne. **~ing** *n.* canotage *m.*

boatswain /'bəʊsn/ *n.* maître d'équipage *m.*

bob[1] /bɒb/ *v.i.* (*p.t.* **bobbed**). **~ up and down**, monter et descendre.

bob[2] /bɒb/ *n. invar.* (*sl.*) shilling *m.*

bobby /'bɒbɪ/ *n.* (*fam.*) flic *m.*

bobsleigh /ˈbɒbsleɪ/ *n.* bob-(sleigh) *m.*

bode /bəʊd/ *v.i.* ~ **well/ill**, être de bon/mauvais augure.

bodily /ˈbɒdɪlɪ/ *a.* physique, corporel. ● *adv.* physiquement; (*in person*) en personne.

body /ˈbɒdɪ/ *n.* corps *m.*; (*mass*) masse *f.*; (*organization*) organisme *m.* ~**(work)**, (*auto.*) carrosserie *f.* **the main** ~ **of**, le gros de. ~**builder** *n.* culturiste *m./f.* ~**building** *n.* culturisme *m.*

bodyguard /ˈbɒdɪɡɑːd/ *n.* garde du corps *m.*

bog /bɒɡ/ *n.* marécage *m.* ● *v.t.* (*p.t.* **bogged**) **get** ~**ged down**, s'embourber.

boggle /ˈbɒɡl/ *v.i.* **the mind** ~**s**, on est stupéfait.

bogus /ˈbəʊɡəs/ *a.* faux.

bogy /ˈbəʊɡɪ/ *n.* (*annoyance*) embêtement *m.* ~**(man)**, croquemitaine *m.*

boil¹ /bɔɪl/ *n.* furoncle *m.*

boil² /bɔɪl/ *v.t./i.* (faire) bouillir. **bring to the** ~, porter à ébullition. ~ **down to**, se ramener à. ~ **over**, déborder. ~**ing hot**, bouillant. ~**ing point**, point d'ébullition *m.* ~**ed** *a.* (*egg*) à la coque; (*potatoes*) à l'eau.

boiler /ˈbɔɪlə(r)/ *n.* chaudière *f.* ~ **suit**, bleu (de travail) *m.*

boisterous /ˈbɔɪstərəs/ *a.* tapageur.

bold /bəʊld/ *a.* (**-er, -est**) hardi; (*cheeky*) effronté; (*type*) gras. ~**ness** *n.* hardiesse *f.*

Bolivia /bəˈlɪvɪə/ *n.* Bolivie *f.* ~**n** *a. & n.* bolivien(ne) (*m.* (*f.*)).

bollard /ˈbɒləd/ *n.* (*on road*) borne *f.*

bolster /ˈbəʊlstə(r)/ *n.* traversin *m.* ● *v.t.* soutenir.

bolt /bəʊlt/ *n.* verrou *m.*; (*for nut*) boulon *m.*; (*lightning*) éclair *m.* ● *v.t.* (*door etc.*) verrouiller; (*food*) engouffrer. ● *v.i.* se sauver. ~ **upright**, tout droit.

bomb /bɒm/ *n.* bombe *f.* ● *v.t.* bombarder. ~ **scare**, alerte à la bombe *f.* ~**er** *n.* (*aircraft*) bombardier *m.*; (*person*) plastiqueur *m.*

bombard /bɒmˈbɑːd/ *v.t.* bombarder.

bombastic /bɒmˈbæstɪk/ *a.* grandiloquent.

bombshell /ˈbɒmʃel/ *n.* **be a** ~, tomber comme une bombe.

bona fide /bəʊnəˈfaɪdɪ/ *a.* de bonne foi.

bond /bɒnd/ *n.* (*agreement*) engagement *m.*; (*link*) lien *m.*; (*comm.*) obligation *f.*, bon *m.* **in** ~, (entreposé) en douane.

bondage /ˈbɒndɪdʒ/ *n.* esclavage *m.*

bone /bəʊn/ *n.* os *m.*; (*of fish*) arête *f.* ● *v.t.* désosser. ~**-dry** *a.* tout à fait sec. ~ **idle**, paresseux comme une couleuvre.

bonfire /ˈbɒnfaɪə(r)/ *n.* feu *m.*; (*for celebration*) feu de joie *m.*

bonnet /ˈbɒnɪt/ *n.* (*hat*) bonnet *m.*; (*of vehicle*) capot *m.*

bonus /ˈbəʊnəs/ *n.* prime *f.*

bony /ˈbəʊnɪ/ *a.* (**-ier, -iest**) (*thin*) osseux; (*meat*) plein d'os; (*fish*) plein d'arêtes.

boo /buː/ *int.* hou. ● *v.t./i.* huer. ● *n.* huée *f.*

boob /buːb/ *n.* (*blunder: sl.*) gaffe *f.* ● *v.i.* (*sl.*) gaffer.

booby-trap /ˈbuːbɪtræp/ *n.* engin piégé *m.* ● *v.t.* (*p.t.* **-trapped**) piéger.

book /bʊk/ *n.* livre *m.*; (*of tickets etc.*) carnet *m.* ~**s**, (*comm.*) comptes *m. pl.* ● *v.t.* (*reserve*) réserver; (*driver*) dresser un P.V. à; (*player*) prendre le nom de; (*write down*) inscrire. ● *v.i.* retenir des places. ~**able** *a.* qu'on peut retenir. **(fully)** ~**ed**, complet. ~**ing office**, guichet *m.*

bookcase /ˈbʊkkeɪs/ *n.* bibliothèque *f.*

bookkeeping /ˈbʊkkiːpɪŋ/ *n.* comptabilité *f.*

booklet /ˈbʊklɪt/ *n.* brochure *f.*

bookmaker /ˈbʊkmeɪkə(r)/ *n.* bookmaker *m.*

bookseller /ˈbʊkselə(r)/ *n.* libraire *m./f.*

bookshop /ˈbʊkʃɒp/ *n.* librairie *f.*

bookstall /ˈbʊkstɔːl/ *n.* kiosque (à journaux) *m.*

boom /buːm/ *v.i.* (*gun, wind, etc.*) gronder; (*trade*) prospérer. ● *n.* grondement *m.*; (*comm.*) boom *m.*, prospérité *f.*

boon /buːn/ *n.* (*benefit*) aubaine *f.*

boost /buːst/ *v.t.* stimuler; (*morale*) remonter; (*price*) augmenter; (*publicize*) faire de la réclame pour. ● *n.* **give a** ~ **to**, = **boost**.

boot /buːt/ *n.* (*knee-length*); botte *f.*; (*ankle-length*) chaussure (montante) *f.*; (*for walking*) chaussure de marche *f.*; (*sport*) chaussure de sport *f.*; (*of vehicle*) coffre *m.*

● *v.t./i.* ~ **up**, (*comput.*) démarrer, lancer (le programme). **get the** ~, (*sl.*) être mis à la porte.

booth /buːð/ *n.* (*for telephone*) cabine *f.*; (*at fair*) baraque *f.*

booty /'buːtɪ/ *n.* butin *m.*

booze /buːz/ *v.i.* (*fam.*) boire (beaucoup). ● *n.* (*fam.*) alcool *m.*; (*spree*) beuverie *f.*

border /'bɔːdə(r)/ *n.* (*edge*) bord *m.*; (*frontier*) frontière *f.*; (*in garden*) bordure *f.* ● *v.i.* ~ **on**, (*be next to, come close to*) être voisin de, avoisiner.

borderline /'bɔːdəlaɪn/ *n.* ligne de démarcation *f.* ~ **case**, cas limite *m.*

bore [1] /bɔː(r)/ *see* bear [2].

bore [2] /bɔː(r)/ *v.t./i.* (*techn.*) forer.

bore [3] /bɔː(r)/ *v.t.* ennuyer. ● *n.* raseu|r, -se *m.*, *f.*; (*thing*) ennui *m.* **be** ~**d**, s'ennuyer. ~**dom** *n.* ennui *m.* **boring** *a.* ennuyeux.

born /bɔːn/ *a.* né. **be** ~, naître.

borne /bɔːn/ *see* bear [2].

borough /'bʌrə/ *n.* municipalité *f.*

borrow /'bɒrəʊ/ *v.t.* emprunter (**from**, à). ~**ing** *n.* emprunt *m.*

bosom /'bʊzəm/ *n.* sein *m.* ~ **friend**, ami(e) intime *m.* (*f.*).

boss /bɒs/ *n.* (*fam.*) patron(ne) *m.* (*f.*) ● *v.t.* ~ (**about**), (*fam.*) donner des ordres à, régenter.

bossy /'bɒsɪ/ *a.* autoritaire.

botan|y /'bɒtənɪ/ *n.* botanique *f.* ~**ical** /bə'tænɪkl/ *a.* botanique. ~**ist** *n.* botaniste *m./f.*

botch /bɒtʃ/ *v.t.* bâcler, saboter.

both /bəʊθ/ *a.* les deux. ● *pron.* tous *or* toutes (les) deux, l'un(e) et l'autre. ● *adv.* à la fois. ~ **the books**, les deux livres. **we** ~ **agree**, nous sommes tous les deux d'accord. **I bought** ~ (**of them**), j'ai acheté les deux. **I saw** ~ **of you**, je vous ai vus tous les deux. ~ **Paul and Anne**, (et) Paul et Anne.

bother /'bɒðə(r)/ *v.t.* (*annoy, worry*) ennuyer; (*disturb*) déranger. ● *v.i.* se déranger. ● *n.* ennui *m.*; (*effort*) peine *f.* **don't** ~ (**calling**), ce n'est pas la peine d'appeler). **don't** ~ **about us**, ne t'inquiète pas pour nous. **I can't be** ~**ed**, j'ai la flemme. **it's no** ~, ce n'est rien.

bottle /'bɒtl/ *n.* bouteille *f.*; (*for baby*) biberon *m.* ● *v.t.* mettre en bouteille(s). ~ **bank**, collecteur de verre usagé *m.* ~**-opener** *n.* ouvre-bouteille(s) *m.* ~ **up**, contenir.

bottleneck /'bɒtlnek/ *n.* (*traffic jam*) bouchon *m.*

bottom /'bɒtəm/ *n.* fond *m.*; (*of hill, page, etc.*) bas *m.*; (*buttocks*) derrière *m.* ● *a.* inférieur, du bas. ~**less** *a.* insondable.

bough /baʊ/ *n.* rameau *m.*

bought /bɔːt/ *see* buy.

boulder /'bəʊldə(r)/ *n.* rocher *m.*

boulevard /'buːləvɑːd/ *n.* boulevard *m.*

bounce /baʊns/ *v.i.* rebondir; (*person*) faire des bonds, bondir; (*cheques: sl.*) être refusé. ● *v.t.* faire rebondir. ● *n.* rebond *m.*

bouncer /'baʊnsə(r)/ *n.* videur *m.*

bound [1] /baʊnd/ *v.i.* (*leap*) bondir. ● *n.* bond *m.*

bound [2] /baʊnd/ *see* bind. ● *a.* **be** ~ **for**, être en route pour, aller vers. ~ **to**, (*obliged*) obligé de; (*certain*) sûr de.

boundary /'baʊndrɪ/ *n.* limite *f.*

bound|s /baʊndz/ *n. pl.* limites *f. pl.* **out of** ~**s**, interdit. ~**ed by**, limité par. ~**less** *a.* sans bornes.

bouquet /bʊ'keɪ/ *n.* bouquet *m.*

bout /baʊt/ *n.* période *f.*; (*med.*) accès *m.*; (*boxing*) combat *m.*

boutique /buːˈtiːk/ *n.* boutique (de mode) *f.*

bow [1] /bəʊ/ *n.* (*weapon*) arc *m.*; (*mus.*) archet *m.*; (*knot*) nœud *m.* ~**-legged** *a.* aux jambes arquées. ~**tie** *n.* nœud papillon *m.*

bow [2] /baʊ/ *n.* (*with head*) salut *m.*; (*with body*) révérence *f.* ● *v.t./i.* (s')incliner.

bow [3] /baʊ/ *n.* (*naut.*) proue *f.*

bowels /'baʊəlz/ *n. pl.* intestins *m. pl.*; (*fig.*) entrailles *f. pl.*

bowl [1] /bəʊl/ *n.* cuvette *f.*; (*for food*) bol *m.*; (*for soup etc.*) assiette creuse *f.*

bowl [2] /bəʊl/ *n.* (*ball*) boule *f.* ● *v.t./ i.* (*cricket*) lancer. ~ **over**, bouleverser. ~**ing** *n.* jeu de boules *m.* ~**ing-alley** *n.* bowling *m.*

bowler [1] /'bəʊlə(r)/ *n.* (*cricket*) lanceur *m.*

bowler [2] /'bəʊlə(r)/ *n.* ~ (*hat*), (chapeau) melon *m.*

box [1] /bɒks/ *n.* boîte *f.*; (*cardboard*) carton *m.* (*theatre*) loge *f.* ● *v.t.* mettre en boîte. **the** ~, (*fam.*) la télé. ~ **in**, enfermer. ~**-office** *n.* bureau de location *m.* **Boxing Day**, le lendemain de Noël.

box 285 **break**

box ^{2} /bɒks/ v.t./i. (sport) boxer. ~
s.o.'s ears, gifler qn. ~**ing** n. boxe f.;
a. de boxe.

boy /bɔɪ/ n. garçon m. ~**-friend** n.
(petit) ami m. ~**hood** n. enfance f.
~**ish** a. enfantin, de garçon.

boycott /'bɔɪkɒt/ v.t. boycotter. ● n.
boycottage m.

bra /brɑː/ n. soutien-gorge m.

brace /breɪs/ n. (fastener) attache f.;
(dental) appareil m.; (for bit) vilbre-
quin m. ~**s**, (for trousers) bretelles f.
pl. ● v.t. soutenir. ~ **o.s.**, rassembler ses forces.

bracelet /'breɪslɪt/ n. bracelet m.

bracing /'breɪsɪŋ/ a. vivifiant.

bracken /'brækən/ n. fougère f.

bracket /'brækɪt/ n. (for shelf etc.)
tasseau m., support m.; (group)
tranche f. (**round**) ~, (printing
sign) parenthèse f. (**square**) ~,
crochet m. ● v.t. (p.t. **bracketed**)
mettre entre parenthèses or crochets.

brag /bræg/ v.i. (p.t. **bragged**) se
vanter.

braid /breɪd/ n. (trimming) galon m.;
(of hair) tresse f.

Braille /breɪl/ n. braille m.

brain /breɪn/ n. cerveau m. ~**s**, (fig.)
intelligence f. ● v.t. assommer. ~**-
child** n. invention personnelle f. ~**-
drain** n. exode des cerveaux m.
~**less** a. stupide.

brainwash /'breɪnwɒʃ/ v.t. faire un
lavage de cerveau à.

brainwave /'breɪnweɪv/ n. idée gé-
niale f., trouvaille f.

brainy /'breɪnɪ/ a. (**-ier, -iest**) intelligent.

braise /breɪz/ v.t. braiser.

brake /breɪk/ n. (auto & fig.) frein
m. ● v.t./i. freiner. ~ **fluid**, liquide
de frein m. ~ **light**, feu de stop m. ~
lining, garniture de frein f.

bramble /'bræmbl/ n. ronce f.

bran /bræn/ n. (husks) son m.

branch /brɑːntʃ/ n. branche f.; (of
road) embranchement m.; (comm.)
succursale f.; (of bank) agence f.
● v.i. ~ (**off**), bifurquer.

brand /brænd/ n. marque f. ● v.t. ~
s.o. as, donner à qn. la réputation
de. ~**-new** a. tout neuf.

brandish /'brændɪʃ/ v.t. brandir.

brandy /'brændɪ/ n. cognac m.

brash /bræʃ/ a. effronté.

brass /brɑːs/ n. cuivre m. **get down
to** ~ **tacks**, en venir aux choses

sérieuses. **the** ~, (mus.) les cuivres
m. pl. **top** ~, (sl.) gros bonnets m.
pl.

brassière /'bræsɪə(r), Amer. brə'zɪər/
n. soutien-gorge m.

brat /bræt/ n. (child: pej.) môme m./
f.; (ill-behaved) garnement m.

bravado /brə'vɑːdəʊ/ n. bravade f.

brave /breɪv/ a. (**-er, -est**) courageux,
brave. ● n. (American Indian)
brave m. ● v.t. braver. ~**ry** /-ərɪ/
n. courage m.

bravo /'brɑːvəʊ/ int. bravo.

brawl /brɔːl/ n. bagarre f. ● v.i. se
bagarrer.

brawn /brɔːn/ n. muscles m. pl. ~**y** a.
musclé.

bray /breɪ/ n. braiment m. ● v.i.
braire.

brazen /'breɪzn/ a. effronté.

brazier /'breɪzɪə(r)/ n. brasero m.

Brazil /brə'zɪl/ n. Brésil m. ~**ian** a. &
n. brésilien(ne) (m. (f.)).

breach /briːtʃ/ n. violation f.; (of
contract) rupture f.; (gap) brèche f.
● v.t. ouvrir une brèche dans.

bread /bred/ n. pain m. ~ **and
butter**, tartine f. ~**-bin**, (Amer.)
~**-box** ns. boîte à pain f. ~**-winner**
n. soutien de famille m.

breadcrumbs /'bredkrʌmz/ n. pl.
(culin.) chapelure f.

breadline /'bredlaɪn/ n. **on the** ~,
dans l'indigence.

breadth /bretθ/ n. largeur f.

break /breɪk/ v.t. (p.t. **broke**, p.p.
broken) casser; (smash into pieces)
briser; (vow, silence, rank, etc.)
rompre; (law) violer; (a record)
battre; (news) révéler; (journey)
interrompre; (heart, strike, ice)
briser. ● v.i. (se) casser; se briser.
● n. cassure f., rupture f.; (in
relationship, continuity) rupture f.;
(interval) interruption f.; (at school)
récréation f., récré f.; (for coffee)
pause f.; (luck: fam.) chance f. ~
one's arm, se casser le bras. ~
away from, quitter. ~ **down** v.i.
(collapse) s'effondrer; (fail) échouer;
(machine) tomber en panne; v.t.
(door) enfoncer; (analyse) analyser. ~ **even**, rentrer dans ses
frais. ~**-in** n. cambriolage m. ~
into, cambrioler.. ~ **off**, se détacher; (suspend) rompre; (stop talking) s'interrompre. ~ **out**, (fire,
war, etc.) éclater. ~ **up**, (end) (faire)
cesser; (couple) rompre; (marriage)

(se) briser; (*crowd*) (se) disperser; (*schools*) entrer en vacances. ~**able** *a*. cassable. ~**age** *n*. casse *f*.

breakdown /'breɪkdaʊn/ *n*. (*techn.*) panne *f*.; (*med.*) dépression *f*.; (*of figures*) analyse *f*. ● *a*. (*auto.*) de dépannage.

breaker /'breɪkə(r)/ *n*. (*wave*) brisant *m*.

breakfast /'brekfəst/ *n*. petit déjeuner *m*.

breakthrough /'breɪkθruː/ *n*. percée *f*.

breakwater /'breɪkwɔːtə(r)/ *n*. brise-lames *m*. *invar*.

breast /brest/ *n*. sein *m*.; (*chest*) poitrine *f*. ~**-feed** *v.t*. (*p.t.* -**fed**) allaiter. ~**-stroke** *n*. brasse *f*.

breath /breθ/ *n*. souffle *m*., haleine *f*. **out of** ~, essoufflé. **under one's** ~, tout bas. ~**less** *a*. essoufflé.

breathalyser /'breθəlaɪzə(r)/ *n*. alcootest *m*.

breath|**e** /briːð/ *v.t./i*. respirer. ~ **in**, inspirer. ~ **out**, expirer. ~**ing** *n*. respiration *f*.

breather /'briːðə(r)/ *n*. moment de repos *m*.

breathtaking /'breθteɪkɪŋ/ *a*. à vous couper le souffle.

bred /bred/ *see* breed.

breeches /'brɪtʃɪz/ *n. pl*. culotte *f*.

breed /briːd/ *v.t*. (*p.t.* **bred**) élever; (*give rise to*) engendrer. ● *v.i*. se reproduire. ● *n*. race *f*. ~**er** *n*. éleveur *m*. ~**ing** *n*. élevage *m*.; (*fig.*) éducation *f*.

breez|**e** /briːz/ *n*. brise *f*. ~**y** *a*. (*weather*) frais; (*cheerful*) jovial; (*casual*) désinvolte.

Breton /'bretn/ *a. & n*. breton(ne) (*m*. (*f*.)).

brevity /'brevətɪ/ *n*. brièveté *f*.

brew /bruː/ *v.t*. (*beer*) brasser; (*tea*) faire infuser. ● *v.i*. fermenter; infuser; (*fig.*) se préparer. ● *n*. décoction *f*. ~**er** *n*. brasseur *m*. ~**ery** *n*. brasserie *f*.

bribe /braɪb/ *n*. pot-de-vin *m*. ● *v.t*. soudoyer, acheter. ~**ry** /-ərɪ/ *n*. corruption *f*.

brick /brɪk/ *n*. brique *f*.

bricklayer /'brɪkleɪə(r)/ *n*. maçon *m*.

bridal /'braɪdl/ *a*. nuptial.

bride /braɪd/ *n*. mariée *f*.

bridegroom /'braɪdɡrʊm/ *n*. marié *m*.

bridesmaid /'braɪdzmeɪd/ *n*. demoiselle d'honneur *f*.

bridge[1] /brɪdʒ/ *n*. pont *m*.; (*naut.*) passerelle *f*.; (*of nose*) arête *f*. ● *v.t*. ~ **a gap**, combler une lacune.

bridge[2] /brɪdʒ/ *n*. (*cards*) bridge *m*.

bridle /'braɪdl/ *n*. bride *f*. ● *v.t*. brider. ~**-path** *n*. allée cavalière *f*.

brief[1] /briːf/ *a*. (-**er**, -**est**) bref. ~**ly** *adv*. brièvement. ~**ness** *n*. brièveté *f*.

brief[2] /briːf/ *n*. instructions *f. pl*.; (*jurid.*) dossier *m*. ● *v.t*. donner des instructions à. ~**ing** *n*. briefing *m*.

briefcase /'briːfkeɪs/ *n*. serviette *f*.

briefs /briːfs/ *n. pl*. slip *m*.

brigad|**e** /brɪ'ɡeɪd/ *n*. brigade *f*. ~**ier** /-ə'dɪə(r)/ *n*. général de brigade *m*.

bright /braɪt/ *a*. (-**er**, -**est**) brillant, vif; (*day, room*) clair; (*cheerful*) gai; (*clever*) intelligent. ~**ly** *adv*. brillamment. ~**ness** *n*. éclat *m*.

brighten /'braɪtn/ *v.t*. égayer. ● *v.i*. (*weather*) s'éclaircir; (*of face*) s'éclairer.

brillian|**t** /'brɪljənt/ *a*. brillant; (*light*) éclatant; (*very good*: *fam*.) super. ~**ce** *n*. éclat *m*.

brim /brɪm/ *n*. bord *m*. ● *v.i*. (*p.t.* **brimmed**). ~ **over**, déborder.

brine /braɪn/ *n*. saumure *f*.

bring /brɪŋ/ *v.t*. (*p.t.* **brought**) (*thing*) apporter; (*person, vehicle*) amener. ~ **about**, provoquer. ~ **back**, rapporter; ramener. ~ **down**, faire tomber; (*shoot down, knock down*) abattre. ~ **forward**, avancer. ~ **off**, réussir. ~ **out**, (*take out*) sortir; (*show*) faire ressortir; (*book*) publier. ~ **round** *or* **to**, ranimer. ~ **to bear**, (*pressure etc.*) exercer. ~ **up**, élever; (*med.*) vomir; (*question*) soulever.

brink /brɪŋk/ *n*. bord *m*.

brisk /brɪsk/ *a*. (-**er**, -**est**) vif. ~**ness** *n*. vivacité *f*.

bristl|**e** /'brɪsl/ *n*. poil *m*. ● *v.i*. se hérisser. ~**ing with**, hérissé de.

Britain /'brɪtn/ *n*. Grande-Bretagne *f*.

British /'brɪtɪʃ/ *a*. britannique. **the** ~, les Britanniques *m. pl*.

Briton /'brɪtn/ *n*. Britannique *m./f*.

Brittany /'brɪtənɪ/ *n*. Bretagne *f*.

brittle /'brɪtl/ *a*. fragile.

broach /brəʊtʃ/ *v.t*. entamer.

broad /brɔːd/ *a*. (-**er**, -**est**) large; (*daylight, outline*) grand. ~ **bean**, fève *f*. ~**-minded** *a*. large d'esprit. ~**ly** *adv*. en gros.

broadcast /'brɔːdkɑːst/ *v.t./i*. (*p.t.* **broadcast**) diffuser; (*person*) parler à la télévision *or* à la radio. ● *n.* émission *f.*

broaden /'brɔːdn/ *v.t./i.* (s')élargir.

broccoli /'brɒkəlɪ/ *n. invar.* brocoli *m.*

brochure /'brəʊʃə(r)/ *n.* brochure *f.*

broke /brəʊk/ *see* break. ● *a.* (*penniless: sl.*) fauché.

broken /'brəʊkən/ *see* break. ● *a.* ~ **English**, mauvais anglais *m.* ~-**hearted** *a.* au cœur brisé.

broker /'brəʊkə(r)/ *n.* courtier *m.*

brolly /'brɒlɪ/ *n.* (*fam.*) pépin *m.*

bronchitis /brɒŋ'kaɪtɪs/ *n.* bronchite *f.*

bronze /brɒnz/ *n.* bronze *m.* ● *v.t./i.* (se) bronzer.

brooch /brəʊtʃ/ *n.* broche *f.*

brood /bruːd/ *n.* nichée *f.*, couvée *f.* ● *v.i.* couver; (*fig.*) méditer tristement.~**y** *a.* mélancolique.

brook[1] /brʊk/ *n.* ruisseau *m.*

brook[2] /brʊk/ *v.t.* souffrir.

broom /bruːm/ *n.* balai *m.*

broomstick /'bruːmstɪk/ *n.* manche à balai *m.*

broth /brɒθ/ *n.* bouillon *m.*

brothel /'brɒθl/ *n.* maison close *f.*

brother /'brʌðə(r)/ *n.* frère *m.* ~**hood** *n.* fraternité *f.* ~-**in-law** *n.* (*pl.* ~**s-in-law**) beau-frère *m.* ~**ly** *a.* fraternel.

brought /brɔːt/ *see* bring.

brow /braʊ/ *n.* front *m.*; (*of hill*) sommet *m.*

browbeat /'braʊbiːt/ *v.t.* (*p.t.* -**beat**, *p.p.* -**beaten**) intimider.

brown /braʊn/ *a.* (-**er**, -**est**) marron (*invar.*); (*cheveux*) brun. ● *n.* marron *m.*; brun *m.* ● *v.t./i.* brunir; (*culin.*) (faire) dorer. **be ~ed off**, (*sl.*) en avoir ras le bol. ~ **bread**, pain bis *m.* ~ **sugar**, cassonade *f.*

Brownie /'braʊnɪ/ *n.* jeannette *f.*

browse /braʊz/ *v.i.* feuilleter; (*animal*) brouter.

bruise /bruːz/ *n.* bleu *m.* ● *v.t.* (*hurt*) faire un bleu à; (*fruit*) abîmer. ~**d** *a.* couvert de bleus.

brunch /brʌntʃ/ *n.* petit déjeuner copieux *m.* (*pris comme déjeuner*).

brunette /bruː'net/ *n.* brunette *f.*

brunt /brʌnt/ *n.* **the ~ of**, le plus fort de.

brush /brʌʃ/ *n.* brosse *f.*; (*skirmish*) accrochage *m.*; (*bushes*) broussailles *f. pl.* ● *v.t.* brosser. ~ **against**, effleurer. ~ **aside**, écarter. **give s.o. the ~-off**, (*reject: fam.*) en-

voyer promener qn. ~ **up (on)**, se remettre à.

Brussels /'brʌslz/ *n.* Bruxelles *m./f.* ~ **sprouts**, choux de Bruxelles *m. pl.*

brutal /'bruːtl/ *a.* brutal. ~**ity** /-'tælətɪ/ *n.* brutalité *f.*

brute /bruːt/ *n.* brute *f.* **by ~ force**, par la force.

B.Sc. *abbr. see* Bachelor of Science.

bubble /'bʌbl/ *n.* bulle *f.* ● *v.i.* bouillonner. ~ **bath**, bain moussant *m.* ~ **over**, déborder.

buck[1] /bʌk/ *n.* mâle *m.* ● *v.i.* ruer. ~ **up**, (*sl.*) prendre courage; (*hurry: sl.*) se grouiller.

buck[2] /bʌk/ *n.* (*Amer., sl.*) dollar *m.*

buck[3] /bʌk/ *n.* **pass the ~**, rejeter la responsabilité (**to**, sur).

bucket /'bʌkɪt/ *n.* seau *m.* ~ **shop**, agence de charters *f.*

buckle /'bʌkl/ *n.* boucle *f.* ● *v.t./i.* (*fasten*) (se) boucler; (*bend*) voiler. ~ **down to**, s'atteler à.

bud /bʌd/ *n.* bourgeon *m.* ● *v.i.* (*p.t.* **budded**) bourgeonner.

Buddhis|t /'bʊdɪst/ *a. & n.* bouddhiste (*m./f.*) ~**m** /-ɪzəm/ *n.* bouddhisme *m.*

budding /'bʌdɪŋ/ *a.* (*talent etc.*) naissant; (*film star etc.*) en herbe.

buddy /'bʌdɪ/ *n.* (*fam.*) copain *m.*

budge /bʌdʒ/ *v.t./i.* (faire) bouger.

budgerigar /'bʌdʒərɪgɑː(r)/ *n.* perruche *f.*

budget /'bʌdʒɪt/ *n.* budget *m.* ● *v.i.* (*p.t.* **budgeted**). ~ **for**, prévoir (dans son budget).

buff /bʌf/ *n.* (*colour*) chamois *m.*; (*fam.*) fanatique *m./f.*

buffalo /'bʌfələʊ/ *n.* (*pl.* -**oes** *or* -**o**) buffle *m.*; (*Amer.*) bison *m.*

buffer /'bʌfə(r)/ *n.* tampon *m.* ~ **zone**, zone tampon *f.*

buffet[1] /'bʊfeɪ/ *n.* (*meal, counter*) buffet *m.* ~ **car**, buffet *m.*

buffet[2] /'bʌfɪt/ *n.* (*blow*) soufflet *m.* ● *v.t.* (*p.t.* **buffeted**) souffleter.

buffoon /bə'fuːn/ *n.* bouffon *m.*

bug /bʌg/ *n.* (*insect*) punaise *f.*; (*any small insect*) bestiole *f.*; (*germ: sl.*) microbe *m.*; (*device: sl.*) micro *m.*; (*defect: sl.*) défaut *m.* ● *v.t.* (*p.t.* **bugged**) mettre des micros dans; (*Amer., sl.*) embêter.

buggy /'bʌgɪ/ *n.* (*child's*) poussette *f.*

bugle /'bjuːgl/ *n.* clairon *m.*

build /bɪld/ *v.t./i.* (*p.t.* **built**) bâtir, construire. ● *n.* carrure *f.* ~ **up**, (*increase*) augmenter, monter; (*ac-*

cumulate (s')accumuler. **~-up** n. accumulation f.; (fig.) publicité f. **~er** n. entrepreneur m.; (workman) ouvrier m.

building /'bɪldɪŋ/ n. bâtiment m.; (dwelling) immeuble m. **~ society,** caisse d'épargne-logement f.

built /bɪlt/ see build. **~-in** a. encastré. **~-up area,** agglomération f., zone urbanisée f.

bulb /bʌlb/ n. oignon m.; (electr.) ampoule f. **~ous** a. bulbeux.

Bulgaria /bʌl'ɡeərɪə/ n. Bulgarie f. **~n** a. & n. bulgare (m./f.).

bulg|e /bʌldʒ/ n. renflement m. ● v.i. se renfler, être renflé. **be ~ing with,** être gonflé or bourré de.

bulimia /bjuː'lɪmɪə/ n. boulimie f.

bulk /bʌlk/ n. grosseur f. **in ~,** en gros; (loose) en vrac. **the ~ of,** la majeure partie de. **~y** a. gros.

bull /bʊl/ n. taureau m. **~'s-eye** n. centre (de la cible) m.

bulldog /'bʊldɒɡ/ n. bouledogue m.

bulldoze /'bʊldəʊz/ v.t. raser au bulldozer. **~r** /-ə(r)/ n. bulldozer m.

bullet /'bʊlɪt/ n. balle f. **~-proof** a. pare-balles invar.; (vehicle) blindé.

bulletin /'bʊlətɪn/ n. bulletin m.

bullfight /'bʊlfaɪt/ n. corrida f. **~er** n. torero m.

bullion /'bʊljən/ n. or or argent en lingots m.

bullring /'bʊlrɪŋ/ n. arène f.

bully /'bʊlɪ/ n. brute f.; tyran m. ● v.t. (treat badly) brutaliser; (persecute) tyranniser; (coerce) forcer (into, à).

bum [1] /bʌm/ n. (sl.) derrière m.

bum [2] /bʌm/ n. (Amer., sl.) vagabond(e) m. (f.).

bumble-bee /'bʌmblbiː/ n. bourdon m.

bump /bʌmp/ n. choc m.; (swelling) bosse f. ● v.t./i. cogner, heurter. **~ along,** cahoter. **~ into,** (hit) rentrer dans; (meet) tomber sur. **~y** a. cahoteux.

bumper /'bʌmpə(r)/ n. pare-chocs m. invar. ● a. exceptionnel.

bumptious /'bʌmpʃəs/ a. prétentieux.

bun /bʌn/ n. (cake) petit pain au lait m.; (hair) chignon m.

bunch /bʌntʃ/ n. (of flowers) bouquet m.; (of keys) trousseau m.; (of people) groupe m.; (of bananas) régime m. **~ of grapes,** grappe de raisin f.

bundle /'bʌndl/ n. paquet m. ● v.t. mettre en paquet; (push) pousser.

bung /bʌŋ/ n. bonde f. ● v.t. boucher; (throw: sl.) flanquer.

bungalow /'bʌŋɡələʊ/ n. bungalow m.

bungle /'bʌŋɡl/ v.t. gâcher.

bunion /'bʌnjən/ n. (med.) oignon m.

bunk [1] /bʌŋk/ n. couchette f. **~-beds** n. pl. lits superposés m. pl.

bunk [2] /bʌŋk/ n. (nonsense: sl.) foutaise(s) f. (pl.).

bunker /'bʌŋkə(r)/ n. (mil.) bunker m.

bunny /'bʌnɪ/ n. (children's use) (Jeannot) lapin m.

buoy /bɔɪ/ n. bouée f. ● v.t. **~ up,** (hearten) soutenir, encourager.

buoyan|t /'bɔɪənt/ a. (cheerful) gai. **~cy** n. gaieté f.

burden /'bɜːdn/ n. fardeau m. ● v.t. accabler. **~some** a. lourd.

bureau /'bjʊərəʊ/ n. (pl. **-eaux** /-əʊz/) bureau m.

bureaucracy /bjʊə'rɒkrəsɪ/ n. bureaucratie f.

bureaucrat /'bjʊərəkræt/ n. bureaucrate m./f. **~ic** /-'krætɪk/ a. bureaucratique.

burglar /'bɜːɡlə(r)/ n. cambrioleur m. **~ize** v.t. (Amer.) cambrioler. **~ alarm,** alarme f. **~y** n. cambriolage m.

burgle /'bɜːɡl/ v.t. cambrioler.

Burgundy /'bɜːɡəndɪ/ n. (wine) bourgogne m.

burial /'berɪəl/ n. enterrement m.

burlesque /bɜː'lesk/ n. (imitation) parodie f.

burly /'bɜːlɪ/ a. (**-ier, -iest**) costaud, solidement charpenté.

Burm|a /'bɜːmə/ n. Birmanie f. **~ese** /-'miːz/ a. & n. birman(e) (m. (f.)).

burn /bɜːn/ n. v.t./i. (p.t. **burned** or **burnt**) brûler. ● n. brûlure f. **~ down** or **be ~ed down,** être réduit en cendres. **~er** n. brûleur m. **~ing** a. (fig.) brûlant.

burnish /'bɜːnɪʃ/ v.t. polir.

burnt /bɜːnt/ see burn.

burp /bɜːp/ n. (fam.) rot m. ● v.i. (fam.) roter.

burrow /'bʌrəʊ/ n. terrier m. ● v.t. creuser.

bursar /'bɜːsə(r)/ n. économe m./f.

bursary /'bɜːsərɪ/ n. bourse f.

burst /bɜːst/ v.t./i. (p.t. **burst**) crever, (faire) éclater. ● n. explosion f.; (of laughter) éclat m.; (surge) élan m.

be ~**ing with,** déborder de. ~ **into,** faire irruption dans. ~ **into tears,** fondre en larmes. ~ **out laughing,** éclater de rire. ~ **pipe,** conduite qui a éclaté f.

bury /'berɪ/ v.t. (person etc.) enterrer; (hide, cover) enfouir; (engross, thrust) plonger.

bus /bʌs/ n. (pl. **buses**) (auto)bus m. ● v.t. transporter en bus. ● v.i. (p.t. **bussed**) prendre l'autobus m. ~**-stop** n. arrêt d'autobus m.

bush /bʊʃ/ n. buisson m.; (land) brousse f. ~**y** a. broussailleux.

business /'bɪznɪs/ n. (task, concern) affaire f.; (commerce) affaires f. pl.; (line of work) métier m.; (shop) commerce m. **he has no** ~ **to,** il n'a pas le droit de. **mean** ~, être sérieux. **that's none of your** ~!, ça ne vous regarde pas! ~**man,** homme d'affaires m.

businesslike /'bɪznɪslaɪk/ a. sérieux.

busker /'bʌskə(r)/ n. musicien(ne) des rues m. (f.).

bust[1] /bʌst/ n. buste m.; (bosom) poitrine f.

bust[2] /bʌst/ v.t./i. (p.t. **busted** or **bust**) (burst: sl.) crever; (break: sl.) (se) casser. ● a. (broken, finished: sl.) fichu. ~**-up** n. (sl.) engueulade f. **go** ~, (sl.) faire faillite.

bustl|e /'bʌsl/ v.i. s'affairer. ● n. affairement m., remue-ménage m. ~**ing** a. (place) bruyant, animé.

bus|y /'bɪzɪ/ a. (**-ier, -iest**) occupé; (street) animé; (day) chargé. ● v.t. ~**y o.s. with,** s'occuper à. ~**ily** adv. activement.

busybody /'bɪzɪbɒdɪ/ n. **be a** ~, faire la mouche du coche.

but /bʌt, unstressed bət/ conj. mais. ● prep. sauf. ● adv. (only) seulement. ~ **for,** sans. **nobody** ~, personne d'autre que. **nothing** ~, rien que.

butane /'bjuːteɪn/ n. butane m.

butcher /'bʊtʃə(r)/ n. boucher m. ● v.t. massacrer. ~**y** n. boucherie f., massacre m.

butler /'bʌtlə(r)/ n. maître d'hôtel m.

butt /bʌt/ n. (of gun) crosse f.; (of cigarette) mégot m.; (target) cible f.; (barrel) tonneau m.; (Amer., fam.) derrière m. ● v.i. ~ **in,** interrompre.

butter /'bʌtə(r)/ n. beurre m. ● v.t. beurrer. ~**-bean** n. haricot blanc m. ~**-fingers** n. maladroit(e) m. (f.).

buttercup /'bʌtəkʌp/ n. bouton-d'or m.

butterfly /'bʌtəflaɪ/ n. papillon m.

buttock /'bʌtək/ n. fesse f.

button /'bʌtn/ n. bouton m. ● v.t./i. ~ **(up),** (se) boutonner.

buttonhole /'bʌtnhəʊl/ n. boutonnière f. ● v.t. accrocher.

buttress /'bʌtrɪs/ n. contrefort m. ● v.t. soutenir.

buxom /'bʌksəm/ a. bien en chair.

buy /baɪ/ v.t. (p.t. **bought**) acheter (**from,** à); (believe: sl.) croire, avaler. ● n. achat m. ~ **sth for s.o.** acheter qch. à qn., prendre qch. pour qn. ~**er** n. acheteu|r, -se m., f.

buzz /bʌz/ n. bourdonnement m. ● v.i. bourdonner. ~ **off,** (sl.) ficher le camp. ~**er** n. sonnerie f.

by /baɪ/ prep. par, de; (near) à côté de; (before) avant; (means) en, à, par. **by bike,** à vélo. **by car,** en auto. **by day,** de jour. **by the kilo,** au kilo. **by running**/etc., en courant/etc. **by sea,** par mer. **by that time,** à ce moment-là. ~ **the way,** à propos. ● adv. (near) tout près. **by and large,** dans l'ensemble. **by-election** n. élection partielle f. ~**-law** n. arrêté m.; (of club etc.) statut m. **by o.s.,** tout seul. ~**-product** n. sous-produit m.; (fig.) conséquence f. **by-road** n. chemin de traverse m.

bye(-bye) /baɪ('baɪ)/ int. (fam.) au revoir, salut.

bypass /'baɪpɑːs/ n. (auto.) route qui contourne f.; (med.) pontage m. ● v.t. contourner.

bystander /'baɪstændə(r)/ n. specta|teur, -trice m., f.

byte /baɪt/ n. octet m.

byword /'baɪwɜːd/ n. **be a** ~ **for,** être connu pour.

C

cab /kæb/ n. taxi m.; (of lorry, train) cabine f.

cabaret /'kæbəreɪ/ n. spectacle (de cabaret) m.

cabbage /'kæbɪdʒ/ n. chou m.

cabin /'kæbɪn/ n. (hut) cabane f.; (in ship, aircraft) cabine f.

cabinet /'kæbɪnɪt/ n. (petite) armoire f., meuble de rangement m.; (for *filing*) classeur *m*. **C~**, (*pol*.) cabinet *m*. **~-maker** *n*. ébéniste *m*.

cable /'keɪbl/ *n*. câble *m*. ● *v.t.* câbler. **~-car** *n*. téléphérique *m*. **~ railway**, funiculaire *m*.

caboose /kə'buːs/ *n*. (rail., Amer.) fourgon *m*.

cache /kæʃ/ *n*. (place) cachette *f*. **a ~ of arms**, des armes cachées.

cackle /'kækl/ *n*. caquet *m*. ● *v.i.* caqueter.

cactus /'kæktəs/ *n*. (pl. **-ti** /-taɪ/ or **-tuses**) cactus *m*.

caddie /'kædɪ/ *n*. (golf) caddie *m*.

caddy /'kædɪ/ *n*. boîte à thé *f*.

cadence /'keɪdns/ *n*. cadence *f*.

cadet /kə'det/ *n*. élève officier *m*.

cadge /kædʒ/ *v.t.* se faire payer, écornifler. ● *v.i.* quémander. **~ money from**, taper. **~r** /-ə(r)/ *n*. écornifleu|r, -se *m*., *f*.

Caesarean /sɪ'zeərɪən/ *a*. **~ (section)**, césarienne *f*.

café /'kæfeɪ/ *n*. café(-restaurant) *m*.

cafeteria /kæfɪ'tɪərɪə/ *n*. cafétéria *f*.

caffeine /'kæfiːn/ *n*. caféine *f*.

cage /keɪdʒ/ *n*. cage *f*. ● *v.t.* mettre en cage.

cagey /'keɪdʒɪ/ *a*. (secretive: fam.) peu communicatif.

cagoule /kə'guːl/ *n*. K-way *m*. (P.).

Cairo /'kaɪərəʊ/ *n*. le Caire *m*.

cajole /kə'dʒəʊl/ *v.t.* **~ s.o. into doing**, faire l'enjôleur pour que qn. fasse.

cake /keɪk/ *n*. gâteau *m*. **~d** *a*. durci. **~d with**, raidi par.

calamit|y /kə'læmətɪ/ *n*. calamité *f*. **~ous** *a*. désastreux.

calcium /'kælsɪəm/ *n*. calcium *m*.

calculat|e /'kælkjʊleɪt/ *v.t./i.* calculer; (Amer.) supposer. **~ed** *a*. (action) délibéré. **~ing** *a*. calculateur. **~ion** /-'leɪʃn/ *n*. calcul *m*. **~or** *n*. calculatrice *f*.

calculus /'kælkjʊləs/ *n*. (pl. **-li** /-laɪ/ or **-luses**) calcul *m*.

calendar /'kælɪndə(r)/ *n*. calendrier *m*.

calf[1] /kɑːf/ *n*. (pl. **calves**) (young cow or bull) veau *m*.

calf[2] /kɑːf/ *n*. (pl. **calves**) (of leg) mollet *m*.

calibre /'kælɪbə(r)/ *n*. calibre *m*.

calico /'kælɪkəʊ/ *n*. calicot *m*.

call /kɔːl/ *v.t./i.* appeler. **~ (in or round)**, (visit) passer. ● *n*. appel *m*.; (of bird) cri *m*.; visite *f*. **be ~ed**, (named) s'appeler. **be on ~**, être de garde. **~ back**, rappeler; (visit) repasser. **~-box** *n*. cabine téléphonique *f*. **~ for**, (require) demander; (fetch) passer prendre. **~-girl** *n*. call-girl *f*. **~ off**, annuler. **~ out (to)**, appeler. **~ on**, (visit) passer chez; (appeal to) faire appel à. **~ up**, appeler (au téléphone); (mil.) mobiliser, appeler. **~er** *n*. visiteu|r, -se *m*., *f*.; (on phone) personne qui appelle *f*. **~ing** *n*. vocation *f*.

callous /'kæləs/ *a*. **~ly** *adv*. sans pitié. **~ness** *n*. manque de pitié *m*.

callow /'kæləʊ/ *a*. (**-er**, **-est**) inexpérimenté.

calm /kɑːm/ *a*. (**-er**, **-est**) calme. ● *n*. calme *m*. ● *v.t./i.* **~ (down)**, (se) calmer. **~ness** *n*. calme *m*.

calorie /'kælərɪ/ *n*. calorie *f*.

camber /'kæmbə(r)/ *n*. (of road) bombement *m*.

camcorder /'kæmkɔːdə(r)/ *n*. caméscope *m*.

came /keɪm/ see **come**.

camel /'kæml/ *n*. chameau *m*.

cameo /'kæmɪəʊ/ *n*. (pl. **-os**) camée *m*.

camera /'kæmərə/ *n*. appareil (-photo) *m*.; (for moving pictures) caméra *f*. **in ~**, à huis clos. **~man** *n*. (pl. **-men**) caméraman *m*.

camouflage /'kæməflɑːʒ/ *n*. camouflage *m*. ● *v.t.* camoufler.

camp[1] /kæmp/ *n*. camp *m*. ● *v.i.* camper. **~-bed** *n*. lit de camp *m*. **~er** *n*. campeu|r, -se *m*., *f*. **~er (-van)**, camping-car *m*. **~ing** *n*. camping *m*.

camp[2] /kæmp/ *a*. (mannered) affecté; (vulgar) de mauvais goût.

campaign /kæm'peɪn/ *n*. campagne *f*. ● *v.i.* faire campagne.

campsite /'kæmpsaɪt/ *n*. (for holidaymakers) camping *m*.

campus /'kæmpəs/ *n*. (pl. **-puses**) campus *m*.

can[1] /kæn/ *n*. bidon *m*.; (sealed container for food) boîte *f*. ● *v.t.* (p.t. **canned**) mettre en boîte. **~ it!**, (Amer., sl.) ferme-la! **~ned music**, musique de fond enregistrée *f*. **~-opener** *n*. ouvre-boîte(s) *m*.

can[2] /kæn, unstressed kən/ *v. aux.* (be able to) pouvoir; (know how to) savoir.

Canad|a /'kænədə/ *n*. Canada *m*. **~ian** /kə'neɪdɪən/ *a*. & *n*. canadien(ne) (*m*. (*f*.)).

canal /kə'næl/ *n*. canal *m*.

canary /kə'neərɪ/ *n.* canari *m.*

cancel /'kænsl/ *v.t./i.* (*p.t.* **cancelled**) (*call off, revoke*) annuler; (*cross out*) barrer; (*a stamp*) oblitérer. **~ out**, (se) neutraliser. **~lation** /-ə'leɪʃn/ *n.* annulation *f.*; oblitération *f.*

cancer /'kænsə(r)/ *n.* cancer *m.* **~ous** *a.* cancéreux.

Cancer /'kænsə(r)/ *n.* le Cancer.

candid /'kændɪd/ *a.* franc. **~ness** *n.* franchise *f.*

candida|te /'kændɪdeɪt/ *n.* candidat(e) *m.* (*f.*). **~cy** /-əsɪ/ *n.* candidature *f.*

candle /'kændl/ *n.* bougie *f.*, chandelle *f.*; (*in church*) cierge *m.*

candlestick /'kændlstɪk/ *n.* bougeoir *m.*, chandelier *m.*

candour, (*Amer.*) **candor** /'kændə(r)/ *n.* franchise *f.*

candy /'kændɪ/ *n.* (*Amer.*) bonbon(s) *m.* (*pl.*). **~-floss** *n.* barbe à papa *f.*

cane /keɪn/ *n.* canne *f.*; (*for baskets*) rotin *m.*; (*for punishment*: *schol.*) baguette *f.*, bâton *m.* ● *v.t.* donner des coups de baguette *or* de bâton à, fustiger.

canine /'keɪnaɪn/ *a.* canin.

canister /'kænɪstə(r)/ *n.* boîte *f.*

cannabis /'kænəbɪs/ *n.* cannabis *m.*

cannibal /'kænɪbl/ *n.* cannibale *m./f.* **~ism** *n.* cannibalisme *m.*

cannon /'kænən/ *n.* (*pl.* **~** *or* **~s**) canon *m.* **~-ball** *n.* boulet de canon *m.*

cannot /'kænət/ = **can not**.

canny /'kænɪ/ *a.* rusé, madré.

canoe /kə'nu:/ *n.* (*sport*) canoë *m.*, kayak *m.* ● *v.i.* faire du canoë *or* du kayak. **~ist** *n.* canoéiste *m./f.*

canon /'kænən/ *n.* (*clergyman*) chanoine *m.*; (*rule*) canon *m.*

canonize /'kænənaɪz/ *v.t.* canoniser.

canopy /'kænəpɪ/ *n.* dais *m.*; (*over doorway*) marquise *f.*

can't /kɑ:nt/ = **can not**.

cantankerous /kæn'tæŋkərəs/ *a.* acariâtre, grincheux.

canteen /kæn'ti:n/ *n.* (*restaurant*) cantine *f.*; (*flask*) bidon *m.*

canter /'kæntə(r)/ *n.* petit galop *m.* ● *v.i.* aller au petit galop.

canvas /'kænvəs/ *n.* toile *f.*

canvass /'kænvəs/ *v.t./i.* (*comm., pol.*) solliciter des commandes *or* des voix (de). **~ing** *n.* (*comm.*) démarchage *m.*; (*pol.*) démarchage électoral *m.* **~ opinion,** sonder l'opinion.

canyon /'kænjən/ *n.* cañon *m.*

cap /kæp/ *n.* (*hat*) casquette *f.*; (*of bottle, tube*) bouchon *m.*; (*of beer or milk bottle*) capsule *f.*; (*of pen*) capuchon *m.*; (*for toy gun*) amorce *f.* ● *v.t.* (*p.t.* **capped**) (*bottle*) capsuler; (*outdo*) surpasser. **~ped with,** coiffé de.

capab|le /'keɪpəbl/ *a.* (*person*) capable (**of,** de), compétent. **be ~le of,** (*of situation, text, etc.*) être susceptible de. **~ility** /-'bɪlətɪ/ *n.* capacité *f.* **~ly** *adv.* avec compétence.

capacity /kə'pæsətɪ/ *n.* capacité *f.* **in one's ~,** en sa qualité de.

cape [1] /keɪp/ *n.* (*cloak*) cape *f.*

cape [2] /keɪp/ *n.* (*geog.*) cap *m.*

caper [1] /'keɪpə(r)/ *v.i.* gambader. ● *n.* (*prank*) farce *f.*; (*activity*: *sl.*) affaire *f.*

caper [2] /'keɪpə(r)/ *n.* (*culin.*) câpre *f.*

capital /'kæpɪtl/ *a.* capital. ● *n.* (*town*) capitale *f.*; (*money*) capital *m.* **~ (letter),** majuscule *f.*

capitalis|t /'kæpɪtəlɪst/ *a.* & *n.* capitaliste (*m./f.*). **~m** /-zəm/ *n.* capitalisme *m.*

capitalize /'kæpɪtəlaɪz/ *v.i.* **~ on,** tirer profit de.

capitulat|e /kə'pɪtʃʊleɪt/ *v.i.* capituler. **~ion** /-'leɪʃn/ *n.* capitulation *f.*

capricious /kə'prɪʃəs/ *a.* capricieux.

Capricorn /'kæprɪkɔ:n/ *n.* le Capricorne.

capsize /kæp'saɪz/ *v.t./i.* (faire) chavirer.

capsule /'kæpsju:l/ *n.* capsule *f.*

captain /'kæptɪn/ *n.* capitaine *m.*

caption /'kæpʃn/ *n.* (*for illustration*) légende *f.*; (*heading*) sous-titre *m.*

captivate /'kæptɪveɪt/ *v.t.* captiver.

captiv|e /'kæptɪv/ *a.* & *n.* capti|f, -ve (*m., f.*). **~ity** /-'tɪvətɪ/ *n.* captivité *f.*

capture /'kæptʃə(r)/ *v.t.* (*person, animal*) prendre, capturer; (*attention*) retenir. ● *n.* capture *f.*

car /kɑ:(r)/ *n.* voiture *f.* **~ ferry,** ferry *m.* **~-park** *n.* parking *m.* **~ phone,** téléphone de voiture *m.* **~-wash** *n.* station de lavage *f.*, lave-auto *m.*

carafe /kə'ræf/ *n.* carafe *f.*

caramel /'kærəmel/ *n.* caramel *m.*

carat /'kærət/ *n.* carat *m.*

caravan /'kærəvæn/ *n.* caravane *f.*

carbohydrate /kɑ:bəʊ'haɪdreɪt/ *n.* hydrate de carbone *m.*

carbon /'kɑ:bən/ *n.* carbone *m.* **~ copy, ~ paper,** carbone *m.*

carburettor, (*Amer.*) **carburetor** /kɑːbjʊˈretə(r)/ *n.* carburateur *m.*

carcass /ˈkɑːkəs/ *n.* carcasse *f.*

card /kɑːd/ *n.* carte *f.* **~-index** *n.* fichier *m.*

cardboard /ˈkɑːdbɔːd/ *n.* carton *m.*

cardiac /ˈkɑːdɪæk/ *a.* cardiaque.

cardigan /ˈkɑːdɪgən/ *n.* cardigan *m.*

cardinal /ˈkɑːdɪnl/ *a.* cardinal. ● *n.* (*relig.*) cardinal *m.*

care /keə(r)/ *n.* (*attention*) soin *m.*, attention *f.*; (*worry*) souci *m.*; (*protection*) garde *f.* ● *v.i.* ~ about, s'intéresser à. ~ for, s'occuper de; (*invalid*) soigner. ~ to *or* for, aimer, vouloir. **I don't** ~, ça m'est égal. **take ~ of**, s'occuper de. **take ~ (of yourself)**, prends soin de toi. **take ~ to do sth.**, faire bien attention à faire qch.

career /kəˈrɪə(r)/ *n.* carrière *f.* ● *v.i.* aller à toute vitesse.

carefree /ˈkeəfriː/ *a.* insouciant.

careful /ˈkeəfl/ *a.* soigneux; (*cautious*) prudent. **(be) ~!**, (fais) attention! **~ly** *adv.* avec soin.

careless /ˈkeəlɪs/ *a.* négligent; (*work*) peu soigné. ~ **about**, peu soucieux de. **~ly** *adv.* négligemment. **~ness** *n.* négligence *f.*

caress /kəˈres/ *n.* caresse *f.* ● *v.t.* caresser.

caretaker /ˈkeəteɪkə(r)/ *n.* gardien(ne) *m.* (*f.*). ● *a.* (*president*) par intérim.

cargo /ˈkɑːgəʊ/ *n.* (*pl.* **-oes**) cargaison *f.* ~ **boat**, cargo *m.*

Caribbean /kærɪˈbiːən/ *a.* caraïbe. ● *n.* **the ~**, (*sea*) la mer des Caraïbes; (*islands*) les Antilles *f. pl.*

caricature /ˈkærɪkətjʊə(r)/ *n.* caricature *f.* ● *v.t.* caricaturer.

caring /ˈkeərɪŋ/ *a.* (*mother, son, etc.*) aimant. ● *n.* affection *f.*

carnage /ˈkɑːnɪdʒ/ *n.* carnage *m.*

carnal /ˈkɑːnl/ *a.* charnel.

carnation /kɑːˈneɪʃn/ *n.* œillet *m.*

carnival /ˈkɑːnɪvl/ *n.* carnaval *m.*

carol /ˈkærəl/ *n.* chant de (Noël) *m.*

carp¹ /kɑːp/ *n. invar.* carpe *f.*

carp² /kɑːp/ *v.i.* ~ **(at)**, critiquer.

carpenter /ˈkɑːpɪntə(r)/ *n.* charpentier *m.*; (*for light woodwork, furniture*) menuisier *m.* **~ry** *n.* charpenterie *f.*; menuiserie *f.*

carpet /ˈkɑːpɪt/ *n.* tapis *m.* ● *v.t.* (*p.t.* **carpeted**) recouvrir d'un tapis. **~-sweeper** *n.* balai mécanique *m.* **on the ~**, (*fam.*) sur la sellette.

carriage /ˈkærɪdʒ/ *n.* (*rail & horse-drawn*) voiture *f.*; (*of goods*) transport *m.*; (*cost*) port *m.*

carriageway /ˈkærɪdʒweɪ/ *n.* chaussée *f.*

carrier /ˈkærɪə(r)/ *n.* transporteur *m.*; (*med.*) porteu|r, -se *m., f.* ~ **(bag)**, sac en plastique *m.*

carrot /ˈkærət/ *n.* carotte *f.*

carry /ˈkærɪ/ *v.t./i.* porter; (*goods*) transporter; (*involve*) comporter; (*motion*) voter. **be carried away**, s'emballer. **~-cot** *n.* porte-bébé *m.* ~ **off**, enlever; (*prize*) remporter. ~ **on**, continuer; (*behave: fam.*) se conduire (mal). ~ **out**, (*an order, plan*) exécuter; (*duty*) accomplir; (*task*) effectuer.

cart /kɑːt/ *n.* charrette *f.* ● *v.t.* transporter; (*heavy object: sl.*) trimballer.

cartilage /ˈkɑːtɪlɪdʒ/ *n.* cartilage *m.*

carton /ˈkɑːtn/ *n.* (*box*) carton *m.*; (*of yoghurt, cream*) pot *m.*; (*of cigarettes*) cartouche *f.*

cartoon /kɑːˈtuːn/ *n.* dessin (humoristique) *m.*; (*cinema*) dessin animé *m.* **~ist** *n.* dessina|teur, -trice *m., f.*

cartridge /ˈkɑːtrɪdʒ/ *n.* cartouche *f.*

carve /kɑːv/ *v.t.* tailler; (*meat*) découper.

cascade /kæsˈkeɪd/ *n.* cascade *f.* ● *v.i.* tomber en cascade.

case¹ /keɪs/ *n.* cas *m.*; (*jurid.*) affaire *f.*; (*phil.*) arguments *m. pl.* **in ~ he comes**, au cas où il viendrait. **in ~ of fire**, en cas d'incendie. **in ~ of any problems**, au cas où il y aurait un problème. **in that ~**, à ce moment-là.

case² /keɪs/ *n.* (*crate*) caisse *f.*; (*for camera, cigarettes, spectacles, etc.*) étui *m.*; (*suitcase*) valise *f.*

cash /kæʃ/ *n.* argent *m.* ● *a.* (*price etc.*) (au) comptant. ● *v.t.* encaisser. ~ **a cheque**, (*person*) encaisser un chèque; (*bank*) payer un chèque. **pay ~**, payer comptant. **in ~**, en espèces. ~ **desk**, caisse *f.* ~ **dispenser**, distributeur de billets *m.* **~-flow** *n.* cash-flow *m.* **~ in (on)**, profiter (de). ~ **register**, caisse enregistreuse *f.*

cashew /ˈkæʃuː/ *n.* noix de cajou *f.*

cashier /kæˈʃɪə(r)/ *n.* caiss|ier, -ière *m., f.*

cashmere /ˈkæʃmɪə(r)/ *n.* cachemire *m.*

casino /kəˈsiːnəʊ/ *n.* (*pl.* **-os**) casino *m.*

cask /kɑːsk/ n. tonneau m.

casket /'kɑːskɪt/ n. (box) coffret m.; (coffin: Amer.) cercueil m.

casserole /'kæsərəʊl/ n. (utensil) cocotte f.; (stew) daube f.

cassette /kə'set/ n. cassette f.

cast /kɑːst/ v.t. (p.t. **cast**) (throw) jeter; (glance, look) jeter; (shadow) projeter; (vote) donner; (metal) couler. ~ (off), (shed) se dépouiller de. ● n. (theatre) distribution f.; (of dice) coup m.; (mould) moule m.; (med.) plâtre m. ~ **iron**, fonte f. ~-**iron** a. de fonte; (fig.) solide. ~-**offs** n. pl. vieux vêtements m. pl.

castanets /kæstə'nets/ n. pl. castagnettes f. pl.

castaway /'kɑːstəweɪ/ n. naufragé(e) m. (f.).

caste /kɑːst/ n. caste f.

castle /'kɑːsl/ n. château m.; (chess) tour f.

castor /'kɑːstə(r)/ n. (wheel) roulette f. ~ **sugar**, sucre en poudre m.

castrat|e /kæ'streɪt/ v.t. châtrer. ~**ion** /-ʃn/ n. castration f.

casual /'kæʒʊəl/ a. (remark) fait au hasard; (meeting) fortuit; (attitude) désinvolte; (work) temporaire; (clothes) sport invar. ~**ly** adv. par hasard; (carelessly) avec désinvolture.

casualty /'kæʒʊəltɪ/ n. (dead) mort(e) m. (f.); (injured) blessé(e) m. (f.); (accident victim) accidenté(e) m. (f.).

cat /kæt/ n. chat m. **C**~'s-**eyes** n. pl. (P.) catadioptres m. pl.

catalogue /'kætəlɒg/ n. catalogue m. ● v.t. cataloguer.

catalyst /'kætəlɪst/ n. catalyseur m.

catapult /'kætəpʌlt/ n. lance-pierres m. invar. ● v.t. catapulter.

cataract /'kætərækt/ n. (waterfall & med.) cataracte f.

catarrh /kə'tɑː(r)/ n. rhume m., catarrhe m.

catastroph|e /kə'tæstrəfɪ/ n. catastrophe f. ~**ic** /kætə'strɒfɪk/ a. catastrophique.

catch /kætʃ/ v.t. (p.t. **caught**) attraper; (grab) prendre, saisir; (catch unawares) surprendre; (jam, trap) prendre; (understand) saisir. ● v.i. prendre; (get stuck) se prendre (in, dans). ● n. capture f., prise f.; (on door) loquet m.; (fig.) piège m. ~ **fire**, prendre feu. ~ **on**, (fam.) prendre, devenir populaire. ~ **out**, prendre en faute. ~-**phrase** n. slo-

gan m. ~ **sight of**, apercevoir. ~ **s.o.'s eye**, attirer l'attention de qn. ~ **up**, se rattraper. ~ **up (with)**, rattraper.

catching /'kætʃɪŋ/ a. contagieux.

catchment /'kætʃmənt/ n. ~ **area**, région desservie f.

catchy /'kætʃɪ/ a. facile à retenir.

categorical /kætɪ'gɒrɪkl/ a. catégorique.

category /'kætɪgərɪ/ n. catégorie f.

cater /'keɪtə(r)/ v.i. s'occuper de la nourriture. ~ **for**, (pander to) satisfaire; (of magazine etc.) s'adresser à. ~**er** n. traiteur m.

caterpillar /'kætəpɪlə(r)/ n. chenille f.

cathedral /kə'θiːdrəl/ n. cathédrale f.

catholic /'kæθəlɪk/ a. universel. **C**~ a. & n. catholique (m./f.). **C**~**ism** /kə'θɒlɪsɪzəm/ n. catholicisme m.

cattle /'kætl/ n. pl. bétail m.

catty /'kætɪ/ a. méchant.

caucus /'kɔːkəs/ n. comité électoral m.

caught /kɔːt/ see catch.

cauliflower /'kɒlɪflaʊə(r)/ n. chou-fleur m.

cause /kɔːz/ n. cause f.; (reason) raison f., motif m. ● v.t. causer. ~ **sth. to grow/move**/etc., faire pousser/bouger/etc. qch.

causeway /'kɔːzweɪ/ n. chaussée f.

cauti|on /'kɔːʃn/ n. prudence f.; (warning) avertissement m. ● v.t. avertir. ~**ous** a. prudent. ~**ously** adv. prudemment.

cavalier /kævə'lɪə(r)/ a. cavalier.

cavalry /'kævəlrɪ/ n. cavalerie f.

cave /keɪv/ n. caverne f., grotte f. ● v.i. ~ **in**, s'effondrer; (agree) céder.

caveman /'keɪvmæn/ n. (pl. -men) homme des cavernes m.

cavern /'kævən/ n. caverne f.

caviare, Amer. **caviar** /'kævɪɑː(r)/ n. caviar m.

caving /'keɪvɪŋ/ n. spéléologie f.

cavity /'kævətɪ/ n. cavité f.

cavort /kə'vɔːt/ v.i. gambader.

CD /siː'diː/ n. compact disc m.

cease /siːs/ v.t./i. cesser. ~-**fire** n. cessez-le-feu m. invar. ~**less** a. incessant.

cedar /'siːdə(r)/ n. cèdre m.

cede /siːd/ v.t. céder.

cedilla /sɪ'dɪlə/ n. cédille f.

ceiling /'siːlɪŋ/ n. plafond m.

celebrat|e /'selɪbreɪt/ v.t. (perform, glorify) célébrer; (event) fêter, célébrer. ● *v.i.* **we shall** ~**e**, on va fêter ça. ~**ion** /-'breɪʃn/ *n.* fête *f.*

celebrated /'selɪbreɪtɪd/ *a.* célèbre.

celebrity /sɪ'lebrətɪ/ *n.* célébrité *f.*

celery /'selərɪ/ *n.* céleri *m.*

cell /sel/ *n.* cellule *f.*; (*electr.*) élément *m.*

cellar /'selə(r)/ *n.* cave *f.*

cell|o /'tʃeləʊ/ *n.* (*pl.* -**os**) violoncelle *m.* ~**ist** *n.* violoncelliste *m./f.*

Cellophane /'seləfeɪn/ *n.* (P.) cellophane *f.* (P.).

Celt /kelt/ *n.* Celte *m./f.* ~**ic** *a.* celtique, celte.

cement /sɪ'ment/ *n.* ciment *m.* ● *v.t.* cimenter. ~**-mixer** *n.* bétonnière *f.*

cemetery /'semətrɪ/ *n.* cimetière *m.*

censor /'sensə(r)/ *n.* censeur *m.* ● *v.t.* censurer. **the** ~, la censure. ~**ship** *n.* censure *f.*

censure /'senʃə(r)/ *n.* blâme *m.* ● *v.t.* blâmer.

census /'sensəs/ *n.* recensement *m.*

cent /sent/ *n.* (*coin*) cent *m.*

centenary /sen'tiːnərɪ, *Amer.* 'sentənərɪ/ *n.* centenaire *m.*

centigrade /'sentɪɡreɪd/ *a.* centigrade.

centilitre, *Amer.* **centiliter** /'sentɪliːtə(r)/ *n.* centilitre *m.*

centimetre, *Amer.* **centimeter** /'sentɪmiːtə(r)/ *n.* centimètre *m.*

centipede /'sentɪpiːd/ *n.* millepattes *m. invar.*

central /'sentrəl/ *a.* central. ~ **heating**, chauffage central *m.* ~**ize** *v.t.* centraliser. ~**ly** *adv.* (*situated*) au centre.

centre /'sentə(r)/ *n.* centre *m.* ● *v.t.* (*p.t.* centred) centrer. ● *v.i.* ~ **on**, tourner autour de.

centrifugal /sen'trɪfjʊɡl/ *a.* centrifuge.

century /'sentʃərɪ/ *n.* siècle *m.*

ceramic /sɪ'ræmɪk/ *a.* (*art*) céramique; (*object*) en céramique.

cereal /'sɪərɪəl/ *n.* céréale *f.*

cerebral /'serɪbrəl, *Amer.* sə'riːbrəl/ *a.* cérébral.

ceremonial /serɪ'məʊnɪəl/ *a.* de cérémonie. ● *n.* cérémonial *m.*

ceremon|y /'serɪmənɪ/ *n.* cérémonie *f.* ~**ious** /-'məʊnɪəs/ *a.* solennel.

certain /'sɜːtn/ *a.* certain. **for** ~, avec certitude. **make** ~ **of**, s'assurer de. ~**ly** *adv.* certainement. ~**ty** *n.* certitude *f.*

certificate /sə'tɪfɪkət/ *n.* certificat *m.*

certify /'sɜːtɪfaɪ/ *v.t.* certifier.

cervical /sɜː'vaɪkl/ *a.* cervical.

cessation /se'seɪʃn/ *n.* cessation *f.*

cesspit, cesspool /'sespɪt, 'sespuːl/ *ns.* fosse d'aisances *f.*

chafe /tʃeɪf/ *v.t.* frotter (contre).

chaff /tʃɑːf/ *v.t.* taquiner.

chaffinch /'tʃæfɪntʃ/ *n.* pinson *m.*

chagrin /'ʃæɡrɪn/ *n.* vif dépit *m.*

chain /tʃeɪn/ *n.* chaîne *f.* ● *v.t.* enchaîner. ~ **reaction**, réaction en chaîne *f.* ~**-smoke** *v.i.* fumer de manière ininterrompue. ~ **store**, magasin à succursales multiples *m.*

chair /tʃeə(r)/ *n.* chaise *f.*; (*armchair*) fauteuil *m.*; (*univ.*) chaire *f.* ● *v.t.* (*preside over*) présider.

chairman /'tʃeəmən/ *n.* (*pl.* -**men**) président(e) *m.* (*f.*).

chalet /'ʃæleɪ/ *n.* chalet *m.*

chalk /tʃɔːk/ *n.* craie *f.* ~**y** *a.* crayeux.

challeng|e /'tʃælɪndʒ/ *n.* défi *m.*; (*task*) gageure *f.* ● *v.t.* (*summon*) défier (**to do**, de faire); (*question truth of*) contester. ~**er** *n.* (*sport*) challenger *m.* ~**ing** *a.* stimulant.

chamber /'tʃeɪmbə(r)/ *n.* (*old use*) chambre *f.* ~ **music**, musique de chambre *f.* ~**-pot** *n.* pot de chambre *m.*

chambermaid /'tʃeɪmbəmeɪd/ *n.* femme de chambre *f.*

chamois /'ʃæmɪ/ *n.* ~**(-leather)**, peau de chamois *f.*

champagne /ʃæm'peɪn/ *n.* champagne *m.*

champion /'tʃæmpɪən/ *n.* champion(ne) *m.* (*f.*). ● *v.t.* défendre. ~**ship** *n.* championnat *m.*

chance /tʃɑːns/ *n.* (*luck*) hasard *m.*; (*opportunity*) occasion *f.*; (*likelihood*) chances *f. pl.*; (*risk*) risque *m.* ● *a.* fortuit. ● *v.t.* ~ **doing**, prendre le risque de faire. ~ **it**, risquer le coup. **by** ~, par hasard. **by any** ~, par hasard. ~**s are that**, il est probable que.

chancellor /'tʃɑːnsələ(r)/ *n.* chancelier *m.* **C**~ **of the Exchequer**, Chancelier de l'Échiquier *m.*

chancy /'tʃɑːnsɪ/ *a.* risqué.

chandelier /ʃændə'lɪə(r)/ *n.* lustre *m.*

change /tʃeɪndʒ/ *v.t.* (*alter*) changer; (*exchange*) échanger (**for**, contre); (*money*) changer. ~ **trains/one's dress/***etc.*, (*by substitution*) changer de train/de robe/*etc.* ● *v.i.* changer; (*change clothes*) se changer. ● *n.* changement *m.*; (*money*) monnaie *f.* **a** ~ **for the better**, une amélioration. **a ~ for the worse**, un changement en pire. **~ into**, se transformer en; (*clothes*) mettre. **a ~ of clothes**, des vêtements de rechange. **~ one's mind**, changer d'avis. **~ over**, passer (**to**, à). **for a ~**, pour changer. **~-over** *n.* passage *m.* **~able** *a.* changeant; (*weather*) variable. **~ing** *a.* changeant. **~ing room**, (*in shop*) cabine d'essayage *f.*; (*sport.*) vestiaire *m.*

channel /'tʃænl/ *n.* chenal *m.*; (*TV*) chaîne *f.*; (*medium, agency*) canal *m.*; (*groove*) rainure *f.* ● *v.t.* (*p.t.* **channelled**) (*direct*) canaliser. **the (English) C~**, la Manche. **the C~ Islands**, les îles anglo-normandes *f. pl.*

chant /tʃɑ:nt/ *n.* (*relig.*) psalmodie *f.*; (*of demonstrators*) chant (scandé) *m.* ● *v.t./i.* psalmodier; scander (des slogans).

chao|s /'keɪɒs/ *n.* chaos *m.* **~tic** /-'ɒtɪk/ *a.* chaotique.

chap /tʃæp/ *n.* (*man: fam.*) type *m.*

chapel /'tʃæpl/ *n.* chapelle *f.*; (*Non-conformist*) église (non-conformiste) *f.*

chaperon /'ʃæpərəʊn/ *n.* chaperon *m.* ● *v.t.* chaperonner.

chaplain /'tʃæplɪn/ *n.* aumônier *m.*

chapped /tʃæpt/ *a.* gercé.

chapter /'tʃæptə(r)/ *n.* chapitre *m.*

char [1] /tʃɑ:(r)/ *n.* (*fam.*) femme de ménage *f.*

char [2] /tʃɑ:(r)/ *v.t.* (*p.t.* **charred**) carboniser.

character /'kærəktə(r)/ *n.* caractère *m.*; (*in novel, play*) personnage *m.* **of good ~**, de bonne réputation. **~ize** *v.t.* caractériser.

characteristic /kærəktə'rɪstɪk/ *a.* & *n.* caractéristique (*f.*). **~ally** *adv.* typiquement.

charade /ʃə'rɑːd/ *n.* charade *f.*

charcoal /'tʃɑːkəʊl/ *n.* charbon (de bois) *m.*

charge /tʃɑ:dʒ/ *n.* prix *m.*; (*mil.*) charge *f.*; (*jurid.*) inculpation *f.*, accusation *f.*; (*task, custody*) charge *f.* **~s**, frais *m. pl.* ● *v.t.* faire payer; (*ask*) demander (**for**, pour); (*enemy, gun*) charger; (*jurid.*) inculper, accuser (**with**, de). ● *v.i.* foncer, se précipiter. **~ card**, carte d'achat *f.* **~ it to my account**, mettez-le sur mon compte. **in ~ of**, responsable de. **take ~ of**, prendre en charge, se

charger de. **~able to**, (*comm.*) aux frais de.

charisma /kə'rɪzmə/ *n.* magnétisme *m.* **~tic** /kærɪz'mætɪk/ *a.* charismatique.

charit|y /'tʃærətɪ/ *n.* charité *f.*; (*society*) fondation charitable *f.* **~able** *a.* charitable.

charlatan /'ʃɑːlətən/ *n.* charlatan *m.*

charm /tʃɑːm/ *n.* charme *m.*; (*trinket*) amulette *f.* ● *v.t.* charmer. **~ing** *a.* charmant.

chart /tʃɑːt/ *n.* (*naut.*) carte (marine) *f.*; (*table*) tableau *m.*, graphique *m.* ● *v.t.* (*route*) porter sur la carte.

charter /'tʃɑːtə(r)/ *n.* charte *f.* ● *v.t.* affréter. **~ (flight)**, charter *m.* **~ed accountant**, expert-comptable *m.*

charwoman /'tʃɑːwʊmən/ *n.* (*pl.* **-women**) femme de ménage *f.*

chase /tʃeɪs/ *v.t.* poursuivre. ● *v.i.* courir (**after**, après). ● *n.* chasse *f.* **~ away** *or* **off**, chasser.

chasm /'kæzəm/ *n.* abîme *m.*

chassis /'ʃæsɪ/ *n.* châssis *m.*

chaste /tʃeɪst/ *a.* chaste.

chastise /tʃæ'staɪz/ *v.t.* châtier.

chastity /'tʃæstətɪ/ *n.* chasteté *f.*

chat /tʃæt/ *n.* causette *f.* ● *v.i.* (*p.t.* **chatted**) bavarder. **have a ~**, bavarder. **~ show**, talk-show *m.* **~ up**, (*fam.*) draguer. **~ty** *a.* bavard.

chatter /'tʃætə(r)/ *n.* bavardage *m.* ● *v.i.* bavarder. **his teeth are ~ing**, il claque des dents.

chatterbox /'tʃætəbɒks/ *n.* bavard(e) *m.* (*f.*).

chauffeur /'ʃəʊfə(r)/ *n.* chauffeur (de particulier) *m.*

chauvinis|t /'ʃəʊvɪnɪst/ *n.* chauvin(e) *m.* (*f.*). **male ~t**, (*pej.*) phallocrate *m.* **~m** /-zəm/ *n.* chauvinisme *m.*

cheap /tʃiːp/ *a.* (**-er, -est**) bon marché *invar.*; (*fare, rate*) réduit; (*worthless*) sans valeur. **~er**, meilleur marché *invar.* **~(ly)** *adv.* à bon marché. **~ness** *n.* bas prix *m.*

cheapen /'tʃiːpən/ *v.t.* déprécier.

cheat /tʃiːt/ *v.i.* tricher; (*by fraud*) frauder. ● *v.t.* (*defraud*) frauder; (*deceive*) tromper. ● *n.* escroc *m.*

check [1] /tʃek/ *v.t./i.* vérifier; (*tickets*) contrôler; (*stop*) enrayer, arrêter; (*restrain*) contenir; (*rebuke*) réprimander; (*tick off: Amer.*) cocher. ● *n.* vérification *f.*; contrôle *m.*; (*curb*) frein *m.*; (*chess*) échec *m.*; (*bill: Amer.*) addition *f.*; (*cheque*:

Amer.) chèque m. ~ in, signer le registre; (at airport) passer à l'enregistrement. ~-in n. enregistrement m. ~-list n. liste récapitulative f. ~ out, régler sa note. ~-out n. caisse f. ~-point n. contrôle m. ~ up, vérifier. ~ up on, (detail) vérifier; (situation) s'informer sur. ~-up n. examen médical m.

check² /tʃek/ n. (pattern) carreaux m. pl. ~ed a. à carreaux.

checking /'tʃekɪŋ/ a. ~ account, (Amer.) compte courant m.

checkmate /'tʃekmeɪt/ n. échec et mat m.

checkroom /'tʃekrʊm/ n. (Amer.) vestiaire m.

cheek /tʃiːk/ n. joue f.; (impudence) culot m. ~y a. effronté.

cheer /tʃɪə(r)/ n. gaieté f. ~s, acclamations f. pl.; (when drinking) à votre santé. ● v.t. acclamer, applaudir. ~ (up), (gladden) remonter le moral à. ~ up, prendre courage. ~ful à gai. ~fulness n. gaieté f.

cheerio /tʃɪərɪ'əʊ/ int. (fam.) salut.

cheese /tʃiːz/ n. fromage m.

cheetah /'tʃiːtə/ n. guépard m.

chef /ʃef/ n. (cook) chef m.

chemical /'kemɪkl/ a. chimique. ● n. produit chimique m.

chemist /'kemɪst/ n. pharmacien(ne) m. (f.); (scientist) chimiste m./f. ~'s shop, pharmacie f. ~ry n. chimie f.

cheque /tʃek/ n. chèque m. ~-book n. chéquier m. ~ card, carte bancaire f.

chequered /'tʃekəd/ a. (pattern) à carreaux; (fig.) mouvementé.

cherish /'tʃerɪʃ/ v.t. chérir; (hope) nourrir, caresser.

cherry /'tʃerɪ/ n. cerise f.

chess /tʃes/ n. échecs m. pl. ~-board n. échiquier m.

chest /tʃest/ n. (anat.) poitrine f.; (box) coffre m. ~ of drawers, commode f.

chestnut /'tʃesnʌt/ n. châtaigne f.; (edible) marron m., châtaigne f.

chew /tʃuː/ v.t. mâcher. ~ing-gum n. chewing-gum m.

chic /ʃiːk/ a. chic invar.

chick /tʃɪk/ n. poussin m.

chicken /'tʃɪkɪn/ n. poulet m. ● a. (sl.) froussard. ● v.i. ~ out, (sl.) se dégonfler. ~-pox n. varicelle f.

chick-pea /'tʃɪkpiː/ n. pois chiche m.

chicory /'tʃɪkərɪ/ n. (for salad) endive f.; (in coffee) chicorée f.

chief /tʃiːf/ n. chef m. ● a. principal. ~ly adv. principalement.

chilblain /'tʃɪlbleɪn/ n. engelure f.

child /tʃaɪld/ n. (pl. children /'tʃɪldrən/) enfant m./f. ~hood n. enfance f. ~ish a. enfantin. ~less a. sans enfants. ~like a. innocent, candide. ~-minder n. nourrice f.

childbirth /'tʃaɪldbɜːθ/ n. accouchement m.

Chile /'tʃɪlɪ/ n. Chili m. ~an a. & n. chilien(ne) (m. (f.)).

chill /tʃɪl/ n. froid m.; (med.) refroidissement m. ● a. froid. ● v.t. (person) donner froid à; (wine) rafraîchir; (food) mettre au frais. ~y a. froid; (sensitive to cold) frileux. be or feel ~y, avoir froid.

chilli /'tʃɪlɪ/ n. (pl. -ies) piment m.

chime /tʃaɪm/ n. carillon m. ● v.t./i. carillonner.

chimney /'tʃɪmnɪ/ n. cheminée f. ~-sweep n. ramoneur m.

chimpanzee /tʃɪmpæn'ziː/ n. chimpanzé m.

chin /tʃɪn/ n. menton m.

china /'tʃaɪnə/ n. porcelaine f.

Chin|a /'tʃaɪnə/ n. Chine f. ~ese /-'niːz/ a. & n. chinois(e) (m. (f.)).

chink¹ /tʃɪŋk/ n. (slit) fente f.

chink² /tʃɪŋk/ n. tintement m. ● v.t./ i. (faire) tinter.

chip /tʃɪp/ n. (on plate etc.) ébréchure f.; (piece) éclat m.; (of wood) copeau m.; (culin.) frite f.; (microchip) microplaquette f., puce f. ● v.t. (p.t. chipped) (s')ébrécher. ~ in, (fam.) dire son mot; (with money: fam.) contribuer. (potato) ~s, (Amer.) chips f. pl.

chipboard /'tʃɪpbɔːd/ n. aggloméré m.

chiropodist /kɪ'rɒpədɪst/ n. pédicure m./f.

chirp /tʃɜːp/ n. pépiement m. ● v.i. pépier.

chirpy /'tʃɜːpɪ/ a. gai.

chisel /'tʃɪzl/ n. ciseau m. ● v.t. (p.t. chiselled) ciseler.

chit /tʃɪt/ n. note f., mot m.

chit-chat /'tʃɪttʃæt/ n. bavardage m.

chivalr|y /'ʃɪvlrɪ/ n. galanterie f. ~ous a. chevaleresque.

chives /tʃaɪvz/ n. pl. ciboulette f.

chlorine /'klɔːriːn/ n. chlore m.

choc-ice /'tʃɒkaɪs/ n. esquimau m.

chock /tʃɒk/ n. cale f. **~-a-block, ~-full** adjs. archiplein.

chocolate /'tʃɒklət/ n. chocolat m.

choice /tʃɔɪs/ n. choix m. ● a. de choix.

choir /'kwaɪə(r)/ n. chœur m.

choirboy /'kwaɪəbɔɪ/ n. jeune choriste m.

choke /tʃəʊk/ v.t./i. (s')étrangler. ● n. starter m. **~ (up),** boucher.

cholera /'kɒlərə/ n. choléra m.

cholesterol /kə'lestərɒl/ n. cholestérol m.

choose /tʃuːz/ v.t./i. (p.t. **chose,** p.p. **chosen**) choisir. **~ to do,** décider de faire.

choosy /'tʃuːzɪ/ a. (fam.) exigeant.

chop /tʃɒp/ v.t./i. (p.t. **chopped**) (wood) couper (à la hache); (food) hacher. ● n. (meat) côtelette f. **~ down,** abattre. **~per** n. hachoir m.; (sl.) hélicoptère m. **~ping-board** n. planche à découper f.

choppy /'tʃɒpɪ/ a. (sea) agité.

chopstick /'tʃɒpstɪk/ n. baguette f.

choral /'kɔːrəl/ a. choral.

chord /kɔːd/ n. (mus.) accord m.

chore /tʃɔː(r)/ n. travail (routinier) m.; (unpleasant task) corvée f.

choreography /kɒrɪ'ɒgrəfɪ/ n. chorégraphie f.

chortle /'tʃɔːtl/ n. gloussement m. ● v.i. glousser.

chorus /'kɔːrəs/ n. chœur m.; (of song) refrain m.

chose, chosen /tʃəʊz, 'tʃəʊzn/ see choose.

Christ /kraɪst/ n. le Christ.

christen /'krɪsn/ v.t. baptiser. **~ing** n. baptême m.

Christian /'krɪstʃən/ a. & n. chrétien(ne) (m. (f.)). **~ name,** prénom m. **~ity** /-stɪ'ænətɪ/ n. christianisme m.

Christmas /'krɪsməs/ n. Noël m. ● a. (card, tree, etc.) de Noël. **~-box** n. étrennes f. pl. **~ Day/Eve,** le jour/la veille de Noël.

chrome /krəʊm/ n. chrome m.

chromium /'krəʊmɪəm/ n. chrome m.

chromosome /'krəʊməsəʊm/ n. chromosome m.

chronic /'krɒnɪk/ a. (situation, disease) chronique; (bad: fam.) affreux.

chronicle /'krɒnɪkl/ n. chronique f.

chronolog|y /krə'nɒlədʒɪ/ n. chronologie f. **~ical** /krɒnə'lɒdʒɪkl/ a. chronologique.

chrysanthemum /krɪ'sænθəməm/ n. chrysanthème m.

chubby /'tʃʌbɪ/ a. (-ier, -iest) dodu, potelé.

chuck /tʃʌk/ v.t. (fam.) lancer. **~ away** or **out,** (fam.) balancer.

chuckle /'tʃʌkl/ n. gloussement m. ● v.i. glousser, rire.

chuffed /tʃʌft/ a. (sl.) bien content.

chum /tʃʌm/ n. cop|ain, -ine m., f. **~my** a. amical. **~my with,** copain avec.

chunk /tʃʌŋk/ n. (gros) morceau m.

chunky /'tʃʌŋkɪ/ a. trapu.

church /tʃɜːtʃ/ n. église f.

churchyard /'tʃɜːtʃjɑːd/ n. cimetière m.

churlish /'tʃɜːlɪʃ/ a. grossier.

churn /tʃɜːn/ n. baratte f.; (milk-can) bidon m. ● v.t. baratter. **~ out,** produire (en série).

chute /ʃuːt/ n. glissière f.; (for rubbish) vide-ordures m. invar.

chutney /'tʃʌtnɪ/ n. condiment (de fruits) m.

cider /'saɪdə(r)/ n. cidre m.

cigar /sɪ'gɑː(r)/ n. cigare m.

cigarette /sɪgə'ret/ n. cigarette f. **~ end,** mégot m. **~-holder** n. fume-cigarette m. invar.

cinder /'sɪndə(r)/ n. cendre f.

cine-camera /'sɪnɪkæmərə/ n. caméra f.

cinema /'sɪnəmə/ n. cinéma m.

cinnamon /'sɪnəmən/ n. cannelle f.

cipher /'saɪfə(r)/ n. (numeral, code) chiffre m.; (person) nullité f.

circle /'sɜːkl/ n. cercle m.; (theatre) balcon m. ● v.t. (go round) faire le tour de; (word, error, etc.) entourer d'un cercle. ● v.i. décrire des cercles.

circuit /'sɜːkɪt/ n. circuit m. **~-breaker** n. disjoncteur m.

circuitous /sɜː'kjuːɪtəs/ a. indirect.

circular /'sɜːkjʊlə(r)/ a. & n. circulaire (f.).

circulat|e /'sɜːkjʊleɪt/ v.t./i. (faire) circuler. **~ion** /-'leɪʃn/ n. circulation f.; (of newspaper) tirage m.

circumcis|e /'sɜːkəmsaɪz/ v.t. circoncire. **~ion** /-'sɪʒn/ n. circoncision f.

circumference /sɜː'kʌmfərəns/ n. circonférence f.

circumflex /'sɜːkəmfleks/ n. circonflexe m.

circumspect /'sɜːkəmspekt/ a. circonspect.

circumstance /'sɜːkəmstəns/ *n.* circonstance *f.* **~s,** (*financial*) situation financière *f.*

circus /'sɜːkəs/ *n.* cirque *m.*

cistern /'sɪstən/ *n.* réservoir *m.*

citadel /'sɪtədel/ *n.* citadelle *f.*

cit|e /saɪt/ *v.t.* citer. **~ation** /-'teɪʃn/ *n.* citation *f.*

citizen /'sɪtɪzn/ *n.* citoyen(ne) *m.* (*f.*); (*of town*) habitant(e) *m.* (*f.*). **~ship** *n.* citoyenneté *f.*

citrus /'sɪtrəs/ *a.* **~ fruit(s),** agrumes *m. pl.*

city /'sɪtɪ/ *n.* (grande) ville *f.* **the C~,** la Cité de Londres.

civic /'sɪvɪk/ *a.* civique. **~ centre,** centre administratif *m.* **~s** *n. pl.* instruction civique *f.*

civil /'sɪvl/ *a.* civil; (*rights*) civique; (*defence*) passif. **~ engineer,** ingénieur civil *m.* **C~ Servant,** fonctionnaire *m./f.* **C~ Service,** fonction publique *f.* **~ war,** guerre civile *f.* **~ity** /sɪ'vɪlətɪ/ *n.* civilité *f.*

civilian /sɪ'vɪlɪən/ *a. & n.* civil(e) (*m.* (*f.*)).

civiliz|e /'sɪvəlaɪz/ *v.t.* civiliser. **~ation** /-'zeɪʃn/ *n.* civilisation *f.*

civvies /'sɪvɪz/ *n. pl.* **in ~,** (*sl.*) en civil.

clad /klæd/ *a.* **~ in,** vêtu de.

claim /kleɪm/ *v.t.* revendiquer, réclamer; (*assert*) prétendre. ● *n.* revendication *f.*, prétention *f.*; (*assertion*) affirmation *f.*; (*for insurance*) réclamation *f.*; (*right*) droit *m.*

claimant /'kleɪmənt/ *n.* (*of social benefits*) demandeur *m.*

clairvoyant /kleə'vɔɪənt/ *n.* voyant(e) *m.* (*f.*).

clam /klæm/ *n.* palourde *f.*

clamber /'klæmbə(r)/ *v.i.* grimper.

clammy /'klæmɪ/ *a.* (**-ier, -iest**) moite.

clamour /'klæmə(r)/ *n.* clameur *f.*, cris *m. pl.* ● *v.i.* **~ for,** demander à grands cris.

clamp /klæmp/ *n.* agrafe *f.*; (*large*) crampon *m.*; (*for carpentry*) serre-joint(s) *m.*; (*for car*) sabot de Denver *m.* ● *v.t.* serrer; (*car*) mettre un sabot de Denver à. **~ down on,** sévir contre.

clan /klæn/ *n.* clan *m.*

clandestine /klæn'destɪn/ *a.* clandestin.

clang /klæŋ/ *n.* son métallique *m.*

clanger /'klæŋə(r)/ *n.* (*sl.*) bévue *f.*

clap /klæp/ *v.t./i.* (*p.t.* **clapped**) applaudir; (*put forcibly*) mettre. ● *n.*

applaudissement *m.*; (*of thunder*) coup *m.* **~ one's hands,** battre des mains.

claptrap /'klæptræp/ *n.* baratin *m.*

claret /'klærət/ *n.* bordeaux rouge *m.*

clarif|y /'klærɪfaɪ/ *v.t./i.* (se) clarifier. **~ication** /-ɪ'keɪʃn/ *n.* clarification *f.*

clarinet /klærɪ'net/ *n.* clarinette *f.*

clarity /'klærətɪ/ *n.* clarté *f.*

clash /klæʃ/ *n.* choc *m.*; (*fig.*) conflit *m.* ● *v.i.* (*metal objects*) s'entrechoquer; (*fig.*) se heurter.

clasp /klɑːsp/ *n.* (*fastener*) fermoir *m.*, agrafe *f.* ● *v.t.* serrer.

class /klɑːs/ *n.* classe *f.* ● *v.t.* classer.

classic /'klæsɪk/ *a. & n.* classique (*m.*). **~s,** (*univ.*) les humanités *f. pl.* **~al** *a.* classique.

classif|y /'klæsɪfaɪ/ *v.t.* classifier. **~ication** /-ɪ'keɪʃn/ *n.* classification *f.* **~ied** *a.* (*information etc.*) secret. **~ied advertisement,** petite annonce *f.*

classroom /'klɑːsrʊm/ *n.* salle de classe *f.*

classy /'klɑːsɪ/ *a.* (*sl.*) chic *invar.*

clatter /'klætə(r)/ *n.* cliquetis *m.* ● *v.i.* cliqueter.

clause /klɔːz/ *n.* clause *f.*; (*gram.*) proposition *f.*

claustrophob|ia /klɔːstrə'fəʊbɪə/ *n.* claustrophobie *f.* **~ic** *a. & n.* claustrophobe (*m./f.*).

claw /klɔː/ *n.* (*of animal, small bird*) griffe *f.*; (*of bird of prey*) serre *f.*; (*of lobster*) pince *f.* ● *v.t.* griffer.

clay /kleɪ/ *n.* argile *f.*

clean /kliːn/ *a.* (**-er, -est**) propre; (*shape, stroke, etc.*) net. ● *adv.* complètement. ● *v.t.* nettoyer. ● *v.i.* **~ up,** faire le nettoyage. **~ one's teeth,** se brosser les dents. **~-shaven** *a.* glabre. **~er** *n.* (*at home*) femme de ménage *f.*; (*industrial*) agent de nettoyage *m./f.*; (*of clothes*) teintur|ier, -ière *m.*, *f.* **~ly** *adv.* proprement; (*sharply*) nettement.

cleanliness /'klenlɪnɪs/ *n.* propreté *f.*

cleans|e /klenz/ *v.t.* nettoyer; (*fig.*) purifier. **~ing cream,** crème démaquillante *f.*

clear /klɪə(r)/ *a.* (**-er, -est**) clair; (*glass*) transparent; (*profit*) net; (*road*) dégagé. ● *adv.* complètement. ● *v.t.* dégager (**of,** de); (*table*) débarrasser; (*building*) évacuer; (*cheque*) encaisser; (*jump over*) franchir; (*debt*) liquider; (*jurid.*) disculper. **~ (away or**

off), (*remove*) enlever. ● *v.i.* (*fog*) se dissiper. ~ **of,** (*away from*) à l'écart de. ~ **off** or **out,** (*sl.*) décamper. ~ **out,** (*clean*) nettoyer. ~ **up,** (*tidy*) ranger; (*mystery*) éclaircir; (*of weather*) s'éclaircir. **make shift. ~,** être très clair sur qch. **~-cut** *a.* net. **~ly** *adv.* clairement.

clearance /'klɪərəns/ *n.* (*permission*) autorisation *f.*; (*space*) dégagement *m.* ~ **sale,** liquidation *f.*

clearing /'klɪərɪŋ/ *n.* clairière *f.*

clearway /'klɪəweɪ/ *n.* route à stationnement interdit *f.*

cleavage /'kliːvɪdʒ/ *n.* clivage *m.*; (*breasts*) décolleté *m.*

clef /klef/ *n.* (*mus.*) clé *f.*

cleft /kleft/ *n.* fissure *f.*

clemen|t /'klemənt/ *a.* clément. **~cy** *n.* clémence *f.*

clench /klentʃ/ *v.t.* serrer.

clergy /'klɜːdʒɪ/ *n.* clergé *m.* **~man** *n.* (*pl.* **-men**) ecclésiastique *m.*

cleric /'klerɪk/ *n.* clerc *m.* **~al** *a.* (*relig.*) clérical; (*of clerks*) de bureau, d'employé.

clerk /klɑːk, *Amer.* klɜːk/ *n.* employé(e) de bureau *m.* (*f.*). (*Amer.*) (*sales*) **~,** vendeu|r, -se *m.*, *f.*.

clever /'klevə(r)/ *a.* (**-er, -est**) intelligent; (*skilful*) habile. **~ly** *adv.* intelligemment; habilement. **~ness** *n.* intelligence *f.*

cliché /'kliːʃeɪ/ *n.* cliché *m.*

click /klɪk/ *n.* déclic *m.* ● *v.i.* faire un déclic; (*people: sl.*) s'entendre, se plaire. ● *v.t.* (*heels, tongue*) faire claquer.

client /'klaɪənt/ *n.* client(e) *m.* (*f.*).

clientele /kliːɒn'tel/ *n.* clientèle *f.*

cliff /klɪf/ *n.* falaise *f.*

climat|e /'klaɪmɪt/ *n.* climat *m.* **~ic** /-'mætɪk/ *a.* climatique.

climax /'klaɪmæks/ *n.* point culminant *m.*; (*sexual*) orgasme *m.*

climb /klaɪm/ *v.t.* (*stairs*) monter, grimper; (*tree, ladder*) monter or grimper à; (*mountain*) faire l'ascension de. ● *v.i.* monter, grimper. ● *n.* montée *f.* ~ **down,** (*fig.*) reculer. **~-down,** *n.* recul *m.* **~er** *n.* (*sport*) alpiniste *m./f.*

clinch /klɪntʃ/ *v.t.* (*a deal*) conclure.

cling /klɪŋ/ *v.i.* (*p.t.* **clung**) se cramponner (**to,** à); (*stick*) coller. **~-film** *n.* (P.) film adhésif *m.*

clinic /'klɪnɪk/ *n.* centre médical *m.*; (*private*) clinique *f.*

clinical /'klɪnɪkl/ *a.* clinique.

clink /klɪŋk/ *n.* tintement *m.* ● *v.t./i.* (faire) tinter.

clinker /'klɪŋkə(r)/ *n.* mâchefer *m.*

clip [1] /klɪp/ *n.* (*for paper*) trombone *m.*; (*for hair*) barrette *f.*; (*for tube*) collier *m.* ● *v.t.* (*p.t.* **clipped**) attacher (**to,** à).

clip [2] /klɪp/ *v.t.* (*p.t.* **clipped**) (*cut*) couper. ● *n.* coupe *f.*; (*of film*) extrait *m.*; (*blow: fam.*) taloche *f.* **~ping** *n.* coupure *f.*

clippers /'klɪpəz/ *n. pl.* tondeuse *f.*; (*for nails*) coupe-ongles *m.*

clique /kliːk/ *n.* clique *f.*

cloak /kləʊk/ *n.* (grande) cape *f.*, manteau ample *m.*

cloakroom /'kləʊkrʊm/ *n.* vestiaire *m.*; (*toilet*) toilettes *f. pl.*

clobber /'klɒbə(r)/ *n.* (*sl.*) affaires *f. pl.* ● *v.t.* (*hit: sl.*) tabasser.

clock /klɒk/ *n.* pendule *f.*; (*large*) horloge *f.* ● *v.i.* ~ **up,** (*miles etc.: fam.*) faire. **~-tower** *n.* clocher *m.*

clockwise /'klɒkwaɪz/ *a.* & *adv.* dans le sens des aiguilles d'une montre.

clockwork /'klɒkwɜːk/ *n.* mécanisme *m.* ● *a.* mécanique.

clog /klɒg/ *n.* sabot *m.* ● *v.t./i.* (*p.t.* **clogged**) (se) boucher.

cloister /'klɔɪstə(r)/ *n.* cloître *m.*

close [1] /kləʊs/ *a.* (**-er, -est**) (*near*) proche (**to,** de); (*link, collaboration*) étroit; (*examination*) attentif; (*friend*) intime; (*order, match*) serré; (*weather*) lourd. ~ **together,** (*crowded*) serrés. ● *adv.* (*tout*) près. ● *n.* (*street*) impasse *f.* ~ **by,** ~ **at hand,** tout près. **~-up** *n.* gros plan *m.* **have a ~ shave,** l'échapper belle. **keep a ~ watch on,** surveiller de près. **~ly** *adv.* (*follow*) de près. **~ness** *n.* proximité *f.*

close [2] /kləʊz/ *v.t.* fermer. ● *v.i.* se fermer; (*of shop etc.*) fermer; (*end*) (se) terminer. ● *n.* fin *f.* **~d shop,** organisation qui exclut les travailleurs non syndiqués *f.*

closet /'klɒzɪt/ *n.* (*Amer.*) placard *m.*

closure /'kləʊʒə(r)/ *n.* fermeture *f.*

clot /klɒt/ *n.* (*of blood*) caillot *m.*; (*in sauce*) grumeau *m.* ● *v.t./i.* (*p.t.* **clotted**) se coaguler.

cloth /klɒθ/ *n.* tissu *m.*; (*duster*) linge *m.*; (*table-cloth*) nappe *f.*

cloth|e /kləʊð/ *v.t.* vêtir. **~ing** *n.* vêtements *m. pl.*

clothes /kləʊðz/ *n. pl.* vêtements *m. pl.*, habits *m. pl.* **~-brush** *n.* brosse à habits *f.* **~-hanger** *n.* cintre *m.* **~-line** *n.* corde à linge *f.* **~-peg**, (*Amer.*) **~-pin** *ns.* pince à linge *f.*

cloud /klaʊd/ *n.* nuage *m.* ● *v.i.* se couvrir (de nuages); (*become gloomy*) s'assombrir. **~y** *a.* (*sky*) couvert; (*liquid*) trouble.

cloudburst /'klaʊdbɜːst/ *n.* trombe d'eau *f.*

clout /klaʊt/ *n.* (*blow*) coup de poing *m.*; (*power: fam.*) pouvoir effectif *m.* ● *v.t.* frapper.

clove /kləʊv/ *n.* clou de girofle *m.* **~ of garlic**, gousse d'ail *f.*

clover /'kləʊvə(r)/ *n.* trèfle *m.*

clown /klaʊn/ *n.* clown *m.* ● *v.i.* faire le clown.

cloy /klɔɪ/ *v.t.* écœurer.

club /klʌb/ *n.* (*group*) club *m.*; (*weapon*) massue *f.* **~s**, (*cards*) trèfle *m.* ● *v.t./i.* (*p.t.* **clubbed**) matraquer. **(golf) ~**, club (de golf) *m.* **~ together**, (*share costs*) se cotiser.

cluck /klʌk/ *v.i.* glousser.

clue /kluː/ *n.* indice *m.*; (*in crossword*) définition *f.* **I haven't a ~**, (*fam.*) je n'en ai pas la moindre idée.

clump /klʌmp/ *n.* massif *m.*

clums|y /'klʌmzɪ/ *a.* (**-ier, -iest**) maladroit; (*tool*) peu commode. **~iness** *n.* maladresse *f.*

clung /klʌŋ/ *see* cling.

cluster /'klʌstə(r)/ *n.* (petit) groupe *m.* ● *v.i.* se grouper.

clutch /klʌtʃ/ *v.t.* (*hold*) serrer fort; (*grasp*) saisir. ● *v.i.* (*try to grasp*) essayer de saisir. ● *n.* étreinte *f.*; (*auto.*) embrayage *m.*

clutter /'klʌtə(r)/ *n.* désordre *m.*, fouillis *m.* ● *v.t.* encombrer.

coach /kəʊtʃ/ *n.* autocar *m.*; (*of train*) wagon *m.*; (*horse-drawn*) carrosse *m.*; (*sport*) entraîneu|r, -se *m.*, *f.* ● *v.t.* donner des leçons (particulières) à; (*sport*) entraîner.

coagulate /kəʊ'ægjʊleɪt/ *v.t./i.* (se) coaguler.

coal /kəʊl/ *n.* charbon *m.* **~-mine** *n.* mine de charbon *f.*

coalfield /'kəʊlfiːld/ *n.* bassin houiller *m.*

coalition /kəʊə'lɪʃn/ *n.* coalition *f.*

coarse /kɔːs/ *a.* (**-er, -est**) grossier. **~ness** *n.* caractère grossier *m.*

coast /kəʊst/ *n.* côte *f.* ● *v.i.* (*car, bicycle*) descendre en roue libre. **~al** *a.* côtier.

coaster /'kəʊstə(r)/ *n.* (*ship*) caboteur *m.*; (*mat*) dessous de verre *m.*

coastguard /'kəʊstgɑːd/ *n.* gardecôte *m.*

coastline /'kəʊstlaɪn/ *n.* littoral *m.*

coat /kəʊt/ *n.* manteau *m.*; (*of animal*) pelage *m.*; (*of paint*) couche *f.* ● *v.t.* enduire, couvrir; (*with chocolate*) enrober (**with**, de). **~-hanger** *n.* cintre *m.* **~ of arms**, armoiries *f. pl.* **~ing** *n.* couche *f.*

coax /kəʊks/ *v.t.* amadouer.

cob /kɒb/ *n.* (*of corn*) épi *m.*

cobble¹ /'kɒbl/ *n.* pavé *m.* **~-stone** *n.* pavé *m.*

cobble² /'kɒbl/ *v.t.* rapetasser.

cobbler /'kɒblə(r)/ *n.* (*old use*) cordonnier *m.*

cobweb /'kɒbweb/ *n.* toile d'araignée *f.*

cocaine /kəʊ'keɪn/ *n.* cocaïne *f.*

cock /kɒk/ *n.* (*oiseau*) mâle *m.*; (*rooster*) coq *m.* ● *v.t.* (*gun*) armer; (*ears*) dresser. **~-and-bull story**, histoire à dormir debout *f.* **~-eyed** *a.* (*askew: sl.*) de travers. **~-up** *n.* (*sl.*) pagaille *f.*

cockerel /'kɒkərəl/ *n.* jeune coq *m.*

cockle /'kɒkl/ *n.* (*culin.*) coque *f.*

cockney /'kɒknɪ/ *n.* Cockney *m./f.*

cockpit /'kɒkpɪt/ *n.* poste de pilotage *m.*

cockroach /'kɒkrəʊtʃ/ *n.* cafard *m.*

cocksure /kɒk'ʃʊə(r)/ *a.* sûr de soi.

cocktail /'kɒkteɪl/ *n.* cocktail *m.* **~ party**, cocktail *m.* **fruit ~**, macédoine (de fruits) *f.*

cocky /'kɒkɪ/ *a.* (**-ier, -iest**) trop sûr de soi, arrogant.

cocoa /'kəʊkəʊ/ *n.* cacao *m.*

coconut /'kəʊkənʌt/ *n.* noix de coco *f.*

cocoon /kə'kuːn/ *n.* cocon *m.*

COD *abbr.* (*cash on delivery*) paiement à la livraison *m.*

cod /kɒd/ *n. invar.* morue *f.* **~-liver oil**, huile de foie de morue *f.*

coddle /'kɒdl/ *v.t.* dorloter.

code /kəʊd/ *n.* code *m.* ● *v.t.* coder.

codify /'kəʊdɪfaɪ/ *v.t.* codifier.

coeducational /kəʊedʒʊ'keɪʃənl/ *a.* (*school, teaching*) mixte.

coerc|e /kəʊ'ɜːs/ *v.t.* contraindre. **~ion** /-ʃn/ *n.* contrainte *f.*

coexist /kəʊɪg'zɪst/ *v.i.* coexister. **~ence** *n.* coexistence *f.*

coffee /ˈkɒfɪ/ n. café m. ~ **bar**, café m., cafétéria f. ~**pot** n. cafetière f. ~**table** n. table basse f.

coffer /ˈkɒfə(r)/ n. coffre m.

coffin /ˈkɒfɪn/ n. cercueil m.

cog /kɒg/ n. dent f.; (fig.) rouage m.

cogent /ˈkəʊdʒənt/ a. convaincant; (relevant) pertinent.

cognac /ˈkɒnjæk/ n. cognac m.

cohabit /kəʊˈhæbɪt/ v.i. vivre en concubinage.

coherent /kəʊˈhɪərənt/ a. cohérent.

coil /kɔɪl/ v.t./i. (s')enrouler. ● n. rouleau m.; (one ring) spire f.; (contraceptive) stérilet m.

coin /kɔɪn/ n. pièce (de monnaie) f. ● v.t. (word) inventer. ~**age** n. monnaie f.; (fig.) invention f. ~**box** n. téléphone public m.

coincide /kəʊɪnˈsaɪd/ v.i. coïncider.

coinciden|ce /kəʊˈɪnsɪdəns/ n. coïncidence f. ~**tal** /-ˈdentl/ a. dû à une coïncidence.

coke /kəʊk/ n. coke m.

colander /ˈkʌləndə(r)/ n. passoire f.

cold /kəʊld/ a. (-er, -est) froid. be or feel ~, avoir froid. it is ~, il fait froid. ● n. froid m.; (med.) rhume m. ~-**blooded** a. sans pitié. ~-**cream**, crème de beauté f. get ~ **feet**, se dégonfler. ~-**shoulder** v.t. snober. ~ **sore**, bouton de fièvre m. ~**ness** n. froideur f.

coleslaw /ˈkəʊlslɔː/ n. salade de chou cru f.

colic /ˈkɒlɪk/ n. coliques f. pl.

collaborat|e /kəˈlæbəreɪt/ v.i. collaborer. ~**ion** /-ˈreɪʃn/ n. collaboration f. ~**or** n. collabora|teur, -trice m., f.

collage /ˈkɒlɑːʒ/ n. collage m.

collapse /kəˈlæps/ v.i. s'effondrer; (med.) avoir un malaise. ● n. effondrement m.

collapsible /kəˈlæpsəbl/ a. pliant.

collar /ˈkɒlə(r)/ n. col m.; (of dog) collier m. ● v.t. (take: sl.) piquer. ~-**bone** n. clavicule f.

collateral /kəˈlætərəl/ n. nantissement m.

colleague /ˈkɒliːg/ n. collègue m./f.

collect /kəˈlekt/ v.t. rassembler; (pick up) ramasser; (call for) passer prendre; (money, rent) encaisser; (taxes) percevoir; (as hobby) collectionner. ● v.i. se rassembler; (dust) s'amasser. ● adv. call ~, (Amer.) téléphoner en PCV. ~**ion** /-kʃn/ n. collection f.; (in church) quête f.; (of mail) levée f. ~**or** n. (as hobby) collectionneu|r, -se m., f.

collective /kəˈlektɪv/ a. collectif.

college /ˈkɒlɪdʒ/ n. (for higher education) institut m., école f.; (within university) collège m. be at ~, être en faculté.

collide /kəˈlaɪd/ v.i. entrer en collision (with, avec).

colliery /ˈkɒlɪərɪ/ n. houillère f.

collision /kəˈlɪʒn/ n. collision f.

colloquial /kəˈləʊkwɪəl/ a. familier. ~**ism** n. expression familière f.

collusion /kəˈluːʒn/ n. collusion f.

colon /ˈkəʊlən/ n. (gram.) deux-points m. invar.; (anat.) côlon m.

colonel /ˈkɜːnl/ n. colonel m.

colonize /ˈkɒlənaɪz/ v.t. coloniser.

colon|y /ˈkɒlənɪ/ n. colonie f. ~**ial** /kəˈləʊnɪəl/ a. & n. colonial(e) (m. (f.)).

colossal /kəˈlɒsl/ a. colossal.

colour /ˈkʌlə(r)/ n. couleur f. ● a. (photo etc.) en couleur; (TV set) couleur invar. ● v.t. colorer; (with crayon) colorier. ~-**blind** a. daltonien. ~-**fast** a. grand teint. invar. ~**ful** a. coloré; (person) haut en couleur. ~**ing** n. (of skin) teint m.; (in food) colorant m.

coloured /ˈkʌləd/ a. (person, pencil) de couleur. ● n. personne de couleur f.

colt /kəʊlt/ n. poulain m.

column /ˈkɒləm/ n. colonne f.

columnist /ˈkɒləmnɪst/ n. journaliste chroniqueur m.

coma /ˈkəʊmə/ n. coma m.

comb /kəʊm/ n. peigne m. ● v.t. peigner; (search) ratisser. ~ **one's hair**, se peigner.

combat /ˈkɒmbæt/ n. combat m. ● v.t. (p.t. **combated**) combattre. ~**ant** /-ətənt/ n. combattant(e) m. (f.).

combination /kɒmbɪˈneɪʃn/ n. combinaison f.

combine¹ /kəmˈbaɪn/ v.t./i. (se) combiner, (s')unir.

combine² /ˈkɒmbaɪn/ n. (comm.) trust m., cartel m. ~ **harvester**, moissonneuse-batteuse f.

combustion /kəmˈbʌstʃən/ n. combustion f.

come /kʌm/ v.i. (p.t. **came**, p.p. **come**) venir; (occur) arriver; (sexually) jouir. ~ **about**, arriver. ~ **across**, rencontrer or trouver par hasard. ~ **away** or **off**, se détacher,

partir. ~ **back**, revenir. ~**-back** n.
rentrée f.; (*retort*) réplique f. ~ **by**,
obtenir. ~ **down**, descendre; (*price*)
baisser. ~**-down** n. humiliation f. ~
forward, se présenter. ~ **from**, être
de. ~ **in**, entrer. ~ **in for**, recevoir.
~ **into**, (*money*) hériter de. ~ **off**,
(*succeed*) réussir; (*fare*) s'en tirer. ~
on, (*actor*) entrer en scène; (*light*)
s'allumer; (*improve*) faire des
progrès. ~ **on!**, allez! ~ **out**,
sortir. ~ **round** *or* **to**, revenir à
soi. ~ **through**, s'en tirer (indemne
de). ~ **to**, (*amount*) revenir à;
(*decision, conclusion*) arriver à. ~
up, monter; (*fig.*) se présenter. ~ **up
against**, rencontrer. ~ **get one's** ~**-
uppance** n. (*fam.*) finir par recevoir
ce qu'on mérite. ~ **up with**, (*find*)
trouver; (*produce*) produire.

comedian /kə'mi:dɪən/ n. comique
m.

comedy /'kɒmədɪ/ n. comédie f.

comely /'kʌmlɪ/ a. (**-ier, -iest**) (*old
use*) avenant, beau.

comet /'kɒmɪt/ n. comète f.

comfort /'kʌmfət/ n. confort m.;
(*consolation*) réconfort m. ● v.t.
consoler. **one's** ~**s**, ses aises.
~**able** a. (*chair, car, etc.*) confortable; (*person*) à l'aise, bien; (*wealthy*)
aisé.

comforter /'kʌmfətə(r)/ n. (*baby's
dummy*) sucette f.; (*quilt: Amer.*)
édredon m.

comfy /'kʌmfɪ/ a. (*fam.*) = **comfortable.**

comic /'kɒmɪk/ a. comique. ● n.
(*person*) comique m.; (*periodical*)
comic m. ~ **strip**, bande dessinée f.
~**al** a. comique.

coming /'kʌmɪŋ/ n. arrivée f. ● a. à
venir. ~**s and goings**, allées et
venues f. pl.

comma /'kɒmə/ n. virgule f.

command /kə'mɑːnd/ n. (*authority*)
commandement m.; (*order*) ordre
m.; (*mastery*) maîtrise f. ● v.t. commander (**s.o. to**, à qn. de); (*be able to
use*) disposer de; (*require*) nécessiter; (*respect*) inspirer. ~**er** n. commandant m. ~**ing** a. imposant.

commandeer /kɒmən'dɪə(r)/ v.t. réquisitionner.

commandment /kə'mɑːndmənt/ n.
commandement m.

commando /kə'mɑːndəʊ/ n. (pl. **-os**)
commando m.

commemorat|e /kə'meməreɪt/ v.t.
commémorer. ~**ion** /-'reɪʃn/ n. com-
mémoration f. ~**ive** /-ətɪv/ a. commémoratif.

commence /kə'mens/ v.t./i.
commencer. ~**ment** n. commencement m.; (*univ., Amer.*) cérémonie
de distribution des diplômes f.

commend /kə'mend/ v.t. (*praise*)
louer; (*entrust*) confier. ~**able** a.
louable. ~**ation** /kɒmen'deɪʃn/ n.
éloge m.

commensurate /kə'menʃərət/ a.
proportionné.

comment /'kɒment/ n. commentaire
m. ● v.i. faire des commentaires. ~
on, commenter.

commentary /'kɒməntrɪ/ n. commentaire m.; (*radio, TV*) reportage
m.

commentat|e /'kɒmənteɪt/ v.i. faire
un reportage. ~**or** n. commenta|-
teur, -trice m., f.

commerce /'kɒmɜːs/ n. commerce m.

commercial /kə'mɜːʃl/ a. commercial; (*traveller*) de commerce. ● n.
publicité f. ~**ize** v.t. commercialiser.

commiserat|e /kə'mɪzəreɪt/ v.i. com-
patir (**with**, avec). ~**ion** /-'reɪʃn/ n.
commisération f.

commission /kə'mɪʃn/ n. commission f.; (*order for work*) commande
f. ● v.t. (*order*) commander; (*mil.*)
nommer officier. ~ **to do**, charger
de faire. **out of** ~, hors service. ~**er**
n. préfet (de police) m.; (*in E.C.*)
commissaire m.

commissionaire /kəmɪʃə'neə(r)/ n.
commissionnaire m.

commit /kə'mɪt/ v.t. (p.t. **committed**) commettre; (*entrust*)
confier. ~ **o.s.**, s'engager. ~ **perjury**, se parjurer. ~ **suicide**, se
suicider. ~ **to memory**, apprendre
par cœur. ~**ment** n. engagement m.

committee /kə'mɪtɪ/ n. comité m.

commodity /kə'mɒdətɪ/ n. produit
m., article m.

common /'kɒmən/ a. (**-er, -est**)
(*shared by all*) commun; (*usual*)
courant, commun; (*vulgar*) vulgaire, commun. ● n. terrain communal m. ~ **law**, droit coutumier m.
C~ Market, Marché Commun m. ~**-
room** n. (*schol.*) salle commune f. ~
sense, bon sens m. **House of C~s**,
Chambre des Communes f. **in** ~, en
commun. ~**ly** adv. communément.

commoner /'kɒmənə(r)/ *n.* rotur|ier, -ière *m.*, *f.*

commonplace /'kɒmənpleɪs/ *a.* banal. ● *n.* banalité *f.*

Commonwealth /'kɒmənwelθ/ *n.* **the ~**, le Commonwealth *m.*

commotion /kə'məʊʃn/ *n.* agitation *f.*, remue-ménage *m. invar.*

communal /'kɒmjʊnl/ *a.* (*shared*) commun; (*life*) collectif.

commune /'kɒmjuːn/ *n.* (*group*) communauté *f.*

communicat|e /kə'mjuːnɪkeɪt/ *v.t./i.* communiquer. **~ion** /-'keɪʃn/ *n.* communication *f.* **~ive** /-ətɪv/ *a.* communicatif.

communion /kə'mjuːnɪən/ *n.* communion *f.*

communiqué /kə'mjuːnɪkeɪ/ *n.* communiqué *m.*

Communis|t /'kɒmjʊnɪst/ *a. & n.* communiste (*m.*/*f.*). **~m** /-zəm/ *n.* communisme *m.*

community /kə'mjuːnətɪ/ *n.* communauté *f.*

commutation /kɒmjuː'teɪʃn/ *n.* **~ ticket**, carte d'abonnement *f.*

commute /kə'mjuːt/ *v.i.* faire la navette. ● *v.t.* (*jurid.*) commuer. **~r** /-ə(r)/ *n.* banlieusard(e) *m.* (*f.*).

compact[1] /kəm'pækt/ *a.* compact. **~ disc**, (disque) compact *m.*

compact[2] /'kɒmpækt/ *n.* (*lady's case*) poudrier *m.*

companion /kəm'pænjən/ *n.* comp|agnon, -agne *m.*, *f.* **~ship** *n.* camaraderie *f.*

company /'kʌmpənɪ/ *n.* (*companionship, firm*) compagnie *f.*; (*guests*) invité(e)s *m.* (*f.*) *pl.*

comparable /'kɒmpərəbl/ *a.* comparable.

compar|e /kəm'peə(r)/ *v.t.* comparer (**with, to**, à). **~ed with** *or* **to**, en comparaison de. ● *v.i.* être comparable. **~ative** /-'pærətɪv/ *a.* (*study, form*) comparatif; (*comfort etc.*) relatif. **~atively** /-'pærətɪvlɪ/ *adv.* relativement.

comparison /kəm'pærɪsn/ *n.* comparaison *f.*

compartment /kəm'pɑːtmənt/ *n.* compartiment *m.*

compass /'kʌmpəs/ *n.* (*for direction*) boussole *f.*; (*scope*) portée *f.* **~(es)**, (*for drawing*) compas *m.*

compassion /kəm'pæʃn/ *n.* compassion *f.* **~ate** *a.* compatissant.

compatib|le /kəm'pætəbl/ *a.* compatible. **~ility** /-'bɪlətɪ/ *n.* compatibilité *f.*

compatriot /kəm'pætrɪət/ *n.* compatriote *m.*/*f.*

compel /kəm'pel/ *v.t.* (*p.t.* **compelled**) contraindre. **~ling** *a.* irrésistible.

compendium /kəm'pendɪəm/ *n.* abrégé *m.*, résumé *m.*

compensat|e /'kɒmpənseɪt/ *v.t./i.* (*financially*) dédommager (**for**, de). **~e for sth.**, compenser qch. **~ion** /-'seɪʃn/ *n.* compensation *f.*; (*financial*) dédommagement *m.*

compete /kəm'piːt/ *v.i.* concourir. **~ with**, rivaliser avec.

competen|t /'kɒmpɪtənt/ *a.* compétent. **~ce** *n.* compétence *f.*

competition /kɒmpə'tɪʃn/ *n.* (*contest*) concours *m.*; (*sport*) compétition *f.*; (*comm.*) concurrence *f.*

competitive /kəm'petətɪv/ *a.* (*prices*) concurrentiel, compétitif. **~ examination**, concours *m.*

competitor /kəm'petɪtə(r)/ *n.* concurrent(e) *m.* (*f.*).

compile /kəm'paɪl/ *v.t.* (*list*) dresser; (*book*) rédiger. **~r** /-ə(r)/ *n.* rédacteur, -trice *m.*, *f.*

complacen|t /kəm'pleɪsnt/ *a.* content de soi. **~cy** *n.* contentement de soi *m.*

complain /kəm'pleɪn/ *v.i.* se plaindre (**about, of**, de).

complaint /kəm'pleɪnt/ *n.* plainte *f.*; (*in shop etc.*) réclamation *f.*; (*illness*) maladie *f.*

complement /'kɒmplɪmənt/ *n.* complément *m.* ● *v.t.* compléter. **~ary** /-'mentrɪ/ *a.* complémentaire.

complet|e /kəm'pliːt/ *a.* complet; (*finished*) achevé; (*downright*) parfait. ● *v.t.* achever; (*a form*) remplir. **~ely** *adv.* complètement. **~ion** /-ʃn/ *n.* achèvement *m.*

complex /'kɒmpleks/ *a.* complexe. ● *n.* (*psych., archit.*) complexe *m.* **~ity** /kəm'pleksətɪ/ *n.* complexité *f.*

complexion /kəm'plekʃn/ *n.* (*of face*) teint *m.*; (*fig.*) caractère *m.*

compliance /kəm'plaɪəns/ *n.* (*agreement*) conformité *f.*

complicat|e /'kɒmplɪkeɪt/ *v.t.* compliquer. **~ed** *a.* compliqué. **~ion** /-'keɪʃn/ *n.* complication *f.*

complicity /kəm'plɪsətɪ/ *n.* complicité *f.*

compliment /'kɒmplɪmənt/ n. compliment m. ● v.t. /'kɒmplɪment/ complimenter.

complimentary /kɒmplɪ'mentrɪ/ a. (offert) à titre gracieux; (praising) flatteur.

comply /kəm'plaɪ/ v.i. ~ with, se conformer à, obéir à.

component /kəm'pəʊnənt/ n. (of machine etc.) pièce f.; (chemical substance) composant m.; (element: fig.) composante f. ● a. constituant.

compose /kəm'pəʊz/ v.t. composer. ~ o.s., se calmer. ~d a. calme. ~r /-ə(r)/ n. (mus.) compositeur m.

composition /kɒmpə'zɪʃn/ n. composition f.

compost /'kɒmpɒst, Amer. 'kɒmpəʊst/ n. compost m.

composure /kəm'pəʊʒə(r)/ n. calme m.

compound[1] /'kɒmpaʊnd/ n. (substance, word) composé m.; (enclosure) enclos m. ● a. composé.

compound[2] /kəm'paʊnd/ v.t. (problem etc.) aggraver.

comprehen|d /kɒmprɪ'hend/ v.t. comprendre. ~sion n. compréhension f.

comprehensive /kɒmprɪ'hensɪv/ a. étendu, complet; (insurance) tous-risques invar. ~ school, collège d'enseignement secondaire m.

compress /kəm'pres/ v.t. comprimer. ~ion /-ʃn/ n. compression f.

comprise /kəm'praɪz/ v.t. comprendre, inclure.

compromise /'kɒmprəmaɪz/ n. compromis m. ● v.t. compromettre. ● v.i. transiger, trouver un compromis. not ~ on, ne pas transiger sur.

compulsion /kəm'pʌlʃn/ n. contrainte f.

compulsive /kəm'pʌlsɪv/ a. (psych.) compulsif; (liar, smoker) invétéré.

compulsory /kəm'pʌlsərɪ/ a. obligatoire.

compunction /kəm'pʌŋkʃn/ n. scrupule m.

computer /kəm'pjuːtə(r)/ n. ordinateur m. ~ science, informatique f. ~ize v.t. informatiser.

comrade /'kɒmr(e)ɪd/ n. camarade m./f. ~ship n. camaraderie f.

con[1] /kɒn/ v.t. (p.t. conned) (sl.) rouler, escroquer (out of, de). ● n. (sl.) escroquerie f. ~ s.o. into doing, arnaquer qn. en lui faisant faire. ~ man, (sl.) escroc m.

con[2] /kɒn/ see pro.

concave /'kɒŋkeɪv/ a. concave.

conceal /kən'siːl/ v.t. dissimuler. ~ment n. dissimulation f.

concede /kən'siːd/ v.t. concéder. ● v.i. céder.

conceit /kən'siːt/ n. suffisance f. ~ed a. suffisant.

conceivabl|e /kən'siːvəbl/ a. concevable. ~y adv. this may ~y be done, il est concevable que cela puisse se faire.

conceive /kən'siːv/ v.t./i. concevoir. ~ of, concevoir.

concentrat|e /'kɒnsntreɪt/ v.t./i. (se) concentrer. ~ion /-'treɪʃn/ n. concentration f.

concept /'kɒnsept/ n. concept m. ~ual /kən'septʃʊəl/ a. notionnel.

conception /kən'sepʃn/ n. conception f.

concern /kən'sɜːn/ n. (interest, business) affaire f.; (worry) inquiétude f.; (firm: comm.) entreprise f., affaire f. ● v.t. concerner. ~ o.s. with, be ~ed with, s'occuper de. ~ing prep. en ce qui concerne.

concerned /kən'sɜːnd/ a. inquiet.

concert /'kɒnsət/ n. concert m. in ~, ensemble.

concerted /kən'sɜːtɪd/ a. concerté.

concertina /kɒnsə'tiːnə/ n. concertina m.

concerto /kən'tʃeətəʊ/ n. (pl. -os) concerto m.

concession /kən'seʃn/ n. concession f.

conciliation /kənsɪlɪ'eɪʃn/ n. conciliation f.

concise /kən'saɪs/ a. concis. ~ly adv. avec concision. ~ness n. concision f.

conclu|de /kən'kluːd/ v.t. conclure. ● v.i. se terminer. ~ding a. final. ~sion n. conclusion f.

conclusive /kən'kluːsɪv/ a. concluant. ~ly adv. de manière concluante.

concoct /kən'kɒkt/ v.t. confectionner; (invent: fig.) fabriquer. ~ion /-kʃn/ n. mélange m.

concourse /'kɒnkɔːs/ n. (rail.) hall m.

concrete /'kɒŋkriːt/ n. béton m. ● a. concret. ● v.t. bétonner. ~-mixer n. bétonnière f.

concur /kən'kɜ:(r)/ v.i. (p.t. con-curred) être d'accord.

concurrently /kən'kʌrəntlɪ/ adv. si-multanément.

concussion /kən'kʌʃn/ n. commotion (cérébrale) f.

condemn /kən'dem/ v.t. condamner. **~ation** /kɒndem'neɪʃn/ n. condam-nation f.

condens|e /kən'dens/ v.t./i. (se) condenser. **~ation** /kɒnden'seɪʃn/ n. condensation f.; (mist) buée f.

condescend /kɒndɪ'send/ v.i. condes-cendre.

condiment /'kɒndɪmənt/ n. condi-ment m.

condition /kən'dɪʃn/ n. condition f. ● v.t. conditionner. **on ~ that**, à condition que. **~al** a. conditionnel. **be ~al upon**, dépendre de. **~er** n. après-shampooing m.

condolences /kən'dəʊlənsɪz/ n. pl. condoléances f. pl.

condom /'kɒndɒm/ n. préservatif m.

condominium /kɒndə'mɪnɪəm/ n. (Amer.) copropriété f.

condone /kən'dəʊn/ v.t. pardonner, fermer les yeux sur.

conducive /kən'dju:sɪv/ a. ~ to, favorable à.

conduct[1] /kən'dʌkt/ v.t. conduire; (orchestra) diriger.

conduct[2] /'kɒndʌkt/ n. conduite f.

conduct|or /kən'dʌktə(r)/ n. chef d'orchestre m.; (of bus) receveur m.; (on train: Amer.) chef de train m.; (electr.) conducteur m. **~ress** n. receveuse f.

cone /kəʊn/ n. cône m.; (of ice-cream) cornet m.

confectioner /kən'fekʃənə(r)/ n. confiseur, -se m., f. **~y** n. confiserie f.

confederation /kənfedə'reɪʃn/ n. confédération f.

confer /kən'fɜ:(r)/ v.t./i. (p.t. con-ferred) conférer.

conference /'kɒnfərəns/ n. confé-rence f.

confess /kən'fes/ v.t./i. avouer; (re-lig.) (se) confesser. **~ion** /-ʃn/ n. confession f.; (of crime) aveu m.

confessional /kən'feʃənl/ n. confes-sionnal m.

confetti /kən'fetɪ/ n. confettis m. pl.

confide /kən'faɪd/ v.t. confier. ● v.i. **~ in**, se confier à.

confiden|t /'kɒnfɪdənt/ a. sûr. **~ce** n. (trust) confiance f.; (boldness) con-fiance en soi f.; (secret) confidence f.

~ce trick, escroquerie f. **in ~ce**, en confidence.

confidential /kɒnfɪ'denʃl/ a. confi-dentiel.

configure /kən'fɪgə(r)/ v.t. (comput.) configurer.

confine /kən'faɪn/ v.t. enfermer; (limit) limiter. **~d space**, espace réduit m. **~d to**, limité à. **~ment** n. détention f.; (med.) couches f. pl.

confines /'kɒnfaɪnz/ n. pl. confins m. pl.

confirm /kən'fɜ:m/ v.t. confirmer. **~ation** /kɒnfə'meɪʃn/ n. confirma-tion f. **~ed** a. (bachelor) endurci; (smoker) invétéré.

confiscat|e /'kɒnfɪskeɪt/ v.t. con-fisquer. **~ion** /-'keɪʃn/ n. confisca-tion f.

conflagration /kɒnflə'greɪʃn/ n. in-cendie m.

conflict[1] /'kɒnflɪkt/ n. conflit m.

conflict[2] /kən'flɪkt/ v.i. (statements, views) être en contradiction (with, avec); (appointments) tomber en même temps (with, que). **~ing** a. contradictoire.

conform /kən'fɔ:m/ v.t./i. (se) conformer. **~ist** n. conformiste m./f.

confound /kən'faʊnd/ v.t. confondre. **~ed** a. (fam.) sacré.

confront /kən'frʌnt/ v.t. affronter. **~ with**, confronter avec. **~ation** /kɒnfrʌn'teɪʃn/ n. confrontation f.

confus|e /kən'fju:z/ v.t. embrouiller; (mistake, confound) confondre. **be-come ~ed**, s'embrouiller. **I am ~ed**, je m'y perds. **~ing** a. dé-routant. **~ion** /-ʒn/ n. confusion f.

congeal /kən'dʒi:l/ v.t./i. (se) figer.

congenial /kən'dʒi:nɪəl/ a. sympathi-que.

congenital /kən'dʒenɪtl/ a. congéni-tal.

congest|ed /kən'dʒestɪd/ a. encom-bré; (med.) congestionné. **~ion** /-stʃən/ n. (traffic) encombrement(s) m. (pl.); (med.) congestion f.

conglomerate /kən'glɒmərət/ n. (comm.) conglomérat m.

congratulat|e /kən'grætjʊleɪt/ v.t. féliciter (on, de). **~ions** /-'leɪʃnz/ n. pl. félicitations f. pl.

congregat|e /'kɒngrɪgeɪt/ v.i. se rassembler. **~ion** /-'geɪʃn/ n. assem-blée f.

congress /'kɒngres/ n. congrès m. **C~**, (Amer.) le Congrès.

conic(al) /'kɒnɪk(l)/ a. conique.

conifer /ˈkɒnɪfə(r)/ n. conifère m.

conjecture /kənˈdʒektʃə(r)/ n. conjecture f. ● v.t./i. conjecturer.

conjugal /ˈkɒndʒʊgl/ a. conjugal.

conjugat|e /ˈkɒndʒʊgeɪt/ v.t. conjuguer. **~ion** /-ˈgeɪʃn/ n. conjugaison f.

conjunction /kənˈdʒʌŋkʃn/ n. conjonction f. **in ~ with,** conjointement avec.

conjunctivitis /kɒndʒʌŋktɪˈvaɪtɪs/ n. conjonctivite f.

conjur|e /ˈkʌndʒə(r)/ v.i. faire des tours de passe-passe. ● v.t. **~e up,** faire apparaître. **~or** n. prestidigita|teur, -trice m., f.

conk /kɒŋk/ v.i. **~ out,** (sl.) tomber en panne.

conker /ˈkɒŋkə(r)/ n. (horse-chestnut fruit: fam.) marron m.

connect /kəˈnekt/ v.t./i. (se) relier; (in mind) faire le rapport entre; (install, wire up to mains) brancher. **~ with,** (of train) assurer la correspondance avec. **~ed** a. lié. **be ~ed with,** avoir rapport à; (deal with) avoir des rapports avec.

connection /kəˈnekʃn/ n. rapport m.; (rail.) correspondance f.; (phone call) communication f.; (electr.) contact m.; (joining piece) raccord m. **~s,** (comm.) relations f. pl.

conniv|e /kəˈnaɪv/ v.i. **~e at,** se faire le complice de. **~ance** n. connivence f.

connoisseur /kɒnəˈsɜː(r)/ n. connaisseur m.

connot|e /kəˈnəʊt/ v.t. connoter. **~ation** /kɒnəˈteɪʃn/ n. connotation f.

conquer /ˈkɒŋkə(r)/ v.t. vaincre; (country) conquérir. **~or** n. conquérant m.

conquest /ˈkɒŋkwest/ n. conquête f.

conscience /ˈkɒnʃəns/ n. conscience f.

conscientious /kɒnʃɪˈenʃəs/ a. consciencieux.

conscious /ˈkɒnʃəs/ a. conscient; (deliberate) voulu. **~ly** adv. consciemment. **~ness** n. conscience f.; (med.) connaissance f.

conscript[1] /kənˈskrɪpt/ v.t. recruter par conscription. **~ion** /-pʃn/ n. conscription f.

conscript[2] /ˈkɒnskrɪpt/ n. conscrit m.

consecrate /ˈkɒnsɪkreɪt/ v.t. consacrer.

consecutive /kənˈsekjʊtɪv/ a. consécutif. **~ly** adv. consécutivement.

consensus /kənˈsensəs/ n. consensus m.

consent /kənˈsent/ v.i. consentir (to, à). ● n. consentement m.

consequence /ˈkɒnsɪkwəns/ n. conséquence f.

consequent /ˈkɒnsɪkwənt/ a. résultant. **~ly** adv. par conséquent.

conservation /kɒnsəˈveɪʃn/ n. préservation f. **~ area,** zone classée f.

conservationist /kɒnsəˈveɪʃənɪst/ n. défenseur de l'environnement m.

conservative /kənˈsɜːvətɪv/ a. conservateur; (estimate) modeste. **C~** a. & n. conserva|teur, -trice (m. (f.)).

conservatory /kənˈsɜːvətrɪ/ n. (greenhouse) serre f.; (room) véranda f.

conserve /kənˈsɜːv/ v.t. conserver; (energy) économiser.

consider /kənˈsɪdə(r)/ v.t. considérer; (allow for) tenir compte de; (possibility) envisager (doing, de faire). **~ation** /-ˈreɪʃn/ n. considération f.; (respect) égard(s) m. (pl.). **~ing** prep. compte tenu de.

considerabl|e /kənˈsɪdərəbl/ a. considérable; (much) beaucoup de. **~y** adv. beaucoup, considérablement.

considerate /kənˈsɪdərət/ a. prévenant, attentionné.

consign /kənˈsaɪn/ v.t. (entrust) confier; (send) expédier. **~ment** n. envoi m.

consist /kənˈsɪst/ v.i. consister (of, en; in doing, à faire).

consisten|t /kənˈsɪstənt/ a. cohérent. **~t with,** conforme à. **~cy** n. (of liquids) consistance f.; (of argument) cohérence f. **~tly** adv. régulièrement.

consol|e /kənˈsəʊl/ v.t. consoler. **~ation** /kɒnsəˈleɪʃn/ n. consolation f.

consolidat|e /kənˈsɒlɪdeɪt/ v.t./i. (se) consolider. **~ion** /-ˈdeɪʃn/ n. consolidation f.

consonant /ˈkɒnsənənt/ n. consonne f.

consort[1] /ˈkɒnsɔːt/ n. époux m., épouse f.

consort[2] /kənˈsɔːt/ v.i. **~ with,** fréquenter.

consortium /kənˈsɔːtɪəm/ n. (pl.-tia) consortium m.

conspicuous /kənˈspɪkjʊəs/ a. (*easily seen*) en évidence; (*showy*) voyant; (*noteworthy*) remarquable.

conspiracy /kənˈspɪrəsɪ/ n. conspiration f.

conspire /kənˈspaɪə(r)/ v.i. (*person*) comploter (**to do**, de faire), conspirer; (*events*) conspirer (**to do**, à faire).

constable /ˈkʌnstəbl/ n. agent de police m., gendarme m.

constant /ˈkɒnstənt/ a. incessant; (*unchanging*) constant; (*friend*) fidèle. ● n. constante f. **~ly** adv. constamment.

constellation /kɒnstəˈleɪʃn/ n. constellation f.

consternation /kɒnstəˈneɪʃn/ n. consternation f.

constipat|e /ˈkɒnstɪpeɪt/ v.t. constiper. **~ion** /-ˈpeɪʃn/ n. constipation f.

constituency /kənˈstɪtjʊənsɪ/ n. circonscription électorale f.

constituent /kənˈstɪtjʊənt/ a. constitutif. ● n. élément constitutif m.; (*pol.*) élec|teur, -trice m., f.

constitut|e /ˈkɒnstɪtjuːt/ v.t. constituer. **~ion** /-ˈtjuːʃn/ n. constitution f. **~ional** /-ˈtjuːʃənl/ a. constitutionnel; n. promenade f.

constrain /kənˈstreɪn/ v.t. contraindre.

constraint /kənˈstreɪnt/ n. contrainte f.

constrict /kənˈstrɪkt/ v.t. resserrer; (*movement*) gêner. **~ion** /-kʃn/ n. resserrement m.

construct /kənˈstrʌkt/ v.t. construire. **~ion** /-kʃn/ n. construction f. **~ion worker**, ouvrier du bâtiment m.

constructive /kənˈstrʌktɪv/ a. constructif.

construe /kənˈstruː/ v.t. interpréter.

consul /ˈkɒnsl/ n. consul m. **~ar** /-jʊlə(r)/ a. consulaire.

consulate /ˈkɒnsjʊlət/ n. consulat m.

consult /kənˈsʌlt/ v.t. consulter. ● v.i. **~ with**, conférer avec. **~ation** /kɒnslˈteɪʃn/ n. consultation f.

consultant /kənˈsʌltənt/ n. conseill|er, -ère m., f.; (*med.*) spécialiste m./f.

consume /kənˈsjuːm/ v.t. consommer; (*destroy*) consumer. **~r** /-ə(r)/ n. consomma|teur, -trice m., f. a. (*society*) de consommation.

consumerism /kənˈsjuːmərɪzəm/ n. protection des consommateurs f.

consummate /ˈkɒnsəmeɪt/ v.t. consommer.

consumption /kənˈsʌmpʃn/ n. consommation f.; (*med.*) phtisie f.

contact /ˈkɒntækt/ n. contact m.; (*person*) relation f. ● v.t. contacter. **~ lenses**, lentilles (de contact) f. pl.

contagious /kənˈteɪdʒəs/ a. contagieux.

contain /kənˈteɪn/ v.t. contenir. **~ o.s.**, se contenir. **~er** n. récipient m.; (*for transport*) container m.

contaminat|e /kənˈtæmɪneɪt/ v.t. contaminer. **~ion** /-ˈneɪʃn/ n. contamination f.

contemplat|e /ˈkɒntəmpleɪt/ v.t. (*gaze at*) contempler; (*think about*) envisager. **~ion** /-ˈpleɪʃn/ n. contemplation f.

contemporary /kənˈtemprərɪ/ a. & n. contemporain(e) (m. (f.)).

contempt /kənˈtempt/ n. mépris m. **~ible** a. méprisable. **~uous** /-tʃʊəs/ a. méprisant.

contend /kənˈtend/ v.t. soutenir. ● v.i. **~ with**, (*compete*) rivaliser avec; (*face*) faire face à. **~er** n. adversaire m./f.

content [1] /kənˈtent/ a. satisfait. ● v.t. contenter. **~ed** a. satisfait. **~ment** n. contentement m.

content [2] /ˈkɒntent/ n. (*of letter*) contenu m.; (*amount*) teneur f. **~s**, contenu m.

contention /kənˈtenʃn/ n. dispute f.; (*claim*) affirmation f.

contest [1] /ˈkɒntest/ n. (*competition*) concours m.; (*fight*) combat m.

contest [2] /kənˈtest/ v.t. contester; (*compete for or in*) disputer. **~ant** n. concurrent(e) (m. (f.).

context /ˈkɒntekst/ n. contexte m.

continent /ˈkɒntɪnənt/ n. continent m. **the C~**, l'Europe (continentale) f. **~al** /-ˈnentl/ a. continental; européen. **~al quilt**, couette f.

contingen|t /kənˈtɪndʒənt/ a. **be ~t upon**, dépendre de. ● n. (*mil.*) contingent m. **~cy** n. éventualité f. **~cy plan**, plan d'urgence m.

continual /kənˈtɪnjʊəl/ a. continuel. **~ly** adv. continuellement.

continu|e /kənˈtɪnjuː/ v.t./i. continuer; (*resume*) reprendre. **~ance** n. continuation f. **~ation** /-ʊˈeɪʃn/ n. continuation f.; (*after interrup-*

tion) reprise *f*.; (*new episode*) suite *f*. **~ed** *a*. continu.

continuity /kɒntɪˈnjuːətɪ/ *n*. continuité *f*.

continuous /kənˈtɪnjʊəs/ *a*. continu. **~ stationery,** papier continu *m*. **~ly** *adv*. sans interruption, continûment.

contort /kənˈtɔːt/ *v.t.* tordre. **~ o.s.,** se contorsionner. **~ion** /-ʃn/ *n*. torsion *f*.; contorsion *f*. **~ionist** /-ʃənɪst/ *n*. contorsionniste *m./f*.

contour /ˈkɒntʊə(r)/ *n*. contour *m*.

contraband /ˈkɒntrəbænd/ *n*. contrebande *f*.

contraception /kɒntrəˈsepʃn/ *n*. contraception *f*.

contraceptive /kɒntrəˈseptɪv/ *a. & n*. contraceptif (*m.*).

contract¹ /ˈkɒntrækt/ *n*. contrat *m*.

contract² /kənˈtrækt/ *v.t./i.* (se) contracter. **~ion** /-kʃn/ *n*. contraction *f*.

contractor /kənˈtræktə(r)/ *n*. entrepreneur *m*.

contradict /kɒntrəˈdɪkt/ *v.t.* contredire. **~ion** /-kʃn/ *n*. contradiction *f*. **~ory** *a*. contradictoire.

contralto /kənˈtræltəʊ/ *n*. (*pl.* -os) contralto *m*.

contraption /kənˈtræpʃn/ *n*. (*fam.*) engin *m.*, truc *m*.

contrary¹ /ˈkɒntrərɪ/ *a*. contraire (**to,** à). ● *n*. contraire *m*. ● *adv*. **~ to,** contrairement à. **on the ~,** au contraire.

contrary² /kənˈtreərɪ/ *a*. entêté.

contrast¹ /ˈkɒntrɑːst/ *n*. contraste *m*.

contrast² /kənˈtrɑːst/ *v.t./i.* contraster. **~ing** *a*. contrasté.

contraven|e /kɒntrəˈviːn/ *v.t.* enfreindre. **~tion** /-ˈvenʃn/ *n*. infraction *f*.

contribut|e /kənˈtrɪbjuːt/ *v.t.* donner. ● *v.i.* **~e to,** contribuer à; (*take part*) participer à; (*newspaper*) collaborer à. **~ion** /kɒntrɪˈbjuːʃn/ *n*. contribution *f*. **~or** *n*. collabora|teur, -trice *m.,f*.

contrivance /kənˈtraɪvəns/ *n*. (*device*) appareil *m.*, truc *m*.

contrive /kənˈtraɪv/ *v.t.* imaginer. **~ to do,** trouver moyen de faire. **~d** *a*. tortueux.

control /kənˈtrəʊl/ *v.t.* (*p.t.* **controlled**) (*a firm etc.*) diriger; (*check*) contrôler; (*restrain*) maîtriser. ● *n*. contrôle *m.*; (*mastery*) maîtrise *f*. **~s,** commandes *f. pl.*; (*knobs*) bou-

tons *m. pl.* **~ tower,** tour de contrôle *f*. **have under ~,** (*event*) avoir en main. **in ~ of,** maître de.

controversial /kɒntrəˈvɜːʃl/ *a*. discutable, discuté.

controversy /ˈkɒntrəvɜːsɪ/ *n*. controverse *f*.

conurbation /kɒnɜːˈbeɪʃn/ *n*. agglomération *f.*, conurbation *f*.

convalesce /kɒnvəˈles/ *v.i.* être en convalescence. **~nce** *n*. convalescence *f*. **~nt** *a. & n*. convalescent(e) (*m.* (*f.*)). **~nt home,** maison de convalescence *f*.

convector /kənˈvektə(r)/ *n*. convecteur *m*.

convene /kənˈviːn/ *v.t.* convoquer. ● *v.i.* se réunir.

convenience /kənˈviːnɪəns/ *n*. commodité *f*. **~s,** toilettes *f. pl.* **all modern ~s,** tout le confort moderne. **at your ~,** quand cela vous conviendra, à votre convenance. **~ foods,** plats tout préparés *m. pl*.

convenient /kənˈviːnɪənt/ *a*. commode, pratique; (*time*) bien choisi. **be ~ for,** convenir à. **~ly** *adv*. (*arrive*) à propos. **~ly situated,** bien situé.

convent /ˈkɒnvənt/ *n*. couvent *m*.

convention /kənˈvenʃn/ *n*. (*assembly, agreement*) convention *f.*; (*custom*) usage *m*. **~al** *a*. conventionnel.

converge /kənˈvɜːdʒ/ *v.i.* converger.

conversant /kənˈvɜːsnt/ *a*. **be ~ with,** connaître; (*fact*) savoir; (*machinery*) s'y connaître en.

conversation /kɒnvəˈseɪʃn/ *n*. conversation *f*. **~al** *a*. (*tone etc.*) de la conversation; (*French etc.*) de tous les jours. **~alist** *n*. causeu|r, -se *m.,f*.

converse¹ /kənˈvɜːs/ *v.i.* s'entretenir, converser (**with,** avec).

converse² /ˈkɒnvɜːs/ *a. & n*. inverse (*m.*). **~ly** *adv*. inversement.

conver|t¹ /kənˈvɜːt/ *v.t.* convertir; (*house*) aménager. ● *v.i.* **~t into,** se transformer en. **~sion** /-ʃn/ *n*. conversion *f*. **~tible** *a*. convertible. ● *n*. (*car*) décapotable *f*.

convert² /ˈkɒnvɜːt/ *n*. converti(e) *m*. (*f.*).

convex /ˈkɒnveks/ *a*. convexe.

convey /kənˈveɪ/ *v.t.* (*wishes, order*) transmettre; (*goods, people*) transporter; (*idea, feeling*) communiquer

~ance *n.* transport *m.* ~or belt, tapis roulant *m.*

convict[1] /kən'vɪkt/ *v.t.* déclarer coupable. ~ion /-kʃn/ *n.* condamnation *f.*; (*opinion*) conviction *f.*

convict[2] /'kɒnvɪkt/ *n.* prisonni|er, -ère *m., f.*

convinc|e /kən'vɪns/ *v.t.* convaincre. ~ing *a.* convaincant.

convivial /kən'vɪvɪəl/ *a.* joyeux.

convoke /kən'vəʊk/ *v.t.* convoquer.

convoluted /'kɒnvəluːtɪd/ *a.* (*argument etc.*) compliqué.

convoy /'kɒnvɔɪ/ *n.* convoi *m.*

convuls|e /kən'vʌls/ *v.t.* convulser; (*fig.*) bouleverser. be ~ed with laughter, se tordre de rire. ~ion /-ʃn/ *n.* convulsion *f.*

coo /kuː/ *v.i.* roucouler.

cook /kʊk/ *v.t./i.* (faire) cuire; (*of person*) faire la cuisine. ● *n.* cuisin|ier, -ière *m., f.* ~ up, (*fam.*) fabriquer. ~ing *n.* cuisine *f.*; *a.* de cuisine.

cooker /'kʊkə(r)/ *n.* (*stove*) cuisinière *f.*; (*apple*) pomme à cuire *f.*

cookery /'kʊkərɪ/ *n.* cuisine *f.* ~ book, livre de cuisine *m.*

cookie /'kʊkɪ/ *n.* (*Amer.*) biscuit *m.*

cool /kuːl/ *a.* (-er, -est) frais; (*calm*) calme; (*unfriendly*) froid. ● *n.* fraîcheur *f.*; (*calmness: sl.*) sang-froid *m.* ● *v.t./i.* rafraîchir. in the ~, au frais. ~ box, glacière *f.* ~er *n.* (*for food*) glacière *f.*; ~ly *adv.* calmement; froidement. ~ness *n.* fraîcheur *f.*; froideur *f.*

coop /kuːp/ *n.* poulailler *m.* ● *v.t.* ~ up, enfermer.

co-operat|e /kəʊ'ɒpəreɪt/ *v.i.* coopérer. ~ion /-'reɪʃn/ *n.* coopération *f.*

co-operative /kəʊ'ɒpərətɪv/ *a.* coopératif. ● *n.* coopérative *f.*

co-opt /kəʊ'ɒpt/ *v.t.* coopter.

co-ordinat|e /kəʊ'ɔːdɪneɪt/ *v.t.* coordonner. ~ion /-'neɪʃn/ *n.* coordination *f.*

cop /kɒp/ *v.t.* (*p.t.* copped) (*sl.*) piquer. ● *n.* (*policeman: sl.*) flic *m.* ~ out, (*sl.*) se dérober. ~-out *n.* (*sl.*) dérobade *f.*

cope /kəʊp/ *v.i.* assurer. ~ with, s'en sortir avec.

copious /'kəʊpɪəs/ *a.* copieux.

copper[1] /'kɒpə(r)/ *n.* cuivre *m.*; (*coin*) sou *m.* ● *a.* de cuivre.

copper[2] /'kɒpə(r)/ *n.* (*sl.*) flic *m.*

coppice, copse /'kɒpɪs, kɒps/ *ns.* taillis *m.*

copulat|e /'kɒpjʊleɪt/ *v.i.* s'accoupler. ~ion /-'leɪʃn/ *n.* copulation *f.*

copy /'kɒpɪ/ *n.* copie *f.*; (*of book, newspaper*) exemplaire *m.*; (*print: photo.*) épreuve *f.* ● *v.t./i.* copier. ~-writer *n.* rédacteur-concepteur *m.*, rédactrice-conceptrice *f.*

copyright /'kɒpɪraɪt/ *n.* droit d'auteur *m.*, copyright *m.*

coral /'kɒrəl/ *n.* corail *m.*

cord /kɔːd/ *n.* (petite) corde *f.*; (*of curtain, pyjamas, etc.*) cordon *m.*; (*electr.*) cordon électrique *m.*; (*fabric*) velours côtelé *m.*

cordial /'kɔːdɪəl/ *a.* cordial. ● *n.* (*fruit-flavoured drink*) sirop *m.*

cordon /'kɔːdn/ *n.* cordon *m.* ● *v.t.* ~ off, mettre un cordon autour de.

corduroy /'kɔːdərɔɪ/ *n.* velours côtelé *m.*, velours à côtes *m.*

core /kɔː(r)/ *n.* (*of apple*) trognon *m.*; (*of problem*) cœur *m.*; (*techn.*) noyau *m.* ● *v.t.* vider.

cork /kɔːk/ *n.* liège *m.*; (*for bottle*) bouchon *m.* ● *v.t.* boucher.

corkscrew /'kɔːkskruː/ *n.* tire-bouchon *m.*

corn[1] /kɔːn/ *n.* blé *m.*; (*maize: Amer.*) maïs *m.*; (*seed*) grain *m.* ~-cob *n.* épi de maïs *m.*

corn[2] /kɔːn/ *n.* (*hard skin*) cor *m.*

cornea /'kɔːnɪə/ *n.* cornée *f.*

corned /kɔːnd/ *a.* ~ beef, corned-beef *m.*

corner /'kɔːnə(r)/ *n.* coin *m.*; (*bend in road*) virage *m.*; (*football*) corner *m.* ● *v.t.* coincer, acculer; (*market*) accaparer. ● *v.i.* prendre un virage. ~-stone *n.* pierre angulaire *f.*

cornet /'kɔːnɪt/ *n.* cornet *m.*

cornflakes /'kɔːnfleɪks/ *n. pl.* corn flakes *m. pl.*

cornflour /'kɔːnflaʊə(r)/ *n.* farine de maïs *f.*

cornice /'kɔːnɪs/ *n.* corniche *f.*

cornstarch /kɔːnstɑːtʃ/ *n. Amer.* = cornflour.

cornucopia /kɔːnjʊ'kəʊpɪə/ *n.* corne d'abondance *f.*

Corn|wall /'kɔːnwəl/ *n.* Cornouailles *f.* ~ish *a.* de Cornouailles.

corny /'kɔːnɪ/ *a.* (-ier, -iest) (*trite: fam.*) rebattu; (*mawkish: fam.*) à l'eau de rose.

corollary /kə'rɒlərɪ, *Amer.* 'kɒrələrɪ/ *n.* corollaire *m.*

coronary /'kɒrənərɪ/ n. infarctus m.

coronation /kɒrə'neɪʃn/ n. couronnement m.

coroner /'kɒrənə(r)/ n. coroner m.

corporal¹ /'kɔːpərəl/ n. caporal m.

corporal² /'kɔːpərəl/ a. ~ punishment, châtiment corporel m.

corporate /'kɔːpərət/ a. en commun; (body) constitué.

corporation /kɔːpə'reɪʃn/ n. (comm.) société f.; (of town) municipalité f.

corps /kɔː(r)/ n. (pl. corps /kɔːz/) corps m.

corpse /kɔːps/ n. cadavre m.

corpulent /'kɔːpjʊlənt/ a. corpulent.

corpuscle /'kɔːpʌsl/ n. globule m.

corral /kə'rɑːl/ n. (Amer.) corral m.

correct /kə'rekt/ a. (right) exact, juste, ~, correct; (proper) correct. **you are ~,** vous avez raison. ● v.t. corriger. **~ion** /-kʃn/ n. correction f.

correlate /'kɒrəleɪt/ v.t./i. (faire) correspondre. **~ion** /-'leɪʃn/ n. corrélation f.

correspond /kɒrɪ'spɒnd/ v.i. correspondre. **~ence** n. correspondance f. **~ence course,** cours par correspondance m. **~ent** n. correspondant(e) m.(f.).

corridor /'kɒrɪdɔː(r)/ n. couloir m.

corroborate /kə'rɒbəreɪt/ v.t. corroborer.

corrode /kə'rəʊd/ v.t./i. (se) corroder. **~sion** n. corrosion f.

corrosive /kə'rəʊsɪv/ a. corrosif.

corrugated /'kɒrəgeɪtɪd/ a. ondulé. **~ iron,** tôle ondulée f.

corrupt /kə'rʌpt/ a. corrompu. ● v.t. corrompre. **~ion** /-pʃn/ n. corruption f.

corset /'kɔːsɪt/ n. (boned) corset m.; (elasticated) gaine f.

Corsica /'kɔːsɪkə/ n. Corse f.

cortisone /'kɔːtɪzəʊn/ n. cortisone f.

cos /kɒs/ n. laitue romaine f.

cosh /kɒʃ/ n. matraque f. ● v.t. matraquer.

cosmetic /kɒz'metɪk/ n. produit de beauté m. ● a. cosmétique; (fig., pej.) superficiel.

cosmic /'kɒzmɪk/ a. cosmique.

cosmonaut /'kɒzmənɔːt/ n. cosmonaute m./f.

cosmopolitan /kɒzmə'pɒlɪt(ə)n/ a. & n. cosmopolite (m./f.).

cosmos /'kɒzmɒs/ n. cosmos m.

Cossack /'kɒsæk/ n. cosaque m.

cosset /'kɒsɪt/ v.t. (p.t. **cosseted**) dorloter.

cost /kɒst/ v.t. (p.t. cost) coûter; (p.t. costed) établir le prix de. ● n. coût m. ~s, (jurid.) dépens m. pl. **at all ~s,** à tout prix. **to one's ~,** à ses dépens. **~-effective** a. rentable. **~-effectiveness** n. rentabilité f. **~ price,** prix de revient m. **~ of living,** coût de la vie m.

co-star /'kəʊstɑː(r)/ n. partenaire m./f.

costly /'kɒstlɪ/ a. (-ier, -iest) coûteux; (valuable) précieux.

costume /'kɒstjuːm/ n. costume m.; (for swimming) maillot m. **~ jewellery,** bijoux de fantaisie m. pl.

cos|y /'kəʊzɪ/ a. (-ier, -iest) confortable, intime. ● n. couvre-théière m. **~iness** n. confort m.

cot /kɒt/ n. lit d'enfant m.; (camp-bed: Amer.) lit de camp m.

cottage /'kɒtɪdʒ/ n. petite maison de campagne f.; (thatched) chaumière f. **~ cheese,** fromage blanc (maigre) m. **~ industry,** activité artisanale f. **~ pie,** hachis Parmentier m.

cotton /'kɒtn/ n. coton m.; (for sewing) fil (à coudre) m. ● v.i. ~ on, (sl.) piger. **~ candy,** (Amer.) barbe à papa f. **~ wool,** coton hydrophile m.

couch /kaʊtʃ/ n. divan m. ● v.t. (express) formuler.

couchette /kuː'ʃet/ n. couchette f.

cough /kɒf/ v.i. tousser. ● n. toux f. **~ up,** (sl.) cracher, payer.

could /kʊd, unstressed kəd/ p.t. of **can**².

couldn't /'kʊdnt/ = could not.

council /'kaʊnsl/ n. conseil m. **~ house,** maison construite par la municipalité f., (approx.) H.L.M. m./f.

councillor /'kaʊnsələ(r)/ n. conseill|er, -ère municipal(e) m., f.

counsel /'kaʊnsl/ n. conseil m. ● n. invar. (jurid.) avocat(e) m. (f.). **~lor** n. conseill|er, -ère m., f.

count¹ /kaʊnt/ v.t./i. compter. ● n. compte m. **~ on,** compter sur.

count² /kaʊnt/ n. (nobleman) comte m.

countdown /'kaʊntdaʊn/ n. compte à rebours m.

countenance /'kaʊntɪnəns/ n. mine f. ● v.t. admettre, approuver.

counter /'kaʊntə(r)/ n. comptoir m.; (in bank etc.) guichet m.; (token) jeton m.

counter[2] /'kaʊntə(r)/ adv. ~ **to**, à l'encontre de. ● a. opposé. ● v.t. opposer; (blow) parer. ● v.i. riposter.

counter- /'kaʊntə(r)/ pref. contre-.

counteract /kaʊntər'ækt/ v.t. neutraliser.

counter-attack /'kaʊntərətæk/ n. contre-attaque f. ● v.t./i. contreattaquer.

counterbalance /'kaʊntəbæləns/ n. contrepoids m. ● v.t. contrebalancer.

counter-clockwise /kaʊntə'klɒkwaɪz/ a. & adv. (Amer.) dans le sens inverse des aiguilles d'une montre.

counterfeit /'kaʊntəfɪt/ a. & n. faux (m.). ● v.t. contrefaire.

counterfoil /'kaʊntəfɔɪl/ n. souche f.

countermand /kaʊntə'mɑːnd/ v.t. annuler.

counterpart /'kaʊntəpɑːt/ n. équivalent m.; (person) homologue m./f.

counter-productive /kaʊntəprə'dʌktɪv/ a. (measure) qui produit l'effet contraire.

countersign /'kaʊntəsaɪn/ v.t. contresigner.

counter-tenor /'kaʊntətenə(r)/ n. haute-contre m.

countess /'kaʊntɪs/ n. comtesse f.

countless /'kaʊntlɪs/ a. innombrable.

countrified /'kʌntrɪfaɪd/ a. rustique.

country /'kʌntrɪ/ n. (land, region) pays m.; (homeland) patrie f.; (countryside) campagne f. ~ **dance**, danse folklorique f.

countryman /'kʌntrɪmən/ n. (pl. -men) campagnard m.; (fellow citizen) compatriote m.

countryside /'kʌntrɪsaɪd/ n. campagne f.

county /'kaʊntɪ/ n. comté m.

coup /kuː/ n. (achievement) joli coup m.; (pol.) coup d'état m.

coupé /'kuːpeɪ/ n. (car) coupé m.

couple /'kʌpl/ n. (people, animals) couple m. ● v.t./i. (s')accoupler. **a** ~ **(of)**, (two or three) deux ou trois.

coupon /'kuːpɒn/ n. coupon m.; (for shopping) bon or coupon de réduction m.

courage /'kʌrɪdʒ/ n. courage m. ~**ous** /kə'reɪdʒəs/ a. courageux.

courgette /kʊə'ʒet/ n. courgette f.

courier /'kʊrɪə(r)/ n. messag|er, -ère m., f.; (for tourists) guide m.

course /kɔːs/ n. cours m.; (for training) stage m.; (series) série f.; (culin.) plat m.; (for golf) terrain m.; (at sea) itinéraire m. **change** ~, changer de cap. ~ **(of action)**, façon de faire f. **during the** ~ **of**, pendant. **in due** ~, en temps utile. **of** ~, bien sûr.

court /kɔːt/ n. cour f.; (tennis) court m. ● v.t. faire la cour à; (danger) rechercher. ~ **martial**, (pl. **courts martial**) conseil de guerre m. ~-**martial** v.t. (p.t. -**martialled**) faire passer en conseil de guerre. ~-**house** n. (Amer.) palais de justice m. ~ **shoe**, escarpin m. **go to** ~, aller devant les tribunaux.

courteous /'kɜːtɪəs/ a. courtois.

courtesy /'kɜːtəsɪ/ n. courtoisie f. **by** ~ **of**, avec la permission de.

courtier /'kɔːtɪə(r)/ n. (old use) courtisan m.

courtroom /'kɔːtrʊm/ n. salle de tribunal f.

courtyard /'kɔːtjɑːd/ n. cour f.

cousin /'kʌzn/ n. cousin(e) m. (f.). **first** ~, cousin(e) germain(e) m. (f.).

cove /kəʊv/ n. anse f., crique f.

covenant /'kʌvənənt/ n. convention f.

Coventry /'kɒvntrɪ/ n. **send to** ~, mettre en quarantaine.

cover /'kʌvə(r)/ v.t. couvrir. ● n. (for bed, book, etc.) couverture f.; (lid) couvercle m.; (for furniture) housse f.; (shelter) abri m. ~ **charge**, couvert m. ~ **up**, cacher; (crime) couvrir. ~ **up for**, couvrir. ~-**up** n. tentative pour cacher la vérité f. **take** ~, se mettre à l'abri. ~**ing** n. enveloppe f. ~**ing letter**, lettre f. (jointe à un document).

coverage /'kʌvərɪdʒ/ n. reportage m.

coveralls /'kʌvərɔːlz/ (Amer.) bleu de travail m.

covert /'kʌvət, Amer. /'kəʊvɜːrt/ a. (activity) secret; (threat) voilé (look) dérobé.

covet /'kʌvɪt/ v.t. convoiter.

cow /kaʊ/ n. vache f.

coward /'kaʊəd/ n. lâche m./f. ~**ly** a. lâche.

cowardice /'kaʊədɪs/ n. lâcheté f.

cowboy /'kaʊbɔɪ/ n. cow-boy m.

cower /'kaʊə(r)/ v.i. se recroqueviller (sous l'effet de la peur).

cowshed /'kaʊʃed/ n. étable f.

cox /kɒks/ n. barreur m. ● v.t. barrer.

coxswain /'kɒksn/ *n.* barreur *m.*

coy /kɔɪ/ *a.* (**-er, -est**) (faussement) timide, qui fait le *or* la timide.

cozy /'kəʊzɪ/ *Amer.* = **cosy.**

crab /kræb/ *n.* crabe *m.* ● *v.i.* (*p.t.* **crabbed**) rouspéter. **~-apple** *n.* pomme sauvage *f.*

crack /kræk/ *n.* fente *f.*; (*in glass*) fêlure *f.*; (*noise*) craquement *m.*; (*joke*) plaisanterie *f.* ● *a.* (*fam.*) d'élite. ● *v.t./i.* (*break partially*) (se) fêler; (*split*) (se) fendre; (*nut*) casser; (*joke*) raconter; (*problem*) résoudre. **~ down on,** (*fam.*) sévir contre. **~ up,** (*fam.*) craquer. **get ~ing,** (*fam.*) s'y mettre.

cracked /krækt/ *a.* (*sl.*) cinglé.

cracker /'krækə(r)/ *n.* pétard *m.*; (*culin.*) biscuit (salé) *m.*

crackers /'krækəz/ *a.* (*sl.*) cinglé.

crackle /'krækl/ *v.i.* crépiter. ● *n.* crépitement *m.*

crackpot /'krækpɒt/ *n.* (*sl.*) cinglé(e) *m.* (*f.*).

cradle /'kreɪdl/ *n.* berceau *m.* ● *v.t.* bercer.

craft[1] /krɑːft/ *n.* métier artisanal *m.*; (*technique*) art *m.*; (*cunning*) ruse *f.*

craft[2] /krɑːft/ *n. invar.* (*boat*) bateau *m.*

craftsman /'krɑːftsmən/ *n.* (*pl.* **-men**) artisan *m.* **~ship** *n.* art *m.*

crafty /'krɑːftɪ/ *a.* (**-ier, -iest**) rusé.

crag /kræg/ *n.* rocher à pic *m.* **~gy** *a.* à pic; (*face*) rude.

cram /kræm/ *v.t./i.* (*p.t.* **crammed**). **~ (for an exam),** bachoter. **~ into,** (*pack*) (s')entasser dans. **~ with,** (*fill*) bourrer de.

cramp /kræmp/ *n.* crampe *f.*

cramped /kræmpt/ *a.* à l'étroit.

cranberry /'krænbərɪ/ *n.* canneberge *f.*

crane /kreɪn/ *n.* grue *f.* ● *v.t.* (*neck*) tendre.

crank[1] /kræŋk/ *n.* (*techn.*) manivelle *f.*

crank[2] /kræŋk/ *n.* excentrique *m./f.* **~y** *a.* excentrique; (*Amer.*) grincheux.

cranny /'krænɪ/ *n.* fissure *f.*

craps /kræps/ *n.* **shoot ~,** (*Amer.*) jouer aux dés.

crash /kræʃ/ *n.* accident *m.*; (*noise*) fracas *m.*; (*of thunder*) coup *m.*; (*of firm*) faillite *f.* ● *v.t./i.* avoir un accident (avec); (*two vehicles*) se percuter. ● *a.* (*course*) intensif. **~-helmet** *n.* cas-

que (anti-choc) *m.* **~ into,** rentrer dans. **~-land** *v.i.* atterrir en catastrophe.

crass /kræs/ *a.* grossier.

crate /kreɪt/ *n.* cageot *m.*

crater /'kreɪtə(r)/ *n.* cratère *m.*

cravat /krə'væt/ *n.* foulard *m.*

crav|e /kreɪv/ *v.t./i.* **~e (for),** désirer ardemment. **~ing** *n.* envie irrésistible *f.*

crawl /krɔːl/ *v.i.* ramper; (*vehicle*) se traîner. ● *n.* (*pace*) pas *m.*; (*swimming*) crawl *m.* **be ~ing with,** grouiller de.

crayfish /'kreɪfɪʃ/ *n. invar.* écrevisse *f.*

crayon /'kreɪən/ *n.* crayon *m.*

craze /kreɪz/ *n.* engouement *m.*

crazed /kreɪzd/ *a.* affolé.

craz|y /'kreɪzɪ/ *a.* (**-ier, -iest**) fou. **~y about,** (*person*) fou de; (*thing*) fana *or* fou de. **~iness** *n.* folie *f.* **~y paving,** dallage irrégulier *m.*

creak /kriːk/ *n.* grincement *m.* ● *v.i.* grincer. **~y** *a.* grinçant.

cream /kriːm/ *n.* crème *f.* ● *a.* crème *invar.* ● *v.t.* écrémer. **~ cheese,** fromage frais *m.* **~ off,** se servir en prenant. **~y** *a.* crémeux.

crease /kriːs/ *n.* pli *m.* ● *v.t./i.* (se) froisser.

creat|e /kriː'eɪt/ *v.t.* créer. **~ion** /-ʃn/ *n.* création *f.* **~ive** *a.* créateur. **~or** *n.* créa|teur, -trice *m.,f.*

creature /'kriːtʃə(r)/ *n.* créature *f.*

crèche /kreʃ/ *n.* garderie *f.*

credence /'kriːdns/ *n.* **give ~ to,** ajouter foi à.

credentials /krɪ'denʃlz/ *n. pl.* (*identity*) pièces d'identité *f. pl.*; (*competence*) références *f. pl.*

credib|le /'kredəbl/ *a.* (*excuse etc.*) croyable, plausible. **~ility** /-'bɪlətɪ/ *n.* crédibilité *f.*

credit /'kredɪt/ *n.* crédit *m.*; (*honour*) honneur *m.* **in ~,** créditeur. **~s,** (*cinema*) générique *m.* ● *a.* (*balance*) créditeur. ● *v.t.* (*p.t.* **credited**) croire; (*comm.*) créditer. **~ card,** carte de crédit *f.* **~ note,** avoir *m.* **~ s.o. with,** attribuer à qn. **~-worthy** *a.* solvable. **~or** *n.* créan|cier, -ière *m.,f.*

creditable /'kredɪtəbl/ *a.* méritoire, honorable.

credulous /'kredjʊləs/ *a.* crédule.

creed /kriːd/ *n.* credo *m.*

creek /kri:k/ *n.* crique *f.*; (*Amer.*) ruisseau *m.* **up the ~,** (*sl.*) dans le pétrin.

creep /kri:p/ *v.i.* (*p.t.* **crept**) ramper; (*fig.*) se glisser. ● *n.* (*person: sl.*) pauvre type *m.* **give s.o. the ~s,** faire frissonner qn. **~er** *n.* liane *f.* **~y** *a.* qui fait frissonner.

cremat|e /krɪˈmeɪt/ *v.t.* incinérer. **~ion** /-ʃn/ *n.* incinération *f.*

crematorium /kreməˈtɔːrɪəm/ *n.* (*pl.* **-ia**) crématorium *m.*

Creole /ˈkriːəʊl/ *n.* créole *m./f.*

crêpe /kreɪp/ *n.* crêpe *m.* **~ paper,** papier crêpon *m.*

crept /krept/ *see* creep.

crescendo /krɪˈʃendəʊ/ *n.* (*pl.* **-os**) crescendo *m.*

crescent /ˈkresnt/ *n.* croissant *m.*; (*fig.*) rue en demi-lune *f.*

cress /kres/ *n.* cresson *m.*

crest /krest/ *n.* crête *f.*; (*coat of arms*) armoiries *f. pl.*

Crete /kri:t/ *n.* Crète *f.*

cretin /ˈkretɪn, Amer.* ˈkri:tɪn/ *n.* crétin(e) *m.* (*f.*). **~ous** *a.* crétin.

crevasse /krɪˈvæs/ *n.* crevasse *f.*

crevice /ˈkrevɪs/ *n.* fente *f.*

crew /kru:/ *n.* équipage *m.*; (*gang*) équipe *f.* **~ cut,** coupe en brosse *f.* **~ neck,** (col) ras du cou *m.*

crib¹ /krɪb/ *n.* lit d'enfant *m.*

crib² /krɪb/ *v.t./i.* (*p.t.* **cribbed**) copier. ● *n.* (*schol.: fam.*) traduction *f.*, aide-mémoire *m. invar.*

crick /krɪk/ *n.* (*in neck*) torticolis *m.*

cricket¹ /ˈkrɪkɪt/ *n.* (*sport*) cricket *m.* **~er** *n.* joueur de cricket *m.*

cricket² /ˈkrɪkɪt/ *n.* (*insect*) grillon *m.*

crime /kraɪm/ *n.* crime *m.*; (*minor*) délit *m.*; (*acts*) criminalité *f.*

criminal /ˈkrɪmɪnl/ *a. & n.* criminel(le) (*m.* (*f.*)).

crimp /krɪmp/ *v.t.* (*hair*) friser.

crimson /ˈkrɪmzn/ *a./n.* cramoisi (*m.*).

cring|e /krɪndʒ/ *v.i.* reculer; (*fig.*) s'humilier. **~ing** *a.* servile.

crinkle /ˈkrɪŋkl/ *v.t./i.* (se) froisser. ● *n.* pli *m.*

cripple /ˈkrɪpl/ *n.* infirme *m./f.* ● *v.t.* estropier; (*fig.*) paralyser.

crisis /ˈkraɪsɪs/ *n.* (*pl.* **crises** /-si:z/) crise *f.*

crisp /krɪsp/ *a.* (**-er, -est**) (*culin.*) croquant; (*air, reply*) vif. **~s** *n. pl.* chips *f. pl.*

criss-cross /ˈkrɪskrɒs/ *a.* entrecroisé. ● *v.t./i.* (s')entrecroiser.

criterion /kraɪˈtɪərɪən/ *n.* (*pl.* **-ia**) critère *m.*

critic /ˈkrɪtɪk/ *n.* critique *m.* **~al** *a.* critique. **~ally** *adv.* d'une manière critique; (*ill*) gravement.

criticism /ˈkrɪtɪsɪzəm/ *n.* critique *f.*

criticize /ˈkrɪtɪsaɪz/ *v.t./i.* critiquer.

croak /krəʊk/ *n.* (*bird*) croassement *m.*; (*frog*) coassement *m.* ● *v.i.* croasser; coasser.

crochet /ˈkrəʊʃeɪ/ *n.* crochet *m.* ● *v.t.* faire au crochet.

crockery /ˈkrɒkərɪ/ *n.* vaisselle *f.*

crocodile /ˈkrɒkədaɪl/ *n.* crocodile *m.*

crocus /ˈkrəʊkəs/ *n.* (*pl.* **-uses**) crocus *m.*

crony /ˈkrəʊnɪ/ *n.* cop|ain, -ine *m.*, *f.*

crook /krʊk/ *n.* (*criminal: fam.*) escroc *m.*; (*stick*) houlette *f.*

crooked /ˈkrʊkɪd/ *a.* tordu; (*winding*) tortueux; (*askew*) de travers; (*dishonest: fig.*) malhonnête. **~ly** *adv.* de travers.

croon /kru:n/ *v.t./i.* chantonner.

crop /krɒp/ *n.* récolte *f.*; (*fig.*) quantité *f.* ● *v.t.* (*p.t.* **cropped**) couper. ● *v.i.* **~ up,** se présenter.

croquet /ˈkrəʊkeɪ/ *n.* croquet *m.*

croquette /krəʊˈket/ *n.* croquette *f.*

cross /krɒs/ *n.* croix *f.*; (*hybrid*) hybride *m.* ● *v.t./i.* traverser; (*legs, animals*) croiser; (*cheque*) barrer; (*paths*) se croiser. ● *a.* en colère, fâché (**with,** contre). **~-check** *v.t.* vérifier (pour confirmer). **~-country** (*running*), cross *m.* **~ off** *or* **out,** rayer. **~ s.o.'s mind,** venir à l'esprit de qn. **talk at ~ purposes,** parler sans se comprendre. **~ly** *adv.* avec colère.

crossbar /ˈkrɒsbɑː(r)/ *n.* barre transversale *f.*

cross-examine /krɒsɪɡˈzæmɪn/ *v.t.* faire subir un contre-interrogatoire à.

cross-eyed /ˈkrɒsaɪd/ *a.* **be ~,** loucher.

crossfire /ˈkrɒsfaɪə(r)/ *n.* feux croisés *m. pl.*

crossing /ˈkrɒsɪŋ/ *n.* (*by boat*) traversée *f.*; (*on road*) passage clouté *m.*

cross-reference /krɒsˈrefrəns/ *n.* renvoi *m.*

crossroads /ˈkrɒsrəʊdz/ *n.* carrefour *m.*

cross-section /krɒsˈsekʃn/ *n.* coupe transversale *f.*; (*sample: fig.*) échantillon *m.*

cross-wind /'krɒswɪnd/ *n.* vent de travers *m.*

crosswise /'krɒswaɪz/ *adv.* en travers.

crossword /'krɒswɜːd/ *n.* mots croisés *m. pl.*

crotch /krɒtʃ/ *n.* (*of garment*) entrejambes *m. invar.*

crotchet /'krɒtʃɪt/ *n.* (*mus.*) noire *f.*

crotchety /'krɒtʃɪtɪ/ *a.* grincheux.

crouch /kraʊtʃ/ *v.i.* s'accroupir.

crow /krəʊ/ *n.* corbeau *m.* ● *v.i.* (*of cock*) (*p.t.* **crew**) chanter; (*fig.*) jubiler. **as the ~ flies,** à vol d'oiseau. **~'s feet,** pattes d'oie *f. pl.*

crowbar /'krəʊbɑː(r)/ *n.* pied-de-biche *m.*

crowd /kraʊd/ *n.* foule *f.* ● *v.i.* affluer. ● *v.t.* remplir. **~ into,** (s')entasser dans. **~ed** *a.* plein.

crown /kraʊn/ *n.* couronne *f.*; (*top part*) sommet *m.* ● *v.t.* couronner. **C~ Court,** Cour d'assises *f.* **C~ prince,** prince héritier *m.*

crucial /'kruːʃl/ *a.* crucial.

crucifix /'kruːsɪfɪks/ *n.* crucifix *m.*

crucif|y /'kruːsɪfaɪ/ *v.t.* crucifier. **~ixion** /-'fɪkʃn/ *n.* crucifixion *f.*

crude /kruːd/ *a.* (**-er, -est**) (*raw*) brut; (*rough, vulgar*) grossier.

cruel /krʊəl/ *a.* (**crueller, cruellest**) cruel. **~ty** *n.* cruauté *f.*

cruet /'kruːɪt/ *n.* huilier *m.*

cruis|e /kruːz/ *n.* croisière *f.* ● *v.i.* (*ship*) croiser; (*tourists*) faire une croisière; (*vehicle*) rouler. **~er** *n.* croiseur *m.* **~ing speed,** vitesse de croisière *f.*

crumb /krʌm/ *n.* miette *f.*

crumble /'krʌmbl/ *v.t./i.* (s')effriter; (*bread*) (s')émietter; (*collapse*) s'écrouler.

crummy /'krʌmɪ/ *a.* (**-ier, -iest**) (*sl.*) moche, minable.

crumpet /'krʌmpɪt/ *n.* (*culin.*) petite crêpe (grillée) *f.*

crumple /'krʌmpl/ *v.t./i.* (se) froisser.

crunch /krʌntʃ/ *v.t.* croquer. ● *n.* (*event*) moment critique *m.* **when it comes to the ~,** quand ça devient sérieux.

crusade /kruː'seɪd/ *n.* croisade *f.* **~r** /-ə(r)/ *n.* (*knight*) croisé *m.*; (*fig.*) militant(e) *m.* (*f.*).

crush /krʌʃ/ *v.t.* écraser; (*clothes*) froisser. ● *n.* (*crowd*) presse *f.* **a ~ on,** (*sl.*) le béguin pour.

crust /krʌst/ *n.* croûte *f.* **~y** *a.* croustillant.

crutch /krʌtʃ/ *n.* béquille *f.*; (*crotch*) entrejambes *m. invar.*

crux /krʌks/ *n.* **the ~ of,** (*problem etc.*) le nœud de.

cry /kraɪ/ *n.* cri *m.* ● *v.i.* (*weep*) pleurer; (*call out*) crier. **~-baby** *n.* pleurnicheu|r, -se *m., f.* **~ off,** abandonner.

crying /'kraɪɪŋ/ *a.* (*evil etc.*) flagrant. **a ~ shame,** une vraie honte.

crypt /krɪpt/ *n.* crypte *f.*

cryptic /'krɪptɪk/ *a.* énigmatique.

crystal /'krɪstl/ *n.* cristal *m.* **~-clear** *a.* parfaitement clair. **~lize** *v.t./i.* (se) cristalliser.

cub /kʌb/ *n.* petit *m.* **Cub (Scout),** louveteau *m.*

Cuba /'kjuːbə/ *n.* Cuba *m.* **~n** *a.* & *n.* cubain(e) (*m.* (*f.*)).

cubby-hole /'kʌbɪhəʊl/ *n.* cagibi *m.*

cub|e /kjuːb/ *n.* cube *m.* **~ic** *a.* cubique; (*metre etc.*) cube.

cubicle /'kjuːbɪkl/ *n.* (*in room, hospital, etc.*) box *m.*; (*at swimming-pool*) cabine *f.*

cuckoo /'kʊkuː/ *n.* coucou *m.*

cucumber /'kjuːkʌmbə(r)/ *n.* concombre *m.*

cuddl|e /'kʌdl/ *v.t.* câliner. ● *v.i.* (*kiss and*) **~e,** s'embrasser. ● *n.* caresse *f.* **~y** *a.* câlin, caressant.

cudgel /'kʌdʒl/ *n.* gourdin *m.*

cue ¹ /kjuː/ *n.* signal *m.*; (*theatre*) réplique *f.*

cue ² /kjuː/ *n.* (*billiards*) queue *f.*

cuff /kʌf/ *n.* manchette *f.*; (*Amer.*) revers *m.* ● *v.t.* gifler. **~-link** *n.* bouton de manchette *m.* **off the ~,** impromptu.

cul-de-sac /'kʌldəsæk/ *n.* (*pl.* **culs-de-sac**) impasse *f.*

culinary /'kʌlɪnərɪ/ *a.* culinaire.

cull /kʌl/ *v.t.* (*select*) choisir; (*kill*) abattre sélectivement.

culminat|e /'kʌlmɪneɪt/ *v.i.* **~e in,** se terminer par. **~ion** /-'neɪʃn/ *n.* point culminant *m.*

culprit /'kʌlprɪt/ *n.* coupable *m./f.*

cult /kʌlt/ *n.* culte *m.* **~ movie,** film culte.

cultivat|e /'kʌltɪveɪt/ *v.t.* cultiver. **~ion** /-'veɪʃn/ *n.* culture *f.*

cultural /'kʌltʃərəl/ *a.* culturel.

culture /'kʌltʃə(r)/ *n.* culture *f.* **~d** *a.* cultivé.

cumbersome /'kʌmbəsəm/ *a.* encombrant.

cumulative /'kjuːmjʊlətɪv/ *a.* cumulatif.

cunning /'kʌnɪŋ/ a. rusé. ● n. astuce f., ruse f.

cup /kʌp/ n. tasse f.; (prize) coupe f. **Cup final**, finale de la coupe f. **~ size**, profondeur de bonnet f. **~-tie** n. match de coupe m.

cupboard /'kʌbəd/ n. placard m., armoire f.

cupful /'kʌpful/ n. tasse f.

Cupid /'kjuːpɪd/ n. Cupidon m.

curable /'kjʊərəbl/ a. guérissable.

curate /'kjʊərət/ n. vicaire m.

curator /kjʊə'reɪtə(r)/ n. (of museum) conservateur m.

curb[1] /kɜːb/ n. (restraint) frein m. ● v.t. (desires etc.) refréner; (price increase etc.) freiner.

curb[2] (Amer.) **kerb** /kɜːb/ n. bord de trottoir m.

curdle /'kɜːdl/ v.t./i. (se) cailler.

curds /kɜːdz/ n. pl. lait caillé m.

cure[1] /kjʊə(r)/ v.t. guérir; (fig.) éliminer. ● n. (recovery) guérison f.; (remedy) remède m.

cure[2] /kjʊə(r)/ v.t. (culin.) fumer; (in brine) saler.

curfew /'kɜːfjuː/ n. couvre-feu m.

curio /'kjʊərɪəʊ/ n. (pl. -os) curiosité f., bibelot m.

curi|ous /'kjʊərɪəs/ a. curieux. **~osity** /-'ɒsətɪ/ n. curiosité f.

curl /kɜːl/ v.t./i. (hair) boucler. ● n. boucle f. **~ up**, se pelotonner; (shrivel) se racornir.

curler /'kɜːlə(r)/ n. bigoudi m.

curly /'kɜːlɪ/ a. (-ier, -iest) bouclé.

currant /'kʌrənt/ n. raisin de Corinthe m.; (berry) groseille f.

currency /'kʌrənsɪ/ n. (money) monnaie f.; (acceptance) cours m. **foreign ~**, devises étrangères f. pl.

current /'kʌrənt/ a. (common) courant; (topical) actuel; (year etc.) en cours. ● n. courant m. **~ account**, compte courant m. **~ events**, l'actualité f. **~ly** adv. actuellement.

curriculum /kə'rɪkjʊləm/ n. (pl. -la) programme scolaire m. **~ vitae**, curriculum vitae m.

curry[1] /'kʌrɪ/ n. curry m., cari m.

curry[2] /'kʌrɪ/ v.t. **~ favour with**, chercher les bonnes grâces de.

curse /kɜːs/ n. malédiction f.; (oath) juron m. ● v.t. maudire. ● v.i. (swear) jurer.

cursor /'kɜːsə(r)/ n. curseur m.

cursory /'kɜːsərɪ/ a. (trop) rapide.

curt /kɜːt/ a. brusque.

curtail /kɜː'teɪl/ v.t. écourter, raccourcir; (expenses etc.) réduire.

curtain /'kɜːtn/ n. rideau m.

curtsy /'kɜːtsɪ/ n. révérence f. ● v.i. faire une révérence.

curve /kɜːv/ n. courbe f. ● v.t./i. (se) courber; (of road) tourner.

cushion /'kʊʃn/ n. coussin m. ● v.t. (a blow) amortir; (fig.) protéger.

cushy /'kʊʃɪ/ a. (-ier, -iest) (job etc.: fam.) pépère.

custard /'kʌstəd/ n. crème anglaise f.; (set) crème renversée f.

custodian /kʌ'stəʊdɪən/ n. gardien(ne) m. (f.).

custody /'kʌstədɪ/ n. garde f.; (jurid.) détention préventive f.

custom /'kʌstəm/ n. coutume f.; (patronage: comm.) clientèle f. **~-built**, **~-made** adjs. fait etc. sur commande. **~ary** a. d'usage.

customer /'kʌstəmə(r)/ n. client(e) m. (f.); (fam.) **an odd/a difficult ~**, un individu curieux/difficile.

customize /'kʌstəmaɪz/ v.t. personnaliser.

customs /'kʌstəmz/ n. pl. douane f. ● a. douanier. **~ officer**, douanier m.

cut /kʌt/ v.t./i. (p.t. **cut**, pres. p. **cutting**) couper; (hedge, jewel) tailler; (prices etc.) réduire. ● n. coupure f.; (of clothes) coupe f.; (piece) morceau m.; réduction f. **~ back** or **down (on)**, réduire. **~-back** n. réduction f. **~ in**, (auto.) se rabattre. **~ off**, couper; (fig.) isoler. **~ out**, découper; (leave out) supprimer. **~-price** a. à prix réduit. **~ short**, (visit) écourter. **~ up**, couper; (carve) découper. **~ up about**, démoraliser par.

cute /kjuːt/ a. (-er, -est) (fam.) astucieux; (Amer.) mignon.

cuticle /'kjuːtɪkl/ n. petites peaux f. pl. (de l'ongle).

cutlery /'kʌtlərɪ/ n. couverts m. pl.

cutlet /'kʌtlɪt/ n. côtelette f.

cutting /'kʌtɪŋ/ a. cinglant. ● n. (from newspaper) coupure f.; (plant) bouture f. **~ edge**, tranchant m.

CV abbr. see curriculum vitae.

cyanide /'saɪənaɪd/ n. cyanure m.

cybernetics /saɪbə'netɪks/ n. cybernétique f.

cycl|e /'saɪkl/ n. cycle m.; (bicycle) vélo m. ● v.i. aller à vélo. **~ing** n. cyclisme m. **~ist** n. cycliste m./f.

cyclic(al) /'saɪklɪk(l)/ a. cyclique.

cyclone /'saɪkləʊn/ n. cyclone m.

cylind|er /'sɪlɪndə(r)/ n. cylindre m. **~rical** /-'lɪndrɪkl/ a. cylindrique.

cymbal /'sɪmbl/ n. cymbale f.

cynic /'sɪnɪk/ n. cynique m./f. **~al** a. cynique. **~ism** /-sɪzəm/ n. cynisme m.

cypress /'saɪprəs/ n. cyprès m.

Cypr|us /'saɪprəs/ n. Chypre f. **~iot** /'sɪprɪət/ a. & n. cypriote (m./f.).

cyst /sɪst/ n. kyste m. **~ic fibrosis**, mucoviscidose f.

cystitis /sɪst'aɪtɪs/ n. cystite f.

czar /zɑː(r)/ n. tsar m.

Czech /tʃek/ a. & n. tchèque (m./f.).

Czechoslovak /tʃekə'sləʊvæk/ a. & n. tchécoslovaque (m./f.). **~ia** /-slə'vækɪə/ n. Tchécoslovaquie f.

D

dab /dæb/ v.t. (p.t. **dabbed**) tamponner. ● n. a **~ of**, un petit coup de; (fam.) be a **~ hand at**, avoir le coup de main pour. **~ sth. on**, appliquer qch. à petits coups sur.

dabble /'dæbl/ v.i. **~ in**, se mêler un peu de. **~r** /-ə(r)/ n. amateur m.

dad /dæd/ n. (fam.) papa m. **~dy** n. (children's use) papa m.

daffodil /'dæfədɪl/ n. jonquille f.

daft /dɑːft/ a. (-er, -est) idiot.

dagger /'dægə(r)/ n. poignard m.

dahlia /'deɪlɪə/ n. dahlia m.

daily /'deɪlɪ/ a. quotidien. ● adv. tous les jours. ● n. (newspaper) quotidien m.; (charwoman: fam.) femme de ménage f.

dainty /'deɪntɪ/ a. (-ier, -iest) délicat.

dairy /'deərɪ/ n. (on farm) laiterie f.; (shop) crémerie f. ● a. laitier.

daisy /'deɪzɪ/ n. pâquerette f. **~ wheel**, marguerite f.

dale /deɪl/ n. vallée f.

dam /dæm/ n. barrage m. ● v.t. (p.t. **dammed**) endiguer.

damag|e /'dæmɪdʒ/ n. dégâts m. pl., dommages m. pl.; (harm: fig.) préjudice m. **~es**, (jurid.) dommages et intérêts m. pl. ● v.t. abîmer; (fig.) nuire à. **~ing** a. nuisible.

dame /deɪm/ n. (old use) dame f.; (Amer., sl.) fille f.

damn /dæm/ v.t. (relig.) maudire; (swear at) maudire; (condemn: fig.) condamner. ● int. zut, merde. ● n.

not care a **~**, s'en foutre. ● a. sacré. ● adv. rudement. **~ation** /-'neɪʃn/ n. damnation f.

damp /dæmp/ n. humidité f. ● a. (-er, -est) humide. ● v.t. humecter; (fig.) refroidir. **~en** v.t. = damp. **~ness** n. humidité f.

dance /dɑːns/ v.t./i. danser. ● n. danse f.; (gathering) bal m. **~ hall**, dancing m., salle de danse f. **~r** /-ə(r)/ n. danseu|r, -se m., f.

dandelion /'dændɪlaɪən/ n. pissenlit m.

dandruff /'dændrʌf/ n. pellicules f. pl.

dandy /'dændɪ/ n. dandy m.

Dane /deɪn/ n. Danois(e) m. (f.).

danger /'deɪndʒə(r)/ n. danger m.; (risk) risque m. **be in ~ of**, risquer de. **~ous** a. dangereux.

dangle /'dæŋgl/ v.t./i. (se) balancer, (laisser) pendre. **~ sth. in front of s.o.**, (fig.) faire miroiter qch. à qn.

Danish /'deɪnɪʃ/ a. danois. ● n. (lang.) danois m.

dank /dæŋk/ a. (-er, -est) humide et froid.

dapper /'dæpə(r)/ a. élégant.

dare /deə(r)/ v.t. **~ (to) do**, oser faire. **~ s.o. to do**, défier qn de faire. ● n. défi m. **I ~ say**, je suppose (that, que).

daredevil /'deədevl/ n. casse-cou m. invar.

daring /'deərɪŋ/ a. audacieux.

dark /dɑːk/ a. (-er, -est) obscur, sombre, noir; (colour) foncé, sombre; (skin) brun, foncé; (gloomy) sombre. ● n. noir m.; (nightfall) tombée de la nuit f. **~ horse**, individu aux talents inconnus m. **~-room** n. chambre noire f. **in the ~**, (fig.) dans l'ignorance (about, de). **~ness** n. obscurité f.

darken /'dɑːkən/ v.t./i. (s')assombrir.

darling /'dɑːlɪŋ/ a. & n. chéri(e) (m. (f.)).

darn /dɑːn/ v.t. repriser.

dart /dɑːt/ n. fléchette f. **~s**, (game) fléchettes f. pl. ● v.i. s'élancer.

dartboard /'dɑːtbɔːd/ n. cible f.

dash /dæʃ/ v.i. (hurry) se dépêcher; (forward etc.) se précipiter. ● v.t. jeter (avec violence); (hopes) briser. ● n. ruée f.; (stroke) tiret m. a **~ of**, un peu de. **~ off**, (leave) partir en vitesse.

dashboard /'dæʃbɔːd/ n. tableau de bord m.

dashing /'dæʃɪŋ/ a. fringant.

data /'deɪtə/ n. pl. données f. pl. **~ processing**, traitement des données m.

database /'deɪtəbeɪs/ n. base de données f.

date [1] /deɪt/ n. date f.; (*meeting: fam.*) rendez-vous m. ● v.t./i. dater; (*go out with: fam.*) sortir avec. **~ from**, dater de. **out of ~**, (*old-fashioned*) démodé; (*passport*) périmé. **to ~**, à ce jour. **up to ~**, (*modern*) moderne; (*list*) à jour. **~d** /-ɪd/ a. démodé.

date [2] /deɪt/ n. (*fruit*) datte f.

daub /dɔːb/ v.t. barbouiller.

daughter /'dɔːtə(r)/ n. fille f. **~-in-law** n. (*pl.* **~s-in-law**) belle-fille f.

daunt /dɔːnt/ v.t. décourager.

dauntless /'dɔːntlɪs/ a. intrépide.

dawdle /'dɔːdl/ v.i. lambiner. **~r** /-ə(r)/ n. lambin(e) m. (f.).

dawn /dɔːn/ n. aube f. ● v.i. poindre; (*fig.*) naître. **it ~ed on me**, je m'en suis rendu compte.

day /deɪ/ n. jour m.; (*whole day*) journée f.; (*period*) époque f. **~-break** n. point du jour m. **~-dream** n. rêverie f.; v.i. rêvasser. **the ~ before**, la veille. **the following** or **next ~**, le lendemain.

daylight /'deɪlaɪt/ n. jour m.

daytime /'deɪtaɪm/ n. jour m., journée f.

daze /deɪz/ v.t. étourdir; (*with drugs*) hébéter. ● n. **in a ~**, étourdi; hébété.

dazzle /'dæzl/ v.t. éblouir.

deacon /'diːkən/ n. diacre m.

dead /ded/ a. mort; (*numb*) engourdi. ● adv. complètement. ● n. **in the ~ of**, au cœur de. **the ~**, les morts. **~ beat**, éreinté. **~ end**, impasse f. **~-end job**, travail sans avenir m. **a ~ loss**, (*thing*) une perte de temps; (*person*) une catastrophe. **~-pan** a. impassible. **in ~ centre**, au beau milieu. **stop ~**, s'arrêter net. **the race was a ~ heat**, ils ont été classés ex aequo.

deaden /'dedn/ v.t. (*sound, blow*) amortir; (*pain*) calmer.

deadline /'dedlaɪn/ n. date limite f.

deadlock /'dedlɒk/ n. impasse f.

deadly /'dedlɪ/ a. (**-ier, -iest**) mortel; (*weapon*) meurtrier.

deaf /def/ a. (**-er, -est**) sourd. **the ~ and dumb**, les sourds-muets. **~-aid** n. appareil acoustique m. **~ness** n. surdité f.

deafen /'defn/ v.t. assourdir.

deal /diːl/ v.t. (*p.t.* **dealt**) donner; (*a blow*) porter. ● v.i. (*trade*) commercer. ● n. affaire f. **a great** or **good ~ (of, de)**, beaucoup (of, de). **~ in**, faire le commerce de. **~ with**, (*handle, manage*) s'occuper de; (*be about*) traiter de. **~er** n. marchand(e) m. (f.); (*agent*) concessionnaire m./f.

dealings /'diːlɪŋz/ n. pl. relations f. pl.

dean /diːn/ n. doyen m.

dear /dɪə(r)/ a. (**-er, -est**) cher. ● n. (**my**) **~**, mon cher, ma chère; (*darling*) (mon) chéri, (ma) chérie. ● adv. cher. ● int. **oh ~!**, oh mon Dieu! **~ly** adv. tendrement; (*pay*) cher.

dearth /dɜːθ/ n. pénurie f.

death /deθ/ n. mort f. **~ certificate**, acte de décès m. **~ duty**, droits de succession m. pl. **~ penalty**, peine de mort f. **it is a ~-trap**, (*place, vehicle*) il y a un danger de mort. **~ly** a. de mort, mortel.

debar /dɪ'bɑː(r)/ v.t. (*p.t.* **debarred**) exclure.

debase /dɪ'beɪs/ v.t. avilir.

debat|e /dɪ'beɪt/ n. discussion f., débat m. ● v.t. discuter. **~e whether**, se demander si. **~able** a. discutable.

debauch /dɪ'bɔːtʃ/ v.t. débaucher. **~ery** n. débauche f.

debilitate /dɪ'bɪlɪteɪt/ v.t. débiliter.

debility /dɪ'bɪlətɪ/ n. débilité f.

debit /'debɪt/ n. débit m. **in ~**, débiteur. ● a. (*balance*) débiteur. ● v.t. (*p.t.* **debited**) débiter.

debris /'deɪbriː/ n. débris m. pl.

debt /det/ n. dette f. **in ~**, endetté. **~or** n. débi|teur, -trice m., f.

debunk /diː'bʌŋk/ v.t. (*fam.*) démythifier.

decade /'dekeɪd/ n. décennie f.

decaden|t /'dekədənt/ a. décadent. **~ce** n. décadence f.

decaffeinated /diː'kæfɪneɪtɪd/ a. décaféiné.

decanter /dɪ'kæntə(r)/ n. carafe f.

decathlon /dɪ'kæθlən/ n. décathlon m.

decay /dɪ'keɪ/ v.i. se gâter, pourrir; (*fig.*) décliner. ● n. pourriture f.; (*of tooth*) carie f.; (*fig.*) déclin m.

deceased /dɪ'siːst/ a. décédé. ● n. défunt(e) m. (f.).

deceit /dɪˈsiːt/ n. tromperie f. ~**ful** a. trompeur. ~**fully** adv. d'une manière trompeuse.

deceive /dɪˈsiːv/ v.t. tromper.

December /dɪˈsembə(r)/ n. décembre m.

decent /ˈdiːsnt/ a. décent, convenable; (good: fam.) (assez) bon; (kind: fam.) gentil. ~**cy** n. décence f. ~**tly** adv. décemment.

decentralize /diːˈsentrəlaɪz/ v.t. décentraliser.

decept|ive /dɪˈseptɪv/ a. trompeur. ~**ion** n. -pʃn/ n. tromperie f.

decibel /ˈdesɪbel/ n. décibel m.

decide /dɪˈsaɪd/ v.t./i. décider; (question) régler. ~ **on**, se décider pour. ~ **to do**, décider de faire. ~**d** /-ɪd/ a. (firm) résolu; (clear) net. ~**dly** /-ɪdlɪ/ adv. résolument; nettement.

deciduous /dɪˈsɪdjʊəs/ a. à feuillage caduc.

decimal /ˈdesɪml/ a. décimal. ● n. décimale f. ~ **point**, virgule f.

decimate /ˈdesɪmeɪt/ v.t. décimer.

decipher /dɪˈsaɪfə(r)/ v.t. déchiffrer.

decision /dɪˈsɪʒn/ n. décision f.

decisive /dɪˈsaɪsɪv/ a. (conclusive) décisif; (firm) décidé. ~**ly** adv. d'une façon décidée.

deck /dek/ n. pont m.; (of cards: Amer.) jeu m. ~-**chair** n. chaise longue f. ~ **top** ~, (of bus) impériale f.

declar|e /dɪˈkleə(r)/ v.t. déclarer. ~**ation** /dekləˈreɪʃn/ n. déclaration f.

decline /dɪˈklaɪn/ v.t./i. refuser (politement); (deteriorate) décliner; (fall) baisser. ● n. déclin m.; baisse f.

decode /diːˈkəʊd/ v.t. décoder.

decompos|e /diːkəmˈpəʊz/ v.t./i. (se) décomposer. ~**ition** /-ɒmpəˈzɪʃn/ n. décomposition f.

décor /ˈdeɪkɔː(r)/ n. décor m.

decorat|e /ˈdekəreɪt/ v.t. décorer; (room) peindre or tapisser. ~**ion** /-ˈreɪʃn/ n. décoration f. ~**ive** /-ətɪv/ a. décoratif.

decorator /ˈdekəreɪtə(r)/ n. peintre en bâtiment m. **(interior)** ~, décora|teur, -trice d'appartements m., f.

decorum /dɪˈkɔːrəm/ n. décorum m.

decoy[1] /ˈdiːkɔɪ/ n. (bird) appeau m.; (trap) piège m., leurre f.

decoy[2] /dɪˈkɔɪ/ v.t. attirer, appâter.

decrease /dɪˈkriːs/ v.t./i. diminuer. ● n. /ˈdiːkriːs/ diminution f.

decree /dɪˈkriː/ n. (pol., relig.) décret m.; (jurid.) jugement m. ● v.t. (p.t. **decreed**) décréter.

decrepit /dɪˈkrepɪt/ a. (building) délabré; (person) décrépit.

decry /dɪˈkraɪ/ v.t. dénigrer.

dedicat|e /ˈdedɪkeɪt/ v.t. dédier. ~**e o.s. to**, se consacrer à. ~**ed** a. dévoué. ~**ion** /-ˈkeɪʃn/ n. dévouement m.; (in book) dédicace f.

deduce /dɪˈdjuːs/ v.t. déduire.

deduct /dɪˈdʌkt/ v.t. déduire; (from wages) retenir. ~**ion** /-kʃn/ n. déduction f.; retenue f.

deed /diːd/ n. acte m.

deem /diːm/ v.t. juger.

deep /diːp/ a. (-er, -est) profond. ● adv. profondément. ~ **in thought**, absorbé dans ses pensées. ~ **into the night**, tard dans la nuit. ~-**freeze** n. congélateur m.; v.t. congeler. ~-**fry**, frire. ~**ly** adv. profondément.

deepen /ˈdiːpən/ v.t. approfondir. ● v.i. devenir plus profond; (mystery, night) s'épaissir.

deer /dɪə(r)/ n. invar. cerf m.; (doe) biche f.

deface /dɪˈfeɪs/ v.t. dégrader.

defamation /defəˈmeɪʃn/ n. diffamation f.

default /dɪˈfɔːlt/ v.i. (jurid.) faire défaut. ● n. défaut m. **by** ~, (jurid.) par défaut. **win by** ~, gagner par forfait. ● a. (comput.) par défaut.

defeat /dɪˈfiːt/ v.t. vaincre; (thwart) faire échouer. ● n. défaite f.; (of plan etc.) échec m.

defect[1] /ˈdiːfekt/ n. défaut m. ~**ive** /dɪˈfektɪv/ a. défectueux.

defect[2] /dɪˈfekt/ v.i. faire défection. ~ **to**, passer à. ~**or** n. transfuge m./f.

defence /dɪˈfens/ n. défense f. ~**less** a. sans défense.

defend /dɪˈfend/ v.t. défendre. ~**ant** n. (jurid.) accusé(e) m. (f.). ~**er**, défenseur m.

defense /dɪˈfens/ n. Amer. = **defence**.

defensive /dɪˈfensɪv/ a. défensif. ● n. défensive f.

defer /dɪˈfɜː(r)/ v.t. (p.t. **deferred**) (postpone) différer, remettre.

deferen|ce /ˈdefərəns/ n. déférence f. ~**tial** /-ˈrenʃl/ a. déférent.

defian|ce /dɪˈfaɪəns/ n. défi m. **in** ~**ce of**, au mépris de. ~**t** a. de défi. ~**tly** adv. d'un air de défi.

deficien|t /dɪˈfɪʃnt/ a. insuffisant. be ~**t in**, manquer de. ~**cy** n. insuffisance f.; (fault) défaut m.

deficit /ˈdefɪsɪt/ n. déficit m.

defile /dɪˈfaɪl/ v.t. souiller.

define /dɪˈfaɪn/ v.t. définir.

definite /ˈdefɪnɪt/ a. précis; (obvious) net; (firm) catégorique; (certain) certain. ~**ly** adv. certainement; (clearly) nettement.

definition /defɪˈnɪʃn/ n. définition f.

definitive /dɪˈfɪnɪtɪv/ a. définitif.

deflat|e /dɪˈfleɪt/ v.t. dégonfler. ~**ion** /-ʃn/ n. dégonflement m.; (comm.) déflation f.

deflect /dɪˈflekt/ v.t./i. (faire) dévier.

deforestation /diːˌfɒrɪˈsteɪʃn/ n. déforestation f.

deform /dɪˈfɔːm/ v.t. déformer. ~**ed** a. difforme. ~**ity** n. difformité f.

defraud /dɪˈfrɔːd/ v.t. (state, customs) frauder. ~ **s.o. of sth.**, escroquer qch. à qn.

defray /dɪˈfreɪ/ v.t. payer.

defrost /diːˈfrɒst/ v.t. dégivrer.

deft /deft/ a. (-er, -est) adroit. ~**ness** n. adresse f.

defunct /dɪˈfʌŋkt/ a. défunt.

defuse /diːˈfjuːz/ v.t. désamorcer.

defy /dɪˈfaɪ/ v.t. défier; (attempts) résister à.

degenerate[1] /dɪˈdʒenəreɪt/ v.i. dégénérer (**into**, en).

degenerate[2] /dɪˈdʒenərət/ a. & n. dégénéré(e) (m. (f.)).

degrad|e /dɪˈgreɪd/ v.t. dégrader. ~**ation** /degrəˈdeɪʃn/ n. dégradation f.; (state) déchéance f.

degree /dɪˈgriː/ n. degré m.; (univ.) diplôme universitaire m.; (Bachelor's degree) licence f. **higher** ~, (univ.) maîtrise f. or doctorat m. **to such a ~ that**, à tel point que.

dehydrate /diːˈhaɪdreɪt/ v.t./i. (se) déshydrater.

de-ice /diːˈaɪs/ v.t. dégivrer.

deign /deɪn/ v.t. ~ **to do**, daigner faire.

deity /ˈdiːɪtɪ/ n. divinité f.

deject|ed /dɪˈdʒektɪd/ a. abattu. ~**ion** /-kʃn/ n. abattement m.

delay /dɪˈleɪ/ v.t. retarder. ● v.i. tarder. ● n. (lateness, time overdue) retard m.; (waiting) délai m. ~ **doing**, attendre pour faire.

delectable /dɪˈlektəbl/ a. délectable, très agréable.

delegate[1] /ˈdelɪgət/ n. délégué(e) m. (f.).

delegate[2] /ˈdelɪgeɪt/ v.t. déléguer. ~**ion** /-ˈgeɪʃn/ n. délégation f.

delet|e /dɪˈliːt/ v.t. effacer; (with line) barrer. ~**ion** /-ʃn/ n. suppression f.; (with line) rature f.

deliberate[1] /dɪˈlɪbərət/ a. délibéré; (steps, manner) mesuré. ~**ly** adv. exprès, délibérément.

deliberate[2] /dɪˈlɪbəreɪt/ v.i. délibérer. ● v.t. considérer. ~**ion** /-ˈreɪʃn/ n. délibération f.

delica|te /ˈdelɪkət/ a. délicat. ~**cy** n. délicatesse f.; (food) mets délicat or raffiné m.

delicatessen /delɪkəˈtesn/ n. épicerie fine f., charcuterie f.

delicious /dɪˈlɪʃəs/ a. délicieux.

delight /dɪˈlaɪt/ n. grand plaisir m., joie f., délice m. (f. in pl.); (thing) délice m. (f. in pl.). ● v.t. réjouir. ● v.i. ~ **in**, prendre plaisir à. ~**ed** a. ravi. ~**ful** a. charmant, très agréable.

delinquen|t /dɪˈlɪŋkwənt/ a. & n. délinquant(e) (m. (f.)). ~**cy** n. délinquance f.

deliri|ous /dɪˈlɪrɪəs/ a. **be** ~**ous**, délirer. ~**um** n. délire m.

deliver /dɪˈlɪvə(r)/ v.t. (message) remettre; (goods) livrer; (letters) distribuer; (free) délivrer; (utter) prononcer; (med.) accoucher; (a blow) porter. ~**ance** n. délivrance f. ~**y** n. livraison f.; distribution f.; accouchement m.

delta /ˈdeltə/ n. delta m.

delu|de /dɪˈluːd/ v.t. tromper. ~**de o.s.**, se faire des illusions. ~**sion** /-ʒn/ n. illusion f.

deluge /ˈdeljuːdʒ/ n. déluge m. ● v.t. inonder (**with**, de).

de luxe /dəˈlʌks/ a. de luxe.

delve /delv/ v.i. fouiller.

demagogue /ˈdeməgɒg/ n. démagogue m./f.

demand /dɪˈmɑːnd/ v.t. exiger; (in negotiations) réclamer. ● n. exigence f.; (claim) revendication f.; (comm.) demande f. **in** ~, recherché. **on** ~, à la demande. ~**ing** a. exigeant.

demarcation /diːmɑːˈkeɪʃn/ n. démarcation f.

demean /dɪˈmiːn/ v.t. ~ **o.s.**, s'abaisser, s'avilir.

demeanour, (Amer.) **demeanor** /dɪˈmiːnə(r)/ n. comportement m.

demented /dɪˈmentɪd/ a. dément.

demerara /deməˈreərə/ n. (*brown sugar*) cassonade f.

demise /dɪˈmaɪz/ n. décès m.

demo /ˈdeməʊ/ n. (pl. **-os**) (*demonstration: fam.*) manif f.

demobilize /diːˈməʊbəlaɪz/ v.t. démobiliser.

democracy /dɪˈmɒkrəsɪ/ n. démocratie f.

democrat /ˈdeməkræt/ n. démocrate m./f. **~ic** /-ˈkrætɪk/ a. démocratique.

demolish /dɪˈmɒlɪʃ/ v.t. démolir. **~tion** /demə'lɪʃn/ n. démolition f.

demon /ˈdiːmən/ n. démon m.

demonstrat|e /ˈdemənstreɪt/ v.t. démontrer. ● v.i. (*pol.*) manifester. **~ion** /-ˈstreɪʃn/ n. démonstration f.; (*pol.*) manifestation f. **~or** n. manifestant(e) m. (f.).

demonstrative /dɪˈmɒnstrətɪv/ a. démonstratif.

demoralize /dɪˈmɒrəlaɪz/ v.t. démoraliser.

demote /dɪˈməʊt/ v.t. rétrograder.

demure /dɪˈmjʊə(r)/ a. modeste.

den /den/ n. antre m.

denial /dɪˈnaɪəl/ n. dénégation f.; (*statement*) démenti m.

denigrate /ˈdenɪgreɪt/ v.t. dénigrer.

denim /ˈdenɪm/ n. toile de coton f. **~s**, (*jeans*) blue-jeans m. pl.

Denmark /ˈdenmɑːk/ n. Danemark m.

denomination /dɪnɒmɪˈneɪʃn/ n. (*relig.*) confession f.; (*money*) valeur f.

denote /dɪˈnəʊt/ v.t. dénoter.

denounce /dɪˈnaʊns/ v.t. dénoncer.

dens|e /dens/ a. (**-er, -est**) dense; (*person*) obtus. **~ely** adv. (*packed etc.*) très. **~ity** n. densité f.

dent /dent/ n. bosse f. ● v.t. cabosser. **there is a ~ in the car door**, la portière est cabossée.

dental /ˈdentl/ a. dentaire. **~ floss**, fil dentaire m. **~ surgeon**, dentiste m./f.

dentist /ˈdentɪst/ n. dentiste m./f. **~ry** n. art dentaire m.

dentures /ˈdentʃəz/ n. pl. dentier m.

denude /dɪˈnjuːd/ v.t. dénuder.

denunciation /dɪnʌnsɪˈeɪʃn/ n. dénonciation f.

deny /dɪˈnaɪ/ v.t. nier (**that**, que); (*rumour*) démentir; (*disown*) renier; (*refuse*) refuser.

deodorant /diːˈəʊdərənt/ n. & a. déodorant (m.).

depart /dɪˈpɑːt/ v.i. partir. **~ from**, (*deviate*) s'écarter de.

department /dɪˈpɑːtmənt/ n. département m.; (*in shop*) rayon m.; (*in office*) service m. **D~ of Health**, ministère de la santé m. **~ store**, grand magasin m.

departure /dɪˈpɑːtʃə(r)/ n. départ m. **a ~ from**, (*custom, diet, etc.*) une entorse à.

depend /dɪˈpend/ v.i. dépendre (**on**, de). **it (all) ~s**, ça dépend. **~ on**, (*rely on*) compter sur. **~ing on the weather**, selon le temps qu'il fera. **~able** a. sûr. **~ence** n. dépendance f. **~ent** a. dépendant. **be ~ent on**, dépendre de.

dependant /dɪˈpendənt/ n. personne à charge f.

depict /dɪˈpɪkt/ v.t. (*describe*) dépeindre; (*in picture*) représenter.

deplete /dɪˈpliːt/ v.t. (*reduce*) réduire; (*use up*) épuiser.

deplor|e /dɪˈplɔː(r)/ v.t. déplorer. **~able** a. déplorable.

deploy /dɪˈplɔɪ/ v.t. déployer.

depopulate /diːˈpɒpjʊleɪt/ v.t. dépeupler.

deport /dɪˈpɔːt/ v.t. expulser. **~ation** /diːpɔːˈteɪʃn/ n. expulsion f.

depose /dɪˈpəʊz/ v.t. déposer.

deposit /dɪˈpɒzɪt/ v.t. (p.t. **deposited**) déposer. ● n. dépôt m.; (*of payment*) acompte m.; (*to reserve*) arrhes f. pl.; (*against damage*) caution f.; (*on bottle etc.*) consigne f.; (*of mineral*) gisement m. **~ account**, compte de dépôt m. **~or** n. (*comm.*) déposant(e) m. (f.), épargnant(e) m. (f.).

depot /ˈdepəʊ, Amer. ˈdiːpəʊ/ n. dépôt m.; (*Amer.*) gare (routière) f.

deprav|e /dɪˈpreɪv/ v.t. dépraver. **~ity** /-ˈprævətɪ/ n. dépravation f.

deprecate /ˈdeprɪkeɪt/ v.t. désapprouver.

depreciat|e /dɪˈpriːʃɪeɪt/ v.t./i. (se) déprécier. **~ion** /-ˈeɪʃn/ n. dépréciation f.

depress /dɪˈpres/ v.t. (*sadden*) déprimer; (*push down*) appuyer sur. **become ~ed**, déprimer. **~ing** a. déprimant. **~ion** /-ʃn/ n. dépression f.

deprivation /deprɪˈveɪʃn/ n. privation f.

depriv|e /dɪˈpraɪv/ v.t. **~ of**, priver de. **~d** a. (*child etc.*) déshérité.

depth /depθ/ n. profondeur f. **be out of one's ~**, (*fig.*) être perdu. **in the ~s of**, au plus profond de.

deputation /depjʊ'teɪʃn/ n. députation f.

deputize 'depjʊtaɪz/ v.i. assurer l'intérim (**for**, de). ● v.t. (Amer.) déléguer, nommer.

deputy 'depjʊtɪ/ n. suppléant(e) m. (f.) ● a. adjoint. **~ chairman**, vice-président m.

derail /dɪ'reɪl/ v.t. faire dérailler. **be ~ed**, dérailler. **~ment** n. déraillement m.

deranged /dɪ'reɪndʒd/ a. (mind) dérangé.

derelict 'derəlɪkt/ a. abandonné.

deri|de /dɪ'raɪd/ v.t. railler. **~sion** /-'rɪʒn/ n. dérision f. **~sive** a. (laughter, person) railleur.

derisory /dɪ'raɪsərɪ/ a. (scoffing) railleur; (offer etc.) dérisoire.

derivative /dɪ'rɪvətɪv/ a. & n. dérivé (m.).

deriv|e /dɪ'raɪv/ v.t. **~e from**, tirer de. ● v.i. **~e from**, dériver de. **~ation** /derɪ'veɪʃn/ n. dérivation f.

derogatory /dɪ'rɒgətrɪ/ a. (word) péjoratif; (remark) désobligeant.

derv /dɜːv/ n. gas-oil m., gazole m.

descend /dɪ'send/ v.t./i. descendre. **be ~ed from**, descendre de. **~ant** n. descendant(e) m. (f.).

descent /dɪ'sent/ n. descente f.; (lineage) origine f.

descri|be /dɪ'skraɪb/ v.t. décrire. **~ption** /-'skrɪpʃn/ n. description f. **~ptive** /-'skrɪptɪv/ a. descriptif.

desecrat|e 'desɪkreɪt/ v.t. profaner. **~ion** /-'kreɪʃn/ n. profanation f.

desert¹ 'dezət/ n. désert m. ● a. désertique. **~ island**, île déserte f.

desert² /dɪ'zɜːt/ v.t./i. déserter. **~ed** a. désert. **~er** n. déserteur m. **~ion** /-ʃn/ n. désertion f.

deserts /dɪ'zɜːts/ n. pl. **one's ~**, ce qu'on mérite.

deserv|e /dɪ'zɜːv/ v.t. mériter (**to**, de). **~edly** /-ɪdlɪ/ adv. à juste titre. **~ing** a. (person) méritant; (action) méritoire.

design /dɪ'zaɪn/ n. (sketch) dessin m., plan m.; (construction) conception f.; (pattern) motif m.; (style of dress) modèle m.; (aim) dessein m. ● v.t. (sketch) dessiner; (devise, intend) concevoir. **~er** n. dessina|teur, - trice m.; (of fashion) styliste m./f.

designat|e 'dezɪgneɪt/ v.t. désigner. **~ion** /-'neɪʃn/ n. désignation f.

desir|e /dɪ'zaɪə(r)/ n. désir m. ● v.t. désirer. **~able** a. désirable. **~ability** /-ə'bɪlətɪ/ n. attrait m.

desk /desk/ n. bureau m.; (of pupil) pupitre m.; (in hotel) réception f.; (in bank) caisse f.

desolat|e 'desələt/ a. (place) désolé; (bleak: fig.) morne. **~ion** /-'leɪʃn/ n. désolation f.

despair /dɪ'speə(r)/ n. désespoir m. ● v.i. désespérer (**of**, de).

despatch /dɪ'spætʃ/ v.t. **= dispatch**.

desperate 'despərət/ a. désespéré; (criminal) prêt à tout. **be ~ for**, avoir une envie folle de. **~ly** adv. désespérément; (worried) terriblement; (ill) gravement.

desperation /despə'reɪʃn/ n. désespoir m. **in** or **out of ~**, en désespoir de cause.

despicable /dɪ'spɪkəbl/ a. méprisable, infâme.

despise /dɪ'spaɪz/ v.t. mépriser.

despite /dɪ'spaɪt/ prep. malgré.

desponden|t /dɪ'spɒndənt/ a. découragé. **~cy** n. découragement m.

despot 'despɒt/ n. despote m.

dessert /dɪ'zɜːt/ n. dessert m. **~spoon** n. cuiller à dessert f. **~spoonful** n. cuillerée à soupe f.

destination /destɪ'neɪʃn/ n. destination f.

destine 'destɪn/ v.t. destiner.

destiny 'destɪnɪ/ n. destin m.

destitute 'destɪtjuːt/ a. indigent. **~ of**, dénué de.

destr|oy /dɪ'strɔɪ/ v.t. détruire; (animal) abattre. **~uction** n. destruction f. **~uctive** a. destructeur.

destroyer /dɪ'strɔɪə(r)/ n. (warship) contre-torpilleur m.

detach /dɪ'tætʃ/ v.t. détacher. **~able** a. détachable. **~ed** a. détaché. **~ed house**, maison individuelle f.

detachment /dɪ'tætʃmənt/ n. détachement m.

detail 'diːteɪl/ n. détail m. ● v.t. exposer en détail; (troops) détacher. **go into ~**, entrer dans le détail. **~ed** a. détaillé.

detain /dɪ'teɪn/ v.t. retenir; (in prison) détenir. **~ee** /diːteɪ'niː/ n. détenu(e) m. (f.).

detect /dɪ'tekt/ v.t. découvrir; (perceive) distinguer; (tumour) dépister; (mine) détecter. **~ion** /-kʃn/ n. découverte f.; dépistage m.; détection f. **~or** n. détecteur m.

detective /dɪ'tektɪv/ n. policier m.; (*private*) détective m.

detention /dɪ'tenʃn/ n. détention f.; (*schol.*) retenue f.

deter /dɪ'tɜ:(r)/ v.t. (p.t. **deterred**) dissuader (**from**, de).

detergent /dɪ'tɜ:dʒənt/ a. & n. détergent (m.).

deteriorat|e /dɪ'tɪərɪəreɪt/ v.i. se détériorer. ~**ion** /-'reɪʃn/ n. détérioration f.

determin|e /dɪ'tɜ:mɪn/ v.t. déterminer. ~**e to do**, décider de faire. ~**ation** /-'neɪʃn/ n. détermination f. ~**ed** a. déterminé. ~**ed to do**, décidé à faire.

deterrent /dɪ'terənt, *Amer.* dɪ'tɜ:rənt/ n. force de dissuasion f.

detest /dɪ'test/ v.t. détester. ~**able** a. détestable.

detonat|e /'detəneɪt/ v.t./i. (faire) détoner. ~**ion** /-'neɪʃn/ n. détonation f. ~**or** n. détonateur m.

detour /'di:tʊə(r)/ n. détour m.

detract /dɪ'trækt/ v.i. ~ **from**, (*lessen*) diminuer.

detriment /'detrɪmənt/ n. détriment m. ~**al** /-'mentl/ a. préjudiciable (**to**, à).

devalu|e /di:'vælju:/ v.t. dévaluer. ~**ation** /-jʊ'eɪʃn/ n. dévaluation f.

devastat|e /'devəsteɪt/ v.t. dévaster; (*overwhelm: fig.*) accabler. ~**ing** a. accablant.

develop /dɪ'veləp/ v.t./i. (p.t. **developed**) (se) développer; (*contract*) contracter; (*build on, transform*) exploiter, aménager; (*change*) évoluer; (*appear*) se manifester. ~ **into**, devenir. ~**ing country**, pays en voie de développement m. ~**ment** n. développement m. (**housing**) ~, lotissement m. (**new**) ~**ment**, fait nouveau m.

deviant /'di:vɪənt/ a. anormal. ● n. (*psych.*) déviant m.

deviat|e /'di:vɪeɪt/ v.i. dévier. ~**e from**, (*norm*) s'écarter de. ~**ion** /-'eɪʃn/ n. déviation f.

device /dɪ'vaɪs/ n. appareil m.; (*scheme*) procédé m.

devil /'devl/ n. diable m. ~**ish** a. diabolique.

devious /'di:vɪəs/ a. tortueux. **he is** ~, il a l'esprit tortueux.

devise /dɪ'vaɪz/ v.t. inventer; (*plan, means*) combiner, imaginer.

devoid /dɪ'vɔɪd/ a. ~ **of**, dénué de.

devolution /di:və'lu:ʃn/ n. décentralisation f.; (*of authority, power*) délégation f. (**to**, à).

devot|e /dɪ'vəʊt/ v.t. consacrer. ~**ed** a. dévoué. ~**edly** adv. avec dévouement. ~**ion** /-ʃn/ n. dévouement m.; (*relig.*) dévotion f. ~**ions** f. pl.

devotee /devə'ti:/ n. ~ **of**, passionné(e) de m. (f.).

devour /dɪ'vaʊə(r)/ v.t. dévorer.

devout /dɪ'vaʊt/ a. fervent.

dew /dju:/ n. rosée f.

dexterity /dek'sterətɪ/ n. dextérité f.

diabet|es /daɪə'bi:ti:z/ n. diabète m. ~**ic** /-'betɪk/ a. & n. diabétique (m./f.).

diabolical /daɪə'bɒlɪkl/ a. diabolique; (*bad: fam.*) atroce.

diagnose /'daɪəgnəʊz/ v.t. diagnostiquer.

diagnosis /daɪəg'nəʊsɪs/ n. (pl. -**oses** /-si:z/) diagnostic m.

diagonal /daɪ'ægənl/ a. diagonal. ● n. diagonale f. ~**ly** adv. en diagonale.

diagram /'daɪəgræm/ n. schéma m.

dial /'daɪəl/ n. cadran m. ● v.t. (p.t. **dialled**) (*number*) faire; (*person*) appeler. ~**ling code**, (*Amer.*) ~ **code**, indicatif m. ~**ling tone**, (*Amer.*) ~ **tone**, tonalité f.

dialect /'daɪəlekt/ n. dialecte m.

dialogue /'daɪəlɒg/ n. dialogue m.

diameter /daɪ'æmɪtə(r)/ n. diamètre m.

diamond /'daɪəmənd/ n. diamant m.; (*shape*) losange m.; (*baseball*) terrain m. ~**s**, (*cards*) carreau m.

diaper /'daɪəpə(r)/ n. (*baby's nappy: Amer.*) couche f.

diaphragm /'daɪəfræm/ n. diaphragme m.

diarrhoea, (*Amer.*) **diarrhea** /daɪə'rɪə/ n. diarrhée f.

diary /'daɪərɪ/ n. (*for appointments etc.*) agenda m.; (*appointments*) emploi du temps m. (*for private thoughts*) journal intime m.

dice /daɪs/ n. invar. dé m. ● v.t. (*food*) couper en dés.

dicey /'daɪsɪ/ a. (*fam.*) risqué.

dictat|e /dɪk'teɪt/ v.t./i. dicter. ~**ion** /-ʃn/ n. dictée f.

dictates /'dɪkteɪts/ n. pl. préceptes m. pl.

dictator /dɪk'teɪtə(r)/ n. dictateur m. ~**ship** n. dictature f.

dictatorial /dɪktəˈtɔːrɪəl/ a. dictatorial.

diction /ˈdɪkʃn/ n. diction f.

dictionary /ˈdɪkʃənrɪ/ n. dictionnaire m.

did /dɪd/ see do.

diddle /ˈdɪdl/ v.t. (sl.) escroquer.

didn't /ˈdɪdnt/ = did not.

die [1] /daɪ/ v.i. (pres. p. dying) mourir. ~ **down**, diminuer. ~ **out**, disparaître. **be dying to do/for,** mourir d'envie de faire/de.

die [2] /daɪ/ n. (metal mould) matrice f., étampe f.

die-hard /ˈdaɪhɑːd/ n. réactionnaire m./f.

diesel /ˈdiːzl/ n. diesel m. ~ **engine,** moteur diesel m.

diet /ˈdaɪət/ n. (habitual food) alimentation f.; (restricted) régime m. ● v.i. suivre un régime.

diet|etic /daɪəˈtetɪk/ a. diététique. ~**ician** n. diététicien(ne) m. (f.).

differ /ˈdɪfə(r)/ v.i. différer (**from,** de); (disagree) ne pas être d'accord.

differen|t /ˈdɪfrənt/ a. différent. ~**ce** n. différence f.; (disagreement) différend m. ~**tly** adv. différemment (**from,** de).

differential /dɪfəˈrenʃl/ a. & n. différentiel (m.).

differentiate /dɪfəˈrenʃɪeɪt/ v.t. différencier. ● v.i. faire la différence (**between,** entre).

difficult /ˈdɪfɪkəlt/ a. difficile. ~**y** n. difficulté f.

diffiden|t /ˈdɪfɪdənt/ a. qui manque d'assurance. ~**ce** n. manque d'assurance m.

diffuse [1] /dɪˈfjuːs/ a. diffus.

diffus|e [2] /dɪˈfjuːz/ v.t. diffuser. ~**ion** /-ʒn/ n. diffusion f.

dig /dɪg/ v.t./i. (p.t. **dug,** pres. p. **digging**) creuser; (thrust) enfoncer. ● n. (poke) coup de coude m.; (remark) coup de patte m.; (archaeol.) fouilles f. pl. ~**s,** (lodgings: fam.) chambre meublée f. ~ **(over),** bêcher. ~ **up,** déterrer.

digest [1] /dɪˈdʒest/ v.t./i. digérer. ~**ible** a. digestible. ~**ion** /-stʃən/ n. digestion f.

digest [2] /ˈdaɪdʒest/ n. sommaire m.

digestive /dɪˈdʒestɪv/ a. digestif.

digger /ˈdɪgə(r)/ n. (techn.) pelleteuse f., excavateur m.

digit /ˈdɪdʒɪt/ n. chiffre m.

digital /ˈdɪdʒɪtl/ a. (clock) numérique, à affichage numérique; (recording) numérique.

dignif|y /ˈdɪgnɪfaɪ/ v.t. donner de la dignité à. ~**ied** a. digne.

dignitary /ˈdɪgnɪtərɪ/ n. dignitaire m.

dignity /ˈdɪgnɪtɪ/ n. dignité f.

digress /daɪˈgres/ v.i. faire une digression. ~ **from,** s'écarter de. ~**ion** /-ʃn/ n. digression f.

dike /daɪk/ n. digue f.

dilapidated /dɪˈlæpɪdeɪtɪd/ a. délabré.

dilat|e /daɪˈleɪt/ v.t./i. (se) dilater. ~**ion** /-ʃn/ n. dilatation f.

dilatory /ˈdɪlətərɪ/ a. dilatoire.

dilemma /dɪˈlemə/ n. dilemme m.

dilettante /dɪlɪˈtæntɪ/ n. dilettante m./f.

diligen|t /ˈdɪlɪdʒənt/ a. assidu. ~**ce** n. assiduité f.

dilly-dally /ˈdɪlɪdælɪ/ v.i. (fam.) lanterner.

dilute /daɪˈljuːt/ v.t. diluer.

dim /dɪm/ a. (**dimmer, dimmest**) (weak) faible; (dark) sombre; (indistinct) vague; (fam.) stupide. ● v.t./i. (p.t. **dimmed**) (light) (s')atténuer. ~**ly** adv. (shine) faiblement; (remember) vaguement. ~**mer** n. ~ **(switch),** variateur d'intensité m. ~**ness** n. faiblesse f.; (of room etc.) obscurité f.

dime /daɪm/ n. (in USA, Canada) pièce de dix cents f.

dimension /daɪˈmenʃn/ n. dimension f.

diminish /dɪˈmɪnɪʃ/ v.t./i. diminuer.

diminutive /dɪˈmɪnjʊtɪv/ a. minuscule. ● n. diminutif m.

dimple /ˈdɪmpl/ n. fossette f.

din /dɪn/ n. vacarme m.

dine /daɪn/ v.i. dîner. ~**r** /-ə(r)/ n. dîneu|r, -se m., f.; (rail.) wagonrestaurant m.; (Amer.) restaurant à service rapide m.

dinghy /ˈdɪŋgɪ/ n. canot m.; (inflatable) canot pneumatique m.

ding|y /ˈdɪndʒɪ/ a. (-**ier, -iest**) miteux, minable. ~**iness** n. aspect miteux or minable m.

dining-room /ˈdaɪnɪŋrʊm/ n. salle à manger f.

dinner /ˈdɪnə(r)/ n. (evening meal) dîner m.; (lunch) déjeuner m. ~-**jacket** n. smoking m. ~ **party,** dîner m.

dinosaur /ˈdaɪnəsɔː(r)/ n. dinosaure m.

dint /dɪnt/ n. by ~ of, à force de.

diocese /'daɪəsɪs/ n. diocèse m.

dip /dɪp/ v.t./i. (p.t. **dipped**) plonger. ● n. (slope) déclivité f.; (in sea) bain rapide m. ~ **into**, (book) feuilleter; (savings) puiser dans. ~ **one's headlights**, se mettre en code.

diphtheria /dɪf'θɪərɪə/ n. diphtérie f.

diphthong /'dɪfθɒŋ/ n. diphtongue f.

diploma /dɪ'pləʊmə/ n. diplôme m.

diplomacy /dɪ'pləʊməsɪ/ n. diplomatie f.

diplomat /'dɪpləmæt/ n. diplomate m./f. ~**ic** /-'mætɪk/ a. (pol.) diplomatique; (tactful) diplomate.

dire /daɪə(r)/ a. (-er, -est) affreux; (need, poverty) extrême.

direct /dɪ'rekt/ a. direct. ● adv. directement. ● v.t. diriger; (letter, remark) adresser; (a play) mettre en scène. ~ **s.o. to**, indiquer à qn. le chemin de; (order) signifier à qn. de. ~**ness** n. franchise f.

direction /dɪ'rekʃn/ n. direction f.; (theatre) mise en scène f. ~**s**, indications f. pl. **ask** ~**s**, demander le chemin. ~**s for use**, mode d'emploi m.

directly /dɪ'rektlɪ/ adv. directement; (at once) tout de suite. ● conj. dès que.

director /dɪ'rektə(r)/ n. direc|teur, -trice m., f.; (theatre) metteur en scène m.

directory /dɪ'rektərɪ/ n. (phone book) annuaire m.

dirt /dɜːt/ n. saleté f.; (earth) terre f. ~ **cheap**, (sl.) très bon marché invar. ~**-track** n. (sport) cendrée f.

dirty /'dɜːtɪ/ a. (-ier, -iest) sale; (word) grossier. **get** ~, se salir. ● v.t./i. (se) salir.

disability /dɪsə'bɪlətɪ/ n. handicap m.

disable /dɪs'eɪbl/ v.t. rendre infirme. ~**d** a. handicapé.

disadvantage /dɪsəd'vɑːntɪdʒ/ n. désavantage m. ~**d** a. déshérité.

disagree /dɪsə'griː/ v.i. ne pas être d'accord (with, avec). ~ **with s.o.**, (food, climate) ne pas convenir à qn. ~**ment** n. désaccord m.; (quarrel) différend m.

disagreeable /dɪsə'griːəbl/ a. désagréable.

disappear /dɪsə'pɪə(r)/ v.i. disparaître. ~**ance** n. disparition f.

disappoint /dɪsə'pɔɪnt/ v.t. décevoir. ~**ing** a. décevant. ~**ed** a. déçu. ~**ment** n. déception f.

disapprov|e /dɪsə'pruːv/ v.i. ~**e (of)**, désapprouver. ~**al** n. désapprobation f.

disarm /dɪs'ɑːm/ v.t./i. désarmer. ~**ament** n. désarmement m.

disarray /dɪsə'reɪ/ n. désordre m.

disassociate /dɪsə'səʊʃɪeɪt/ v.t. = **dissociate**.

disast|er /dɪ'zɑːstə(r)/ n. désastre m. ~**rous** a. désastreux.

disband /dɪs'bænd/ v.t./i. (se) disperser.

disbelief /dɪsbɪ'liːf/ n. incrédulité f.

disc /dɪsk/ n. disque m.; (comput.) = **disk**. ~ **brake**, frein à disque m. ~ **jockey**, disc-jockey m., animateur m.

discard /dɪ'skɑːd/ v.t. se débarrasser de; (beliefs etc.) abandonner.

discern /dɪ'sɜːn/ v.t. discerner. ~**ible** a. perceptible. ~**ing** a. perspicace.

discharge[1] /dɪs'tʃɑːdʒ/ v.t. (unload) décharger; (liquid) déverser; (duty) remplir; (dismiss) renvoyer; (prisoner) libérer. ● v.i. (of pus) s'écouler.

discharge[2] /'dɪstʃɑːdʒ/ n. (med.) écoulement m.; (dismissal) renvoi m.; (electr.) décharge m.

disciple /dɪ'saɪpl/ n. disciple m.

disciplin|e /'dɪsɪplɪn/ n. discipline f. ● v.t. discipliner; (punish) punir. ~**ary** a. disciplinaire.

disclaim /dɪs'kleɪm/ v.t. désavouer. ~**er** n. correctif m., précision f.

disclos|e /dɪs'kləʊz/ v.t. révéler. ~**ure** /-ʒə(r)/ n. révélation f.

disco /'dɪskəʊ/ n. (pl. -os) (club; fam.) discothèque f., disco m.

discol|our /dɪs'kʌlə(r)/ v.t./i. (se) décolorer. ~**oration** /-'reɪʃn/ n. décoloration f.

discomfort /dɪs'kʌmfət/ n. gêne f.

disconcert /dɪskən'sɜːt/ v.t. déconcerter.

disconnect /dɪskə'nekt/ v.t. détacher; (unplug) débrancher; (cut off) couper.

discontent /dɪskən'tent/ n. mécontentement m. ~**ed** a. mécontent.

discontinue /dɪskən'tɪnjuː/ v.t. interrompre, cesser.

discord /'dɪskɔːd/ n. discorde f.; (mus.) dissonance f. ~**ant** /-'skɔːdənt/ a. discordant.

discothèque /'dɪskətek/ n. discothèque f.

discount[1] /'dɪskaʊnt/ n. rabais m.

discount[2] /dɪs'kaʊnt/ v.t. ne pas tenir compte de.

discourage /dɪsˈkʌrɪdʒ/ v.t. décourager.

discourse /ˈdɪskɔːs/ n. discours m.

discourteous /dɪsˈkɜːtɪəs/ a. impoli, peu courtois.

discover /dɪsˈkʌvə(r)/ v.t. découvrir. **~y** n. découverte f.

discredit /dɪsˈkredɪt/ v.t. (p.t. **discredited**) discréditer. ● n. discrédit m.

discreet /dɪsˈkriːt/ a. discret. **~ly** adv. discrètement.

discrepancy /dɪsˈkrepənsɪ/ n. contradiction f., incohérence f.

discretion /dɪsˈkreʃn/ n. discrétion f.

discriminat|e /dɪsˈkrɪmɪneɪt/ v.t./i. distinguer. **~e against,** faire de la discrimination contre. **~ing** a. (person) qui a du discernement. **~ion** /-ˈneɪʃn/ n. discernement m.; (bias) discrimination f.

discus /ˈdɪskəs/ n. disque m.

discuss /dɪsˈkʌs/ v.t. (talk about) discuter de; (argue about, examine critically) discuter. **~ion** /-ʃn/ n. discussion f.

disdain /dɪsˈdeɪn/ n. dédain m. **~ful** a. dédaigneux.

disease /dɪˈziːz/ n. maladie f. **~d** a. malade.

disembark /dɪsɪmˈbɑːk/ v.t./i. débarquer.

disembodied /dɪsɪmˈbɒdɪd/ a. désincarné.

disenchant /dɪsɪnˈtʃɑːnt/ v.t. désenchanter. **~ment** n. désenchantement m.

disengage /dɪsɪnˈɡeɪdʒ/ v.t. dégager; (mil.) retirer. ● v.i. (mil.) retirer; (auto.) débrayer. **~ment** n. dégagement m.

disentangle /dɪsɪnˈtæŋɡl/ v.t. démêler.

disfavour, (Amer.) **disfavor** /dɪsˈfeɪvə(r)/ n. défaveur f.

disfigure /dɪsˈfɪɡə(r)/ v.t. défigurer.

disgrace /dɪsˈɡreɪs/ n. (shame) honte f.; (disfavour) disgrâce f. ● v.t. déshonorer. **~d** a. (in disfavour) disgracié. **~ful** a. honteux.

disgruntled /dɪsˈɡrʌntld/ a. mécontent.

disguise /dɪsˈɡaɪz/ v.t. déguiser. ● n. déguisement m. **in ~,** déguisé.

disgust /dɪsˈɡʌst/ n. dégoût m. ● v.t. dégoûter. **~ing** a. dégoûtant.

dish /dɪʃ/ n. plat m. ● v.t. **~ out,** (fam.) distribuer. **~ up,** servir. **the ~es,** (crockery) la vaisselle.

dishcloth /ˈdɪʃklɒθ/ n. lavette f.; (for drying) torchon m.

dishearten /dɪsˈhɑːtn/ v.t. décourager.

dishevelled /dɪˈʃevld/ a. échevelé.

dishonest /dɪsˈɒnɪst/ a. malhonnête. **~y** n. malhonnêteté f.

dishonour, (Amer.) **dishonor** /dɪsˈɒnə(r)/ n. déshonneur m. ● v.t. déshonorer. **~able** a. déshonorant. **~ably** adv. avec déshonneur.

dishwasher /ˈdɪʃwɒʃə(r)/ n. lave-vaisselle m. invar.

disillusion /dɪsɪˈluːʒn/ v.t. désillusionner. **~ment** n. désillusion f.

disincentive /dɪsɪnˈsentɪv/ n. **be a ~ to,** décourager.

disinclined /dɪsɪnˈklaɪnd/ a. **~ to,** peu disposé à.

disinfect /dɪsɪnˈfekt/ v.t. désinfecter. **~ant** n. désinfectant m.

disinherit /dɪsɪnˈherɪt/ v.t. déshériter.

disintegrate /dɪsˈɪntɪɡreɪt/ v.t./i. (se) désintégrer.

disinterested /dɪsˈɪntrəstɪd/ a. désintéressé.

disjointed /dɪsˈdʒɔɪntɪd/ a. (talk) décousu.

disk /dɪsk/ n. (Amer.) = **disc;** (comput.) disque m. **~ drive,** drive m., lecteur de disquettes m.

diskette /dɪˈsket/ n. disquette f.

dislike /dɪsˈlaɪk/ n. aversion f. ● v.t. ne pas aimer.

dislocat|e /ˈdɪsləkeɪt/ v.t. (limb) disloquer. **~ion** /-ˈkeɪʃn/ n. dislocation f.

dislodge /dɪsˈlɒdʒ/ v.t. (move) déplacer; (drive out) déloger.

disloyal /dɪsˈlɔɪəl/ a. déloyal. **~ty** n. déloyauté f.

dismal /ˈdɪzməl/ a. morne, triste.

dismantle /dɪsˈmæntl/ v.t. démonter, défaire.

dismay /dɪsˈmeɪ/ n. consternation f. ● v.t. consterner.

dismiss /dɪsˈmɪs/ v.t. renvoyer; (appeal) rejeter; (from mind) écarter. **~al** n. renvoi m.

dismount /dɪsˈmaʊnt/ v.i. descendre, mettre pied à terre.

disobedien|t /dɪsəˈbiːdɪənt/ a. désobéissant. **~ce** n. désobéissance f.

disobey /dɪsəˈbeɪ/ v.t. désobéir à ● v.i. désobéir.

disorder /dɪsˈɔːdə(r)/ n. désordre m.; (ailment) trouble(s) m. (pl.). ~ly a. désordonné.

disorganize /dɪsˈɔːɡənaɪz/ v.t. désorganiser.

disorientate /dɪsˈɔːrɪənteɪt/ v.t. désorienter.

disown /dɪsˈəʊn/ v.t. renier.

disparaging /dɪsˈpærɪdʒɪŋ/ a. désobligeant. ~ly adv. de façon désobligeante.

disparity /dɪˈspærətɪ/ n. disparité f., écart m.

dispassionate /dɪsˈpæʃənət/ a. impartial; (unemotional) calme.

dispatch /dɪsˈpætʃ/ v.t. (send, complete) expédier; (troops) envoyer. ● n. expédition f.; envoi m.; (report) dépêche f. ~-rider n. estafette f.

dispel /dɪsˈpel/ v.t. (p.t. dispelled) dissiper.

dispensary /dɪsˈpensərɪ/ n. pharmacie f., officine f.

dispense /dɪsˈpens/ v.t. distribuer; (medicine) préparer. ● v.i. ~ with, se passer de. ~r /-ə(r)/ n. (container) distributeur m.

dispers|e /dɪsˈpɜːs/ v.t./i. (se) disperser. ~al n. dispersion f.

dispirited /dɪsˈpɪrɪtɪd/ a. découragé, abattu.

displace /dɪsˈpleɪs/ v.t. déplacer.

display /dɪsˈpleɪ/ v.t. montrer, exposer; (feelings) manifester. ● n. exposition f.; manifestation f.; (comm.) étalage m.; (of computer) visuel m.

displeas|e /dɪsˈpliːz/ v.t. déplaire à. ~ed with, mécontent de. ~ure /-ˈpleʒə(r)/ n. mécontentement m.

disposable /dɪsˈpəʊzəbl/ a. à jeter.

dispos|e /dɪsˈpəʊz/ v.t. disposer. ● v.i. ~e of, se débarrasser de. well ~ed to, bien disposé envers. ~al n. (of waste) évacuation f. at s.o.'s ~al, à la disposition de qn.

disposition /dɪspəˈzɪʃn/ n. disposition f.; (character) naturel m.

disproportionate /dɪsprəˈpɔːʃənət/ a. disproportionné.

disprove /dɪsˈpruːv/ v.t. réfuter.

dispute /dɪsˈpjuːt/ v.t. contester. ● n. discussion f.; (pol.) conflit m. in ~, contesté.

disqualif|y /dɪsˈkwɒlɪfaɪ/ v.t. rendre inapte; (sport) disqualifier. ~y from driving, retirer le permis à. ~ication /-ɪˈkeɪʃn/ n. disqualification f.

disquiet /dɪsˈkwaɪət/ n. inquiétude f. ~ing a. inquiétant.

disregard /dɪsrɪˈɡɑːd/ v.t. ne pas tenir compte de. ● n. indifférence f. (for, à).

disrepair /dɪsrɪˈpeə(r)/ n. mauvais état m., délabrement m.

disreputable /dɪsˈrepjʊtəbl/ a. peu recommendable.

disrepute /dɪsrɪˈpjuːt/ n. discrédit m.

disrespect /dɪsrɪˈspekt/ n. manque de respect m. ~ful a. irrespectueux.

disrupt /dɪsˈrʌpt/ v.t. (disturb, break up) perturber; (plans) déranger. ~ion /-pʃn/ n. perturbation f. ~ive a. perturbateur.

dissatisf|ied /dɪsˈsætɪsfaɪd/ a. mécontent. ~action /dɪsætɪsˈfækʃn/ n. mécontentement m.

dissect /dɪˈsekt/ v.t. disséquer. ~ion /-kʃn/ n. dissection f.

disseminate /dɪˈsemɪneɪt/ v.t. disséminer.

dissent /dɪˈsent/ v.i. différer (from, de). ● n. dissentiment m.

dissertation /dɪsəˈteɪʃn/ n. (univ.) mémoire m.

disservice /dɪsˈsɜːvɪs/ n. mauvais service m.

dissident /ˈdɪsɪdənt/ a. & n. dissident(e) (m. (f.)).

dissimilar /dɪˈsɪmɪlə(r)/ a. dissemblable, différent.

dissipate /ˈdɪsɪpeɪt/ v.t./i. (se) dissiper; (efforts) gaspiller. ~d /-ɪd/ a. (person) débauché.

dissociate /dɪˈsəʊʃɪeɪt/ v.t. dissocier. ~ o.s. from, se désolidariser de.

dissolute /ˈdɪsəljuːt/ a. dissolu.

dissolution /dɪsəˈluːʃn/ n. dissolution f.

dissolve /dɪˈzɒlv/ v.t./i. (se) dissoudre.

dissuade /dɪˈsweɪd/ v.t. dissuader.

distance /ˈdɪstəns/ n. distance f. from a ~, de loin. in the ~, au loin.

distant /ˈdɪstənt/ a. éloigné, lointain; (relative) éloigné; (aloof) distant.

distaste /dɪsˈteɪst/ n. dégoût m. ~ful a. désagréable.

distemper /dɪsˈtempə(r)/ n. (paint) badigeon m.; (animal disease) maladie f. ● v.t. badigeonner.

distend /dɪsˈtend/ v.t./i. (se) distendre.

distil /dɪsˈtɪl/ v.t. (p.t. distilled) distiller. ~lation /-ˈleɪʃn/ n. distillation f.

distillery /drˈstɪlərɪ/ *n.* distillerie *f.*

distinct /drˈstɪŋkt/ *a.* distinct; (*marked*) net. **as ~ from,** par opposition à. **~ion** /-kʃn/ *n.* distinction *f.*; (*in exam*) mention très bien *f.* **~ive** *a.* distinctif. **~ly** *adv.* (*see*) distinctement; (*forbid*) expressément; (*markedly*) nettement.

distinguish /drˈstɪŋgwɪʃ/ *v.t./i.* distinguer. **~ed** *a.* distingué.

distort /drˈstɔːt/ *v.t.* déformer. **~ion** /-ʃn/ *n.* distorsion *f.*; (*of facts*) déformation *f.*

distract /drˈstrækt/ *v.t.* distraire. **~ed** *a.* (*distraught*) éperdu. **~ing** *a.* gênant. **~ion** /-kʃn/ *n.* (*lack of attention, entertainment*) distraction *f.*

distraught /drˈstrɔːt/ *a.* éperdu.

distress /drˈstres/ *n.* douleur *f.*; (*poverty, danger*) détresse *f.* ● *v.t.* peiner. **~ing** *a.* pénible.

distribut|e /drˈstrɪbjuːt/ *v.t.* distribuer. **~ion** /-ˈbjuːʃn/ *n.* distribution *f.* **~or** *n.* distributeur *m.*

district /ˈdɪstrɪkt/ *n.* région *f.*; (*of town*) quartier *m.*

distrust /dɪsˈtrʌst/ *n.* méfiance *f.* ● *v.t.* se méfier de.

disturb /drˈstɜːb/ *v.t.* déranger; (*alarm, worry*) troubler. **~ance** *n.* dérangement *m.* (**of,** de); (*noise*) tapage *m.* **~ances** *n. pl.* (*pol.*) troubles *m. pl.* **~ed** *a.* troublé; (*psychologically*) perturbé. **~ing** *a.* troublant.

disused /dɪsˈjuːzd/ *a.* désaffecté.

ditch /dɪtʃ/ *n.* fossé *m.* ● *v.t.* (*sl.*) abandonner.

dither /ˈdɪðə(r)/ *v.i.* hésiter.

ditto /ˈdɪtəʊ/ *adv.* idem.

divan /drˈvæn/ *n.* divan *m.*

div|e /daɪv/ *v.i.* plonger; (*rush*) se précipiter. ● *n.* plongeon *m.*; (*of plane*) piqué *m.*; (*place: sl.*) bouge *m.* **~er** *n.* plongeu|r, -se *m., f.* **~ing-board** *n.* plongeoir *m.* **~ing-suit** *n.* tenue de plongée *f.*

diverge /daɪˈvɜːdʒ/ *v.i.* diverger.

divergent /daɪˈvɜːdʒənt/ *a.* divergent.

diverse /daɪˈvɜːs/ *a.* divers.

diversify /daɪˈvɜːsɪfaɪ/ *v.t.* diversifier.

diversity /daɪˈvɜːsətɪ/ *n.* diversité *f.*

diver|t /daɪˈvɜːt/ *v.t.* détourner; (*traffic*) dévier. **~sion** /-ʃn/ *n.* détournement *m.*; (*distraction*) diversion *f.*; (*of traffic*) déviation *f.*

divest /daɪˈvest/ *v.t.* **~ of,** (*strip of*) priver de, déposséder de.

divide /drˈvaɪd/ *v.t./i.* (se) diviser.

dividend /ˈdɪvɪdend/ *n.* dividende *m.*

divine /drˈvaɪn/ *a.* divin.

divinity /drˈvɪnətɪ/ *n.* divinité *f.*

division /drˈvɪʒn/ *n.* division *f.*

divorce /drˈvɔːs/ *n.* divorce *m.* (**from,** d'avec). ● *v.t./i.* divorcer (d'avec). **~d** *a.* divorcé.

divorcee /dɪvɔːˈsiː/, *Amer.* dɪvɔːˈseɪ/ *n.* divorcé(e) *m.* (*f.*).

divulge /daɪˈvʌldʒ/ *v.t.* divulguer.

DIY *abbr. see* **do-it-yourself.**

dizz|y /ˈdɪzɪ/ *a.* (**-ier, -iest**) vertigineux. **be** *or* **feel ~y,** avoir le vertige. **~iness** *n.* vertige *m.*

do /duː/ *v.t./i.* (*3 sing. present tense* **does**/ *p.t.* **did;** *p.p.* **done**) faire; (*progress, be suitable*) aller; (*be enough*) suffire; (*swindle: sl.*) avoir. **do well/badly,** se débrouiller bien/mal. **do the house,** peindre *ou* nettoyer *etc.* la maison. **well done!,** bravo! **well done,** (*culin.*) bien cuit. **done for,** (*fam.*) fichu. ● *v. aux.* **do you see?,** voyez-vous? **do you live here?,** est-ce que vous habitez ici? **I do live here,** si, j'habite ici. **I do not smoke,** je ne fume pas. **don't you?, doesn't he?,** *etc.*, n'est-ce pas? ● *n.* (*pl.* **dos** *or* **do's**) soirée *f.*, fête *f.* **dos and don'ts,** choses à faire et à ne pas faire. **do away with,** supprimer. **do in,** (*sl.*) tuer. **do-it-yourself** *n.* bricolage *m.*; *a.* (*shop, book*) de bricolage. **do out,** (*clean*) nettoyer. **do up,** (*fasten*) fermer; (*house*) refaire. **it's to ~ with the house,** c'est à propos de la maison. **it's nothing to do with me,** ça n'a rien à voir avec moi. **I could do with a holiday,** j'aurais bien besoin de vacances. **~ without,** se passer de.

docile /ˈdəʊsaɪl/ *a.* docile.

dock[1] /dɒk/ *n.* dock *m.* ● *v.t./i.* (se) mettre à quai. **~er** *n.* docker *m.*

dock[2] /dɒk/ *n.* (*jurid.*) banc des accusés *m.*

dock[3] /dɒk/ *v.t.* (*money*) retrancher.

dockyard /ˈdɒkjɑːd/ *n.* chantier naval *m.*

doctor /ˈdɒktə(r)/ *n.* médecin *m.*, docteur *m.*; (*univ.*) docteur *m.* ● *v.t.* (*cat*) châtrer; (*fig.*) altérer.

doctorate /ˈdɒktərət/ *n.* doctorat *m.*

doctrine /ˈdɒktrɪn/ *n.* doctrine *f.*

document /ˈdɒkjʊmənt/ *n.* document *m.* **~ary** /-ˈmentrɪ/ *a. & n.* documentaire (m.). **~ation** /-'eɪʃn/ n. documentation f.

doddering /'dɒdərɪŋ/ a. gâteux.

dodge /dɒdʒ/ v.t. esquiver. ● v.i. faire un saut de côté. ● n. (fam.) truc m.

dodgems /'dɒdʒəmz/ n. pl. autos tamponneuses f. pl.

dodgy /'dɒdʒɪ/ a. (-ier, -iest) (fam.: difficult) épineux, délicat; (dangerous) douteux.

doe /dəʊ/ n. (deer) biche f.

does /dʌz/ see do.

doesn't /'dʌznt/ = does not.

dog /dɒg/ n. chien m. ● v.t. (p.t. dogged) poursuivre. **~-collar** n. (fam.) (faux) col d'ecclésiastique m. **~-eared** a. écorné.

dogged /'dɒgɪd/ a. obstiné.

dogma /'dɒgmə/ n. dogme m. **~tic** /-'mætɪk/ a. dogmatique.

dogsbody /'dɒgzbɒdɪ/ n. factotum m., bonne à tout faire f.

doily /'dɔɪlɪ/ n. napperon m.

doings /'du:ɪŋz/ n. pl. (fam.) activités f. pl., occupations f. pl.

doldrums /'dɒldrəmz/ n. pl. be in the **~**, (person) avoir le cafard.

dole /dəʊl/ v.t. **~ out**, distribuer. ● n. (fam.) indemnité de chômage f. on the **~**, (fam.) au chômage.

doleful /'dəʊlfl/ a. triste, morne.

doll /dɒl/ n. poupée f. ● v.t. **~ up**, (fam.) bichonner.

dollar /'dɒlə(r)/ n. dollar m.

dollop /'dɒləp/ n. (of food etc.: fam.) gros morceau m.

dolphin /'dɒlfɪn/ n. dauphin m.

domain /də'meɪn/ n. domaine m.

dome /dəʊm/ n. dôme m.

domestic /də'mestɪk/ a. familial; (trade, flights, etc.) intérieur; (animal) domestique. **~ science**, arts ménagers m. pl. **~ated** a. (animal) domestique.

domesticity /dɒme'stɪsətɪ/ n. vie de famille f.

dominant /'dɒmɪnənt/ a. dominant.

dominat|e /'dɒmɪneɪt/ v.t./i. dominer. **~ion** /-'neɪʃn/ n. domination f.

domineering /dɒmɪ'nɪərɪŋ/ a. dominateur, autoritaire.

dominion /də'mɪnjən/ n. (British pol.) dominion m.

domino /'dɒmɪnəʊ/ n. (pl. -oes) domino m. **~es**, (game) dominos m. pl.

don[1] /dɒn/ v.t. (p.t. donned) revêtir, endosser.

don[2] /dɒn/ n. professeur d'université m.

donat|e /dəʊ'neɪt/ v.t. faire don de. **~ion** /-ʃn/ n. don m.

done /dʌn/ see do.

donkey /'dɒŋkɪ/ n. âne m. the **~-work** le sale boulot.

donor /'dəʊnə(r)/ n. dona|teur, -trice m., f.; (of blood) donneu|r, -se m., f.

don't /dəʊnt/ = do not.

doodle /'du:dl/ v.i. griffonner.

doom /du:m/ n. (ruin) ruine f.; (fate) destin m. ● v.t. be **~ed** to, être destiné or condamné à. **~ed (to failure),** voué à l'échec.

door /dɔ:(r)/ n. porte f.; (of vehicle) portière f., porte f.

doorbell /'dɔ:bel/ n. sonnette f.

doorman /'dɔ:mæn/ n. (pl. -men) portier m.

doormat /'dɔ:mæt/ n. paillasson m.

doorstep /'dɔ:step/ n. pas de (la) porte m., seuil m.

doorway /'dɔ:weɪ/ n. porte f.

dope /dəʊp/ n. (fam.) drogue f.; (idiot: sl.) imbécile m./f. ● v.t. doper. **~y** a. (foolish: sl.) imbécile.

dormant /'dɔ:mənt/ a. en sommeil.

dormitory /'dɔ:mɪtrɪ, Amer. 'dɔ:mɪtɔ:rɪ/ n. dortoir m.; (univ., Amer.) résidence f.

dormouse /'dɔ:maʊs/ n. (pl. -mice) loir m.

dos|e /dəʊs/ n. dose f. **~age** n. dose f.; (on label) posologie f.

doss /dɒs/ v.i. (sl.) roupiller. **~-house** n. asile de nuit m.

dossier /'dɒsɪə(r)/ n. dossier m.

dot /dɒt/ n. point m. on the **~**, (fam.) à l'heure pile. **~-matrix** a. (printer) matriciel.

dote /dəʊt/ v.i. **~ on**, être gaga de.

dotted /'dɒtɪd/ a. (fabric) à pois. **~ line**, ligne en pointillés f. **~ with**, parsemé de.

dotty /'dɒtɪ/ a. (-ier, -iest) (fam.) cinglé, dingue.

double /'dʌbl/ a. double; (room, bed) pour deux personnes. ● adv. deux fois. ● n. double m.; (stuntman) doublure f. **~s**, (tennis) double m. ● v.t./i. doubler; (fold) plier en deux. at or on the **~**, au pas de course. **~ the size**, deux fois plus grand: pay **~**, payer le double. **~-bass** n. (mus.) contrebasse f. **~-breasted** a. croisé. **~-check** v.t. revérifier. **~ chin**, double menton m. **~-cross** v.t. tromper. **~-dealing** n. double jeu *m.* **~-decker** *n.* autobus à impériale *m.* **~ Dutch**, de l'hébreu *m.*

doubly /'dʌblɪ/ *adv.* doublement.

doubt /daʊt/ *n.* doute *m.* ● *v.t.* douter de. **~ if** *or* **that**, douter que. **~ful** *a.* incertain, douteux; (*person*) qui a des doutes. **~less** *adv.* sans doute.

dough /dəʊ/ *n.* pâte *f.*; (*money: sl.*) fric *m.*

doughnut /'dəʊnʌt/ *n.* beignet *m.*

douse /daʊs/ *v.t.* arroser; (*light, fire*) éteindre.

dove /dʌv/ *n.* colombe *f.*

Dover /'dəʊvə(r)/ *n.* Douvres *m./f.*

dovetail /'dʌvteɪl/ *v.t./i.* (s')ajuster.

dowdy /'daʊdɪ/ *a.* (**-ier**, **-iest**) (*clothes*) sans chic, monotone.

down [1] /daʊn/ *n.* (*fluff*) duvet *m.*

down [2] /daʊn/ *adv.* en bas; (*of sun*) couché; (*lower*) plus bas. ● *prep.* en bas de; (*along*) le long de. ● *v.t.* (*knock down, shoot down*) abattre; (*drink*) vider. **come** *or* **go ~**, descendre. **go ~ to the post office**, aller à la poste. **~-and-out** *a.* clochard(e) *m.* (*f.*). **~-hearted** *a.* découragé. **~-market** *a.* bas de gamme. **~ payment**, acompte *m.* **~-to-earth** *a.* terre-à-terre *invar.* **~ under**, aux antipodes. **~ with**, à bas.

downcast /'daʊnkɑːst/ *a.* démoralisé.

downfall /'daʊnfɔːl/ *n.* chute *f.*

downgrade /daʊn'greɪd/ *v.t.* déclasser.

downhill /daʊn'hɪl/ *adv.* **go ~**, descendre; (*pej.*) baisser.

downpour /'daʊnpɔː(r)/ *n.* grosse averse *f.*

downright /'daʊnraɪt/ *a.* (*utter*) véritable; (*honest*) franc. ● *adv.* carrément.

downs /daʊnz/ *n. pl.* région de collines *f.*

downstairs /daʊn'steəz/ *adv.* en bas. ● *a.* d'en bas.

downstream /'daʊnstriːm/ *adv.* en aval.

downtown /'daʊntaʊn/ *a.* (*Amer.*) du centre de la ville. **~ Boston**/*etc.*, le centre de Boston/*etc.*

downtrodden /'daʊntrɒdn/ *a.* opprimé.

downward /'daʊnwəd/ *a. & adv.*, **~s** *adv.* vers le bas.

dowry /'daʊərɪ/ *n.* dot *f.*

doze /dəʊz/ *v.i.* sommeiller. **~ off**, s'assoupir. ● *n.* somme *m.*

dozen /'dʌzn/ *n.* douzaine *f.* **a ~ eggs**, une douzaine d'œufs. **~s of**, (*fam.*) des dizaines de.

Dr *abbr.* (*Doctor*) Docteur.

drab /dræb/ *a.* terne.

draft [1] /drɑːft/ *n.* (*outline*) brouillon *m.*; (*comm.*) traite *f.* ● *v.t.* faire le brouillon de; (*draw up*) rédiger. **the ~**, (*mil., Amer.*) la conscription. **a ~ treaty**, un projet de traité.

draft [2] /drɑːft/ *n.* (*Amer.*) = **draught**.

drag /dræg/ *v.t./i.* (*p.t.* **dragged**) traîner; (*river*) draguer; (*pull away*) arracher. ● *n.* (*task: fam.*) corvée *f.*; (*person: fam.*) raseu|r, -se *m., f.* **in ~**, en travesti. **~ on**, s'éterniser.

dragon /'drægən/ *n.* dragon *m.*

dragon-fly /'drægənflaɪ/ *n.* libellule *f.*

drain /dreɪn/ *v.t.* (*land*) drainer; (*vegetables*) égoutter; (*tank, glass*) vider; (*use up*) épuiser. **~ (off)**, (*liquid*) faire écouler. ● *v.i.* **~ (off)**, (*liquid*) s'écouler. **~** *n.* (*sewer*) égout *m.* **~(-pipe)**, tuyau d'écoulement *m.* **be a ~ on**, pomper. **~ing-board** *n.* égouttoir *m.*

drama /'drɑːmə/ *n.* art dramatique *m.*, théâtre *m.*; (*play, event*) drame *m.* **~tic** /drə'mætɪk/ *a.* (*situation*) dramatique; (*increase*) spectaculaire. **~tist** /'dræmətɪst/ *n.* dramaturge *m.* **~tize** /'dræmətaɪz/ *v.t.* adapter pour la scène; (*fig.*) dramatiser.

drank /dræŋk/ *see* **drink**.

drape /dreɪp/ *v.t.* draper. **~s** *n. pl.* (*Amer.*) rideaux *m. pl.*

drastic /'dræstɪk/ *a.* sévère.

draught /drɑːft/ *n.* courant d'air *m.* **~s**, (*game*) dames *f. pl.* **~ beer**, bière (à la) pression *f.* **~y** *a.* plein de courants d'air.

draughtsman /'drɑːftsmən/ *n.* (*pl.* **-men**) dessina|teur, -trice industriel(le) *m., f.*

draw /drɔː/ *v.t.* (*p.t.* **drew**, *p.p.* **drawn**) (*pull*) tirer; (*attract*) attirer; (*pass*) passer; (*picture*) dessiner; (*line*) tracer. ● *v.i.* dessiner; (*sport*) faire match nul; (*come, move*) venir. ● *n.* (*sport*) match nul *m.*; (*in lottery*) tirage au sort *m.* **~ back**, (*recoil*) reculer. **~ in**, (*days*) diminuer. **~ near**, (s')approcher (**to**, de). **~ out**, (*money*) retirer. **~ up** *v.i.* (*stop*) s'arrêter;

v.t. (*document*) dresser; (*chair*) approcher.

drawback /'drɔːbæk/ *n.* inconvénient *m.*

drawbridge /'drɔːbrɪdʒ/ *n.* pont-levis *m.*

drawer /drɔː(r)/ *n.* tiroir *m.*

drawers /drɔːz/ *n. pl.* culotte *f.*

drawing /'drɔːɪŋ/ *n.* dessin *m.* **~-board** *n.* planche à dessin *f.* **~-pin** *n.* punaise *f.* **~-room** *n.* salon *m.*

drawl /drɔːl/ *n.* voix traînante *f.*

drawn /drɔːn/ *see* draw. ● *a.* (*features*) tiré; (*match*) nul.

dread /dred/ *n.* terreur *f.*, crainte *f.* ● *v.t.* redouter.

dreadful /'dredfl/ *a.* épouvantable, affreux. **~ly** *adv.* terriblement.

dream /driːm/ *n.* rêve *m.* ● *v.t./i.* (*p.t.* **dreamed** *or* **dreamt**) rêver. ● *a.* (*ideal*) de ses rêves. **~ up**, imaginer. **~er** *n.* rêveu|r, -se *m., f.* **~y** *a.* rêveur.

drear|y /'drɪərɪ/ *a.* (**-ier, -iest**) triste; (*boring*) monotone. **~iness** *n.* tristesse *f.*; monotonie *f.*

dredge /dredʒ/ *n.* drague *f.* ● *v.t./i.* draguer. **~r** /-ə(r)/ *n.* dragueur *m.*

dregs /dregz/ *n. pl.* lie *f.*

drench /drentʃ/ *v.t.* tremper.

dress /dres/ *n.* robe *f.*; (*clothing*) tenue *f.* ● *v.t./i.* (s')habiller; (*food*) assaisonner; (*wound*) panser. **~ circle**, premier balcon *m.* **~ rehearsal**, répétition générale *f.* **~ up as**, se déguiser en. **get ~ed**, s'habiller.

dresser /'dresə(r)/ *n.* buffet *m.*; (*actor's*) habilleu|r, -se *m., f.*

dressing /'dresɪŋ/ *n.* (*sauce*) assaisonnement *m.*; (*bandage*) pansement *m.* **~-gown** *n.* robe de chambre *f.* **~-room** *n.* (*sport*) vestiaire *m.*; (*theatre*) loge *f.* **~-table** *n.* coiffeuse *f.*

dressmak|er /'dresmeɪkə(r)/ *n.* couturière *f.* **~ing** *n.* couture *f.*

dressy /'dresɪ/ *a.* (**-ier, -iest**) chic *invar.*

drew /druː/ *see* draw.

dribble /'drɪbl/ *v.i.* couler goutte à goutte; (*person*) baver; (*football*) dribbler.

dribs and drabs /drɪbzn'dræbz/ *n. pl.* petites quantités *f. pl.*

dried /draɪd/ *a.* (*fruit etc.*) sec.

drier /'draɪə(r)/ *n.* séchoir *m.*

drift /drɪft/ *v.i.* aller à la dérive; (*pile up*) s'amonceler. ● *n.* dérive *f.*; amoncellement *m.*; (*of events*) tour-

nure *f.*; (*meaning*) sens *m.* **~ towards**, glisser vers. (*snow*) **~**, congère *f.* **~er** *n.* personne sans but dans la vie *f.*

driftwood /'drɪftwʊd/ *n.* bois flotté *m.*

drill /drɪl/ *n.* (*tool*) perceuse *f.*; (*for teeth*) roulette *f.*; (*training*) exercice *m.*; (*procedure: fam.*) marche à suivre *f.* **(pneumatic) ~**, marteau piqueur *m.* ● *v.t.* percer; (*train*) entraîner. ● *v.i.* être à l'exercice.

drily /'draɪlɪ/ *adv.* sèchement.

drink /drɪŋk/ *v.t./i.* (*p.t.* **drank**, *p.p.* **drunk**) boire. ● *n.* (*liquid*) boisson *f.*; (*glass of alcohol*) verre *m.* **a ~ of water**, un verre d'eau. **~able** *a.* (*not unhealthy*) potable; (*palatable*) buvable. **~er** *n.* buveu|r, -se *m., f.* **~ing water** *n.* eau potable *f.*

drip /drɪp/ *v.i.* (*p.t.* **dripped**) (é)goutter; (*washing*) s'égoutter. ● *n.* goutte *f.*; (*person: sl.*) lavette *f.* **~-dry** *v.t.* laisser égoutter; *a.* sans repassage.

dripping /'drɪpɪŋ/ *n.* (*Amer.* **~s**) graisse de rôti *f.*

drive /draɪv/ *v.t.* (*p.t.* **drove**, *p.p.* **driven**) chasser, pousser; (*vehicle*) conduire; (*machine*) actionner. ● *v.i.* conduire. ● *n.* promenade en voiture *f.*; (*private road*) allée *f.*; (*fig.*) énergie *f.*; (*psych.*) instinct *m.*; (*pol.*) campagne *f.*; (*auto.*) traction *f.*; (*golf, comput.*) drive *m.* **it's a two-hour ~**, c'est deux heures en voiture. **~ at**, en venir à. **~ away**, (*of car*) partir. **~ in**, (*force in*) enfoncer. **~ mad**, rendre fou. **left-hand ~**, conduite à gauche *f.*

drivel /'drɪvl/ *n.* radotage *m.*

driver /'draɪvə(r)/ *n.* conduc|teur, -trice *m.,f.*, chauffeur *m.* **~'s license** (*Amer.*), permis de conduire *m.*

driving /'draɪvɪŋ/ *n.* conduite *f.* **~ licence**, permis de conduire *m.* **~ rain**, pluie battante *f.* **~ school**, auto-école *f.* **take one's ~ test**, passer son permis.

drizzle /'drɪzl/ *n.* bruine *f.* ● *v.i.* bruiner.

dromedary /'drɒmədərɪ/, (*Amer.*) /'drɒmɪderɪ/ *n.* dromadaire *m.*

drone /drəʊn/ *n.* (*noise*) bourdonnement *m.*; (*bee*) faux bourdon *m.* ● *v.i.* bourdonner; (*fig.*) parler d'une voix monotone.

drool /druːl/ *v.i.* baver (**over**, sur).

droop /druːp/ *v.i.* pencher, tomber.

drop /drɒp/ n. goutte f.; (*fall, lowering*) chute f. ● v.t./i. (p.t. **dropped**) (*laisser*) tomber; (*decrease, lower*) baisser. ~ **(off)**, (*person from car*) déposer. ~ **a line**, écrire un mot (**to**, à). ~ **in**, passer (**on**, chez). ~ **off**, (*doze*) s'assoupir. ~ **out**, se retirer (**of**, de); (*of student*) abandonner. ~**out** n. marginal(e) m. (f.), raté(e) m. (f.).

droppings /'drɒpɪŋz/ n. pl. crottes f. pl.

dross /drɒs/ n. déchets m. pl.

drought /draʊt/ n. sécheresse f.

drove /drəʊv/ see **drive**.

droves /drəʊvz/ n. pl. foule(s) f. (pl.).

drown /draʊn/ v.t./i. (se) noyer.

drowsy /'draʊzɪ/ a. somnolent. **be or feel** ~, avoir envie de dormir.

drudge /drʌdʒ/ n. esclave du travail m. ~**ry** /-ərɪ/ n. travail pénible et ingrat m.

drug /drʌg/ n. drogue f.; (*med.*) médicament m. ● v.t. (p.t. **drugged**) droguer. ~ **addict**, drogué(e) m. (f.). ~**gist** n. pharmacien (-ne) m. (f.).

drugstore /'drʌgstɔː(r)/ n. (*Amer.*) drugstore m.

drum /drʌm/ n. tambour m.; (*for oil*) bidon m. ~**s**, batterie f. ● v.i. (p.t. **drummed**) tambouriner. ● v.t. ~ **into s.o.**, répéter sans cesse à qn. ~ **up**, (*support*) susciter; (*business*) créer. ~**mer** n. tambour m.; (*in pop group*) batteur m.

drumstick /'drʌmstɪk/ n. baguette de tambour f.; (*of chicken*) pilon m.

drunk /drʌŋk/ see **drink**. ● a. ivre. **get** ~, s'enivrer. ● n. ~**ard** n. ivrogne(sse) m. (f.). ~**en** a. ivre; (*habitually*) ivrogne. ~**enness** n. ivresse f.

dry /draɪ/ a. (**drier, driest**) sec; (*day*) sans pluie. ● v.t./i. (faire) sécher. **be or feel** ~, avoir soif. ~**-clean** v.t. nettoyer à sec. ~-**cleaner** n. teinturier m. ~ **run**, galop d'essai m. ~ **up**, (*dry dishes*) essuyer la vaisselle; (*of supplies*) (se) tarir; (*be silent: fam.*) se taire. ~**ness** n. sécheresse f.

dual /'djuːəl/ a. double. ~ **carriageway**, route à quatre voies f. ~-**purpose** a. qui fait double emploi.

dub /dʌb/ v.t. (p.t. **dubbed**) (*film*) doubler; (*nickname*) surnommer.

dubious /'djuːbɪəs/ a. (*pej.*) douteux. **be** ~ **about sth.**, (*person*) avoir des doutes sur qch.

duchess /'dʌtʃɪs/ n. duchesse f.

duck /dʌk/ n. canard m. ● v.i. se baisser subitement. ● v.t. (*head*) baisser; (*person*) plonger dans l'eau. ~**ling** n. caneton m.

duct /dʌkt/ n. conduit m.

dud /dʌd/ a. (*tool etc.: sl.*) mal fichu; (*coin: sl.*) faux; (*cheque: sl.*) sans provision. ● n. **be a** ~, (*not work: sl.*) ne pas marcher.

dude /duːd/ n. (*Amer.*) dandy m.

due /djuː/ a. (*owing*) dû; (*expected*) attendu; (*proper*) qui convient. ● adv. ~ **east**/*etc.*, droit vers l'est/ *etc.* ● n. dû m. ~**s**, droits m. pl.; (*of club*) cotisation f. ~ **to**, à cause de; (*caused by*) dû à. **she's** ~ **to leave now**, c'est prévu qu'elle parte maintenant. **in** ~ **course**, (*eventually*) avec le temps; (*at the right time*) en temps et lieu.

duel /'djuːəl/ n. duel m.

duet /djuː'et/ n. duo m.

duffle /'dʌfl/ a. ~ **bag**, sac de marin m. ~ **coat**, duffel-coat m.

dug /dʌg/ see **dig**.

duke /djuːk/ n. duc m.

dull /dʌl/ a. (**-er, -est**) ennuyeux; (*colour*) terne; (*weather*) morne; (*sound*) sourd; (*stupid*) bête; (*blunt*) émoussé. ● v.t. (*pain*) amortir; (*mind*) engourdir.

duly /'djuːlɪ/ adv. comme il convient; (*in due time*) en temps voulu.

dumb /dʌm/ a. (**-er, -est**) muet; (*stupid: fam.*) bête.

dumbfound /dʌm'faʊnd/ v.t. sidérer, ahurir.

dummy /'dʌmɪ/ n. (*comm.*) article factice m.; (*of tailor*) mannequin m.; (*of baby*) sucette f. ● a. factice. ~ **run**, galop d'essai m.

dump /dʌmp/ v.t. déposer; (*abandon: fam.*) se débarrasser de; (*comm.*) dumper. ● n. tas d'ordures m.; (*refuse tip*) décharge f.; (*mil.*) dépôt m.; (*dull place: fam.*) trou m. **be in the** ~**s**, (*fam.*) avoir le cafard.

dumpling /'dʌmplɪŋ/ n. boulette de pâte f.

dumpy /'dʌmpɪ/ a. (**-ier, -iest**) boulot, rondelet.

dunce /dʌns/ n. cancre m., âne m.

dune /djuːn/ n. dune f.

dung /dʌŋ/ n. (*excrement*) bouse f., crotte f.; (*manure*) fumier m.

dungarees /dʌŋgə'riːz/ n. pl. (*overalls*) salopette f.; (*jeans: Amer.*) jean m.

dungeon /'dʌndʒən/ n. cachot m.

dunk /dʌŋk/ v.t. tremper.

dupe /dju:p/ v.t. duper. ● n. dupe f.

duplex /'dju:pleks/ n. duplex m.

duplicate[1] /'dju:plɪkət/ n. double m.
● a. identique.

duplicate[2] /'dju:plɪkeɪt/ v.t. faire un double de; (*on machine*) polycopier.
~**or** n. duplicateur m.

duplicity /dju:'plɪsətɪ/ n. duplicité f.

durable /'djʊərəbl/ a. (*tough*) résistant; (*enduring*) durable.

duration /djʊ'reɪʃn/ n. durée f.

duress /djʊ'res/ n. contrainte f.

during /'djʊərɪŋ/ prep. pendant.

dusk /dʌsk/ n. crépuscule m.

dusky /'dʌskɪ/ a. (-**ier**, -**iest**) foncé.

dust /dʌst/ n. poussière f. ● v.t.
épousseter; (*sprinkle*) saupoudrer
(**with**, de). ~-**jacket** n. jaquette f.

dustbin /'dʌstbɪn/ n. poubelle f.

duster /'dʌstə(r)/ n. chiffon m.

dustman /'dʌstmən/ n. (pl. -**men**)
éboueur m.

dustpan /'dʌstpæn/ n. pelle à poussière f.

dusty /'dʌstɪ/ a. (-**ier**, -**iest**) poussiéreux.

Dutch /dʌtʃ/ a. hollandais. ● n.
(*lang.*) hollandais m. **go** ~, partager
les frais. ~**man** n. Hollandais m.
~**woman** n. Hollandaise f.

dutiful /'dju:tɪfl/ a. obéissant.

dut|**y** /'dju:tɪ/ n. devoir m.; (*tax*) droit
m. ~**ies**, (*of official etc.*) fonctions f.
pl. ~**y-free** a. hors-taxe. **on** ~**y**, de
service.

duvet /'du:veɪ/ n. couette f.

dwarf /dwɔ:f/ n. (pl. -**fs**) nain(e) m.
(f.). ● v.t. rapetisser.

dwell /dwel/ v.i. (p.t. **dwelt**)
demeurer. ~ **on**, s'étendre sur.
~**er** n. habitant(e) m. (f.). ~**ing** n.
habitation f.

dwindle /'dwɪndl/ v.i. diminuer.

dye /daɪ/ v.t. (pres. p. **dyeing**)
teindre. ● n. teinture f.

dying /'daɪɪŋ/ a. mourant; (*art*) qui
se perd.

dynamic /daɪ'næmɪk/ a. dynamique.

dynamism /'daɪnəmɪzəm/ n. dynamisme m.

dynamite /'daɪnəmaɪt/ n. dynamite
f. ● v.t. dynamiter.

dynamo /'daɪnəməʊ/ n. (pl. -**os**)
dynamo f.

dynasty /'dɪnəstɪ, Amer. 'daɪnəstɪ/ n.
dynastie f.

dysentery /'dɪsəntrɪ/ n. dysenterie f.

dyslexi|**a** /dɪs'leksɪə/ n. dyslexie f. ~**c**
a. & n. dyslexique (m./f.).

E

each /i:tʃ/ a. chaque. ● pron.
chacun(e). ~ **one**, chacun(e). ~
other, l'un(e) l'autre, les un(e)s les
autres. **know** ~ **other**, se connaître.
love ~ **other**, s'aimer. **a pound** ~,
(*get*) une livre chacun; (*cost*) une
livre chaque.

eager /'i:gə(r)/ a. impatient (**to**, de);
(*supporter, desire*) ardent. **be** ~ **to**,
(*want*) avoir envie de. ~ **for**, avide
de. ~**ly** adv. avec impatience or
ardeur. ~**ness** n. impatience f.,
désir m., ardeur f.

eagle /'i:gl/ n. aigle m.

ear[1] /ɪə(r)/ n. oreille f. ~-**drum** n.
tympan m. ~-**ring** n. boucle d'oreille
f.

ear[2] /ɪə(r)/ n. (*of corn*) épi m.

earache /'ɪəreɪk/ n. mal à l'oreille m.,
mal d'oreille m.

earl /ɜ:l/ n. comte m.

earlier /'ɜ:lɪə(r)/ a. (*in series*) précédent; (*in history*) plus ancien, antérieur; (*in future*) plus avancé.
● adv. précédemment; antérieurement; avant.

early /'ɜ:lɪ/ a. (-**ier**, -**iest**) adv. tôt, de
bonne heure; (*ahead of time*) en
avance. ● a. premier; (*hour*) matinal; (*fruit*) précoce; (*retirement*)
anticipé. **have an** ~ **dinner**, dîner
tôt. **in** ~ **summer**, au début de l'été.

earmark /'ɪəmɑ:k/ v.t. destiner, réserver (**for**, à).

earn /ɜ:n/ v.t. gagner; (*interest:
comm.*) rapporter. ~ **s.o. sth.**,
(*bring*) valoir qch. à qn.

earnest /'ɜ:nɪst/ a. sérieux. **in** ~,
sérieusement.

earnings /'ɜ:nɪŋz/ n. pl. salaire m.;
(*profits*) bénéfices m. pl.

earphone /'ɪəfəʊn/ n. écouteur m.

earshot /'ɪəʃɒt/ n. **within** ~, à portée
de voix.

earth /ɜ:θ/ n. terre f. ● v.t. (*electr.*)
mettre à la terre. **why/how/where
on** ~ . . . ?, pourquoi/comment/où
diable . . . ? ~**ly** a. terrestre.

earthenware /'ɜ:θnweə(r)/ n. faïence
f.

earthquake /'ɜːθkweɪk/ *n.* tremblement de terre *m.*

earthy /'ɜːθɪ/ *a.* (*of earth*) terreux; (*coarse*) grossier.

earwig /'ɪəwɪg/ *n.* perce-oreille *m.*

ease /iːz/ *n.* aisance *f.*, facilité *f.*; (*comfort*) bien-être *m.* ● *v.t./i.* (se) calmer; (*relax*) (se) détendre; (*slow down*) ralentir; (*slide*) glisser. **at ~,** à l'aise; (*mil.*) au repos. **with ~,** aisément.

easel /'iːzl/ *n.* chevalet *m.*

east /iːst/ *n.* est *m.* ● *a.* d'est. ● *adv.* vers l'est. **the E~,** (*Orient*) l'Orient *m.* **~erly** *a.* d'est. **~ern** *a.* de l'est, oriental. **~ward** *a.* à l'est. **~wards** *adv.* vers l'est.

Easter /'iːstə(r)/ *n.* Pâques *f. pl.* (*or m. sing.*). **~ egg,** œuf de Pâques *m.*

easy /'iːzɪ/ *a.* (**-ier, -iest**) facile; (*relaxed*) aisé. **~ chair,** fauteuil *m.* **go ~ with,** (*fam.*) y aller doucement avec. **take it ~,** ne pas se fatiguer. **easily** *adv.* facilement.

easygoing /iːzɪ'gəʊɪŋ/ *a.* (*with people*) accommodant; (*relaxed*) décontracté.

eat /iːt/ *v.t./i.* (*p.t.* **ate,** *p.p.* **eaten**) manger. **~ into,** ronger. **~able** *a.* mangeable. **~er** *n.* mangeur, -se *m., f.*

eau-de-Cologne /əʊdəkə'ləʊn/ *n.* eau de Cologne *f.*

eaves /iːvz/ *n. pl.* avant-toit *m.*

eavesdrop /'iːvzdrɒp/ *v.i.* (*p.t.* **-dropped**). **~ (on),** écouter en cachette.

ebb /eb/ *n.* reflux *m.* ● *v.i.* refluer; (*fig.*) décliner.

ebony /'ebənɪ/ *n.* ébène *f.*

ebullient /ɪ'bʌlɪənt/ *a.* exubérant.

EC *abbr.* (*European Community*) CE.

eccentric /ɪk'sentrɪk/ *a. & n.* excentrique (*m./f.*). **~ity** /eksən'trɪsətɪ/ *n.* excentricité *f.*

ecclesiastical /ɪkliːzɪ'æstɪkl/ *a.* ecclésiastique.

echo /'ekəʊ/ *n.* (*pl.* **-oes**) écho *m.* ● *v.t./i.* (*p.t.* **echoed,** *pres. p.* **echoing**) (se) répercuter; (*fig.*) répéter.

eclipse /ɪ'klɪps/ *n.* éclipse *f.* ● *v.t.* éclipser.

ecolog|y /iː'kɒlədʒɪ/ *n.* écologie *f.* **~ical** /iːkə'lɒdʒɪkl/ *a.* écologique.

economic /iːkə'nɒmɪk/ *a.* économique; (*profitable*) rentable. **~al** *a.* économique; (*person*) économe. **~s** *n.* économie politique *f.*

economist /ɪ'kɒnəmɪst/ *n.* économiste *m./f.*

economy /ɪ'kɒnəmɪ/ *n.* économie *f.* **~ize** *v.i.* **~ (on),** économiser.

ecosystem /'iːkəʊsɪstəm/ *n.* écosystème *m.*

ecstasy /'ekstəsɪ/ *n.* extase *f.*

ECU /'eɪkjuː/ *n.* ÉCU *m.*

eczema /'eksɪmə/ *n.* eczéma *m.*

eddy /'edɪ/ *n.* tourbillon *m.*

edge /edʒ/ *n.* bord *m.*; (*of town*) abords *m. pl.*; (*of knife*) tranchant *m.* ● *v.t.* border. ● *v.i.* (*move*) se glisser. **have the ~ on,** (*fam.*) l'emporter sur. **on ~,** énervé.

edgeways /'edʒweɪz/ *adv.* de côté. **I can't get a word in ~,** je ne peux pas placer un mot.

edging /'edʒɪŋ/ *n.* bordure *f.*

edgy /'edʒɪ/ *a.* énervé.

edible /'edɪbl/ *a.* mangeable; (*not poisonous*) comestible.

edict /'iːdɪkt/ *n.* décret *m.*

edifice /'edɪfɪs/ *n.* édifice *m.*

edify /'edɪfaɪ/ *v.t.* édifier.

edit /'edɪt/ *v.t.* (*p.t.* **edited**) (*newspaper*) diriger; (*prepare text of*) mettre au point, préparer; (*write*) rédiger; (*cut*) couper.

edition /ɪ'dɪʃn/ *n.* édition *f.*

editor /'edɪtə(r)/ *n.* (*writer*) rédacteur, -trice *m., f.*; (*annotator*) éditeur, -trice *m., f.* **the ~ (in chief),** le rédacteur en chef. **~ial** /-'tɔːrɪəl/ *a.* de la rédaction; *n.* éditorial *m.*

educat|e /'edʒʊkeɪt/ *v.t.* instruire; (*mind, public*) éduquer. **~ed** *a.* instruit. **~ion** /-'keɪʃn/ *n.* éducation *f.*; (*schooling*) enseignement *m.* **~ional** /-'keɪʃənl/ *a.* pédagogique, éducatif.

EEC *abbr.* (*European Economic Community*) CEE *f.*

eel /iːl/ *n.* anguille *f.*

eerie /'ɪərɪ/ *a.* (**-ier, -iest**) sinistre.

effect /ɪ'fekt/ *n.* effet *m.* ● *v.t.* effectuer. **come into ~,** entrer en vigueur. **in ~,** effectivement. **take ~,** agir.

effective /ɪ'fektɪv/ *a.* efficace; (*striking*) frappant; (*actual*) effectif. **~ly** *adv.* efficacement; de manière frappante; effectivement. **~ness** *n.* efficacité *f.*

effeminate /ɪ'femɪnət/ *a.* efféminé.

effervescent /efə'vesnt/ *a.* effervescent.

efficien|t /ɪˈfɪʃnt/ a. efficace; (*person*) compétent. **~cy** n. efficacité f.; compétence f. **~tly** adv. efficacement.

effigy /ˈefɪdʒɪ/ n. effigie f.

effort /ˈefət/ n. effort m. **~less** a. facile.

effrontery /ɪˈfrʌntərɪ/ n. effronterie f.

effusive /ɪˈfjuːsɪv/ a. expansif.

e.g. /iːˈdʒiː/ abbr. par exemple.

egalitarian /ɪˌɡælɪˈteərɪən/ a. égalitaire. ● n. égalitariste m./f.

egg [1] /eɡ/ n. œuf m. **~-cup** n. coquetier m. **~-plant** n. aubergine f.

egg [2] /eɡ/ v.t. **~ on**, (fam.) inciter.

eggshell /ˈeɡʃel/ n. coquille d'œuf f.

ego /ˈiːɡəʊ/ n. (pl. **-os**) moi m. **~(t)ism** n. égoïsme m. **~(t)ist** n. égoïste m./f.

Egypt /ˈiːdʒɪpt/ n. Égypte f. **~ian** /ɪˈdʒɪpʃn/ a. & n. égyptien(ne) (m. (f.)).

eh /eɪ/ int. (fam.) hein.

eiderdown /ˈaɪdədaʊn/ n. édredon f.

eight /eɪt/ a. & n. huit (m.). **eighth** /eɪtθ/ a. & n. huitième (m./f.).

eighteen /eɪˈtiːn/ a. & n. dix-huit (m.). **~th** a. & n. dix-huitième (m./f.).

eight|y /ˈeɪtɪ/ a. & n. quatre-vingts (m.). **~ieth** a. & n. quatre-vingtième (m./f.).

either /ˈaɪðə(r)/ a. & pron. l'un(e) ou l'autre; (with negative) ni l'un(e) ni l'autre; (each) chaque. ● adv. non plus. ● conj. **~ ... or**, ou (bien) ... ou (bien); (with negative) ni ... ni.

eject /ɪˈdʒekt/ v.t. éjecter. **~or seat**, siège éjectable m.

eke /iːk/ v.t. **~ out**, faire durer; (living) gagner difficilement.

elaborate [1] /ɪˈlæbərət/ a. compliqué, recherché.

elaborate [2] /ɪˈlæbəreɪt/ v.t. élaborer. ● v.i. préciser. **~ on**, s'étendre sur.

elapse /ɪˈlæps/ v.i. s'écouler.

elastic /ɪˈlæstɪk/ a. & n. élastique (m.). **~ band**, élastique m. **~ity** /elæˈstɪsətɪ/ n. élasticité f.

elated /ɪˈleɪtɪd/ a. fou de joie.

elbow /ˈelbəʊ/ n. coude m. **~ room**, possibilité de manœuvrer f.

elder [1] /ˈeldə(r)/ a. & n. aîné(e) (m. (f.)).

elder [2] /ˈeldə(r)/ n. (tree) sureau m.

elderly /ˈeldəlɪ/ a. (assez) âgé.

eldest /ˈeldɪst/ a. & n. aîné(e) (m. (f.)).

elect /ɪˈlekt/ v.t. élire. ● a. (president etc.) futur. **~ to do**, choisir de faire. **~ion** /-kʃn/ n. élection f.

elector /ɪˈlektə(r)/ n. élec|teur, -trice m., f. **~al** a. électoral. **~ate** n. électorat m.

electric /ɪˈlektrɪk/ a. électrique. **~ blanket**, couverture chauffante f. **~al** a. électrique.

electrician /ɪlekˈtrɪʃn/ n. électricien m.

electricity /ɪlekˈtrɪsətɪ/ n. électricité f.

electrify /ɪˈlektrɪfaɪ/ v.t. électrifier; (excite) électriser.

electrocute /ɪˈlektrəkjuːt/ v.t. électrocuter.

electron /ɪˈlektrɒn/ n. électron m.

electronic /ɪlekˈtrɒnɪk/ a. électronique. **~s** n. électronique f.

elegan|t /ˈelɪɡənt/ a. élégant. **~ce** n. élégance f. **~tly** adv. élégamment.

element /ˈelɪmənt/ n. élément m.; (of heater etc.) résistance f. **~ary** /-ˈmentrɪ/ a. élémentaire.

elephant /ˈelɪfənt/ n. éléphant m.

elevat|e /ˈelɪveɪt/ v.t. élever. **~ion** /-ˈveɪʃn/ n. élévation f.

elevator /ˈelɪveɪtə(r)/ n. (Amer.) ascenseur m.

eleven /ɪˈlevn/ a. & n. onze (m.). **~th** a. & n. onzième (m./f.).

elf /elf/ (pl. **elves**) lutin m.

elicit /ɪˈlɪsɪt/ v.t. obtenir (**from**, de).

eligible /ˈelɪdʒəbl/ a. admissible (**for**, à). **be ~ for**, (entitled to) avoir droit à.

eliminat|e /ɪˈlɪmɪneɪt/ v.t. éliminer. **~ion** /-ˈneɪʃn/ n. élimination f.

élit|e /eɪˈliːt/ n. élite f. **~ist** a. & n. élitiste (m./f.).

ellip|se /ɪˈlɪps/ n. ellipse f. **~tical** a. elliptique.

elm /elm/ n. orme m.

elocution /eləˈkjuːʃn/ n. élocution f.

elongate /ˈiːlɒŋɡeɪt/ v.t. allonger.

elope /ɪˈləʊp/ v.i. s'enfuir. **~ment** n. fugue (amoureuse) f.

eloquen|t /ˈeləkwənt/ a. éloquent. **~ce** n. éloquence f. **~tly** adv. avec éloquence.

else /els/ adv. d'autre. **everybody ~**, tous les autres. **nobody ~**, personne d'autre. **nothing ~**, rien d'autre. **or ~**, ou bien. **somewhere ~**, autre part. **~where** adv. ailleurs.

elucidate /ɪˈluːsɪdeɪt/ v.t. élucider.

elude /ɪˈluːd/ v.t. échapper à; (question) éluder.

elusive /ɪˈluːsɪv/ *a.* insaisissable.

emaciated /ɪˈmeɪʃɪeɪtɪd/ *a.* émacié.

emanate /ˈeməneɪt/ *v.i.* émaner.

emancipat|e /ɪˈmænsɪpeɪt/ *v.t.* émanciper. **~ion** /-ˈpeɪʃn/ *n.* émancipation *f.*

embalm /ɪmˈbɑːm/ *v.t.* embaumer.

embankment /ɪmˈbæŋkmənt/ *n.* (*of river*) quai *m.*; (*of railway*) remblai *m.*, talus *m.*

embargo /ɪmˈbɑːgəʊ/ *n.* (*pl.* -**oes**) embargo *m.*

embark /ɪmˈbɑːk/ *v.t./i.* (s')embarquer. **~ on**, (*business etc.*) se lancer dans; (*journey*) commencer. **~ation** /embɑːˈkeɪʃn/ *n.* embarquement *m.*

embarrass /ɪmˈbærəs/ *v.t.* embarrasser, gêner. **~ment** *n.* embarras *m.*, gêne *f.*

embassy /ˈembəsɪ/ *n.* ambassade *f.*

embed /ɪmˈbed/ *v.t.* (*p.t.* **embedded**) encastrer.

embellish /ɪmˈbelɪʃ/ *v.t.* embellir. **~ment** *n.* enjolivement *m.*

embers /ˈembəz/ *n. pl.* braise *f.*

embezzle /ɪmˈbezl/ *v.t.* détourner. **~ment** *n.* détournement de fonds *m.* **~ r** /-ə(r)/ *n.* escroc *m.*

embitter /ɪmˈbɪtə(r)/ *v.t.* (*person*) aigrir; (*situation*) envenimer.

emblem /ˈembləm/ *n.* emblème *m.*

embod|y /ɪmˈbɒdɪ/ *v.t.* incarner, exprimer; (*include*) contenir. **~iment** *n.* incarnation *f.*

emboss /ɪmˈbɒs/ *v.t.* (*metal*) repousser; (*paper*) gaufrer.

embrace /ɪmˈbreɪs/ *v.t./i.* (s')embrasser. ● *n.* étreinte *f.*

embroider /ɪmˈbrɔɪdə(r)/ *v.t.* broder. **~y** *n.* broderie *f.*

embroil /ɪmˈbrɔɪl/ *v.t.* mêler (**in**, à).

embryo /ˈembrɪəʊ/ *n.* (*pl.* -**os**) embryon *m.* **~nic** /-ˈɒnɪk/ *a.* embryonnaire.

emend /ɪˈmend/ *v.t.* corriger.

emerald /ˈemərəld/ *n.* émeraude *f.*

emerge /ɪˈmɜːdʒ/ *v.i.* apparaître. **~nce** /-əns/ *n.* apparition *f.*

emergency /ɪˈmɜːdʒənsɪ/ *n.* (*crisis*) crise *f.*; (*urgent case: med.*) urgence *f.* ● *a.* d'urgence. **~ exit**, sortie de secours *f.* **~ landing**, atterrissage forcé *m.* **in an ~**, en cas d'urgence.

emery /ˈemərɪ/ *n.* émeri *m.*

emigrant /ˈemɪgrənt/ *n.* émigrant(e) *m.* (*f.*).

emigrat|e /ˈemɪgreɪt/ *v.i.* émigrer. **~ion** /-ˈgreɪʃn/ *n.* émigration *f.*

eminen|t /ˈemɪnənt/ *a.* éminent. **~ce** *n.* éminence *f.* **~tly** *adv.* éminemment, parfaitement.

emissary /ˈemɪsərɪ/ *n.* émissaire *m.*

emi|t /ɪˈmɪt/ *v.t.* (*p.t.* **emitted**) émettre. **~ssion** *n.* émission *f.*

emotion /ɪˈməʊʃn/ *n.* émotion *f.* **~al** *a.* (*person, shock*) émotif; (*speech, scene*) émouvant.

emotive /ɪˈməʊtɪv/ *a.* émotif.

emperor /ˈempərə(r)/ *n.* empereur *m.*

emphasis /ˈemfəsɪs/ *n.* (*on word*) accent *m.* **lay ~ on**, mettre l'accent sur.

emphasize /ˈemfəsaɪz/ *v.t.* souligner; (*syllable*) insister sur.

emphatic /ɪmˈfætɪk/ *a.* catégorique; (*manner*) énergique.

empire /ˈempaɪə(r)/ *n.* empire *m.*

employ /ɪmˈplɔɪ/ *v.t.* employer. **~er** *n.* employeu|r, -se *m.*, *f.* **~ment** *n.* emploi *m.* **~ment agency**, agence de placement *f.*

employee /emplɔɪˈiː/ *n.* employé(e) *m.* (*f.*).

empower /ɪmˈpaʊə(r)/ *v.t.* autoriser (**to do**, à faire).

empress /ˈemprɪs/ *n.* impératrice *f.*

empt|y /ˈemptɪ/ *a.* (-**ier**, -**est**) vide; (*promise*) vain. ● *v.t./i.* (se) vider. **~y-handed** *a.* les mains vides. **on an ~y stomach**, à jeun. **~ies** *n. pl.* bouteilles vides *f. pl.* **~iness** *n.* vide *m.*

emulat|e /ˈemjʊleɪt/ *v.t.* imiter. **~ion** /-ˈleɪʃn/ *n.* (*comput.*) émulation *f.*

emulsion /ɪˈmʌlʃn/ *n.* émulsion *f.* **~ (paint)**, peinture-émulsion *f.*

enable /ɪˈneɪbl/ *v.t.* **~ s.o. to**, permettre à qn. de.

enact /ɪˈnækt/ *v.t.* (*law*) promulguer; (*scene*) représenter.

enamel /ɪˈnæml/ *n.* émail *m.* ● *v.t.* (*p.t.* **enamelled**) émailler.

enamoured /ɪˈnæməd/ *a.* **be ~ of**, aimer beaucoup, être épris de.

encampment /ɪnˈkæmpmənt/ *n.* campement *m.*

encase /ɪnˈkeɪs/ *v.t.* (*cover*) recouvrir (**in**, de); (*enclose*) enfermer (**in**, dans).

enchant /ɪnˈtʃɑːnt/ *v.t.* enchanter. **~ing** *a.* enchanteur. **~ment** *n.* enchantement *m.*

encircle /ɪnˈsɜːkl/ *v.t.* encercler.

enclave /ˈenkleɪv/ *n.* enclave *f.*

enclose /ɪnˈkləʊz/ *v.t.* (*land*) clôturer; (*with letter*) joindre. **~d** *a.*

(*space*) clos; (*market*) couvert; (*with letter*) ci-joint.

enclosure /ɪnˈkləʊʒə(r)/ *n.* enceinte *f.*; (*comm.*) pièce jointe *f.*

encompass /ɪnˈkʌmpəs/ *v.t.* (*include*) inclure.

encore /ˈɒŋkɔː(r)/ *int. & n.* bis (*m.*).

encounter /ɪnˈkaʊntə(r)/ *v.t.* rencontrer. ● *n.* rencontre *f.*

encourage /ɪnˈkʌrɪdʒ/ *v.t.* encourager. **~ment** *n.* encouragement *m.*

encroach /ɪnˈkrəʊtʃ/ *v.i.* ~ **upon**, empiéter sur.

encumber /ɪnˈkʌmbə(r)/ *v.t.* encombrer.

encyclical /ɪnˈsɪklɪkl/ *n.* encyclique *f.*

encyclopaedia, **encyclopedia** /ɪnsaɪkləˈpiːdɪə/ *n.* encyclopédie *f.* **~ic** *a.* encyclopédique.

end /end/ *n.* fin *f.*; (*farthest part*) bout *m.* ● *v.t./i.* (se) terminer. ~ **up doing**, finir par faire. **come to an ~**, prendre fin. **~-product**, produit fini *m.* **in the ~**, finalement. **no ~ of**, (*fam.*) énormément de. **on ~**, (*upright*) debout; (*in a row*) de suite. **put an ~ to**, mettre fin à.

endanger /ɪnˈdeɪndʒə(r)/ *v.t.* mettre en danger.

endear|ing /ɪnˈdɪərɪŋ/ *a.* attachant. **~ment** *n.* parole tendre *f.*

endeavour, (*Amer.*) **endeavor** /ɪnˈdevə(r)/ *n.* effort *m.* ● *v.i.* s'efforcer (**to**, de).

ending /ˈendɪŋ/ *n.* fin *f.*

endive /ˈendɪv/ *n.* chicorée *f.*

endless /ˈendlɪs/ *a.* interminable; (*times*) innombrable; (*patience*) infini.

endorse /ɪnˈdɔːs/ *v.t.* (*document*) endosser; (*action*) approuver. **~ment** *n.* (*auto.*) contravention *f.*

endow /ɪnˈdaʊ/ *v.t.* doter. **~ed with**, doté de. **~ment** *n.* dotation *f.* (**of**, de).

endur|e /ɪnˈdjʊə(r)/ *v.t.* supporter. ● *v.i.* durer. **~able** *a.* supportable. **~ance** *n.* endurance *f.* **~ing** *a.* durable.

enemy /ˈenəmɪ/ *n. & a.* ennemi(e) (*m.* (*f.*)).

energetic /enəˈdʒetɪk/ *a.* énergique.

energy /ˈenədʒɪ/ *n.* énergie *f.*

enforce /ɪnˈfɔːs/ *v.t.* appliquer, faire respecter; (*impose*) imposer (**on**, à). **~d** *a.* forcé.

engage /ɪnˈɡeɪdʒ/ *v.t.* engager. ● *v.i.* ~ **in**, prendre part à. **~d** *a.* fiancé;

(*busy*) occupé. **get ~d**, se fiancer. **~ment** *n.* fiançailles *f. pl.*; (*meeting*) rendez-vous *m.*; (*undertaking*) engagement *m.*

engaging /ɪnˈɡeɪdʒɪŋ/ *a.* engageant, séduisant.

engender /ɪnˈdʒendə(r)/ *v.t.* engendrer.

engine /ˈendʒɪn/ *n.* moteur *m.*; (*of train*) locomotive *f.*; (*of ship*) machine *f.* **~-driver** *n.* mécanicien *m.*

engineer /endʒɪˈnɪə(r)/ *n.* ingénieur *m.*; (*appliance repairman*) dépanneur *m.* ● *v.t.* (*contrive*: *fam.*) machiner. **~ing** *n.* (*mechanical*) mécanique *f.*; (*road-building etc.*) génie *m.*

England /ˈɪŋɡlənd/ *n.* Angleterre *f.*

English /ˈɪŋɡlɪʃ/ *a.* anglais. ● *n.* (*lang.*) anglais *m.* **~-speaking** *a.* anglophone. **the ~,** les Anglais *m. pl.* **~man** *n.* Anglais *m.* **~woman** *n.* Anglaise *f.*

engrav|e /ɪnˈɡreɪv/ *v.t.* graver. **~ing** *n.* gravure *f.*

engrossed /ɪnˈɡrəʊst/ *a.* absorbé (**in**, par).

engulf /ɪnˈɡʌlf/ *v.t.* engouffrer.

enhance /ɪnˈhɑːns/ *v.t.* rehausser; (*price, value*) augmenter.

enigma /ɪˈnɪɡmə/ *n.* énigme *f.* **~tic** /enɪɡˈmætɪk/ *a.* énigmatique.

enjoy /ɪnˈdʒɔɪ/ *v.t.* aimer (*doing*, faire); (*benefit from*) jouir de. ~ **o.s.,** s'amuser. ~ **your meal,** bon appétit! **~able** *a.* agréable. **~ment** *n.* plaisir *m.*

enlarge /ɪnˈlɑːdʒ/ *v.t./i.* (s')agrandir. ~ **upon**, s'étendre sur. **~ment** *n.* agrandissement *m.*

enlighten /ɪnˈlaɪtn/ *v.t.* éclairer. **~ment** *n.* édification *f.*; (*information*) éclaircissements *m. pl.*

enlist /ɪnˈlɪst/ *v.t.* (*person*) recruter; (*fig.*) obtenir. ● *v.i.* s'engager.

enliven /ɪnˈlaɪvn/ *v.t.* animer.

enmity /ˈenmətɪ/ *n.* inimitié *f.*

enormity /ɪˈnɔːmətɪ/ *n.* énormité *f.*

enormous /ɪˈnɔːməs/ *a.* énorme. **~ly** *adv.* énormément.

enough /ɪˈnʌf/ *adv. & n.* assez. ● *a.* assez de. ~ **glasses/time/***etc.,* assez de verres/de temps/*etc.* **have ~ of**, en avoir assez de.

enquir|e /ɪnˈkwaɪə(r)/ *v.t./i.* demander. **~e about**, se renseigner sur. **~y** *n.* demande de renseignements *f.*

enrage /ɪnˈreɪdʒ/ v.t. mettre en rage, rendre furieux.

enrich /ɪnˈrɪtʃ/ v.t. enrichir.

enrol, (*Amer.*) **enroll** /ɪnˈrəʊl/ v.t./i. (*p.t.* **enrolled**) (s')inscrire. ~**ment** n. inscription f.

ensconce /ɪnˈskɒns/ v.t. ~ **o.s.,** bien s'installer.

ensemble /ɒnˈsɒmbl/ n. (*clothing & mus.*) ensemble m.

ensign /ˈensən, ˈensaɪn/ n. (*flag*) pavillon m.

enslave /ɪnˈsleɪv/ v.t. asservir.

ensue /ɪnˈsjuː/ v.i. s'ensuivre.

ensure /ɪnˈʃʊə(r)/ v.t. assurer. ~ **that,** (*ascertain*) s'assurer que.

entail /ɪnˈteɪl/ v.t. entraîner.

entangle /ɪnˈtæŋgl/ v.t. emmêler.

enter /ˈentə(r)/ v.t. entrer dans; (*room, club, race, etc.*) entrer dans; (*note down, register*) inscrire; (*data*) entrer, saisir. ● v.i. entrer (**into,** dans). ~ **for,** s'inscrire à.

enterprise /ˈentəpraɪz/ n. entreprise f.; (*boldness*) initiative f.

enterprising /ˈentəpraɪzɪŋ/ a. entreprenant.

entertain /entəˈteɪn/ v.t. amuser, divertir; (*guests*) recevoir; (*ideas*) considérer. ~**er** n. artiste m./f. ~**ing** a. divertissant. ~**ment** n. amusement m., divertissement m.; (*performance*) spectacle m.

enthral, (*Amer.*) **enthrall** /ɪnˈθrɔːl/ v.t. (*p.t.* **enthralled**) captiver.

enthuse /ɪnˈθjuːz/ v.i. ~ **over,** s'enthousiasmer pour.

enthusiasm /ɪnˈθjuːzɪæzəm/ n. enthousiasme m.

enthusiast /ɪnˈθjuːzɪæst/ n. fervent(e) m. (f.), passionné(e) m. (f.) (**for,** de). ~**ic** /-ˈæstɪk/ a. (*supporter*) enthousiaste. **be** ~**ic about,** être enthousiasmé par. ~**ically** adv. /-ˈæstɪklɪ/ adv. avec enthousiasme.

entice /ɪnˈtaɪs/ v.t. attirer. ~ **to do,** entraîner à faire. ~**ment** n. (*attraction*) attrait m.

entire /ɪnˈtaɪə(r)/ a. entier. ~**ly** adv. entièrement.

entirety /ɪnˈtaɪərətɪ/ n. **in its** ~, en entier.

entitle /ɪnˈtaɪtl/ v.t. donner droit à (**to sth.,** à qch.; **to do,** de faire). ~**d** a. (*book*) intitulé. **be** ~**d to sth.,** avoir droit à qch. ~**ment** n. droit m.

entity /ˈentɪtɪ/ n. entité f.

entrails /ˈentreɪlz/ n. pl. entrailles f. pl.

entrance[1] /ˈentrəns/ n. (*entering, way in*) entrée f. (**to,** de); (*right to enter*) admission f. ● a. (*charge, exam*) d'entrée.

entrance[2] /ɪnˈtrɑːns/ v.t. transporter.

entrant /ˈentrənt/ n. (*sport*) concurrent(e) m. (f.); (*in exam*) candidat(e) m. (f.).

entreat /ɪnˈtriːt/ v.t. supplier.

entrenched /ɪnˈtrentʃt/ a. ancré.

entrepreneur /ɒntrəprəˈnɜː(r)/ n. entrepreneur m.

entrust /ɪnˈtrʌst/ v.t. confier.

entry /ˈentrɪ/ n. (*entrance*) entrée f.; (*word on list*) mot inscrit m. ~ **form,** feuille d'inscription f.

enumerate /ɪˈnjuːməreɪt/ v.t. énumérer.

enunciate /ɪˈnʌnsɪeɪt/ v.t. (*word*) articuler; (*ideas*) énoncer.

envelop /ɪnˈveləp/ v.t. (*p.t.* **enveloped**) envelopper.

envelope /ˈenvələʊp/ n. enveloppe f.

enviable /ˈenvɪəbl/ a. enviable.

envious /ˈenvɪəs/ a. envieux (**of sth.,** de qch.). ~ **of s.o.,** jaloux de qn. ~**ly** adv. avec envie.

environment /ɪnˈvaɪərənmənt/ n. milieu m.; (*ecological*) environnement m. ~**al** /-ˈmentl/ a. du milieu; de l'environnement. ~**alist** n. spécialiste de l'environnement m./f.

envisage /ɪnˈvɪzɪdʒ/ v.t. envisager.

envoy /ˈenvɔɪ/ n. envoyé(e) m. (f.).

envy /ˈenvɪ/ n. envie f. ● v.t. envier.

enzyme /ˈenzaɪm/ n. enzyme m.

ephemeral /ɪˈfemərəl/ a. éphémère.

epic /ˈepɪk/ n. épopée f. ● a. épique.

epidemic /epɪˈdemɪk/ n. épidémie f.

epileps|y /ˈepɪlepsɪ/ n. épilepsie f. ~**tic** /-ˈleptɪk/ a. & n. épileptique (m./f.).

episode /ˈepɪsəʊd/ n. épisode m.

epistle /ɪˈpɪsl/ n. épître f.

epitaph /ˈepɪtɑːf/ n. épitaphe f.

epithet /ˈepɪθet/ n. épithète f.

epitom|e /ɪˈpɪtəmɪ/ n. (*embodiment*) modèle m.; (*summary*) résumé m. ~**ize** v.t. incarner.

epoch /ˈiːpɒk/ n. époque f. ~-**making** a. qui fait époque.

equal /ˈiːkwəl/ a. & n. égal(e) (m.f.). ● v.t. (*p.t.* **equalled**) égaler. ~ **opportunities/rights,** égalité des chances/droits f. ~ **to,** (*task*) à la hauteur de. ~**ity** /ɪˈkwɒlətɪ/ n. égalité f. ~**ly** adv. également; (*just as*) tout aussi.

equalize /'i:kwəlaɪz/ v.t./i. égaliser. **~r** /-ə(r)/ n. (goal) but égalisateur m.

equanimity /ekwə'nɪmətɪ/ n. égalité d'humeur f., calme m.

equate /ɪ'kweɪt/ v.t. assimiler, égaler (**with**, à).

equation /ɪ'kweɪʒn/ n. équation f.

equator /ɪ'kweɪtə(r)/ n. équateur m. **~ial** /ekwə'tɔːrɪəl/ a. équatorial.

equilibrium /i:kwɪ'lɪbrɪəm/ n. équilibre m.

equinox /'i:kwɪnɒks/ n. équinoxe m.

equip /ɪ'kwɪp/ v.t. (p.t. **equipped**) équiper (**with**, de). **~ment** n. équipement m.

equitable /'ekwɪtəbl/ a. équitable.

equity /'ekwətɪ/ n. équité f.

equivalent /ɪ'kwɪvələnt/ a. & n. équivalent (m.). **~ce** n. équivalence f.

equivocal /ɪ'kwɪvəkl/ a. équivoque.

era /'ɪərə/ n. ère f., époque f.

eradicate /ɪ'rædɪkeɪt/ v.t. supprimer, éliminer.

erase /ɪ'reɪz/ v.t. effacer. **~r** /-ə(r)/ n. (rubber) gomme f.

erect /ɪ'rekt/ a. droit. ● v.t. ériger. **~ion** /-kʃn/ n. érection f.

ermine /'ɜːmɪn/ n. hermine f.

ero|de /ɪ'rəʊd/ v.t. ronger. **~sion** n. érosion f.

erotic /ɪ'rɒtɪk/ a. érotique. **~ism** /-sɪzəm/ n. érotisme m.

err /ɜː(r)/ v.i. (be mistaken) se tromper; (sin) pécher.

errand /'erənd/ n. course f.

erratic /ɪ'rætɪk/ a. (uneven) irrégulier; (person) capricieux.

erroneous /ɪ'rəʊnɪəs/ a. erroné.

error /'erə(r)/ n. erreur f.

erudit|e /'eruːdaɪt, Amer. 'erjʊdaɪt/ a. érudit. **~ion** /-'dɪʃn/ n. érudition f.

erupt /ɪ'rʌpt/ v.i. (volcano) entrer en éruption; (fig.) éclater. **~ion** /-pʃn/ n. éruption f.

escalat|e /'eskəleɪt/ v.t./i. (s')intensifier; (of prices) monter en flèche. **~ion** /-'leɪʃn/ n. escalade f.

escalator /'eskəleɪtə(r)/ n. escalier mécanique m., escalator m.

escapade /eskə'peɪd/ n. fredaine f.

escape /ɪ'skeɪp/ v.i. s'échapper (**from a place**, d'un lieu); (prisoner) s'évader. ● v.t. échapper à. ● n. fuite f., évasion f.; (of gas etc.) fuite f. **~ from s.o.**, échapper à qn. **~ to**, s'enfuir dans. **have a lucky** or **narrow ~**, l'échapper belle.

escapism /ɪ'skeɪpɪzəm/ n. évasion (de la réalité) f.

escort[1] /'eskɔːt/ n. (guard) escorte f.; (of lady) cavalier m.

escort[2] /ɪ'skɔːt/ v.t. escorter.

Eskimo /'eskɪməʊ/ n. (pl. **-os**) Esquimau(de) m. (f.).

especial /ɪ'speʃl/ a. particulier. **~ly** adv. particulièrement.

espionage /'espɪənɑːʒ/ n. espionnage m.

esplanade /esplə'neɪd/ n. esplanade f.

espresso /e'spresəʊ/ n. (pl. **-os**) (café) express m.

essay /'eseɪ/ n. essai m.; (schol.) rédaction f.; (univ.) dissertation f.

essence /'esns/ n. essence f.; (main point) essentiel m.

essential /ɪ'senʃl/ a. essentiel. ● n. pl. **the ~s**, l'essentiel m. **~ly** adv. essentiellement.

establish /ɪ'stæblɪʃ/ v.t. établir; (business, state) fonder. **~ment** n. établissement m.; fondation f. **the E~ment**, les pouvoirs établis m.pl.

estate /ɪ'steɪt/ n. (land) propriété f.; (possessions) biens m. pl.; (inheritance) succession f.; (district) cité f., complexe m. **~ agent**, agent immobilier m. **~ car**, break m.

esteem /ɪ'stiːm/ v.t. estimer. ● n. estime f.

esthetic /es'θetɪk/ a. (Amer.) = **aesthetic**.

estimate[1] /'estɪmət/ n. (calculation) estimation f.; (comm.) devis m.

estimat|e[2] /'estɪmeɪt/ v.t. estimer. **~ion** /-'meɪʃn/ n. jugement m.; (high regard) estime f.

estuary /'estʃʊərɪ/ n. estuaire m.

etc. /et'setərə/ adv. etc.

etching /'etʃɪŋ/ n. eau-forte f.

eternal /ɪ'tɜːnl/ a. éternel.

eternity /ɪ'tɜːnətɪ/ n. éternité f.

ether /'iːθə(r)/ n. éther m.

ethic /'eθɪk/ n. éthique f. **~s**, moralité f. **~al** a. éthique.

ethnic /'eθnɪk/ a. ethnique.

ethos /'iːθɒs/ n. génie m.

etiquette /'etɪket/ n. étiquette f.

etymology /etɪ'mɒlədʒɪ/ n. étymologie f.

eucalyptus /juːkə'lɪptəs/ n. (pl. **-tuses**) eucalyptus m.

eulogy /'juːlədʒɪ/ n. éloge m.

euphemism /'juːfəmɪzəm/ n. euphémisme m.

euphoria /juː'fɔːrɪə/ n. euphorie f.

eurocheque /'jʊərəʊtʃek/ *n.* euro-chèque *m.*

Europe /'jʊərəp/ *n.* Europe *f.* **~an** /-'pɪən/ *a.* & *n.* européen(ne) (*m.* (*f.*)). **E~an Community,** Communauté Européenne *f.*

euthanasia /ju:θə'neɪzɪə/ *n.* euthanasie *f.*

evacuat|e /ɪ'vækjʊeɪt/ *v.t.* évacuer. **~ion** /-'eɪʃn/ *n.* évacuation *f.*

evade /ɪ'veɪd/ *v.t.* esquiver. **~ tax,** frauder le fisc.

evaluate /ɪ'væljʊeɪt/ *v.t.* évaluer.

evangelical /i:væn'dʒelɪkl/ *a.* évangélique.

evangelist /ɪ'vændʒəlɪst/ *n.* évangéliste *m.*

evaporat|e /ɪ'væpəreɪt/ *v.i.* s'évaporer. **~ed milk,** lait concentré *m.* **~ion** /-'reɪʃn/ *n.* évaporation *f.*

evasion /ɪ'veɪʒn/ *n.* fuite *f.* (**of,** devant); (*excuse*) subterfuge *m.* **tax ~,** fraude fiscale.

evasive /ɪ'veɪsɪv/ *a.* évasif.

eve /i:v/ *n.* veille *f.* (**of,** de).

even /'i:vn/ *a.* régulier; (*surface*) uni; (*equal, unvarying*) égal; (*number*) pair. ● *v.t./i.* **~ (out** *or* **up),** (s')égaliser. ● *adv.* même. **~ better/**etc.*, (still)* encore mieux/etc.* **get ~ with,** se venger de. **~ly** *adv.* régulièrement; (*equally*) de manière égale.

evening /'i:vnɪŋ/ *n.* soir *m.*; (*whole evening, event*) soirée *f.*

event /ɪ'vent/ *n.* événement *m.*; (*sport*) épreuve *f.* **in the ~ of,** en cas de. **~ful** *a.* mouvementé.

eventual /ɪ'ventʃʊəl/ *a.* final, définitif. **~ity** /-'ælətɪ/ *n.* éventualité *f.* **~ly** *adv.* en fin de compte; (*in future*) un jour ou l'autre.

ever /'evə(r)/ *adv.* jamais; (*at all times*) toujours. **~ since** *prep.* & *adv.* depuis (ce moment-là); *conj.* depuis que. **~ so,** (*fam.*) vraiment.

evergreen /'evəgri:n/ *n.* arbre à feuilles persistantes *m.*

everlasting /evə'lɑ:stɪŋ/ *a.* éternel.

every /'evrɪ/ *a.* chaque. **~ one,** chacun(e). **~ other day,** un jour sur deux, tous les deux jours.

everybody /'evrɪbɒdɪ/ *pron.* tout le monde.

everyday /'evrɪdeɪ/ *a.* quotidien.

everyone /'evrɪwʌn/ *pron.* tout le monde.

everything /'evrɪθɪŋ/ *pron.* tout.

everywhere /'evrɪweə(r)/ *adv.* partout. **~ he goes,** partout où il va.

evict /ɪ'vɪkt/ *v.t.* expulser. **~ion** /-kʃn/ *n.* expulsion *f.*

evidence /'evɪdəns/ *n.* (*proof*) preuve(s) *f.* (*pl.*); (*certainty*) évidence *f.*; (*signs*) signes *m. pl.*; (*testimony*) témoignage *m.* **give ~,** témoigner. **in ~,** en vue.

evident /'evɪdənt/ *a.* évident. **~ly** *adv.* de toute évidence.

evil /'i:vl/ *a.* mauvais. ● *n.* mal *m.*

evo|ke /ɪ'vəʊk/ *v.t.* évoquer. **~cative** /ɪ'vɒkətɪv/ *a.* évocateur.

evolution /i:və'lu:ʃn/ *n.* évolution *f.*

evolve /ɪ'vɒlv/ *v.i.* se développer, évoluer. ● *v.t.* développer.

ewe /ju:/ *n.* brebis *f.*

ex- /eks/ *pref.* ex-, ancien.

exacerbate /ɪg'zæsəbeɪt/ *v.t.* exacerber.

exact¹ /ɪg'zækt/ *a.* exact. **~ly** *adv.* exactement. **~ness** *n.* exactitude *f.*

exact² /ɪg'zækt/ *v.t.* exiger (**from,** de). **~ing** *a.* exigeant.

exaggerat|e /ɪg'zædʒəreɪt/ *v.t./i.* exagérer. **~ion** /-'reɪʃn/ *n.* exagération *f.*

exalted /ɪg'zɔ:ltɪd/ *a.* (*in rank*) de haut rang; (*ideal*) élevé.

exam /ɪg'zæm/ *n.* (*fam.*) examen *m.*

examination /ɪgzæmɪ'neɪʃn/ *n.* examen *m.*

examine /ɪg'zæmɪn/ *v.t.* examiner; (*witness etc.*) interroger. **~r** /-ə(r)/ *n.* examina|teur, -trice *m., f.*

example /ɪg'zɑ:mpl/ *n.* exemple *m.* **for ~,** par exemple. **make an ~ of,** punir pour l'exemple.

exasperat|e /ɪg'zæspəreɪt/ *v.t.* exaspérer. **~ion** /-'reɪʃn/ *n.* exaspération *f.*

excavat|e /'ekskəveɪt/ *v.t.* creuser; (*uncover*) déterrer. **~ions** /-'veɪʃnz/ *n. pl.* (*archaeol.*) fouilles *f. pl.*

exceed /ɪk'si:d/ *v.t.* dépasser. **~ingly** *adv.* extrêmement.

excel /ɪk'sel/ *v.i.* (*p.t.* **excelled**) exceller. ● *v.t.* surpasser.

excellen|t /'eksələnt/ *a.* excellent. **~ce** *n.* excellence *f.* **~tly** *adv.* admirablement, parfaitement.

except /ɪk'sept/ *prep.* sauf, excepté. ● *v.t.* excepter. **~ for,** à part. **~ing** *prep.* sauf, excepté.

exception /ɪk'sepʃn/ *n.* exception *f.* **take ~ to,** s'offenser de.

exceptional /ɪkˈsepʃənl/ *a.* exceptionnel. **~ly** *adv.* exceptionnellement.

excerpt /ˈeksɜːpt/ *n.* extrait *m.*

excess [1] /ɪkˈses/ *n.* excès *m.*

excess [2] /ˈekses/ *a.* excédentaire. **~ fare,** supplément *m.* **~ luggage,** excédent de bagages *m.*

excessive /ɪkˈsesɪv/ *a.* excessif. **~ly** *adv.* excessivement.

exchange /ɪksˈtʃeɪndʒ/ *v.t.* échanger. ● *n.* échange *m.*; (*between currencies*) change *m.* **~ rate,** taux d'échange *m.* **(telephone) ~,** central (téléphonique) *m.*

exchequer /ɪksˈtʃekə(r)/ *n.* (*British pol.*) Échiquier *m.*

excise /ˈeksaɪz/ *n.* impôt (indirect) *m.*

excit|e /ɪkˈsaɪt/ *v.t.* exciter; (*enthuse*) enthousiasmer. **~able** *a.* excitable. **~ed** *a.* excité. **get ~ed,** s'exciter. **~ement** *n.* excitation *f.* **~ing** *a.* passionnant.

exclaim /ɪkˈskleɪm/ *v.t./i.* exclamer, s'écrier.

exclamation /ekskləˈmeɪʃn/ *n.* exclamation *f.* **~ mark** *or* **point** (*Amer.*), point d'exclamation *m.*

exclu|de /ɪkˈskluːd/ *v.t.* exclure. **~sion** *n.* exclusion *f.*

exclusive /ɪkˈskluːsɪv/ *a.* (*rights etc.*) exclusif; (*club etc.*) sélect; (*news item*) en exclusivité. **~ of service/** *etc.,* service/*etc.* non compris. **~ly** *adv.* exclusivement.

excrement /ˈekskrəmənt/ *n.* excrément(s) *m.* (*pl.*).

excruciating /ɪkˈskruːʃɪeɪtɪŋ/ *a.* atroce, insupportable.

excursion /ɪkˈskɜːʃn/ *n.* excursion *f.*

excus|e [1] /ɪkˈskjuːz/ *v.t.* excuser. **~e from,** (*exempt*) dispenser de. **~e me!,** excusez-moi!, pardon! **~able** *a.* excusable.

excuse [2] /ɪkˈskjuːs/ *n.* excuse *f.*

ex-directory /eksdɪˈrektərɪ/ *a.* qui n'est pas dans l'annuaire.

execute /ˈeksɪkjuːt/ *v.t.* exécuter.

execution /eksɪˈkjuːʃn/ *n.* exécution *f.* **~er** *n.* bourreau *m.*

executive /ɪgˈzekjʊtɪv/ *n.* (pouvoir) exécutif *m.*; (*person*) cadre *m.* ● *a.* exécutif.

exemplary /ɪgˈzemplərɪ/ *a.* exemplaire.

exemplify /ɪgˈzemplɪfaɪ/ *v.t.* illustrer.

exempt /ɪgˈzempt/ *a.* exempt (**from,** de). ● *v.t.* exempter. **~ion** /-pʃn/ *n.* exemption *f.*

exercise /ˈeksəsaɪz/ *n.* exercice *m.* ● *v.t.* exercer; (*restraint, patience*) faire preuve de. ● *v.i.* prendre de l'exercice. **~ book,** cahier *m.*

exert /ɪgˈzɜːt/ *v.t.* exercer. **~ o.s.,** se dépenser, faire des efforts. **~ion** /-ʃn/ *n.* effort *m.*

exhaust /ɪgˈzɔːst/ *v.t.* épuiser. ● *n.* (*auto.*) (pot d')échappement *m.* **~ed** *a.* épuisé. **~ion** /-stʃən/ *n.* épuisement *m.*

exhaustive /ɪgˈzɔːstɪv/ *a.* complet.

exhibit /ɪgˈzɪbɪt/ *v.t.* exposer; (*fig.*) faire preuve de. ● *n.* objet exposé *m.* **~or** *n.* exposant(e) *m.* (*f.*).

exhibition /eksɪˈbɪʃn/ *n.* exposition *f.*; (*act of showing*) démonstration *f.* **~ist** *n.* exhibitionniste *m./f.*

exhilarat|e /ɪgˈzɪləreɪt/ *v.t.* transporter de joie; (*invigorate*) vivifier. **~ing** *a.* euphorisant. **~ion** /-ˈreɪʃn/ *n.* joie *f.*

exhort /ɪgˈzɔːt/ *v.t.* exhorter (**to,** à).

exhume /eksˈhjuːm/ *v.t.* exhumer.

exile /ˈeksaɪl/ *n.* exil *m.*; (*person*) exilé(e) *m.* (*f.*). ● *v.t.* exiler.

exist /ɪgˈzɪst/ *v.i.* exister. **~ence** *n.* existence *f.* **be in ~ence,** exister. **~ing** *a.* actuel.

exit /ˈeksɪt/ *n.* sortie *f.* ● *v.t./i.* (*comput.*) sortir (de).

exodus /ˈeksədəs/ *n.* exode *m.*

exonerate /ɪgˈzɒnəreɪt/ *v.t.* disculper, innocenter.

exorbitant /ɪgˈzɔːbɪtənt/ *a.* exorbitant.

exorcize /ˈeksɔːsaɪz/ *v.t.* exorciser.

exotic /ɪgˈzɒtɪk/ *a.* exotique.

expan|d /ɪkˈspænd/ *v.t./i.* (*develop*) (se) développer; (*extend*) (s')étendre; (*metal, liquid*) (se) dilater. **~sion** *n.* développement *m.*; dilatation *f.*; (*pol., comm.*) expansion *f.*

expanse /ɪkˈspæns/ *n.* étendue *f.*

expatriate /eksˈpætrɪət, *Amer.* eksˈpeɪtrɪət/ *a. & n.* expatrié(e) (*m. (f.)*).

expect /ɪkˈspekt/ *v.t.* attendre, s'attendre à; (*suppose*) supposer; (*demand*) exiger; (*baby*) attendre. **~ to do,** compter faire. **~ation** /ekspekˈteɪʃn/ *n.* attente *f.*

expectan|t /ɪkˈspektənt/ *a.* **~t look,** air d'attente *m.* **~t mother,** future maman *f.* **~cy** *n.* attente *f.*

expedient /ɪkˈspiːdɪənt/ *a.* opportun. ● *n.* expédient *m.*

expedite /ˈekspɪdaɪt/ *v.t.* hâter.

expedition /ekspɪˈdɪʃn/ *n.* expédition *f.*

expel /ɪkˈspel/ *v.t.* (*p.t.* **expelled**) expulser; (*from school*) renvoyer.

expend /ɪkˈspend/ *v.t.* dépenser. **~able** *a.* remplaçable.

expenditure /ɪkˈspendɪtʃə(r)/ *n.* dépense(s) *f.* (*pl.*).

expense /ɪkˈspens/ *n.* dépense *f.*; frais *m. pl.* **at s.o.'s ~,** aux dépens de qn. **~ account,** note de frais *f.*

expensive /ɪkˈspensɪv/ *a.* cher, coûteux; (*tastes, habits*) de luxe. **~ly** *adv.* coûteusement.

experience /ɪkˈspɪərɪəns/ *n.* expérience *f.*; (*adventure*) aventure *f.* ● *v.t.* (*undergo*) connaître; (*feel*) éprouver. **~d** *a.* expérimenté.

experiment /ɪkˈsperɪmənt/ *n.* expérience *f.* ● *v.i.* faire une expérience. **~al** /-ˈmentl/ *a.* expérimental.

expert /ˈekspɜːt/ *n.* expert(e) *m.* (*f.*). ● *a.* expert. **~ly** *adv.* habilement.

expertise /eksˈpɜːˈtiːz/ *n.* compétence *f.* (**in,** en).

expir|e /ɪkˈspaɪə(r)/ *v.i.* expirer. **~ed** *a.* périmé. **~y** *n.* expiration *f.*

expl|ain /ɪkˈsplem/ *v.t.* expliquer. **~anation** /ekspləˈneɪʃn/ *n.* explication *f.* **~anatory** /-ˈænətərɪ/ *a.* explicatif.

expletive /ɪkˈspliːtɪv, *Amer.* ˈeksplətɪv/ *n.* juron *m.*

explicit /ɪkˈsplɪsɪt/ *a.* explicite.

explo|de /ɪkˈspləʊd/ *v.t./i.* (faire) exploser. **~sion** *n.* explosion *f.* **~sive** *a. & n.* explosif (*m.*).

exploit[1] /ˈeksplɔɪt/ *n.* exploit *m.*

exploit[2] /ɪkˈsplɔɪt/ *v.t.* exploiter. **~ation** /eksplɔɪˈteɪʃn/ *n.* exploitation *f.*

exploratory /ɪkˈsplɒrətrɪ/ *a.* (*talks; pol.*) exploratoire.

explor|e /ɪkˈsplɔː(r)/ *v.t.* explorer; (*fig.*) examiner. **~ation** /ekspləˈreɪʃn/ *n.* exploration *f.* **~er** *n.* explora|teur, -trice *m.,f.*

exponent /ɪkˈspəʊnənt/ *n.* interprète *m.* (**of,** de).

export[1] /ɪkˈspɔːt/ *v.t.* exporter. **~er** *n.* exportateur *m.*

export[2] /ˈekspɔːt/ *n.* exportation *f.*

expos|e /ɪkˈspəʊz/ *v.t.* exposer; (*disclose*) dévoiler. **~ure** /-ʒə(r)/ *n.* exposition *f.*; (*photo.*) pose *f.* **die of ~ure,** mourir de froid.

expound /ɪkˈspaʊnd/ *v.t.* exposer.

express[1] /ɪkˈspres/ *a.* formel, exprès; (*letter*) exprès *invar.* ● *adv.* (*by express post*) (par) exprès. ● *n.* (*train*) rapide *m.*; (*less fast*) express *m.* **~ly** *adv.* expressément.

express[2] /ɪkˈspres/ *v.t.* exprimer. **~ion** -ʃn/ *n.* expression *f.* **~ive** *a.* expressif.

expressway /ɪkˈspreswei/ *n.* voie express *f.*

expulsion /ɪkˈspʌlʃn/ *n.* expulsion *f.*; (*from school*) renvoi *m.*

expurgate /ˈekspɜːgeɪt/ *v.t.* expurger.

exquisite /ˈekskwɪzɪt/ *a.* exquis. **~ly** *adv.* d'une façon exquise.

ex-serviceman /eksˈsɜːvɪsmən/ *n.* (*pl.* **-men**) ancien combattant *m.*

extant /ekˈstænt/ *a.* existant.

extempore /ekˈstempərɪ/ *a. & adv.* impromptu.

exten|d /ɪkˈstend/ *v.t.* (*increase*) étendre, agrandir; (*arm, leg*) étendre; (*prolong*) prolonger; (*house*) agrandir; (*grant*) offrir. ● *v.i.* (*stretch*) s'étendre; (*in time*) se prolonger. **~sion** *n.* (*of line, road*) prolongement *m.*; (*in time*) prolongation *f.*; (*building*) annexe *f.*; (*of phone*) appareil supplémentaire *m.*; (*phone number*) poste *m.*; (*cable, hose, etc.*) rallonge *f.*

extensive /ɪkˈstensɪv/ *a.* vaste; (*study*) profond; (*damage etc.*) important. **~ly** *adv.* (*much*) beaucoup; (*very*) très.

extent /ɪkˈstent/ *n.* (*size, scope*) étendue *f.*; (*degree*) mesure *f.* **to some ~,** dans une certaine mesure. **to such an ~ that,** à tel point que.

extenuating /ɪkˈstenjʊeɪtɪŋ/ *a.* **~ circumstances,** circonstances atténuantes.

exterior /ɪkˈstɪərɪə(r)/ *a. & n.* extérieur (*m.*).

exterminat|e /ɪkˈstɜːmɪneɪt/ *v.t.* exterminer. **~ion** /-ˈneɪʃn/ *n.* extermination *f.*

external /ɪkˈstɜːnl/ *a.* extérieur; (*cause, medical use*) externe. **~ly** *adv.* extérieurement.

extinct /ɪkˈstɪŋkt/ *a.* (*species*) disparu; (*volcano, passion*) éteint. **~ion** /-kʃn/ *n.* extinction *f.*

extinguish /ɪkˈstɪŋgwɪʃ/ *v.t.* éteindre. **~er** *n.* extincteur *m.*

extol /ɪkˈstəʊl/ *v.t.* (*p.t.* **extolled**) exalter, chanter les louanges de.

extort /ɪkˈstɔːt/ *v.t.* extorquer (**from,** à). **~ion** /-ʃn/ *n.* (*jurid.*) extorsion (de fonds) *f.*

extortionate /ɪk'stɔːʃənət/ a. exorbitant.

extra /'ekstrə/ a. de plus, supplémentaire. ● adv. plus (que d'habitude). ~ **strong,** extra-fort. ● n. (additional thing) supplément m.; (cinema) figurant(e) m. (f.). ~ **charge,** supplément m. ~ **time,** (football) prolongation f.

extra- /'ekstrə/ pref. extra-.

extract[1] /ɪk'strækt/ v.t. extraire; (promise, tooth) arracher; (fig.) obtenir. **~ion** /-kʃn/ n. extraction f.

extract[2] /'ekstrækt/ n. extrait m.

extra-curricular /ekstrəkə'rɪkjʊlə(r)/ a. parascolaire.

extradit|e /'ekstrədaɪt/ v.t. extrader. **~ion** /-'dɪʃn/ n. extradition f.

extramarital /ekstrə'mærɪtl/ a. extra-conjugal.

extramural /ekstrə'mjʊərəl/ a. (univ.) hors faculté.

extraordinary /ɪk'strɔːdnrɪ/ a. extraordinaire.

extravagan|t /ɪk'strævəgənt/ a. extravagant; (wasteful) prodigue. **~ce** n. extravagance f.; prodigalité f.

extrem|e /ɪk'striːm/ a. & n. extrême (m.). **~ely** adv. extrêmement. **~ist** n. extrémiste m./f.

extremity /ɪk'stremətɪ/ n. extrémité f.

extricate /'ekstrɪkeɪt/ v.t. dégager.

extrovert /'ekstrəvɜːt/ n. extraverti(e) m. (f.).

exuberan|t /ɪg'zjuːbərənt/ a. exubérant. **~ce** n. exubérance f.

exude /ɪg'zjuːd/ v.t. (charm etc.) dégager.

exult /ɪg'zʌlt/ v.i. exulter.

eye /aɪ/ n. œil m. (pl. yeux). ● v.t. (p.t. **eyed,** pres. p. **eyeing**) regarder. **keep an ~ on,** surveiller. **~-catching** a. qui attire l'attention. **~-opener** n. révélation f. **~-shadow** n. ombre à paupières f.

eyeball /'aɪbɔːl/ n. globe oculaire m.

eyebrow /'aɪbraʊ/ n. sourcil m.

eyeful /'aɪfʊl/ n. **get an ~,** (fam.) se rincer l'œil.

eyelash /'aɪlæʃ/ n. cil m.

eyelet /'aɪlɪt/ n. œillet m.

eyelid /'aɪlɪd/ n. paupière f.

eyesight /'aɪsaɪt/ n. vue f.

eyesore /'aɪsɔː(r)/ n. horreur f.

eyewitness /'aɪwɪtnɪs/ n. témoin oculaire m.

F

fable /'feɪbl/ n. fable f.

fabric /'fæbrɪk/ n. (cloth) tissu m.

fabrication /fæbrɪ'keɪʃn/ n. (invention) invention f.

fabulous /'fæbjʊləs/ a. fabuleux; (marvellous: fam.) formidable.

façade /fə'sɑːd/ n. façade f.

face /feɪs/ n. visage m., figure f.; (aspect) face f.; (of clock) cadran m. ● v.t. être en face de; (risk) devoir affronter; (confront) faire face à, affronter. ● v.i. se tourner; (of house) être exposé. **~-flannel** n. gant de toilette m. **~-lift** n. lifting m. **give a ~-lift to,** donner un coup de neuf à. ~ **value,** (comm.) valeur nominale. **take sth. at ~ value,** prendre qch. au premier degré. ~ **to face,** face à face. ~ **up/down,** tourné vers le haut/bas. ~ **up to,** faire face à. **in the ~ of,** ~d **with,** face à. **make a (funny) ~,** faire une grimace.

faceless /'feɪslɪs/ a. anonyme.

facet /'fæsɪt/ n. facette f.

facetious /fə'siːʃəs/ a. facétieux.

facial /'feɪʃl/ a. de la face, facial. ● n. soin du visage m.

facile /'fæsaɪl, Amer. 'fæsl/ a. facile, superficiel.

facilitate /fə'sɪlɪteɪt/ v.t. faciliter.

facilit|y /fə'sɪlətɪ/ n. facilité f. **~ies,** (equipment) équipements m. pl.

facing /'feɪsɪŋ/ n. parement m. ● prep. en face de. ● a. en face.

facsimile /fæk'sɪmɪlɪ/ n. facsimilé m. ~ **transmission,** télécopie f.

fact /fækt/ n. fait m. **as a matter of ~, in ~,** en fait.

faction /'fækʃn/ n. faction f.

factor /'fæktə(r)/ n. facteur m.

factory /'fæktərɪ/ n. usine f.

factual /'fæktʃʊəl/ a. basé sur les faits.

faculty /'fækltɪ/ n. faculté f.

fad /fæd/ n. manie f., folie f.

fade /feɪd/ v.i. (sound) s'affaiblir; (memory) s'évanouir; (flower) se faner; (material) déteindre; (colour) passer.

fag /fæg/ n. (chore: fam.) corvée f.; (cigarette: sl.) sèche f.; (homosexual: Amer., sl.) pédé m.

fagged /fægd/ a. (tired) éreinté.

fail /feɪl/ v.i. échouer; (grow weak) (s'af)faiblir; (run short) manquer; (engine etc.) tomber en panne. ● v.t. (exam) échouer à; (candidate) refuser, recaler; (disappoint) décevoir. ~ s.o., (of words etc.) manquer à qn. ~ to do, (not do) ne pas faire; (not be able) ne pas réussir à faire. without ~, à coup sûr.

failing /ˈfeɪlɪŋ/ n. défaut m. ● prep. à défaut de.

failure /ˈfeɪljə(r)/ n. échec m.; (person) raté(e) m. (f.); (breakdown) panne f. ~ to do, (inability) incapacité de faire f.

faint /feɪnt/ a. (-er, -est) léger, faible. ● v.i. s'évanouir. ● n. évanouissement m. feel ~, (ill) se trouver mal. I haven't the ~est idea, je n'en ai pas la moindre idée. ~-hearted a. timide. ~ly adv. (weakly) faiblement; (slightly) légèrement. ~ness n. faiblesse f.

fair¹ /feə(r)/ n. foire f. ~-ground n. champ m. de foire.

fair² /feə(r)/ a. (-er, -est) (hair, person) blond; (skin etc.) clair; (just) juste, équitable; (weather) beau; (amount, quality) raisonnable. ● adv. (play) loyalement. ~ play, le fair-play. ~ly adv. (justly) équitablement; (rather) assez. ~ness n. justice f.

fairy /ˈfeərɪ/ n. fée f. ~ story, ~-tale n. conte m. de fées.

faith /feɪθ/ n. foi. f. ~-healer n. guérisseu|r, -se m., f.

faithful /ˈfeɪθfl/ a. fidèle. ~ly adv. fidèlement. ~ness n. fidélité f.

fake /feɪk/ n. (forgery) faux m.; (person) imposteur m. it is a ~, c'est faux. ● a. faux. ● v.t. (copy) faire un faux de; (alter) falsifier, truquer; (illness) simuler.

falcon /ˈfɔːlkən/ n. faucon m.

fall /fɔːl/ v.i. (p.t. fell, p.p. fallen) tomber. ● n. chute f.; (autumn: Amer.) automne m. Niagara F~s, chutes de Niagara. ~ back on, se rabattre sur. ~ behind, prendre du retard. ~ down or off, tomber. ~ for, (person: fam.) tomber amoureux de; (a trick: fam.) se laisser prendre à. ~ in, (mil.) se mettre en rangs. ~ off, (decrease) diminuer. ~ out, se brouiller (with, avec). ~-out n. retombées f. pl. ~ over, tomber (par terre). ~ short, être

insuffisant. ~ through, (plans) tomber à l'eau.

fallacy /ˈfæləsɪ/ n. erreur f.

fallible /ˈfæləbl/ a. faillible.

fallow /ˈfæləʊ/ a. en jachère.

false /fɔːls/ a. faux. ~hood n. mensonge m. ~ly adv. faussement. ~ness n. fausseté f.

falsetto /fɔːlˈsetəʊ/ n. (pl. -os) fausset m.

falsify /ˈfɔːlsɪfaɪ/ v.t. falsifier.

falter /ˈfɔːltə(r)/ v.i. vaciller; (nerve) faire défaut.

fame /feɪm/ n. renommée f.

famed /feɪmd/ a. renommé.

familiar /fəˈmɪlɪə(r)/ a. familier. be ~ with, connaître. ~ity /-ˈærətɪ/ n. familiarité f. ~ize v.t. familiariser.

family /ˈfæməlɪ/ n. famille f. ● a. de famille, familial.

famine /ˈfæmɪn/ n. famine f.

famished /ˈfæmɪʃt/ a. affamé.

famous /ˈfeɪməs/ a. célèbre. ~ly adv. (very well: fam.) à merveille.

fan¹ /fæn/ n. ventilateur m.; (hand-held) éventail m. ● v.t. (p.t. fanned) éventer; (fig.) attiser. ● v.i. ~ out, se déployer en éventail. ~ belt, courroie de ventilateur f.

fan² /fæn/ n. (of person) fan m./f., admira|teur, -trice m., f.; (enthusiast) fervent(e) m. (f.), passionné(e) m. (f.).

fanatic /fəˈnætɪk/ n. fanatique m./f. ~al a. fanatique. ~ism /-sɪzəm/ n. fanatisme m.

fancier /ˈfænsɪə(r)/ n. (dog/etc.) ~, amateur (de chiens/etc.) m.

fanciful /ˈfænsɪfl/ a. fantaisiste.

fancy /ˈfænsɪ/ n. (whim, fantasy) fantaisie f.; (liking) goût m. ● a. (buttons etc.) fantaisie invar.; (prices) extravagant; (impressive) impressionnant. ● v.t. s'imaginer; (want: fam.) avoir envie de; (like: fam.) aimer. take a ~ to s.o., se prendre d'affection pour qn. it took my ~, ça m'a plu. ~ dress, déguisement m.

fanfare /ˈfænfeə(r)/ n. fanfare f.

fang /fæŋ/ n. (of dog etc.) croc m.; (of snake) crochet m.

fanlight /ˈfænlaɪt/ n. imposte f.

fantastic /fænˈtæstɪk/ a. fantastique.

fantas|y /ˈfæntəsɪ/ n. fantaisie f.; (day-dream) fantasme m. ~ize v.i. fantasmer.

far /fɑ:(r)/ adv. loin; (*much*) beaucoup; (*very*) très. ● a. lointain; (*end*, *side*) autre. ~ **away**, ~ **off**, au loin. **as** ~ **as**, (*up to*) jusqu'à. **as** ~ **as I know**, autant que je sache. ~ **away** a. lointain. **by** ~, de loin. ~ **from**, loin de. **the Far East**, l'Extrême-Orient *m*. ~**-fetched** a. bizarre, exagéré. ~**-reaching** a. de grande portée.

farc|e /fɑ:s/ n. farce f. ~**ical** a. ridicule, grotesque.

fare /feə(r)/ n. (prix du) billet *m*.; (*food*) nourriture f. ● v.i. (*progress*) aller; (*manage*) se débrouiller.

farewell /feə'wel/ int. & n. adieu (*m*.).

farm /fɑ:m/ n. ferme f. ● v.t. cultiver. ● v.i. être fermier. ~ **out**, céder en sous-traitance. ~ **worker**, ouvri|er, -ère agricole *m*., f. ~**er** n. fermier *m*. ~**ing** n. agriculture f.

farmhouse /'fɑ:mhaus/ n. ferme f.

farmyard /'fɑ:mjɑ:d/ n. basse-cour f.

fart /fɑ:t/ v.i. péter. ● n. pet *m*.

farth|er /'fɑ:ðə(r)/ adv. plus loin. ● a. plus éloigné. ~**est** adv. le plus loin; a. le plus éloigné.

fascinat|e /'fæsɪneɪt/ v.t. fasciner. ~**ion** /-'neɪʃn/ n. fascination f.

Fascis|t /'fæʃɪst/ n. fasciste *m*./f. ~**m** /-zəm/ n. fascisme *m*.

fashion /'fæʃn/ n. (*current style*) mode f.; (*manner*) façon f. ● v.t. façonner. ~ **designer**, styliste *m*./f. **in** ~, à la mode. **out of** ~, démodé. ~**able** a., ~**ably** adv. à la mode.

fast[1] /fɑ:st/ a. (**-er**, **-est**) rapide; (*colour*) grand teint *invar.*, fixe; (*firm*) fixe, solide. ● adv. vite; (*firmly*) ferme. **be** ~, (*clock etc.*) avancer. ~ **asleep**, profondément endormi. ~ **food**, fast food *m*. restauration rapide f.

fast[2] /fɑ:st/ v.i. (*go without food*) jeûner. ● n. jeûne *m*.

fasten /'fɑ:sn/ v.t./i. (s')attacher. ~**er**, ~**ing** ns. attache f., fermeture f.

fastidious /fə'stɪdɪəs/ a. difficile.

fat /fæt/ n. graisse f.; (*on meat*) gras *m*. ● a. (**fatter**, **fattest**) gros, gras; (*meat*) gras; (*sum*, *volume*: *fig.*) gros. **a** ~ **lot**, (*sl.*) bien peu (**of**, de). ~**head** n. (*fam.*) imbécile *m*./f. ~**ness** n. corpulence f.

fatal /'feɪtl/ a. mortel; (*fateful*, *disastrous*) fatal. ~**ity** /fə'tælətɪ/ n. mort *m*. ~**ly** adv. mortellement.

fatalist /'feɪtəlɪst/ n. fataliste *m*./f.

fate /feɪt/ n. (*controlling power*) destin *m*., sort *m*.; (*one's lot*) sort *m*. ~**ful** a. fatidique.

fated /'feɪtɪd/ a. destiné (**to**, à).

father /'fɑ:ðə(r)/ n. père *m*. ~**-in-law** n. (*pl.* ~**s-in-law**) beau-père *m*. ~**hood** n. paternité f. ~**ly** a. paternel.

fathom /'fæðəm/ n. brasse f. (= *1.8 m.*). ● v.t. ~ (**out**), comprendre.

fatigue /fə'ti:g/ n. fatigue f. ● v.t. fatiguer.

fatten /'fætn/ v.t./i. engraisser. ~**ing** a. qui fait grossir.

fatty /'fætɪ/ a. gras; (*tissue*) adipeux. ● n. (*person*: *fam.*) gros(se) *m*. (f.).

fatuous /'fætʃʊəs/ a. stupide.

faucet /'fɔ:sɪt/ n. (*Amer.*) robinet *m*.

fault /fɔ:lt/ n. (*defect*, *failing*) défaut *m*.; (*blame*) faute f.; (*geol.*) faille f. ● v.t. ~ **sth./s.o.**, trouver des défauts à qch./chez qn. **at** ~, fautif. ~**less** a. irréprochable. ~**y** a. défectueux.

fauna /'fɔ:nə/ n. faune f.

favour, (*Amer.*) **favor** /'feɪvə(r)/ n. faveur f. ● v.t. favoriser; (*support*) être en faveur de; (*prefer*) préférer. **do s.o. a** ~, rendre service à qn. **in** ~ **of**, pour. ~**able** a. favorable. ~**ably** adv. favorablement.

favourit|e /'feɪvərɪt/ a. & n. favori(te) (*m*. (f.)). ~**ism** n. favoritisme *m*.

fawn[1] /fɔ:n/ n. faon *m*. ● a. fauve.

fawn[2] /fɔ:n/ v.i. ~ **on**, flatter bassement, flagorner.

fax /fæks/ n. fax *m*., télécopie f. ● v.t. faxer, envoyer par télécopie. ~ **machine**, télécopieur *m*.

FBI abbr. (*Federal Bureau of Investigation*) (*Amer.*) service d'enquêtes du Ministère de la Justice *m*.

fear /fɪə(r)/ n. crainte f., peur f.; (*fig.*) risque *m*. ● v.t. craindre. **for** ~ **of/that**, de peur de/que. ~**ful** a. (*terrible*) affreux; (*timid*) craintif. ~**less** a. intrépide. ~**lessness** n. intrépidité f.

fearsome /'fɪəsəm/ a. redoutable.

feasib|le /'fi:zəbl/ a. faisable; (*likely*) plausible. ~**ility** /-'bɪlətɪ/ n. possibilité f.; plausibilité f.

feast /fi:st/ n. festin *m*.; (*relig.*) fête f. ● v.i. festoyer. ● v.t. régaler. ~ **on**, se régaler de.

feat /fi:t/ n. exploit *m*.

feather /'feðə(r)/ n. plume f. ● v.t. ~ **one's nest**, s'enrichir. ~ **duster**, plumeau *m*.

featherweight /ˈfeðəweɪt/ n. poids plume m. invar.

feature /ˈfiːtʃə(r)/ n. caractéristique f.; (of person, face) trait m.; (film) long métrage m.; (article) article vedette m. ● v.t. représenter; (give prominence to) mettre en vedette. ● v.i. figurer (**in**, dans).

February /ˈfebruəri/ n. février m.

feckless /ˈfekləs/ a. inepte.

fed /fed/ see **feed**. ● a. **be ~ up**, (fam.) en avoir marre (**with**, de).

federa|**l** /ˈfedərəl/ a. fédéral. **~tion** /-ˈreɪʃn/ n. fédération f.

fee /fiː/ n. (for entrance) prix m.; (of doctor etc.) honoraires m. pl.; (of actor, artist) cachet m.; (for tuition) frais m. pl.; (for enrolment) droits m. pl.

feeble /ˈfiːbl/ a. (-**er**, -**est**) faible. **~-minded** a. faible d'esprit.

feed /fiːd/ v.t. (p.t. **fed**) nourrir, donner à manger à; (suckle) allaiter; (supply) alimenter. ● v.i. se nourrir (**on**, de). ● n. nourriture f.; (of baby) tétée f. **~ in information**, rentrer des données. **~er** n. alimentation f.

feedback /ˈfiːdbæk/ n. réaction(s) f. (pl.); (med., techn.) feed-back m.

feel /fiːl/ v.t. (p.t. **felt**) (touch) tâter; (be conscious of) sentir; (emotion) ressentir; (experience) éprouver; (think) estimer. ● v.i. (tired, lonely, etc.) se sentir. **~ hot/thirsty**/etc., avoir chaud/soif/etc. **~ as if**, avoir l'impression que. **~ awful**, (ill) se sentir malade. **~ like**, (want: fam.) avoir envie de.

feeler /ˈfiːlə(r)/ n. antenne f. **put out a ~**, lancer un ballon d'essai.

feeling /ˈfiːlɪŋ/ n. sentiment m.; (physical) sensation f.

feet /fiːt/ see **foot**.

feign /feɪn/ v.t. feindre.

feint /feɪnt/ n. feinte f.

felicitous /fəˈlɪsɪtəs/ a. heureux.

feline /ˈfiːlaɪn/ a. félin.

fell [1] /fel/ v.t. (cut down) abattre.

fell [2] /fel/ see **fall**.

fellow /ˈfeləʊ/ n. compagnon m., camarade m.; (of society) membre m.; (man: fam.) type m. **~-countryman** n. compatriote m. **~-passenger**, **~-traveller** n. compagnon de voyage m. **~ship** n. camaraderie f.; (group) association f.

felony /ˈfeləni/ n. crime m.

felt [1] /felt/ n. feutre m. **~-tip** n. feutre m.

felt [2] /felt/ see **feel**.

female /ˈfiːmeɪl/ a. (animal etc.) femelle; (voice, sex, etc.) féminin. ● n. femme f.; (animal) femelle f.

feminin|**e** /ˈfemənɪn/ a. & n. féminin (m.). **~ity** /-ˈnɪnɪti/ n. féminité f.

feminist /ˈfemɪnɪst/ n. féministe m./f.

fenc|**e** /fens/ n. barrière f.; (person: jurid.) receleu|r, -se m., f. ● v.t. **~e (in)**, clôturer. ● v.i. (sport) faire de l'escrime. **~er** n. escrimeu|r, -se m., f. **~ing** n. escrime f.

fend /fend/ v.i. **~ for o.s.**, se débrouiller tout seul. ● v.t. **~ off**, (blow, attack) parer.

fender /ˈfendə(r)/ n. (for fireplace) garde-feu m. invar.; (mudguard: Amer.) garde-boue m. invar.

fennel /ˈfenl/ n. (culin.) fenouil m.

ferment [1] /fəˈment/ v.t./i. (faire) fermenter. **~ation** /fɜːmenˈteɪʃn/ n. fermentation f.

ferment [2] /ˈfɜːment/ n. ferment m.; (excitement: fig.) agitation f.

fern /fɜːn/ n. fougère f.

feroc|**ious** /fəˈrəʊʃəs/ a. féroce. **~ity** /-ˈrɒsəti/ n. férocité f.

ferret /ˈferɪt/ n. (animal) furet m. ● v.i. (p.t. **ferreted**) fureter. ● v.t. **~ out**, dénicher.

ferry /ˈferi/ n. ferry m., bac m. ● v.t. transporter.

fertil|**e** /ˈfɜːtaɪl, Amer. ˈfɜːtl/ a. fertile; (person, animal) fécond. **~ity** /fəˈtɪləti/ n. fertilité f.; fécondité f. **~ize** /-əlaɪz/ v.t. fertiliser; féconder.

fertilizer /ˈfɜːtəlaɪzə(r)/ n. engrais m.

fervent /ˈfɜːvənt/ a. fervent.

fervour /ˈfɜːvə(r)/ n. ferveur f.

fester /ˈfestə(r)/ v.i. (wound) suppurer; (fig.) rester sur le cœur.

festival /ˈfestɪvl/ n. festival m.; (relig.) fête f.

festiv|**e** /ˈfestɪv/ a. de fête, gai. **~e season**, période des fêtes f. **~ity** /feˈstɪvəti/ n. réjouissances f. pl.

festoon /feˈstuːn/ v.i. **~ with**, orner de.

fetch /fetʃ/ v.t. (go for) aller chercher; (bring person) amener; (bring thing) apporter; (be sold for) rapporter.

fête /feɪt/ n. fête f. ● v.t. fêter.

fetid /ˈfetɪd/ a. fétide.

fetish /ˈfetɪʃ/ n. (object) fétiche m.; (psych.) obsession f.

fetter /ˈfetə(r)/ v.t. enchaîner. **~s** n. pl. chaînes f. pl.

feud /fjuːd/ n. querelle f.

feudal /ˈfjuːdl/ a. féodal.

fever /ˈfiːvə(r)/ n. fièvre f. **~ish** a. fiévreux.

few /fjuː/ a. & n. peu (de). **~ books**, peu de livres. **they are ~**, ils sont peu nombreux. **a ~** a. quelques; n. quelques-un(e)s. **a good ~**, **quite a ~**, (fam.) bon nombre (de). **~er** a. & n. moins (de). **be ~er**, être moins nombreux (**than**, que). **~est** a. & n. le moins (de).

fiancé /frˈɒnseɪ/ n. fiancé m.

fiancée /frˈɒnseɪ/ n. fiancée f.

fiasco /frˈæskəʊ/ n. (pl. -os) fiasco m.

fib /fɪb/ n. mensonge m. **~ber** n. menteu|r, -se m., f.

fibre, Amer. **fiber** /ˈfaɪbə(r)/ n. fibre f. **~ optics**, fibres optiques.

fibreglass, Amer. **fiberglass** /ˈfaɪbəglɑːs/ n. fibre de verre f.

fickle /ˈfɪkl/ a. inconstant.

fiction /ˈfɪkʃn/ n. fiction f. **(works of) ~**, romans m. pl. **~al** a. fictif.

fictitious /fɪkˈtɪʃəs/ a. fictif.

fiddle /ˈfɪdl/ n. (fam.) violon m.; (swindle: sl.) combine f. ● v.i. (sl.) frauder. ● v.t. (sl.) falsifier. **~ with**, (fam.) tripoter. **~r** /-ə(r)/ n. (fam.) violoniste m./f.

fidelity /frˈdelətɪ/ n. fidélité f.

fidget /ˈfɪdʒɪt/ v.i. (p.t. **fidgeted**) remuer sans cesse. ● n. **be a ~**, être remuant. **~ with**, tripoter. **~y** a. remuant.

field /fiːld/ n. champ m.; (sport) terrain m.; (fig.) domaine m. ● v.t. (ball: cricket) bloquer. **~-day** n. grande occasion f. **~-glasses** n. pl. jumelles f. pl. **F~ Marshal**, maréchal m.

fieldwork /ˈfiːldwɜːk/ n. travaux pratiques m. pl.

fiend /fiːnd/ n. démon m. **~ish** a. diabolique.

fierce /fɪəs/ a. (-er, -est) féroce; (storm, attack) violent. **~ness** n. férocité f.; violence f.

fiery /ˈfaɪərɪ/ a. (-ier, -iest) (hot) ardent; (spirited) fougueux.

fiesta /frˈestə/ n. fiesta f.

fifteen /fɪfˈtiːn/ a. & n. quinze (m.). **~th** a. & n. quinzième (m./f.).

fifth /fɪfθ/ a. & n. cinquième (m./f.). **~ column**, cinquième colonne f.

fift|y /ˈfɪftɪ/ a. & n. cinquante (m.). **~ieth** a. & n. cinquantième (m./f.).

a ~y-fifty chance, (equal) une chance sur deux.

fig /fɪg/ n. figue f.

fight /faɪt/ v.i. (p.t. **fought**) se battre; (struggle: fig.) lutter; (quarrel) se disputer. ● v.t. se battre avec; (evil etc.: fig.) lutter contre. ● n. (struggle) lutte f.; (quarrel) dispute f.; (brawl) bagarre f.; (mil.) combat m. **~ back**, se défendre. **~ off**, surmonter. **~ over sth.**, se disputer qch. **~ shy of**, fuir devant. **~er** n. (brawler, soldier) combattant m.; (fig.) battant m.; (aircraft) chasseur m. **~ing** n. combats m. pl.

figment /ˈfɪgmənt/ n. invention f.

figurative /ˈfɪgjərətɪv/ a. figuré.

figure /ˈfɪgə(r)/ n. (number) chiffre m.; (diagram) figure f.; (shape) forme f.; (body) ligne f. **~s**, arithmétique f. ● v.t. s'imaginer. ● v.i. (appear) figurer. **~ out**, comprendre. **~-head** n. (person with no real power) prête-nom m. **~ of speech**, façon de parler f. **that ~s**, (Amer., fam.) c'est logique.

filament /ˈfɪləmənt/ n. filament m.

filch /fɪltʃ/ v.t. voler, piquer.

file[1] /faɪl/ n. (tool) lime f. ● v.t. limer. **~ings** n. pl. limaille f.

file[2] /faɪl/ n. dossier m.; classeur m.; (comput.) fichier m.; (row) file f. ● v.t. (papers) classer; (jurid.) déposer. ● v.i. **~ in**, entrer en file. **~ past**, défiler devant. **~ing cabinet**, classeur m.

fill /fɪl/ v.t./i. remplir. ● n. **eat one's ~**, manger à sa faim. **have had one's ~**, en avoir assez. **~ in**, (form) remplir. **~ out**, (get fat) grossir. **~ up**, (auto.) faire le plein (d'essence).

fillet /ˈfɪlɪt, Amer. frˈleɪ/ n. filet m. ● v.t. (p.t. **filleted**) découper en filets.

filling /ˈfɪlɪŋ/ n. (of tooth) plombage m.; (of sandwich) garniture f. **~ station**, station-service f.

filly /ˈfɪlɪ/ n. pouliche f.

film /fɪlm/ n. film m.; (photo.) pellicule f. ● v.t. filmer. **~-goer** n. cinéphile m./f. **~ star**, vedette de cinéma f.

filter /ˈfɪltə(r)/ n. filtre m.; (traffic signal) flèche f. ● v.t./i.p. filtrer; (of traffic) suivre la flèche. **~ coffee**, café-filtre m. **~-tip** n. bout filtre m.

filth /fɪlθ/, **~iness** /fɪlθ, fɪlθɪnəs/ n. saleté f. **~y** a. sale.

fin /fɪn/ *n.* (*of fish, seal*) nageoire *f.*; (*of shark*) aileron *m.*

final /faml/ *a.* dernier; (*conclusive*) définitif. ● *n.* (*sport*) finale *f.* ~**ist** *n.* finaliste *m./f.* ~**ly** *adv.* (*lastly, at last*) enfin, finalement; (*once and for all*) définitivement.

finale /fɪ'nɑːlɪ/ *n.* (*mus.*) final(e) *m.*

finalize /'faɪnəlaɪz/ *v.t.* mettre au point, fixer.

financ|e /'faɪnæns/ *n.* finance *f.* ● *a.* financier. ● *v.t.* financer. ~**ier** /-'nænsɪə(r)/ *n.* financier *m.*

financial /faɪ'nænʃl/ *a.* financier. ~**ly** *adv.* financièrement.

find /faɪnd/ *v.t.* (*p.t.* **found**) trouver; (*sth. lost*) retrouver. ● *n.* trouvaille *f.* ~ **out** *v.t.* découvrir; *v.i.* se renseigner (**about**, sur). ~**ings** *n. pl.* conclusions *f. pl.*

fine[1] /faɪn/ *n.* amende *f.* ● *v.t.* condamner à une amende.

fine[2] /faɪn/ *a.* (**-er, -est**) fin; (*excellent*) beau. ● *adv.* (très) bien; (*small*) fin. ~ **arts**, beaux-arts *m. pl.* ~**ly** *adv.* (*admirably*) magnifiquement; (*cut*) fin.

finery /'faɪnərɪ/ *n.* atours *m. pl.*

finesse /fɪ'nes/ *n.* finesse *f.*

finger /'fɪŋgə(r)/ *n.* doigt *m.* ● *v.t.* palper. ~**-nail** *n.* ongle *m.* ~**-stall** *n.* doigtier *m.*

fingerprint /'fɪŋgəprɪnt/ *n.* empreinte digitale *f.*

fingertip /'fɪŋgətɪp/ *n.* bout du doigt *m.*

finicking, finicky /'fɪnɪkɪŋ, 'fɪnɪkɪ/ *adjs.* méticuleux.

finish /'fɪnɪʃ/ *v.t./i.* finir. ● *n.* fin *f.*; (*of race*) arrivée *f.*; (*appearance*) finition *f.* ~ **doing**, finir de faire. ~ **up doing**, finir par faire. ~ **up in**, (*land up in*) se retrouver à.

finite /'faɪnaɪt/ *a.* fini.

Fin|land /'fɪnlənd/ *n.* Finlande *f.* ~**n** *n.* Finlandais(e) *m.* (*f.*). ~**nish** *a.* finlandais; *n.* (*lang.*) finnois *m.*

fir /fɜː(r)/ *n.* sapin *m.*

fire /faɪə(r)/ *n.* feu *m.*; (*conflagration*) incendie *m.*; (*heater*) radiateur *m.* ● *v.t.* (*bullet etc.*) tirer; (*dismiss*) renvoyer; (*fig.*) enflammer. ● *v.i.* tirer (**at**, sur). ~ **a gun**, tirer un coup de revolver *or* de fusil. **set ~ to**, mettre le feu à. ~ **alarm**, avertisseur d'incendie *m.* ~ **brigade**, pompiers *m. pl.* ~**-engine** *n.* voiture de pompiers *m.* ~**-escape** *n.* escalier de secours *m.* ~ **extinguisher**, ex-

tincteur d'incendie *m.* ~ **station**, caserne de pompiers *f.*

firearm /'faɪərɑːm/ *n.* arme à feu *f.*

firecracker /'faɪəkrækə(r)/ *n.* (*Amer.*) pétard *m.*

firelight /'faɪəlaɪt/ *n.* lueur du feu *f.*

fireman /'faɪəmən/ *n.* (*pl.* **-men**) pompier *m.*

fireplace /'faɪəpleɪs/ *n.* cheminée *f.*

fireside /'faɪəsaɪd/ *n.* coin du feu *m.*

firewood /'faɪəwʊd/ *n.* bois de chauffage *m.*

firework /'faɪəwɜːk/ *n.* feu d'artifice *m.*

firing-squad /'faɪərɪŋskwɒd/ *n.* peloton d'exécution *m.*

firm[1] /fɜːm/ *n.* firme *f.*, société *f.*

firm[2] /fɜːm/ *a.* (**-er, -est**) ferme; (*belief*) solide. ~**ly** *adv.* fermement. ~**ness** *n.* fermeté *f.*

first /fɜːst/ *a.* premier. ● *n.* prem|ier, -ière *m.,f.* ● *adv.* d'abord, premièrement; (*arrive etc.*) le premier, la première. **at ~**, d'abord. **at ~ hand**, de première main. **at ~ sight**, à première vue. ~ **aid**, premiers soins *m. pl.* ~**-class** *a.* de première classe. ~ **floor**, (*Amer.*) rez-de-chaussée *m. invar.* ~ **(gear)**, première (vitesse) *f.* **F~ Lady**, (*Amer.*) épouse du Président *f.* ~ **name**, prénom *m.* ~ **of all**, tout d'abord. ~**-rate** *a.* de premier ordre. ~**ly** *adv.* premièrement.

fiscal /'fɪskl/ *a.* fiscal.

fish /fɪʃ/ *n.* (*usually invar.*) poisson *m.* ● *v.i.* pêcher. ~ **for**, (*cod etc.*) pêcher. ~ **out**, (*from water*) repêcher; (*take out: fam.*) sortir. ~ **shop**, poissonnerie *f.* ~**ing** *n.* pêche *f.* **go ~ing**, aller à la pêche. ~**ing rod**, canne à pêche *f.* ~**y** *a.* de poisson; (*fig.*) louche.

fisherman /'fɪʃəmən/ *n.* (*pl.* **-men**) *n.* pêcheur *m.*

fishmonger /'fɪʃmʌŋgə(r)/ *n.* pois-sonn|ier, -ière *m.,f.*

fission /'fɪʃn/ *n.* fission *f.*

fist /fɪst/ *n.* poing *m.*

fit[1] /fɪt/ *n.* (*bout*) accès *m.*, crise *f.*

fit[2] /fɪt/ *a.* (**fitter, fittest**) en bonne santé; (*proper*) convenable; (*good enough*) bon; (*able*) capable. ● *v.t./i.* (*p.t.* **fitted**) (*clothes*) aller (à); (*match*) s'accorder (avec); (*put or go in or on*) (s')adapter (**to**, à); (*into space*) aller; (*install*) poser. ● *n.* **be a good ~**, (*dress*) être à la bonne taille. **in no ~ state to do**, pas en état de faire. **~ in**, v.t. caser; v.i. (newcomer) s'intégrer. **~ out, ~ up**, équiper. **~ness** n. santé f.; (of remark) justesse f.

fitful /'fɪtfl/ a. irrégulier.

fitment /'fɪtmənt/ n. meuble fixe m.

fitted /'fɪtɪd/ a. (wardrobe) encastré. **~ carpet**, moquette f.

fitting /'fɪtɪŋ/ a. approprié. ● n. essayage m. **~ room**, cabine d'essayage f.

fittings /'fɪtɪŋz/ n. pl. (in house) installations f. pl.

five /faɪv/ a. & n. cinq (m.).

fiver /'faɪvə(r)/ n. (fam.) billet de cinq livres m.

fix /fɪks/ v.t. (make firm, attach, decide) fixer; (mend) réparer; (deal with) arranger. ● n. **in a ~**, dans le pétrin. **~ s.o. up with sth.**, trouver qch. à qn. **~ed** a. fixe.

fixation /fɪk'seɪʃn/ n. fixation f.

fixture /'fɪkstʃə(r)/ n. (sport) match m. **~s**, (in house) installations f. pl.

fizz /fɪz/ v.i. pétiller. ● n. pétillement m. **~y** a. gazeux.

fizzle /'fɪzl/ v.i. pétiller. **~ out**, (plan etc.) finir en queue de poisson.

flab /flæb/ n. (fam.) corpulence f. **~by** /'flæbɪ/ a. flasque.

flabbergast /'flæbəgɑːst/ v.t. sidérer, ahurir.

flag[1] /flæg/ n. drapeau m.; (naut.) pavillon m. ● v.t. (p.t. flagged). **~ (down)**, faire signe de s'arrêter à. **~-pole** n. mât m.

flag[2] /flæg/ v.i. (p.t. flagged) (weaken) faiblir; (sick person) s'affaiblir; (droop) dépérir.

flagon /'flægən/ n. bouteille f.

flagrant /'fleɪgrənt/ a. flagrant.

flagstone /'flægstəʊn/ n. dalle f.

flair /fleə(r)/ n. flair m.

flak /flæk/ n. (fam.) critiques f. pl.

flak|e /fleɪk/ n. flocon m.; (of paint, metal) écaille f. ● v.i. s'écailler. **~y** a. (paint) écailleux.

flamboyant /flæm'bɔɪənt/ a. (colour) éclatant; (manner) extravagant.

flame /fleɪm/ n. flamme f. ● v.i. flamber. **burst into ~s**, exploser. **go up in ~s**, brûler.

flamingo /flə'mɪŋgəʊ/ n. (pl. -os) flamant (rose) m.

flammable /'flæməbl/ a. inflammable.

flan /flæn/ n. tarte f.; (custard tart) flan m.

flank /flæŋk/ n. flanc m. ● v.t. flanquer.

flannel /'flænl/ n. flannelle f.; (for face) gant de toilette m.

flannelette /flænə'let/ n. pilou m.

flap /flæp/ v.i. (p.t. flapped) battre. ● v.t. **its wings**, battre des ailes. ● n. (of pocket) rabat m.; (of table) abattant m. **get into a ~**, (fam.) s'affoler.

flare /fleə(r)/ v.i. **~ up**, s'enflammer, flamber; (fighting) éclater; (person) s'emporter. ● n. flamboiement m.; (mil.) fusée éclairante f.; (in skirt) évasement m. **~d** a. (skirt) évasé.

flash /flæʃ/ v.i. briller; (on and off) clignoter. ● v.t. faire briller; (aim torch) diriger (at, sur); (flaunt) étaler. ● n. éclair m., éclat m.; (of news, camera) flash m. **in a ~**, en un éclair. **~ one's headlights**, faire un appel de phares. **~ past**, passer à toute vitesse.

flashback /'flæʃbæk/ n. retour en arrière m.

flashlight /'flæʃlaɪt/ n. (torch) lampe électrique f.

flashy /'flæʃɪ/ a. voyant.

flask /flɑːsk/ n. flacon m.; (vacuum flask) thermos m./f. invar. (P.).

flat /flæt/ a. (flatter, flattest) plat; (tyre) à plat; (refusal) catégorique; (fare, rate) fixe. ● adv. (say) carrément. ● n. (rooms) appartement m.; (tyre: fam.) crevaison f.; (mus.) bémol m. **~ out**, (drive) à toute vitesse; (work) d'arrache-pied. **~-pack** a. en kit. **~ly** adv. catégoriquement. **~ness** n. égalité f.

flatten /'flætn/ v.t./i. (s')aplatir.

flatter /'flætə(r)/ v.t. flatter. **~er** n. flatteu|r, -se m., f. **~ing** a. flatteur. **~y** n. flatterie f.

flatulence /'flætjʊləns/ n. flatulence f.

flaunt /flɔːnt/ v.t. étaler, afficher.

flautist /'flɔːtɪst/ n. flûtiste m./f.

flavour, (Amer.) **flavor** /'fleɪvə(r)/ n. goût m.; (of ice-cream etc.) parfum m. ● v.t. parfumer, assaisonner. **~ing** n. arôme artificiel m.

flaw /flɔː/ n. défaut m. **~ed** a. imparfait. **~less** a. parfait.

flax /flæks/ n. lin m. **~en** a. de lin.

flea /fliː/ n. puce f. **~ market**, marché aux puces m.

fleck /flek/ n. petite tache f.

fled /fled/ see flee.

fledged /fledʒd/ a. fully-~, (*doctor etc.*) diplômé; (*member, citizen*) à part entière.

flee /fliː/ v.i. (*p.t.* **fled**) s'enfuir. ● v.t. s'enfuir de; (*danger*) fuir.

fleece /fliːs/ n. toison f. ● v.t. voler.

fleet /fliːt/ n. (*naut., aviat.*) flotte f. **a ~ of vehicles**, un parc automobile.

fleeting /ˈfliːtɪŋ/ a. très bref.

Flemish /ˈflemɪʃ/ a. flamand. ● n. (*lang.*) flamand m.

flesh /fleʃ/ n. chair f. **one's (own) ~ and blood**, les siens m. pl. **~y** a. charnu.

flew /fluː/ *see* fly².

flex /fleks/ v.t. (*knee etc.*) fléchir; (*muscle*) faire jouer.

flex² /fleks/ n. (*electr.*) fil souple m.

flexib|le /ˈfleksəbl/ a. flexible. **~ility** /-ˈbɪlətɪ/ n. flexibilité f.

flexitime /ˈfleksɪtaɪm/ n. horaire variable m.

flick /flɪk/ n. petit coup m. ● v.t. donner un petit coup à. **~-knife** n. couteau à cran d'arrêt m. **~ through**, feuilleter.

flicker /ˈflɪkə(r)/ v.i. vaciller. ● n. vacillement m.; (*light*) lueur f.

flier /ˈflaɪə(r)/ n. = **flyer**.

flies /flaɪz/ n. pl. (*on trousers: fam.*) braguette f.

flight¹ /flaɪt/ n. (*of bird, plane, etc.*) vol m. **~-deck** n. poste de pilotage m. **~ of stairs**, escalier m.

flight² /flaɪt/ n. (*fleeing*) fuite f. **put to ~**, mettre en fuite. **take ~**, prendre la fuite.

flimsy /ˈflɪmzɪ/ a. (**-ier, -iest**) (*pej.*) mince, peu solide.

flinch /flɪntʃ/ v.i. (*wince*) broncher; (*draw back*) reculer.

fling /flɪŋ/ v.t. (*p.t.* **flung**) jeter. ● n. **have a ~**, faire la fête.

flint /flɪnt/ n. silex m.; (*for lighter*) pierre f.

flip /flɪp/ v.t. (*p.t.* **flipped**) donner un petit coup à. ● n. chiquenaude f. **~ through**, feuilleter. **~-flops** n. pl. tongs f. pl.

flippant /ˈflɪpənt/ a. désinvolte.

flipper /ˈflɪpə(r)/ n. (*of seal etc.*) nageoire f.; (*of swimmer*) palme f.

flirt /flɜːt/ v.i. flirter. ● n. flirteu|r, -se m., f. **~ation** /-ˈteɪʃn/ n. flirt m.

flit /flɪt/ v.i. (*p.t.* **flitted**) voltiger.

float /fləʊt/ v.t./i. (faire) flotter. ● n. flotteur m.; (*cart*) char m.

flock /flɒk/ n. (*of sheep etc.*) troupeau m.; (*of people*) foule f. ● v.i. venir en foule.

flog /flɒg/ v.t. (*p.t.* **flogged**) (*beat*) fouetter; (*sell: sl.*) vendre.

flood /flʌd/ n. inondation f.; (*fig.*) flot m. ● v.t. inonder. ● v.i. (*building etc.*) être inondé; (*river*) déborder; (*people: fig.*) affluer.

floodlight /ˈflʌdlaɪt/ n. projecteur m. ● v.t. (*p.t.* **floodlit**) illuminer.

floor /flɔː(r)/ n. sol m., plancher m.; (*for dancing*) piste f.; (*storey*) étage m. ● v.t. (*knock down*) terrasser; (*baffle*) stupéfier. **~-board** n. planche f.

flop /flɒp/ v.i. (*p.t.* **flopped**) s'agiter faiblement; (*drop*) s'affaler; (*fail: sl.*) échouer. ● n. (*sl.*) échec m., fiasco m. **~py** a. lâche, flasque. **~py (disk)**, disquette f.

flora /ˈflɔːrə/ n. flore f.

floral /ˈflɔːrəl/ a. floral.

florid /ˈflɒrɪd/ a. fleuri.

florist /ˈflɒrɪst/ n. fleuriste m./f.

flounce /flaʊns/ n. volant m.

flounder¹ /ˈflaʊndə(r)/ v.i. patauger (avec difficulté).

flounder² /ˈflaʊndə(r)/ n. (*fish: Amer.*) carrelet m., plie f.

flour /ˈflaʊə(r)/ n. farine f. **~y** a. farineux.

flourish /ˈflʌrɪʃ/ v.i. prospérer. ● v.t. brandir. ● n. geste élégant m.; (*curve*) fioriture f.

flout /flaʊt/ v.t. faire fi de.

flow /fləʊ/ v.i. couler; (*circulate*) circuler; (*traffic*) s'écouler; (*hang loosely*) flotter. ● n. (*of liquid, traffic*) écoulement m.; (*of tide*) flux m.; (*of orders, words: fig.*) flot m. **~ chart**, organigramme m. **~ in**, affluer. **~ into**, (*of river*) se jeter dans.

flower /ˈflaʊə(r)/ n. fleur f. ● v.i. fleurir. **~-bed** n. plate-bande f. **~ed** a. à fleurs. **~y** a. fleuri.

flown /fləʊn/ *see* fly².

flu /fluː/ n. (*fam.*) grippe f.

fluctuat|e /ˈflʌktʃʊeɪt/ v.i. varier. **~ion** /-ˈeɪʃn/ n. variation f.

flue /fluː/ n. (*duct*) tuyau m.

fluen|t /ˈfluːənt/ a. (*style*) aisé. **be ~t (in a language)**, parler (une langue) couramment. **~cy** n. facilité f. **~tly** adv. avec facilité; (*lang.*) couramment.

fluff /flʌf/ n. peluche(s) f. (*pl.*); (*down*) duvet m. **~y** a. pelucheux.

fluid /'fluːɪd/ *a. & n.* fluide (*m.*).

fluke /fluːk/ *n.* coup de chance *m.*

flung /flʌŋ/ *see* fling.

flunk /flʌŋk/ *v.t./i.* (*Amer., fam.*) être collé (à).

fluorescent /flʊə'resnt/ *a.* fluorescent.

fluoride /'flɔːraɪd/ *n.* (*in toothpaste, water*) fluor *m.*

flurry /'flʌrɪ/ *n.* (*squall*) rafale *f.*; (*fig.*) agitation *f.*

flush¹ /flʌʃ/ *v.i.* rougir. ● *v.t.* nettoyer à grande eau. ● *n.* (*blush*) rougeur *f.*; (*fig.*) excitation *f.* ● *a.* ~ **with**, (*level with*) au ras de. ~ **the toilet**, tirer la chasse d'eau.

flush² /flʌʃ/ *v.t.* ~ **out**, chasser.

fluster /'flʌstə(r)/ *v.t.* énerver.

flute /fluːt/ *n.* flûte *f.*

flutter /'flʌtə(r)/ *v.i.* voleter (*of wings*) battre. ● *n.* (*of wings*) battement *m.*; (*fig.*) agitation *f.*; (*bet: fam.*) pari *m.*

flux /flʌks/ *n.* changement continuel *m.*

fly¹ /flaɪ/ *n.* mouche *f.*

fly² /flaɪ/ *v.i.* (*p.t.* flew, *p.p.* flown) voler; (*of passengers*) voyager en avion; (*of flag*) flotter; (*rush*) filer. ● *v.t.* (*aircraft*) piloter; (*passengers, goods*) transporter par avion; (*flag*), arborer. ● *n.* (*of trousers*) braguette *f.* ~ **off**, s'envoler.

flyer /'flaɪə(r)/ *n.* aviateur *m.*; (*circular: Amer.*) prospectus *m.*

flying /'flaɪɪŋ/ *a.* (*saucer etc.*) volant. ● *n.* (*activity*) aviation *f.* ~ **buttress**, arc-boutant *m.* ~ **with** ~ **colours**, haut la main. ~ **start**, excellent départ *m.* ~ **visit**, visite éclair *f.* (*a. invar.*).

flyover /'flaɪəʊvə(r)/ *n.* (*road*) toboggan *m.*, saut-de-mouton *m.*

flyweight /'flaɪweɪt/ *n.* poids mouche *m.*

foal /fəʊl/ *n.* poulain *m.*

foam /fəʊm/ *n.* écume *f.*, mousse *f.* ● *v.i.* écumer, mousser. ~ (**rubber**) *n.* caoutchouc mousse *m.*

fob /fɒb/ *v.t.* (*p.t.* fobbed) ● ~ **off on (to) s.o.**, (*palm off*) refiler à qn. ~ **s.o. off with**, forcer qn. à se contenter de.

focal /'fəʊkl/ *a.* focal.

focus /'fəʊkəs/ *n.* (*pl.* -cuses *or* -ci /-saɪ/) foyer *m.*; (*fig.*) centre *m.* ● *v.t./i.* (*p.t.* focused) (faire) converger; (*instrument*) mettre au point; (*with camera*) faire la mise au point (**on,**

sur; (*fig.*) (se) concentrer. **be in/out of** ~, être/ne pas être au point.

fodder /'fɒdə(r)/ *n.* fourrage *m.*

foe /fəʊ/ *n.* ennemi(e) *m.(f.).*

foetus /'fiːtəs/ *n.* (*pl.* -tuses) fœtus *m.*

fog /fɒg/ *n.* brouillard *m.* ● *v.t./i.* (*p.t.* fogged) (*window etc.*) (s')embuer. ~-**horn** *n.* (*naut.*) corne de brume *f.* ~**gy** *a.* brumeux. **it is** ~**gy**, il fait du brouillard.

fog(e)y /'fəʊgɪ/ *n.* (**old**) ~, vieille baderne *f.*

foible /'fɔɪbl/ *n.* faiblesse *f.*

foil¹ /fɔɪl/ *n.* (*tin foil*) papier d'aluminium *m.*; (*fig.*) repoussoir *m.*

foil² /fɔɪl/ *v.t.* (*thwart*) déjouer.

foist /fɔɪst/ *v.t.* imposer (**on,** à).

fold¹ /fəʊld/ *v.t./i.* (se) plier; (*arms*) croiser; (*fail*) s'effondrer. ● *n.* pli *m.* ~**er** *n.* (*file*) chemise *f.*; (*leaflet*) dépliant *m.* ~**ing** *a.* pliant.

fold² /fəʊld/ *n.* (*for sheep*) parc à moutons *m.*; (*relig.*) bercail *m.*

foliage /'fəʊlɪɪdʒ/ *n.* feuillage *m.*

folk /fəʊk/ *n.* gens *m. pl.* ~**s**, parents *m. pl.* ● *a.* folklorique.

folklore /'fəʊklɔː(r)/ *n.* folklore *m.*

follow /'fɒləʊ/ *v.t./i.* suivre. **it** ~**s that**, il s'ensuit que. ~ **suit**, en faire autant. ~ **up**, (*letter etc.*) donner suite à. ~**er** *n.* partisan *m.* ~**ing** *n.* partisans *m. pl.*; *a.* suivant; *prep.* à la suite de.

folly /'fɒlɪ/ *n.* sottise *f.*

foment /fəʊ'ment/ *v.t.* fomenter.

fond /fɒnd/ *a.* (-**er**, -**est**) (*loving*) affectueux; (*hope*) cher. **be** ~ **of,** aimer. ~**ness** *n.* affection *f.*; (*for things*) attachement *m.*

fondle /'fɒndl/ *v.t.* caresser.

food /fuːd/ *n.* nourriture *f.* ● *a.* alimentaire. **French** ~, la cuisine française. ~ **processor**, robot (ménager) *m.*

fool /fuːl/ *n.* idiot(e) *m.* (*f.*). ● *v.t.* duper. ● *v.i.* ~ **around**, faire l'idiot.

foolhardy /'fuːlhɑːdɪ/ *a.* téméraire.

foolish /'fuːlɪʃ/ *a.* idiot. ~**ly** *adv.* sottement. ~**ness** *n.* sottise *f.*

foolproof /'fuːlpruːf/ *a.* infaillible.

foot /fʊt/ *n.* (*pl.* **feet**) pied *m.*; (*measure*) pied *m.* (= 30.48 cm.); (*of stairs, page*) bas *m.* ● *v.t.* (*bill*) payer. ~-**bridge** *n.* passerelle *f.* **on** ~, à pied. **on** *or* **to one's feet**, debout. **under s.o.'s feet**, dans les jambes de qn.

footage /'fʊtɪdʒ/ *n.* (*of film*) métrage *m.*

football /'fʊtbɔːl/ *n.* (*ball*) ballon *m.*; (*game*) football *m.* **~ pools**, paris sur les matchs de football *m. pl.* **~er** *n.* footballeur *m.*

foothills /'fʊthɪlz/ *n. pl.* contreforts *m. pl.*

foothold /'fʊthəʊld/ *n.* prise *f.*

footing /'fʊtɪŋ/ *n.* prise (de pied) *f.*, équilibre *m.*; (*fig.*) situation *f.* **on an equal ~**, sur un pied d'égalité.

footlights /'fʊtlaɪts/ *n. pl.* rampe *f.*

footman /'fʊtmən/ *n.* (*pl.* **-men**) valet de pied *m.*

footnote /'fʊtnəʊt/ *n.* note (en bas de la page) *f.*

footpath /'fʊtpɑːθ/ *n.* sentier *m.*; (*at the side of the road*) chemin *m.*

footprint /'fʊtprɪnt/ *n.* empreinte (de pied) *f.*

footsore /'fʊtsɔː(r)/ *a.* **be ~**, avoir les pieds douloureux.

footstep /'fʊtstep/ *n.* pas *m.*

footwear /'fʊtweə(r)/ *n.* chaussures *f. pl.*

for /fɔː(r), *unstressed* fə(r)/ *prep.* pour; (*during*) pendant; (*before*) avant. ● *conj.* car. **a liking ~**, look **~**, chercher. **pay ~**, payer. **he has been away ~**, il est absent depuis. **he stopped ~ ten minutes**, il s'est arrêté (pendant) dix minutes. **it continues ~ ten kilometres**, ça continue pendant dix kilomètres. **~ ever**, pour toujours. **~ good**, pour de bon. **~ all my work**, malgré mon travail.

forage /'fɒrɪdʒ/ *v.i.* fourrager. ● *n.* fourrage *m.*

foray /'fɒreɪ/ *n.* incursion *f.*

forbade /fə'bæd/ *see* forbid.

forbear /fɔː'beə(r)/ *v.t./i.* (*p.t.* **forbore**, *p.p.* **forborne**) s'abstenir. **~ance** *n.* patience *f.*

forbid /fə'bɪd/ *v.t.* (*p.t.* **forbade**, *p.p.* **forbidden**) interdire, défendre (**s.o. to do**, à qn. de faire). **~ s.o. sth.**, interdire *or* défendre qch. à qn. **you are ~den to leave**, il vous est interdit de partir.

forbidding /fə'bɪdɪŋ/ *a.* menaçant.

force /fɔːs/ *n.* force *f.* ● *v.t.* forcer. **~ into**, faire entrer de force. **~ on**, imposer à. **come into ~**, entrer en vigueur, **the ~s**, les forces armées *f. pl.* **~d** *a.* forcé. **~ful** *a.* énergique.

force-feed /'fɔːsfiːd/ *v.t.* (*p.t.* **-fed**) nourrir de force.

forceps /'fɔːseps/ *n. invar.* forceps *m.*

forcibl|e /'fɔːsəbl/ *a.*, **~y** *adv.* de force.

ford /fɔːd/ *n.* gué *m.* ● *v.t.* passer à gué.

fore /fɔː(r)/ *a.* antérieur. ● *n.* **to the ~**, en évidence.

forearm /'fɔːrɑːm/ *n.* avant-bras *m. invar.*

foreboding /fɔː'bəʊdɪŋ/ *n.* pressentiment *m.*

forecast /'fɔːkɑːst/ *v.t.* (*p.t.* **forecast**) prévoir. ● *n.* prévision *f.*

forecourt /'fɔːkɔːt/ *n.* (*of garage*) devant *m.*; (*of station*) cour *f.*

forefathers /'fɔːfɑːðəz/ *n. pl.* aïeux *m. pl.*

forefinger /'fɔːfɪŋɡə(r)/ *n.* index *m.*

forefront /'fɔːfrʌnt/ *n.* premier rang *m.*

foregone /'fɔːɡɒn/ *a.* **~ conclusion**, résultat à prévoir *m.*

foreground /'fɔːɡraʊnd/ *n.* premier plan *m.*

forehead /'fɒrɪd/ *n.* front *m.*

foreign /'fɒrən/ *a.* étranger; (*trade*) extérieur; (*travel*) à l'étranger. **~er** *n.* étrang|er, -ère *m., f.*

foreman /'fɔːmən/ *n.* (*pl.* **-men**) contremaître *m.*

foremost /'fɔːməʊst/ *a.* le plus éminent. ● *adv.* **first and ~**, tout d'abord.

forename /'fɔːneɪm/ *n.* prénom *m.*

forensic /fə'rensɪk/ *a.* médico-légal. **~ medicine**, médecine légale *f.*

foreplay /'fɔːpleɪ/ *n.* préliminaires *m. pl.*

forerunner /'fɔːrʌnə(r)/ *n.* précurseur *m.*

foresee /fɔː'siː/ *v.t.* (*p.t.* **-saw**, *p.p.* **-seen**) prévoir. **~able** *a.* prévisible.

foreshadow /fɔː'ʃædəʊ/ *v.t.* présager, laisser prévoir.

foresight /'fɔːsaɪt/ *n.* prévoyance *f.*

forest /'fɒrɪst/ *n.* forêt *f.*

forestall /fɔː'stɔːl/ *v.t.* devancer.

forestry /'fɒrɪstrɪ/ *n.* sylviculture *f.*

foretaste /'fɔːteɪst/ *n.* avant-goût *m.*

foretell /fɔː'tel/ *v.t.* (*p.t.* **foretold**) prédire.

forever /fə'revə(r)/ *adv.* toujours.

forewarn /fɔː'wɔːn/ *v.t.* avertir.

foreword /'fɔːwɜːd/ *n.* avant-propos *m. invar.*

forfeit /'fɔːfɪt/ *n.* (*penalty*) peine *f.*; (*in game*) gage *m.* ● *v.t.* perdre.

forgave /fə'ɡeɪv/ *see* forgive.

forge ¹ /fɔːdʒ/ v.i. ~ **ahead**, aller de l'avant, avancer.

forge ² /fɔːdʒ/ n. forge f. ● v.t. (*metal, friendship*) forger; (*copy*) contrefaire, falsifier. ~**r** /-ə(r)/ n. faussaire m. ~**ry** /-ərɪ/ n. faux m., contrefaçon f.

forget /fə'get/ v.t./i. (*p.t.* **forgot**, *p.p.* **forgotten**) oublier. ~-**me-not** n. myosotis m. ~ **o.s.**, s'oublier. ~**ful** a. distrait. ~**ful of**, oublieux de.

forgive /fə'gɪv/ v.t. (*p.t.* **forgave**, *p.p.* **forgiven**) pardonner (**s.o. for sth.**, qch. à qn.). ~**ness** n. pardon m.

forgo /fɔː'gəʊ/ v.t. (*p.t.* **forwent**, *p.p.* **forgone**) renoncer à.

fork /fɔːk/ n. fourchette f.; (*for digging etc.*) fourche f.; (*in road*) bifurcation f. ● v.i. (*road*) bifurquer. ~-**lift truck**, chariot élévateur m. ~ **out**, (*sl.*) payer. ~**ed** a. fourchu.

forlorn /fə'lɔːn/ a. triste, abandonné. ~ **hope**, mince espoir m.

form /fɔːm/ n. forme f.; (*document*) formulaire m.; (*schol.*) classe f. ● v.t./i. (se) former. **on** ~, en forme.

formal /'fɔːml/ a. officiel, en bonne et due forme; (*person*) compassé, cérémonieux; (*dress*) de cérémonie; (*denial, grammar*) formel; (*language*) soutenu. ~**ity** /-'mælətɪ/ n. cérémonial m.; (*requirement*) formalité f. ~**ly** adv. officiellement.

format /'fɔːmæt/ n. format m. ● v.t. (*p.t.* **formatted**) (*disk*) initialiser, formater.

formation /fɔː'meɪʃn/ n. formation f.

formative /'fɔːmətɪv/ a. formateur.

former /'fɔːmə(r)/ a. ancien; (*first of two*) premier. ● n. **the** ~, celui-là, celle-là. ~**ly** adv. autrefois.

formidable /'fɔːmɪdəbl/ a. redoutable, terrible.

formula /'fɔːmjʊlə/ n. (*pl.* -**ae** /-iː/ or -**as**) formule f.

formulate /'fɔːmjʊleɪt/ v.t. formuler.

forsake /fə'seɪk/ v.t. (*p.t.* **forsook**, *p.p.* **forsaken**) abandonner.

fort /fɔːt/ n. (*mil.*) fort m.

forte /'fɔːteɪ/ n. (*talent*) fort m.

forth /fɔːθ/ adv. en avant. **and so** ~, et ainsi de suite. **go back and** ~, aller et venir.

forthcoming /fɔːθ'kʌmɪŋ/ a. à venir, prochain; (*sociable: fam.*) communicatif.

forthright /'fɔːθraɪt/ a. direct.

forthwith /fɔːθ'wɪθ/ adv. sur-le-champ.

fortify /'fɔːtɪfaɪ/ v.t. fortifier. ~**ication** /-ɪ'keɪʃn/ n. fortification f.

fortitude /'fɔːtɪtjuːd/ n. courage m.

fortnight /'fɔːtnaɪt/ n. quinze jours m. pl., quinzaine f. ~**ly** a. bimensuel; adv. tous les quinze jours.

fortress /'fɔːtrɪs/ n. forteresse f.

fortuitous /fɔː'tjuːɪtəs/ a. fortuit.

fortunate /'fɔːtʃənət/ a. heureux. **be** ~, avoir de la chance. ~**ly** adv. heureusement.

fortune /'fɔːtʃuːn/ n. fortune f. ~-**teller** n. diseuse de bonne aventure f. **have the good** ~ **to**, avoir la chance de.

fort|y /'fɔːtɪ/ a. & n. quarante (m.). ~**y winks**, un petit somme. ~**ieth** a. & n. quarantième (m./f.).

forum /'fɔːrəm/ n. forum m.

forward /'fɔːwəd/ a. en avant; (*advanced*) précoce; (*pert*) effronté. ● n. (*sport*) avant m. ● adv. en avant. ● v.t. (*letter*) faire suivre; (*goods*) expédier; (*fig.*) favoriser. **come** ~, se présenter. **go** ~, avancer. ~**ness** n. précocité f.

forwards /'fɔːwədz/ adv. en avant.

fossil /'fɒsl/ n. & a. fossile (m.).

foster /'fɒstə(r)/ v.t. (*promote*) encourager; (*child*) élever. ~-**child** n. enfant adoptif m. ~-**mother** n. mère adoptive f.

fought /fɔːt/ see **fight**.

foul /faʊl/ a. (-**er**, -**est**) (*smell, weather, etc.*) infect; (*place, action*) immonde; (*language*) ordurier. ● n. (*football*) faute f. ● v.t. souiller, encrasser. ~-**mouthed** a. au langage ordurier. ~ **play**, jeu irrégulier m.; (*crime*) acte criminel m. ~ **up**, (*sl.*) gâcher.

found ¹ /faʊnd/ see **find**.

found ² /faʊnd/ v.t. fonder. ~**ation** /-'deɪʃn/ n. fondation f.; (*basis*) fondement m.; (*make-up*) fond de teint m. ~**er** ¹ n. fondateur, -trice m., f.

founder ² /'faʊndə(r)/ v.i. sombrer.

foundry /'faʊndrɪ/ n. fonderie f.

fountain /'faʊntɪn/ n. fontaine f. ~-**pen** n. stylo à encre m.

four /fɔː(r)/ a. & n. quatre (m.). ~**fold** a. quadruple; adv. au quadruple. ~**th** a. & n. quatrième (m./f.). ~-**wheel drive**, quatre roues motrices; (*car*) quatre-quatre m.

foursome /'fɔːsəm/ n. partie à quatre f.

fourteen /fɔːˈtiːn/ a. & n. quatorze (m.). **~th** a. & n. quatorzième (m./ f.).

fowl /faʊl/ n. volaille f.

fox /fɒks/ n. renard m. ● v.t. (baffle) mystifier; (deceive) tromper.

foyer /ˈfɔɪeɪ/ n. (hall) foyer m.

fraction /ˈfrækʃn/ n. fraction f.

fracture /ˈfræktʃə(r)/ n. fracture f. ● v.t./i. (se) fracturer.

fragile /ˈfrædʒaɪl, Amer. ˈfrædʒəl/ a. fragile.

fragment /ˈfrægmənt/ n. fragment m. **~ary** a. fragmentaire.

fragrant /ˈfreɪɡrənt/ a. parfumé. **~ce** n. parfum m.

frail /freɪl/ a. (-er, -est) frêle.

frame /freɪm/ n. charpente f.; (of picture) cadre m.; (of window) châssis m.; (of spectacles) monture f. ● v.t. encadrer; (fig.) formuler; (jurid., sl.) monter un coup contre. **~ of mind**, humeur f.

framework /ˈfreɪmwɜːk/ n. structure f.; (context) cadre m.

franc /fræŋk/ n. franc m.

France /frɑːns/ n. France f.

franchise /ˈfræntʃaɪz/ n. (pol.) droit de vote m.; (comm.) franchise f.

Franco- /ˈfræŋkəʊ/ pref. franco-.

frank [1] /fræŋk/ a. franc. **~ly** adv. franchement. **~ness** n. franchise f.

frank [2] /fræŋk/ v.t. affranchir.

frantic /ˈfræntɪk/ a. frénétique. **~ with**, fou de.

fratern|al /frəˈtɜːnl/ a. fraternel. **~ity** n. (bond) fraternité f.; (group, club) confrérie f.

fraternize /ˈfrætənaɪz/ v.i. fraterniser (with, avec).

fraud /frɔːd/ n. (deception) fraude f.; (person) imposteur m. **~ulent** a. frauduleux.

fraught /frɔːt/ a. (tense) tendu. **~ with**, chargé de.

fray [1] /freɪ/ n. rixe f.

fray [2] /freɪ/ v.t./i. (s')effilocher.

freak /friːk/ n. phénomène m. ● a. anormal. **~ish** a. anormal.

freckle /ˈfrekl/ n. tache de rousseur f. **~d** a. couvert de taches de rousseur.

free /friː/ a. (**freer** /ˈfriːə(r)/, **freest** /ˈfriːɪst/) libre; (gratis) gratuit; (lavish) généreux. ● v.t. (p.t. **freed**) libérer; (clear) dégager. **~ enterprise**, la libre entreprise. **a ~ hand**, carte blanche f. **~ kick**, coup franc m. **~lance** a. & n. free-lance (m./f.), indépendant(e) m., f. **~ (of charge)**,

gratuit(ement). **~-range** a. (eggs) de ferme. **~-wheel** v.i. descendre en roue libre. **~-wheeling** a. sans contraintes. **~ly** adv. librement.

freedom /ˈfriːdəm/ n. liberté f.

Freemason /ˈfriːmeɪsn/ n. franc-maçon m. **~ry** n. francmaçonnerie f.

freeway /ˈfriːweɪ/ n. (Amer.) autoroute f.

freez|e /friːz/ v.t./i. (p.t. **froze**, p.p. **frozen**) geler; (culin.) (se) congeler; (wages etc.) bloquer. ● n. gel m.; blocage m. **~e-dried** a. lyophilisé. **~er** n. congélateur m. **~ing** a. glacial. **below ~ing**, au-dessous de zéro.

freight /freɪt/ n. fret m. **~er** n. (ship) cargo m.

French /frentʃ/ a. français. ● n. (lang.) français m. **~ bean**, haricot vert m. **~ fries**, frites f. pl. **~-speaking** a. francophone. **~ window** n. porte-fenêtre f. **the ~**, les Français m. pl. **~man** n. Français m. **~woman** n. Française f.

frenz|y /ˈfrenzɪ/ n. frénésie f. **~ied** a. frénétique.

frequen|t [1] /ˈfriːkwənt/ a. fréquent. **~cy** n. fréquence f. **~tly** adv. fréquemment.

frequent [2] /frɪˈkwent/ v.t. fréquenter.

fresco /ˈfreskəʊ/ n. (pl. **-os**) fresque f.

fresh /freʃ/ a. (-er, -est) frais; (different, additional) nouveau; (cheeky: fam.) culotté. **~ly** adv. nouvellement. **~ness** n. fraîcheur f.

freshen /ˈfreʃn/ v.i. (weather) fraîchir. **~ up**, (person) se rafraîchir.

fresher /ˈfreʃə(r)/ n., **freshman** /ˈfreʃmən/ n. (pl. **-men**) bizuth m./f.

freshwater /ˈfreʃwɔːtə(r)/ a. d'eau douce.

fret /fret/ v.i. (p.t. **fretted**) se tracasser. **~ful** a. ronchon, insatisfait.

friar /ˈfraɪə(r)/ n. moine m., frère m.

friction /ˈfrɪkʃn/ n. friction f.

Friday /ˈfraɪdɪ/ n. vendredi m.

fridge /frɪdʒ/ n. frigo m.

fried /fraɪd/ see **fry**. ● a. frit. **~ eggs**, œufs sur le plat m. pl.

friend /frend/ n. ami(e) m. (f.). **~ship** n. amitié f.

friend|ly /ˈfrendlɪ/ a. (-ier, -iest) amical, gentil. **F~y Society**, mutuelle f., société de prévoyance f. **~iness** n. gentillesse f.

frieze /friːz/ n. frise f.

frigate /'frɪgət/ n. frégate f.

fright /fraɪt/ n. peur f.; (person, thing) horreur f. **~ful** a. affreux. **~fully** adv. affreusement.

frighten /'fraɪtn/ v.t. effrayer. **~ off**, faire fuir. **~ed** a. effrayé. **be ~ed**, avoir peur (**of**, de). **~ing** a. effrayant.

frigid /'frɪdʒɪd/ a. froid, glacial; (psych.) frigide. **~ity** /-'dʒɪdətɪ/ n. frigidité f.

frill /frɪl/ n. (trimming) fanfreluche f. **with no ~s**, très simple.

fringe /frɪndʒ/ n. (edging, hair) frange f.; (of area) bordure f.; (of society) marge f. **~ benefits**, avantages sociaux m. pl.

frisk /frɪsk/ v.t. (search) fouiller.

frisky /'frɪskɪ/ a. (**-ier, -iest**) fringant, frétillant.

fritter [1] /'frɪtə(r)/ n. beignet m.

fritter [2] /'frɪtə(r)/ v.t. **~ away**, gaspiller.

frivol|ous /'frɪvələs/ a. frivole. **~ity** /-'vɒlɪtɪ/ n. frivolité f.

frizzy /'frɪzɪ/ a. crépu, crêpelé.

fro /frəʊ/ see to and fro.

frock /frɒk/ n. robe f.

frog /frɒg/ n. grenouille f. **a ~ in one's throat**, un chat dans la gorge.

frogman /'frɒgmən/ n. (pl. **-men**) homme-grenouille m.

frolic /'frɒlɪk/ v.i. (p.t. **frolicked**) s'ébattre. ● n. ébats m. pl.

from /frɒm, unstressed frəm/ prep. de; (with time, prices, etc.) à partir de, de; (habit, conviction, etc.) par; (according to) d'après. **take ~ s.o.**, prendre à qn. **take ~ one's pocket**, prendre dans sa poche.

front /frʌnt/ n. (of car, train, etc.) avant m.; (of garment, building) devant m.; (mil., pol.) front m.; (of book, pamphlet, etc.) début m.; (appearance: fig.) façade f. ● a. de devant, avant invar.; (first) premier. **~ door**, porte d'entrée f. **~-wheel drive**, traction avant f. **in ~ (of)**, devant. **~age** n. façade f. **~al** a. frontal; (attack) de front.

frontier /'frʌntɪə(r)/ n. frontière f.

frost /frɒst/ n. gel m., gelée f.; (on glass etc.) givre m. ● v.t./i. (se) givrer. **~-bite** n. gelure f. **~-bitten** a. gelé. **~ed** a. (glass) dépoli. **~ing** n. (icing: Amer.) glace f. **~y** a. (weather, welcome) glacial; (window) givré.

froth /frɒθ/ n. mousse f., écume f. ● v.i. mousser, écumer. **~y** a. mousseux.

frown /fraʊn/ v.i. froncer les sourcils. ● n. froncement de sourcils m. **~ on**, désapprouver.

froze /frəʊz/ see freeze.

frozen /'frəʊzn/ see freeze. ● a. congelé.

frugal /'fruːgl/ a. (person) économe; (meal, life) frugal. **~ly** adv. (live) simplement.

fruit /fruːt/ n. fruit m.; (collectively) fruits m. pl. **~ machine**, machine à sous f. **~ salad**, salade de fruits f. **~erer** n. fruit|ier, -ière m., f. **~y** a. (taste) fruité.

fruit|ful /'fruːtfl/ a. (discussions) fructueux. **~less** a. stérile.

fruition /fruː'ɪʃn/ n. **come to ~**, se réaliser.

frustrat|e /frʌ'streɪt/ v.t. (plan) faire échouer; (person: psych.) frustrer; (upset: fam.) exaspérer. **~ion** /-ʃn/ n. (psych.) frustration f.; (disappointment) déception f.

fry [1] /fraɪ/ v.t./i. (p.t. **fried**) (faire) frire. **~ing-pan** n. poêle (à frire) f.

fry [2] /fraɪ/ n. **the small ~**, le menu fretin.

fuddy-duddy /'fʌdɪdʌdɪ/ n. **be a ~**, (sl.) être vieux jeu invar.

fudge /fʌdʒ/ n. (sorte de) caramel mou m. ● v.t. se dérober à.

fuel /'fjuːəl/ n. combustible m.; (for car engine) carburant m. ● v.t. (p.t. **fuelled**) alimenter en combustible.

fugitive /'fjuːdʒətɪv/ n. & a. fugiti|f, -ve (m., f.).

fugue /fjuːg/ n. (mus.) fugue f.

fulfil /fʊl'fɪl/ v.t. (p.t. **fulfilled**) accomplir, réaliser; (condition) remplir. **~ o.s.**, s'épanouir. **~ling** a. satisfaisant. **~ment** n. réalisation f.; épanouissement m.

full /fʊl/ a. (**-er, -est**) plein (**of**, de); (bus, hotel) complet; (programme) chargé; (name) complet; (skirt) ample. ● n. **in ~**, intégral(ement). **to the ~**, complètement. **be ~ (up)**, n'avoir plus faim. **~ back**, (sport) arrière m. **~ moon**, pleine lune f. **~-scale** a. (drawing etc.) grandeur nature invar.; (fig.) de grande envergure. **at ~ speed**, à toute vitesse. **~ stop**, point m. **~-time** a. & adv. à plein temps. **~y** adv. complètement.

fulsome /'fʊlsəm/ a. excessif.

fumble /'fʌmbl/ v.i. tâtonner, fouiller. ~ **with**, tripoter.

fume /fjuːm/ v.i. rager. ~**s** n. pl. exhalaisons f. pl., vapeurs f. pl.

fumigate /'fjuːmɪɡeɪt/ v.t. désinfecter.

fun /fʌn/ n. amusement m. be ~, être chouette. for ~, pour rire. ~-**fair** n. fête foraine f. **make** ~ **of**, se moquer de.

function /'fʌŋkʃn/ n. (purpose, duty) fonction f.; (event) réception f. ● v.i. fonctionner. ~**al** a. fonctionnel.

fund /fʌnd/ n. fonds m. ● v.t. fournir les fonds pour.

fundamental /fʌndə'mentl/ a. fondamental. ~**ist** n. intégriste m./f. ~**ism** n. intégrisme m.

funeral /'fjuːnərəl/ n. enterrement m., funérailles f. pl. ● a. funèbre.

fungus /'fʌŋɡəs/ n. (pl. -**gi** /-ɡaɪ/) (plant) champignon m.; (mould) moisissure f.

funicular /fjuː'nɪkjʊlə(r)/ n. funiculaire m.

funk /fʌŋk/ m. be in a ~, (afraid: sl.) avoir la frousse; (depressed: Amer., sl.) être déprimé.

funnel /'fʌnl/ n. (for pouring) entonnoir m.; (of ship) cheminée f.

funn|y /'fʌnɪ/ a. (-**ier**, -**iest**) drôle; (odd) bizarre. ~**y business**, quelque chose de louche. ~**ily** adv. drôlement; bizarrement.

fur /fɜː(r)/ n. fourrure f.; (in kettle) tartre m.

furious /'fjʊərɪəs/ a. furieux. ~**ly** adv. furieusement.

furnace /'fɜːnɪs/ n. fourneau m.

furnish /'fɜːnɪʃ/ v.t. (with furniture) meubler; (supply) fournir. ~**ings** n. pl. ameublement m.

furniture /'fɜːnɪtʃə(r)/ n. meubles m. pl., mobilier m.

furrow /'fʌrəʊ/ n. sillon m.

furry /'fɜːrɪ/ a. (animal) à fourrure; (toy) en peluche.

furth|er /'fɜːðə(r)/ a. plus éloigné; (additional) supplémentaire. ● adv. plus loin; (more) davantage. ● v.t. avancer. ~**er education**, formation continue f. ~**est** a. le plus éloigné; adv. le plus loin.

furthermore /'fɜːðəmɔː(r)/ adv. en outre, de plus.

furtive /'fɜːtɪv/ a. furtif.

fury /'fjʊərɪ/ n. fureur f.

fuse¹ /fjuːz/ v.t./i. (melt) fondre; (unite: fig.) fusionner. ● n. fusible m., plomb m. ~ **the lights** etc., faire sauter les plombs.

fuse² /fjuːz/ n. (of bomb) amorce f.

fuselage /'fjuːzəlɑːʒ/ n. fuselage m.

fusion /'fjuːʒn/ n. fusion f.

fuss /fʌs/ n. (when upset) histoire(s) f. (pl.); (when excited) agitation f. ● v.i. s'agiter. **make a** ~, faire des histoires; s'agiter; (about food) faire des chichis. **make a** ~ **of**, faire grand cas de. ~**y** a. (finicky) tatillon; (hard to please) difficile.

futile /'fjuːtaɪl/ a. futile, vain.

future /'fjuːtʃə(r)/ a. futur. ● n. avenir m.; (gram.) futur m. **in** ~, à l'avenir.

fuzz /fʌz/ n. (fluff, growth) duvet m.; (police: sl.) flics m. pl.

fuzzy /'fʌzɪ/ a. (hair) crépu; (photograph) flou; (person: fam.) à l'esprit confus.

G

gabardine /ɡæbə'diːn/ n. gabardine f.

gabble /'ɡæbl/ v.t./i. bredouiller. ● n. baragouin m.

gable /'ɡeɪbl/ n. pignon m.

gad /ɡæd/ v.i. (p.t. **gadded**). ~ **about**, se promener, aller çà et là.

gadget /'ɡædʒɪt/ n. gadget m.

Gaelic /'ɡeɪlɪk/ n. gaélique m.

gaffe /ɡæf/ n. (blunder) gaffe f.

gag /ɡæɡ/ n. bâillon m.; (joke) gag m. ● v.t. (p.t. **gagged**) bâillonner.

gaiety /'ɡeɪətɪ/ n. gaieté f.

gaily /'ɡeɪlɪ/ adv. gaiement.

gain /ɡeɪn/ v.t. gagner; (speed, weight) prendre. ● v.i. (of clock) avancer. ● n. acquisition f.; (profit) gain m. ~**ful** a. profitable.

gait /ɡeɪt/ n. démarche f.

gala /'ɡɑːlə/ n. (festive occasion) gala m.; (sport) concours m.

galaxy /'ɡæləksɪ/ n. galaxie f.

gale /ɡeɪl/ n. tempête f.

gall /ɡɔːl/ n. bile f.; (fig.) fiel m.; (impudence: sl.) culot m. ~-**bladder** n. vésicule biliaire f.

gallant /'ɡælənt/ a. (brave) courageux; (chivalrous) galant. ~**ry** n. courage m.

galleon /'ɡælɪən/ n. galion m.

gallery /'ɡælərɪ/ n. galerie f. (**art**) ~, (public) musée m.

galley /'gælɪ/ *n.* (*ship*) galère *f.*; (*kitchen*) cambuse *f.*

Gallic /'gælɪk/ *a.* français. **~ism** /-sɪzəm/ *n.* gallicisme *m.*

gallivant /gælɪ'vænt/ *v.i.* (*fam.*) se promener, aller çà et là.

gallon /'gælən/ *n.* gallon *m.* (*imperial* = 4.546 litres; *Amer.* = 3.785 litres).

gallop /'gæləp/ *n.* galop *m.* ● *v.i.* (*p.t.* **galloped**) galoper.

gallows /'gæləʊz/ *n.* potence *f.*

galore /gə'lɔː(r)/ *adv.* en abondance, à gogo.

galosh /gə'lɒʃ/ *n.* (*overshoe*) caoutchouc *m.*

galvanize /'gælvənaɪz/ *v.t.* galvaniser.

gambit /'gæmbɪt/ *n.* (**opening**) **~**, (*move*) première démarche *f.*; (*ploy*) stratagème *m.*

gamble /'gæmbl/ *v.t./i.* jouer. ● *n.* (*venture*) entreprise risquée *f.*; (*bet*) pari *m.*; (*risk*) risque *m.* **~e on**, miser sur. **~er** *n.* joueu|r, -se *m., f.* **~ing** *n.* le jeu.

game[^1] /geɪm/ *n.* jeu *m.*; (*football*) match *m.*; (*tennis*) partie *f.*; (*animals, birds*) gibier *m.* ● *a.* (*brave*) brave. **~ for**, prêt à.

game[^2] /geɪm/ *a.* (*lame*) estropié.

gamekeeper /'geɪmkiːpə(r)/ *n.* garde-chasse *m.*

gammon /'gæmən/ *n.* jambon fumé *m.*

gamut /'gæmət/ *n.* gamme *f.*

gamy /'geɪmɪ/ *a.* faisandé.

gang /gæŋ/ *n.* bande *f.*; (*of workmen*) équipe *f.* ● *v.i.* **~ up**, se liguer (**on**, **against**, contre).

gangling /'gæŋglɪŋ/ *a.* dégingandé, grand et maigre.

gangrene /'gæŋgriːn/ *n.* gangrène *f.*

gangster /'gæŋstə(r)/ *n.* gangster *m.*

gangway /'gæŋweɪ/ *n.* passage *m.*; (*aisle*) allée *f.*; (*of ship*) passerelle *f.*

gaol /dʒeɪl/ *n. & v.t.* = **jail**.

gap /gæp/ *n.* trou *m.*, vide *m.*; (*in time*) intervalle *m.*; (*in education*) lacune *f.*; (*difference*) écart *m.*

gaple /geɪp/ *v.i.* rester bouche bée. **~ing** *a.* béant.

garage /'gærɑːʒ, *Amer.* gə'rɑːʒ/ *n.* garage *m.* ● *v.t.* mettre au garage.

garb /gɑːb/ *n.* costume *m.*

garbage /'gɑːbɪdʒ/ *n.* ordures *f. pl.*

garble /'gɑːbl/ *v.t.* déformer.

garden /'gɑːdn/ *n.* jardin *m.* ● *v.i.* jardiner. **~er** *n.* jardin|ier, -ière *m., f.* **~ing** *n.* jardinage *m.*

gargle /'gɑːgl/ *v.i.* se gargariser. ● *n.* gargarisme *m.*

gargoyle /'gɑːgɔɪl/ *n.* gargouille *f.*

garish /'geərɪʃ/ *a.* voyant, criard.

garland /'gɑːlənd/ *n.* guirlande *f.*

garlic /'gɑːlɪk/ *n.* ail *m.*

garment /'gɑːmənt/ *n.* vêtement *m.*

garnish /'gɑːnɪʃ/ *v.t.* garnir (**with**, de). ● *n.* garniture *f.*

garret /'gærət/ *n.* mansarde *f.*

garrison /'gærɪsn/ *n.* garnison *f.*

garrulous /'gærələs/ *a.* loquace.

garter /'gɑːtə(r)/ *n.* jarretière *f.* **~-belt** *n.* porte-jarretelles *n.m. invar.*

gas /gæs/ *n.* (*pl.* **gases**) gaz *m.*; (*med.*) anesthésique *m.*; (*petrol: Amer. fam.*) essence *f.* ● *a.* (*mask, pipe*) à gaz. ● *v.t.* asphyxier; (*mil.*) gazer. ● *v.i.* (*fam.*) bavarder.

gash /gæʃ/ *n.* entaille *f.* ● *v.t.* entailler.

gasket /'gæskɪt/ *n.* (*auto.*) joint de culasse *m.*; (*for pressure cooker*) rondelle *f.*

gasoline /'gæsəliːn/ *n.* (*petrol: Amer.*) essence *f.*

gasp /gɑːsp/ *v.i.* haleter; (*in surprise: fig.*) avoir le souffle coupé. ● *n.* halètement *m.*

gassy /'gæsɪ/ *a.* gazeux.

gastric /'gæstrɪk/ *a.* gastrique.

gastronomy /gæ'strɒnəmɪ/ *n.* gastronomie *f.*

gate /geɪt/ *n.* porte *f.*; (*of metal*) grille *f.*; (*barrier*) barrière *f.*

gatecrash /'geɪtkræʃ/ *v.t./i.* venir sans invitation (à). **~er** *n.* intrus(e) *m.(f).*

gateway /'geɪtweɪ/ *n.* porte *f.*

gather /'gæðə(r)/ *v.t.* (*people, objects*) rassembler; (*pick up*) ramasser; (*flowers*) cueillir; (*fig.*) comprendre; (*sewing*) froncer. ● *v.i.* (*people*) se rassembler; (*crowd*) se former; (*pile up*) s'accumuler. **~ speed**, prendre de la vitesse. **~ing** *n.* rassemblement *m.*

gaudy /'gɔːdɪ/ *a.* (**-ier, -iest**) voyant, criard.

gauge /geɪdʒ/ *n.* jauge *f.*, indicateur *m.* ● *v.t.* jauger, évaluer.

gaunt /gɔːnt/ *a.* (*lean*) émacié; (*grim*) lugubre.

gauntlet /'gɔːntlɪt/ *n.* **run the ~ of**, subir (l'assaut de).

gauze /gɔːz/ *n.* gaze *f.*

gave /geɪv/ *see* give.

gawky /'gɔːkɪ/ *a.* (**-ier, -iest**) gauche, maladroit.

[^1]: game¹
[^2]: game²

gawp (*or* **gawk**) /gɔ:p, gɔ:k/ *v.i.* ~ **(at)**, regarder bouche bée.

gay /geɪ/ *a.* (**-er**, **-est**) (*joyful*) gai; (*fam.*) gay *invar.* ● *n.* gay *m./f.*

gaze /geɪz/ *v.i.* ~ **(at)**, regarder (fixement). ● *n.* regard (fixe) *m.*

gazelle /ɡəˈzel/ *n.* gazelle *f.*

gazette /ɡəˈzet/ *n.* journal (officiel) *m.*

GB *abbr. see* Great Britain.

gear /ɡɪə(r)/ *n.* équipement *m.*; (*techn.*) engrenage *m.*; (*auto.*) vitesse *f.* ● *v.t.* adapter. ~**-lever**, (*Amer.*) ~**-shift** *ns.* levier de vitesse *m.* **in** ~, en prise. **out of** ~, au point mort.

gearbox /ˈɡɪəbɒks/ *n.* (*auto.*) boîte de vitesses *f.*

geese /ɡi:s/ *see* goose.

gel /dʒel/ *n.* gelée *f.*; (*for hair*) gel *m.*

gelatine /ˈdʒeləti:n/ *n.* gélatine *f.*

gelignite /ˈdʒelɪɡnaɪt/ *n.* nitroglycérine *f.*

gem /dʒem/ *n.* pierre précieuse *f.*

Gemini /ˈdʒemɪnaɪ/ *n.* les Gémeaux *m. pl.*

gender /ˈdʒendə(r)/ *n.* genre *m.*

gene /dʒi:n/ *n.* gène *m.*

genealogy /dʒi:nɪˈælədʒɪ/ *n.* généalogie *f.*

general /ˈdʒenrəl/ *a.* général. ● *n.* général *m.* ~ **election**, élections législatives *f. pl.* ~ **practitioner**, (*med.*) généraliste *m.* **in** ~, en général. ~**ly** *adv.* généralement.

generalize /ˈdʒenrəlaɪz/ *v.t./i.* généraliser. ~**ation** /-ˈzeɪʃn/ *n.* généralisation *f.*

generate /ˈdʒenəreɪt/ *v.t.* produire.

generation /dʒenəˈreɪʃn/ *n.* génération *f.*

generator /ˈdʒenəreɪtə(r)/ *n.* (*electr.*) groupe électrogène *m.*

generous /ˈdʒenərəs/ *a.* généreux; (*plentiful*) copieux. ~**osity** /-ˈrɒsətɪ/ *n.* générosité *f.*

genetic /dʒɪˈnetɪk/ *a.* génétique. ~**s** *n.* génétique *f.*

Geneva /dʒɪˈni:və/ *n.* Genève *m./f.*

genial /ˈdʒi:nɪəl/ *a.* affable, sympathique; (*climate*) doux.

genital /ˈdʒenɪtl/ *a.* génital. ~**s** *n. pl.* organes génitaux *m. pl.*

genius /ˈdʒi:nɪəs/ *n.* (*pl.* **-uses**) génie *m.*

genocide /ˈdʒenəsaɪd/ *n.* génocide *m.*

gent /dʒent/ *n.* (*sl.*) monsieur *m.*

genteel /dʒenˈti:l/ *a.* distingué.

gentle /ˈdʒentl/ *a.* (**-er**, **-est**) (*mild*, *kind*) doux; (*slight*) léger; (*hint*) discret. ~**eness** *n.* douceur *f.* ~**y** *adv.* doucement.

gentleman /ˈdʒentlmən/ *n.* (*pl.* **-men**) (*man*) monsieur *m.*; (*wellbred*) gentleman *m.*

genuine /ˈdʒenjʊɪn/ *a.* (*true*) véritable; (*person*, *belief*) sincère.

geography /dʒɪˈɒɡrəfɪ/ *n.* géographie *f.* ~**er** *n.* géographe *m./f.* ~**ical** /dʒɪəˈɡræfɪkl/ *a.* géographique.

geology /dʒɪˈɒlədʒɪ/ *n.* géologie *f.* ~**ical** /dʒɪəˈlɒdʒɪkl/ *a.* géologique. ~**ist** *n.* géologue *m./f.*

geometry /dʒɪˈɒmətrɪ/ *n.* géométrie *f.* ~**ic(al)** /dʒɪəˈmetrɪk(l)/ *a.* géométrique.

geranium /dʒəˈreɪnɪəm/ *n.* géranium *m.*

geriatric /dʒerɪˈætrɪk/ *a.* gériatrique.

germ /dʒɜ:m/ *n.* (*rudiment*, *seed*) germe *m.*; (*med.*) microbe *m.*

German /ˈdʒɜ:mən/ *a. & n.* allemand(e) (*m.* (*f.*)); (*lang.*) allemand *m.* ~ **measles**, rubéole *f.* ~ **shepherd**, (*dog: Amer.*) berger allemand *m.* ~**ic** /dʒəˈmænɪk/ *a.* germanique. ~**y** *n.* Allemagne *f.*

germinate /ˈdʒɜ:mɪneɪt/ *v.t./i.* (faire) germer.

gestation /dʒeˈsteɪʃn/ *n.* gestation *f.*

gesticulate /dʒeˈstɪkjʊleɪt/ *v.i.* gesticuler.

gesture /ˈdʒestʃə(r)/ *n.* geste *m.*

get /get/ *v.t.* (*p.t. & p.p.* **got**, *p.p. Amer.* **gotten**, *pres. p.* **getting**) avoir, obtenir, recevoir; (*catch*) prendre; (*buy*) acheter, prendre; (*find*) trouver; (*fetch*) aller chercher; (*understand: sl.*) comprendre. ~ **s.o. to do sth.**, faire faire qch. à qn. ~ **sth. done**, faire faire qch. **did you** ~ **that number?**, tu as relevé le numéro? ● *v.i.* aller, arriver (**to**, à); (*become*) devenir; (*start*) se mettre (**to**, à); (*manage*) parvenir (**to**, à). ~ **married/ready**/*etc.*, se marier/se préparer/*etc.* ~ **promoted/hurt**/*etc.*, être promu/ blessé/*etc.* ~ **arrested/robbed**/ *etc.*, se faire arrêter/voler/*etc.* **you** ~ **to use the computer**, vous utilisez l'ordinateur. **it's** ~**ting to be annoying**, ça commence a être agaçant. ~ **about**, (*person*) se déplacer. ~ **across**, (*cross*) traverser. ~ **along** *or* **by**, (*manage*) se débrouiller. ~ along *or* on, (*progress*) avancer. ~ along *or* on with, s'entendre avec. ~ at, (*reach*) parvenir à. what are you ~ting at?, où veux-tu en venir? ~ away, partir; (*escape*) s'échapper. ~ back *v.i.* revenir; *v.t.* (*recover*) récupérer. ~ by *or* through, (*pass*) passer. ~ down *v.t./i.* descendre; (*depress*) déprimer. ~ in, entrer, arriver. ~ into, (*car*) monter dans; (*dress*) mettre. ~ into trouble, avoir des ennuis. ~ off *v.i.* (*from bus etc.*) descendre; (*leave*) partir; (*jurid.*) être acquitté; *v.t.* (*remove*) enlever. ~ on, (*on train etc.*) monter; (*succeed*) réussir. ~ on with, (*job*) attaquer; (*person*) s'entendre avec. ~ out, sortir. ~ out of, (*fig.*) se soustraire à. ~ over, (*illness*) se remettre de. ~ round, (*rule*) contourner; (*person*) entortiller. ~ through, (*finish*) finir. ~ up *v.i.* se lever; *v.t.* (*climb, bring*) monter. ~up *n.* (*clothes: fam.*) mise *f.*

getaway /'getəweɪ/ *n.* fuite *f.*

geyser /'giːzə(r)/ *n.* chauffe-eau *m. invar.*; (*geol.*) geyser *m.*

Ghana /'gɑːnə/ *n.* Ghana *m.*

ghastly /'gɑːstlɪ/ *a.* (-ier, -iest) affreux; (*pale*) blême.

gherkin /'gɜːkɪn/ *n.* cornichon *m.*

ghetto /'getəʊ/ *n.* (*pl.* -os) ghetto *m.*

ghost /ɡəʊst/ *n.* fantôme *m.* ~ly *a.* spectral.

giant /'dʒaɪənt/ *n. & a.* géant (*m.*).

gibberish /'dʒɪbərɪʃ/ *n.* baragouin *m.*, charabia *m.*

gibe /dʒaɪb/ *n.* raillerie *f.* ● *v.i.* ~ (at), railler.

giblets /'dʒɪblɪts/ *n. pl.* abattis *m. pl.*, abats *m. pl.*

giddy /'ɡɪdɪ/ *a.* (-ier, -iest) vertigineux. be *or* feel ~y, avoir le vertige. ~iness *n.* vertige *m.*

gift /ɡɪft/ *n.* cadeau *m.*; (*ability*) don *m.* ~-wrap *v.t.* (*p.t.* -wrapped) faire un paquet-cadeau de.

gifted /'ɡɪftɪd/ *a.* doué.

gig /ɡɪɡ/ *n.* (*fam.*) concert *m.*

gigantic /dʒaɪˈɡæntɪk/ *a.* gigantesque.

giggle /'ɡɪɡl/ *v.i.* ricaner (sottement), glousser. ● *n.* ricanement *m.* the ~s, le fou rire.

gild /ɡɪld/ *v.t.* dorer.

gill /dʒɪl/ *n.* (*approx.*) décilitre (*imperial = 0.15 litre; Amer. = 0.12 litre*).

gills /ɡɪlz/ *n. pl.* ouïes *f. pl.*

gilt /ɡɪlt/ *a.* doré. ● *n.* dorure *f.* ~-edged *a.* (*comm.*) de tout repos.

gimmick /'ɡɪmɪk/ *n.* truc *m.*

gin /dʒɪn/ *n.* gin *m.*

ginger /'dʒɪndʒə(r)/ *n.* gingembre *m.* ● *a.* roux. ~ ale, ~ beer, boisson gazeuse au gingembre *f.*

gingerbread /'dʒɪndʒəbred/ *n.* pain d'épice *m.*

gingerly /'dʒɪndʒəlɪ/ *adv.* avec précaution.

gipsy /'dʒɪpsɪ/ *n.* = gypsy.

giraffe /dʒɪˈrɑːf/ *n.* girafe *f.*

girder /'ɡɜːdə(r)/ *n.* poutre *f.*

girdle /'ɡɜːdl/ *n.* (*belt*) ceinture *f.*; (*corset*) gaine *f.*

girl /ɡɜːl/ *n.* (petite) fille *f.*; (*young woman*) (jeune) fille *f.* ~-friend *n.* amie *f.*; (*of boy*) petite amie *f.* ~hood *n.* enfance *f.*, jeunesse *f.* ~ish *a.* de (jeune) fille.

giro /'dʒaɪərəʊ/ *n.* (*pl.* -os) virement bancaire *m.*; (*cheque: fam.*) mandat *m.*

girth /ɡɜːθ/ *n.* circonférence *f.*

gist /dʒɪst/ *n.* essentiel *m.*

give /ɡɪv/ *v.t.* (*p.t.* gave, *p.p.* given) donner; (*gesture*) faire; (*laugh, sigh, etc.*) pousser. ~ s.o. sth., donner qch. à qn. ● *v.i.* donner; (*yield*) céder; (*stretch*) se détendre. ● *n.* élasticité *f.* ~ away, donner; (*secret*) trahir. ~ back, rendre. ~ in, (*yield*) se rendre. ~ off, dégager. ~ out *v.t.* distribuer; *v.i.* (*become used up*) s'épuiser. ~ over, (*devote*) consacrer; (*stop: fam.*) cesser. ~ up *v.t./i.* (*renounce*) renoncer (à); (*yield*) céder. ~ o.s. up, se rendre. ~ way, céder; (*collapse*) s'effondrer.

given /'ɡɪvn/ *see* give. ● *a.* donné. ~ name, prénom *m.*

glacier /'ɡlæsɪə(r)/, *Amer.* 'ɡleɪʃər/ *n.* glacier *m.*

glad /ɡlæd/ *a.* content. ~ly *adv.* avec plaisir.

gladden /'ɡlædn/ *v.t.* réjouir.

gladiolus /ˌɡlædɪˈəʊləs/ *n.* (*pl.* -li /-laɪ/) glaïeul *m.*

glamour /'ɡlæmə(r)/ *n.* enchantement *m.*, séduction *f.* ~orize *v.t.* rendre séduisant. ~orous *a.* séduisant, ensorcelant.

glance /ɡlɑːns/ *n.* coup d'œil *m.* ● *v.i.* ~ at, jeter un coup d'œil à.

gland /ɡlænd/ *n.* glande *f.*

glare /ɡleə(r)/ *v.i.* briller très fort. ● *n.* éclat (aveuglant) *m.*; (*stare: fig.*) regard furieux *m.* ~e at, regarder d'un air furieux. ~ing a. éblouissant; (*obvious*) flagrant.

glass /glɑːs/ n. verre m.; (*mirror*) miroir m. ~es, (*spectacles*) lunettes f. pl. ~y a. vitreux.

glaze /gleɪz/ v.t. (*door etc.*) vitrer; (*pottery*) vernisser. ● n. vernis m.

gleam /gliːm/ n. lueur f. ● v.i. luire.

glean /gliːn/ v.t. glaner.

glee /gliː/ n. joie f. ~ **club,** chorale f. ~**ful** a. joyeux.

glen /glen/ n. vallon m.

glib /glɪb/ a. (*person: pej.*) qui a la parole facile or du bagou; (*reply*, *excuse*) désinvolte, spécieux. ~**ly** adv. avec désinvolture.

glide /glaɪd/ v.i. glisser; (*of plane*) planer. ~**r** /-ə(r)/ n. planeur m.

glimmer /ˈglɪmə(r)/ n. lueur f. ● v.i. luire.

glimpse /glɪmps/ n. aperçu m. **catch a ~ of,** entrevoir.

glint /glɪnt/ n. éclair m. ● v.i. étinceler.

glisten /ˈglɪsn/ v.i. briller, luire.

glitter /ˈglɪtə(r)/ v.i. scintiller. ● n. scintillement m.

gloat /gləʊt/ v.i. jubiler (**over,** à l'idée de).

global /ˈgləʊbl/ a. (*world-wide*) mondial; (*all-embracing*) global.

globe /gləʊb/ n. globe m.

gloom /gluːm/ n. obscurité f.; (*sadness: fig.*) tristesse f. ~**y** a. triste; (*pessimistic*) pessimiste.

glorif|**y** /ˈglɔːrɪfaɪ/ v.t. glorifier. a ~**ied** waitress/etc., à peine plus qu'une serveuse/etc.

glorious /ˈglɔːrɪəs/ a. splendide; (*deed, hero, etc.*) glorieux.

glory /ˈglɔːrɪ/ n. gloire f.; (*beauty*) splendeur f. ● v.i. ~ **in,** s'enorgueillir de.

gloss /glɒs/ n. lustre m., brillant m. ● a. brillant. ● v.i. ~ **over,** (*make light of*) glisser sur; (*cover up*) dissimuler. ~**y** a. brillant.

glossary /ˈglɒsərɪ/ n. glossaire m.

glove /glʌv/ n. gant m. ~ **compartment,** (*auto.*) vide-poches m. invar. ~**d** a. ganté.

glow /gləʊ/ v.i. rougeoyer; (*person, eyes*) rayonner. ● n. rougeoiement m., éclat m. ~**ing** a. (*account etc.*) enthousiaste.

glucose /ˈgluːkəʊs/ n. glucose m.

glue /gluː/ n. colle f. ● v.t. (*pres. p.* **gluing**) coller.

glum /glʌm/ a. (**glummer, glummest**) triste, morne.

glut /glʌt/ n. surabondance f.

glutton /ˈglʌtn/ n. glouton(ne) m. (f.). ~**ous** a. glouton. ~**y** n. gloutonnerie f.

glycerine /ˈglɪsəriːn/ n. glycérine f.

gnarled /nɑːld/ a. noueux.

gnash /næʃ/ v.t. ~ **one's teeth,** grincer des dents.

gnat /næt/ n. (*fly*) cousin m.

gnaw /nɔː/ v.t./i. ronger.

gnome /nəʊm/ n. gnome m.

go /gəʊ/ v.i. (*p.t.* **went,** *p.p.* **gone**) aller; (*leave*) partir; (*work*) marcher; (*become*) devenir; (*be sold*) se vendre; (*vanish*) disparaître. **my coat's gone,** mon manteau n'est plus là. ~ **via Paris,** passer par Paris. ~ **by car/on foot,** aller en voiture/à pied. ~ **for a walk/ride,** aller se promener/faire un tour en voiture. **go red/dry/etc.,** rougir/tarir/etc. **don't ~ telling him,** ne va pas lui dire. ~ **riding/ shopping/etc.,** faire du cheval/les courses/etc. ● n. (*pl.* **goes**) (*try*) coup m.; (*success*) réussite f.; (*turn*) tour m.; (*energy*) dynamisme m. **have a ~,** essayer. **be ~ing to do,** aller faire. ~ **across,** traverser. ~ **ahead!,** allez-y! ~**-ahead** n. feu vert m.; a. dynamique. ~ **away,** s'en aller. ~ **back,** retourner; (*go home*) rentrer. ~ **back on,** (*promise etc.*) revenir sur. ~ **bad or off,** se gâter. ~**-between** n. intermédiaire m./f. ~ **by,** (*pass*) passer. ~ **down,** descendre; (*sun*) se coucher. ~ **for,** aller chercher; (*like*) aimer; (*attack: sl.*) attaquer. ~ **in,** (r)entrer. ~ **in for,** (*exam*) se présenter à. ~ **into,** entrer dans; (*subject*) examiner. ~**-kart** n. kart m. ~ **off,** partir; (*explode*) sauter; (*ring*) sonner; (*take place*) se dérouler; (*dislike*) revenir de. ~ **on,** continuer; (*happen*) se passer. ~ **out,** sortir; (*light, fire*) s'éteindre. ~ **over,** (*cross*) traverser; (*pass*) passer. ~ **over or through,** (*check*) vérifier; (*search*) fouiller. ~ **round,** (*be enough*) suffire. ~**-slow** n. grève perlée f. ~ **through,** (*suffer*) subir. ~ **under,** (*sink*) couler; (*fail*) échouer. ~ **up,** monter. ~ **without,** se passer de. **on the ~,** actif.

goad /gəʊd/ v.t. aiguillonner.

goal /gəʊl/ n. but m. **~-post** n. poteau de but m.

goalkeeper /'gəʊlkiːpə(r)/ n. gardien de but m.

goat /gəʊt/ n. chèvre f.

goatee /gəʊ'tiː/ n. barbiche f.

gobble /'gɒbl/ v.t. engouffrer.

goblet /'gɒblɪt/ n. verre à pied m.

goblin /'gɒblɪn/ n. lutin m.

God /gɒd/ n. Dieu m. **~-forsaken** a. perdu.

god /gɒd/ n. dieu m. **~dess** n. déesse f. **~ly** a. dévot.

god|child /'gɒdtʃaɪld/ n. (pl. **-children**) filleul(e) m. (f.). **~daughter** n. filleule f. **~father** n. parrain m. **~mother** n. marraine f. **~son** n. filleul m.

godsend /'gɒdsend/ n. aubaine f.

goggle /'gɒgl/ v.i. **~ (at)**, regarder avec de gros yeux.

goggles /'gɒglz/ n. pl. lunettes (protectrices) f. pl.

going /'gəʊɪŋ/ n. it is slow/hard ~, c'est lent/difficile. ● a. (price, rate) actuel. **~s-on** n. pl. activités (bizarres) f. pl.

gold /gəʊld/ n. or m. ● a. en or, d'or. **~-mine** n. mine d'or f.

golden /'gəʊldən/ a. d'or; (in colour) doré; (opportunity) unique. ~ **wedding**, noces d'or f. pl.

goldfish /'gəʊldfɪʃ/ n. invar. poisson rouge m.

gold-plated /gəʊld'pleɪtɪd/ a. plaqué or.

goldsmith /'gəʊldsmɪθ/ n. orfèvre m.

golf /gɒlf/ n. golf m. ~ **ball**, balle de golf f.; (on typewriter) boule f. **~-course** n. terrain de golf m. **~er** n. joueur|r, -se de golf m. f.

gondol|a /'gɒndələ/ n. gondole f. **~ier** /-'lɪə(r)/ n. gondolier m.

gone /gɒn/ see go. ● a. parti. ~ six o'clock, six heures passées. the butter's all ~, il n'y a plus de beurre.

gong /gɒŋ/ n. gong m.

good /gʊd/ a. (**better, best**) bon; (weather) beau; (well-behaved) sage. ● n. bien m. as ~ as, (almost) pratiquement. that's ~ of you, c'est gentil (de ta part). be ~ with, savoir s'y prendre avec. do ~, faire du bien. feel ~, se sentir bien. **~-for-nothing** a. & n. propre à rien (m./f.). G~ **Friday**, Vendredi saint m. **~-afternoon**, **~-morning** ints. bonjour. **~-evening** int. bonsoir.

~-looking a. beau. **~-natured** a. gentil. ~ **name**, réputation f. **~-night** int. bonsoir, bonne nuit. it is ~ **for you**, ça vous fait du bien. is it any ~?, est-ce que c'est bien? it's no ~, ça ne vaut rien. it is no ~ **shouting**/etc., ça ne sert à rien de crier/etc. **for** ~, pour toujours. **~ness** n. bonté f. **my ~ness!**, mon Dieu!

goodbye /gʊd'baɪ/ int. & n. au revoir (m. invar.).

goods /gʊdz/ n. pl. marchandises f. pl.

goodwill /gʊd'wɪl/ n. bonne volonté f.

goody /'gʊdɪ/ n. (fam.) bonne chose f. **~-goody** n. petit(e) saint(e) m. (f.).

gooey /'guːɪ/ a. (sl.) poisseux.

goof /guːf/ v.i. (Amer.) gaffer.

goose /guːs/ n. (pl. **geese**) oie f. **~-flesh**, **~-pimples** ns. chair de poule f.

gooseberry /'gʊzbərɪ/ n. groseille à maquereau f.

gore¹ /gɔː(r)/ n. (blood) sang m.

gore² /gɔː(r)/ v.t. encorner.

gorge /gɔːdʒ/ n. (geog.) gorge f. ● v.t. ~ o.s., se gorger.

gorgeous /'gɔːdʒəs/ a. magnifique, splendide, formidable.

gorilla /gə'rɪlə/ n. gorille m.

gormless /'gɔːmlɪs/ a. (sl.) stupide.

gorse /gɔːs/ n. invar. ajonc(s) m. (pl.).

gory /'gɔːrɪ/ a. (**-ier, -iest**) sanglant; (horrific: fig.) horrible.

gosh /gɒʃ/ int. mince (alors).

gospel /'gɒspl/ n. évangile m. **the G~**, l'Évangile m.

gossip /'gɒsɪp/ n. bavardage(s) m. (pl.), commérage(s) m. (pl.); (person) bavard(e) m. (f.). ● v.i. (p.t. **gossiped**) bavarder. **~y** a. bavard.

got /gɒt/ see get. ● have ~, avoir. have ~ to do, devoir faire.

Gothic /'gɒθɪk/ a. gothique.

gouge /gaʊdʒ/ v.t. ~ **out**, arracher.

gourmet /'gʊəmeɪ/ n. gourmet m.

gout /gaʊt/ n. (med.) goutte f.

govern /'gʌvn/ v.t./i. gouverner. **~ess** /-ənɪs/ n. gouvernante f. **~or** /-ənə(r)/ n. gouverneur m.

government /'gʌvənmənt/ n. gouvernement m. **~al** /-'mentl/ a. gouvernemental.

gown /gaʊn/ n. robe f.; (of judge, teacher) toge f.

GP abbr. see general practitioner.

grab /græb/ v.t. (p.t. **grabbed**) saisir.

grace /greɪs/ n. grâce f. ● v.t. (*honour*) honorer; (*adorn*) orner. **~ful** a. gracieux.

gracious /'greɪʃəs/ a. (*kind*) bienveillant; (*elegant*) élégant.

gradation /grə'deɪʃn/ n. gradation f.

grade /greɪd/ n. catégorie f.; (*of goods*) qualité f.; (*on scale*) grade m.; (*school mark*) note f.; (*class: Amer.*) classe f. ● v.t. classer; (*school work*) noter. **~ crossing**, (*Amer.*) passage à niveau m. **~ school**, (*Amer.*) école primaire f.

gradient /'greɪdɪənt/ n. (*slope*) inclinaison f.

gradual /'grædʒʊəl/ a. progressif, graduel. **~ly** adv. progressivement, peu à peu.

graduate[1] /'grædʒʊət/ n. (*univ.*) diplômé(e) m. (f.).

graduate[2] /'grædʒʊeɪt/ v.i. obtenir son diplôme. ● v.t. graduer. **~ion** /-'eɪʃn/ n. remise de diplômes f.

graffiti /grə'fiːtiː/ n. pl. graffiti m. pl.

graft[1] /grɑːft/ n. (*med., bot.*) greffe f. (*work*) boulot m. ● v.t. greffer; (*work*) trimer.

graft[2] /grɑːft/ n. (*bribery: fam.*) corruption f.

grain /greɪn/ n. (*seed, quantity, texture*) grain m.; (*in wood*) fibre f.

gram /græm/ n. gramme m.

grammar /'græmə(r)/ n. grammaire f. **~atical** /grə'mætɪkl/ a. grammatical.

grand /grænd/ a. (**-er, -est**) magnifique; (*duke, chorus*) grand. **~ piano**, piano à queue m.

grandad /'grændæd/ n. (*fam.*) papy m.

grand|child /'græn(d)tʃaɪld/ n. (*pl. -children*) petit(e)-enfant m. (f.). **~daughter** n. petite-fille f. **~father** n. grand-père m. **~mother** n. grand-mère f. **~parents** n. pl. grands-parents m. pl. **~son** n. petit-fils m.

grandeur /'grændʒə(r)/ n. grandeur f.

grandiose /'grændɪəʊs/ a. grandiose.

grandma /'grændmɑː/ n. = **granny**.

grandstand /'græn(d)stænd/ n. tribune f.

granite /'grænɪt/ n. granit m.

granny /'grænɪ/ n. (*fam.*) grandmaman f., mémé f., mamie f.

grant /grɑːnt/ v.t. (*give*) accorder; (*request*) accéder à; (*admit*) admettre (**that**, que). ● n. subvention f.; (*univ.*) bourse f. **take sth. for ~ed**, considérer qch. comme une chose acquise.

granulated /'grænjʊleɪtɪd/ a. **~ sugar**, sucre semoule m.

granule /'grænjuːl/ n. granule m.

grape /greɪp/ n. grain de raisin m. **~s**, raisin(s) m. (pl.).

grapefruit /'greɪpfruːt/ n. invar. pamplemousse m.

graph /grɑːf/ n. graphique m.

graphic /'græfɪk/ a. (*arts etc.*) graphique; (*fig.*) vivant, explicite. **~s** n. pl. (*comput.*) graphiques m. pl.

grapple /'græpl/ v.i. **~ with**, affronter, être aux prises avec.

grasp /grɑːsp/ v.t. saisir. ● n. (*hold*) prise f.; (*strength of hand*) poigne f.; (*reach*) portée f.; (*fig.*) compréhension f.

grasping /'grɑːspɪŋ/ a. rapace.

grass /grɑːs/ n. herbe f.; (*pol.*) base f. **~-roots** a. populaire. **~y** a. herbeux.

grasshopper /'grɑːshɒpə(r)/ n. sauterelle f.

grassland /'grɑːslænd/ n. prairie f.

grate[1] /greɪt/ n. (*fireplace*) foyer m.; (*frame*) grille f.

grate[2] /greɪt/ v.t. râper. ● v.i. grincer. **~r** /-ə(r)/ n. râpe f.

grateful /'greɪtfl/ a. reconnaissant. **~ly** adv. avec reconnaissance.

gratify /'grætɪfaɪ/ v.t. satisfaire; (*please*) faire plaisir à **~ied** a. très heureux. **~ying** a. agréable.

grating /'greɪtɪŋ/ n. grille f.

gratis /'greɪtɪs, 'grætɪs/ a. & adv. gratis (a. invar.).

gratitude /'grætɪtjuːd/ n. gratitude f.

gratuitous /grə'tjuːɪtəs/ a. gratuit.

gratuity /grə'tjuːətɪ/ n. (*tip*) pourboire m.; (*bounty: mil.*) prime f.

grave[1] /greɪv/ n. tombe f. **~-digger** n. fossoyeur m.

grave[2] /greɪv/ a. (**-er, -est**) (*serious*) grave. **~ly** adv. gravement.

grave[3] /grɑːv/ a. **~ accent**, accent grave m.

gravel /'grævl/ n. gravier m.

gravestone /'greɪvstəʊn/ n. pierre tombale f.

graveyard /'greɪvjɑːd/ n. cimetière m.

gravitate /'grævɪteɪt/ v.i. graviter. **~ion** /-'teɪʃn/ n. gravitation f.

gravity /'grævɪtɪ/ n. (*seriousness*) gravité f.; (*force*) pesanteur f.

gravy /'greɪvɪ/ n. jus (de viande) m.

gray /greɪ/ a. & n. = **grey**.

graze[1] /greɪz/ *v.t./i.* (*eat*) paître.

graze[2] /greɪz/ *v.t.* (*touch*) frôler; (*scrape*) écorcher. ● *n.* écorchure *f.*

greas|e /griːs/ *n.* graisse *f.* ● *v.t.* graisser. ~**e-proof paper**, papier sulfurisé *m.* ~**y** *a.* graisseux.

great /greɪt/ *a.* (-er, -est) grand; (*very good*: *fam.*) magnifique. ~ **Britain**, Grande-Bretagne *f.* ~**-grandfather** *n.* arrière-grand-père *m.* ~**-grandmother** *n.* arrière-grand-mère *f.* ~**ly** *adv.* (*very*) très; (*much*) beaucoup. ~**ness** *n.* grandeur *f.*

Greece /griːs/ *n.* Grèce *f.*

greed /griːd/ *n.* avidité *f.*; (*for food*) gourmandise *f.* ~**y** *a.* avide; gourmand.

Greek /griːk/ *a. & n.* grec(que) (*m. (f.)*); (*lang.*) grec *m.*

green /griːn/ *a.* (-er, -est) vert; (*fig.*) naïf. ● *n.* vert *m.*; (*grass*) pelouse *f.*; (*golf*) green *m.* ~**s**, légumes verts *m. pl.* ~ **belt**, ceinture verte *f.* ~ **light**, feu vert *m.* ~**ery** *n.* verdure *f.*

greengage /ˈgriːngeɪdʒ/ *n.* (*plum*) reine-claude *f.*

greengrocer /ˈgriːngrəʊsə(r)/ *n.* marchand(e) de fruits et légumes *m. (f.).*

greenhouse /ˈgriːnhaʊs/ *n.* serre *f.*

greet /griːt/ *v.t.* (*receive*) accueillir; (*address politely*) saluer. ~**ing** *n.* accueil *m.* ~**ings** *n. pl.* compliments *m. pl.*; (*wishes*) vœux *m. pl.* ~**ings card**, carte de vœux *f.*

gregarious /grɪˈgeərɪəs/ *a.* (*instinct*) grégaire; (*person*) sociable.

grenade /grɪˈneɪd/ *n.* grenade *f.*

grew /gruː/ *see* **grow**.

grey /greɪ/ *a.* (-er, -est) gris; (*fig.*) triste. ● *n.* gris *m.* **go** ~, (*hair, person*) grisonner.

greyhound /ˈgreɪhaʊnd/ *n.* lévrier *m.*

grid /grɪd/ *n.* grille *f.*; (*network*: *electr.*) réseau *m.*; (*culin.*) gril *m.*

grief /griːf/ *n.* chagrin *m.* **come to** ~, (*person*) avoir un malheur; (*fail*) tourner mal.

grievance /ˈgriːvns/ *n.* grief *m.*

grieve /griːv/ *v.t./i.* (s')affliger. ~ **for**, pleurer.

grill /grɪl/ *n.* (*cooking device*) gril *m.*; (*food*) grillade *f.*; (*auto.*) calandre *f.* ● *v.t./i.* griller; (*interrogate*) cuisiner.

grille /grɪl/ *n.* grille *f.*

grim /grɪm/ *a.* (**grimmer, grimmest**) sinistre.

grimace /grɪˈmeɪs/ *n.* grimace *f.* ● *v.i.* grimacer.

grim|e /graɪm/ *n.* crasse *f.* ~**y** *a.* crasseux.

grin /grɪn/ *v.i.* (*p.t.* **grinned**) sourire. ● *n.* (large) sourire *m.*

grind /graɪnd/ *v.t.* (*p.t.* **ground**) écraser; (*coffee*) moudre; (*sharpen*) aiguiser. ● *n.* corvée *f.* ~ **one's teeth**, grincer des dents. ~ **to a halt**, devenir paralysé.

grip /grɪp/ *v.t.* (*p.t.* **gripped**) saisir; (*interest*) passionner. ● *n.* prise *f.*; (*strength of hand*) poigne *f.*; (*bag*) sac de voyage *m.* **come to** ~**s**, en venir aux prises.

gripe /graɪp/ *n.* ~**s**, (*med.*) coliques *f. pl.* ● *v.i.* (*grumble*: *sl.*) râler.

grisly /ˈgrɪzlɪ/ *a.* (-ier, -iest) macabre, horrible.

gristle /ˈgrɪsl/ *n.* cartilage *m.*

grit /grɪt/ *n.* gravillon *m.*, sable *m.*; (*fig.*) courage *m.* ● *v.t.* (*p.t.* **gritted**) (*road*) sabler; (*teeth*) serrer.

grizzle /ˈgrɪzl/ *v.i.* (*cry*) pleurnicher.

groan /grəʊn/ *v.i.* gémir. ● *n.* gémissement *m.*

grocer /ˈgrəʊsə(r)/ *n.* épic|ier, -ière *m., f.* ~**ies** *n. pl.* (*goods*) épicerie *f.* ~**y** *n.* (*shop*) épicerie *f.*

grog /grɒg/ *n.* grog *m.*

groggy /ˈgrɒgɪ/ *a.* (*weak*) faible; (*unsteady*) chancelant; (*ill*) mal fichu.

groin /grɔɪn/ *n.* aine *f.*

groom /gruːm/ *n.* marié *m.*; (*for horses*) valet d'écurie *m.* ● *v.t.* (*horse*) panser; (*fig.*) préparer.

groove /gruːv/ *n.* (*for door etc.*) rainure *f.*; (*in record*) sillon *m.*

grope /grəʊp/ *v.i.* tâtonner. ~ **for**, chercher à tâtons.

gross /grəʊs/ *a.* (-er, -est) (*coarse*) grossier; (*comm.*) brut. ● *n. invar.* grosse *f.* ~**ly** *adv.* grossièrement; (*very*) extrêmement.

grotesque /grəʊˈtesk/ *a.* grotesque, horrible.

grotto /ˈgrɒtəʊ/ *n.* (*pl.* -oes) grotte *f.*

grotty /ˈgrɒtɪ/ *a.* (*sl.*) moche.

grouch /graʊtʃ/ *v.i.* (*grumble*: *fam.*) rouspéter, râler.

ground[1] /graʊnd/ *n.* terre *f.*, sol *m.*; (*area*) terrain *m.*; (*reason*) raison *f.*; (*electr.*, *Amer.*) masse *f.* ~**s**, terres *f. pl.*, parc *m.*; (*of coffee*) marc *m.* ● *v.t./i.* (*naut.*) échouer; (*aircraft*) retenir au sol. **on the** ~, par terre. **lose** ~, perdre du terrain. ~ **floor**, rez-de-chaussée *m. invar.* ~ **rule,** règle de base *f.* **~less** *a.* sans fondement. ~ **swell,** lame de fond *f.*

ground [²](graʊnd/ *see* grind. ● *a.* ~ **beef,** (*Amer.*) bifteck haché *m.*

grounding /'graʊndɪŋ/ *n.* connaissances (de base) *f. pl.*

groundsheet /'graʊndʃiːt/ *n.* tapis de sol *m.*

groundwork /'graʊndwɜːk/ *n.* travail préparatoire *m.*

group /gruːp/ *n.* groupe *m.* ● *v.t./i.* (se) grouper.

grouse [¹](graʊs/ *n. invar.* (*bird*) coq de bruyère *m.*, grouse *f.*

grouse [²](graʊs/ *v.i.* (*grumble: fam.*) rouspéter, râler.

grove /grəʊv/ *n.* bocage *m.*

grovel /'grɒvl/ *v.i.* (*p.t.* **grovelled**) ramper. **~ling** *a.* rampant.

grow /grəʊ/ *v.i.* (*p.t.* **grew**, *p.p.* **grown**) grandir; (*of plant*) pousser; (*become*) devenir. ● *v.t.* cultiver. ~ **up,** devenir adulte, grandir. **~er** *n.* cultiva|teur, -trice *m., f.* **~ing** *a.* grandissant.

growl /graʊl/ *v.i.* grogner. ● *n.* grognement *m.*

grown /grəʊn/ *see* grow. ● *a.* adulte. **~-up** *a. & n.* adulte (*m./f.*).

growth /grəʊθ/ *n.* croissance *f.*; (*in numbers*) accroissement *m.*; (*of hair, tooth*) pousse *f.*; (*med.*) tumeur *f.*

grub /grʌb/ *n.* (*larva*) larve *f.*; (*food: sl.*) bouffe *f.*

grubby /'grʌbɪ/ *a.* (**-ier, -iest**) sale.

grudge /grʌdʒ/ *v.t.* ~ **doing,** faire à contrecœur. ~ **s.o. sth.,** (*success, wealth*) en vouloir à qn. de qch. ● *n.* rancune *f.* **have a ~ against,** en vouloir à. **grudgingly** *adv.* à contrecœur.

gruelling /'gruːəlɪŋ/ *a.* exténuant.

gruesome /'gruːsəm/ *a.* macabre.

gruff /grʌf/ *a.* (**-er, -est**) bourru.

grumble /'grʌmbl/ *v.i.* ronchonner, grogner (**at,** après).

grumpy /'grʌmpɪ/ *a.* (**-ier, -iest**) grincheux, grognon.

grunt /grʌnt/ *v.i.* grogner. ● *n.* grognement *m.*

guarant|ee /ˌgærən'tiː/ *n.* garantie *f.* ● *v.t.* garantir. **~or** *n.* garant(e) *m.* (*f.*).

guard /gɑːd/ *v.t.* protéger; (*watch*) surveiller. ● *v.i.* ~ **against,** se protéger contre. ● *n.* (*vigilance, mil., group*) garde *f.*; (*person*) garde *m.*; (*on train*) chef de train *m.* **~ian**

n. gardien(ne) *m.* (*f.*); (*of orphan*) tu|teur, -trice *m., f.*

guarded /'gɑːdɪd/ *a.* prudent.

guerrilla /gə'rɪlə/ *n.* guérillero *m.* ~ **warfare,** guérilla *f.*

guess /ges/ *v.t./i.* deviner; (*suppose*) penser. ● *n.* conjecture *f.*

guesswork /'geswɜːk/ *n.* conjectures *f. pl.*

guest /gest/ *n.* invité(e) *m.* (*f.*); (*in hotel*) client(e) *m.* (*f.*). **~-house** *n.* pension *f.* **~-room** *n.* chambre d'ami *f.*

guffaw /gə'fɔː/ *n.* gros rire *m.* ● *v.i.* s'esclaffer, rire bruyamment.

guidance /'gaɪdns/ *n.* (*advice*) conseils *m. pl.*; (*information*) information *f.*

guide /gaɪd/ *n.* (*person, book*) guide *m.* ● *v.t.* guider. **~d** /-ɪd/ *a.* **~d missile,** missile téléguidé *m.* **~-dog** *n.* chien d'aveugle *m.* **~-lines** *n. pl.* grandes lignes *f. pl.*

Guide /gaɪd/ *n.* (*girl*) guide *f.*

guidebook /'gaɪdbʊk/ *n.* guide *m.*

guild /gɪld/ *n.* corporation *f.*

guile /gaɪl/ *n.* ruse *f.*

guillotine /'gɪlətiːn/ *n.* guillotine *f.*; (*for paper*) massicot *m.*

guilt /gɪlt/ *n.* culpabilité *f.* **~y** *a.* coupable.

guinea-pig /'gɪnɪpɪg/ *n.* cobaye *m.*

guinea-fowl /'gɪnɪfaʊl/ *n.* pintade *f.*

guise /gaɪz/ *n.* apparence *f.*

guitar /gɪ'tɑː(r)/ *n.* guitare *f.* **~ist** *n.* guitariste *m./f.*

gulf /gʌlf/ *n.* (*part of sea*) golfe *m.*; (*hollow*) gouffre *m.*

gull /gʌl/ *n.* mouette *f.*, goéland *m.*

gullet /'gʌlɪt/ *n.* gosier *m.*

gullible /'gʌləbl/ *a.* crédule.

gully /'gʌlɪ/ *n.* (*ravine*) ravine *f.*; (*drain*) rigole *f.*

gulp /gʌlp/ *v.t.* ~ (**down**), avaler en vitesse. ● *v.i.* (*from fear etc.*) avoir un serrement de gorge. ● *n.* gorgée *f.*

gum [¹](gʌm/ *n.* (*anat.*) gencive *f.*

gum [²](gʌm/ *n.* (*from tree*) gomme *f.*; (*glue*) colle *f.*; (*for chewing*) chewing-gum *m.* ● *v.t.* (*p.t.* **gummed**) gommer.

gumboil /'gʌmbɔɪl/ *n.* abcès dentaire *m.*

gumboot /'gʌmbuːt/ *n.* botte de caoutchouc *f.*

gumption /'gʌmpʃn/ *n.* (*fam.*) initiative *f.*, courage *m.*, audace *f.*

gun /gʌn/ n. (*pistol*) revolver m.; (*rifle*) fusil m.; (*large*) canon m. ● v.t. (*p.t.* gunned). ~ **down**, abattre. ~ner n. artilleur m.

gunfire /'gʌnfaɪə(r)/ n. fusillade f.

gunge /gʌndʒ/ n. (*sl.*) crasse f.

gunman /'gʌnmən/ n. (*pl.* -men) bandit armé m.

gunpowder /'gʌnpaʊdə(r)/ n. poudre à canon f.

gunshot /'gʌnʃɒt/ n. coup de feu m.

gurgle /'gɜːgl/ n. glouglou m. ● v.i. glouglouter.

guru /'gʊruː/ n. (*pl.* -us) gourou m.

gush /gʌʃ/ v.i. ~ (out), jaillir. ● n. jaillissement m.

gust /gʌst/ n. rafale f.; (*of smoke*) bouffée f. ~y a. venteux.

gusto /'gʌstəʊ/ n. enthousiasme m.

gut /gʌt/ n. boyau m. ~s, boyaux m. pl., ventre m.; (*courage: fam.*) cran m. ● v.t. (*p.t.* gutted) (*fish*) vider; (*of fire*) dévaster.

gutter /'gʌtə(r)/ n. (*on roof*) gouttière f.; (*in street*) caniveau m.

guttural /'gʌtərəl/ a. guttural.

guy /gaɪ/ n. (*man: fam.*) type m.

guzzle /'gʌzl/ v.t./i. (*eat*) bâfrer; (*drink: Amer.*) boire d'un trait.

gym /dʒɪm/ n. (*fam.*) gymnase m.; (*fam.*) gym(nastique) f. ~-slip n. tunique f. ~nasium n. gymnase m.

gymnast /'dʒɪmnæst/ n. gymnaste m./f. ~ics /-'næstɪks/ n. pl. gymnastique f.

gynaecolog|y /gaɪnɪ'kɒlədʒɪ/ n. gynécologie f. ~ist n. gynécologue m./f.

gypsy /'dʒɪpsɪ/ n. bohémien(ne) m. (f.).

gyrate /dʒaɪ'reɪt/ v.i. tournoyer.

H

haberdashery /hæbə'dæʃərɪ/ n. mercerie f.

habit /'hæbɪt/ n. habitude f.; (*costume: relig.*) habit m. **be in/get into the ~ of**, avoir/prendre l'habitude de.

habit|able /'hæbɪtəbl/ a. habitable. ~ation /-'teɪʃn/ n. habitation f.

habitat /'hæbɪtæt/ n. habitat m.

habitual /hə'bɪtʃʊəl/ a. (*usual*) habituel; (*smoker, liar*) invétéré. ~ly adv. habituellement.

hack[1] /hæk/ n. (*old horse*) haridelle f.; (*writer*) nègre m., écrivailleu|r, -se m., f.

hack[2] /hæk/ v.t. hacher, tailler.

hackneyed /'hæknɪd/ a. rebattu.

had /hæd/ see have.

haddock /'hædək/ n. invar. églefin m. **smoked ~**, haddock m.

haemorrhage /'hemərɪdʒ/ n. hémorragie f.

haemorrhoids /'hemərɔɪdz/ n. pl. hémorroïdes f. pl.

hag /hæg/ n. (vieille) sorcière f.

haggard /'hægəd/ a. (*person*) qui a le visage défait; (*face, look*) défait, hagard.

haggle /'hægl/ v.i. marchander. ~ **over**, (*object*) marchander; (*price*) discuter.

Hague (The) /(ðə)'heɪg/ n. La Haye f.

hail[1] /heɪl/ v.t. (*greet*) saluer; (*taxi*) héler. ● v.i. ~ **from**, venir de.

hail[2] /heɪl/ n. grêle f. ● v.i. grêler.

hailstone /'heɪlstəʊn/ n. grêlon m.

hair /heə(r)/ n. (*on head*) cheveux m. pl.; (*on body, of animal*) poils m. pl.; (*single strand on head*) cheveu m.; (*on body*) poil m. ~-**do** n. (*fam.*) coiffure f. ~-**drier** n. séchoir (à cheveux) m. ~-**grip** n. pince à cheveux f. ~-**raising** a. horrifiant. ~-**remover**, dépilatoire m. ~-**style** n. coiffure f.

hairbrush /'heəbrʌʃ/ n. brosse à cheveux f.

haircut /'heəkʌt/ n. coupe de cheveux f. **have a ~**, se faire couper les cheveux.

hairdresser /'heədresə(r)/ n. coiffeu|r, -se m., f.

hairpin /'heəpɪn/ n. épingle à cheveux f.

hairy /'heərɪ/ a. (-ier, -iest) poilu; (*terrifying: sl.*) horrifiant.

hake /heɪk/ n. invar. colin m.

hale /heɪl/ a. vigoureux.

half /hɑːf/ n. (*pl.* halves) moitié f., demi(e) m. (f.). ● a. demi. ● adv. à moitié. ~ **a dozen**, une demi-douzaine. ~ **an hour**, une demi-heure. **four and a ~**, quatre et demi(e). ~ **and half**, moitié moitié. **in ~**, en deux. ~-**back** n. (*sport*) demi m. ~-**caste** n. métis(se) m. (f.). ~-**hearted** a. tiède. **at ~-mast** adv. en berne. ~-**measure**, demi-mesure f. ~-**price**, moitié prix. ~-**term** n. congé de (de)mi-trimestre m. ~-**time**

n. mi-temps *f.* **~-way** *adv.* à mi-chemin. **~-wit** *n.* imbécile *m./f.*

halibut /'hælɪbət/ *n. invar. (fish)* flétan *m.*

hall /hɔːl/ *n. (room)* salle *f.; (entrance)* vestibule *m.; (mansion)* manoir *m.; (corridor)* couloir *m.* **~ of residence,** foyer d'étudiants *m.*

hallelujah /hælɪ'luːjə/ *int. & n.* = **alleluia.**

hallmark /'hɔːlmɑːk/ *n. (on gold etc.)* poinçon *m.; (fig.)* sceau *m.*

hallo /hə'ləʊ/ *int. & n.* bonjour *(m.).* **~!,** *(on telephone)* allô!; *(in surprise)* tiens!

hallow /'hæləʊ/ *v.t.* sanctifier.

Hallowe'en /hæləʊ'iːn/ *n.* la veille de la Toussaint.

hallucination /həluːsɪ'neɪʃn/ *n.* hallucination *f.*

halo /'heɪləʊ/ *n. (pl. -oes)* auréole *f.*

halt /hɔːlt/ *n.* halte *f.* ● *v.t./i.* (s')arrêter.

halve /hɑːv/ *v.t.* diviser en deux; *(time etc.)* réduire de moitié.

ham /hæm/ *n.* jambon *m.; (theatre: sl.)* cabotin(e) *m. (f.).* **~-fisted** *a.* maladroit.

hamburger /'hæmbɜːgə(r)/ *n.* hamburger *m.*

hamlet /'hæmlɪt/ *n.* hameau *m.*

hammer /'hæmə(r)/ *n.* marteau *m.* ● *v.t./i.* marteler, frapper; *(defeat)* battre à plate couture. **~ out,** *(differences)* arranger; *(agreement)* arriver à.

hammock /'hæmək/ *n.* hamac *m.*

hamper [1] /'hæmpə(r)/ *n.* panier *m.*

hamper [2] /'hæmpə(r)/ *v.t.* gêner.

hamster /'hæmstə(r)/ *n.* hamster *m.*

hand /hænd/ *n.* main *f.; (of clock)* aiguille *f.; (writing)* écriture *f.; (worker)* ouvr|ier, -ière *m., f.; (cards)* jeu *m.* ● *v.t.* donner. **at ~,** proche. **~-baggage** *n.* bagages à main *m. pl.* **give s.o. a ~,** donner un coup de main à qn. **in** *or* **over,** remettre. **~ out,** distribuer. **~-out** *n.* prospectus *m.; (money)* aumône *f.* **on ~,** disponible. **on one's ~s,** *(fig.)* sur les bras. **on the one ~ ... on the other ~,** d'une part ... d'autre part. **to ~,** à portée de la main.

handbag /'hændbæg/ *n.* sac à main *m.*

handbook /'hændbʊk/ *n.* manuel *m.*

handbrake /'hændbreɪk/ *n.* frein à main *m.*

handcuffs /'hændkʌfs/ *n. pl.* menottes *f. pl.*

handful /'hændfʊl/ *n.* poignée *f.;* **he's a ~!,** c'est du boulot!

handicap /'hændɪkæp/ *n.* handicap *m.* ● *v.t. (p.t.* **handicapped)** handicaper.

handicraft /'hændɪkrɑːft/ *n.* travaux manuels *m. pl.,* artisanat *m.*

handiwork /'hændɪwɜːk/ *n.* ouvrage *m.*

handkerchief /'hæŋkətʃɪf/ *n. (pl. -fs)* mouchoir *m.*

handle /'hændl/ *n. (of door etc.)* poignée *f.; (of implement)* manche *m.; (of cup etc.)* anse *f.; (of pan etc.)* queue *f.; (for turning)* manivelle *f.* ● *v.t.* manier; *(deal with)* s'occuper de; *(touch)* toucher à.

handlebar /'hændlbɑː(r)/ *n.* guidon *m.*

handshake /'hændʃeɪk/ *n.* poignée de main *f.*

handsome /'hænsəm/ *a. (goodlooking)* beau; *(generous)* généreux; *(large)* considérable.

handwriting /'hændraɪtɪŋ/ *n.* écriture *f.*

handy /'hændɪ/ *a.* **(-ier, -iest)** *(useful)* commode, utile; *(person)* adroit; *(near)* accessible.

handyman /'hændɪmæn/ *n. (pl. -men)* bricoleur *m.; (servant)* homme à tout faire *m.*

hang /hæŋ/ *v.t. (p.t.* **hung)** suspendre, accrocher; *(p.t.* **hanged)** *(criminal)* pendre. ● *v.i.* pendre. ● *n.* **get the ~ of doing,** trouver le truc pour faire. **~ about,** traîner. **~-gliding** *n.* vol libre *m.* **~ on,** *(hold out)* tenir bon; *(wait: sl.)* attendre. **~ out** *v.i.* pendre; *(live: sl.)* crécher; *(spend time: sl.)* passer son temps; *v.t. (washing)* étendre. **~ up,** *(telephone)* raccrocher. **~-up** *n. (sl.)* complexe *m.*

hangar /'hæŋə(r)/ *n.* hangar *m.*

hanger /'hæŋə(r)/ *n. (for clothes)* cintre *m.* **~-on** *n.* parasite *m.*

hangover /'hæŋəʊvə(r)/ *n. (after drinking)* gueule de bois *f.*

hanker /'hæŋkə(r)/ *v.i.* **~ after,** avoir envie de. **~ing** *n.* envie *f.*

hanky-panky /'hæŋkɪpæŋkɪ/ *n. (trickery: sl.)* manigances *f. pl.*

haphazard /hæp'hæzəd/ *a.,* **~ly** *adv.* au petit bonheur, au hasard.

hapless /'hæplɪs/ *a.* infortuné.

happen /'hæpən/ v.i. arriver, se passer. it so ~s that, il se trouve que. he ~s to know that, il se trouve qu'il sait que. ~ing n. événement m.

happ|y /'hæpɪ/ a. (-ier, -iest) heureux. I'm not ~y about the idea, je n'aime pas trop l'idée. ~y with sth., satisfait de qch. ~y medium or mean, juste milieu m. ~ily adv. joyeusement; (fortunately) heureusement; ~iness n. bonheur m. ~y-go-lucky a. insouciant.

harass /'hærəs/ v.t. harceler. ~ment n. harcèlement m.

harbour, (Amer.) **harbor** /'hɑːbə(r)/ n. port m. ● v.t. (shelter) héberger.

hard /hɑːd/ a. (-er, -est) dur; (difficult) difficile, dur. ● adv. dur; (think) sérieusement; (pull) fort. ~ and fast, concret. ~-boiled egg, œuf dur m. ~ by, tout près. ~ disk, disque dur m. ~ done by, mal traité. ~-headed a. réaliste. ~ of hearing, dur d'oreille. the ~ of hearing, les malentendants m. pl. ~-line a. pur et dur. ~ shoulder, accotement stabilisé m. ~ up, (fam.) fauché. ~-wearing a. solide. ~-working a. travailleur. ~ness n. dureté f.

hardboard /'hɑːdbɔːd/ n. Isorel m. (P.).

harden /'hɑːdn/ v.t./i. durcir.

hardly /'hɑːdlɪ/ adv. à peine. ~ ever, presque jamais.

hardship /'hɑːdʃɪp/ n. ~(s), épreuves f. pl., souffrance f.

hardware /'hɑːdweə(r)/ n. (metal goods) quincaillerie f.; (machinery, of computer) matériel m.

hardy /'hɑːdɪ/ a. (-ier, iest) résistant.

hare /heə(r)/ n. lièvre m. ~-around, courir partout. ~-brained a. écervelé.

hark /hɑːk/ v.i. écouter. ~ back to, revenir sur.

harm /hɑːm/ n. (hurt) mal m.; (wrong) tort m. ● v.t. (hurt) faire du mal à; (wrong) faire du tort à; (object) endommager. there is no ~ in, il n'y a pas de mal à. ~ful a. nuisible. ~less a. inoffensif.

harmonica /hɑː'mɒnɪkə/ n. harmonica m.

harmon|y /'hɑːmənɪ/ n. harmonie f. ~ious /-'məʊnɪəs/ a. harmonieux. ~ize v.t./i. (s')harmoniser.

harness /'hɑːnɪs/ n. harnais m. ● v.t. (horse) harnacher; (control) maîtriser; (use) exploiter.

harp /hɑːp/ n. harpe f. ● v.i. ~ on (about), rabâcher. ~ist n. harpiste m./f.

harpoon /hɑː'puːn/ n. harpon m.

harpsichord /'hɑːpsɪkɔːd/ n. clavecin m.

harrowing /'hærəʊɪŋ/ a. déchirant, qui déchire le cœur.

harsh /hɑːʃ/ a. (-er, -est) dur, rude; (taste) âpre; (sound) rude, âpre. ~ly adv. durement. ~ness n. dureté f.

harvest /'hɑːvɪst/ n. moisson f., récolte f. the wine ~, les vendanges f. pl. ● v.t. moissonner, récolter. ~er n. moissonneuse f.

has /hæz/ see have.

hash /hæʃ/ n. (culin.) hachis m.; (fig.) gâchis m. make a ~ of, (bungle: sl.) saboter.

hashish /'hæʃiːʃ/ n. ha(s)chisch m.

hassle /'hæsl/ n. (fam.) difficulté(s) f. (pl.); (bother, effort: fam.) mal m., peine f.; (quarrel: fam.) chamaillerie f. ● v.t. (harass: fam.) harceler.

haste /heɪst/ n. hâte f. in ~, à la hâte. make ~, se hâter.

hasten /'heɪsn/ v.t./i. (se) hâter.

hast|y /'heɪstɪ/ a. (-ier, -iest) précipité. ~ily adv. à la hâte.

hat /hæt/ n. chapeau m. ~ trick, trois succès consécutifs.

hatch[1] /hætʃ/ n. (for food) passeplat m.; (naut.) écoutille f.

hatch[2] /hætʃ/ v.t./i. (faire) éclore.

hatchback /'hætʃbæk/ n. voiture avec hayon arrière f.

hatchet /'hætʃɪt/ n. hachette f.

hate /heɪt/ n. haine f. ● v.t. haïr. ~ful a. haïssable.

hatred /'heɪtrɪd/ n. haine f.

haughty /'hɔːtɪ/ a. (-ier, -iest) hautain.

haul /hɔːl/ v.t. traîner, tirer. ● n. (of thieves) butin m.; (catch) prise f.; (journey) voyage m. ~age m. camionnage m. ~ier n. camionneur m.

haunch /hɔːntʃ/ n. on one's ~es, accroupi.

haunt /hɔːnt/ v.t. hanter. ● n. endroit favori m.

have /hæv/ v.t. (3 sing. present tense has; p.t. had) avoir; (meal, bath, etc.) prendre; (walk, dream, etc.) faire. ● v. aux. avoir; (with aller, partir, etc. & pronominal verbs) être. ~ it out with, s'expliquer avec. ~ just

done, venir de faire. ~ sth. done, faire faire qch. ~ to do, devoir faire. **the ~s and have-nots**, les riches et les pauvres *m. pl.*

haven /'heɪvn/ *n.* havre *m.*, abri *m.*

haversack /'hævəsæk/ *n.* musette *f.*

havoc /'hævək/ *n.* ravages *m. pl.*

haw /hɔː/ *see* hum.

hawk¹ /hɔːk/ *n.* faucon *m.*

hawk² /hɔːk/ *v.t.* colporter. **~er** *n.* colporteu|r, -se *m., f.*

hawthorn /'hɔːθɔːn/ *n.* aubépine *f.*

hay /heɪ/ *n.* foin *m.* **~ fever**, rhume des foins *m.*

haystack /'heɪstæk/ *n.* meule de foin *f.*

haywire /'heɪwaɪə(r)/ *a.* **go ~**, (*plans*) se désorganiser; (*machine*) se détraquer.

hazard /'hæzəd/ *n.* risque *m.* ● *v.t.* risquer, hasarder. **~ warning lights**, feux de détresse *m. pl.* **~ous** *a.* hasardeux, risqué.

haze /heɪz/ *n.* brume *f.*

hazel /'heɪzl/ *n.* (*bush*) noisetier *m.* **~-nut** *n.* noisette *f.*

hazy /'heɪzɪ/ *a.* (**-ier, -iest**) (*misty*) brumeux; (*fig.*) flou, vague.

he /hiː/ *pron.* il; (*emphatic*) lui. ● *n.* mâle *m.*

head /hed/ *n.* tête *f.*; (*leader*) chef *m.*; (*of beer*) mousse *f.* ● *a.* principal. ● *v.t.* être à la tête de. ● *v.i.* **~ for**, se diriger vers. **~-dress** *n.* coiffure *f.*; (*lady's*) coiffe *f.* **~-on** *a. & adv.* de plein fouet. **~ first**, la tête la première. **~s or tails?**, pile ou face? **~ office**, siège *m.* **~ rest**, appui-tête *m.* **~ the ball**, faire une tête. **~ waiter**, maître d'hôtel *m.* **~er** *n.* (*football*) tête *f.*

headache /'hedeɪk/ *n.* mal de tête *m.*

heading /'hedɪŋ/ *n.* titre *m.*; (*subject category*) rubrique *f.*

headlamp /'hedlæmp/ *n.* phare *m.*

headland /'hedlənd/ *n.* cap *m.*

headlight /'hedlaɪt/ *n.* phare *m.*

headline /'hedlaɪn/ *n.* titre *m.*

headlong /'hedlɒŋ/ *adv.* (*in a rush*) à toute allure.

head|master /hed'mɑːstə(r)/ *n.* (*of school*) directeur *m.* **~mistress** *n.* directrice *f.*

headphone /'hedfəʊn/ *n.* écouteur *m.* **~s**, casque (à écouteurs) *m.*

headquarters /'hedkwɔːtəz/ *n. pl.* siège *m.*, bureau central *m.*; (*mil.*) quartier général *m.*

headstrong /'hedstrɒŋ/ *a.* têtu.

headway /'hedweɪ/ *n.* progrès *m.* (*pl.*) **make ~**, faire des progrès.

heady /'hedɪ/ *a.* (**-ier, -iest**) (*wine*) capiteux; (*exciting*) grisant.

heal /hiːl/ *v.t./i.* guérir.

health /helθ/ *n.* santé *f.* **~ centre**, dispensaire *m.* **~ foods**, aliments diététiques *m. pl.* **~ insurance**, assurance médicale *f.* **~y** *a.* sain; (*person*) en bonne santé.

heap /hiːp/ *n.* tas *m.* ● *v.t.* entasser. **~s of**, (*fam.*) des tas de.

hear /hɪə(r)/ *v.t./i.* (*p.t.* **heard** /hɜːd/) entendre. **hear, hear!**, bravo! **~ from**, recevoir des nouvelles de. **~ of** *or* **about**, entendre parler de. **not ~ of**, (*refuse to allow*) ne pas entendre parler de. **~ing** *n.* ouïe *f.*; (*of witness*) audition *f.*; (*of case*) audience *f.* **~ing-aid** *n.* appareil acoustique *m.*

hearsay /'hɪəseɪ/ *n.* ouï-dire *m. invar.* **from ~**, par ouï-dire.

hearse /hɜːs/ *n.* corbillard *m.*

heart /hɑːt/ *n.* cœur *m.* **~s**, (*cards*) cœur *m.* **at ~**, au fond. **by ~**, par cœur. **~ attack**, crise cardiaque *f.* **~-break** *n.* chagrin *m.* **~-breaking** *a.* navrant. **be ~-broken**, avoir le cœur brisé. **~-to-heart** *a.* à cœur ouvert. **lose ~**, perdre courage.

heartache /'hɑːteɪk/ *n.* chagrin *m.*

heartburn /'hɑːtbɜːn/ *n.* brûlures d'estomac *f. pl.*

hearten /'hɑːtn/ *v.t.* encourager.

heartfelt /'hɑːtfelt/ *a.* sincère.

hearth /hɑːθ/ *n.* foyer *m.*

heartless /'hɑːtlɪs/ *a.* cruel.

heart|y /'hɑːtɪ/ *a.* (**-ier, -iest**) (*sincere*) chaleureux; (*meal*) gros. **~ily** *adv.* (*eat*) avec appétit.

heat /hiːt/ *n.* chaleur *f.*; (*excitement: fig.*) feu *m.*; (*contest*) éliminatoire *f.* ● *v.t./i.* chauffer. **~ stroke**, insolation *f.* **~ up**, (*food*) réchauffer. **~ wave**, vague de chaleur *f.* **~er** *n.* radiateur *m.* **~ing** *n.* chauffage *m.*

heated /'hiːtɪd/ *a.* (*fig.*) passionné.

heath /hiːθ/ *n.* (*area*) lande *f.*

heathen /'hiːðn/ *n.* païen(ne) *m.* (*f.*).

heather /'heðə(r)/ *n.* bruyère *f.*

heave /hiːv/ *v.t./i.* (*lift*) (se) soulever; (*a sigh*) pousser; (*throw: fam.*) lancer; (*retch*) avoir des nausées.

heaven /'hevn/ *n.* ciel *m.* **~ly** *a.* céleste; (*pleasing: fam.*) divin.

heav|y /'hevɪ/ *a.* (**-ier, -iest**) lourd; (*cold, work, etc.*) gros; (*traffic*) dense. **~y goods vehicle**, poids

lourd *m.* **~y-handed** *a.* maladroit.
~ily *adv.* lourdement; (*smoke,
drink*) beaucoup.
heavyweight /'heviweit/ *n.* poids
lourd *m.*
Hebrew /'hi:bru:/ *a.* hébreu (*m.
only*), hébraïque. ● *n.* (*lang.*) hébreu *m.*
heckle /'hekl/ *v.t.* (*speaker*) interrompre, interpeller.
hectic /'hektɪk/ *a.* très bousculé, tré-
pidant, agité.
hedge /hedʒ/ *n.* haie *f.* ● *v.t.*
entourer. ● *v.i.* (*in answering*) répondre évasivement. **~ one's bets**,
protéger ses arrières.
hedgehog /'hedʒhɒg/ *n.* hérisson *m.*
heed /hi:d/ *v.t.* faire attention à. ● *n.*
pay ~ to, faire attention à. **~less** *a.*
~less of, inattentif à.
heel /hi:l/ *n.* talon *m.*; (*man: sl.*)
salaud *m.* **down at ~**, (*Amer.*)
down at the ~s, miteux.
hefty /'hefti/ *a.* (**-ier, -iest**) gros,
lourd.
heifer /'hefə(r)/ *n.* génisse *f.*
height /hait/ *n.* hauteur *f.*; (*of person*) taille *f.*; (*of plane, mountain*)
altitude *f.*; (*of fame, glory*) apogée
m.; (*of joy, folly, pain*) comble *m.*
heighten /'haitn/ *v.t.* (*raise*) rehausser; (*fig.*) augmenter.
heinous /'heinəs/ *a.* atroce.
heir /eə(r)/ *n.* héritier *m.* **~ess** *n.*
héritière *f.*
heirloom /'eəlu:m/ *n.* bijou (meuble,
tableau, *etc.*) de famille *m.*
held /held/ *see* **hold** [1].
helicopter /'helikɒptə(r)/ *n.* hélicoptère *m.*
heliport /'helipɔ:t/ *n.* héliport *m.*
hell /hel/ *n.* enfer *m.* **~-bent** *a.*
acharné (**on**, à). **~ish** *a.* infernal.
hello /hə'ləʊ/ *int.* & *n.* = **hallo.**
helm /helm/ *n.* (*of ship*) barre *f.*
helmet /'helmɪt/ *n.* casque *m.*
help /help/ *v.t./i.* aider. ● *n.* aide *f.*;
(*employees*) personnel *m.*; (*charwoman*) femme de ménage *f.* **~ o.s.
to**, se servir de. **he cannot ~ laughing**, il ne peut pas s'empêcher de
rire. **~er** *n.* aide *m./f.* **~ful** *a.* utile;
(*person*) serviable. **~less** *a.* impuissant.
helping /'helpɪŋ/ *n.* portion *f.*
helter-skelter /heltə'skeltə(r)/ *n.* toboggan *m.* ● *adv.* pêle-mêle.
hem /hem/ *n.* ourlet *m.* ● *v.t.* (*p.t.*
hemmed) ourler. **~ in**, enfermer.

hemisphere /'hemisfɪə(r)/ *n.* hémisphère *m.*
hemorrhage /'hemərɪdʒ/ *n.* (*Amer.*)
= **haemorrhage.**
hemorrhoids /'hemərɔɪdz/ *n. pl.*
(*Amer.*) = **haemorrhoids.**
hen /hen/ *n.* poule *f.*
hence /hens/ *adv.* (*for this reason*)
d'où; (*from now*) d'ici. **~forth** *adv.*
désormais.
henchman /'hentʃmən/ *n.* (*pl.* **-men**)
acolyte *m.*, homme de main *m.*
henpecked /'henpekt/ *a.* dominé *or*
harcelé par sa femme.
hepatitis /hepə'taɪtɪs/ *n.* hépatite *f.*
her /hɜ:(r)/ *pron.* la, l'*; (*after prep.*)
elle. **(to) ~**, lui. **I know ~**, je la
connais. ● *a.* son, sa, *pl.* ses.
herald /'herəld/ *v.t.* annoncer.
herb /hɜ:b, *Amer.* ɜ:b/ *n.* herbe *f.* **~s**,
(*culin.*) fines herbes *f. pl.*
herd /hɜ:d/ *n.* troupeau *m.* ● *v.t./i.* **~
together**, (s')entasser.
here /hɪə(r)/ *adv.* ici. **~!**, (*take this*)
tenez! **~ is**, **~ are**, voici. **I'm ~**, je
suis là. **~abouts** *adv.* par ici.
hereafter /hɪər'ɑ:ftə(r)/ *adv.* après;
(*in book*) ci-après.
hereby /hɪə'baɪ/ *adv.* par le présent
acte; (*in letter*) par la présente.
hereditary /hə'redɪtərɪ/ *a.* hérédi-
taire.
heredity /hə'redətɪ/ *n.* hérédité *f.*
here|sy /'herəsɪ/ *n.* hérésie *f.* **~tic** *n.*
hérétique *m./f.*
herewith /hɪə'wɪð/ *adv.* (*comm.*)
avec ceci, ci-joint.
heritage /'herɪtɪdʒ/ *n.* patrimoine *m.*,
héritage *m.*
hermit /'hɜ:mɪt/ *n.* ermite *m.*
hernia /'hɜ:nɪə/ *n.* hernie *f.*
hero /'hɪərəʊ/ *n.* (*pl.* **-oes**) héros *m.*
~ine /'herəʊɪn/ *n.* héroïne *f.* **~ism**
/'herəʊɪzəm/ *n.* héroïsme *m.*
heroic /hɪ'rəʊɪk/ *a.* héroïque.
heroin /'herəʊɪn/ *n.* héroïne *f.*
heron /'herən/ *n.* héron *m.*
herpes /'hɜ:pi:z/ *n.* herpès *m.*
herring /'herɪŋ/ *n.* hareng *m.*
hers /hɜ:z/ *poss. pron.* le sien, la
sienne, les sien(ne)s. **it is ~**, c'est à
elle *or* le sien.
herself /hɜ:'self/ *pron.* elle-même;
(*reflexive*) se; (*after prep.*) elle.
hesitant /'hezɪtənt/ *a.* hésitant.
hesitat|e /'hezɪteɪt/ *v.i.* hésiter. **~ion**
/-'teɪʃn/ *n.* hésitation *f.*
het /het/ *a.* **~ up**, (*sl.*) énervé.

heterosexual /hetərəʊ'seksjʊəl/ a. & n. hétérosexuel(le) (m. (f.)).

hexagon /'heksəgən/ n. hexagone m. **~al** /-'ægənl/ a. hexagonal.

hey /heɪ/ int. dites donc.

heyday /'heɪdeɪ/ n. apogée m.

HGV abbr. see heavy goods vehicle.

hi /haɪ/ int. (greeting: Amer.) salut.

hibernat|e /'haɪbəneɪt/ v.i. hiberner. **~ion** /-'neɪʃn/ n. hibernation f.

hiccup /'hɪkʌp/ n. hoquet m. ● v.i. hoqueter. **(the) ~s**, le hoquet.

hide[1] /haɪd/ v.t. (p.t. hid, p.p. hidden) cacher (from, à). ● v.i. se cacher (from, de). **go into hiding**, se cacher. **~out** n. (fam.) cachette f.

hide[2] /haɪd/ n. (skin) peau f.

hideous /'hɪdɪəs/ a. (dreadful) atroce; (ugly) hideux.

hiding /'haɪdɪŋ/ n. (thrashing: fam.) correction f.

hierarchy /'haɪərɑːkɪ/ n. hiérarchie f.

hi-fi /'haɪfaɪ/ a. & n. hi-fi a. & f. invar.; (machine) chaîne hi-fi f.

high /haɪ/ a. (-er, -est) haut; (price, number) élevé; (priest, speed) grand; (voice) aigu. ● n. **a (new) ~**, (recorded level) un record. ● adv. haut. **~ chair**, chaise haute f. **~-handed** a. autoritaire. **~-jump**, saut en hauteur m. **~-level** a. de haut niveau. **~-rise building**, tour f. **~ road**, grand-route f. **~ school**, lycée m. **in the ~ season**, en pleine saison. **~-speed** a. ultra-rapide. **~ spot**, (fam.) point culminant m. **~ street**, grand-rue f. **~-strung** a. (Amer.) nerveux. **~ tea**, goûter-dîner m. **~er education**, enseignement supérieur m.

highbrow /'haɪbraʊ/ a. & n. intellectuel(le) (m. (f.)).

highlight /'haɪlaɪt/ n. (vivid moment) moment fort m. **~s**, (in hair) balayage m. recorded **~s**, extraits enregistrés m. pl. ● v.t. (emphasize) souligner.

highly /'haɪlɪ/ adv. extrêmement; (paid) très bien. **~-strung** a. nerveux. **speak/think ~ of**, dire/penser du bien de.

Highness /'haɪnɪs/ n. Altesse f.

highway /'haɪweɪ/ n. route nationale f. **~ code**, code de la route m.

hijack /'haɪdʒæk/ v.t. détourner. ● n. détournement m. **~er** n. pirate (de l'air) m.

hike /haɪk/ n. randonnée f. ● v.i. faire de la randonnée. **price ~**,

hausse de prix f. **~r** /-ə(r)/ n. randonneu|r, -se m., f.

hilarious /hɪ'leərɪəs/ a. (funny) désopilant.

hill /hɪl/ n. colline f.; (slope) côte f. **~y** a. accidenté.

hillside /'hɪlsaɪd/ n. coteau m.

hilt /hɪlt/ n. (of sword) garde f. **to the ~**, tout à fait, au maximum.

him /hɪm/ pron. le, l*; (after prep.) lui. **(to) ~**, lui. **I know ~**, je le connais.

himself /hɪm'self/ pron. lui-même; (reflexive) se; (after prep.) lui.

hind /haɪnd/ a. de derrière.

hind|er /'haɪndə(r)/ v.t. (hamper) gêner; (prevent) empêcher. **~rance** n. obstacle m., gêne f.

hindsight /'haɪndsaɪt/ n. **with ~**, rétrospectivement.

Hindu /hɪn'duː/ a. & n. hindou(e) (m. (f.)). **~ism** /'hɪnduːɪzəm/ n. hindouisme m.

hinge /hɪndʒ/ n. charnière f. ● v.i. **~ on**, (depend on) dépendre de.

hint /hɪnt/ n. allusion f.; (advice) conseil m. ● v.t. laisser entendre. ● v.i. **~ at**, faire allusion à.

hip /hɪp/ n. hanche f.

hippie /'hɪpɪ/ n. hippie m./f.

hippopotamus /hɪpə'pɒtəməs/ n. (pl. -muses) hippopotame m.

hire /'haɪə(r)/ v.t. (thing) louer; (person) engager. ● n. location f. **~-car** n. voiture de location f. **~-purchase** n. achat à crédit m., vente à crédit f.

his /hɪz/ a. son, sa, pl. ses. ● poss. pron. le sien, la sienne, les sien(ne)s. **it is ~**, c'est à lui or le sien.

hiss /hɪs/ n. sifflement m. ● v.t./i. siffler.

historian /hɪ'stɔːrɪən/ n. historien(ne) m. (f.).

histor|y /'hɪstərɪ/ n. histoire f. **make ~y**, entrer dans l'histoire. **~ic(al)** /hɪ'stɒrɪk(l)/ a. historique.

hit /hɪt/ v.t. (p.t. hit, pres. p. hitting) frapper; (knock against, collide with) heurter; (find) trouver; (affect, reach) toucher. ● v.i. **~ on**, (find) tomber sur. ● n. (blow) coup m.; (fig.) succès m.; (song) tube m. **~ it off**, s'entendre bien (with, avec). **~-or-miss** a. fait au petit bonheur.

hitch /hɪtʃ/ v.t. (fasten) accrocher. ● n. (snag) anicroche f. **~ a lift**, **~-hike** v.i. faire de l'auto-stop. **~-hiker** n. auto-stoppeu|r, -se m., f. **~ up**, (pull up) remonter.

hi-tech /haɪˈtek/ a. & n. high-tech (m.) invar.

hitherto /hɪðəˈtuː/ adv. jusqu'ici.

HIV abbr. HIV. **~-positive** a. séropositif.

hive /haɪv/ n. ruche f. ● v.t. ~ off, séparer; (industry) vendre.

hoard /hɔːd/ v.t. amasser. ● n. réserve(s) f. (pl.); (of money) magot m., trésor m.

hoarding /ˈhɔːdɪŋ/ n. panneau d'affichage m.

hoar-frost /ˈhɔːfrɒst/ n. givre m.

hoarse /hɔːs/ a. (-er, -est) enroué. **~ness** n. enrouement m.

hoax /həʊks/ n. canular m. ● v.t. faire un canular à.

hob /hɒb/ n. plaque chauffante f.

hobble /ˈhɒbl/ v.i. clopiner.

hobby /ˈhɒbɪ/ n. passe-temps m. invar. **~-horse** n. (fig.) dada m.

hob-nob /ˈhɒbnɒb/ v.i. (p.t. hob-nobbed) ~ with, frayer avec.

hock¹ /hɒk/ n. vin du Rhin m.

hock² /hɒk/ v.t. (pawn: sl.) mettre au clou.

hockey /ˈhɒkɪ/ n. hockey m.

hoe /həʊ/ n. binette f. ● v.t. (pres. p. hoeing) biner.

hog /hɒg/ n. cochon m. ● v.t. (p.t. hogged) (fam.) accaparer.

hoist /hɔɪst/ v.t. hisser. ● n. palan m.

hold¹ /həʊld/ v.t. (p.t. held) tenir; (contain) contenir; (interest, breath, etc.) retenir; (possess) avoir; (believe) maintenir. ● v.i. (of rope, weather, etc.) tenir. ● n. prise f. get ~ of, saisir; (fig.) trouver. on ~, en suspens. ~ back, (contain) retenir; (hide) cacher. ~ down, (job) garder; (in struggle) retenir. ~ on, (stand firm) tenir bon; (wait) attendre. ~ on to, (keep) garder; (cling to) se cramponner à. ~ one's tongue, se taire. ~ out v.t. (offer) offrir; v.i. (resist) tenir le coup. ~ (the line), please, ne quittez pas. ~ up, (support) soutenir; (delay) retarder; (rob) attaquer. **~-up** n. retard m.; (of traffic) bouchon m.; (robbery) hold-up m. invar. not ~ with, désapprouver. **~er** n. détenteur, -trice m., f.; (of post) titulaire m./f.; (for object) support m.

hold² /həʊld/ n. (of ship) cale f.

holdall /ˈhəʊldɔːl/ n. (bag) fourretout m. invar.

holding /ˈhəʊldɪŋ/ n. (possession, land) possession f. ~ company, holding m.

hole /həʊl/ n. trou m. ● v.t. trouer.

holiday /ˈhɒlədeɪ/ n. vacances f. pl.; (public) jour férié m.; (day off) congé m. ● v.i. passer ses vacances. ● a. de vacances. **~maker** n. vacancier, -ière m., f.

holiness /ˈhəʊlɪnɪs/ n. sainteté f.

holistic /həʊˈlɪstɪk/ a. holistique.

Holland /ˈhɒlənd/ n. Hollande f.

hollow /ˈhɒləʊ/ a. creux; (fig.) faux. ● n. creux m. ● v.t. creuser.

holly /ˈhɒlɪ/ n. houx m.

holster /ˈhəʊlstə(r)/ n. étui de revolver m.

holy /ˈhəʊlɪ/ a. (-ier, -iest) saint, sacré; (water) bénit. **H~ Ghost**, **H~ Spirit**, Saint-Esprit m.

homage /ˈhɒmɪdʒ/ n. hommage m.

home /həʊm/ n. maison f., foyer m.; (institution) maison f.; (for soldiers, workers) foyer m.; (country) pays natal m. ● a. de la maison, du foyer; (of family) de famille; (pol.) national, intérieur; (match, visit) à domicile. ● adv. (at) ~, à la maison, chez soi. come or go ~, rentrer; (from abroad) rentrer dans son pays. feel at ~ with, être à l'aise avec. **H~ Counties**, région autour de Londres f. **~-made** a. (food) fait maison; (clothes) fait à la maison. **H~ Office**, ministère de l'Intérieur m. **H~ Secretary**, ministre de l'Intérieur m. ~ town, ville natale f. ~ truth, vérité bien sentie f. **~less** a. sans abri.

homeland /ˈhəʊmlænd/ n. patrie f.

homely /ˈhəʊmlɪ/ a. (-ier, -iest) simple; (person: Amer.) assez laid.

homesick /ˈhəʊmsɪk/ a. be ~, avoir le mal du pays.

homeward /ˈhəʊmwəd/ a. (journey) de retour.

homework /ˈhəʊmwɜːk/ n. devoirs m. pl.

homicide /ˈhɒmɪsaɪd/ n. homicide m.

homœopath|**y** /həʊmɪˈɒpəθɪ/ n. homéopathie f. **~ic** a. homéopathique.

homogeneous /hɒməˈdʒiːnɪəs/ a. homogène.

homosexual /hɒməˈsekʃʊəl/ a. & n. homosexuel(le) (m. (f.)).

honest /ˈɒnɪst/ a. honnête; (frank) franc. **~ly** adv. honnêtement; franchement. **~y** n. honnêteté f.

honey /'hʌnɪ/ n. miel m.; (person: fam.) chéri(e) m. (f.).

honeycomb /'hʌnɪkəʊm/ n. rayon de miel m.

honeymoon /'hʌnɪmuːn/ n. lune de miel f.

honk /hɒŋk/ v.i. klaxonner.

honorary /'ɒnərərɪ/ a. (person) honoraire; (duties) honorifique.

honour, (Amer.) **honor** /'ɒnə(r)/ n. honneur m. ● v.t. honorer. ~**able** a. honorable.

hood /hʊd/ n. capuchon m.; (car roof) capote f.; (car engine cover: Amer.) capot m.

hoodlum /'huːdləm/ n. voyou m.

hoodwink /'hʊdwɪŋk/ v.t. tromper.

hoof /huːf/ n. (pl. -fs) sabot m.

hook /hʊk/ n. crochet m.; (on garment) agrafe f.; (for fishing) hameçon m. ● v.t./i. (s')accrocher; (garment) (s')agrafer. **off the ~,** tiré d'affaire; (phone) décroché.

hooked /hʊkt/ a. crochu. ~ **on,** (sl.) adonné à.

hooker /'hʊkə(r)/ n. (rugby) talonneur m.; (Amer., sl.) prostituée f.

hookey /'hʊkɪ/ n. **play ~,** (Amer., sl.) faire l'école buissonnière.

hooligan /'huːlɪgən/ n. houligan m.

hoop /huːp/ n. (toy etc.) cerceau m.

hooray /hʊ'reɪ/ int. & n. = **hurrah.**

hoot /huːt/ n. (h)ululement m.; coup de klaxon m.; huée f. ● v.i. (owl) (h)ululer; (of car) klaxonner; (jeer) huer. ~**er** n. klaxon m. (P.); (of factory) sirène f.

Hoover /'huːvə(r)/ n. (P.) aspirateur m. ● v.t. passer à l'aspirateur.

hop[1] /hɒp/ v.i. (p.t. **hopped**) sauter (à cloche-pied). ● n. saut m.; (flight) étape f. ~ **in,** (fam.) monter. ~ **it,** (sl.) décamper. ~ **out,** (fam.) descendre.

hop[2] /hɒp/ n. ~**(s),** houblon m.

hope /həʊp/ n. espoir m. ● v.t./i. espérer. ~ **for,** espérer (avoir). **I ~ so,** je l'espère. ~**ful** a. encourageant. **be ~ful (that),** avoir bon espoir (que). ~**fully** adv. avec espoir; (it is hoped) on l'espère. ~**less** a. sans espoir; (useless: fig.) nul. ~**lessly** adv. sans espoir m.

hopscotch /'hɒpskɒtʃ/ n. marelle f.

horde /hɔːd/ n. horde f., foule f.

horizon /hə'raɪzn/ n. horizon m.

horizontal /hɒrɪ'zɒntl/ a. horizontal.

hormone /'hɔːməʊn/ n. hormone f.

horn /hɔːn/ n. corne f.; (of car) klaxon m. (P.); (mus.) cor m. ● v.i. ~ **in,** (sl.) interrompre. ~**y** a. (hands) calleux.

hornet /'hɔːnɪt/ n. frelon m.

horoscope /'hɒrəskəʊp/ n. horoscope m.

horrible /'hɒrəbl/ a. horrible.

horrid /'hɒrɪd/ a. horrible.

horrific /hə'rɪfɪk/ a. horrifiant.

horr|or /'hɒrə(r)/ n. horreur f. ● a. (film etc.) d'épouvante. ~**ify** v.t. horrifier.

hors-d'œuvre /ɔː'dɜːvrə/ n. hors-d'œuvre m. invar.

horse /hɔːs/ n. cheval m. ~**-chestnut** n. marron (d'Inde) m. ~**-race** n. course de chevaux f. ~**-radish** n. raifort m. ~ **sense,** (fam.) bon sens m.

horseback /'hɔːsbæk/ n. **on ~,** à cheval.

horseman /'hɔːsmən/ n. (pl. -men) cavalier m.

horsepower /'hɔːspaʊə(r)/ n. (unit) cheval (vapeur) m.

horseshoe /'hɔːsʃuː/ n. fer à cheval m.

horsy /'hɔːsɪ/ a. (face etc.) chevalin.

horticultur|e /'hɔːtɪkʌltʃə(r)/ n. horticulture f. ~**al** /-'kʌltʃərəl/ a. horticole.

hose /həʊz/ n. (tube) tuyau m. ● v.t. arroser. ~**-pipe** n. tuyau m.

hosiery /'həʊzɪərɪ/ n. bonneterie f.

hospice /'hɒspɪs/ n. hospice m.

hospit|able /hɒ'spɪtəbl/ a. hospitalier. ~**ably** adv. avec hospitalité. ~**ality** /-'tælɪtɪ/ n. hospitalité f.

hospital /'hɒspɪtl/ n. hôpital m.

host[1] /həʊst/ n. (to guests) hôte m.; (on TV) animateur m. ~**ess** n. hôtesse f.

host[2] /həʊst/ n. **a ~ of,** une foule de.

host[3] /həʊst/ n. (relig.) hostie f.

hostage /'hɒstɪdʒ/ n. otage m.

hostel /'hɒstl/ n. foyer m. **(youth) ~,** auberge (de jeunesse) f.

hostile /'hɒstaɪl, Amer. /'hɒstl/ a. hostile. ~**ity** /hɒ'stɪlətɪ/ n. hostilité f.

hot /hɒt/ a. (**hotter, hottest**) chaud; (culin.) épicé; (news) récent. **be or feel ~,** avoir chaud. **it is ~,** il fait chaud. ● v.t./i. (p.t. **hotted**) ~ **up,** (fam.) chauffer. ~ **dog,** hot-dog m. ~ **line,** téléphone rouge m. ~ **shot,** (Amer., sl.) crack m. ~**-water bot-**

tle, bouillotte *f.* **in ~ water,** (*fam.*) dans le pétrin. **~ly** *adv.* vivement.

hotbed /'hɒtbed/ *n.* foyer *m.*

hotchpotch /'hɒtʃpɒtʃ/ *n.* fatras *m.*

hotel /həʊ'tel/ *n.* hôtel *m.* **~ier** /-ɪeɪ/ *n.* hôtel|ier, -ière *m., f.*

hothead /'hɒthed/ *n.* tête brûlée *f.* **~ed** *a.* impétueux.

hotplate /'hɒtpleɪt/ *n.* plaque chauffante *f.*

hound /haʊnd/ *n.* chien courant *m.* ● *v.t.* poursuivre.

hour /'aʊə(r)/ *n.* heure *f.* **~ly** *a.* & *adv.* toutes les heures. **~ly rate,** tarif horaire *m.* **paid ~ly,** payé à l'heure.

house¹ /haʊs/ *n.* (*pl.* **-s** /'haʊzɪz/) maison *f.*; (*theatre*) salle *f.*; (*pol.*) chambre *f.* **~-proud** *a.* méticuleux. **~-warming** *n.* pendaison de la crémaillère *f.*

house² /haʊz/ *v.t.* loger; (*of building*) abriter; (*keep*) garder.

housebreaking /'haʊsbreɪkɪŋ/ *n.* cambriolage *m.*

housecoat /'haʊskəʊt/ *n.* blouse *f.*, tablier *m.*

household /'haʊshəʊld/ *n.* (*house, family*) ménage *m.* ● *a.* ménager. **~er** *n.* occupant(e) *m.* (*f.*); (*owner*) propriétaire *m./f.*

housekeep|er /'haʊskiːpə(r)/ *n.* gouvernante *f.* **~ing** *n.* ménage *m.*

housewife /'haʊswaɪf/ *n.* (*pl.* **-wives**) ménagère *f.*

housework /'haʊswɜːk/ *n.* ménage *m.* travaux de ménage *m. pl.*

housing /'haʊzɪŋ/ *n.* logement *m.* **~ association,** service de logement *m.* **~ development,** cité *f.*

hovel /'hɒvl/ *n.* taudis *m.*

hover /'hɒvə(r)/ *v.i.* (*bird, threat, etc.*) planer; (*loiter*) rôder.

hovercraft /'hɒvəkrɑːft/ *n.* aéroglisseur *m.*

how /haʊ/ *adv.* comment. **~ long/ tall is . . .?,** quelle est la longueur/ hauteur de . . .? **~ pretty!,** comme *or* que c'est joli! **~ about a walk?,** si on faisait une promenade? **~ are you?,** comment allez-vous? **~ do you do?,** (*introduction*) enchanté. **~ many?,** **~ much?,** combien?

however /haʊ'evə(r)/ *adv.* de quelque manière que; (*nevertheless*) cependant. **~ small/delicate/etc. it may be,** quelque petit/délicat/*etc.* que ce soit.

howl /haʊl/ *n.* hurlement *m.* ● *v.i.* hurler.

howler /'haʊlə(r)/ *n.* (*fam.*) bévue *f.*

HP *abbr. see* hire-purchase.

hp *abbr. see* horsepower.

HQ *abbr. see* headquarters.

hub /hʌb/ *n.* moyeu *m.*; (*fig.*) centre *m.* **~-cap** *n.* enjoliveur *m.*

hubbub /'hʌbʌb/ *n.* vacarme *m.*

huddle /'hʌdl/ *v.i.* se blottir.

hue¹ /hjuː/ *n.* (*colour*) teinte *f.*

hue² /hjuː/ *n.* **~ and cry,** clameur *f.*

huff /hʌf/ *n.* **in a ~,** fâché, vexé.

hug /hʌg/ *v.t.* (*p.t.* **hugged**) serrer dans ses bras; (*keep close to*) serrer. ● *n.* étreinte *f.*

huge /hjuːdʒ/ *a.* énorme. **~ly** *adv.* énormément.

hulk /hʌlk/ *n.* (*of ship*) épave *f.*; (*person*) mastodonte *m.*

hull /hʌl/ *n.* (*of ship*) coque *f.*

hullo /hə'ləʊ/ *int.* & *n.* = **hallo.**

hum /hʌm/ *v.t./i.* (*p.t.* **hummed**) (*person*) fredonner; (*insect*) bourdonner; (*engine*) vrombir. ● *n.* bourdonnement *m.*; vrombissement *m.* **~ and haw,** hésiter.

human /'hjuːmən/ *a.* humain. ● *n.* être humain *m.* **~itarian** /-mænɪ'teərɪən/ *a.* humanitaire.

humane /hjuː'meɪn/ *a.* humain, plein d'humanité.

humanity /hjuː'mænətɪ/ *n.* humanité *f.*

humbl|e /'hʌmbl/ *a.* (**-er, -est**) humble. ● *v.t.* humilier. **~y** *adv.* humblement.

humbug /'hʌmbʌg/ *n.* (*false talk*) hypocrisie *f.*

humdrum /'hʌmdrʌm/ *a.* monotone.

humid /'hjuːmɪd/ *a.* humide. **~ity** /-'mɪdətɪ/ *n.* humidité *f.*

humiliat|e /hjuː'mɪlɪeɪt/ *v.t.* humilier. **~ion** /-'eɪʃn/ *n.* humiliation *f.*

humility /hjuː'mɪlətɪ/ *n.* humilité *f.*

humorist /'hjuːmərɪst/ *n.* humoriste *m./f.*

hum|our (*Amer.*) **humor** /'hjuːmə(r)/ *n.* humour *m.*; (*mood*) humeur *f.* ● *v.t.* ménager. **~orous** *a.* humoristique; (*person*) plein d'humour. **~orously** *adv.* avec humour.

hump /hʌmp/ *n.* bosse *f.* ● *v.t.* voûter. **the ~,** (*sl.*) le cafard.

hunch¹ /hʌntʃ/ *v.t.* voûter.

hunch² /hʌntʃ/ *n.* petite idée *f.*

hunchback /'hʌntʃbæk/ *n.* bossu(e) *m.* (*f.*).

hundred /ˈhʌndrəd/ a. & n. cent (m.). **~s of**, des centaines de. **~fold** a. `centuple; adv.` au centuple. **~th** a. & n. centième (m./f.).

hundredweight /ˈhʌndrədweɪt/ n. 50.8 kg.; (Amer.) 45.36 kg.

hung /hʌŋ/ see hang.

Hungar|y /ˈhʌŋgərɪ/ n. Hongrie f. **~ian** /-ˈgeərɪən/ a. & n. hongrois(e) (m. (f.)).

hunger /ˈhʌŋgə(r)/ n. faim f. ● v.i. **~ for**, avoir faim de. **~-strike** n. grève de la faim f.

hungr|y /ˈhʌŋgrɪ/ a. (-ier, -iest) affamé. **be ~y**, avoir faim. **~ily** adv. avidement.

hunk /hʌŋk/ n. gros morceau m.

hunt /hʌnt/ v.t./i. chasser. ● n. chasse f. **~ for**, chercher. **~er** n. chasseur m. **~ing** n. chasse f.

hurdle /ˈhɜːdl/ n. (sport) haie f.; (fig.) obstacle m.

hurl /hɜːl/ v.t. lancer.

hurrah, hurray /hʊˈrɑː, hʊˈreɪ/ int. & n. hourra (m.).

hurricane /ˈhʌrɪkən, Amer. ˈhʌrɪkeɪn/ n. ouragan m.

hurried /ˈhʌrɪd/ a. précipité. **~ly** adv. précipitamment.

hurry /ˈhʌrɪ/ v.i. se dépêcher, se presser. ● v.t. presser, activer. ● n. hâte f. **in a ~**, pressé.

hurt /hɜːt/ v.t./i. (p.t. hurt) faire mal (à); (injure, offend) blesser. ● a. blessé. ● n. mal m. **~ful** a. blessant.

hurtle /ˈhɜːtl/ v.t. lancer. ● v.i. **~ along**, avancer à toute vitesse.

husband /ˈhʌzbənd/ n. mari m.

hush /hʌʃ/ v.t. faire taire. ● n. silence m. **~-hush** a. (fam.) ultrasecret. **~ up**, (news etc.) étouffer.

husk /hʌsk/ n. (of grain) enveloppe f.

husky /ˈhʌskɪ/ a. (-ier, -iest) (hoarse) rauque; (burly) costaud. ● n. chien de traîneau m.

hustle /ˈhʌsl/ v.t. (push, rush) bousculer. ● v.i. (work busily; Amer.) se démener. ● n. bousculade f. **~ and bustle**, agitation f.

hut /hʌt/ n. cabane f.

hutch /hʌtʃ/ n. clapier m.

hyacinth /ˈhaɪəsɪnθ/ n. jacinthe f.

hybrid /ˈhaɪbrɪd/ a. & n. hybride (m.).

hydrangea /haɪˈdreɪndʒə/ n. hortensia m.

hydrant /ˈhaɪdrənt/ n. **(fire) ~**, bouche d'incendie f.

hydraulic /haɪˈdrɔːlɪk/ a. hydraulique.

hydroelectric /haɪdrəʊˈlektrɪk/ a. hydro-électrique.

hydrofoil /ˈhaɪdrəʊfɔɪl/ n. hydroptère m.

hydrogen /ˈhaɪdrədʒən/ n. hydrogène m. **~ bomb**, bombe à hydrogène f.

hyena /haɪˈiːnə/ n. hyène f.

hygiene /ˈhaɪdʒiːn/ n. hygiène f.

hygienic /haɪˈdʒiːnɪk/ a. hygiénique.

hymn /hɪm/ n. cantique m., hymne m.

hype /haɪp/ n. tapage publicitaire m. ● v.t. faire du tapage autour de.

hyper- /ˈhaɪpə(r)/ pref. hyper-.

hypermarket /ˈhaɪpəmɑːkɪt/ n. hypermarché m.

hyphen /ˈhaɪfn/ n. trait d'union m. **~ate** v.t. mettre un trait d'union à.

hypno|sis /hɪpˈnəʊsɪs/ n. hypnose f. **~tic** /-ˈnɒtɪk/ a. hypnotique.

hypnot|ize /ˈhɪpnətaɪz/ v.t. hypnotiser. **~ism** n. hypnotisme m.

hypochondriac /haɪpəˈkɒndrɪæk/ n. malade imaginaire m./f.

hypocrisy /hɪˈpɒkrəsɪ/ n. hypocrisie f.

hypocrit|e /ˈhɪpəkrɪt/ n. hypocrite m./f. **~ical** /-ˈkrɪtɪkl/ a. hypocrite.

hypodermic /haɪpəˈdɜːmɪk/ a. hypodermique. ● n. seringue hypodermique f.

hypothermia /haɪpəˈθɜːmɪə/ n. hypothermie f.

hypothe|sis /haɪˈpɒθəsɪs/ n. (pl. -theses /-siːz/) hypothèse f. **~tical** /-əˈθetɪkl/ a. hypothétique.

hyster|ia /hɪˈstɪərɪə/ n. hystérie f. **~ical** /-erɪkl/ a. hystérique; (person) surexcité.

hysterics /hɪˈsterɪks/ n. pl. crise de nerfs or de rire f.

I

I /aɪ/ pron. je, j'*; (stressed) moi.

ice /aɪs/ n. glace f.; (on road) verglas m. ● v.t. (cake) glacer. ● v.i. **~ (up)**, (window) se givrer; (river) geler. **~-cream** n. glace f. **~-cube** n. glaçon m. **~ hockey**, hockey sur glace m. **~ lolly**, glace (sur bâtonnet) f. **~ rink**, patinoire f. **~ skate**, patin à glace m.

iceberg /ˈaɪsbɜːg/ n. iceberg m.

icebox /'aɪsbɒks/ n. (Amer.) réfrigérateur m.

Iceland /'aɪslənd/ n. Islande f. ~er n. Islandais(e) m. (f.). ~ic /-'lændɪk/ a. islandais; n. (lang.) islandais m.

icicle /'aɪsɪkl/ n. glaçon m.

icing /'aɪsɪŋ/ n. (sugar) glace f.

icon /'aɪkɒn/ n. icône f.

icy /'aɪsɪ/ a. (-ier, -iest) (hands, wind) glacé; (road) verglacé; (manner, welcome) glacial.

idea /aɪ'dɪə/ n. idée f.

ideal /aɪ'dɪəl/ a. idéal. ● n. idéal m. ~ize v.t. idéaliser. ~ly adv. idéalement.

idealis|t /aɪ'dɪəlɪst/ n. idéaliste m./f. ~m /-zəm/ n. idéalisme m. ~tic /-'lɪstɪk/ a. idéaliste.

identical /aɪ'dentɪkl/ a. identique.

identif|y /aɪ'dentɪfaɪ/ v.t. identifier. ● v.i. ~y with, s'identifier à. ~ication /-ɪ'keɪʃn/ n. identification f.; (papers) une pièce d'identité.

identikit /aɪ'dentɪkɪt/ n. ~ picture, portrait-robot m.

identity /aɪ'dentətɪ/ n. identité f.

ideolog|y /aɪdɪ'ɒlədʒɪ/ n. idéologie f. ~ical /-ə'lɒdʒɪkl/ a. idéologique.

idiocy /'ɪdɪəsɪ/ n. idiotie f.

idiom /'ɪdɪəm/ n. expression idiomatique f.; (language) idiome m. ~atic /-'mætɪk/ a. idiomatique.

idiosyncrasy /ɪdɪə'sɪŋkrəsɪ/ n. particularité f.

idiot /'ɪdɪət/ n. idiot(e) m. (f.). ~ic /-'ɒtɪk/ a. idiot.

idle /'aɪdl/ a. (-er, -est) désœuvré, oisif; (lazy) paresseux; (unemployed) sans travail; (machine) au repos; (fig.) vain. ● v.i. (engine) tourner au ralenti. ● v.t. ~ away, gaspiller. ~ness n. oisiveté f. ~r /-ə(r)/ n. oisif,-ive m., f.

idol /'aɪdl/ n. idole f. ~ize v.t. idolâtrer.

idyllic /ɪ'dɪlɪk, Amer. aɪ'dɪlɪk/ a. idyllique.

i.e. abbr. c'est-à-dire.

if /ɪf/ conj. si.

igloo /'ɪgluː/ n. igloo m.

ignite /ɪg'naɪt/ v.t./i. (s')enflammer.

ignition /ɪg'nɪʃn/ n. (auto.) allumage m. ~ key, clé de contact f. ~ (switch), contact m.

ignoran|t /'ɪgnərənt/ a. ignorant (of, de). ~ce n. ignorance f. ~tly adv. par ignorance.

ignore /ɪg'nɔː(r)/ v.t. ne faire or prêter aucune attention à; (person in

street etc.) faire semblant de ne pas voir; (facts) ne pas tenir compte de.

ilk /ɪlk/ n. (kind: fam.) acabit m.

ill /ɪl/ a. malade; (bad) mauvais. ● adv. mal. ● n. mal m. ~-advised a. peu judicieux. ~ at ease, mal à l'aise. ~-bred a. mal élevé. ~-fated a. malheureux. ~ feeling, ressentiment m. ~-gotten a. mal acquis. ~-natured a. désagréable. ~-treat v.t. maltraiter. ~ will, malveillance f.

illegal /ɪ'liːgl/ a. illégal.

illegible /ɪ'ledʒəbl/ a. illisible.

illegitima|te /ɪlɪ'dʒɪtɪmət/ a. illégitime. ~cy n. illégitimité f.

illitera|te /ɪ'lɪtərət/ a. & n. illettré(e) (m. (f.)), analphabète m./f. ~cy n. analphabétisme m.

illness /'ɪlnɪs/ n. maladie f.

illogical /ɪ'lɒdʒɪkl/ a. illogique.

illuminat|e /ɪ'luːmɪneɪt/ v.t. éclairer; (decorate with lights) illuminer. ~ion /-'neɪʃn/ n. éclairage m.; illumination f.

illusion /ɪ'luːʒn/ n. illusion f.

illusory /ɪ'luːsərɪ/ a. illusoire.

illustrat|e /'ɪləstreɪt/ v.t. illustrer. ~ion /-'streɪʃn/ n. illustration f. ~ive /-ətɪv/ a. qui illustre.

illustrious /ɪ'lʌstrɪəs/ a. illustre.

image /'ɪmɪdʒ/ n. image f. (public) ~, (of firm, person) image de marque f. ~ry /-ərɪ/ n. images f. pl.

imaginary /ɪ'mædʒɪnərɪ/ a. imaginaire.

imaginat|ion /ɪmædʒɪ'neɪʃn/ n. imagination f. ~ive /ɪ'mædʒɪnətɪv/ a. plein d'imagination.

imagin|e /ɪ'mædʒɪn/ v.t. (picture to o.s.) (s')imaginer; (suppose) imaginer. ~able a. imaginable.

imbalance /ɪm'bæləns/ n. déséquilibre m.

imbecile /'ɪmbəsiːl/ n. & a. imbécile (m./f.).

imbue /ɪm'bjuː/ v.t. imprégner.

imitat|e /'ɪmɪteɪt/ v.t. imiter. ~ion /-'teɪʃn/ n. imitation f. ~or n. imitateur, -trice m., f.

immaculate /ɪ'mækjʊlət/ a. (room, dress, etc.) impeccable.

immaterial /ɪmə'tɪərɪəl/ a. sans importance (to, pour; that, que).

immature /ɪmə'tjʊə(r)/ a. pas mûr; (person) immature.

immediate /ɪ'miːdɪət/ a. immédiat. ~ly adv. immédiatement; conj. dès que.

immens|e /ɪˈmens/ a. immense. **~ely** adv. extrêmement, immensément. **~ity** n. immensité f.

immers|e /ɪˈmɜːs/ v.t. plonger, immerger. **~ion** /-ʒn/ n. immersion f. **~ion heater,** chauffe-eau (électrique) m. invar.

immigr|ate /ˈɪmɪɡreɪt/ v.i. immigrer. **~ant** n. & a. immigré(e) (m. (f.)); (newly-arrived) immigrant(e) (m. (f.)). **~ation** /-ˈɡreɪʃn/ n. immigration f. **go through ~ation,** passer le contrôle des passeports.

imminen|t /ˈɪmɪnənt/ a. imminent. **~ce** n. imminence f.

immobil|e /ɪˈməʊbaɪl, Amer. ˈɪməʊbl/ a. immobile. **~ize** /-əlaɪz/ v.t. immobiliser.

immoderate /ɪˈmɒdərət/ a. immodéré.

immoral /ɪˈmɒrəl/ a. immoral. **~ity** /ɪməˈrælətɪ/ n. immoralité f.

immortal /ɪˈmɔːtl/ a. immortel. **~ity** /-ˈtælətɪ/ n. immortalité f. **~ize** v.t. immortaliser.

immun|e /ɪˈmjuːn/ a. immunisé (from, to, contre). **~ity** n. immunité f.

immuniz|e /ˈɪmjʊnaɪz/ v.t. immuniser. **~ation** /-ˈzeɪʃn/ n. immunisation f.

imp /ɪmp/ n. lutin m.

impact /ˈɪmpækt/ n. impact m.

impair /ɪmˈpeə(r)/ v.t. détériorer.

impart /ɪmˈpɑːt/ v.t. communiquer, transmettre.

impartial /ɪmˈpɑːʃl/ a. impartial. **~ity** /-ɪˈælətɪ/ n. impartialité f.

impassable /ɪmˈpɑːsəbl/ a. (barrier etc.) infranchissable; (road) impraticable.

impasse /ˈæmpɑːs, Amer. ˈɪmpæs/ n. impasse f.

impassioned /ɪmˈpæʃnd/ n. passionné.

impassive /ɪmˈpæsɪv/ a. impassible.

impatien|t /ɪmˈpeɪʃnt/ a. impatient. **get ~t,** s'impatienter. **~ce** n. impatience f. **~tly** adv. impatiemment.

impeccable /ɪmˈpekəbl/ a. impeccable.

impede /ɪmˈpiːd/ v.t. gêner.

impediment /ɪmˈpedɪmənt/ n. obstacle m. **(speech) ~,** défaut d'élocution m.

impel /ɪmˈpel/ v.t. (p.t. impelled) pousser, forcer (to do, à faire).

impending /ɪmˈpendɪŋ/ a. imminent.

impenetrable /ɪmˈpenɪtrəbl/ a. impénétrable.

imperative /ɪmˈperətɪv/ a. nécessaire; (need etc.) impérieux. ● n. (gram.) impératif m.

imperceptible /ɪmpəˈseptɪbl/ a. imperceptible.

imperfect /ɪmˈpɜːfɪkt/ a. imparfait; (faulty) défectueux. **~ion** /-əˈfekʃn/ n. imperfection f.

imperial /ɪmˈpɪərɪəl/ a. impérial; (measure) légal (au Royaume-Uni). **~ism** n. impérialisme m.

imperil /ɪmˈperəl/ v.t. (p.t. imperilled) mettre en péril.

imperious /ɪmˈpɪərɪəs/ a. impérieux.

impersonal /ɪmˈpɜːsənl/ a. impersonnel.

impersonat|e /ɪmˈpɜːsəneɪt/ v.t. se faire passer pour; (mimic) imiter. **~ion** /-ˈneɪʃn/ n. imitation f. **~or** n. imita|teur, -trice m., f.

impertinen|t /ɪmˈpɜːtɪnənt/ a. impertinent. **~ce** n. impertinence f. **~tly** adv. avec impertinence.

impervious /ɪmˈpɜːvɪəs/ a. **~ to,** imperméable à.

impetuous /ɪmˈpetʃʊəs/ a. impétueux.

impetus /ˈɪmpɪtəs/ n. impulsion f.

impinge /ɪmˈpɪndʒ/ v.i. **~ on,** affecter; (encroach) empiéter sur.

impish /ˈɪmpɪʃ/ a. espiègle.

implacable /ɪmˈplækəbl/ a. implacable.

implant /ɪmˈplɑːnt/ v.t. implanter. ● n. implant m.

implement[1] /ˈɪmplɪmənt/ n. (tool) outil m.; (utensil) ustensile m.

implement[2] /ˈɪmplɪmənt/ v.t. exécuter, mettre en pratique.

implicat|e /ˈɪmplɪkeɪt/ v.t. impliquer. **~ion** /-ˈkeɪʃn/ n. implication f.

implicit /ɪmˈplɪsɪt/ a. (implied) implicite; (unquestioning) absolu.

implore /ɪmˈplɔː(r)/ v.t. implorer.

impl|y /ɪmˈplaɪ/ v.t. (assume, mean) impliquer; (insinuate) laisser entendre. **~ied** a. implicite.

impolite /ɪmpəˈlaɪt/ a. impoli.

imponderable /ɪmˈpɒndərəbl/ a. & n. impondérable (m.).

import[1] /ɪmˈpɔːt/ v.t. importer. **~ation** /-ˈteɪʃn/ n. importation f. **~er** n. importa|teur, -trice m., f.

import[2] /ˈɪmpɔːt/ n. (article) importation f.; (meaning) sens m.

importan|t /ɪmˈpɔːtnt/ a. important. **~ce** n. importance f.

impos|e /ɪm'pəʊz/ *v.t.* imposer. ● *v.i.* ~e on, abuser de l'amabilité de. ~**ition** /-ə'zɪʃn/ *n.* imposition *f.*; (*fig.*) dérangement *m.*

imposing /ɪm'pəʊzɪŋ/ *a.* imposant.

impossib|le /ɪm'pɒsəbl/ *a.* impossible. ~**ility** /-'bɪlətɪ/ *n.* impossibilité *f.*

impostor /ɪm'pɒstə(r)/ *n.* imposteur *m.*

impoten|t /'ɪmpətənt/ *a.* impuissant. ~**ce** *n.* impuissance *f.*

impound /ɪm'paʊnd/ *v.t.* confisquer, saisir.

impoverish /ɪm'pɒvərɪʃ/ *v.t.* appauvrir.

impracticable /ɪm'præktɪkəbl/ *a.* impraticable.

impractical /ɪm'præktɪkl/ *a.* peu pratique.

imprecise /ɪmprɪ'saɪs/ *a.* imprécis.

impregnable /ɪm'pregnəbl/ *a.* imprenable; (*fig.*) inattaquable.

impregnate /'ɪmpregneɪt/ *v.t.* imprégner (**with**, de).

impresario /ɪmprɪ'sɑːrɪəʊ/ *n.* (*pl.* -os) imprésario *m.*

impress /ɪm'pres/ *v.t.* impressionner; (*imprint*) imprimer. ~ **on s.o.**, faire comprendre à qn.

impression /ɪm'preʃn/ *n.* impression *f.* ~**able** *a.* impressionnable.

impressive /ɪm'presɪv/ *a.* impressionnant.

imprint[1] /'ɪmprɪnt/ *n.* empreinte *f.*

imprint[2] /ɪm'prɪnt/ *v.t.* imprimer.

imprison /ɪm'prɪzn/ *v.t.* emprisonner. ~**ment** *n.* emprisonnement *m.*, prison *f.*

improbab|le /ɪm'prɒbəbl/ *a.* (*not likely*) improbable; (*incredible*) invraisemblable. ~**ility** /-'bɪlətɪ/ *n.* improbabilité *f.*

impromptu /ɪm'prɒmptjuː/ *a. & adv.* impromptu.

improp|er /ɪm'prɒpə(r)/ *a.* inconvenant, indécent; (*wrong*) incorrect. ~**riety** /-ə'praɪətɪ/ *n.* inconvenance *f.*

improve /ɪm'pruːv/ *v.t./i.* (s')améliorer. ~**ment** *n.* amélioration *f.*

improvis|e /'ɪmprəvaɪz/ *v.t./i.* improviser. ~**ation** /-'zeɪʃn/ *n.* improvisation *f.*

imprudent /ɪm'pruːdnt/ *a.* imprudent.

impuden|t /'ɪmpjʊdənt/ *a.* impudent. ~**ce** *n.* impudence *f.*

impulse /'ɪmpʌls/ *n.* impulsion *f.* **on ~**, sur un coup de tête.

impulsive /ɪm'pʌlsɪv/ *a.* impulsif. ~**ly** *adv.* par impulsion.

impunity /ɪm'pjuːnətɪ/ *n.* impunité *f.* **with ~**, impunément.

impur|e /ɪm'pjʊə(r)/ *a.* impur. ~**ity** *n.* impureté *f.*

impute /ɪm'pjuːt/ *v.t.* imputer.

in /ɪn/ *prep.* dans, à, en. (*inside*) dedans; (*at home*) là, à la maison; (*in fashion*) à la mode. **in the box/garden**, dans la boîte/le jardin. **in Paris/school**, à Paris/l'école. **in town**, en ville. **in the country**, à la campagne. **in English**, en anglais. **in India**, en Inde. **in Japan**, au Japon. **in a firm manner/voice**, d'une manière/voix ferme. **in blue**, en bleu. **in ink**, à l'encre. **in uniform**, en uniforme. **in a skirt**, en jupe. **in a whisper**, en chuchotant. **in a loud voice**, d'une voix forte. **in winter**, en hiver. **in spring**, au printemps. **in an hour**, (*at end of*) au bout d'une heure. **in an hour('s time)**, dans une heure. **in (the space of) an hour**, en une heure. **in doing**, en faisant. **in the evening**, le soir. **one in ten**, un sur dix. **in between**, entre les deux; (*time*) entretemps. **the best in**, le meilleur de. **we are in for**, on va avoir. **in-laws** *n. pl.* (*fam.*) beaux-parents *m. pl.* ~**-patient** *n.* malade hospitalisé(e) *m.(f.).* **the ins and outs of**, les tenants et aboutissants de. **in so far as**, dans la mesure où.

inability /ɪnə'bɪlətɪ/ *n.* incapacité *f.* (**to do**, de faire).

inaccessible /ɪnæk'sesəbl/ *a.* inaccessible.

inaccurate /ɪn'ækjərət/ *a.* inexact.

inaction /ɪn'ækʃn/ *n.* inaction *f.*

inactiv|e /ɪn'æktɪv/ *a.* inactif. ~**ity** /-'tɪvətɪ/ *n.* inaction *f.*

inadequa|te /ɪn'ædɪkwət/ *a.* insuffisant. ~**cy** *n.* insuffisance *f.*

inadmissible /ɪnəd'mɪsəbl/ *a.* inadmissible.

inadvertently /ɪnəd'vɜːtəntlɪ/ *adv.* par mégarde.

inadvisable /ɪnəd'vaɪzəbl/ *a.* déconseillé, pas recommandé.

inane /ɪ'neɪn/ *a.* inepte.

inanimate /ɪn'ænɪmət/ *a.* inanimé.

inappropriate /ɪnə'prəʊprɪət/ *a.* inopportun; (*term*) inapproprié.

inarticulate /mɑ:'tɪkjʊlət/ a. qui a du mal à s'exprimer.

inasmuch as /məz'mʌtʃəz/ adv. en ce sens que; (because) vu que.

inattentive /məˈtentɪv/ a. inattentif.

inaudible /ɪnˈɔ:dɪbl/ a. inaudible.

inaugural /ɪˈnɔ:gjʊrəl/ a. inaugural.

inaugurat|e /ɪˈnɔ:gjʊreɪt/ v.t. (open, begin) inaugurer; (person) investir. ~ion /-ˈreɪʃn/ n. inauguration f.; investiture f.

inauspicious /mɔ:ˈspɪʃəs/ a. peu propice.

inborn /mˈbɔ:n/ a. inné.

inbred /mˈbred/ a. (inborn) inné.

inc. abbr. (incorporated) S.A.

incalculable /mˈkælkjʊləbl/ a. incalculable.

incapable /mˈkeɪpəbl/ a. incapable.

incapacit|y /mkəˈpæsətɪ/ n. incapacité f. ~ate v.t. rendre incapable (de travailler etc.).

incarcerate /mˈkɑ:səreɪt/ v.t. incarcérer.

incarnat|e /mˈkɑ:neɪt/ a. incarné. ~ion /-ˈneɪʃn/ n. incarnation f.

incendiary /mˈsendɪərɪ/ a. incendiaire. ● n. (bomb) bombe incendiaire f.

incense¹ /ˈmsens/ n. encens m.

incense² /mˈsens/ v.t. mettre en fureur.

incentive /mˈsentɪv/ n. motivation f.; (payment) prime (d'encouragement) f.

inception /mˈsepʃn/ n. début m.

incessant /mˈsesnt/ a. incessant. ~ly adv. sans cesse.

incest /ˈmsest/ n. inceste m. ~uous /mˈsestjʊəs/ a. incestueux.

inch /mtʃ/ n. pouce m. (= 2.54 cm.). ● v.i. avancer doucement.

incidence /ˈmsɪdəns/ n. fréquence f.

incident /ˈmsɪdənt/ n. incident m.; (in play, film, etc.) épisode m.

incidental /msɪˈdentl/ a. accessoire. ~ly adv. accessoirement; (by the way) à propos.

incinerat|e /mˈsɪnəreɪt/ v.t. incinérer. ~or n. incinérateur m.

incipient /mˈsɪpɪənt/ a. naissant.

incision /mˈsɪʒn/ n. incision f.

incisive /mˈsaɪsɪv/ a. incisif.

incite /mˈsaɪt/ v.t. inciter, pousser. ~ment n. incitation f.

inclement /mˈklemənt/ a. inclément, rigoureux.

inclination /mklɪˈneɪʃn/ n. (propensity, bowing) inclination f.

incline¹ /mˈklaɪn/ v.t./i. incliner. be ~d to, avoir tendance à.

incline² /ˈmklaɪn/ n. pente f.

inclu|de /mˈklu:d/ v.t. comprendre, inclure. ~ding prep. (y) compris. ~sion n. inclusion f.

inclusive /mˈklu:sɪv/ a. & adv. inclus, compris. be ~ of, comprendre, inclure.

incognito /mknɒgˈni:təʊ/ adv. incognito.

incoherent /mkəʊˈhɪərənt/ a. incohérent.

income /ˈmkʌm/ n. revenu m. ~ tax, impôt sur le revenu m.

incoming /ˈmkʌmɪŋ/ a. (tide) montant; (tenant etc.) nouveau.

incomparable /mˈkɒmprəbl/ a. incomparable.

incompatible /mkəmˈpætəbl/ a. incompatible.

incompeten|t /mˈkɒmpɪtənt/ a. incompétent. ~ce n. incompétence f.

incomplete /mkəmˈpli:t/ a. incomplet.

incomprehensible /mkɒmprɪˈhensəbl/ a. incompréhensible.

inconceivable /mkənˈsi:vəbl/ a. inconcevable.

inconclusive /mkənˈklu:sɪv/ a. peu concluant.

incongruous /mˈkɒŋgrʊəs/ a. déplacé, incongru.

inconsequential /mkɒnsɪˈkwenʃl/ a. sans importance.

inconsiderate /mkənˈsɪdərət/ a. (person) qui ne se soucie pas des autres; (act) irréfléchi.

inconsisten|t /mkənˈsɪstənt/ a. (treatment) sans cohérence, inconséquent; (argument) contradictoire; (performance) irrégulier. ~t with, incompatible avec. ~cy n. inconséquence f., contradiction f.; irrégularité f.

inconspicuous /mkənˈspɪkjʊəs/ a. peu en évidence.

incontinen|t /mˈkɒntɪnənt/ a. incontinent. ~ce n. incontinence f.

inconvenien|t /mkənˈvi:nɪənt/ a. incommode, peu pratique; (time) mal choisi. be ~t for, ne pas convenir à. ~ce n. dérangement m.; (drawback) inconvénient m.; v.t. déranger.

incorporate /mˈkɔ:pəreɪt/ v.t. incorporer; (include) contenir.

incorrect /mkəˈrekt/ a. inexact.

incorrigible /ɪn'kɒrɪdʒəbl/ a. incorrigible.

incorruptible /ɪnkə'rʌptəbl/ a. incorruptible.

increase¹ /ɪn'kri:s/ v.t./i. augmenter. ~ing a. croissant. ~ingly adv. de plus en plus.

increase² /'ɪnkri:s/ n. augmentation f. (in, of, de). be on the ~, augmenter.

incredible /ɪn'kredəbl/ a. incroyable.

incredulous /ɪn'kredjʊləs/ a. incrédule.

increment /'ɪnkrəmənt/ n. augmentation f.

incriminat|e /ɪn'krɪmɪneɪt/ v.t. incriminer. ~ing a. compromettant.

incubat|e /'ɪnkjʊbeɪt/ v.t. (eggs) couver. ~ion /-'beɪʃn/ n. incubation f. ~or n. couveuse f.

inculcate /'ɪnkʌlkeɪt/ v.t. inculquer.

incumbent /ɪn'kʌmbənt/ n. (pol., relig.) titulaire m./f.

incur /ɪn'kɜ:(r)/ v.t. (p.t. incurred) encourir; (debts) contracter; (anger) s'exposer à.

incurable /ɪn'kjʊərəbl/ a. incurable.

incursion /ɪn'kɜ:ʃn/ n. incursion f.

indebted /ɪn'detɪd/ a. ~ to s.o., redevable à qn. (for, de).

indecen|t /ɪn'di:snt/ a. indécent. ~cy n. indécence f.

indecision /ɪndɪ'sɪʒn/ n. indécision f.

indecisive /ɪndɪ'saɪsɪv/ a. indécis; (ending) peu concluant.

indeed /ɪn'di:d/ adv. en effet, vraiment.

indefensible /ɪndɪ'fensɪbl/ a. indéfendable.

indefinable /ɪndɪ'faɪnəbl/ a. indéfinissable.

indefinite /ɪn'defnɪt/ a. indéfini; (time) indéterminé. ~ly adv. indéfiniment.

indelible /ɪn'deləbl/ a. indélébile.

indemni|fy /ɪn'demnɪfaɪ/ v.t. (compensate) indemniser (for, de); (safeguard) garantir. ~ty /-nətɪ/ n. indemnité f.; garantie f.

indent /ɪn'dent/ v.t. (text) renfoncer. ~ation /-'teɪʃn/ n. (outline) découpure f.

independen|t /ɪndɪ'pendənt/ a. indépendant. ~ce n. indépendance f. ~tly adv. de façon indépendante. ~tly of, indépendamment de.

indescribable /ɪndɪ'skraɪbəbl/ a. indescriptible.

indestructible /ɪndɪ'strʌktəbl/ a. indestructible.

indeterminate /ɪndɪ'tɜ:mɪnət/ a. indéterminé.

index /'ɪndeks/ n. (pl. indexes) (figure) indice m.; (in book) index m.; (in library) catalogue m. ● v.t. classer. ~ card, fiche f. ~ finger index m. ~-linked a. indexé.

India /'ɪndɪə/ n. Inde f. ~n a. & n. indien(ne) (m. (f.)). ~n summer, été de la Saint-Martin m.

indicat|e /'ɪndɪkeɪt/ v.t. indiquer. ~ion /-'keɪʃn/ n. indication f. ~or n. (device) indicateur m.; (on vehicle) clignotant m.; (board) tableau m.

indicative /ɪn'dɪkətɪv/ a. indicatif. ● n. (gram.) indicatif m.

indict /ɪn'daɪt/ v.t. accuser. ~ment n. accusation f.

indifferen|t /ɪn'dɪfrənt/ a. indifférent; (not good) médiocre. ~ce n. indifférence f.

indigenous /ɪn'dɪdʒɪnəs/ a. indigène.

indigest|ion /ɪndɪ'dʒestʃən/ n. indigestion f. ~ible /-təbl/ a. indigeste.

indign|ant /ɪn'dɪgnənt/ a. indigné. ~ation /-'neɪʃn/ n. indignation f.

indigo /'ɪndɪgəʊ/ n. indigo m.

indirect /ɪndɪ'rekt/ a. indirect. ~ly adv. indirectement.

indiscr|eet /ɪndɪ'skri:t/ a. indiscret; (not wary) imprudent. ~etion /-eʃn/ n. indiscrétion f.

indiscriminate /ɪndɪ'skrɪmɪnət/ a. qui manque de discernement; (random) fait au hasard. ~ly adv. sans discernement; au hasard.

indispensable /ɪndɪ'spensəbl/ a. indispensable.

indispos|ed /ɪndɪ'spəʊzd/ a. indisposé, souffrant. ~ition /-ə'zɪʃn/ n. indisposition f.

indisputable /ɪndɪ'spju:təbl/ a. incontestable.

indistinct /ɪndɪ'stɪŋkt/ a. indistinct.

indistinguishable /ɪndɪ'stɪŋgwɪʃəbl/ a. indifférenciable.

individual /ɪndɪ'vɪdʒʊəl/ a. individuel. ● n. individu m. ~ist n. individualiste m./f. ~ity /-'ælətɪ/ n. individualité f. ~ly adv. individuellement.

indivisible /ɪndɪ'vɪzəbl/ a. indivisible.

indoctrinat|e /ɪn'dɒktrɪneɪt/ v.t. endoctriner. ~ion /-'neɪʃn/ n. endoctrinement m.

indolen|t /'ɪndələnt/ a. indolent. ~ce n. indolence f.

indomitable /ɪn'dɒmɪtəbl/ a. indomptable.

Indonesia /ɪndəʊ'niːzɪə/ n. Indonésie f. ~n a. & n. indonésien(ne) (m. (f.)).

indoor /'ɪndɔː(r)/ a. (clothes etc.) d'intérieur; (under cover) couvert. ~s /ɪn'dɔːz/ adv. à l'intérieur.

induce /ɪn'djuːs/ v.t. (influence) persuader; (cause) provoquer. ~ment n. encouragement m.

induct /ɪn'dʌkt/ v.t. investir, installer; (mil., Amer.) incorporer.

indulge /ɪn'dʌldʒ/ v.t. (desires) satisfaire; (person) se montrer indulgent pour, gâter. • v.i. ~ in, se livrer à, s'offrir.

indulgen|t /ɪn'dʌldʒənt/ a. indulgent. ~ce n. indulgence f.; (treat) gâterie f.

industrial /ɪn'dʌstrɪəl/ a. industriel; (unrest etc.) ouvrier; (action) revendicatif; (accident) du travail. ~ist n. industriel(le) m.(f.). ~ized a. industrialisé.

industrious /ɪn'dʌstrɪəs/ a. travailleur, appliqué.

industry /'ɪndəstrɪ/ n. industrie f.; (zeal) application f.

inebriated /ɪ'niːbrɪeɪtɪd/ a. ivre.

inedible /ɪn'edɪbl/ a. (food) immangeable.

ineffective /ɪnɪ'fektɪv/ a. inefficace; (person) incapable.

ineffectual /ɪnɪ'fektʃʊəl/ a. inefficace; (person) incapable.

inefficien|t /ɪnɪ'fɪʃnt/ a. inefficace; (person) incompétent. ~cy n. inefficacité f.; incompétence f.

ineligible /ɪn'elɪdʒəbl/ a. inéligible. be ~ for, ne pas avoir droit à.

inept /ɪ'nept/ a. (absurd) inepte; (out of place) mal à propos.

inequality /ɪnɪ'kwɒlətɪ/ n. inégalité f.

inert /ɪ'nɜːt/ a. inerte.

inertia /ɪ'nɜːʃə/ n. inertie f.

inescapable /ɪnɪ'skeɪpəbl/ a. inéluctable.

inevitabl|e /ɪn'evɪtəbl/ a. inévitable. ~y adv. inévitablement.

inexact /ɪnɪg'zækt/ a. inexact.

inexcusable /ɪnɪk'skjuːzəbl/ a. inexcusable.

inexhaustible /ɪnɪg'zɔːstəbl/ a. inépuisable.

inexorable /ɪn'eksərəbl/ a. inexorable.

inexpensive /ɪnɪk'spensɪv/ a. bon marché invar., pas cher.

inexperience /ɪnɪk'spɪərɪəns/ n. inexpérience f. ~d a. inexpérimenté.

inexplicable /ɪnɪk'splɪkəbl/ a. inexplicable.

inextricable /ɪnɪk'strɪkəbl/ a. inextricable.

infallib|le /ɪn'fæləbl/ a. infaillible. ~ility /-'bɪlətɪ/ n. infaillibilité f.

infam|ous /'ɪnfəməs/ a. infâme. ~y n. infamie f.

infan|t /'ɪnfənt/ n. (baby) nourrisson m.; (at school) petit(e) enfant m.(f.). ~cy n. petite enfance f.; (fig.) enfance f.

infantile /'ɪnfəntaɪl/ a. infantile.

infantry /'ɪnfəntrɪ/ n. infanterie f.

infatuat|ed /ɪn'fætʃʊeɪtɪd/ a. ~ed with, engoué de. ~ion /-'eɪʃn/ n. engouement m., béguin m.

infect /ɪn'fekt/ v.t. infecter. ~ with, communiquer à qn. ~ion /-kʃn/ n. infection f.

infectious /ɪn'fekʃəs/ a. (med.) infectieux; (fig.) contagieux.

infer /ɪn'fɜː(r)/ v.t. (p.t. inferred) déduire. ~ence /'ɪnfərəns/ n. déduction f.

inferior /ɪn'fɪərɪə(r)/ a. inférieur (to, à); (work, product) de qualité inférieure. • n. inférieur(e) m. (f.). ~ity /-'ɒrətɪ/ n. infériorité f.

infernal /ɪn'fɜːnl/ a. infernal. ~ly adv. (fam.) atrocement.

inferno /ɪn'fɜːnəʊ/ n. (pl. -os) (hell) enfer m.; (blaze) incendie m.

infertil|e /ɪn'fɜːtaɪl, Amer. ɪn'fɜːtl/ a. infertile. ~ity /-ə'tɪlətɪ/ n. infertilité f.

infest /ɪn'fest/ v.t. infester.

infidelity /ɪnfɪ'delətɪ/ n. infidélité f.

infighting /'ɪnfaɪtɪŋ/ n. querelles internes f. pl.

infiltrat|e /'ɪnfɪltreɪt/ v.t./i. s'infiltrer (dans). ~ion /-'treɪʃn/ n. infiltration f.

infinite /'ɪnfɪnɪt/ a. infini. ~ly adv. infiniment.

infinitesimal /ɪnfɪnɪ'tesɪml/ a. infinitésimal.

infinitive /ɪn'fɪnətɪv/ n. infinitif m.

infinity /ɪn'fɪnətɪ/ n. infinité f.

infirm /ɪn'fɜːm/ a. infirme. ~ity n. infirmité f.

infirmary /ɪn'fɜːmərɪ/ n. hôpital m.; (sick-bay) infirmerie f.

inflam|e /ɪn'fleɪm/ v.t. enflammer. ~mable /-æməbl/ a. inflammable.

~mation /-ə'meɪʃn/ *n.* inflammation *f.*

inflammatory /ɪn'flæmətrɪ/ *a.* incendiaire.

inflat|e /ɪn'fleɪt/ *v.t.* (*balloon, prices, etc.*) gonfler. **~able** *a.* gonflable.

inflation /ɪn'fleɪʃn/ *n.* inflation *f.* **~ary** *a.* inflationniste.

inflection /ɪn'flekʃn/ *n.* inflexion *f.*; (*suffix: gram.*) désinence *f.*

inflexible /ɪn'fleksəbl/ *a.* inflexible.

inflict /ɪn'flɪkt/ *v.t.* infliger (**on**, à).

influence /'ɪnfluəns/ *n.* influence *f.* ● *v.t.* influencer. **under the ~,** (*drunk: fam.*) en état d'ivresse.

influential /ɪnflʊ'enʃl/ *a.* influent.

influenza /ɪnflʊ'enzə/ *n.* grippe *f.*

influx /'ɪnflʌks/ *n.* afflux *m.*

inform /ɪn'fɔːm/ *v.t.* informer (**of**, de). **keep ~ed,** tenir au courant. **~ant** *n.* informa|teur, -trice *m., f.* **~er** *n.* indica|teur, -trice *m., f.*

informal /ɪn'fɔːml/ *a.* (*simple*) simple, sans cérémonie; (*unofficial*) officieux; (*colloquial*) familier. **~ity** /-'mælətɪ/ *n.* simplicité *f.* **~ly** *adv.* sans cérémonie.

information /ɪnfə'meɪʃn/ *n.* renseignement(s) *m.* (*pl.*), information(s) *f.* (*pl.*). **some ~,** un renseignement. **~ technology,** informatique *f.*

informative /ɪn'fɔːmətɪv/ *a.* instructif.

infra-red /ɪnfrə'red/ *a.* infrarouge.

infrastructure /'ɪnfrəstrʌktʃə(r)/ *n.* infrastructure *f.*

infrequent /ɪn'friːkwənt/ *a.* peu fréquent. **~ly** *adv.* rarement.

infringe /ɪn'frɪndʒ/ *v.t.* contrevenir à. **~ on,** empiéter sur. **~ment** *n.* infraction *f.*

infuriate /ɪn'fjʊərɪeɪt/ *v.t.* exaspérer, rendre furieux.

infus|e /ɪn'fjuːz/ *v.t.* infuser. **~ion** /-ʒn/ *n.* infusion *f.*

ingen|ious /ɪn'dʒiːnɪəs/ *a.* ingénieux. **~uity** /-ɪ'njuːətɪ/ *n.* ingéniosité *f.*

ingenuous /ɪn'dʒenjʊəs/ *a.* ingénu.

ingot /'ɪŋgət/ *n.* lingot *m.*

ingrained /ɪn'greɪnd/ *a.* enraciné.

ingratiate /ɪn'greɪʃɪeɪt/ *v.t.* **~ o.s. with,** gagner les bonnes grâces de.

ingratitude /ɪn'grætɪtjuːd/ *n.* ingratitude *f.*

ingredient /ɪn'griːdɪənt/ *n.* ingrédient *m.*

inhabit /ɪn'hæbɪt/ *v.t.* habiter. **~able** *a.* habitable. **~ant** *n.* habitant(e) *m.* (*f.*).

inhale /ɪn'heɪl/ *v.t.* inhaler; (*tobacco smoke*) avaler. **~r** *n.* spray *m.*

inherent /ɪn'hɪərənt/ *a.* inhérent. **~ly** *adv.* en soi, intrinsèquement.

inherit /ɪn'herɪt/ *v.t.* hériter (de). **~ance** *n.* héritage *m.*

inhibit /ɪn'hɪbɪt/ *v.t.* (*hinder*) gêner; (*prevent*) empêcher. **be ~ed,** avoir des inhibitions. **~ion** /-'bɪʃn/ *n.* inhibition *f.*

inhospitable /ɪnhɒ'spɪtəbl/ *a.* inhospitalier.

inhuman /ɪn'hjuːmən/ *a.* (*brutal, not human*) inhumain. **~ity** /-'mænətɪ/ *n.* inhumanité *f.*

inhumane /ɪnhjuː'meɪn/ *a.* (*unkind*) inhumain.

inimitable /ɪ'nɪmɪtəbl/ *a.* inimitable.

iniquit|ous /ɪ'nɪkwɪtəs/ *a.* inique. **~y** /-ətɪ/ *n.* iniquité *f.*

initial /ɪ'nɪʃl/ *n.* initiale *f.* ● *v.t.* (*p.t.* **initialled**) parapher. ● *a.* initial. **~ly** *adv.* initialement.

initiat|e /ɪ'nɪʃɪeɪt/ *v.t.* (*begin*) amorcer; (*scheme*) lancer; (*person*) initier (**into**, à). **~ion** /-'eɪʃn/ *n.* initiation *f.*; (*start*) amorce *f.*

initiative /ɪ'nɪʃətɪv/ *n.* initiative *f.*

inject /ɪn'dʒekt/ *v.t.* injecter; (*new element: fig.*) insuffler. **~ion** /-kʃn/ *n.* injection *f.*, piqûre *f.*

injunction /ɪn'dʒʌŋkʃn/ *n.* (*court order*) ordonnance *f.*

injure /'ɪndʒə(r)/ *v.t.* blesser; (*do wrong to*) nuire à.

injury /'ɪndʒərɪ/ *n.* (*physical*) blessure *f.*; (*wrong*) préjudice *m.*

injustice /ɪn'dʒʌstɪs/ *n.* injustice *f.*

ink /ɪŋk/ *n.* encre *f.* **~-well** *n.* encrier *m.* **~y** *a.* taché d'encre.

inkling /'ɪŋklɪŋ/ *n.* petite idée *f.*

inland /'ɪnlənd/ *a.* à l'intérieur. ● *adv.* /ɪn'lænd/ à l'intérieur. **I~ Revenue,** fisc *m.*

in-laws /'ɪnlɔːz/ *n. pl.* (*parents*) beaux-parents *m. pl.*; (*family*) belle-famille *f.*

inlay [1] /ɪn'leɪ/ *v.t.* (*p.t.* **inlaid**) incruster.

inlay [2] /'ɪnleɪ/ *n.* incrustation *f.*

inlet /'ɪnlet/ *n.* bras de mer *m.*; (*techn.*) arrivée *f.*

inmate /'ɪnmeɪt/ *n.* (*of asylum*) interné(e) *m.* (*f.*); (*of prison*) détenu(e) *m.* (*f.*).

inn /ɪn/ *n.* auberge *f.*

innards /ˈɪnədz/ *n. pl.* (*fam.*) entrailles *f. pl.*

innate /ɪˈneɪt/ *a.* inné.

inner /ˈɪnə(r)/ *a.* intérieur, interne; (*fig.*) profond, intime. ~ **city,** quartiers défavorisés *m. pl.* ~**most** *a.* le plus profond. ~ **tube,** chambre à air *f.*

innings /ˈɪnɪŋz/ *n. invar.* tour de batte *m.*; (*fig.*) tour *m.*

innkeeper /ˈɪnkiːpə(r)/ *n.* aubergiste *m./f.*

innocen|t /ˈɪnəsnt/ *a. & n.* innocent(e) (*m.* (*f.*)). ~**ce** *n.* innocence *f.*

innocuous /ɪˈnɒkjʊəs/ *a.* inoffensif.

innovat|e /ˈɪnəveɪt/ *v.i.* innover. ~**ion** /-ˈveɪʃn/ *n.* innovation *f.* ~**or** *n.* innova|teur, -trice *m., f.*

innuendo /ɪnjuːˈendəʊ/ *n.* (*pl. -oes*) insinuation *f.*

innumerable /ɪˈnjuːmərəbl/ *a.* innombrable.

inoculat|e /ɪˈnɒkjʊleɪt/ *v.t.* inoculer. ~**ion** /-ˈleɪʃn/ *n.* inoculation *f.*

inoffensive /ɪnəˈfensɪv/ *a.* inoffensif.

inoperative /ɪnˈɒpərətɪv/ *a.* inopérant.

inopportune /ɪnˈɒpətjuːn/ *a.* inopportun.

inordinate /ɪˈnɔːdɪnət/ *a.* excessif. ~**ly** *adv.* excessivement.

input /ˈɪnpʊt/ *n.* (*data*) données *f. pl.*; (*computer process*) entrée *f.*; (*power; electr.*) énergie *f.*

inquest /ˈɪnkwest/ *n.* enquête *f.*

inquire /ɪnˈkwaɪə(r)/ *v.t./i.* = **enquire.**

inquiry /ɪnˈkwaɪərɪ/ *n.* enquête *f.*

inquisition /ɪnkwɪˈzɪʃn/ *n.* inquisition *f.*

inquisitive /ɪnˈkwɪzətɪv/ *a.* curieux; (*prying*) indiscret.

inroad /ˈɪnrəʊd/ *n.* incursion *f.*

insan|e /ɪnˈseɪn/ *a.* fou. ~**ity** /ɪnˈsænətɪ/ *n.* folie *f.*, démence *f.*

insanitary /ɪnˈsænɪtrɪ/ *a.* insalubre, malsain.

insatiable /ɪnˈseɪʃəbl/ *a.* insatiable.

inscri|be /ɪnˈskraɪb/ *v.t.* inscrire; (*book*) dédicacer. ~**ption** /-ɪpʃn/ *n.* inscription *f.*; dédicace *f.*

inscrutable /ɪnˈskruːtəbl/ *a.* impénétrable.

insect /ˈɪnsekt/ *n.* insecte *m.*

insecticide /ɪnˈsektɪsaɪd/ *n.* insecticide *m.*

insecur|e /ɪnsɪˈkjʊə(r)/ *a.* (*not firm*) peu solide; (*unsafe*) peu sûr; (*worried*) anxieux. ~**ity** *n.* insécurité *f.*

insemination /ɪnsemɪˈneɪʃn/ *n.* insémination *f.*

insensible /ɪnˈsensəbl/ *a.* insensible; (*unconscious*) inconscient.

insensitive /ɪnˈsensətɪv/ *a.* insensible.

inseparable /ɪnˈseprəbl/ *a.* inséparable.

insert[1] /ɪnˈsɜːt/ *v.t.* insérer. ~**ion** /-ʃn/ *n.* insertion *f.*

insert[2] /ˈɪnsɜːt/ *n.* insertion *f.*; (*advertising*) encart *m.*

in-service /ɪnˈsɜːvɪs/ *a.* (*training*) continu.

inshore /ɪnˈʃɔː(r)/ *a.* côtier.

inside /ɪnˈsaɪd/ *n.* intérieur *m.* ~(**s**), (*fam.*) entrailles *f. pl.* ● *a.* intérieur. ● *adv.* à l'intérieur, dedans. ● *prep.* à l'intérieur de; (*of time*) en moins de. ~ **out,** à l'envers; (*thoroughly*) à fond.

insidious /ɪnˈsɪdɪəs/ *a.* insidieux.

insight /ˈɪnsaɪt/ *n.* (*perception*) perspicacité *f.*; (*idea*) aperçu *m.*

insignia /ɪnˈsɪɡnɪə/ *n. pl.* insignes *m. pl.*

insignificant /ɪnsɪɡˈnɪfɪkənt/ *a.* insignifiant.

insincer|e /ɪnsɪnˈsɪə(r)/ *a.* peu sincère. ~**ity** /-ˈserətɪ/ *n.* manque de sincérité *m.*

insinuat|e /ɪnˈsɪnjʊeɪt/ *v.t.* insinuer. ~**ion** /-ˈeɪʃn/ *n.* insinuation *f.*

insipid /ɪnˈsɪpɪd/ *a.* insipide.

insist /ɪnˈsɪst/ *v.t./i.* insister. ~ **on,** affirmer; (*demand*) exiger. ~ **on doing,** insister pour faire.

insisten|t /ɪnˈsɪstənt/ *a.* insistant. ~**ce** *n.* insistance *f.* ~**tly** *adv.* avec insistance.

insole /ˈɪnsəʊl/ *n.* (*separate*) semelle *f.*

insolen|t /ˈɪnsələnt/ *a.* insolent. ~**ce** *n.* insolence *f.*

insoluble /ɪnˈsɒljʊbl/ *a.* insoluble.

insolvent /ɪnˈsɒlvənt/ *a.* insolvable.

insomnia /ɪnˈsɒmnɪə/ *n.* insomnie *f.* ~**c** /-ɪæk/ *n.* insomniaque *m./f.*

inspect /ɪnˈspekt/ *v.t.* inspecter; (*tickets*) contrôler. ~**ion** /-kʃn/ *n.* inspection *f.*; contrôle *m.* ~**or** *n.* inspec|teur, -trice *m., f.*; (*on train, bus*) contrôleu|r, -se *f., f.*

inspir|e /ɪnˈspaɪə(r)/ *v.t.* inspirer. ~**ation** /-əˈreɪʃn/ *n.* inspiration *f.*

instability /ɪnstəˈbɪlətɪ/ *n.* instabilité *f.*

install /ɪnˈstɔːl/ *v.t.* installer. ~**ation** /-əˈleɪʃn/ *n.* installation *f.*

instalment /ɪn'stɔːlmənt/ *n.* (*payment*) acompte *m.*; versement *m.*; (*of serial*) épisode *m.*

instance /'ɪnstəns/ *n.* exemple *m.*; (*case*) cas *m.* **for ~,** par exemple. **in the first ~,** en premier lieu.

instant /ɪn'stənt/ *a.* immédiat; (*food*) instantané. ● *n.* instant *m.* ~**ly** *adv.* immédiatement.

instantaneous /ɪnstən'teɪnɪəs/ *a.* instantané.

instead /ɪn'sted/ *adv.* plutôt. **~ of doing,** au lieu de faire. **~ of s.o.,** à la place de qn.

instep /'ɪnstep/ *n.* cou-de-pied *m.*

instigat|e /'ɪnstɪɡeɪt/ *v.t.* provoquer. ~**ion** /-'ɡeɪʃn/ *n.* instigation *f.* ~**or** *n.* instiga|teur, -trice *m., f.*

instil /ɪn'stɪl/ *v.t.* (*p.t.* **instilled**) inculquer; (*inspire*) insuffler.

instinct /'ɪnstɪŋkt/ *n.* instinct *m.* ~**ive** /ɪn'stɪŋktɪv/ *a.* instinctif.

institut|e /'ɪnstɪtjuːt/ *n.* institut *m.* ● *v.t.* instituer; (*inquiry etc.*) entamer. ~**ion** /-'tjuːʃn/ *n.* institution *f.*; (*school, hospital*) établissement *m.*

instruct /ɪn'strʌkt/ *v.t.* instruire; (*order*) ordonner. **~ s.o. in sth.,** enseigner qch. à qn. **~ s.o. to do,** ordonner à qn. de faire. ~**ion** /-kʃn/ *n.* instruction *f.* ~**ions** /-kʃnz/ *n. pl.* (*for use*) mode d'emploi *m.* ~**ive** *a.* instructif. ~**or** *n.* professeur *m.*; (*skiing, driving*) moni|teur, -trice *m., f.*

instrument /'ɪnstrʊmənt/ *n.* instrument *m.* **~ panel,** tableau de bord *m.*

instrumental /ɪnstrʊ'mentl/ *a.* instrumental. **be ~ in,** contribuer à. ~**ist** *n.* instrumentaliste *m./f.*

insubordinat|e /ɪnsə'bɔːdɪnət/ *a.* insubordonné. ~**ion** /-'neɪʃn/ *n.* insubordination *f.*

insufferable /ɪn'sʌfrəbl/ *a.* intolérable, insupportable.

insufficient /ɪnsə'fɪʃnt/ *a.* insuffisant. ~**ly** *adv.* insuffisamment.

insular /'ɪnsjʊlə(r)/ *a.* insulaire; (*mind, person: fig.*) borné.

insulat|e /'ɪnsjʊleɪt/ *v.t.* (*room, wire, etc.*) isoler. ~**ing tape,** chatterton *m.* ~**ion** /-'leɪʃn/ *n.* isolation *f.*

insulin /'ɪnsjʊlɪn/ *n.* insuline *f.*

insult[1] /ɪn'sʌlt/ *v.t.* insulter.

insult[2] /'ɪnsʌlt/ *n.* insulte *f.*

insuperable /ɪn'sjuːprəbl/ *a.* insurmontable.

insur|e /ɪn'ʃʊə(r)/ *v.t.* assurer. ~**e that,** (*ensure: Amer.*) s'assurer que. ~**ance** *n.* assurance *f.*

insurmountable /ɪnsə'maʊntəbl/ *a.* insurmontable.

insurrection /ɪnsə'rekʃn/ *n.* insurrection *f.*

intact /ɪn'tækt/ *a.* intact.

intake /'ɪnteɪk/ *n.* admission(s) *f.* (*pl.*); (*techn.*) prise *f.*

intangible /ɪn'tændʒəbl/ *a.* intangible.

integral /'ɪntɪɡrəl/ *a.* intégral. **be an ~ part of,** faire partie intégrante de.

integrat|e /'ɪntɪɡreɪt/ *v.t./i.* (s')intégrer. ~**ion** /-'ɡreɪʃn/ *n.* intégration *f.*; (*racial*) déségrégation *f.*

integrity /ɪn'teɡrətɪ/ *n.* intégrité *f.*

intellect /'ɪntəlekt/ *n.* intelligence *f.* ~**ual** /-'lektʃʊəl/ *a.* & *n.* intellectuel(le) (*m.* (*f.*)).

intelligen|t /ɪn'telɪdʒənt/ *a.* intelligent. ~**ce** *n.* intelligence *f.*; (*mil.*) renseignements *m. pl.* ~**tly** *adv.* intelligemment.

intelligentsia /ɪntelɪ'dʒentsɪə/ *n.* intelligentsia *f.*

intelligible /ɪn'telɪdʒəbl/ *a.* intelligible.

intemperance /ɪn'tempərəns/ *n.* (*drunkenness*) ivrognerie *f.*

intend /ɪn'tend/ *v.t.* destiner. **~ to do,** avoir l'intention de faire. ~**ed** *a.* (*deliberate*) intentionnel; (*planned*) prévu; *n.* (*future spouse: fam.*) promis(e) *m.* (*f.*).

intens|e /ɪn'tens/ *a.* intense; (*person*) passionné. ~**ely** *adv.* (*to live etc.*) intensément; (*very*) extrêmement. ~**ity** *n.* intensité *f.*

intensif|y /ɪn'tensɪfaɪ/ *v.t.* intensifier. ~**ication** /-ɪ'keɪʃn/ *n.* intensification *f.*

intensive /ɪn'tensɪv/ *a.* intensif. **in ~ care,** en réanimation.

intent /ɪn'tent/ *n.* intention *f.* ● *a.* attentif. **~ on,** absorbé par. **~ on doing,** résolu à faire. ~**ly** *adv.* attentivement.

intention /ɪn'tenʃn/ *n.* intention *f.* ~**al** *a.* intentionnel.

inter /ɪn'tɜː(r)/ *v.t.* (*p.t.* **interred**) enterrer.

inter- /'ɪntə(r)/ *pref.* inter-.

interact /ɪntə'rækt/ *v.i.* avoir une action réciproque. ~**ion** /-kʃn/ *n.* interaction *f.*

intercede /ɪntə'siːd/ *v.i.* intercéder.

intercept /ɪntə'sept/ v.t. intercepter. **~ion** /-pʃn/ n. interception f.

interchange /'ɪntətʃeɪndʒ/ n. (road junction) échangeur m.

interchangeable /ɪntə'tʃeɪndʒəbl/ a. interchangeable.

intercom /'ɪntəkɒm/ n. interphone m.

interconnected /ɪntəkə'nektɪd/ a. (facts, events, etc.) lié.

intercourse /'ɪntəkɔːs/ n. (sexual, social) rapports m. pl.

interest /'ɪntrəst/ n. intérêt m.; (stake) intérêts m. pl. ● v.t. intéresser. **~ rates**, taux d'intérêt m. pl. **~ed** a. intéressé. **be ~ed in**, s'intéresser à. **~ing** a. intéressant.

interface /'ɪntəfeɪs/ n. (comput.) interface f.; (fig.) zone de rencontre f.

interfer|e /ɪntə'fɪə(r)/ v.i. se mêler des affaires des autres. **~e in**, s'ingérer dans. **~e with**, (plans) créer un contretemps avec; (work) s'immiscer dans; (radio) faire des interférences avec; (lock) toucher à. **~ence** n. ingérence f.; (radio) parasites m. pl.

interim /'ɪntərɪm/ n. intérim m. ● a. intérimaire.

interior /ɪn'tɪərɪə(r)/ n. intérieur m. ● a. intérieur.

interjection /ɪntə'dʒekʃn/ n. interjection f.

interlinked /ɪntə'lɪŋkt/ a. lié.

interlock /ɪntə'lɒk/ v.t./i. (techn.) (s')emboîter, (s')enclencher.

interloper /'ɪntələʊpə(r)/ n. intrus(e) m. (f.).

interlude /'ɪntəluːd/ n. intervalle m.; (theatre, mus.) intermède m.

intermarr|iage /ɪntə'mærɪdʒ/ n. mariage entre membres de races différentes m. **~y** v.i. se marier (entre eux).

intermediary /ɪntə'miːdɪərɪ/ a. & n. intermédiaire (m./f.).

intermediate /ɪntə'miːdɪət/ a. intermédiaire; (exam etc.) moyen.

interminable /ɪn'tɜːmɪnəbl/ a. interminable.

intermission /ɪntə'mɪʃn/ n. pause f.; (theatre etc.) entracte m.

intermittent /ɪntə'mɪtnt/ a. intermittent. **~ly** adv. par intermittence.

intern[1] /ɪn'tɜːn/ v.t. interner. **~ee** /-'niː/ n. interné(e) m. (f.). **~ment** n. internement m.

intern[2] /'ɪntɜːn/ n. (doctor: Amer.) interne m./f.

internal /ɪn'tɜːnl/ a. interne; (domestic: pol.) intérieur. **I~ Revenue**, (Amer.) fisc m. **~ly** adv. intérieurement.

international /ɪntə'næʃnəl/ a. & n. international (m.).

interplay /'ɪntəpleɪ/ n. jeu m., interaction f.

interpolate /ɪn'tɜːpəleɪt/ v.t. interpoler.

interpret /ɪn'tɜːprɪt/ v.t. interpréter. ● v.i. faire l'interprète. **~ation** /-'teɪʃn/ n. interprétation f. **~er** n. interprète m./f.

interrelated /ɪntərɪ'leɪtɪd/ a. en corrélation, lié.

interrogat|e /ɪn'terəgeɪt/ v.t. interroger. **~ion** /-'geɪʃn/ n. interrogation f. (of, de); (session of questions) interrogatoire m.

interrogative /ɪntə'rɒgətɪv/ a. & n. interrogatif (m.).

interrupt /ɪntə'rʌpt/ v.t. interrompre. **~ion** /-pʃn/ n. interruption f.

intersect /ɪntə'sekt/ v.t./i. (lines, roads) (se) couper. **~ion** /-kʃn/ n. intersection f.; (crossroads) croisement m.

interspersed /ɪntə'spɜːst/ a. (scattered) dispersé. **~ with**, parsemé de.

intertwine /ɪntə'twaɪn/ v.t./i. (s')entrelacer.

interval /'ɪntəvl/ n. intervalle m.; (theatre) entracte m. **at ~s**, par intervalles.

interven|e /ɪntə'viːn/ v.i. intervenir; (of time) s'écouler (**between**, entre); (happen) survenir. **~tion** /-'venʃn/ n. intervention f.

interview /'ɪntəvjuː/ n. (with reporter) interview f.; (for job etc.) entrevue f. ● v.t. interviewer. **~er** n. interviewer m.

intestine /ɪn'testɪn/ n. intestin m. **~al** a. intestinal.

intima|te[1] /'ɪntɪmət/ a. intime; (detailed) profond. **~cy** n. intimité f. **~tely** adv. intimement.

intimate[2] /'ɪntɪment/ v.t. (state) annoncer; (imply) suggérer.

intimidat|e /ɪn'tɪmɪdeɪt/ v.t. intimider. **~ion** /-'deɪʃn/ n. intimidation f.

into /'ɪntuː, unstressed 'ɪntə/ prep. (put, go, fall, etc.) dans; (divide, translate, etc.) en.

intolerable /ɪnˈtɒlərəbl/ a. intolérable.

intoleran|t /ɪnˈtɒlərənt/ a. intolérant. ~ce n. intolérance f.

intonation /ɪntəˈneɪʃn/ n. intonation f.

intoxicat|e /ɪnˈtɒksɪkeɪt/ v.t. enivrer. ~ed a. ivre. ~ion /-ˈkeɪʃn/ n. ivresse f.

intra- /ˈɪntrə/ pref. intra-.

intractable /ɪnˈtræktəbl/ a. très difficile.

intransigent /ɪnˈtrænsɪdʒənt/ a. intransigeant.

intransitive /ɪnˈtrænsətɪv/ a. (verb) intransitif.

intravenous /ɪntrəˈviːnəs/ a. (med.) intraveineux.

intrepid /ɪnˈtrepɪd/ a. intrépide.

intrica|te /ˈɪntrɪkət/ a. complexe. ~cy n. complexité f.

intrigu|e /ɪnˈtriːg/ v.t./i. intriguer. ● n. intrigue f. ~ing a. très intéressant; (curious) curieux.

intrinsic /ɪnˈtrɪnsɪk/ a. intrinsèque. ~ally /-klɪ/ adv. intrinsèquement.

introduce /ɪntrəˈdjuːs/ v.t. (bring in, insert) introduire; (programme, question) présenter. ~ s.o. to, (person) présenter qn. à; (subject) faire connaître à qn.

introduct|ion /ɪntrəˈdʌkʃn/ n. introduction f.; (to person) présentation f. ~ory /-tərɪ/ a. (letter, words) d'introduction.

introspective /ɪntrəˈspektɪv/ a. introspectif.

introvert /ˈɪntrəvɜːt/ n. introverti(e) m. (f.).

intru|de /ɪnˈtruːd/ v.i. (person) s'imposer (on s.o., à qn.), déranger. ~der n. intrus(e) m. (f.). ~sion n. intrusion f.

intuit|ion /ɪntjuːˈɪʃn/ n. intuition f. ~ive a. /ɪnˈtjuːɪtɪv/ a. intuitif.

inundat|e /ˈɪnʌndeɪt/ v.t. inonder (with, de). ~ion /-ˈdeɪʃn/ n. inondation f.

invade /ɪnˈveɪd/ v.t. envahir. ~r /-ə(r)/ n. envahisseu|r, -se m., f.

invalid[1] /ˈɪnvəlɪd/ n. malade m./f.; (disabled) infirme m./f.

invalid[2] /ɪnˈvælɪd/ a. non valable. ~ate v.t. invalider.

invaluable /ɪnˈvæljʊəbl/ a. inestimable.

invariab|le /ɪnˈveərɪəbl/ a. invariable. ~y adv. invariablement.

invasion /ɪnˈveɪʒn/ n. invasion f.

invective /ɪnˈvektɪv/ n. invective f.

inveigh /ɪnˈveɪ/ v.i. invectiver.

inveigle /ɪnˈveɪgl/ v.t. persuader.

invent /ɪnˈvent/ v.t. inventer. ~ion /-enʃn/ n. invention f. ● a. inventif. ~or n. inven|teur, -trice m., f.

inventory /ˈɪnvəntrɪ/ n. inventaire m.

inverse /ɪnˈvɜːs/ a. & n. inverse (m.). ~ly adv. inversement.

inver|t /ɪnˈvɜːt/ v.t. intervertir. ~ted commas, guillemets m. pl. ~sion n. inversion f.

invest /ɪnˈvest/ v.t. investir; (time, effort: fig.) consacrer. ● v.i. faire un investissement. ~ in, (buy: fam.) se payer. ~ment n. investissement m. ~or n. actionnaire m./f.; (saver) épargnant(e) m. (f.).

investigat|e /ɪnˈvestɪgeɪt/ v.t. étudier; (crime etc.) enquêter sur. ~ion /-ˈgeɪʃn/ n. investigation f. under ~ion, à l'étude. ~or n. (police) enquêteu|r, -se m., f.

inveterate /ɪnˈvetərət/ a. invétéré.

invidious /ɪnˈvɪdɪəs/ a. (hateful) odieux; (unfair) injuste.

invigilat|e /ɪnˈvɪdʒɪleɪt/ v.i. (schol.) être de surveillance. ~or n. surveillant(e) m. (f.).

invigorate /ɪnˈvɪgəreɪt/ v.t. vivifier; (encourage) stimuler.

invincible /ɪnˈvɪnsəbl/ a. invincible.

invisible /ɪnˈvɪzəbl/ a. invisible.

invit|e /ɪnˈvaɪt/ v.t. inviter; (ask for) demander. ~ation /ɪnvɪˈteɪʃn/ n. invitation f. ~ing a. (meal, smile, etc.) engageant.

invoice /ˈɪnvɔɪs/ n. facture f. ● v.t. facturer.

invoke /ɪnˈvəʊk/ v.t. invoquer.

involuntary /ɪnˈvɒləntrɪ/ a. involontaire.

involve /ɪnˈvɒlv/ v.t. entraîner; (people) faire participer. ~d a. (complex) compliqué; (at stake) en jeu. be ~d in, (work) participer à; (crime) être mêlé à. ~ment n. participation f.

invulnerable /ɪnˈvʌlnərəbl/ a. invulnérable.

inward /ˈɪnwəd/ a. & adv. vers l'intérieur; (feeling etc.) intérieur. ~ly adv. intérieurement. ~s adv. vers l'intérieur.

iodine /ˈaɪədiːn/ n. iode m.; (antiseptic) teinture d'iode f.

iota /aɪˈəʊtə/ n. (amount) brin m.

IOU /aɪəʊˈjuː/ *abbr.* (*I owe you*) reconnaissance de dette *f.*

IQ /ˈaɪˈkjuː/ *abbr.* (*intelligence quotient*) QI *m.*

Iran /ɪˈrɑːn/ *n.* Iran *m.* ~**ian** /ɪˈreɪnɪən/ *a.* & *n.* iranien(ne) (*m.* (*f.*)).

Iraq /ɪˈrɑːk/ *n.* Irak *m.* ~**i** *a.* & *n.* irakien(ne) (*m.* (*f.*)).

irascible /ɪˈræsəbl/ *a.* irascible.

irate /aɪˈreɪt/ *a.* en colère, furieux.

ire /ˈaɪə(r)/ *n.* courroux *m.*

Ireland /ˈaɪələnd/ *n.* Irlande *f.*

iris /ˈaɪərɪs/ *n.* (*anat.*, *bot.*) iris *m.*

Irish /ˈaɪərɪʃ/ *a.* irlandais. ● *n.* (*lang.*) irlandais *m.* ~**man** *n.* Irlandais *m.* ~**woman** *n.* Irlandaise *f.*

irk /ɜːk/ *v.t.* ennuyer. ~**some** *a.* ennuyeux.

iron /ˈaɪən/ *n.* fer *m.*; (*appliance*) fer (à repasser) *m.* ● *a.* de fer. ● *v.t.* repasser. **I**~ **Curtain,** rideau de fer *m.* ~ **out,** faire disparaître. ~**ing-board** *n.* planche à repasser *f.*

ironic(al) /aɪˈrɒnɪk(l)/ *a.* ironique.

ironmonger /ˈaɪənmʌŋɡə(r)/ *n.* quincaillier *m.* ~**y** *n.* quincaillerie *f.*

ironwork /ˈaɪənwɜːk/ *n.* ferronnerie *f.*

irony /ˈaɪərənɪ/ *n.* ironie *f.*

irrational /ɪˈræʃənl/ *a.* irrationnel; (*person*) pas rationnel.

irreconcilable /ɪˌrekənˈsaɪləbl/ *a.* irréconciliable; (*incompatible*) inconciliable.

irrefutable /ɪˈrefjʊtəbl/ *a.* irréfutable.

irregular /ɪˈreɡjʊlə(r)/ *a.* irrégulier. ~**ity** /-ˈlærɪtɪ/ *n.* irrégularité *f.*

irrelevan|t /ɪˈreləvənt/ *a.* sans rapport (**to,** avec). ~**ce** *n.* manque de rapport *m.*

irreparable /ɪˈrepərəbl/ *a.* irréparable, irrémédiable.

irreplaceable /ɪrɪˈpleɪsəbl/ *a.* irremplaçable.

irrepressible /ɪrɪˈpresəbl/ *a.* irrépressible.

irresistible /ɪrɪˈzɪstəbl/ *a.* irrésistible.

irresolute /ɪˈrezəluːt/ *a.* irrésolu.

irrespective /ɪrɪˈspektɪv/ *a.* ~ **of,** sans tenir compte de.

irresponsible /ɪrɪˈspɒnsəbl/ *a.* irresponsable.

irretrievable /ɪrɪˈtriːvəbl/ *a.* irréparable.

irreverent /ɪˈrevərənt/ *a.* irrévérencieux.

irreversible /ɪrɪˈvɜːsəbl/ *a.* irréversible; (*decision*) irrévocable.

irrevocable /ɪˈrevəkəbl/ *a.* irrévocable.

irrigat|e /ˈɪrɪɡeɪt/ *v.t.* irriguer. ~**ion** /-ˈɡeɪʃn/ *m.* irrigation *f.*

irritable /ˈɪrɪtəbl/ *a.* irritable.

irritat|e /ˈɪrɪteɪt/ *v.t.* irriter. **be** ~**ed by,** être énervé par. ~**ing** *a.* énervant. ~**ion** /-ˈteɪʃn/ *n.* irritation *f.*

is /ɪz/ *see* be.

Islam /ˈɪzlɑːm/ *n.* Islam *m.* ~**ic** /ɪzˈlæmɪk/ *a.* islamique.

island /ˈaɪlənd/ *n.* île *f.* **traffic** ~, refuge *m.* ~**er** *n.* insulaire *m./f.*

isle /aɪl/ *n.* île *f.*

isolat|e /ˈaɪsəleɪt/ *v.t.* isoler. ~**ion** /-ˈleɪʃn/ *n.* isolement *m.*

isotope /ˈaɪsətəʊp/ *n.* isotope *m.*

Israel /ˈɪzreɪl/ *n.* Israël *m.* ~**i** /ɪzˈreɪlɪ/ *a.* & *n.* israélien(ne) (*m.* (*f.*)).

issue /ˈɪʃuː/ *n.* question *f.*; (*outcome*) résultat *m.*; (*of magazine etc.*) numéro *m.*; (*of stamps etc.*) émission *f.*; (*offspring*) descendance *f.* ● *v.t.* distribuer, donner; (*stamps etc.*) émettre; (*book*) publier; (*order*) donner. ● *v.i.* ~ **from,** sortir de. **at** ~, en cause. **take** ~, engager une controverse.

isthmus /ˈɪsməs/ *n.* isthme *m.*

it /ɪt/ *pron.* (*subject*) il, elle; (*object*) le, la, l'*; (*impersonal subject*) il; (*non-specific*) ce, c'*, cela, ça. **it is,** (*quiet, my book, etc.*) c'est. **it is/it's cold/warm/late/** *etc.*, il fait froid/chaud/tard/*etc.* **that's it,** c'est ça. **who is it?,** qui est-ce? **of it, from it,** en. **in it, at it, to it,** y.

IT *abbr. see* information technology.

italic /ɪˈtælɪk/ *a.* italique. ~**s** *n. pl.* italique *m.*

Ital|y /ˈɪtəlɪ/ *n.* Italie *f.* ~**ian** /ɪˈtælɪən/ *a.* & *n.* italien(ne) (*m.* (*f.*)); (*lang.*) italien *m.*

itch /ɪtʃ/ *n.* démangeaison *f.* ● *v.i.* démanger. **my arm** ~**es,** mon bras me démange. **I am** ~**ing to,** ça me démange de. ~**y** *a.* qui démange.

item /ˈaɪtəm/ *n.* article *m.*, chose *f.*; (*on agenda*) question *f.* **news** ~, nouvelle *f.* ~**ize** *v.t.* détailler.

itinerant /aɪˈtɪnərənt/ *a.* itinérant; (*musician, actor*) ambulant.

itinerary /aɪˈtɪnərərɪ/ *n.* itinéraire *m.*

its /ɪts/ *a.* son, sa, *pl.* ses.

it's /ɪts/ = it is, it has.

itself /ɪt'self/ *pron.* lui-même, elle-même; (*reflexive*) se.

IUD *abbr.* (*intrauterine device*) stérilet *m.*

ivory /'aɪvərɪ/ *n.* ivoire *m.* ~ **tower,** tour d'ivoire *f.*

ivy /'aɪvɪ/ *n.* lierre *m.*

J

jab /dʒæb/ *v.t.* (*p.t.* **jabbed**) (*thrust*) enfoncer; (*prick*) piquer. ● *n.* coup *m.*; (*injection*) piqûre *f.*

jabber /'dʒæbə(r)/ *v.i.* jacasser, bavarder; (*indistinctly*) bredouiller. ● *n.* bavardage *m.*

jack /dʒæk/ *n.* (*techn.*) cric *m.*; (*cards*) valet *m.*; (*plug*) fiche *f.* ● *v.t.* ~ **up,** soulever (avec un cric).

jackal /'dʒækɔːl/ *n.* chacal *m.*

jackass /'dʒækæs/ *n.* âne *m.*

jackdaw /'dʒækdɔː/ *n.* choucas *m.*

jacket /'dʒækɪt/ *n.* veste *f.*, veston *m.*; (*of book*) jaquette *f.*

jack-knife /'dʒæknaɪf/ *n.* couteau pliant *m.* ● *v.i.* (*lorry*) faire un tête-à-queue.

jackpot /'dʒækpɒt/ *n.* gros lot *m.* **hit the** ~, gagner le gros lot.

Jacuzzi /dʒə'kuːzɪ/ *n.* (P.) bain à remous *m.*

jade /dʒeɪd/ *n.* (*stone*) jade *m.*

jaded /'dʒeɪdɪd/ *a.* las; (*appetite*) blasé.

jagged /dʒægɪd/ *a.* dentelé.

jail /dʒeɪl/ *n.* prison *f.* ● *v.t.* mettre en prison. ~**er** *n.* geôlier *m.*

jalopy /dʒə'lɒpɪ/ *n.* vieux tacot *m.*

jam¹ /dʒæm/ *n.* confiture *f.*

jam² /dʒæm/ *v.t./i.* (*p.t.* **jammed**) (*wedge, become wedged*) (se) coincer; (*cram*) (s')entasser; (*street etc.*) encombrer; (*thrust*) enfoncer; (*radio*) brouiller. ● *n.* foule *f.*; (*of traffic*) embouteillage *m.*; (*situation: fam.*) pétrin *m.* ~**-packed** *a.* (*fam.*) bourré.

Jamaica /dʒə'meɪkə/ *n.* Jamaïque *f.*

jangle /'dʒæŋgl/ *n.* cliquetis *m.* ● *v.t./i.* (faire) cliqueter.

janitor /'dʒænɪtə(r)/ *n.* concierge *m.*

January /'dʒænjʊərɪ/ *n.* janvier *m.*

Japan /dʒə'pæn/ *n.* Japon *m.* ~**ese** /dʒæpə'niːz/ *a. & n.* japonais(e) (*m.* (*f.*)); (*lang.*) japonais *m.*

jar¹ /dʒɑː(r)/ *n.* pot *m.*, bocal *m.*

jar² /dʒɑː(r)/ *v.i.* (*p.t.* **jarred**) grincer; (*of colours etc.*) détonner. ● *v.t.* ébranler. ● *n.* son discordant *m.* ~**ring** *a.* discordant.

jargon /'dʒɑːgən/ *n.* jargon *m.*

jasmine /'dʒæsmɪn/ *n.* jasmin *m.*

jaundice /'dʒɔːndɪs/ *n.* jaunisse *f.*

jaundiced /'dʒɔːndɪst/ *a.* (*envious*) envieux; (*bitter*) aigri.

jaunt /dʒɔːnt/ *n.* (*trip*) balade *f.*

jaunty /'dʒɔːntɪ/ *a.* (**-ier, -iest**) (*cheerful, sprightly*) allègre.

javelin /'dʒævlɪn/ *n.* javelot *m.*

jaw /dʒɔː/ *n.* mâchoire *f.* ● *v.i.* (*talk: sl.*) jacasser.

jay /dʒeɪ/ *n.* geai *m.* ~**-walk** *v.i.* traverser la chaussée imprudemment.

jazz /dʒæz/ *n.* jazz *m.* ● *v.t.* ~ **up,** animer. ~**y** *a.* tape-à-l'œil *invar.*

jealous /'dʒeləs/ *a.* jaloux. ~**y** *n.* jalousie *f.*

jeans /dʒiːnz/ *n. pl.* (blue-)jean *m.*

jeep /dʒiːp/ *n.* jeep *f.*

jeer /dʒɪə(r)/ *v.t./i.* ~ (**at**), railler; (*boo*) huer. ● *n.* raillerie *f.*; huée *f.*

jell /dʒel/ *v.i.* (*set: fam.*) prendre. ~**ied** *a.* en gelée.

jelly /'dʒelɪ/ *n.* gelée *f.*

jellyfish /'dʒelɪfɪʃ/ *n.* méduse *f.*

jeopardy /'dʒepədɪ/ *n.* péril *m.* ~**ize** *v.t.* mettre en péril.

jerk /dʒɜːk/ *n.* secousse *f.*; (*fool: sl.*) idiot *m.*; (*creep: sl.*) salaud *m.* ● *v.t.* donner une secousse à. ~**ily** *adv.* par saccades. ~**y** *a.* saccadé.

jersey /'dʒɜːzɪ/ *n.* (*garment*) chandail *m.*, tricot *m.*; (*fabric*) jersey *m.*

jest /dʒest/ *n.* plaisanterie *f.* ● *v.i.* plaisanter. ~**er** *n.* bouffon *m.*

Jesus /'dʒiːzəs/ *n.* Jésus *m.*

jet¹ /dʒet/ *n.* (*mineral*) jais *m.* ~-**black** *a.* de jais.

jet² /dʒet/ *n.* (*stream*) jet *m.*; (*plane*) avion à réaction *m.*, jet *m.* ~ **lag,** fatigue due au décalage horaire *f.* ~-**propelled** *a.* à réaction.

jettison /'dʒetɪsn/ *v.t.* jeter à la mer; (*aviat.*) larguer; (*fig.*) abandonner.

jetty /'dʒetɪ/ *n.* (*breakwater*) jetée *f.*

Jew /dʒuː/ *n.* Juif *m.* ~**ess** *n.* Juive *f.*

jewel /'dʒuːəl/ *n.* bijou *m.* ~**led** *a.* orné de bijoux. ~**ler** *n.* bijout|ier, -ière *m.* ~**lery** *n.* bijoux *m. pl.*

Jewish /'dʒuːɪʃ/ *a.* juif.

Jewry /'dʒʊərɪ/ *n.* les Juifs *m. pl.*

jib /dʒɪb/ *v.i.* (*p.t.* **jibbed**) regimber (**at,** devant). ● *n.* (*sail*) foc *m.*

jibe /dʒaɪb/ *n.* = **gibe**.

jiffy /'dʒɪfɪ/ n. (fam.) instant m.

jig /dʒɪg/ n. (dance) gigue f.

jiggle /'dʒɪgl/ v.t. secouer légèrement.

jigsaw /'dʒɪgsɔː/ n. puzzle m.

jilt /dʒɪlt/ v.t. laisser tomber.

jingle /'dʒɪŋgl/ v.t./i. (faire) tinter. ● n. tintement m.; (advertising) jingle m., sonal m.

jinx /dʒɪŋks/ n. (person: fam.) porte-malheur m. invar.; (spell: fig.) mauvais sort m.

jitter|s /'dʒɪtəz/ n. pl. the ~s, (fam.) la frousse f. ~y /-ərɪ/ a. be ~y, (fam.) avoir la frousse.

job /dʒɒb/ n. travail m.; (post) poste m. have a ~ doing, avoir du mal à faire. it is a good ~ that, heureusement que. ~less a. sans travail, au chômage.

jobcentre /'dʒɒbsentə(r)/ n. agence (nationale) pour l'emploi f.

jockey /'dʒɒkɪ/ n. jockey m. ● v.i. (manœuvre) manœuvrer.

jocular /'dʒɒkjʊlə(r)/ a. jovial.

jog /dʒɒg/ v.t. (p.t. jogged) pousser; (memory) rafraîchir. ● v.i. faire du jogging. ~ging n. jogging m.

join /dʒɔɪn/ v.t. joindre, unir; (club) devenir membre de; (political group) adhérer à; (army) s'engager dans. ~ s.o., (in activity) se joindre à qn.; (meet) rejoindre qn. ● v.i. (roads etc.) se rejoindre. ~ joint m. ~ in, participer (à). ~ up, (mil.) s'engager.

joiner /'dʒɔɪnə(r)/ n. menuisier m.

joint /dʒɔɪnt/ a. (account, venture) commun. ● n. (join) joint m.; (anat.) articulation f.; (culin.) rôti m.; (place: sl.) boîte f. ~ author, coauteur m. out of ~, déboîté. ~ly adv. conjointement.

joist /dʒɔɪst/ n. solive f.

joke /dʒəʊk/ n. plaisanterie f.; (trick) farce f. ● v.i. plaisanter. it's no ~e, ce n'est pas drôle. ~er n. blagueu|r, -se m., f.; (pej.) petit malin m.; (cards) joker m. ~ingly adv. pour rire.

joll|y /'dʒɒlɪ/ a. (-ier, -iest) gai. ● adv. (fam.) rudement. ~ification /-fɪ'keɪ-ʃn/, ~ity ns. réjouissances f. pl.

jolt /dʒəʊlt/ v.t./i. (vehicle, passenger) cahoter; (shake) secouer. ● n. cahot m.; secousse f.

Jordan /'dʒɔːdn/ n. Jordanie f.

jostle /'dʒɒsl/ v.t./i. (push) bouscul-er; (push each other) se bousculer.

jot /dʒɒt/ n. brin m. ● v.t. (p.t. jotted) ~ down, noter. ~ter n. (pad) bloc-notes m.

journal /'dʒɜːnl/ n. journal m. ~ism n. journalisme m. ~ist n. journaliste m./f. ~ese /-'liːz/ n. jargon des journalistes m.

journey /'dʒɜːnɪ/ n. voyage m.; (distance) trajet m. ● v.i. voyager.

jovial /'dʒəʊvɪəl/ a. jovial.

joy /dʒɔɪ/ n. joie f. ~-riding n. courses en voitures volées f. pl. ~ful, ~ous adjs. joyeux.

joystick /'dʒɔɪstɪk/ n. (comput.) manette f.

jubil|ant /'dʒuːbɪlənt/ a. débordant de joie. be ~ant, jubiler. ~ation /-'leɪʃn/ n. jubilation f.

jubilee /'dʒuːbɪliː/ n. jubilé m.

Judaism /'dʒuːdeɪɪzəm/ n. judaïsme m.

judder /'dʒʌdə(r)/ v.i. vibrer. ● n. vibration f.

judge /dʒʌdʒ/ n. juge m. ● v.t. juger. **judging by**, à juger de. ~ment n. jugement m.

judic|iary /dʒuː'dɪʃərɪ/ n. magistrature f. ~ial a. judiciaire.

judicious /dʒuː'dɪʃəs/ a. judicieux.

judo /'dʒuːdəʊ/ n. judo m.

jug /dʒʌg/ n. cruche f., pichet m.

juggernaut /'dʒʌgənɔːt/ n. (lorry) poids lourd m., mastodonte m.

juggle /'dʒʌgl/ v.t./i. jongler (avec). ~r /-ə(r)/ n. jongleu|r, -se m., f.

juic|e /dʒuːs/ n. jus m. ~y a. juteux; (details etc.: fam.) croustillant.

juke-box /'dʒuːkbɒks/ n. juke-box m.

July /dʒuː'laɪ/ n. juillet m.

jumble /'dʒʌmbl/ v.t. mélanger. ● n. (muddle) fouillis m. ~ sale, vente (de charité) f.

jumbo /'dʒʌmbəʊ/ a. ~ jet, avion géant m., jumbo-jet m.

jump /dʒʌmp/ v.t./i. sauter; (start) sursauter; (of price etc.) faire un bond. ● n. saut m.; sursaut m.; (increase) hausse f. ~ at, sauter sur. ~-leads n. pl. câbles de démarrage m. pl. ~ the gun, agir prématurément. ~ the queue, resquiller.

jumper /'dʒʌmpə(r)/ n. pull(-over) m.; (dress: Amer.) robe chasuble f.

jumpy /'dʒʌmpɪ/ a. nerveux.

junction /'dʒʌŋkʃn/ n. jonction f.; (of roads etc.) embranchement m.

juncture /'dʒʌŋktʃə(r)/ n. moment m.; (state of affairs) conjoncture f.

June /dʒuːn/ n. juin m.

jungle /'dʒʌŋgl/ n. jungle f.

junior /'dʒuːnɪə(r)/ a. (in age) plus jeune (to, que); (in rank) subalterne; (school) élémentaire; (executive, doctor) jeune. ● n. cadet(te) m. (f.); (schol.) petit(e) élève m.(f.); (sport) junior m./f.

junk /dʒʌŋk/ n. bric-à-brac m. invar.; (poor material) camelote f. ● v.t. (Amer., sl.) balancer. ~ food, saloperies f. pl. ~-shop n. boutique de brocanteur f.

junkie /'dʒʌŋkɪ/ n. (sl.) drogué(e) m. (f.).

junta /'dʒʌntə/ n. junte f.

jurisdiction /dʒʊərɪs'dɪkʃn/ n. juridiction f.

jurisprudence /dʒʊərɪs'pruːdəns/ n. jurisprudence f.

juror /'dʒʊərə(r)/ n. juré m.

jury /'dʒʊərɪ/ n. jury m.

just /dʒʌst/ a. (fair) juste. ● adv. juste, exactement; (only, slightly) juste; (simply) tout simplement. he has/had ~ left/etc., il vient/venait de partir/etc. have ~ missed, avoir manqué de peu. it's ~ a cold, ce n'est qu'un rhume. ~ as tall/etc., tout aussi grand/etc. (as, que). ~ as well, heureusement (que). ~ listen!, écoutez donc! ~ly adv. avec justice.

justice /'dʒʌstɪs/ n. justice f. J~ of the Peace, juge de paix m.

justifiabl|e /dʒʌstɪ'faɪəbl/ a. justifiable. ~y adv. avec raison.

justif|y /'dʒʌstɪfaɪ/ v.t. justifier. ~ication /-ɪ'keɪʃn/ n. justification f.

jut /dʒʌt/ v.i. (p.t. jutted). ~ out, faire saillie, dépasser.

juvenile /'dʒuːvənaɪl/ a. (youthful) juvénile; (childish) puéril; (delinquent) jeune; (court) pour enfants. ● n. jeune m./f.

juxtapose /dʒʌkstə'pəʊz/ v.t. juxtaposer.

K

kaleidoscope /kə'laɪdəskəʊp/ n. kaléidoscope.

kangaroo /kæŋgə'ruː/ n. kangourou m.

karate /kə'rɑːtɪ/ n. karaté m.

kebab /kə'bæb/ n. brochette f.

keel /kiːl/ n. (of ship) quille f. ● v.i. ~ over, chavirer.

keen /kiːn/ a. (-er, -est) (interest, wind, feeling, etc.) vif; (mind, analysis) pénétrant; (edge, appetite) aiguisé; (eager) enthousiaste. be ~ on, (person, thing: fam.) aimer beaucoup. be ~ to do or on doing, tenir beaucoup à faire. ~ly adv. vivement; avec enthousiasme. ~ness n. vivacité f.; enthousiasme m.

keep /kiːp/ v.t. (p.t. kept) garder; (promise, shop, diary, etc.) tenir; (family) entretenir; (animals) élever; (rule etc.) respecter; (celebrate) célébrer; (delay) retenir; (prevent) empêcher; (conceal) cacher. ● v.i. (food) se garder; (remain) rester. ~ (on), continuer (doing, à faire). ● n. subsistance f.; (of castle) donjon m. for ~s, (fam.) pour toujours. ~ back v.t. retenir; v.i. ne pas s'approcher. ~ s.o. from doing, empêcher qn. de faire. ~ in/out, empêcher d'entrer/de sortir. ~ up, (se) maintenir. ~ up (with), suivre. ~er n. gardien(ne) m. (f.). ~-fit n. exercices physiques m. pl.

keeping /'kiːpɪŋ/ n. garde f. in ~ with, en accord avec.

keepsake /'kiːpseɪk/ n. (thing) souvenir m.

keg /keg/ n. tonnelet m.

kennel /'kenl/ n. niche f.

Kenya /'kenjə/ n. Kenya m.

kept /kept/ see keep.

kerb /kɜːb/ n. bord du trottoir m.

kerfuffle /kə'fʌfl/ n. (fuss: fam.) histoire(s) f. (pl.).

kernel /'kɜːnl/ n. amande f.

kerosene /'kerəsiːn/ n. (aviation fuel) kérosène m.; (paraffin) pétrole (lampant) m.

ketchup /'ketʃəp/ n. ketchup m.

kettle /'ketl/ n. bouilloire f.

key /kiː/ n. clef f.; (of piano etc.) touche f. ● a. clef (f. invar.). ~-ring n. porte-clefs m. invar. ● v.t. ~ in, (comput.) saisir. ~ up, surexciter.

keyboard /'kiːbɔːd/ n. clavier m.

keyhole /'kiːhəʊl/ n. trou de la serrure m.

keynote /'kiːnəʊt/ n. (of speech etc.) note dominante f.

keystone /'kiːstəʊn/ n. (archit., fig.) clef de voûte f.

khaki /'kɑːkɪ/ a. kaki invar.

kibbutz /kɪˈbʊts/ n. (pl. **-im** /-iːm/) n. kibboutz m.

kick /kɪk/ v.t./i. donner un coup de pied (à); (of horse) ruer. ● n. coup de pied m.; ruade f.; (of gun) recul m.; (thrill: fam.) (malin) plaisir m. **~-off** n. coup d'envoi m. **~ out**, (fam.) flanquer dehors. **~ up**, (fuss, racket: fam.) faire.

kid /kɪd/ n. (goat, leather) chevreau m.; (child: sl.) gosse m./f. ● v.t./i. (p.t. **kidded**) blaguer.

kidnap /ˈkɪdnæp/ v.t. (p.t. **kidnapped**) enlever, kidnapper. **~ping** n. enlèvement m.

kidney /ˈkɪdnɪ/ n. rein m.; (culin.) rognon m.

kill /kɪl/ v.t. tuer; (fig.) mettre fin à. ● n. mise à mort f. **~er** n. tueu|r, -se m., f. **~ing** n. massacre m.; meurtre m.; a. (funny: fam.) tordant; (tiring: fam.) tuant.

killjoy /ˈkɪldʒɔɪ/ n. rabat-joie m. invar., trouble-fête m./f. invar.

kiln /kɪln/ n. four m.

kilo /ˈkiːləʊ/ n. (pl. **-os**) kilo m.

kilobyte /ˈkɪləbaɪt/ n. kilo-octet m.

kilogram /ˈkɪləgræm/ n. kilogramme m.

kilohertz /ˈkɪləhɜːts/ n. kilohertz m.

kilometre /ˈkɪləmiːtə(r)/ n. kilomètre m.

kilowatt /ˈkɪləwɒt/ n. kilowatt m.

kilt /kɪlt/ n. kilt m.

kin /kɪn/ n. parents m. pl.

kind [1] /kaɪnd/ n. genre m., sorte f., espèce f. **in ~**, en nature f. **~ of**, (somewhat: fam.) un peu. **be two of a ~**, se rassembler.

kind [2] /kaɪnd/ a. (**-er, -est**) gentil, bon. **~-hearted** a. bon. **~ness** n. bonté f.

kindergarten /ˈkɪndəgɑːtn/ n. jardin d'enfants m.

kindle /ˈkɪndl/ v.t./i. (s')allumer.

kindly /ˈkaɪndlɪ/ a. (**-ier, -iest**) bienveillant. ● adv. avec bonté. **~ wait**/etc., voulez-vous avoir la bonté d'attendre/etc.

kindred /ˈkɪndrɪd/ a. apparenté. **~ spirit**, personne qui a les mêmes goûts f., âme sœur f.

kinetic /kɪˈnetɪk/ a. cinétique.

king /kɪŋ/ n. roi m. **~-size(d)** a. géant.

kingdom /ˈkɪŋdəm/ n. royaume m.; (bot.) règne m.

kingfisher /ˈkɪŋfɪʃə(r)/ n. martin-pêcheur m.

kink /kɪŋk/ n. (in rope) entortillement m., déformation f.; (fig.) perversion f. **~y** a. (fam.) perverti.

kiosk /ˈkiːɒsk/ n. kiosque m. **telephone ~**, cabine téléphonique f.

kip /kɪp/ n. (sl.) roupillon m. ● v.i. (p.t. **kipped**) (sl.) roupiller.

kipper /ˈkɪpə(r)/ n. hareng fumé m.

kirby-grip /ˈkɜːbɪgrɪp/ n. pince à cheveux f.

kiss /kɪs/ n. baiser m. ● v.t./i. (s')embrasser.

kit /kɪt/ n. équipement m.; (clothing) affaires f. pl.; (set of tools etc.) trousse f.; (for assembly) kit m. ● v.t. (p.t. **kitted**). **~ out**, équiper.

kitbag /ˈkɪtbæg/ n. sac m. (de marin etc.).

kitchen /ˈkɪtʃɪn/ n. cuisine f. **~ garden**, jardin potager m.

kitchenette /kɪtʃɪˈnet/ n. kitchenette f.

kite /kaɪt/ n. (toy) cerf-volant m.

kith /kɪθ/ n. **~ and kin**, parents et amis m. pl.

kitten /ˈkɪtn/ n. chaton m.

kitty /ˈkɪtɪ/ n. (fund) cagnotte f.

knack /næk/ n. truc m., chic m.

knapsack /ˈnæpsæk/ n. sac à dos m.

knave /neɪv/ n. (cards) valet m.

knead /niːd/ v.t. pétrir.

knee /niː/ n. genou m.

kneecap /ˈniːkæp/ n. rotule f.

kneel /niːl/ v.i. (p.t. **knelt**). **~ (down)**, s'agenouiller.

knell /nel/ n. glas m.

knew /njuː/ see **know**.

knickers /ˈnɪkəz/ n. pl. (woman's undergarment) culotte f., slip m.

knife /naɪf/ n. (pl. **knives**) couteau m. ● v.t. poignarder.

knight /naɪt/ n. chevalier m.; (chess) cavalier m. ● v.t. faire or armer chevalier. **~hood** n. titre de chevalier m.

knit /nɪt/ v.t./i. (p.t. **knitted** or **knit**) tricoter; (bones etc.) (se) souder. **~ one's brow**, froncer les sourcils. **~ting** n. tricot m.

knitwear /ˈnɪtweə(r)/ n. tricots m. pl.

knob /nɒb/ n. bouton m.

knock /nɒk/ v.t./i. frapper, cogner; (criticize: sl.) critiquer. ● n. coup m. **~ about** v.t. malmener; v.i. vadrouiller. **~ down**, (chair, pedestrian) renverser; (demolish) abattre; (reduce) baisser. **~-down** a. (price) très bas. **~-kneed** a. cagneux. **~ off** v.t. faire tomber; (fam.) expédier; v.i.

(*fam.*) s'arrêter de travailler. ~ **out**, (*by blow*) assommer; (*tire*) épuiser. **~-out** *n.* (*boxing*) knock-out *m.* ~ **over**, renverser. ~ **up**, (*meal etc.*) préparer en vitesse. **~er** *n.* heurtoir *m.*

knot /nɒt/ *n.* nœud *m.* ● *v.t.* (*p.t.* **knotted**) nouer. **~ty** /'nɒtɪ/ *a.* noueux; (*problem*) épineux.

know /nəʊ/ *v.t./i.* (*p.t.* **knew**, *p.p.* **known**) savoir (**that**, que); (*person*, *place*) connaître. ~ **how to do**, savoir comment faire. ● *n.* **in the ~**, (*fam.*) dans le secret, au courant. ~ **about**, (*cars etc.*) s'y connaître en. **~-all**, (*Amer.*) **~-it-all** *n.* je-sais-tout *m./f.* **~-how** *n.* technique *f.* ~ **of**, connaître, avoir entendu parler de. **~ingly** *adv.* (*consciously*) sciemment.

knowledge /'nɒlɪdʒ/ *n.* connaissance *f.*; (*learning*) connaissances *f. pl.* **~able** *a.* bien informé.

known /nəʊn/ *see* know. ● *a.* connu; (*recognized*) reconnu.

knuckle /'nʌkl/ *n.* articulation du doigt *f.* ● *v.i.* ~ **under**, se soumettre.

Koran /kə'rɑːn/ *n.* Coran *m.*

Korea /kə'rɪə/ *n.* Corée *f.*

kosher /'kəʊʃə(r)/ *a.* kascher *invar.*

kowtow /kaʊ'taʊ/ *v.i.* se prosterner (**to**, devant).

kudos /'kjuːdɒs/ *n.* (*fam.*) gloire *f.*

Kurd /kɜːd/ *a. & n.* kurde *m./f.*

L

lab /læb/ *n.* (*fam.*) labo *m.*

label /'leɪbl/ *n.* étiquette *f.* ● *v.t.* (*p.t.* **labelled**) étiqueter.

laboratory /lə'bɒrətrɪ, *Amer.* 'læbrətɔːrɪ/ *n.* laboratoire *m.*

laborious /lə'bɔːrɪəs/ *a.* laborieux.

labour /'leɪbə(r)/ *n.* travail *m.*; (*workers*) main-d'œuvre *f.* ● *v.i.* peiner. ● *v.t.* trop insister sur. **in ~**, en train d'accoucher, en couches. **~ed** *a.* laborieux.

Labour /'leɪbə(r)/ *n.* le parti travailliste *m.* ● *a.* travailliste.

labourer /'leɪbərə(r)/ *n.* manœuvre *m.*; (*on farm*) ouvrier agricole *m.*

labyrinth /'læbərɪnθ/ *n.* labyrinthe *m.*

lace /leɪs/ *n.* dentelle *f.*; (*of shoe*) lacet *m.* ● *v.t.* (*fasten*) lacer; (*drink*) arroser. **~-ups** *n. pl.* chaussures à lacets *f. pl.*

lacerate /'læsəreɪt/ *v.t.* lacérer.

lack /læk/ *n.* manque *m.* ● *v.t.* manquer de. **be ~ing**, manquer (**in**, de). **for ~ of**, faute de.

lackadaisical /lækə'deɪzɪkl/ *a.* indolent, apathique.

lackey /'lækɪ/ *n.* laquais *m.*

laconic /lə'kɒnɪk/ *a.* laconique.

lacquer /'lækə(r)/ *n.* laque *f.*

lad /læd/ *n.* garçon *m.*, gars *m.*

ladder /'lædə(r)/ *n.* échelle *f.*; (*in stocking*) maille filée *f.* ● *v.t./i.* (*stocking*) filer.

laden /'leɪdn/ *a.* chargé (**with**, de).

ladle /'leɪdl/ *n.* louche *f.*

lady /'leɪdɪ/ *n.* dame *f.* **~-friend**, amie *f.* **~-in-waiting** *n.* dame d'honneur *f.* **young ~**, jeune femme *or* fille *f.* **~-like** *a.* distingué.

lady|bird /'leɪdɪbɜːd/ *n.* coccinelle *f.* **~bug** *n.* (*Amer.*) coccinelle *f.*

lag¹ /læg/ *v.i.* (*p.t.* **lagged**) traîner. ● *n.* (*interval*) décalage *m.*

lag² /læg/ *v.t.* (*p.t.* **lagged**) (*pipes*) calorifuger.

lager /'lɑːgə(r)/ *n.* bière blonde *f.*

lagoon /lə'guːn/ *n.* lagune *f.*

laid /leɪd/ *see* lay². ● **~-back** *a.* (*fam.*) cool.

lain /leɪn/ *see* lie².

lair /leə(r)/ *n.* tanière *f.*

laity /'leɪətɪ/ *n.* laïques *m. pl.*

lake /leɪk/ *n.* lac *m.*

lamb /læm/ *n.* agneau *m.*

lambswool /'læmzwʊl/ *n.* laine d'agneau *f.*

lame /leɪm/ *a.* (**-er**, **-est**) boiteux; (*excuse*) faible. **~ly** *adv.* (*argue*) sans conviction. ~ **duck**, canard boiteux *m.*

lament /lə'ment/ *n.* lamentation *f.* ● *v.t./i.* se lamenter (**sur**). **~able** *a.* lamentable.

laminated /'læmɪneɪtɪd/ *a.* laminé.

lamp /læmp/ *n.* lampe *f.*

lamppost /'læmppəʊst/ *n.* réverbère *m.*

lampshade /'læmpʃeɪd/ *n.* abat-jour *m. invar.*

lance /lɑːns/ *n.* lance *f.* ● *v.t.* (*med.*) inciser.

lancet /'lɑːnsɪt/ *n.* bistouri *m.*

land /lænd/ *n.* terre *f.*; (*plot*) terrain *m.*; (*country*) pays *m.* ● *a.* terrestre; (*policy*, *reform*) agraire. ● *v.t./i.*

débarquer; (*aircraft*) (se) poser, (faire) atterrir; (*fall*) tomber; (*obtain*) décrocher; (*put*) mettre; (*a blow*) porter. ~-locked *a.* sans accès à la mer. ~ up, se retrouver.

landed /'lændɪd/ *a.* foncier.

landing /'lændɪŋ/ *n.* débarquement *m.*; (*aviat.*) atterrissage *m.*; (*top of stairs*) palier *m.* ~-stage débarcadère *m.*

landlady /'lændleɪdɪ/ *n.* propriétaire *f.*; (*of inn*) patronne *f.* ~lord *n.* propriétaire *m.*; patron *m.*

landmark /'lændmɑːk/ *n.* (point de) repère *m.*

landscape /'læn(d)skeɪp/ *n.* paysage *m.* ● *v.t.* aménager.

landslide /'lændslaɪd/ *n.* glissement de terrain *m.*; (*pol.*) raz-de-marée (électoral) *m. invar.*

lane /leɪn/ *n.* (*path, road*) chemin *m.*; (*strip of road*) voie *f.*; (*of traffic*) file *f.*; (*aviat.*) couloir *m.*

language /'læŋgwɪdʒ/ *n.* langue *f.*; (*speech, style*) langage *m.* ~ laboratory, laboratoire de langue *m.*

languid /'læŋgwɪd/ *a.* languissant.

languish /'læŋgwɪʃ/ *v.i.* languir.

lank /læŋk/ *a.* grand et maigre.

lanky /'læŋkɪ/ *a.* (-ier, -iest) dégingandé, grand et maigre.

lanolin /'lænəʊlɪn/ *n.* lanoline *f.*

lantern /'læntən/ *n.* lanterne *f.*

lap[1] /læp/ *n.* genoux *m. pl.*; (*sport*) tour (de piste) *m.* ● *v.i.* (*p.t.* lapped) ~ over, (se) chevaucher.

lap[2] /læp/ *v.t.* (*p.t.* lapped). ~ up, laper. ● *v.i.* (*waves*) clapoter.

lapel /lə'pel/ *n.* revers *m.*

lapse /læps/ *v.i.* (*decline*) se dégrader; (*expire*) se périmer. ● *n.* défaillance *f.*, erreur *f.*; (*of time*) intervalle *m.* ~ into, retomber dans.

larceny /'lɑːsənɪ/ *n.* vol simple *m.*

lard /lɑːd/ *n.* saindoux *m.*

larder /'lɑːdə(r)/ *n.* garde-manger *m. invar.*

large /lɑːdʒ/ *a.* (-er, -est) grand, gros. at ~, en liberté. by and ~, en général. in ~, en grande mesure. ~ness *n.* grandeur *f.*

lark[1] /lɑːk/ *n.* (*bird*) alouette *f.*

lark[2] /lɑːk/ *n.* (*bit of fun: fam.*) rigolade *f.* ● *v.i.* (*fam.*) rigoler.

larva /'lɑːvə/ *n.* (*pl.* -vae /-viː/) larve *f.*

laryngitis /lærɪn'dʒaɪtɪs/ *n.* laryngite *f.*

larynx /'lærɪŋks/ *n.* larynx *m.*

lasagne /lə'zænjə/ *n.* lasagne *f.*

lascivious /lə'sɪvɪəs/ *a.* lascif.

laser /'leɪzə(r)/ *n.* laser *m.* ~ printer, imprimante laser *f.*

lash /læʃ/ *v.t.* fouetter. ● *n.* coup de fouet *m.*; (*eyelash*) cil *m.* ~ out, (*spend*) dépenser follement. ~ out against, attaquer.

lashings /'læʃɪŋz/ *n. pl.* ~ of, (*cream etc.: sl.*) des masses de.

lass /læs/ *n.* jeune fille *f.*

lasso /læ'suː/ *n.* (*pl.* -os) lasso *m.*

last[1] /lɑːst/ *a.* dernier. ● *adv.* en dernier; (*most recently*) la dernière fois. ● *n.* dern|ier, -ière *m.*, *f.*; (*remainder*) reste *m.* at (long) ~, enfin. ~-ditch *a.* ultime. ~-minute *a.* de dernière minute. ~ night, hier soir. the ~ straw, le comble. the ~ word, le mot de la fin. on its ~ legs, sur le point de rendre l'âme. ~ly *adv.* en dernier lieu.

last[2] /lɑːst/ *v.i.* durer. ~ing *a.* durable.

latch /lætʃ/ *n.* loquet *m.*

late /leɪt/ *a.* (-er, -est) (*not on time*) en retard; (*recent*) récent; (*former*) ancien; (*hour, fruit, etc.*) tardif; (*deceased*) défunt. the ~ Mrs X, feu Mme X. ~st /-ɪst/ (*last*) dernier. ● *adv.* (*not early*) tard; (*not on time*) en retard. in ~ July, fin juillet. of ~, dernièrement. ~ness *n.* retard *m.*; (*of event*) heure tardive *f.*

latecomer /'leɪtkʌmə(r)/ *n.* retardataire *m.*/*f.*

lately /'leɪtlɪ/ *adv.* dernièrement.

latent /'leɪtnt/ *a.* latent.

lateral /'lætərəl/ *a.* latéral.

lathe /leɪð/ *n.* tour *m.*

lather /'lɑːðə(r)/ *n.* mousse *f.* ● *v.t.* savonner. ● *v.i.* mousser.

Latin /'lætɪn/ *n.* (*lang.*) latin *m.* ● *a.* latin. ~ America, Amérique latine *f.*

latitude /'lætɪtjuːd/ *n.* latitude *f.*

latrine /lə'triːn/ *n.* latrines *f. pl.*

latter /'lætə(r)/ *a.* dernier. ● *n.* the ~, celui-ci, celle-ci. ~-day *a.* moderne. ~ly *adv.* dernièrement.

lattice /'lætɪs/ *n.* treillage *m.*

laudable /'lɔːdəbl/ *a.* louable.

laugh /lɑːf/ *v.i.* rire (at, de). ● *n.* rire *m.* ~able *a.* ridicule. ~ing-stock *n.* objet de risée *m.*

laughter /'lɑːftə(r)/ *n.* (*act*) rire *m.*; (*sound of laughs*) rires *m. pl.*

launch[1] /lɔːntʃ/ *v.t.* lancer. ● *n.* lancement *m.* ~ (out) into, se lancer dans. ~ing pad, aire de lancement *f.*

launch[2] /lɔːntʃ/ *n.* (*boat*) vedette *f.*

launder /'lɔːndə(r)/ *v.t.* blanchir.

launderette /lɔ:n'dret/ n. laverie automatique f.

laundry /'lɔ:ndrɪ/ n. (place) blanchisserie f.; (clothes) linge m.

laurel /'lɒrəl/ n. laurier m.

lava /'lɑ:və/ n. lave f.

lavatory /'lævətrɪ/ n. cabinets m. pl.

lavender /'lævəndə(r)/ n. lavande f.

lavish /'lævɪʃ/ a. (person) prodigue; (plentiful) copieux; (lush) somptueux. ● v.t. prodiguer (on, à). **~ly** adv. copieusement.

law /lɔ:/ n. loi f.; (profession, subject of study) droit m. **~-abiding** a. respectueux des lois. **~ and order,** l'ordre public. **~ful** a. légal. **~fully** adv. légalement. **~less** a. sans loi.

lawcourt /'lɔ:kɔ:t/ n. tribunal m.

lawn /lɔ:n/ n. pelouse f., gazon m. **~-mower** n. tondeuse à gazon f. **~ tennis,** tennis (sur gazon) m.

lawsuit /'lɔ:su:t/ n. procès m.

lawyer /'lɔ:jə(r)/ n. avocat m.

lax /læks/ a. négligent; (morals etc.) relâché. **~ity** n. négligence f.

laxative /'læksətɪv/ n. laxatif m.

lay[1] /leɪ/ a. (non-clerical) laïque; (opinion etc.) d'un profane.

lay[2] /leɪ/ v.t. (p.t. **laid**) poser, mettre; (trap) tendre; (table) mettre; (plan) former; (eggs) pondre. ● v.i. pondre. **~ aside,** mettre de côté. **~ down,** (dé)poser; (condition) (im)poser. **~ hold of,** saisir. **~ off** v.t. (worker) licencier; v.i. (fam.) arrêter. **~-off** n. licenciement m. **~ on,** (provide) fournir. **~ out,** (design) dessiner; (display) disposer; (money) dépenser; (store) amasser. **~ waste,** ravager.

lay[3] /leɪ/ see **lie**[2].

layabout /'leɪəbaʊt/ n. fainéant(e) m. (f.).

lay-by /'leɪbaɪ/ n. (pl. **-bys**) petite aire de stationnement f.

layer /'leɪə(r)/ n. couche f.

layman /'leɪmən/ n. (pl. **-men**) profane m.

layout /'leɪaʊt/ n. disposition f.

laze /leɪz/ v.i. paresser.

laz|y /'leɪzɪ/ a. (**-ier, -iest**) paresseux. **~iness** n. paresse f. **~y-bones** n. flemmard(e) m. (f.).

lead[1] /li:d/ v.t./i. (p.t. **led**) mener; (team etc.) diriger; (life) mener; (induce) amener. **~ to,** conduire à, mener à. ● n. avance f.; (clue) indice m.; (leash) laisse f.; (theatre) premier rôle m.; (wire) fil m.; (ex-

ample) exemple m. **in the ~,** en tête. **~ away,** emmener. **~ up to,** (come to) en venir à; (precede) précéder.

lead[2] /led/ n. plomb m.; (of pencil) mine f. **~en** a. (sky) de plomb; (humour) lourd.

leader /'li:də(r)/ n. chef m.; (of country, club, etc.) dirigeant(e) m. (f.); (leading article) éditorial m. **~ship** n. direction f.

leading /'li:dɪŋ/ a. principal. **~ article,** éditorial m.

leaf /li:f/ n. (pl. **leaves**) feuille f.; (of table) rallonge f. ● v.i. **~ through,** feuilleter.

leaflet /'li:flɪt/ n. prospectus m.

league /li:g/ n. ligue f.; (sport) championnat m. **in ~ with,** de mèche avec.

leak /li:k/ n. fuite f. ● v.i. fuir; (news: fig.) s'ébruiter. ● v.t. répandre; (fig.) divulguer. **~age** n. fuite f. **~y** a. qui a une fuite.

lean[1] /li:n/ a. (**-er, -est**) maigre. ● n. (of meat) maigre m. **~ness** n. maigreur f.

lean[2] /li:n/ v.t./i. (p.t. **leaned** or **leant** /lent/) (rest) (s')appuyer; (slope) pencher. **~ out,** se pencher à l'extérieur. **~ over,** (of person) se pencher. **~-to** n. appentis m.

leaning /'li:nɪŋ/ a. penché ● n. tendance f.

leap /li:p/ v.i. (p.t. **leaped** or **leapt** /lept/) bondir. ● n. bond m. **~-frog** n. saute-mouton m. invar.; v.i. (p.t. **-frogged**) sauter (over, par-dessus). **~ year,** année bissextile f.

learn /lɜ:n/ v.t./i. (p.t. **learned** or **learnt**) apprendre (to do, à faire). **~er** n. débutant(e) m. (f.).

learn|ed /'lɜ:nɪd/ a. érudit. **~ing** n. érudition f., connaissances f. pl.

lease /li:s/ n. bail m. ● v.t. louer à bail.

leaseback /'li:sbæk/ n. cession-bail f.

leash /li:ʃ/ n. laisse f.

least /li:st/ a. **the ~,** (smallest amount of) le moins de; (slightest) le or la moindre. ● n. le moins. ● adv. le moins; (with adjective) le or la moins. **at ~,** au moins.

leather /'leðə(r)/ n. cuir m.

leave /li:v/ v.t. (p.t. **left**) laisser; (depart from) quitter. ● v.i. partir. ● n. (holiday) congé m.; (consent) permission f. **be left (over),** rester. **~ alone,** (thing) ne pas toucher à; (person) laisser tranquille. **~ behind,** laisser. **~ out,** omettre. **on ~,** (*mil.*) en permission. **take one's ~,** prendre congé (**of,** de).

leavings /'li:vɪŋz/ *n. pl.* restes *m. pl.*

Leban|on /'lebənən/ *n.* Liban *m.* **~ese** /-'ni:z/ *a. & n.* libanais(e) (*m. (f.)).*

lecher /'letʃə(r)/ *n.* débauché *m.* **~ous** *a.* lubrique. **~y** *n.* lubricité *f.*

lectern /'lektən/ *n.* lutrin *m.*

lecture /'lektʃə(r)/ *n.* cours *m.,* conférence *f.;* (*rebuke*) réprimande *f.* ● *v.t./i.* faire un cours *or* une conférence (à); (*rebuke*) réprimander. **~r** /-ə(r)/ *n.* conférenci|er, -ière *m., f.,* (*univ.*) enseignant(e) *m. (f.).*

led /led/ *see* lead [1].

ledge /ledʒ/ *n.* (*window*) rebord *m.;* (*rock*) saillie *f.*

ledger /'ledʒə(r)/ *n.* grand livre *m.*

lee /li:/ *n.* côté sous le vent *m.*

leech /li:tʃ/ *n.* sangsue *f.*

leek /li:k/ *n.* poireau *m.*

leer /lɪə(r)/ *v.i.* **~ (at),** lorgner. ● *n.* regard sournois *m.*

leeway /'li:weɪ/ *n.* (*naut.*) dérive *f.;* (*fig.*) liberté d'action *f.* **make up ~,** rattraper le retard.

left [1] /left/ *see* leave. **~ luggage (office),** consigne *f.* **~-overs** *n. pl.* restes *m. pl.*

left [2] /left/ *a.* gauche. ● *adv.* à gauche. ● *n.* gauche *f.* **~-hand** *a.* à *or* de gauche. **~-handed** *a.* gaucher. **~-wing** *a.* (*pol.*) de gauche.

leftist /'leftɪst/ *n.* gauchiste *m./f.*

leg /leg/ *n.* jambe *f.;* (*of animal*) patte *f.;* (*of table*) pied *m.;* (*of chicken*) cuisse *f.;* (*of lamb*) gigot *m.;* (*of journey*) étape *f.* **~-room** *n.* place pour les jambes *f.* **~-warmers** *n. pl.* jambières *f. pl.*

legacy /'legəsɪ/ *n.* legs *m.*

legal /'li:gl/ *a.* légal; (*affairs etc.*) juridique. **~ity** /li:'gælɪtɪ/ *n.* légalité *f.* **~ly** *adv.* légalement.

legalize /'li:gəlaɪz/ *v.t.* légaliser.

legend /'ledʒənd/ *n.* légende *f.* **~ary** *a.* légendaire.

leggings /'legɪŋz/ *n. pl.* collant sans pieds *m.*

legib|le /'ledʒəbl/ *a.* lisible. **~ility** /-'bɪlɪtɪ/ *n.* lisibilité *f.* **~ly** *adv.* lisiblement.

legion /'li:dʒən/ *n.* légion *f.* **~naire** *n.* légionnaire *m.* **~naire's disease,** maladie du légionnaire *f.*

legislat|e /'ledʒɪsleɪt/ *v.i.* légiférer. **~ion** /-'leɪʃn/ *n.* (*body of laws*) législation *f.;* (*law*) loi *f.*

legislat|ive /'ledʒɪslətɪv/ *a.* législatif. **~ure** /-eɪtʃə(r)/ *n.* corps législatif *m.*

legitima|te /lɪ'dʒɪtɪmət/ *a.* légitime. **~cy** *n.* légitimité *f.*

leisure /'leʒə(r)/ *n.* loisir(s) *m.* (*pl.*). **at one's ~,** à tête reposée. **~ centre,** centre de loisirs *m.* **~ly** *a.* lent; *adv.* sans se presser.

lemon /'lemən/ *n.* citron *m.*

lemonade /lemə'neɪd/ *n.* (*fizzy*) limonade *f.;* (*still*) citronnade *f.*

lend /lend/ *v.t.* (*p.t.* lent) prêter; (*contribute*) donner. **~ to,** se prêter à. **~er** *n.* prêteu|r, -se *m., f.* **~ing** *n.* prêt *m.*

length /leŋθ/ *n.* longueur *f.;* (*in time*) durée *f.;* (*section*) morceau *m.* **at ~,** (*at last*) enfin. **at (great) ~,** longuement. **~y** *a.* long.

lengthen /'leŋθən/ *v.t./i.* (s')allonger.

lengthways /'leŋθweɪz/ *adv.* dans le sens de la longueur.

lenien|t /'li:nɪənt/ *a.* indulgent. **~cy** *n.* indulgence *f.* **~tly** *adv.* avec indulgence.

lens /lenz/ *n.* lentille *f.;* (*of spectacles*) verre *m.;* (*photo.*) objectif *m.*

lent /lent/ *see* lend.

Lent /lent/ *n.* Carême *m.*

lentil /'lentl/ *n.* (*bean*) lentille *f.*

Leo /'li:əʊ/ *n.* le Lion.

leopard /'lepəd/ *n.* léopard *m.*

leotard /'li:əta:d/ *n.* collant *m.*

leper /'lepə(r)/ *n.* lépreu|x, -se *m., f.*

leprosy /'leprəsɪ/ *n.* lèpre *f.*

lesbian /'lezbɪən/ *n.* lesbienne *f.* ● *a.* lesbien.

lesion /'li:ʒn/ *n.* lésion *f.*

less /les/ *a.* (*in quantity etc.*) moins de (**than,** que). ● *adv., n. & prep.* moins. **~ than,** (*with numbers*) moins de. **work/etc. ~ than,** travailler/etc. moins que. **ten pounds/etc. ~,** dix livres/etc. de moins. **~ and less,** de moins en moins. **~er** *a.* moindre.

lessen /'lesn/ *v.t./i.* diminuer.

lesson /'lesn/ *n.* leçon *f.*

lest /lest/ *conj.* de peur que *or* de.

let /let/ *v.t.* (*p.t.* let, *pres. p.* letting) laisser; (*lease*) louer. ● *v. aux.* **~ us do, ~'s do,** faisons. **~ him do,** qu'il fasse. **~ me know the results,** informe-moi des résultats. ● *n.* location *f.* **~ alone,** (*thing*) ne pas toucher à; (*person*) laisser tranquille; (*never mind*) encore moins. ~ **down**, baisser; (*deflate*) dégonfler; (*fig.*) décevoir. ~**down** *n.* déception *f.* ~ **go** *v.t.* lâcher; *v.i.* lâcher prise. ~ **sb. in/out**, laisser *or* faire entrer/sortir qn. ~ **a dress out**, élargir une robe. ~ **o.s. in for**, (*task*) s'engager à; (*trouble*) s'attirer. ~ **off**, (*explode*, *fire*) faire éclater *or* partir; (*excuse*) dispenser; (*not punish*) ne pas punir. ~ **up**, (*fam.*) s'arrêter. ~**up** *n.* répit *m.*

lethal /'li:θl/ *a.* mortel; (*weapon*) meurtrier.

letharg|y /'leθədʒɪ/ *n.* léthargie *f.* ~**ic** /lɪ'θɑ:dʒɪk/ *a.* léthargique.

letter /'letə(r)/ *n.* lettre *f.* ~**-bomb** *n.* lettre piégée *f.* ~**-box** *n.* boîte à *or* aux lettres *f.* ~**ing** *n.* (*letters*) caractères *m. pl.*

lettuce /'letɪs/ *n.* laitue *f.*, salade *f.*

leukaemia /lu:'ki:mɪə/ *n.* leucémie *f.*

level /'levl/ *a.* plat, uni; (*on surface*) horizontal; (*in height*) au même niveau (**with**, que); (*in score*) à égalité. ● *n.* niveau *m.* (spirit) ~, niveau à bulle *m.* ● *v.t.* (*p.t.* levelled) niveler; (*aim*) diriger. **be on the** ~, (*fam.*) être franc. ~ **crossing**, passage à niveau *m.* ~**-headed** *a.* équilibré.

lever /'li:və(r)/ *n.* levier *m.* ● *v.t.* soulever au moyen d'un levier.

leverage /'li:vərɪdʒ/ *n.* influence *f.*

levity /'levɪtɪ/ *n.* légèreté *f.*

levy /'levɪ/ *v.t.* (*tax*) (pré)lever. ● *n.* impôt *m.*

lewd /lju:d/ *a.* (-er, -est) obscène.

liable /'laɪəbl/ *a.* **be** ~ **to do**, avoir tendance à faire, pouvoir faire. ~ **to**, (*illness etc.*) sujet à; (*fine*) passible de. ~ **for**, responsable de.

liabilit|y /laɪə'bɪlətɪ/ *n.* responsabilité *f.*; (*handicap*) handicap *m.* ~**ies**, (*debts*) dettes *f. pl.*

liais|e /lɪ'eɪz/ *v.i.* (*fam.*) faire la liaison. ~**on** /-ɒn/ *n.* liaison *f.*

liar /'laɪə(r)/ *n.* menteu|r, -se *m.*, *f.*

libel /'laɪbl/ *n.* diffamation *f.* ● *v.t.* (*p.t.* libelled) diffamer.

liberal /'lɪbərəl/ *a.* libéral; (*generous*) généreux, libéral. ~**ly** *adv.* libéralement.

Liberal /'lɪbərəl/ *a.* & *n.* (*pol.*) libéral(e) (*m.* (*f.*)).

liberat|e /'lɪbəreɪt/ *v.t.* libérer. ~**ion** /-'reɪʃn/ *n.* libération *f.*

libert|y /'lɪbətɪ/ *n.* liberté *f.* **at** ~**y to**, libre de. **take** ~**ies**, prendre des libertés.

libido /lɪ'bi:dəʊ/ *n.* libido *f.*

Libra /'li:brə/ *n.* la Balance.

librar|y /'laɪbrərɪ/ *n.* bibliothèque *f.* ~**ian** /-'breərɪən/ *n.* bibliothécaire *m./f.*

libretto /lɪ'bretəʊ/ *n.* (*pl.* -os) (*mus.*) livret *m.*

Libya /'lɪbɪə/ *n.* Libye *f.* ~**n** *a.* & *n.* libyen(ne) (*m.* (*f.*)).

lice /laɪs/ *see* **louse**.

licence, *Amer.* **license** [1] /'laɪsns/ *n.* permis *m.*; (*for television*) redevance *f.*; (*comm.*) licence *f.*; (*liberty: fig.*) licence *f.* ~ **plate**, plaque minéralogique *f.*

license [2] /'laɪsns/ *v.t.* accorder un permis à, autoriser.

licentious /laɪ'senʃəs/ *a.* licencieux.

lichen /'laɪkən/ *n.* lichen *m.*

lick /lɪk/ *v.t.* lécher; (*defeat: sl.*) rosser. ● *n.* coup de langue *m.* ~ **one's chops**, se lécher les babines.

licorice /'lɪkərɪs/ *n.* (*Amer.*) réglisse *f.*

lid /lɪd/ *n.* couvercle *m.*

lido /'laɪdəʊ/ *n.* (*pl.* -os) piscine en plein air *f.*

lie [1] /laɪ/ *n.* mensonge *m.* ● *v.i.* (*p.t.* lied, *pres. p.* lying) (*tell lies*) mentir. **give the** ~ **to**, démentir.

lie [2] /laɪ/ *v.i.* (*p.t.* lay, *p.p.* lain, *pres. p.* lying) s'allonger; (*remain*) rester; (*be*) se trouver, être; (*in grave*) reposer. **be lying**, être allongé. ~ **down**, s'allonger. ~ **in**, **have a** ~**in**, faire la grasse matinée. ~ **low**, se cacher.

lieu /lju:/ *n.* **in** ~ **of**, au lieu de.

lieutenant /lef'tenənt, *Amer.* lu:-'tenənt/ *n.* lieutenant *m.*

life /laɪf/ *n.* (*pl.* **lives**) vie *f.* ~ **cycle**, cycle de vie *m.* ~**-guard** *n.* sauveteur *m.* ~ **insurance**, assurance-vie *f.* ~**-jacket** *n.* gilet de sauvetage *m.* ~ **preserver**, (*Amer.*) gilet de sauvetage *m.* ~ **size(d)** *a.* grandeur nature *invar.* ~**-style** *n.* style de vie *m.*

lifebelt /'laɪfbelt/ *n.* bouée de sauvetage *f.*

lifeboat /'laɪfbəʊt/ *n.* canot de sauvetage *m.*

lifebuoy /'laɪfbɔɪ/ *n.* bouée de sauvetage *f.*

lifeless /'laɪflɪs/ *a.* sans vie.

lifelike /'laɪflaɪk/ *a.* très ressemblant.

lifelong /'laɪflɒŋ/ *a.* de toute la vie.

lifetime /'laɪftaɪm/ n. vie f. **in one's ~**, de son vivant.

lift /lɪft/ v.t. lever; (*steal: fam.*) voler. ● v.i. (*of fog*) se lever. ● n. (*in building*) ascenseur m. **give a ~ to**, emmener (en voiture). **~-off** n. (*aviat.*) décollage m.

ligament /'lɪɡəmənt/ n. ligament m.

light [1] /laɪt/ n. lumière f.; (*lamp*) lampe f.; (*for fire, on vehicle, etc.*) feu m.; (*headlight*) phare m. ● a. (*not dark*) clair. ● v.t. (*p.t.* **lit** *or* **lighted**) allumer; (*room etc.*) éclairer; (*match*) frotter. **bring to ~**, révéler. **come to ~**, être révélé. **have you got a ~?**, vous avez du feu? **~ bulb**, ampoule f. **~ pen**, crayon optique m. **~ up** v.i. s'allumer; v.t. (*room*) éclairer. **~-year** n. année lumière f.

light [2] /laɪt/ a. (**-er, -est**) (*not heavy*) léger. **~-fingered** a. chapardeur. **~-headed** a. (*dizzy*) qui a un vertige; (*frivolous*) étourdi. **~-hearted** a. gai. **~ly** adv. légèrement. **~ness** n. légèreté f.

lighten [1] /'laɪtn/ v.t. (*give light to*) éclairer; (*make brighter*) éclaircir.

lighten [2] /'laɪtn/ v.t. (*make less heavy*) alléger.

lighter /'laɪtə(r)/ n. briquet m.; (*for stove*) allume-gaz m. invar.

lighthouse /'laɪthaʊs/ n. phare m.

lighting /'laɪtɪŋ/ n. éclairage m. **~ technician**, éclairagiste m./f.

lightning /'laɪtnɪŋ/ n. éclair(s) m. (*pl.*). ● a. éclair invar.

lightweight /'laɪtweɪt/ a. léger. ● n. (*boxing*) poids léger m.

like [1] /laɪk/ a. semblable, pareil. ● prep. comme. ● conj. (*fam.*) comme. ● n. pareil m. **be ~-minded**, avoir les mêmes sentiments. **the ~s of you**, des gens comme vous.

like [2] /laɪk/ v.t. aimer (bien). **~s** n. pl. goûts m. pl. **I should ~**, je voudrais, j'aimerais. **would you ~?**, voulez-vous? **~able** a. sympathique.

likel|y /'laɪklɪ/ a. (**-ier, -iest**) probable. ● adv. probablement. **he is ~y to do**, il fera probablement. **not ~y!**, (*fam.*) pas question! **~ihood** n. probabilité f.

liken /'laɪkən/ v.t. comparer.

likeness /'laɪknɪs/ n. ressemblance f.

likewise /'laɪkwaɪz/ adv. de même.

liking /'laɪkɪŋ/ n. (*for thing*) penchant m.; (*for person*) affection f.

lilac /'laɪlək/ n. lilas m. ● a. lilas invar.

lily /'lɪlɪ/ n. lis m., lys m. **~ of the valley**, muguet m.

limb /lɪm/ n. membre m. **out on a ~**, isolé (et vulnérable).

limber /'lɪmbə(r)/ v.i. **~ up**, faire des exercices d'assouplissement.

limbo /'lɪmbəʊ/ n. **be in ~**, (*forgotten*) être tombé dans l'oubli.

lime [1] /laɪm/ n. chaux f.

lime [2] /laɪm/ n. (*fruit*) citron vert m.

lime [3] /laɪm/ n. **~(-tree)**, tilleul m.

limelight /'laɪmlaɪt/ n. **in the ~**, en vedette.

limerick /'lɪmərɪk/ n. poème humoristique m. (*de cinq vers*)

limit /'lɪmɪt/ n. limite f. ● v.t. limiter. **~ed company**, société anonyme f. **~ation** /-'teɪʃn/ n. limitation f. **~less** a. sans limites.

limousine /'lɪməziːn/ n. (*car*) limousine f.

limp [1] /lɪmp/ v.i. boiter. ● n. **have a ~**, boiter.

limp [2] /lɪmp/ a. (**-er, -est**) mou.

limpid /'lɪmpɪd/ a. limpide.

linctus /'lɪŋktəs/ n. sirop m.

line [1] /laɪn/ n. ligne f.; (*track*) voie f.; (*wrinkle*) ride f.; (*row*) rangée f., file f.; (*of poem*) vers m.; (*rope*) corde f.; (*of goods*) gamme f.; (*queue*: Amer.) queue f. ● v.t. (*paper*) régler; (*streets etc.*) border. **be in ~ for**, avoir de bonnes chances d'avoir. **in ~ with**, en accord avec. **stand in ~**, faire la queue. **~ up**, (s')aligner; (*in queue*) faire la queue. **~ sth. up**, prévoir qch.

line [2] /laɪn/ v.t. (*garment*) doubler; (*fill*) remplir, garnir.

lineage /'lɪnɪdʒ/ n. lignée f.

linear /'lɪnɪə(r)/ a. linéaire.

linen /'lɪnɪn/ n. (*sheets etc.*) linge m.; (*material*) lin m., toile de lin f.

liner /'laɪnə(r)/ n. paquebot m.

linesman /'laɪnzmən/ n. (*football*) juge de touche m.

linger /'lɪŋɡə(r)/ v.i. s'attarder; (*smells etc.*) persister.

lingerie /'lænʒərɪ/ n. lingerie f.

lingo /'lɪŋɡəʊ/ n. (*pl.* **-os**) (*hum., fam.*) jargon m.

linguist /'lɪŋɡwɪst/ n. linguiste m./f.

linguistic /lɪŋ'ɡwɪstɪk/ a. linguistique. **~s** n. linguistique f.

lining /'laɪnɪŋ/ n. doublure f.

link /lɪŋk/ n. lien m.; (*of chain*) maillon m. ● v.t. relier; (*relate*) (re)lier. **~ up,** (*of roads*) se rejoindre. **~age** *n.* lien *m.* **~-up** *n.* liaison *f.*

links /lɪŋks/ *n. invar.* terrain de golf *m.*

lino /'laɪnəʊ/ *n.* (*pl.* **-os**) lino *m.*

linoleum /lɪ'nəʊlɪəm/ *n.* linoléum *m.*

lint /lɪnt/ *n.* (*med.*) tissu ouaté *m.*; (*fluff*) peluche(s) *f.* (*pl.*).

lion /'laɪən/ *n.* lion *m.* **take the ~'s share,** se tailler la part du lion. **~ess** *n.* lionne *f.*

lip /lɪp/ *n.* lèvre *f.*; (*edge*) rebord *m.* **~-read** *v.t./i.* lire sur les lèvres. **pay ~-service to,** n'approuver que pour la forme.

lipsalve /'lɪpsælv/ *n.* baume pour les lèvres *m.*

lipstick /'lɪpstɪk/ *n.* rouge (à lèvres) *m.*

liquefy /'lɪkwɪfaɪ/ *v.t./i.* (se) liquéfier.

liqueur /lɪ'kjʊə(r)/ *n.* liqueur *f.*

liquid /'lɪkwɪd/ *n. & a.* liquide (*m.*). **~ize** *v.t.* passer au mixeur. **~izer** *n.* mixeur *m.*

liquidat|e /'lɪkwɪdeɪt/ *v.t.* liquider. **~ion** /-'deɪʃn/ *n.* liquidation *f.* **go into ~ion,** déposer son bilan.

liquor /'lɪkə(r)/ *n.* alcool *m.*

liquorice /'lɪkərɪs/ *n.* réglisse *f.*

lira /'lɪərə/ *n.* (*pl.* **lire** /'lɪəreɪ/ *or* **liras**) lire *f.*

lisp /lɪsp/ *n.* zézaiement *m.* ● *v.i.* zézayer. **with a ~,** en zézayant.

list[1] /lɪst/ *n.* liste *f.* ● *v.t.* dresser la liste de.

list[2] /lɪst/ *v.i.* (*ship*) gîter.

listen /'lɪsn/ *v.i.* écouter. **~ to, ~ in (to),** écouter. **~er** *n.* audi|teur, -trice *m./f.*

listless /'lɪstlɪs/ *a.* apathique.

lit /lɪt/ *see* **light**[1].

litany /'lɪtənɪ/ *n.* litanie *f.*

liter /'li:tə(r)/ *see* **litre**.

literal /'lɪtərəl/ *a.* littéral; (*person*) prosaïque. **~ly** *adv.* littéralement.

literary /'lɪtərərɪ/ *a.* littéraire.

litera|te /'lɪtərət/ *a.* qui sait lire et écrire. **~cy** *n.* capacité de lire et écrire *f.*

literature /'lɪtrətʃə(r)/ *n.* littérature *f.*; (*fig.*) documentation *f.*

lithe /laɪð/ *a.* souple, agile.

litigation /lɪtɪ'geɪʃn/ *n.* litige *m.*

litre, (*Amer.*) **liter** /'li:tə(r)/ *n.* litre *m.*

litter /'lɪtə(r)/ *n.* détritus *m. pl.*, papiers *m. pl.*; (*animals*) portée *f.* ● *v.t.* éparpiller; (*make untidy*) lais-

ser des détritus dans. **~-bin** *n.* poubelle *f.* **~ed with,** jonché de.

little /'lɪtl/ *a.* petit; (*not much*) peu de. ● *n.* peu *m.* ● *adv.* peu. **a ~,** un peu (de).

liturgy /'lɪtədʒɪ/ *n.* liturgie *f.*

live[1] /laɪv/ *a.* vivant; (*wire*) sous tension; (*broadcast*) en direct. **be a ~ wire,** être vif, être dynamique.

live[2] /lɪv/ *v.t./i.* vivre; (*reside*) habiter, vivre. **~ down,** faire oublier. **~ it up,** mener la belle vie. **~ on,** (*feed o.s. on*) vivre de; (*continue*) survivre. **~ up to,** se montrer à la hauteur de.

livelihood /'laɪvlɪhʊd/ *n.* moyens d'existence *m. pl.*

livel|y /'laɪvlɪ/ *a.* (**-ier, -iest**) vif, vivant. **~iness** *n.* vivacité *f.*

liven /'laɪvn/ *v.t./i.* **~ up,** (s')animer; (*cheer up*) (s')égayer.

liver /'lɪvə(r)/ *n.* foie *m.*

livery /'lɪvərɪ/ *n.* livrée *f.*

livestock /'laɪvstɒk/ *n.* bétail *m.*

livid /'lɪvɪd/ *a.* livide; (*angry: fam.*) furieux.

living /'lɪvɪŋ/ *a.* vivant. ● *n.* vie *f.* **make a ~,** gagner sa vie. **~ conditions,** conditions de vie *f. pl.* **~-room** *n.* salle de séjour *f.*

lizard /'lɪzəd/ *n.* lézard *m.*

llama /'lɑ:mə/ *n.* lama *m.*

load /ləʊd/ *n.* charge *f.*; (*loaded goods*) chargement *m.*, charge *f.*; (*weight, strain*) poids *m.* **~s of,** (*fam.*) des masses de. ● *v.t.* charger. **~ed** *a.* (*dice*) pipé; (*wealthy: sl.*) riche.

loaf[1] /ləʊf/ *n.* (*pl.* **loaves**) pain *m.*

loaf[2] /ləʊf/ *v.i.* **~ (about),** fainéanter. **~er** *n.* fainéant(e) *m.* (*f.*).

loam /ləʊm/ *n.* terreau *m.*

loan /ləʊn/ *n.* prêt *m.*; (*money borrowed*) emprunt *m.* ● *v.t.* (*lend: fam.*) prêter.

loath /ləʊθ/ *a.* peu disposé (**to,** à).

loath|e /ləʊð/ *v.t.* détester. **~ing** *n.* dégoût *m.* **~some** *a.* dégoûtant.

lobby /'lɒbɪ/ *n.* entrée *f.*, vestibule *m.*; (*pol.*) lobby *m.*, groupe de pression *m.* ● *v.t.* faire pression sur.

lobe /ləʊb/ *n.* lobe *m.*

lobster /'lɒbstə(r)/ *n.* homard *m.*

local /'ləʊkl/ *a.* local; (*shops etc.*) du quartier. ● *n.* personne du coin *f.*; (*pub: fam.*) pub du coin *m.* **~ government,** administration locale *f.* **~ly** *adv.* localement; (*nearby*) dans les environs.

locale /ləʊˈkɑːl/ *n.* lieu *m.*

locality /ləʊˈkælətɪ/ *n.* (*district*) région *f.*; (*position*) lieu *m.*

localized /ˈləʊkəlaɪzd/ *a.* localisé.

locat|e /ləʊˈkeɪt/ *v.t.* (*situate*) situer; (*find*) repérer. ~**ion** /-ʃn/ *n.* emplacement *m.* **on** ~**ion**, (*cinema*) en extérieur.

lock ¹ /lɒk/ *n.* mèche (de cheveux) *f.*

lock ² /lɒk/ *n.* (*of door etc.*) serrure *f.*; (*on canal*) écluse *f.* ● *v.t./i.* fermer à clef; (*wheels*: *auto.*) (se) bloquer. ~ **in** *or* **up**, enfermer. ~ **out**, (*by mistake*) enfermer dehors. ~**out** *n.* lockout *m. invar.* ~**-up** *n.* (*shop*) boutique *f.*; (*garage*) box *m.*

locker /ˈlɒkə(r)/ *n.* casier *m.*

locket /ˈlɒkɪt/ *n.* médaillon *m.*

locksmith /ˈlɒksmɪθ/ *n.* serrurier *m.*

locomotion /ləʊkəˈməʊʃn/ *n.* locomotion *f.*

locomotive /ˈləʊkəməʊtɪv/ *n.* locomotive *f.*

locum /ˈləʊkəm/ *n.* (*doctor etc.*) remplaçant(e) *m.* (*f.*).

locust /ˈləʊkəst/ *n.* criquet *m.*, sauterelle *f.*

lodge /lɒdʒ/ *n.* (*house*) pavillon (de gardien *or* de chasse) *m.*; (*of porter*) loge *f.* ● *v.t.* loger; (*money, complaint*) déposer. ● *v.i.* être logé (**with**, chez); (*become fixed*) se loger. ~**r** /-ə(r)/ *n.* locataire *m./f.*, pensionnaire *m./f.*

lodgings /ˈlɒdʒɪŋz/ *n.* chambre (meublée) *f.*; (*flat*) logement *m.*

loft /lɒft/ *n.* grenier *m.*

lofty /ˈlɒftɪ/ *a.* (**-ier, -iest**) (*tall, noble*) élevé; (*haughty*) hautain.

log /lɒg/ *n.* (*of wood*) bûche *f.* ~**(-book**), (*naut.*) journal de bord *m.*; (*auto.*) (*équivalent de la*) carte grise *f.* ● *v.t.* (*p.t.* **logged**) noter; (*distance*) parcourir. ~ **on**, entrer. ~ **off**, sortir.

logarithm /ˈlɒgərɪðəm/ *n.* logarithme *m.*

loggerheads /ˈlɒgəhedz/ *n. pl.* **at** ~, en désaccord.

logic ./ˈlɒdʒɪk/ *a.* logique. ~**al** *a.* logique. ~**ally** *adv.* logiquement.

logistics /ləˈdʒɪstɪks/ *n.* logistique *f.*

logo /ˈləʊgəʊ/ *n.* (*pl.* **-os**) (*fam.*) emblème *m.*

loin /lɔɪn/ *n.* (*culin.*) filet *m.* ~**s**, reins *m. pl.*

loiter /ˈlɔɪtə(r)/ *v.i.* traîner.

loll /lɒl/ *v.i.* se prélasser.

loll|ipop /ˈlɒlɪpɒp/ *n.* sucette *f.* ~**y** *n.* (*fam.*) sucette *f.*; (*sl.*) fric *m.*

London /ˈlʌndən/ *n.* Londres *m./f.* ~**er** *n.* Londonien(ne) *m.* (*f.*).

lone /ləʊn/ *a.* solitaire *m./f.* ~**some** *a.* solitaire.

lonely /ˈləʊnlɪ/ *a.* (**-ier, -iest**) solitaire; (*person*) seul, solitaire.

long ¹ /lɒŋ/ *a.* (**-er, -est**) long. ● *adv.* longtemps. **how** ~ **is?**, quelle est la longueur de?; (*in time*) quelle est la durée de? **how** ~**?**, combien de temps? **he will not be** ~, il n'en a pas pour longtemps. **a** ~ **time**, longtemps. **as** *or* **so** ~ **as**, pourvu que. **before** ~, avant peu. **I no** ~**er do**, je ne fais plus. ~**-distance** *a.* (*flight*) sur long parcours; (*phone call*) interurbain. ~ **face**, grimace *f.* ~ **johns**, (*fam.*) caleçon long *m.* ~ **jump**, saut en longueur *m.* ~**-playing record**, microsillon *m.* ~**-range** *a.* à longue portée; (*forecast*) à long terme. ~**-sighted** *a.* presbyte. ~**standing** *a.* de longue date. ~**suffering** *a.* très patient. ~**-term** *a.* à long terme. ~ **wave**, grandes ondes *f. pl.* ~**-winded** *a.* (*speaker etc.*) verbeux.

long ² /lɒŋ/ *v.i.* avoir bien *or* très envie (**for, to,** de). ~ **for s.o.**, (*pine for*) languir après qn. ~**ing** *n.* envie *f.*; (*nostalgia*) nostalgie *f.*

longevity /lɒnˈdʒevətɪ/ *n.* longévité *f.*

longhand /ˈlɒŋhænd/ *n.* écriture courante *f.*

longitude /ˈlɒndʒɪtjuːd/ *n.* longitude *f.*

loo /luː/ *n.* (*fam.*) toilettes *f. pl.*

look /lʊk/ *v.t./i.* regarder; (*seem*) avoir l'air. ● *n.* regard *m.*; (*appearance*) air *m.*, aspect *m.* (**good**) ~**s**, beauté *f.* ~ **after**, s'occuper de, soigner. ~ **at**, regarder. ~ **back on**, repenser à. ~ **down on**, mépriser. ~ **for**, chercher. ~ **forward to**, attendre avec impatience. ~ **in on**, passer voir. ~ **into**, examiner. ~ **like**, ressembler à, avoir l'air de. ~ **out**, faire attention. ~ **out for**, chercher; (*watch*) guetter. ~**-out** *n.* (*mil.*) poste de guet *m.*; (*person*) guetteur *m.* **be on the** ~**-out for**, rechercher. ~ **round**, se retourner. ~ **up**, (*word*) chercher; (*visit*) passer voir. ~ **up to**, respecter. ~**-alike** *n.* sosie *m.* ~**ing-glass** *n.* glace *f.*

loom ¹ /luːm/ *n.* métier à tisser *m.*

loom² /luːm/ v.i. surgir; (event etc.: fig.) paraître imminent.

loony /ˈluːnɪ/ n. & a. (sl.) fou, folle (m., f.).

loop /luːp/ n. boucle f. ● v.t. boucler.

loophole /ˈluːphəʊl/ n. (in rule) échappatoire f.

loose /luːs/ a. (-er, -est) (knot etc.) desserré; (page etc.) détaché; (clothes) ample, lâche; (tooth) qui bouge; (lax) relâché; (not packed) en vrac; (inexact) vague; (pej.) immoral. at a ~ end, désœuvré. come ~, bouger. ~ly adv. sans serrer; (roughly) vaguement.

loosen /ˈluːsn/ v.t. (slacken) desserrer; (untie) défaire.

loot /luːt/ n. butin m. ● v.t. piller. ~er n. pillard(e) m. (f.). ~ing n. pillage m.

lop /lɒp/ v.t. (p.t. lopped). ~ off, couper.

lop-sided /lɒpˈsaɪdɪd/ a. de travers.

lord /lɔːd/ n. seigneur m.; (British title) lord m. the L~, le Seigneur. (good) L~!, mon Dieu! ~ly a. noble; (haughty) hautain.

lore /lɔː(r)/ n. traditions f. pl.

lorry /ˈlɒrɪ/ n. camion m.

lose /luːz/ v.t./i. (p.t. lost) perdre. get lost, se perdre. ~r /-ə(r)/ n. perdant(e) m. (f.).

loss /lɒs/ n. perte f. be at a ~, être perplexe. be at a ~ to, être incapable de. heat ~, déperdition de chaleur f.

lost /lɒst/ see lose. ● a. perdu. ~ property, (Amer.) ~ and found, objets trouvés m. pl.

lot¹ /lɒt/ n. (fate) sort m.; (at auction) lot m.; (land) lotissement m.

lot² /lɒt/ n. the ~, (le) tout m.; (people) tous m. pl., toutes f. pl. a ~ (of), ~s (of), (fam.) beaucoup (de). quite a ~ (of), (fam.) pas mal (de).

lotion /ˈləʊʃn/ n. lotion f.

lottery /ˈlɒtərɪ/ n. loterie f.

loud /laʊd/ a. (-er, -est) bruyant, fort. ● adv. fort. ~ hailer, portevoix m. invar. out ~, tout haut. ~ly adv. fort.

loudspeaker /laʊdˈspiːkə(r)/ n. haut-parleur m.

lounge /laʊndʒ/ v.i. paresser. ● n. salon m. ~ suit, costume m.

louse /laʊs/ n. (pl. lice) pou m.

lousy /ˈlaʊzɪ/ a. (-ier, -iest) pouilleux; (bad: sl.) infect.

lout /laʊt/ n. rustre m.

lovable /ˈlʌvəbl/ a. adorable.

love /lʌv/ n. amour m.; (tennis) zéro m. ● v.t. aimer; (like greatly) aimer (beaucoup) (to do, faire). in ~, amoureux (with, de). ~ affair, liaison amoureuse f. ~ life, vie amoureuse f. make ~, faire l'amour.

lovely /ˈlʌvlɪ/ a. (-ier, -iest) joli; (delightful: fam.) très agréable.

lover /ˈlʌvə(r)/ n. amant m.; (devotee) amateur m. (of, de).

lovesick /ˈlʌvsɪk/ a. ~ amoureux.

loving /ˈlʌvɪŋ/ a. affectueux.

low¹ /ləʊ/ v.i. meugler.

low² /ləʊ/ a. & adv. (-er, -est) bas. ● n. (low pressure) dépression f. reach a (new) ~, atteindre son niveau le plus bas. ~ in sth., à faible teneur en qch. ~-calorie a. basses-calories. ~-cut a. décolleté. ~-down a. méprisable; n. (fam.) renseignements m. pl. ~-fat a. maigre. ~-key a. modéré; (discreet) discret. ~-lying a. à faible altitude.

lowbrow /ˈləʊbraʊ/ a. peu intellectuel.

lower /ˈləʊə(r)/ a. & adv. see low². ● v.t. baisser. ~ o.s., s'abaisser.

lowlands /ˈləʊləndz/ n. pl. plaine(s) f. (pl.).

lowly /ˈləʊlɪ/ a. (-ier, -iest) humble.

loyal /ˈlɔɪəl/ a. loyal. ~ly adv. loyalement. ~ty n. loyauté f.

lozenge /ˈlɒzɪndʒ/ n. (shape) losange m.; (tablet) pastille f.

LP abbr. see long-playing record.

Ltd. abbr. (Limited) SA.

lubricate /ˈluːbrɪkeɪt/ v.t. graisser, lubrifier. ~ant n. lubrifiant m. ~ation /-ˈkeɪʃn/ n. graissage m.

lucid /ˈluːsɪd/ a. lucide. ~ity /luːˈsɪdətɪ/ n. lucidité f.

luck /lʌk/ n. chance f. bad ~, malchance f. good ~!, bonne chance!

lucky /ˈlʌkɪ/ a. (-ier, -iest) qui a de la chance, heureux; (event) heureux; (number) qui porte bonheur. it's ~y that, c'est une chance que. ~ily adv. heureusement.

lucrative /ˈluːkrətɪv/ a. lucratif.

ludicrous /ˈluːdɪkrəs/ a. ridicule.

lug /lʌg/ v.t. (p.t. lugged) traîner.

luggage /ˈlʌgɪdʒ/ n. bagages m. pl. ~-rack n. porte-bagages m. invar.

lukewarm /ˈluːkwɔːm/ a. tiède.

lull /lʌl/ v.t. (soothe, send to sleep) endormir. ● n. accalmie f.
lullaby /'lʌləbaɪ/ n. berceuse f.
lumbago /lʌm'beɪɡəʊ/ n. lumbago m.
lumber /'lʌmbə(r)/ n. bric-à-brac m. invar.; (wood) bois de charpente m. ● v.t. ~ s.o. with, (chore etc.) coller à qn.
lumberjack /'lʌmbədʒæk/ n. (Amer.) bûcheron m.
luminous /'luːmɪnəs/ a. lumineux.
lump /lʌmp/ n. morceau m.; (swelling on body) grosseur f.; (in liquid) grumeau m. ● v.t. ~ together, réunir. ~ sum, somme globale f. ~y a. (sauce) grumeleux; (bumpy) bosselé.
lunacy /'luːnəsɪ/ n. folie f.
lunar /'luːnə(r)/ a. lunaire.
lunatic /'luːnətɪk/ n. fou, folle m., f.
lunch /lʌntʃ/ n. déjeuner m. ● v.i. déjeuner. ~ box, cantine f.
luncheon /'lʌntʃən/ n. déjeuner m. ~ meat, (approx.) saucisson m. ~ voucher, chèque-repas m.
lung /lʌŋ/ n. poumon m.
lunge /lʌndʒ/ n. mouvement brusque en avant m. ● v.i. s'élancer (at, sur).
lurch[1] /lɜːtʃ/ n. leave in the ~, planter là, laisser en plan.
lurch[2] /lɜːtʃ/ v.i. (person) tituber.
lure /lʊə(r)/ v.t. appâter, attirer. ● n. (attraction) attrait m., appât m.
lurid /'lʊərɪd/ a. choquant, affreux; (gaudy) voyant.
lurk /lɜːk/ v.i. se cacher; (in ambush) s'embusquer; (prowl) rôder. a ~ing suspicion, un petit soupçon.
luscious /'lʌʃəs/ a. appétissant.
lush /lʌʃ/ a. luxuriant. ● n. (Amer., fam.) ivrogne(sse) m. (f.).
lust /lʌst/ n. luxure f.; (fig.) convoitise f. ● v.i. ~ after, convoiter.
lustre /'lʌstə(r)/ n. lustre m.
lusty /'lʌstɪ/ a. (-ier, -iest) robuste.
lute /luːt/ n. (mus.) luth m.
Luxemburg /'lʌksəmbɜːɡ/ n. Luxembourg m.
luxuriant /lʌɡ'ʒʊərɪənt/ a. luxuriant.
luxurious /lʌɡ'ʒʊərɪəs/ a. luxueux.
luxury /'lʌkʃərɪ/ n. luxe m. ● a. de luxe.
lying /'laɪɪŋ/ see lie[1], lie[2]. ● n. le mensonge.
lynch /lɪntʃ/ v.t. lyncher.
lynx /lɪŋks/ n. lynx m.
lyric /'lɪrɪk/ a. lyrique. ~s n. pl. paroles f. pl. ~al a. lyrique. ~ism /-sɪzəm/ n. lyrisme m.

M

MA abbr. see Master of Arts
mac /mæk/ n. (fam.) imper m.
macaroni /mækə'rəʊnɪ/ n. macaronis m. pl.
macaroon /mækə'ruːn/ n. macaron m.
mace /meɪs/ n. (staff) masse f.
Mach /mɑːk/ n. ~ (number), (nombre de) Mach m.
machiavellian /mækɪə'velɪən/ a. machiavélique.
machinations /mækɪ'neɪʃnz/ n. pl. machinations f. pl.
machine /mə'ʃiːn/ n. machine f. ● v.t. (sew) coudre à la machine; (techn.) usiner. ~ code, code machine m. ~-gun n. mitrailleuse f.; v.t. (p.t. -gunned) mitrailler. ~-readable a. en langage machine. ~-tool, machine-outil f.
machinery /mə'ʃiːnərɪ/ n. machinerie f.; (working parts & fig.) mécanisme(s) m. (pl.).
machinist /mə'ʃiːnɪst/ n. (operator) opéra|teur, -trice sur machine m., f.; (on sewing-machine) piqueu|r, -se m., f.
macho /'mætʃəʊ/ n. (pl. -os) macho m. ● a. macho invar.
mackerel /'mækrəl/ n. invar. (fish) maquereau m.
mackintosh /'mækɪntɒʃ/ n. imperméable m.
macrobiotic /mækrəʊbaɪ'ɒtɪk/ a. macrobiotique.
mad /mæd/ a. (madder, maddest) fou; (foolish) insensé; (dog etc.) enragé; (angry: fam.) furieux. be ~ about, se passionner pour; (person) être fou de. drive s.o. ~, exaspérer qn. like a ~, comme un fou. ~ly adv. (interested, in love, etc.) follement; (frantically) comme un fou. ~ness n. folie f.
Madagascar /mædə'ɡæskə(r)/ n. Madagascar f.
madam /'mædəm/ n. madame f.; (unmarried) mademoiselle f.
madden /'mædn/ v.t. exaspérer.
made /meɪd/ see make. ~ to measure, fait sur mesure.
Madeira /mə'dɪərə/ n. (wine) madère m.
madhouse /'mædhaʊs/ n. (fam.) maison de fous f.

madman /'mædmən/ n. (pl. -men) fou m.

madrigal /'mædrɪgl/ n. madrigal m.

magazine /mægə'ziːn/ n. revue f., magazine m.; (of gun) magasin m.

magenta /mə'dʒentə/ a. magenta (invar.).

maggot /'mægət/ n. ver m., asticot m. ~y a. véreux.

magic /'mædʒɪk/ n. magie f. ● a. magique. ~al a. magique.

magician /mə'dʒɪʃn/ n. magicien(ne) m. (f.).

magistrate /'mædʒɪstreɪt/ n. magistrat m.

magnanim|ous /mæg'nænɪməs/ a. magnanime. ~ity /-ə'nɪməti/ n. magnanimité f.

magnate /'mægneɪt/ n. magnat m.

magnesia /mæg'niːʃə/ n. magnésie f.

magnet /'mægnɪt/ n. aimant m. ~ic /-'netɪk/ a. magnétique. ~ism n. magnétisme m. ~ize v.t. magnétiser.

magneto /mæg'niːtəʊ/ n. (pl. os) magnéto f.

magnificen|t /mæg'nɪfɪsnt/ a. magnifique. ~ce n. magnificence f.

magnif|y /'mægnɪfaɪ/ v.t. grossir; (sound) amplifier; (fig.) exagérer. ~ication /-ɪ'keɪʃn/ n. grossissement m.; amplification f. ~ier n., ~ying glass, loupe f.

magnitude /'mægnɪtjuːd/ n. (importance) ampleur f.; (size) grandeur f.

magnolia /mæg'nəʊlɪə/ n. magnolia m.

magnum /'mægnəm/ n. magnum m.

magpie /'mægpaɪ/ n. pie f.

mahogany /mə'hɒgənɪ/ n. acajou m.

maid /meɪd/ n. (servant) bonne f.; (girl: old use) jeune fille f.

maiden /'meɪdn/ n. (old use) jeune fille f. ● a. (aunt) célibataire; (voyage) premier. ~ name, nom de jeune fille m. ~hood n. virginité f. ~ly a. virginal.

mail¹ /meɪl/ n. (servant) poste f.; (letters) courrier m. ● a. (bag, van) postal. ● v.t. envoyer par la poste. **mail box**, boîte à lettres f. ~ing list, liste d'adresses f. ~ order, vente par correspondance f. ~ shot, publipostage m.

mail² /meɪl/ n. (armour) cotte de mailles f.

mailman /'meɪlmæn/ n. (pl. -men) (Amer.) facteur m.

maim /meɪm/ v.t. mutiler.

main¹ /meɪn/ a. principal. ● n. in the ~, en général. ~ line, grande ligne f. a ~ road, une grande route. ~ly adv. principalement, surtout.

main² /meɪn/ n. (water/gas) ~, conduite d'eau/de gaz f. the ~s, (electr.) le secteur.

mainframe n. unité centrale f.

mainland /'meɪnlənd/ n. continent m.

mainspring /'meɪnsprɪŋ/ n. ressort principal m.; (motive: fig.) mobile principal m.

mainstay /'meɪnsteɪ/ n. soutien m.

mainstream /'meɪnstriːm/ n. tendance principale f., ligne f.

maintain /meɪn'teɪn/ v.t. (continue, keep, assert) maintenir; (house, machine, family) entretenir; (rights) soutenir.

maintenance /'meɪntənəns/ n. (care) entretien m.; (continuation) maintien m.; (allowance) pension alimentaire f.

maisonette /meɪzə'net/ n. duplex m.

maize /meɪz/ n. maïs m.

majestic /mə'dʒestɪk/ a. majestueux.

majesty /'mædʒəstɪ/ n. majesté f.

major /'meɪdʒə(r)/ a. majeur. ● n. commandant m. ● v.i. ~ in, (univ., Amer.) se spécialiser en. ~ road, route à priorité f.

Majorca /mə'dʒɔːkə/ n. Majorque f.

majority /mə'dʒɒrɪtɪ/ n. majorité f. ● a. majoritaire. the ~ of people, la plupart des gens.

make /meɪk/ v.t./i. (p.t. made) faire; (manufacture) fabriquer; (friends) se faire; (money) gagner, se faire; (decision) prendre; (destination) arriver à; (cause to be) rendre. ~ s.o. do sth., faire faire qch. à qn.; (force) obliger qn. à faire qch. ● n. fabrication f.; (brand) marque f. be made of, être fait de. ~ as if to, mettre à l'aise. ~ s.o. happy, rendre qn. heureux. ~ it, arriver; (succeed) réussir. I ~ it two o'clock, j'ai deux heures. I ~ it 150, d'après moi, ça fait 150. I cannot ~ anything of it, je n'y comprends rien. can you ~ Friday?, vendredi, c'est possible? ~ as if to, faire mine de. ~ believe, faire semblant. ~-believe, a. feint, illusoire; n. fantaisie f. ~ do, (manage) se débrouiller (with, avec). ~ do with, (content o.s.) se contenter de. ~ for, se diriger vers; (cause) tendre à créer. ~ good v.i. réussir;

v.t. compenser; (*repair*) réparer. ~ **off**, filer (**with**, avec). ~ **out** *v.t.* distinguer; (*understand*) comprendre; (*draw up*) faire; (*assert*) prétendre; (*v.i. fam.*) se débrouiller. ~ **over**, céder (**to**, à); (*convert*) transformer. ~ **up** *v.t.* faire, former; (*story*) inventer; (*deficit*) combler; *v.i.* se réconcilier. ~ **up** (**one's face**), se maquiller. **~-up** *n.* maquillage *m.*; (*of object*) constitution *f.*; (*psych.*) caractère *m.* ~ **up for**, compenser; (*time*) rattraper. ~ **up one's mind**, se décider. ~ **up to**, se concilier les bonnes grâces de.

maker /'meɪkə(r)/ *n.* fabricant *m.*

makeshift /'meɪkʃɪft/ *n.* expédient *m.* ● *a.* provisoire.

making /'meɪkɪŋ/ *n.* **be the ~ of**, faire le succès de. **he has the ~s of**, il a l'étoffe de.

maladjusted /mælə'dʒʌstɪd/ *a.* inadapté.

maladministration /mælədmɪnɪ'streɪʃn/ *n.* mauvaise gestion *f.*

malaise /mæ'leɪz/ *n.* malaise *m.*

malaria /mə'leərɪə/ *n.* malaria *f.*

Malay /mə'leɪ/ *a. & n.* malais(e) (*m. (f.)*). **~sia** *n.* Malaisie *f.*

Malaya /mə'leɪə/ *n.* Malaisie *f.*

male /meɪl/ *a.* (*voice, sex*) masculin; (*bot., techn.*) mâle. ● *n.* mâle *m.*

malevolen|t /mə'levələnt/ *a.* malveillant. **~ce** *n.* malveillance *f.*

malform|ation /mælfɔː'meɪʃn/ *n.* malformation *f.* **~ed** *a.* difforme.

malfunction /mæl'fʌŋkʃn/ *n.* mauvais fonctionnement *m.* ● *v.i.* mal fonctionner.

malice /'mælɪs/ *n.* méchanceté *f.*

malicious /mə'lɪʃəs/ *a.* méchant. **~ly** *adv.* méchamment.

malign /mə'laɪn/ *a.* pernicieux. ● *v.t.* calomnier.

malignan|t /mə'lɪɡnənt/ *a.* malveillant; (*tumour*) malin. **~cy** *n.* malveillance *f.*; malignité *f.*

malinger /mə'lɪŋɡə(r)/ *v.i.* feindre la maladie. **~er** *n.* simula|teur, -trice *m., f.*

mall /mɔːl/ *n.* (**shopping**) **~**, centre commercial *m.*

malleable /'mælɪəbl/ *a.* malléable.

mallet /'mælɪt/ *n.* maillet *m.*

malnutrition /mælnjuː'trɪʃn/ *n.* sous-alimentation *f.*

malpractice /mæl'præktɪs/ *n.* faute professionnelle *f.*

malt /mɔːlt/ *n.* malt *m.* **~ whisky**, whisky pur malt *m.*

Malt|a /'mɔːltə/ *n.* Malte *f.* **~ese** /-'tiːz/ *a. & n.* maltais(e) (*m. (f.)*).

maltreat /mæl'triːt/ *v.t.* maltraiter. **~ment** *n.* mauvais traitement *m.*

mammal /'mæml/ *n.* mammifère *m.*

mammoth /'mæməθ/ *n.* mammouth *m.* ● *a.* monstre.

man /mæn/ *n.* (*pl.* **men**) homme *m.*; (*in sports team*) joueur *m.*; (*chess*) pièce *f.* ● *v.t.* (*p.t.* **manned**) pourvoir en hommes; (*guns*) servir; (*be on duty at*) être de service à. **~-hour** *n.* heure de main-d'œuvre *f.* ~ **in the street**, homme de la rue *m.* **~-made** *a.* artificiel. **~-sized** *a.* grand. ~ **to man**, d'homme à homme. **~ned space flight**, vol spatial habité *m.*

manage /'mænɪdʒ/ *v.t.* diriger; (*shop, affairs*) gérer; (*handle*) manier. **I could ~ another drink**, (*fam.*) je prendrais bien encore un verre. **can you ~ Friday?**, vendredi, c'est possible? ● *v.i.* se débrouiller. ~ **to do**, réussir à faire. **~able** *a.* (*tool, size, person, etc.*) maniable; (*job*) faisable. **~ment** *n.* direction *f.*; (*of shop*) gestion *f.* **managing director**, directeur général *m.*

manager /'mænɪdʒə(r)/ *n.* direc|teur, -trice *m., f.*; (*of shop*) gérant(e) *m. (f.)*; (*of actor*) impresario *m.* **~ess** /-'res/ *n.* directrice *f.*; gérante *f.* **~ial** /-'dʒɪərɪəl/ *a.* directorial. **~ial staff**, cadres *m. pl.*

mandarin /'mændərɪn/ *n.* mandarin *m.*; (*orange*) mandarine *f.*

mandate /'mændeɪt/ *n.* mandat *m.*

mandatory /'mændətrɪ/ *a.* obligatoire.

mane /meɪn/ *n.* crinière *f.*

manful /'mænfl/ *a.* courageux.

manganese /mæŋɡə'niːz/ *n.* manganèse *m.*

mangetout /mɒnʒ'tuː/ *n.* mange-tout *m. invar.*

mangle[1] /'mæŋɡl/ *n.* (*for wringing*) essoreuse *f.*; (*for smoothing*) calandre *f.*

mangle[2] /'mæŋɡl/ *v.t.* mutiler.

mango /'mæŋɡəʊ/ *n.* (*pl.* **-oes**) mangue *f.*

manhandle /'mænhændl/ *v.t.* maltraiter, malmener.

manhole /'mænhəʊl/ *n.* trou d'homme *m.*, regard *m.*

manhood /'mænhʊd/ n. âge d'homme m.; (quality) virilité f.

mania /'meɪnɪə/ n. manie f. ~c /-ıæk/ n. maniaque m./f., fou m., folle f.

manic-depressive /'mænɪkdɪ'presɪv/ a & n. maniaco-dépressif(-ive) (m. (f.)).

manicur|e /'mænɪkjʊə(r)/ n. soin des mains m. ● v.t. soigner, manucurer. ~ist n. manucure m./f.

manifest /'mænɪfest/ a. manifeste. ● v.t. manifester. ~ation /-'steɪʃn/ n. manifestation f.

manifesto /mænɪ'festəʊ/ n. (pl. -os) manifeste m.

manifold /'mænɪfəʊld/ a. multiple. ● n. (auto.) collecteur m.

manipulat|e /mə'nɪpjʊleɪt/ v.t. (tool, person) manipuler. ~ion /-'leɪʃn/ n. manipulation f.

mankind /mæn'kaɪnd/ n. genre humain m.

manly /'mænlɪ/ a. viril.

manner /'mænə(r)/ n. manière f.; (attitude) attitude f.; (kind) sorte f. ~s, (social behaviour) manières f. pl. ~ed a. maniéré.

mannerism /'mænərɪzəm/ n. trait particulier m.

manœuvre /mə'nuːvə(r)/ n. manœuvre f. ● v.t./i. manœuvrer.

manor /'mænə(r)/ n. manoir m.

manpower /'mænpaʊə(r)/ n. main-d'œuvre f.

manservant /'mænsɜːvənt/ n. (pl. menservants) domestique m.

mansion /'mænʃn/ n. château m.

manslaughter /'mænslɔːtə(r)/ n. homicide involontaire m.

mantelpiece /'mæntlpiːs/ n. (shelf) cheminée f.

manual /'mænjʊəl/ a. manuel. ● n. (handbook) manuel m.

manufacture /mænjʊ'fæktʃə(r)/ v.t. fabriquer. ● n. fabrication f. ~r /-ə(r)/ n. fabricant m.

manure /mə'njʊə(r)/ n. fumier m.; (artificial) engrais m.

manuscript /'mænjʊskrɪpt/ n. manuscrit m.

many /'menɪ/ a. & n. beaucoup (de). a great or good ~, un grand nombre (de). ~ a, bien des.

Maori /'maʊrɪ/ a. maori. ● n. Maori(e) m. (f.).

map /mæp/ n. carte f.; (of streets etc.) plan m. ● v.t. (p.t. mapped) faire la carte de. ~ out, (route) tracer; (arrange) organiser.

maple /'meɪpl/ n. érable m.

mar /mɑː(r)/ v.t. (p.t. marred) gâter; (spoil beauty of) déparer.

marathon /'mærəθən/ n. marathon m.

marble /'mɑːbl/ n. marbre m.; (for game) bille f.

March /mɑːtʃ/ n. mars m.

march /mɑːtʃ/ v.i. (mil.) marcher (au pas). ~ off/etc., partir/etc. allégrement. ● v.t. ~ off, (lead away) emmener. ● n. marche f. ~-past n. défilé m.

mare /meə(r)/ n. jument f.

margarine /mɑːdʒə'riːn/ n. margarine f.

margin /'mɑːdʒɪn/ n. marge f. ~al a. marginal; (increase etc.) léger, faible. ~al seat, (pol.) siège chaudement disputé m. ~alize v.t. marginaliser. ~ally adv. très légèrement.

marigold /'mærɪgəʊld/ n. souci m.

marijuana /mærɪ'wɑːnə/ n. marijuana f.

marina /mə'riːnə/ n. marina f.

marinate /'mærɪneɪt/ v.t. mariner.

marine /mə'riːn/ a. marin. ● n. (shipping) marine f.; (sailor) fusilier marin m.

marionette /mærɪə'net/ n. marionnette f.

marital /'mærɪtl/ a. conjugal. ~ status, situation de famille f.

maritime /'mærɪtaɪm/ a. maritime.

marjoram /'mɑːdʒərəm/ n. marjolaine f.

mark [1] /mɑːk/ n. (currency) mark m.

mark [2] /mɑːk/ n. marque f.; (trace) trace f., marque f.; (schol.) note f.; (target) but m. ● v.t. marquer; (exam) corriger. ~ out, délimiter; (person) désigner. ~ time, marquer le pas. ~er n. marque f. ~ing n. (marks) marques f.pl.

marked /mɑːkt/ a. marqué. ~ly /-ɪdlɪ/ adv. visiblement.

market /'mɑːkɪt/ n. marché m. ● v.t. (sell) vendre; (launch) commercialiser. ~ garden, jardin maraîcher m. ~-place n. marché m. ~ research, étude de marché f. ~ value, valeur marchande f. on the ~, en vente. ~ing n. marketing m.

marksman /'mɑːksmən/ n. (pl. -men) tireur d'élite m.

marmalade /'mɑːməleɪd/ n. confiture d'oranges f.

maroon /mə'ruːn/ n. bordeaux m. invar. ● a. bordeaux invar.

marooned /mə'ruːnd/ a. abandonné; (snow-bound etc.) bloqué.

marquee /mɑː'kiː/ n. grande tente f.; (awning: Amer.) marquise f.

marquis /'mɑːkwɪs/ n. marquis m.

marriage /'mærɪdʒ/ n. mariage m. ~able a. nubile, mariable.

marrow /'mærəʊ/ n. (of bone) moelle f.; (vegetable) courge f.

marr|y /'mærɪ/ v.t. épouser; (give or unite in marriage) marier. ● v.i. se marier. ~ied a. marié; (life) conjugal. get ~ied, se marier (to, avec).

Mars /mɑːz/ n. (planet) Mars f.

marsh /mɑːʃ/ n. marais m. ~y a. marécageux.

marshal /'mɑːʃl/ n. maréchal m.; (at event) membre du service d'ordre m. ● v.t. (p.t. marshalled) rassembler.

marshmallow /mɑːʃ'mæləʊ/ n. guimauve f.

martial /'mɑːʃl/ a. martial. ~ law, loi martiale f.

martyr /'mɑːtə(r)/ n. martyr(e) m. (f.). ● v.t. martyriser. ~dom n. martyre m.

marvel /'mɑːvl/ n. merveille f. ● v.i. (p.t. marvelled) s'émerveiller (at, de).

marvellous /'mɑːvələs/ a. merveilleux.

Marxis|t /'mɑːksɪst/ a. & n. marxiste (m./f.). ~m /-zəm/ n. marxisme m.

marzipan /'mɑːzɪpæn/ n. pâte d'amandes f.

mascara /mæ'skɑːrə/ n. mascara m.

mascot /'mæskət/ n. mascotte f.

masculin|e /'mæskjulɪn/ a. & n. masculin (m.). ~ity /-'lɪnətɪ/ n. masculinité f.

mash /mæʃ/ n. pâtée f.; (potatoes: fam.) purée f. ● v.t. écraser. ~ed potatoes, purée (de pommes de terre) f.

mask /mɑːsk/ n. masque m. ● v.t. masquer.

masochis|t /'mæsəkɪst/ n. masochiste m./f. ~m /-zəm/ n. masochisme m.

mason /'meɪsn/ n. (builder) maçon m. ~ry n. maçonnerie f.

Mason /'meɪsn/ n. maçon m. ~ic /mə'sɒnɪk/ a. maçonnique

masquerade /mɑːskə'reɪd/ n. mascarade f. ● v.i. ~ as, se faire passer pour.

mass¹ /mæs/ n. (relig.) messe f.

mass² /mæs/ n. masse f. ● v.t./i. (se) masser. ~-produce v.t. fabriquer en série. the ~es, les masses f.pl. the ~ media, les média m.pl.

massacre /'mæsəkə(r)/ n. massacre m. ● v.t. massacrer.

massage /'mæsɑːʒ, Amer. mə'sɑːʒ/ n. massage m. ● v.t. masser.

masseu|r /mæ'sɜː(r)/ n. masseur m. ~se /-ɜːz/ n. masseuse f.

massive /'mæsɪv/ a. (large) énorme; (heavy) massif.

mast /mɑːst/ n. mât m.; (for radio, TV) pylône m.

master /'mɑːstə(r)/ n. maître m.; (in secondary school) professeur m. ● v.t. maîtriser. ~-key n. passepartout m. invar. ~-mind n. (of scheme etc.) cerveau m.; v.t. diriger. M~ of Arts/etc., titulaire d'une maîtrise ès lettres/etc. m./f. ~-stroke n. coup de maître m. ~y n. maîtrise f.

masterly /'mɑːstəlɪ/ a. magistral.

masterpiece /'mɑːstəpiːs/ n. chef-d'œuvre m.

mastiff /'mæstɪf/ n. dogue m.

masturbat|e /'mæstəbeɪt/ v.i. se masturber. ~ion /-'beɪʃn/ n. masturbation f.

mat /mæt/ n. (petit) tapis m., natte f.; (at door) paillasson m.

match¹ /mætʃ/ n. allumette f.

match² /mætʃ/ n. (sport) match m.; (equal) égal(e) m. (f.); (marriage) mariage m.; (s.o. to marry) parti m. ● v.t. opposer; (go with) aller avec; (cups etc.) assortir; (equal) égaler. be a ~ for, pouvoir tenir tête à. ● v.i. (be alike) être assorti. ~ing a. assorti.

matchbox /'mætʃbɒks/ n. boîte à allumettes f.

mate¹ /meɪt/ n. camarade m./f.; (of animal) compagnon m., compagne f.; (assistant) aide m./f. ● v.t./i. (s')accoupler (with, avec).

mate² /meɪt/ n. (chess) mat m.

material /mə'tɪərɪəl/ n. matière f.; (fabric) tissu m.; (documents, for building) matériau(x) m. (pl.). ~s, (equipment) matériel m. ● a. matériel; (fig.) important. ~istic /-'lɪstɪk/ a. matérialiste.

materialize /mə'tɪərɪəlaɪz/ *v.i.* se matérialiser, se réaliser.

maternal /mə'tɜːnl/ *a.* maternel.

maternity /mə'tɜːnətɪ/ *n.* maternité *f.* ● *a.* (*clothes*) de grossesse. ~ **hospital**, maternité *f.* ~ **leave**, congé maternité *m.*

mathematic|s /mæθə'mætɪks/ *n. &* *n. pl.* mathématiques *f. pl.* ~**ian** /-ə'tɪʃn/ *n.* mathématicien(ne) *m.* (*f.*). ~**al** *a.* mathématique.

maths /mæθs/ (*Amer.* **math** /mæθ/) *n. & n. pl.* (*fam.*) maths *f. pl.*

matinée /'mætɪneɪ/ *n.* matinée *f.*

mating /'meɪtɪŋ/ *n.* accouplement *m.* ~ **season**, saison des amours *f.*

matriculat|e /mə'trɪkjʊleɪt/ *v.t./i.* (s')inscrire. ~**ion** /-'leɪʃn/ *n.* inscription *f.*

matrimon|y /'mætrɪmənɪ/ *n.* mariage *m.* ~**ial** /-'məʊnɪəl/ *a.* matrimonial.

matrix /'meɪtrɪks/ *n.* (*pl.* **matrices** /-ɪsiːz/) matrice *f.*

matron /'meɪtrən/ *n.* (*married, elderly*) dame âgée *f.*; (*in hospital: former use*) infirmière-major *f.* ~**ly** *a.* d'âge mûr; (*manner*) très digne.

matt /mæt/ *a.* mat.

matted /'mætɪd/ *a.* (*hair*) emmêlé.

matter /'mætə(r)/ *n.* (*substance*) matière *f.*; (*affair*) affaire *f.*; (*pus*) pus *m.* ● *v.i.* importer. **as a ~ of fact**, en fait. **it does not ~**, ça ne fait rien. ~**-of-fact** *a.* terre à terre *invar.* **no ~ what happens**, quoi qu'il arrive. **what is the ~?**, qu'est-ce qu'il y a?

mattress /'mætrɪs/ *n.* matelas *m.*

matur|e /mə'tjʊə(r)/ *a.* mûr. ● *v.t./i.* (se) mûrir. ~**ity** *n.* maturité *f.*

maul /mɔːl/ *v.t.* déchiqueter.

Mauritius /mə'rɪʃəs/ *n.* île Maurice *f.*

mausoleum /mɔːsə'lɪəm/ *n.* mausolée *m.*

mauve /məʊv/ *a. & n.* mauve *m.*

maverick /'mævərɪk/ *n.* non-conformiste.

maxim /'mæksɪm/ *n.* maxime *f.*

maxim|um /'mæksɪməm/ *a. & n.* (*pl.* **-ima**) maximum (*m.*). ~**ize** *v.t.* porter au maximum.

may /meɪ/ *v. aux.* (*p.t.* **might**) pouvoir. **he ~/might come**, il peut/pourrait venir. **you might have**, vous auriez pu. **you ~ leave**, vous pouvez partir. ~ **I smoke?**, puis-je fumer? ~ **he be happy**, qu'il

soit heureux. **I ~ or might as well stay**, je ferais aussi bien de rester.

May /meɪ/ *n.* mai *m.* ~ **Day**, le Premier Mai.

maybe /'meɪbɪ/ *adv.* peut-être.

mayhem /'meɪhem/ *n.* (*havoc*) ravages *m. pl.*

mayonnaise /meɪə'neɪz/ *n.* mayonnaise *f.*

mayor /meə(r)/ *n.* maire *m.* ~**ess** *n.* (*wife*) femme du maire *f.*

maze /meɪz/ *n.* labyrinthe *m.*

MBA (*abbr.*) (*Master of Business Administration*) magistère en gestion commerciale *m.*

me /miː/ *pron.* me, m'*; (*after prep.*) moi. (**to**) ~, me, m'*. **he knows ~**, il me connaît.

meadow /'medəʊ/ *n.* pré *m.*

meagre /'miːgə(r)/ *a.* maigre.

meal ¹ /miːl/ *n.* repas *m.*

meal ² /miːl/ *n.* (*grain*) farine *f.*

mealy-mouthed /miːlɪ'maʊðd/ *a.* mielleux.

mean ¹ /miːn/ *a.* (**-er, -est**) (*poor*) misérable; (*miserly*) avare; (*unkind*) méchant. ~**ness** *n.* avarice *f.*; méchanceté *f.*

mean ² /miːn/ *a.* moyen. ● *n.* milieu *m.*; (*average*) moyenne *f.* **in the ~ time**, en attendant.

mean ³ /miːn/ *v.t.* (*p.t.* **meant**) vouloir dire; (*involve*) entraîner. **I ~ that!**, je suis sérieux. **be meant for**, être destiné à. ~ **to do**, avoir l'intention de faire.

meander /mɪ'ændə(r)/ *v.i.* faire des méandres.

meaning /'miːnɪŋ/ *n.* sens *m.*, signification *f.* ~**ful** *a.* significatif. ~**less** *a.* denué de sens.

means /miːnz/ *n.* moyen(s) *m.* (*pl.*). **by ~ of sth.**, au moyen de qch. ● *n. pl.* (*wealth*) moyens financiers *m. pl.* **by all ~**, certainement. **by no ~**, nullement.

meant /ment/ *see* **mean** ².

mean|time /'miːntaɪm/, ~**while** *advs.* en attendant.

measles /'miːzlz/ *n.* rougeole *f.*

measly /'miːzlɪ/ *a.* (*sl.*) minable.

measurable /'meʒərəbl/ *a.* mesurable.

measure /'meʒə(r)/ *n.* mesure *f.*; (*ruler*) règle *f.* ● *v.t./i.* mesurer. ~ **up to**, être à la hauteur de. ~**d** *a.* mesuré. ~**ment** *n.* mesure *f.*

meat /miːt/ *n.* viande *f.* ~**y** *a.* de viande; (*fig.*) substantiel.

mechanic /mɪ'kænɪk/ a. mécanicien(ne) m. (f.).

mechanic|al /mɪ'kænɪkl/ d. mécanique. ~s n. (science) mécanique f.; n. pl. mécanisme m.

mechan|ism /'mekənɪzəm/ n. mécanisme m. ~ize v.t. mécaniser.

medal /'medl/ n. médaille f. ~list n. médaillé(e) m. (f.). **be a gold ~list**, être médaille d'or.

medallion /mɪ'dælɪən/ n. (medal, portrait, etc.) médaillon m.

meddle /'medl/ v.i. (interfere) se mêler (**in**, de); (tinker) toucher (**with**, à). ~**some** a. importun.

media /'miːdɪə/ see **medium**. ● n. pl. **the ~**, les média m. pl. **talk to the ~**, parler à la presse.

median /'miːdɪən/ a. médian. ● n. médiane f.

mediat|e /'miːdɪeɪt/ v.i. servir d'intermédiaire. ~**ion** /-'eɪʃn/ n. médiation f. ~**or** or n. média|teur, -trice m., f.

medical /'medɪkl/ a. médical; (student) en médecine. ● n. (fam.) visite médicale f.

medicat|ed /'medɪkeɪtɪd/ a. médical. ~**ion** /-'keɪʃn/ n. médicaments m. pl.

medicin|e /'medsn/ n. (science) médecine f.; (substance) médicament m. ~**al** /mɪ'dɪsnl/ a. médicinal.

medieval /medɪ'iːvl/ a. médiéval.

mediocr|e /miːdɪ'əʊkə(r)/ a. médiocre. ~**ity** /-'ɒkrɪtɪ/ n. médiocrité f.

meditat|e /'medɪteɪt/ v.t./i. méditer. ~**ion** /-'teɪʃn/ n. méditation f.

Mediterranean /medɪtə'reɪnɪən/ a. méditerranéen. ● n. **the ~**, la Méditerranée f.

medium /'miːdɪəm/ n. (pl. **media**) milieu m.; (for transmitting data etc.) support m.; (pl. **mediums**) (person) médium m. ● a. moyen.

medley /'medlɪ/ n. mélange m.; (mus.) pot-pourri m.

meek /miːk/ a. (-er, -est) doux.

meet /miːt/ v.t./i. (p.t. **met**) rencontrer; (see again) retrouver; (fetch) (aller) chercher; (be introduced to) faire la connaissance de; (face) faire face à; (requirement) satisfaire. ● v.i. se rencontrer; (see each other again) se retrouver; (in session) se réunir.

meeting /'miːtɪŋ/ n. réunion f.; (between two people) rencontre f.

megalomania /megələʊ'meɪnɪə/ n. mégalomanie f. ~**c** /-æk/ n. mégalomane m./f.

megaphone /'megəfəʊn/ n. portevoix m. invar.

melamine /'meləmiːn/ n. mélamine f.

melanchol|y /'melənkəlɪ/ n. mélancolie f. ● a. mélancolique. ~**ic** /-'kɒlɪk/ a. mélancolique.

mellow /'meləʊ/ a. (-er, -est) (fruit) mûr; (sound, colour) moelleux, doux; (person) mûri. ● v.t./i. (mature) mûrir; (soften) (s')adoucir.

melodious /mɪ'ləʊdɪəs/ a. mélodieux.

melodrama /'melədrɑːmə/ n. mélodrame m. ~**tic** /-ə'mætɪk/ a. mélodramatique.

melod|y /'melədɪ/ n. mélodie f. ~**ic** /mɪ'lɒdɪk/ a. mélodique.

melon /'melən/ n. melon m.

melt /melt/ v.t./i. (faire) fondre. ~**ing-pot** n. creuset m.

member /'membə(r)/ n. membre m. **M~ of Parliament**, député m. ~**ship** n. adhésion f.; (members) membres m. pl.; (fee) cotisation f.

membrane /'membreɪn/ n. membrane f.

memento /mɪ'mentəʊ/ n. (pl. **-oes**) (object) souvenir m.

memo /'meməʊ/ n. (pl. **-os**) (fam.) note f.

memoir /'memwɑː(r)/ n. (record, essay) mémoire m.

memorable /'memərəbl/ a. mémorable.

memorandum /memə'rændəm/ n. (pl. **-ums**) note f.

memorial /mɪ'mɔːrɪəl/ n. monument m. ● a. commémoratif.

memorize /'meməraɪz/ v.t. apprendre par cœur.

memory /'memərɪ/ n. (mind, in computer) mémoire f.; (thing remembered) souvenir m. **from ~**, de mémoire. **in ~ of**, à la mémoire de.

men /men/ see **man**.

menac|e /'menəs/ n. menace f.; (nuisance) peste f. ● v.t. menacer. ~**ing** a. menaçant.

menagerie /mɪ'nædʒərɪ/ n. ménagerie f.

mend /mend/ v.t. réparer; (darn) raccommoder. ● n. raccommodage m. ~ **one's ways**, s'amender. **on the ~**, en voie de guérison.

menial /'miːnɪəl/ a. servile.

meningitis /menɪn'dʒaɪtɪs/ n. méningite f.

menopause /'menəpɔːz/ n. ménopause f.

menstruation /menstrʊ'eɪʃn/ n. menstruation f.

mental /'mentl/ a. mental; (hospital) psychiatrique. ~ block, blocage m.

mentality /men'tælətɪ/ n. mentalité f.

menthol /'menθɒl/ n. menthol m. ● a. mentholé.

mention /'menʃn/ v.t. mentionner. ● n. mention f. don't ~ it!, il n'y a pas de quoi!, je vous en prie!

mentor /'mentɔː(r)/ n. mentor m.

menu /'menjuː/ n. (food, on computer) menu m.; (list) carte f.

MEP (abbr.) (member of the European Parliament) député européen m.

mercenary /'mɜːsɪnərɪ/ a. & n. mercenaire (m.).

merchandise /'mɜːtʃəndaɪz/ n. marchandises f. pl.

merchant /'mɜːtʃənt/ n. marchand m. ● a. (ship, navy) marchand. ~ bank, banque de commerce f.

merciful /'mɜːsɪfl/ a. miséricordieux. ~ly adv. (fortunately: fam.) Dieu merci.

merciless /'mɜːsɪlɪs/ a. impitoyable, implacable.

mercury /'mɜːkjʊrɪ/ n. mercure m.

mercy /'mɜːsɪ/ n. pitié f. at the ~ of, à la merci de.

mere /mɪə(r)/ a. simple. ~ly adv. simplement.

merest /'mɪərɪst/ a. moindre.

merge /mɜːdʒ/ v.t./i. (se) mêler (with, à); (companies: comm.) fusionner. ~r /-ə(r)/ n. fusion f.

meridian /mə'rɪdɪən/ n. méridien m.

meringue /mə'ræŋ/ n. meringue f.

merit /'merɪt/ n. mérite m. ● v.t. (p.t. merited) mériter.

mermaid /'mɜːmeɪd/ n. sirène f.

merriment /'merɪmənt/ n. gaieté f.

merry /'merɪ/ a. (-ier, -iest) gai. make ~, faire la fête. ~-go-round n. manège m. ~-making n. réjouissances f. pl. merrily adv. gaiement.

mesh /meʃ/ n. maille f.; (fabric) tissu à mailles m.; (network) réseau m.

mesmerize /'mezməraɪz/ v.t. hypnotiser.

mess /mes/ n. désordre m., gâchis m.; (dirt) saleté f.; (mil.) mess m. ● v.t. ~ up, gâcher. ● v.i. ~ about, s'amuser; (dawdle) traîner. ~

with, (tinker with) tripoter. make a ~ of, gâcher.

message /'mesɪdʒ/ n. message m.

messenger /'mesɪndʒə(r)/ n. messager m.

Messrs /'mesəz/ n. pl. ~ Smith, Messieurs or MM. Smith.

messy /'mesɪ/ a. (-ier, -iest) en désordre; (dirty) sale.

met /met/ see meet.

metabolic /metə'bɒlɪk/ adj. métabolique.

metabolism /mɪ'tæbəlɪzəm/ n. métabolisme m.

metal /'metl/ n. métal m. ● a. de métal. ~lic /mɪ'tælɪk/ a. métallique; (paint, colour) métallisé.

metallurgy /mɪ'tælədʒɪ, Amer. 'metələdʒɪ/ n. métallurgie f.

metamorphosis /metə'mɔːfəsɪs/ n. (pl. -phoses /-siːz/) métamorphose f.

metaphor /'metəfə(r)/ n. métaphore f. ~ical /-'fɒrɪkl/ a. métaphorique.

mete /miːt/ v.t. ~ out, donner, distribuer; (justice) rendre.

meteor /'miːtɪə(r)/ n. météore m.

meteorite /'miːtɪəraɪt/ n. météorite m.

meteorolog|y /miːtɪə'rɒlədʒɪ/ n. météorologie f. ~ical /-ə'lɒdʒɪkl/ a. météorologique.

meter¹ /'miːtə(r)/ n. compteur m.

meter² /'miːtə(r)/ n. (Amer.) = metre.

method /'meθəd/ n. méthode f.

methodical /mɪ'θɒdɪkl/ a. méthodique.

Methodist /'meθədɪst/ n. & a. méthodiste (m./f.).

methodology /meθə'dɒlədʒɪ/ n. méthodologie f.

methylated /'meθɪleɪtɪd/ a. ~ spirit, alcool à brûler m.

meticulous /mɪ'tɪkjʊləs/ a. méticuleux.

metre /'miːtə(r)/ n. mètre m.

metric /'metrɪk/ a. métrique. ~ation /-'keɪʃn/ n. adoption du système métrique f.

metropol|is /mə'trɒpəlɪs/ n. (city) métropole f. ~itan /metrə'pɒlɪtən/ a. métropolitain.

mettle /'metl/ n. courage m.

mew /mjuː/ n. miaulement m. ● v.i. miauler.

mews /mjuːz/ n. pl. (dwellings) appartements chic aménagés dans des anciennes écuries m. pl.

Mexic|o /'meksɪkəʊ/ n. Mexique m. **~an** a. & n. mexicain(e) (m. (f.)).

miaow /miːˈaʊ/ n. & v.i. = **mew**.

mice /maɪs/ see **mouse**.

mickey /'mɪkɪ/ n. take the **~** out of, (sl.) se moquer de.

micro- /'maɪkrəʊ/ pref. micro-.

microbe /'maɪkrəʊb/ n. microbe m.

microchip /'maɪkrəʊtʃɪp/ n. micro-plaquette f., puce f.

microclimate /'maɪkrəʊklaɪmət/ n. microclimat n.

microcomputer /maɪkrəʊkəmˈpjuːtə(r)/ n. micro(-ordinateur) m.

microcosm /'maɪkrəʊkɒzm/ n. microcosme m.

microfilm /'maɪkrəʊfɪlm/ n. microfilm m.

microlight /'maɪkrəʊlaɪt/ n. U.L.M. m.

mile /maɪl/ n. mille m. (= 1.6 km.). **~s** too big/etc., (fam.) beaucoup trop grand/etc. **~age** n. (loosely) kilométrage m.

microphone /'maɪkrəfəʊn/ n. microphone m.

microprocessor /maɪkrəʊˈprəʊsesə(r)/ n. microprocesseur m.

microscop|e /'maɪkrəskəʊp/ n. microscope m. **~ic** /-'skɒpɪk/ a. microscopique.

microwave /'maɪkrəʊweɪv/ n. micro-onde f. **~ oven**, four à micro-ondes m.

mid /mɪd/ a. in **~** air/etc., en plein ciel/etc. in **~** March/etc., à la mi-mars/etc. in **~** ocean/etc., au milieu de l'océan/etc.

midday /mɪd'deɪ/ n. midi m.

middle /'mɪdl/ a. du milieu; (quality) moyen. ● n. milieu m. in the **~** of, au milieu de. **~-aged** a. d'un certain âge. **M~ Ages**, moyen âge m. **~ class**, classe moyenne f. **~-class** a. bourgeois. **M~ East**, Proche-Orient m.

middleman /'mɪdlmæn/ n. (pl. -men) intermédiaire m.

middling /'mɪdlɪŋ/ a. moyen.

midge /mɪdʒ/ n. moucheron m.

midget /'mɪdʒɪt/ n. nain(e) m. (f.). ● a. minuscule.

Midlands /'mɪdləndz/ n. pl. région du centre de l'Angleterre f.

midnight /'mɪdnaɪt/ n. minuit f.

midriff /'mɪdrɪf/ n. ventre m.

midst /mɪdst/ n. in the **~** of, au milieu de. in our **~**, parmi nous.

midsummer /mɪd'sʌmə(r)/ n. milieu de l'été m.; (solstice) solstice d'été m.

midway /mɪdweɪ/ adv. à mi-chemin.

midwife /'mɪdwaɪf/ n. (pl. -wives) sage-femme f.

might[1] /maɪt/ n. puissance f. **~y** a. puissant; (very great: fam.) très grand; adv. (fam.) rudement.

might[2] /maɪt/ see **may**.

migraine /'miːgreɪn, Amer. 'maɪgreɪn/ n. migraine f.

migrant /'maɪgrənt/ a. & n. (bird) migrateur (m.); (worker) migrant(e) (m. (f.)).

migrat|e /maɪ'greɪt/ v.i. émigrer. **~ion** /-ʃn/ n. migration f.

mike /maɪk/ n. (fam.) micro m.

mild /maɪld/ a. (-er, -est) doux; (illness) bénin. **~ly** adv. doucement. to put it **~ly**, pour ne rien exagérer. **~ness** n. douceur f.

mildew /'mɪldjuː/ n. moisissure f.

milestone /'maɪlstəʊn/ n. borne f.; (event, stage: fig.) jalon m.

militant /'mɪlɪtənt/ a. & n. militant(e) (m. (f.)).

military /'mɪlɪtrɪ/ a. militaire.

militate /'mɪlɪteɪt/ v.i. militer.

militia /mɪ'lɪʃə/ n. milice f.

milk /mɪlk/ n. lait m. ● a. (product) laitier. ● v.t. (cow etc.) traire; (fig.) exploiter. **~ shake**, milk-shake m. **~y** a. (diet) lacté; (colour) laiteux; (tea etc.) au lait. **M~y Way**, Voie lactée f.

milkman /'mɪlkmən, Amer. 'mɪlkmæn/ n. (pl. -men) laitier m.

mill /mɪl/ n. moulin m.; (factory) usine f. ● v.t. moudre. ● v.i. **~ around**, tourner en rond; (crowd) grouiller. **~er** n. meunier m.

millennium /mɪ'lenɪəm/ n. (pl. -ums) millénaire m.

millet /'mɪlɪt/ n. millet m.

milli- /'mɪlɪ/ pref. milli-.

millimetre /'mɪlɪmiːtə(r)/ n. millimètre m.

milliner /'mɪlɪnə(r)/ n. modiste f.

million /'mɪljən/ n. million m. a **~ pounds**, un million de livres. **~aire** /-'neə(r)/ n. millionnaire m.

millstone /'mɪlstəʊn/ n. meule f.; (burden: fig.) boulet m.

milometer /maɪ'lɒmɪtə(r)/ n. compteur kilométrique m.

mime /maɪm/ n. (actor) mime m./f.; (art) (art du) mime m. ● v.t./i. mimer.

mimic /'mɪmɪk/ v.t. (p.t. **mimicked**) imiter. ● n. imita|teur, -trice m., f. ~**ry** n. imitation f.

mince /mɪns/ v.t. hacher. ● n. viande hachée f. ~ **pie**, tarte aux fruits confits f. **not to ~ matters**, ne pas mâcher ses mots. ~**r** /-ə(r)/ n. (machine) hachoir m.

mincemeat /'mɪnsmiːt/ n. hachis de fruits confits m. **make ~ of**, anéantir, pulvériser.

mind /maɪnd/ n. esprit m.; (sanity) raison f.; (opinion) avis m. ● v.t. (have charge of) s'occuper de; (heed) faire attention à. **be on s.o.'s ~**, préoccuper qn. **bear that in ~**, ne l'oubliez pas. **change one's ~**, changer d'avis. **make up one's ~**, se décider (**to**, à). **I do not ~ the noise/**etc., le bruit/etc. ne me dérange pas. **I do not ~**, ça m'est égal. **would you ~ checking?**, je peux vous demander de vérifier? ~**ful** a. attentif (**of**, à). ~**less** a. irréfléchi.

minder /'maɪndə(r)/ n. (for child) gardien(ne) m. (f.); (for protection) ange gardien m.

mine[1] /maɪn/ poss. pron. le mien, la mienne, les mien(ne)s. **it is ~**, c'est à moi or le mien.

min|e[2] /maɪn/ n. mine f. ● v.t. extraire; (mil.) miner. ~**er** n. mineur m. ~**ing** n. exploitation minière f.; a. minier.

minefield /'maɪnfiːld/ n. champ de mines m.

mineral /'mɪnərəl/ n. & a. minéral (m.). ~ (**water**), (fizzy soft drink) boisson gazeuse f. ~ **water**, (natural) eau minérale f.

minesweeper /'maɪnswiːpə(r)/ n. (ship) dragueur de mines m.

mingle /'mɪŋgl/ v.t./i. (se) mêler (**with**, à).

mingy /'mɪndʒɪ/ a. (fam.) radin.

mini- /'mɪnɪ/ pref. mini-.

miniatur|e /'mɪnɪtʃə(r)/ a. & n. miniature (f.). ~**ize** v.t. miniaturiser.

minibus /'mɪnɪbʌs/ n. minibus m.

minicab /'mɪnɪkæb/ n. taxi m.

minim /'mɪnɪm/ n. blanche f.

minim|um /'mɪnɪməm/ a. & n. (pl. -ima) minimum (m.). ~**al** a. minimal. ~**ize** v.t. minimiser.

minist|er /'mɪnɪstə(r)/ n. ministre m. ~**erial** /-'stɪərɪəl/ a. ministériel. ~**ry** n. ministère m.

mink /mɪŋk/ n. vison m.

minor /'maɪnə(r)/ a. petit, mineur. ● n. (jurid.) mineur(e) m. (f.).

minority /maɪ'nɒrətɪ/ n. minorité f. ● a. minoritaire.

mint[1] /mɪnt/ n. **the M~**, l'Hôtel de la Monnaie m. **a ~**, une fortune. ● v.t. frapper. **in ~ condition**, à l'état neuf.

mint[2] /mɪnt/ n. (plant) menthe f.; (sweet) pastille de menthe f.

minus /'maɪnəs/ prep. moins; (without: fam.) sans. ● n. (sign) moins m. ~ **sign**, moins m.

minute[1] /'mɪnɪt/ n. minute f. ~**s**, (of meeting) procès-verbal m.

minute[2] /maɪ'njuːt/ a. (tiny) minuscule; (detailed) minutieux.

mirac|le /'mɪrəkl/ n. miracle m. ~**ulous** /mɪ'rækjʊləs/ a. miraculeux.

mirage /'mɪrɑːʒ/ n. mirage m.

mire /maɪə(r)/ n. fange f.

mirror /'mɪrə(r)/ n. miroir m., glace f. ● v.t. refléter.

mirth /mɜːθ/ n. gaieté f.

misadventure /mɪsəd'ventʃə(r)/ n. mésaventure f.

misanthropist /mɪs'ænθrəpɪst/ n. misanthrope m./f.

misapprehension /mɪsæprɪ'henʃn/ n. malentendu m.

misbehav|e /mɪsbɪ'heɪv/ v.i. se conduire mal. ~**iour** n. mauvaise conduite f.

miscalculat|e /mɪs'kælkjʊleɪt/ v.t. mal calculer. ● v.i. se tromper. ~**ion** /-'leɪʃn/ n. erreur de calcul f.

miscarr|y /mɪs'kærɪ/ v.i. faire une fausse couche. ~**iage** /-ɪdʒ/ n. fausse couche f. ~**iage of justice**, erreur judiciaire f.

miscellaneous /mɪsə'leɪnɪəs/ a. divers.

mischief /'mɪstʃɪf/ n. (foolish conduct) espièglerie f.; (harm) mal m. **get into ~**, faire des sottises.

mischievous /'mɪstʃɪvəs/ a. espiègle; (malicious) méchant.

misconception /mɪskən'sepʃn/ n. idée fausse f.

misconduct /mɪs'kɒndʌkt/ n. mauvaise conduite f.

misconstrue /mɪskən'struː/ v.t. mal interpréter.

misdeed /mɪs'diːd/ n. méfait m.

misdemeanour /mɪsdɪ'miːnə(r)/ n. (jurid.) délit m.

misdirect /mɪsdɪ'rekt/ v.t. (person) mal renseigner.

miser /'maɪzə(r)/ n. avare m./f. ~ly a. avare.

miserable /'mɪzrəbl/ a. (sad) malheureux; (wretched) misérable; (unpleasant) affreux.

misery /'mɪzərɪ/ n. (unhappiness) malheur m.; (pain) souffrances f. pl.; (poverty) misère f.; (person: fam.) grincheu|x, -se m., f.

misfire /mɪs'faɪə(r)/ v.i. (plan etc.) rater; (engine) avoir des ratés.

misfit /'mɪsfɪt/ n. inadapté(e) m. (f.).

misfortune /mɪs'fɔːtʃuːn/ n. malheur m.

misgiving /mɪs'gɪvɪŋ/ n. (doubt) doute m.; (apprehension) crainte f.

misguided /mɪs'gaɪdɪd/ a. (foolish) imprudent; (mistaken) erroné. be ~, (person) se tromper.

mishap /'mɪshæp/ n. mésaventure f., contretemps m.

misinform /mɪsɪn'fɔːm/ v.t. mal renseigner.

misinterpret /mɪsɪn'tɜːprɪt/ v.t. mal interpréter.

misjudge /mɪs'dʒʌdʒ/ v.t. mal juger.

mislay /mɪs'leɪ/ v.t. (p.t. mislaid) égarer.

mislead /mɪs'liːd/ v.t. (p.t. misled) tromper. ~ing a. trompeur.

mismanage /mɪs'mænɪdʒ/ v.t. mal gérer. ~ment n. mauvaise gestion f.

misnomer /mɪs'nəʊmə(r)/ n. terme impropre m.

misplace /mɪs'pleɪs/ v.t. mal placer; (lose) égarer.

misprint /'mɪsprɪnt/ n. faute d'impression f., coquille f.

misread /mɪs'riːd/ v.t. (p.t. misread /mɪs'red/) mal lire; (intentions) mal comprendre.

misrepresent /mɪsreprɪ'zent/ v.t. présenter sous un faux jour.

miss[1] /mɪs/ v.t./i. manquer; (deceased person etc.) regretter. he ~es her/Paris/etc., elle/Paris/etc. lui manque. I ~ you, tu me manques. you're ~ing the point, vous n'avez rien compris. ● n. coup manqué m. it was a near ~, on l'a échappé belle or de peu. ~ out, omettre. ~ out on sth, rater qch.

miss[2] /mɪs/ n. (pl. misses) mademoiselle f. (pl. mesdemoiselles). M~ Smith, Mademoiselle or Mlle Smith.

misshapen /mɪs'ʃeɪpən/ a. difforme.

missile /'mɪsaɪl/ n. (mil.) missile m.; (object thrown) projectile m.

missing /'mɪsɪŋ/ a. (person) disparu; (thing) qui manque. something's ~, il manque quelque chose.

mission /'mɪʃn/ n. mission f.

missionary /'mɪʃənrɪ/ n. missionnaire m./f.

missive /'mɪsɪv/ n. missive f.

misspell /mɪs'spel/ v.t. (p.t. misspelt or misspelled) mal écrire.

mist /mɪst/ n. brume f.; (on window) buée f. ● v.t./i. (s')embuer.

mistake /mɪ'steɪk/ n. erreur f. ● v.t. (p.t. mistook, p.p. mistaken) mal comprendre; (choose wrongly) se tromper de. by ~, par erreur. make a ~, faire une erreur. ~ for, prendre pour. ~n /-ən/ a. erroné. be ~n, se tromper. ~nly /-ənlɪ/ adv. par erreur.

mistletoe /'mɪsltəʊ/ n. gui m.

mistreat /mɪs'triːt/ v.t. maltraiter.

mistress /'mɪstrɪs/ n. maîtresse f.

mistrust /mɪs'trʌst/ v.t. se méfier de. ● n. méfiance f.

misty /'mɪstɪ/ a. (-ier, -iest) brumeux; (window) embué.

misunderstand /mɪsʌndə'stænd/ v.t. (p.t. -stood) mal comprendre. ~ing n. malentendu m.

misuse[1] /mɪs'juːz/ v.t. mal employer; (power etc.) abuser de.

misuse[2] /mɪs'juːs/ n. mauvais emploi m.; (unfair use) abus m.

mitigat|e /'mɪtɪgeɪt/ v.t. atténuer. ~ing circumstances, circonstances atténuantes f. pl.

mitten /'mɪtn/ n. moufle f.

mix /mɪks/ v.t./i. (se) mélanger. ● n. mélange m. ~ up, mélanger; (bewilder) embrouiller; (mistake, confuse) confondre (with, avec). ~-up n. confusion f. ~ with, (people) fréquenter. ~er n. (culin.) mélangeur m. be a good ~er, être sociable. ~er tap, mélangeur m.

mixed /mɪkst/ a. (school etc.) mixte; (assorted) assorti. be ~-up, (fam.) avoir des problèmes.

mixture /'mɪkstʃə(r)/ n. mélange m.; (for cough) sirop m.

moan /məʊn/ n. gémissement m. ● v.i. gémir; (complain) grogner. ~er n. (grumbler) grognon m.

moat /məʊt/ n. douve(s) f. (pl.).

mob /mɒb/ n. (crowd) cohue f.; (gang: sl.) bande f. ● v.t. (p.t. mobbed) assiéger.

mobil|e /'məʊbaɪl/ a. mobile. ~e
home, caravane f. ● n. mobile m.
~ity /-'bɪlətɪ/ n. mobilité f.

mobiliz|e /'məʊbɪlaɪz/ v.t./i. mo-
biliser. ~ation /-'zeɪʃn/ n. mobili-
sation f.

moccasin /'mɒkəsɪn/ n. mocassin m.

mock /mɒk/ v.t./i. se moquer (de).
● a. faux. ~-up n. maquette f.

mockery /'mɒkərɪ/ n. moquerie f. a
~ of, une parodie de.

mode /məʊd/ n. (way, method) mode
m.; (fashion) mode f.

model /'mɒdl/ n. modèle m.; (of toy)
modèle réduit m.; (artist's) modèle
m.; (for fashion) mannequin m. ● a.
modèle; (car etc.) modèle réduit
invar. ● v.t. (p.t. modelled) modeler; (clothes) présenter. ● v.i. être
mannequin m.; (pose) poser. ~ling n.
métier de mannequin m.

modem /'məʊdem/ n. modem m.

moderate¹ /'mɒdərət/ a. & n. mo-
déré(e) (m. (f.)). ~ly adv. (in moderation) modérément; (fairly) mo-
yennement.

moderate² /'mɒdəreɪt/ v.t./i. (se)
modérer. ~ion /-'reɪʃn/ n. modération f. in ~ion, avec modération.

modern /'mɒdn/ a. moderne. ~ lan-
guages, langues vivantes f. pl. ~ize
v.t. moderniser.

modest /'mɒdɪst/ a. modeste. ~y n.
modestie f.

modicum /'mɒdɪkəm/ n. a ~ of, un
peu de.

modif|y /'mɒdɪfaɪ/ v.t. modifier.
~ication /-ɪ'keɪʃn/ n. modification f.

modular /'mɒdjʊlə(r)/ a. modulaire

modulat|e /'mɒdjʊleɪt/ v.t./i. modu-
ler. ~ion /-'leɪʃn/ n. modulation
f.

module /'mɒdju:l/ n. module m.

mohair /'məʊheə(r)/ n. mohair m.

moist /mɔɪst/ a. (-er, -est) humide,
moite. ~ure /'mɔɪstʃə(r)/ n. humidité f. ~urizer /'mɔɪstʃəraɪzə(r)/ n.
produit hydratant m.

moisten /'mɔɪsn/ v.t. humecter.

molar /'məʊlə(r)/ n. molaire f.

molasses /mə'læsɪz/ n. mélasse f.

mold /məʊld/ (Amer.) = mould.

mole¹ /məʊl/ n. grain de beauté m.

mole² /məʊl/ n. (animal) taupe f.

molecule /'mɒlɪkju:l/ n. molécule f.

molest /mə'lest/ v.t. (pester) impor-
tuner; (ill-treat) molester.

mollusc /'mɒləsk/ n. mollusque m.

mollycoddle /'mɒlɪkɒdl/ v.t. dorloter, chouchouter.

molten /'məʊltən/ a. en fusion.

mom /mɒm/ n. (Amer.) maman f.

moment /'məʊmənt/ n. moment m.

momentar|y /'məʊməntrɪ, Amer.
-terɪ/ a. momentané. ~ily (Amer.
/-'terəlɪ/) adv. momentanément;
(soon: Amer.) très bientôt.

momentous /mə'mentəs/ a. important.

momentum /mə'mentəm/ n. élan m.

Monaco /'mɒnəkəʊ/ n. Monaco f.

monarch /'mɒnək/ n. monarque m.
~y n. monarchie f.

monast|ery /'mɒnəstrɪ/ n. monastère
m. ~ic /mə'næstɪk/ a. monastique.

Monday /'mʌndɪ/ n. lundi m.

monetarist /'mʌnɪtərɪst/ n. monéta-
riste m./f.

monetary /'mʌnɪtrɪ/ a. monétaire.

money /'mʌnɪ/ n. argent m. ~s,
sommes d'argent f. pl. ~-box n.
tirelire f. ~-lender n. prêteu|r, -se
m.,f. ~ order, mandat m. ~-spinner
n. mine d'or f.

mongrel /'mʌŋgrəl/ n. (chien) bâtard
m.

monitor /'mɒnɪtə(r)/ n. (pupil) chef
de classe m.; (techn.) moniteur m.
● v.t. contrôler; (a broadcast) écouter.

monk /mʌŋk/ n. moine m.

monkey /'mʌŋkɪ/ n. singe m. ~-nut
n. cacahuète f. ~-wrench n. clef à
molette f.

mono /'mɒnəʊ/ n. (pl. -os) mono f.
● a. mono invar.

monochrome /'mɒnəkrəʊm/ a. & n.
(en) noir et blanc (m.).

monogram /'mɒnəgræm/ n. monogramme m.

monologue /'mɒnəlɒg/ n. monologue m.

monopol|y /mə'nɒpəlɪ/ n. monopole
m. ~ize v.t. monopoliser.

monotone /'mɒnətəʊn/ n. ton uniforme m.

monoton|ous /mə'nɒtənəs/ a. mo-
notone. ~y n. monotonie f.

monsoon /mɒn'su:n/ n. mousson f.

monst|er /'mɒnstə(r)/ n. monstre m.
~rous a. monstrueux.

monstrosity /mɒn'strɒsətɪ/ n. mons-
truosité f.

month /mʌnθ/ n. mois m.

monthly /'mʌnθlɪ/ a. mensuel.
● adv. mensuellement. ● n. (periodical) mensuel m.

monument /'mɒnjʊmənt/ *n.* monument *m.* ~al /-'mentl/ *a.* monumental.

moo /muː/ *n.* meuglement *m.* ● *v.i.* meugler.

mooch /muːtʃ/ *v.i.* (*sl.*) flâner. ● *v.t.* (*Amer., sl.*) se procurer.

mood /muːd/ *n.* humeur *f.* in a good/bad ~, de bonne/mauvaise humeur. ~y *a.* d'humeur changeante; (*sullen*) maussade.

moon /muːn/ *n.* lune *f.*

moon|light /'muːnlaɪt/ *n.* clair de lune *m.* ~lit *a.* éclairé par la lune.

moonlighting /'muːnlaɪtɪŋ/ *n.* (*fam.*) travail au noir *m.*

moor¹ /mʊə(r)/ *n.* lande *f.*

moor² /mʊə(r)/ *v.t.* amarrer. ~ings *n. pl.* (*chains etc.*) amarres *f. pl.*; (*place*) mouillage *m.*

moose /muːs/ *n. invar.* élan *m.*

moot /muːt/ *a.* discutable. ● *v.t.* (*question*) soulever.

mop /mɒp/ *n.* balai à franges *m.* ● *v.t.* (*p.t.* **mopped**). ~ (**up**), éponger. ~ **of hair**, tignasse *f.*

mope /məʊp/ *v.i.* se morfondre.

moped /'məʊped/ *n.* cyclomoteur *m.*

moral /'mɒrəl/ *a.* moral. ● *n.* morale *f.* ~s, moralité *f.* ~ize *v.i.* moraliser. ~ly *adv.* moralement.

morale /mə'rɑːl/ *n.* moral *m.*

morality /mə'rælətɪ/ *n.* moralité *f.*

morass /mə'ræs/ *n.* marais *m.*

morbid /'mɔːbɪd/ *a.* morbide.

more /mɔː(r)/ *a.* (*a greater amount of*) plus de (**than**, que). ● *n. & adv.* plus (**than**, que). (**some**) ~ **tea/pens/** etc., (*additional*) encore du thé/des stylos/*etc.* no ~ **bread**/etc., plus de pain/*etc.* I want no ~, I do not want any ~, je n'en veux plus. ~ or less, plus ou moins.

moreover /mɔː'rəʊvə(r)/ *adv.* de plus, en outre.

morgue /mɔːg/ *n.* morgue *f.*

moribund /'mɒrɪbʌnd/ *a.* moribond.

morning /'mɔːnɪŋ/ *n.* matin *m.*; (*whole morning*) matinée *f.*

Morocc|o /mə'rɒkəʊ/ *n.* Maroc *m.* ~an *a. & n.* marocain(e) (*m.* (*f.*)).

moron /'mɔːrɒn/ *n.* crétin(e) *m.* (*f.*).

morose /mə'rəʊs/ *a.* morose.

morphine /'mɔːfiːn/ *n.* morphine *f.*

Morse /mɔːs/ *n.* ~ (**code**), morse *m.*

morsel /'mɔːsl/ *n.* petit morceau *m.*; (*of food*) bouchée *f.*

mortal /'mɔːtl/ *a. & n.* mortel(le) (*m.*(*f.*)). ~ity /mɔː'tælətɪ/ *n.* mortalité *f.*

mortar /'mɔːtə(r)/ *n.* mortier *m.*

mortgage /'mɔːgɪdʒ/ *n.* crédit immobilier *m.* ● *v.t.* hypothéquer.

mortify /'mɔːtɪfaɪ/ *v.t.* mortifier.

mortise /'mɔːtɪs/ *n.* ~ **lock** serrure encastrée *f.*

mortuary /'mɔːtʃərɪ/ *n.* morgue *f.*

mosaic /məʊ'zeɪk/ *n.* mosaïque *f.*

Moscow /'mɒskəʊ/ *n.* Moscou *m.*/*f.*

Moses /'məʊzɪz/ *a.* ~ **basket**, moïse *m.*

mosque /mɒsk/ *n.* mosquée *f.*

mosquito /mə'skiːtəʊ/ *n.* (*pl.* **-oes**) moustique *m.*

moss /mɒs/ *n.* mousse *f.* ~y *a.* moussu.

most /məʊst/ *a.* (*the greatest amount of*) le plus de; (*the majority of*) la plupart de. ● *n.* le plus. ● *adv.* (le) plus; (*very*) fort. ~ **of**, la plus grande partie de; (*majority*) la plupart de. at ~, tout au plus. for the ~ part, pour la plupart. make the ~ of, profiter de. ~ly *adv.* surtout.

motel /məʊ'tel/ *n.* motel *m.*

moth /mɒθ/ *n.* papillon de nuit *m.*; (*in cloth*) mite *f.* ~ball *n.* boule de naphtaline *f.*; *v.t.* mettre en réserve. ~-eaten *a.* mité.

mother /'mʌðə(r)/ *n.* mère *f.* ● *v.t.* entourer de soins maternels, materner. ~hood *n.* maternité *f.* ~-in-law *n.* (*pl.* ~s-in-law) belle-mère *f.* ~-of-pearl *n.* nacre *f.* M~'s Day, la fête des mères. ~-to-be *n.* future maman *f.* ~ tongue, langue maternelle *f.*

motherly /'mʌðəlɪ/ *a.* maternel.

motif /məʊ'tiːf/ *n.* motif *m.*

motion /'məʊʃn/ *n.* mouvement *m.*; (*proposal*) motion *f.* ● *v.t./i.* ~ (to) s.o. to, faire signe à qn. de. ~less *a.* immobile. ~ picture, (*Amer.*) film *m.*

motivate /'məʊtɪveɪt/ *v.t.* motiver. ~ion /-'veɪʃn/ *n.* motivation *f.*

motive /'məʊtɪv/ *n.* motif *m.*

motley /'mɒtlɪ/ *a.* bigarré.

motor /'məʊtə(r)/ *n.* moteur *m.*; (*car*) auto *f.* ● *a.* (*anat.*) moteur; (*boat*) à moteur. ● *v.i.* aller en auto. ~ **bike**, (*fam.*) moto *f.* ~ **car**, auto *f.* ~ **cycle**, motocyclette *f.* ~-**cyclist** *n.* motocycliste *m.*/*f.* ~ **home**, (*Amer.*) camping-car *m.* ~ing *n.* (*sport*)

l'automobile *f.* **~ized** *a.* motorisé **~
vehicle,** véhicule automobile *m.*

motorist /ˈməʊtərɪst/ *n.* automobiliste *m./f.*

motorway /ˈməʊtəweɪ/ *n.* autoroute *f.*

mottled /ˈmɒtld/ *a.* tacheté.

motto /ˈmɒtəʊ/ *n.* (*pl.* **-oes**) devise *f.*

mould¹ /məʊld/ *n.* moule *m.* ● *v.t.*
mouler; (*influence*) former. **~ing** *n.*
(*on wall etc.*) moulure *f.*

mould² /məʊld/ *n.* (*fungus, rot*) moisissure *f.* **~y** *a.* moisi.

moult /məʊlt/ *v.i.* muer.

mound /maʊnd/ *n.* monticule *m.,*
tertre *m.;* (*pile: fig.*) tas *m.*

mount¹ /maʊnt/ *n.* (*hill*) mont *m.*

mount² /maʊnt/ *v.t./i.* monter. ● *n.*
monture *f.* **~ up,** s'accumuler; (*add
up*) chiffrer (**to,** à).

mountain /ˈmaʊntɪn/ *n.* montagne *f.*
~ bike, (vélo) tout terrain *m.,* vtt *m.*
~ous *a.* montagneux.

mountaineer /maʊntɪˈnɪə(r)/ *n.* alpiniste *m./f.* **~ing** *n.* alpinisme *m.*

mourn /mɔːn/ *v.t./i.* **~ (for),** pleurer.
~er *n.* personne qui suit le cortège
funèbre *f.* **~ing** *n.* deuil *m.*

mournful /ˈmɔːnfl/ *a.* triste.

mouse /maʊs/ *n.* (*pl.* **mice**) souris *f.*

mousetrap /ˈmaʊstræp/ *n.* souricière *f.*

mousse /muːs/ *n.* mousse *f.*

moustache /məˈstɑːʃ, *Amer.* ˈmʌstæʃ/ *n.* moustache *f.*

mousy /ˈmaʊsɪ/ *a.* (*hair*) d'un brun
terne; (*fig.*) timide.

mouth /maʊθ/ *n.* bouche *f.;* (*of dog,
cat, etc.*) gueule *f.* **~-organ** *n.* harmonica *m.*

mouthful /ˈmaʊθfʊl/ *n.* bouchée *f.*

mouthpiece /ˈmaʊθpiːs/ *n.* (*mus.*)
embouchure *f.;* (*person: fig.*) porteparole *m. invar.*

mouthwash /ˈmaʊθwɒʃ/ *n.* eau dentifrice *f.*

mouthwatering /ˈmaʊθwɔːtrɪŋ/ *a.*
qui fait venir l'eau à la bouche.

movable /ˈmuːvəbl/ *a.* mobile.

move /muːv/ *v.t./i.* remuer, (dé)placer, bouger; (*incite*) pousser;
(*emotionally*) émouvoir; (*propose*)
proposer; (*depart*) partir; (*act*)
agir. **~ (out),** déménager. ● *n.*
mouvement *m.;* (*in game*) coup *m.;*
(*player's turn*) tour *m.;* (*procedure:
fig.*) démarche *f.;* (*house change*)
déménagement *m.* **~ back,** (faire)
reculer. **~ forward** *or* **on,** (faire)

avancer. **~ in,** emménager. **~ over,**
se pousser. **on the ~,** en marche.

movement /ˈmuːvmənt/ *n.* mouvement *m.*

movie /ˈmuːvɪ/ *n.* (*Amer.*) film *m.* **the
~s,** le cinéma. **~ camera,** (*Amer.*)
caméra *f.*

moving /ˈmuːvɪŋ/ *a.* en mouvement;
(*touching*) émouvant.

mow /məʊ/ *v.t.* (*p.p.* **mowed** *or*
mown) (*corn etc.*) faucher; (*lawn*)
tondre. **~ down,** faucher. **~er** *n.*
(*for lawn*) tondeuse *f.*

MP *abbr. see* Member of Parliament.

Mr /ˈmɪstə(r)/ *n.* (*pl.* **Messrs**). **~**
Smith, Monsieur *or* M. Smith.

Mrs /ˈmɪsɪz/ *n.* (*pl.* **Mrs**). **~ Smith,**
Madame *or* Mme Smith. **the ~
Smith,** Mesdames *or* Mmes Smith.

Ms /mɪz/ *n.* (*title of married or
unmarried woman*). **~ Smith,** Madame *or* Mme Smith.

much /mʌtʃ/ *a.* beaucoup de. ● *adv.*
& *n.* beaucoup.

muck /mʌk/ *n.* fumier *m.;* (*dirt: fam.*)
saleté *f.* ● *v.i.* **~ about,** (*sl.*)
s'amuser. **~ about with,** (*sl.*)
tripoter. **~ in,** (*sl.*) participer.
● *v.t.* **~ up,** (*sl.*) gâcher. **~y** *a.* sale.

mucus /ˈmjuːkəs/ *n.* mucus *m.*

mud /mʌd/ *n.* boue *f.* **~dy** *a.* couvert
de boue.

muddle /ˈmʌdl/ *v.t.* embrouiller.
● *v.i.* **~ through,** se débrouiller.
● *n.* désordre *m.,* confusion *f.;* (*mix-
up*) confusion *f.*

mudguard /ˈmʌdɡɑːd/ *n.* garde-boue
m. invar.

muff /mʌf/ *n.* manchon *m.*

muffin /ˈmʌfɪn/ *n.* muffin *m.* (*petit
pain rond et plat*)

muffle /ˈmʌfl/ *v.t.* emmitoufler;
(*sound*) assourdir. **~r** /-ə(r)/ *n.*
(*scarf*) cache-nez *m. invar.;* (*Amer.:
auto.*) silencieux *m.*

mug /mʌɡ/ *n.* tasse *f.;* (*in plastic,
metal*) gobelet *m.;* (*for beer*) chope *f.;*
(*face: sl.*) gueule *f.;* (*fool: sl.*) idiot(e)
m.(f.) ● *v.t.* (*p.t.* **mugged**) agresser.
~ger *n.* agresseur *m.* **~ging** *n.*
agression *f.*

muggy /ˈmʌɡɪ/ *a.* lourd.

mule /mjuːl/ *n.* (*male*) mulet *m.;*
(*female*) mule *f.*

mull¹ /mʌl/ *v.t.* (*wine*) chauffer.

mull² /mʌl/ *v.t.* **~ over,** ruminer.

multi- /ˈmʌltɪ/ *pref.* multi-.

multicoloured /ˈmʌltɪkʌləd/ *a.* multicolore.

multifarious /mʌltɪ'feərɪəs/ a. divers.

multinational /mʌltɪ'næʃnəl/ a. & n. multinational(e) (f.).

multiple /'mʌltɪpl/ a. & n. multiple (m.). ~ **sclerosis**, sclérose en plaques f.

multipl|y /'mʌltɪplaɪ/ v.t./i. (se) multiplier. ~**ication** /-ɪ'keɪʃn/ n. multiplication f.

multistorey /mʌltɪ'stɔːrɪ/ a. (car park) à étages.

multitude /'mʌltɪtjuːd/ n. multitude f.

mum¹ /mʌm/ a. **keep** ~, (fam.) garder le silence.

mum² /mʌm/ n. (fam.) maman f.

mumble /'mʌmbl/ v.t./i. marmotter, marmonner.

mummy¹ /'mʌmɪ/ n. (embalmed body) momie f.

mummy² /'mʌmɪ/ n. (mother: fam.) maman f.

mumps /mʌmps/ n. oreillons m. pl.

munch /mʌntʃ/ v.t./i. mastiquer.

mundane /mʌn'deɪn/ a. banal.

municipal /mjuː'nɪsɪpl/ a. municipal. ~**ity** /-'pælətɪ/ n. municipalité f.

munitions /mjuː'nɪʃnz/ n. pl. munitions f. pl.

mural /'mjʊərəl/ a. mural. ● n. peinture murale f.

murder /'mɜːdə(r)/ n. meurtre m. ● v.t. assassiner; (ruin: fam.) massacrer. ~**er** n. meurtrier m., assassin m. ~**ous** a. meurtrier.

murky /'mɜːkɪ/ a. (-ier, -iest) (night, plans, etc.) sombre, ténébreux; (liquid) épais, sale.

murmur /'mɜːmə(r)/ n. murmure m. ● v.t./i. murmurer.

muscle /'mʌsl/ n. muscle m. ● v.i. ~ **in**, (sl.) s'introduire de force (on, dans).

muscular /'mʌskjʊlə(r)/ a. musculaire; (brawny) musclé.

muse /mjuːz/ v.i. méditer.

museum /mjuː'zɪəm/ n. musée m.

mush /mʌʃ/ n. (pulp, soft food) bouillie f. ~**y** a. mou.

mushroom /'mʌʃrʊm/ n. champignon m. ● v.i. pousser comme des champignons.

music /'mjuːzɪk/ n. musique f. ~**al** a. musical; (instrument) de musique; (talented) doué pour la musique; n. comédie musicale f.

musician /mjuː'zɪʃn/ n. musicien(ne) m. (f.).

musk /mʌsk/ n. musc m.

Muslim /'mʊzlɪm/ a. & n. musulman(e) (m. (f.)).

muslin /'mʌzlɪn/ n. mousseline f.

mussel /'mʌsl/ n. moule f.

must /mʌst/ v. aux. devoir. **you** ~ **go**, vous devez partir, il faut que vous partiez. **he** ~ **be old**, il doit être vieux. **I** ~ **have done it**, j'ai dû le faire. ● n. **be a** ~, (fam.) être un must.

mustard /'mʌstəd/ n. moutarde f.

muster /'mʌstə(r)/ v.t./i. (se) rassembler.

musty /'mʌstɪ/ a. (-ier, -iest) (room, etc.) qui sent le moisi; (smell, taste) de moisi.

mutant /'mjuːtənt/ a. & n. mutant. (m.).

mutation /mjuː'teɪʃn/ n. mutation f.

mute /mjuːt/ a. & n. muet(te) (m. (f.)). ~**d** /-ɪd/ a. (colour, sound) sourd, atténué; (criticism) voilé.

mutilat|e /'mjuːtɪleɪt/ v.t. mutiler. ~**ion** /-'leɪʃn/ n. mutilation f.

mutin|y /'mjuːtɪnɪ/ n. mutinerie f. ● v.i. se mutiner. ~**ous** a. (sailor etc.) mutiné; (fig.) rebelle.

mutter /'mʌtə(r)/ v.t./i. marmonner, murmurer.

mutton /'mʌtn/ n. mouton m.

mutual /'mjuːtʃʊəl/ a. mutuel; (common to two or more: fam.) commun. ~**ly** adv. mutuellement.

muzzle /'mʌzl/ n. (snout) museau m.; (device) muselière f.; (of gun) gueule f. ● v.t. museler.

my /maɪ/ a. mon, ma, pl. mes.

myopic /maɪ'ɒpɪk/ a. myope.

myself /maɪ'self/ pron. moi-même; (reflexive) me, m'*; (after prep.) moi.

mysterious /mɪ'stɪərɪəs/ a. mystérieux.

mystery /'mɪstərɪ/ n. mystère m.

mystic /'mɪstɪk/ a. & n. mystique (m./f.). ~**al** a. mystique. ~**ism** /-sɪzəm/ n. mysticisme m.

mystify /'mɪstɪfaɪ/ v.t. laisser perplexe.

mystique /mɪ'stiːk/ n. mystique f.

myth /mɪθ/ n. mythe m. ~**ical** a. mythique.

mythology /mɪ'θɒlədʒɪ/ n. mythologie f.

N

nab /næb/ v.t. (p.t. **nabbed**) (arrest: sl.) épingler, attraper.

nag /næg/ v.t./i. (p.t. **nagged**) critiquer; (pester) harceler.

nagging /'nægɪŋ/ a. persistant.

nail /neɪl/ n. clou m.; (of finger, toe) ongle m. ● v.t. clouer. ~-brush n. brosse à ongles f. ~-file n. lime à ongles f. ~ polish, vernis à ongles m. on the ~, (pay) sans tarder, tout de suite.

naïve /naɪ'iːv/ a. naïf.

naked /'neɪkɪd/ a. nu. to the ~ eye, à l'œil nu. ~ly adv. à nu. ~ness n. nudité f.

name /neɪm/ n. nom m.; (fig.) réputation f. ● v.t. nommer; (fix) fixer. be ~d after, porter le nom de. ~less a. sans nom, anonyme.

namely /'neɪmlɪ/ adv. à savoir.

namesake /'neɪmseɪk/ n. (person) homonyme m.

nanny /'nænɪ/ n. nounou f. ~-goat n. chèvre f.

nap /næp/ n. somme m. ● v.i. (p.t. **napped**) faire un somme. catch ~ping, prendre au dépourvu.

nape /neɪp/ n. nuque f.

napkin /'næpkɪn/ n. (at meals) serviette f.; (for baby) couche f.

nappy /'næpɪ/ n. couche f.

narcotic /nɑː'kɒtɪk/ a. & n. narcotique (m.).

narrat|e /nə'reɪt/ v.t. raconter. ~ion /-ʃn/ n. narration f. ~or n. narrateur, -trice m., f.

narrative /'nærətɪv/ n. récit m.

narrow /'nærəʊ/ a. (-er, -est) étroit. ● v.t./i. (se) rétrécir; (limit) (se) limiter. ~ down the choices, limiter les choix. ~ly adv. étroitement; (just) de justesse. ~-minded a. à l'esprit étroit; (ideas etc.) étroit. ~ness n. étroitesse f.

nasal /'neɪzl/ a. nasal.

nast|y /'nɑːstɪ/ a. (-ier, -iest) mauvais, désagréable; (malicious) méchant. ~ily adv. désagréablement; méchamment. ~iness n. (malice) méchanceté f.

nation /'neɪʃn/ n. nation f. ~-wide a. dans l'ensemble du pays.

national /'næʃnəl/ a. national. ● n. ressortissant(e) m. (f.). ~ anthem, hymne national m. ~ism n. natio-

nalisme m. ~ize v.t. nationaliser. ~ly adv. à l'échelle nationale.

nationality /næʃə'nælətɪ/ n. nationalité f.

native /'neɪtɪv/ n. (local inhabitant) autochtone m./f.; (non-European) indigène m./f. ● a. indigène; (country) natal; (inborn) inné. be a ~ of, être originaire de. ~ language, langue maternelle f. ~ speaker of French, personne de langue maternelle française f.

Nativity /nə'tɪvətɪ/ n. the ~, la Nativité f.

natter /'nætə(r)/ v.i. bavarder.

natural /'nætʃrəl/ a. naturel. ~ history, histoire naturelle f. ~ist n. naturaliste m./f. ~ly adv. (normally, of course) naturellement; (by nature) de nature.

naturaliz|e /'nætʃrəlaɪz/ v.t. naturaliser. ~ation /-'zeɪʃn/ n. naturalisation f.

nature /'neɪtʃə(r)/ n. nature f.

naught /nɔːt/ n. (old use) rien m.

naught|y /'nɔːtɪ/ a. (-ier, -iest) vilain, méchant; (indecent) grivois. ~ily adv. mal.

nause|a /'nɔːsɪə/ n. nausée f. ~ous a. nauséabond.

nauseate /'nɔːsɪeɪt/ v.t. écœurer.

nautical /'nɔːtɪkl/ a. nautique.

naval /'neɪvl/ a. (battle etc.) naval; (officer) de marine.

nave /neɪv/ n. (of church) nef f.

navel /'neɪvl/ n. nombril m.

navigable /'nævɪɡəbl/ a. navigable.

navigat|e /'nævɪɡeɪt/ v.t. (sea etc.) naviguer sur; (ship) piloter. ● v.i. naviguer. ~ion /-'ɡeɪʃn/ n. navigation f. ~or n. navigateur m.

navvy /'nævɪ/ n. terrassier m.

navy /'neɪvɪ/ n. marine f. ~ (blue), bleu marine invar.

near /nɪə(r)/ adv. près. ● prep. près de. ● a. proche. ● v.t. approcher de. draw ~, (s')approcher (to, de). ~ by adv. tout près. N~ East, Proche-Orient m. ~ to, près de. ~ness n. proximité f. ~-sighted a. myope.

nearby /nɪə'baɪ/ a. proche.

nearly /'nɪəlɪ/ adv. presque. I ~ forgot, j'ai failli oublier. not ~ as pretty/etc. as, loin d'être aussi joli/etc. que.

nearside /'nɪəsaɪd/ a. (auto.) du côté du passager.

neat /niːt/ a. (-er, -est) soigné, net; (room etc.) bien rangé; (clever) habile; (*whisky, brandy, etc.*) sec. ~ly adv. avec soin; habilement. ~ness n. netteté f.

nebulous /'nebjʊləs/ a. nébuleux.

necessar|y /'nesəsərɪ/ a. nécessaire. ~ies n. pl. nécessaire m. ~ily adv. nécessairement.

necessitate /nɪ'sesɪteɪt/ v.t. nécessiter.

necessity /nɪ'sesətɪ/ n. nécessité f.; (*thing*) chose indispensable f.

neck /nek/ n. cou m.; (*of dress*) encolure f. ~ and neck, à égalité.

necklace /'neklɪs/ n. collier m.

neckline /'neklaɪn/ n. encolure f.

necktie /'nektaɪ/ n. cravate f.

nectarine /'nektərɪn/ n. brugnon m., nectarine f.

need /niːd/ n. besoin m. ● v.t. avoir besoin de; (*demand*) demander. you ~ not come, vous n'êtes pas obligé de venir. ~less a. inutile. ~lessly adv. inutilement.

needle /'niːdl/ n. aiguille f. ● v.t. (*annoy. fam.*) asticoter, agacer.

needlework /'niːdlwɜːk/ n. couture f.; (*object*) ouvrage (à l'aiguille) m.

needy /'niːdɪ/ a. (-ier, -iest) nécessiteux, indigent.

negation /nɪ'geɪʃn/ n. négation f.

negative /'negətɪv/ a. négatif. ● n. (*of photograph*) négatif m.; (*word: gram.*) négation f. in the ~, (*answer*) par la négative; (*gram.*) à la forme négative. ~ly adv. négativement.

neglect /nɪ'glekt/ v.t. négliger, laisser à l'abandon. ● n. manque de soins m. (state of) ~, abandon m. ~ to do, négliger de faire. ~ful a. négligent.

négligé /'neglɪʒeɪ/ n. négligé m.

negligen|t /'neglɪdʒənt/ a. négligent. ~ce a. négligence f.

negligible /'neglɪdʒəbl/ a. négligeable.

negotiable /nɪ'gəʊʃəbl/ a. négociable.

negotiat|e /nɪ'gəʊʃɪeɪt/ v.t./i. négocier. ~or /-'eɪʃn/ n. négociation f. ~or n. négocia|teur, -trice m., f.

Negr|o /'niːgrəʊ/ n. (pl. -oes) Noir m. ● a. noir; (*art, music*) nègre. ~ess n. Noire f.

neigh /neɪ/ n. hennissement m. ● v.i. hennir.

neighbour, Amer. **neighbor** /'neɪbə(r)/ n. voisin(e) m. (f.). ~hood n. voisinage m., quartier m. in the ~hood of, aux alentours de. ~ing a. voisin.

neighbourly /'neɪbəlɪ/ a. amical.

neither /'naɪðə(r)/ a. & pron. aucun(e) des deux, ni l'un(e) ni l'autre. ● adv. ni. ● conj. (ne) non plus. ~ big nor small, ni grand ni petit. ~ am I coming, je ne viendrai pas non plus.

neon /'niːɒn/ n. néon m. ● a. (*lamp etc.*) au néon.

nephew /'nevjuː, Amer. 'nefjuː/ n. neveu m.

nerve /nɜːv/ n. nerf m.; (*courage*) courage m.; (*calm*) sang-froid m.; (*impudence: fam.*) culot m. ~s, (*before exams etc.*) le trac ~-racking a. éprouvant.

nervous /'nɜːvəs/ a. nerveux. be or feel ~, (*afraid*) avoir peur. ~ breakdown, dépression nerveuse f. ~ly adv. (*tensely*) nerveusement; (*timidly*) craintivement. ~ness n. nervosité f.; (*fear*) crainte f.

nervy /'nɜːvɪ/ a. = nervous; (Amer., fam.) effronté.

nest /nest/ n. nid m. ● v.i. nicher. ~-egg n. pécule m.

nestle /'nesl/ v.i. se blottir.

net[1] /net/ n. filet m. ● v.t. (p.t. netted) prendre au filet. ~ting n. (*nets*) filets m. pl.; (*wire*) treillis m.; (*fabric*) voile m.

net[2] /net/ a. (*weight etc.*) net.

netball /'netbɔːl/ n. netball m.

Netherlands /'neðələndz/ n. pl. the ~, les Pays-Bas m. pl.

nettle /'netl/ n. ortie f.

network /'netwɜːk/ n. réseau m.

neuralgia /njʊə'rældʒə/ n. névralgie f.

neuro|sis /njʊə'rəʊsɪs/ n. (pl. -oses /-siːz/) névrose f. ~tic /-'rɒtɪk/ a. & n. névrosé(e) (m. (f.)).

neuter /'njuːtə(r)/ a. & n. neutre (m.). ● v.t. (*castrate*) castrer.

neutral /'njuːtrəl/ a. neutre. ~ (gear), (*auto.*) point mort m. ~ity /-'trælətɪ/ n. neutralité f.

neutron /'njuːtrɒn/ n. neutron m. ~ bomb, bombe à neutrons f.

never /'nevə(r)/ adv. (ne) jamais; (*not: fam.*) (ne) pas. he ~ refuses, il ne refuse jamais. I ~ saw him, (*fam.*) je ne l'ai pas vu. ~ again, plus jamais. ~ mind, (*don't worry*) ne vous en faites pas; (*it doesn't*

matter) peu importe. **~-ending** *a.*
interminable.

nevertheless /ˌnevəðə'les/ *adv.* néanmoins, toutefois.

new /njuː/ *a.* (**-er, -est**) nouveau;
(*brand-new*) neuf. ● *a.* nou-
veau-né. **~-laid egg,** œuf frais *m.* **~**
moon, nouvelle lune *f.* **~ year,**
nouvel an *m.* **New Year's Day,** le
jour de l'an. **New Year's Eve,** la
Saint-Sylvestre. **New Zealand,** Nou-
velle-Zélande *f.* **New Zealander,**
Néo-Zélandais(e) *m.* (*f.*). **~ness** *n.*
nouveauté *f.*

newcomer /'njuːkʌmə(r)/ *n.* nouveau venu *m.*, nouvelle venue *f.*

newfangled /njuː'fæŋgld/ *a.* (*pej.*)
moderne, neuf.

newly /'njuːlɪ/ *adv.* nouvellement. **~-**
weds *n. pl.* nouveaux mariés *m. pl.*

news /njuːz/ *n.* nouvelle(s) *f.* (*pl.*);
(*radio, press*) informations *f. pl.*;
(*TV*) actualités *f. pl.*, informations
f. pl. **~ agency,** agence de presse *f.*
~caster, ~-reader *ns.* présentateur, trice *m.f.*

newsagent /'njuːzeɪdʒənt/ *n.* mar-
chand(e) de journaux *m.(f.).*

newsletter /'njuːzletə(r)/ *n.* bulletin
m.

newspaper /'njuːzpeɪpə(r)/ *n.* journal *m.*

newsreel /'njuːzriːl/ *n.* actualités *f.*
pl.

newt /njuːt/ *n.* triton *m.*

next /nekst/ *a.* prochain; (*adjoining*)
voisin; (*following*) suivant. ● *adv.*
la prochaine fois; (*afterwards*)
ensuite. ● *n.* suivant(e) *m.(f.).* **~-**
door (**to,** de). **~-door** *a.* d'à
côté. **~ of kin,** parent le plus proche
m. **~ to,** à côté de.

nib /nɪb/ *n.* bec *m.*, plume *f.*

nibble /'nɪbl/ *v.t./i.* grignoter.

nice /naɪs/ *a.* (**-er, -est**) agréable, bon;
(*kind*) gentil; (*pretty*) joli; (*respectable*) bien *invar.*; (*subtle*) délicat.
~ly *adv.* agréablement; gentiment;
(*well*) bien.

nicety /'naɪsətɪ/ *n.* subtilité *f.*

niche /nɪtʃ, niːʃ/ *n.* (*recess*) niche *f.*;
(*fig.*) place *f.*, situation *f.*

nick /nɪk/ *n.* petite entaille *f.* ● *v.t.*
(*steal, arrest: sl.*) piquer. **in the ~ of**
time, juste à temps.

nickel /'nɪkl/ *n.* nickel *m.*; (*Amer.*)
pièce de cinq cents *f.*

nickname /'nɪkneɪm/ *n.* surnom *m.*;
(*short form*) diminutif *m.* ● *v.t.*
surnommer.

nicotine /'nɪkətiːn/ *n.* nicotine *f.*

niece /niːs/ *n.* nièce *f.*

nifty /'nɪftɪ/ *a.* (*sl.*) chic *invar.*

Nigeria /naɪ'dʒɪərɪə/ *n.* Nigéria *m./f.*
~n *a. & n.* nigérian(e) (*m. (f.*)).

niggardly /'nɪgədlɪ/ *a.* chiche.

niggling /'nɪglɪŋ/ *a.* (*person*) tatillon;
(*detail*) insignifiant.

night /naɪt/ *n.* nuit *f.*; (*evening*) soir
m. ● *a.* de nuit. **~-cap** *n.* boisson *f.*
(*avant d'aller se coucher*). **~-club** *n.*
boîte de nuit *f.* **~-dress, ~-gown,**
~ie *ns.* chemise de nuit *f.* **~-life** *n.*
vie nocturne *f.* **~-school** *n.* cours du
soir *m. pl.* **~-time** *n.* nuit *f.* **~-**
watchman *n.* veilleur de nuit *m.*

nightfall /'naɪtfɔːl/ *n.* tombée de la
nuit *f.*

nightingale /'naɪtɪŋgeɪl/ *n.* rossignol
m.

nightly /'naɪtlɪ/ *a. & adv.* (de) chaque
nuit *or* soir.

nightmare /'naɪtmeə(r)/ *n.* cauchemar *m.*

nil /nɪl/ *n.* rien *m.*; (*sport*) zéro *m.*
● *a.* (*chances, risk, etc.*) nul.

nimble /'nɪmbl/ *a.* (**-er, -est**) agile.

nine /naɪn/ *a. & n.* neuf (*m.*). **~th** *a.*
& n. neuvième (*m./f.*).

nineteen /naɪn'tiːn/ *a. & n.* dix-neuf
(*m.*). **~th** *a. & n.* dix-neuvième (*m./*
f.).

ninety /'naɪntɪ/ *a. & n.* quatre-vingt-
dix (*m.*). **~tieth** *a. & n.* quatre-
vingt-dixième (*m./f.*).

nip /nɪp/ *v.t./i.* (*p.t.* **nipped**) (*pinch*)
pincer; (*rush: sl.*) courir. **~ out/**
back/etc., sortir/rentrer/*etc.* rapidement. ● *n.* pincement *m.*; (*cold*)
fraîcheur *f.*

nipper /'nɪpə(r)/ *n.* (*sl.*) gosse *m./f.*

nipple /'nɪpl/ *n.* bout de sein *m.*; (*of*
baby's bottle) tétine *f.*

nippy /'nɪpɪ/ *a.* (**-ier, -iest**) (*fam.*)
alerte; (*chilly: fam.*) frais.

nitrogen /'naɪtrədʒən/ *n.* azote *m.*

nitwit /'nɪtwɪt/ *n.* (*fam.*) imbécile *m./*
f.

no /nəʊ/ *a.* aucun(e); pas de. ● *adv.*
non. ● *n.* (*pl.* **noes**) non *m. invar.* **~**
man/etc., aucun homme/*etc.* **~**
money/time/etc., pas d'argent/de
temps/*etc.* **~ man's land,** no man's
land *m.* **~ one = nobody. ~ smok-**
ing/entry, défense de fumer/

d'entrer. ~ **way!**, (*fam.*) pas question!

nob|le /'nəʊbl/ a. (**-er, -est**) noble. **~ility** /-'bɪlətɪ/ n. noblesse f.

nobleman /'nəʊblmən/ n. (*pl.* **-men**) noble m.

nobody /'nəʊbədɪ/ *pron.* (ne) personne. ● n. nullité f. **he knows ~**, il ne connaît personne. **~ is there**, personne n'est là.

nocturnal /nɒk'tɜːnl/ a. nocturne.

nod /nɒd/ v.t./i. (*p.t.* **nodded**). ~ **(one's head)**, faire un signe de tête. ~ **off**, s'endormir. ● n. signe de tête m.

noise /nɔɪz/ n. bruit m. **~less** a. silencieux.

nois|y /'nɔɪzɪ/ a. (**-ier, -iest**) bruyant. **~ily** adv. bruyamment.

nomad /'nəʊmæd/ n. nomade m./f. **~ic** /-'mædɪk/ a. nomade.

nominal /'nɒmɪnl/ a. symbolique, nominal; (*value*) nominal. **~ly** adv. nominalement.

nominat|e /'nɒmɪneɪt/ v.t. nommer; (*put forward*) proposer. **~ion** /-'neɪʃn/ n. nomination f.

non- /nɒn/ *pref.* non-. **~-iron** a. qui ne se repasse pas. **~-skid** a. antidérapant. **~-stick** a. à revêtement antiadhésif.

non-commissioned /nɒnkə'mɪʃnd/ a. ~ **officer**, sous-officier m.

non-committal /nɒnkə'mɪtl/ a. évasif.

nondescript /'nɒndɪskrɪpt/ a. indéfinissable.

none /nʌn/ *pron.* aucun(e). ~ **of us**, aucun de nous. **I have ~**, je n'en ai pas. ~ **of the money was used**, l'argent n'a pas du tout été utilisé. ● adv. **too**, (ne) pas tellement. **he is ~ the happier**, il n'en est pas plus heureux.

nonentity /nɒ'nentətɪ/ n. nullité f.

non-existent /nɒnɪg'zɪstənt/ a. inexistant.

nonplussed /nɒn'plʌst/ a. perplexe, déconcerté.

nonsens|e /'nɒnsəns/ n. absurdités f. pl. **~ical** /-'sensɪkl/ a. absurde.

non-smoker /nɒn'sməʊkə(r)/ n. nonfumeur m.

non-stop /nɒn'stɒp/ a. (*train, flight*) direct. ● adv. sans arrêt.

noodles /'nuːdlz/ n. pl. nouilles f. pl.

nook /nʊk/ n. (re)coin m.

noon /nuːn/ n. midi m.

noose /nuːs/ n. nœud coulant m.

nor /nɔː(r)/ adv. ni. ● *conj.* (ne) plus. ~ **shall I come**, je ne viendrai pas non plus.

norm /nɔːm/ n. norme f.

normal /'nɔːml/ a. normal. **~ity** /nɔː'mælətɪ/ n. normalité f. **~ly** adv. normalement.

Norman /'nɔːmən/ a. & n. normand(e) (m.(f.)). **~dy** n. Normandie f.

north /nɔːθ/ n. nord m. ● a. nord invar., du nord. ● adv. vers le nord. **N~ America**, Amérique du Nord f. **N~ American** a. & n. nord-américain(e) (m. (f.)). **~-east** n. nord-est m. **~erly** /'nɔːðəlɪ/ a. du nord. **~ward** a. au nord. **~wards** adv. vers le nord. **~-west** n. nord-ouest m.

northern /'nɔːðən/ a. du nord. **~er** n. habitant(e) du nord m. (f.).

Norw|ay /'nɔːweɪ/ n. Norvège f. **~egian** /nɔː'wiːdʒən/ a. & n. norvégien(ne) (m. (f.)).

nose /nəʊz/ n. nez m. ● v.i. ~ **about**, fouiner.

nosebleed /'nəʊzbliːd/ n. saignement de nez m.

nosedive /'nəʊzdaɪv/ n. piqué m. ● v.i. descendre en piqué.

nostalg|ia /nɒ'stældʒə/ n. nostalgie f. **~ic** a. nostalgique.

nostril /'nɒstrəl/ n. narine f.; (*of horse*) naseau m.

nosy /'nəʊzɪ/ a. (**-ier, -iest**) (*fam.*) curieux, indiscret.

not /nɒt/ adv. (ne) pas. **I do ~ know**, je ne sais pas. ~ **at all**, pas du tout. ~ **yet**, pas encore. **I suppose ~**, je suppose que non.

notable /'nəʊtəbl/ a. notable. ● n. (*person*) notable m.

notably /'nəʊtəblɪ/ adv. notamment.

notary /'nəʊtərɪ/ n. notaire m.

notation /nəʊ'teɪʃn/ n. notation f.

notch /nɒtʃ/ n. entaille f. ● v.t. ~ **up**, (*score etc.*) marquer.

note /nəʊt/ n. note f.; (*banknote*) billet m.; (*short letter*) mot m. ● v.t. noter; (*notice*) remarquer.

notebook /'nəʊtbʊk/ n. carnet m.

noted /'nəʊtɪd/ a. connu (**for**, pour).

notepaper /'nəʊtpeɪpə(r)/ n. papier à lettres m.

noteworthy /'nəʊtwɜːðɪ/ a. remarquable.

nothing /'nʌθɪŋ/ *pron.* (ne) rien. ● n. rien m.; (*person*) nullité f. ● adv. nullement. **he eats ~**, il ne mange rien. ~ **big**/*etc.*, rien de grand/*etc.* ~ **else**, rien d'autre. ~ **much**, pas grand-chose. **for** ~, pour rien, gratis.

notice /'nəʊtɪs/ *n.* avis *m.*, annonce *f.*; (*poster*) affiche *f.* (**advance**) ~, préavis *m.* **at short** ~, dans des délais très brefs. **give in one's** ~, donner sa démission. ● *v.t.* remarquer, observer. ~**board** *n.* tableau d'affichage *m.* **take** ~, faire attention (**of, à**).

noticeabl|e /'nəʊtɪsəbl/ *a.* visible. ~**y** *adv.* visiblement.

notif|y /'nəʊtɪfaɪ/ *v.t.* (*inform*) aviser; (*make known*) notifier. ~**ication** /-ɪ'keɪʃn/ *n.* avis *m.*

notion /'nəʊʃn/ *n.* idée *f.*, notion *f.* ~**s**, (*sewing goods etc.: Amer.*) mercerie *f.*

notor|ious /nəʊ'tɔ:rɪəs/ *a.* (tristement) célèbre. ~**iety** /-ə'raɪətɪ/ *n.* notoriété *f.* ~**iously** *adv.* notoirement.

notwithstanding /nɒtwɪθ'stændɪŋ/ *prep.* malgré. ● *adv.* néanmoins.

nougat /'nu:gɑː/ *n.* nougat *m.*

nought /nɔːt/ *n.* zéro *m.*

noun /naʊn/ *n.* nom *m.*

nourish /'nʌrɪʃ/ *v.t.* nourrir. ~**ing** *a.* nourrissant. ~**ment** *n.* nourriture *f.*

novel /'nɒvl/ *n.* roman *m.* ● *a.* nouveau. ~**ist** *n.* roman|cier, -ière *m., f.* ~**ty** *n.* nouveauté *f.*

November /nəʊ'vembə(r)/ *n.* novembre *m.*

novice /'nɒvɪs/ *n.* novice *m./f.*

now /naʊ/ *adv.* maintenant. ● *conj.* maintenant que. **just** ~, maintenant; (*a moment ago*) tout à l'heure. ~ **and again**, ~ **and then**, de temps à autre.

nowadays /'naʊədeɪz/ *adv.* de nos jours.

nowhere /'nəʊweə(r)/ *adv.* nulle part.

nozzle /'nɒzl/ *n.* (*tip*) embout *m.*; (*of hose*) lance *f.*

nuance /'nju:ɑːns/ *n.* nuance *f.*

nuclear /'nju:klɪə(r)/ *a.* nucléaire.

nucleus /'nju:klɪəs/ *n.* (*pl.* -**lei** /-lɪaɪ/) noyau *m.*

nud|e /nju:d/ *a.* nu. ● *n.* nu *m.* **in the** ~**e**, tout nu. ~**ity** *n.* nudité *f.*

nudge /nʌdʒ/ *v.t.* pousser du coude. ● *n.* coup de coude *m.*

nudis|t /'nju:dɪst/ *n.* nudiste *m./f.* ~**m** /-zəm/ *n.* nudisme *m.*

nuisance /'nju:sns/ *n.* (*thing, event*) ennui *m.*; (*person*) peste *f.* **be a** ~, être embêtant.

null /nʌl/ *a.* nul. ~**ify** *v.t.* infirmer.

numb /nʌm/ *a.* engourdi. ● *v.t.* engourdir.

number /'nʌmbə(r)/ *n.* nombre *m.*; (*of ticket, house, page, etc.*) numéro *m.* ● *v.t.* numéroter; (*count, include*) compter. **a** ~ **of people**, plusieurs personnes. ~-**plate** *n.* plaque d'immatriculation *f.*

numeral /'nju:mərəl/ *n.* chiffre *m.*

numerate /'nju:mərət/ *a.* qui sait calculer.

numerical /nju:'merɪkl/ *a.* numérique.

numerous /'nju:mərəs/ *a.* nombreux.

nun /nʌn/ *n.* religieuse *f.*

nurs|e /nɜːs/ *n.* infirmière *f.*, infirmier *m.*; (*nanny*) nurse *f.* ● *v.t.* soigner; (*hope etc.*) nourrir. ~**ing home**, clinique *f.*

nursemaid /'nɜːsmeɪd/ *n.* bonne d'enfants *f.*

nursery /'nɜːsərɪ/ *n.* chambre d'enfants *f.*; (*for plants*) pépinière *f.* (**day**) ~, crèche *f.* ~ **rhyme**, chanson enfantine *f.*, comptine *f.* ~ **school**, (école) maternelle *f.* ~ **slope**, piste facile *f.*

nurture /'nɜːtʃə(r)/ *v.t.* élever.

nut /nʌt/ *n.* (*walnut, Brazil nut, etc.*) noix *f.*; (*hazelnut*) noisette *f.*; (*peanut*) cacahuète *f.*; (*techn.*) écrou *m.*; (*sl.*) idiot(e) *m.* (*f.*).

nutcrackers /'nʌtkrækəz/ *n. pl.* casse-noix *m. invar.*

nutmeg /'nʌtmeg/ *n.* muscade *f.*

nutrient /'nju:trɪənt/ *n.* substance nutritive *f.*

nutrit|ion /nju:'trɪʃn/ *n.* nutrition *f.* ~**ious** *a.* nutritif.

nuts /nʌts/ *a.* (*crazy: sl.*) cinglé.

nutshell /'nʌtʃel/ *n.* coquille de noix *f.* **in a** ~, en un mot.

nuzzle /'nʌzl/ *v.i.* ~ **up to**, coller son museau à.

nylon /'naɪlɒn/ *n.* nylon *m.* ~**s**, bas nylon *m. pl.*

O

oaf /əʊf/ *n.* (*pl.* **oafs**) lourdaud(e) *m.* (*f.*).

oak /əʊk/ *n.* chêne *m.*

OAP abbr. (old-age pensioner) retraité(e) m. (f.), personne âgée f.

oar /ɔː(r)/ n. aviron m., rame f.

oasis /əʊˈeɪsɪs/ n. (pl. oases /-siːz/) oasis f.

oath /əʊθ/ n. (promise) serment m.; (swear-word) juron m.

oatmeal /ˈəʊtmiːl/ n. farine d'avoine f., flocons d'avoine m. pl.

oats /əʊts/ n. pl. avoine f.

obedien|t /əˈbiːdɪənt/ a. obéissant. ~ce n. obéissance f. ~tly adv. docilement, avec soumission.

obes|e /əʊˈbiːs/ a. obèse. ~ity n. obésité f.

obey /əˈbeɪ/ v.t./i. obéir (à).

obituary /əˈbɪtʃʊərɪ/ n. nécrologie f.

object[1] /ˈɒbdʒɪkt/ n. (thing) objet m.; (aim) but m., objet m.; (gram.) complément (d'objet) m. money/etc. is no ~, l'argent/etc. ne pose pas de problèmes.

object[2] /əbˈdʒekt/ v.i. protester. ● v.t. ~ that, objecter que. ~ to, (behaviour) désapprouver; (plan) protester contre. ~ion /-kʃn/ n. objection f.; (drawback) inconvénient m.

objectionable /əbˈdʒekʃnəbl/ a. désagréable.

objectiv|e /əbˈdʒektɪv/ a. objectif. ● n. objectif m. ~ity /ɒbdʒekˈtɪvətɪ/ n. objectivité f.

obligat|e /ˈɒblɪɡeɪt/ v.t. obliger. ~ion /-ˈɡeɪʃn/ n. obligation f. under an ~ion to s.o., redevable à qn. (for, de).

obligatory /əˈblɪɡətrɪ/ a. obligatoire.

oblig|e /əˈblaɪdʒ/ v.t. obliger. ~e to do, obliger à faire. ~ed a. obligé (to, de). ~ed to s.o., redevable à qn. ~ing a. obligeant. ~ingly adv. obligeamment.

oblique /əˈbliːk/ a. oblique; (reference etc.: fig.) indirect.

obliterat|e /əˈblɪtəreɪt/ v.t. effacer. ~ion /-ˈreɪʃn/ n. effacement m.

oblivion /əˈblɪvɪən/ n. oubli m.

oblivious /əˈblɪvɪəs/ a. (unaware) inconscient (to, of, de).

oblong /ˈɒblɒŋ/ a. oblong. ● n. rectangle m.

obnoxious /əbˈnɒkʃəs/ a. odieux.

oboe /ˈəʊbəʊ/ n. hautbois m.

obscen|e /əbˈsiːn/ a. obscène. ~ity /-enətɪ/ n. obscénité f.

obscur|e /əbˈskjʊə(r)/ a. obscur. ● v.t. obscurcir; (conceal) cacher. ~ely adv. obscurément. ~ity n. obscurité f.

obsequious /əbˈsiːkwɪəs/ a. obséquieux.

observan|t /əbˈzɜːvənt/ a. observateur. ~ce n. observance f.

observatory /əbˈzɜːvətrɪ/ n. observatoire m.

observ|e /əbˈzɜːv/ v.t. observer; (remark) remarquer. ~ation /ɒbzəˈveɪʃn/ n. observation f. ~er n. observa|teur, -trice m., f.

obsess /əbˈses/ v.t. obséder. ~ion /-ʃn/ n. obsession f. ~ive a. obsédant; (psych.) obsessionnel.

obsolete /ˈɒbsəliːt/ a. dépassé.

obstacle /ˈɒbstəkl/ n. obstacle m.

obstetric|s /əbˈstetrɪks/ n. obstétrique f. ~ian /ɒbstɪˈtrɪʃn/ n. médecin accoucheur m.

obstina|te /ˈɒbstɪnət/ a. obstiné. ~cy n. obstination f. ~tely adv. obstinément.

obstruct /əbˈstrʌkt/ v.t. (block) boucher; (congest) encombrer; (hinder) entraver. ~ion /-kʃn/ n. (act) obstruction f.; (thing) obstacle m.; (traffic jam) encombrement m.

obtain /əbˈteɪn/ v.t. obtenir. ● v.i. avoir cours. ~able a. disponible.

obtrusive /əbˈtruːsɪv/ a. importun; (thing) trop en évidence.

obtuse /əbˈtjuːs/ a. obtus.

obviate /ˈɒbvɪeɪt/ v.t. éviter.

obvious /ˈɒbvɪəs/ a. évident, manifeste. ~ly adv. manifestement.

occasion /əˈkeɪʒn/ n. occasion f.; (big event) événement m. ● v.t. occasionner. on ~, à l'occasion.

occasional /əˈkeɪʒənl/ a. fait, pris, etc. de temps en temps; (visitor etc.) qui vient de temps en temps. ~ly adv. de temps en temps. very ~ly, rarement.

occult /ɒˈkʌlt/ a. occulte.

occupation /ɒkjʊˈpeɪʃn/ n. (activity, occupying) occupation f.; (job) métier m., profession f. ~al a. professionnel, du métier. ~al therapy ergothérapie f.

occup|y /ˈɒkjʊpaɪ/ v.t. occuper. ~ant, ~ier ns. occupant(e) m. (f.).

occur /əˈkɜː(r)/ v.i. (p.t. occurred) se produire; (arise) se présenter. ~ to s.o., venir à l'esprit de qn.

occurrence /əˈkʌrəns/ n. événement m. a frequent ~, une chose qui arrive souvent.

ocean /ˈəʊʃn/ n. océan m.

o'clock /ə'klɒk/ *adv.* **it is six ~**/*etc.*, il est six heures/*etc.*

octagon /'ɒktəgən/ *n.* octogone *m.*

octane /'ɒkteɪn/ *n.* octane *m.*

octave /'ɒktɪv/ *n.* octave *f.*

October /ɒk'təʊbə(r)/ *n.* octobre *m.*

octopus /'ɒktəpəs/ *n.* (*pl.* **-puses**) pieuvre *f.*

odd /ɒd/ *a.* (**-er**, **-est**) bizarre; (*number*) impair; (*left over*) qui reste; (*not of set*) dépareillé; (*occasional*) fait, pris, *etc.* de temps en temps. **~ jobs**, menus travaux *m. pl.* **twenty ~**, vingt et quelques. **~ity** *n.* bizarrerie *f.*; (*thing*) curiosité *f.* **~ly** *adv.* bizarrement.

oddment /'ɒdmənt/ *n.* fin de série *f.*

odds /ɒdz/ *n. pl.* chances *f. pl.*; (*in betting*) cote *f.* (**on**, de). **at ~**, en désaccord. **it makes no ~**, ça ne fait rien. **~ and ends**, des petites choses.

ode /əʊd/ *n.* ode *f.*

odious /'əʊdɪəs/ *a.* odieux.

odour, *Amer.* **odor** /'əʊdə(r)/ *n.* odeur *f.* **~less** *a.* inodore.

of /ɒv, *unstressed* əv/ *prep.* de. **of the**, du, de la, *pl.* des. **of it, of them**, en. **a friend of mine**, un de mes amis. **six of them**, six d'entre eux. **the fifth of June**/*etc.*, le cinq juin/*etc.* **a litre of water**, un litre d'eau; **made of steel**, en acier.

off /ɒf/ *adv.* parti, absent; (*switched off*) éteint; (*tap*) fermé; (*taken off*) enlevé, détaché; (*cancelled*) annulé. ● *prep.* de; (*distant from*) éloigné de. **go ~**, (*leave*) partir; (*milk*) tourner; (*food*) s'abîmer. **be better ~**, (*in a better position, richer*) être mieux. **a day ~**, un jour de congé. **20% ~**, une réduction de 20%. **take sth. ~**, (*a surface*) prendre qch. sur. **~-beat** *a.* original. **on the ~ chance (that)**, au cas où. **~ colour**, (*ill*) patraque. **~ color**, (*improper: Amer.*) scabreux. **~-licence** *n.* débit de vins *m.* **~-line** *a.* autonome; (*switched off*) déconnecté. **~-load** *v.t.* décharger. **~-peak** *a.* (*hours*) creux; (*rate*) des heures creuses. **~-putting** *a.* (*fam.*) rebutant. **~-stage** *a.* & *adv.* dans les coulisses. **~-white** *a.* blanc cassé *invar.*

offal /'ɒfl/ *n.* abats *m. pl.*

offence /ə'fens/ *n.* délit *m.* **give ~ to**, offenser. **take ~**, s'offenser (**at**, de).

offend /ə'fend/ *v.t.* offenser; (*fig.*) choquer. **be ~ed**, s'offenser (**at**, de). **~er** *n.* délinquant(e) *m. (f.).*

offensive /ə'fensɪv/ *a.* offensant; (*disgusting*) dégoûtant; (*weapon*) offensif. ● *n.* offensive *f.*

offer /'ɒfə(r)/ *v.t.* (*p.t.* **offered**) offrir. ● *n.* offre *f.* **on ~**, en promotion. **~ing** *n.* offrande *f.*

offhand /ɒf'hænd/ *a.* désinvolte. ● *adv.* à l'improviste.

office /'ɒfɪs/ *n.* bureau *m.*; (*surgery: Amer.*) cabinet *m.* ● *a.* de bureau. **good ~s**, bons offices *m. pl.* **in ~**, au pouvoir. **~ building**, immeuble de bureaux *m.*

officer /'ɒfɪsə(r)/ *n.* (*army etc.*) officier *m.*; (*policeman*) agent *m.*

official /ə'fɪʃl/ *a.* officiel. ● *n.* officiel *m.*; (*civil servant*) fonctionnaire *m./f.* **~ly** *adv.* officiellement.

officiate /ə'fɪʃɪeɪt/ *v.i.* (*priest*) officier; (*president*) présider.

officious /ə'fɪʃəs/ *a.* trop zélé.

offing /'ɒfɪŋ/ *n.* **in the ~**, en perspective.

offset /'ɒfset/ *v.t.* (*p.t.* **-set**, *pres. p.* **-setting**) compenser.

offshoot /'ɒfʃuːt/ *n.* (*bot.*) rejeton *m.*; (*fig.*) ramification *f.*

offshore /ɒf'ʃɔː(r)/ *a.* (*waters*) côtier; (*exploration*) en mer; (*banking*) dans les paladis fiscaux.

offside /ɒf'saɪd/ *a.* (*sport*) hors jeu *invar.*; (*auto.*) du côté du conducteur.

offspring /'ɒfsprɪŋ/ *n. invar.* progéniture *f.*

often /'ɒfn/ *adv.* souvent. **how ~?**, combien de fois? **every so ~**, de temps en temps.

ogle /'əʊgl/ *v.t.* lorgner.

ogre /'əʊgə(r)/ *n.* ogre *m.*

oh /əʊ/ *int.* oh, ah.

oil /ɔɪl/ *n.* huile *f.*; (*petroleum*) pétrole *m.*; (*for heating*) mazout *m.* ● *v.t.* graisser. **~-painting** *n.* peinture à l'huile *f.* **~-tanker** *n.* pétrolier *m.* **~y** *a.* graisseux.

oilfield /'ɔɪlfiːld/ *n.* gisement pétrolifère *m.*

oilskins /'ɔɪlskɪnz/ *n. pl.* ciré *m.*

ointment /'ɔɪntmənt/ *n.* pommade *f.*, onguent *m.*

OK /əʊ'keɪ/ *a.* & *adv.* (*fam.*) bien.

old /əʊld/ *a.* (**-er**, **-est**) vieux; (*person*) vieux, âgé; (*former*) ancien. **how ~ is he?**, quel âge a-t-il? **he is eight years ~**, il a huit ans. **of ~**, jadis. **~ age**, vieillesse *f.* **~-age** pensioner, retraité(e) *m. (f.).* **~ boy**, ancien élève *m.*; (*fellow: fam.*) vieux *m.*

~er, ~est, (*son etc.*) aîné. ~-fashioned *a.* démodé. ~ maid, vieille fille *f.* ~ man, vieillard *m.*, vieux *m.* ~-time *a.* ancien. ~ woman, vieille *f.*

olive /'ɒlɪv/ *n.* olive *f.* ● *a.* olive *invar.* ~ oil, huile d'olive *f.*

Olympic /ə'lɪmpɪk/ *a.* olympique. ~s *n. pl.*, ~ Games, Jeux olympiques *m. pl.*

omelette /'ɒmlɪt/ *n.* omelette *f.*

omen /'əʊmen/ *n.* augure *m.*

ominous /'ɒmɪnəs/ *a.* de mauvais augure; (*fig.*) menaçant.

omi|t /ə'mɪt/ *v.t.* (*p.t.* **omitted**) omettre. ~**ssion** *n.* omission *f.*

on /ɒn/ *prep.* sur. ● *adv.* en avant. (*switched on*) allumé; (*tap*) ouvert; (*machine*) en marche; (*put on*) mis. **on foot/time/**etc., à pied/l'heure/ *etc.* **on arriving**, en arrivant. **on Tuesday**, mardi. **on Tuesdays**, le mardi. **walk/**etc. **on**, continuer à marcher/*etc.* **be on**, (*of film*) passer. **the meeting/deal is still on**, la réunion/le marché est maintenu(e). **be on at**, (*fam.*) être après. **on and off**, de temps en temps.

once /wʌns/ *adv.* une fois; (*formerly*) autrefois. ● *conj.* une fois que. **all at ~**, tout à coup. ~**-over** *n.* (*fam.*) coup d'œil rapide *m.*

oncoming /'ɒnkʌmɪŋ/ *a.* (*vehicle etc.*) qui approche.

one /wʌn/ *a. & n.* un(e) (*m.* (*f.*)). ● *pron.* un(e) *m.* (*f.*); (*impersonal*) on. ~ **(and only)**, seul (et unique). **a big/red/**etc.. ~, un(e) grand(e)/ rouge/*etc.* **this/that ~**, celui-ci/-là, celle-ci/-là. ~ **another**, l'un(e) l'autre. ~**-eyed**, borgne. ~**-off** *a.* (*fam.*), ~ **of a kind**, (*Amer.*) unique, exceptionnel. ~**-sided** *a.* (*biased*) partial; (*unequal*) inégal. ~**-way** *a.* ·(*street*) à sens unique; (*ticket*) simple.

oneself /wʌn'self/ *pron.* soi-même; (*reflexive*) se.

ongoing /'ɒngəʊɪŋ/ *a.* qui continue à évoluer.

onion /'ʌnjən/ *n.* oignon *m.*

onlooker /'ɒnlʊkə(r)/ *n.* specta|teur, -trice *m., f.*

only /'əʊnlɪ/ *a.* seul. **an ~ son/** etc., un fils/*etc.* unique. ● *adv. & conj.* seulement. **he ~ has six**, il n'en a que six, il en a six seulement. ~ **too**, extrêmement.

onset /'ɒnset/ *n.* début *m.*

onslaught /'ɒnslɔːt/ *n.* attaque *f.*

onus /'əʊnəs/ *n.* **the ~ is on me/**etc., c'est ma/*etc.* responsabilité (**to**, de).

onward(s) /'ɒnwəd(z)/ *adv.* en avant.

onyx /'ɒnɪks/ *n.* onyx *m.*

ooze /uːz/ *v.i.* suinter.

opal /'əʊpl/ *n.* opale *f.*

opaque /əʊ'peɪk/ *a.* opaque.

open /'əʊpən/ *a.* ouvert; (*view*) dégagé; (*free to all*) public; (*undisguised*) manifeste; (*question*) en attente. ● *v.t./i.* (s')ouvrir; (*of shop, play*) ouvrir. **in the ~ air**, en plein air. ~**-ended** *a.* sans limite (*de durée etc.*); (*system*) qui peut évoluer. ~**-heart** *a.* (*surgery*) à cœur ouvert. **keep ~ house**, tenir table ouverte. ~ **out** or **up**, (s')ouvrir. ~**-minded** *a.* à l'esprit ouvert. ~**-plan** *a.* sans cloisons. ~ **secret**, secret de Polichinelle *m.*

opener /'əʊpənə(r)/ *n.* ouvre-boite(s) *m.*, ouvre-bouteille(s) *m.*

opening /'əʊpənɪŋ/ *n.* ouverture *f.*; (*job*) débouché *m.*, poste vacant *m.*

openly /'əʊpənlɪ/ *adv.* ouvertement.

opera /'ɒpərə/ *n.* opéra *m.* ~**-glasses** *n. pl.* jumelles *f. pl.* ~**tic** /ɒpə'rætɪk/ *a.* d'opéra.

operat|e /'ɒpəreɪt/ *v.t./i.* opérer; (*techn.*) (faire) fonctionner. ~**e on**, (*med.*) opérer. ~**ing theatre**, salle d'opération *f.* ~**ion** /-'reɪʃn/ *n.* opération *f.* **have an ~ion**, se faire opérer. **in ~ion**, en vigueur; (*techn.*) en service. ~**or** *n.* opéra|teur, -trice *m., f.*; (*telephonist*) standardiste *m./ f.*

operational /ɒpə'reɪʃənl/ *a.* opérationnel.

operative /'ɒpərətɪv/ *a.* (*med.*) opératoire; (*law etc.*) en vigueur.

operetta /ɒpə'retə/ *n.* opérette *f.*

opinion /ə'pɪnjən/ *n.* opinion *f.*, avis *m.* ~**ated** *a.* dogmatique.

opium /'əʊpɪəm/ *n.* opium *m.*

opponent /ə'pəʊnənt/ *n.* adversaire *m./f.*

opportune /'ɒpətjuːn/ *a.* opportun.

opportunist /ɒpə'tjuːnɪst/ *n.* opportuniste *m./f.*

opportunity /ɒpə'tjuːnətɪ/ *n.* occasion *f.* (**to do**, de faire).

oppos|e /ə'pəʊz/ *v.t.* s'opposer à. ~**ed to**, opposé à. ~**ing** *a.* opposé.

opposite /'ɒpəzɪt/ *a.* opposé. ● *n.* contraire *m.*, opposé *m.* ● *adv.* en face. ● *prep.* ~ **(to)**, en face de.

one's ~ number, son homologue
m./f.

opposition /ɒpə'zɪʃn/ *n.* opposition
f.; (*mil.*) résistance *f.*

oppress /ə'pres/ *v.t.* opprimer. ~ion
/-ʃn/ *n.* oppression *f.* ~ive *a.* (*cruel*)
oppressif; (*heat*) oppressant. ~or *n.*
oppresseur *m.*

opt /ɒpt/ *v.i.* ~ for, opter pour. ~
out, refuser de participer (of, à). ~
to do, choisir de faire.

optical /'ɒptɪkl/ *a.* optique. ~ illusion, illusion d'optique *f.*

optician /ɒp'tɪʃn/ *n.* opticien(ne) *m.*
(*f.*).

optimis|t /'ɒptɪmɪst/ *n.* optimiste *m./
f.* ~m /-zəm/ *n.* optimisme *m.* ~tic
/-'mɪstɪk/ *a.* optimiste. ~tically
/-'mɪstɪklɪ/ *adv.* avec optimisme.

optimum /'ɒptɪməm/ *a.* & *n.* (*pl.*
-ima) optimum (*m.*).

option /'ɒpʃn/ *n.* choix *m.*, option *f.*

optional /'ɒpʃənl/ *a.* facultatif. ~
extras, accessoires en option *m. pl.*

opulen|t /'ɒpjʊlənt/ *a.* opulent. ~ce
n. opulence *f.*

or /ɔ:(r)/ *conj.* ou; (*with negative*) ni.

oracle /'ɒrəkl/ *n.* oracle *m.*

oral /'ɔ:rəl/ *a.* oral. ● *n.* (*examination: fam.*) oral *m.*

orange /'ɒrɪndʒ/ *n.* (*fruit*) orange *f.*
● *a.* (*colour*) orange *invar.*

orangeade /ɒrɪndʒ'eɪd/ *n.* orangeade
f.

orator /'ɒrətə(r)/ *n.* ora|teur, -trice
m., f. ~y /-trɪ/ *n.* rhétorique *f.*

oratorio /ɒrə'tɔ:rɪəʊ/ *n.* (*pl.* -os)
oratorio *m.*

orbit /'ɔ:bɪt/ *n.* orbite *f.* ● *v.t.* graviter autour de, orbiter.

orchard /'ɔ:tʃəd/ *n.* verger *m.*

orchestra /'ɔ:kɪstrə/ *n.* orchestre *m.*
~ stalls (*Amer.*), fauteuils d'orchestre *m. pl.* ~l /-'kestrəl/ *a.* orchestral.

orchestrate /'ɔ:kɪstreɪt/ *v.t.* orches-
trer.

orchid /'ɔ:kɪd/ *n.* orchidée *f.*

ordain /ɔ:'deɪn/ *v.t.* décréter (that,
que); (*relig.*) ordonner.

ordeal /ɔ:'di:l/ *n.* épreuve *f.*

order /'ɔ:də(r)/ *n.* ordre *m.*; (*comm.*)
commande *f.* ● *v.t.* ordonner;
(*goods etc.*) commander. in ~,
(*tidy*) en ordre; (*document*) en règle;
(*fitting*) de règle. in ~ that, pour
que. in ~ to, pour. ~ s.o. to,
ordonner à qn. de.

orderly /'ɔ:dəlɪ/ *a.* (*tidy*) ordonné;
(*not unruly*) discipliné. ● *n.* (*mil.*)
planton *m.*; (*med.*) garçon de salle *m.*

ordinary /'ɔ:dɪnrɪ/ *a.* (*usual*) ordinaire; (*average*) moyen.

ordination /ɔ:dɪ'neɪʃn/ *n.* (*relig.*)
ordination *f.*

ore /ɔ:(r)/ *n.* mineral *m.*

organ /'ɔ:gən/ *n.* organe *m.*; (*mus.*)
orgue *m.* ~ist *n.* organiste *m./f.*

organic /ɔ:'gænɪk/ *a.* organique.

organism /'ɔ:gənɪzəm/ *n.* organisme
m.

organiz|e /'ɔ:gənaɪz/ *v.t.* organiser.
~ation /-'zeɪʃn/ *n.* organisation *f.*
~er *n.* organisa|teur, -trice *m., f.*

orgasm /'ɔ:gæzəm/ *n.* orgasme *m.*

orgy /'ɔ:dʒɪ/ *n.* orgie *f.*

Orient /'ɔ:rɪənt/ *n.* the ~, l'Orient *m.*
~al /-'entl/ *n.* Oriental(e) *m.* (*f.*).

oriental /ɔ:rɪ'entl/ *a.* oriental.

orient(at|e) /'ɔ:rɪənt(eɪt)/ *v.t.*
orienter. ~ion /-'teɪʃn/ *n.* orientation *f.*

orifice /'ɒrɪfɪs/ *n.* orifice *m.*

origin /'ɒrɪdʒɪn/ *n.* origine *f.*

original /ə'rɪdʒənl/ *a.* (*first*) originel;
(*not copied*) original. ~ity /-'nælətɪ/
n. originalité *f.* ~ly *adv.* (*at the
outset*) à l'origine; (*write etc.*) origi-
nalement.

originat|e /ə'rɪdʒɪneɪt/ *v.i.* (*plan*)
prendre naissance. ● *v.t.* être l'auteur de. ~e from, provenir de;
(*person*) venir de. ~or *n.* auteur *m.*

ornament /'ɔ:nəmənt/ *n.* (*decoration*) ornement *m.*; (*object*) objet
décoratif *m.* ~al /-'mentl/ *a.*
ornemental. ~ation /-en'teɪʃn/ *n.*
ornementation *f.*

ornate /ɔ:'neɪt/ *a.* richement orné.

ornithology /ɔ:nɪ'θɒlədʒɪ/ *n.* ornithologie *f.*

orphan /'ɔ:fn/ *n.* orphelin(e) *m.* (*f.*).
● *v.t.* rendre orphelin. ~age *n.*
orphelinat *m.*

orthodox /'ɔ:θədɒks/ *a.* orthodoxe.
~y *n.* orthodoxie *f.*

orthopaedic /ɔ:θə'pi:dɪk/ *a.* orthopédique.

oscillate /'ɒsɪleɪt/ *v.i.* osciller.

ostensibl|e /ɒs'tensəbl/ *a.* apparent,
prétendu. ~y *adv.* apparemment,
prétendument.

ostentati|on /ɒsten'teɪʃn/ *n.* ostenta-
tion *f.* ~ous *a.* prétentieux.

osteopath /'ɒstɪəpæθ/ *n.* ostéopathe
m./f.

ostracize /ˈɒstrəsaɪz/ v.t. frapper d'ostracisme.

ostrich /ˈɒstrɪtʃ/ n. autruche f.

other /ˈʌðə(r)/ a. autre. ● n. & pron. autre m./f. ● adv. ~ than, autrement que; (except) à part. **(some)** ~s, d'autres. **the** ~ **one**, l'autre m./f.

otherwise /ˈʌðəwaɪz/ adv. autrement.

otter /ˈɒtə(r)/ n. loutre f.

ouch /aʊtʃ/ int. aïe!

ought /ɔːt/ v. aux. devoir. **you** ~ **to stay**, vous devriez rester. **he** ~ **to succeed**, il devrait réussir. **I** ~ **to have done it**, j'aurais dû le faire.

ounce /aʊns/ n. once f. (= 28.35 g.).

our /ˈaʊə(r)/ a. notre, pl. nos.

ours /ˈaʊəz/ poss. le or la nôtre, les nôtres.

ourselves /aʊəˈselvz/ pron. nous-mêmes; (reflexive & after prep.) nous.

oust /aʊst/ v.t. évincer.

out /aʊt/ adv. dehors; (sun) levé. **be** ~, (person, book) être sorti; (light) être éteint; (flower) être épanoui; (tide) être bas; (secret) se savoir; (wrong) se tromper. **be** ~ **to do**, être résolu à faire. **run**/etc. ~, sortir en courant/etc. **~-and-out** a. absolu. ~ **of**, hors de; (without) sans, à court de. ~ **of pity**/etc., par pitié/etc. **made** ~ **of**, fait en or de. **take** ~ **of**, prendre dans. **5** ~ **of 6**, 5 sur 6. ~ **of date**, démodé; (not valid) périmé. ~ **of doors**, dehors. ~ **of hand**, (situation) dont on n'est plus maître. ~ **of line**, (impertinent: Amer.) incorrect. ~ **of one's mind**, fou. ~ **of order**, (broken) en panne. ~ **of place**, (object, remark) déplacé. ~ **of the way**, écarté. **get** ~ **of the way!** écarte-toi! ~ **of work**, sans travail. **~-patient** n. malade en consultation externe m./f.

outbid /aʊtˈbɪd/ v.t. (p.t. **-bid**, pres. p. **-bidding**) enchérir sur.

outboard /ˈaʊtbɔːd/ a. (motor) hors-bord invar.

outbreak /ˈaʊtbreɪk/ n. (of war etc.) début m.; (of violence, boils) éruption f.

outburst /ˈaʊtbɜːst/ n. explosion f.

outcast /ˈaʊtkɑːst/ n. paria m.

outclass /aʊtˈklɑːs/ v.t. surclasser.

outcome /ˈaʊtkʌm/ n. résultat m.

outcrop /ˈaʊtkrɒp/ n. affleurement m.

outcry /ˈaʊtkraɪ/ n. tollé m.

outdated /aʊtˈdeɪtɪd/ a. démodé.

outdo /aʊtˈduː/ v.t. (p.t. **-did**, p.p. **-done**) surpasser.

outdoor /ˈaʊtdɔː(r)/ a. de or en plein air. ~**s** /-ˈdɔːz/ adv. dehors.

outer /ˈaʊtə(r)/ a. extérieur. ~ **space**, espace (cosmique) m.

outfit /ˈaʊtfɪt/ n. (articles) équipement m.; (clothes) tenue f.; (group: fam.) équipe f. ~**ter** n. spécialiste de confection m./f.

outgoing /ˈaʊtgəʊɪŋ/ a. (minister, tenant) sortant; (sociable) ouvert. ~**s** n. pl. dépenses f. pl.

outgrow /aʊtˈgrəʊ/ v.t. (p.t. **-grew**, p.p. **-grown**) (clothes) devenir trop grand pour; (habit) dépasser.

outhouse /ˈaʊthaʊs/ n. appentis m.; (of mansion) dépendance f.; (Amer.) cabinets extérieurs m. pl.

outing /ˈaʊtɪŋ/ n. sortie f.

outlandish /aʊtˈlændɪʃ/ a. bizarre, étrange.

outlaw /ˈaʊtlɔː/ n. hors-la-loi m. invar. ● v.t. proscrire.

outlay /ˈaʊtleɪ/ n. dépenses f. pl.

outlet /ˈaʊtlet/ n. (for water, gases) sortie f.; (for goods) débouché m.; (for feelings) exutoire m.

outline /ˈaʊtlaɪn/ n. contour m.; (summary) esquisse f. (main) ~**s**, grandes lignes f. pl. ● v.t. tracer le contour de; (summarize) exposer sommairement.

outlive /aʊtˈlɪv/ v.t. survivre à.

outlook /ˈaʊtlʊk/ n. perspective f.

outlying /ˈaʊtlaɪɪŋ/ a. écarté.

outmoded /aʊtˈməʊdɪd/ a. démodé.

outnumber /aʊtˈnʌmbə(r)/ v.t. surpasser en nombre.

outpost /ˈaʊtpəʊst/ n. avant-poste m.

output /ˈaʊtpʊt/ n. rendement m.; (comput.) sortie f. ● v.t./i. (comput.) sortir.

outrage /ˈaʊtreɪdʒ/ n. atrocité f.; (scandal) scandale m. ● v.t. (morals) outrager; (person) scandaliser.

outrageous /aʊtˈreɪdʒəs/ a. scandaleux, atroce.

outright /aʊtˈraɪt/ adv. complètement; (at once) sur le coup; (frankly) carrément. ● a. /ˈaʊtraɪt/ complet; (refusal) net.

outset /ˈaʊtset/ n. début m.

outside [1] /aʊtˈsaɪd/ n. extérieur m. ● adv. (au) dehors. ● prep. en dehors de; (in front of) devant.

outside [2] /ˈaʊtsaɪd/ a. extérieur.

outsider /aʊtˈsaɪdə(r)/ *n.* étranger, -ère *m., f.*; (*sport*) outsider *m.*

outsize /ˈaʊtsaɪz/ *a.* grande taille *invar.*

outskirts /ˈaʊtskɜːts/ *n. pl.* banlieue *f.*

outspoken /aʊtˈspəʊkən/ *a.* franc.

outstanding /aʊtˈstændɪŋ/ *a.* exceptionnel; (*not settled*) en suspens.

outstretched /aʊtˈstretʃt/ *a.* (*arm*) tendu.

outstrip /aʊtˈstrɪp/ *v.t.* (*p.t.* -stripped) devancer, surpasser.

outward /ˈaʊtwəd/ *a. & adv.* vers l'extérieur; (*sign etc.*) extérieur; (*journey*) d'aller. ~ly *adv.* extérieurement. ~s *adv.* vers l'extérieur.

outweigh /aʊtˈweɪ/ *v.t.* (*exceed in importance*) l'emporter sur.

outwit /aʊtˈwɪt/ *v.t.* (*p.t.* -witted) duper, être plus malin que.

oval /ˈəʊvl/ *n. & a.* ovale (*m.*).

ovary /ˈəʊvərɪ/ *n.* ovaire *m.*

ovation /əˈveɪʃn/ *n.* ovation *f.*

oven /ˈʌvn/ *n.* four *m.*

over /ˈəʊvə(r)/ *prep.* sur, au-dessus de; (*across*) de l'autre côté de; (*during*) pendant; (*more than*) plus de. ● *adv.* (par-)dessus; (*ended*) fini; (*past*) passé; (*too*) trop; (*more*) plus. **jump**/*etc.* ~, sauter/*etc.* par-dessus. ~ **the radio**, à la radio. **ask** ~, inviter chez soi. **he has some** ~, il lui en reste. **all** ~ (**the table**), partout (sur la table). ~ **and above**, en plus de. ~ **and over**, à maintes reprises. ~ **here**, par ici. ~ **there**, là-bas.

over- /ˈəʊvə(r)/ *pref.* sur-, trop.

overall¹ /ˈəʊvərɔːl/ *n.* blouse *f.* ~s, bleu(s) de travail *m.* (*pl.*).

overall² /əʊvərˈɔːl/ *a.* global, d'ensemble; (*length, width*) total. ● *adv.* globalement.

overawe /əʊvərˈɔː/ *v.t.* intimider.

overbalance /əʊvəˈbæləns/ *v.t./i.* (faire) basculer.

overbearing /əʊvəˈbeərɪŋ/ *a.* autoritaire.

overboard /ˈəʊvəbɔːd/ *adv.* par-dessus bord.

overbook /əʊvəˈbʊk/ *v.t.* accepter trop de réservations pour.

overcast /ˈəʊvəkɑːst/ *a.* couvert.

overcharge /əʊvəˈtʃɑːdʒ/ *v.t.* ~ s.o. (**for**), faire payer trop cher à qn.

overcoat /ˈəʊvəkəʊt/ *n.* pardessus *m.*

overcome /əʊvəˈkʌm/ *v.t.* (*p.t.* -came, *p.p.* -come) triompher de; (*difficulty*) surmonter, triompher de. ~ **by**, accablé de.

overcrowded /əʊvəˈkraʊdɪd/ *a.* bondé; (*country*) surpeuplé.

overdo /əʊvəˈduː/ *v.t.* (*p.t.* -did, *p.p.* -done) exagérer; (*culin.*) trop cuire. ~ **it**, (*overwork*) se surmener.

overdose /ˈəʊvədəʊs/ *n.* overdose *f.*, surdose *f.*

overdraft /ˈəʊvədrɑːft/ *n.* découvert *m.*

overdraw /əʊvəˈdrɔː/ *v.t.* (*p.t.* -drew, *p.p.* -drawn) (*one's account*) mettre à découvert.

overdrive /ˈəʊvədraɪv/ *n.* surmultipliée *f.*

overdue /əʊvəˈdjuː/ *a.* en retard; (*belated*) tardif; (*bill*) impayé.

overestimate /əʊvərˈestɪmeɪt/ *v.t.* surestimer.

overexposed /əʊvərɪkˈspəʊzd/ *a.* surexposé.

overflow¹ /əʊvəˈfləʊ/ *v.i.* déborder.

overflow² /ˈəʊvəfləʊ/ *n.* (*outlet*) trop-plein *m.*

overgrown /əʊvəˈgrəʊn/ *a.* (*garden etc.*) envahi par la végétation.

overhang /əʊvəˈhæŋ/ *v.t.* (*p.t.* -hung) surplomber. ● *v.i.* faire saillie.

overhaul¹ /əʊvəˈhɔːl/ *v.t.* réviser.

overhaul² /ˈəʊvəhɔːl/ *n.* révision *f.*

overhead¹ /əʊvəˈhed/ *adv.* au-dessus; (*in sky*) dans le ciel.

overhead² /ˈəʊvəhed/ *a.* aérien. ~s *n. pl.* frais généraux *m. pl.* ~ **projector**, rétroprojecteur *m.*

overhear /əʊvəˈhɪə(r)/ *v.t.* (*p.t.* -heard) surprendre, entendre.

overjoyed /əʊvəˈdʒɔɪd/ *a.* ravi.

overland *a.* /ˈəʊvəlænd/, *adv.* /əʊvəˈlænd/ par voie de terre.

overlap /əʊvəˈlæp/ *v.t./i.* (*p.t.* -lapped) (se) chevaucher.

overleaf /əʊvəˈliːf/ *adv.* au verso.

overload /əʊvəˈləʊd/ *v.t.* surcharger.

overlook /əʊvəˈlʊk/ *v.t.* oublier, négliger; (*of window, house*) donner sur; (*of tower*) dominer.

overly /ˈəʊvəlɪ/ *adv.* excessivement.

overnight /əʊvəˈnaɪt/ *adv.* (pendant) la nuit; (*instantly; fig.*) du jour au lendemain. ● *a.* /ˈəʊvənaɪt/ (*train etc.*) de nuit; (*stay etc.*) d'une nuit; (*fig.*) soudain.

overpay /əʊvəˈpeɪ/ *v.t.* (*p.t.* -paid) (*person*) surpayer.

overpower /əʊvəˈpaʊə(r)/ *v.t.* subjuguer; (*opponent*) maîtriser; (*fig.*)

accabler. **~ing** *a.* irrésistible; (*heat, smell*) accablant.

overpriced /əʊvə'praɪst/ *a.* trop cher.

overrate /əʊvə'reɪt/ *v.t.* surestimer. **~d** /-ɪd/ *a.* surfait.

overreach /əʊvə'riːtʃ/ *v. pr.* **~ o.s.**, trop entreprendre.

overreact /əʊvərɪ'ækt/ *v.i.* réagir excessivement.

overrid|e /əʊvə'raɪd/ *v.t.* (*p.t.* **-rode,** *p.p.* **-ridden**) passer outre à. **~ing** *a.* prépondérant; (*importance*) majeur.

overripe /'əʊvəraɪp/ *a.* trop mûr.

overrule /əʊvə'ruːl/ *v.t.* rejeter.

overrun /əʊvə'rʌn/ *v.t.* (*p.t.* **-ran,** *p.p.* **-run,** *pres. p.* **-running**) envahir; (*a limit*) aller au-delà de. ● *v.i.* (*meeting*) durer plus longtemps que prévu.

overseas /əʊvə'siːz/ *a.* d'outre-mer, étranger. ● *adv.* outre-mer, à l'étranger.

oversee /əʊvə'siː/ *v.t.* (*p.t.* **-saw,** *p.p.* **-seen**) surveiller. **~r** /'əʊvəsɪə(r)/ *n.* contremaître *m.*

overshadow /əʊvə'ʃædəʊ/ *v.t.* (*darken*) assombrir; (*fig.*) éclipser.

overshoot /əʊvə'ʃuːt/ *v.t.* (*p.t.* **-shot**) dépasser.

oversight /'əʊvəsaɪt/ *n.* omission *f.*

oversleep /əʊvə'sliːp/ *v.i.* (*p.t.* **-slept**) se réveiller trop tard.

overt /'əʊvɜːt/ *a.* manifeste.

overtake /əʊvə'teɪk/ *v.t./i.* (*p.t.* **-took,** *p.p.* **-taken**) dépasser; (*vehicle*) doubler, dépasser; (*surprise*) surprendre.

overtax /əʊvə'tæks/ *v.t.* (*strain*) fatiguer; (*taxpayer*) surimposer.

overthrow /əʊvə'θrəʊ/ *v.t.* (*p.t.* **-threw,** *p.p.* **-thrown**) renverser.

overtime /'əʊvətaɪm/ *n.* heures supplémentaires *f. pl.*

overtone /'əʊvətəʊn/ *n.* nuance *f.*

overture /'əʊvətjʊə(r)/ *n.* ouverture *f.*

overturn /əʊvə'tɜːn/ *v.t./i.* (se) renverser.

overweight /əʊvə'weɪt/ *a.* **be ~,** peser trop.

overwhelm /əʊvə'welm/ *v.t.* accabler; (*defeat*) écraser; (*amaze*) bouleverser. **~ing** *a.* accablant; (*victory*) écrasant; (*urge*) irrésistible.

overwork /əʊvə'wɜːk/ *v.t./i.* (se) surmener. ● *n.* surmenage *m.*

overwrought /əʊvə'rɔːt/ *a.* à bout.

ow|e /əʊ/ *v.t.* devoir. **~ing** *a.* dû. **~ing to,** à cause de.

owl /aʊl/ *n.* hibou *m.*

own [1] /əʊn/ *a.* propre. **a house/etc. of one's ~,** sa propre maison/*etc.*, une maison/*etc.* à soi. **get one's ~ back,** (*fam.*) prendre sa revanche. **hold one's ~,** bien se défendre. **on one's ~,** tout seul.

own [2] /əʊn/ *v.t.* posséder. **~ up (to),** (*fam.*) avouer. **~er** *n.* propriétaire *m./f.* **~ership** *n.* possession *f.* (*of, de*); (*right*) propriété *f.*

ox /ɒks/ *n.* (*pl.* **oxen**) bœuf *m.*

oxygen /'ɒksɪdʒən/ *n.* oxygène *m.*

oyster /'ɔɪstə(r)/ *n.* huître *f.*

ozone /'əʊzəʊn/ *n.* ozone *m.* **~ layer,** couche d'ozone *f.*

P

pace /peɪs/ *n.* pas *m.*; (*speed*) allure *f.*; (*room etc.*) arpenter. ● *v.i.* **~ (up and down),** faire les cent pas. **keep ~ with,** suivre.

pacemaker /'peɪsmeɪkə(r)/ *n.* (*med.*) stimulateur cardiaque *m.*

Pacific /pə'sɪfɪk/ *a.* pacifique. ● *n.* **~ (Ocean),** Pacifique *m.*

pacifist /'pæsɪfɪst/ *n.* pacifiste *m./f.*

pacif|y /'pæsɪfaɪ/ *v.t.* (*country*) pacifier; (*person*) apaiser. **~ier** *n.* (*Amer.*) sucette *f.*

pack /pæk/ *n.* paquet *m.*; (*mil.*) sac *m.*; (*of hounds*) meute *f.*; (*of thieves*) bande *f.*; (*of lies*) tissu *m.* ● *v.t.* emballer; (*suitcase*) faire; (*box, room*) remplir; (*press down*) tasser. ● *v.i.* **~ (one's bags),** faire ses valises. **~ into,** (*cram*) (s')entasser dans. **~ off,** expédier. **send ~ing,** envoyer promener. **~ed** *a.* (*crowded*) bondé. **~ed lunch,** repas froid *m.* **~ing** *n.* (*action, material*) emballage *m.* **~ing case,** caisse *f.*

package /'pækɪdʒ/ *n.* paquet *m.* ● *v.t.* empaqueter. **~ deal,** forfait *m.* **~ tour,** voyage organisé *m.*

packet /'pækɪt/ *n.* paquet *m.*

pact /pækt/ *n.* pacte *m.*

pad [1] /pæd/ *n.* bloc(-notes) *m.*; (*for ink*) tampon *m.* **(launching) ~,** rampe (de lancement) *f.* ● *v.t.* (*p.t.* **padded**) rembourrer; (*text: fig.*) délayer. **~ding** *n.* rembourrage *m.*; délayage *m.*

pad [2] /pæd/ *v.i.* (*p.t.* **padded**) (*walk*) marcher à pas feutrés.

paddle [1] /'pædl/ n. pagaie f. ● v.t. ~ a canoe, pagayer. ~-steamer n. bateau à roues m.

paddl|e [2] /'pædl/ v.i. barboter, se mouiller les pieds. ~ing pool, pataugeoire f.

paddock /'pædək/ n. paddock m.

paddy(-field) /'pædɪ(fiːld)/ n. rizière f.

padlock /'pædlɒk/ n. cadenas m. ● v.t. cadenasser.

paediatrician /piːdɪə'trɪʃn/ n. pédiatre m./f.

pagan /'peɪɡən/ a. & n. païen(ne) (m. (f.)).

page [1] /peɪdʒ/ n. (of book etc.) page f.

page [2] /peɪdʒ/ n. (in hotel) chasseur m. (at wedding) page m. ● v.t. (faire) appeler.

pageant /'pædʒənt/ n. spectacle (historique) m. ~ry n. pompe f.

pagoda /pə'ɡəʊdə/ n. pagode f.

paid /peɪd/ see pay. ● a. put ~ to, (fam.) mettre fin à.

pail /peɪl/ n. seau m.

pain /peɪn/ n. douleur f. ~s, efforts m. pl. ● v.t. (grieve) peiner. be in ~, souffrir. take ~s to, se donner du mal pour. ~-killer n. analgésique m. ~less a. indolore.

painful /'peɪnfl/ a. douloureux; (laborious) pénible.

painstaking /'peɪnzteɪkɪŋ/ a. assidu, appliqué.

paint /peɪnt/ n. peinture f. ~s, (in tube, box) couleurs f. pl. ● v.t./i. peindre. ~er n. peintre m. ~ing n. peinture f.

paintbrush /'peɪntbrʌʃ/ n. pinceau m.

paintwork /'peɪntwɜːk/ n. peintures f. pl.

pair /peə(r)/ n. paire f.; (of people) couple m. a ~ of trousers, un pantalon. ● v.i. ~ off, (at dance etc.) former un couple.

pajamas /pə'dʒɑːməz/ n.pl. (Amer.) pyjama m.

Pakistan /pɑːkɪ'stɑːn/ n. Pakistan. m. ~i a. & n. pakistanais(e) (m. (f.)).

pal /pæl/ n. (fam.) copain, -ine m., f.

palace /'pælɪs/ n. palais m.

palat|e /'pælət/ n. (of mouth) palais m. ~able a. agréable au goût.

palatial /pə'leɪʃl/ a. somptueux.

palaver /pə'lɑːvə(r)/ n. (fuss: fam.) histoire(s) f. (pl.).

pale /peɪl/ a. (-er, -est) pâle. ● v.i. pâlir. ~ness n. pâleur f.

Palestin|e /'pælɪstam/ n. Palestine f. ~ian /-'stɪnɪən/ a. & n. palestinien(ne) (m. (f.)).

palette /'pælɪt/ n. palette f.

pall /pɔːl/ v.i. devenir insipide.

pallet /'pælɪt/ n. palette f.

pallid /'pælɪd/ a. pâle.

palm /pɑːm/ n. (of hand) paume f.; (tree) palmier m.; (symbol) palme f. ● v.t. ~ off, (thing) refiler, coller (on, à); (person) coller. P~ Sunday, dimanche des Rameaux m.

palmist /'pɑːmɪst/ n. chiromancien(ne) m. (f.).

palpable /'pælpəbl/ a. manifeste.

palpitat|e /'pælpɪteɪt/ v.i. palpiter. ~ion /-'teɪʃn/ n. palpitation f.

paltry /'pɔːltrɪ/ a. (-ier, -iest) dérisoire, piètre.

pamper /'pæmpə(r)/ v.t. dorloter.

pamphlet /'pæmflɪt/ n. brochure f.

pan /pæn/ n. casserole f.; (for frying) poêle f.; (of lavatory) cuvette f. (p.t. panned) (fam.) critiquer.

panacea /pænə'siːə/ n. panacée f.

panache /pə'næʃ/ n. panache m.

pancake /'pænkeɪk/ n. crêpe f.

pancreas /'pæŋkrɪəs/ n. pancréas m.

panda /'pændə/ n. panda m. ~ car, voiture pie (de la police) f.

pandemonium /pændɪ'məʊnɪəm/ n. tumulte m., chaos m.

pander /'pændə(r)/ v.i. ~ to, (person, taste) flatter bassement.

pane /peɪn/ n. carreau m., vitre f.

panel /'pænl/ n. (of door etc.) panneau m.; (jury) jury m.; (speakers: TV) invités m. pl. (instrument) ~, tableau de bord m. ~ of experts, groupe d'experts m. ~led a. lambrissé. ~ling n. lambrissage m. ~list n. (TV) invité(e) (de tribune) m. (f.).

pang /pæŋ/ n. pincement au cœur m. ~s, (of hunger, death) affres f. pl. ~s of conscience, remords m. pl.

panic /'pænɪk/ n. panique f. ● v.t./ i. (p.t. panicked) (s')affoler, paniquer. ~-stricken a. pris de panique, affolé.

panorama /pænə'rɑːmə/ n. panorama m.

pansy /'pænzɪ/ n. (bot.) pensée f.

pant /pænt/ v.i. haleter.

panther /'pænθə(r)/ n. panthère f.

panties /'pæntɪz/ n. pl. (fam.) slip m., culotte f. (de femme).

pantihose /'pæntɪhəʊz/ n. (Amer.) collant m.

pantomime /'pæntəmaɪm/ *n.* (*show*) spectacle de Noël *m.*; (*mime*) pantomime *f.*

pantry /'pæntrɪ/ *n.* office *m.*

pants /pænts/ *n. pl.* (*underwear*: *fam.*) slip *m.*; (*trousers*: *fam. & Amer.*) pantalon *m.*

papacy /'peɪpəsɪ/ *n.* papauté *f.*

papal /'peɪpl/ *a.* papal.

paper /'peɪpə(r)/ *n.* papier *m.*; (*newspaper*) journal *m.*; (*exam*) épreuve *f.*; (*essay*) exposé *m.*; (*wallpaper*) papier peint *m.* (*identity*) ~s papiers (d'identité) *m. pl.* ● *v.t.* (*room*) tapisser. **on ~**, par écrit. **~-clip** *n.* trombone *m.*

paperback /'peɪpəbæk/ *a. & n.* ~ (book), livre broché *m.*

paperweight /'peɪpəweɪt/ *n.* presse-papiers *m. invar.*

paperwork /'peɪpəwɜːk/ *n.* paperasserie *f.*

paprika /'pæprɪkə/ *n.* paprika *m.*

par /pɑː(r)/ *n.* **be below ~**, ne pas être en forme. **on a ~ with**, à égalité avec.

parable /'pærəbl/ *n.* parabole *f.*

parachut|e /'pærəʃuːt/ *n.* parachute *m.* ● *v.i.* descendre en parachute. **~ist** *n.* parachutiste *m./f.*

parade /pə'reɪd/ *n.* (*procession*) défilé *m.*; (*ceremony, display*) parade *f.*; (*street*) avenue *f.* ● *v.i.* défiler. ● *v.t.* faire parade de.

paradise /'pærədaɪs/ *n.* paradis *m.*

paradox /'pærədɒks/ *n.* paradoxe *m.* **~ical** /-'dɒksɪkl/ *a.* paradoxal.

paraffin /'pærəfɪn/ *n.* pétrole (lampant) *m.*; (*wax*) paraffine *f.*

paragon /'pærəgən/ *n.* modèle *m.*

paragraph /'pærəgrɑːf/ *n.* paragraphe *m.*

parallel /'pærəlel/ *a.* parallèle. ● *n.* (*line*) parallèle *f.*; (*comparison & geog.*) parallèle *m.* ● *v.t.* (*p.t.* **paralleled**) être semblable à; (*match*) égaler.

paralyse /'pærəlaɪz/ *v.t.* paralyser.

paraly|sis /pə'ræləsɪs/ *n.* paralysie *f.* **~tic** /pærə'lɪtɪk/ *a. & n.* paralytique (*m./f.*).

paramedic /pærə'medɪk/ *n.* auxiliaire médical(e) *m.* (*f.*).

parameter /pə'ræmɪtə(r)/ *n.* paramètre *m.*

paramount /'pærəmaʊnt/ *a.* primordial, fondamental.

paranoi|a /pærə'nɔɪə/ *n.* paranoïa *f.* **~d** *a.* paranoïaque; (*fam.*) parano *invar.*

parapet /'pærəpɪt/ *n.* parapet *m.*

paraphernalia /pærəfə'neɪlɪə/ *n.* attirail *m.*, équipement *m.*

paraphrase /'pærəfreɪz/ *n.* paraphrase *f.* ● *v.t.* paraphraser.

parasite /'pærəsaɪt/ *n.* parasite *m.*

parasol /'pærəsɒl/ *n.* ombrelle *f.*; (*on table, at beach*) parasol *m.*

paratrooper /'pærətruːpə(r)/ *n.* (*mil.*) parachutiste *m/f.*

parcel /'pɑːsl/ *n.* colis *m.*, paquet *m.* ● *v.t.* (*p.t.* **parcelled**). **~ out**, diviser en parcelles.

parch /pɑːtʃ/ *v.t.* dessécher. **be ~ed**, (*person*) avoir très soif.

parchment /'pɑːtʃmənt/ *n.* parchemin *m.*

pardon /'pɑːdn/ *n.* pardon *m.*; (*jurid.*) grâce *m.* ● *v.t.* (*p.t.* **pardoned**) pardonner (s.o. for sth., qch. à qn.); gracier. **I beg your ~**, pardon.

pare /peə(r)/ *v.t.* (*clip*) rogner; (*peel*) éplucher.

parent /'peərənt/ *n.* père *m.*, mère *f.* **~s**, parents *m. pl.* **~al** /pə'rentl/ *a.* des parents. **~hood** *n.* l'état de parent *m.*

parenthesis /pə'renθəsɪs/ *n.* (*pl.* -**theses** /-siːz/) parenthèse *f.*

Paris /'pærɪs/ *n.* Paris *m./f.* **~ian** /pə'rɪzɪən, Amer.* pə'riːʒn/ *a. & n.* parisien(ne) (*m.* (*f.*)).

parish /'pærɪʃ/ *n.* (*relig.*) paroisse *f.*; (*municipal*) commune *f.* **~ioner** /pə'rɪʃənə(r)/ *n.* paroissien(ne) *m.* (*f.*).

parity /'pærətɪ/ *n.* parité *f.*

park /pɑːk/ *n.* parc *m.* ● *v.t./i.* (se) garer; (*remain parked*) stationner. **~ing-lot** *n.* (*Amer.*) parking *m.* **~ing-meter** *n.* parcmètre *m.* **~ing ticket**, procès-verbal *m.*

parka /'pɑːkə/ *n.* parka *m./f.*

parlance /'pɑːləns/ *n.* langage *m.*

parliament /'pɑːləmənt/ *n.* parlement *m.* **~ary** /-'mentrɪ/ *a.* parlementaire.

parlour /'pɑːlə(r)/ *n.* (*Amer.*) **parlor** salon *m.*

parochial /pə'rəʊkɪəl/ *a.* (*relig.*) paroissial; (*fig.*) borné, provincial.

parody /'pærədɪ/ *n.* parodie *f.* ● *v.t.* parodier.

parole /pə'rəʊl/ *n.* **on ~**, en liberté conditionnelle.

parquet /'pɑːkeɪ/ *n.* parquet *m.*

parrot /'pærət/ *n.* perroquet *m.*

parry /'pærɪ/ v.t. (sport) parer; (question etc.) esquiver. ● n. parade f.

parsimonious /pɑːsɪ'məʊnɪəs/ a. parcimonieux.

parsley /'pɑːslɪ/ n. persil m.

parsnip /'pɑːsnɪp/ n. panais m.

parson /'pɑːsn/ n. pasteur m.

part /pɑːt/ n. partie f.; (of serial) épisode m.; (of machine) pièce f.; (theatre) rôle m.; (side in dispute) parti m. ● a. partiel. ● adv. en partie. ● v.t./i. (separate) (se) séparer. in ~, en partie. on the ~ of, de la part de. ~-exchange n. reprise f. ~ of speech, catégorie grammaticale f. ~-time a. & adv. à temps partiel. ~ with, se séparer de. take ~ in, participer à. in these ~s, dans la région, dans le coin.

partake /pɑː'teɪk/ v.i. (p.t. -took, p.p. -taken) participer (in, à).

partial /'pɑːʃl/ a. partiel; (biased) partial. be ~ to, avoir une prédilection pour. ~ity /-ɪ'ælətɪ/ n. (bias) partialité f.; (fondness) prédilection f. ~ly adv. partiellement.

particip|ate /pɑː'tɪsɪpeɪt/ v.i. participer (in, à). ~ant n. participant(e) m. (f.). ~ation /-'peɪʃn/ n. participation f.

participle /'pɑːtɪsɪpl/ n. participe m.

particle /'pɑːtɪkl/ n. particule f.

particular /pə'tɪkjʊlə(r)/ a. particulier; (fussy) difficile; (careful) méticuleux. that ~ man, cet homme-là en particulier. ~s n. pl. détails m. pl. in ~, en particulier. ~ly adv. particulièrement.

parting /'pɑːtɪŋ/ n. séparation f.; (in hair) raie f. ● a. d'adieu.

partisan /pɑː'tɪzæn, Amer. 'pɑːtɪzn/ n. partisan(e) m. (f.).

partition /pɑː'tɪʃn/ n. (of room) cloison f.; (pol.) partage m., partition f. ● v.t. (room) cloisonner; (country) partager.

partly /'pɑːtlɪ/ adv. en partie.

partner /'pɑːtnə(r)/ n. associé(e) m. (f.); (sport) partenaire m./f. ~ship n. association f.

partridge /'pɑːtrɪdʒ/ n. perdrix f.

party /'pɑːtɪ/ n. fête f.; (formal) réception f.; (for young people) boum f.; (group) groupe m., équipe f.; (pol.) parti m.; (jurid.) partie f. ~ line, (telephone) ligne commune f.

pass /pɑːs/ v.t./i. (p.t. passed) passer; (overtake) dépasser; (in exam) être reçu (à); (approve) accepter, autori-

ser; (remark) faire; (judgement) prononcer; (law, bill) voter. ~ (by), (building) passer devant; (person) croiser. ● n. (permit) laissez-passer m. invar.; (ticket) carte (d'abonnement) f.; (geog.) col m.; (sport) passe f. ~ (mark), (in exam) moyenne f. make a ~ at, (fam.) faire des avances à. ~ away, mourir. ~ out or round, distribuer. ~ out, (faint: fam.) s'évanouir. ~ over, (overlook) passer sur. ~ up, (forego: fam.) laisser passer.

passable /'pɑːsəbl/ a. (adequate) passable; (road) praticable.

passage /'pæsɪdʒ/ n. (way through, text, etc.) passage m.; (voyage) traversée f.; (corridor) couloir m.

passenger /'pæsɪndʒə(r)/ n. passag|er, -ère m., f.; (in train) voyageu|r, -se m., f.

passer-by /pɑːsə'baɪ/ n. (pl. passers-by) passant(e) m. (f.).

passing /'pɑːsɪŋ/ a. (fleeting) fugitif, passager.

passion /'pæʃn/ n. passion f. ~ate a. passionné. ~ately adv. passionnément.

passive /'pæsɪv/ a. passif. ~ness n. passivité f.

Passover /'pɑːsəʊvə(r)/ n. Pâque f.

passport /'pɑːspɔːt/ n. passeport m.

password /'pɑːswɜːd/ n. mot de passe m.

past /pɑːst/ a. passé; (former) ancien. ● n. passé m. ● prep. au-delà de; (in front of) devant. ● adv. devant. the ~ months, ces derniers mois. ~ midnight, minuit passé. 10 ~ 6, six heures dix.

pasta /'pæstə/ n. pâtes f. pl.

paste /peɪst/ n. (glue) colle f.; (dough) pâte f.; (of fish, meat) pâté m.; (jewellery) strass m. ● v.t. coller.

pastel /'pæstl/ n. pastel m. ● a. pastel invar.

pasteurize /'pæstʃəraɪz/ v.t. pasteuriser.

pastiche /pæ'stiːʃ/ n. pastiche m.

pastille /'pæstɪl/ n. pastille f.

pastime /'pɑːstaɪm/ n. passetemps m. invar.

pastoral /'pɑːstərəl/ a. pastoral.

pastry /'peɪstrɪ/ n. (dough) pâte f.; (tart) pâtisserie f.

pasture /'pɑːstʃə(r)/ n. pâturage m.

pasty[1] /'pæstɪ/ n. petit pâté m.

pasty[2] /'peɪstɪ/ a. pâteux.

pat /pæt/ v.t. (p.t. **patted**) tapoter. ● n. petite tape f. ● adv. & a. à propos; (ready) tout prêt.

patch /pætʃ/ n. pièce f.; (over eye) bandeau m.; (spot) tache f.; (of vegetables) carré m. ● v.t. ~ up, rapiécer; (fig.) régler. bad ~, période de difficile f. not be a ~ on, ne pas arriver à la cheville de. ~y a. inégal.

patchwork /'pætʃwɜːk/ n. patchwork m.

pâté /'pæteɪ/ n. pâté m.

patent /'peɪtnt/ a. patent. ● n. brevet (d'invention) m. ● v.t. breveter. ~ leather, cuir verni m. ~ly adv. manifestement.

paternal /pə'tɜːnl/ a. paternel.

paternity /pə'tɜːnətɪ/ n. paternité f.

path /pɑːθ/ n. (pl. -s /pɑːðz/) sentier m., chemin m.; (in park) allée f.; (of rocket) trajectoire f.

pathetic /pə'θetɪk/ a. pitoyable; (bad: fam.) minable.

pathology /pə'θɒlədʒɪ/ n. pathologie f.

pathos /'peɪθɒs/ n. pathétique m.

patience /'peɪʃns/ n. patience f.

patient /'peɪʃnt/ a. patient. ● n. malade m./f., patient(e) m. (f.). ~ly adv. patiemment.

patio /'pætɪəʊ/ n. (pl. -os) patio m.

patriot /'pætrɪət, 'peɪtrɪət/ n. patriote m./f. ~ic /-'ɒtɪk/ a. patriotique; (person) patriote. ~ism n. patriotisme m.

patrol /pə'trəʊl/ n. patrouille f. ● v.t./i. patrouiller (dans). ~ car, voiture de police f.

patrolman /pə'trəʊlmən/ n. (pl. -men /-men/) (Amer.) agent de police m.

patron /'peɪtrən/ n. (of the arts) mécène m. (customer) client(e) m. (f.). ~ saint, saint(e) patron(ne) m. (f.).

patron|age /'pætrənɪdʒ/ n. clientèle f.; (support) patronage m. ~ize v.t. être client de; (fig.) traiter avec condescendance.

patter[1] /'pætə(r)/ n. (of steps) bruit m.; (of rain) crépitement m.

patter[2] /'pætə(r)/ n. (speech) baratin m.

pattern /'pætn/ n. motif m., dessin m.; (for sewing) patron m.; (procedure, type) schéma m.; (example) exemple m.

paunch /pɔːntʃ/ n. panse f.

pauper /'pɔːpə(r)/ n. indigent(e) m. (f.), pauvre m., pauvresse f.

pause /pɔːz/ n. pause f. ● v.i. faire une pause; (hesitate) hésiter.

pav|e /peɪv/ v.t. paver. ~e the way, ouvrir la voie (for, à). ~ing-stone n. pavé m.

pavement /'peɪvmənt/ n. trottoir m.; (Amer.) chaussée f.

pavilion /pə'vɪljən/ n. pavillon m.

paw /pɔː/ n. patte f. ● v.t. (of animal) donner des coups de patte à; (touch: fam.) tripoter.

pawn[1] /pɔːn/ n. (chess & fig.) pion m.

pawn[2] /pɔːn/ v.t. mettre en gage. ● n. in ~, en gage. ~-shop n. mont-de-piété m.

pawnbroker /'pɔːnbrəʊkə(r)/ n. prêteur sur gages m.

pay /peɪ/ v.t./i. (p.t. **paid**) payer; (yield: comm.) rapporter; (compliment, visit) faire. ● n. salaire m., paie f. in the ~ of, à la solde de. ~ attention, faire attention (to, à). ~ back, rembourser. ~ for, payer. ~ homage, rendre hommage (to, à). ~ in, verser (to, à). ~ off, (finir de) payer; (succeed: fam.) être payant. ~ out, payer, verser.

payable /'peɪəbl/ a. payable.

payment /'peɪmənt/ n. paiement m.; (regular) versement m. (reward) récompense f.

payroll /'peɪrəʊl/ n. registre du personnel m. be on the ~ of, être membre du personnel de.

pea /piː/ n. (petit) pois m. ~-shooter n. sarbacane f.

peace /piːs/ n. paix f. ~ of mind, tranquillité d'esprit f. ~able a. pacifique.

peaceful /'piːsfl/ a. paisible; (intention, measure) pacifique.

peacemaker /'piːsmeɪkə(r)/ n. concilia|teur, -trice m., f.

peach /piːtʃ/ n. pêche f.

peacock /'piːkɒk/ n. paon m.

peak /piːk/ n. sommet m.; (of mountain) pic m.; (maximum) maximum m. ~ hours, heures de pointe f. pl. ~ed cap, casquette f.

peaky /'piːkɪ/ a. (pale) pâlot; (puny) chétif; (ill) patraque.

peal /piːl/ n. (of bells) carillon m.; (of laughter) éclat m.

peanut /'piːnʌt/ n. cacahuète f. ~s, (money: sl.) une bagatelle.

pear /peə(r)/ n. poire f.

pearl /pɜːl/ n. perle f. ~y a. nacré.

peasant /'peznt/ n. paysan(ne) m. (f.).

peat /pi:t/ n. tourbe f.

pebble /'pebl/ n. caillou m.; (on beach) galet m.

peck /pek/ v.t./i. (food etc.) picorer; (attack) donner des coups de bec (à). ● n. coup de bec m. a ~ on the cheek, une bise.

peckish /'pekɪʃ/ a. be ~, (fam.) avoir faim.

peculiar /pɪ'kju:lɪə(r)/ a. (odd) bizarre; (special) particulier (to, à). ~ity /-'ærətɪ/ n. bizarrerie f.

pedal /'pedl/ n. pédale f. ● v.i. pédaler.

pedantic /pɪ'dæntɪk/ a. pédant.

peddle /'pedl/ v.t. colporter; (drugs) revendre.

pedestal /'pedɪstl/ n. piédestal m.

pedestrian /pɪ'destrɪən/ n. piéton m. ● a. (precinct, street) piétonnier; (fig.) prosaïque. ~ crossing, passage piétons m.

pedigree /'pedɪgri:/ n. (of person) ascendance f.; (of animal) pedigree m. ● a. (cattle etc.) de race.

pedlar /'pedlə(r)/ n. camelot m.; (door-to-door) colporteu|r, -se m., f.

pee /pi:/ v.i. (fam.) faire pipi.

peek /pi:k/ v.i. & n. = peep¹.

peel /pi:l/ n. épluchure(s) f. (pl.); (of orange) écorce f. ● v.t. (fruit, vegetables) éplucher. ● v.i. (of skin) peler; (of paint) s'écailler. ~ings n. pl. épluchures f. pl.

peep¹ /pi:p/ v.i. jeter un coup d'œil (furtif) (at, à). ● n. coup d'œil (furtif) m. ~-hole n. judas m. P~ing Tom, voyeur m.

peep² /pi:p/ v.i. (chirp) pépier.

peer¹ /pɪə(r)/ v.i. ~ (at), regarder attentivement, scruter.

peer² /pɪə(r)/ n. (equal, noble) pair m. ~age n. pairie f.

peeved /pi:vd/ a. (sl.) irrité.

peevish /'pi:vɪʃ/ a. grincheux.

peg /peg/ n. cheville f.; (for clothes) pince à linge f.; (to hang coats etc.) patère f.; (for tent) piquet m. ● v.t. (p.t. pegged) (prices) stabiliser. buy off the ~, acheter en prêt-à-porter.

pejorative /pɪ'dʒɒrətɪv/ a. péjoratif.

pelican /'pelɪkən/ n. pélican m. ~ crossing, passage clouté (avec feux de signalisation).

pellet /'pelɪt/ n. (round mass) boulette f.; (for gun) plomb m.

pelt¹ /pelt/ n. (skin) peau f.

pelt² /pelt/ v.t. bombarder (with, de). ● v.i. pleuvoir à torrents.

pelvis /'pelvɪs/ n. (anat.) bassin m.

pen¹ /pen/ n. (for sheep etc.) enclos m.; (for baby, cattle) parc m.

pen² /pen/ n. stylo m.; (to be dipped in ink) plume f. ● v.t. (p.t. penned) écrire. ~-friend n. correspondant(e) m. (f.). ~-name n. pseudonyme m.

penal /'pi:nl/ a. pénal. ~ize v.t. pénaliser; (fig.) handicaper.

penalty /'penltɪ/ n. peine f.; (fine) amende f.; (sport) pénalité f.

penance /'penəns/ n. pénitence f.

pence /pens/ see penny.

pencil /'pensl/ n. crayon m. ● v.t. (p.t. pencilled) crayonner. ~ in, noter provisoirement. ~-sharpener n. taille-crayon(s) m.

pendant /'pendənt/ n. pendentif m.

pending /'pendɪŋ/ a. en suspens. ● prep. (until) en attendant.

pendulum /'pendjʊləm/ n. pendule m.; (of clock) balancier m.

penetrat|e /'penɪtreɪt/ v.t. (enter) pénétrer dans; (understand, permeate) pénétrer. ● v.i. pénétrer. ~ing a. pénétrant. ~ion /-'treɪʃn/ n. pénétration f.

penguin /'peŋgwɪn/ n. manchot m., pingouin m.

penicillin /penɪ'sɪlɪn/ n. pénicilline f.

peninsula /pə'nɪnsjʊlə/ n. péninsule f.

penis /'pi:nɪs/ n. pénis m.

penitent /'penɪtənt/ a. & n. pénitent(e) (m. (f.)). ~ce n. pénitence f.

penitentiary /penɪ'tenʃərɪ/ n. (Amer.) prison f., pénitencier m.

penknife /'pennaɪf/ n. (pl. -knives) canif m.

pennant /'penənt/ n. flamme f.

penniless /'penɪlɪs/ a. sans le sou.

penny /'penɪ/ n. (pl. pennies or pence) penny m.; (fig.) sou m.

pension /'penʃn/ n. pension f.; (for retirement) retraite f. ● v.t. ~ off, mettre à la retraite. ~ scheme, caisse de retraite f. ~able a. qui a droit à une retraite. ~er n. (old-age) ~er, retraité(e) m. (f.), personne âgée f.

pensive /'pensɪv/ a. pensif.

Pentecost /'pentɪkɒst/ n. Pentecôte f. ~al a. pentecôtiste.

penthouse /'penthaʊs/ n. appartement de luxe m. (sur le toit d'un immeuble).

pent-up /pent'ʌp/ a. refoulé.

penultimate /pen'ʌltɪmət/ a. avant-dernier.

people /'piːpl/ n. pl. gens m. pl., personnes f. pl. ● n. peuple m. ● v.t. peupler. **English**/*etc.* ~, les Anglais/ *etc. m. pl.* ~ **say**, on dit.

pep /pep/ n. entrain m. ● v.t. ~ **up**, donner de l'entrain à. ~ **talk**, discours d'encouragement m.

pepper /'pepə(r)/ n. poivre m.; (*vegetable*) poivron m. ● v.t. (*culin.*) poivrer. ~**y** a. poivré.

peppermint /'pepəmɪnt/ n. (*plant*) menthe poivrée f.; (*sweet*) bonbon à la menthe m.

per /pɜː(r)/ prep. par. ~ **annum**, par an. ~ **cent**, pour cent. ~ **kilo**/*etc.*, le kilo/*etc.* **ten km**. ~ **hour**, dix km à l'heure.

perceive /pə'siːv/ v.t. percevoir; (*notice*) s'apercevoir de. ~ **that**, s'apercevoir que.

percentage /pə'sentɪdʒ/ n. pourcentage m.

perceptible /pə'septəbl/ a. perceptible.

percept|ion /pə'sepʃn/ n. perception f. ~**ive** /-tɪv/ a. pénétrant.

perch /pɜːtʃ/ n. (*of bird*) perchoir m. ● v.i. (se) percher.

percolat|e /'pɜːkəleɪt/ v.t. passer. ● v.i. filtrer. ~**or** n. cafetière f.

percussion /pə'kʌʃn/ n. percussion f.

peremptory /pə'remptərɪ/ a. péremptoire.

perennial /pə'renɪəl/ a. perpétuel; (*plant*) vivace.

perfect[1] /'pɜːfɪkt/ a. parfait. ~**ly** adv. parfaitement.

perfect[2] /pə'fekt/ v.t. parfaire, mettre au point. ~**ion** /-kʃn/ n. perfection f. **to** ~**ion**, à la perfection. ~**ionist** /-kʃənɪst/ n. perfectionniste m./f.

perforat|e /'pɜːfəreɪt/ v.t. perforer. ~**ion** /-'reɪʃn/ n. perforation f.; (*line of holes*) pointillé m.

perform /pə'fɔːm/ v.t. exécuter, faire; (*a function*) remplir; (*mus., theatre*) interpréter, jouer. ● v.i. jouer; (*behave, function*) se comporter. ~**ance** n. exécution f.; interprétation f.; (*of car, team*) performance f.; (*show*) représentation f.; séance f.; (*fuss*) histoire f. ~**er** n. artiste m./f.

perfume /'pɜːfjuːm/ n. parfum m.

perfunctory /pə'fʌŋktərɪ/ a. négligent, superficiel.

perhaps /pə'hæps/ adv. peut-être.

peril /'perəl/ n. péril m. ~**ous** a. périlleux.

perimeter /pə'rɪmɪtə(r)/ n. périmètre m.

period /'pɪərɪəd/ n. période f., époque f.; (*era*) époque f.; (*lesson*) cours m.; (*gram.*) point m.; (*med.*) règles f. pl. ● a. d'époque. ~**ic** /-'ɒdɪk/ a. périodique. ~**ically** /-'ɒdɪklɪ/ adv. périodiquement.

periodical /pɪərɪ'ɒdɪkl/ n. périodique m.

peripher|y /pə'rɪfərɪ/ n. périphérie f. ~**al** a. périphérique; (*of lesser importance:* fig.) accessoire; n. (*comput.*) périphérique m.

periscope /'perɪskəʊp/ n. périscope m.

perish /'perɪʃ/ v.i. périr; (*rot*) se détériorer. ~**able** a. périssable.

perjur|e /'pɜːdʒə(r)/ v. pr. ~**e o.s.**, se parjurer. ~**y** n. parjure m.

perk[1] /pɜːk/ v.t./i. ~ **up**, (*fam.*) (se) remonter. ~**y** a. (*fam.*) gai.

perk[2] /pɜːk/ n. (*fam.*) avantage m.

perm /pɜːm/ n. permanente f. ● v.t. **have one's hair** ~**ed**, se faire faire une permanente.

permanen|t /'pɜːmənənt/ a. permanent. ~**ce** n. permanence f. ~**tly** adv. à titre permanent.

permeable /'pɜːmɪəbl/ a. perméable.

permeate /'pɜːmɪeɪt/ v.t. imprégner, se répandre dans.

permissible /pə'mɪsəbl/ a. permis.

permission /pə'mɪʃn/ n. permission f.

permissive /pə'mɪsɪv/ a. tolérant, laxiste. ~**ness** n. laxisme m.

permit[1] /pə'mɪt/ v.t. (*p.t.* **permitted**) permettre (**s.o. to**, à qn. de), autoriser (**s.o. to**, qn. à).

permit[2] /'pɜːmɪt/ n. permis m.; (*pass*) laissez-passer m. invar.

permutation /pɜːmjʊ'teɪʃn/ n. permutation f.

pernicious /pə'nɪʃəs/ a. nocif, pernicieux; (*med.*) pernicieux.

peroxide /pə'rɒksaɪd/ n. eau oxygénée f.

perpendicular /pɜːpən'dɪkjʊlə(r)/ a. & n. perpendiculaire (f.).

perpetrat|e /'pɜːpɪtreɪt/ v.t. perpétrer. ~**or** n. auteur m.

perpetual /pə'petʃʊəl/ a. perpétuel.

perpetuate /pə'petʃʊeɪt/ v.t. perpétuer.

perplex /pə'pleks/ v.t. rendre perplexe. ~ed a. perplexe. ~ing a. déroutant. ~ity n. perplexité f.

persecut|e /'pɜ:sɪkju:t/ v.t. persécuter. ~ion /-'kju:ʃn/ n. persécution f.

persever|e /pɜ:sɪ'vɪə(r)/ v.i. persévérer. ~ance n. persévérance f.

Persian /'pɜ:ʃn/ a. & n. (lang.) persan (m.). ~ **Gulf**, golfe persique m.

persist /pə'sɪst/ v.i. persister (**in** doing, à faire). ~ence n. persistance f. ~ent a. (cough, snow, etc.) persistant; (obstinate) obstiné; (continual) continuel. ~ently adv. avec persistance.

person /'pɜ:sn/ n. personne f. **in ~**, en personne. ~able a. beau.

personal /'pɜ:sənl/ a. personnel; (hygiene, habits) intime; (secretary) particulier. ~ly adv. personnellement. ~ **stereo**, baladeur m.

personality /pɜ:sə'næləti/ n. personnalité f.; (on TV) vedette f.

personify /pə'sɒnɪfaɪ/ v.t. personnifier.

personnel /pɜ:sə'nel/ n. personnel m.

perspective /pə'spektɪv/ n. perspective f.

Perspex /'pɜ:speks/ n. (P.) plexiglas m. (P.).

perspir|e /pə'spaɪə(r)/ v.i. transpirer. ~ation /-ə'reɪʃn/ n. transpiration f.

persua|de /pə'sweɪd/ v.t. persuader (**to**, de). ~sion /-eɪʒn/ n. persuasion f.

persuasive /pə'sweɪsɪv/ a. (person, speech, etc.) persuasif. ~ly adv. d'une manière persuasive.

pert /pɜ:t/ a. (saucy) impertinent; (lively) plein d'entrain. ~ly adv. avec impertinence.

pertain /pə'teɪn/ v.i. ~ **to**, se rapporter à.

pertinent /'pɜ:tɪnənt/ a. pertinent. ~ly adv. pertinemment.

perturb /pə'tɜ:b/ v.t. troubler.

Peru /pə'ru:/ n. Pérou m. ~vian a. & n. péruvien(ne) (m. (f.)).

peruse /pə'ru:z/ v.t. lire (attentivement). ~al n. lecture f.

perva|de /pə'veɪd/ v.t. imprégner, envahir. ~sive a. (mood, dust) envahissant.

pervers|e /pə'vɜ:s/ a. (stubborn) entêté; (wicked) pervers. ~ity n. perversité f.

pervert[1] /pə'vɜ:t/ v.t. pervertir.

~sion n. perversion f.

pervert[2] /'pɜ:vɜ:t/ n. perverti(e) m. (f.), dépravé(e) m. (f.).

peseta /pə'seɪtə/ n. peseta f.

pessimis|t /'pesɪmɪst/ n. pessimiste m./f. ~m /-zəm/ n. pessimisme m. ~tic /-'mɪstɪk/ a. pessimiste. ~tically /-'mɪstɪklɪ/ adv. avec pessimisme.

pest /pest/ n. insecte or animal nuisible m.; (person: fam.) enquiquineu|r, -se m., f.

pester /'pestə(r)/ v.t. harceler.

pesticide /'pestɪsaɪd/ n. pesticide m., insecticide m.

pet /pet/ n. animal (domestique) m.; (favourite) chouchou(te) m. (f.). ● a. (tame) apprivoisé. ● v.t. (p.t. petted) caresser; (sexually) peloter. ~ **hate**, bête noire f. ~ **name**, diminutif m.

petal /'petl/ n. pétale m.

peter /'pi:tə(r)/ v.i. ~ **out**, (supplies) s'épuiser; (road) finir.

petite /pə'ti:t/ a. (woman) menue.

petition /pɪ'tɪʃn/ n. pétition f. ● v.t. adresser une pétition à.

petrify /'petrɪfaɪ/ v.t. pétrifier; (scare: fig.) pétrifier de peur.

petrol /'petrəl/ n. essence f. ~ **bomb**, cocktail molotov m. ~ **station**, station-service f. ~ **tank**, réservoir d'essence m.

petroleum /pɪ'trəʊlɪəm/ n. pétrole m.

petticoat /'petɪkəʊt/ n. jupon m.

petty /'petɪ/ a. (-ier, -iest) (minor) petit; (mean) mesquin. ~ **cash**, petite caisse f.

petulan|t /'petjʊlənt/ a. irritable. ~ce n. irritabilité f.

pew /pju:/ n. banc d'église) m.

pewter /'pju:tə(r)/ n. étain m.

phallic /'fælɪk/ a. phallique.

phantom /'fæntəm/ n. fantôme m.

pharmaceutical /fɑ:mə'sju:tɪkl/ a. pharmaceutique.

pharmac|y /'fɑ:məsɪ/ n. pharmacie f. ~ist n. pharmacien(ne) m. (f.).

pharyngitis /færɪn'dʒaɪtɪs/ n. pharyngite f.

phase /feɪz/ n. phase f. ● v.t. ~ **in/out**, introduire/retirer progressivement.

pheasant /'feznt/ n. faisan m.

phenomen|on /fɪ'nɒmɪnən/ n. (pl. -ena) phénomène m. ~al a. phénoménal.

phew /fju:/ int. ouf.

phial /ˈfaɪəl/ n. fiole f.

philanderer /fɪˈlændərə(r)/ n. coureur (de femmes) m.

philanthrop|ist /fɪˈlænθrəpɪst/ n. philanthrope m./f. ~**ic** /-ənˈθrɒpɪk/ a. philanthropique.

philatel|y /fɪˈlætəlɪ/ n. philatélie f. ~**ist** n. philatéliste m./f.

philharmonic /fɪlaːˈmɒnɪk/ a. philharmonique.

Philippines /ˈfɪlɪpiːnz/ n. pl. the ~, les Philippines f. pl.

philistine /ˈfɪlɪstaɪn, Amer. ˈfɪlɪstiːn/ n. philistin m.

philosoph|y /fɪˈlɒsəfɪ/ n. philosophie f. ~**er** n. philosophe m./f. ~**ical** /-əˈsɒfɪkl/ a. philosophique; (resigned) philosophe.

phlegm /flem/ n. (med.) mucosité f.

phlegmatic /flegˈmætɪk/ a. flegmatique.

phobia /ˈfəʊbɪə/ n. phobie f.

phone /fəʊn/ n. téléphone m. ● v.t. (person) téléphoner à; (message) téléphoner. ● v.i. téléphoner. ~ **back**, rappeler. **on the** ~, au téléphone. ~ **book**, annuaire m. ~ **box**, ~ **booth**, cabine téléphonique f. ~ **call**, coup de fil m. ~**-in** n. émission à ligne ouverte f.

phonecard /ˈfəʊnkaːd/ n. télécarte f.

phonetic /fəˈnetɪk/ a. phonétique.

phoney /ˈfəʊnɪ/ a. (**-ier, -iest**) (sl.) faux. ● n. (person: sl.) charlatan m. **it's a** ~, (sl.) c'est faux.

phosphate /ˈfɒsfeɪt/ n. phosphate m.

phosphorus /ˈfɒsfərəs/ n. phosphore m.

photo /ˈfəʊtəʊ/ n. (pl. -os) (fam.) photo f.

photocop|y /ˈfəʊtəʊkɒpɪ/ n. photocopie f. ● v.t. photocopier. ~**ier** n. photocopieuse f.

photogenic /fəʊtəʊˈdʒenɪk/ a. photogénique.

photograph /ˈfəʊtəgraːf/ n. photographie f. ● v.t. photographier. ~**er** /fəˈtɒgrəfə(r)/ n. photographe m./f. ~**ic** /-ˈgræfɪk/ a. photographique. ~**y** /fəˈtɒgrəfɪ/ n. (activity) photographie f.

phrase /freɪz/ n. expression f.; (idiom & gram.) locution f. ● v.t. exprimer, formuler. ~**-book** n. guide de conversation m.

physical /ˈfɪzɪkl/ a. physique. ~**ly** adv. physiquement.

physician /fɪˈzɪʃn/ n. médecin m.

physicist /ˈfɪzɪsɪst/ n. physicien(ne) m. (f.).

physics /ˈfɪzɪks/ n. physique f.

physiology /fɪzɪˈɒlədʒɪ/ n. physiologie f.

physiotherap|y /fɪzɪəʊˈθerəpɪ/ n. kinésithérapie f. ~**ist** n. kinésithérapeute m./f.

physique /fɪˈziːk/ n. constitution f.; (appearance) physique m.

pian|o /pɪˈænəʊ/ n. (pl. -os) piano m. ~**ist** /ˈpɪənɪst/ n. pianiste m./f.

piazza /pɪˈætsə/ n. (square) place f.

pick [1] /pɪk/ (tool) n. pioche f.

pick [2] /pɪk/ v.t. (flower etc.) cueillir; (lock) crocheter; (nose) se curer; (pockets) faire. ~ (**off**), enlever. ● n. choix m.; (best) meilleur(e) m. (f.). ~ **a quarrel with**, chercher querelle à. ~ **holes in**, relever les défauts de. **the** ~ **of**, ce qu'il y a de mieux dans. ~ **off**, (mil.) abattre un à un. ~ **on**, harceler. ~ **out**, choisir; (identify) distinguer. ~ **up** v.t. ramasser; (sth. fallen) relever; (weight) soulever; (habit, passenger, speed, etc.) prendre; (learn) apprendre; v.i. s'améliorer. ~**-me-up** n. remontant m. ~**-up** n. partenaire de rencontre m./f.; (truck, stylus-holder) pick-up m.

pickaxe /ˈpɪkæks/ n. pioche f.

picket /ˈpɪkɪt/ n. (single striker) gréviste m./f.; (stake) piquet m. ~ (**line**), piquet de grève m. ● v.t. (p.t. **picketed**) mettre un piquet de grève devant.

pickings /ˈpɪkɪŋz/ n. pl. restes m. pl.

pickle /ˈpɪkl/ n. vinaigre m.; (brine) saumure f. ~**s**, pickles m. pl.; (Amer.) concombres m.pl. ● v.t. conserver dans du vinaigre or de la saumure. **in a** ~, (fam.) dans le pétrin.

pickpocket /ˈpɪkpɒkɪt/ n. (thief) pickpocket m.

picnic /ˈpɪknɪk/ n. pique-nique m. ● v.i. (p.t. **picnicked**) piqueniquer.

pictorial /pɪkˈtɔːrɪəl/ a. illustré.

picture /ˈpɪktʃə(r)/ n. image f.; (painting) tableau m.; (photograph) photo f.; (drawing) dessin m.; (film) film m.; (fig.) description f., tableau m. ● v.t. s'imaginer; (describe) dépeindre. **the** ~**s**, (cinema) le cinéma. ~ **book**, livre d'images m.

picturesque /pɪktʃəˈresk/ a. pittoresque.

piddling /'pɪdlɪŋ/ a. (fam.) dérisoire.

pidgin /'pɪdʒɪn/ a. ~ English, pidgin m.

pie /paɪ/ n. tarte f.; (of meat) pâté en croûte m. ~ chart, camembert m.

piebald /'paɪbɔːld/ a. pie invar.

piece /piːs/ n. morceau m.; (of currency, machine, etc.) pièce f. ● v.t. ~ (together), (r)assembler. a ~ of advice/furniture/etc., un conseil/meuble/etc. ~-work n. travail à la pièce m. go to ~s, (fam.) s'effondrer. take to ~s, démonter.

piecemeal /'piːsmiːl/ a. par bribes.

pier /pɪə(r)/ n. (promenade) jetée f.

pierce /pɪəs/ v.t. percer. ~ing a. perçant; (cold) glacial.

piety /'paɪətɪ/ n. piété f.

piffl|e /'pɪfl/ n. (sl.) fadaises f. pl. ~ing a. (sl.) insignifiant.

pig /pɪg/ n. cochon m. ~-headed a. entêté.

pigeon /'pɪdʒɪn/ n. pigeon m. ~-hole n. casier m.; v.t. classer.

piggy /'pɪgɪ/ a. porcin; (greedy: fam.) goinfre. ~-back adv. sur le dos. ~ bank, tirelire f.

pigment /'pɪgmənt/ n. pigment m. ~ation /-en'teɪʃn/ n. pigmentation f.

pigsty /'pɪgstaɪ/ n. porcherie f.

pigtail /'pɪgteɪl/ n. natte f.

pike /paɪk/ n. invar. (fish) brochet m.

pilchard /'pɪltʃəd/ n. pilchard m.

pile /paɪl/ n. pile f., tas m.; (of carpet) poils m.pl. ● v.t. ~ (up), (stack) empiler. ● v.i. ~ into, s'empiler dans. ~ up, (accumulate) (s')accumuler. a ~ of, (fam.) un tas de. ~-up n. (auto.) carambolage m.

piles /paɪlz/ n. pl. (fam.) hémorroïdes f. pl.

pilfer /'pɪlfə(r)/ v.t. chaparder. ~age n. chapardage m.

pilgrim /'pɪlgrɪm/ n. pèlerin m. ~age n. pèlerinage m.

pill /pɪl/ n. pilule f.

pillage /'pɪlɪdʒ/ n. pillage m. ● v.t. piller. ● v.i. se livrer au pillage.

pillar /'pɪlə(r)/ n. pilier m. ~-box n. boîte à or aux lettres f.

pillion /'pɪljən/ n. siège arrière m. ride ~, monter derrière.

pillory /'pɪlərɪ/ n. pilori m.

pillow /'pɪləʊ/ n. oreiller m.

pillowcase /'pɪləʊkeɪs/ n. taie d'oreiller f.

pilot /'paɪlət/ n. pilote m. ● a. pilote. ● v.t. (p.t. piloted) piloter. ~-light n. veilleuse f.

pimento /pɪ'mentəʊ/ n. (pl. -os) piment m.

pimp /pɪmp/ n. souteneur m.

pimpl|e /'pɪmpl/ n. bouton m. ~y a. boutonneux.

pin /pɪn/ n. épingle f.; (techn.) goupille f. ● v.t. (p.t. pinned) épingler, attacher; (hold down) clouer. have ~s and needles, avoir des fourmis. ~ s.o. down, (fig.) forcer qn. à se décider. ~-point v.t. repérer, définir. ~ up, afficher. ~-up n. (fam.) pin-up f. invar.

pinafore /'pɪnəfɔː(r)/ n. tablier m.

pincers /'pɪnsəz/ n. pl. tenailles f. pl.

pinch /pɪntʃ/ v.t. pincer; (steal: sl.) piquer. ● v.i. (be too tight) serrer. ● n. (mark) pinçon m.; (of salt) pincée f. at a ~, au besoin.

pincushion /'pɪnkʊʃn/ n. pelote à épingles f.

pine [1] /paɪn/ n. (tree) pin m. ~-cone n. pomme de pin f.

pine [2] /paɪn/ v.i. ~ away, dépérir. ~ for, languir après.

pineapple /'paɪnæpl/ n. ananas m.

ping /pɪŋ/ n. bruit métallique m.

ping-pong /'pɪŋpɒŋ/ n. ping-pong m.

pink /pɪŋk/ a. & n. rose (m.).

pinnacle /'pɪnəkl/ n. pinacle m.

pint /paɪnt/ n. pinte f. (imperial = 0.57 litre; Amer. = 0.47 litre).

pioneer /paɪə'nɪə(r)/ n. pionnier m. ● v.t. être le premier à faire, utiliser, étudier, etc.

pious /'paɪəs/ a. pieux.

pip [1] /pɪp/ n. (seed) pépin m.

pip [2] /pɪp/ n. (sound) top m.

pipe /paɪp/ n. tuyau m.; (of smoker) pipe f.; (mus.) pipeau m. ● v.t. transporter par tuyau. ~-cleaner n. cure-pipe m. ~ down, se taire. ~-dream n. chimère f.

pipeline /'paɪplaɪn/ n. pipeline m. in the ~, en route.

piping /'paɪpɪŋ/ n. tuyau(x) m. (pl.). ~ hot, très chaud.

piquant /'piːkənt/ a. piquant.

pique /piːk/ n. dépit m.

pira|te /'paɪərət/ n. pirate m. ● v.t. pirater. ~cy n. piraterie f.

Pisces /'paɪsiːz/ n. les Poissons m. pl.

pistachio /pɪ'stæʃɪəʊ/ n. (pl. -os) pistache f.

pistol /'pɪstl/ n. pistolet m.

piston /'pɪstən/ n. piston m.

pit /pɪt/ n. fosse f., trou m.; (mine) puits m.; (quarry) carrière f.; (for orchestra) fosse f.; (of stomach) creux *m.*; (*of cherry etc.*: *Amer.*) noyau *m.* ● *v.t.* (*p.t.* pitted) trouer; (*fig.*) opposer. ~ o.s. against, se mesurer à.

pitch ¹ /pɪtʃ/ *n.* (*tar*) poix *f.* ~-black *a.* d'un noir d'ébène.

pitch ² /pɪtʃ/ *v.t.* lancer; (*tent*) dresser. ● *v.i.* (*of ship*) tanguer. ● *n.* degré *m.*; (*of voice*) hauteur *f.*; (*mus.*) ton *m.*; (*sport*) terrain *m.* ~ed battle, bataille rangée *f.* a high-~ed voice, une voix aiguë. ~ in, (*fam.*) contribuer. ~ into, (*fam.*) s'attaquer à.

pitcher /ˈpɪtʃə(r)/ *n.* cruche *f.*

pitchfork /ˈpɪtʃfɔːk/ *n.* fourche à foin *f.*

pitfall /ˈpɪtfɔːl/ *n.* piège *m.*

pith /pɪθ/ *n.* (*of orange*) peau blanche *f.*; (*essence*; *fig.*) moelle *f.*

pithy /ˈpɪθɪ/ *a.* (-ier, -iest) (*terse*) concis; (*forceful*) vigoureux.

piti|**ful** /ˈpɪtɪfl/ *a.* pitoyable. ~less *a.* impitoyable.

pittance /ˈpɪtns/ *n.* revenu *or* salaire dérisoire *m.*

pity /ˈpɪtɪ/ *n.* pitié *f.*; (*regrettable fact*) dommage *m.* ● *v.t.* plaindre. take ~ on, avoir pitié de. what a ~, quel dommage. it's a ~, c'est dommage.

pivot /ˈpɪvət/ *n.* pivot *m.* ● *v.i.* (*p.t.* pivoted) pivoter.

pixie /ˈpɪksɪ/ *n.* lutin *m.*

pizza /ˈpiːtsə/ *n.* pizza *f.*

placard /ˈplækɑːd/ *n.* affiche *f.*

placate /pləˈkeɪt, *Amer.* ˈpleɪkeɪt/ *v.t.* calmer.

place /pleɪs/ *n.* endroit *m.*, lieu *m.*; (*house*) maison *f.*; (*seat, rank, etc.*) place *f.* ● *v.t.* placer; (*an order*) passer; (*remember*) situer. at *or* to my ~, chez moi. be ~d, (*in race*) se placer. change ~s, changer de place. in the first ~, d'abord. out of ~, déplacé. take ~, avoir lieu. ~-mat *n.* set *m.*

placenta /pləˈsentə/ *n.* placenta *m.*

placid /ˈplæsɪd/ *a.* placide.

plagiar|**ize** /ˈpleɪdʒəraɪz/ *v.t.* plagier. ~ism *n.* plagiat *m.*

plague /pleɪg/ *n.* peste *f.*; (*nuisance*: *fam.*) fléau *m.* ● *v.t.* harceler.

plaice /pleɪs/ *n. invar.* carrelet *m.*

plaid /plæd/ *n.* tissu écossais *m.*

plain /pleɪn/ *a.* (-er, -est) clair; (*candid*) franc; (*simple*) simple; (*not pretty*) sans beauté; (*not patterned*) uni. ● *adv.* franchement. ● *n.* plaine *f.* ~ chocolate, chocolat

noir *m.* in ~ clothes, en civil. ~ly *adv.* clairement; franchement; simplement. ~ness *n.* simplicité *f.*

plaintiff /ˈpleɪntɪf/ *n.* plaignant(e) *m.* (*f.*).

plaintive /ˈpleɪntɪv/ *a.* plaintif.

plait /plæt/ *v.t.* tresser, natter. ● *n.* tresse *f.*, natte *f.*

plan /plæn/ *n.* projet *m.*, plan *m.*; (*diagram*) plan *m.* ● *v.t.* (*p.t.* planned) prévoir, projeter; (*arrange*) organiser; (*design*) concevoir; (*economy, work*) planifier. ● *v.i.* faire des projets. ~ to do, avoir l'intention de faire.

plane ¹ /pleɪn/ *n.* (*tree*) platane *m.*

plane ² /pleɪn/ *n.* (*level*) plan *m.*; (*aeroplane*) avion *m.* ● *a.* plan.

plane ³ /pleɪn/ *n.* (*tool*) rabot *m.* ● *v.t.* raboter.

planet /ˈplænɪt/ *n.* planète *f.* ~ary *a.* planétaire.

plank /plæŋk/ *n.* planche *f.*

plankton /ˈplæŋktn/ *n.* plancton *m.*

planning /ˈplænɪŋ/ *n.* (*pol., comm.*) planification *f.* family ~, planning familial *m.* ~ permission, permis de construire *m.*

plant /plɑːnt/ *n.* plante *f.*; (*techn.*) matériel *m.*; (*factory*) usine *f.* ● *v.t.* planter; (*bomb*) (dé)poser. ~ation /-ˈteɪʃn/ *n.* plantation *f.*

plaque /plɑːk/ *n.* plaque *f.*

plasma /ˈplæzmə/ *n.* plasma *m.*

plaster /ˈplɑːstə(r)/ *n.* plâtre *m.*; (*adhesive*) sparadrap *m.* ● *v.t.* plâtrer; (*cover*) tapisser (with, de). in ~, dans le plâtre. ~ of Paris, plâtre à mouler *m.* ~er *n.* plâtrier *m.*

plastic /ˈplæstɪk/ *a.* en plastique; (*art, substance*) plastique. ● *n.* plastique *m.* ~ surgery, chirurgie esthétique *f.*

Plasticine /ˈplæstɪsiːn/ *n.* (P.) pâte à modeler *f.*

plate /pleɪt/ *n.* assiette *f.*; (*of metal*) plaque *f.*; (*gold or silver dishes*) vaisselle plate *f.*; (*in book*) gravure *f.* ● *v.t.* (*metal*) plaquer. ~ful *n.* (*pl.* -fuls) assiettée *f.*

plateau /ˈplætəʊ/ *n.* (*pl.* -eaux /-əʊz/) plateau *m.*

platform /ˈplætfɔːm/ *n.* (*in classroom, hall, etc.*) estrade *f.*; (*for speaking*) tribune *f.*; (*rail.*) quai *m.*; (*of bus & pol.*) plate-forme *f.*

platinum /ˈplætɪnəm/ *n.* platine *m.*

platitude /ˈplætɪtjuːd/ *n.* platitude *f.*

platonic /pləˈtɒnɪk/ *a.* platonique.

platoon /plə'tuːn/ n. (mil.) section f.

platter /'plætə(r)/ n. plat m.

plausible /'plɔːzəbl/ a. plausible.

play /pleɪ/ v.t./i. jouer; (instrument) jouer de; (record) passer; (game) jouer à; (opponent) jouer contre; (match) disputer. ● n. jeu m.; (theatre) pièce f. ~-act v.i. jouer la comédie. ~ down, minimiser. ~-group ns. garderie f. ~-off n. (sport) belle f. ~ on, (take advantage of) jouer sur. ~ on words, jeu de mots m. ~ed out, épuisé. ~-pen n. parc m. ~ safe, ne pas prendre de risques. ~ up, (fam.) créer des problèmes (à). ~ up to, flatter. ~er n. joueu|r, -se m., f.

playboy /'pleɪbɔɪ/ n. play-boy m.

playful /'pleɪfl/ a. enjoué; (child) joueur. ~ly adv. avec espièglerie.

playground /'pleɪgraʊnd/ n. cour de récréation f.

playing /'pleɪɪŋ/ n. jeu m. ~-card n. carte à jouer f. ~-field n. terrain de sport m.

playmate /'pleɪmeɪt/ n. camarade m./f., cop|ain, -ine m., f.

plaything /'pleɪθɪŋ/ n. jouet m.

playwright /'pleɪraɪt/ n. dramaturge m./f.

plc abbr. (public limited company) SA.

plea /pliː/ n. (entreaty) supplication f.; (reason) excuse f.; (jurid.) défense f.

plead /pliːd/ v.t./i. (jurid.) plaider; (as excuse) alléguer. ~ for, (beg for) implorer. ~ with, (beg) implorer.

pleasant /'pleznt/ a. agréable. ~ly adv. agréablement.

please /pliːz/ v.t./i. plaire (à), faire plaisir (à). ● adv. s'il vous or te plaît. ~ o.s., do as one ~s, faire qu'on veut. ~d a. content (with, de). **pleasing** a. agréable.

pleasur|e /'pleʒə(r)/ n. plaisir m. ~able a. très agréable.

pleat /pliːt/ n. pli m. ● v.t. plisser.

plebiscite /'plebɪsɪt/ n. plébiscite m.

pledge /pledʒ/ n. (token) gage m.; (fig.) promesse f. ● v.t. promettre; (pawn) engager.

plentiful /'plentɪfl/ a. abondant.

plenty /'plentɪ/ n. abondance f. ~ (of), (a great deal) beaucoup (de); (enough) assez (de).

pleurisy /'plʊərəsɪ/ n. pleurésie f.

pliable /'plaɪəbl/ a. souple.

pliers /'plaɪəz/ n. pl. pince(s) f. (pl.).

plight /plaɪt/ n. triste situation f.

plimsoll /'plɪmsəl/ n. chaussure de gym f.

plinth /plɪnθ/ n. socle m.

plod /plɒd/ v.i. (p.t. plodded) avancer péniblement or d'un pas lent; (work) bûcher. ~der n. bûcheu|r, -se m., f. ~ding a. lent.

plonk /plɒŋk/ n. (sl.) pinard m. ● v.t. ~ down, poser lourdement.

plot /plɒt/ n. complot m.; (of novel etc.) intrigue f. ~ (of land), terrain m. ● v.t./i. (p.t. plotted) comploter; (mark out) tracer.

plough /plaʊ/ n. charrue f. ● v.t./i. labourer. ~ back, réinvestir. ~ into, rentrer dans. ~ through, avancer péniblement dans.

plow /plaʊ/ n. & v.t./i. (Amer.) = plough.

ploy /plɔɪ/ n. (fam.) stratagème m.

pluck /plʌk/ v.t. cueillir; (bird) plumer; (eyebrows) épiler; (strings: mus.) pincer. ● n. courage m. ~ up courage, prendre son courage à deux mains. ~y a. courageux.

plug /plʌg/ n. (of cloth, paper, etc.) tampon m.; (for sink etc.) bonde f.; (electr.) fiche f., prise f. ● v.t. (p.t. plugged) (hole) boucher; (publicize: fam.) faire du battage autour de. ● v.i. ~ away, (work: fam.) bosser. ~ in, brancher. ~-hole n. vidange f.

plum /plʌm/ n. prune f. ~ job, travail en or m. ~ pudding, (plum-) pudding m.

plumb /plʌm/ adv. tout à fait. ● v.t. (probe) sonder. ~-line n. fil à plomb m.

plumb|er /'plʌmə(r)/ n. plombier m. ~ing n. plomberie f.

plum|e /pluːm/ n. plume(s) f. (pl.). ~age n. plumage m.

plummet /'plʌmɪt/ v.i. (p.t. plummeted) tomber, plonger.

plump /plʌmp/ a. (-er, -est) potelé, dodu. ● v.i. ~ for, choisir. ~ness n. rondeur f.

plunder /'plʌndə(r)/ v.t. piller. ● n. (act) pillage m.; (goods) butin m.

plunge /plʌndʒ/ v.t./i. (dive, thrust) plonger; (fall) tomber. ● n. plongeon m.; (fall) chute f. take the ~, se jeter à l'eau.

plunger /'plʌndʒə(r)/ n. (for sink etc.) ventouse f., débouchoir m.

plural /'plʊərəl/ a. pluriel; (noun) au pluriel. ● n. pluriel m.

plus /plʌs/ prep. plus. ● a. (electr. & fig.) positif. ● n. signe plus m.; (fig.) atout m. ten ~, plus de dix.

plush(y) /plʌʃ(ɪ)/ a. somptueux.

ply /plaɪ/ v.t. (tool) manier; (trade) exercer. ● v.i. faire la navette. ~ s.o. with drink, offrir continuellement à boire à qn.

plywood /'plaɪwʊd/ n. contreplaqué m.

p.m. /pi:'em/ adv. de l'après-midi or du soir.

pneumatic /nju:'mætɪk/ a. pneumatique. ~ drill, marteau-piqueur m.

pneumonia /nju:'məʊnɪə/ n. pneumonie f.

PO abbr. see Post Office.

poach /pəʊtʃ/ v.t./i. (game) braconner; (staff) débaucher; (culin.) pocher. ~er n. braconnier m.

pocket /'pɒkɪt/ n. poche f. ● a. de poche. ● v.t. empocher. be out of ~, avoir perdu de l'argent. ~-book n. (notebook) carnet m.; (wallet: Amer.) portefeuille m.; (handbag: Amer.) sac à main m. ~-money n. argent de poche m.

pock-marked /'pɒkmɑːkt/ a. (face etc.) grêlé.

pod /pɒd/ n. (peas etc.) cosse f.; (vanilla) gousse f.

podgy /'pɒdʒɪ/ a. (-ier, -iest) dodu.

poem /'pəʊɪm/ n. poème m.

poet /'pəʊɪt/ n. poète m. ~ic /-'etɪk/ a. poétique.

poetry /'pəʊɪtrɪ/ n. poésie f.

poignant /'pɔɪnjənt/ a. poignant.

point /pɔɪnt/ n. point m.; (tip) pointe f.; (decimal point) virgule f.; (meaning) sens m., intérêt m.; (remark) remarque f. ~s, (rail.) aiguillage m. ● v.t. (aim) braquer; (show) indiquer. ● v.i. indiquer du doigt (at or to s.o., qn.). ~ out that, make the ~ that, faire remarquer que. good ~s, qualités f. pl. make a ~ of doing, ne pas manquer de faire. on the ~ of, sur le point de. ~-blank a. & adv. à bout portant. ~ in time, moment m. ~ of view, point de vue m. ~ out, signaler. to the ~, pertinent. what is the ~?, à quoi bon?

pointed /'pɔɪntɪd/ a. pointu; (remark) lourd de sens.

pointer /'pɔɪntə(r)/ n. (indicator) index m.; (dog) chien d'arrêt m.; (advice: fam.) tuyau m.

pointless /'pɔɪntlɪs/ a. inutile.

poise /pɔɪz/ n. équilibre m.; (carriage) maintien m.; (fig.) assurance f. ~d a. en équilibre; (confident) assuré. ~d for, prêt à.

poison /'pɔɪzn/ n. poison m. ● v.t. empoisonner. ~ous a. (substance etc.) toxique; (plant) vénéneux; (snake) venimeux.

poke /pəʊk/ v.t./i. (push) pousser; (fire) tisonner; (thrust) fourrer. ● n. (petit) coup m. ~ about, fureter. ~ fun at, se moquer de. ~ out, (head) sortir.

poker[1] /'pəʊkə(r)/ n. tisonnier m.

poker[2] /'pəʊkə(r)/ n. (cards) poker m.

poky /'pəʊkɪ/ a. (-ier, -iest) (small) exigu; (slow: Amer.) lent.

Poland /'pəʊlənd/ n. Pologne f.

polar /'pəʊlə(r)/ a. polaire. ~ bear, ours blanc m.

polarize /'pəʊləraɪz/ v.t. polariser.

Polaroid /'pəʊlərɔɪd/ n. (P.) polaroïd (P.) m.

pole[1] /pəʊl/ n. (fixed) poteau m.; (rod) perche f.; (for flag) mât m. ~-vault n. saut à la perche m.

pole[2] /pəʊl/ n. (geog.) pôle m.

Pole /pəʊl/ n. Polonais(e) m. (f.).

polemic /pə'lemɪk/ n. polémique f.

police /pə'li:s/ n. police f. ● v.t. faire la police dans. ~ state, état policier m. ~ station, commissariat de police m.

police|man /pə'li:smən/ n. (pl. -men) agent de police m. ~woman (pl. -women) femme-agent f.

policy[1] /'pɒlɪsɪ/ n. politique f.

policy[2] /'pɒlɪsɪ/ n. (insurance) police (d'assurance) f.

polio(myelitis) /'pəʊlɪəʊ(maɪə-'laɪtɪs)/ n. polio(myélite) f.

polish /'pɒlɪʃ/ v.t. polir; (shoes, floor) cirer. ● n. (for shoes) cirage m.; (for floor) encaustique f.; (for nails) vernis m.; (shine) poli m.; (fig.) raffinement m. ~ off, finir en vitesse. ~ up, (language) perfectionner. ~ed a. raffiné.

Polish /'pəʊlɪʃ/ a. polonais. ● n. (lang.) polonais m.

polite /pə'laɪt/ a. poli. ~ly adv. poliment. ~ness n. politesse f.

political /pə'lɪtɪkl/ a. politique.

politician /pɒlɪ'tɪʃn/ n. homme politique m., femme politique f.

politics /'pɒlətɪks/ n. politique f.

polka /'pɒlkə, *Amer.* 'pəʊlkə/ *n.* polka *f.* **~ dots,** pois *m. pl.*

poll /pəʊl/ *n.* scrutin *m.*; (*survey*) sondage *m.* ● *v.t.* (*votes*) obtenir. **go to the ~s,** aller aux urnes. **~ing-booth** *n.* isoloir *m.* **~ing station,** bureau de vote *m.*

pollen /'pɒlən/ *n.* pollen *m.*

pollut|e /pə'lu:t/ *v.t.* polluer. **~ion** /-ʃn/ *n.* pollution *f.*

polo /'pəʊləʊ/ *n.* polo *m.* **~ neck,** col roulé *m.* **~ shirt,** polo *m.*

polyester /pɒlɪ'estə(r)/ *n.* polyester *m.*

polygamy /pə'lɪgəmɪ/ *n.* polygamie *f.*

polytechnic /pɒlɪ'teknɪk/ *n.* institut universitaire de technologie *m.*

polythene /'pɒlɪθi:n/ *n.* polythène *m.*, polyéthylène *m.*

pomegranate /'pɒmɪgrænɪt/ *n.* (*fruit*) grenade *f.*

pomp /pɒmp/ *n.* pompe *f.*

pompon /'pɒmpɒn/ *n.* pompon *m.*

pomp|ous /'pɒmpəs/ *a.* pompeux. **~osity** /-'pɒsətɪ/ *n.* solennité *f.*

pond /pɒnd/ *n.* étang *m.*; (*artificial*) bassin *m.*; (*stagnant*) mare *f.*

ponder /'pɒndə(r)/ *v.t./i.* réfléchir (à), méditer (sur).

ponderous /'pɒndərəs/ *a.* pesant.

pong /pɒŋ/ *n.* (*stink: sl.*) puanteur *f.* ● *v.i.* (*sl.*) puer.

pony /'pəʊnɪ/ *n.* poney *m.* **~-tail** *n.* queue de cheval *f.*

poodle /'pu:dl/ *n.* caniche *m.*

pool[1] /pu:l/ *n.* (*puddle*) flaque *f.*; (*pond*) étang *m.*; (*of blood*) mare *f.*; (*for swimming*) piscine *f.*

pool[2] /pu:l/ *n.* (*fund*) fonds commun *m.*; (*of ideas*) réservoir *m.*; (*of typists*) pool *m.*; (*snooker*) billard américain *m.* **~s,** pari mutuel sur le football *m.* ● *v.t.* mettre en commun.

poor /pɔː(r)/ *a.* (-er, -est) pauvre; (*not good*) médiocre, mauvais. **~ly** *adv.* mal; *a.* malade.

pop[1] /pɒp/ *n.* (*noise*) bruit sec *m.* ● *v.t./i.* (*p.t.* **popped**) (*burst*) crever; (*put*) mettre. **~ in/out/off,** entrer/sortir/partir. **~ over,** faire un saut (**to see s.o.,** chez qn.). **~ up,** surgir.

pop[2] /pɒp/ *n.* (*mus.*) musique pop *f.* ● *a.* pop *invar.*

popcorn /'pɒpkɔːn/ *n.* pop-corn *m.*

pope /pəʊp/ *n.* pape *m.*

poplar /'pɒplə(r)/ *n.* peuplier *m.*

poppy /'pɒpɪ/ *n.* pavot *m.*; (*wild*) coquelicot *m.*

popsicle /'pɒpsɪkl/ *n.* (P.) (*Amer.*) glace à l'eau *f.*

popular /'pɒpjʊlə(r)/ *a.* populaire; (*in fashion*) en vogue. **be ~ with,** plaire à. **~ity** /-'lærətɪ/ *n.* popularité *f.* **~ize** *v.t.* populariser. **~ly** *adv.* communément.

populat|e /'pɒpjʊleɪt/ *v.t.* peupler. **~ion** /-'leɪʃn/ *n.* population *f.*

populous /'pɒpjʊləs/ *a.* populeux.

porcelain /'pɔːsəlɪn/ *n.* porcelaine *f.*

porch /pɔːtʃ/ *n.* porche *m.*

porcupine /'pɔːkjʊpaɪn/ *n.* (*rodent*) porc-épic *m.*

pore[1] /pɔː(r)/ *n.* pore *m.*

pore[2] /pɔː(r)/ *v.i.* **~ over,** étudier minutieusement.

pork /pɔːk/ *n.* (*food*) porc *m.*

pornograph|y /pɔː'nɒgrəfɪ/ *n.* pornographie *f.* **~ic** /-ə'græfɪk/ *a.* pornographique.

porous /'pɔːrəs/ *a.* poreux.

porpoise /'pɔːpəs/ *n.* marsouin *m.*

porridge /'pɒrɪdʒ/ *n.* porridge *m.*

port[1] /pɔːt/ *n.* (*harbour*) port *m.* **~ of call,** escale *f.*

port[2] /pɔːt/ *n.* (*left: naut.*) bâbord *m.*

port[3] /pɔːt/ *n.* (*wine*) porto *m.*

portable /'pɔːtəbl/ *a.* portatif.

portal /'pɔːtl/ *n.* portail *m.*

porter[1] /'pɔːtə(r)/ *n.* (*carrier*) porteur *m.*

porter[2] /'pɔːtə(r)/ *n.* (*door-keeper*) portier *m.*

portfolio /pɔːt'fəʊlɪəʊ/ *n.* (*pl.* -os) (*pol., comm.*) portefeuille *m.*

porthole /'pɔːthəʊl/ *n.* hublot *m.*

portico /'pɔːtɪkəʊ/ *n.* (*pl.* -oes) portique *m.*

portion /'pɔːʃn/ *n.* (*share, helping*) portion *f.*; (*part*) partie *f.*

portly /'pɔːtlɪ/ *a.* (-ier, -iest) corpulent (et digne).

portrait /'pɔːtrɪt/ *n.* portrait *m.*

portray /pɔː'treɪ/ *v.t.* représenter. **~al** *n.* portrait *m.*, peinture *f.*

Portug|al /'pɔːtjʊgl/ *n.* Portugal *m.* **~uese** /-'giːz/ *a.* & *n. invar.* portugais(e) (*m.* (*f.*)).

pose /pəʊz/ *v.t./i.* poser. ● *n.* pose *f.* **~ as,** (*expert etc.*) se poser en.

poser /'pəʊzə(r)/ *n.* colle *f.*

posh /pɒʃ/ *a.* (*sl.*) chic *invar.*

position /pə'zɪʃn/ *n.* position *f.*; (*job, state*) situation *f.* ● *v.t.* placer.

positive /'pɒzətɪv/ *a.* (*test, help, etc.*) positif; (*sure*) sûr, certain; (*real*)

réel, vrai. **~ly** *adv.* positivement; (*absolutely*) complètement.
possess /pə'zes/ *v.t.* posséder. **~ion** /-ʃn/ *n.* possession *f.* **take ~ion of**, prendre possession de. **~or** *n.* possesseur *m.*
possessive /pə'zesɪv/ *a.* possessif.
possib|le /'pɒsəbl/ *a.* possible. **~ility** /-'bɪlətɪ/ *n.* possibilité *f.*
possibly /'pɒsəblɪ/ *adv.* peut-être. **if I ~ can**, si cela m'est possible. **I cannot ~ leave**, il m'est impossible de partir.
post[1] /pəʊst/ *n.* (*pole*) poteau *m.* ● *v.t.* **~ (up)**, (*a notice*) afficher.
post[2] /pəʊst/ *n.* (*station, job*) poste *m.* ● *v.t.* poster; (*appoint*) affecter.
post[3] /pəʊst/ *n.* (*mail service*) poste *f.*; (*letters*) courrier *m.* ● *a.* postal. ● *v.t.* (*put in box*) poster; (*send*) envoyer (par la poste). **catch the last ~**, attraper la dernière levée. **keep ~ed**, tenir au courant. **~box** *n.* boîte à *or* aux lettres *f.* **~ code** *n.* code postal *m.* **P~ Office**, postes *f. pl.*; (*in France*) Postes et Télécommunications *f. pl.* **~ office**, bureau de poste *m.*, poste *f.*
post- /pəʊst/ *pref.* post-.
postage /'pəʊstɪdʒ/ *n.* tarif postal *m.*, frais de port *m.pl.*
postal /'pəʊstl/ *a.* postal. **~ order**, mandat *m.* **~ worker**, employé(e) des postes *m.* (*f.*).
postcard /'pəʊstkɑːd/ *n.* carte postale *f.*
poster /'pəʊstə(r)/ *n.* affiche *f.*; (*for decoration*) poster *m.*
posterior /pɒ'stɪərɪə(r)/ *n.* postérieur *m.*
posterity /pɒ'sterətɪ/ *n.* postérité *f.*
postgraduate /pəʊst'grædʒʊət/ *n.* étudiant(e) de troisième cycle *m.* (*f.*).
posthumous /'pɒstjʊməs/ *a.* posthume. **~ly** *adv.* à titre posthume.
postman /'pəʊstmən/ *n.* (*pl.* **-men**) facteur *m.*
postmark /'pəʊstmɑːk/ *n.* cachet de la poste *m.*
postmaster /'pəʊstmɑːstə(r)/ *n.* receveur des postes *m.*
post-mortem /pəʊst'mɔːtəm/ *n.* autopsie *f.*
postpone /pə'spəʊn/ *v.t.* remettre. **~ment** *n.* ajournement *m.*
postscript /'pəʊskrɪpt/ *n.* (*to letter*) post-scriptum *m. invar.*
postulate /'pɒstjʊleɪt/ *v.t.* postuler.

posture /'pɒstʃə(r)/ *n.* posture *f.* ● *v.i.* (*affectedly*) prendre des poses.
post-war /'pəʊstwɔː(r)/ *a.* d'après-guerre.
pot /pɒt/ *n.* pot *m.*; (*for cooking*) marmite *f.*; (*drug: sl.*) marie-jeanne *f.* ● *v.t.* (*plants*) mettre en pot. **go to ~**, (*sl.*) aller à la ruine. **~-belly** *n.* gros ventre *m.* **take ~ luck**, tenter sa chance. **take a ~-shot at**, faire un carton sur.
potato /pə'teɪtəʊ/ *n.* (*pl.* **-oes**) pomme de terre *f.*
poten|t /'pəʊtnt/ *a.* puissant; (*drink*) fort. **~cy** *n.* puissance *f.*
potential /pə'tenʃl/ *a. & n.* potentiel (*m.*). **~ly** *adv.* potentiellement.
pot-hol|e /'pɒthəʊl/ *n.* (*in rock*) caverne *f.*; (*in road*) nid de poule *m.* **~ing** *n.* spéléologie *f.*
potion /'pəʊʃn/ *n.* potion *f.*
potted /'pɒtɪd/ *a.* (*plant etc.*) en pot; (*preserved*) en conserve; (*abridged*) condensé.
potter[1] /'pɒtə(r)/ *n.* potier *m.* **~y** *n.* (*art*) poterie *f.*; (*objects*) poteries *f.pl.*
potter[2] /'pɒtə(r)/ *v.i.* bricoler.
potty /'pɒtɪ/ *a.* (**-ier, -iest**) (*crazy: sl.*) toqué. ● *n.* pot *m.*
pouch /paʊtʃ/ *n.* poche *f.*; (*for tobacco*) blague *f.*
pouffe /puːf/ *n.* pouf *m.*
poultice /'pəʊltɪs/ *n.* cataplasme *m.*
poult|ry /'pəʊltrɪ/ *n.* volaille *f.* **~erer** *n.* marchand de volailles *m.*
pounce /paʊns/ *v.i.* bondir (**on**, sur). ● *n.* bond *m.*
pound[1] /paʊnd/ *n.* (*weight*) livre *f.* (= 454 g.); (*money*) livre *f.*
pound[2] /paʊnd/ *n.* (*for dogs, cars*) fourrière *f.*
pound[3] /paʊnd/ *v.t.* (*crush*) piler; (*bombard*) pilonner. ● *v.i.* frapper fort; (*of heart*) battre fort; (*walk*) marcher à pas lourds.
pour /pɔː(r)/ *v.t.* verser. ● *v.i.* couler, ruisseler (**from**, de); (*rain*) pleuvoir à torrents. **~ in/out**, (*people*) arriver/sortir en masse. **~ off** *or* **out**, vider. **~ing rain**, pluie torrentielle *f.*
pout /paʊt/ *v.t./i.* **~ (one's lips)**, faire la moue. ● *n.* moue *f.*
poverty /'pɒvətɪ/ *n.* misère *f.*, pauvreté *f.*
powder /'paʊdə(r)/ *n.* poudre *f.* ● *v.t.* poudrer. **~ed** *a.* en poudre. **~y** *a.* poudreux. **~-room** *n.* toilettes pour dames *f. pl.*

power /'pauə(r)/ *n.* puissance *f.*; (*ability*, *authority*) pouvoir *m.*; (*energy*) énergie *f.*; (*electr.*) courant *m.* ~ **cut,** coupure de courant *f.* ~**ed by,** fonctionner à; (*jet etc.*) propulsé par. ~**less** *a.* impuissant. ~ **point,** prise de courant *f.* ~**-station** *n.* centrale électrique *f.*

powerful /'pauəfl/ *a.* puissant. ~**ly** *adv.* puissamment.

practicable /'præktɪkəbl/ *a.* praticable.

practical /'præktɪkl/ *a.* pratique. ~**ity** /-'kæləti/ *n.* sens *or* aspect pratique *m.* ~ **joke,** farce *f.*

practically /'præktɪklɪ/ *adv.* pratiquement.

practice /'præktɪs/ *n.* pratique *f.*; (*of profession*) exercice *m.*; (*sport*) entraînement *m.*; (*clients*) clientèle *f.* **be in** ~, (*doctor, lawyer*) exercer. **in** ~, (*in fact*) en pratique; (*well-trained*) en forme. **out of** ~, rouillé. **put into** ~, mettre en pratique.

practis|e /'præktɪs/ *v.t./i.* (*musician, typist, etc.*) s'exercer (à); (*sport*) s'entraîner (à); (*put into practice*) pratiquer; (*profession*) exercer. ~**ed** *a.* expérimenté. ~**ing** *a.* (*Catholic etc.*) pratiquant.

practitioner /præk'tɪʃənə(r)/ *n.* praticien(ne) *m.* (*f.*).

pragmatic /præg'mætɪk/ *a.* pragmatique.

prairie /'preərɪ/ *n.* (*in North America*) prairie *f.*

praise /preɪz/ *v.t.* louer. ● *n.* éloge(s) *m.* (*pl.*), louange(s) *f.* (*pl.*).

praiseworthy /'preɪzwɜːðɪ/ *a.* digne d'éloges.

pram /præm/ *n.* voiture d'enfant *f.*, landau *m.*

prance /prɑːns/ *v.i.* caracoler.

prank /præŋk/ *n.* farce *f.*

prattle /'prætl/ *v.i.* jaser.

prawn /prɔːn/ *n.* crevette rose *f.*

pray /preɪ/ *v.i.* prier.

prayer /preə(r)/ *n.* prière *f.*

pre- /priː/ *pref.* pré-.

preach /priːtʃ/ *v.t./i.* prêcher. ~ **at** *or* **to,** prêcher. ~**er** *n.* prédicateur *m.*

preamble /priː'æmbl/ *n.* préambule *m.*

pre-arrange /priːə'reɪndʒ/ *v.t.* fixer à l'avance.

precarious /prɪ'keərɪəs/ *a.* précaire.

precaution /prɪ'kɔːʃn/ *n.* précaution *f.* ~**ary** *a.* de précaution.

preced|e /prɪ'siːd/ *v.t.* précéder. ~**ing** *a.* précédent.

precedence /'presɪdəns/ *n.* priorité *f.*; (*in rank*) préséance *f.*

precedent /'presɪdənt/ *n.* précédent *m.*

precept /'priːsept/ *n.* précepte *m.*

precinct /'priːsɪŋkt/ *n.* enceinte *f.*; (*pedestrian area*) zone *f.*; (*district: Amer.*) circonscription *f.*

precious /'preʃəs/ *a.* précieux. ● *adv.* (*very: fam.*) très.

precipice /'presɪpɪs/ *n.* (*geog.*) à-pic *m. invar.*; (*fig.*) précipice *m.*

precipitat|e /prɪ'sɪpɪteɪt/ *v.t.* (*person, event, chemical*) précipiter. ● *a.* /-ɪtət/ précipité. ~**ion** /-'teɪʃn/ *n.* précipitation *f.*

précis /'preɪsiː/ *n. invar.* précis *m.*

precis|e /prɪ'saɪs/ *a.* précis; (*careful*) méticuleux. ~**ely** *adv.* précisément. ~**ion** /-'sɪʒn/ *n.* précision *f.*

preclude /prɪ'kluːd/ *v.t.* (*prevent*) empêcher; (*rule out*) exclure.

precocious /prɪ'kəuʃəs/ *a.* précoce.

preconc|eived /priːkən'siːvd/ *a.* préconçu. ~**eption** *n.* préconception *f.*

pre-condition /priːkən'dɪʃn/ *n.* condition requise *f.*

predator /'predətə(r)/ *n.* prédateur *m.* ~**y** *a.* rapace.

predecessor /'priːdɪsesə(r)/ *n.* prédécesseur *m.*

predicament /prɪ'dɪkəmənt/ *n.* mauvaise situation *or* passe *f.*

predict /prɪ'dɪkt/ *v.t.* prédire. ~**able** *a.* prévisible. ~**ion** /-kʃn/ *n.* prédiction *f.*

predispose /priːdɪ'spəuz/ *v.t.* prédisposer (**to do,** à faire).

predominant /prɪ'dɒmɪnənt/ *a.* prédominant. ~**ly** *adv.* pour la plupart.

predominate /prɪ'dɒmɪneɪt/ *v.i.* prédominer.

pre-eminent /priː'emɪnənt/ *a.* prééminent.

pre-empt /priː'empt/ *v.t.* (*buy*) acquérir d'avance; (*stop*) prévenir. ~**ive** *a.* preventif.

preen /priːn/ *v.t.* (*bird*) lisser. ~ **o.s.,** (*person*) se bichonner.

prefab /'priːfæb/ *n.* (*fam.*) bâtiment préfabriqué *m.* ~**ricated** /-'fæbrɪkeɪtɪd/ *a.* préfabriqué.

preface /'prefɪs/ *n.* préface *f.*

prefect /'pri:fekt/ *n.* (*pupil*) élève chargé(e) de la discipline *m.(f.)*; (*official*) préfet *m.*

prefer /prɪ'fɜ:(r)/ *v.t.* (*p.t.* **preferred**) préférer (**to do**, faire). **~able** /'prefrəbl/ *a.* préférable. **~ably** *adv.* de préférence.

preferen|ce /'prefrəns/ *n.* préférence *f.* **~tial** /-ə'renʃl/ *a.* préférentiel.

prefix /'pri:fɪks/ *n.* préfixe *m.*

pregnan|t /'pregnənt/ *a.* (*woman*) enceinte; (*animal*) pleine. **~cy** *n.* (*of woman*) grossesse *f.*

prehistoric /pri:hɪ'stɒrɪk/ *a.* préhistorique.

prejudge /pri:'dʒʌdʒ/ *v.t.* préjuger de; (*person*) juger d'avance.

prejudice /'predʒʊdɪs/ *n.* préjugé(s) *m.* (*pl.*); (*harm*) préjudice *m.* ● *v.t.* (*claim*) porter préjudice à; (*person*) prévenir. **~d** *a.* partial; (*person*) qui a des préjugés.

preliminar|y /prɪ'lɪmɪnərɪ/ *a.* préliminaire. **~ies** *n. pl.* préliminaires *m. pl.*

prelude /'prelju:d/ *n.* prélude *m.*

pre-marital /pri:'mærɪtl/ *a.* avant le mariage.

premature /'premətjʊə(r)/ *a.* prématuré.

premeditated /pri:'medɪteɪtɪd/ *a.* prémédité.

premier /'premɪə(r)/ *a.* premier. ● *n.* premier ministre *m.*

première /'premɪeə(r)/ *n.* première *f.*

premises /'premɪsɪz/ *n. pl.* locaux *m. pl.* **on the ~,** sur les lieux.

premiss /'premɪs/ *n.* prémisse *f.*

premium /'pri:mɪəm/ *n.* prime *f.* **be at a ~,** faire prime.

premonition /pri:mə'nɪʃn/ *n.* prémonition *f.*, pressentiment *m.*

preoccup|ation /pri:ɒkjʊ'peɪʃn/ *n.* préoccupation *f.* **~ied** /-'ɒkjʊpaɪd/ *a.* préoccupé.

prep /prep/ *n.* (*work*) devoirs *m.pl.* **~ school = preparatory school**.

preparation /prepə'reɪʃn/ *n.* préparation *f.* **~s,** préparatifs *m. pl.*

preparatory /prɪ'pærətrɪ/ *a.* préparatoire. **~ school**, école primaire privée *f.*; (*Amer.*) école secondaire privée *f.*

prepare /prɪ'peə(r)/ *v.t./i.* (se) préparer (**for,** à). **be ~d for,** (*expect*) s'attendre à **~d to,** prêt à.

prepay /pri:'peɪ/ *v.t.* (*p.t.* **-paid**) payer d'avance.

preponderance /prɪ'pɒndərəns/ *n.* prédominance *f.*

preposition /prepə'zɪʃn/ *n.* préposition *f.*

preposterous /prɪ'pɒstərəs/ *a.* absurde, ridicule.

prerequisite /pri:'rekwɪzɪt/ *n.* condition préalable *f.*

prerogative /prɪ'rɒgətɪv/ *n.* prérogative *f.*

Presbyterian /prezbɪ'tɪərɪən/ *a. & n.* presbytérien(ne) (*m.* (*f.*)).

prescri|be /prɪ'skraɪb/ *v.t.* prescrire. **~ption** /-ɪpʃn/ *n.* prescription *f.*; (*med.*) ordonnance *f.*

presence /'prezns/ *n.* présence *f.* **~ of mind,** présence d'esprit *f.*

present[1] /'preznt/ *a.* présent. ● *n.* présent *m.* **at ~,** à présent. **for the ~,** pour le moment. **~-day** *a.* actuel.

present[2] /'preznt/ *n.* (*gift*) cadeau *m.*

present[3] /prɪ'zent/ *v.t.* présenter; (*film, concert, etc.*) donner. **~ s.o. with,** offrir à qn. **~able** *a.* présentable. **~ation** /prezn'teɪʃn/ *n.* présentation *f.* **~er** *n.* présentateur, -trice *m., f.*

presently /'prezntlɪ/ *adv.* bientôt; (*now: Amer.*) en ce moment.

preservative /prɪ'zɜ:vətɪv/ *n.* (*culin.*) agent de conservation *m.*

preserv|e /prɪ'zɜ:v/ *v.t.* conserver; (*maintain & culin.*) conserver. ● *n.* réserve *f.*; (*fig.*) domaine *m.*; (*jam*) confiture *f.* **~ation** /prezə'veɪʃn/ *n.* conservation *f.*

preside /prɪ'zaɪd/ *v.i.* présider. **~ over,** présider.

presiden|t /'prezɪdənt/ *n.* président(e) *m.* (*f.*). **~cy** *n.* présidence *f.* **~tial** /-'denʃl/ *a.* présidentiel.

press /pres/ *v.t./i.* (*button etc.*) appuyer (sur); (*squeeze*) presser; (*iron*) repasser; (*pursue*) poursuivre. ● *n.* (*newspapers, machine*) presse *f.*; (*for wine*) pressoir *m.* **be ~ed for,** (*time etc.*) manquer de. **~ for sth.,** faire pression pour avoir qch. **~ s.o. to do sth.,** pousser qn. à faire qch. **~ conference/cutting,** conférence/coupure de presse *f.* **~ on,** continuer (**with sth.,** qch.). **~ release,** communiqué de presse *m.* **~-stud** *n.* bouton-pression *m.* **~-up** *n.* traction *f.*

pressing /'presɪŋ/ *a.* pressant.

pressure /'preʃə(r)/ *n.* pression *f.* ● *v.t.* faire pression sur. **~-cooker**

n. cocotte-minute *f.* ~ group, groupe de pression *m.*

pressurize /ˈpreʃəraɪz/ *v.t.* (*cabin etc.*) pressuriser; (*person*) faire pression sur.

prestige /preˈstiːʒ/ *n.* prestige *m.*

prestigious /preˈstɪdʒəs/ *a.* prestigieux.

presumably /prɪˈzjuːməblɪ/ *adv.* vraisemblablement.

presum|e /prɪˈzjuːm/ *v.t.* (*suppose*) présumer. ~e to, (*venture*) se permettre de. ~ption /-ˈzʌmpʃn/ *n.* présomption *f.*

presumptuous /prɪˈzʌmptʃʊəs/ *a.* présomptueux.

pretence, (*Amer.*) **pretense** /prɪˈtens/ *n.* feinte *f.*, simulation *f.*; (*claim*) prétention *f.*; (*pretext*) prétexte *m.*

pretend /prɪˈtend/ *v.t./i.* faire semblant (to do, de faire). ~ to, (*lay claim to*) prétendre à.

pretentious /prɪˈtenʃəs/ *a.* prétentieux.

pretext /ˈpriːtekst/ *n.* prétexte *m.*

pretty /ˈprɪtɪ/ *a.* (-ier, -iest) joli. ● *adv.* assez. ~ much, presque.

prevail /prɪˈveɪl/ *v.i.* prédominer; (*win*) prévaloir. ~ on, persuader (to do, de faire). ~ing *a.* actuel; (*wind*) dominant.

prevalen|t /ˈprevələnt/ *a.* répandu. ~ce *n.* fréquence *f.*

prevent /prɪˈvent/ *v.t.* empêcher (from doing, de faire). ~able *a.* évitable. ~ion /-enʃn/ *n.* prévention *f.* ~ive *a.* préventif.

preview /ˈpriːvjuː/ *n.* avant-première *f.*; (*fig.*) aperçu *m.*

previous /ˈpriːvɪəs/ *a.* précédent, antérieur. ~ to, avant. ~ly *adv.* précédemment, auparavant.

pre-war /ˈpriːwɔː(r)/ *a.* d'avant-guerre.

prey /preɪ/ *n.* proie *f.* ● *v.i.* ~ on, faire sa proie de; (*worry*) préoccuper. bird of ~, rapace *m.*

price /praɪs/ *n.* prix *m.* ● *v.t.* fixer le prix de. ~less *a.* inestimable; (*amusing: sl.*) impayable.

pricey /ˈpraɪsɪ/ *a.* (*fam.*) coûteux.

prick /prɪk/ *v.t.* (*with pin etc.*) piquer. ● *n.* piqûre *f.* ~ up one's ears, dresser l'oreille.

prickl|e /ˈprɪkl/ *n.* piquant *m.*; (*sensation*) picotement *m.* ~y *a.* piquant; (*person*) irritable.

pride /praɪd/ *n.* orgueil *m.*; (*satisfaction*) fierté *f.* ● *v. pr.* ~ o.s. on, s'enorgueillir de. ~ of place, place d'honneur *f.*

priest /priːst/ *n.* prêtre *m.* ~hood *n.* sacerdoce *m.* ~ly *a.* sacerdotal.

prig /prɪg/ *n.* petit saint *m.*, pharisien(ne) *m.* (*f.*). ~gish *a.* pharisaïque.

prim /prɪm/ *a.* (primmer, primmest) guindé, méticuleux.

primary /ˈpraɪmərɪ/ *a.* (*school, elections, etc.*) primaire; (*chief, basic*) premier, fondamental. ● *n.* (*pol.: Amer.*) primaire *m.* ~ily /-ˈmerɪlɪ/ *Amer.* /ˈmerɪlɪ/ *adv.* essentiellement.

prime [1] /praɪm/ *a.* principal, premier; (*first-rate*) excellent. P~ Minister, Premier Ministre *m.* the ~ of life, la force de l'âge.

prime [2] /praɪm/ *v.t.* (*pump, gun*) amorcer; (*surface*) apprêter. ~r [1] /-ə(r)/ *n.* (*paint etc.*) apprêt *m.*

primer [2] /ˈpraɪmə(r)/ *n.* (*school-book*) premier livre *m.*

primeval /praɪˈmiːvl/ *a.* primitif.

primitive /ˈprɪmɪtɪv/ *a.* primitif.

primrose /ˈprɪmrəʊz/ *n.* primevère (jaune) *f.*

prince /prɪns/ *n.* prince *m.* ~ly *a.* princier.

princess /prɪnˈses/ *n.* princesse *f.*

principal /ˈprɪnsəpl/ *a.* principal. ● *n.* (*of school etc.*) direc|teur, -trice *m.*, *f.* ~ly *adv.* principalement.

principle /ˈprɪnsəpl/ *n.* principe *m.* in/on ~, en/par principe.

print /prɪnt/ *v.t.* imprimer; (*write in capitals*) écrire en majuscules. ● *n.* (*of foot etc.*) empreinte *f.*; (*letters*) caractères *m. pl.*; (*photograph*) épreuve *f.*; (*engraving*) gravure *f.* in ~, disponible. out of ~, épuisé. ~-out *n.* listage *m.* ~ed matter, imprimés *m. pl.*

print|er /ˈprɪntə(r)/ *n.* (*person*) imprimeur *m.*; (*comput.*) imprimante *f.* ~ing *n.* impression *f.*

prior [1] /ˈpraɪə(r)/ *a.* précédent. ~ to, *prep.* avant (de).

prior [2] /ˈpraɪə(r)/ *n.* (*relig.*) prieur *m.* ~y *n.* prieuré *m.*

priority /praɪˈɒrətɪ/ *n.* priorité *f.* take ~, avoir la priorité (over, sur).

prise /praɪz/ *v.t.* forcer. ~ open, ouvrir en forçant.

prism /ˈprɪzəm/ *n.* prisme *m.*

prison /ˈprɪzn/ *n.* prison *f.* ~er *n.* prisonn|ier, -ière *m.*, *f.* ~ officer, gardien(ne) de prison *m.* (*f.*).

pristine /'prɪstiːn/ a. primitif; (*condition*) parfait.

privacy /'prɪvəsɪ/ n. intimité f., solitude f.

private /'praɪvɪt/ a. privé; (*confidential*) personnel; (*lessons, house, etc.*) particulier; (*ceremony*) intime. ● n. (*soldier*) simple soldat m. in ~, en privé; (*of ceremony*) dans l'intimité. ~ly adv. en privé; dans l'intimité. (*inwardly*) intérieurement.

privation /praɪ'veɪʃn/ n. privation f.

privet /'prɪvɪt/ n. (*bot.*) troène m.

privilege /'prɪvəlɪdʒ/ n. privilège m. ~d a. privilégié. be ~d to, avoir le privilège de.

privy /'prɪvɪ/ a. ~ to, au fait de.

prize /praɪz/ n. prix m. ● a. (*entry etc.*) primé; (*fool etc.*) parfait. ● v.t. (*value*) priser. ~-fighter n. boxeur professionnel m. ~-winner n. lauréat(e) m. (f.); (*in lottery etc.*) gagnant(e) m. (f.).

pro /prəʊ/ n. the ~s and cons, le pour et le contre.

pro- /prəʊ/ pref. pro-.

probab|le /'prɒbəbl/ a. probable. ~ility /-'bɪlətɪ/ n. probabilité f. ~ly adv. probablement.

probation /prə'beɪʃn/ n. (*testing*) essai m.; (*jurid.*) liberté surveillée f. ~ary a. d'essai.

probe /prəʊb/ n. (*device*) sonde f.; (*fig.*) enquête f. ● v.t. sonder. ● v.i. ~ into, sonder.

problem /'prɒbləm/ n. problème m. ● a. difficile. ~atic /-'mætɪk/ a. problématique.

procedure /prə'siːdʒə(r)/ n. procédure f.; (*way of doing sth.*) démarche à suivre f.

proceed /prə'siːd/ v.i. (*go*) aller, avancer; (*pass*) passer (to, à); (*act*) procéder. ~ (with), (*continue*) continuer. ~ to do, se mettre à faire. ~ing n. procédé m.

proceedings /prə'siːdɪŋz/ n. pl. (*discussions*) débats m. pl.; (*meeting*) réunion f.; (*report*) actes m. pl.; (*jurid.*) poursuites f. pl.

proceeds /'prəʊsiːdz/ n. pl. (*profits*) produit m., bénéfices m. pl.

process /'prəʊses/ n. processus m.; (*method*) procédé m. ● v.t. (*material, data*) traiter. in ~, en cours. in the ~ of doing, en train de faire.

procession /prə'seʃn/ n. défilé m.

procl|aim /prə'kleɪm/ v.t. proclamer. ~amation /prɒklə'meɪʃn/ n. proclamation f.

procrastinate /prə'kræstɪneɪt/ v.i. différer, tergiverser.

procreation /prəʊkrɪ'eɪʃn/ n. procréation f.

procure /prə'kjʊə(r)/ v.t. obtenir.

prod /prɒd/ v.t./i. (p.t. prodded) pousser. ● n. poussée f., coup m.

prodigal /'prɒdɪgl/ a. prodigue.

prodigious /prə'dɪdʒəs/ a. prodigieux.

prodigy /'prɒdɪdʒɪ/ n. prodige m.

produc|e¹ /prə'djuːs/ v.t./i. produire; (*bring out*) sortir; (*show*) présenter; (*cause*) provoquer; (*theatre, TV*) mettre en scène; (*radio*) réaliser; (*cinema*) produire. ~er n. metteur en scène m.; réalisateur m.; producteur m. ~tion /-'dʌkʃn/ n. production f.; mise en scène f.; réalisation f.

produce² /'prɒdjuːs/ n. (*food etc.*) produits m. pl.

product /'prɒdʌkt/ n. produit m.

productiv|e /prə'dʌktɪv/ a. productif. ~ity /prɒdʌk'tɪvətɪ/ n. productivité f.

profan|e /prə'feɪn/ a. sacrilège; (*secular*) profane. ~ity /-'fænətɪ/ n. (*oath*) juron m.

profess /prə'fes/ v.t. professer. ~ to do, prétendre faire.

profession /prə'feʃn/ n. profession f. ~al a. professionnel; (*of high quality*) de professionnel; (*person*) qui exerce une profession libérale; n. professionnel(le) m. (f.).

professor /prə'fesə(r)/ n. professeur (titulaire d'une chaire) m.

proficien|t /prə'fɪʃnt/ a. compétent. ~cy n. compétence f.

profile /'prəʊfaɪl/ n. profil m.

profit /'prɒfɪt/ n. profit m., bénéfice m. ● v.i. (p.t. profited) ~ by, tirer profit de. ~able a. rentable.

profound /prə'faʊnd/ a. profond. ~ly adv. profondément.

profus|e /prə'fjuːs/ a. abondant. ~e in, (*lavish in*) prodigue de. ~ely adv. en abondance; (*apologize*) avec effusion. ~ion /-ʒn/ n. profusion f.

progeny /'prɒdʒənɪ/ n. progéniture f.

program /'prəʊgræm/ n. (*Amer.*) = programme. (computer) ~, programme m. ● v.t. (p.t. programmed) programmer. ~mer n. programmeu|r, -se m., f. ~ming n. (*on computer*) programmation f.

programme /ˈprəʊɡræm/ n. programme m.; (broadcast) émission f.

progress /ˈprəʊɡres/ n. progrès m. (pl.). in ~, en cours. make ~, faire des progrès. ~ report, compte-rendu m.

progress /prəˈɡres/ v.i. (advance, improve) progresser. ~ion /-ʃn/ n. progression f.

progressive /prəˈɡresɪv/ a. progressif; (reforming) progressiste. ~ly adv. progressivement.

prohibit /prəˈhɪbɪt/ v.t. interdire (s.o. from doing, à qn. de faire).

prohibitive /prəˈhɪbətɪv/ a. (price etc.) prohibitif.

project /prəˈdʒekt/ v.t. projeter. ● v.i. (jut out) être en saillie. ~ion /-kʃn/ n. projection f.; saillie f.

project /ˈprɒdʒekt/ n. (plan) projet m.; (undertaking) entreprise f.; (schol.) dossier m.

projectile /prəˈdʒektaɪl/ n. projectile m.

projector /prəˈdʒektə(r)/ n. (cinema etc.) projecteur m.

proletari|at /prəʊlɪˈteərɪət/ n. prolétariat m. ~an a. prolétarien; prolétaire m./f.

proliferat|e /prəˈlɪfəreɪt/ v.i. proliférer. ~ion /-ˈreɪʃn/ n. prolifération f.

prolific /prəˈlɪfɪk/ a. prolifique.

prologue /ˈprəʊlɒɡ/ n. prologue m.

prolong /prəˈlɒŋ/ v.t. prolonger.

promenade /prɒməˈnɑːd/ n. promenade f. ● v.t./i. (se) promener.

prominen|t /ˈprɒmɪnənt/ a. (projecting) proéminent; (conspicuous) bien en vue; (fig.) important. ~ce n. proéminence f.; importance f. ~tly adv. bien en vue.

promiscu|ous /prəˈmɪskjʊəs/ a. qui a plusieurs partenaires; (pej.) de mœurs faciles. ~ity /prɒmɪˈskjuːətɪ/ n. les partenaires multiples; (pej.) liberté de mœurs f.

promis|e /ˈprɒmɪs/ n. promesse f. ● v.t./i. promettre. ~ing a. prometteur; (person) qui promet.

promot|e /prəˈməʊt/ v.t. promouvoir; (advertise) faire la promotion de. ~ion /-ˈməʊʃn/ n. (of person, sales, etc.) promotion f.

prompt /prɒmpt/ a. rapide; (punctual) à l'heure, ponctuel. ● adv. (on the dot) pile. ● v.t. inciter; (cause) provoquer; (theatre) souffler (son rôle) à. ~er n. souffleu|r, -se m., f.

~ly adv. rapidement; ponctuellement. ~ness n. rapidité f.

prone /prəʊn/ a. couché sur le ventre. ~ to, prédisposé à.

prong /prɒŋ/ n. (of fork) dent f.

pronoun /ˈprəʊnaʊn/ n. pronom m.

pron|ounce /prəˈnaʊns/ v.t. prononcer. ~ouncement n. déclaration f. ~unciation /-ʌnsɪˈeɪʃn/ n. prononciation f.

pronounced /prəˈnaʊnst/ a. (noticeable) prononcé.

proof /pruːf/ n. (evidence) preuve f.; (test, trial copy) épreuve f.; (of liquor) teneur en alcool f. ● a. ~ against, à l'épreuve de.

prop /prɒp/ n. support m. ● v.t. (p.t. propped). ~ (up), (support) étayer; (lean) appuyer.

prop /prɒp/ n. (theatre, fam.) accessoire m.

propaganda /prɒpəˈɡændə/ n. propagande f.

propagat|e /ˈprɒpəɡeɪt/ v.t./i. (se) propager. ~ion /-ˈɡeɪʃn/ n. propagation f.

propane /ˈprəʊpeɪn/ n. propane m.

propel /prəˈpel/ v.t. (p.t. propelled) propulser. ~ling pencil, porte-mine m. invar.

propeller /prəˈpelə(r)/ n. hélice f.

proper /ˈprɒpə(r)/ a. correct, bon; (seemly) convenable; (real) vrai; (thorough: fam.) parfait. ● noun. ~ noun, nom propre m. ~ly adv. correctement, comme il faut; (rightly) avec raison.

property /ˈprɒpətɪ/ n. propriété f.; (things owned) biens m. pl., propriété f. ● a. immobilier, foncier.

prophecy /ˈprɒfəsɪ/ n. prophétie f.

prophesy /ˈprɒfɪsaɪ/ v.t./i. prophétiser. ~ that, prédire que.

prophet /ˈprɒfɪt/ n. prophète m. ~ic /prəˈfetɪk/ a. prophétique.

proportion /prəˈpɔːʃn/ n. (ratio, dimension) proportion f.; (amount) partie f. ~al, ~ate adjs. proportionnel.

proposal /prəˈpəʊzl/ n. proposition f.; (of marriage) demande en mariage f.

propos|e /prəˈpəʊz/ v.t. proposer. ● v.i. ~e to, faire une demande en mariage à. ~e to do, se proposer de faire. ~ition /prɒpəˈzɪʃn/ n. proposition f.; (matter: fam.) affaire f.; v.t. (fam.) faire des propositions malhonnêtes à.

propound /prə'paʊnd/ v.t. (theory etc.) proposer.

proprietor /prə'praɪətə(r)/ n. propriétaire m./f.

propriety /prə'praɪətɪ/ n. (correct behaviour) bienséance f.

propulsion /prə'pʌlʃn/ n. propulsion f.

prosaic /prə'zeɪɪk/ a. prosaïque.

proscribe /prə'skraɪb/ v.t. proscrire.

prose /prəʊz/ n. prose f.; (translation) thème m.

prosecut|e /'prɒsɪkjuːt/ v.t. poursuivre. ~ion /-'kjuːʃn/ n. poursuites f. pl. ~or n. procureur m.

prospect [1] /'prɒspekt/ n. perspective f.; (chance) espoir m. **a job with ~s,** un travail avec des perspectives d'avenir.

prospect [2] /prə'spekt/ v.t./i. prospecter. ~or n. prospecteur m.

prospective /prə'spektɪv/ a. (future) futur; (possible) éventuel.

prospectus /prə'spektəs/ n. prospectus m.; (univ.) guide m.

prosper /'prɒspə(r)/ v.i. prospérer.

prosper|ous /'prɒspərəs/ a. prospère. ~ity /-'sperətɪ/ n. prospérité f.

prostate /'prɒsteɪt/ n. prostate f.

prostitut|e /'prɒstɪtjuːt/ n. prostituée f. ~ion /-'tjuːʃn/ n. prostitution f.

prostrate /'prɒstreɪt/ a. (prone) à plat ventre; (submissive) prosterné; (exhausted) prostré.

protagonist /prə'tægənɪst/ n. protagoniste m.

protect /prə'tekt/ v.t. protéger. ~ion /-kʃn/ n. protection f. ~or n. protec|teur, -trice m., f.

protective /prə'tektɪv/ a. protecteur; (clothes) de protection.

protégé /'prɒtɪʒeɪ/ n. protégé m. ~e n. protégée f.

protein /'prəʊtiːn/ n. protéine f.

protest [1] /'prəʊtest/ n. protestation f. **under ~,** en protestant.

protest [2] /prə'test/ v.t./i. protester. ~er n. (pol.) manifestant(e) m. (f.).

Protestant /'prɒtɪstənt/ a. & n. protestant(e) (m. (f.)).

protocol /'prəʊtəkɒl/ n. protocole m.

prototype /'prəʊtətaɪp/ n. prototype m.

protract /prə'trækt/ v.t. prolonger, faire traîner. ~ed a. prolongé.

protractor /prə'træktə(r)/ n. (for measuring) rapporteur m.

protrude /prə'truːd/ v.i. dépasser.

proud /praʊd/ a. (-er, -est) fier, orgueilleux. ~ly adv. fièrement.

prove /pruːv/ v.t. prouver. ● v.i. ~ (to be) easy/etc., se révéler facile/ etc. ~ o.s., faire ses preuves. ~n a. prouvé.

proverb /'prɒvɜːb/ n. proverbe m. ~ial /prə'vɜːbɪəl/ a. proverbial.

provide /prə'vaɪd/ v.t. fournir (s.o. with sth., qch. à qn.). ● v.i. ~ for, (allow for) prévoir; (guard against) parer à; (person) pourvoir aux besoins de.

provided /prə'vaɪdɪd/ conj. ~ that, à condition que.

providence /'prɒvɪdəns/ n. providence f.

providing /prə'vaɪdɪŋ/ conj. = provided.

provinc|e /'prɒvɪns/ n. province f.; (fig.) compétence f. ~ial /prə'vɪnʃl/ a. & n. provincial(e) (m. (f.)).

provision /prə'vɪʒn/ n. (stock) provision f.; (supplying) fourniture f.; (stipulation) disposition f. ~s, (food) provisions f. pl.

provisional /prə'vɪʒənl/ a. provisoire. ~ly adv. provisoirement.

proviso /prə'vaɪzəʊ/ n. (pl. -os) condition f., stipulation f.

provo|ke /prə'vəʊk/ v.t. provoquer. ~cation /prɒvə'keɪʃn/ n. provocation f. ~cative /-'vɒkətɪv/ a. provocant.

prow /praʊ/ n. proue f.

prowess /'praʊɪs/ n. prouesse f.

prowl /praʊl/ v.i. rôder. ● n. **be on the ~,** rôder. ~er n. rôdeu|r, -se m., f.

proximity /prɒk'sɪmətɪ/ n. proximité f.

proxy /'prɒksɪ/ n. **by ~,** par procuration.

prud|e /pruːd/ n. prude f. ~ish a. prude.

pruden|t /'pruːdnt/ a. prudent. ~ce n. prudence f. ~tly adv. prudemment.

prune [1] /pruːn/ n. pruneau m.

prune [2] /pruːn/ v.t. (cut) tailler.

pry [1] /praɪ/ v.i. être indiscret. ~ into, fourrer son nez dans.

pry [2] /praɪ/ v.t. (Amer.) = prise.

psalm /sɑːm/ n. psaume m.

pseudo- /'sjuːdəʊ/ pref. pseudo-.

pseudonym /'sjuːdənɪm/ n. pseudonyme m.

psoriasis /sə'raɪəsɪs/ n. psoriasis m.

psyche /'saɪkɪ/ n. psyché f.

psychiatr|y /saɪ'kaɪətrɪ/ n. psychiatrie f. ~**ic** /-ɪ'rætrɪk/ a. psychiatrique. ~**ist** n. psychiatre m./f.

psychic /'saɪkɪk/ a. (phenomenon etc.) métapsychique; (person) doué de télépathie.

psychoanalys|e /saɪkəʊ'ænəlaɪz/ v.t. psychanalyser. ~**t** /-ɪst/ n. psychanalyste m./f.

psychoanalysis /saɪkəʊə'næləsɪs/ n. psychanalyse f.

psycholog|y /saɪ'kɒlədʒɪ/ n. psychologie f. ~**ical** /-ə'lɒdʒɪkl/ a. psychologique. ~**ist** n. psychologue m./f.

psychopath /'saɪkəʊpæθ/ n. psychopathe m./f.

psychosomatic /saɪkəʊsə'mætɪk/ a. psychosomatique.

psychotherap|y /saɪkəʊ'θerəpɪ/ n. psychothérapie f. ~**ist** n. psychothérapeute m./f.

pub /pʌb/ n. pub m.

puberty /'pju:bətɪ/ n. puberté f.

public /'pʌblɪk/ a. public; (library etc.) municipal. **in ~,** en public. ~ **address system,** sonorisation f. (dans un lieu public). ~ **house,** pub m. ~ **relations,** relations publiques f. pl. ~ **school,** école privée f.; (Amer.) école publique f. ~ **servant,** fonctionnaire m./f. ~-**spirited** a. dévoué au bien public. ~ **transport,** transports en commun m. pl. ~**ly** adv. publiquement.

publican /'pʌblɪkən/ n. patron(ne) de pub m. (f.).

publication /pʌblɪ'keɪʃn/ n. publication f.

publicity /pʌb'lɪsətɪ/ n. publicité f.

publicize /'pʌblɪsaɪz/ v.t. faire connaître au public.

publish /'pʌblɪʃ/ v.t. publier. ~**er** n. éditeur m. ~**ing** n. édition f.

puck /pʌk/ n. (ice hockey) palet m.

pucker /'pʌkə(r)/ v.t./i. (se) plisser.

pudding /'pʊdɪŋ/ n. dessert m.; (steamed) pudding m. **black ~,** boudin m. **rice ~,** riz au lait m.

puddle /'pʌdl/ n. flaque d'eau f.

pudgy /'pʌdʒɪ/ a. (-ier, -iest) dodu.

puerile /'pjʊəraɪl/ a. puéril.

puff /pʌf/ n. bouffée f. ● v.t./i. souffler. ~ **at,** (cigar) tirer sur. ~ **out,** (swell) (se) gonfler.

puffy /'pʌfɪ/ a. gonflé.

pugnacious /pʌg'neɪʃəs/ a. batailleur, combatif.

pug-nosed /'pʌgnəʊzd/ a. camus.

pull /pʊl/ v.t./i. tirer; (muscle) se froisser. ● n. traction f.; (fig.) attraction f.; (influence) influence f. **give a ~,** tirer. ~ **a face,** faire une grimace. ~ **one's weight,** faire sa part du travail. ~ **s.o.'s leg,** faire marcher qn. ~ **apart,** mettre en morceaux. ~ **away,** (auto.) démarrer. ~ **back** or **out,** (withdraw) (se) retirer. ~ **down,** baisser; (building) démolir. ~ **in,** (enter) entrer; (stop) s'arrêter. ~ **off,** enlever; (fig.) réussir. ~ **out,** (from bag etc.) sortir; (extract) arracher; (auto.) déboîter. ~ **over,** (auto.) se ranger. ~ **round** or **through,** s'en tirer. ~ **o.s. together,** se ressaisir. ~ **up,** remonter; (uproot) déraciner; (auto.) (s')arrêter.

pulley /'pʊlɪ/ n. poulie f.

pullover /'pʊləʊvə(r)/ n. pull(-over) m.

pulp /pʌlp/ n. (of fruit) pulpe f.; (for paper) pâte à papier f.

pulpit /'pʊlpɪt/ n. chaire f.

pulsate /pʌl'seɪt/ v.i. battre.

pulse /pʌls/ n. (med.) pouls m.

pulverize /'pʌlvəraɪz/ v.t. (grind, defeat) pulvériser.

pummel /'pʌml/ v.t. (p.t. pummelled) bourrer de coups.

pump [1] /pʌmp/ n. pompe f. ● v.t./i. pomper; (person) soutirer des renseignements à. ~ **up,** gonfler.

pump [2] /pʌmp/ n. (plimsoll) tennis m.; (for dancing) escarpin m.

pumpkin /'pʌmpkɪn/ n. potiron m.

pun /pʌn/ n. jeu de mots m.

punch [1] /pʌntʃ/ v.t. donner un coup de poing à; (perforate) poinçonner; (a hole) faire. ● n. coup de poing m.; (vigour: sl.) punch m.; (device) poinçonneuse f. ~-**drunk** a. sonné. ~-**line,** chute f. ~-**up** n. (fam.) bagarre f.

punch [2] /pʌntʃ/ n. (drink) punch m.

punctual /'pʌŋktʃʊəl/ a. à l'heure; (habitually) ponctuel. ~**ity** /-'ælətɪ/ n. ponctualité f. ~**ly** adv. à l'heure; ponctuellement.

punctuat|e /'pʌŋktʃʊeɪt/ v.t. ponctuer. ~**ion** /-'eɪʃn/ n. ponctuation f.

puncture /'pʌŋktʃə(r)/ n. (in tyre) crevaison f. ● v.t./i. crever.

pundit /'pʌndɪt/ n. expert m.

pungent /'pʌndʒənt/ a. âcre.

punish /'pʌnɪʃ/ *v.t.* punir (**for sth.**, de qch.). **~able** *a.* punissable (**by**, de). **~ment** *n.* punition *f.*

punitive /'pju:nɪtɪv/ *a.* punitif.

punk /pʌŋk/ *n.* (*music, fan*) punk *m.*; (*person: Amer., fam.*) salaud *m.*

punt[1] /pʌnt/ *n.* (*boat*) bachot *m.*

punt[2] /pʌnt/ *v.i.* (*bet*) parier.

puny /'pju:nɪ/ *a.* (**-ier, -iest**) chétif.

pup(py) /'pʌp(ɪ)/ *n.* chiot *m.*

pupil /'pju:pl/ *n.* (*person*) élève *m./f.*; (*of eye*) pupille *f.*

puppet /'pʌpɪt/ *n.* marionnette *f.*

purchase /'pɜːtʃəs/ *v.t.* acheter (**from s.o.**, à qn.). ● *n.* achat *m.* **~r** /-ə(r)/ *n.* acheteu|r, -se *m., f.*

pur|e /pjʊə(r)/ *a.* (**-er, -est**) pur. **~ely** *adv.* purement. **~ity** *n.* pureté *f.*

purgatory /'pɜːgətrɪ/ *n.* purgatoire *m.*

purge /pɜːdʒ/ *v.t.* purger (**of**, de). ● *n.* purge *f.*

purif|y /'pjʊərɪfaɪ/ *v.t.* purifier. **~ication** /-ɪ'keɪʃn/ *n.* purification *f.*

purist /'pjʊərɪst/ *n.* puriste *m./f.*

puritan /'pjʊərɪtən/ *n.* puritain(e) *m. (f.).* **~ical** /-'tænɪkl/ *a.* puritain.

purple /'pɜːpl/ *a. & n.* violet (*m.*).

purport /pə'pɔːt/ *v.t.* **~ to be,** (*claim*) prétendre être.

purpose /'pɜːpəs/ *n.* but *m.*; (*fig.*) résolution *f.* **on ~,** exprès. **~-built** *a.* construit spécialement. **to no ~,** sans résultat.

purr /pɜː(r)/ *n.* ronronnement *m.* ● *v.i.* ronronner.

purse /pɜːs/ *n.* porte-monnaie *m.* *invar.*; (*handbag: Amer.*) sac à main *m.* ● *v.t.* (*lips*) pincer.

pursue /pə'sjuː/ *v.t.* poursuivre. **~r** /-ə(r)/ *n.* poursuivant(e) *m. (f.).*

pursuit /pə'sjuːt/ *n.* poursuite *f.*; (*fig.*) activité *f.*, occupation *f.*

purveyor /pə'veɪə(r)/ *n.* fournisseur *m.*

pus /pʌs/ *n.* pus *m.*

push /pʊʃ/ *v.t./i.* pousser; (*button*) appuyer sur; (*thrust*) enfoncer; (*recommend: sl.*) proposer avec insistance. ● *n.* poussée *f.*; (*effort*) gros effort *m.*; (*drive*) dynamisme *m.* **be ~ed for,** (*time etc.*) manquer de. **be ~ing thirty/** etc., (*fam.*) friser la trentaine/*etc.* **give the ~ to,** (*sl.*) flanquer à la porte. **~ s.o. around,** bousculer qn. **~ back,** repousser. **~-chair** *n.* poussette *f.* **~er** *n.* reven-deu|r, -se (de drogue) *m., f.* **~ off,** (*sl.*) filer. **~ on,** continuer. **~-over**

n. jeu d'enfant *m.* **~ up,** (*lift*) relever; (*prices*) faire monter. **~-up** *n.* (*Amer.*) traction *f.* **~y** *a.* (*fam.*) autoritaire.

pushing /'pʊʃɪŋ/ *a.* arriviste.

puss /pʊs/ *n.* (*cat*) minet(te) *m. (f.).*

put /pʊt/ *v.t./i.* (*p.t.* put, *pres. p.* **putting**) mettre, placer, poser; (*question*) poser. **~ the damage at a million,** estimer les dégâts à un million; **I'd ~ it at a thousand,** je dirais un millier. **~ sth. tactfully,** dire qch. avec tact. **~ across,** communiquer. **~ away,** ranger; (*fig.*) enfermer. **~ back,** remettre; (*delay*) retarder. **~ by,** mettre de côté. **~ down,** (dé)poser; (*write*) inscrire; (*pay*) verser; (*suppress*) réprimer. **~ forward,** (*plan*) soumettre. **~ in,** (*insert*) introduire; (*fix*) installer; (*submit*) soumettre. **~ in for,** faire une demande de. **~ off,** (*postpone*) renvoyer à plus tard; (*disconcert*) déconcerter; (*displease*) rebuter. **~ s.o. off sth.,** dégoûter qn. de qch. **~ on,** (*clothes, radio*) mettre; (*light*) allumer; (*speed, accent, weight*) prendre. **~ out,** sortir; (*stretch*) (é)tendre; (*extinguish*) éteindre; (*disconcert*) déconcerter; (*inconvenience*) déranger. **~ up,** lever, remonter; (*building*) construire; (*notice*) mettre; (*price*) augmenter; (*guest*) héberger; (*offer*) offrir. **~-up job,** coup monté *m.* **~ up with,** supporter.

putt /pʌt/ *n.* (*golf*) putt *m.*

putter /'pʌtə(r)/ *v.i.* (*Amer.*) bricoler.

putty /'pʌtɪ/ *n.* mastic *m.*

puzzle /'pʌzl/ *n.* énigme *f.*; (*game*) casse-tête *m. invar.*; (*jigsaw*) puzzle *m.* ● *v.t.* rendre perplexe. ● *v.i.* se creuser la tête.

pygmy /'pɪgmɪ/ *n.* pygmée *m.*

pyjamas /pə'dʒɑːməz/ *n. pl.* pyjama *m.*

pylon /'paɪlən/ *n.* pylône *m.*

pyramid /'pɪrəmɪd/ *n.* pyramide *f.*

Pyrenees /pɪrə'niːz/ *n. pl.* **the ~,** les Pyrénées *f. pl.*

python /'paɪθn/ *n.* python *m.*

Q

quack[1] /kwæk/ *n.* (*of duck*) coin-coin *m. invar.*

quack² /kwæk/ *n.* charlatan *m.*

quad /kwɒd/ (*fam.*) = **quadrangle, quadruplet**.

quadrangle /'kwɒdræŋgl/ (*of college*) *n.* cour *f.*

quadruped /'kwɒdruped/ *n.* quadrupède *m.*

quadruple /kwɒ'dru:pl/ *a. & n.* quadruple (*m.*). ● *v.t./i.* quadrupler. ~ts /-plɪts/ *n. pl.* quadruplé(e)s *m. (f.) pl.*

quagmire /'kwægmaɪə(r)/ *n.* (*bog*) bourbier *m.*

quail /kweɪl/ *n.* (*bird*) caille *f.*

quaint /kweɪnt/ *a.* (-er, -est) pittoresque; (*old*) vieillot; (*odd*) bizarre. ~ness *n.* pittoresque *m.*

quake /kweɪk/ *v.i.* trembler. ● *n.* (*fam.*) tremblement de terre *m.*

Quaker /'kweɪkə(r)/ *n.* quaker(esse) *m. (f.).*

qualification /kwɒlɪfɪ'keɪʃn/ *n.* diplôme *m.*; (*ability*) compétence *f.*; (*fig.*) réserve *f.*, restriction *f.*

qualif|y /'kwɒlɪfaɪ/ *v.t.* qualifier; (*modify: fig.*) mettre des réserves à; (*statement*) nuancer. ● *v.i.* obtenir son diplôme (as, de); (*sport*) se qualifier; (*fig.*) remplir les conditions requises. ~ied *a.* diplômé; (*able*) qualifié (to do, pour faire); (*fig.*) conditionnel; (*success*) modéré. ~ying *a.* (*round*) éliminatoire; (*candidates*) qualifiés.

qualit|y /'kwɒlətɪ/ *n.* qualité *f.* ~ative /-ɪtətɪv/ *a.* qualitatif.

qualm /kwɑ:m/ *n.* scrupule *m.*

quandary /'kwɒndərɪ/ *n.* embarras *m.*, dilemme *m.*

quantit|y /'kwɒntətɪ/ *n.* quantité *f.* ~ative /-ɪtətɪv/ *a.* quantitatif.

quarantine /'kwɒrənti:n/ *n.* (*isolation*) quarantaine *f.*

quarrel /'kwɒrəl/ *n.* dispute *f.*, querelle *f.* ● *v.i.* (*p.t.* quarrelled) se disputer. ~some *a.* querelleur.

quarry¹ /'kwɒrɪ/ *n.* (*prey*) proie *f.*

quarry² /'kwɒrɪ/ *n.* (*excavation*) carrière *f.* ● *v.t.* extraire.

quart /kwɔ:t/ *n.* (*approx.*) litre *m.*

quarter /'kwɔ:tə(r)/ *n.* quart *m.*; (*of year*) trimestre *m.*; (*25 cents: Amer.*) quart de dollar *m.*; (*district*) quartier *m.* ~s, logement(s) *m.* (*pl.*) ● *v.t.* diviser en quatre; (*mil.*) cantonner. from all ~s, de toutes parts. ~-final *n.* quart de finale *m.* ~ly *a.* trimestriel; *adv.* trimestriellement.

quartermaster /'kwɔ:təma:stə(r)/ *n.* (*mil.*) intendant *m.*

quartet /kwɔ:'tet/ *n.* quatuor *m.*

quartz /kwɔ:ts/ *n.* quartz *m.* ● *a.* (*watch etc.*) à quartz.

quash /kwɒʃ/ *v.t.* (*suppress*) étouffer; (*jurid.*) annuler.

quasi- /'kweɪsaɪ/ *pref.* quasi-.

quaver /'kweɪvə(r)/ *v.i.* trembler, chevroter. ● *n.* (*mus.*) croche *f.*

quay /ki:/ *n.* (*naut.*) quai *m.* ~side *n.* (*edge of quay*) quai *m.*

queasy /'kwi:zɪ/ *a.* (*stomach*) délicat. feel ~, avoir mal au cœur.

queen /kwi:n/ *n.* reine *f.*; (*cards*) dame *f.* ~ mother, reine mère *f.*

queer /kwɪə(r)/ *a.* (-er, -est) étrange; (*dubious*) louche; (*ill*) patraque. ● *n.* (*sl.*) homosexuel *m.*

quell /kwel/ *v.t.* réprimer.

quench /kwentʃ/ *v.t.* éteindre; (*thirst*) étancher; (*desire*) étouffer.

query /'kwɪərɪ/ *n.* question *f.* ● *v.t.* mettre en question.

quest /kwest/ *n.* recherche *f.*

question /'kwestʃən/ *n.* question *f.* ● *v.t.* interroger; (*doubt*) mettre en question, douter de. a ~ of money, une question d'argent. in ~, en question. no ~ of, pas question de. out of the ~, hors de question. ~ mark, point d'interrogation *m.*

questionable /'kwestʃənəbl/ *a.* discutable.

questionnaire /kwestʃə'neə(r)/ *n.* questionnaire *m.*

queue /kju:/ *n.* queue *f.* ● *v.i.* (*pres. p.* queuing) faire la queue.

quibble /'kwɪbl/ *v.i.* ergoter.

quick /kwɪk/ *a.* (-er, -est) rapide. ● *adv.* vite. ● *n.* a ~ one, (*fam.*) un petit verre. cut to the ~, piquer au vif. be ~, (*hurry*) se dépêcher. have a ~ temper, s'emporter facilement. ~ly *adv.* rapidement, vite. ~-witted *a.* vif.

quicken /'kwɪkən/ *v.t./i.* (s')accélérer.

quicksand /'kwɪksænd/ *n.* ~(s), sables mouvants *m. pl.*

quid /kwɪd/ *n. invar.* (*sl.*) livre *f.*

quiet /'kwaɪət/ *a.* (-er, -est) (*calm, still*) tranquille; (*silent*) silencieux; (*gentle*) doux; (*discreet*) discret. ● *n.* tranquillité *f.* keep ~, se taire. on the ~, en cachette. ~ly *adv.* tranquillement; silencieusement; doucement; discrètement. ~ness *n.* tranquillité *f.*

quieten /'kwaɪətn/ *v.t./i.* (se) calmer.

quill /kwɪl/ *n.* plume (d'oie) *f.*

quilt /kwɪlt/ *n.* édredon **m.** (**continental**) ∼, couette *f.* ● *v.t.* matelasser.

quinine /'kwɪniːn, *Amer.* 'kwaɪnaɪn/ *n.* quinine *f.*

quintet /kwɪn'tet/ *n.* quintette *m.*

quintuplets /kwɪn'tjuːplɪts/ *n. pl.* quintuplé(e)s *m.* (*f.*) *pl.*

quip /kwɪp/ *n.* mot piquant *m.*

quirk /kwɜːk/ *n.* bizarrerie *f.*

quit /kwɪt/ *v.t.* (*p.t.* **quitted**) quitter. ● *v.i.* abandonner; (*resign*) démissionner. ∼ **doing**, (*cease*: *Amer.*) cesser de faire.

quite /kwaɪt/ *adv.* tout à fait, vraiment; (*rather*) assez. ∼ (**so**)!, parfaitement! ∼ **a few**, un assez grand nombre (de).

quits /kwɪts/ *a.* quitte (**with**, envers). **call it** ∼, en rester là.

quiver /'kwɪvə(r)/ *v.i.* trembler.

quiz /kwɪz/ *n.* (*pl.* **quizzes**) test *m.*; (*game*) jeu-concours *m.* ● *v.t.* (*p.t.* **quizzed**) questionner.

quizzical /'kwɪzɪkl/ *a.* moqueur.

quorum /'kwɔːrəm/ *n.* quorum *m.*

quota /'kwəʊtə/ *n.* quota *m.*

quotation /kwəʊ'teɪʃn/ *n.* citation *f.*; (*price*) devis *m.*; (*stock exchange*) cotation *f.* ∼ **marks**, guillemets *m. pl.*

quote /kwəʊt/ *v.t.* citer; (*reference*: *comm.*) rappeler; (*price*) indiquer; (*share price*) coter. ● *v.i.* ∼ **for**, faire un devis pour. ∼ **from**, citer. ● *n.* (*estimate*) devis; (*fam.*) = quotation. **in** ∼**s**, (*fam.*) entre guillemets.

quotient /'kwəʊʃnt/ *n.* quotient *m.*

R

rabbi /'ræbaɪ/ *n.* rabbin *m.*

rabbit /'ræbɪt/ *n.* lapin *m.*

rabble /'ræbl/ *n.* (*crowd*) cohue *f.* **the** ∼, (*pej.*) la populace.

rabid /'ræbɪd/ *a.* enragé.

rabies /'reɪbiːz/ *n.* (*disease*) rage *f.*

race [1] /reɪs/ *n.* course *f.* ● *v.t.* (*horse*) faire courir; (*engine*) emballer. ∼ (**against**), faire la course à. ● *v.i.* courir; (*rush*) foncer. ∼**-track** *n.* piste *f.*; (*for horses*) champ de courses *m.*

race [2] /reɪs/ *n.* (*group*) race *f.* ● *a.* racial; (*relations*) entre les races.

racecourse /'reɪskɔːs/ *n.* champ de courses *m.*

racehorse /'reɪshɔːs/ *n.* cheval de course *m.*

racial /'reɪʃl/ *a.* racial.

racing /'reɪsɪŋ/ *n.* courses *f. pl.* ∼ **car**, voiture de course *f.*

racis|**t** /'reɪsɪst/ *a. & n.* raciste (*m./f.*). ∼**m** /-zəm/ *n.* racisme *m.*

rack [1] /ræk/ *n.* (*shelf*) étagère *f.*; (*pigeon-holes*) casier *m.*; (*for luggage*) porte-bagages *m. invar.*; (*for dishes*) égouttoir *m.*; (*on car roof*) galerie *f.* ∼ **one's brains**, se creuser la cervelle.

rack [2] /ræk/ *n.* **go to** ∼ **and ruin**, aller à la ruine; (*building*) tomber en ruine.

racket [1] /'rækɪt/ *n.* raquette *f.*

racket [2] /'rækɪt/ *n.* (*din*) tapage *m.*; (*dealings*) combine *f.*; (*crime*) racket *m.* ∼**eer** /-ə'tɪə(r)/ *n.* racketteur *m.*

racy /'reɪsɪ/ *a.* (**-ier, -iest**) fougueux, piquant; (*Amer.*) risqué.

radar /'reɪdɑː(r)/ *n.* radar *m.* ● *a.* (*system etc.*) radar *invar.*

radial /'reɪdɪəl/ *a.* (*tyre*) à carcasse radiale.

radian|**t** /'reɪdɪənt/ *a.* rayonnant. ∼**ce** *n.* éclat *m.* ∼**tly** *adv.* avec éclat.

radiat|**e** /'reɪdɪeɪt/ *v.t.* dégager. ● *v.i.* rayonner (**from**, de). ∼**ion** /-'eɪʃn/ *n.* rayonnement *m.*; (*radioactivity*) radiation *f.*

radiator /'reɪdɪeɪtə(r)/ *n.* radiateur *m.*

radical /'rædɪkl/ *a.* radical. ● *n.* (*person*: *pol.*) radical(e) *m.* (*f.*).

radio /'reɪdɪəʊ/ *n.* (*pl.* **-os**) radio *f.* ● *v.t.* (*message*) envoyer par radio; (*person*) appeler par radio.

radioactiv|**e** /reɪdɪəʊ'æktɪv/ *a.* radioactif. ∼**ity** /-'tɪvəti/ *n.* radioactivité *f.*

radiographer /reɪdɪ'ɒɡrəfə(r)/ *n.* radiologue *m./f.*

radish /'rædɪʃ/ *n.* radis *m.*

radius /'reɪdɪəs/ *n.* (*pl.* **-dii** /-dɪaɪ/) rayon *m.*

raffle /'ræfl/ *n.* tombola *f.*

raft /rɑːft/ *n.* radeau *m.*

rafter /'rɑːftə(r)/ *n.* chevron *m.*

rag [1] /ræɡ/ *n.* lambeau *m.*, loque *f.*; (*for wiping*) chiffon *m.*; (*newspaper*) torchon *m.* **in** ∼**s**, (*person*) en haillons; (*clothes*) en lambeaux. ∼ **doll**, poupée de chiffon *f.*

rag [2] /ræg/ v.t. (p.t. ragged) (tease: sl.) taquiner. ● n. (univ., sl.) carnaval m. (pour une œuvre de charité).

ragamuffin /'rægəmʌfɪn/ n. va-nu-pieds m. invar.

rage /reɪdʒ/ n. rage f., fureur f. ● v.i. rager; (storm, battle) faire rage. be all the ~, faire fureur.

ragged /'rægɪd/ a. (clothes, person) loqueteux; (edge) déchiqueté.

raging /'reɪdʒɪŋ/ a. (storm, fever, etc.) violent.

raid /reɪd/ n. (mil.) raid m.; (by police) rafle f.; (by criminals) hold-up m. invar. ● v.t. faire un raid or une rafle or un hold-up dans. ~er n. (person) bandit m., pillard m. ~ers n. pl. (mil.) commando m.

rail /reɪl/ n. (on balcony) balustrade f.; (stairs) main courante f., rampe f.; (for train) rail m.; (for curtain) tringle f. by ~, par chemin de fer.

railing /'reɪlɪŋ/ n. ~s, grille f.

railroad /'reɪlrəʊd/ n. (Amer.) = railway.

railway /'reɪlweɪ/ n. chemin de fer m. ~ line, voie ferrée f. ~man n. (pl. -men) cheminot m. ~ station, gare f.

rain /reɪn/ n. pluie f. ● v.i. pleuvoir. ~ forest, forêt (humide) tropicale f. ~-storm n. trombe d'eau f. ~-water n. eau de pluie f.

rainbow /'reɪnbəʊ/ n. arc-en-ciel m.

raincoat /'reɪnkəʊt/ n. imperméable m.

rainfall /'reɪnfɔːl/ n. précipitation f.

rainy /'reɪnɪ/ a. (-ier, -iest) pluvieux; (season) des pluies.

raise /reɪz/ v.t. lever; (breed, build) élever; (question etc.) soulever; (price etc.) relever; (money etc.) obtenir; (voice) élever. ● n. (Amer.) augmentation f.

raisin /'reɪzn/ n. raisin sec m.

rake [1] /reɪk/ n. râteau m. ● v.t. (garden) ratisser; (search) fouiller dans. ~ in, (money) amasser. ~-off n. (fam.) profit m. ~ up, (memories, past) remuer.

rake [2] /reɪk/ n. (man) débauché m.

rally /'rælɪ/ v.t./i. (se) rallier; (strength) reprendre; (after illness) aller mieux. ● n. rassemblement m.; (auto.) rallye m.; (tennis) échange m. ~ round, venir en aide.

ram /ræm/ n. bélier m. ● v.t. (p.t. rammed) (thrust) enfoncer; (crash into) emboutir, percuter.

RAM /ræm/ abbr. (random access memory) mémoire vive f.

rambl|e /'ræmbl/ n. randonnée f. ● v.i. faire une randonnée. ~e on, parler (sans cesse), divaguer. ~er n. randonneu|r, -se, m., f. ~ing a. (speech) décousu.

ramification /ræmɪfɪ'keɪʃn/ n. ramification f.

ramp /ræmp/ n. (slope) rampe f.; (in garage) pont de graissage m.

rampage [1] /ræm'peɪdʒ/ v.i. se livrer à des actes de violence, se déchaîner.

rampage [2] /'ræmpeɪdʒ/ n. go on the ~ = rampage [1].

rampant /'ræmpənt/ a. be ~, (disease etc.) sévir, être répandu.

rampart /'ræmpɑːt/ n. rempart m.

ramshackle /'ræmʃækl/ a. délabré.

ran /ræn/ see run.

ranch /rɑːntʃ/ n. ranch m.

rancid /'rænsɪd/ a. rance.

rancour /'ræŋkə(r)/ n. rancœur f.

random /'rændəm/ a. fait, pris, etc. au hasard, aléatoire (techn.). ● n. at ~, au hasard.

randy /'rændɪ/ a. (-ier, -iest) (fam.) excité, en chaleur.

rang /ræŋ/ see ring [2].

range /reɪndʒ/ n. (distance) portée f.; (of aircraft etc.) rayon d'action m.; (series) gamme f.; (scale) échelle f.; (choice) choix m.; (domain) champ m.; (of mountains) chaîne f.; (stove) cuisinière f. ● v.i. s'étendre; (vary) varier.

ranger /'reɪndʒə(r)/ n. garde forestier m.

rank [1] /ræŋk/ n. rang m.; (grade: mil.) grade m., rang m. ● v.t./i. ~ among, compter parmi. the ~ and file, les gens ordinaires.

rank [2] /ræŋk/ a. (-er, -est) (plants: pej.) luxuriant; (smell) fétide; (complete) absolu.

rankle /'ræŋkl/ v.i. ~ with s.o., rester sur le cœur à qn.

ransack /'rænsæk/ v.t. (search) fouiller; (pillage) saccager.

ransom /'rænsəm/ n. rançon f. ● v.t. rançonner; (redeem) racheter. hold to ~, rançonner.

rant /rænt/ v.i. tempêter.

rap /ræp/ n. petit coup sec m. ● v.t./i. (p.t. rapped) frapper.

rape /reɪp/ v.t. violer. ● n. viol m.

rapid /'ræpɪd/ a. rapide. ~ity /rə'pɪdətɪ/ n. rapidité f. ~s n. pl. (of river) rapides m. pl.

rapist /'reɪpɪst/ n. violeur m.

rapport /ræ'pɔː(r)/ n. rapport m.

rapt /ræpt/ a. (attention) profond. ~ in, plongé dans.

rapture /'ræptʃə(r)/ n. extase f. ~ous a. (person) en extase; (welcome etc.) frénétique.

rare[1] /reə(r)/ a. (-er, -est) rare. ~ly adv. rarement. ~ity n. rareté f.

rare[2] /reə(r)/ a. (-er, -est) (culin.) saignant.

rarefied /'reərɪfaɪd/ a. raréfié.

raring /'reərɪŋ/ a. ~ to, (fam.) impatient de.

rascal /'rɑːskl/ n. coquin(e) m. (f.).

rash[1] /ræʃ/ n. (med.) éruption f., rougeurs f. pl.

rash[2] /ræʃ/ a. (-er, -est) imprudent. ~ly adv. imprudemment. ~ness n. imprudence f.

rasher /'ræʃə(r)/ n. tranche (de lard) f.

raspberry /'rɑːzbrɪ/ n. framboise f.

rasping /'rɑːspɪŋ/ a. grinçant.

rat /ræt/ n. rat m. ● v.i. (p.t. ratted). ~ on, (desert) lâcher; (inform on) dénoncer. ~ race, foire d'empoigne f.

rate /reɪt/ n. (ratio, level) taux m.; (speed) allure f.; (price) tarif m. ~s, (taxes) impôts locaux m. pl. ● v.t. évaluer; (consider) considérer; (deserve: Amer.) mériter. ● v.i. ~ as, être considéré comme. at any ~, en tout cas. at the ~ of, (on the basis of) à raison de.

ratepayer /'reɪtpeɪə(r)/ n. contribuable m./f.

rather /'rɑːðə(r)/ adv. (by preference) plutôt; (fairly) assez, plutôt; (a little) un peu. I would ~ go, j'aimerais mieux partir. ~ than go, plutôt que de partir.

ratify /'rætɪfaɪ/ v.t. ratifier. ~ication /-ɪ'keɪʃn/ n. ratification f.

rating /'reɪtɪŋ/ n. classement m.; (sailor) matelot m.; (number) indice m. the ~s, (TV) l'audimat (P.).

ratio /'reɪʃɪəʊ/ n. (pl. -os) proportion f.

ration /'ræʃn/ n. ration f. ● v.t. rationner.

rational /'ræʃənl/ a. rationnel; (person) raisonnable.

rationalize /'ræʃənəlaɪz/ v.t. tenter de justifier; (organize) rationaliser.

rattle /'rætl/ v.i. faire du bruit; (of bottles) cliqueter. ● v.t. secouer; (sl.) agacer. ● n. bruit (de ferraille) m.; cliquetis m.; (toy) hochet m. ~ off, débiter en vitesse.

rattlesnake /'rætlsneɪk/ n. serpent à sonnette m., crotale m.

raucous /'rɔːkəs/ a. rauque.

raunchy /'rɔːntʃɪ/ a. (-ier, -iest) (Amer., sl.) cochon.

ravage /'rævɪdʒ/ v.t. ravager. ~s /-ɪz/ n. pl. ravages m. pl.

rav|**e** /reɪv/ v.i. divaguer; (in anger) tempêter. ~e about, s'extasier sur. ~ings n. pl. divagations f. pl.

raven /'reɪvn/ n. corbeau m.

ravenous /'rævənəs/ a. vorace. I am ~, je meurs de faim.

ravine /rə'viːn/ n. ravin m.

raving /'reɪvɪŋ/ a. ~ lunatic, fou furieux m., folle furieuse f.

ravioli /rævɪ'əʊlɪ/ n. ravioli m. pl.

ravish /'rævɪʃ/ v.t. (rape) ravir. ~ing a. (enchanting) ravissant.

raw /rɔː/ a. (-er, -est) cru; (not processed) brut; (wound) à vif; (immature) inexpérimenté. get a ~ deal, être mal traité. ~ materials, matières premières f. pl.

ray /reɪ/ n. (of light etc.) rayon m. ~ of hope, lueur d'espoir f.

raze /reɪz/ v.t. (destroy) raser.

razor /'reɪzə(r)/ n. rasoir m. ~-blade n. lame de rasoir f.

re /riː/ prep. concernant.

re- /riː/ pref. re-, ré-, r-.

reach /riːtʃ/ v.t. atteindre, arriver à; (contact) joindre; (hand over) passer. ● v.i. s'étendre. ● n. portée f. ~ for, tendre la main pour prendre. within ~ of, à portée de; (close to) à proximité de.

react /rɪ'ækt/ v.i. réagir.

reaction /rɪ'ækʃn/ n. réaction f. ~ary a. & n. réactionnaire (m./f.).

reactor /rɪ'æktə(r)/ n. réacteur m.

read /riːd/ v.t./i. (p.t. read /red/) lire; (fig.) comprendre; (study) étudier; (of instrument) indiquer. ● n. (fam.) lecture f. ~ about s.o., lire un article sur qn. ~ out, lire à haute voix. ~able a. agréable or facile à lire. ~ing n. lecture f.; indication f. ~ing-glasses n. pl. lunettes pour lire f. pl. ~ing-lamp n. lampe de bureau f. ~-out n. affichage m.

reader /'riːdə(r)/ n. lec|teur, -trice m., f. ~ship n. lecteurs m. pl.

readily /'redɪlɪ/ adv. (willingly) volontiers; (easily) facilement.

readiness /'redɪnɪs/ n. empressement m. in ~, prêt (for, à).

readjust /ri:ə'dʒʌst/ v.t. rajuster.
● v.i. se réadapter (to, à).

ready /'redɪ/ a. (-ier, -iest) prêt;
(quick) prompt. ● n. at the ~,
tout prêt. ~-made a. tout fait. ~
money, (argent) liquide m. ~ reck-
oner, barème m. ~-to-wear a. prêt-
à-porter.

real /rɪəl/ a. vrai, véritable, réel.
● adv. (Amer., fam.) vraiment. ~
estate, biens fonciers m. pl.

realis|t /'rɪəlɪst/ n. réaliste m./f. ~m
/-zəm/ n. réalisme m. ~tic /-'lɪstɪk/
a. réaliste. ~tically /-'lɪstɪklɪ/ adv.
avec réalisme.

reality /rɪ'ælətɪ/ n. réalité f.

realize /'rɪəlaɪz/ v.t. se rendre compte
de, comprendre; (fulfil, turn into
cash) réaliser; (price) atteindre.
~ation /-'zeɪʃn/ n. prise de conscience f.; réalisation f.

really /'rɪəlɪ/ adv. vraiment.

realtor /'rɪəltə(r)/ n. (Amer.) agent
immobilier m.

realm /relm/ n. royaume m.

reap /ri:p/ v.t. (crop, field) moissonner; (fig.) récolter.

reappear /ri:ə'pɪə(r)/ v.i. réapparaître, reparaître.

reappraisal /ri:ə'preɪzl/ n. réévalua-
tion f.

rear¹ /rɪə(r)/ n. arrière m., derrière
m. ● a. arrière invar., de derrière.
~-view mirror, rétroviseur m.

rear² /rɪə(r)/ v.t. (bring up, breed)
élever. ● v.i. (horse) se cabrer. ~
one's head, dresser la tête.

rearguard /'rɪəgɑ:d/ n. (mil.) arrière-
garde f.

rearm /ri:'ɑ:m/ v.t./i. réarmer.

rearrange /ri:ə'reɪndʒ/ v.t. réarran-
ger.

reason /'ri:zn/ n. raison f. ● v.i.
raisonner. it stands to ~ that, de
toute évidence. we have ~ to
believe that, on a tout lieu de croire
que. there is no ~ to panic, il n'y a
pas de raison de paniquer. ~ with,
raisonner. everything within ~,
tout dans les limites normales.
~ing n. raisonnement m.

reasonable /'ri:znəbl/ a. raisonnable.

reassur|e /ri:ə'ʃʊə(r)/ v.t. rassurer.
~ance n. réconfort m.

rebate /'ri:beɪt/ n. remboursement
(partiel) m.; (discount) rabais m.

rebel¹ /'rebl/ n. & a. rebelle (m./f.).

rebel² /rɪ'bel/ v.i. (p.t. rebelled) se
rebeller. ~lion n. rébellion f.
~lious a. rebelle.

rebound /rɪ'baʊnd/ v.i. rebondir. ~
on, (backfire) se retourner contre.
● n. /'ri:baʊnd/ n. rebond m.

rebuff /rɪ'bʌf/ v.t. repousser. ● n.
rebuffade f.

rebuild /ri:'bɪld/ v.t. reconstruire.

rebuke /rɪ'bju:k/ v.t. réprimander.
● n. réprimande f., reproche m.

rebuttal /rɪ'bʌtl/ n. réfutation f.

recall /rɪ'kɔ:l/ v.t. (to s.o., call back)
rappeler; (remember) se rappeler.
● n. rappel m.

recant /rɪ'kænt/ v.i. se rétracter.

recap /'ri:kæp/ v.t./i. (p.t. recapped)
(fam.) récapituler. ● n. (fam.) réca-
pitulation f.

recapitulate /ri:kə'pɪtʃʊleɪt/ v.t./i.
récapituler. ~ion /-'leɪʃn/ n. récapi-
tulation f.

recapture /ri:'kæptʃə(r)/ v.t. reprendre; (recall) recréer.

reced|e /rɪ'si:d/ v.i. s'éloigner. his
hair is ~ing, son front se dégarnit.
~ing a. (forehead) fuyant.

receipt /rɪ'si:t/ n. (written) reçu m.;
(of letter) réception f. ~s, (money:
comm.) recettes f. pl.

receive /rɪ'si:v/ v.t. recevoir. ~r
/-ə(r)/ n. (of stolen goods) receleu|r,
-se m., f.; (telephone) combiné m.

recent /'ri:snt/ a. récent. ~ly adv.
récemment.

receptacle /rɪ'septəkl/ n. récipient m.

reception /rɪ'sepʃn/ n. réception f.
give s.o. a warm ~, donner un
accueil chaleureux à qn. ~ist n.
réceptionniste m./f.

receptive /rɪ'septɪv/ a. réceptif.

recess /rɪ'ses/ n. (alcove) renforcement m.; (nook) recoin m.; (holiday)
vacances f. pl.; (schol., Amer.) récréation f.

recession /rɪ'seʃn/ n. récession f.

recharge /ri:'tʃɑ:dʒ/ v.t. recharger.

recipe /'resəpɪ/ n. recette f.

recipient /rɪ'sɪpɪənt/ n. (of honour)
récipiendaire m.; (of letter) destinataire m./f.

reciprocal /rɪ'sɪprəkl/ a. réciproque.

reciprocate /rɪ'sɪprəkeɪt/ v.t. offrir
en retour. ● v.i. en faire autant.

recital /rɪ'saɪtl/ n. récital m.

recite /rɪ'saɪt/ v.t. (poem, lesson, etc.)
réciter; (list) énumérer.

reckless /'reklɪs/ a. imprudent. ~ly
adv. imprudemment.

reckon /'rekən/ v.t./i. calculer; (*judge*) considérer; (*think*) penser. ~ **on/with**, compter sur/avec. ~**ing** n. calcul(s) m. (pl.).

reclaim /rɪ'kleɪm/ v.t. (*seek return of*) réclamer; (*land*) défricher; (*flooded land*) assécher.

reclin|e /rɪ'klaɪn/ v.i. être étendu. ~**ing** a. (*person*) étendu; (*seat*) à dossier réglable.

recluse /rɪ'kluːs/ n. reclus(e) m. (f.), ermite m.

recognition /rekəg'nɪʃn/ n. reconnaissance f. **beyond** ~, méconnaissable. **gain** ~, être reconnu.

recognize /'rekəgnaɪz/ v.t. reconnaître.

recoil /rɪ'kɔɪl/ v.i. reculer (**from**, devant).

recollect /rekə'lekt/ v.t. se souvenir de, se rappeler. ~**ion** /-kʃn/ n. souvenir m.

recommend /rekə'mend/ v.t. recommander. ~**ation** /-'deɪʃn/ n. recommandation f.

recompense /'rekəmpens/ v.t. (ré)compenser. ● n. récompense f.

reconcil|e /'rekənsaɪl/ v.t. (*people*) réconcilier; (*facts*) concilier. ~**e o.s. to**, se résigner à. ~**iation** /-sɪlɪ'eɪʃn/ n. réconciliation f.

recondition /riːkən'dɪʃn/ v.t. remettre à neuf, réviser.

reconn|oitre /rekə'nɔɪtə(r)/ v.t. (*pres. p.* -**tring**) (*mil.*) reconnaître. ~**aissance** /rɪ'kɒnɪsns/ n. reconnaissance f.

reconsider /riːkən'sɪdə(r)/ v.t. reconsidérer. ● v.i. se déjuger.

reconstruct /riːkən'strʌkt/ v.t. reconstruire; (*crime*) reconstituer.

record¹ /rɪ'kɔːd/ v.t./i. (*in register, on tape, etc.*) enregistrer; (*in diary*) noter. ~ **that**, rapporter que. ~**ing** n. enregistrement m.

record² /'rekɔːd/ n. (*report*) rapport m.; (*register*) registre m.; (*mention*) mention f.; (*file*) dossier m.; (*fig.*) résultats m. pl.; (*mus.*) disque m.; (*sport*) record m. (*criminal*) ~, casier judiciaire m. ● a. record invar. **off the** ~, officieusement. ~**holder** n. déten|teur, -trice du record m., f. ~**player** n. électrophone m.

recorder /rɪ'kɔːdə(r)/ n. (*mus.*) flûte à bec f.

recount /rɪ'kaʊnt/ v.t. raconter.

re-count /riː'kaʊnt/ v.t. recompter.

recoup /rɪ'kuːp/ v.t. récupérer.

recourse /rɪ'kɔːs/ n. recours m. **have** ~ **to**, avoir recours à.

recover /rɪ'kʌvə(r)/ v.t. récupérer. ● v.i. se remettre; (*med.*) se rétablir; (*economy*) se redresser. ~**y** n. récupération f.; (*med.*) rétablissement m.

recreation /rekrɪ'eɪʃn/ n. récréation f. ~**al** a. de récréation.

recrimination /rɪkrɪmɪ'neɪʃn/ n. contre-accusation f.

recruit /rɪ'kruːt/ n. recrue f. ● v.t. recruter. ~**ment** n. recrutement m.

rectang|le /'rektæŋgl/ n. rectangle m. ~**ular** /-'tæŋgjʊlə(r)/ a. rectangulaire.

rectif|y /'rektɪfaɪ/ v.t. rectifier. ~**ication** /-ɪ'keɪʃn/ n. rectification f.

recuperate /rɪ'kjuːpəreɪt/ v.t. récupérer. ● v.i. (*med.*) se rétablir.

recur /rɪ'kɜː(r)/ v.i. (*p.t.* **recurred**) revenir, se répéter.

recurren|t /rɪ'kʌrənt/ a. fréquent. ~**ce** n. répétition f., retour m.

recycle /riː'saɪkl/ v.t. recycler.

red /red/ a. (**redder, reddest**) rouge; (*hair*) roux. ● n. rouge m. **in the** ~, en déficit. **roll out the** ~ **carpet for,** recevoir en grande pompe. **Red Cross,** Croix-Rouge f. ~**handed** a. en flagrant délit. ~ **herring,** fausse piste f. ~**hot** a. brûlant. the ~ **light,** le feu rouge m. ~ **tape,** paperasserie f., bureaucratie f.

redcurrant /red'kʌrənt/ n. groseille f.

redden /'redn/ v.t./i. rougir.

reddish /'redɪʃ/ a. rougeâtre.

redecorate /riː'dekəreɪt/ v.t. (*repaint etc.*) repeindre, refaire.

redeem /rɪ'diːm/ v.t. racheter. ~**ing quality,** qualité qui rachète les défauts f.

redemption n. /rɪ'dempʃn/ rachat m.

redeploy /riːdɪ'plɔɪ/ v.t. réorganiser; (*troops*) répartir.

redirect /riːdaɪə'rekt/ v.t. (*letter*) faire suivre.

redness /'rednɪs/ n. rougeur f.

redo /riː'duː/ v.t. (*p.t.* **-did**, *p.p.* **-done**) refaire.

redolent /'redələnt/ a. ~ **of**, qui évoque.

redouble /rɪ'dʌbl/ v.t. redoubler.

redress /rɪ'dres/ v.t. (*wrong etc.*) redresser. ● n. réparation f.

reduc|e /rɪ'dju:s/ v.t. réduire; (*temperature etc.*) faire baisser. **~tion** /rɪ'dʌkʃn/ n. réduction f.

redundan|t /rɪ'dʌndənt/ a. superflu; (*worker*) licencié. **make ~,** licencier. **~cy** n. licenciement m.; (*word, phrase*) pléonasme m.

reed /ri:d/ n. (*plant*) roseau m.; (*mus.*) anche f.

reef /ri:f/ n. récif m., écueil m.

reek /ri:k/ n. puanteur f. ● v.i. ~ (**of**), puer.

reel /ri:l/ n. (*of thread*) bobine f.; (*of film*) bande f.; (*winding device*) dévidoir m. ● v.i. chanceler. ● v.t. ~ **off,** réciter.

refectory /rɪ'fektərɪ/ n. réfectoire m.

refer /rɪ'fɜ:(r)/ v.t./i. (*p.t.* referred). ~ **to,** (*allude to*) faire allusion à; (*concern*) s'appliquer à; (*consult*) consulter; (*submit*) soumettre à; (*direct*) renvoyer à.

referee /refə'ri:/ n. arbitre m.; (*for job*) répondant(e) m. (f.). ● v.t. (*p.t.* refereed) arbitrer.

reference /'refrəns/ n. référence f.; (*mention*) allusion f.; (*person*) répondant(e) m. (f.). **in** or **with ~ to,** en ce qui concerne; (*comm.*) suite à. ~ **book,** ouvrage de référence m.

referendum /refə'rendəm/ n. (*pl.* -ums) référendum m.

refill[1] /ri:'fɪl/ v.t. remplir (à nouveau); (*pen etc.*) recharger.

refill[2] /'ri:fɪl/ n. (*of pen, lighter, lipstick*) recharge f.

refine /rɪ'faɪn/ v.t. raffiner. **~d** a. raffiné. **~ment** n. raffinement m.; (*techn.*) raffinage m. **~ry** /-ərɪ/ n. raffinerie f.

reflate /ri:'fleɪt/ v.t. relancer.

reflect /rɪ'flekt/ v.t. refléter; (*of mirror*) réfléchir, refléter. ● v.i. réfléchir (**on,** à). ~ **on s.o.,** (*glory etc.*) (faire) rejaillir sur qn.; (*pej.*) donner une mauvaise impression de qn. **~ion** /-kʃn/ n. réflexion f.; (*image*) reflet m. **on ~ion,** réflexion faite. **~or** n. réflecteur m.

reflective /rɪ'flektɪv/ a. réfléchissant.

reflex /'ri:fleks/ n. & a. réflexe (m.).

reflexive /rɪ'fleksɪv/ a. (*gram.*) réfléchi.

reform /rɪ'fɔ:m/ v.t. réformer. ● v.i. (*person*) s'amender. ● n. réforme f. **~er** n. réforma|teur, -trice m., f.

refract /rɪ'frækt/ v.t. réfracter.

refrain[1] /rɪ'freɪn/ n. refrain m.

refrain[2] /rɪ'freɪn/ v.i. s'abstenir (**from,** de).

refresh /rɪ'freʃ/ v.t. rafraîchir; (*of rest etc.*) ragaillardir, délasser. **~ing** a. (*drink*) rafraîchissant; (*sleep*) réparateur. **~ments** n. pl. rafraîchissements m. pl.

refresher /rɪ'freʃə(r)/ a. (*course*) de perfectionnement.

refrigerat|e /rɪ'frɪdʒəreɪt/ v.t. réfrigérer. **~or** n. réfrigérateur m.

refuel /ri:'fju:əl/ v.t./i. (*p.t.* refuelled) (se) ravitailler.

refuge /'refju:dʒ/ n. refuge m. **take ~,** se réfugier.

refugee /refjo'dʒi:/ n. réfugié(e) m. (f.).

refund /rɪ'fʌnd/ v.t. rembourser. ● n. /'ri:fʌnd/ remboursement m.

refurbish /ri:'fɜ:bɪʃ/ v.t. remettre à neuf.

refus|e[1] /rɪ'fju:z/ v.t./i. refuser. **~al** n. refus m.

refuse[2] /'refju:s/ n. ordures f. pl.

refute /rɪ'fju:t/ v.t. réfuter.

regain /rɪ'geɪn/ v.t. retrouver; (*lost ground*) regagner.

regal /'ri:gl/ a. royal, majestueux.

regalia /rɪ'geɪlɪə/ n. pl. (*insignia*) insignes (royaux) m. pl.

regard /rɪ'gɑ:d/ v.t. considérer. ● n. considération f., estime f. **~s,** amitiés f. pl. **in this ~,** à cet égard. **as ~s, ~ing** prep. en ce qui concerne.

regardless /rɪ'gɑ:dlɪs/ adv. quand même. ~ **of,** sans tenir compte de.

regatta /rɪ'gætə/ n. régates f. pl.

regenerat|e /rɪ'dʒenəreɪt/ v.t. régénérer. **~ion** /-'reɪʃn/ n. régénération f.

regen|t /'ri:dʒənt/ n. régent(e) m. (f.). **~cy** n. régence f.

regime /reɪ'ʒi:m/ n. régime m.

regiment /'redʒɪmənt/ n. régiment m. **~al** /-'mentl/ a. d'un régiment. **~ation** /-en'teɪʃn/ n. discipline excessive f.

region /'ri:dʒən/ n. région f. **in the ~ of,** environ. **~al** a. régional.

regist|er /'redʒɪstə(r)/ n. registre m. ● v.t. enregistrer; (*vehicle*) immatriculer; (*birth*) déclarer; (*letter*) recommander; (*indicate*) indiquer; (*express*) exprimer. ● v.i. (*enrol*) s'inscrire; (*fig.*) être compris. **~er office,** bureau d'état civil m. **~ration** /-'streɪʃn/ n. enregistrement m.; inscription f.; (*vehicle document*) carte grise f. **~ration**

(number), (*auto.*) numéro d'immatriculation *m*.

registrar /redʒɪ'strɑ:(r)/ *n*. officier de l'état civil *m*.; (*univ.*) secrétaire général *m*.

regret /rɪ'gret/ *n*. regret *m*. ● *v.t.* (*p.t.* **regretted**) regretter (**to do**, de faire). ~**fully** *adv*. à regret. ~**table** *a*. regrettable, fâcheux. ~**tably** *adv*. malheureusement; (*small, poor, etc.*) fâcheusement.

regroup /ri:'gru:p/ *v.t./i.* (se) regrouper.

regular /'regjʊlə(r)/ *a*. régulier; (*usual*) habituel; (*thorough*: *fam.*) vrai. ● *n*. (*fam.*) habitué(e) *m*. (*f*.). ~**ity** /-'lærətɪ/ *n*. régularité *f*. ~**ly** *adv*. régulièrement.

regulat|e /'regjʊleɪt/ *v.t.* régler. ~**ion** /-'leɪʃn/ *n*. réglage *m*.; (*rule*) règlement *m*.

rehabilitat|e /ri:ə'bɪlɪteɪt/ *v.t.* réadapter; (*in public esteem*) réhabiliter. ~**ion** /-'teɪʃn/ *n*. réadaptation *f*.; réhabilitation *f*.

rehash[1] /ri:'hæʃ/ *v.t.* remanier.

rehash[2] /'ri:hæʃ/ *n*. réchauffé *m*.

rehears|e /rɪ'hɜ:s/ *v.t./i.* (*theatre*) répéter. ~**al** *n*. répétition *f*.

re-heat /ri:'hi:t/ *v.t.* réchauffer.

reign /reɪn/ *n*. règne *m*. ● *v.i.* régner (**over**, sur).

reimburse /ri:ɪm'bɜ:s/ *v.t.* rembourser.

rein /reɪn/ *n*. rêne *f*.

reindeer /'reɪndɪə(r)/ *n. invar.* renne *m*.

reinforce /ri:ɪn'fɔ:s/ *v.t.* renforcer. ~**ment** *n*. renforcement *m*. ~**ments** *n. pl.* renforts *m. pl.* ~**d concrete**, béton armé *m*.

reinstate /ri:ɪn'steɪt/ *v.t.* réintégrer, rétablir.

reiterate /ri:'ɪtəreɪt/ *v.t.* réitérer.

reject[1] /rɪ'dʒekt/ *v.t.* (*offer, plea, etc.*) rejeter; (*book, goods, etc.*) refuser. ~**ion** /-kʃn/ *n*. rejet *m*.; refus *m*.

reject[2] /'ri:dʒekt/ *n*. (article de) rebut *m*.

rejoic|e /rɪ'dʒɔɪs/ *v.i.* se réjouir. ~**ing** *n*. réjouissance *f*.

rejuvenate /rɪ'dʒu:vəneɪt/ *v.t.* rajeunir.

relapse /rɪ'læps/ *n*. rechute *f*. ● *v.i.* rechuter. ~ **into**, retomber dans.

relate /rɪ'leɪt/ *v.t.* raconter; (*associate*) rapprocher. ● *v.i.* ~ **to**, se rapporter à; (*get on with*) s'entendre

avec. ~**d** /-ɪd/ *a*. (*ideas etc.*) lié. ~**d to s.o.**, parent(e) de qn.

relation /rɪ'leɪʃn/ *n*. rapport *m*.; (*person*) parent(e) *m*. (*f*.). ~**ship** *n*. lien de parenté *m*.; (*link*) rapport *m*.; (*affair*) liaison *f*.

relative /'relətɪv/ *n*. parent(e) *m*. (*f*.). ● *a*. relatif; (*respective*) respectif. ~**ly** *adv*. relativement.

relax /rɪ'læks/ *v.t./i.* (*less tense*) (se) relâcher; (*for pleasure*) (se) détendre. ~**ation** /ri:læk'seɪʃn/ *n*. relâchement *m*.; détente *f*. ~**ing** *a*. délassant.

relay[1] /'ri:leɪ/ *n*. relais *m*. ~ **race**, course de relais *f*.

relay[2] /rɪ'leɪ/ *v.t.* relayer.

release /rɪ'li:s/ *v.t.* libérer; (*bomb*) lâcher; (*film*) sortir; (*news*) publier; (*smoke*) dégager; (*spring*) déclencher. ● *n*. libération *f*.; sortie *f*.; (*record*) nouveau disque *m*. (*of pollution*) émission *f*.

relegate /'relɪgeɪt/ *v.t.* reléguer.

relent /rɪ'lent/ *v.i.* se laisser fléchir. ~**less** *a*. impitoyable.

relevan|t /'reləvənt/ *a*. pertinent. **be ~t to**, avoir rapport à. ~**ce** *n*. pertinence *f*., rapport *m*.

reliab|le /rɪ'laɪəbl/ *a*. sérieux, sûr; (*machine*) fiable. ~**ility** /-'bɪlətɪ/ *n*. sérieux *m*.; fiabilité *f*.

reliance /rɪ'laɪəns/ *n*. dépendance *f*.; (*trust*) confiance *f*.

relic /'relɪk/ *n*. relique *f*. ~**s**, (*of past*) vestiges *m. pl.*

relief /rɪ'li:f/ *n*. soulagement *m*. (**from**, à); (*assistance*) secours *m*.; (*outline, design*) relief *m*. ~ **road**, route de délestage *f*.

relieve /rɪ'li:v/ *v.t.* soulager; (*help*) secourir; (*take over from*) relayer.

religion /rɪ'lɪdʒən/ *n*. religion *f*.

religious /rɪ'lɪdʒəs/ *a*. religieux.

relinquish /rɪ'lɪŋkwɪʃ/ *v.t.* abandonner; (*relax hold of*) lâcher.

relish /'relɪʃ/ *n*. plaisir *m*., goût *m*.; (*culin.*) assaisonnement *m*. ● *v.t.* savourer; (*idea etc.*) aimer.

relocate /ri:ləʊ'keɪt/ *v.t.* (*company*) déplacer; (*employee*) muter. ● *v.i.* se déplacer, déménager.

reluctan|t /rɪ'lʌktənt/ *a*. fait, donné, *etc.* à contrecœur. ~**t to**, peu disposé à. ~**ce** *n*. répugnance *f*. ~**tly** *adv*. à contrecœur.

rely /rɪ'laɪ/ *v.i.* ~ **on**, compter sur; (*financially*) dépendre de.

remain /rɪ'mem/ v.i. rester. ~s n. pl. restes m. pl.

remainder /rɪ'memdə(r)/ n. reste m.; (book) invendu soldé m.

remand /rɪ'mɑːnd/ v.t. mettre en détention préventive. ● n. on ~, en détention préventive.

remark /rɪ'mɑːk/ n. remarque f. ● v.t. remarquer. ● v.i. ~ on, faire des commentaires sur. ~able a. remarquable.

remarry /riː'mærɪ/ v.i. se remarier.

remed|y /'remədɪ/ n. remède m. ● v.t. remédier à. ~ial /rɪ'miːdɪəl/ a. (class etc.) de rattrapage; (treatment: med.) curatif.

rememb|er /rɪ'membə(r)/ v.t. se souvenir de, se rappeler. ~er to do, ne pas oublier de faire. ~rance n. souvenir m.

remind /rɪ'maɪnd/ v.t. rappeler (s.o. of sth., qch. à qn.). ~ s.o. to do, rappeler à qn. qu'il doit faire. ~er n. (letter, signal) rappel m.

reminisce /remɪ'nɪs/ v.i. évoquer ses souvenirs. ~nces n. pl. réminiscences f. pl.

reminiscent /remɪ'nɪsnt/ a. ~ of, qui rappelle, qui évoque.

remiss /rɪ'mɪs/ a. négligent.

remission /rɪ'mɪʃn/ n. rémission f.; (jurid.) remise de peine f.

remit /rɪ'mɪt/ v.t. (p.t. remitted) (money) envoyer; (debt) remettre. ~tance n. paiement m.

remnant /'remnənt/ n. reste m., débris m.; (trace) vestige m.; (of cloth) coupon m.

remodel /riː'mɒdel/ v.t. (p.t. remodelled) remodeler.

remorse /rɪ'mɔːs/ n. remords m. (pl.). ~ful a. plein de remords. ~less a. implacable.

remote /rɪ'məʊt/ a. (place, time) lointain; (person) distant; (slight) vague. ~ control, télécommande f. ~ly adv. au loin; vaguement. ~ness n. éloignement m.

removable /rɪ'muːvəbl/ a. (detachable) amovible.

remov|e /rɪ'muːv/ v.t. enlever; (lead away) emmener; (dismiss) renvoyer; (do away with) supprimer. ~al n. enlèvement m.; renvoi m.; suppression f.; (from house) déménagement m. ~al men, déménageurs m. pl. ~er n. (for paint) décapant m.

remunerat|e /rɪ'mjuːnəreɪt/ v.t. rémunérer. ~ion /-'reɪʃn/ n. rémunération f.

rename /riː'neɪm/ v.t. rebaptiser.

render /'rendə(r)/ v.t. (give, make) rendre; (mus.) interpréter. ~ing n. interprétation f.

rendezvous /'rɒndeɪvuː/ n. (pl. -vous /-vuːz/) rendez-vous m. invar.

renegade /'renɪgeɪd/ n. renégat(e) m. (f.).

renew /rɪ'njuː/ v.t. renouveler; (resume) reprendre. ~able a. renouvelable. ~al n. renouvellement m.; reprise f.

renounce /rɪ'naʊns/ v.t. renoncer à; (disown) renier.

renovat|e /'renəveɪt/ v.t. rénover. ~ion /-'veɪʃn/ n. rénovation f.

renown /rɪ'naʊn/ n. renommée f. ~ed a. renommé.

rent /rent/ n. loyer m. ● v.t. louer. for ~, à louer. ~al n. prix de location m.

renunciation /rɪnʌnsɪ'eɪʃn/ n. renonciation f.

reopen /riː'əʊpən/ v.t./i. rouvrir. ~ing n. réouverture f.

reorganize /riː'ɔːgənaɪz/ v.t. réorganiser.

rep /rep/ n. (comm., fam.) représentant(e) m. (f.).

repair /rɪ'peə(r)/ v.t. réparer. ● n. réparation f. in good/bad ~, en bon/mauvais état. ~er n. réparateur m.

repartee /repɑː'tiː/ n. repartie f.

repatriat|e /riː'pætrɪeɪt/ v.t. rapatrier. ~ion /-'eɪʃn/ n. rapatriement m.

repay /riː'peɪ/ v.t. (p.t. repaid) rembourser; (reward) récompenser. ~ment n. remboursement m.; récompense f. monthly ~ments, mensualités f. pl.

repeal /rɪ'piːl/ v.t. abroger, annuler. ● n. abrogation f.

repeat /rɪ'piːt/ v.t./i. répéter; (renew) renouveler. ● n. répétition f.; (broadcast) reprise f. ~ itself, ~ o.s., se répéter.

repeatedly /rɪ'piːtɪdlɪ/ adv. à maintes reprises.

repel /rɪ'pel/ v.t. (p.t. repelled) repousser. ~lent a. repoussant.

repent /rɪ'pent/ v.i. se repentir (of, de). ~ance n. repentir m. ~ant a. repentant.

repercussion /riːpəˈkʌʃn/ n. répercussion f.

repertoire /ˈrepətwɑː(r)/ n. répertoire m.

repertory /ˈrepətrɪ/ n. répertoire m. **~ (theatre)**, théâtre de répertoire m.

repetit|ion /repɪˈtɪʃn/ n. répétition f. **~ious** /-ˈtɪʃəs/, **~ive** /rɪˈpetətɪv/ adjs. plein de répétitions.

replace /rɪˈpleɪs/ v.t. remettre; (take the place of) remplacer. **~ment** n. remplacement m. (**of**, de); (person) remplaçant(e) m. (f.); (new part) pièce de rechange f.

replay /ˈriːpleɪ/ n. (sport) match rejoué m.; (recording) répétition immédiate f.

replenish /rɪˈplenɪʃ/ v.t. (refill) remplir; (renew) renouveler.

replica /ˈreplɪkə/ n. copie exacte f.

reply /rɪˈplaɪ/ v.t./i. répondre. ● n. réponse f.

report /rɪˈpɔːt/ v.t. rapporter, annoncer (**that**, que); (notify) signaler; (denounce) dénoncer. ● v.i. faire un rapport. **~ (on)**, (news item) faire un reportage sur. **~ to**, (go) se présenter chez. ● n. rapport m.; (in press) reportage m.; (schol.) bulletin m.; (sound) détonation f. **~edly** adv. selon ce qu'on dit.

reporter /rɪˈpɔːtə(r)/ n. reporter m.

repose /rɪˈpəʊz/ n. repos m.

repossess /riːpəˈzes/ v.t. reprendre.

represent /reprɪˈzent/ v.t. représenter. **~ation** /-ˈteɪʃn/ n. représentation f. **make ~ations to**, protester auprès de.

representative /reprɪˈzentətɪv/ a. représentatif, typique (**of**, de). ● n. représentant(e) m. (f.).

repress /rɪˈpres/ v.t. réprimer. **~ion** /-ʃn/ n. répression f. **~ive** a. répressif.

reprieve /rɪˈpriːv/ n. (delay) sursis m.; (pardon) grâce f. ● v.t. accorder un sursis à; gracier.

reprimand /ˈreprɪmɑːnd/ v.t. réprimander. ● n. réprimande f.

reprint /ˈriːprɪnt/ n. réimpression f.; (offprint) tiré à part m.

reprisals /rɪˈpraɪzlz/ n. pl. représailles f. pl.

reproach /rɪˈprəʊtʃ/ v.t. reprocher (**s.o. for sth.**, qch. à qn.). ● n. reproche m. **~ful** a. de reproche, réprobateur. **~fully** adv. avec reproche.

reproduc|e /riːprəˈdjuːs/ v.t./i. (se) reproduire. **~tion** /-ˈdʌkʃn/ n. reproduction f. **~tive** /-ˈdʌktɪv/ a. reproducteur.

reptile /ˈreptaɪl/ n. reptile m.

republic /rɪˈpʌblɪk/ n. république f. **~an** a. & n. républicain(e) (m. (f.)).

repudiate /rɪˈpjuːdɪeɪt/ v.t. répudier; (treaty) refuser d'honorer.

repugnan|t /rɪˈpʌɡnənt/ a. répugnant. **~ce** n. répugnance f.

repuls|e /rɪˈpʌls/ v.t. repousser. **~ion** /-ʃn/ n. répulsion f. **~ive** a. repoussant.

reputable /ˈrepjʊtəbl/ a. honorable, de bonne réputation.

reputation /repjʊˈteɪʃn/ n. réputation f.

repute /rɪˈpjuːt/ n. réputation f. **~d** /-ɪd/ a. réputé. **~dly** /-ɪdlɪ/ adv. d'après ce qu'on dit.

request /rɪˈkwest/ n. demande f. ● v.t. demander (**of**, **from**, à). **~ stop**, arrêt facultatif m.

requiem /ˈrekwɪem/ n. requiem m.

require rɪˈkwaɪə(r) v.t. (of thing) demander; (of person) avoir besoin de; (demand, order) exiger. **~d** a. requis. **~ment** n. exigence f.; (condition) condition (requise) f.

requisite /ˈrekwɪzɪt/ a. nécessaire. ● n. chose nécessaire f. **~s**, (for travel etc.) articles m. pl.

requisition /rekwɪˈzɪʃn/ n. réquisition f. ● v.t. réquisitionner.

re-route /riːˈruːt/ v.t. dérouter.

resale /ˈriːseɪl/ n. revente f.

rescind /rɪˈsɪnd/ v.t. annuler.

rescue /ˈreskjuː/ v.t. sauver. ● n. sauvetage m. (**of**, de); (help) secours m. **~r** /-ə(r)/ n. sauveteur m.

research /rɪˈsɜːtʃ/ n. recherche(s) f.(pl.). ● v.t./i. faire des recherches (sur). **~er** n. chercheu|r, -se m., f.

resembl|e /rɪˈzembl/ v.t. ressembler à. **~ance** n. ressemblance f.

resent /rɪˈzent/ v.t. être indigné de, s'offenser de. **~ful** a. plein de ressentiment, indigné. **~ment** n. ressentiment m.

reservation /rezəˈveɪʃn/ n. réserve f.; (booking) réservation f.; (Amer.) réserve (indienne) f. **make a ~**, réserver.

reserve /rɪˈzɜːv/ v.t. réserver. ● n. (reticence, stock, land) réserve f.; (sport) remplaçant(e) m. (f.). **in ~**, en réserve. **the ~s**, (mil.) les ré-

serves f. pl. ~d a. (person, room)
réservé.

reservist /rɪ'zɜ:vɪst/ n. (mil.) réserviste m.

reservoir /'rezəvwɑ:(r)/ n. (lake, supply, etc.) réservoir m.

reshape /ri:'ʃeɪp/ v.t. remodeler.

reshuffle /ri:'ʃʌfl/ v.t. (pol.) remanier. ● n. (pol.) remaniement (ministériel) m.

reside /rɪ'zaɪd/ v.i. résider.

residen|t /'rezɪdənt/ a. résidant. be ~t, résider. ● n. habitant(e) m. (f.); (foreigner) résident(e) m. (f.); (in hotel) pensionnaire m./f. ~ce n. résidence f.; (of students) foyer m. in ~ce, (doctor) résidant; (students) au foyer.

residential /rezɪ'denʃl/ a. résidentiel.

residue /'rezɪdju:/ n. résidu m.

resign /rɪ'zaɪn/ v.t. abandonner; (job) démissionner de. ● v.i. démissionner. ~ o.s. to, se résigner à. ~ation /rezɪg'neɪʃn/ n. résignation f.; (from job) démission f. ~ed a. résigné.

resilien|t /rɪ'zɪlɪənt/ a. élastique; (person) qui a du ressort. ~ce n. élasticité f.; ressort m.

resin /'rezɪn/ n. résine f.

resist /rɪ'zɪst/ v.t./i. résister (à). ~ance n. résistance f. ~ant a. (med.) rebelle; (metal) résistant.

resolut|e /'rezəluːt/ a. résolu. ~ion /-'lu:ʃn/ n. résolution f.

resolve /rɪ'zɒlv/ v.t. résoudre (to do, de faire). ● n. résolution f. ~d a. résolu (to do, à faire).

resonan|t /'rezənənt/ a. résonnant. ~ce n. résonance f.

resort /rɪ'zɔ:t/ v.i. ~ to, avoir recours à. ● n. (recourse) recours m.; (place) station f. in the last ~, en dernier ressort.

resound /rɪ'zaʊnd/ v.i. retentir (with, de). ~ing a. retentissant.

resource /rɪ'sɔ:s/ n. (expedient) ressource f. ~s, (wealth etc.) ressources f. pl. ~ful a. ingénieux. ~fulness n. ingéniosité f.

respect /rɪ'spekt/ n. respect m.; (aspect) égard m. ● v.t. respecter. with ~ to, à l'égard de, relativement à. ~ful a. respectueux.

respectab|le /rɪ'spektəbl/ a. respectable. ~ility /-'bɪlətɪ/ n. respectabilité f. ~ly adv. convenablement.

respective /rɪ'spektɪv/ a. respectif. ~ly adv. respectivement.

respiration /respə'reɪʃn/ n. respiration f.

respite /'resp(a)ɪt/ n. répit m.

resplendent /rɪ'splendənt/ a. resplendissant.

respond /rɪ'spɒnd/ v.i. répondre (to, à) ~ to, (react to) réagir à.

response /rɪ'spɒns/ n. réponse f.

responsib|le /rɪ'spɒnsəbl/ a. responsable: (job) qui comporte des responsabilités. ~ility /-'bɪlətɪ/ n. responsabilité f. ~ly adv. de façon responsable.

responsive /rɪ'spɒnsɪv/ a. qui réagit bien. ~ to, sensible à.

rest[1] /rest/ v.t./i. (se) reposer; (lean) (s')appuyer (on, sur); (be buried, lie) reposer. ● n. (repose) repos m.; (support) support m. have a ~, se reposer; (at work) prendre une pause. ~-room n. (Amer.) toilettes f. pl.

rest[2] /rest/ v.i. (remain) demeurer. ● n. (remainder) reste m. (of, de). the ~ (of the), (others, other) les autres. it ~s with him to, il lui appartient de.

restaurant /'restərɒnt/ n. restaurant m.

restful /'restfl/ a. reposant.

restitution /restɪ'tju:ʃn/ n. (for injury) compensation f.

restive /'restɪv/ a. rétif.

restless /'restlɪs/ a. agité. ~ly adv. avec agitation, fébrilement.

restor|e /rɪ'stɔ:(r)/ v.t. rétablir; (building) restaurer. ~ sth. to s.o., restituer qch. à qn. ~ation /restə'reɪʃn/ n. rétablissement m.; restauration f. ~er n. (art) restaura|teur, -trice m., f.

restrain /rɪ'streɪn/ v.t. contenir. ~ s.o. from, retenir qn. de. ~ed a. (moderate) mesuré; (in control of self) maître de soi. ~t n. contrainte f.; (moderation) retenue f.

restrict /rɪ'strɪkt/ v.t. restreindre. ~ion /-kʃn/ n. restriction f. ~ive a. restrictif.

restructure /ri:'strʌktʃə(r)/ v.t. restructurer.

result /rɪ'zʌlt/ n. résultat m. ● v.i. résulter. ~ in, aboutir à.

resum|e /rɪ'zju:m/ v.t./i. reprendre. ~ption /rɪ'zʌmpʃn/ n. reprise f.

résumé /'rezjuːmeɪ/ *n.* résumé *m.*; (*of career*: *Amer.*) CV *m.*, curriculum vitae *m.*

resurgence /rɪ'sɜːdʒəns/ *n.* réapparition *f.*

resurrect /rezə'rekt/ *v.t.* ressusciter. ~**ion** /-kʃn/ *n.* résurrection *f.*

resuscitate /rɪ'sʌsɪteɪt/ *v.t.* réanimer.

retail /'riːteɪl/ *n.* détail *m.* ● *a.* & *adv.* au détail. ● *v.t./i.* (se) vendre (au détail). ~**er** *n.* détaillant(e) *m.* (*f.*).

retain /rɪ'teɪn/ *v.t.* (*hold back, remember*) retenir; (*keep*) conserver.

retaliat|e /rɪ'tælɪeɪt/ *v.i.* riposter. ~**ion** /-'eɪʃn/ *n.* représailles *f. pl.*

retarded /rɪ'tɑːdɪd/ *a.* arriéré.

retch /retʃ/ *v.i.* avoir un haut-le-cœur.

retentive /rɪ'tentɪv/ *a.* (*memory*) fidèle. ~ **of**, qui retient.

rethink /riː'θɪŋk/ *v.t.* (*p.t.* **rethought**) repenser.

reticen|t /'retɪsnt/ *a.* réticent. ~**ce** *n.* réticence *f.*

retina /'retɪnə/ *n.* rétine *f.*

retinue /'retɪnjuː/ *n.* suite *f.*

retire /rɪ'taɪə(r)/ *v.i.* (*from work*) prendre sa retraite; (*withdraw*) se retirer; (*go to bed*) se coucher. ● *v.t.* mettre à la retraite. ~**d** *a.* retraité. ~**ment** *n.* retraite *f.*

retiring /rɪ'taɪərɪŋ/ *a.* réservé.

retort /rɪ'tɔːt/ *v.t./i.* répliquer. ● *n.* réplique *f.*

retrace /riː'treɪs/ *v.t.* ~ **one's steps**, revenir sur ses pas.

retract /rɪ'trækt/ *v.t./i.* (se) rétracter.

retrain /riː'treɪn/ *v.t./i.* (se) recycler.

retread /riː'tred/ *n.* pneu rechapé *m.*

retreat /rɪ'triːt/ *v.i.* (*mil.*) battre en retraite. ● *n.* retraite *f.*

retrial /riː'traɪəl/ *n.* nouveau procès *m.*

retribution /retrɪ'bjuːʃn/ *n.* châtiment *m.*; (*vengeance*) vengeance *f.*

retriev|e /rɪ'triːv/ *v.t.* (*recover*) récupérer; (*restore*) rétablir; (*put right*) réparer. ~**al** *n.* récupération *f.*; (*of information*) recherche documentaire *f.* ~**er** *n.* (*dog*) chien d'arrêt *m.*

retrograde /'retrəgreɪd/ *a.* rétrograde. ● *v.i.* rétrograder.

retrospect /'retrəspekt/ *n.* **in** ~, rétrospectivement.

return /rɪ'tɜːn/ *v.i.* (*come back*) revenir; (*go back*) retourner; (*go home*) rentrer. ● *v.t.* (*give back*) rendre; (*bring back*) rapporter; (*send back*) renvoyer; (*put back*) remettre. ● *n.*

retour *m.*; (*yield*) rapport *m.* ~**s**, (*comm.*) bénéfices *m. pl.* **in** ~ **for**, en échange de. ~ **journey**, voyage de retour *m.* ~ **match**, match retour *m.* ~ **ticket**, aller-retour *m.*

reunion /riː'juːnɪən/ *n.* réunion *f.*

reunite /riːjuː'naɪt/ *v.t.* réunir.

rev /rev/ *n.* (*auto.*, *fam.*) tour *m.* ● *v.t./i.* (*p.t.* **revved**). ~ (**up**), (*engine*: *fam.*) (s')emballer.

revamp /riː'væmp/ *v.t.* rénover.

reveal /rɪ'viːl/ *v.t.* révéler; (*allow to appear*) laisser voir. ~**ing** *a.* révélateur.

revel /'revl/ *v.i.* (*p.t.* **revelled**) faire bombance. ~ **in**, se délecter de. ~**ry** *n.* festivités *f. pl.*

revelation /revə'leɪʃn/ *n.* révélation *f.*

revenge /rɪ'vendʒ/ *n.* vengeance *f.*; (*sport*) revanche *f.* ● *v.t.* venger.

revenue /'revənjuː/ *n.* revenu *m.*

reverberate /rɪ'vɜːbəreɪt/ *v.i.* (*sound, light*) se répercuter.

revere /rɪ'vɪə(r)/ *v.t.* révérer. ~**nce** /'revərəns/ *n.* vénération *f.*

reverend /'revərənd/ *a.* révérend.

reverent /'revərənt/ *a.* respectueux.

reverie /'revərɪ/ *n.* rêverie *f.*

revers|e /rɪ'vɜːs/ *a.* contraire, inverse. ● *n.* contraire *m.*; (*back*) revers *m.*, envers *m.*; (*gear*) marche arrière *f.* ● *v.t.* (*situation, bracket, etc.*) renverser; (*order*) inverser; (*decision*) annuler. ● *v.i.* (*auto.*) faire marche arrière. ~**al** *n.* renversement *m.*; (*of view*) revirement *m.*

revert /rɪ'vɜːt/ *v.i.* ~ **to**, revenir à.

review /rɪ'vjuː/ *n.* (*inspection, magazine*) revue *f.*; (*of book etc.*) critique *f.* ● *v.t.* passer en revue; (*situation*) réexaminer; faire la critique de. ~**er** *n.* critique *m.*

revis|e /rɪ'vaɪz/ *v.t.* réviser; (*text*) revoir. ~**ion** /-ɪʒn/ *n.* révision *f.*

revitalize /riː'vaɪtəlaɪz/ *v.t.* revitaliser, revivifier.

reviv|e /rɪ'vaɪv/ *v.t.* (*person, hopes*) ranimer; (*play*) reprendre; (*custom*) rétablir. ● *v.i.* se ranimer. ~**al** *n.* (*resumption*) reprise *f.*; (*of faith*) renouveau *m.*

revoke /rɪ'vəʊk/ *v.t.* révoquer.

revolt /rɪ'vəʊlt/ *v.t./i.* (se) révolter. ● *n.* révolte *f.*

revolting /rɪ'vəʊltɪŋ/ *a.* dégoûtant.

revolution /revə'luːʃn/ *n.* révolution *f.* ~**ary** *a.* & *n.* révolutionnaire (*m./f.*). ~**ize** *v.t.* révolutionner.

revolve /rɪ'vɒlv/ v.i. tourner. ~ing door, tambour m.

revolver /rɪ'vɒlvə(r)/ n. revolver m.

revulsion /rɪ'vʌlʃn/ n. dégoût m.

reward /rɪ'wɔːd/ n. récompense f. ● v.t. récompenser (for, de). ~ing a. rémunérateur; (worthwhile) qui (en) vaut la peine.

rewind /riː'waɪnd/ v.t. (p.t. rewound) (tape, film) rembobiner.

rewire /riː'waɪə(r)/ v.t. refaire l'installation électrique de.

reword /riː'wɜːd/ v.t. reformuler.

rewrite /riː'raɪt/ v.t. récrire.

rhapsody /'ræpsədɪ/ n. rhapsodie f.

rhetoric /'retərɪk/ n. rhétorique f. ~al /rɪ'tɒrɪkl/ a. (de) rhétorique; (question) de pure forme.

rheumati|c /ruː'mætɪk/ a. (pain) rhumatismal; (person) rhumatisant. ~sm /'ruːmətɪzəm/ n. rhumatisme m.

rhinoceros /raɪ'nɒsərəs/ n. (pl. -oses) rhinocéros m.

rhubarb /'ruːbɑːb/ n. rhubarbe f.

rhyme /raɪm/ n. rime f.; (poem) vers m. pl. ● v.t./i. (faire) rimer.

rhythm /'rɪðəm/ n. rythme m. ~ic(al) /'rɪðmɪk(l)/ a. rythmique.

rib /rɪb/ n. côte f.

ribald /'rɪbld/ a. grivois.

ribbon /'rɪbən/ n. ruban m. in ~s, (torn pieces) en lambeaux.

rice /raɪs/ n. riz m.

rich /rɪtʃ/ a. (-er, -est) riche. ~es n. pl. richesses f. pl. ~ly adv. richement. ~ness n. richesse f.

rickety /'rɪkətɪ/ a. branlant.

ricochet /'rɪkəʃeɪ/ n. ricochet m. ● v.i. (p.t. ricocheted /-ʃeɪd/) ricocher.

rid /rɪd/ v.t. (p.t. rid, pres. p. ridding) débarrasser (of, de). get ~ of, se débarrasser de.

riddance /'rɪdns/ n. good ~!, bon débarras!

ridden /'rɪdn/ see ride.

riddle [1] /'rɪdl/ n. énigme f.

riddle [2] /'rɪdl/ v.t. ~ with, (bullets) cribler de; (mistakes) bourrer de.

ride /raɪd/ v.i. (p.t. rode, p.p. ridden) aller (à bicyclette, à cheval, etc.); (in car) rouler. ~ (a horse), (go riding as sport) monter (à cheval). ● v.t. (a particular horse) monter; (distance) parcourir. ● n. promenade f., tour m.; (distance) trajet m. give s.o. a ~, (Amer.) prendre qn. en voiture. go for a ~, aller faire un tour (à

bicyclette, à cheval, etc.). ~r /-ə(r)/ n. caval|ier, -ière m., f.; (in horse race) jockey m.; (cyclist) cycliste m./ f.; (motorcyclist) motocycliste m./f.; (in document) annexe f.

ridge /rɪdʒ/ n. arête f., crête f.

ridicule /'rɪdɪkjuːl/ n. ridicule m. ● v.t. ridiculiser.

ridiculous /rɪ'dɪkjʊləs/ a. ridicule.

riding /'raɪdɪŋ/ n. équitation f.

rife /raɪf/ a. be ~, être répandu, sévir. ~ with, abondant en.

riff-raff /'rɪfræf/ n. canaille f.

rifle /'raɪfl/ n. fusil m. ● v.t. (rob) dévaliser.

rift /rɪft/ n. (crack) fissure f.; (between people) désaccord m.

rig [1] /rɪg/ v.t. (p.t. rigged) (equip) équiper. ● n. (for oil) derrick m. ~ out, habiller. ~-out n. (fam.) tenue f. ~ up, (arrange) arranger.

rig [2] /rɪg/ v.t. (p.t. rigged) (election, match, etc.) truquer.

right /raɪt/ a. (morally) bon; (fair) juste; (best) bon, qu'il faut; (not left) droit. be ~, (person) avoir raison (to, de); (calculation, watch) être exact. ● n. (entitlement) droit m.; (not left) droite f.; (not evil) le bien. ● v.t. (a wrong, sth. fallen, etc.) redresser. ● adv. (not left) à droite; (directly) tout droit; (exactly) bien, juste; (completely) tout (à fait). be in the ~, avoir raison. by ~s, normalement. on the ~, à droite. put ~, arranger, rectifier. ~ angle, angle droit m. ~ away, tout de suite. ~-hand a. à or de droite. ~-hand man, bras droit m. ~-handed a. droitier. ~ now, (at once) tout de suite; (at present) en ce moment. ~ of way, (auto.) priorité f. ~-wing a. (pol.) de droite.

righteous /'raɪtʃəs/ a. (person) vertueux; (cause, anger) juste.

rightful /'raɪtfl/ a. légitime. ~ly adv. à juste titre.

rightly /'raɪtlɪ/ adv. correctement; (with reason) à juste titre.

rigid /'rɪdʒɪd/ a. rigide. ~ity /rɪ'dʒɪdətɪ/ n. rigidité f.

rigmarole /'rɪgmərəʊl/ n. charabia m.; (procedure) comédie f.

rig|our /'rɪgə(r)/ n. rigueur f. ~orous a. rigoureux.

rile /raɪl/ v.t. (fam.) agacer.

rim /rɪm/ n. bord m.; (of wheel) jante f. ~med a. bordé.

rind /raɪnd/ n. (on cheese) croûte f.; (on bacon) couenne f.; (on fruit) écorce f.

ring [1] /rɪŋ/ n. anneau m.; (with stone) bague f.; (circle) cercle m.; (boxing) ring m.; (arena) piste f. ● v.t. entourer; (word in text etc.) entourer d'un cercle. (wedding) ~, alliance f. ~ road, périphérique m.

ring [2] /rɪŋ/ v.t./i. (p.t. rang, p.p. rung) sonner; (of bells etc.) retentir. ~ n. sonnerie f. give s.o. a ~, donner un coup de fil à qn. ~ the bell, sonner. ~ back, rappeler. ~ off, raccrocher. ~ up, téléphoner (à). ~ing n. (of bell) sonnerie f. ~ing tone, tonalité f.

ringleader /'rɪŋliːdə(r)/ n. chef m.

rink /rɪŋk/ n. patinoire f.

rinse /rɪns/ v.t. rincer. ~ out, rincer. ● n. rinçage m.

riot /'raɪət/ n. émeute f.; (of colours) orgie f. ● v.i. faire une émeute. run ~, se déchaîner. ~er n. émeut|ier, -ière m., f.

riotous /'raɪətəs/ a. turbulent.

rip /rɪp/ v.t./i. (p.t. ripped) (se) déchirer. ● n. déchirure f. let ~, (not check) laisser courir. ~ off, (sl.) rouler. ~-off n. (sl.) vol m.

ripe /raɪp/ a. (-er, -est) mûr. ~ness n. maturité f.

ripen /'raɪpən/ v.t./i. mûrir.

ripple /'rɪpl/ n. ride f., ondulation f.; (sound) murmure m. ● v.t./i. (water) (se) rider.

rise /raɪz/ v.i. (p.t. rose, p.p. risen) (go upwards, increase) monter, s'élever; (stand up, get up from bed) se lever; (rebel) se soulever; (sun, curtain) se lever; (water) monter. ● n. (slope) pente f.; (of curtain) lever m.; (increase) hausse f.; (in pay) augmentation f.; (progress, boom) essor m. give ~ to, donner lieu à. ~ up, se soulever. ~r /-ə(r)/ n. be an early ~r, se lever tôt.

rising /'raɪzɪŋ/ n. (revolt) soulèvement m. ● a. (increasing) croissant; (price) qui monte; (tide) montant; (sun) levant. ~ generation, nouvelle génération f.

risk /rɪsk/ n. risque m. ● v.t. risquer. at ~, menacé. ~ doing, (venture) se risquer à faire. ~y a. risqué.

rissole /'rɪsəʊl/ n. croquette f.

rite /raɪt/ n. rite m. last ~s, derniers sacrements m. pl.

ritual /'rɪtʃʊəl/ a. & n. rituel (m.).

rival /'raɪvl/ n. rival(e) m. (f.). ● a. rival; (claim) opposé. ● v.t. (p.t. rivalled) rivaliser avec. ~ry n. rivalité f.

river /'rɪvə(r)/ n. rivière f.; (flowing into sea & fig.) fleuve m. ● a. (fishing, traffic, etc.) fluvial.

rivet /'rɪvɪt/ n. (bolt) rivet m. ● v.t. (p.t. riveted) river, riveter. ~ing a. fascinant.

Riviera /rɪvɪ'eərə/ n. the (French) ~, la Côte d'Azur.

road /rəʊd/ n. route f.; (in town) rue f.; (small) chemin m. ● a. (sign, safety) routier. the ~ to, (glory etc.: fig.) le chemin de. ~-block n. barrage routier m. ~-hog n. chauffard m. ~-map n. carte routière f. ~works n. pl. travaux m. pl.

roadside /'rəʊdsaɪd/ n. bord de la route m.

roadway /'rəʊdweɪ/ n. chaussée f.

roadworthy /'rəʊdwɜːðɪ/ a. en état de marche.

roam /rəʊm/ v.i. errer. ● v.t. (streets, seas, etc.) parcourir.

roar /rɔː(r)/ n. hurlement m.; rugissement m.; grondement m. ● v.t./i. hurler; (of lion, wind) rugir; (of lorry, thunder) gronder. ~ with laughter, rire aux éclats.

roaring /'rɔːrɪŋ/ a. (trade, success) très gros. ~ fire, belle flambée f.

roast /rəʊst/ v.t./i. rôtir. ● n. (roast or roasting meat) rôti m. ● a. rôti. ~ beef, rôti de bœuf m.

rob /rɒb/ v.t. (p.t. robbed) voler (s.o. of sth., qch. à qn.); (bank, house) dévaliser; (deprive) priver (of, de). ~ber n. voleu|r, -se m., f. ~bery n. vol m.

robe /rəʊb/ n. (of judge etc.) robe f.; (dressing-gown) peignoir m.

robin /'rɒbɪn/ n. rouge-gorge m.

robot /'rəʊbɒt/ n. robot m.

robust /rəʊ'bʌst/ a. robuste.

rock [1] /rɒk/ n. roche f.; (rock face, boulder) rocher m.; (hurled stone) pierre f.; (sweet) sucre d'orge m. on the ~s, (drink) avec des glaçons; (marriage) en crise. ~-bottom a. (fam.) très bas. ~-climbing n. varappe f.

rock [2] /rɒk/ v.t./i. (se) balancer; (shake) (faire) trembler; (child) bercer. ● n. (mus.) rock m. ~ing-chair n. fauteuil à bascule m.

rockery /'rɒkərɪ/ n. rocaille f.

rocket /'rɒkɪt/ n. fusée f.

rocky /'rɒkɪ/ a. (**-ier, -iest**) (*ground*) rocailleux; (*hill*) rocheux; (*shaky*: *fig.*) branlant.

rod /rɒd/ n. (*metal*) tige f.; (*for certain*) tringle f.; (*wooden*) baguette f.; (*for fishing*) canne à pêche f.

rode /rəʊd/ *see* ride.

rodent /'rəʊdnt/ n. rongeur m.

rodeo /rəʊ'deɪəʊ, *Amer.* 'rəʊdɪəʊ/ n. (*pl.* **-os**) rodéo m.

roe¹ /rəʊ/ n. œufs de poisson m. *pl.*

roe² /rəʊ/ n. (*pl.* **roe** or **roes**) (*deer*) chevreuil m.

rogue /rəʊg/ n. (*dishonest*) bandit m., voleur, -se m., f.; (*mischievous*) coquin(e) m. (f.). **~ish** a. coquin.

role /rəʊl/ n. rôle m. **~-playing** n. jeu de rôle m.

roll /rəʊl/ v.t./i. rouler. **~** (**about**), (*child, dog*) se rouler. ● n. rouleau m.; (*list*) liste f.; (*bread*) petit pain m.; (*of drum, thunder*) roulement m.; (*of ship*) roulis m. **be ~ing** (**in money**), (*fam.*) rouler sur l'or. **~-bar** n. arceau de sécurité m. **~-call** n. appel m. **~ing-pin** n. rouleau à pâtisserie m. **~ out**, étendre. **~ over**, (*turn over*) se retourner. **~ up** v.t. (*sleeves*) retrousser; v.i. (*fam.*) s'amener.

roller /'rəʊlə(r)/ n. rouleau m. **~-blind** n. store m. **~-coaster** n. montagnes russes f. *pl.* **~-skate** n. patin à roulettes m.

rollicking /'rɒlɪkɪŋ/ a. exubérant.

rolling /'rəʊlɪŋ/ a. onduleux.

ROM (*abbr.*) (*read-only memory*) mémoire morte f.

Roman /'rəʊmən/ a. & n. romain(e) (m. (f.)). **~ Catholic** a. & n. catholique (m./f.). **~ numerals**, chiffres romains m. *pl.*

romance /rə'mæns/ n. roman d'amour m.; (*love*) amour m.; (*affair*) idylle f.; (*fig.*) poésie f.

Romania /rəʊ'meɪnɪə/ n. Roumanie f. **~n** a. & n. roumain(e) (m. (f.)).

romantic /rə'mæntɪk/ a. (*of love etc.*) romantique; (*of the imagination*) romanesque. **~ally** adv. (*behave*) en romantique.

romp /rɒmp/ v.i. s'ébattre; (*fig.*) réussir. ● n. have a **~**, s'ébattre.

roof /ruːf/ n. (*pl.* **roofs**) toit m.; (*of tunnel*) plafond m.; (*of mouth*) palais m. ● v.t. recouvrir. **~ing** n. toiture f. **~-rack** n. galerie f. **~-top** n. toit m.

rook¹ /rʊk/ n. (*bird*) corneille f.

rook² /rʊk/ n. (*chess*) tour f.

room /ruːm/ n. pièce f.; (*bedroom*) chambre f.; (*large hall*) salle f.; (*space*) place f. **~-mate** n. camarade de chambre m./f. **~y** a. spacieux; (*clothes*) ample.

roost /ruːst/ n. perchoir m. ● v.i. percher. **~er** /'ruːstə(r)/ n. coq m.

root¹ /ruːt/ n. racine f.; (*source*) origine f. ● v.t./i. (s')enraciner. **~out**, extirper. **take ~**, prendre racine. **~less** a. sans racines.

root² /ruːt/ v.i. **~ about**, fouiller. **~ for**, (*Amer., fam.*) encourager.

rope /rəʊp/ n. corde f. ● v.t. attacher. **know the ~s**, être au courant. **~ in**, (*person*) enrôler.

rosary /'rəʊzərɪ/ n. chapelet m.

rose¹ /rəʊz/ n. (*flower*) rose f.; (*colour*) rose m.; (*nozzle*) pomme f.

rose² /rəʊz/ *see* rise.

rosé /'rəʊzeɪ/ n. rosé m.

rosette /rəʊ'zet/ n. (*sport*) cocarde f.; (*officer's*) rosette f.

roster /'rɒstə(r)/ n. liste (de service) f., tableau (de service) m.

rostrum /'rɒstrəm/ n. (*pl.* **-tra**) tribune f.; (*sport*) podium m.

rosy /'rəʊzɪ/ a. (**-ier, -iest**) rose; (*hopeful*) plein d'espoir.

rot /rɒt/ v.t./i. (*p.t.* **rotted**) pourrir. ● n. pourriture f.; (*nonsense*: *sl.*) bêtises f. *pl.*, âneries f. *pl.*

rota /'rəʊtə/ n. liste (de service) f.

rotary /'rəʊtərɪ/ a. rotatif.

rotate /rəʊ'teɪt/ v.t./i. (faire) tourner; (*change round*) alterner. **~ing** a. tournant. **~ion** /-ʃn/ n. rotation f.

rote /rəʊt/ n. **by ~**, machinalement.

rotten /'rɒtn/ a. pourri; (*tooth*) gâté; (*bad*: *fam.*) mauvais, sale.

rotund /rəʊ'tʌnd/ a. rond.

rouge /ruːʒ/ n. rouge (à joues) m.

rough /rʌf/ a. (**-er, -est**) (*manners*) rude; (*to touch*) rugueux; (*ground*) accidenté; (*violent*) brutal; (*bad*) mauvais; (*estimate etc.*) approximatif; (*diamond*) brut. ● adv. (*live*) à la dure; (*play*) brutalement. ● n. (*ruffian*) voyou m. ● v.t. **~ it**, vivre à la dure. **~-and-ready** a. (*solution etc.*) grossier (mais efficace). **~-and-tumble** n. mêlée f. **~ out**, ébaucher. **~ paper**, papier brouillon m. **~ly** adv. rudement; (*approximately*) à peu près. **~ness** n. rudesse f.; brutalité f.

roughage /'rʌfɪdʒ/ n. fibres (alimentaires) f. *pl.*

roulette /ruːˈlet/ n. roulette f.
round /raʊnd/ a. (-er, -est) rond. ● n. (circle) rond m.; (slice) tranche f.; (of visits, drinks) tournée f.; (mil.) ronde f.; (competition) partie f., manche f.; (boxing) round m.; (of talks) série f. ● prep. autour de. ● adv. autour. ● v.t. (object) arrondir; (corner) tourner. **go** or **come ~ to**, (a friend etc.) passer chez. **I'm going ~ the corner**, je vais juste à côté. **enough to go ~**, assez pour tout le monde. **go the ~ s**, circuler. **she lives ~ here** elle habite par ici. **~ about**, (near by) par ici; (fig.) à peu près. **~ of applause**, applaudissements m. pl. **~ off**, terminer. **~ the clock**, vingt-quatre heures sur vingt-quatre. **~ trip**, voyage aller-retour m. **~ up**, rassembler. **~-up** n. rassemblement m.; (of suspects) rafle f.
roundabout /ˈraʊndəbaʊt/ n. manège m.; (for traffic) rond-point (à sens giratoire) m. ● a. indirect.
rounders /ˈraʊndəz/ n. sorte de baseball f.
roundly /ˈraʊndlɪ/ adv. (bluntly) franchement.
rouse /raʊz/ v.t. éveiller; (wake up) réveiller. **be ~ed**, (angry) être en colère. **~ing** a. (speech, music) excitant; (cheers) frénétique.
rout /raʊt/ n. (defeat) déroute f. ● v.t. mettre en déroute.
route /ruːt/ n. itinéraire m., parcours m.; (naut., aviat.) route f.
routine /ruːˈtiːn/ n. routine f. ● a. de routine. **daily ~**, travail quotidien m.
rov|e /rəʊv/ v.t./i. errer (dans). **~ing** a. (life) vagabond.
row[1] /rəʊ/ n. rangée f., rang m. **in a ~**, (consecutive) consécutif.
row[2] /rəʊ/ v.i. ramer; (sport) faire de l'aviron. ● v.t. faire aller à la rame. **~ing** n. aviron m. **~(ing)-boat** n. bateau à rames m.
row[3] /raʊ/ n. (noise: fam.) tapage m.; (quarrel; fam.) engueulade f. ● v.i. (fam.) s'engueuler.
rowdy /ˈraʊdɪ/ a. (-ier, -iest) tapageur. ● n. voyou m.
royal /ˈrɔɪəl/ a. royal. **~ly** adv. (treat, live, etc.) royalement.
royalt|y /ˈrɔɪəltɪ/ n. famille royale f. **~ies**, droits d'auteur m. pl.
rub /rʌb/ v.t./i. (p.t. rubbed) frotter. ● n. friction f. **~ it in**, insister là-dessus. **~ off on**, déteindre sur. **~ out**, (s')effacer.
rubber /ˈrʌbə(r)/ n. caoutchouc m.; (eraser) gomme f. **~ band**, élastique m. **~ stamp**, tampon m. **~-stamp** v.t. approuver. **~y** a. caoutchouteux.
rubbish /ˈrʌbɪʃ/ n. (refuse) ordures f. pl.; (junk) saletés f. pl.; (fig.) bêtises f. pl. **~y** a. sans valeur.
rubble /ˈrʌbl/ n. décombres m. pl.
ruby /ˈruːbɪ/ n. rubis m.
rucksack /ˈrʌksæk/ n. sac à dos m.
rudder /ˈrʌdə(r)/ n. gouvernail m.
ruddy /ˈrʌdɪ/ a. (-ier, -iest) coloré, rougeâtre; (damned: sl.) fichu.
rude /ruːd/ a. (-er, -est) impoli, grossier; (improper) indécent; (shock, blow) brutal. **~ly** adv. impoliment. **~ness** n. impolitesse f.; indécence f.; brutalité f.
rudiment /ˈruːdɪmənt/ n. rudiment m. **~ary** /-ˈmentrɪ/ a. rudimentaire.
rueful /ˈruːfl/ a. triste.
ruffian /ˈrʌfɪən/ n. voyou m.
ruffle /ˈrʌfl/ v.t. (hair) ébouriffer; (clothes) froisser; (person) contrarier. ● n. (frill) ruche f.
rug /rʌɡ/ n. petit tapis m.
Rugby /ˈrʌɡbɪ/ n. **~ (football)**, rugby m.
rugged /ˈrʌɡɪd/ a. (surface) rude, rugueux; (ground) accidenté; (character, features) rude.
ruin /ˈruːɪn/ n. ruine f. ● v.t. (destroy) ruiner; (damage) abîmer; (spoil) gâter. **~ous** a. ruineux.
rule /ruːl/ n. règle f.; (regulation) règlement m.; (pol.) gouvernement m. ● v.t. gouverner; (master) dominer; (decide) décider. ● v.i. régner. **as a ~**, en règle générale. **~ out**, exclure. **~d paper**, papier réglé m. **~r** /-ə(r)/ n. dirigeant(e) m. (f.), gouvernant m.; (measure) règle f.
ruling /ˈruːlɪŋ/ a. (class) dirigeant; (party) au pouvoir. ● n. décision f.
rum /rʌm/ n. rhum m.
rumble /ˈrʌmbl/ v.i. gronder; (stomach) gargouiller. ● n. grondement m.; gargouillement m.
rummage /ˈrʌmɪdʒ/ v.i. fouiller.
rumour, (Amer.) **rumor** /ˈruːmə(r)/ n. bruit m., rumeur f. **there's a ~ that**, le bruit court que.
rump /rʌmp/ n. (of horse etc.) croupe f.; (of fowl) croupion m.; (steak) romsteck m.
rumpus /ˈrʌmpəs/ n. (uproar: fam.) chahut m.

run /rʌn/ v.i. (p.t. ran, p.p. run, pres. p. running) courir; (flow) couler; (pass) passer; (function) marcher; (melt) fondre; (extend) s'étendre; (of bus etc.) circuler; (of play) se jouer; (last) durer; (of colour in washing) déteindre; (in election) être candidat. ● v.t. (manage) diriger; (event) organiser; (risk, race) courir; (house) tenir; (blockade) forcer; (temperature, errand) faire; (comput.) exécuter. ● n. course f.; (journey) parcours m.; (outing) promenade f.; (rush) ruée f.; (series) série f.; (in cricket) point m. have the ~ of, avoir à sa disposition. in the long ~, avec le temps. on the ~, en fuite. ~ across, rencontrer par hasard. ~ away, s'enfuir. ~ down, descendre en courant; (of vehicle) renverser; (production) réduire progressivement; (belittle) dénigrer. be ~ down, (weak etc.) être sans forces or mal fichu. ~ in, (vehicle) roder. ~ into, (hit) heurter. ~ off, (copies) tirer. ~-of-the-mill a. ordinaire. ~ out, (be used up) s'épuiser; (of lease) expirer. ~ out of, manquer de. ~ over, (of vehicle) écraser; (details) revoir. ~ through sth., regarder qch. rapidement. ~ sth. through sth., passer qch. à travers qch. ~ up, (bill) accumuler. the ~-up to, la période qui précède.

runaway /'rʌnəweɪ/ n. fugitif|f, -ve m., f. ● a. fugitif; (horse, vehicle) fou; (inflation) galopant.

rung¹ /rʌŋ/ n. (of ladder) barreau m.

rung² /rʌŋ/ see ring².

runner /'rʌnə(r)/ n. coureur|r, -se m., f. ~ bean, haricot (grimpant) m. ~-up n. second(e) m. (f.).

running /'rʌnɪŋ/ n. course f.; (of business) gestion f.; (of machine) marche f. ● a. (commentary) suivi; (water) courant. be in the ~ for, être sur les rangs pour. four days etc. ~, quatre jours/etc. de suite.

runny /'rʌnɪ/ a. (nose) qui coule.

runt /rʌnt/ n. avorton m.

runway /'rʌnweɪ/ n. piste f.

rupture /'rʌptʃə(r)/ n. (breaking, breach) rupture f.; (med.) hernie f. ● v.t./i. (se) rompre. ~ o.s., se donner une hernie.

rural /'rʊərəl/ a. rural.

ruse /ruːz/ n. (trick) ruse f.

rush¹ /rʌʃ/ n. (plant) jonc m.

rush² /rʌʃ/ v.i. (move) se précipiter; (be in a hurry) se dépêcher. ● v.t. faire, envoyer, etc. en vitesse; (person) bousculer; (mil.) prendre d'assaut. ● n. ruée f.; (haste) bousculade f. in a ~, pressé. ~-hour n. heure de pointe f.

rusk /rʌsk/ n. biscotte f.

russet /'rʌsɪt/ a. roussâtre, roux.

Russia /'rʌʃə/ n. Russie f. ~n a. & n. russe (m./f.); (lang.) russe m.

rust /rʌst/ n. rouille f. ● v.t./i. rouiller. ~-proof a. inoxydable. ~y a. (tool, person, etc.) rouillé.

rustic /'rʌstɪk/ a. rustique.

rustle /'rʌsl/ v.t./i. (leaves) (faire) bruire; (steal: Amer.) voler. ~ up, (food etc.: fam.) préparer.

rut /rʌt/ n. ornière f. be in a ~, rester dans l'ornière.

ruthless /'ruːθlɪs/ a. impitoyable. ~ness n. cruauté f.

rye /raɪ/ n. seigle m.; (whisky) whisky m. (à base de seigle).

S

sabbath /'sæbəθ/ n. (Jewish) sabbat m.; (Christian) dimanche m.

sabbatical /sə'bætɪkl/ a. (univ.) sabbatique.

sabot|age /'sæbətɑːʒ/ n. sabotage m. ● v.t. saboter. ~eur /-'tɜː(r)/ n. saboteu|r, -se m., f.

saccharin /'sækərɪn/ n. saccharine f.

sachet /'sæʃeɪ/ n. sachet m.

sack¹ /sæk/ n. (bag) sac m. ● v.t. (fam.) renvoyer. get the ~, (fam.) être renvoyé. ~ing n. toile à sac f.; (dismissal: fam.) renvoi m.

sack² /sæk/ v.t. (plunder) saccager.

sacrament /'sækrəmənt/ n. sacrement m.

sacred /'seɪkrɪd/ a. sacré.

sacrifice /'sækrɪfaɪs/ n. sacrifice m. ● v.t. sacrifier.

sacrileg|e /'sækrɪlɪdʒ/ n. sacrilège m. ~ious /-'lɪdʒəs/ a. sacrilège.

sad /sæd/ a. (sadder, saddest) triste. ~ly adv. tristement; (unfortunately) malheureusement. ~ness n. tristesse f.

sadden /'sædn/ v.t. attrister.

saddle /'sædl/ n. selle f. ● v.t. (horse) seller. ~ s.o. with, (task, *person*) coller à qn. **in the ~,** bien en selle. **~-bag** n. sacoche f.

sadis|t /'seɪdɪst/ n. sadique m./f. **~m** /-zəm/ n. sadisme m. **~tic** /sə'dɪstɪk/ a. sadique.

safari /sə'fɑːrɪ/ n. safari m.

safe /seɪf/ a. (**-er, -est**) (*not dangerous*) sans danger; (*reliable*) sûr; (*out of danger*) en sécurité; (*after accident*) sain et sauf; (*wise: fig.*) prudent. ● n. coffre-fort m. **to be on the ~ side,** pour être sûr. **in ~ keeping,** en sécurité. **~ conduct,** sauf-conduit m. **~ from,** à l'abri de. **~ly** adv. sans danger; (*in safe place*) en sûreté.

safeguard /'seɪfgɑːd/ n. sauvegarde f. ● v.t. sauvegarder.

safety /'seɪftɪ/ n. sécurité f. **~-belt** n. ceinture de sécurité f. **~-pin** n. épingle de sûreté f. **~-valve** n. soupape de sûreté f.

saffron /'sæfrən/ n. safran m.

sag /sæg/ v.i. (*p.t.* **sagged**) s'affaisser, fléchir. **~ging** a. affaissé.

saga /'sɑːgə/ n. saga f.

sage¹ /seɪdʒ/ n. (*herb*) sauge f.

sage² /seɪdʒ/ a. & n. sage (m.).

Sagittarius /sædʒɪ'teərɪəs/ n. le Sagittaire.

said /sed/ *see* say.

sail /seɪl/ n. voile f.; (*journey*) tour en bateau m. ● v.i. naviguer; (*leave*) partir; (*sport*) faire de la voile; (*glide*) glisser. ● v.t. (*boat*) piloter. **~ing-boat, ~ing-ship** ns. bateau à voiles m.

sailor /'seɪlə(r)/ n. marin m.

saint /seɪnt/ n. saint(e) m. (f.). **~ly** a. (*person, act, etc.*) saint.

sake /seɪk/ n. **for the ~ of,** pour, pour l'amour de.

salad /'sæləd/ n. salade f. **~-dressing** n. vinaigrette f.

salami /sə'lɑːmɪ/ n. salami m.

salar|y /'sælərɪ/ n. traitement m., salaire m. **~ied** a. salarié.

sale /seɪl/ n. vente f. **~s,** (*at reduced prices*) soldes m. pl. **~s assistant,** (*Amer.*) **~s clerk,** vendeu|r, -se m., f. **for ~,** à vendre. **on ~,** en vente; (*at a reduced price: Amer.*) en solde. **~-room** n. salle des ventes f.

saleable /'seɪləbl/ a. vendable.

sales|man /'seɪlzmən/ n. (*pl.* **-men**) (*in shop*) vendeur m.; (*traveller*) représentant m. **~woman** n. (*pl.* **-women**) vendeuse f.; représentante f.

salient /'seɪlɪənt/ a. saillant.

saline /'seɪlaɪn/ a. salin. ● n. sérum physiologique m.

saliva /sə'laɪvə/ n. salive f.

sallow /'sæləʊ/ a. (**-er, -est**) (*complexion*) jaunâtre.

salmon /'sæmən/ n. invar. saumon m.

salon /'sælɒn/ n. salon m.

saloon /sə'luːn/ n. (*on ship*) salon m.; (*bar: Amer.*) bar m., saloon m. **~ (car),** berline f.

salt /sɔːlt/ n. sel m. ● a. (*culin.*) salé; (*water*) de mer. ● v.t. saler. **~-cellar** n. salière f. **~y** a. salé.

salutary /'sæljʊtrɪ/ a. salutaire.

salute /sə'luːt/ n. (*mil.*) salut m. ● v.t. saluer. ● v.i. faire un salut.

salvage /'sælvɪdʒ/ n. sauvetage m.; (*of waste*) récupération f.; (*goods*) objets sauvés m. pl. ● v.t. sauver; (*for re-use*) récupérer.

salvation /sæl'veɪʃn/ n. salut m.

salvo /'sælvəʊ/ n. (*pl.* **-oes**) salve f.

same /seɪm/ a. même (**as, que**). ● pron. **the ~,** le *or* la même, les mêmes. **at the ~ time,** en même temps. **the ~ (thing),** la même chose.

sample /'sɑːmpl/ n. échantillon m.; (*of blood*) prélèvement m. ● v.t. essayer; (*food*) goûter.

sanatorium /sænə'tɔːrɪəm/ n. (*pl.* **-iums**) sanatorium m.

sanctify /'sæŋktɪfaɪ/ v.t. sanctifier.

sanctimonious /sæŋktɪ'məʊnɪəs/ a. (*person*) bigot; (*air, tone*) de petit saint.

sanction /'sæŋkʃn/ n. sanction f. ● v.t. sanctionner.

sanctity /'sæŋktətɪ/ n. sainteté f.

sanctuary /'sæŋktʃʊərɪ/ n. (*relig.*) sanctuaire m.; (*for animals*) réserve f.; (*refuge*) asile m.

sand /sænd/ n. sable m. **~s,** (*beach*) plage f. ● v.t. sabler. **~-castle** n. château de sable m. **~-pit** n. (*Amer.*) **~-box** n. bac à sable m.

sandal /'sændl/ n. sandale f.

sandpaper /'sændpeɪpə(r)/ n. papier de verre m. ● v.t. poncer.

sandstone /'sændstəʊn/ n. grès m.

sandwich /'sænwɪdʒ/ n. sandwich m. ● v.t. **~ed between,** pris en sandwich entre. **~ course,** stage de formation continue à mi-temps m.

sandy /'sændɪ/ a. sablonneux, de sable; (*hair*) blond roux *invar.*

sane /seɪn/ a. (-er, -est) (*view etc.*) sain; (*person*) sain d'esprit. **~ly** adv. sainement.

sang /sæŋ/ *see* sing.

sanitary /'sænɪtrɪ/ a. (*clean*) hygiénique; (*system etc.*) sanitaire. **~ towel**, (*Amer.*) **~ napkin**, serviette hygiénique f.

sanitation /sænɪ'teɪʃn/ n. hygiène (publique) f.; (*drainage etc.*) système sanitaire m.

sanity /'sænətɪ/ n. santé mentale f.; (*good sense: fig.*) bon sens m.

sank /sæŋk/ *see* sink.

Santa Claus /'sæntəklɔːz/ n. le père Noël.

sap /sæp/ n. (*of plants*) sève f. ● v.t. (*p.t.* **sapped**) (*undermine*) saper.

sapphire /'sæfaɪə(r)/ n. saphir m.

sarcas|m /'sɑːkæzəm/ n. sarcasme m. **~tic** /sɑːˈkæstɪk/ a. sarcastique.

sardine /sɑːˈdiːn/ n. sardine f.

Sardinia /sɑːˈdɪnɪə/ n. Sardaigne f.

sardonic /sɑːˈdɒnɪk/ a. sardonique.

sash /sæʃ/ n. (*on uniform*) écharpe f.; (*on dress*) ceinture f. **~-window** n. fenêtre à guillotine f.

sat /sæt/ *see* sit.

satanic /sə'tænɪk/ a. satanique.

satchel /'sætʃl/ n. cartable m.

satellite /'sætəlaɪt/ n. & a. satellite (m.). **~ dish**, antenne parabolique f.

satin /'sætɪn/ n. satin m.

satir|e /'sætaɪə(r)/ n. satire f. **~ical** /sə'tɪrɪkl/ a. satirique.

satisfactor|y /sætɪs'fæktərɪ/ a. satisfaisant. **~ily** adv. d'une manière satisfaisante.

satisf|y /'sætɪsfaɪ/ v.t. satisfaire; (*convince*) convaincre. **~action** /-'fæk-ʃn/ n. satisfaction f. **~ying** a. satisfaisant.

satsuma /sæt'suːmə/ n. mandarine f.

saturat|e /'sætʃəreɪt/ v.t. saturer. **~ed** a. (*wet*) trempé. **~ion** /-'reɪ-ʃn/ n. saturation f.

Saturday /'sætədɪ/ n. samedi m.

sauce /sɔːs/ n. sauce f.; (*impudence: sl.*) toupet m.

saucepan /'sɔːspən/ n. casserole f.

saucer /'sɔːsə(r)/ n. soucoupe f.

saucy /'sɔːsɪ/ a. (-ier, -iest) impertinent; (*boldly smart*) coquin.

Saudi Arabia /saʊdɪə'reɪbɪə/ n. Arabie Séoudite f.

sauna /'sɔːnə/ n. sauna m.

saunter /'sɔːntə(r)/ v.i. flâner.

sausage /'sɒsɪdʒ/ n. saucisse f.; (*pre-cooked*) saucisson m.

savage /'sævɪdʒ/ a. (*fierce*) féroce; (*wild*) sauvage. ● n. sauvage m./f. ● v.t. attaquer férocement. **~ry** n. sauvagerie f.

sav|e /seɪv/ v.t. sauver; (*money*) économiser; (*time*) (faire) gagner; (*keep*) garder; (*prevent*) éviter (**from**, de). ● n. (*football*) arrêt m. ● prep. sauf. **~er** n. épargnant(e) m. (f.). **~ing** n. (*of time, money*) économie f. **~ings** n. pl. économies f. pl.

saviour, (*Amer.*) **savior** /'seɪvɪə(r)/ n. sauveur m.

savour, (*Amer.*) **savor** /'seɪvə(r)/ n. saveur f. ● v.t. savourer. **~y** a. (*tasty*) savoureux; (*culin.*) salé.

saw[1] /sɔː/ *see* see[1].

saw[2] /sɔː/ n. scie f. ● v.t. (*p.t.* **sawed**, *p.p.* **sawn** /sɔːn/ or **sawed**) scier.

sawdust /'sɔːdʌst/ n. sciure f.

saxophone /'sæksəfəʊn/ n. saxophone m.

say /seɪ/ v.t./i. (*p.t.* **said** /sed/) dire; (*prayer*) faire. ● n. have a ~, dire son mot; (*in decision*) avoir voix au chapitre. **I ~!**, dites donc!

saying /'seɪɪŋ/ n. proverbe m.

scab /skæb/ n. (*on sore*) croûte f.; (*blackleg: fam.*) jaune m.

scaffold /'skæfəʊld/ n. (*gallows*) échafaud m. **~ing** /-əldɪŋ/ n. (*for workmen*) échafaudage m.

scald /skɔːld/ v.t. (*injure, cleanse*) ébouillanter. ● n. brûlure f.

scale[1] /skeɪl/ n. (*of fish*) écaille f.

scale[2] /skeɪl/ n. (*for measuring, size, etc.*) échelle f.; (*mus.*) gamme f.; (*of salaries, charges*) barème m. **on a small/etc. ~**, sur une petite etc. échelle. **~ model**, maquette f. ● v.t. (*climb*) escalader. **~ down**, réduire (proportionnellement).

scales /skeɪlz/ n. pl. (*for weighing*) balance f.

scallop /'skɒləp/ n. coquille Saint-Jacques f.

scalp /skælp/ n. cuir chevelu m. ● v.t. (*mutilate*) scalper.

scalpel /'skælp(ə)l/ n. scalpel m.

scamper /'skæmpə(r)/ v.i. courir, trotter. **~ away**, détaler.

scampi /'skæmpɪ/ n. pl. grosses crevettes f. pl., gambas f. pl.

scan /skæn/ v.t. (*p.t.* **scanned**) scruter; (*quickly*) parcourir; (*poetry*) scander; (*of radar*) balayer. ● n. (*ultrasound*) échographie f.

scandal /'skændl/ *n.* (*disgrace, outrage*) scandale *m.*; (*gossip*) cancans *m. pl.* ~**ous** *a.* scandaleux.

scandalize /'skændəlaız/ *v.t.* scandaliser.

Scandinavia /skændɪ'neɪvɪə/ *n.* Scandinavie *f.* ~**n** *a. & n.* scandinave (*m./f.*).

scant /skænt/ *a.* insuffisant.

scant|y /'skæntɪ/ *a.* (-**ier**, -**iest**) insuffisant; (*clothing*) sommaire. ~**ily** *adv.* insuffisamment. ~**ily dressed**, à peine vêtu.

scapegoat /'skeɪpɡəʊt/ *n.* bouc émissaire *m.*

scar /skɑː(r)/ *n.* cicatrice *f.* ● *v.t.* (*p.t.* scarred) marquer d'une cicatrice; (*fig.*) marquer.

scarc|e /skeəs/ *a.* (-**er**, -**est**) rare. make o.s. ~**e**, (*fam.*) se sauver. ~**ity** *n.* rareté *f.*, pénurie *f.*

scarcely /'skeəslɪ/ *adv.* à peine.

scare /skeə(r)/ *v.t.* faire peur à. ● *n.* peur *f.* be ~**d**, avoir peur. **bomb** ~, alerte à la bombe *f.*

scarecrow /'skeəkrəʊ/ *n.* épouvantail *m.*

scarf /skɑːf/ *n.* (*pl.* scarves) écharpe *f.*; (*over head*) foulard *m.*

scarlet /'skɑːlət/ *a.* écarlate. ~ **fever**, scarlatine *f.*

scary /'skeərɪ/ *a.* (-**ier**, -**iest**) (*fam.*) qui fait peur, effrayant.

scathing /'skeɪðɪŋ/ *a.* cinglant.

scatter /'skætə(r)/ *v.t.* (*throw*) éparpiller, répandre; (*disperse*) disperser. ● *v.i.* se disperser. ~**brain** *n.* écervelé(e) *m.* (*f.*).

scavenge /'skævɪndʒ/ *v.i.* fouiller (dans les ordures). ~**r** /-ə(r)/ *n.* (*vagrant*) personne qui fouille dans les ordures *f.*

scenario /sɪ'nɑːrɪəʊ/ *n.* (*pl.* -**os**) scénario *m.*

scene /siːn/ *n.* scène *f.*; (*of accident, crime*) lieu(x) *m.* (*pl.*); (*sight*) spectacle *m.*; (*incident*) incident *m.* **behind the** ~**s**, en coulisse. **to make a** ~, faire une esclandre.

scenery /'siːnərɪ/ *n.* paysage *m.*; (*theatre*) décor(s) *m.* (*pl.*).

scenic /'siːnɪk/ *a.* pittoresque.

scent /sent/ *n.* (*perfume*) parfum *m.*; (*trail*) piste *f.* ● *v.t.* flairer; (*make fragrant*) parfumer.

sceptic /'skeptɪk/ *n.* sceptique *m./f.* ~**al** *a.* sceptique. ~**ism** /-sɪzəm/ *n.* scepticisme *m.*

schedule /'ʃedjuːl, *Amer.* 'skedʒʊl/ *n.* horaire *m.*; (*for job*) planning *m.* ● *v.t.* prévoir. **behind** ~, en retard. **on** ~, (*train*) à l'heure; (*work*) dans les temps. ~**d flight**, vol régulier *m.*

scheme /skiːm/ *n.* plan *m.*; (*dishonest*) combine *f.*; (*fig.*) arrangement *m.* ● *v.i.* intriguer. **pension** ~, caisse de retraite *f.* ~**r** /-ə(r)/ *n.* intrigant(e) *m.* (*f.*).

schism /'sɪzəm/ *n.* schisme *m.*

schizophrenic /skɪtsəʊ'frenɪk/ *a. & n.* schizophrène (*m./f.*).

scholar /'skɒlə(r)/ *n.* érudit(e) *m.* (*f.*) ~**ly** *a.* érudit. ~**ship** *n.* érudition *f.*; (*grant*) bourse *f.*

school /skuːl/ *n.* école *f.*; (*secondary*) lycée *m.*; (*of university*) faculté *f.* ● *a.* (*age, year, holidays*) scolaire. ● *v.t.* (*person*) éduquer; (*animal*) dresser. ~**ing** *n.* (*education*) instruction *f.*; (*attendance*) scolarité *f.*

school|boy /'skuːlbɔɪ/ *n.* écolier *m.* ~**girl** *n.* écolière *f.*

school|master /'skuːlmɑːstə(r)/, ~**mistress**, ~**teacher** *ns.* (*primary*) institu|teur, -trice *m.*, *f.*; (*secondary*) professeur *m.*

schooner /'skuːnə(r)/ *n.* goélette *f.*

sciatica /saɪ'ætɪkə/ *n.* sciatique *f.*

scien|ce /'saɪəns/ *n.* science *f.* ~**ce fiction**, science-fiction *f.* ~**tific** /-'tɪfɪk/ *a.* scientifique.

scientist /'saɪəntɪst/ *n.* scientifique *m./f.*

scintillate /'sɪntɪleɪt/ *v.i.* scintiller; (*person: fig.*) briller.

scissors /'sɪzəz/ *n. pl.* ciseaux *m. pl.*

scoff[1] /skɒf/ *v.i.* ~ **at**, se moquer de.

scoff[2] /skɒf/ *v.t.* (*eat: sl.*) bouffer.

scold /skəʊld/ *v.t.* réprimander. ~**ing** *n.* réprimande *f.*

scone /skɒn/ *n.* petit pain au lait *m.*, galette *f.*

scoop /skuːp/ *n.* (*for grain, sugar*) pelle (à main) *f.*; (*for food*) cuiller *f.*; (*ice cream*) boule *f.*; (*news*) exclusivité *f.* ● *v.t.* (*pick up*) ramasser. ~ **out**, creuser. ~ **up**, ramasser.

scoot /skuːt/ *v.i.* (*fam.*) filer.

scooter /'skuːtə(r)/ *n.* (*child's*) trottinette *f.*; (*motor cycle*) scooter *m.*

scope /skəʊp/ *n.* étendue *f.*; (*competence*) compétence *f.*; (*opportunity*) possibilité(s) *f.* (*pl.*).

scorch /skɔːtʃ/ *v.t.* brûler, roussir. ~**ing** *a.* brûlant, très chaud.

score /skɔː(r)/ *n.* score *m.*; (*mus.*) partition *f.* ● *v.t.* marquer; (*suc-*

cess) remporter. ● v.i. marquer un point; (football) marquer un but; (keep score) compter les points. a ~ (of), (twenty) vingt. on that ~, à cet égard. ~ out, rayer. ~-board n. tableau m. ~r /-ə(r)/ n. (sport) marqueur m.

scorn /skɔːn/ n. mépris m. ● v.t. mépriser. ~ful a. méprisant. ~fully adv. avec mépris.

Scorpio /'skɔːpɪəʊ/ n. le Scorpion.

scorpion /'skɔːpɪən/ n. scorpion m.

Scot /skɒt/ n. Écossais(e) m. (f.). ~tish a. écossais.

Scotch /skɒtʃ/ a. écossais. ● n. whisky m., scotch m.

scotch /skɒtʃ/ v.t. mettre fin à.

scot-free /skɒt'friː/ a. & adv. sans être puni; (gratis) sans payer.

Scotland /'skɒtlənd/ n. Écosse f.

Scots /skɒts/ a. écossais. ~man n. Écossais m. ~woman n. Écossaise f.

scoundrel /'skaʊndrəl/ n. vaurien m., bandit m., gredin(e) m. (f.).

scour[1] /'skaʊə(r)/ v.t. (pan) récurer. ~er n. tampon à récurer m.

scour[2] /'skaʊə(r)/ v.t. (search) parcourir.

scourge /skɜːdʒ/ n. fléau m.

scout /skaʊt/ n. (mil.) éclaireur m. ● v.i. ~ around (for), chercher.

Scout /skaʊt/ n. (boy) scout m., éclaireur m. ~ing n. scoutisme m.

scowl /skaʊl/ n. air renfrogné m. ● v.i. faire la tête (at, à).

scraggy /'skrægɪ/ a. (-ier, -iest) décharné, efflanqué.

scram /skræm/ v.i. (sl.) se tirer.

scramble /'skræmbl/ v.i. (clamber) grimper. ● v.t. (eggs) brouiller. ● n. bousculade f., ruée f. ~ for, se bousculer pour avoir.

scrap[1] /skræp/ n. petit morceau m. ~s, (of metal, fabric, etc.) déchets m. pl.; (of food) restes m. pl. ● v.t. (p.t. scrapped) mettre au rebut; (plan etc.) abandonner. ~-book n. album m. on the ~-heap, mis au rebut. ~-iron n. ferraille f. ~-paper n. brouillon m. ~py a. fragmentaire.

scrap[2] /skræp/ n. (fight: fam.) bagarre f., dispute f.

scrape /skreɪp/ v.t. racler, gratter; (graze) érafler. ● v.i. (rub) frotter. ● n. raclement m.; éraflure f. in a ~, dans une mauvaise passe. ~ through, réussir de justesse. ~ together, réunir. ~r /-ə(r)/ n. racloir m.

scratch /skrætʃ/ v.t./i. (se) gratter; (with claw, nail) griffer; (graze) érafler; (mark) rayer. ● n. éraflure f. start from ~, partir de zéro. up to ~, au niveau voulu.

scrawl /skrɔːl/ n. gribouillage m. ● v.t./i. gribouiller.

scrawny /'skrɔːnɪ/ a. (-ier, -iest) décharné, émacié.

scream /skriːm/ v.t./i. crier, hurler. ● n. cri (perçant) m.

scree /skriː/ n. éboulis m.

screech /skriːtʃ/ v.i. (scream) hurler; (of brakes) grincer. ● n. hurlement m.; grincement m.

screen /skriːn/ n. écran m.; (folding) paravent m. ● v.t. masquer; (protect) protéger; (film) projeter; (candidates) filtrer; (med.) faire subir un test de dépistage. ~ing n. projection f.

screenplay /'skriːnpleɪ/ n. scénario m.

screw /skruː/ n. vis f. ● v.t. visser. ~ up, (eyes) plisser; (ruin: sl.) bousiller.

screwdriver /'skruːdraɪvə(r)/ n. tournevis m.

screwy /'skruːɪ/ a. (-ier, -iest) (crazy: sl.) cinglé.

scribble /'skrɪbl/ v.t./i. griffonner. ● n. griffonnage m.

scribe /skraɪb/ n. scribe m.

script /skrɪpt/ n. écriture f.; (of film) scénario m.; (of play) texte m. ~writer n. scénariste m./f.

Scriptures /'skrɪptʃəz/ n. pl. the ~, l'Écriture (sainte) f.

scroll /skrəʊl/ n. rouleau m. ● v.t./i. (comput.) (faire) défiler.

scrounge /skraʊndʒ/ v.t. (meal) se faire payer; (steal) chiper. ● v.i. (beg) quémander. ~ money from, taper. ~r /-ə(r)/ n. parasite m.; (of money) tapeu|r, -se m., f.

scrub[1] /skrʌb/ n. (land) broussailles f. pl.

scrub[2] /skrʌb/ v.t./i. (p.t. scrubbed) nettoyer (à la brosse), frotter. ● n. nettoyage m.

scruff /skrʌf/ n. by the ~ of the neck, par la peau du cou.

scruffy /'skrʌfɪ/ a. (-ier, -iest) (fam.) miteux, sale.

scrum /skrʌm/ n. (Rugby) mêlée f.

scruple /'skruːpl/ n. scrupule m.

scrupulous /'skruːpjʊləs/ a. scrupuleux. ~ly adv. scrupuleusement. **~ly clean**, impeccable.

scrutiny /'skru:tɪnɪ/ n. examen minutieux m. **~ize** v.t. scruter.

scuba-diving /'sku:bədaɪvɪŋ/ n. plongée sous-marine f.

scuff /skʌf/ v.t. (scratch) érafler.

scuffle /'skʌfl/ n. bagarre f.

sculpt /skʌlpt/ v.t./i. sculpter. **~or** n. sculpteur m. **~ure** /-tʃə(r)/ n. sculpture f.; v.t./i. sculpter.

scum /skʌm/ n. (on liquid) écume f.; (people: pej.) racaille f.

scurf /skɜːf/ n. pellicules f. pl.

scurrilous /'skʌrɪləs/ a. grossier, injurieux, venimeux.

scurry /'skʌrɪ/ v.i. courir (for, pour chercher). **~ off**, filer.

scuttle[1] /'skʌtl/ v.t. (ship) saborder.

scuttle[2] /'skʌtl/ v.i. **~ away**, se sauver, filer.

scythe /saɪð/ n. faux f.

sea /si:/ n. mer f. ● a. de (la) mer, marin. **at ~**, en mer. **by ~**, par mer. **~-green** a. vert glauque invar. **~-level** n. niveau de la mer m. **~ shell**, coquillage m. **~shore** n. rivage m.

seaboard /'si:bɔːd/ n. littoral m.

seafarer /'si:feərə(r)/ n. marin m.

seafood /'si:fu:d/ n. fruits de mer m. pl.

seagull /'si:gʌl/ n. mouette f.

seal[1] /si:l/ n. (animal) phoque m.

seal[2] /si:l/ n. sceau m.; (with wax) cachet m. ● v.t. sceller; cacheter; (stick down) coller. **~ing-wax** n. cire à cacheter f. **~ off**, (area) boucler.

seam /si:m/ n. (in cloth etc.) couture f.; (of coal) veine f.

seaman /'si:mən/ n. (pl. **-men**) marin m.

seamy /'si:mɪ/ a. **~ side**, côté sordide m.

seance /'seɪɑːns/ n. séance de spiritisme f.

seaplane /'si:pleɪn/ n. hydravion m.

seaport /'si:pɔːt/ n. port de mer m.

search /sɜːtʃ/ v.t./i. fouiller; (study) examiner. ● n. fouille f.; (quest) recherche(s) f. (pl.). **in ~ of**, à la recherche de. **~ for**, chercher. **~-party** n. équipe de secours f. **~-warrant** n. mandat de perquisition m. **~ing** a. (piercing) pénétrant.

searchlight /'sɜːtʃlaɪt/ n. projecteur m.

seasick /'si:sɪk/ a. **be ~**, avoir le mal de mer.

seaside /'si:saɪd/ n. bord de la mer m.

season /'si:zn/ n. saison f. ● v.t. assaisonner. **in ~**, de saison. **~able** a. qui convient à la saison. **~al** a. saisonnier. **~ing** n. assaisonnement m. **~-ticket** n. carte d'abonnement f.

seasoned /'si:znd/ a. expérimenté.

seat /si:t/ n. siège m.; (place) place f.; (of trousers) fond m. ● v.t. (put) placer; (have seats for) avoir des places assises pour. **be ~ed**, **take a ~**, s'asseoir. **~-belt** n. ceinture de sécurité f.

seaweed /'si:wi:d/ n. algues f. pl.

seaworthy /'si:wɜːðɪ/ a. en état de naviguer.

secateurs /sekə'tɜːz/ n. pl. sécateur m.

sece|de /sɪ'si:d/ v.i. faire sécession. **~ssion** /-eʃn/ n. sécession f.

seclu|de /sɪ'klu:d/ v.t. isoler. **~ded** a. isolé. **~sion** /-ʒn/ n. solitude f.

second[1] /'sekənd/ a. deuxième, second. ● n. deuxième m./f.; second(e) m. (f.); (unit of time) seconde f. **~s**, (goods) articles de second choix m. pl. ● adv. (in race etc.) en seconde place. ● v.t. (proposal) appuyer. **~-best** a. de second choix, numéro deux invar. **~-class** a. de deuxième classe. **at ~ hand**, de seconde main. **~-hand** a. & adv. d'occasion; n. (on clock) trotteuse f. **~-rate** a. médiocre. **have ~ thoughts**, avoir des doutes, changer d'avis. **on ~ thoughts**, (Amer.) **on ~ thought**, à la réflexion. **~ly** adv. deuxièmement.

second[2] /sɪ'kɒnd/ v.t. (transfer) détacher (**to**, à). **~ment** n. détachement m.

secondary /'sekəndrɪ/ a. secondaire. **~ school**, lycée m., collège m.

secrecy /'si:krəsɪ/ n. secret m.

secret /'si:krɪt/ a. secret. ● n. secret m. **in ~**, en secret. **~ly** adv. en secret, secrètement.

secretariat /sekrə'teərɪət/ n. secrétariat m.

secretar|y /'sekrətrɪ/ n. secrétaire m./f. **S~y of State**, ministre m.; (Amer.) ministre des Affaires étrangères m. **~ial** /-'teərɪəl/ a. (work etc.) de secrétaire.

secre|te /sɪ'kri:t/ v.t. (med.) sécréter. **~ion** /-ʃn/ n. sécrétion f.

secretive /'si:krətɪv/ a. cachottier.

sect /sekt/ *n.* secte *f.* **~arian** /-'teərɪən/ *a.* sectaire.

section /'sekʃn/ *n.* section *f.*; (*of country, town*) partie *f.*; (*in store*) rayon *m.*; (*newspaper column*) rubrique *f.*

sector /'sektə(r)/ *n.* secteur *m.*

secular /'sekjʊlə(r)/ *a.* (*school etc.*) laïque; (*art, music, etc.*) profane.

secure /sɪ'kjʊə(r)/ *a.* (*safe*) en sûreté; (*in mind*) tranquille; (*psychologically*) sécurisé; (*firm*) solide; (*against attack*) sûr; (*window etc.*) bien fermé. ● *v.t.* attacher; (*ensure*) assurer. **~ly** *adv.* solidement; (*safely*) en sûreté.

security /sɪ'kjʊərətɪ/ *n.* sécurité *f.*; (*for loan*) caution *f.* **~ guard**, vigile *m.*

sedan /sɪ'dæn/ *n.* (*Amer.*) berline *f.*

sedate[1] /sɪ'deɪt/ *a.* calme.

sedate[2] /sɪ'deɪt/ *v.t.* donner un sédatif à. **~ion** /-ʃn/ *n.* sédation *f.*

sedative /'sedətɪv/ *n.* sédatif *m.*

sedentary /'sedntrɪ/ *a.* sédentaire.

sediment /'sedɪmənt/ *n.* sédiment *m.*

sedition /sɪ'dɪʃn/ *n.* sédition *f.*

seduce /sɪ'dju:s/ *v.t.* séduire. **~r** /-ə(r)/ *n.* séduc|teur, -trice *m., f.*

seduct|ion /sɪ'dʌkʃn/ *n.* séduction *f.* **~ive** /-tɪv/ *a.* séduisant.

see[1] /si:/ *v.t./i.* (*p.t.* saw, *p.p.* seen) voir; (*escort*) (r)accompagner. **~ about** *or* to, s'occuper de. **~ through**, (*task*) mener à bonne fin; (*person*) deviner (le jeu de). **~ (to it) that**, veiller à ce que. **see you (soon)!**, à bientôt! **~ing that**, vu que.

see[2] /si:/ *n.* (*of bishop*) évêché *m.*

seed /si:d/ *n.* graine *f.*; (*collectively*) graines *f. pl.*; (*origin: fig.*) germe *m.*; (*tennis*) tête de série *f.* **go to ~**, (*plant*) monter en graine; (*person*) se laisser aller. **~ling** *n.* plant *m.*

seedy /'si:dɪ/ *a.* (-ier, -iest) miteux.

seek /si:k/ *v.t.* (*p.t.* sought) chercher. **~ out**, aller chercher.

seem /si:m/ *v.i.* sembler. **~ingly** *adv.* apparemment.

seemly /'si:mlɪ/ *adv.* convenable.

seen /si:n/ *see* see[1].

seep /si:p/ *v.i.* (*ooze*) suinter. **~ into**, s'infiltrer dans. **~age** *n.* suintement *m.*; infiltration *f.*

see-saw /'si:sɔ:/ *n.* balançoire *f.*, tapecul *m.* ● *v.i.* osciller.

seethe /si:ð/ *v.i.* **~ with**, (*anger*) bouillir de; (*people*) grouiller de.

segment /'segmənt/ *n.* segment *m.*; (*of orange*) quartier *m.*

segregat|e /'segrɪgeɪt/ *v.t.* séparer. **~ion** /-'geɪʃn/ *n.* ségrégation *f.*

seize /si:z/ *v.t.* saisir; (*take possession of*) s'emparer de. ● *v.i.* **~ on**, (*chance etc.*) saisir. **~ up**, (*engine etc.*) se gripper.

seizure /'si:ʒə(r)/ *n.* (*med.*) crise *f.*

seldom /'seldəm/ *adv.* rarement.

select /sɪ'lekt/ *v.t.* choisir, sélectionner. ● *a.* choisi; (*exclusive*) sélect. **~ion** /-kʃn/ *n.* sélection *f.*

selective /sɪ'lektɪv/ *a.* sélectif.

self /self/ *n.* (*pl.* selves) (*on cheque*) moi-même, le ~, le moi *m. invar.* **your good ~**, vous-même.

self- /self/ *pref.* **~-assurance** *n.* assurance *f.* **~-assured** *a.* sûr de soi. **~-catering** *a.* où l'on fait la cuisine soi-même. **~-centred**, (*Amer.*) **~-entered** *a.* égocentrique. **~-coloured**, (*Amer.*) **~-colored** *a.* uni. **~-confidence** *n.* confiance en soi *f.* **~-confident** *a.* sûr de soi. **~-conscious** *a.* gêné, timide. **~-contained** *a.* (*flat*) indépendant. **~-control** *n.* maîtrise de soi *f.* **~-defence** *n.* autodéfense *f.*; (*jurid.*) légitime défense *f.* **~-denial** *n.* abnégation *f.* **~-employed** *a.* qui travaille à son compte. **~-esteem** *n.* amour-propre *m.* **~-evident** *a.* évident. **~-government** *n.* autonomie *f.* **~-indulgent** *a.* qui se permet tout. **~-interest** *n.* intérêt personnel *m.* **~-portrait** *n.* autoportrait *m.* **~-possessed** *a.* assuré. **~-reliant** *a.* indépendant. **~-respect** *n.* respect de soi *m.*, dignité *f.* **~-righteous** *a.* satisfait de soi. **~-sacrifice** *n.* abnégation *f.* **~-satisfied** *a.* content de soi. **~-seeking** *a.* égoïste. **~-service** *n. & a.* libre-service (*m.*). **~-styled** *a.* soi-disant. **~-sufficient** *a.* indépendant. **~-willed** *a.* entêté.

selfish /'selfɪʃ/ *a.* égoïste; (*motive*) intéressé. **~ness** *n.* égoïsme *m.*

selfless /'selflɪs/ *a.* désintéressé.

sell /sel/ *v.t./i.* (*p.t.* sold) (se) vendre. **~-by date**, date limite de vente *f.* **be sold out of**, n'avoir plus de. **~ off**, liquider. **~-out**, *n.* trahison *f.* **it was a ~-out**, on a vendu tous les billets. **~ up**, vendre son fonds, sa maison, *etc.* **~er** *n.* vendeu|r, -se *m., f.*

Sellotape /'seləʊteɪp/ *n.* (P.) scotch *m.* (P.).

semantic /sɪˈmæntɪk/ a. sémantique. **~s** n. sémantique f.

semaphore /ˈseməfɔː(r)/ n. signaux à bras m. pl.; (device: rail.) sémaphore m.

semblance /ˈsembləns/ n. semblant m.

semen /ˈsiːmən/ n. sperme m.

semester /sɪˈmestə(r)/ n. (univ., Amer.) semestre m.

semi- /ˈsemɪ/ pref. semi-, demi-.

semibreve /ˈsemɪbriːv/ n. (mus.) ronde f.

semicircle /ˈsemɪsɜːkl/ n. demi-cercle m. **~ular** /-ˈsɜːkjʊlə(r)/ a. en demi-cercle.

semicolon /semɪˈkəʊlən/ n. point-virgule m.

semiconductor /semɪkənˈdʌktə(r)/ n. semi-conducteur n.

semi-detached /semɪdɪˈtætʃt/ a. **~ house**, maison jumelée f.

semifinal /semɪˈfaɪnl/ n. demi-finale f.

seminar /ˈsemɪnɑː(r)/ n. séminaire m.

seminary /ˈsemɪnərɪ/ n. séminaire m.

semiquaver /ˈsemɪkweɪvə(r)/ n. (mus.) double croche f.

Semite /ˈsiːmaɪt, Amer. ˈsemaɪt/ n. Sémite m./f. **~ic** /sɪˈmɪtɪk/ a. sémite; (lang.) sémitique.

semolina /seməˈliːnə/ n. semoule f.

senate /ˈsenɪt/ n. sénat m. **~or** /-ətə(r)/ n. sénateur m.

send /send/ v.t./i. (p.t. sent) envoyer. **~ away**, (dismiss) renvoyer. **~ (away or off) for**, commander (par la poste). **~ back**, renvoyer. **~ for**, (person, help) envoyer chercher. **~ a player off**, renvoyer un joueur. **~-off** n. adieux chaleureux m. pl. **~ up**, (fam.) parodier. **~er** n. expéditeur, -trice m., f.

senile /ˈsiːnaɪl/ a. sénile. **~ity** /sɪˈnɪlətɪ/ n. sénilité f.

senior /ˈsiːnɪə(r)/ a. plus âgé (to, que); (in rank) supérieur; (teacher, partner) principal. ● n. aîné(e) m. (f.); (schol.) grand(e) m. (f.). **~ citizen**, personne âgée f. **~ity** /-ˈɒrətɪ/ n. priorité d'âge f.; supériorité f.; (in service) ancienneté f.

sensation /senˈseɪʃn/ n. sensation f. **~al** a. (event) qui fait sensation; (wonderful) sensationnel.

sense /sens/ n. sens m.; (sensation) sensation f.; (mental impression) sentiment m.; (common sense) bon sens m. **~s**, (mind) raison f. ● v.t.

(pres)sentir. **make ~**, avoir du sens. **make ~ of**, comprendre. **~less** a. stupide; (med.) sans connaissance.

sensibility /sensɪˈbɪlətɪ/ n. sensibilité f. **~ies**, susceptibilité f.

sensible /ˈsensəbl/ a. raisonnable, sensé; (clothing) fonctionnel.

sensitive /ˈsensɪtɪv/ a. sensible (to, à); (touchy) susceptible. **~ity** /-ˈtɪvətɪ/ n. sensibilité f.

sensory /ˈsensərɪ/ a. sensoriel.

sensual /ˈsenʃʊəl/ a. sensuel. **~ity** /-ˈælətɪ/ n. sensualité f.

sensuous /ˈsenʃʊəs/ a. sensuel.

sent /sent/ see send.

sentence /ˈsentəns/ n. phrase f.; (decision: jurid.) jugement m., condamnation f.; (punishment) peine f. ● v.t. **~ to**, condamner à.

sentiment /ˈsentɪmənt/ n. sentiment m.

sentimental /sentɪˈmentl/ a. sentimental. **~ity** /-ˈtælətɪ/ n. sentimentalité f.

sentry /ˈsentrɪ/ n. sentinelle f.

separable /ˈsepərəbl/ a. séparable.

separate[1] /ˈseprət/ a. séparé, différent; (independent) indépendant. **~s** n. pl. coordonnés m. pl. **~ly** adv. séparément.

separate[2] /ˈsepəreɪt/ v.t./i. (se) séparer. **~ion** /-ˈreɪʃn/ n. séparation f.

September /sepˈtembə(r)/ n. septembre m.

septic /ˈseptɪk/ a. (wound) infecté. **~ tank**, fosse septique f.

sequel /ˈsiːkwəl/ n. suite f.

sequence /ˈsiːkwəns/ n. (order) ordre m.; (series) suite f.; (of film) séquence f.

sequin /ˈsiːkwɪn/ n. paillette f.

serenade /serəˈneɪd/ n. sérénade f. ● v.t. donner une sérénade à.

serene /sɪˈriːn/ a. serein. **~ity** /-enətɪ/ n. sérénité f.

sergeant /ˈsɑːdʒənt/ n. (mil.) sergent m.; (policeman) brigadier m.

serial /ˈsɪərɪəl/ n. (story) feuilleton m. ● a. (number) de série.

series /ˈsɪəriːz/ n. invar. série f.

serious /ˈsɪərɪəs/ a. sérieux; (very bad, critical) grave, sérieux. **~ly** adv. sérieusement, gravement. **take ~ly**, prendre au sérieux. **~ness** n. sérieux m.

sermon /ˈsɜːmən/ n. sermon m.

serpent /ˈsɜːpənt/ n. serpent m.

serrated /sɪˈreɪtɪd/ a. (*edge*) en dents de scie.

serum /ˈsɪərəm/ n. (*pl.* -a) sérum m.

servant /ˈsɜːvənt/ n. domestique m./ f.; (*of God etc.*) serviteur m.

serve /sɜːv/ v.t./i. servir; (*undergo, carry out*) faire; (*of transport*) desservir. ● n. (*tennis*) service m. ~ **as/to**, servir de/à. ~ **its purpose**, remplir sa fonction.

service /ˈsɜːvɪs/ n. service m.; (*maintenance*) révision f.; (*relig.*) office m. ~**s**, (*mil.*) forces armées f. pl. ● v.t. (*car etc.*) réviser. **of ~ to**, utile à. ~ **area**, (*auto.*) aire de services f. ~ **charge**, service m. ~ **station**, station-service f.

serviceable /ˈsɜːvɪsəbl/ a. (*usable*) utilisable; (*useful*) commode; (*durable*) solide.

serviceman /ˈsɜːvɪsmən/ n. (*pl.* -men) militaire m.

serviette /ˌsɜːvɪˈet/ n. serviette f.

servile /ˈsɜːvaɪl/ a. servile.

session /ˈseʃn/ n. séance f.; (*univ.*) année (universitaire) f.; (*univ., Amer.*) semestre m.

set /set/ v.t. (*p.t.* set, *pres. p.* setting) mettre; (*put down*) poser, mettre; (*limit etc.*) fixer; (*watch, clock*) régler; (*example, task*) donner; (*for printing*) composer; (*in plaster*) plâtrer. ● v.i. (*of sun*) se coucher; (*of jelly*) prendre. ● n. (*of chairs, stamps, etc.*) série f.; (*of knives, keys, etc.*) jeu m.; (*of people*) groupe m.; (*TV, radio*) poste m.; (*style of hair*) mise en plis f.; (*theatre*) décor m.; (*tennis*) set m.; (*mathematics*) ensemble m. ● a. fixe; (*in habits*) régulier; (*meal*) à prix fixe; (*book*) au programme. ~ **against sth.**, opposé à. **be ~ on doing**, être résolu à faire. ~ **about or to**, se mettre à. ~ **back**, (*delay*) retarder; (*cost: sl.*) coûter. ~**-back** n. revers m. ~ **fire to**, mettre le feu à. ~ **free**, libérer. ~ **in**, (*take hold*) s'installer. ~ **off** *or* **out**, partir. ~ **off**, (*mechanism, activity*) déclencher; (*bomb*) faire éclater. ~ **out**, (*state*) exposer; (*arrange*) disposer. ~ **out to do sth.**, entreprendre de faire qch. ~ **sail**, partir. ~ **square**, équerre f. ~ **to**, (*about to*) sur le point de. ~**-to** n. querelle f. ~ **to music**, mettre en musique. ~ **up**, (*establish*) fonder, établir; (*launch*) lancer. ~**-up** n. (*fam.*) affaire f.

settee /seˈtiː/ n. canapé m.

setting /ˈsetɪŋ/ n. cadre m.

settle /ˈsetl/ v.t. (*arrange, pay*) régler; (*date*) fixer; (*nerves*) calmer. ● v.i. (*come to rest*) se poser; (*live*) s'installer. ~ **down**, se calmer; (*become orderly*) se ranger. ~ **for**, accepter. ~ **in**, s'installer. ~ **up** (**with**), régler. ~**r** /-ə(r)/ n. colon m.

settlement /ˈsetlmənt/ n. règlement m. (of, de); (*agreement*) accord m.; (*place*) colonie f.

seven /ˈsevn/ a. & n. sept (m.). ~**th** a. & n. septième (m./f.).

seventeen /sevnˈtiːn/ a. & n. dix-sept (m.). ~**th** a. & n. dix-septième (m./f.).

sevent|y /ˈsevntɪ/ a. & n. soixante-dix (m.). ~**ieth** a. & n. soixante-dixième (m./f.).

sever /ˈsevə(r)/ v.t. (*cut*) couper; (*relations*) rompre. ~**ance** n. (*breaking off*) rupture f. ~**ance pay**, indemnité de licenciement f.

several /ˈsevrəl/ a. & pron. plusieurs.

sever|e /sɪˈvɪə(r)/ a. (-er, -est) sévère; (*violent*) violent; (*serious*) grave. ~**ely** adv. sévèrement; gravement. ~**ity** /sɪˈverətɪ/ n. sévérité f.; violence f.; gravité f.

sew /səʊ/ v.t./i. (*p.t.* sewed, *p.p.* sewn *or* sewed) coudre. ~**ing** n. couture f. ~**ing-machine** n. machine à coudre f.

sewage /ˈsjuːɪdʒ/ n. eaux d'égout f. pl., vidanges f. pl.

sewer /ˈsuːə(r)/ n. égout m.

sewn /səʊn/ *see* sew.

sex /seks/ n. sexe m. ● a. sexuel. **have ~**, avoir des rapports (sexuels). ~ **maniac**, obsédé(e) sexuel(le) m. (f.). ~**y** a. sexy *invar*.

sexist /ˈseksɪst/ a. & n. sexiste (m./f.).

sextet /seksˈtet/ n. sextuor m.

sexual /ˈsekʃʊəl/ a. sexuel. ~ **intercourse**, rapports sexuels m. pl. ~**ity** /-ˈælətɪ/ n. sexualité f.

shabb|y /ˈʃæbɪ/ a. (-ier, -iest) (*place, object*) minable, miteux; (*person*) pauvrement vêtu; (*mean*) mesquin. ~**ily** adv. (*dress*) pauvrement; (*act*) mesquinement.

shack /ʃæk/ n. cabane f.

shackles /ˈʃæklz/ n. pl. chaînes f. pl.

shade /ʃeɪd/ n. ombre f.; (*of colour, opinion*) nuance f.; (*for lamp*) abat-jour m.; (*blind: Amer.*) store m. **a ~**

bigger/*etc.*, légèrement plus grand/ *etc.* ● *v.t.* (*of person etc.*) abriter; (*of tree*) ombrager.

shadow /'ʃædəʊ/ *n.* ombre *f.* ● *v.t.* (*follow*) filer. **S~ Cabinet**, cabinet fantôme *m.* **~y** *a.* ombragé; (*fig.*) vague.

shady /'ʃeɪdɪ/ *a.* (**-ier, -iest**) ombragé; (*dubious: fig.*) louche.

shaft /ʃɑːft/ *n.* (*of arrow*) hampe *f.*; (*axle*) arbre *m.*; (*of mine*) puits *m.*; (*of light*) rayon *m.*

shaggy /'ʃægɪ/ *a.* (**-ier, -iest**) (*beard*) hirsute; (*hair*) broussailleux; (*animal*) à longs poils.

shake /ʃeɪk/ *v.t.* (*p.t.* **shook**, *p.p.* **shaken**) secouer; (*bottle*) agiter; (*house, belief, etc.*) ébranler. ● *v.i.* trembler. ● *n.* secousse *f.* **~ hands with**, serrer la main à. **~ off**, (*get rid of*) se débarrasser de. **~ one's head**, (*in refusal*) dire non de la tête. **~ up**, (*disturb, rouse, mix contents of*) secouer. **~-up** *n.* (*upheaval*) remaniement *m.*

shaky /'ʃeɪkɪ/ *a.* (**-ier, -iest**) (*hand, voice*) tremblant; (*table etc.*) branlant; (*weak: fig.*) faible.

shall /ʃæl, *unstressed* ʃ(ə)l/ *v. aux.* **I ~ do**, je ferai. **we ~ do**, nous ferons.

shallot /ʃə'lɒt/ *n.* échalote *f.*

shallow /'ʃæləʊ/ *a.* (**-er, -est**) peu profond; (*fig.*) superficiel.

sham /ʃæm/ *n.* comédie *f.*; (*person*) imposteur *m.*; (*jewel*) imitation *f.* ● *a.* faux; (*affected*) feint. ● *v.t.* (*p.t.* **shammed**) feindre.

shambles /'ʃæmblz/ *n. pl.* (*mess: fam.*) désordre *m.*, pagaille *f.*

shame /ʃeɪm/ *n.* honte *f.* ● *v.t.* faire honte à. **it's a ~**, c'est dommage. **~ful** *a.* honteux. **~fully** *adv.* honteusement. **~less** *a.* éhonté.

shamefaced /'ʃeɪmfeɪst/ *a.* honteux.

shampoo /ʃæm'puː/ *n.* shampooing *m.* ● *v.t.* faire un shampooing à, shampooiner.

shandy /'ʃændɪ/ *n.* panaché *m.*

shan't /ʃɑːnt/ = shall not.

shanty /'ʃæntɪ/ *n.* (*shack*) baraque *f.* **~ town**, bidonville *m.*

shape /ʃeɪp/ *n.* forme *f.* ● *v.t.* (*fashion, mould*) façonner; (*future etc.: fig.*) déterminer. ● *v.i.* **~ up**, (*plan etc.*) prendre tournure or forme; (*person etc.*) faire des progrès. **~less** *a.* informe.

shapely /'ʃeɪplɪ/ *a.* (**-ier, -iest**) (*leg, person*) bien tourné.

share /ʃeə(r)/ *n.* part *f.*; (*comm.*) action *f.* ● *v.t./i.* partager; (*feature*) avoir en commun. **~-out** *n.* partage *m.*

shareholder /'ʃeəhəʊldə(r)/ *n.* actionnaire *m./f.*

shark /ʃɑːk/ *n.* requin *m.*

sharp /ʃɑːp/ *a.* (**-er, -est**) (*knife etc.*) tranchant; (*pin etc.*) pointu; (*point*) aigu; (*acute*) vif; (*sudden*) brusque; (*dishonest*) peu scrupuleux. ● *adv.* (*stop*) net. **six o'clock/etc.**, six heures/*etc.* pile. ● *n.* (*mus.*) dièse *m.* **~ly** *adv.* (*harshly*) vivement; (*suddenly*) brusquement.

sharpen /'ʃɑːpən/ *v.t.* aiguiser; (*pencil*) tailler. **~er** *n.* (*for pencil*) taille-crayon(s) *m.*

shatter /'ʃætə(r)/ *v.t./i.* (*glass etc.*) (faire) voler en éclats, (se) briser; (*upset, ruin*) anéantir.

shav|e /ʃeɪv/ *v.t./i.* (se) raser. ● *n.* **have a ~e**, se raser. **~en** *a.* rasé. **~er** *n.* rasoir électrique *m.* **~ing-brush** *n.* blaireau *m.* **~ing-cream** *n.* crème à raser *f.*

shaving /'ʃeɪvɪŋ/ *n.* copeau *m.*

shawl /ʃɔːl/ *n.* châle *m.*

she /ʃiː/ *pron.* elle. ● *n.* femelle *f.*

sheaf /ʃiːf/ *n.* (*pl.* **sheaves**) gerbe *f.*

shear /ʃɪə(r)/ *v.t.* (*p.p.* **shorn** or **sheared**) (*sheep etc.*) tondre. **~ off**, se détacher.

shears /ʃɪəz/ *n. pl.* cisaille(s) *f.* (*pl.*).

sheath /ʃiːθ/ *n.* (*pl.* **-s** /ʃiːðz/) gaine *f.*, fourreau *m.*; (*contraceptive*) préservatif *m.*

sheathe /ʃiːð/ *v.t.* rengainer.

shed[1] /ʃed/ *n.* remise *f.*

shed[2] /ʃed/ *v.t.* (*p.t.* **shed**, *pres. p.* **shedding**) perdre; (*light, tears*) répandre.

sheen /ʃiːn/ *n.* lustre *m.*

sheep /ʃiːp/ *n. invar.* mouton *m.* **~-dog** *n.* chien de berger *m.*

sheepish /'ʃiːpɪʃ/ *a.* penaud. **~ly** *adv.* d'un air penaud.

sheepskin /'ʃiːpskɪn/ *n.* peau de mouton *f.*

sheer /ʃɪə(r)/ *a.* pur (*et simple*); (*steep*) à pic; (*fabric*) très fin. ● *adv.* à pic, verticalement.

sheet /ʃiːt/ *n.* drap *m.*; (*of paper*) feuille *f.*; (*of glass, ice*) plaque *f.*

sheikh /ʃeɪk/ *n.* cheik *m.*

shelf /ʃelf/ *n.* (*pl.* **shelves**) rayon *m.* étagère *f.* **on the ~**, (*person*) laissé pour compte.

shell /ʃel/ n. coquille f.; (on beach) coquillage m.; (of building) carcasse f.; (explosive) obus m. ● v.t. (nut etc.) décortiquer; (peas) écosser; (mil.) bombarder.

shellfish /'ʃelfɪʃ/ n. invar. (lobster etc.) crustacé(s) m. (pl.); (mollusc) coquillage(s) m. (pl.).

shelter /'ʃeltə(r)/ n. abri m. ● v.t./i. (s')abriter; (give lodging to) donner asile à. ~ed a. (life etc.) protégé.

shelve /ʃelv/ v.t. laisser en suspens, remettre à plus tard.

shelving /'ʃelvɪŋ/ n. (shelves) rayonnage(s) m. (pl.).

shepherd /'ʃepəd/ n. berger m. ● v.t. (people) guider. ~'s pie, hachis Parmentier m.

sherbet /'ʃɜːbət/ n. jus de fruits m.; (powder) poudre acidulée f.; (water-ice: Amer.) sorbet m.

sheriff /'ʃerɪf/ n. shérif m.

sherry /'ʃerɪ/ n. xérès m.

shield /ʃiːld/ n. bouclier m.; (screen) écran m. ● v.t. protéger.

shift /ʃɪft/ v.t./i. (se) déplacer, bouger; (exchange, alter) changer de. ● n. changement m.; (workers) équipe f.; (work) poste m.; (auto.: Amer.) levier de vitesse m. make ~, se débrouiller. ~ work, travail par roulement m.

shiftless /'ʃɪftlɪs/ a. paresseux.

shifty /'ʃɪftɪ/ a. (-ier, -iest) louche.

shilling /'ʃɪlɪŋ/ n. shilling m.

shilly-shally /'ʃɪlɪʃælɪ/ v.i. hésiter, balancer.

shimmer /'ʃɪmə(r)/ v.i. chatoyer. ● n. chatoiement m.

shin /ʃɪn/ n. tibia m.

shine /ʃaɪn/ v.t./i. (p.t. shone /ʃɒn/) (faire) briller. ● n. éclat m., brillant m. ~ one's torch or the light (on), éclairer.

shingle /'ʃɪŋgl/ n. (pebbles) galets m. pl.; (on roof) bardeau m.

shingles /'ʃɪŋglz/ n. pl. (med.) zona m.

shiny /'ʃaɪnɪ/ a. (-ier, -iest) brillant.

ship /ʃɪp/ n. bateau m., navire m. ● v.t. (p.t. shipped) transporter; (send) expédier; (load) embarquer. ~ment n. cargaison f., envoi m. ~per n. expéditeur m. ~ping n. (ships) navigation f., navires m. pl.

shipbuilding /'ʃɪpbɪldɪŋ/ n. construction navale f.

shipshape /'ʃɪpʃeɪp/ adv. & a. parfaitement en ordre.

shipwreck /'ʃɪprek/ n. naufrage m. ~ed a. naufragé. be ~ed, faire naufrage.

shipyard /'ʃɪpjɑːd/ n. chantier naval m.

shirk /ʃɜːk/ v.t. esquiver. ~er n. tire-au-flanc m. invar.

shirt /ʃɜːt/ n. chemise f.; (of woman) chemisier m. in ~-sleeves, en bras de chemise.

shiver /'ʃɪvə(r)/ v.i. frissonner. ● n. frisson m.

shoal /ʃəʊl/ n. (of fish) banc m.

shock /ʃɒk/ n. choc m., secousse f.; (electr.) décharge f.; (med.) choc m. ● a. (result) choc invar.; (tactics) de choc. ● v.t. choquer. ~ absorber, amortisseur m. be a ~er, (fam.) être affreux. ~ing a. choquant; (bad: fam.) affreux. ~ingly adv. (fam.) affreusement.

shodd|y /'ʃɒdɪ/ a. (-ier, -iest) mal fait, mauvais. ~ily adv. mal.

shoe /ʃuː/ n. chaussure f., soulier m.; (of horse) fer (à cheval) m.; (in vehicle) sabot (de frein) m. ● v.t. (p.t. shod /ʃɒd/, pres. p. shoeing) (horse) ferrer. ~ repairer, cordonnier m. on a ~string, avec très peu d'argent.

shoehorn /'ʃuːhɔːn/ n. chausse-pied m.

shoelace /'ʃuːleɪs/ n. lacet m.

shoemaker /'ʃuːmeɪkə(r)/ n. cordonnier m.

shone /ʃɒn/ see shine.

shoo /ʃuː/ v.t. chasser.

shook /ʃʊk/ see shake.

shoot /ʃuːt/ v.t. (p.t. shot) (gun) tirer un coup de; (missile, glance) lancer; (kill, wound) tuer, blesser d'un coup de fusil, de pistolet, etc.); (execute) fusiller; (hunt) chasser; (film) tourner. ● v.i. tirer (at, sur). ● n. (bot.) pousse f. ~ down, abattre. ~ out, (rush) sortir en vitesse. ~ up, (spurt) jaillir; (grow) pousser vite. hear ~ing, entendre des coups de feu. ~ing-range n. stand de tir m. ~ing star, étoile filante f.

shop /ʃɒp/ n. magasin m., boutique f.; (workshop) atelier m. ● v.i. (p.t. shopped) faire ses courses. ~ around, comparer les prix. ~ assistant, vendeu|r, -se m., f. ~- floor n. (workers) ouvriers m. pl. ~per n. acheteu|r, -se m., f. ~-soiled, (Amer.) ~-worn adjs. abîmé. ~

steward, délégué(e) syndical(e) m. (f.). ~ window, vitrine f.

shopkeeper /'ʃɒpkiːpə(r)/ n. commerçant(e) m. (f.).

shoplift|er /'ʃɒplɪftə(r)/ n. voleu|r, -se à l'étalage m., f. ~ing n. vol à l'étalage m.

shopping /'ʃɒpɪŋ/ n. (goods) achats m. pl. go ~, faire ses courses. ~ bag, sac à provisions m. ~ centre, centre commercial m.

shore /ʃɔː(r)/ n. rivage m.

shorn /ʃɔːn/ see shear. ● a. ~ of, dépouillé de.

short /ʃɔːt/ a. (-er, -est) court; (person) petit; (brief) court, bref; (curt) brusque. be ~ (of), (lack) manquer (de). ● adv. (stop) net. in ~. (electr.) court-circuit m.; (film) court-métrage m. ~s, (trousers) short m. ~ of money, à court d'argent. I'm two ~, il m'en manque deux. ~ of doing sth, à moins de faire qch. everything ~ of, tout sauf. nothing ~ of, rien de moins que. cut ~, écourter. cut s.o. ~, couper court à qn. fall ~ of, ne pas arriver à. he is called Tom for ~, son diminutif est Tom. in ~, en bref. ~-change v.t. (cheat) rouler. ~-circuit, court-circuit m. ~-circuit v.t. court-circuiter. ~-cut, raccourci m. ~-handed a. à court de personnel. ~ list, liste des candidats choisis f. ~-lived a. éphémère. ~-sighted a. myope. ~-staffed a. à court de personnel. ~ story, nouvelle f. ~-term a. à court terme. ~ wave, ondes courtes f. pl.

shortage /'ʃɔːtɪdʒ/ n. manque m.

shortbread /'ʃɔːtbred/ n. sablé m.

shortcoming /'ʃɔːtkʌmɪŋ/ n. défaut m.

shorten /'ʃɔːtn/ v.t. raccourcir.

shortfall /'ʃɔːtfɔːl/ n. déficit m.

shorthand /'ʃɔːthænd/ n. sténo(-graphie) f. ~ typist, sténodactylo f.

shortly /'ʃɔːtlɪ/ adv. bientôt.

shot /ʃɒt/ see shoot. ● n. (firing, attempt, etc.) coup de feu m.; (person) tireur m.; (bullet) balle f.; (photograph) photo f.; (injection) piqûre f. like a ~, comme une flèche. ~-gun n. fusil de chasse m.

should /ʃʊd, unstressed ʃəd/ v.aux. devoir. I ~ help me, vous devriez m'aider. I ~ have stayed, j'aurais dû rester. I ~ like to, j'aimerais bien. if he ~ come, s'il vient.

shoulder /'ʃəʊldə(r)/ n. épaule f. ● v.t. (responsibility) endosser; (burden) se charger de. ~-bag, sac à bandoulière m. ~-blade n. omoplate f. ~-pad n. épaulette f.

shout /ʃaʊt/ n. cri m. ● v.t./i. crier. ~ at, engueuler. ~ down, huer.

shove /ʃʌv/ n. poussée f. ● v.t./i. pousser; (put: fam.) ficher. ~ off, (depart: fam.) se tirer.

shovel /'ʃʌvl/ n. pelle f. ● v.t. (p.t. shovelled) pelleter.

show /ʃəʊ/ v.t. (p.t. showed, p.p. shown) montrer; (of dial, needle) indiquer; (put on display) exposer; (film) donner; (conduct) conduire. ● v.i. (be visible) se voir. ● n. démonstration f.; (ostentation) parade f.; (exhibition) exposition f., salon m.; (theatre) spectacle m.; (cinema) séance f. for ~, pour l'effet. on ~, exposé. ~-down n. épreuve de force f. ~-jumping n. concours hippique m. ~ off v.t. étaler; v.i. poser, crâner. ~-off n. poseu|r, -se m., f. ~-piece n. modèle du genre m. ~ s.o. in/out, faire entrer/sortir qn. ~ up, (faire) ressortir; (appear: fam.) se montrer. ~ing n. performance f.; (cinema) séance f.

shower /'ʃaʊə(r)/ n. (of rain) averse f.; (of blows etc.) grêle f.; (for washing) douche f. ● v.t. ~ with, couvrir de. ● v.i. se doucher. ~y a. pluvieux.

showerproof /'ʃaʊəpruːf/ a. imperméable.

showmanship /'ʃəʊmənʃɪp/ n. art de la mise en scène m.

shown /ʃəʊn/ see show.

showroom /'ʃəʊrʊm/ n. salle d'exposition f.

showy /'ʃəʊɪ/ a. (-ier, -iest) voyant; (manner) prétentieux.

shrank /ʃræŋk/ see shrink.

shrapnel /'ʃræpn(ə)l/ n. éclats d'obus m. pl.

shred /ʃred/ n. lambeau m.; (least amount: fig.) parcelle f. ● v.t. (p.t. shredded) déchiqueter; (culin.) râper. ~der n. destructeur de documents m.

shrew /ʃruː/ n. (woman) mégère f.

shrewd /ʃruːd/ a. (-er, -est) astucieux. ~ness n. astuce f.

shriek /ʃriːk/ n. hurlement m. ● v.t./i. hurler.

shrift /ʃrɪft/ n. give s.o. short ~, traiter qn. sans ménagement.

shrill /ʃrɪl/ a. strident, aigu.

shrimp /ʃrɪmp/ n. crevette f.

shrine /ʃraɪn/ n. (place) lieu saint m.; (tomb) châsse f.

shrink /ʃrɪŋk/ v.t./i. (p.t. shrank, p.p. shrunk) rétrécir; (lessen) diminuer. ~ from, reculer devant. ~age n. rétrécissement m.

shrivel /ʃrɪvl/ v.t./i. (p.t. shrivelled) (se) ratatiner.

shroud /ʃraʊd/ n. linceul m. ● v.t. (veil) envelopper.

Shrove /ʃrəʊv/ n. ~ Tuesday, Mardi gras m.

shrub /ʃrʌb/ n. arbuste m. ~bery n. arbustes m. pl.

shrug /ʃrʌg/ v.t. (p.t. shrugged). ~ one's shoulders, hausser les épaules. ● n. haussement d'épaules m. ~ sth. off, réagir avec indifférence à qch.

shrunk /ʃrʌŋk/ see shrink. ~en a. rétréci; (person) ratatiné.

shudder /ʃʌdə(r)/ v.i. frémir. ● n. frémissement m.

shuffle /ʃʌfl/ v.t. (feet) traîner; (cards) battre. ● v.i. traîner les pieds. ● n. démarche traînante f.

shun /ʃʌn/ v.t. (p.t. shunned) éviter, fuir.

shunt /ʃʌnt/ v.t. (train) aiguiller.

shush /ʃʊʃ/ int. (fam.) chut.

shut /ʃʌt/ v.t. (p.t. shut, pres. p. shutting) fermer. ● v.i. se fermer; (of shop, bank, etc.) fermer. ~ down or up, fermer. ~-down n. fermeture f. ~ in or up, enfermer. ~ up v.i. (fam.) se taire; v.t. (fam.) faire taire.

shutter /ʃʌtə(r)/ n. volet m.; (photo.) obturateur m.

shuttle /ʃʌtl/ n. (bus etc.) navette f. ● v.i. faire la navette. ● v.t. transporter. ~ service, navette f.

shuttlecock /ʃʌtlkɒk/ n. (badminton) volant m.

shy /ʃaɪ/ a. (-er, -est) timide. ● v.i. reculer. ~ness n. timidité f.

Siamese /saɪəˈmiːz/ a. siamois.

sibling /sɪblɪŋ/ n. frère m., sœur f.

Sicily /sɪslɪ/ n. Sicile f.

sick /sɪk/ a. malade; (humour) macabre. be ~, (vomit) vomir. be ~ of, en avoir assez or marre de. feel ~, avoir mal au cœur. ~-bay n. infirmerie f. ~-leave n. congé mala-

die m. ~-pay n. assurance-maladie f. ~room n. chambre de malade f.

sicken /sɪkən/ v.t. écœurer. ● v.i. be ~ing for, (illness) couver.

sickle /sɪkl/ n. faucille f.

sickly /sɪklɪ/ a. (-ier, -iest) (person) maladif; (taste, smell, etc.) écœurant.

sickness /sɪknɪs/ n. maladie f.

side /saɪd/ n. côté m.; (of road, river) bord m.; (of hill) flanc m.; (sport) équipe f. ● a. latéral. ● v.i. ~ with, (extra) du côté de. on the ~, (extra) en plus; (secretly) en catimini. ~ by side, côte à côte. ~-car n. side-car m. ~-effect n. effet secondaire m. ~-saddle adv. en amazone. ~-show n. petite attraction f. ~-step n. (p.t. -stepped) éviter. ~-street n. rue latérale f. ~-track v.t. faire dévier de son sujet.

sideboard /saɪdbɔːd/ n. buffet m. ~s, (whiskers: sl.) pattes f. pl.

sideburns /saɪdbɜːnz/ n. pl. pattes f. pl., rouflaquettes f. pl.

sidelight /saɪdlaɪt/ n. (auto.) veilleuse f., lanterne f.

sideline /saɪdlaɪn/ n. activité secondaire f.

sidewalk /saɪdwɔːk/ n. (Amer.) trottoir m.

side|ways /saɪdweɪz/, ~long adv. & a. de côté.

siding /saɪdɪŋ/ n. voie de garage f.

sidle /saɪdl/ v.i. avancer furtivement (up to, vers).

siege /siːdʒ/ n. siège m.

siesta /sɪˈestə/ n. sieste f.

sieve /sɪv/ n. tamis m.; (for liquids) passoire f. ● v.t. tamiser.

sift /sɪft/ v.t. tamiser. ● v.i. ~ through, examiner.

sigh /saɪ/ n. soupir m. ● v.t./i. soupirer.

sight /saɪt/ n. vue f.; (scene) spectacle m.; (on gun) mire f. ● v.t. apercevoir. at or on ~, à vue. catch ~ of, apercevoir. in ~, visible. lose ~ of, perdre de vue.

sightsee|ing /saɪtsiːŋ/ n. tourisme m. ~r /-ə(r)/ n. touriste m./f.

sign /saɪn/ n. signe m.; (notice) panneau m. ● v.t./i. signer. ~ language, (for deaf) langage des sourds-muets m. ~ on, (when unemployed) s'inscrire au chômage. ~ up, (s')enrôler.

signal /sɪɡnəl/ n. signal m. ● v.t. (p.t. signalled) communiquer (par signaux); (*person*) faire signe à. **~-box** *n.* poste d'aiguillage *m.*

signalman /'sɪgnəlmən/ *n.* (*pl.* **-men**) (*rail.*) aiguilleur *m.*

signatory /'sɪgnətrɪ/ *n.* signataire *m./f.*

signature /'sɪgnətʃə(r)/ *n.* signature *f.* **~ tune**, indicatif musical *m.*

signet-ring /'sɪgnɪtrɪŋ/ *n.* chevalière *f.*

significan|t /sɪg'nɪfɪkənt/ *a.* important; (*meaningful*) significatif. **~ce** *n.* importance *f.*; (*meaning*) signification *f.* **~tly** *adv.* (*much*) sensiblement.

signify /'sɪgnɪfaɪ/ *v.t.* signifier.

signpost /'saɪnpəʊst/ *n.* poteau indicateur *m.*

silence /'saɪləns/ *n.* silence *m.* ● *v.t.* faire taire. **~r** /-ə(r)/ *n.* (*on gun, car*) silencieux *m.*

silent /'saɪlənt/ *a.* silencieux; (*film*) muet. **~ly** *adv.* silencieusement.

silhouette /sɪlu:'et/ *n.* silhouette *f.* ● *v.t.* be **~d against**, se profiler contre.

silicon /'sɪlɪkən/ *n.* silicium *m.* **~ chip**, microplaquette *f.*

silk /sɪlk/ *n.* soie *f.* **~en**, **~y** *adjs.* soyeux.

sill /sɪl/ *n.* rebord *m.*

silly /'sɪlɪ/ *a.* (**-ier**, **-iest**) bête, idiot.

silo /'saɪləʊ/ *n.* (*pl.* **-os**) silo *m.*

silt /sɪlt/ *n.* vase *f.*

silver /'sɪlvə(r)/ *n.* argent *m.*; (*silverware*) argenterie *f.* ● *a.* en argent, d'argent. **~ wedding**, noces d'argent *f. pl.* **~y** *a.* argenté; (*sound*) argentin.

silversmith /'sɪlvəsmɪθ/ *n.* orfèvre *m.*

silverware /'sɪlvəweə(r)/ *n.* argenterie *f.*

similar /'sɪmɪlə(r)/ *a.* semblable (**to**, à). **~ity** /-ə'lærətɪ/ *n.* ressemblance *f.* **~ly** *adv.* de même.

simile /'sɪmɪlɪ/ *n.* comparaison *f.*

simmer /'sɪmə(r)/ *v.t./i.* (*soup etc.*) mijoter; (*water*) (laisser) frémir; (*smoulder: fig.*) couver. **~ down**, se calmer.

simper /'sɪmpə(r)/ *v.i.* minauder. **~ing** *a.* minaudier.

simpl|e /'sɪmpl/ *a.* (**-er**, **-est**) simple. **~e-minded** *a.* simple d'esprit. **~icity** /-'plɪsətɪ/ *n.* simplicité *f.* **~y** *adv.* simplement; (*absolutely*) absolument.

simplif|y /'sɪmplɪfaɪ/ *v.t.* simplifier. **~ication** /-ɪ'keɪʃn/ *n.* simplification *f.*

simplistic /sɪm'plɪstɪk/ *a.* simpliste.

simulat|e /'sɪmjʊleɪt/ *v.t.* simuler. **~ion** /-'leɪʃn/ *n.* simulation *f.*

simultaneous /sɪml'teɪnɪəs, *Amer.* saɪml'teɪnɪəs/ *a.* simultané. **~ly** *adv.* simultanément.

sin /sɪn/ *n.* péché *m.* ● *v.i.* (*p.t.* **sinned**) pécher.

since /sɪns/ *prep. & adv.* depuis. ● *conj.* depuis que; (*because*) puisque. **~ then**, depuis.

sincer|e /sɪn'sɪə(r)/ *a.* sincère. **~ely** *adv.* sincèrement. **~ity** /-'serətɪ/ *n.* sincérité *f.*

sinew /'sɪnju:/ *n.* tendon *m.* **~s**, muscles *m. pl.*

sinful /'sɪnfl/ *a.* (*act*) coupable, qui constitue un péché; (*shocking*) scandaleux.

sing /sɪŋ/ *v.t./i.* (*p.t.* **sang**, *p.p.* **sung**) chanter. **~er** *n.* chanteu|r, -se *m., f.*

singe /sɪndʒ/ *v.t.* (*pres. p.* **singeing**) brûler légèrement, roussir.

single /'sɪŋgl/ *a.* seul; (*not double*) simple; (*unmarried*) célibataire; (*room, bed*) pour une personne; (*ticket*) simple. ● *n.* (*ticket*) aller simple *m.*; (*record*) 45 tours *m. invar.* **~s**, (*tennis*) simple *m.* **~s bar**, bar pour les célibataires *m.* ● *v.t.* **~ out**, choisir. **in ~ file**, en file indienne. **~-handed** *a.* sans aide. **~-minded** *a.* tenace. **~ parent**, parent seul *m.* **singly** *adv.* un à un.

singlet /'sɪŋglɪt/ *n.* maillot de corps *m.*

singsong /'sɪŋsɒŋ/ *n.* **have a ~**, chanter en chœur. ● *a.* (*voice*) monotone.

singular /'sɪŋgjʊlə(r)/ *n.* singulier *m.* ● *a.* (*uncommon & gram.*) singulier; (*noun*) au singulier. **~ly** *adv.* singulièrement.

sinister /'sɪnɪstə(r)/ *a.* sinistre.

sink /sɪŋk/ *v.t./i.* (*p.t.* **sank**, *p.p.* **sunk**) (faire) couler; (*of ground, person*) s'affaisser; (*well*) creuser; (*money*) investir. ● *n.* (*in kitchen*) évier *m.*; (*wash-basin*) lavabo *m.* **in**, (*fig.*) être compris. **~ into** *v.t.* (*thrust*) enfoncer dans; *v.i.* (*go deep*) s'enfoncer dans. **~ unit**, bloc-évier *m.*

sinner /'sɪnə(r)/ *n.* péch|eur, -eresse *m., f.*

sinuous /'sɪnjʊəs/ *a.* sinueux.

sinus /'saɪnəs/ n. (pl. **-uses**) (anat.) sinus m.

sip /sɪp/ n. petite gorgée f. ● v.t. (p.t. **sipped**) boire à petites gorgées.

siphon /'saɪfn/ n. siphon m. ● v.t. ~ **off**, siphonner.

sir /sɜː(r)/ n. monsieur m. **Sir**, (title) Sir m.

siren /'saɪərən/ n. sirène f.

sirloin /'sɜːlɔɪn/ n. faux-filet m., aloyau m.; (Amer.) romsteck m.

sissy /'sɪsɪ/ n. personne efféminée f.; (coward) dégonflé(e) m. (f.).

sister /'sɪstə(r)/ n. sœur f.; (nurse) infirmière en chef f. ~**-in-law** /~s-in-law/ belle-sœur f. ~**ly** a. fraternel.

sit /sɪt/ v.t./i. (p.t. **sat**, pres. p. **sitting**) (s')asseoir; (of committee etc.) siéger. ~ **(for)**, (exam) se présenter à. be ~**ting**, être assis. ~ **around**, ne rien faire. ~ **down**, s'asseoir. ~ **in on a meeting**, assister à une réunion pour écouter. ~**-in** n. sit-in m. invar. ~**ting** n. séance f.; (in restaurant) service m. ~**ting-room** n. salon m.

site /saɪt/ n. emplacement m. (**building**) ~, chantier m. ● v.t. placer, construire, situer.

situate /'sɪtʃʊeɪt/ v.t. situer. be ~**ed**, être situé. ~**ion** /-'eɪʃn/ n. situation f.

six /sɪks/ a. & n. six (m.). ~**th** a. & n. sixième (m.).

sixteen /sɪk'stiːn/ a. & n. seize (m.). ~**th** a. & n. seizième (m./f.).

sixty /'sɪkstɪ/ a. & n. soixante (m.). ~**ieth** a. & n. soixantième (m./f.).

size /saɪz/ n. dimension f.; (of person, garment, etc.) taille f.; (of shoes) pointure f.; (of sum, salary) montant m.; (extent) ampleur f. ● v.t. ~ **up**, (fam.) jauger, juger. ~**able** a. assez grand.

sizzle /'sɪzl/ v.i. grésiller.

skate[1] /skeɪt/ n. invar. (fish) raie f.

skate[2] /skeɪt/ n. patin m. ● v.i. patiner. ~**er** n. patineu|r, -se m., f. ~**ing** n. patinage m. ~**ing-rink** n. patinoire f.

skateboard /'skeɪtbɔːd/ n. skateboard m., planche à roulettes f.

skeleton /'skelɪtən/ n. squelette m. ~**on crew** or **staff**, effectifs minimums m. pl. ~**al** a. squelettique.

sketch /sketʃ/ n. esquisse f., croquis m.; (theatre) sketch m. ● v.t. faire un croquis de, esquisser. ● v.i. faire des esquisses. ~ **out**, esquisser. ~ **pad**, bloc à dessins m.

sketchy /'sketʃɪ/ a. (**-ier**, **-iest**) sommaire, incomplet.

skew /skjuː/ n. **on the** ~, de travers. ~**-whiff** a. (fam.) de travers.

skewer /'skjʊə(r)/ n. brochette f.

ski /skiː/ n. (pl. **-is**) ski m. ● a. de ski. ● v.i. (p.t. **ski'd** or **skied**, pres. p. **skiing**) skier; (go skiing) faire du ski. ~ **jump**, saut à skis m. ~ **lift**, remonte-pente m. ~**er** n. skieu|r, -se m., f. ~**ing** n. ski m.

skid /skɪd/ v.i. (p.t. **skidded**) déraper. ● n. dérapage m.

skilful /'skɪlfl/ a. habile.

skill /skɪl/ n. habileté f.; (craft) métier m. ~**s**, aptitudes f. pl. ~**ed** a. habile; (worker) qualifié.

skim /skɪm/ v.t. (p.t. **skimmed**) écumer; (milk) écrémer; (pass or glide over) effleurer. ● v.i. ~ **through**, parcourir.

skimp /skɪmp/ v.t./i. ~ **(on)**, lésiner (sur).

skimpy /'skɪmpɪ/ a. (**-ier**, **-iest**) (clothes) étriqué; (meal) chiche.

skin /skɪn/ n. peau f. ● v.t. (p.t. **skinned**) (animal) écorcher; (fruit) éplucher. ~**-diving** n. plongée sous-marine f. ~**-tight** a. collant.

skinflint /'skɪnflɪnt/ n. avare m./f.

skinny /'skɪnɪ/ a. (**-ier**, **-iest**) maigre, maigrichon.

skint /skɪnt/ a. (sl.) fauché.

skip[1] /skɪp/ v.i. (p.t. **skipped**) sautiller; (with rope) sauter à la corde. ● v.t. (page, class, etc.) sauter. ● n. petit saut m. ~**ping-rope** n. corde à sauter f.

skip[2] /skɪp/ n. (container) benne f.

skipper /'skɪpə(r)/ n. capitaine m.

skirmish /'skɜːmɪʃ/ n. escarmouche f., accrochage m.

skirt /skɜːt/ n. jupe f. ● v.t. contourner. ~**ing-board** n. plinthe f.

skit /skɪt/ n. sketch satirique m.

skittle /'skɪtl/ n. quille f.

skive /skaɪv/ v.i. (sl.) tirer au flanc.

skivvy /'skɪvɪ/ n. (fam.) boniche f.

skulk /skʌlk/ v.i. (move) rôder furtivement; (hide) se cacher.

skull /skʌl/ n. crâne m. ~**-cap** n. calotte f.

skunk /skʌŋk/ n. (animal) mouffette f.; (person: sl.) salaud m.

sky /skaɪ/ n. ciel m. ~**-blue** a. & n. bleu ciel m. invar.

skylight /ˈskaɪlaɪt/ n. lucarne f.

skyscraper /ˈskaɪskreɪpə(r)/ n. gratte-ciel m. invar.

slab /slæb/ n. plaque f., bloc m.; (of paving-stone) dalle f.

slack /slæk/ a. (-er, -est) (rope) lâche; (person) négligent; (business) stagnant; (period) creux. ● n. the ~, (in rope) du mou ● v.t./i. (se) relâcher.

slacken /ˈslækən/ v.t./i. (se) relâcher; (slow) (se) ralentir.

slacks /slæks/ n. pl. pantalon m.

slag /slæg/ n. scories f. pl. ~-heap n. crassier m.

slain /sleɪn/ see slay.

slake /sleɪk/ v.t. étancher.

slalom /ˈslɑːləm/ n. slalom m.

slam /slæm/ v.t./i. (p.t. slammed) (door etc.) claquer; (throw) flanquer; (criticize: sl.) critiquer. ● n. (noise) claquement m.

slander /ˈslɑːndə(r)/ n. diffamation f., calomnie f. ● v.t. diffamer, calomnier. ~ous a. diffamatoire.

slang /slæŋ/ n. argot m. ~y a. argotique.

slant /slɑːnt/ v.t./i. (faire) pencher; (news) présenter sous un certain jour. ● n. inclinaison f.; (bias) angle m. ~ed a. partial. be ~ing, être penché.

slap /slæp/ v.t. (p.t. slapped) (strike) donner une claque à; (face) gifler; (put) flanquer. ● n. claque f.; gifle f. ● adv. tout droit. ~-happy a. (carefree: fam.) insouciant; (dazed: fam.) abruti. ~-up meal, (sl.) gueuleton m.

slapdash /ˈslæpdæʃ/ a. fait, qui travaille etc. n'importe comment.

slapstick /ˈslæpstɪk/ n. grosse farce f.

slash /slæʃ/ v.t. (cut) taillader; (sever) trancher; (fig.) réduire (radicalement). ● n. taillade f.

slat /slæt/ n. (in blind) lamelle f.; (on bed) latte f.

slate /sleɪt/ n. ardoise f. ● v.t. (fam.) critiquer, éreinter.

slaughter /ˈslɔːtə(r)/ v.t. massacrer; (animals) abattre. ● n. massacre m.; abattage m.

slaughterhouse /ˈslɔːtəhaʊs/ n. abattoir m.

Slav /slɑːv/ a. & n. slave (m./f.). ~onic /sləˈvɒnɪk/ a. (lang.) slave.

slave /sleɪv/ n. esclave m./f. ● v.i. trimer. ~-driver n. négr|ier, -ière m., f. ~ry /-ərɪ/ n. esclavage m.

slavish /ˈsleɪvɪʃ/ a. servile.

slay /sleɪ/ v.t. (p.t. slew, p.p. slain) tuer.

sleazy /ˈsliːzɪ/ a. (-ier, -iest) (fam.) sordide, miteux.

sledge /sledʒ/ n. luge f.; (horse-drawn) traîneau m. ~-hammer n. marteau de forgeron m.

sleek /sliːk/ a. (-er, -est) lisse, brillant; (manner) onctueux.

sleep /sliːp/ n. sommeil m. ● v.i. (p.t. slept) dormir; (spend the night) coucher. ● v.t. loger. go to ~, s'endormir. ~ in, faire la grasse matinée. ~er n. dormeu|r, -se m., f.; (beam: rail) traverse f.; (berth) couchette f. ~ing-bag n. sac de couchage m. ~ing pill, somnifère m. ~less a. sans sommeil. ~-walker n. somnambule m./f.

sleep|y /ˈsliːpɪ/ a. (-ier, -iest) somnolent. be ~y, avoir sommeil. ~ily adv. à moitié endormi.

sleet /sliːt/ n. neige fondue f.; (coat of ice: Amer.) verglas m. ● v.i. tomber de la neige fondue.

sleeve /sliːv/ n. manche f.; (of record) pochette f. up one's ~, en réserve. ~less a. sans manches.

sleigh /sleɪ/ n. traîneau m.

sleight /slaɪt/ n. ~ of hand, prestidigitation f.

slender /ˈslendə(r)/ a. mince, svelte; (scanty: fig.) faible.

slept /slept/ see sleep.

sleuth /sluːθ/ n. limier m.

slew[1] /sluː/ v.i. (turn) virer.

slew[2] /sluː/ see slay.

slice /slaɪs/ n. tranche f. ● v.t. couper (en tranches).

slick /slɪk/ a. (unctuous) mielleux; (cunning) astucieux. ● n. (oil) ~, nappe de pétrole f., marée noire f.

slide /slaɪd/ v.t./i. (p.t. slid) glisser. ● n. glissade f.; (fall: fig.) baisse f.; (in playground) toboggan m.; (for hair) barrette f.; (photo.) diapositive f. ~ into, (go silently) se glisser dans. ~-rule n. règle à calcul f. **sliding** a. (door, panel) à glissière, à coulisse. **sliding scale,** échelle mobile f.

slight /slaɪt/ a. (-er, -est) petit, léger; (slender) mince; (frail) frêle. ● v.t. (insult) offenser. ● n. affront m. ~est a. moindre. ~ly adv. légèrement, un peu.

slim /slɪm/ a. (**slimmer, slimmest**) mince. ● *v.i.* (*p.t.* **slimmed**) maigrir. ~**ness** n. minceur f.

slim|e /slaɪm/ n. boue (visqueuse) f.; (*on river-bed*) vase f. ~**y** a. boueux; vaseux; (*sticky, servile*) visqueux.

sling /slɪŋ/ n. (*weapon, toy*) fronde f.; (*bandage*) écharpe f. ● *v.t.* (*p.t.* **slung**) jeter, lancer.

slip /slɪp/ *v.t./i.* (*p.t.* **slipped**) glisser. ● n. faux pas m.; (*mistake*) erreur f.; (*petticoat*) combinaison f.; (*paper*) fiche f. **give the ~ to**, fausser compagnie à. ~ **away**, s'esquiver. ~**-cover** n. (*Amer.*) housse f. ~ **into**, (*go*) se glisser dans; (*clothes*) mettre. ~ **of the tongue**, lapsus m. ~**ped disc**, hernie discale f. ~**-road** n. bretelle f. ~ **s.o.'s mind**, échapper à qn. ~**-stream** n. sillage m. ~ **up**, (*fam.*) gaffer. ~**-up** n. (*fam.*) gaffe f.

slipper /'slɪpə(r)/ n. pantoufle f.

slippery /'slɪpərɪ/ a. glissant.

slipshod /'slɪpʃɒd/ a. (*person*) négligent; (*work*) négligé.

slit /slɪt/ n. fente f. ● *v.t* (*p.t.* **slit**, *pres. p.* **slitting**) couper, fendre.

slither /'slɪðə(r)/ *v.i.* glisser.

sliver /'slɪvə(r)/ n. (*of cheese etc.*) lamelle f.; (*splinter*) éclat m.

slob /slɒb/ n. (*fam.*) rustre m.

slobber /'slɒbə(r)/ *v.i.* baver.

slog /slɒg/ *v.t.* (*p.t.* **slogged**) (*hit*) frapper dur. ● *v.i.* (*work*) trimer. ● n. (*work*) travail dur m.; (*effort*) gros effort m.

slogan /'sləʊgən/ n. slogan m.

slop /slɒp/ *v.t./i.* (*p.t.* **slopped**) (se) répandre. ~**s** n. pl. eaux sales f. pl.

slop|e /sləʊp/ *v.i.* être en pente; (*of handwriting*) pencher. ● n. pente f.; (*of mountain*) flanc m. ~**ing** a. en pente.

sloppy /'slɒpɪ/ a. (**-ier, -iest**) (*ground*) détrempé; (*food*) liquide; (*work*) négligé; (*person*) négligent; (*fig.*) sentimental.

slosh /slɒʃ/ *v.t.* (*fam.*) répandre; (*hit sl.*) frapper. ● *v.i.* patauger.

slot /slɒt/ n. fente f. ● *v.t./i.* (*p.t.* **slotted**) (s')insérer. ~**-machine** n. distributeur automatique m.; (*for gambling*) machine à sous f.

sloth /sləʊθ/ n. paresse f.

slouch /slaʊtʃ/ *v.i.* avoir le dos voûté; (*move*) marcher le dos voûté.

sloven|ly /'slʌvnlɪ/ a. débraillé. ~**iness** n. débraillé m.

slow /sləʊ/ a. (**-er, -est**) lent. ● *adv.* lentement. ● *v.t./i.* ralentir. **be ~**, (*clock etc.*) retarder. **in ~ motion**, au ralenti. ~**ly** adv. lentement. ~**ness** n. lenteur f.

slow|coach /'sləʊkəʊtʃ/, (*Amer.*) ~**poke** ns. lambin(e) m. (f.).

sludge /slʌdʒ/ n. gadoue f., boue f.

slug /slʌg/ n. (*mollusc*) limace f.; (*bullet*) balle f.; (*blow*) coup m.

sluggish /'slʌgɪʃ/ a. lent, mou.

sluice /slu:s/ n. (*gate*) vanne f.

slum /slʌm/ n. taudis m.

slumber /'slʌmbə(r)/ n. sommeil. m. ● *v.i.* dormir.

slump /slʌmp/ n. effondrement m.; baisse f.; (*in business*) marasme m. ● *v.i.* (*collapse, fall limply*) s'effondrer; (*decrease*) baisser.

slung /slʌŋ/ *see* sling.

slur /slɜ:(r)/ *v.t./i.* (*p.t.* **slurred**) (*spoken words*) mal articuler. ● n. bredouillement m.; (*discredit*) atteinte f. (**on**, à).

slush /slʌʃ/ n. (*snow*) neige fondue f. ~ **fund**, fonds servant à des pots-de-vin m. ~**y** a. (*road*) couvert de neige fondue.

slut /slʌt/ n. (*dirty*) souillon f.; (*immoral*) dévergondée f.

sly /slaɪ/ a. (**slyer, slyest**) (*crafty*) rusé; (*secretive*) sournois. ● n. **on the ~**, en cachette. ~**ly** adv. sournoisement.

smack[1] /smæk/ n. tape f.; (*on face*) gifle f. ● *v.t.* donner une tape à; gifler. ● adv. (*fam.*) tout droit.

smack[2] /smæk/ *v.i.* ~ **of sth.**, (*have flavour*) sentir qch.

small /smɔ:l/ a. (**-er, -est**) petit. ● n. ~ **of the back**, creux des reins m. ● adv. (*cut etc.*) menu. ~**ness** n. petitesse f. ~ **ads**, petites annonces f. pl. ~ **businesses**, les petites entreprises. ~ **change**, petite monnaie f. ~ **talk**, menus propos m. pl. ~**-time** a. petit, peu important.

smallholding /'smɔ:lhəʊldɪŋ/ n. petite ferme f.

smallpox /'smɔ:lpɒks/ n. variole f.

smarmy /'smɑ:mɪ/ a. (**-ier, -iest**) (*fam.*) obséquieux, patelin.

smart /smɑ:t/ a. (**-er, -est**) élégant; (*clever*) astucieux, intelligent; (*brisk*) rapide. ● *v.i.* (*of wound etc.*) brûler. ~**ly** adv. élégamment. ~**ness** n. élégance f.

smarten /'smɑːtn/ v.t./i. ~ (up), embellir. ~ (o.s.) up, se faire beau; (tidy) s'arranger.

smash /smæʃ/ v.t./i. (se) briser, (se) fracasser; (opponent, record) pulvériser. ● n. (noise) fracas m.; (blow) coup m.; (fig.) collision f.

smashing /'smæʃɪŋ/ a. (fam.) formidable, épatant.

smattering /'smætərɪŋ/ n. a ~ of, des notions de.

smear /smɪə(r)/ v.t. (stain) tacher; (coat) enduire; (discredit: fig.) entacher. ● n. tache f. ~ test, frottis m.

smell /smel/ n. odeur f.; (sense) odorat m. ● v.t./i. (p.t. smelt or smelled) sentir. ~ of, sentir. ~y a. malodorant, qui pue.

smelt[1] /smelt/ see smell

smelt[2] /smelt/ v.t. (ore) fondre.

smile /smaɪl/ n. sourire. ● v.i. sourire. ~ing a. souriant.

smirk /smɜːk/ n. sourire affecté m.

smith /smɪθ/ n. forgeron m.

smithereens /smɪðə'riːnz/ n. pl. to or in ~, en mille morceaux.

smitten /'smɪtn/ a. (in love) épris (with, de).

smock /smɒk/ n. blouse f.

smog /smɒg/ n. brouillard mélangé de fumée m., smog m.

smoke /sməʊk/ n. fumée f. ● v.t./i. fumer. have a ~, fumer. ~d a. fumé. ~less a. (fuel) non polluant. ~r /-ə(r)/ n. fumeur, -se m., f. ~-screen n. écran de fumée m.; (fig.) manœuvre de diversion f. smoky a. (air) enfumé.

smooth /smuːð/ a. (-er, -est) lisse; (movement) régulier; (manners, cream) onctueux; (flight) sans turbulence; (changes) sans heurt. ● v.t. lisser. ~ out, (fig.) faire disparaître. ~ly adv. facilement, doucement.

smother /'smʌðə(r)/ v.t. (stifle) étouffer; (cover) couvrir.

smoulder /'sməʊldə(r)/ v.i. (fire, discontent, etc.) couver.

smudge /smʌdʒ/ n. tache f. ● v.t./i. (se) salir, (se) tacher.

smug /smʌg/ a. (smugger, smuggest) suffisant. ~ly adv. avec suffisance. ~ness n. suffisance f.

smuggle /'smʌgl/ v.t. passer (en contrebande). ~er n. contrebandier, -ière m., f. ~ing n. contrebande f.

smut /smʌt/ n. saleté f. ~ty a. indécent.

snack /snæk/ n. casse-croûte m. invar. ~-bar n. snack(-bar) m.

snag /snæg/ n. difficulté f., inconvénient m.; (in cloth) accroc m.

snail /sneɪl/ n. escargot m. at a ~'s pace, à un pas de tortue.

snake /sneɪk/ n. serpent m.

snap /snæp/ v.t./i. (p.t. snapped) (whip, fingers, etc.) (faire) claquer; (break) (se) casser net; (say) dire sèchement. ● n. claquement m.; (photograph) instantané m.; (press-stud: Amer.) bouton-pression m. ● a. soudain. ~ at, (bite) happer; (angrily) être cassant avec. ~ up, (buy) sauter sur.

snappy /'snæpɪ/ a. (-ier, -iest) (brisk: fam.) prompt, rapide. make it ~, (fam.) se dépêcher.

snapshot /'snæpʃɒt/ n. instantané m., photo f.

snare /sneə(r)/ n. piège m.

snarl /snɑːl/ v.i. gronder (en montrant les dents). ● n. grondement m. ~-up, n. embouteillage m.

snarl /snɑːl/ v.i. gronder (en montrant les dents). ● n. grondement m. ~-up n. embouteillage m.

snatch /snætʃ/ v.t. (grab) saisir; (steal) voler. ~ from s.o., arracher à qn. ● n. (theft) vol m.; (short part) fragment m.

sneak /sniːk/ v.i. aller furtivement. ● n. (schol., sl.) rapporteur, -se m., f. ~y a. sournois.

sneakers /'sniːkəz/ n. pl. (shoes) tennis m. pl.

sneaking /'sniːkɪŋ/ a. caché.

sneer /snɪə(r)/ n. ricanement m. ● v.i. ricaner.

sneeze /sniːz/ n. éternuement m. ● v.i. éternuer.

snide /snaɪd/ a. (fam.) narquois.

sniff /snɪf/ v.t./i. renifler. ● n. reniflement m.

snigger /'snɪgə(r)/ n. ricanement m. ● v.i. ricaner.

snip /snɪp/ v.t. (p.t. snipped) couper. ● n. morceau coupé m.; (bargain: sl.) bonne affaire f.

snipe /snaɪp/ v.i. canarder. ~r /-ə(r)/ n. tireur embusqué m.

snippet /'snɪpɪt/ n. bribe f.

snivel /'snɪvl/ v.i. (p.t. snivelled) pleurnicher.

snob /snɒb/ n. snob m./f. ~bery n. snobisme m. ~bish a. snob invar.

snooker /'snu:kə(r)/ n. (sorte de) jeu de billard m.

snoop /snu:p/ v.i. (fam.) fourrer son nez partout. ~ on, espionner.

snooty /'snu:tɪ/ a. (-ier, -iest) (fam.) snob invar., hautain.

snooze /snu:z/ n. petit somme m. ● v.i. faire un petit somme.

snore /snɔ:(r)/ n. ronflement m. ● v.i. ronfler.

snorkel /'snɔ:kl/ n. tuba m.

snort /snɔ:t/ n. grognement m. ● v.i. (person) grogner; (horse) s'ébrouer.

snotty /'snotɪ/ a. morveux.

snout /snaʊt/ n. museau m.

snow /snəʊ/ n. neige f. ● v.i. neiger. be ~ed under with, être submergé de. ~-bound a. bloqué par la neige. ~-drift n. congère f. ~-plough n. chasse-neige m. invar. ~-shoe n. raquette f. ~y a. neigeux.

snowball /'snəʊbɔ:l/ n. boule de neige f. ● v.i. faire boule de neige.

snowdrop /'snəʊdrɒp/ n. perce-neige m./f. invar.

snowfall /'snəʊfɔ:l/ n. chute de neige f.

snowflake /'snəʊfleɪk/ n. flocon de neige m.

snowman /'snəʊmæn/ n. (pl. -men) bonhomme de neige m.

snowstorm /'snəʊstɔ:m/ n. tempête de neige f.

snub /snʌb/ v.t. (p.t. snubbed) (person) snober; (offer) repousser. ● n. rebuffade f.

snub-nosed /'snʌbnəʊzd/ a. au nez retroussé.

snuff¹ /snʌf/ n. tabac à priser m.

snuff² /snʌf/ v.t. (candle) moucher.

snuffle /'snʌfl/ v.i. renifler.

snug /snʌg/ a. (snugger, snuggest) (cosy) confortable; (tight) bien ajusté; (safe) sûr.

snuggle /'snʌgl/ v.i. se pelotonner.

so /səʊ/ adv. si, tellement; (thus) ainsi. ● conj. donc, alors. so am I, moi aussi. so good/etc. as, aussi bon/etc. que. so does he, lui aussi. that is so, c'est ça. I think so, je pense que oui. five or so, environ cinq. so-and-so n. un(e) tel(le) m. (f.). so as to, de manière à. so-called a. soi-disant invar. ~ far, jusqu'ici. so long!, (fam.) à bientôt! so many, so much, tant (de). so-so a. & adv. comme ci comme ça. so that, pour que.

soak /səʊk/ v.t./i. (faire) tremper (in, dans). ~ in or up, absorber. ~ing a. trempé.

soap /səʊp/ n. savon m. ● v.t. savonner. ~ opera, feuilleton m. ~ powder, lessive f. ~y a. savonneux.

soar /sɔ:(r)/ v.i. monter (en flèche).

sob /sɒb/ n. sanglot m. ● v.i. (p.t. sobbed) sangloter.

sober /'səʊbə(r)/ a. qui n'est pas ivre; (serious) sérieux; (colour) sobre. ● v.t./i. ~ up, dessoûler.

soccer /'sɒkə(r)/ n. (fam.) football m.

sociable /'səʊʃəbl/ a. sociable.

social /'səʊʃl/ a. social; (gathering, life) mondain. ● n. réunion (amicale) f., fête f. ~ly adv. socialement; (meet) en société. ~ security, aide sociale f.; (for old age: Amer.) pension (de retraite) f.; ~ worker, assistant(e) social(e) m. (f.).

socialis|t /'səʊʃəlɪst/ n. socialiste m./ f. ~m /-zəm/ n. socialisme m.

socialize /'səʊʃəlaɪz/ v.i. se mêler aux autres. ~ with, fréquenter.

society /sə'saɪətɪ/ n. société f.

sociolog|y /səʊsɪ'ɒlədʒɪ/ n. sociologie f. ~ical /-ə'lɒdʒɪkl/ a. sociologique. ~ist n. sociologue m./f.

sock¹ /sɒk/ n. chaussette f.

sock² /sɒk/ v.t. (hit: sl.) flanquer un coup (de poing) à.

socket /'sɒkɪt/ n. cavité f.; (for lamp) douille f.; (electr.) prise (de courant) f.; (of tooth) alvéole f.

soda /'səʊdə/ n. soude f. ~(-pop), (Amer.) soda m. ~(-water), soda m., eau de Seltz f.

sodden /'sɒdn/ a. détrempé.

sodium /'səʊdɪəm/ n. sodium m.

sofa /'səʊfə/ n. canapé m., sofa m.

soft /sɒft/ a. (-er, -est) (gentle, lenient) doux; (not hard) doux, mou; (heart, wood) tendre; (silly) ramolli; (easy: sl.) facile. ~ drink, boisson non alcoolisée f. ~ly adv. doucement. ~ness n. douceur f. ~ spot, faible m.

soften /'sɒfn/ v.t./i. ramollir; (tone down, lessen) (s')adoucir.

software /'sɒftweə(r)/ n. (for computer) logiciel m.

softwood /'sɒftwʊd/ n. bois tendre m.

soggy /'sɒgɪ/ a. (-ier, -iest) détrempé; (bread etc.) ramolli.

soil¹ /sɔɪl/ n. sol m., terre f.

soil² /sɔɪl/ v.t./i. (se) salir.

solar /'səʊlə(r)/ a. solaire.

sold /səʊld/ *see* sell. ● *a.* ~ **out**, épuisé.

solder /'sɒldə(r), *Amer.* 'sɒdər/ *n.* soudure *f.* ● *v.t.* souder. ~**ing iron**, fer à souder *m.*

soldier /'səʊldʒə(r)/ *n.* soldat *m.* ● *v.i.* ~ **on**, (*fam.*) persévérer.

sole¹ /səʊl/ *n.* (*of foot*) plante *f.*; (*of shoe*) semelle *f.*

sole² /səʊl/ *n.* (*fish*) sole *f.*

sole³ /səʊl/ *a.* unique, seul. ~**ly** *adv.* uniquement.

solemn /'sɒləm/ *a.* (*formal*) solennel; (*not cheerful*) grave. ~**ity** /sə'lemnəti/ *n.* solennité *f.* ~**ly** *adv.* solennellement; gravement.

solicit /sə'lɪsɪt/ *v.t.* (*seek*) solliciter. ● *v.i.* (*of prostitute*) racoler.

solicitor /sə'lɪsɪtə(r)/ *n.* avoué *m.*

solid /'sɒlɪd/ *a.* solide, (*not hollow*) plein; (*gold*) massif; (*mass*) compact; (*meal*) substantiel. ● *n.* solide *m.* ~**s**, (*food*) aliments solides *m. pl.* ~**-state** *a.* à circuits intégrés. ~**ity** /sə'lɪdətɪ/ *n.* solidité *f.* ~**ly** *adv.* solidement.

solidarity /sɒlɪ'dærətɪ/ *n.* solidarité *f.*

solidify /sə'lɪdɪfaɪ/ *v.t./i.* (se) solidifier.

soliloquy /sə'lɪləkwɪ/ *n.* monologue *m.*, soliloque *m.*

solitary /'sɒlɪtrɪ/ *a.* (*alone, lonely*) solitaire; (*only, single*) seul.

solitude /'sɒlɪtjuːd/ *n.* solitude *f.*

solo /'səʊləʊ/ *n.* (*pl.* -os) solo *m.* ● *a.* (*mus.*) solo *invar.*; (*flight*) en solitaire. ~**ist** *n.* soliste *m./f.*

solstice /'sɒlstɪs/ *n.* solstice *m.*

soluble /'sɒljʊbl/ *a.* soluble.

solution /sə'luːʃn/ *n.* solution *f.*

solv|e /sɒlv/ *v.t.* résoudre. ~**able** *a.* soluble.

solvent /'sɒlvənt/ *a.* (*comm.*) solvable. ● *n.* (dis)solvant *m.*

sombre /'sɒmbə(r)/ *a.* sombre.

some /sʌm/ *a.* (*quantity, number*) du, de l'*, de la, des; (*unspecified, some or other*) un(e), quelque; (*a little*) un peu de; (*a certain*) un(e) certain(e), quelque; (*contrasted with others*) quelques, certain(e)s. ● *pron.* quelques-un(e)s; (*certain quantity of it or them*) en; (*a little*) un peu. ● *adv.* (*approximately*) quelque. **pour** ~ **milk**, versez du lait. **buy** ~ **flowers**, achetez des fleurs. ~ **people like them**, il y a des gens qui les aiment. ~ **of my friends**, quelques amis à moi. **he wants** ~, il en veut. ~

book (or other), un livre (quelconque), quelque livre. ~ **time ago**, il y a un certain temps.

somebody /'sʌmbədɪ/ *pron.* quelqu'un. ● *n.* **be a** ~, être quelqu'un.

somehow /'sʌmhaʊ/ *adv.* d'une manière ou d'une autre; (*for some reason*) je ne sais pas pourquoi.

someone /'sʌmwʌn/ *pron. & n.* = somebody.

someplace /'sʌmpleɪs/ *adv.* (*Amer.*) = somewhere.

somersault /'sʌməsɔːlt/ *n.* culbute *f.* ● *v.i.* faire la culbute.

something /'sʌmθɪŋ/ *pron. & n.* quelque chose (*m.*). ~ **good/etc.**, quelque chose de bon/etc. ~ **like**, un peu comme.

sometime /'sʌmtaɪm/ *adv.* un jour. ● *a.* (*former*) ancien. ~ **in June**, en juin.

sometimes /'sʌmtaɪmz/ *adv.* quelquefois, parfois.

somewhat /'sʌmwɒt/ *adv.* quelque peu, un peu.

somewhere /'sʌmweə(r)/ *adv.* quelque part.

son /sʌn/ *n.* fils *m.* ~**-in-law** *n.* (*pl.* ~**s-in-law**) beau-fils *m.*, gendre *m.*

sonar /'səʊnɑː(r)/ *n.* sonar *m.*

sonata /sə'nɑːtə/ *n.* sonate *f.*

song /sɒŋ/ *n.* chanson *f.* **going for a** ~, à vendre pour une bouchée de pain.

sonic /'sɒnɪk/ *a.* ~ **boom**, bang supersonique *m.*

sonnet /'sɒnɪt/ *n.* sonnet *m.*

sonny /'sʌnɪ/ *n.* (*fam.*) fiston *m.*

soon /suːn/ *adv.* (-er, -est) bientôt; (*early*) tôt. **I would** ~**er stay**, j'aimerais mieux rester. ~ **after**, peu après. ~**er or later**, tôt ou tard.

soot /sʊt/ *n.* suie *f.* ~**y** *a.* couvert de suie.

soothe /suːð/ *v.t.* calmer. ~**ing** *a.* (*remedy, words, etc.*) calmant.

sophisticated /sə'fɪstɪkeɪtɪd/ *a.* raffiné; (*machine etc.*) sophistiqué.

sophomore /'sɒfəmɔː(r)/ *n.* (*Amer.*) étudiant(e) de seconde année *m.* (*f.*).

soporific /sɒpə'rɪfɪk/ *a.* soporifique.

sopping /'sɒpɪŋ/ *a.* trempé.

soppy /'sɒpɪ/ *a.* (-ier, -iest) (*fam.*) sentimental; (*silly: fam.*) bête.

soprano /sə'prɑːnəʊ/ *n.* (*pl.* -os) (*voice*) soprano *m.*; (*singer*) soprano *m./f.*

sorcerer /'sɔːsərə(r)/ *n.* sorcier *m.*

sordid /'sɔːdɪd/ a. sordide.

sore /'sɔː(r)/ a. (-er, -est) douloureux; (vexed) en rogne (at, with, contre). ● n. plaie f.

sorely /'sɔːlɪ/ adv. fortement.

sorrow /'sɒrəʊ/ n. chagrin m. ~ful a. triste.

sorry /'sɒrɪ/ a. (-ier, -iest) (regretful) désolé (to, de; that, que); (wretched) triste (about, de). feel ~ for, plaindre. ~!, pardon!

sort /sɔːt/ n. genre m., sorte f., espèce f.; (person: fam.) type m. ● v.t. (out), (classify) trier. what ~ of?, quel genre de? be out of ~s, ne pas être dans son assiette. ~ out, (tidy) ranger; (arrange) arranger; (problem) régler.

SOS /esəʊˈes/ n. SOS m.

soufflé /'suːfleɪ/ n. soufflé m.

sought /sɔːt/ see seek.

soul /səʊl/ n. âme f. ~-destroying a. démoralisant.

soulful /'səʊlfl/ a. plein de sentiment, très expressif.

sound¹ /saʊnd/ n. son m., bruit m. ● v.t./i. sonner; (seem) sembler (as if, que). ~ a horn, klaxonner. ~ barrier, mur du son m. ~ like, sembler être. ~-proof a. insonorisé; v.t. insonoriser. ~-track n. bande sonore f.

sound² /saʊnd/ a. (-er, -est) solide; (healthy) sain; (sensible) sensé. ~ asleep, profondément endormi. ~ly adv. solidement; (sleep) profondément.

sound³ /saʊnd/ v.t. (test) sonder. ~ out, sonder.

soup /suːp/ n. soupe f., potage m. in the ~, (sl.) dans le pétrin.

sour /'saʊə(r)/ a. (-er, -est) aigre. ● v.t./i. (s')aigrir.

source /sɔːs/ n. source f.

south /saʊθ/ n. sud m. ● a. sud invar., du sud. ● adv. vers le sud. S~ Africa/America, Afrique/Amérique du Sud f. S~ African a. & n. sud-africain(e) (m. (f.)). S~ American a. & n. sud-américain(e) (m. (f.)). ~-east n. sud-est m. ~erly /'sʌðəlɪ/ a. du sud. ~ward a. au sud. ~wards adv. vers le sud. ~-west n. sud-ouest m.

southern /'sʌðən/ a. du sud. ~er n. habitant(e) du sud.

souvenir /suːvəˈnɪə(r)/ n. (thing) souvenir m.

sovereign /'sɒvrɪn/ n. & a. souverain(e) (m. (f.)). ~ty n. souveraineté f.

Soviet /'səʊvɪət/ a. soviétique. the ~ Union, l'Union soviétique f.

sow¹ /səʊ/ v.t. (p.t. sowed, p.p. sowed or sown) (seed etc.) semer; (land) ensemencer.

sow² /saʊ/ n. (pig) truie f.

soya, soy /'sɔɪə, sɔɪ/ n. soja. ~ bean, graine de soja f. ~ sauce, sauce soja f.

spa /spɑː/ n. station thermale f.

space /speɪs/ n. espace m.; (room) place f.; (period) période f. ● a. (research etc.) spatial. ● v.t. (out), espacer.

space|craft /'speɪskrɑːft/ n. invar., ~ship n. engin spatial m.

spacesuit /'speɪssuːt/ n. scaphandre m.

spacious /'speɪʃəs/ a. spacieux.

spade¹ /speɪd/ n. (large, for garden) bêche f.; (child's) pelle f.

spade² /speɪd/ n. (cards) pique m.

spadework /'speɪdwɜːk/ n. (fig.) travail préparatoire m.

spaghetti /spəˈgetɪ/ n. spaghetti m. pl.

Spa|in /speɪn/ n. Espagne f. ~niard /'spænɪəd/ n. Espagnol(e) m. (f.). ~nish /'spænɪʃ/ a. espagnol; n. (lang.) espagnol m.

span¹ /spæn/ n. (of arch) portée f.; (of wings) envergure f.; (of time) durée f. ● v.t. (p.t. spanned) enjamber; (in time) embrasser.

span² /spæn/ see spick.

spaniel /'spænɪəl/ n. épagneul m.

spank /spæŋk/ v.t. donner une fessée à. ~ing n. fessée f.

spanner /'spænə(r)/ n. (tool) clé (plate) f.; (adjustable) clé à molette f.

spar /spɑː(r)/ v.i. (p.t. sparred) s'entraîner (à la boxe).

spare /speə(r)/ v.t. épargner; (do without) se passer de; (afford to give) donner, accorder; (use with restraint) ménager. ● a. en réserve; (surplus) de trop; (tyre, shoes, etc.) de rechange; (room, bed) d'ami. ● n. ~ (part), pièce de rechange f. ~ time, loisirs m. pl. are there any ~ tickets? y a-t-il encore des places?

sparing /'speərɪŋ/ a. frugal. ~ of, avare de. ~ly adv. en petite quantité.

spark /spɑːk/ n. étincelle f. ● v.t. ~
off, (initiate) provoquer. ~**(ing)-
plug** n. bougie f.

sparkle /'spɑːkl/ v.i. étinceler. ● n.
étincellement m.

sparkling /'spɑːklɪŋ/ a. (wine) mousseux, pétillant; (eyes) pétillant.

sparrow /'spærəʊ/ n. moineau m.

sparse /spɑːs/ a. clairsemé. ~**ly** adv.
(furnished etc.) peu.

spartan /'spɑːtn/ a. spartiate.

spasm /'spæzəm/ n. (of muscle)
spasme m.; (of coughing, anger,
etc.) accès m.

spasmodic /spæz'mɒdɪk/ a. intermittent.

spastic /'spæstɪk/ n. handicapé(e)
moteur m. (f.).

spat /spæt/ see spit¹.

spate /speɪt/ n. a ~ of, (letters etc.)
une avalanche de.

spatter /'spætə(r)/ v.t. éclabousser
(with, de).

spatula /'spætjʊlə/ n. spatule f.

spawn /spɔːn/ n. frai m., œufs m. pl.
● v.t. pondre. ● v.i. frayer.

speak /spiːk/ v.i. (p.t. **spoke,** p.p.
spoken) parler. ● v.t. (say) dire;
(language) parler. ~ **up,** parler plus
fort.

speaker /'spiːkə(r)/ n. (in public)
orateur m.; (pol.) président m.;
(loudspeaker) baffle m. **be a
French/a good**/etc. ~, parler fran-
çais/bien/ etc.

spear /spɪə(r)/ n. lance f.

spearhead /'spɪəhed/ n. fer de lance
m. ● v.t. (lead) mener.

spearmint /'spɪəmɪnt/ n. menthe
verte f. ● a. à la menthe.

spec /spek/ n. on ~, (as speculation:
fam.) à tout hasard.

special /'speʃl/ a. spécial; (exceptional) exceptionnel. ~**ity** /-ɪ'ræləti/,
(Amer.) ~**ty** n. spécialité f. ~**ly** adv.
spécialement.

specialist /'speʃəlɪst/ n. spécialiste
m./f.

specialize /'speʃəlaɪz/ v.i. se spécialiser (in, en). ~**d** a. spécialisé.

species /'spiːʃiːz/ n. invar. espèce f.

specific /spə'sɪfɪk/ a. précis, explicite.
~**ally** adv. explicitement; (exactly)
précisément.

specif|y /'spesɪfaɪ/ v.t. spécifier.
~**ication** /-ɪ'keɪʃn/ n. spécification
f.; (details) prescriptions f. pl.

specimen /'spesɪmɪn/ n. spécimen
m., échantillon m.

speck /spek/ n. (stain) (petite) tache
f.; (particle) grain m.

speckled /'spekld/ a. tacheté.

specs /speks/ n. pl. (fam.) lunettes f.
pl.

spectacle /'spektəkl/ n. spectacle m.
~**s,** lunettes f. pl.

spectacular /spek'tækjʊlə(r)/ a. spectaculaire.

spectator /spek'teɪtə(r)/ n. specta|
teur, -trice m., f.

spectre /'spektə(r)/ n. spectre m.

spectrum /'spektrəm/ n. (pl. -tra)
spectre m.; (of ideas etc.) gamme f.

speculat|e /'spekjʊleɪt/ v.i. s'interro-
ger (about, sur); (comm.) spéculer.
~**ion** /-'leɪʃn/ n. conjectures f. pl.;
(comm.) spéculation f. ~**or** n. spé-
cula|teur, -trice m., f.

speech /spiːtʃ/ n. (faculty) parole f.;
(diction) élocution f.; (dialect) langage m.; (address) discours m. ~**less**
a. muet (with, de).

speed /spiːd/ n. (of movement) vitesse
f.; (swiftness) rapidité f. ● v.i. (p.t.
sped /sped/) aller vite; (p.t.
speeded) (drive too fast) aller trop
vite. ~ **limit,** limitation de vitesse
f. ~ **up,** accélérer; (of pace)
s'accélérer. ~**ing** n. excès de vitesse
m.

speedboat /'spiːdbəʊt/ n. vedette f.

speedometer /spiː'dɒmɪtə(r)/ n.
compteur (de vitesse) m.

speedway /'spiːdweɪ/ n. piste pour
motos f.; (Amer.) autodrome m.

speed|y /'spiːdɪ/ a. (-ier, -iest) rapide.
~**ily** adv. rapidement.

spell¹ /spel/ n. (magic) charme m.,
sortilège m.; (curse) sort m.

spell² /spel/ v.t./i. (p.t. **spelled** or
spelt) écrire; (mean) signifier. ~
out, épeler; (explain) expliquer.
~**ing** n. orthographe f. ~**ing mistake,** faute d'orthographe f.

spell³ /spel/ n. (courte) période f.

spend /spend/ v.t. (p.t. **spent**)
(money) dépenser (on, pour); (time,
holiday) passer; (energy) consacrer
(on, à). ● v.i. dépenser.

spendthrift /'spendθrɪft/ n. dépen-
s|ier, -ière m., f.

spent /spent/ see spend. ● a. (used)
utilisé; (person) épuisé.

sperm /spɜːm/ n. (pl. **sperms** or
sperm) (semen) sperme m.; (cell)
spermatozoïde m. ~**icide** n. spermi-
cide m.

spew /spjuː/ v.t./i. vomir.

sphere /sfɪə(r)/ *n.* sphère *f.*

spherical /'sferɪkl/ *a.* sphérique.

spic|e /spaɪs/ *n.* épice *f.*; (*fig.*) piquant *m.* **~y** *a.* épicé; piquant.

spick /spɪk/ *a.* **~ and span**, impeccable, d'une propreté parfaite.

spider /'spaɪdə(r)/ *n.* araignée *f.*

spiel /ʃpiːl/ (*Amer.*) spiːl/ *n.* baratin *m.*

spik|e /spaɪk/ *n.* (*of metal etc.*) pointe *f.* **~y** *a.* garni de pointes.

spill /spɪl/ *v.t.* (*p.t.* **spilled** *or* **spilt**) renverser, répandre. ● *v.i.* se répandre. **~ over**, déborder.

spin /spɪn/ *v.t./i.* (*p.t.* **spun**, *pres. p.* **spinning**) (*wool, web, of spinner*) filer; (*turn*) (faire) tourner; (*story*) débiter. ● *n.* (*movement, excursion*) tour *m.* **~ out**, faire durer. **~-drier** *n.* essoreuse *f.* **~ning-wheel** *n.* rouet *m.* **~-off** *n.* avantage accessoire *m.*; (*by-product*) dérivé *m.*

spinach /'spɪnɪdʒ/ *n.* (*plant*) épinard *m.*; (*as food*) épinards *m. pl.*

spinal /'spaɪnl/ *a.* vertébral. **~ cord**, moelle épinière *f.*

spindl|e /'spɪndl/ *n.* fuseau *m.* **~y** *a.* filiforme, grêle.

spine /spaɪn/ *n.* colonne vertébrale *f.*; (*prickle*) piquant *m.*

spineless /'spaɪnlɪs/ *a.* (*fig.*) sans caractère, mou, lâche.

spinster /'spɪnstə(r)/ *n.* célibataire *f.*; (*pej.*) vieille fille *f.*

spiral /'spaɪərəl/ *a.* en spirale; (*staircase*) en colimaçon. ● *n.* spirale *f.* ● *v.i.* (*p.t.* **spiralled**) (*prices*) monter (en flèche).

spire /'spaɪə(r)/ *n.* flèche *f.*

spirit /'spɪrɪt/ *n.* esprit *m.*; (*boldness*) courage *m.* **~s**, (*morale*) moral *m.*; (*drink*) spiritueux *m. pl.* ● *v.t.* **~ away**, faire disparaître. **~-level** *n.* niveau à bulle *m.*

spirited /'spɪrɪtɪd/ *a.* fougueux.

spiritual /'spɪrɪtʃʊəl/ *a.* spirituel. ● *n.* (*song*) (negro-)spiritual *m.*

spit[1] /spɪt/ *v.t./i.* (*p.t.* **spat** *or* **spit**, *pres. p.* **spitting**) cracher; (*of rain*) crachiner. ● *n.* crachat(s) *m.* (*pl.*) **~ out**, cracher. **the ~ting image of**, le portrait craché *or* vivant de.

spit[2] /spɪt/ *n.* (*for meat*) broche *f.*

spite /spaɪt/ *n.* rancune *f.* ● *v.t.* contrarier. **in ~ of**, malgré. **~ful** *a.* méchant, rancunier. **~fully** *adv.* méchamment.

spittle /'spɪtl/ *n.* crachat(s) *m.* (*pl.*).

splash /splæʃ/ *v.t.* éclabousser. ● *v.i.* faire des éclaboussures. **~ (about)**, patauger. ● *n.* (*act, mark*) éclaboussure *f.*; (*sound*) plouf *m.*; (*of colour*) tache *f.*

spleen /spliːn/ *n.* (*anat.*) rate *f.*

splendid /'splendɪd/ *a.* magnifique, splendide.

splendour /'splendə(r)/ *n.* splendeur *f.*, éclat *m.*

splint /splɪnt/ *n.* (*med.*) attelle *f.*

splinter /'splɪntə(r)/ *n.* éclat *m.*; (*in finger*) écharde *f.* **~ group**, groupe dissident *m.*

split /splɪt/ *v.t./i.* (*p.t.* **split**, *pres. p.* **splitting**) (se) fendre; (*tear*) (se) déchirer; (*divide*) (se) diviser; (*share*) partager. ● *n.* fente *f.*; déchirure *f.*; (*share*: *fam.*) part *f.*, partage *m.*; (*quarrel*) rupture *f.*; (*pol.*) scission *f.* **~ up**, (*couple*) rompre. **a ~ second**, un rien de temps. **~ one's sides**, se tordre (de rire).

splurge /splɜːdʒ/ *v.i.* (*fam.*) faire de folles dépenses.

splutter /'splʌtə(r)/ *v.i.* crachoter; (*stammer*) bafouiller; (*engine*) tousser; (*fat*) crépiter.

spoil /spɔɪl/ *v.t.* (*p.t.* **spoilt** *or* **spoiled**) (*pamper*) gâter; (*ruin*) abîmer; (*mar*) gâcher, gâter. **~(s)**, (*plunder*) butin *m.* **~-sport** *n.* trouble-fête *m./f. invar.*

spoke[1] /spəʊk/ *n.* rayon *m.*

spoke[2], **spoken** /spəʊk, 'spəʊkən/ *see* speak.

spokesman /'spəʊksmən/ *n.* (*pl.* **-men**) porte-parole *m. invar.*

sponge /spʌndʒ/ *n.* éponge *f.* ● *v.t.* éponger. ● *v.i.* **~ on**, vivre aux crochets de. **~-bag** *n.* trousse de toilette *f.* **~-cake** *n.* génoise *f.* **~r** /-ə(r)/ *n.* parasite *m.* **spongy** *a.* spongieux.

sponsor /'spɒnsə(r)/ *n.* (*of concert*) parrain *m.*, sponsor *m.*; (*surety*) garant *m.*; (*for membership*) parrain *m.*, marraine *f.* ● *v.t.* parrainer, sponsoriser; (*member*) parrainer. **~ship** *n.* patronage *m.*; parrainage *m.*

spontane|ous /spɒn'teɪnɪəs/ *a.* spontané. **~ity** /-tə'niːətɪ/ *n.* spontanéité *f.* **~ously** *adv.* spontanément.

spoof /spuːf/ *n.* (*fam.*) parodie *f.*

spool /spuːl/ *n.* bobine *f.*

spoon /spuːn/ *n.* cuiller *f.* **~-feed** *v.t.* (*p.t.* **-fed**) nourrir à la cuiller; (*help*:

fig.) mâcher la besogne à. **~ful** *n.* (*pl.* **-fuls**) cuillerée *f.*

sporadic /spə'rædɪk/ *a.* sporadique.

sport /spɔːt/ *n.* sport *m.* (**good**) **~**, (*person:* sl.) chic type *m.* ● *v.t.* (*display*) exhiber, arborer. **~s car/coat,** voiture/veste de sport *f.* **~y** *a.* (*fam.*) sportif.

sporting /'spɔːtɪŋ/ *a.* sportif. **a ~ chance,** une assez bonne chance.

sports|man /'spɔːtsmən/ *n.* (*pl.* -**men**) sportif *m.* **~manship** *n.* sportivité *f.* **~woman** *n.* (*pl.* -**women**) sportive *f.*

spot /spɒt/ *n.* (*mark, stain*) tache *f.*; (*dot*) point *m.*; (*in pattern*) pois *m.*; (*drop*) goutte *f.*; (*place*) endroit *m.*; (*pimple*) bouton *m.* ● *v.t.* (*p.t.* **spotted**) (*fam.*) apercevoir. **a ~ of,** (*fam.*) un peu de. **be in a ~,** (*fam.*) avoir un problème. **on the ~,** sur place; (*without delay*) sur le coup. **~ check,** contrôle à l'improviste *m.* **~ted** *a.* tacheté; (*fabric*) à pois. **~ty** *a.* (*skin*) boutonneux.

spotless /'spɒtlɪs/ *a.* impeccable.

spotlight /'spɒtlaɪt/ *n.* (*lamp*) projecteur *m.*, spot *m.*

spouse /spaʊs/ *n.* époux *m.*, épouse *f.*

spout /spaʊt/ *n.* (*of vessel*) bec *m.*; (*of liquid*) jet *m.* ● *v.i.* jaillir. **up the ~,** (*ruined:* sl.) fichu.

sprain /spreɪn/ *n.* entorse *f.*, foulure *f.* ● *v.t.* **~ one's wrist**/*etc.*, se fouler le poignet/*etc.*

sprang /spræŋ/ *see* spring.

sprawl /sprɔːl/ *v.i.* (*town, person, etc.*) s'étaler. ● *n.* étalement *m.*

spray¹ /spreɪ/ *n.* (*of flowers*) gerbe *f.*

spray² /spreɪ/ *n.* (*water*) gerbe d'eau *f.*; (*from sea*) embruns *m. pl.*; (*device*) bombe *f.*, atomiseur *m.* ● *v.t.* (*surface, insecticide*) vaporiser; (*plant etc.*) arroser; (*crops*) traiter.

spread /spred/ *v.t./i.* (*p.t.* **spread**) (*stretch, extend*) (s')étendre; (*news, fear, etc.*) (se) répandre; (*illness*) (se) propager; (*butter etc.*) (s')étaler. ● *n.* propagation *f.*; (*of population*) distribution *f.*; (*paste*) pâte à tartiner *f.*; (*food*) belle table *f.* **~-eagled** *a.* bras et jambes écartés.

spreadsheet /'spredʃiːt/ *n.* tableur *m.*

spree /spriː/ *n.* **go on a ~,** (*have fun:* fam.) faire la noce.

sprig /sprɪg/ *n.* (*shoot*) brin *m.*; (*twig*) brindille *f.*

sprightly /'spraɪtlɪ/ *a.* (-**ier**, -**iest**) alerte, vif.

spring /sprɪŋ/ *v.i.* (*p.t.* **sprang**, *p.p.* **sprung**) bondir. ● *v.t.* (*news, annoncer, etc.*) à l'improviste (**on,** à). ● *n.* bond *m.*; (*device*) ressort *m.*; (*season*) printemps *m.*; (*of water*) source *f.* **~-clean** *v.t.* nettoyer de fond en comble. **~ from,** provenir de. **~ onion,** oignon blanc *m.* **~ up,** surgir.

springboard /'sprɪŋbɔːd/ *n.* tremplin *m.*

springtime /'sprɪŋtaɪm/ *n.* printemps *m.*

springy /'sprɪŋɪ/ *a.* (-**ier**, -**iest**) élastique.

sprinkle /'sprɪŋkl/ *v.t.* (*with liquid*) arroser (**with,** de); (*with salt, flour*) saupoudrer (**with,** de). **~ sand**/*etc.*, répandre du sable/*etc.* **~r** /-ə(r)/ *n.* (*in garden*) arroseur *m.*; (*for fires*) extincteur (à déclenchement) automatique *m.*

sprinkling /'sprɪŋklɪŋ/ *n.* (*amount*) petite quantité *f.*

sprint /sprɪnt/ *v.i.* (*sport*) sprinter. ● *n.* sprint *m.* **~er** *n.* sprinteu|r, -se *m., f.*

sprout /spraʊt/ *v.t./i.* pousser. ● *n.* (*on plant etc.*) pousse *f.* (**Brussels**) **~s,** choux de Bruxelles *m. pl.*

spruce¹ /spruːs/ *a.* pimpant. ● *v.t.* **~ o.s. up,** se faire beau.

spruce² /spruːs/ *n.* (*tree*) épicéa *m.*

sprung /sprʌŋ/ *see* spring. ● *a.* (*mattress etc.*) à ressorts.

spry /spraɪ/ *a.* (**spryer**, **spryest**) alerte, vif.

spud /spʌd/ *n.* (sl.) patate *f.*

spun /spʌn/ *see* spin.

spur /spɜː(r)/ *n.* (*of rider, cock, etc.*) éperon *m.*; (*stimulus*) aiguillon *m.* ● *v.t.* (*p.t.* **spurred**) éperonner. **on the ~ of the moment,** sous l'impulsion du moment.

spurious /'spjʊərɪəs/ *a.* faux.

spurn /spɜːn/ *v.t.* repousser.

spurt /spɜːt/ *v.i.* jaillir; (*fig.*) accélérer. ● *n.* jet *m.*; (*at work*) coup de collier *m.*

spy /spaɪ/ *n.* espion(ne) *m.* (*f.*). ● *v.i.* espionner. ● *v.t.* apercevoir. **~ on,** espionner. **~ out,** reconnaître.

squabble /'skwɒbl/ *v.i.* se chamailler. ● *n.* chamaillerie *f.*

squad /skwɒd/ *n.* (*of soldiers etc.*) escouade *f.*; (*sport*) équipe *f.*

squadron /'skwɒdrən/ n. (mil.) escadron m.; (aviat.) escadrille f.; (naut.) escadre f.

squalid /'skwɒlɪd/ a. sordide. **~or** n. conditions sordides f. pl.

squall /skwɔːl/ n. rafale f.

squander /'skwɒndə(r)/ v.t. (money, time, etc.) gaspiller.

square /skweə(r)/ n. carré m.; (open space in town) place f.; (instrument) équerre f. ● a. carré; (honest) honnête; (meal) solide; (fam.) ringard. **(all) ~**, (quits) quitte. ● v.t. (settle) régler. ● v.i. (agree) cadrer (with, avec). **~ up to**, faire face à. **~ metre**, mètre carré m. **~ly** adv. carrément.

squash /skwɒʃ/ v.t. écraser; (crowd) serrer. ● n. (game) squash m.; (marrow: Amer.) courge f. **lemon ~**, citronnade f. **orange ~**, orangeade f. **~y** a. mou.

squat /skwɒt/ v.i. (p.t. **squatted**) s'accroupir. ● a. (dumpy) trapu. **~ in a house**, squatteriser une maison. **~ter** n. squatter m.

squawk /skwɔːk/ n. cri rauque m. ● v.i. pousser un cri rauque.

squeak /skwiːk/ n. petit cri m.; (of door etc.) grincement m. ● v.i. crier; grincer. **~y** a. grinçant.

squeal /skwiːl/ n. cri aigu m. ● v.i. pousser un cri aigu. **~ on**, (inform on: sl.) dénoncer.

squeamish /'skwiːmɪʃ/ a. (trop) délicat, facilement dégoûté.

squeeze /skwiːz/ v.t. presser; (hand, arm) serrer; (extract) exprimer (from, de); (extort) soutirer (from, à). ● v.i. (force one's way) se glisser. ● n. pression f.; (comm.) restrictions de crédit f. pl.

squelch /skweltʃ/ v.i. faire flic flac. ● v.t. (suppress) supprimer.

squid /skwɪd/ n. calmar m.

squiggle /'skwɪgl/ n. ligne onduleuse f.

squint /skwɪnt/ v.i. loucher; (with half-shut eyes) plisser les yeux. ● n. (med.) strabisme m.

squire /'skwaɪə(r)/ n. propriétaire terrien m.

squirm /skwɜːm/ v.i. se tortiller.

squirrel /'skwɪrəl, Amer. 'skwɜːrəl/ n. écureuil m.

squirt /skwɜːt/ v.t./i. (faire) jaillir. ● n. jet m.

stab /stæb/ v.t. (p.t. **stabbed**) (with knife etc.) poignarder. ● n. coup (de couteau) m. **have a ~ at sth.**, essayer de faire qch.

stabilize /'steɪbəlaɪz/ v.t. stabiliser.

stable[1] /'steɪbl/ a. (**-er, -est**) stable. **~ility** /stə'bɪlətɪ/ n. stabilité f.

stable[2] /'steɪbl/ n. écurie f. **~-boy** n. lad m.

stack /stæk/ n. tas m. ● v.t. **~ (up)**, entasser, empiler.

stadium /'steɪdɪəm/ n. stade m.

staff /stɑːf/ n. personnel m.; (in school) professeurs m. pl.; (mil.) état-major m.; (stick) bâton m. ● v.t. pourvoir en personnel.

stag /stæg/ n. cerf m. **have a ~ party**, enterrer sa vie de garçon.

stage /steɪdʒ/ n. (theatre) scène f.; (phase) stade m., étape f.; (platform in hall) estrade f. ● v.t. mettre en scène; (fig.) organiser. **go on the ~**, faire du théâtre. **~-coach** n. (old use) diligence f. **~ door**, entrée des artistes f. **~ fright**, trac m. **~-manage** v.t. monter, organiser. **~-manager** n. régisseur m.

stagger /'stægə(r)/ v.i. chanceler. ● v.t. (shock) stupéfier; (holidays etc.) étaler. **~ing** a. stupéfiant.

stagnant /'stægnənt/ a. stagnant.

stagnat|e /stæg'neɪt/ v.i. stagner. **~ion** /-ʃn/ n. stagnation f.

staid /steɪd/ a. sérieux.

stain /steɪn/ v.t. tacher; (wood etc.) colorer. ● n. tache f.; (colouring) colorant m. **~ed glass window**, vitrail m. **~less steel**, acier inoxydable m. **~ remover**, détachant m.

stair /steə(r)/ n. marche f. **the ~s**, l'escalier m.

stair|case /'steəkeɪs/, **~way** ns. escalier m.

stake /steɪk/ n. (post) pieu m.; (wager) enjeu m. ● v.t. (area) jalonner; (wager) jouer. **at ~**, en jeu. **~ a claim to**, revendiquer.

stale /steɪl/ a. (**-er, -est**) pas frais; (bread) rassis; (smell) de renfermé; (news) vieux. **~ness** n. manque de fraîcheur m.

stalemate /'steɪlmeɪt/ n. (chess) pat m.; (fig.) impasse f.

stalk[1] /stɔːk/ n. (of plant) tige f.

stalk[2] /stɔːk/ v.i. marcher de façon guindée. ● v.t. (prey) traquer.

stall /stɔːl/ n. (in stable) stalle f.; (in market) éventaire m. **~s**, (theatre) orchestre m. ● v.t./i. (auto.) caler. **~ (for time)**, temporiser.

stallion /'stælɪən/ n. étalon m.

stalwart /'stɔːlwət/ n. (*supporter*) partisan(e) fidèle m. (f.).

stamina /'stæmɪnə/ n. résistance f.

stammer /'stæmə(r)/ v.t./i. bégayer. ● n. bégaiement m.

stamp /stæmp/ v.t./i. ~ (one's foot), taper du pied. ● v.t. (*letter etc.*) timbrer. ● n. (*for postage, marking*) timbre m.; (*mark: fig.*) sceau m. ~-collecting n. philatélie f. ~ out, supprimer.

stampede /stæm'piːd/ n. fuite désordonnée f.; (*rush: fig.*) ruée f. ● v.i. s'enfuir en désordre; se ruer.

stance /stæns/ n. position f.

stand /stænd/ v.i. (*p.t.* stood) être or se tenir (debout); (*rise*) se lever; (*be situated*) se trouver; (*rest*) reposer; (*pol.*) être candidat (for, à). ● v.t. mettre (debout); (*tolerate*) supporter. ● n. position f.; (*mil.*) résistance f.; (*for lamp etc.*) support m.; (*at fair*) stand m.; (*in street*) kiosque m.; (*for spectators*) tribune f.; (*jurid., Amer.*) barre f. make a ~, prendre position. ~ a chance, avoir une chance. ~ back, reculer. ~ by or around, ne rien faire. ~ by, (*be ready*) se tenir prêt; (*promise, person*) rester fidèle à. ~-by a. de réserve; n. be a ~-by, être de réserve. ~ down, se désister. ~ for, représenter; (*fam.*) supporter. ~ in for, remplacer. ~-in n. remplaçant(e) m. (f.). ~ in line, (*Amer.*) faire la queue. ~-offish a. (*fam.*) distant. ~ out, (*be conspicuous*) ressortir. ~ to reason, être logique. ~ up, se lever. ~ up for, défendre. ~ up to, résister à.

standard /'stændəd/ n. norme f.; (*level*) niveau (voulu) m.; (*flag*) étendard m. ~s, (*morals*) principes m. pl. ● a. ordinaire. ~ lamp, lampadaire m. ~ of living, niveau de vie m.

standardize /'stændədaɪz/ v.t. standardiser.

standing /'stændɪŋ/ a. debout *invar.*; (*army, offer*) permanent. ● n. position f., réputation f.; (*duration*) durée f. ~ order, prélèvement bancaire m. ~ room, places debout f. pl.

standpoint /'stændpɔɪnt/ n. point de vue m.

standstill /'stændstɪl/ n. at a ~, immobile. bring/come to a ~, (s')immobiliser.

stank /stæŋk/ see stink.

stanza /'stænzə/ n. strophe f.

staple[1] /'steɪpl/ n. agrafe f. ● v.t. agrafer. ~r /-ə(r)/ n. agrafeuse f.

staple[2] /'steɪpl/ a. principal, de base.

star /stɑː(r)/ n. étoile f.; (*famous person*) vedette f. ● v.t. (*p.t.* starred) (*of film*) avoir pour vedette. ● v.i. ~ in, être la vedette de. ~dom n. célébrité f.

starboard /'stɑːbəd/ n. tribord m.

starch /stɑːtʃ/ n. amidon m.; (*in food*) fécule f. ● v.t. amidonner. ~y a. féculent; (*stiff*) guindé.

stare /steə(r)/ v.i. ~ at, regarder fixement. ● n. regard fixe m.

starfish /'stɑːfɪʃ/ n. étoile de mer f.

stark /stɑːk/ a. (-er, -est) (*desolate*) désolé; (*severe*) austère; (*utter*) complet; (*fact etc.*) brutal. ● adv. complètement.

starling /'stɑːlɪŋ/ n. étourneau m.

starlit /'stɑːlɪt/ a. étoilé.

starry /'stɑːrɪ/ a. étoilé. ~-eyed a. naïf, (trop) optimiste.

start /stɑːt/ v.t./i. commencer; (*machine*) (se) mettre en marche; (*fashion etc.*) lancer; (*cause*) provoquer; (*jump*) sursauter; (*of vehicle*) démarrer. ● n. commencement m., début m.; (*of race*) départ m.; (*lead*) avance f.; (*jump*) sursaut m. ~ to do, commencer or se mettre à faire. ~ off doing, commencer par faire. ~ out, partir. ~ up a business, lancer une affaire. ~er n. (*auto.*) démarreur m.; (*runner*) partant m.; (*culin.*) entrée f. ~ing point, point de départ m. ~ing tomorrow, à partir de demain.

startle /'stɑːtl/ v.t. (*make jump*) faire tressaillir; (*shock*) alarmer.

starv|e /stɑːv/ v.i. mourir de faim. ● v.t. affamer; (*deprive*) priver. ~ation /-'veɪʃn/ n. faim f.

stash /stæʃ/ v.t. (*hide: sl.*) cacher.

state /steɪt/ n. état m.; (*pomp*) apparat m. S~, (*pol.*) État m. ● a. d'État, de l'État; (*school*) public. ● v.t. affirmer (that, que); (*views*) exprimer; (*fix*) fixer. the S~s, les États-Unis. get into a ~, s'affoler.

stateless /'steɪtlɪs/ a. apatride.

stately /'steɪtlɪ/ a. (-ier, -iest) majestueux. ~ home, château m.

statement /'steɪtmənt/ n. déclaration f.; (*of account*) relevé m.

statesman /'steɪtsmən/ n. (*pl.* -men) homme d'État m.

static /'stætɪk/ *a.* statique. ● *n.* (*radio, TV*) parasites *m. pl.*

station /'steɪʃn/ *n.* station *f.*; (*rail.*) gare *f.*; (*mil.*) poste *m.*; (*rank*) condition *f.* ● *v.t.* poster, placer. **~ed at** *or* **in**, (*mil.*) en garnison à. **~ wagon**, (*Amer.*) break *m.*

stationary /'steɪʃənrɪ/ *a.* immobile, stationnaire; (*vehicle*) à l'arrêt.

stationer /'steɪʃnə(r)/ *n.* papet|ier, -ière *m., f.* **~'s shop**, papeterie *f.* **~y** *n.* papeterie *f.*

statistic /stə'tɪstɪk/ *n.* statistique *f.* **~s**, statistique *f.* **~al** *a.* statistique.

statue /'stætʃuː/ *n.* statue *f.*

stature /'stætʃə(r)/ *n.* stature *f.*

status /'steɪtəs/ *n.* (*pl.* **-uses**) situation *f.*, statut *m.*; (*prestige*) standing *m.* **~ quo**, statu quo *m.*

statut|e /'stætʃuːt/ *n.* loi *f.* **~es**, (*rules*) statuts *m. pl.* **~ory** /-ʊtrɪ/ *a.* statutaire; (*holiday*) légal.

staunch /stɔːntʃ/ *a.* (**-er, -est**) (*friend etc.*) loyal, fidèle.

stave /steɪv/ *n.* (*mus.*) portée *f.* ● *v.t.* **~ off**, éviter, conjurer.

stay /steɪ/ *v.i.* rester, (*spend time*) séjourner; (*reside*) loger. ● *v.t.* (*hunger*) tromper. ● *n.* séjour *m.* **~ away from**, (*school etc.*) ne pas aller à. **~ behind/on/late/etc.**, rester. **~ in/out**, rester à la maison/dehors. **~ up** (*late*), veiller, se coucher tard.

stead /sted/ *n.* **stand s.o. in good ~**, être bien utile à qn.

steadfast /'stedfɑːst/ *a.* ferme.

stead|y /'stedɪ/ *a.* (**-ier, -iest**) stable; (*hand, voice*) ferme; (*regular*) régulier; (*staid*) sérieux. ● *v.t.* maintenir, assurer; (*calm*) calmer. **~ily** *adv.* fermement; régulièrement.

steak /steɪk/ *n.* steak *m.*, bifteck *m.*; (*of fish*) darne *f.*

steal /stiːl/ *v.t./i.* (*p.t.* **stole**, *p.p.* **stolen**) voler (**from s.o.**, à qn.).

stealth /stelθ/ *n.* **by ~**, furtivement. **~y** *a.* furtif.

steam /stiːm/ *n.* vapeur *f.*; (*on glass*) buée *f.* ● *v.t.* (*cook*) cuire à la vapeur; (*window*) embuer. ● *v.i.* fumer. **~-engine** *n.* locomotive à vapeur *f.* **~ iron**, fer à vapeur *m.* **~y** *a.* humide.

steam|er /'stiːmə(r)/ *n.* (*culin.*) cuit-vapeur *m.*; (*also* **~ship**) (bateau à) vapeur *m.*

steamroller /'stiːmrəʊlə(r)/ *n.* rouleau compresseur *m.*

steel /stiːl/ *n.* acier *m.* ● *v. pr.* **~ o.s.**, s'endurcir, se cuirasser. **~ industry**, sidérurgie *f.*

steep[1] /stiːp/ *v.t.* (*soak*) tremper. **~ed in**, (*fig.*) imprégné de.

steep[2] /stiːp/ *a.* (**-er, -est**) raide, rapide; (*price: fam.*) excessif. **~ly** *adv.* **rise ~ly**, (*slope, price*) monter rapidement.

steeple /'stiːpl/ *n.* clocher *m.*

steeplechase /'stiːpltʃeɪs/ *n.* (*race*) steeple(-chase) *m.*

steer[1] /stɪə(r)/ *n.* (*ox*) bouvillon *m.*

steer[2] /stɪə(r)/ *v.t.* diriger; (*ship*) gouverner; (*fig.*) guider. ● *v.i.* (*in ship*) gouverner. **~ clear of**, éviter. **~ing** *n.* (*auto.*) direction *f.* **~ing-wheel** *n.* volant *m.*

stem[1] /stem/ *n.* tige *f.*; (*of glass*) pied *m.* ● *v.i.* (*p.t.* **stemmed**). **~ from**, provenir de.

stem[2] /stem/ *v.t.* (*p.t.* **stemmed**) (*check, stop*) endiguer, contenir.

stench /stentʃ/ *n.* puanteur *f.*

stencil /'stensl/ *n.* pochoir *m.*; (*for typing*) stencil *m.* ● *v.t.* (*p.t.* **stencilled**) (*document*) polycopier.

stenographer /ste'nɒgrəfə(r)/ *n.* (*Amer.*) sténodactylo *f.*

step /step/ *v.i.* (*p.t.* **stepped**) marcher, aller. ● *v.t.* **~ up**, augmenter. ● *n.* pas *m.*; (*stair*) marche *f.*; (*of train*) marchepied *m.*; (*action*) mesure *f.* **~s**, (*ladder*) escabeau *m.* **in ~**, au pas; (*fig.*) conforme (**with**, à). **~ down**, (*resign*) démissionner; (*from ladder*) descendre. **~ forward**, (faire un) pas en avant. **~ up**, (*pressure*) augmenter. **~ in**, (*intervene*) intervenir. **~-ladder** *n.* escabeau *m.* **~ping-stone** *n.* (*fig.*) tremplin *m.*

step|brother /'stepbrʌðə(r)/ *n.* demi-frère *m.* **~daughter** *n.* belle-fille *f.* **~father** *n.* beau-père *m.* **~mother** *n.* belle-mère *f.* **~sister** *n.* demi-sœur *f.* **~son** *n.* beau-fils *m.*

stereo /'sterɪəʊ/ *n.* (*pl.* **-os**) stéréo *f.*; (*record-player*) chaîne stéréo *f.* ● *a.* stéréo *invar.* **~phonic** /-ə'fɒnɪk/ *a.* stéréophonique.

stereotype /'sterɪətaɪp/ *n.* stéréotype *m.* **~d** *a.* stéréotypé.

steril|e /'steraɪl, *Amer.* 'sterəl/ *a.* stérile. **~ity** /stə'rɪlətɪ/ *n.* stérilité *f.*

steriliz|e /'sterəlaɪz/ *v.t.* stériliser. **~ation** /-'zeɪʃn/ *n.* stérilisation *f.*

sterling /'stɜːlɪŋ/ n. livre(s) sterling f. (pl.). ● a. sterling invar.; (silver) fin; (fig.) excellent.

stern [1] /stɜːn/ a. (-er, -est) sévère.

stern [2] /stɜːn/ n. (of ship) arrière m.

steroid /'steroid/ n. stéroïde m.

stethoscope /'steθəskəup/ n. stéthoscope m.

stew /stjuː/ v.t./i. cuire à la casserole. ● n. ragoût m. ~ed fruit, compote f. ~ed tea, thé trop infusé m. ~-pan n. cocotte f.

steward /stjuəd/ n. (of club etc.) intendant m.; (on ship etc.) steward m. ~ess /-'des/ n. hôtesse f.

stick [1] /stɪk/ n. bâton m.; (for walking) canne f.

stick [2] /stɪk/ v.t. (p.t. stuck) (glue) coller; (thrust) enfoncer; (put: fam.) mettre; (endure: sl.) supporter. ● v.i. (adhere) coller, adhérer; (to pan) attacher; (remain: fam.) rester; (be jammed) être coincé. **be stuck with s.o.,** (fam.) se farcir qn. ~-in-the-mud n. encroûté(e)n m. (f.). ~ at, persévérer dans. ~ out v.t. (head etc.) sortir; (tongue) tirer; v.i. (protrude) dépasser. ~ to, (promise etc.) rester fidèle à. ~ up for, (fam.) défendre. ~ing-plaster n. sparadrap m.

sticker /'stɪkə(r)/ n. autocollant m.

stickler /'stɪklə(r)/ n. **be a ~ for,** insister sur.

sticky /'stɪkɪ/ a. (-ier, -iest) poisseux; (label, tape) adhésif.

stiff /stɪf/ a. (-er, -est) raide; (limb, joint) ankylosé; (tough) dur; (drink) fort; (price) élevé; (manner) guindé. ~ **neck,** torticolis m. ~ness n. raideur f.

stiffen /'stɪfn/ v.t./i. (se) raidir.

stifle /'staɪfl/ v.t./i. étouffer.

stigma /'stɪgmə/ n. (pl. -as) stigmate m. ~tize v.t. stigmatiser.

stile /staɪl/ n. échalier m.

stiletto /stɪ'letəu/ a. & n. (pl. -os) ~s, ~ **heels** talons aiguille m. pl.

still [1] /stɪl/ a. immobile; (quiet) calme, tranquille. ● n. silence m. ● adv. encore, toujours; (even) encore; (nevertheless) tout de même. **keep ~!,** arrête de bouger! ~ **life,** nature morte f.

still [2] /stɪl/ n. (apparatus) alambic m.

stillborn /'stɪlbɔːn/ a. mort-né.

stilted /'stɪltɪd/ a. guindé.

stilts /stɪlts/ n. pl. échasses f. pl.

stimullate /'stɪmjuleɪt/ v.t. stimuler. ~ant n. stimulant m. ~ation /-'leɪʃn/ n. stimulation f.

stimulus /'stɪmjuləs/ n. (pl. -li /-laɪ/) (spur) stimulant m.

sting /stɪŋ/ n. piqûre f.; (organ) dard m. ● v.t./i. (p.t. stung) piquer. ~ing a. (fig.) cinglant.

stingy /'stɪndʒɪ/ a. (-ier, -iest) avare (with, de).

stink /stɪŋk/ n. puanteur f. ● v.i. (p.t. stank or stunk, p.p. stunk). ~ (of), puer. ● v.t. ~ **out,** (room etc.) empester.

stinker /'stɪŋkə(r)/ n. (thing: sl.) vacherie f.; (person: sl.) vache f.

stint /stɪnt/ v.i. ~ **on,** lésiner sur. ● n. (work) tour m.

stipulate /'stɪpjuleɪt/ v.t. stipuler. ~ion /-'leɪʃn/ n. stipulation f.

stir /stɜː(r)/ v.t./i. (p.t. stirred) (move) remuer; (excite) exciter. ● n. agitation f. ~ **up,** (trouble etc.) provoquer.

stirrup /'stɪrəp/ n. étrier m.

stitch /stɪtʃ/ n. point m.; (in knitting) maille f.; (med.) point de suture m.; (muscle pain) point de côté m. ● v.t. coudre. **be in ~es,** (fam.) avoir le fou rire.

stoat /stəut/ n. hermine f.

stock /stɒk/ n. réserve f.; (comm.) stock m.; (financial) valeurs f. pl.; (family) souche f.; (soup) bouillon m. ● a. (goods) courant. ● v.t. (shop etc.) approvisionner; (sell) vendre. ● v.i. ~ **up,** s'approvisionner (with, de). ~-car n. stock-car m. ~ **cube,** bouillon-cube m. S~ **Exchange,** ~ **market,** Bourse f. ~ **phrase,** cliché m. ~-taking n. (comm.) inventaire m. **in ~,** en stock. **we're out of ~,** il n'y en a plus. **take ~,** (fig.) faire le point.

stockbroker /'stɒkbrəukə(r)/ n. agent de change m.

stocking /'stɒkɪŋ/ n. bas m.

stockist /'stɒkɪst/ n. stockiste m.

stockpile /'stɒkpaɪl/ n. stock m. ● v.t. stocker; (arms) amasser.

stocky /'stɒkɪ/ a. (-ier, -iest) trapu.

stodglle /'stɒdʒ/ n. (fam.) aliment(s) lourd(s) m. (pl.). ~y a. lourd.

stoic /'stəuɪk/ n. stoïque m./f. ~al a. stoïque. ~ism /-sɪzəm/ n. stoïcisme m.

stoke /stəuk/ v.t. (boiler, fire) garnir, alimenter.

stole [1] /stəul/ n. (garment) étole f.

stole², **stolen** /stəʊl, 'stəʊlən/ see steal.

stolid /'stɒlɪd/ a. flegmatique.

stomach /'stʌmək/ n. estomac m.; (*abdomen*) ventre m. ● v.t. (*put up with*) supporter. **~-ache** n. mal à l'estomac or au ventre m.

ston|e /stəʊn/ n. pierre f.; (*pebble*) caillou m.; (*in fruit*) noyau m.; (*weight*) 6.350 kg. ● a. de pierre. ● v.t. lapider; (*fruit*) dénoyauter. **~e-cold/-deaf,** complètement froid/sourd. **~y** a. pierreux. **~y-broke** a. (*sl.*) fauché.

stonemason /'stəʊnmeɪsn/ n. maçon m., tailleur de pierre m.

stood /stʊd/ see stand.

stooge /stuːdʒ/ n. (*actor*) comparse m./f.; (*fig.*) fantoche m., laquais m.

stool /stuːl/ n. tabouret m.

stoop /stuːp/ v.i. (*bend*) se baisser; (*condescend*) s'abaisser. ● n. have a ~, être voûté.

stop /stɒp/ v.t./i. (*p.t. stopped*) arrêter (**doing,** de faire); (*moving, talking*) s'arrêter; (*prevent*) empêcher (**from,** de); (*hole, leak, etc.*) boucher; (*of pain, noise, etc.*) cesser; (*stay: fam.*) rester. ● n. arrêt m.; (*full stop*) point m. ~ **off,** s'arrêter. ~ **up,** boucher. **~(-over),** halte f.; (*port of call*) escale f. **~-light** n. (*on vehicle*) stop m. **~-watch** n. chronomètre m.

stopgap /'stɒpgæp/ n. bouche-trou m. ● a. intérimaire.

stoppage /'stɒpɪdʒ/ n. arrêt m.; (*of work*) arrêt de travail m.; (*of pay*) retenue f.

stopper /'stɒpə(r)/ n. bouchon m.

storage /'stɔːrɪdʒ/ n. (*of goods, food, etc.*) emmagasinage m. ~ **heater,** radiateur électrique à accumulation m. ~ **space,** espace de rangement m.

store /stɔː(r)/ n. réserve f.; (*warehouse*) entrepôt m.; (*shop*) grand magasin m.; (*Amer.*) magasin m. ● v.t. (*for future*) mettre en réserve; (*in warehouse, mine*) emmagasiner. **have in ~ for,** réserver à. **set ~ by,** attacher du prix à. **~-room** n. réserve f.

storey /'stɔːrɪ/ n. étage m.

stork /stɔːk/ n. cigogne f.

storm /stɔːm/ n. tempête f., orage m. ● v.t. prendre d'assaut. ● v.i. (*rage*) tempêter. **~y** a. orageux.

story /'stɔːrɪ/ n. histoire f.; (*in press*) article m.; (*storey: Amer.*) étage m. ~

book, livre d'histoires m. **~-teller** n. conteu|r, -se m., f.; (*liar: fam.*) menteu|r, -se m., f.

stout /staʊt/ a. (-er, -est) corpulent; (*strong*) solide. ● n. bière brune f. **~ness** n. corpulence f.

stove /stəʊv/ n. (*for cooking*) cuisinière f.; (*heater*) poêle m.

stow /stəʊ/ v.t. ~ **away,** (*put away*) ranger; (*hide*) cacher. ● v.i. voyager clandestinement.

stowaway /'stəʊəweɪ/ n. passag|er, -ère clandestin(e) m., f.

straddle /'strædl/ v.t. être à cheval sur, enjamber.

straggle /'strægl/ v.i. (*lag behind*) traîner en désordre. **~r** /-ə(r)/ n. traînard(e) m. (f.).

straight /streɪt/ a. (-er, -est) droit; (*tidy*) en ordre; (*frank*) franc. ● adv. (*in straight line*) droit; (*direct*) tout droit. ~ **ahead** or **on,** tout droit. ~ **away,** tout de suite. ~ **face,** visage sérieux m. **get sth. ~,** mettre qch. au clair. ~ **off,** (*fam.*) sans hésiter.

straighten /'streɪtn/ v.t. (*nail, situation, etc.*) redresser; (*tidy*) arranger.

straightforward /streɪt'fɔːwəd/ a. honnête; (*easy*) simple.

strain¹ /streɪn/ n. (*breed*) race f.; (*streak*) tendance f.

strain² /streɪn/ v.t. (*rope, ears*) tendre; (*limb*) fouler; (*eyes*) fatiguer; (*muscle*) froisser; (*filter*) passer; (*vegetables*) égoutter; (*fig.*) mettre à l'épreuve. ● v.i. fournir des efforts. ● n. tension f.; (*fig.*) effort m. **~s,** (*tune: mus.*) accents m. pl. **~ed** a. forcé; (*relations*) tendu. **~er** n. passoire f.

strait /streɪt/ n. détroit m. **~s,** détroit m.; (*fig.*) embarras m. **~-jacket** n. camisole de force f. **~-laced** a. collet monté invar.

strand /strænd/ n. (*thread*) fil m., brin m.; (*lock of hair*) mèche f.

stranded /'strændɪd/ a. (*person*) en rade; (*ship*) échoué.

strange /streɪndʒ/ a. (-er, -est) étrange; (*unknown*) inconnu. **~ly** adv. étrangement. **~ness** n. étrangeté f.

stranger /'streɪndʒə(r)/ n. inconnu(e) m. (f.).

strangle /'stræŋgl/ v.t. étrangler.

stranglehold /'stræŋglhəʊld/ n. **have a ~ on,** tenir à la gorge.

strap /stræp/ n. (of leather etc.) courroie f.; (of dress) bretelle f.; (of watch) bracelet m. ● v.t. (p.t. **strapped**) attacher.

strapping /'stræpɪŋ/ a. costaud.

stratagem /'strætədʒəm/ n. stratagème m.

strategic /strə'tiːdʒɪk/ a. stratégique.

strategy /'strætədʒɪ/ n. stratégie f.

stratum /'strɑːtəm/ n. (pl. **strata**) couche f.

straw /strɔː/ n. paille f. **the last ~**, le comble.

strawberry /'strɔːbrɪ/ n. fraise f.

stray /streɪ/ v.i. s'égarer; (deviate) s'écarter. ● a. perdu; (isolated) isolé. ● n. animal perdu m.

streak /striːk/ n. raie f., bande f.; (trace) trace f.; (period) période f.; (tendency) tendance f. ● v.t. (mark) strier. ● v.i. filer à toute allure. **~y** a. strié.

stream /striːm/ n. ruisseau m.; (current) courant m.; (flow) flot m.; (in schools) classe (de niveau) f. ● v.i. ruisseler (**with**, de); (eyes, nose) couler.

streamer /'striːmə(r)/ n. (of paper) serpentin m.; (flag) banderole f.

streamline /'striːmlaɪn/ v.t. rationaliser. **~d** a. (shape) aérodynamique.

street /striːt/ n. rue f. **~ lamp**, réverbère m. **~ map**, plan des rues m.

streetcar /'striːtkɑː(r)/ n. (Amer.) tramway m.

strength /streŋθ/ n. force f.; (of wall, fabric, etc.) solidité f. **on the ~ of**, en vertu de.

strengthen /'streŋθn/ v.t. renforcer, fortifier.

strenuous /'strenjʊəs/ a. énergique; (arduous) ardu; (tiring) fatigant. **~ly** adv. énergiquement.

stress /stres/ n. accent m.; (pressure) pression f.; (med.) stress m. ● v.t. souligner, insister sur.

stretch /stretʃ/ v.t. (pull taut) tendre; (arm, leg) étendre; (neck) tendre; (clothes) étirer; (truth etc.) forcer. ● v.i. s'étendre; (of person, clothes) s'étirer. ● n. étendue f.; (period) période f.; (of road) tronçon m. ● a. (fabric) extensible. **~ one's legs**, se dégourdir les jambes. **at a ~**, d'affilée.

stretcher /'stretʃə(r)/ n. brancard m.

strew /struː/ v.t. (p.t. **strewed**, p.p. **strewed** or **strewn**) (scatter) répandre; (cover) joncher.

stricken /'strɪkən/ a. **~ with**, frappé or atteint de.

strict /strɪkt/ a. (-er, -est) strict. **~ly** adv. strictement. **~ness** n. sévérité f.

stride /straɪd/ v.i. (p.t. **strode**, p.p. **stridden**) faire de grands pas. ● n. grand pas m.

strident /'straɪdnt/ a. strident.

strife /straɪf/ n. conflit(s) m. (pl.).

strike /straɪk/ v.t. (p.t. **struck**) frapper; (blow) donner; (match) frotter; (gold etc.) trouver. ● v.i. faire grève; (attack) attaquer; (clock) sonner. ● n. (of workers) grève f.; (mil.) attaque f.; (find) découverte f. **on ~**, en grève. **~ off** or **out**, rayer. **~ up a friendship**, lier amitié (**with**, avec).

striker /'straɪkə(r)/ n. gréviste m./f.; (football) buteur m.

striking /'straɪkɪŋ/ a. frappant.

string /strɪŋ/ n. ficelle f.; (of violin, racket, etc.) corde f.; (of pearls) collier m.; (of lies etc.) chapelet m. ● v.t. (p.t. **strung**) (thread) enfiler. **the ~s**, (mus.) les cordes. **~ bean**, haricot vert m. **pull ~s**, faire jouer ses relations, faire marcher le piston. **~ out**, (s')échelonner. **~ed** a. (instrument) à cordes. **~y** a. filandreux.

stringent /'strɪndʒənt/ a. rigoureux, strict.

strip¹ /strɪp/ v.t./i. (p.t. **stripped**) (undress) (se) déshabiller; (machine) démonter; (deprive) dépouiller. **~per** n. strip-teaseuse f.; (solvent) décapant m. **~-tease** n. strip-tease m.

strip² /strɪp/ n. bande f. **comic ~**, bande dessinée f. **~ light**, néon m.

stripe /straɪp/ n. rayure f., raie f. **~d** a. rayé.

strive /straɪv/ v.i. (p.t. **strove**, p.p. **striven**) s'efforcer (**to**, de).

strode /strəʊd/ see stride.

stroke¹ /strəʊk/ n. coup m.; (of pen) trait m.; (swimming) nage f.; (med.) attaque f., congestion f. **at a ~**, d'un seul coup.

stroke² /strəʊk/ v.t. (with hand) caresser. ● n. caresse f.

stroll /strəʊl/ v.i. flâner. ● n. petit tour m. **~ in/etc.**, entrer/etc.

tranquillement. **~er** n. (*Amer.*) poussette f.

strong /strɒŋ/ a. (**-er**, **-est**) fort; (*shoes, fabric, etc.*) solide. **be fifty/ etc. ~**, être au nombre de cinquante/ *etc.* **~-box** n. coffre-fort m. **~-minded** a. résolu. **~- room** n. chambre forte f. **~ly** adv. (*greatly*) fortement; (*with energy*) avec force; (*deeply*) profondément.

stronghold /'strɒŋhəʊld/ n. bastion m.

strove /strəʊv/ see strive.

struck /strʌk/ see strike. ● a. **~ on**, (*sl.*) impressionné par.

structure /'strʌktʃə(r)/ n. (*of cell, poem, etc.*) structure f.; (*building*) construction f. **~al** a. structural; de (la) construction.

struggle /'strʌgl/ v.i. lutter, se battre. ● n. lutte f.; (*effort*) effort m. **have a ~ to**, avoir du mal à.

strum /strʌm/ v.t. (*p.t.* **strummed**) (*banjo etc.*) gratter de.

strung /strʌŋ/ see string. ● a. **~ up**, (*tense*) nerveux.

strut /strʌt/ n. (*support*) étai m. ● v.i. (*p.t.* **strutted**) se pavaner.

stub /stʌb/ n. bout m.; (*of tree*) souche f.; (*counterfoil*) talon m. ● v.t. (*p.t.* **stubbed**). **~ one's toe**, se cogner le doigt de pied. **~ out**, écraser.

stubble /'stʌbl/ n. (*on chin*) barbe de plusieurs jours f.; (*remains of wheat*) chaume m.

stubborn /'stʌbən/ a. opiniâtre, obstiné. **~ly** adv. obstinément. **~ness** n. opiniâtreté f.

stubby /'stʌbɪ/ a. (**-ier**, **-iest**) (*finger*) épais; (*person*) trapu.

stuck /stʌk/ see stick². ● a. (*jammed*) coincé. **I'm ~**, (*for answer*) je sèche. **~-up** a. (*sl.*) prétentieux.

stud¹ /stʌd/ n. clou m.; (*for collar*) bouton m. ● v.t. (*p.t.* **studded**) clouter. **~ded with**, parsemé de.

stud² /stʌd/ n. (*horses*) écurie f. **~ (-farm)** n. haras m.

student /'stju:dnt/ n. (*univ.*) étudiant(e) m. (f.); (*schol.*) élève m./f. ● a. (*restaurant, life, residence*) universitaire.

studied /'stʌdɪd/ a. étudié.

studio /'stju:dɪəʊ/ n. (*pl.* **-os**) studio m. **~ flat**, studio m.

studious /'stju:dɪəs/ a. (*person*) studieux; (*deliberate*) étudié. **~ly** adv. (*carefully*) avec soin.

study /'stʌdɪ/ n. étude f.; (*office*) bureau m. ● v.t./i. étudier.

stuff /stʌf/ n. substance f.; (*sl.*) chose(s) f. (*pl.*). ● v.t. rembourrer; (*animal*) empailler; (*cram*) bourrer; (*culin.*) farcir; (*block up*) boucher; (*put*) fourrer. **~ing** n. bourre f.; (*culin.*) farce f.

stuffy /'stʌfɪ/ a. (**-ier**, **-iest**) mal aéré; (*dull: fam.*) vieux jeu *invar.*

stumble /'stʌmbl/ v.i. trébucher. **~e across** *or* **on**, tomber sur. **~ing-block** n. pierre d'achoppement f.

stump /stʌmp/ n. (*of tree*) souche f.; (*of limb*) moignon m.; (*of pencil*) bout m.

stumped /stʌmpt/ a. (*baffled: fam.*) embarrassé.

stun /stʌn/ v.t. (*p.t.* **stunned**) étourdir; (*bewilder*) stupéfier.

stung /stʌŋ/ see sting.

stunk /stʌŋk/ see stink.

stunning /'stʌnɪŋ/ a. (*delightful: fam.*) sensationnel.

stunt¹ /stʌnt/ v.t. (*growth*) retarder. **~ed** a. (*person*) rabougri.

stunt² /stʌnt/ n. (*feat: fam.*) tour de force m.; (*trick: fam.*) truc m.; (*dangerous*) cascade f. **~man** n. cascadeur m.

stupefy /'stju:pɪfaɪ/ v.t. abrutir; (*amaze*) stupéfier.

stupendous /stju:'pendəs/ a. prodigieux, formidable.

stupid /'stju:pɪd/ a. stupide, bête. **~ity** /-'pɪdətɪ/ n. stupidité f. **~ly** adv. stupidement, bêtement.

stupor /'stju:pə(r)/ n. stupeur f.

sturdy /'stɜ:dɪ/ a. (**-ier**, **-iest**) robuste. **~iness** n. robustesse f.

stutter /'stʌtə(r)/ v.i. bégayer. ● n. bégaiement m.

sty¹ /staɪ/ n. (*pigsty*) porcherie f.

sty² /staɪ/ n. (*on eye*) orgelet m.

style /staɪl/ n. style m.; (*fashion*) mode f.; (*sort*) genre m.; (*pattern*) modèle m. ● v.t. (*design*) créer. **do sth. in ~e**, faire qch. avec classe. **~e s.o.'s hair**, coiffer qn. **~ist** n. (*of hair*) coiffeur, -se m., f.

stylish /'staɪlɪʃ/ a. élégant.

stylized /'staɪlaɪzd/ a. stylisé.

stylus /'staɪləs/ n. (*pl.* **-uses**) (*of record-player*) saphir m.

suave /swɑ:v/ a. (*urbane*) courtois; (*smooth: pej.*) doucereux.

sub- /sʌb/ *pref.* sous-, sub-.

subconscious /sʌbˈkɒnʃəs/ *a. & n.* inconscient (*m.*), subconscient (*m.*). **~ly** *adv.* inconsciemment.

subcontract /sʌbkənˈtrækt/ *v.t.* sous-traiter.

subdivide /sʌbdɪˈvaɪd/ *v.t.* subdiviser.

subdue /səbˈdjuː/ *v.t.* (*feeling*) maîtriser; (*country*) subjuguer. **~d** *a.* (*weak*) faible; (*light*) tamisé; (*person, criticism*) retenu.

subject[1] /ˈsʌbdʒɪkt/ *a.* (*state etc.*) soumis. ● *n.* sujet *m.*; (*schol., univ.*) matière *f.*; (*citizen*) ressortissant(e) *m.* (*f.*), sujet(te) *m.* (*f.*). **~-matter** *n.* contenu *m.* **~ to**, soumis à; (*liable to, dependent on*) sujet à.

subject[2] /səbˈdʒekt/ *v.t.* soumettre. **~ion** /-kʃn/ *n.* soumission *f.*

subjective /səbˈdʒektɪv/ *a.* subjectif.

subjunctive /səbˈdʒʌŋktɪv/ *a. & n.* subjonctif (*m.*).

sublet /sʌbˈlet/ *v.t.* sous-louer.

sublime /səˈblaɪm/ *a.* sublime.

submarine /sʌbməˈriːn/ *n.* sous-marin *m.*

submerge /səbˈmɜːdʒ/ *v.t.* submerger. ● *v.i.* plonger.

submissive /səbˈmɪsɪv/ *a.* soumis.

submi|t /səbˈmɪt/ *v.t./i.* (*p.t.* **submitted**) (se) soumettre (**to**, à). **~ssion** *n.* soumission *f.*

subordinate[1] /səˈbɔːdɪnət/ *a.* subalterne; (*gram.*) subordonné. ● *n.* subordonné(e) *m.* (*f.*).

subordinate[2] /səˈbɔːdɪneɪt/ *v.t.* subordonner (**to**, à).

subpoena /səbˈpiːnə/ *n.* (*pl.* **-as**) (*jurid.*) citation *f.*, assignation *f.*

subroutine /ˈsʌbruːtiːn/ *n.* sous-programme *m.*

subscribe /səbˈskraɪb/ *v.t./i.* verser (de l'argent) (**to**, à). **~ to**, (*loan, theory*) souscrire à; (*newspaper*) s'abonner à, être abonné à. **~r** /-ə(r)/ *n.* abonné(e) *m.* (*f.*).

subscription /səbˈskrɪpʃn/ *n.* souscription *f.*; abonnement *m.*; (*membership dues*) cotisation *f.*

subsequent /ˈsʌbsɪkwənt/ *a.* (*later*) ultérieur; (*next*) suivant. **~ly** *adv.* par la suite.

subside /səbˈsaɪd/ *v.i.* (*land etc.*) s'affaisser; (*flood, wind*) baisser. **~nce** /-əns/ *n.* affaissement *m.*

subsidiary /səbˈsɪdɪərɪ/ *a.* accessoire. ● *n.* (*comm.*) filiale *f.*

subsid|y /ˈsʌbsədɪ/ *n.* subvention *f.* **~ize** /-ɪdaɪz/ *v.t.* subventionner.

subsist /səbˈsɪst/ *v.i.* subsister. **~ence** *n.* subsistance *f.*

substance /ˈsʌbstəns/ *n.* substance *f.*

substandard /sʌbˈstændəd/ *a.* de qualité inférieure.

substantial /səbˈstænʃl/ *a.* considérable; (*meal*) substantiel. **~ly** *adv.* considérablement.

substantiate /səbˈstænʃɪeɪt/ *v.t.* justifier, prouver.

substitut|e /ˈsʌbstɪtjuːt/ *n.* succédané *m.*; (*person*) remplaçant(e) *m.* (*f.*). ● *v.t.* substituer (**for**, à). **~ion** /-ˈtjuːʃn/ *n.* substitution *f.*

subterfuge /ˈsʌbtəfjuːdʒ/ *n.* subterfuge *m.*

subterranean /sʌbtəˈreɪnɪən/ *a.* souterrain.

subtitle /ˈsʌbtaɪtl/ *n.* sous-titre *m.*

subtle /ˈsʌtl/ *a.* (**-er, -est**) subtil. **~ty** *n.* subtilité *f.*

subtotal /ˈsʌbtəʊtl/ *n.* total partiel *m.*

subtract /səbˈtrækt/ *v.t.* soustraire. **~ion** /-kʃn/ *n.* soustraction *f.*

suburb /ˈsʌbɜːb/ *n.* faubourg *m.*, banlieue *f.* **~s**, banlieue *f.* **~an** /səˈbɜːbən/ *a.* de banlieue.

suburbia /səˈbɜːbɪə/ *n.* la banlieue.

subversive /səbˈvɜːsɪv/ *a.* subversif.

subver|t /səbˈvɜːt/ *v.t.* renverser. **~sion** /-ʃn/ *n.* subversion *f.*

subway /ˈsʌbweɪ/ *n.* passage souterrain *m.*; (*Amer.*) métro *m.*

succeed /səkˈsiːd/ *v.i.* réussir (**in doing**, à faire). ● *v.t.* (*follow*) succéder à. **~ing** *a.* suivant.

success /səkˈses/ *n.* succès *m.*, réussite *f.*

successful /səkˈsesfl/ *a.* réussi, couronné de succès; (*favourable*) heureux; (*in exam*) reçu. **be ~ in doing**, réussir à faire. **~ly** *adv.* avec succès.

succession /səkˈseʃn/ *n.* succession *f.* **in ~**, de suite.

successive /səkˈsesɪv/ *a.* successif. **six ~ days**, six jours consécutifs.

successor /səkˈsesə(r)/ *n.* successeur *m.*

succinct /səkˈsɪŋkt/ *a.* succinct.

succulent /ˈsʌkjʊlənt/ *a.* succulent.

succumb /səˈkʌm/ *v.i.* succomber.

such /sʌtʃ/ *a. & pron.* tel(le), tel(le)s; (*so much*) tant (de). ● *adv.* si. **~ a book**/*etc.*, un tel livre/*etc.* **~ books**/*etc.*, de tels livres/*etc.* **~ courage**/*etc.*, tant de courage/ *etc.* **~ a big house**, une si grande maison. **~ as**, comme, tel que. **as ~,** en tant que tel. **there's no ~ thing,** ça n'existe pas. **~-and-such** a. tel ou tel.

suck /sʌk/ v.t. sucer. **~ in** or **up,** aspirer. **~er** n. (*rubber pad*) ventouse f.; (*person: sl.*) dupe f.

suction /'sʌkʃn/ n. succion f.

sudden /'sʌdn/ a. soudain, subit. **all of a ~,** tout à coup. **~ly** adv. subitement, brusquement. **~ness** n. soudaineté f.

suds /sʌdz/ n. pl. (*froth*) mousse de savon f.

sue /suː/ v.t. (*pres. p.* **suing**) poursuivre (en justice).

suede /sweɪd/ n. daim m.

suet /'suːɪt/ n. graisse de rognon f.

suffer /'sʌfə(r)/ v.t./i. souffrir; (*loss, attack, etc.*) subir. **~er** n. victime f., malade m./f. **~ing** n. souffrance(s) f. (*pl.*).

suffice /sə'faɪs/ v.i. suffire.

sufficient /sə'fɪʃnt/ a. (*enough*) suffisamment de; (*big enough*) suffisant. **~ly** adv. suffisamment.

suffix /'sʌfɪks/ n. suffixe m.

suffocat|e /'sʌfəkeɪt/ v.t./i. suffoquer. **~ion** /-'keɪʃn/ n. suffocation f.; (*med.*) asphyxie f.

suffused /sə'fjuːzd/ a. **~ with,** (*light, tears*) baigné de.

sugar /'ʃʊɡə(r)/ n. sucre m. ● v.t. sucrer. **~y** a. sucré.

suggest /sə'dʒest/ v.t. suggérer. **~ion** /-tʃn/ n. suggestion f.

suggestive /sə'dʒestɪv/ a. suggestif. **be ~ of,** suggérer.

suicid|e /'suːɪsaɪd/ n. suicide m. **commit ~e,** se suicider. **~al** /-'saɪdl/ a. suicidaire.

suit /suːt/ n. costume m.; (*woman's*) tailleur m.; (*cards*) couleur f. ● v.t. convenir à; (*of garment, style, etc.*) aller à; (*adapt*) adapter. **~ability** n. (*of action etc.*) à-propos m.; (*of candidate*) aptitude f. (*pl.*). **~able** a. qui convient (**for,** à), convenable. **~ably** adv. convenablement. **~ed** a. (**well**) **~ed,** (*matched*) bien assorti. **~ed to,** fait pour, apte à.

suitcase /'suːtkeɪs/ n. valise f.

suite /swiːt/ n. (*rooms, retinue*) suite f.; (*furniture*) mobilier m.

suitor /'suːtə(r)/ n. soupirant m.

sulfur /'sʌlfər/ n. (*Amer.*) = **sulphur.**

sulk /sʌlk/ v.i. bouder. **~y** a. boudeur, maussade.

sullen /'sʌlən/ a. maussade. **~ly** adv. d'un air maussade.

sulphur /'sʌlfə(r)/ n. soufre m. **~ic** /-'fjʊərɪk/ a. **~ic acid,** acide sulfurique m.

sultan /'sʌltən/ n. sultan m.

sultana /sʌl'tɑːnə/ n. raisin de Smyrne m., raisin sec m.

sultry /'sʌltrɪ/ a. (**-ier, -iest**) étouffant, lourd; (*fig.*) sensuel.

sum /sʌm/ n. somme f.; (*in arithmetic*) calcul m. ● v.t./i. (*p.t.* **summed**). **~ up,** résumer, récapituler; (*assess*) évaluer.

summar|y /'sʌmərɪ/ n. résumé m. ● a. sommaire. **~ize** v.t. résumer.

summer /'sʌmə(r)/ n. été m. ● a. d'été. **~-time** n. (*season*) été m. **~y** a. estival.

summit /'sʌmɪt/ n. sommet m. **~ (conference),** (*pol.*) (conférence f. au) sommet m.

summon /'sʌmən/ v.t. appeler; (*meeting, s.o. to meeting*) convoquer. **~ up,** (*strength, courage, etc.*) rassembler.

summons /'sʌmənz/ n. (*jurid.*) assignation f. ● v.t. assigner.

sump /sʌmp/ n. (*auto.*) carter m.

sumptuous /'sʌmptʃʊəs/ a. somptueux, luxueux.

sun /sʌn/ n. soleil m. ● v.t. (*p.t.* **sunned**). **~ o.s.,** se chauffer au soleil. **~-glasses** n. pl. lunettes de soleil f. pl. **~-roof** n. toit ouvrant m. **~-tan** n. bronzage m. **~-tanned** a. bronzé.

sunbathe /'sʌnbeɪð/ v.i. prendre un bain de soleil.

sunburn /'sʌnbɜːn/ n. coup de soleil m. **~t** a. brûlé par le soleil.

Sunday /'sʌndɪ/ n. dimanche m. **~ school,** catéchisme m.

sundial /'sʌndaɪəl/ n. cadran solaire m.

sundown /'sʌndaʊn/ n. = sunset.

sundr|y /'sʌndrɪ/ a. divers. **~ies** n. pl. articles divers m. pl. **all and ~y,** tout le monde.

sunflower /'sʌnflaʊə(r)/ n. tournesol m.

sung /sʌŋ/ see sing.

sunk /sʌŋk/ see sink.

sunken /'sʌŋkən/ a. (*ship etc.*) submergé; (*eyes*) creux.

sunlight /'sʌnlaɪt/ n. soleil m.

sunny /'sʌnɪ/ a. (**-ier, -iest**) (*room, day, etc.*) ensoleillé.

sunrise /'sʌnraɪz/ n. lever du soleil m.

sunset /'sʌnset/ n. coucher du soleil m.

sunshade /'sʌnʃeɪd/ n. (lady's) ombrelle f.; (awning) parasol m.

sunshine /'sʌnʃaɪn/ n. soleil m.

sunstroke /'sʌnstrəʊk/ n. insolation f.

super /'su:pə(r)/ a. (sl.) formidable.

superb /su:'pɜ:b/ a. superbe.

supercilious /su:pə'sɪlɪəs/ a. hautain, dédaigneux.

superficial /su:pə'fɪʃl/ a. superficiel. ~ity /-ɪ'ælətɪ/ n. caractère superficiel m. ~ly adv. superficiellement.

superfluous /su:'pɜ:flʊəs/ a. superflu.

superhuman /su:pə'hju:mən/ a. surhumain.

superimpose /su:pərɪm'pəʊz/ v.t. superposer (on, à).

superintendent /su:pərɪn'tendənt/ n. direc|teur, -trice m., f.; (of police) commissaire m.

superior /su:'pɪərɪə(r)/ a. & n. supérieur(e) (m. (f.)). ~ity /-'ɒrətɪ/ n. supériorité f.

superlative /su:'pɜ:lətɪv/ a. suprême. ● n. (gram.) superlatif m.

superman /'su:pəmæn/ n. (pl. -men) surhomme m.

supermarket /'su:pəmɑ:kɪt/ n. supermarché m.

supernatural /su:pə'nætʃrəl/ a. surnaturel.

superpower /'su:pəpaʊə(r)/ n. superpuissance f.

supersede /su:pə'si:d/ v.t. remplacer, supplanter.

supersonic /su:pə'sɒnɪk/ a. supersonique.

superstiti|on /su:pə'stɪʃn/ n. superstition f. ~ous a. superstitieux.

superstore /'su:pəstɔ:(r)/ n. hypermarché m.

supertanker /'su:pətæŋkə(r)/ n. pétrolier géant m.

supervis|e /'su:pəvaɪz/ v.t. surveiller, diriger. ~ion /-'vɪʒn/ n. surveillance f. ~or n. surveillant(e) m. (f.); (shop) chef de rayon m.; (firm) chef de service m. ~ory /-'vaɪzərɪ/ a. de surveillance.

supper /'sʌpə(r)/ n. dîner m.; (late at night) souper m.

supple /'sʌpl/ a. souple.

supplement[1] /'sʌplɪmənt/ n. supplément m. ~ary /-'mentrɪ/ a. supplémentaire.

supplement[2] /'sʌplɪment/ v.t. compléter.

supplier /sə'plaɪə(r)/ n. fournisseur m.

suppl|y /sə'plaɪ/ v.t. fournir; (equip) pourvoir; (feed) alimenter (with, en). ● n. provision f.; (of gas etc.) alimentation f. ~ies, (food) vivres m. pl.; (material) fournitures f. pl. ~y teacher, (professeur) suppléant(e) m. (f.).

support /sə'pɔ:t/ v.t. soutenir; (family) assurer la subsistance de; (endure) supporter. ● n. soutien m., appui m.; (techn.) support m. ~er n. partisan(e) m. (f.); (sport) supporter m. ~ive a. qui soutient et encourage.

suppos|e /sə'pəʊz/ v.t./i. supposer. be ~ed to do, être censé faire, devoir faire. ~ing he comes, supposons qu'il vienne. ~ition /sʌpə'zɪʃn/ n. supposition f.

supposedly /sə'pəʊzɪdlɪ/ adv. soi-disant, prétendument.

suppress /sə'pres/ v.t. (put an end to) supprimer; (restrain) réprimer; (stifle) étouffer. ~ion /-ʃn/ n. suppression f.; répression f.

suprem|e /su:'pri:m/ a. suprême. ~acy /-eməsɪ/ n. suprématie f.

surcharge /'sɜ:tʃɑ:dʒ/ n. prix supplémentaire m.; (tax) surtaxe f.; (on stamp) surcharge f.

sure /ʃɔ:(r)/ a. (-er, -est) sûr. ● adv. (Amer., fam.) pour sûr. make ~ of, s'assurer de. make ~ that, vérifier que. ~ly adv. sûrement.

surety /'ʃɔ:rətɪ/ n. caution f.

surf /sɜ:f/ n. (waves) ressac m. ~ing n. surf m.

surface /'sɜ:fɪs/ n. surface f. ● a. superficiel. ● v.t. revêtir. ● v.i. faire surface; (fig.) réapparaître. ~ mail, courrier maritime m.

surfboard /'sɜ:fbɔ:d/ n. planche de surf f.

surfeit /'sɜ:fɪt/ n. excès m. (of, de).

surge /sɜ:dʒ/ v.i. (of crowd) déferler; (of waves) s'enfler; (increase) monter. ● n. (wave) vague f.; (rise) montée f.

surgeon /'sɜ:dʒən/ n. chirurgien m.

surg|ery /'sɜ:dʒərɪ/ n. chirurgie f.; (office) cabinet m.; (session) consultation f. need ~ery, devoir être opéré. ~ical a. chirurgical. ~ical spirit, alcool à 90 degrés m.

surly /'sɜ:lɪ/ a. (-ier, -iest) bourru.

surmise /sə'maɪz/ v.t. conjecturer. ● n. conjecture f.

surmount /sə'maʊnt/ v.t. (overcome, cap) surmonter.

surname /'sɜ:neɪm/ n. nom de famille m.

surpass /sə'pɑ:s/ v.t. surpasser.

surplus /'sɜ:pləs/ n. surplus m. ● a. en surplus.

surpris|**e** /sə'praɪz/ n. surprise f. ● v.t. surprendre. ~**ed** a. surpris (**at**, de). ~**ing** a. surprenant. ~**ingly** adv. étonnamment.

surrender /sə'rendə(r)/ v.i. se rendre. ● v.t. (hand over) remettre; (mil.) rendre. ● n. (mil.) reddition f.; (of passport etc.) remise f.

surreptitious /sʌrəp'tɪʃəs/ a. subreptice, furtif.

surround /sə'raʊnd/ v.t. entourer; (mil.) encercler. ~**ing** a. environnant. ~**ings** n. pl. environs m. pl.; (setting) cadre m.

surveillance /sɜ:'veɪləns/ n. surveillance f.

survey[1] /sə'veɪ/ v.t. (review) passer en revue; (inquire into) enquêter sur; (building) inspecter. ~**or** n. expert (géomètre) m.

survey[2] /'sɜ:veɪ/ n. (inquiry) enquête f.; inspection f.; (general view) vue d'ensemble f.

survival /sə'vaɪvl/ n. survie f.; (relic) vestige m.

surviv|**e** /sə'vaɪv/ v.t./i. survivre (à). ~**or** n. survivant(e) m. (f.).

susceptib|**le** /sə'septəbl/ a. sensible (**to**, à). ~**le to**, (prone to) prédisposé à. ~**ility** /-'bɪlətɪ/ n. sensibilité f.; prédisposition f.

suspect[1] /sə'spekt/ v.t. soupçonner; (doubt) douter de.

suspect[2] /'sʌspekt/ n. & a. suspect(e) (m. (f.)).

suspen|**d** /sə'spend/ v.t. (hang, stop) suspendre; (licence) retirer provisoirement. ~**ded sentence**, condamnation avec sursis f. ~**sion** n. suspension f.; retrait provisoire m. ~**sion bridge**, pont suspendu m.

suspender /sə'spendə(r)/ n. jarretelle f. ~**s**, (braces: Amer.) bretelles f. pl. ~ **belt**, porte-jarretelles m.

suspense /sə'spens/ n. attente f.; (in book etc.) suspense m.

suspicion /sə'spɪʃn/ n. soupçon m.; (distrust) méfiance f.

suspicious /sə'spɪʃəs/ a. soupçonneux; (causing suspicion) suspect.

be ~ of, (distrust) se méfier de. ~**ly** adv. de façon suspecte.

sustain /sə'steɪn/ v.t. supporter; (effort etc.) soutenir; (suffer) subir.

sustenance /'sʌstɪnəns/ n. (food) nourriture f.; (quality) valeur nutritive f.

swab /swɒb/ n. (pad) tampon m.

swagger /'swægə(r)/ v.i. (walk) se pavaner, parader.

swallow[1] /'swɒləʊ/ v.t./i. avaler. ~ **up**, (absorb, engulf) engloutir.

swallow[2] /'swɒləʊ/ n. hirondelle f.

swam /swæm/ see swim.

swamp /swɒmp/ n. marais m. ● v.t. (flood, overwhelm) submerger. ~**y** a. marécageux.

swan /swɒn/ n. cygne m. ~**-song** n. (fig.) chant du cygne m.

swank /swæŋk/ n. (behaviour: fam.) épate f., esbroufe f.; (person: fam.) crâneu|r, -se m., f. ● v.i. (show off: fam.) crâner.

swap /swɒp/ v.t./i. (p.t. **swapped**) (fam.) échanger. ● n. (fam.) échange m.

swarm /swɔ:m/ n. (of insects, people) essaim m. ● v.i. fourmiller. ~ **into** or **round**, (crowd) envahir.

swarthy /'swɔ:ðɪ/ a. (-ier, -iest) noiraud; (complexion) basané.

swastika /'swɒstɪkə/ n. (Nazi) croix gammée f.

swat /swɒt/ v.t. (p.t. **swatted**) (fly etc.) écraser.

sway /sweɪ/ v.t./i. (se) balancer; (influence) influencer. ● n. balancement m.; (rule) empire m.

swear /sweə(r)/ v.t./i. (p.t. **swore**, p.p. **sworn**) jurer (**to sth.**, de qch.). ~ **at**, injurier. ~ **by sth.**, (fam.) ne jurer que par qch. ~**-word** n. juron m.

sweat /swet/ n. sueur f. ● v.i. suer. ~**-shirt** n. sweat-shirt m. ~**y** a. en sueur.

sweater /'swetə(r)/ n. pull-over m.

swede /swi:d/ n. rutabaga m.

Swed|**e** /swi:d/ n. Suédois(e) m. (f.). ~**en** n. Suède f. ~**ish** a. suédois; n. (lang.) suédois m.

sweep /swi:p/ v.t./i. (p.t. **swept**) (carry away) emporter, entraîner; (chimney) ramoner. ● n. coup de balai m.; (curve) courbe f.; (movement) geste m., mouvement m.; (for chimneys) ramoneur m. ~ **by**, passer rapidement or majestueusement. ~ **out**, balayer.

~er n. (for carpet) balai mécanique m.; (football) arrière volant m. ~ing a. (gesture) large; (action) qui va loin; (statement) trop général.

sweet /swiːt/ a. (-er, -est) (not sour, pleasant) doux; (not savoury) sucré; (charming. fam.) gentil. ● n. bonbon m.; (dish) dessert m.; (person) chéri(e) m. (f.). **have a ~ tooth,** aimer les sucreries. **~ corn,** maïs m. **~ pea,** pois de senteur m. **~ shop,** confiserie f. **~ly** adv. gentiment. **~ness** n. douceur f.; goût sucré m.

sweeten /swiːtn/ v.t. sucrer; (fig.) adoucir. **~er** n. édulcorant m.

sweetheart /swiːthaːt/ n. petit(e) ami(e) m. (f.); (term of endearment) chéri(e) m. (f.).

swell /swel/ v.t./i. (p.t. swelled, p.p. swollen or swelled) (increase) grossir; (expand) (se) gonfler; (of hand, face) enfler. ● n. (of sea) houle f. ● a. (fam.) formidable. **~ing** n. (med.) enflure f.

swelter /sweltə(r)/ v.i. étouffer. **~ing** a. étouffant.

swept /swept/ see sweep.

swerve /swɜːv/ v.i. faire un écart.

swift /swift/ a. (-er, -est) rapide. ● n. (bird) martinet m. **~ly** adv. rapidement. **~ness** n. rapidité f.

swig /swig/ v.t. (p.t. swigged) (drink: fam.) lamper. ● n. (fam.) lampée f., coup m.

swill /swil/ v.t. rincer; (drink) lamper. ● n. (pig-food) pâtée f.

swim /swim/ v.i. (p.t. swam, p.p. swum, pres. p. swimming) nager; (be dizzy) tourner. ● v.t. traverser à la nage; (distance) nager. ● n. baignade f. **go for a ~,** aller se baigner. **~mer** n. nageu|r, -se m.,f. **~ming** n. natation f. **~ming-bath, ~ming-pool** ns. piscine f. **~-suit** n. maillot (de bain) m.

swindle /swindl/ v.t. escroquer. ● n. escroquerie f. **~r** /-ə(r)/ n. escroc m.

swine /swain/ n. pl. (pigs) pourceaux m. pl. ● n. invar. (person: fam.) salaud m.

swing /swiŋ/ v.t./i. (p.t. swung) (se) balancer; (turn round) tourner; (of pendulum) osciller. ● n. balancement m.; (seat) balançoire f. (of opinion) revirement m. (towards, en faveur de); (mus.) rythme m. **be in full ~,** battre son plein. **~ round,** (of person) se retourner.

swingeing /swindʒɪŋ/ a. écrasant.

swipe /swaip/ v.t. (hit: fam.) frapper; (steal: fam.) piquer. ● n. (hit: fam.) grand coup m.

swirl /swɜːl/ v.i. tourbillonner. ● n. tourbillon m.

swish /swiʃ/ v.i. (hiss) siffler, cingler l'air. ● a. (fam.) chic invar.

Swiss /swis/ a. suisse. ● n. invar. Suisse(sse) m. (f.).

switch /switʃ/ n. bouton (électrique) m., interrupteur m.; (shift) changement m.; revirement m. ● v.t. (transfer) transférer; (exchange) échanger (for, contre); (reverse positions of) changer de place. **~ trains/** etc., (change) changer de train/etc. ● v.i. (go over) passer. **~ off,** éteindre. **~ on,** mettre, allumer.

switchback /switʃbæk/ n. montagnes russes f. pl.

switchboard /switʃbɔːd/ n. (telephone) standard m.

Switzerland /switsələnd/ n. Suisse f.

swivel /swivl/ v.t./i. (p.t. swivelled) (faire) pivoter.

swollen /swəʊlən/ see swell.

swoon /swuːn/ v.i. se pâmer.

swoop /swuːp/ v.i. (bird) fondre; (police) faire une descente, foncer. ● n. (police raid) descente f.

sword /sɔːd/ n. épée f.

swore /swɔː(r)/ see swear.

sworn /swɔːn/ see swear. ● a. (enemy) juré; (ally) dévoué.

swot /swɒt/ v.t./i. (p.t. swotted) (study: sl.) bûcher. ● n. (sl.) bûcheu|r, -se m.,f.

swum /swʌm/ see swim.

swung /swʌŋ/ see swing.

sycamore /sɪkəmɔː(r)/ n. (maple) sycomore m.; (Amer.) platane m.

syllable /sɪləbl/ n. syllabe f.

syllabus /sɪləbəs/ n. (pl. -uses) (schol., univ.) programme m.

symbol /sɪmbl/ n. symbole m. **~ic(al)** /-bɒlɪk(l)/ a. symbolique. **~ism** n. symbolisme m.

symbolize /sɪmbəlaiz/ v.t. symboliser.

symmetr|y /sɪmətrɪ/ n. symétrie f. **~ical** /sɪmetrɪkl/ a. symétrique.

sympathize /sɪmpəθaiz/ v.i. **~ with,** (pity) plaindre; (fig.) comprendre les sentiments de. **~r** /-ə(r)/ n. sympathisant(e) m. (f.).

sympath|y /sɪmpəθɪ/ n. (pity) compassion f.; (fig.) compréhension f.; (solidarity) solidarité f.; (condo-

lences) condoléances *f. pl.* **be in ~y with**, comprendre, être en accord avec. **~etic** /-'θetɪk/ *a.* compatissant; (*fig.*) compréhensif. **~etically** /-'θetɪklɪ/ *adv.* avec compassion; (*fig.*) avec compréhension.

symphon|y /'sɪmfənɪ/ *n.* symphonie *f.* ● *a.* symphonique. **~ic** /-'fɒnɪk/ *a.* symphonique.

symposium /sɪm'pəʊzɪəm/ *n.* (*pl.* **-ia**) symposium *m.*

symptom /'sɪmptəm/ *n.* symptôme *m.* **~atic** /-'mætɪk/ *a.* symptomatique (**of**, de).

synagogue /'sɪnəgɒg/ *n.* synagogue *f.*

synchronize /'sɪŋkrənaɪz/ *v.t.* synchroniser.

syndicate /'sɪndɪkət/ *n.* syndicat *m.*

syndrome /'sɪndrəʊm/ *n.* syndrome *m.*

synonym /'sɪnənɪm/ *n.* synonyme *m.* **~ous** /sɪ'nɒnɪməs/ *a.* synonyme.

synopsis /sɪ'nɒpsɪs/ *n.* (*pl.* **-opses** /-siːz/) résumé *m.*

syntax /'sɪntæks/ *n.* syntaxe *f.*

synthesis /'sɪnθəsɪs/ *n.* (*pl.* **-theses** /-siːz/) synthèse *f.*

synthetic /sɪn'θetɪk/ *a.* synthétique.

syphilis /'sɪfɪlɪs/ *n.* syphilis *f.*

Syria /'sɪrɪə/ *n.* Syrie *f.* **~n** *a. & n.* syrien(ne) (*m. (f.)*).

syringe /sɪ'rɪndʒ/ *n.* seringue *f.*

syrup /'sɪrəp/ *n.* (*liquid*) sirop *m.*; (*treacle*) mélasse raffinée *f.* **~y** *a.* sirupeux.

system /'sɪstəm/ *n.* système *m.*; (*body*) organisme *m.*; (*order*) méthode *f.* **~s analyst**, analyste-programmeu|r, -se *m., f.* **~s disk**, disque système *m.*

systematic /sɪstə'mætɪk/ *a.* systématique.

T

tab /tæb/ *n.* (*flap*) languette *f.*, patte *f.*; (*loop*) attache *f.*; (*label*) étiquette *f.*; (*Amer., fam.*) addition *f.* **keep ~s on**, (*fam.*) surveiller.

table /'teɪbl/ *n.* table *f.* ● *v.t.* présenter; (*postpone*) ajourner. ● *a.* (*lamp, wine*) de table. **at ~**, à table. **lay or set the ~**, mettre la table. **~-cloth** *n.* nappe *f.* **~-mat** *n.* dessous-de-plat *m. invar.*; (*cloth*) set *m.* **~ of**

contents, table des matières *f.* **~ tennis**, ping-pong *m.*

tablespoon /'teɪblspuːn/ *n.* cuiller à soupe *f.* **~ful** *n.* (*pl.* **~fuls**) cuillerée à soupe *f.*

tablet /'tæblɪt/ *n.* (*of stone*) plaque *f.*; (*drug*) comprimé *m.*

tabloid /'tæblɔɪd/ *n.* tabloïd *m.* **the ~ press**, la presse populaire.

taboo /tə'buː/ *n. & a.* tabou (*m.*).

tabulator /'tæbjʊleɪtə(r)/ *n.* (*on typewriter*) tabulateur *m.*

tacit /'tæsɪt/ *a.* tacite.

taciturn /'tæsɪtɜːn/ *a.* taciturne.

tack /tæk/ *n.* (*nail*) brouquette *f.*; (*stitch*) point de bâti *m.*; (*course of action*) voie *f.* ● *v.t.* (*nail*) clouer; (*stitch*) bâtir; (*add*) ajouter. ● *v.i.* (*naut.*) louvoyer.

tackle /'tækl/ *n.* équipement *m.*, matériel *m.*; (*football*) plaquage *m.* ● *v.t.* (*problem etc.*) s'attaquer à; (*football player*) plaquer.

tacky /'tækɪ/ *a.* (**-ier, -iest**) poisseux, pas sec; (*shabby, mean: Amer.*) moche.

tact /tækt/ *n.* tact *m.* **~ful** *a.* plein de tact. **~fully** *adv.* avec tact. **~less** *a.* qui manque de tact. **~lessly** *adv.* sans tact.

tactic /'tæktɪk/ *n.* tactique *f.* **~s** *n. & n. pl.* tactique *f.* **~al** *a.* tactique.

tactile /'tæktaɪl/ *a.* tactile.

tadpole /'tædpəʊl/ *n.* têtard *m.*

tag /tæg/ *n.* (*label*) étiquette *f.*; (*end piece*) bout *m.*; (*phrase*) cliché *m.* ● *v.t.* (*p.t.* **tagged**) étiqueter; (*join*) ajouter. ● *v.i.* **~ along**, (*fam.*) suivre.

tail /teɪl/ *n.* queue *f.*; (*of shirt*) pan *m.* **~s**, (*coat*) habit *m.* **~s!**, (*tossing coin*) pile! ● *v.t.* (*follow*) filer. ● *v.i.* **~ away or off**, diminuer. **~-back** *n.* (*traffic*) bouchon *m.* **~-end** *n.* fin *f.*, bout *m.* **~-gate** *n.* hayon arrière *m.*

tailcoat /'teɪlkəʊt/ *n.* habit *m.*

tailor /'teɪlə(r)/ *n.* tailleur *m.* ● *v.t.* (*garment*) façonner; (*fig.*) adapter. **~-made** *a.* fait sur mesure. **~-made for**, (*fig.*) fait pour.

tainted /'teɪntɪd/ *a.* (*infected*) infecté; (*decayed*) gâté; (*fig.*) souillé.

take /teɪk/ *v.t./i.* (*p.t.* **took**, *p.p.* **taken**) prendre; (*carry*) (ap)porter (**to**, à); (*escort*) accompagner, amener; (*contain*) contenir; (*tolerate*) supporter; (*prize*) remporter; (*exam*) passer; (*choice*) faire; (*precedence*) avoir. **~ sth. from s.o.**, prendre qch. à qn. ~ **sth. from a place,** prendre qch. d'un endroit. ~ **s.o. home,** ramener qn. chez lui. **be ~n by** *or* **with,** être impressionné par. **be ~n ill,** tomber malade. **it ~s time/courage**/*etc.* **to,** il faut du temps/du courage/*etc.* pour. ~ **after,** ressembler à. ~ **apart,** démonter. ~ **away,** (*object*) emporter; (*person*) emmener; (*remove*) enlever (**from,** à). **~-away** *n.* (*meal*) plat à emporter *m.*; (*shop*) restaurant qui fait des plats à emporter *m.* ~ **back,** reprendre; (*return*) rendre; (*accompany*) raccompagner; (*statement*) retirer. ~ **down,** (*object*) descendre; (*notes*) prendre. ~ **in,** (*object*) rentrer; (*include*) inclure; (*cheat*) tromper; (*grasp*) saisir. ~ **it that,** supposer que. ~ **off** *v.t.* enlever; (*mimic*) imiter; *v.i.* (*aviat.*) décoller. **~-off** *n.* imitation *f.*; (*aviat.*) décollage *m.* ~ **on,** (*task, staff, passenger, etc.*) prendre; (*challenger*) relever le défi de. ~ **out,** sortir; (*stain etc.*) enlever. ~ **over** *v.t.* (*factory, country, etc.*) prendre la direction de; (*firm: comm.*) racheter; *v.i.* (*of dictator*) prendre le pouvoir. ~ **over from,** (*relieve*) prendre la relève de; (*succeed*) prendre la succession de. **~-over** *n.* (*pol.*) prise de pouvoir *f.*; (*comm.*) rachat *m.* ~ **part,** participer (**in,** à). ~ **place,** avoir lieu. ~ **sides,** prendre parti (**with,** pour). ~ **to,** se prendre d'amitié pour; (*activity*) prendre goût à. ~ **to doing,** se mettre à faire. ~ **up,** (*object*) monter; (*hobby*) se mettre à; (*occupy*) prendre; (*resume*) reprendre. ~ **up with,** se lier avec.

takings /ˈteɪkɪŋz/ *n. pl.* recette *f.*

talcum /ˈtælkəm/ *n.* talc *m.* ~ **powder,** talc *m.*

tale /teɪl/ *n.* conte *m.*; (*report*) récit *m.*; (*lie*) histoire *f.*

talent /ˈtælənt/ *n.* talent *m.* **~ed** *a.* doué, qui a du talent.

talk /tɔːk/ *v.t./i.* parler; (*say*) dire; (*chat*) bavarder. ● *n.* conversation *f.*, entretien *m.*; (*words*) propos *m. pl.*; (*lecture*) exposé *m.* ~ **into doing,** persuader de faire. ~ **over,** discuter (de). **~-show** *n.* talk-show *m.* **~er** *n.* causeu|r, -se *m.*/*f.* **~ing-to** *n.* (*fam.*) réprimande *f.*

talkative /ˈtɔːkətɪv/ *a.* bavard.

tall /tɔːl/ *a.* (**-er, -est**) (*high*) haut; (*person*) grand. ~ **story,** (*fam.*) histoire invraisemblable *f.*

tallboy /ˈtɔːlbɔɪ/ *n.* commode *f.*

tally /ˈtælɪ/ *v.i.* correspondre (**with,** à), s'accorder (**with,** avec).

tambourine /tæmbəˈriːn/ *n.* tambourin *m.*

tame /teɪm/ *a.* (**-er, -est**) apprivoisé; (*dull*) insipide. ● *v.t.* apprivoiser; (*lion*) dompter. **~r** /-ə(r)/ *n.* dompteu|r, -se *m.*, *f.*

tamper /ˈtæmpə(r)/ *v.i.* ~ **with,** toucher à; tripoter; (*text*) altérer.

tampon /ˈtæmpɒn/ *n.* (*med.*) tampon hygiénique *m.*

tan /tæn/ *v.t./i.* (*p.t.* **tanned**) bronzer; (*hide*) tanner. ● *n.* bronzage *m.* ● *a.* marron clair *invar.*

tandem /ˈtændəm/ *n.* (*bicycle*) tandem *m.* **in ~,** en tandem.

tang /tæŋ/ *n.* (*taste*) saveur forte *f.*; (*smell*) odeur forte *f.*

tangent /ˈtændʒənt/ *n.* tangente *f.*

tangerine /tændʒəˈriːn/ *n.* mandarine *f.*

tangible /ˈtændʒəbl/ *a.* tangible.

tangle /ˈtæŋgl/ *v.t.* enchevêtrer. ● *n.* enchevêtrement *m.* **become ~d,** s'enchevêtrer.

tango /ˈtæŋgəʊ/ *n.* (*pl.* **-os**) tango *m.*

tank /tæŋk/ *n.* réservoir *m.*; (*vat*) cuve *f.*; (*for fish*) aquarium *m.*; (*mil.*) char *m.*, tank *m.*

tankard /ˈtæŋkəd/ *n.* chope *f.*

tanker /ˈtæŋkə(r)/ *n.* camion-citerne *m.*; (*ship*) pétrolier *m.*

tantaliz|**e** /ˈtæntəlaɪz/ *v.t.* tourmenter. **~ing** *a.* tentant.

tantamount /ˈtæntəmaʊnt/ *a.* **be ~ to,** équivaloir à.

tantrum /ˈtæntrəm/ *n.* crise de colère *or* de rage *f.*

tap[1] /tæp/ *n.* (*for water etc.*) robinet *m.* ● *v.t.* (*p.t.* **tapped**) (*resources*) exploiter; (*telephone*) mettre sur table d'écoute. **on ~,** (*fam.*) disponible.

tap[2] /tæp/ *v.t./i.* (*p.t.* **tapped**) frapper (doucement). ● *n.* petit coup *m.* **~-dance** *n.* claquettes *f. pl*

tape /teɪp/ *n.* ruban *m.*; (*sticky*) ruban adhésif *m.* (*magnetic*) bande (magnétique) *f.* ● *v.t.* (*tie*) attacher; (*stick*) coller; (*record*) enregistrer. **~-measure,** mètre (à) ruban *m.* ~ **recorder,** magnétophone *m.*

taper /'teɪpə(r)/ n. (*for lighting*) bougie f. ● v.t./i. (s')effiler. ~ **off**, (*diminish*) diminuer. ~**ed**, ~**ing** adjs. (*fingers etc.*) effilé, fuselé; (*trousers*) étroit du bas.

tapestry /'tæpɪstrɪ/ n. tapisserie f.

tapioca /tæpɪ'əʊkə/ n. tapioca m.

tar /tɑ:(r)/ n. goudron m. ● v.t. (*p.t.* **tarred**) goudronner.

tardy /'tɑ:dɪ/ a. (**-ier, -iest**) (*slow*) lent; (*belated*) tardif.

target /'tɑ:gɪt/ n. cible f.; (*objective*) objectif m. ● v.t. prendre pour cible.

tariff /'tærɪf/ n. (*charges*) tarif m.; (*on imports*) tarif douanier m.

Tarmac /'tɑ:mæk/ n. (P.) macadam (goudronné) m.; (*runway*) piste f.

tarnish /'tɑ:nɪʃ/ v.t./i. (se) ternir.

tarpaulin /tɑ:'pɔ:lɪn/ n. bâche goudronnée f.

tarragon /'tærəgən/ n. estragon m.

tart[1] /tɑ:t/ a. (**-er, -est**) acide.

tart[2] /tɑ:t/ n. tarte f.; (*prostitute*; *sl.*) poule f. ● v.t. ~ **up**, (*pej.*, *sl.*) embellir (sans le moindre goût).

tartan /'tɑ:tn/ n. tartan m. ● a. écossais.

tartar /'tɑ:tə(r)/ n. tartre m. ~ **sauce**, sauce tartare f.

task /tɑ:sk/ n. tâche f., travail m. **take to** ~, réprimander. ~ **force**, détachement spécial m.

tassel /'tæsl/ n. gland m., pompon m.

taste /teɪst/ n. goût m. ● v.t. (*eat, enjoy*) goûter; (*try*) goûter à; (*perceive taste of*) sentir le goût de. ● v.i. ~ **of** or **like**, avoir un goût de. **have a** ~ **of**, (*experience*) goûter de. ~**less** a. sans goût; (*fig.*) de mauvais goût.

tasteful /'teɪstfl/ a. de bon goût. ~**ly** adv. avec goût.

tasty /'teɪstɪ/ a. (**-ier, -iest**) délicieux, savoureux.

tat /tæt/ see tit[2].

tatter|**s** /'tætəz/ n. pl. lambeaux m. pl. ~**ed** /'tætəd/ a. en lambeaux.

tattoo[1] /tə'tu:/ n. (*mil.*) spectacle militaire m.

tattoo[2] /tə'tu:/ v.t. tatouer. ● n. tatouage m.

tatty /'tætɪ/ a. (**-ier, -iest**) (*shabby*: *fam.*) miteux, minable.

taught /tɔ:t/ see teach.

taunt /tɔ:nt/ v.t. railler. ● n. raillerie f. ~**ing** a. railleur.

Taurus /'tɔ:rəs/ n. le Taureau.

taut /tɔ:t/ a. tendu.

tavern /'tævn/ n. taverne f.

tawdry /'tɔ:drɪ/ a. (**-ier, -iest**) (*showy*) tape-à-l'œil invar.

tax /tæks/ n. taxe f., impôt m.; (*on income*) impôts m. pl. ● v.t. imposer; (*put to test*: *fig.*) mettre à l'épreuve. ~**able** a. imposable. ~**ation** /-'seɪʃn/ n. imposition f.; (*taxes*) impôts m. pl. ~**-collector** n. percepteur m. ~**-deductible** a. déductible d'impôts. ~ **disc**, vignette f. ~**-free** a. exempt d'impôts. ~**ing** a. (*fig.*) éprouvant. ~ **haven** paradis fiscal m. ~ **inspector**, inspecteur des impôts m. ~ **relief**, dégrèvement fiscal m. ~ **return**, déclaration d'impôts f.

taxi /'tæksɪ/ n. (*pl.* **-is**) taxi m. ● v.i. (*p.t.* **taxied**, *pres. p.* **taxiing**) (*aviat.*) rouler au sol. ~**-cab** n. taxi m. ~ **rank**, (*Amer.*) ~ **stand**, station de taxi f.

taxpayer /'tækspeɪə(r)/ n. contribuable m./f.

tea /ti:/ n. thé m.; (*snack*) goûter m. ~**-bag** n. sachet de thé m. ~**-break** n. pause-thé f. ~**-leaf** n. feuille de thé f. ~**-set** n. service à thé m. ~**-shop** n. salon de thé m. ~**-towel** n. torchon m.

teach /ti:tʃ/ v.t. (*p.t.* **taught**) apprendre (**s.o. sth.**, qch. à qn.); (*in school*) enseigner (**s.o. sth.**, qch. à qn.). ● v.i. enseigner. ~**er** n. professeur m.; (*primary*) institu|teur, -trice m., f.; (*member of teaching profession*) enseignant(e) m. (f.). ~**ing** n. enseignement m.; a. pédagogique; (*staff*) enseignant.

teacup /'ti:kʌp/ n. tasse à thé f.

teak /ti:k/ n. (*wood*) teck m.

team /ti:m/ n. équipe f.; (*of animals*) attelage m. ● v.i. ~ **up**, faire équipe (**with**, avec). ~**- work** n. travail d'équipe m.

teapot /'ti:pɒt/ n. théière f.

tear[1] /teə(r)/ v.t./i. (*p.t.* **tore**, *p.p.* **torn**) (se) déchirer; (*snatch*) arracher (**from**, à); (*rush*) aller à toute vitesse. ● n. déchirure f.

tear[2] /tɪə(r)/ n. larme f. **in** ~**s**, en larmes. ~**-gas** n. gaz lacrymogène m.

tearful /'tɪəfl/ a. (*voice*) larmoyant; (*person*) en larmes. ~**ly** adv. en pleurant, les larmes aux yeux.

tease /ti:z/ v.t. taquiner. ● n. (*person*: *fam.*) taquin(e) m. f.

teaspoon /'ti:spu:n/ n. petite cuiller f. ~**ful** n. (*pl.* **-fuls**) cuillerée à café f.

teat /tiːt/ *n.* (*of bottle, animal*) tétine *f.*

technical /ˈteknɪkl/ *a.* technique. **~ity** /-ˈkælətɪ/ *n.* détail technique *m.* **~ly** *adv.* techniquement.

technician /tekˈnɪʃn/ *n.* technicien(ne) *m.* (*f.*).

technique /tekˈniːk/ *n.* technique *f.*

technolog|y /tekˈnɒlədʒɪ/ *n.* technologie *f.* **~ical** /-əˈlɒdʒɪkl/ *a.* technologique.

teddy /ˈtedɪ/ *a.* **~ bear,** ours en peluche *m.*

tedious /ˈtiːdɪəs/ *a.* fastidieux.

tedium /ˈtiːdɪəm/ *n.* ennui *m.*

tee /tiː/ *n.* (*golf*) tee *m.*

teem¹ /tiːm/ *v.i.* (*swarm*) grouiller (**with,** de).

teem² /tiːm/ *v.i.* **~ (with rain),** pleuvoir à torrents.

teenage /ˈtiːneɪdʒ/ *a.* (d')adolescent. **~d** *a.* adolescent. **~r** /-ə(r)/ *n.* adolescent(e) *m.* (*f.*).

teens /tiːnz/ *n. pl.* **in one's ~,** adolescent.

teeny /ˈtiːnɪ/ *a.* (**-ier, -iest**) (*tiny: fam.*) minuscule.

teeter /ˈtiːtə(r)/ *v.i.* chanceler.

teeth /tiːθ/ *see* tooth.

teeth|e /tiːð/ *v.i.* faire ses dents. **~ing troubles,** (*fig.*) difficultés initiales *f. pl.*

teetotaller /tiːˈtəʊtlə(r)/ *n.* personne qui ne boit pas d'alcool *f.*

telecommunications /telɪkəmjuː-nɪˈkeɪʃnz/ *n. pl.* télécommunications *f. pl.*

telegram /ˈtelɪgræm/ *n.* télégramme *m.*

telegraph /ˈtelɪgrɑːf/ *n.* télégraphe *m.* ● *a.* télégraphique. **~ic** /-ˈgræfɪk/ *a.* télégraphique.

telepath|y /tɪˈlepəθɪ/ *n.* télépathie *f.* **~ic** /telɪˈpæθɪk/ *a.* télépathique.

telephone /ˈtelɪfəʊn/ *n.* téléphone *m.* ● *v.t.* (*person*) téléphoner à; (*message*) téléphoner. ● *v.i.* téléphoner. **~ book,** annuaire *m.* **~ box** *n.,* **~ booth,** cabine téléphonique *f.* **~ call,** coup de téléphone *m.* **~ number,** numéro de téléphone *m.*

telephonist /tɪˈlefənɪst/ *n.* (*in exchange*) téléphoniste *m./f.*

telephoto /telɪˈfəʊtəʊ/ *a.* **~ lens,** téléobjectif *m.*

telescop|e /ˈtelɪskəʊp/ *n.* télescope *m.* ● *v.t./i.* (se) télescoper. **~ic** /-ˈskɒpɪk/ *a.* télescopique.

teletext /ˈtelɪtekst/ *n.* télétexte *m.*

televise /ˈtelɪvaɪz/ *v.t.* téléviser.

television /ˈtelɪvɪʒn/ *n.* télévision *f.* **~ set,** poste de télévision *m.*

telex /ˈteleks/ *n.* télex *m.* ● *v.t.* envoyer par télex.

tell /tel/ *v.t.* (*p.t.* **told**) dire (**s.o. sth.,** qch. à qn.); (*story*) raconter; (*distinguish*) distinguer. ● *v.i.* avoir un effet; (*know*) savoir. **~ of,** parler de. **~ off,** (*fam.*) gronder. **~-tale** *n.* rapporteu|r, -se *m., f.*; *a.* révélateur. **~ tales,** rapporter.

teller /ˈtelə(r)/ *n.* (*in bank*) caiss|ier, -ière *m., f.*

telling /ˈtelɪŋ/ *a.* révélateur.

telly /ˈtelɪ/ *n.* (*fam.*) télé *f.*

temerity /tɪˈmerətɪ/ *n.* témérité *f.*

temp /temp/ *n.* (*temporary employee: fam.*) intérimaire *m./f.* ● *v.i.* faire de l'intérim.

temper /ˈtempə(r)/ *n.* humeur *f.*; (*anger*) colère *f.* ● *v.t.* (*metal*) tremper; (*fig.*) tempérer. **lose one's ~,** se mettre en colère.

temperament /ˈtemprəmənt/ *n.* tempérament *m.* **~al** /-ˈmentl/ *a.* capricieux; (*innate*) inné.

temperance /ˈtempərəns/ *n.* (*in drinking*) tempérance *f.*

temperate /ˈtempərət/ *a.* tempéré.

temperature /ˈtemprətʃə(r)/ *n.* température *f.* **have a ~,** avoir (de) la fièvre *or* de la température.

tempest /ˈtempɪst/ *n.* tempête *f.*

tempestuous /temˈpestʃʊəs/ *a.* (*meeting etc.*) orageux.

template /ˈtempl(e)ɪt/ *n.* patron *m.*

temple¹ /ˈtempl/ *n.* temple *m.*

temple² /ˈtempl/ *n.* (*of head*) tempe *f.*

tempo /ˈtempəʊ/ *n.* (*pl.* **-os**) tempo *m.*

temporal /ˈtempərəl/ *a.* temporel.

temporar|y /ˈtemprərɪ/ *a.* temporaire, provisoire. **~ily** *adv.* temporairement, provisoirement.

tempt /tempt/ *v.t.* tenter. **~ s.o. to do,** donner envie à qn. de faire. **~ation** /-ˈteɪʃn/ *n.* tentation *f.* **~ing** *a.* tentant.

ten /ten/ *a. & n.* dix (*m.*).

tenable /ˈtenəbl/ *a.* défendable.

tenac|ious /tɪˈneɪʃəs/ *a.* tenace. **~ity** /-ˈæsətɪ/ *n.* ténacité *f.*

tenancy /ˈtenənsɪ/ *n.* location *f.*

tenant /ˈtenənt/ *n.* locataire *m./f.*

tend¹ /tend/ *v.t.* s'occuper de.

tend² /tend/ *v.i.* **~ to,** (*be apt to*) avoir tendance à.

tendency /ˈtendənsɪ/ *n.* tendance *f.*

tender¹ /'tendə(r)/ a. tendre; (*sore*, *painful*) sensible. **~ly** adv. tendrement. **~ness** n. tendresse f.

tender² /'tendə(r)/ v.t. offrir, donner. ● v.i. faire une soumission. ● n. (*comm.*) soumission f. **be legal ~**, (*money*) avoir cours. **put sth. out to ~**, faire un appel d'offres pour qch.

tendon /'tendən/ n. tendon m.

tenement /'tenəmənt/ n. maison de rapport f., H.L.M. m./f.; (*slum*: *Amer.*) taudis m.

tenet /'tenɪt/ n. principe m.

tenner /'tenə(r)/ n. (*fam.*) billet de dix livres m.

tennis /'tenɪs/ n. tennis m. ● a. de tennis **~ shoes**, tennis m. pl.

tenor /'tenə(r)/ n. (*meaning*) sens général m.; (*mus.*) ténor m.

tense¹ /tens/ n. (*gram.*) temps m.

tense² /tens/ a. (**-er, -est**) tendu. ● v.t. (*muscles*) tendre, raidir. ● v.i. (*of face*) se crisper. **~ness** n. tension f.

tension /'tenʃn/ n. tension f.

tent /tent/ n. tente f.

tentacle /'tentəkl/ n. tentacule m.

tentative /'tentətɪv/ a. provisoire; (*hesitant*) timide. **~ly** adv. provisoirement; timidement.

tenterhooks /'tentəhʊks/ n. pl. **on ~**, sur des charbons ardents.

tenth /tenθ/ a. & n. dixième (m./f.).

tenuous /'tenjʊəs/ a. ténu.

tenure /'tenjʊə(r)/ n. (*in job*, *office*) (période de) jouissance f. **have ~**, être titulaire.

tepid /'tepɪd/ a. tiède.

term /tɜːm/ n. (*word*, *limit*) terme m.; (*of imprisonment*) temps m.; (*in school etc.*) trimestre m.; (*Amer.*) semestre m. **~s**, conditions f. pl. ● v.t. appeler, **on good/bad ~s**, en bons/mauvais termes. **in the short/long ~**, à court/long terme **come to ~s**, arriver à un accord. **come to ~s with sth.**, accepter qch. **~ of office**, (*pol.*) mandat m.

terminal /'tɜːmɪnl/ a. terminal, final; (*med.*) en phase terminale. ● n. (*oil*, *computer*) terminal m.; (*rail.*) terminus m.; (*electr.*) borne f. (**air**) **~**, aérogare f.

terminate /'tɜːmɪneɪt/ v.t. mettre fin à. ● v.i. prendre fin. **~ion** /-'neɪʃn/ n. fin f.

terminology /tɜːmɪ'nɒlədʒɪ/ n. terminologie f.

terminus /'tɜːmɪnəs/ n. (pl. **-ni** /-naɪ/) (*station*) terminus m.

terrace /'terəs/ n. terrasse f.; (*houses*) rangée de maisons contiguës f. **the ~s**, (*sport*) les gradins m. pl.

terracotta /terə'kɒtə/ n. terre cuite f.

terrain /te'reɪn/ n. terrain m.

terrible /'terəbl/ a. affreux, atroce. **~y** adv. affreusement; (*very*) terriblement.

terrier /'terɪə(r)/ n. (*dog*) terrier m.

terrific /tə'rɪfɪk/ a. (*fam.*) terrible. **~ally** /-klɪ/ adv. (*very*: *fam.*) terriblement; (*very well*: *fam.*) terriblement bien.

terrify /'terɪfaɪ/ v.t. terrifier. **be ~ied of**, avoir très peur de.

territorial /terɪ'tɔːrɪəl/ a. territorial.

territory /'terɪtərɪ/ n. territoire m.

terror /'terə(r)/ n. terreur f.

terrorist /'terərɪst/ n. terroriste m./f. **~m** /-zəm/ n. terrorisme m.

terrorize /'terəraɪz/ v.t. terroriser.

terse /tɜːs/ a. concis, laconique.

test /test/ n. examen m., analyse f.; (*of goods*) contrôle m.; (*of machine etc.*) essai m.; (*in school*) interrogation f.; (*of strength etc.*: *fig.*) épreuve f. ● v.t. examiner, analyser; (*check*) contrôler; (*try*) essayer; (*pupil*) donner une interrogation à; (*fig.*) éprouver. **driving ~**, (épreuve f. du) permis de conduire m. **~ match**, match international m. **~ pilot** pilote d'essai m. **~-tube** n. éprouvette f.

testament /'testəmənt/ n. testament m. **Old/New T~**, Ancien/Nouveau Testament m.

testicle /'testɪkl/ n. testicule m.

testify /'testɪfaɪ/ v.t./i. témoigner (**to**, de). **~ that**, témoigner que.

testimony /'testɪmənɪ/ n. témoignage m.

testy /'testɪ/ a. grincheux.

tetanus /'tetənəs/ n. tétanos m.

tetchy /'tetʃɪ/ a. grincheux.

tether /'teðə(r)/ v.t. attacher. ● n. **at the end of one's ~**, à bout.

text /tekst/ n. texte m.

textbook /'tekstbʊk/ n. manuel m.

textile /'tekstaɪl/ n. & a. textile (m.).

texture /'tekstʃə(r)/ n. (*of paper etc.*) grain m.; (*of fabric*) texture f.

Thai /taɪ/ a. & n. thaïlandais(e) (m. (f.)). **~land** n. Thaïlande f.

Thames /temz/ n. Tamise f.

than /ðæn, *unstressed* ðən/ *conj.* que, qu'*; (*with numbers*) de. **more/less ~ ten**, plus/moins de dix.

thank /θæŋk/ *v.t.* remercier. **~s** *n. pl.* remerciements *m. pl.* **~ you!**, merci! **~s!**, (*fam.*) merci! **~s to**, grâce à. **T~sgiving (Day)**, (*Amer.*) jour d'action de grâces *m.* (*fête nationale*).

thankful /'θæŋkfl/ *a.* reconnaissant (**for**, de). **~ly** *adv.* (*happily*) heureusement.

thankless /'θæŋklɪs/ *a.* ingrat.

that /ðæt, *unstressed* ðet/ *a. pl.* **those** ce *or* c*. cette. **those**, ces. ● *pron.* ce *or* c*, cela, ça. **~ (one)**, celui-là, celle-là. **those (ones)**, ceux-là, celles-là. ● *adv.* si, aussi. ● *rel. pron.* (*subject*) qui; (*object*) que, qu'*. ● *conj.* que, qu'*. ● **boy**, ce garçon (*with emphasis*) ce garçon-là. **~ is**, c'est. **~ is (to say)**, c'est-à-dire. **after ~**, après ça *or* cela. **the day ~**, le jour où. **the man ~ married her**, l'homme qui l'a épousée. **the man ~ she married**, l'homme qu'elle a épousé. **the car ~ I came in**, la voiture dans laquelle je suis venu. **~ big**, grand comme ça. **~ many**, **~ much**, tant que ça.

thatch /θætʃ/ *n.* chaume *m.* **~ed** *a.* en chaume. **~ed cottage**, chaumière *f.*

thaw /θɔː/ *v.t./i.* (faire) dégeler; (*snow*) (faire) fondre. ● *n.* dégel *m.*

the /*before vowel* ðɪ, *before consonant* ðə, *stressed* ðiː/ *a.* le *or* l'*, la *or* l'*, *pl.* les. **of ~, from ~**, du, de l'*, de la, *pl.* des. **to ~, at ~**, au, à l'*, à la, *pl.* aux. **~ third of June**, le trois juin.

theatre /'θɪətə(r)/ *n.* théâtre *m.*

theatrical /θɪ'ætrɪkl/ *a.* théâtral.

theft /θeft/ *n.* vol *m.*

their /ðeə(r)/ *a.* leur, *pl.* leurs.

theirs /ðeəz/ *poss. pron.* le *or* la leur, les leurs.

them /ðem, *unstressed* ðəm/ *pron.* les; (*after prep.*) eux, elles. **(to) ~**, leur. **I know ~**, je les connais.

theme /θiːm/ *n.* thème *m.* **~ song**, (*in film etc.*) chanson principale *f.*

themselves /ðəm'selvz/ *pron.* eux-mêmes, elles-mêmes; (*reflexive*) se; (*after prep.*) eux, elles.

then /ðen/ *adv.* alors; (*next*) ensuite, puis; (*therefore*) alors, donc. ● *a.* d'alors. **from ~ on**, dès lors.

theology /θɪ'ɒlədʒɪ/ *n.* théologie *f.* **~ian** /θɪə'ləʊdʒən/ *n.* théologien(ne) *m.* (*f.*).

theorem /'θɪərəm/ *n.* théorème *m.*

theory /'θɪərɪ/ *n.* théorie *f.* **~etical** /-'retɪkl/ *a.* théorique.

therapeutic /θerə'pjuːtɪk/ *a.* thérapeutique.

therapy /'θerəpɪ/ *n.* thérapie *f.*

there /ðeə(r)/ *adv.* là; (*with verb*) y; (*over there*) là-bas. ● *int.* allez. **he goes**, il y va. **on ~**, là-dessus. **~ is**, **~ are**, il y a; (*pointing*) voilà. **~, ~!**, allons, allons! **~abouts** *adv.* par là. **~after** *adv.* par la suite. **~by** *adv.* de cette manière.

therefore /'ðeəfɔː(r)/ *adv.* donc.

thermal /'θɜːml/ *a.* thermique.

thermometer /θə'mɒmɪtə(r)/ *n.* thermomètre *m.*

thermonuclear /θɜːməʊ'njuːklɪə(r)/ *a.* thermonucléaire.

Thermos /'θɜːməs/ *n.* (P.) thermos *m./ f. invar.* (P.).

thermostat /'θɜːməstæt/ *n.* thermostat *m.*

thesaurus /θɪ'sɔːrəs/ *n.* (*pl.* **-ri** /-raɪ/) dictionnaire de synonymes *m.*

these /ðiːz/ *see* this.

thesis /'θiːsɪs/ *n.* (*pl.* **theses** /-siːz/) thèse *f.*

they /ðeɪ/ *pron.* ils, elles; (*emphatic*) eux, elles; (*people in general*) on.

thick /θɪk/ *a.* (**-er, -est**) épais; (*stupid*) bête; (*friends: fam.*) très lié. ● *adv.* = **thickly**. ● *n.* **in the ~ of**, au plus gros de. **~ly** *adv.* (*grow*) dru; (*spread*) en couche épaisse. **~ness** *n.* épaisseur *f.* **~-skinned** *a.* peu sensible.

thicken /'θɪkən/ *v.t./i.* (s')épaissir.

thickset /θɪk'set/ *a.* trapu.

thief /θiːf/ *n.* (*pl.* **thieves**) voleu|r, -se *m.*, *f.*

thigh /θaɪ/ *n.* cuisse *f.*

thimble /'θɪmbl/ *n.* dé (à coudre) *m.*

thin /θɪn/ *a.* (**thinner, thinnest**) mince; (*person*) maigre, mince; (*sparse*) clairsemé; (*fine*) fin. ● *adv.* = **thinly**. ● *v.t./i.* (*p.t.* **thinned**) (*liquid*) (s')éclaircir. **~ out**, (*in quantity*) (s')éclaircir. **~ly** *adv.* (*slightly*) légèrement. **~ner** *n.* diluant *m.* **~ness** *n.* minceur *f.*; maigreur *f.*

thing /θɪŋ/ *n.* chose *f.* **~s**, (*belongings*) affaires *f. pl.* **the best ~ is to**, le mieux est de. **the (right) ~**, ce qu'il faut (**for s.o.**, à qn.).

think /θɪŋk/ *v.t./i.* (*p.t.* **thought**) penser (**about, of**, à); (*carefully*) réfléchir (**about, of**, à); (*believe*) croire. **I ~ so**, je crois que oui. **~ better of it**, se raviser. **~ nothing of**, trouver naturel de. **~ of**, (*hold opinion of*) penser de. **I'm ~ing of going**, je pense que j'irai peut-être. **~ over**, bien réfléchir à. **~tank** n. comité d'experts m. **~ up**, inventer. **~er** n. penseu|r, -se m., f.

third /θɜːd/ a. troisième. ● n. troisième m./f.; (*fraction*) tiers m. **~ly** adv. troisièmement. **~-rate** a. très inférieur. **T~ World**, Tiers-Monde m.

thirst /θɜːst/ n. soif f. **~y** a. **be ~y**, avoir soif. **make ~y**, donner soif à.

thirteen /θɜːˈtiːn/ a. & n. treize (m.). **~th** a. & n. treizième (m./f.).

thirt|y /ˈθɜːtɪ/ a. & n. trente (m.). **~ieth** a. & n. trentième (m./f.).

this /ðɪs/ a. (pl. **these**) ce or cet*, cette. **these**, ces. ● pron. ce or c*, ceci. **~ (one)**, celui-ci, celle-ci. **these (ones)**, ceux-ci, celles-ci. **~ boy**, ce garçon; (*with emphasis*) ce garçon-ci. **~ is a mistake**, c'est une erreur. **~ is the book**, voici le livre. **~ is my son**, je vous présente mon fils. **~ is Anne speaking**, c'est Anne à l'appareil. **after ~**, après ceci.

thistle /ˈθɪsl/ n. chardon m.

thorn /θɔːn/ n. épine f. **~y** a. épineux.

thorough /ˈθʌrə/ a. consciencieux; (*deep*) profond; (*cleaning, washing*) à fond. **~ly** adv. (*clean, study, etc.*) à fond; (*very*) tout à fait.

thoroughbred /ˈθʌrəbred/ n. (*horse etc.*) pur-sang m. invar.

thoroughfare /ˈθʌrəfeə(r)/ n. grande artère f.

those /ðəʊz/ see that.

though /ðəʊ/ conj. bien que. ● adv. (*fam.*) cependant.

thought /θɔːt/ see think. ● n. pensée f.; (*idea*) idée f.

thoughtful /ˈθɔːtfl/ a. pensif; (*considerate*) attentionné. **~ly** adv. pensivement; avec considération.

thoughtless /ˈθɔːtlɪs/ a. étourdi. **~ly** adv. étourdiment.

thousand /ˈθaʊznd/ a. & n. mille (m. invar.). **~s of**, des milliers de.

thrash /θræʃ/ v.t. rosser; (*defeat*) écraser. **~ about**, se débattre. **~ out**, discuter à fond.

thread /θred/ n. (*yarn & fig.*) fil m.; (*of screw*) pas m. ● v.t. enfiler. **~ one's way**, se faufiler.

threadbare /ˈθredbeə(r)/ a. râpé.

threat /θret/ n. menace f.

threaten /ˈθretn/ v.t./i. menacer (**with**, de). **~ingly** adv. d'un air menaçant.

three /θriː/ a. & n. trois (m.). **~-dimensional** a. en trois dimensions.

thresh /θreʃ/ v.t. (*corn etc.*) battre.

threshold /ˈθreʃəʊld/ n. seuil m.

threw /θruː/ see throw.

thrift /θrɪft/ n. économie f. **~y** a. économe.

thrill /θrɪl/ n. émotion f., frisson m. ● v.t. transporter (de joie). ● v.i. frissonner (de joie). **be ~ed**, être ravi. **~ing** a. excitant.

thriller /ˈθrɪlə(r)/ n. livre or film à suspense m.

thriv|e /θraɪv/ v.i. (p.t. **thrived** or **throve**, p.p. **thrived** or **thriven**) prospérer. **he ~es on it**, cela lui réussit. **~ing** a. prospère.

throat /θrəʊt/ n. gorge f. **have a sore ~**, avoir mal à la gorge.

throb /θrɒb/ v.i. (p.t. **throbbed**) (*wound*) causer des élancements; (*heart*) palpiter; (*fig.*) vibrer. ● n. (*pain*) élancement m.; palpitation f. **~bing** a. (*pain*) lancinant.

throes /θrəʊz/ n. pl. **in the ~ of**, au milieu de, aux prises avec.

thrombosis /θrɒmˈbəʊsɪs/ n. thrombose f.

throne /θrəʊn/ n. trône m.

throng /θrɒŋ/ n. foule f. ● v.t. (*streets etc.*) se presser dans. ● v.i. (*arrive*) affluer.

throttle /ˈθrɒtl/ n. (*auto.*) accélérateur m. ● v.t. étrangler.

through /θruː/ prep. à travers; (*during*) pendant; (*by means or way of, out of*) par; (*by reason of*) grâce à, à cause de. ● adv. à travers; (*entirely*) jusqu'au bout. ● a. (*train etc.*) direct. **be ~**, (*finished*) avoir fini. **come** or **go ~**, (*cross, pierce*) traverser. **I'm putting you ~**, je vous passe votre correspondant.

throughout /θruːˈaʊt/ prep. **~ the country**/etc., dans tout le pays/etc. **~ the day**/etc., pendant toute la journée/etc. ● adv. (*place*) partout; (*time*) tout le temps.

throw /θrəʊ/ v.t. (p.t. **threw**, p.p. **thrown**) jeter, lancer; (*baffle: fam.*) déconcerter. ● n. jet m.; (*of dice*) coup m. **~ a party**, (*fam.*) faire une fête. **~ away**, jeter. **~-away** a. à jeter. **~ off**, (*get rid of*) se débarrasser de. **~ out**, jeter; (*person*) expulser; (*reject*) rejeter. **~ over**, (*desert*) plaquer. ~ **up,** (*one's arms*) lever; (*resign from*) abandonner; (*vomit: fam.*) vomir.

thru /θru:/ *prep., adv. & a.* (*Amer.*) = **through.**

thrush /θrʌʃ/ *n.* (*bird*) grive *f.*

thrust /θrʌst/ *v.t.* (*p.t.* **thrust**) pousser. ● *n.* poussée *f.* ~ **into,** (*put*) enforcer dans, mettre dans. ~ **upon,** (*force on*) imposer à.

thud /θʌd/ *n.* bruit sourd *m.*

thug /θʌg/ *n.* voyou *m.*, bandit *m.*

thumb /θʌm/ *n.* pouce *m.* ● *v.t.* (*book*) feuilleter. ~ **a lift,** faire de l'auto-stop. ~**-index,** répertoire à onglets *m.*

thumbtack /'θʌmtæk/ *n.* (*Amer.*) punaise *f.*

thump /θʌmp/ *v.t./i.* cogner (sur); (*of heart*) battre fort. ● *n.* grand coup *m.* ~**ing** *a.* (*fam.*) énorme.

thunder /'θʌndə(r)/ *n.* tonnerre *m.* ● *v.i.* (*weather, person, etc.*) tonner. ~ **past,** passer dans un bruit de tonnerre. ~**y** *a.* orageux.

thunderbolt /'θʌndəbəʊlt/ *n.* coup de foudre *m.*; (*event: fig.*) coup de tonnerre *m.*

thunderstorm /'θʌndəstɔːm/ *n.* orage *m.*

Thursday /'θɜːzdɪ/ *n.* jeudi *m.*

thus /ðʌs/ *adv.* ainsi.

thwart /θwɔːt/ *v.t.* contrecarrer.

thyme /taɪm/ *n.* thym *m.*

thyroid /'θaɪrɔɪd/ *n.* thyroïde *f.*

tiara /tɪ'ɑːrə/ *n.* diadème *m.*

tic /tɪk/ *n.* tic (nerveux) *m.*

tick[1] /tɪk/ *n.* (*sound*) tic-tac *m.*; (*mark*) coche *f.*; (*moment: fam.*) instant *m.* ● *v.i.* faire tic-tac. ● *v.t.* ~ **(off),** cocher. ~ **off,** (*fam.*) réprimander. ~ **over,** (*engine, factory*) tourner au ralenti.

tick[2] /tɪk/ *n.* (*insect*) tique *f.*

ticket /'tɪkɪt/ *n.* billet *m.*; (*for bus, cloakroom, etc.*) ticket *m.*; (*label*) étiquette *f.* ~**-collector** *n.* contrôleu|r, -se *m., f.* ~**-office** *n.* guichet *m.*

tickle /'tɪkl/ *v.t.* chatouiller; (*amuse: fig.*) amuser. ● *n.* chatouillement *m.*

ticklish /'tɪklɪʃ/ *a.* chatouilleux.

tidal /'taɪdl/ *a.* qui a des marées. ~ **wave,** raz-de-marée *m. invar.*

tiddly-winks /'tɪdlɪwɪŋks/ *n.* (*game*) jeu de puce *m.*

tide /taɪd/ *n.* marée *f.*; (*of events*) cours *m.* ● *v.t.* ~ **over,** dépanner.

tidings /'taɪdɪŋz/ *n. pl.* nouvelles *f. pl.*

tid|y /'taɪdɪ/ *a.* (**-ier, -iest**) (*room*) rangé; (*appearance, work*) soigné; (*methodical*) ordonné; (*amount: fam.*) joli. ● *v.t./i.* ranger. ~**y o.s.,** s'arranger. ~**ily** *adv.* avec soin. ~**iness** *n.* ordre *m.*

tie /taɪ/ *v.t.* (*pres. p.* **tying**) attacher, nouer; (*a knot*) faire; (*link*) lier. ● *v.i.* (*darts etc.*) finir à égalité de points; (*football*) faire match nul; (*in race*) être ex aequo. ● *n.* attache *f.*; (*necktie*) cravate *f.*; (*link*) lien *m.*; égalité (de points) *f.*; match nul *m.* ~ **down,** attacher; (*job*) bloquer. ~ **s.o. down to,** (*date*) forcer qn. à respecter. ~ **in with,** être lié à. ~ **up,** attacher; (*money*) immobiliser; (*occupy*) occuper. ~**-up** *n.* (*link*) lien *m.*; (*auto., Amer.*) bouchon *m.*

tier /tɪə(r)/ *n.* étage *m.*, niveau *m.*; (*in stadium etc.*) gradin *m.*

tiff /tɪf/ *n.* petite querelle *f.*

tiger /'taɪgə(r)/ *n.* tigre *m.*

tight /taɪt/ *a.* (**-er, -est**) (*clothes*) étroit, juste; (*rope*) tendu; (*lid*) solidement fixé; (*control*) strict; (*knot, collar, schedule*) serré; (*drunk: fam.*) ivre. ● *adv.* (*hold, sleep, etc.*) bien; (*squeeze*) fort. ~ **corner,** situation difficile *f.* ~**-fisted** *a.* avare. ~**ly** *adv.* bien; (*squeeze*) fort.

tighten /'taɪtn/ *v.t./i.* (se) tendre; (*bolt etc.*) (se) resserrer; (*control etc.*) renforcer. ~ **up on,** se montrer plus strict à l'égard de

tightrope /'taɪtrəʊp/ *n.* corde raide *f.* ~ **walker,** funambule *m./f.*

tights /taɪts/ *n. pl.* collant *m.*

tile /taɪl/ *n.* (*on wall, floor*) carreau *m.*; (*on roof*) tuile *f.* ● *v.t.* carreler; couvrir de tuiles.

till[1] /tɪl/ *v.t.* (*land*) cultiver.

till[2] /tɪl/ *prep. & conj.* = **until.**

till[3] /tɪl/ *n.* caisse (enregistreuse) *f.*

tilt /tɪlt/ *v.i./i.* pencher. ● *n.* (*slope*) inclinaison *f.* **(at) full ~,** à toute vitesse.

timber /'tɪmbə(r)/ *n.* bois (de construction) *m.*; (*trees*) arbres *m. pl.*

time /taɪm/ *n.* temps *m.*; (*moment*) moment *m.*; (*epoch*) époque *f.*; (*by clock*) heure *f.*; (*occasion*) fois *f.*; (*rhythm*) mesure *f.* ~**s,** (*multiplying*) fois *f. pl.* ● *v.t.* choisir le moment de; (*measure*) mesurer; (*sport*) chronométrer. **any ~,** n'importe quand. **behind the ~s,** en retard sur son temps. **for the ~ being**, pour le moment. **from ~ to time**, de temps en temps. **have a good ~**, s'amuser. **in no ~**, en un rien de temps. **in ~**, à temps; (*eventually*) avec le temps. **a long ~**, longtemps. **on ~**, à l'heure. **what's the ~?**, quelle heure est-il? **~ bomb**, bombe à retardement *f.* **~-honoured** *a.* consacré (par l'usage). **~-lag** *n.* décalage *m.* **~-limit** *n.* délai *m.* **~-scale** *n.* délais fixés par. **~ pl.* **~ off**, du temps libre. **~ zone**, fuseau horaire *m.*

timeless /'taɪmlɪs/ *a.* éternel.

timely /'taɪmlɪ/ *a.* à propos.

timer /'taɪmə(r)/ *n.* (*for cooker etc.*) minuteur *m.*; (*on video*) programmateur; (*culin.*) compte-minutes *m. invar.*; (*with sand*) sablier *m.*

timetable /'taɪmteɪbl/ *n.* horaire *m.*

timid /'tɪmɪd/ *a.* timide; (*fearful*) peureux. **~ly** *adv.* timidement.

timing /'taɪmɪŋ/ *n.* (*measuring*) minutage *m.*; (*moment*) moment *m.*; (*of artist*) rythme *m.*

tin /tɪn/ *n.* étain *m.*; (*container*) boîte *f.* **~(plate)**, fer-blanc *m.* ● *v.t.* (*p.t.* **tinned**) mettre en boîte. **~ foil**, papier d'aluminium *m.* **~ny** *a.* métallique. **~-opener** *n.* ouvre-boîte(s) *m.*

tinge /tɪndʒ/ *v.t.* teinter (**with**, de). ● *n.* teinte *f.*

tingle /'tɪŋgl/ *v.i.* (*prickle*) picoter. ● *n.* picotement *m.*

tinker /'tɪŋkə(r)/ *n.* rétameur *m.* ● *v.i.* **~ (with)**, bricoler.

tinkle /'tɪŋkl/ *n.* tintement *m.*; (*fam.*) coup de téléphone *m.*

tinsel /'tɪnsl/ *n.* cheveux d'ange *m. pl.*, guirlandes de Noël *f. pl.*

tint /tɪnt/ *n.* teinte *f.*; (*for hair*) shampooing colorant *m.* ● *v.t.* (*glass, paper*) teinter.

tiny /'taɪnɪ/ *a.* (**-ier, -iest**) minuscule, tout petit.

tip [1] /tɪp/ *n.* bout *m.*; (*cover*) embout *m.* **~ped cigarette**, cigarette (à bout) filtre *f.*

tip [2] /tɪp/ *v.t./i.* (*p.t.* **tipped**) (*tilt*) pencher; (*overturn*) (faire) basculer; (*pour*) verser; (*empty*) déverser; (*give money*) donner un pourboire à. ● *n.* (*money*) pourboire *m.*; (*advice*) tuyau *m.*; (*for rubbish*) décharge *f.* **~ off**, prévenir. **~-off** *n.* tuyau *m.* (*pour prévenir*).

tipsy /'tɪpsɪ/ *a.* un peu ivre, gris.

tiptoe /'tɪptəʊ/ *n.* **on ~**, sur la pointe des pieds.

tiptop /'tɪptɒp/ *a.* (*fam.*) excellent.

tir|**e** [1] /'taɪə(r)/ *v.t./i.* (se) fatiguer. **~e of**, se lasser de. **~eless** *a.* infatigable. **~ing** *a.* fatigant.

tire [2] /'taɪə(r)/ *n.* (*Amer.*) pneu *m.*

tired /'taɪəd/ *a.* fatigué. **be ~ of**, en avoir assez de.

tiresome /'taɪəsəm/ *a.* ennuyeux.

tissue /'tɪʃuː/ *n.* tissu *m.*; (*handkerchief*) mouchoir en papier *m.* **~-paper** *n.* papier de soie *m.*

tit [1] /tɪt/ *n.* (*bird*) mésange *f.*

tit [2] /tɪt/ *n.* **give ~ for tat**, rendre coup pour coup.

titbit /'tɪtbɪt/ *n.* friandise *f.*

titillate /'tɪtɪleɪt/ *v.t.* exciter.

title /'taɪtl/ *n.* titre *m.* **~-deed** *n.* titre de propriété *m.* **~-role** *n.* rôle principal *m.*

titter /'tɪtə(r)/ *v.i.* rigoler.

titular /'tɪtjʊlə(r)/ *a.* (*ruler etc.*) nominal.

to /tuː, *unstressed* tə/ *prep.* à; (*towards*) vers; (*of attitude*) envers. ● *adv.* **push** *or* **pull to**, (*close*) fermer. **to France**/*etc.*, en France/ *etc.* **to town**, en ville. **to Canada**/ *etc.*, au Canada/*etc.* **to the baker's**/ *etc.*, chez le boulanger/*etc.* **the road**/ **door**/ *etc.* **to**, la route/porte/*etc.* de. **to me**/**her**/*etc.*, me/lui/etc. **to do**/ **sit**/*etc.*, faire/s'asseoir/*etc.* **I wrote to tell her**, j'ai écrit pour lui dire. **I tried to help you**, j'ai essayé de t'aider. **ten to six**, (*by clock*) six heures moins dix. **go to and fro**, aller et venir. **husband**/*etc.***-to-be** *n.* futur mari/ *etc. m.*

toad /təʊd/ *n.* crapaud *m.*

toadstool /'təʊdstuːl/ *n.* champignon (vénéneux) *m.*

toast /təʊst/ *n.* pain grillé *m.*, toast *m.*; (*drink*) toast *m.* ● *v.t.* (*bread*) faire griller; (*drink to*) porter un toast à; (*event*) arroser. **~er** *n.* grille-pain *m. invar.*

tobacco /tə'bækəʊ/ *n.* tabac *m.*

tobacconist /tə'bækənɪst/ *n.* marchand(e) de tabac *m.* (*f.*). **~'s shop**, tabac *m.*

toboggan /tə'bɒgən/ *n.* toboggan *m.*, luge *f.*

today /tə'deɪ/ *n. & adv.* aujourd'hui (*m.*).

toddler /'tɒdlə(r)/ *n.* tout(e) petit(e) enfant *m.(f.)*.

toddy /'tɒdɪ/ *n.* (*drink*) grog *m.*

toe /təʊ/ n. orteil m.; (of shoe) bout m. ● v.t. ~ the line, se conformer. **on one's ~s**, vigilant. **~-hold** n. prise (précaire) f.

toffee /'tɒfɪ/ n. caramel m. **~-apple** n. pomme caramélisée f.

together /tə'geðə(r)/ adv. ensemble; (at same time) en même temps. **~ with**, avec. **~ness** n. camaraderie f.

toil /tɔɪl/ v.i. peiner. ● n. labeur m.

toilet /'tɔɪlɪt/ n. toilettes f. pl.; (grooming) toilette f. **~-paper** n. papier hygiénique m. **~-roll** n. rouleau de papier hygiénique m. **~ water**, eau de toilette f.

toiletries /'tɔɪlɪtrɪz/ n. pl. articles de toilette m. pl.

token /'təʊkən/ n. témoignage m., marque f.; (voucher) bon m.; (coin) jeton m. ● a. symbolique.

told /təʊld/ see **tell**. ● a. **all ~**, (all in all) en tout.

tolerab|le /'tɒlərəbl/ a. tolérable; (not bad) passable. **~y** adv. (work, play, etc.) passablement.

toleran|t /'tɒlərənt/ a. tolérant (of, à l'égard de). **~ce** n. tolérance f. **~tly** adv. avec tolérance.

tolerate /'tɒləreɪt/ v.t. tolérer.

toll¹ /təʊl/ n. péage m. **death ~**, nombre de morts m. **take its ~**, (of age) faire sentir son poids.

toll² /təʊl/ v.i. (of bell) sonner.

tom /tɒm/, **~-cat** ns. matou m.

tomato /tə'mɑːtəʊ, Amer. tə'meɪtəʊ/ n. (pl. -oes) tomate f.

tomb /tuːm/ n. tombeau m.

tombola /tɒm'bəʊlə/ n. tombola f.

tomboy /'tɒmbɔɪ/ n. garçon manqué m.

tombstone /'tuːmstəʊn/ n. pierre tombale f.

tomfoolery /tɒm'fuːlərɪ/ n. âneries f. pl., bêtises f. pl.

tomorrow /tə'mɒrəʊ/ n. & adv. demain (m.). **~ morning/night**, demain matin/soir. **the day after ~**, après-demain.

ton /tʌn/ n. tonne f. (= 1016 kg.). **(metric) ~**, tonne f. (= 1000 kg.). **~s of**, (fam.) des masses de.

tone /təʊn/ n. ton m.; (of radio, telephone, etc.) tonalité f. ● v.t. **~ down**, atténuer. ● v.i. **~ in**, s'harmoniser (with, avec). **~-deaf** a. qui n'a pas d'oreille. **~ up**, (muscles) tonifier.

tongs /tɒŋz/ n. pl. pinces f. pl.; (for sugar) pince f.; (for hair) fer m.

tongue /tʌŋ/ n. langue f. **~-tied** a. muet. **~-twister** n. phrase difficile à prononcer f. **with one's ~ in one's cheek**, ironiquement.

tonic /'tɒnɪk/ n. (med.) tonique m. ● a. (effect, accent) tonique. **~ (water)**, tonic m.

tonight /tə'naɪt/ n. & adv. cette nuit (f.); (evening) ce soir (m.).

tonne /tʌn/ n. (metric) tonne f.

tonsil /'tɒnsl/ n. amygdale f.

tonsillitis /tɒnsɪ'laɪtɪs/ n. amygdalite f.

too /tuː/ adv. trop; (also) aussi. **~ many** a. trop de; n. trop de; adv. & n. trop. **~ much** a. trop de; adv. & n. trop.

took /tʊk/ see **take**.

tool /tuːl/ n. outil m. **~-bag** n. trousse à outils f.

toot /tuːt/ n. coup de klaxon m. ● v.t./i. **~ (the horn)**, klaxonner.

tooth /tuːθ/ n. (pl. **teeth**) dent f. **~less** a. édenté.

toothache /'tuːθeɪk/ n. mal de dents m.

toothbrush /'tuːθbrʌʃ/ n. brosse à dents f.

toothcomb /'tuːθkəʊm/ n. peigne fin m.

toothpaste /'tuːθpeɪst/ n. dentifrice m., pâte dentifrice f.

toothpick /'tuːθpɪk/ n. cure-dent m.

top¹ /tɒp/ n. (highest point) sommet m.; (upper part) haut m.; (upper surface) dessus m.; (lid) couvercle m.; (of bottle, tube) bouchon m.; (of beer bottle) capsule f.; (of list) tête f. ● a. (shelf etc.) du haut; (floor) dernier; (in rank) premier; (best) meilleur; (distinguished) éminent; (maximum) maximum. ● v.t. (p.t. **topped**) (exceed) dépasser; (list) venir en tête de. **from ~ to bottom**, de fond en comble. **on ~ of**, sur; (fig.) en plus de. **~ hat**, haut-de-forme m. **~-heavy** a. trop lourd du haut. **~-level** a. du plus haut niveau. **~-notch** a. excellent. **~ quality** a. de la plus haute qualité. **~ secret**, ultra-secret. **~ up**, remplir. **~ped with**, surmonté de; (cream etc.: culin.) nappé de.

top² /tɒp/ n. (toy) toupie f.

topic /'tɒpɪk/ n. sujet m.

topical /'tɒpɪkl/ a. d'actualité.

topless /'tɒplɪs/ a. aux seins nus.

topple /'tɒpl/ v.t./i. (faire) tomber, (faire) basculer.

topsy-turvy /ˌtɒpsɪˈtɜːvɪ/ *adv.* & *a.* sens dessus dessous.

torch /tɔːtʃ/ *n.* (*electric*) lampe de poche *f.*; (*flaming*) torche *f.*

tore /tɔː(r)/ *see* tear[1].

torment[1] /ˈtɔːment/ *n.* tourment *m.*

torment[2] /tɔːˈment/ *v.t.* tourmenter; (*annoy*) agacer.

torn /tɔːn/ *see* tear[1].

tornado /tɔːˈneɪdəʊ/ *n.* (*pl.* **-oes**) tornade *f.*

torpedo /tɔːˈpiːdəʊ/ *n.* (*pl.* **-oes**) torpille *f.* ● *v.t.* torpiller.

torrent /ˈtɒrənt/ *n.* torrent *m.* **~ial** /təˈrenʃl/ *a.* torrentiel.

torrid /ˈtɒrɪd/ *a.* (*climate etc.*) torride; (*fig.*) passionné.

torso /ˈtɔːsəʊ/ *n.* (*pl.* **-os**) torse *m.*

tortoise /ˈtɔːtəs/ *n.* tortue *f.*

tortoiseshell /ˈtɔːtəsʃel/ *n.* (*for ornaments etc.*) écaille *f.*

tortuous /ˈtɔːtʃʊəs/ *a.* tortueux.

torture /ˈtɔːtʃə(r)/ *n.* torture *f.*, supplice *m.* ● *v.t.* torturer. **~r** /-ə(r)/ *n.* tortionnaire *m.*

Tory /ˈtɔːrɪ/ *n.* tory *m.* ● *a.* tory (*invar.*).

toss /tɒs/ *v.t.* jeter, lancer; (*shake*) agiter. ● *v.i.* s'agiter. **~ a coin,** **~ up,** tirer à pile ou face (**for,** pour).

tot[1] /tɒt/ *n.* petit(e) enfant *m.(f.*; (*glass: fam.*) petit verre *m.*

tot[2] /tɒt/ *v.t.* (*p.t.* **totted**). **~ up,** (*fam.*) additionner.

total /ˈtəʊtl/ *a.* total. ● *n.* total *m.* ● *v.t.* (*p.t.* **totalled**) (*find total of*) totaliser; (*amount to*) s'élever à. **~ity** /-ˈtælɪtɪ/ *n.* totalité *f.* **~ly** *adv.* totalement.

totalitarian /ˌtəʊtælɪˈteərɪən/ *a.* totalitaire.

totter /ˈtɒtə(r)/ *v.i.* chanceler.

touch /tʌtʃ/ *v.t./i.* toucher; (*of ends, gardens, etc.*) se toucher; (*tamper with*) toucher à. ● *n.* (*sense*) toucher *m.*; (*contact*) contact *m.*; (*of colour*) touche *f.*; (*football*) touche *f.* **a ~ of,** (*small amount*) un peu de. **get in ~ with,** contacter. **lose ~,** perdre contact. **be out of ~,** ne plus être dans le coup. **~-and-go** *a.* douteux. **~ down,** (*aviat.*) atterrir. **~-line** *n.* (ligne de) touche *f.* **~ off,** (*explode*) faire partir; (*cause*) déclencher. **~ on,** (*mention*) aborder. **~ up,** retoucher.

touchdown /ˈtʌtʃdaʊn/ *n.* atterrissage *m.*; (*sport, Amer.*) but *m.*

touching /ˈtʌtʃɪŋ/ *a.* touchant.

touchstone /ˈtʌtʃstəʊn/ *n.* pierre de touche *f.*

touchy /ˈtʌtʃɪ/ *a.* susceptible.

tough /tʌf/ *a.* (**-er, -est**) (*hard, difficult*) dur; (*strong*) solide; (*relentless*) acharné. ● *n.* **~ (guy),** dur *m.* **~ luck!,** (*fam.*) tant pis! **~ness** *n.* dureté *f.*; solidité *f.*

toughen /ˈtʌfn/ *v.t.* (*strengthen*) renforcer; (*person*) endurcir.

toupee /ˈtuːpeɪ/ *n.* postiche *m.*

tour /tʊə(r)/ *n.* voyage *m.*; (*visit*) visite *f.*; (*by team etc.*) tournée *f.* ● *v.t.* visiter. **on ~,** en tournée. **~ operator,** voyagiste *m.*

tourism /ˈtʊərɪzəm/ *n.* tourisme *m.*

tourist /ˈtʊərɪst/ *n.* touriste *m./f.* ● *a.* touristique. **~ office,** syndicat d'initiative *m.*

tournament /ˈtɔːnəmənt/ *n.* (*sport* & *medieval*) tournoi *m.*

tousle /ˈtaʊzl/ *v.t.* ébouriffer.

tout /taʊt/ *v.i.* **~ (for),** racoler. ● *v.t.* (*sell*) revendre. ● *n.* racoleu|r, -se *m.*, *f.*; revendeu|r, -se *m.*, *f.*

tow /təʊ/ *v.t.* remorquer. ● *n.* remorque *f.* **on ~,** en remorque. **~ away,** (*vehicle*) (faire) enlever. **~-path** *n.* chemin de halage *m.* **~-truck,** dépanneuse *f.*

toward(s) /təˈwɔːd(z), *Amer.* tɔːd(z)/ *prep.* vers; (*of attitude*) envers.

towel /ˈtaʊəl/ *n.* serviette *f.*; (*teatowel*) torchon *m.* **~ling** *n.* tissuéponge *m.*

tower /ˈtaʊə(r)/ *n.* tour *f.* ● *v.i.* **~ above,** dominer. **~ block,** tour *f.*, immeuble *m.* **~ing** *a.* très haut.

town /taʊn/ *n.* ville *f.* **go to ~,** (*fam.*) mettre le paquet. **~ council,** conseil municipal *m.* **~ hall,** hôtel de ville *m.*

toxic /ˈtɒksɪk/ *a.* toxique.

toxin /ˈtɒksɪn/ *n.* toxine *f.*

toy /tɔɪ/ *n.* jouet *m.* ● *v.i.* **~ with,** (*object*) jouer avec; (*idea*) caresser.

toyshop /ˈtɔɪʃɒp/ *n.* magasin de jouets *m.*

trace /treɪs/ *n.* trace *f.* ● *v.t.* suivre *or* retrouver la trace de; (*draw*) tracer; (*with tracing-paper*) décalquer; (*relate*) retracer.

tracing /ˈtreɪsɪŋ/ *n.* calque *m.* **~-paper** *n.* papier-calque *m. invar.*

track /træk/ *n.* (*of person etc.*) trace *f.*, piste *f.*; (*path, race-track* & *of tape*) piste *f.*; (*on disc*) plage *f.*; (*of rocket etc.*) trajectoire *f.*; (*rail.*) voie *f.* ● *v.t.* suivre la trace *or* la trajectoire de. **keep ~ of**, suivre. **~ down**, (find) retrouver; (hunt) traquer. **~ suit**, survêtement m.; (with sweat-shirt) jogging m.

tract[1] /trækt/ n. (land) étendue f.; (anat.) appareil m.

tract[2] /trækt/ n. (pamphlet) tract m.

tractor /'træktə(r)/ n. tracteur m.

trade /treɪd/ n. commerce m.; (job) métier m.; (swap) échange m. ● v.i. faire du commerce. ● v.t. échanger. **~ deficit**, déficit commercial m. **~ in**, (used article) faire reprendre. **~ in** reprise f. **~ mark**, marque de fabrique f.; (name) marque déposée f. **~-off** n. (fam.) compromis m. **~ on**, (exploit) abuser de. **~ union**, syndicat m. **~-unionist** n. syndicaliste m./f. **~r** /-ə(r)/ n. négociant(e) m. (f.), commerçant(e) m. (f.).

tradesman /'treɪdzmən/ n. (pl. -men) commerçant m.

trading /'treɪdɪŋ/ n. commerce m. **~ estate**, zone industrielle f.

tradition /trə'dɪʃn/ n. tradition f. **~al** a. traditionnel.

traffic /'træfɪk/ n. trafic m.; (on road) circulation f. ● v.i. (p.t. **trafficked**) trafiquer (**in**, de). **~ circle**, (Amer.) rond-point m. **~ cone**, cône de délimitation de voie m. **~ jam**, embouteillage m. **~-lights** n. pl. feux (de circulation) m. pl. **~ warden**, contractuel(le) m. (f.).

tragedy /'trædʒədɪ/ n. tragédie f.

tragic /'trædʒɪk/ a. tragique.

trail /treɪl/ v.t./i. traîner; (of plant) ramper; (track) suivre. ● n. (of powder etc.) traînée f.; (track) piste f.; (beaten path) sentier m. **~ behind**, traîner.

trailer /'treɪlə(r)/ n. remorque f.; (caravan: Amer.) caravane f.; (film) bande-annonce f.

train /treɪn/ n. (rail.) train m.; (underground) rame f.; (procession) file f.; (of dress) traîne f. ● v.t. (instruct, develop) former; (sportsman) entraîner; (animal) dresser; (ear) exercer; (aim) braquer. ● v.i. recevoir une formation; s'entraîner. **~ed** a. (skilled) qualifié; (doctor etc.) diplômé. **~er** n. (sport) entraîneu|r, -se m./f. **~ers**, (shoes) chaussures de sport f. pl. **~ing** n. formation f.; entraînement m.; dressage m.

trainee /treɪ'niː/ n. stagiaire m./f.

traipse /treɪps/ v.i. (fam.) traîner.

trait /treɪ(t)/ n. trait m.

traitor /'treɪtə(r)/ n. traître m.

tram /træm/ n. tram(way) m.

tramp /træmp/ v.i. marcher (d'un pas lourd). ● v.t. parcourir. ● n. pas lourds m. pl.; (vagrant) clochard(e) m. (f.); (Amer., sl.) dévergondée f.; (hike) randonnée f.

trample /'træmpl/ v.t./i. **~ (on)**, piétiner; (fig.) fouler aux pieds.

trampoline /'træmpəliːn/ n. (canvas sheet) trampoline m.

trance /trɑːns/ n. transe f.

tranquil /'træŋkwɪl/ a. tranquille. **~lity** /-'kwɪlətɪ/ n. tranquillité f.

tranquillizer /'træŋkwɪlaɪzə(r)/ n. (drug) tranquillisant m.

transact /træn'zækt/ v.t. traiter. **~ion** /-kʃn/ n. transaction f.

transatlantic /trænzət'læntɪk/ a. transatlantique.

transcend /træn'send/ v.t. transcender. **~ent** a. transcendant.

transcript /'trænskrɪpt/ n. (written copy) transcription f.

transfer[1] /træns'fɜː(r)/ v.t. (p.t. **transferred**) transférer; (power) faire passer. ● v.i. être transféré. **~ the charges**, (telephone) téléphoner en PCV.

transfer[2] /'trænsfɜː(r)/ n. transfert m.; (of power) passation f.; (image) décalcomanie f.; (sticker) autocollant m.

transform /træns'fɔːm/ v.t. transformer. **~ation** /-ə'meɪʃn/ n. transformation f. **~er** n. (electr.) transformateur m.

transfusion /træns'fjuːʒn/ n. (of blood) transfusion f.

transient /'trænzɪənt/ a. transitoire, éphémère.

transistor /træn'zɪstə(r)/ n. (device, radio set) transistor m.

transit /'trænsɪt/ n. transit m.

transition /træn'zɪʃn/ n. transition f. **~al** a. transitoire.

transitive /'trænsətɪv/ a. transitif.

transitory /'trænsɪtərɪ/ a. transitoire.

translat|e /trænz'leɪt/ v.t. traduire. **~ion** /-ʃn/ n. traduction f. **~or** n. traduc|teur, -trice m., f.

translucent /trænz'luːsnt/ a. translucide.

transmi|t /trænz'mɪt/ v.t. (p.t. **transmitted**) (pass on etc.) transmettre; (broadcast) émettre. **~ssion** n. transmission f.; émission f. **~tter** n. émetteur m.

transparen|t /træns'pærənt/ *a.*
transparent. **~cy** *n.* transparence *f.*;
(*photo.*) diapositive *f.*

transpire /træn'spaɪə(r)/ *v.i.*
s'avérer; (*happen: fam.*) arriver.

transplant[1] /træns'plɑːnt/ *v.t.* trans-
planter; (*med.*) greffer.

transplant[2] /'trænsplɑːnt/ *n.* trans-
plantation *f.*; greffe *f.*

transport[1] /træn'spɔːt/ *v.t.* (*carry,
delight*) transporter. **~ation** /-'teɪ-
ʃn/ *n.* transport *m.*

transport[2] /'trænspɔːt/ *n.* (*of goods,
delight, etc.*) transport *m.*

transpose /træn'spəʊz/ *v.t.* transposer.

transverse /'trænzvɜːs/ *a.* transver-
sal.

transvestite /trænz'vestaɪt/ *n.* tra-
vesti(e) *m.* (*f.*).

trap /træp/ *n.* piège *m.* ● *v.t.* (*p.t.*
trapped) (*jam, pin down*) coincer;
(*cut off*) bloquer; (*snare*) prendre au
piège. **~per** *n.* trappeur *m.*

trapdoor /træp'dɔː(r)/ *n.* trappe *f.*

trapeze /trə'piːz/ *n.* trapèze *m.*

trappings /'træpɪŋz/ *n. pl.* (*fig.*)
signes extérieurs *m. pl.*, apparat *m.*

trash /træʃ/ *n.* (*junk*) saleté(s) *f.*
(*pl.*); (*refuse*) ordures *f. pl.*; (*nonsense*) idioties *f. pl.* **~can** *n.*
(*Amer.*) poubelle *f.* **~y** *a.* qui ne
vaut rien, de mauvaise qualité.

trauma /'trɔːmə/ *n.* traumatisme *m.*
~tic /-'mætɪk/ *a.* traumatisant.

travel /'trævl/ *v.i.* (*p.t.* **travelled**,
Amer. **traveled**) voyager; (*of
vehicle, bullet, etc.*) aller. ● *v.t.*
parcourir. ● *n.* voyage(s) *m.* (*pl.*).
~ agent, agent de voyage *m.* **~ler** *n.*
voyageu|r, -se *m.*, *f.* **~ler's cheque,**
chèque de voyage *m.* **~ling**
voyage(s) *m.* (*pl.*). **~ sickness,** mal
des transports *m.*

travesty /'trævəstɪ/ *n.* parodie *f.*,
simulacre *m.* ● *v.t.* travestir.

trawler /'trɔːlə(r)/ *n.* chalutier *m.*

tray /treɪ/ *n.* plateau *m.*; (*on office
desk*) corbeille *f.*

treacherous /'tretʃərəs/ *a.* traître.
~ly *adv.* traîtreusement.

treachery /'tretʃərɪ/ *n.* traîtrise *f.*

treacle /'triːkl/ *n.* mélasse *f.*

tread /tred/ *v.i.* (*p.t.* **trod**, *p.p.* **trodden**) marcher (**on,** sur). ● *v.t.* parcourir (à pied); (*soil: fig.*) fouler.
● *n.* démarche *f.*; (*sound*) (bruit *m.*
de) pas *m. pl.*; (*of tyre*) chape *f.* **~**

sth. into, (*carpet*) étaler qch. sur
(avec les pieds).

treason /'triːzn/ *n.* trahison *f.*

treasure /'treʒə(r)/ *n.* trésor *m.* ● *v.t.*
attacher une grande valeur à; (*store*)
conserver. **~r** /-ə(r)/ *n.* trésor|ier,
-ière *m.*, *f.*

treasury /'treʒərɪ/ *n.* trésorerie *f.* **the
T~,** le ministère des Finances.

treat /triːt/ *v.t.* traiter; (*consider*)
considérer. ● *n.* (*pleasure*) plaisir
m., régal *m.*; (*present*) gâterie *f.*;
(*food*) régal *m.* **~ s.o. to sth.,** offrir
qch. à qn.

treatise /'triːtɪz/ *n.* traité *m.*

treatment /'triːtmənt/ *n.* traitement
m.

treaty /'triːtɪ/ *n.* (*pact*) traité *m.*

trebl|e /'trebl/ *a.* triple. ● *v.t./i.*
tripler. ● *n.* (*voice: mus.*) soprano
m. **~e clef,** clé de sol *f.* **~y** *adv.*
triplement.

tree /triː/ *n.* arbre *m.* **~-top** *n.* cime
(d'un arbre) *f.*

trek /trek/ *n.* voyage pénible *m.*;
(*sport*) randonnée *f.* ● *v.i.* (*p.t.*
trekked) voyager (péniblement);
(*sport*) faire de la randonnée.

trellis /'trelɪs/ *n.* treillage *m.*

tremble /'trembl/ *v.i.* trembler.

tremendous /trɪ'mendəs/ *a.* énorme;
(*excellent: fam.*) fantastique. **~ly**
adv. fantastiquement.

tremor /'tremə(r)/ *n.* tremblement *m.*
(**earth**) **~,** secousse (sismique) *f.*

trench /trentʃ/ *n.* tranchée *f.*

trend /trend/ *n.* tendance *f.*; (*fashion*)
mode *f.* **~-setter** *n.* lanceu|r, -se de
mode *m.*, *f.* **~y** *a.* (*fam.*) dans le vent.

trepidation /trepɪ'deɪʃn/ *n.* (*fear*)
inquiétude *f.*

trespass /'trespəs/ *v.i.* s'introduire
sans autorisation (**on,** dans). **~er** *n.*
intrus(e) *m.* (*f.*).

tresses /'tresɪz/ *n. pl.* chevelure *f.*

trestle /'tresl/ *n.* tréteau *m.* **~-table**
n. table à tréteaux *f.*

tri- /traɪ/ *pref.* tri-.

trial /'traɪəl/ *n.* (*jurid.*) procès *m.*;
(*test*) essai *m.*; (*ordeal*) épreuve *f.*
go on ~, passer en jugement. **~
and error,** tâtonnements *m. pl.* **~
run,** galop d'essai *m.*

triang|le /'traɪæŋgl/ *n.* triangle *m.*
~ular /-'æŋgjʊlə(r)/ *a.* triangulaire.

trib|e /traɪb/ *n.* tribu *f.* **~al** *a.* tribal.

tribulation /trɪbjʊ'leɪʃn/ *n.* tribulation *f.*

tribunal /traɪˈbjuːnl/ n. tribunal m.; (mil.) commission f.

tributary /ˈtrɪbjʊtərɪ/ n. affluent m.

tribute /ˈtrɪbjuːt/ n. tribut m. **pay ~ to**, rendre hommage à.

trick /trɪk/ n. astuce f., ruse f.; (joke, feat of skill) tour m.; (habit) manie f. ● v.t. tromper. **do the ~**, (fam.) faire l'affaire.

trickery /ˈtrɪkərɪ/ n. ruse f.

trickle /ˈtrɪkl/ v.i. dégouliner. **~ in/out**, arriver or partir en petit nombre. ● n. filet m.; (fig.) petit nombre m.

tricky /ˈtrɪkɪ/ a. (crafty) rusé; (problem) délicat, difficile.

tricycle /ˈtraɪsɪkl/ n. tricycle m.

trifle /ˈtraɪfl/ n. bagatelle f.; (cake) diplomate m. ● v.i. **~ with**, jouer avec. **a ~**, (small amount) un peu.

trifling /ˈtraɪflɪŋ/ a. insignifiant.

trigger /ˈtrɪgə(r)/ n. (of gun) gâchette f., détente f. ● v.t. **~ (off)**, (initiate) déclencher.

trilby /ˈtrɪlbɪ/ n. (hat) feutre m.

trim /trɪm/ a. (**trimmer, trimmest**) net, soigné; (figure) svelte. ● v.t. (p.t. **trimmed**) (cut) couper légèrement; (hair) rafraîchir; (budget) réduire. ● n. (cut) coupe légère f.; (decoration) garniture f. **in ~**, en bon ordre; (fit) en forme. **~ with**, (decorate) orner de. **~ming(s)** n. (pl.) garniture(s) f. (pl.).

Trinity /ˈtrɪnətɪ/ n. Trinité f.

trinket /ˈtrɪŋkɪt/ n. colifichet m.

trio /ˈtriːəʊ/ n. (pl. **-os**) trio m.

trip /trɪp/ v.t./i. (p.t. **tripped**) (faire) trébucher; (go lightly) marcher d'un pas léger. ● n. (journey) voyage m.; (outing) excursion f.; (stumble) faux pas m.

tripe /traɪp/ n. (food) tripes f. pl.; (nonsense: sl.) bêtises f. pl.

triple /ˈtrɪpl/ a. triple. ● v.t./i. tripler. **~ts** /-plɪts/ n. pl. triplé(e)s m. (f.) pl.

tripod /ˈtraɪpɒd/ n. trépied m.

trite /traɪt/ a. banal.

triumph /ˈtraɪəmf/ n. triomphe m. ● v.i. triompher (**over**, de). **~al** /-ˈʌmfl/ a. triomphal. **~ant** /-ˈʌmfənt/ a. triomphant, triomphal. **~antly** /-ˈʌmfəntlɪ/ adv. en triomphe.

trivial /ˈtrɪvɪəl/ a. insignifiant. **~ize** v.t. considérer comme insignifiant.

trod, trodden /trɒd, ˈtrɒdn/ see tread.

trolley /ˈtrɒlɪ/ n. chariot m. (**tea-)~**, table roulante f. **~-bus** n. trolleybus m.

trombone /trɒmˈbəʊn/ n. (mus.) trombone m.

troop /truːp/ n. bande f. **~s**, (mil.) troupes f. pl. ● v.i. **~ in/out**, entrer/sortir en bande. **~er** n. soldat de cavalerie m. **~ing the colour**, le salut au drapeau.

trophy /ˈtrəʊfɪ/ n. trophée m.

tropic /ˈtrɒpɪk/ n. tropique m. **~s**, tropiques m. pl. **~al** a. tropical.

trot /trɒt/ n. trot m. ● v.i. (p.t. **trotted**) trotter. **on the ~**, (fam.) de suite. **~ out**, (produce: fam.) sortir; (state: fam.) formuler.

trouble /ˈtrʌbl/ n. ennui(s) m. (pl.); difficulté(s) f. (pl.); (pains, effort) mal m., peine f. **~(s)**, ennuis m. pl.; (unrest) conflits m. pl. ● v.t./i. (bother) (se) déranger; (worry) ennuyer. **be in ~**, avoir des ennuis. **go to a lot of ~**, se donner du mal. **what's the ~?**, quel est le problème? **~d** a. inquiet; (period) agité. **~-maker** n. provoca|teur, -trice m., f. **~-shooter** n. personne appelée pour désamorcer une crise.

troublesome /ˈtrʌblsəm/ a. ennuyeux, pénible.

trough /trɒf/ n. (drinking) abreuvoir m.; (feeding) auge f. **~ (of low pressure)**, dépression f.

trounce /traʊns/ v.t. (defeat) écraser; (thrash) rosser.

troupe /truːp/ n. (theatre) troupe f.

trousers /ˈtraʊzəz/ n. pl. pantalon m. **short ~**, culotte courte f.

trousseau /ˈtruːsəʊ/ n. (pl. **-s** /-əʊz/) (of bride) trousseau m.

trout /traʊt/ n. invar. truite f.

trowel /ˈtraʊəl/ n. (garden) déplantoir m.; (for mortar) truelle f.

truan|t /ˈtruːənt/ n. absentéiste m./f.; (schol.) élève absent(e) sans permission m.(f.). **play ~t**, sécher les cours. **~cy** n. absentéisme m.

truce /truːs/ n. trêve f.

truck /trʌk/ n. (lorry) camion m.; (cart) chariot m.; (rail.) wagon m., plateforme f. **~-driver** n. camionneur m.

truculent /ˈtrʌkjʊlənt/ a. agressif.

trudge /trʌdʒ/ v.i. marcher péniblement, se traîner.

true /truː/ a. (**-er, -est**) vrai; (accurate) exact; (faithful) fidèle.

truffle /ˈtrʌfl/ n. truffe f.

truly /'truːlɪ/ *adv.* vraiment; (*faithfully*) fidèlement; (*truthfully*) sincèrement.

trump /trʌmp/ *n.* atout *m.* ● *v.t.* ~ up, inventer. ~ card, atout *m.*

trumpet /'trʌmpɪt/ *n.* trompette *f.*

truncate /trʌŋ'keɪt/ *v.t.* tronquer.

trundle /'trʌndl/ *v.t./i.* rouler bruyamment.

trunk /trʌŋk/ *n.* (*of tree, body*) tronc *m.*; (*of elephant*) trompe *f.*; (*box*) malle *f.*; (*auto., Amer.*) coffre *m.* ~s, (*for swimming*) slip de bain *m.* ~-call *n.* communication interurbaine *f.* ~-road *n.* route nationale *f.*

truss /trʌs/ *n.* (*med.*) bandage herniaire *m.* ● *v.t.* (*fowl*) trousser.

trust /trʌst/ *n.* confiance *f.*; (*association*) trust *m.* ● *v.t.* avoir confiance en. ● *v.i.* ~ in or to, s'en remettre à. in ~, en dépôt. on ~, de confiance. ~ s.o. with, confier à qn. ~ed *a.* (*friend etc.*) éprouvé, sûr. ~ful, ~ing *adjs.* confiant. ~y *a.* fidèle.

trustee /trʌs'tiː/ *n.* administra|teur, -trice *m.,f.*

trustworthy /'trʌstwɜːðɪ/ *a.* digne de confiance.

truth /truːθ/ *n.* (*pl.* -s /truːðz/) vérité *f.* ~ful *a.* (*account etc.*) véridique; (*person*) qui dit la vérité. ~fully *adv.* sincèrement.

try /traɪ/ *v.t./i.* (*p.t.* **tried**) essayer; (*be a strain on*) éprouver; (*jurid.*) juger. ● *n.* (*attempt*) essai *m.*; (*Rugby*) essai *m.* ~ on or out, essayer. ~ to do, essayer de faire. ~ing *a.* éprouvant.

tsar /zɑː(r)/ *n.* tsar *m.*

T-shirt /'tiːʃɜːt/ *n.* tee-shirt *m.*

tub /tʌb/ *n.* baquet *m.*, cuve *f.*; (*bath: fam.*) baignoire *f.*

tuba /'tjuːbə/ *n.* tuba *m.*

tubby /'tʌbɪ/ *a.* (-**ier**, -**iest**) dodu.

tub|e /tjuːb/ *n.* tube *m.*; (*railway: fam.*) métro *m.*; (*in tyre*) chambre à air *f.* ~**ing** *n.* tubes *m. pl.*

tuberculosis /tjuːbɜːkjʊ'ləʊsɪs/ *n.* tuberculose *f.*

tubular /'tjuːbjʊlə(r)/ *a.* tubulaire.

tuck /tʌk/ *n.* (*fold*) rempli *m.*, (re)pli *m.* ● *v.t.* (*put away, place*) ranger; (*hide*) cacher. ● *v.i.* ~ in or into, (*eat: sl.*) attaquer. ~ in, (*shirt*) rentrer; (*blanket, person*) border. ~-shop *n.* (*schol.*) boutique à provisions *f.*

Tuesday /'tjuːzdɪ/ *n.* mardi *m.*

tuft /tʌft/ *n.* (*of hair etc.*) touffe *f.*

tug /tʌɡ/ *v.t.* (*p.t.* **tugged**) tirer fort (sur). ● *v.i.* tirer fort. ● *n.* (*boat*) remorqueur *m.* ~ **of war**, jeu de la corde tirée *m.*

tuition /tjuː'ɪʃn/ *n.* cours *m. pl.*; (*fee*) frais de scolarité *m. pl.*

tulip /'tjuːlɪp/ *n.* tulipe *f.*

tumble /'tʌmbl/ *v.i.* (*fall*) dégringoler. ● *n.* chute *f.* ~-**drier** *n.* séchoir à linge (à air chaud) *m.* ~ **to**, (*realize: fam.*) piger.

tumbledown /'tʌmbldaʊn/ *a.* délabré, en ruine.

tumbler /'tʌmblə(r)/ *n.* gobelet *m.*

tummy /'tʌmɪ/ *n.* (*fam.*) ventre *m.*

tumour /'tjuːmə(r)/ *n.* tumeur *f.*

tumult /'tjuːmʌlt/ *n.* tumulte *m.* ~**uous** /-'mʌltʃʊəs/ *a.* tumultueux.

tuna /'tjuːnə/ *n. invar.* thon *m.*

tune /tjuːn/ *n.* air *m.* ● *v.t.* (*engine*) régler; (*mus.*) accorder. ● *v.i.* ~ **in (to)**, (*radio, TV*) écouter. **be in** ~/**out of** ~, (*instrument*) être accordé/désaccordé; (*singer*) chanter juste/faux. ~**ful** *a.* mélodieux. **tuning-fork** *n.* diapason *m.* ~ **up**, (*orchestra*) accorder leurs instruments.

tunic /'tjuːnɪk/ *n.* tunique *f.*

Tunisia /tjuː'nɪzɪə/ *n.* Tunisie *f.* ~**n** *a.* & *n.* tunisien(ne) (*m.* (*f.*)).

tunnel /'tʌnl/ *n.* tunnel *m.*; (*in mine*) galerie *f.* ● *v.i.* (*p.t.* **tunnelled**) creuser un tunnel (**into**, dans).

turban /'tɜːbən/ *n.* turban *m.*

turbine /'tɜːbaɪn/ *n.* turbine *f.*

turbo /'tɜːbəʊ/ *n.* turbo *m.*

turbulen|t /'tɜːbjʊlənt/ *a.* turbulent. ~**ce** *n.* turbulence *f.*

tureen /tjʊ'riːn/ *n.* soupière *f.*

turf /tɜːf/ *n.* (*pl.* **turf** or **turves**) gazon *m.* ● *v.t.* ~ **out**, (*sl.*) jeter dehors. **the** ~, (*racing*) le turf.

turgid /'tɜːdʒɪd/ *a.* (*speech, style*) boursouflé, ampoulé.

Turk /tɜːk/ *n.* Turc *m.*, Turque *f.* ~**ey** *n.* Turquie *f.* ~**ish** *a.* turc; *n.* (*lang.*) turc *m.*

turkey /'tɜːkɪ/ *n.* dindon *m.*, dinde *f.*; (*as food*) dinde *f.*

turmoil /'tɜːmɔɪl/ *n.* trouble *m.*, chaos *m.* **in** ~, en ébullition.

turn /tɜːn/ *v.t./i.* tourner; (*of person*) se tourner; (*to other side*) retourner; (*change*) (se) transformer (**into**, en); (*become*) devenir; (*deflect*) détourner; (*milk*) tourner. ● *n.* tour *m.*; (*in road*) tournant *m.*; (*of mind*, *events*) tournure *f.*; (*illness*: *fam.*) crise *f.* **do a good ~**, rendre service. **in ~**, à tour de rôle. **speak out of ~**, commettre une indiscrétion. **take ~s**, se relayer. **~ against**, se retourner contre. **~ away** *v.i.* se détourner; *v.t.* (*avert*) détourner; (*refuse*) refuser; (*send back*) renvoyer. **~ back** *v.i.* (*return*) retourner; (*vehicle*) faire demi-tour; *v.t.* (*fold*) rabattre. **~ down**, refuser; (*fold*) rabattre; (*reduce*) baisser. **~ in**, (*go to bed*: *fam.*) se coucher. **~ off**, (*light etc.*) éteindre; (*engine*) arrêter; (*tap*) fermer; (*of driver*) tourner. **~-off** *n.* (*auto.*) embranchement *m.* **~ on**, (*light etc.*) allumer; (*engine*) allumer; (*tap*) ouvrir. **~ out** *v.t.* (*light*) éteindre; (*empty*) vider; (*produce*) produire; *v.i.* (*transpire*) s'avérer; (*come*: *fam.*) venir. **~-out** *n.* assistance *f.* **~ over**, (se) retourner. **~ round**, (*person*) se retourner. **~-round** *n.* revirement *m.* **~ up** *v.i.* arriver; (*be found*) se retrouver; *v.t.* (*find*) déterrer; (*collar*) remonter. **~- up** *n.* (*of trousers*) revers *m.*

turning /'tɜːnɪŋ/ *n.* rue (latérale) *f.*; (*bend*) tournant *m.* **~-point** *n.* tournant *m.*

turnip /'tɜːnɪp/ *n.* navet *m.*

turnover /'tɜːnəʊvə(r)/ *n.* (*pie*, *tart*) chausson *m.*; (*money*) chiffre d'affaires *m.*

turnpike /'tɜːnpaɪk/ *n.* (*Amer.*) autoroute à péage *f.*

turnstile /'tɜːnstaɪl/ *n.* (*gate*) tourniquet *m.*

turntable /'tɜːnteɪbl/ *n.* (*for record*) platine *f.*, plateau *m.*

turpentine /'tɜːpəntaɪn/ *n.* térébenthine *f.*

turquoise /'tɜːkwɔɪz/ *a.* turquoise *invar.*

turret /'tʌrɪt/ *n.* tourelle *f.*

turtle /'tɜːtl/ *n.* tortue (de mer) *f.* **~-neck** *a.* à col montant, roulé.

tusk /tʌsk/ *n.* (*tooth*) défense *f.*

tussle /'tʌsl/ *n.* bagarre *f.*, lutte *f.*

tutor /'tjuːtə(r)/ *n.* précep|teur, -trice *m.*, *f.*; (*univ.*) direc|teur, -trice d'études *m.*, *f.*

tutorial /tjuːˈtɔːrɪəl/ *n.* (*univ.*) séance d'études *or* de travaux pratiques *f.*

tuxedo /tʌkˈsiːdəʊ/ *n.* (*pl.* **-os**) (*Amer.*) smoking *m.*

TV /tiːˈviː/ *n.* télé *f.*

twaddle /'twɒdl/ *n.* fadaises *f. pl.*

twang /twæŋ/ *n.* (*son*: *mus.*) pincement *m.*; (*in voice*) nasillement *m.* ● *v.t./i.* (faire) vibrer.

tweed /twiːd/ *n.* tweed *m.*

tweezers /'twiːzəz/ *n. pl.* pince (à épiler) *f.*

twel|ve /twelv/ *a. & n.* douze (*m.*). **~fth** *a. & n.* douzième (*m./f.*). **~ve (o'clock)**, midi *m. or* minuit *m.*

twent|y /'twentɪ/ *a. & n.* vingt (*m.*). **~ieth** *a. & n.* vingtième (*m./f.*).

twice /twaɪs/ *adv.* deux fois.

twiddle /'twɪdl/ *v.t./i.* **~ (with)**, (*fiddle with*) tripoter. **~ one's thumbs**, se tourner les pouces.

twig[1] /twɪg/ *n.* brindille *f.*

twig[2] /twɪg/ *v.t./i.* (*p.t.* **twigged**) (*understand*: *fam.*) piger.

twilight /'twaɪlaɪt/ *n.* crépuscule *m.* ● *a.* crépusculaire.

twin /twɪn/ *n. & a.* jum|eau, -elle (*m.*, *f.*). ● *v.t.* (*p.t.* **twinned**) jumeler. **~ning** *n.* jumelage *m.*

twine /twaɪn/ *n.* ficelle *f.* ● *v.t./i.* (*wind*) (s')enlacer.

twinge /twɪndʒ/ *n.* élancement *m.*; (*remorse*) remords *m.*

twinkle /'twɪŋkl/ *v.i.* (*star etc.*) scintiller; (*eye*) pétiller. ● *n.* scintillement *m.*; pétillement *m.*

twirl /twɜːl/ *v.t./i.* (faire) tournoyer.

twist /twɪst/ *v.t.* tordre; (*weave together*) entortiller; (*roll*) enrouler; (*distort*) déformer. ● *v.i.* (*rope etc.*) s'entortiller; (*road*) zigzaguer. ● *n.* torsion *f.*; (*in rope*) tortillon *m.*; (*in road*) tournant *m.*; (*of events*) tournure *f.*, tour *m.*

twit /twɪt/ *n.* (*fam.*) idiot(e) *m.* (*f.*).

twitch /twɪtʃ/ *v.t./i.* (se) contracter nerveusement. ● *n.* (*tic*) tic *m.*; (*jerk*) secousse *f.*

two /tuː/ *a. & n.* deux (*m.*). **in** *or* **of ~ minds**, indécis. **put ~ and two together**, faire le rapport. **~-faced** *a.* hypocrite. **~-fold** *a.* double; *adv.* au double. **~-piece** *n.* (*garment*) deux-pièces *m. invar.*

twosome /'tuːsəm/ *n.* couple *m.*

tycoon /taɪˈkuːn/ *n.* magnat *m.*

tying /'taɪɪŋ/ *see* tie.

type /taɪp/ *n.* (*example*) type *m.*; (*kind*) genre *m.*, sorte *f.*; (*person*: *fam.*) type *m.*; (*print*) caractères *m. pl.* ● *v.t./i.* (*write*) taper (à la machine). **~-cast** *a.* catégorisé (**as**, comme).

typescript /'taɪpskrɪpt/ *n.* manuscrit dactylographié *m.*

typewrit|er /'taɪpraɪtə(r)/ *n.* machine
à écrire *f.* ~ten /-ɪtn/ *a.* dactylographié.

typhoid /'taɪfɔɪd/ *n.* ~ (fever), typhoïde *f.*

typhoon /tar'fuːn/ *n.* typhon *m.*

typical /'tɪpɪkl/ *a.* typique. ~ly *adv.*
typiquement.

typify /'tɪpɪfaɪ/ *v.t.* être typique de.

typing /'taɪpɪŋ/ *n.* dactylo(graphie) *f.*

typist /'taɪpɪst/ *n.* dactylo *f.*

tyrann|y /'tɪrənɪ/ *n.* tyrannie *f.* ~ical
/tɪ'rænɪkl/ *a.* tyrannique.

tyrant /'taɪərənt/ *n.* tyran *m.*

tyre /'taɪə(r)/ *n.* pneu *m.*

U

ubiquitous /juː'bɪkwɪtəs/ *a.* omnipré-
sent, qu'on trouve partout.

udder /'ʌdə(r)/ *n.* pis *m.*, mamelle *f.*

UFO /'juːfəʊ/ *n.* (*pl.* -Os) OVNI *m.*

Uganda /juː'gændə/ *n.* Ouganda *m.*

ugl|y /'ʌglɪ/ *a.* (-ier, -iest) laid. ~iness
n. laideur *f.*

UK *abbr. see* United Kingdom.

ulcer /'ʌlsə(r)/ *n.* ulcère *m.*

ulterior /ʌl'tɪərɪə(r)/ *a.* ultérieur. ~
motive, arrière-pensée *f.*

ultimate /'ʌltɪmət/ *a.* dernier, ultime; (*definitive*) définitif; (*basic*)
fondamental. ~ly *adv.* à la fin; (*in
the last analysis*) en fin de compte.

ultimatum /ʌltɪ'meɪtəm/ *n.* (*pl.*
-ums) ultimatum *m.*

ultra- /'ʌltrə/ *pref.* ultra-.

ultrasound /'ʌltrəsaʊnd/ *n.* ultrason
m.

ultraviolet /ʌltrə'vaɪələt/ *a.* ultraviolet.

umbilical /ʌm'bɪlɪkl/ *a.* ~ cord,
cordon ombilical *m.*

umbrella /ʌm'brelə/ *n.* parapluie *m.*

umpire /'ʌmpaɪə(r)/ *n.* (*sport*) arbitre
m. ● *v.t.* arbitrer.

umpteen /'ʌmptiːn/ *a.* (*many: sl.*) un
tas de. ~th *a.* (*fam.*) énième.

UN *abbr.* (*United Nations*) ONU *f.*

un- /ʌn/ *pref.* in-, dé(s)-, non, peu, mal,
sans.

unabated /ʌnə'beɪtɪd/ *a.* non di-
minué, aussi fort qu'avant.

unable /ʌn'eɪbl/ *a.* incapable;
(*through circumstances*) dans l'impossibilité (to do, de faire).

unacceptable /ʌnək'septəbl/ *a.* inacceptable, inadmissible.

unaccountabl|e /ʌnə'kaʊntəbl/ *a.*
(*strange*) inexplicable. ~y *adv.*
inexplicablement.

unaccustomed /ʌnə'kʌstəmd/ *a.*
inaccoutumé. ~ to, peu habitué à.

unadulterated /ʌnə'dʌltəreɪtɪd/ *a.*
(*pure, sheer*) pur.

unaided /ʌn'eɪdɪd/ *a.* sans aide.

unanim|ous /juː'nænɪməs/ *a.* una-
nime. ~ity /-ə'nɪmətɪ/ *n.* unanimité
f. ~ously *adv.* à l'unanimité.

unarmed /ʌn'ɑːmd/ *a.* non armé.

unashamed /ʌnə'ʃeɪmd/ *a.* éhonté.
~ly /-ɪdlɪ/ *adv.* sans vergogne.

unassuming /ʌnə'sjuːmɪŋ/ *a.* modeste, sans prétention.

unattached /ʌnə'tætʃt/ *a.* libre.

unattainable /ʌnə'teɪnəbl/ *a.* inaccessible.

unattended /ʌnə'tendɪd/ *a.* (laissé)
sans surveillance.

unattractive /ʌnə'træktɪv/ *a.* peu
séduisant, laid; (*offer*) peu intéressant.

unauthorized /ʌn'ɔːθəraɪzd/ *a.* non
autorisé.

unavailable /ʌnə'veɪləbl/ *a.* pas disponible.

unavoidabl|e /ʌnə'vɔɪdəbl/ *a.* iné-
vitable. ~y *adv.* inévitablement.

unaware /ʌnə'weə(r)/ *a.* be ~ of,
ignorer. ~s /-eəz/ *adv.* au dépourvu.

unbalanced /ʌn'bælənst/ *a.* (*mind,
person*) déséquilibré.

unbearable /ʌn'beərəbl/ *a.* insupportable.

unbeat|able /ʌn'biːtəbl/ *a.* im-
battable. ~en *a.* non battu.

unbeknown(st) /ʌnbɪ'nəʊn(st)/ *a.*
~(st) to, (*fam.*) à l'insu de.

unbelievable /ʌnbɪ'liːvəbl/ *a.* incroyable.

unbend /ʌn'bend/ *v.i.* (*p.t.* unbent)
(*relax*) se détendre.

unbiased /ʌn'baɪəst/ *a.* impartial.

unblock /ʌn'blɒk/ *v.t.* déboucher.

unborn /ʌn'bɔːn/ *a.* futur, à venir.

unbounded /ʌn'baʊndɪd/ *a.* illimité.

unbreakable /ʌn'breɪkəbl/ *a.* incassable.

unbridled /ʌn'braɪdld/ *a.* débridé.

unbroken /ʌn'brəʊkən/ *a.* (*intact*)
intact; (*continuous*) continu.

unburden /ʌn'bɜːdn/ *v. pr.* ~ o.s.,
(*open one's heart*) s'épancher.

unbutton /ʌn'bʌtn/ *v.t.* déboutonner.

uncalled-for /ʌnˈkɔːldfɔː(r)/ a. injustifié, superflu.

uncanny /ʌnˈkænɪ/ a. (**-ier, -iest**) étrange, mystérieux.

unceasing /ʌnˈsiːsɪŋ/ a. incessant.

unceremonious /ʌnserɪˈməʊnɪəs/ a. sans façon, brusque.

uncertain /ʌnˈsɜːtn/ a. incertain. **be ~ whether**, ne pas savoir exactement si (**to do**, on doit faire). **~ty** n. incertitude f.

unchanged /ʌnˈtʃeɪndʒd/ a. inchangé. **~ing** a. immuable.

uncivilized /ʌnˈsɪvɪlaɪzd/ a. barbare.

uncle /ˈʌŋkl/ n. oncle m.

uncomfortable /ʌnˈkʌmftəbl/ a. (*thing*) peu confortable; (*unpleasant*) désagréable. **feel** *or* **be ~**, (*person*) être mal à l'aise.

uncommon /ʌnˈkɒmən/ a. rare. **~ly** adv. remarquablement.

uncompromising /ʌnˈkɒmprəmaɪzɪŋ/ a. intransigeant.

unconcerned /ʌnkənˈsɜːnd/ a. (*indifferent*) indifférent (**by**, à).

unconditional /ʌnkənˈdɪʃənl/ a. inconditionnel.

unconscious /ʌnˈkɒnʃəs/ a. sans connaissance, inanimé; (*not aware*) inconscient (**of**, de) ● n. inconscient m. **~ly** adv. inconsciemment.

unconventional /ʌnkənˈvenʃənl/ a. peu conventionnel.

uncooperative /ʌnkəʊˈɒpərətɪv/ a. peu coopératif.

uncork /ʌnˈkɔːk/ v.t. déboucher.

uncouth /ʌnˈkuːθ/ a. grossier.

uncover /ʌnˈkʌvə(r)/ v.t. découvrir.

undecided /ʌndɪˈsaɪdɪd/ a. indécis.

undefinable /ʌndɪˈfaɪnəbl/ a. indéfinissable.

undeniable /ʌndɪˈnaɪəbl/ a. indéniable, incontestable.

under /ˈʌndə(r)/ prep. sous; (*less than*) moins de; (*according to*) selon. ● adv. au-dessous de, mineur. **~ it/there**, là-dessous. **~side** n. dessous m. **~ way**, (*in progress*) en cours; (*on the way*) en route.

under- /ˈʌndə(r)/ pref. sous-.

undercarriage /ˈʌndəkærɪdʒ/ n. (*aviat.*) train d'atterrissage m.

underclothes /ˈʌndəkləʊðz/ n. pl. sous-vêtements m. pl.

undercoat /ˈʌndəkəʊt/ n. (*of paint*) couche de fond f.

undercover /ʌndəˈkʌvə(r)/ (*agent, operation*) a. secret.

undercurrent /ˈʌndəkʌrənt/ n. courant (profond) m.

undercut /ʌndəˈkʌt/ v.t. (p.t. **undercut**, pres. p. **undercutting**) (*comm.*) vendre moins cher que.

underdeveloped /ʌndədɪˈveləpt/ a. sous-développé.

underdog /ˈʌndədɒg/ n. (*pol.*) opprimé(e) m. (f.); (*socially*) déshérité(e) m. (f.).

underdone /ʌndəˈdʌn/ a. pas assez cuit; (*steak*) saignant.

underestimate /ʌndərˈestɪmeɪt/ v.t. sous-estimer.

underfed /ʌndəˈfed/ a. sous-alimenté.

underfoot /ʌndəˈfʊt/ adv. sous les pieds.

undergo /ʌndəˈgəʊ/ v.t. (p.t. **-went**, pp. **-gone**) subir.

undergraduate /ʌndəˈgrædʒʊət/ n. étudiant(e) (qui prépare la licence) m. (f.).

underground¹ /ʌndəˈgraʊnd/ adv. sous terre.

underground² /ˈʌndəgraʊnd/ a. souterrain; (*secret*) clandestin. ● n. (*rail.*) métro m.

undergrowth /ˈʌndəgrəʊθ/ n. sousbois m. invar.

underhand /ˈʌndəhænd/ a. (*deceitful*) sournois.

under|lie /ʌndəˈlaɪ/ v.t. (p.t. **-lay**, p.p. **-lain**, pres. p. **-lying**) sous-tendre. **~lying** a. fondamental.

underline /ʌndəˈlaɪn/ v.t. souligner.

undermine /ʌndəˈmaɪn/ v.t. (*cliff, society, etc.*) miner, saper.

underneath /ʌndəˈniːθ/ prep. sous. ● adv. (en) dessous.

underpaid /ʌndəˈpeɪd/ a. sous-payé.

underpants /ˈʌndəpænts/ n. pl. (*man's*) slip m.

underpass /ˈʌndəpɑːs/ n. (*for cars, people*) passage souterrain m.

underprivileged /ʌndəˈprɪvɪlɪdʒd/ a. défavorisé.

underrate /ʌndəˈreɪt/ v.t. sous-estimer.

undershirt /ˈʌndəʃɜːt/ n. (*Amer.*) maillot (de corps) m.

undershorts /ˈʌndəʃɔːts/ n. pl. (*Amer.*) caleçon m.

underskirt /ˈʌndəskɜːt/ n. jupon m.

understand /ʌndəˈstænd/ v.t./i. (p.t. **-stood**) comprendre. **~able** a. compréhensible. **~ing** a. compréhensif; n. compréhension f.; (*agreement*) entente f.

understatement /'ʌndəsteɪtmənt/ *n.* litote *f.* **that's an ~,** c'est en deçà de la vérité.

understudy /'ʌndəstʌdɪ/ *n.* (*theatre*) doublure *f.*

undertak|e /ʌndə'teɪk/ *v.t.* (*p.t.* **-took,** *p.p.* **-taken**) entreprendre; (*responsibility*) assumer. **~e to,** s'engager à. **~ing** *n.* (*task*) entreprise *f.*; (*promise*) promesse *f.*

undertaker /'ʌndəteɪkə(r)/ *n.* entrepreneur de pompes funèbres *m.*

undertone /'ʌndətəʊn/ *n.* **in an ~,** à mi-voix.

undervalue /ʌndə'væljuː/ *v.t.* sous-évaluer.

underwater /ʌndə'wɔːtə(r)/ *a.* sous-marin. ● *adv.* sous l'eau.

underwear /'ʌndəweə(r)/ *n.* sous-vêtements *m. pl.*

underwent /ʌndə'went/ *see* undergo.

underworld /'ʌndəwɜːld/ *n.* (*of crime*) milieu *m.*, pègre *f.*

undeserved /ʌndɪ'zɜːvd/ *a.* immérité.

undesirable /ʌndɪ'zaɪərəbl/ *a.* peu souhaitable; (*person*) indésirable.

undies /'ʌndɪz/ *n. pl.* (*female underwear. fam.*) dessous *m. pl.*

undignified /ʌn'dɪgnɪfaɪd/ *a.* qui manque de dignité, sans dignité.

undisputed /ʌndɪ'spjuːtɪd/ *a.* incontesté.

undistinguished /ʌndɪ'stɪŋgwɪʃt/ *a.* médiocre.

undo /ʌn'duː/ *v.t.* (*p.t.* **-did,** *p.p.* **-done** /-dʌn/) défaire, détacher; (*a wrong*) réparer. **leave ~ne,** ne pas faire.

undoubted /ʌn'daʊtɪd/ *a.* indubitable. **~ly** *adv.* indubitablement.

undreamt /ʌn'dremt/ *a.* **~ of,** insoupçonné, inimaginable.

undress /ʌn'dres/ *v.t./i.* (se) déshabiller. **get ~ed,** se déshabiller.

undu|e /ʌn'djuː/ *a.* excessif. **~ly** *adv.* excessivement.

undulate /'ʌndjʊleɪt/ *v.i.* onduler.

undying /ʌn'daɪɪŋ/ *a.* éternel.

unearth /ʌn'ɜːθ/ *v.t.* déterrer.

unearthly /ʌn'ɜːθlɪ/ *a.* mystérieux. **~ hour,** (*fam.*) heure indue *f.*

uneasy /ʌn'iːzɪ/ *a.* (*ill at ease*) mal à l'aise; (*worried*) inquiet; (*situation*) difficile.

uneducated /ʌn'edjʊkeɪtɪd/ *a.* (*person*) inculte; (*speech*) populaire.

unemploy|ed /ʌnɪm'plɔɪd/ *a.* en chômage. **~ment** *n.* chômage *m.* **~ment benefit,** allocations de chômage *f. pl.*

unending /ʌn'endɪŋ/ *a.* interminable, sans fin.

unequal /ʌn'iːkwəl/ *a.* inégal. **~led** *a.* inégalé.

unerring /ʌn'ɜːrɪŋ/ *a.* infaillible.

uneven /ʌn'iːvn/ *a.* inégal.

uneventful /ʌnɪ'ventfl/ *a.* sans incident.

unexpected /ʌnɪk'spektɪd/ *a.* inattendu, imprévu. **~ly** *adv.* subitement; (*arrive*) à l'improviste.

unfailing /ʌn'feɪlɪŋ/ *a.* constant, continuel; (*loyal*) fidèle.

unfair /ʌn'feə(r)/ *a.* injuste. **~ness** *n.* injustice *f.*

unfaithful /ʌn'feɪθfl/ *a.* infidèle.

unfamiliar /ʌnfə'mɪlɪə(r)/ *a.* inconnu, peu familier. **be ~ with,** ne pas connaître.

unfashionable /ʌn'fæʃənəbl/ *a.* (*clothes*) démodé. **it's ~ to,** ce n'est pas à la mode de.

unfasten /ʌn'fɑːsn/ *v.t.* défaire.

unfavourable /ʌn'feɪvərəbl/ *a.* défavorable.

unfeeling /ʌn'fiːlɪŋ/ *a.* insensible.

unfinished /ʌn'fɪnɪʃt/ *a.* inachevé.

unfit /ʌn'fɪt/ *a.* (*med.*) peu en forme; (*unsuitable*) impropre (**for,** à). **~ to,** (*unable*) pas en état de.

unflinching /ʌn'flɪntʃɪŋ/ *a.* (*fearless*) intrépide.

unfold /ʌn'fəʊld/ *v.t.* déplier; (*expose*) exposer. ● *v.i.* se dérouler.

unforeseen /ʌnfɔː'siːn/ *a.* imprévu.

unforgettable /ʌnfə'getəbl/ *a.* inoubliable.

unforgivable /ʌnfə'gɪvəbl/ *a.* impardonnable, inexcusable.

unfortunate /ʌn'fɔːtʃʊnət/ *a.* malheureux; (*event*) fâcheux. **~ly** *adv.* malheureusement.

unfounded /ʌn'faʊndɪd/ *a.* (*rumour etc.*) sans fondement.

unfriendly /ʌn'frendlɪ/ *a.* peu amical, froid.

ungainly /ʌn'geɪnlɪ/ *a.* gauche.

ungodly /ʌn'gɒdlɪ/ *a.* impie. **~ hour,** (*fam.*) heure indue *f.*

ungrateful /ʌn'greɪtfl/ *a.* ingrat.

unhapp|y /ʌn'hæpɪ/ *a.* (**-ier, -iest**) malheureux, triste; (*not pleased*) mécontent (**with,** de). **~ily** *adv.* malheureusement. **~iness** *n.* tristesse *f.*

unharmed /ʌnˈhɑːmd/ a. indemne, sain et sauf.

unhealthy /ʌnˈhelθɪ/ a. (-ier, -iest) (climate etc.) malsain; (person) en mauvaise santé.

unheard-of /ʌnˈhɜːdɒv/ a. inouï.

unhinge /ʌnˈhɪndʒ/ v.t. (person, mind) déséquilibrer.

unholy /ʌnˈhəʊlɪ/ a. (-ier, -iest) (person, act, etc.) impie; (great; fam.) invraisemblable.

unhook /ʌnˈhʊk/ v.t. décrocher; (dress) dégrafer.

unhoped /ʌnˈhəʊpt/ a. ~ for, inespéré.

unhurt /ʌnˈhɜːt/ a. indemne.

unicorn /ˈjuːnɪkɔːn/ n. licorne f.

uniform /ˈjuːnɪfɔːm/ n. uniforme m. ● a. uniforme. ~ity /-ˈfɔːmətɪ/ n. uniformité f. ~ly adv. uniformément.

unify /ˈjuːnɪfaɪ/ v.t. unifier. ~ication /-ɪˈkeɪʃn/ n. unification f.

unilateral /juːnɪˈlætrəl/ a. unilatéral.

unimaginable /ʌnɪˈmædʒməbl/ a. inimaginable.

unimportant /ʌnɪmˈpɔːtnt/ a. peu important.

uninhabited /ʌnɪnˈhæbɪtɪd/ a. inhabité.

unintentional /ʌnɪmˈtenʃənl/ a. involontaire.

uninterest|ed /ʌnˈɪntrəstɪd/ a. indifférent (in, à). ~ing a. peu intéressant.

union /ˈjuːnɪən/ n. union f.; (trade union) syndicat m. ~ist n. syndiqué(e) m. (f.). U~ Jack, drapeau britannique m.

unique /juːˈniːk/ a. unique. ~ly adv. exceptionnellement.

unisex /ˈjuːnɪseks/ a. unisexe.

unison /ˈjuːnɪsn/ n. in ~, à l'unisson.

unit /ˈjuːnɪt/ n. unité f.; (of furniture etc.) élément m., bloc m. ~ trust, (équivalent d'une) SICAV f.

unite /juːˈnaɪt/ v.t./i. (s')unir. U~d Kingdom, Royaume-Uni m. U~d Nations, Nations Unies f. pl. U~d States (of America), États-Unis (d'Amérique) m. pl.

unity /ˈjuːnətɪ/ n. unité f.; (harmony; fig.) harmonie f.

universal /juːnɪˈvɜːsl/ a. universel.

universe /ˈjuːnɪvɜːs/ n. univers m.

university /juːnɪˈvɜːsətɪ/ n. université f. ● a. universitaire; (student, teacher) d'université.

unjust /ʌnˈdʒʌst/ a. injuste.

unkempt /ʌnˈkempt/ a. négligé.

unkind /ʌnˈkaɪnd/ a. pas gentil, méchant. ~ly adv. méchamment.

unknowingly /ʌnˈnəʊɪŋlɪ/ adv. sans le savoir, inconsciemment.

unknown /ʌnˈnəʊn/ a. inconnu. ● n. the ~, l'inconnu m.

unleash /ʌnˈliːʃ/ v.t. déchaîner.

unless /ənˈles/ conj. à moins que.

unlike /ʌnˈlaɪk/ a. (brothers etc.) différents. ● prep. à la différence de; (different from) très différent de.

unlikl|y /ʌnˈlaɪklɪ/ a. improbable. ~ihood n. improbabilité f.

unlimited /ʌnˈlɪmɪtɪd/ a. illimité.

unlisted /ʌnˈlɪstɪd/ a. (comm.) non inscrit à la cote; (Amer.) qui n'est pas dans l'annuaire.

unload /ʌnˈləʊd/ v.t. décharger.

unlock /ʌnˈlɒk/ v.t. ouvrir.

unlucky /ʌnˈlʌkɪ/ a. (-ier, -iest) malheureux; (number) qui porte malheur. ~ily adv. malheureusement.

unmarried /ʌnˈmærɪd/ a. célibataire, qui n'est pas marié.

unmask /ʌnˈmɑːsk/ v.t. démasquer.

unmistakable /ʌnmɪˈsteɪkəbl/ a. (voice etc.) facilement reconnaissable; (clear) très net.

unmitigated /ʌnˈmɪtɪgeɪtɪd/ a. (absolute) absolu.

unmoved /ʌnˈmuːvd/ a. indifférent (by, à), insensible (by, à).

unnatural /ʌnˈnætʃrəl/ a. pas naturel, anormal.

unnecessary /ʌnˈnesəsərɪ/ a. inutile; (superfluous) superflu.

unnerve /ʌnˈnɜːv/ v.t. troubler.

unnoticed /ʌnˈnəʊtɪst/ a. inaperçu.

unobtainable /ʌnəbˈteɪnəbl/ n. impossible à obtenir.

unobtrusive /ʌnəbˈtruːsɪv/ a. (person, object) discret.

unofficial /ʌnəˈfɪʃl/ a. officieux.

unorthodox /ʌnˈɔːθədɒks/ a. peu orthodoxe.

unpack /ʌnˈpæk/ v.t. (suitcase etc.) défaire; (contents) déballer. ● v.i. défaire sa valise.

unpalatable /ʌnˈpælətəbl/ a. (food, fact, etc.) désagréable.

unparalleled /ʌnˈpærəleld/ a. incomparable.

unpleasant /ʌnˈpleznt/ a. désagréable (to, avec).

unplug /ʌnˈplʌg/ v.t. (electr.) débrancher; (unblock) déboucher.

unpopular /ʌnˈpɒpjʊlə(r)/ a. impopulaire. ~ **with**, mal vu de.

unprecedented /ʌnˈpresɪdentɪd/ a. sans précédent.

unpredictable /ʌnprɪˈdɪktəbl/ a. imprévisible.

unprepared /ʌnprɪˈpeəd/ a. non préparé; (*person*) qui n'a rien préparé. **be ~ for**, (*not expect*) ne pas s'attendre à.

unpretentious /ʌnprɪˈtenʃəs/ a. sans prétention(s).

unprincipled /ʌnˈprɪnsəpld/ a. sans scrupules.

unprofessional /ʌnprəˈfeʃənl/ a. (*work*) d'amateur; (*conduct*) contraire au code professionnel.

unpublished /ʌnˈpʌblɪʃt/ a. inédit.

unqualified /ʌnˈkwɒlɪfaɪd/ a. non diplômé; (*success etc.*) total. **be ~ to**, ne pas être qualifié pour.

unquestionabl|e /ʌnˈkwestʃənəbl/ a. incontestable. **~y** adv. incontestablement.

unravel /ʌnˈrævl/ v.t. (*p.t.* **unravelled**) démêler, débrouiller.

unreal /ʌnˈrɪəl/ a. irréel.

unreasonable /ʌnˈriːznəbl/ a. déraisonnable, peu raisonnable.

unrecognizable /ʌnrekəɡˈnaɪzəbl/ a. méconnaissable.

unrelated /ʌnrɪˈleɪtɪd/ a. (*facts*) sans rapport (**to**, avec).

unreliable /ʌnrɪˈlaɪəbl/ a. peu sérieux; (*machine*) peu fiable.

unremitting /ʌnrɪˈmɪtɪŋ/ a. (*effort*) acharné; (*emotion*) inaltérable.

unreserved /ʌnrɪˈzɜːvɪdlɪ/ adv. sans réserve.

unrest /ʌnˈrest/ n. troubles m. pl.

unrivalled /ʌnˈraɪvld/ a. sans égal, incomparable.

unroll /ʌnˈrəʊl/ v.t. dérouler.

unruffled /ʌnˈrʌfld/ a. (*person*) qui n'a pas perdu son calme.

unruly /ʌnˈruːlɪ/ a. indiscipliné.

unsafe /ʌnˈseɪf/ a. (*dangerous*) dangereux; (*person*) en danger.

unsaid /ʌnˈsed/ a. **leave ~**, passer sous silence.

unsatisfactory /ʌnsætɪsˈfæktərɪ/ a. peu satisfaisant.

unsavoury /ʌnˈseɪvərɪ/ a. désagréable, répugnant.

unscathed /ʌnˈskeɪðd/ a. indemne.

unscheduled /ʌnˈʃedjuːld, *Amer.* ʌnˈskedʒuːld/ a. pas prévu.

unscrew /ʌnˈskruː/ v.t. dévisser.

unscrupulous /ʌnˈskruːpjʊləs/ a. sans scrupules, malhonnête.

unseemly /ʌnˈsiːmlɪ/ a. inconvenant, incorrect, incongru.

unseen /ʌnˈsiːn/ a. inaperçu. ● n. (*translation*) version f.

unsettle /ʌnˈsetl/ v.t. troubler. **~d** a. (*weather*) instable.

unshakeable /ʌnˈʃeɪkəbl/ a. (*person, belief, etc.*) inébranlable.

unshaven /ʌnˈʃeɪvn/ a. pas rasé.

unsightly /ʌnˈsaɪtlɪ/ a. laid.

unskilled /ʌnˈskɪld/ a. inexpert; (*worker*) non qualifié.

unsociable /ʌnˈsəʊʃəbl/ a. insociable, farouche.

unsophisticated /ʌnsəˈfɪstɪkeɪtɪd/ a. peu sophistiqué, simple.

unsound /ʌnˈsaʊnd/ a. peu solide. **of ~ mind**, fou.

unspeakable /ʌnˈspiːkəbl/ a. indescriptible; (*bad*) innommable.

unspecified /ʌnˈspesɪfaɪd/ a. indéterminé.

unstable /ʌnˈsteɪbl/ a. instable.

unsteady /ʌnˈstedɪ/ a. (*step*) chancelant; (*ladder*) instable; (*hand*) mal assuré.

unstuck /ʌnˈstʌk/ a. décollé. **come ~**, (*fail: fam.*) échouer.

unsuccessful /ʌnsəkˈsesfl/ a. (*result, candidate*) malheureux; (*attempt*) infructueux. **be ~**, ne pas réussir (**in doing**, à faire).

unsuit|able /ʌnˈsuːtəbl/ a. qui ne convient pas (**for**, à), peu approprié. **~ed** a. inapte (**to**, à).

unsure /ʌnˈʃʊə(r)/ a. incertain.

unsuspecting /ʌnsəˈspektɪŋ/ a. qui ne se doute de rien.

unsympathetic /ʌnsɪmpəˈθetɪk/ a. (*unhelpful*) peu compréhensif; (*unpleasant*) antipathique.

untangle /ʌnˈtæŋɡl/ v.t. démêler.

untenable /ʌnˈtenəbl/ a. intenable.

unthinkable /ʌnˈθɪŋkəbl/ a. impensable, inconcevable.

untid|y /ʌnˈtaɪdɪ/ a. (**-ier, -iest**) (*person*) désordonné; (*clothes, hair, room*) en désordre; (*work*) mal soigné. **~ily** adv. sans soin.

untie /ʌnˈtaɪ/ v.t. (*knot, parcel*) défaire; (*person*) détacher.

until /ənˈtɪl/ prep. jusqu'à. **not ~**, pas avant. ● conj. jusqu'à ce que; (*before*) avant que.

untimely /ʌnˈtaɪmlɪ/ a. inopportun; (*death*) prématuré.

untold /ʌnˈtəʊld/ a. incalculable.

untoward /ʌntə'wɔːd/ *a.* fâcheux.

untrue /ʌn'truː/ *a.* faux.

unused[1] /ʌn'juːzd/ *a.* (*new*) neuf; (*not in use*) inutilisé.

unused[2] /ʌn'juːst/ *a.* ~ **to**, peu habitué à.

unusual /ʌn'juːʒʊəl/ *a.* exceptionnel; (*strange*) insolite, étrange. **~ly** *adv.* exceptionnellement.

unveil /ʌn'veɪl/ *v.t.* dévoiler.

unwanted /ʌn'wɒntɪd/ *a.* (*useless*) superflu; (*child*) non désiré.

unwelcome /ʌn'welkəm/ *a.* fâcheux; (*guest*) importun.

unwell /ʌn'wel/ *a.* indisposé.

unwieldy /ʌn'wiːldɪ/ *a.* difficile à manier.

unwilling /ʌn'wɪlɪŋ/ *a.* peu disposé (**to**, à); (*victim*) récalcitrant. **~ly** *adv.* à contrecœur.

unwind /ʌn'waɪnd/ *v.t./i.* (*p.t.* **unwound** /ʌn'waʊnd/) (se) dérouler; (*relax: fam.*) se détendre.

unwise /ʌn'waɪz/ *a.* imprudent.

unwittingly /ʌn'wɪtɪŋlɪ/ *adv.* involontairement.

unworkable /ʌn'wɜːkəbl/ *a.* (*plan etc.*) irréalisable.

unworthy /ʌn'wɜːðɪ/ *a.* indigne.

unwrap /ʌn'ræp/ *v.t.* (*p.t.* **unwrapped**) ouvrir, défaire.

unwritten /ʌn'rɪtn/ *a.* (*agreement*) verbal, tacite.

up /ʌp/ *adv.* en haut, en l'air; (*sun, curtain*) levé; (*out of bed*) levé, debout; (*finished*) fini. **be up**, (*level, price*) avoir monté. ● *prep.* (*a hill*) en haut de; (*a tree*) dans; (*a ladder*) sur. ● *v.t.* (*p.t.* **upped**) augmenter. **come** *or* **go up**, monter. **up in the bedroom**, là-haut dans la chambre. **up there**, là-haut. **up to**, jusqu'à; (*task*) à la hauteur de. **it is up to you**, ça dépend de vous (**to**, de). **be up to sth.**, (*able*) être capable de qch.; (*do*) faire qch.; (*plot*) préparer qch. **be up to**, (*in book*) en être à. **be up against**, faire face à. **be up in**, (*fam.*) s'y connaître en. **feel up to doing**, (*able*) être de taille à faire. **have ups and downs**, connaître des hauts et des bas. **up-and-coming** *a.* prometteur. **up-market** *a.* haut-de-gamme. **up to date**, moderne; (*news*) récent.

upbringing /'ʌpbrɪŋɪŋ/ *n.* éducation *f.*

update /ʌp'deɪt/ *v.t.* mettre à jour.

upgrade /ʌp'greɪd/ *v.t.* (*person*) promouvoir; (*job*) revaloriser.

upheaval /ʌp'hiːvl/ *n.* bouleversement *m.*

uphill /ʌp'hɪl/ *a.* qui monte; (*fig.*) difficile. ● *adv.* **go** ~, monter.

uphold /ʌp'həʊld/ *v.t.* (*p.t.* **upheld**) maintenir.

upholster /ʌp'həʊlstə(r)/ *v.t.* (*pad*) rembourrer; (*cover*) recouvrir. **~y** *n.* (*in vehicle*) garniture *f.*

upkeep /'ʌpkiːp/ *n.* entretien *m.*

upon /ə'pɒn/ *prep.* sur.

upper /'ʌpə(r)/ *a.* supérieur. ● *n.* (*of shoe*) empeigne *f.* **have the ~ hand**, avoir le dessus. **~ class**, aristocratie *f.* **~most** *a.* (*highest*) le plus haut.

upright /'ʌpraɪt/ *a.* droit. ● *n.* (*post*) montant *m.*

uprising /'ʌpraɪzɪŋ/ *n.* soulèvement *m.*, insurrection *f.*

uproar /'ʌprɔː(r)/ *n.* tumulte *m.*

uproot /ʌp'ruːt/ *v.t.* déraciner.

upset[1] /ʌp'set/ *v.t.* (*p.t.* **upset**, *pres. p.* **upsetting**) (*overturn*) renverser; (*plan, stomach*) déranger; (*person*) contrarier, affliger. ● *a.* peiné.

upset[2] /'ʌpset/ *n.* dérangement *m.*; (*distress*) chagrin *m.*

upshot /'ʌpʃɒt/ *n.* résultat *m.*

upside-down /ʌpsaɪd'daʊn/ *adv.* (*in position, in disorder*) à l'envers, sens dessus dessous.

upstairs /ʌp'steəz/ *adv.* en haut. ● *a.* (*flat etc.*) d'en haut.

upstart /'ʌpstɑːt/ *n.* (*pej.*) parvenu(e) *m.* (*f.*).

upstream /ʌp'striːm/ *adv.* en amont.

upsurge /'ʌpsɜːdʒ/ *n.* recrudescence *f.*; (*of anger*) accès *m.*

uptake /'ʌpteɪk/ *n.* **be quick on the** ~, comprendre vite.

uptight /ʌp'taɪt/ *a.* (*tense: fam.*) crispé; (*angry: fam.*) en colère.

upturn /'ʌptɜːn/ *n.* amélioration *f.*

upward /'ʌpwəd/ *a.* & *adv.*, **~s** *adv.* vers le haut.

uranium /jʊ'reɪnɪəm/ *n.* uranium *m.*

urban /'ɜːbən/ *a.* urbain.

urbane /ɜː'beɪn/ *a.* courtois.

urchin /'ɜːtʃɪn/ *n.* garnement *m.*

urge /ɜːdʒ/ *v.t.* conseiller vivement (**to do**, de faire). ● *n.* forte envie *f.* ~ **on**, (*impel*) encourager.

urgen|t /'ɜːdʒənt/ *a.* urgent; (*request*) pressant. **~cy** *n.* urgence *f.*; (*of request, tone*) insistance *f.* **~tly** *adv.* d'urgence.

urinal /jʊə'raɪnl/ *n.* urinoir *m.*

V.

urin|e /'jʊərm/ n. urine f. ~**ate** v.i. uriner.

urn /ɜːn/ n. urne f.; (for tea, coffee) fontaine f.

us /ʌs, unstressed əs/ pron. nous. **(to) us,** nous.

US abbr. see United States.

USA abbr. see United States of America.

usable /'juːzəbl/ a. utilisable.

usage /'juːsɪdʒ/ n. usage m.

use[1] /juːz/ v.t. se servir de, utiliser; (consume) consommer. ~ **up,** épuiser. ~**r** /-ə(r)/ n. usager m. ~**r-friendly** a. facile d'emploi.

use[2] /juːs/ n. usage m., emploi m. **in** ~, en usage. **it is no** ~ **shouting**/etc., ça ne sert à rien de crier/etc. **make** ~ **of,** se servir de. **of** ~, utile.

used[1] /juːzd/ a. (second-hand) d'occasion.

used[2] /juːst/ p.t. **he** ~ **to do,** il faisait (autrefois), il avait l'habitude de faire. ● a. ~ **to,** habitué à.

use|ful /'juːsfl/ a. utile. ~**fully** adv. utilement. ~**less** a. inutile; (person) incompétent.

usher /'ʌʃə(r)/ n. (in theatre, hall) placeur m. ● v.t. ~ **in,** faire entrer. ~**ette** n. ouvreuse f.

USSR abbr. (Union of Soviet Socialist Republics) URSS f.

usual /'juːʒəl/ a. habituel, normal. **as** ~, comme d'habitude. ~**ly** adv. d'habitude.

usurp /juːˈzɜːp/ v.t. usurper.

utensil /juːˈtensl/ n. ustensile m.

uterus /'juːtərəs/ n. utérus m.

utilitarian /juːtɪlɪˈteərɪən/ a. utilitaire.

utility /juːˈtɪlətɪ/ n. utilité f. **(public)** ~, service public m.

utilize /'juːtɪlaɪz/ v.t. utiliser.

utmost /'ʌtməʊst/ a. (furthest, most intense) extrême. **the** ~ **care**/etc., (greatest) le plus grand soin/etc. ● n. **do one's** ~, faire tout son possible.

Utopia /juːˈtəʊpɪə/ n. utopie f. ~**n** a. utopique.

utter[1] /'ʌtə(r)/ a. complet, absolu. ~**ly** adv. complètement.

utter[2] /'ʌtə(r)/ v.t. proférer; (sigh, shout) pousser. ~**ance** n. déclaration f. **give** ~**ance to,** exprimer.

U-turn /'juːtɜːn/ n. demi-tour m.

vacan|t /'veɪkənt/ a. (post) vacant; (seat etc.) libre; (look) vague. ~**cy** n. (post) poste vacant m.; (room) chambre disponible f.

vacate /vəˈkeɪt, Amer. 'veɪkeɪt/ v.t. quitter.

vacation /vərˈkeɪʃn/ n. (Amer.) vacances f. pl.

vaccinat|e /'væksɪneɪt/ v.t. vacciner. ~**ion** /-'neɪʃn/ n. vaccination f.

vaccine /'væksiːn/ n. vaccin m.

vacuum /'vækjʊəm/ n. (pl. **-cuums** or **-cua**) vide m. ~ **cleaner,** aspirateur m. ~ **flask,** bouteille thermos f. (P.). ~**-packed** a. emballé sous vide.

vagabond /'vægəbɒnd/ n. vagabond(e) m. (f.).

vagina /vəˈdʒaɪnə/ n. vagin m.

vagrant /'veɪgrənt/ n. vagabond(e) m. (f.), clochard(e) m. (f.).

vague /veɪg/ a. (-er, -est) vague; (outline) flou. **be** ~ **about,** ne pas préciser. ~**ly** adv. vaguement.

vain /veɪn/ a. (-er, -est) (conceited) vaniteux; (useless) vain. **in** ~, en vain. ~**ly** adv. en vain.

valentine /'væləntam/ n. (card) carte de la Saint-Valentin f.

valet /'vælɪt, 'væleɪ/ n. (manservant) valet de chambre m.

valiant /'vælɪənt/ a. courageux.

valid /'vælɪd/ a. valable. ~**ity** /və'lɪdətɪ/ n. validité f.

validate /'vælɪdeɪt/ v.t. valider.

valley /'vælɪ/ n. vallée f.

valour, (Amer.) **valor** /'vælə(r)/ n. courage m.

valuable /'væljʊəbl/ a. (object) de valeur; (help etc.) précieux. ~**s** n. pl. objets de valeur m. pl.

valuation /væljʊˈeɪʃn/ n. expertise f.; (of house) évaluation f.

value /'væljuː/ n. valeur f. ● v.t. (appraise) évaluer; (cherish) attacher de la valeur à. ~ **added tax,** taxe à la valeur ajoutée f., TVA f. ~**d** a. estimé. ~**r** /-ə(r)/ n. expert m.

valve /vælv/ n. (techn.) soupape f.; (of tyre) valve f.; (radio) lampe f.

vampire /'væmpaɪə(r)/ n. vampire m.

van /væn/ n. (vehicle) camionnette f.; (rail.) fourgon m.

vandal /'vændl/ n. vandale m./f. ~**ism** /-əlɪzəm/ n. vandalisme m.

vandalize /'vændəlaız/ v.t. abîmer, détruire, saccager.

vanguard /'vængɑ:d/ n. (of army, progress, etc.) avant-garde f.

vanilla /və'nılə/ n. vanille f.

vanish /'vænıʃ/ v.i. disparaître.

vanity /'vænətı/ n. vanité f. **~ case**, mallette de toilette f.

vantage-point /'vɑ:tɪdʒpɔɪnt/ n. (place) excellent point de vue m.

vapour /'veɪpə(r)/ n. vapeur f.

vari|able /'veərɪəbl/ a. variable. **~ation** /-'eɪʃn/ n. variation f. **~ed** /-ɪd/ a. varié.

variance /'veərɪəns/ n. **at ~**, en désaccord (with, avec).

variant /'veərɪənt/ a. différent. ● n. variante f.

varicose /'værɪkəus/ a. **~ veins**, varices f. pl.

variety /və'raɪətı/ n. variété f.; (entertainment) variétés f. pl.

various /'veərɪəs/ a. divers. **~ly** adv. diversement.

varnish /'vɑ:nɪʃ/ n. vernis m. ● v.t. vernir.

vary /'veərɪ/ v.t./i. varier.

vase /vɑ:z, Amer. veɪs/ n. vase m.

vast /vɑ:st/ a. vaste, immense. **~ly** adv. infiniment, extrêmement. **~ness** n. immensité f.

vat /væt/ n. cuve f.

VAT /vi:eɪti:, væt/ abbr. (value added tax) TVA f.

vault[1] /vɔ:lt/ n. (roof) voûte f.; (in bank) chambre forte f.; (tomb) caveau m.; (cellar) cave f.

vault[2] /vɔ:lt/ v.t./i. sauter. ● n. saut m.

vaunt /vɔ:nt/ v.t. vanter.

VCR abbr. see video cassette recorder.

VDU abbr. see visual display unit.

veal /vi:l/ n. (meat) veau m.

veer /vɪə(r)/ v.i. tourner, virer.

vegan /'vi:gən/ a. & n. végétalien(-ne) (m. (f.)).

vegetable /'vedʒtəbl/ n. légume m. ● a. végétal. **~ garden**, (jardin) potager m.

vegetarian /vedʒɪ'teərɪən/ a. & n. végétarien(ne) (m. (f.)).

vegetate /'vedʒɪteɪt/ v.i. végéter.

vegetation /vedʒɪ'teɪʃn/ n. végétation f.

vehement /'vi:əmənt/ a. véhément. **~ly** adv. avec véhémence.

vehicle /'vi:ɪkl/ n. véhicule m.

veil /veɪl/ n. voile m. ● v.t. voiler.

vein /veɪn/ n. (in body, rock) veine f.; (on leaf) nervure f. (mood) esprit m.

velocity /vɪ'lɒsətɪ/ n. vélocité f.

velvet /'velvɪt/ n. velours m.

vending-machine /'vendɪŋməʃi:n/ n. distributeur automatique m.

vendor /'vendə(r)/ n. vendeu|r, -se m., f.

veneer /və'nɪə(r)/ n. placage m.; (appearance: fig.) vernis m.

venerable /'venərəbl/ a. vénérable.

venereal /və'nɪərɪəl/ a. vénérien.

venetian /və'ni:ʃn/ a. **~ blind**, jalousie f.

vengeance /'vendʒəns/ n. vengeance f. **with a ~**, furieusement.

venison /'venɪzn/ n. venaison f.

venom /'venəm/ n. venin m. **~ous** /'venəməs/ a. venimeux.

vent[1] /vent/ n. (in coat) fente f.

vent[2] /vent/ n. (hole) orifice m.; (for air) bouche d'aération f. ● v.t. (anger) décharger (on, sur). **give ~ to**, donner libre cours à.

ventilat|e /'ventɪleɪt/ v.t. ventiler. **~ion** /-'leɪʃn/ n. ventilation f. **~or** n. ventilateur m.

ventriloquist /ven'trɪləkwɪst/ n. ventriloque m./f.

venture /'ventʃə(r)/ n. entreprise f. ● v.t./i. (se) risquer.

venue /'venju:/ n. lieu de rencontre or de rendez-vous m.

veranda /və'rændə/ n. véranda f.

verb /vɜ:b/ n. verbe m.

verbal /'vɜ:bl/ a. verbal.

verbatim /vɜ:'beɪtɪm/ adv. textuellement, mot pour mot.

verdict /'vɜ:dɪkt/ n. verdict m.

verge /vɜ:dʒ/ n. bord m. ● v.i. **~ on**, friser, frôler. **on the ~ of doing**, sur le point de faire.

verif|y /'verɪfaɪ/ v.t. vérifier. **~ication** /-ɪ'keɪʃn/ n. vérification f.

vermicelli /vɜ:mɪ'selɪ/ n. vermicelle(s) m. (pl.).

vermin /'vɜ:mɪn/ n. vermine f.

vermouth /'vɜ:məθ/ n. vermouth m.

vernacular /və'nækjulə(r)/ n. langue f.; (regional) dialecte m.

versatil|e /'vɜ:sətaɪl, Amer. 'vɜ:sətl/ a. (person) aux talents variés; (mind) souple. **~ity** /-'tɪlətɪ/ n. souplesse f. **her ~ity**, la variété de ses talents.

verse /vɜ:s/ n. strophe f.; (of Bible) verset m.; (poetry) vers m. pl.

versed /vɜ:st/ a. **~ in**, versé dans.

version /'vɜ:ʃn/ n. version f.

versus /'vɜ:səs/ prep. contre.

vertebra /'vɜːtɪbrə/ n. (pl. -brae /-briː/) vertèbre f.

vertical /'vɜːtɪkl/ a. vertical. ~ly adv. verticalement.

vertigo /'vɜːtɪgəʊ/ n. vertige m.

verve /vɜːv/ n. fougue f.

very /'verɪ/ adv. très. ● a. (actual) même. the ~ day/etc., le jour/etc. même. at the ~ end, tout à la fin. the ~ first, le tout premier. ~ much, beaucoup.

vessel /'vesl/ n. (duct, ship) vaisseau m.

vest /vest/ n. maillot de corps m.; (waistcoat: Amer.) gilet m.

vested /'vestɪd/ a. ~ interests, droits acquis m. pl., intérêts m. pl.

vestige /'vestɪdʒ/ n. vestige m.

vestry /'vestrɪ/ n. sacristie f.

vet /vet/ n. (fam.) vétérinaire m./f. ● v.t. (p.t. vetted) (candidate etc.) examiner (de près).

veteran /'vetərən/ n. vétéran m. (war) ~, ancien combattant m.

veterinary /'vetərɪnərɪ/ a. vétérinaire. ~ surgeon, vétérinaire m. /f.

veto /'viːtəʊ/ n. (pl. -oes) veto m.; (right) droit de veto m. ● v.t. mettre son veto à.

vex /veks/ v.t. contrarier, irriter. ~ed question, question controversée f.

via /'vaɪə/ prep. via, par.

viable /'vaɪəbl/ a. (baby, plan, firm) viable.

viaduct /'vaɪədʌkt/ n. viaduc m.

vibrant /'vaɪbrənt/ a. vibrant.

vibrat|e /vaɪ'breɪt/ v.t./i. (faire) vibrer. ~ion /-ʃn/ n. vibration f.

vicar /'vɪkə(r)/ n. pasteur m. ~age n. presbytère m.

vicarious /vɪ'keərɪəs/ a. (emotion) ressenti indirectement.

vice[1] /vaɪs/ n. (depravity) vice m.

vice[2] /vaɪs/ n. (techn.) étau m.

vice- /vaɪs/ pref. vice-.

vice versa /'vaɪsɪ'vɜːsə/ adv. vice versa.

vicinity /vɪ'sɪnətɪ/ n. environs m. pl. in the ~ of, aux environs de.

vicious /'vɪʃəs/ a. (spiteful) méchant; (violent) brutal. ~ circle, cercle vicieux m. ~ly adv. méchamment; brutalement.

victim /'vɪktɪm/ n. victime f.

victimiz|e /'vɪktɪmaɪz/ v.t. persécuter, martyriser. ~ation /-'zeɪʃn/ n. persécution f.

victor /'vɪktə(r)/ n. vainqueur m.

Victorian /vɪk'tɔːrɪən/ a. & n. victorien(ne) (m. (f.)).

victor|y /'vɪktərɪ/ n. victoire f. ~ious /-'tɔːrɪəs/ a. victorieux.

video /'vɪdɪəʊ/ a. (game, camera) vidéo invar. ● n. (recorder) magnétoscope m.; (film) vidéo f. ~ cassette, vidéocassette f. ~ (cassette) recorder, magnétoscope m. ● v.t. (programme) enregistrer.

videotape /'vɪdɪəʊteɪp/ n. bande vidéo f. ● v.t. (programme) enregistrer; (wedding) filmer avec une caméra vidéo.

vie /vaɪ/ v.i. (pres. p. vying) rivaliser (with, avec).

view /vjuː/ n. vue f. ● v.t. (watch) regarder; (consider) considérer (as, comme); (house) visiter. in my ~, à mon avis. in ~ of, compte tenu de. on ~, exposé. with a ~ to, dans le but de. ~er n. (TV) téléspecta|teur, -trice m., f.; (for slides) visionneuse f.

viewfinder /'vjuːfaɪndə(r)/ n. viseur m.

viewpoint /'vjuːpɔɪnt/ n. point de vue m.

vigil /'vɪdʒɪl/ n. veille f.; (over sick person, corpse) veillée f.

vigilan|t /'vɪdʒɪlənt/ a. vigilant. ~ce n. vigilance f.

vig|our, (Amer.) **vigor** /'vɪgə(r)/ n. vigueur f. ~orous a. vigoureux.

vile /vaɪl/ a. (base) infâme, vil; (bad) abominable, exécrable.

vilify /'vɪlɪfaɪ/ v.t. diffamer.

villa /'vɪlə/ n. villa f., pavillon m.

village /'vɪlɪdʒ/ n. village m. ~r /-ə(r)/ n. villageois(e) m. (f.).

villain /'vɪlən/ n. scélérat m., bandit m.; (in story etc.) méchant m. ~y n. infamie f.

vindicat|e /'vɪndɪkeɪt/ v.t. justifier. ~ion /-'keɪʃn/ n. justification f.

vindictive /vɪn'dɪktɪv/ a. vindicatif.

vine /vaɪn/ n. vigne f.

vinegar /'vɪnɪgə(r)/ n. vinaigre m.

vineyard /'vɪnjəd/ n. vignoble m.

vintage /'vɪntɪdʒ/ n. (year) année f., millésime m. ● a. (wine) de grand cru; (car) d'époque.

vinyl /'vaɪnɪl/ n. vinyle m.

viola /vɪ'əʊlə/ n. (mus.) alto m.

violat|e /'vaɪəleɪt/ v.t. violer. ~ion /-'leɪʃn/ n. violation f.

violen|t /'vaɪələnt/ a. violent. **~ce** n. violence f. **~tly** adv. violemment, avec violence.

violet /'vaɪələt/ n. (bot.) violette f.; (colour) violet m. ● a. violet.

violin /vaɪə'lɪn/ n. violon m. **~ist** n. violoniste m./f.

VIP /vi:aɪ'pi:/ abbr. (very important person) personnage de marque m.

viper /'vaɪpə(r)/ n. vipère f.

virgin /'vɜːdʒɪn/ n. (woman) vierge f. ● a. vierge. **be a ~,** (woman, man) être vierge. **~ity** /və'dʒɪnətɪ/ n. virginité f.

Virgo /'vɜːgəʊ/ n. la Vierge.

viril|e /'vɪraɪl, Amer. 'vɪrəl/ a. viril. **~ity** /vɪ'rɪlətɪ/ n. virilité f.

virtual /'vɜːtʃʊəl/ a. vrai. **a ~ failure/etc.,** pratiquement un échec/etc. **~ly** adv. pratiquement.

virtue /'vɜːtʃuː/ n. (goodness, chastity) vertu f.; (merit) mérite m. **by** or **in ~ of,** en raison de.

virtuos|o /vɜːtʃʊ'əʊsəʊ/ n. (pl. -si /-siː/) virtuose m./f. **~ity** /-'ɒsətɪ/ n. virtuosité f.

virtuous /'vɜːtʃʊəs/ a. vertueux.

virulent /'vɪrʊlənt/ a. virulent.

virus /'vaɪərəs/ n. (pl. -uses) virus m.

visa /'viːzə/ n. visa m.

viscount /'vaɪkaʊnt/ n. vicomte m.

viscous /'vɪskəs/ a. visqueux.

vise /vaɪs/ n. (Amer.) étau m.

visib|le /'vɪzəbl/ a. (discernible, obvious) visible. **~ility** /-'bɪlətɪ/ n. visibilité f. **~ly** adv. visiblement.

vision /'vɪʒn/ n. vision f.

visionary /'vɪʒənərɪ/ a. & n. visionnaire (m./f.).

visit /'vɪzɪt/ v.t. (p.t. visited) (person) rendre visite à; (place) visiter. ● v.i. être en visite. ● n. (tour, call) visite f.; (stay) séjour m. **~or** n. visiteu|r, -se m., f.; (guest) invité(e) m. (f.); (in hotel) client(e) m. (f.).

visor /'vaɪzə(r)/ n. visière f.

vista /'vɪstə/ n. perspective f.

visual /'vɪʒʊəl/ a. visuel. **~ display unit,** visuel m., console de visualisation f. **~ly** adv. visuellement.

visualize /'vɪʒʊəlaɪz/ v.t. se représenter; (foresee) envisager.

vital /'vaɪtl/ a. vital. **~ statistics,** (fam.) mensurations f. pl.

vitality /vaɪ'tælətɪ/ n. vitalité f.

vitally /'vaɪtəlɪ/ adv. extrêmement.

vitamin /'vɪtəmɪn/ n. vitamine f.

vivaci|ous /vɪ'veɪʃəs/ a. plein d'entrain, animé. **~ity** /-'æsətɪ/ n. vivacité f., entrain m.

vivid /'vɪvɪd/ a. vif; (graphic) vivant. **~ly** adv. vivement; (describe) de façon vivante.

vivisection /vɪvɪ'sekʃn/ n. vivisection f.

vocabulary /və'kæbjʊlərɪ/ n. vocabulaire m.

vocal /'vəʊkl/ a. vocal; (person: fig.) qui s'exprime franchement. **~ cords,** cordes vocales f. pl. **~ist** n. chanteu|r, -se m., f.

vocation /və'keɪʃn/ n. vocation f. **~al** professionnel.

vociferous /və'sɪfərəs/ a. bruyant.

vodka /'vɒdkə/ n. vodka f.

vogue /vəʊg/ n. (fashion, popularity) vogue f. **in ~,** en vogue.

voice /vɔɪs/ n. voix f. ● v.t. (express) formuler.

void /vɔɪd/ a. vide (**of,** de); (not valid) nul. ● n. vide m.

volatile /'vɒlətaɪl, Amer. 'vɒlətl/ a. (person) versatile; (situation) variable.

volcan|o /vɒl'keɪnəʊ/ n. (pl. -oes) volcan m. **~ic** /-ænɪk/ a. volcanique.

volition /və'lɪʃn/ n. **of one's own ~,** de son propre gré.

volley /'vɒlɪ/ n. (of blows etc., in tennis) volée f.; (of gunfire) salve f. **~-ball** n. volley(-ball) m.

volt /vəʊlt/ n. (electr.) volt m. **~age** n. voltage m.

voluble /'vɒljʊbl/ a. volubile.

volume /'vɒljuːm/ n. volume m.

voluntar|y /'vɒləntərɪ/ a. volontaire; (unpaid) bénévole. **~ily** /-trəlɪ, Amer. -'terəlɪ/ adv. volontairement.

volunteer /vɒlən'tɪə(r)/ n. volontaire m./f. ● v.i. s'offrir (**to do,** pour faire); (mil.) s'engager comme volontaire. ● v.t. offrir.

voluptuous /və'lʌptʃʊəs/ a. voluptueux.

vomit /'vɒmɪt/ v.t./i. (p.t. vomited) vomir. ● n. vomi(ssement) m.

voracious /və'reɪʃəs/ a. vorace.

vot|e /vəʊt/ n. vote m.; (right) droit de vote m. ● v.t./i. voter. **~ (in),** (person) élire. **~er** n. élec|teur, -trice m., f. **~ing** n. vote m. (**of,** de); (poll) scrutin m.

vouch /vaʊtʃ/ v.i. **~ for,** se porter garant de, répondre de.

voucher /'vaʊtʃə(r)/ n. bon m.

vow /vaʊ/ n. vœu m. ● v.t. (loyalty etc.) jurer (**to**, à). ~ **to do**, jurer de faire.

vowel /'vaʊəl/ n. voyelle f.

voyage /'vɔɪdʒ/ n. voyage (par mer) m.

vulgar /'vʌlgə(r)/ a. vulgaire. ~**ity** /-'gærətɪ/ n. vulgarité f.

vulnerab|le /'vʌlnərəbl/ a. vulnérable. ~**ility** /-'bɪlətɪ/ n. vulnérabilité f.

vulture /'vʌltʃə(r)/ n. vautour m.

W

wad /wɒd/ n. (pad) tampon m.; (bundle) liasse f.

wadding /'wɒdɪŋ/ n. rembourrage m., ouate f.

waddle /'wɒdl/ v.i. se dandiner.

wade /weɪd/ v.i. ~ **through**, (mud etc.) patauger dans; (book: fig.) avancer péniblement dans.

wafer /'weɪfə(r)/ n. (biscuit) gaufrette f.; (relig.) hostie f.

waffle[1] /'wɒfl/ n. (talk: fam.) verbiage m. ● v.i. (fam.) divaguer.

waffle[2] /'wɒfl/ n. (cake) gaufre f.

waft /wɒft/ v.i. flotter. ● v.t. porter.

wag /wæg/ v.t./i. (p.t. **wagged**) (tail) remuer.

wage[1] /weɪdʒ/ v.t. (campaign) mener. ~ **war**, faire la guerre.

wage[2] /weɪdʒ/ n. (weekly, daily) salaire m. ~**s**, salaire m. ~**-earner** n. salarié(e) m. (f.).

wager /'weɪdʒə(r)/ n. (bet) pari m. ● v.t. parier (**that**, que).

waggle /'wægl/ v.t./i. remuer.

wagon /'wægən/ n. (horse-drawn) chariot m.; (rail.) wagon (de marchandises) m.

waif /weɪf/ n. enfant abandonné(e) m.(f.).

wail /weɪl/ v.i. (utter cry or complaint) gémir. ● n. gémissement m.

waist /weɪst/ n. taille f.

waistcoat /'weɪskəʊt/ n. gilet m.

wait /weɪt/ v.t./i. attendre. ● n. attente f. **I can't ~**, je n'en peux plus d'impatience. **let's ~ and see**, attendons voir. **while you ~**, sur place. ~ **for**, attendre. ~ **on**, servir. ~**ing-list** n. liste d'attente f. ~**ing-room** n. salle d'attente f.

wait|er /'weɪtə(r)/ n. garçon m., serveur m. ~**ress** n. serveuse f.

waive /weɪv/ v.t. renoncer à.

wake[1] /weɪk/ v.t./i. (p.t. **woke**, p.p. **woken**). ~ (**up**), (se) réveiller.

wake[2] /weɪk/ n. (track) sillage m. **in the ~ of**, (after) à la suite de.

waken /'weɪkən/ v.t./i. (se) réveiller, (s')éveiller.

Wales /weɪlz/ n. pays de Galles m.

walk /wɔːk/ v.i. marcher; (not ride) aller à pied; (stroll) se promener. ● v.t. (streets) parcourir; (distance) faire à pied; (dog) promener. ● n. promenade f., tour m.; (gait) démarche f.; (pace) marche f., pas m.; (path) allée f. ~ **of life**, condition sociale f. ~ **out**, (go away) partir; (worker) faire grève. ~**-out** n. grève surprise f. ~ **out on**, abandonner. ~**-over** n. victoire facile f.

walker /'wɔːkə(r)/ n. (person) marcheu|r, -se m., f.

walkie-talkie /wɔːkɪ'tɔːkɪ/ n. talkiewalkie m.

walking /'wɔːkɪŋ/ n. marche (à pied) f. ● a. (corpse, dictionary: fig.) vivant. ~**-stick** n. canne f.

Walkman /'wɔːkmən/ n. (P.) Walkman (P.) m., baladeur m.

wall /wɔːl/ n. mur m.; (of tunnel, stomach, etc.) paroi f. ● a. mural. ● v.t. (city) fortifier. **go to the ~**, (firm) faire faillite.

wallet /'wɒlɪt/ n. portefeuille m.

wallflower /'wɔːlflaʊə(r)/ n. (bot.) giroflée f.

wallop /'wɒləp/ v.t. (p.t. **walloped**) (hit: sl.) taper sur. ● n. (blow: sl.) grand coup m.

wallow /'wɒləʊ/ v.i. se vautrer.

wallpaper /'wɔːlpeɪpə(r)/ n. papier peint m. ● v.t. tapisser.

walnut /'wɔːlnʌt/ n. (nut) noix f.; (tree) noyer m.

walrus /'wɔːlrəs/ n. morse m.

waltz /wɔːls/ n. valse f. ● v.i. valser.

wan /wɒn/ a. pâle, blême.

wand /wɒnd/ n. baguette (magique) f.

wander /'wɒndə(r)/ v.i. errer; (stroll) flâner; (digress) s'écarter du sujet; (in mind) divaguer. ~**er** n. vagabond(e) m. (f.).

wane /weɪn/ v.i. décroître. ● n. **on the ~**, (strength, fame, etc.) en déclin; (person) sur son déclin.

wangle /'wæŋgl/ v.t. (obtain: sl.) se débrouiller pour avoir.

want /wɒnt/ *v.t.* vouloir (**to do**, faire); (*need*) avoir besoin de (**doing**, d'être fait); (*ask for*) demander. ● *v.i.* ~ **for**, manquer de. ● *n.* (*need, poverty*) besoin *m.*; (*desire*) désir *m.*; (*lack*) manque *m.* **I** ~ **you to do it**, je veux que vous le fassiez. **for** ~ **of**, faute de. ~**ed** *a.* (*criminal*) recherché par la police.

wanting /ˈwɒntɪŋ/ *a.* **be** ~, manquer (**in**, de).

wanton /ˈwɒntən/ *a.* (*cruelty*) gratuit; (*woman*) impudique.

war /wɔː(r)/ *n.* guerre *f.* **at** ~, en guerre. **on the** ~**-path**, sur le sentier de la guerre.

ward /wɔːd/ *n.* (*in hospital*) salle *f.*; (*minor; jurid.*) pupille *m./f.*; (*pol.*) division électorale *f.* ● *v.t.* ~ **off**, (*danger*) prévenir; (*blow, anger*) détourner.

warden /ˈwɔːdn/ *n.* direc|teur, -trice *m.*, *f.*; (*of park*) gardien(ne) *m.* (*f.*). (**traffic**) ~, contractuel(le) *m.* (*f.*).

warder /ˈwɔːdə(r)/ *n.* gardien (de prison) *m.*

wardrobe /ˈwɔːdrəʊb/ *n.* (*place*) armoire *f.*; (*clothes*) garde-robe *f.*

warehouse /ˈweəhaʊs/ *n.* (*pl.* -s /-haʊzɪz/) entrepôt *m.*

wares /weəz/ *n. pl.* (*goods*) marchandises *f. pl.*

warfare /ˈwɔːfeə(r)/ *n.* guerre *f.*

warhead /ˈwɔːhed/ *n.* ogive *f.*

warily /ˈweərɪlɪ/ *adv.* avec prudence.

warm /wɔːm/ *a.* (**-er**, **-est**) chaud; (*hearty*) chaleureux. **be** *or* **feel** ~, avoir chaud. **it is** ~, il fait chaud. ● *v.t./i.* ~ (**up**), (se) réchauffer; (*food*) chauffer; (*liven up*) (s')animer; (*exercise*) s'échauffer. ~**hearted** *a.* chaleureux. ~**ly** *adv.* (*wrap up etc.*) chaudement; (*heartily*) chaleureusement. ~**th** *n.* chaleur *f.*

warn /wɔːn/ *v.t.* avertir, prévenir. ~ **s.o. off sth.**, (*advise against*) mettre qn. en garde contre qch.; (*forbid*) interdire qch. à qn. ~**ing** *n.* avertissement *m.*; (*notice*) avis *m.* **without** ~**ing**, sans prévenir. ~**ing light**, voyant *m.* ~**ing triangle**, triangle de sécurité *m.*

warp /wɔːp/ *v.t./i.* (*wood etc.*) (se) voiler; (*pervert*) pervertir.

warrant /ˈwɒrənt/ *n.* (*for arrest*) mandat (d'arrêt) *m.*; (*comm.*) autorisation *f.* ● *v.t.* justifier.

warranty /ˈwɒrəntɪ/ *n.* garantie *f.*

warring /ˈwɔːrɪŋ/ *a.* en guerre.

warrior /ˈwɒrɪə(r)/ *n.* guerr|ier, -ière *m.*, *f.*

warship /ˈwɔːʃɪp/ *n.* navire de guerre *m.*

wart /wɔːt/ *n.* verrue *f.*

wartime /ˈwɔːtaɪm/ *n.* **in** ~, en temps de guerre.

wary /ˈweərɪ/ *a.* (**-ier**, **-iest**) prudent.

was /wɒz, *unstressed* wəz/ *see* **be**.

wash /wɒʃ/ *v.t./i.* (se) laver; (*flow over*) baigner. ● *n.* lavage *m.*; (*clothes*) lessive *f.*; (*of ship*) sillage *m.* **have a** ~, se laver. ~**-basin** *n.* lavabo *m.* ~**-cloth** *n.* (*Amer.*) gant de toilette *m.* ~ **down**, (*meal*) arroser. ~ **one's hands of**, se laver les mains de. ~ **out**, (*cup etc.*) laver; (*stain*) (faire) partir. ~**-out** *n.* (*sl.*) fiasco *m.* ~**-room** *n.* (*Amer.*) toilettes *f. pl.* ~ **up**, faire la vaisselle; (*Amer.*) se laver. ~**able** *a.* lavable. ~**ing** *n.* lessive *f.* ~**ing-machine** *n.* machine à laver *f.* ~**ing-powder** *n.* lessive *f.* ~**ing-up** *n.* vaisselle *f.*; ~**ing-up liquid**, produit pour la vaisselle *m.*

washed-out /wɒʃt'aʊt/ *a.* (*faded*) délavé; (*tired*) lessivé; (*ruined*) anéanti.

washer /ˈwɒʃə(r)/ *n.* rondelle *f.*

wasp /wɒsp/ *n.* guêpe *f.*

wastage /ˈweɪstɪdʒ/ *n.* gaspillage *m.* **some** ~, (*in goods*, *among candidates, etc.*) du déchet.

waste /weɪst/ *v.t.* (*time*) perdre; (*product*) de rebut. ● *v.i.* ~ **away**, dépérir. ● *a.* superflu; (*product*) de rebut. ● *n.* gaspillage *m.*; (*of time*) perte *f.*; (*rubbish*) déchets *m. pl.* **lay** ~, dévaster. ~ **disposal unit**, broyeur d'ordures *m.* ~ (**land**), (*desolate*) terre désolée *f.*; (*unused*) terre inculte *f.*; (*in town*) terrain vague *m.* ~ **paper**, vieux papiers *m. pl.* ~**-paper basket**, corbeille (à papier) *f.* ~**-pipe** *n.* vidange *f.*

wasteful /ˈweɪstfl/ *a.* peu économique; (*person*) gaspilleur.

watch /wɒtʃ/ *v.t./i.* (*television*) regarder; (*observe*) observer; (*guard, spy on*) surveiller; (*be careful about*) faire attention à. ● *n.* (*for telling time*) montre *f.*; (*naut.*) quart *m.* **be on the** ~, guetter. **keep** ~ **on**, surveiller. ~**-dog** *n.* chien de garde *m.* ~ **out**, (*take care*) faire attention (**for**, à). ~ **out for**, guetter. ~**-tower** *n.* tour de guet *f.* ~**ful** *a.* vigilant.

watchmaker /'wɒtʃmeɪkə(r)/ n. horlog|er, -ère m., f.

watchman /'wɒtʃmən/ n. (pl. -men) (of building) gardien m.

water /'wɔːtə(r)/ n. eau f. ● v.t. arroser. ● v.i. (of eyes) larmoyer. **my/his/etc. mouth ~s**, l'eau me/lui/etc. vient à la bouche. **by ~**, en bateau. **~-bottle** n. bouillotte f. **~-closet** n. waters m. pl. **~-colour** n. couleur pour aquarelle f.; (painting) aquarelle f. **~ down**, couper (d'eau); (tone down) édulcorer. **~ heater**, chauffe-eau m. **~-ice** n. sorbet m. **~-lily** n. nénuphar m. **~-main** n. canalisation d'eau f. **~-melon** n. pastèque f. **~-pistol** n. pistolet à eau m. **~ polo**, water-polo m. **~-power**, énergie hydraulique f. **~-skiing** n. ski nautique m.

watercress /'wɔːtəkres/ n. cresson (de fontaine) m.

waterfall /'wɔːtəfɔːl/ n. chute d'eau f., cascade f.

watering-can /'wɔːtərɪŋkæn/ n. arrosoir m.

waterlogged /'wɔːtəlɒgd/ a. imprégné d'eau; (land) détrempé.

watermark /'wɔːtəmɑːk/ n. (in paper) filigrane m.

waterproof /'wɔːtəpruːf/ a. (material) imperméable.

watershed /'wɔːtəʃed/ n. (in affairs) tournant décisif m.

watertight /'wɔːtətaɪt/ a. étanche.

waterway /'wɔːtəweɪ/ n. voie navigable f.

waterworks /'wɔːtəwɜːks/ n. (place) station hydraulique f.

watery /'wɔːtərɪ/ a. (colour) délavé; (eyes) humide; (soup) trop liquide; (tea) faible.

watt /wɒt/ n. watt m.

wav|e /weɪv/ n. vague f.; (in hair) ondulation f.; (radio) onde f.; (sign) signe m. ● v.t. agiter. ● v.i. faire signe (de la main); (move in wind) flotter. **~y** a. (line) onduleux; (hair) ondulé.

wavelength /'weɪvleŋθ/ n. (radio & fig.) longueur d'ondes f.

waver /'weɪvə(r)/ v.i. vaciller.

wax[1] /wæks/ n. cire f.; (for skis) fart m. ● v.t. cirer; farter; (car) astiquer. **~en, ~y** adjs. cireux.

wax[2] /wæks/ v.i. (of moon) croître.

waxwork /'wækswɜːk/ n. (dummy) figure de cire f.

way /weɪ/ n. (road, path) chemin m. (**to**, de); (distance) distance f.; (direction) direction f.; (manner) façon f.; (means) moyen m.; (particular) égard m. **~s**, (habits) habitudes f. pl. ● adv. (fam.) loin. **be in the ~**, bloquer le passage; (hindrance: fig.) gêner (qn.). **be on one's or the ~**, être sur son or le chemin. **by the ~**, à propos. **by the ~side**, au bord de la route. **by ~ of**, comme; (via) par. **go out of one's ~**, se donner du mal pour. **in a ~**, dans un sens. **make one's ~ somewhere**, se rendre quelque part. **push one's ~ through**, se frayer un passage. **that ~**, par là. **this ~**, par ici. **~ in**, entrée f. **~ out**, sortie f. **~-out** a. (strange: fam.) original.

waylay /'weɪleɪ/ v.t. (p.t. -laid) (assail) assaillir; (stop) accrocher.

wayward /'weɪwəd/ a. capricieux.

WC /dʌb(ə)ljuːˈsiː/ n. w.-c. m. pl.

we /wiː/ pron. nous.

weak /wiːk/ a. (-er, -est) faible; (delicate) fragile. **~ly** adv. faiblement; a. faible. **~ness** n. faiblesse f.; (fault) point faible m. **a ~ness for**, (liking) un faible pour.

weaken /'wiːkən/ v.t. affaiblir ● v.i. s'affaiblir, faiblir.

weakling /'wiːklɪŋ/ n. gringalet m.

wealth /welθ/ n. richesse f.; (riches, resources) richesses f. pl.; (quantity) profusion f.

wealthy /'welθɪ/ a. (-ier, -iest) riche. ● n. **the ~**, les riches m. pl.

wean /wiːn/ v.t. (baby) sevrer.

weapon /'wepən/ n. arme f.

wear /weə(r)/ v.t. (p.t. wore, p.p. worn) porter; (put on) mettre; (expression etc.) avoir. ● v.i. (last) durer. **~ (out)**, (s')user. ● n. usage m.; (damage) usure f.; (clothing) vêtements m. pl. **~ down**, user. **~ off**, (colour, pain) passer. **~ on**, (time) passer. **~ out**, (exhaust) épuiser.

wear|y /'wɪərɪ/ a. (-ier, -iest) fatigué, las; (tiring) fatigant. ● v.i. **~y of**, se lasser de. **~ily** adv. avec lassitude. **~iness** n. lassitude f., fatigue f.

weasel /'wiːzl/ n. belette f.

weather /'weðə(r)/ n. temps m. ● a. météorologique. ● v.t. (survive) réchapper de or à. **under the ~**, patraque. **~-beaten** a. tanné. **~**

forecast, météo *f.* ~**-vane** *n.* girouette *f.*

weathercock /'weðəkɒk/ *n.* girouette *f.*

weave /wiːv/ *v.t./i.* (*p.t.* **wove,** *p.p.* **woven**) tisser; (*basket etc.*) tresser; (*move*) se faufiler. ● *n.* (*style*) tissage *m.* ~**r** /-ə(r)/ *n.* tisserand(e) *m.* (*f.*).

web /web/ *n.* (*of spider*) toile *f.*; (*fabric*) tissu *m.*; (*on foot*) palmure *f.* ~**bed** *a.* (*foot*) palmé. ~**bing** *n.* (*in chair*) sangles *f. pl.*

wed /wed/ *v.t.* (*p.t.* **wedded**) épouser. ● *v.i.* se marier. ~**ded to,** (*devoted to: fig.*) attaché à.

wedding /'wedɪŋ/ *n.* mariage *m.* ~**-ring** *n.* alliance *f.*

wedge /wedʒ/ *n.* coin *m.*; (*under wheel etc.*) cale *f.* ● *v.t.* caler; (*push*) enfoncer; (*crowd*) coincer.

Wednesday /'wenzdɪ/ *n.* mercredi *m.*

wee /wiː/ *a.* (*fam.*) tout petit.

weed /wiːd/ *n.* mauvaise herbe *f.* ● *v.t./i.* désherber. ~**-killer** *n.* désherbant *m.* ~ **out,** extirper. ~**y** *a.* (*person: fig.*) faible, maigre.

week /wiːk/ *n.* semaine *f.* **a ~ today/ tomorrow,** aujourd'hui/demain en huit. ~**ly** *adv.* toutes les semaines; *a. & n.* (*periodical*) hebdomadaire (*m.*).

weekday /'wiːkdeɪ/ *n.* jour de semaine *m.*

weekend /wiːk'end/ *n.* week-end *m.*, fin de semaine *f.*

weep /wiːp/ *v.t./i.* (*p.t.* **wept**) pleurer (**for s.o.,** qn.). ~**ing willow,** saule pleureur *m.*

weigh /weɪ/ *v.t./i.* peser. ~ **anchor,** lever l'ancre. ~ **down,** lester (avec un poids); (*bend*) plier; (*fig.*) accabler. ~ **up,** (*examine: fam.*) calculer.

weight /weɪt/ *n.* poids *m.* **lose/put on ~,** perdre/prendre du poids. ~**lessness** *n.* apesanteur *f.* ~**lifting** *n.* haltérophilie *f.* ~**y** *a.* lourd; (*subject etc.*) de poids.

weighting /'weɪtɪŋ/ *n.* indemnité *f.*

weir /wɪə(r)/ *n.* barrage *m.*

weird /wɪəd/ *a.* (**-er, -est**) mystérieux; (*strange*) bizarre.

welcome /'welkəm/ *a.* agréable; (*timely*) opportun. **be ~,** être le or la bienvenu(e), être les bienvenu(e)s. **you're ~!,** (*after thank you*) il n'y a pas de quoi! ~ **to do,** libre de faire. ● *int.* soyez le *or* la bienvenu(e),

soyez les bienvenu(e)s. ● *n.* accueil *m.* ● *v.t.* accueillir; (*as greeting*) souhaiter la bienvenue à; (*fig.*) se réjouir de.

weld /weld/ *v.t.* souder. ● *n.* soudure *f.* ~**er** *n.* soudeur *m.* ~**ing** *n.* soudure *f.*

welfare /'welfeə(r)/ *n.* bien-être *m.*; (*aid*) aide sociale *f.* **W~ State,** État-providence *m.*

well[1] /wel/ *n.* (*for water, oil*) puits *m.*; (*of stairs*) cage *f.*

well[2] /wel/ *adv.* (**better, best**) bien. ● *a.* bien *invar.* **as ~,** aussi. **be ~,** (*healthy*) aller bien. ● *int.* eh bien; (*surprise*) tiens. **do ~,** (*succeed*) réussir. ~**-behaved** *a.* sage. ~**-being** *n.* bien-être *m.* ~**-built** *a.* bien bâti. ~**-disposed** *a.* bien disposé. ~**-done!** bravo! ~**-dressed** *a.* bien habillé. ~**-heeled** *a.* (*fam.*) nanti. ~**-informed** *a.* bien informé. ~**-known** *a.* (bien) connu. ~**-meaning** *a.* bien intentionné. ~ **off,** aisé, riche. ~**-read** *a.* instruit. ~**-spoken** *a.* qui parle bien. ~**-to-do** *a.* riche. ~**-wisher** *n.* admirateur, -trice *m.*, *f.*

wellington /'welɪŋtən/ *n.* (*boot*) botte de caoutchouc *f.*

Welsh /welʃ/ *a.* gallois. ● *n.* (*lang.*) gallois *m.* ~**man** *n.* Gallois *m.* ~ **rabbit,** croûte au fromage *f.* ~**woman** *n.* Galloise *f.*

welsh /welʃ/ *v.i.* ~ **on,** (*debt, promise*) ne pas honorer.

welterweight /'weltəweɪt/ *n.* poids mi-moyen *m.*

wench /wentʃ/ *n.* (*old use*) jeune fille *f.*

wend /wend/ *v.t.* ~ **one's way,** se diriger, aller son chemin.

went /went/ *see* go.

wept /wept/ *see* weep.

were /wɜː(r), *unstressed* wə(r)/ *see* be.

west /west/ *n.* ouest *m.* **the W~,** (*pol.*) l'Occident *m.* ● *a.* d'ouest. ● *adv.* vers l'ouest. **the W~ Country,** le sud-ouest (de l'Angleterre). **W~ Germany,** Allemagne de l'Ouest *f.* **W~ Indian** *a. & n.* antillais(e) (*m.* (*f.*)). **the W~ Indies,** les Antilles *f. pl.* ~**erly** *a.* d'ouest. ~**ern** *a.* de l'ouest; (*pol.*) occidental; *n.* (*film*) western *m.* ~**erner** *n.* occidental(e) *m.* (*f.*). ~**ward** *a.* à l'ouest. ~**wards** *adv.* vers l'ouest.

westernize /'westənaɪz/ *v.t.* occidentaliser.

wet /wet/ a. (**wetter, wettest**) mouillé; (*damp, rainy*) humide; (*paint*) frais. ● v.t. (*p.t.* **wetted**) mouiller. ● n. the ~, l'humidité f.; (*rain*) la pluie f. **get ~**, se mouiller. ~ **blanket**, rabat-joie m. invar. ~**ness** n. humidité f. ~ **suit**, combinaison de plongée f.

whack /wæk/ n. (*fam.*) grand coup m. ● v.t. (*fam.*) taper sur.

whacked /wækt/ a. (*fam.*) claqué.

whacking /'wækɪŋ/ a. énorme.

whale /weɪl/ n. baleine f.

wham /wæm/ int. vlan.

wharf /wɔ:f/ n. (pl. **wharfs**) (*for ships*) quai m.

what /wɒt/ a. (*in questions*) quel(le), quel(le)s. ● pron. (*in questions*) qu'est-ce qui; (*object*) (qu'est-ce) que or qu'*; (*after prep.*) quoi; (*that which*) ce qui; (*object*) ce que, ce qu'*. ● int. quoi, comment. ~ **date?**, quelle date? ~ **time?**, à quelle heure? ~ **happened?**, qu'est-ce qui s'est passé? ~ **did he say?**, qu'est-ce qu'il a dit? ~ **he said**, ce qu'il a dit. ~ **is important**, ce qui est important. ~ **is it?**, qu'est-ce que c'est? ~ **you need**, ce dont vous avez besoin. ~ **a fool**/etc., quel idiot/etc. ~ **about me**/**him**/etc.?, et moi/lui/etc.? ~ **about doing?**, si on faisait? ~ **for?**, pourquoi?

whatever /wɒt'evə(r)/ a. ~ **book**/ etc., quel que soit le livre/etc. ● pron. (*no matter what*) quoi que, quoi qu'*; (*anything that*) tout ce qui; (*object*) tout ce que or qu'*. ~ **happens**, quoi qu'il arrive. ~ **happened?**, qu'est-ce qui est arrivé? ~ **the problems**, quels que soient les problèmes. ~ **you want**, tout ce que vous voulez. ~ **nothing** ~, rien du tout.

whatsoever /wɒtsəʊ'evər/ a. & pron. = **whatever**.

wheat /wi:t/ n. blé m., froment m.

wheedle /'wi:dl/ v.t. cajoler.

wheel /wi:l/ n. roue f. ● v.t. pousser. ● v.i. tourner. **at the ~**, (*of vehicle*) au volant; (*helm*) au gouvernail. ~ **and deal**, faire des combines.

wheelbarrow /'wi:lbærəʊ/ n. brouette f.

wheelchair /'wi:ltʃeə(r)/ n. fauteuil roulant m.

wheeze /wi:z/ v.i. siffler (en respirant). ● n. sifflement m.

when /wen/ adv. & pron. quand. ● conj. quand, lorsque. **the day**/**moment ~**, le jour/moment où.

whenever /wen'evə(r)/ conj. & adv. (*at whatever time*) quand; (*every time that*) chaque fois que.

where /weə(r)/ adv., conj., & pron. où; (*whereas*) alors que; (*the place that*) là où. ~**abouts** adv. (à peu près) où; n. s.o.'s ~**abouts**, l'endroit où se trouve qn. ~**by** adv. par quoi. ~**upon** adv. sur quoi.

whereas /weər'æz/ conj. alors que.

wherever /weər'evə(r)/ conj. & adv. où que; (*everywhere*) partout où; (*anywhere*) (là) où; (*emphatic where*) où donc.

whet /wet/ v.t. (*p.t.* **whetted**) (*appetite, desire*) aiguiser.

whether /'weðə(r)/ conj. si. **not know ~**, ne pas savoir si. ~ **I go or not**, que j'aille ou non.

which /wɪtʃ/ a. (*in questions*) quel(le), quel(le)s. ● pron. (*in questions*) lequel, laquelle, lesquel(le)s; (*the one or ones that*) celui (celle, ceux, celles) qui; (*object*) celui (celle, ceux, celles) que or qu'*; (*referring to whole sentence,* = *and that*) ce qui; (*object*) ce que, ce qu'*; (*after prep.*) lequel/etc. ● rel. pron. qui; (*object*) que, qu'*. ~ **house?**, quelle maison? ~ **(one) do you want?**, lequel voulez-vous? ~ **are ready?**, lesquels sont prêts? **the bird ~ flies**, l'oiseau qui vole. **the hat ~ he wears**, le chapeau qu'il porte. **of ~, from ~,** duquel/etc. **to ~, at ~,** auquel/etc. **the book of ~**, le livre dont or duquel. **after ~**, après quoi. **she was there, ~ surprised me**, elle était là, ce qui m'a surpris.

whichever /wɪtʃ'evə(r)/ a. ~ **book**/ etc., quel que soit le livre/etc. que or qui. **take ~ book you wish**, prenez le livre que vous voulez. ● pron. celui (celle, ceux, celles) qui or que.

whiff /wɪf/ n. (*puff*) bouffée f.

while /waɪl/ n. moment m. ● conj. (*when*) pendant que; (*although*) bien que; (*as long as*) tant que. ● v.t. ~ **away**, (*time*) passer.

whilst /waɪlst/ conj. = **while**.

whim /wɪm/ n. caprice m.

whimper /'wɪmpə(r)/ v.i. geindre, pleurnicher. ● n. pleurnichement m.

whimsical /'wɪmzɪkl/ a. (*person*) capricieux; (*odd*) bizarre.

whine /waɪn/ v.i. gémir, se plaindre. ● n. gémissement m.

whip /wɪp/ n. fouet m. ● v.t. (p.t. **whipped**) fouetter; (culin.) fouetter, battre; (seize) enlever brusquement. ● v.i. (move) aller en vitesse. **~-round** n. (fam.) collecte f. **~ out**, (gun etc.) sortir. **~ up**, exciter; (cause) provoquer; (meal: fam.) préparer.

whirl /wɜːl/ v.t./i. (faire) tourbillonner. ● n. tourbillon m.

whirlpool /'wɜːlpuːl/ n. (in sea etc.) tourbillon m.

whirlwind /'wɜːlwɪnd/ n. tourbillon (de vent) m.

whirr /wɜː(r)/ v.i. vrombir.

whisk /wɪsk/ v.t. (snatch) enlever or emmener brusquement; (culin.) fouetter. ● n. (culin.) fouet m.; (broom, brush) petit balai m. **~ away**, (brush away) chasser.

whisker /'wɪskə(r)/ n. poil m. **~s**, (man's) barbe f., moustache f.; (sideboards) favoris m. pl.

whisky /'wɪskɪ/ n. whisky m.

whisper /'wɪspə(r)/ v.t./i. chuchoter. ● n. chuchotement m.; (rumour: fig.) rumeur f., bruit m.

whistle /'wɪsl/ n. sifflement m.; (instrument) sifflet m. ● v.t./i. siffler. **~ at or for**, siffler.

Whit /wɪt/ a. **~ Sunday**, dimanche de Pentecôte m.

white /waɪt/ a. (-er, -est) blanc. ● n. blanc m.; (person) blanc(he) m. (f.). **~ coffee**, café au lait m. **~-collar worker**, employé(e) de bureau m. (f.). **~ elephant**, objet, projet, etc. inutile m. **~ lie**, pieux mensonge m. **W~ Paper**, livre blanc m. **~ness** n. blancheur f.

whiten /'waɪtn/ v.t./i. blanchir.

whitewash /'waɪtwɒʃ/ n. blanc de chaux m. ● v.t. blanchir à la chaux; (person: fig.) blanchir.

whiting /'waɪtɪŋ/ n. invar. (fish) merlan m.

Whitsun /'wɪtsn/ n. la Pentecôte.

whittle /'wɪtl/ v.t. **~ down**, tailler (au couteau); (fig.) réduire.

whiz /wɪz/ v.i. (p.t. **whizzed**) (through air) fendre l'air; (hiss) siffler; (rush) aller à toute vitesse. **~-kid** n. jeune prodige m.

who /huː/ pron. qui.

whodunit /huː'dʌnɪt/ n. (story: fam.) roman policier m.

whoever /huː'evə(r)/ pron. (no matter who) qui que ce soit qui or que; (the one who) quiconque. **tell ~ you want**, dites-le à qui vous voulez.

whole /həʊl/ a. entier; (intact) intact. **the ~ house/etc.**, toute la maison/etc. ● n. totalité f.; (unit) tout m. **on the ~**, dans l'ensemble. **~-hearted** a., **~-heartedly** adv. sans réserve.

wholefoods /'həʊlfuːdz/ n. pl. aliments naturels et diététiques m. pl.

wholemeal /'həʊlmiːl/ a. **~ bread**, pain complet m.

wholesale /'həʊlseɪl/ n. gros m. ● a. (firm) de gros; (fig.) systématique. ● adv. (in large quantities) en gros; (buy or sell one item) au prix de gros; (fig.) en masse. **~r** /-ə(r)/ n. grossiste m./f.

wholesome /'həʊlsəm/ a. sain.

wholewheat /'həʊlwiːt/ a. = **wholemeal**.

wholly /'həʊlɪ/ adv. entièrement.

whom /huːm/ pron. (that) que, qu'*; (after prep. & in questions) qui. **of ~**, dont. **with ~**, avec qui.

whooping cough /'huːpɪŋkɒf/ n. coqueluche f.

whopping /'wɒpɪŋ/ a. (sl.) énorme.

whore /hɔː(r)/ n. putain f.

whose /huːz/ pron. & a. à qui, de qui. **~ hat is this?**, **~ is this hat?**, à qui est ce chapeau? **~ son are you?**, de qui êtes-vous le fils? **the man ~ hat I see**, l'homme dont je vois le chapeau.

why /waɪ/ adv. pourquoi. ● int. eh bien, ma parole, tiens. **the reason ~**, la raison pour laquelle.

wick /wɪk/ n. (of lamp etc.) mèche f.

wicked /'wɪkɪd/ a. méchant, mauvais, vilain. **~ly** adv. méchamment. **~ness** n. méchanceté f.

wicker /'wɪkə(r)/ n. osier m. **~work** n. vannerie f.

wicket /'wɪkɪt/ n. guichet m.

wide /waɪd/ a. (-er, -est) large; (ocean etc.) vaste. ● adv. (fall etc.) loin du but. **open ~**, ouvrir tout grand. **~ open**, grand ouvert. **~-angle lens** grand-angle m. **~ awake**, éveillé. **~ly** adv. (spread, space) largement; (travel) beaucoup; (generally) généralement; (extremely) extrêmement.

widen /'waɪdn/ v.t./i. (s')élargir.

widespread /'waɪdspred/ a. très répandu.

widow /'wɪdəʊ/ n. veuve. f. ~**ed** a. (man) veuf; (woman) veuve. **be** ~**ed**, (become widower or widow) devenir veuf or veuve. ~**er** n. veuf m.

width /wɪdθ/ n. largeur f.

wield /wiːld/ v.t. (axe etc.) manier; (power: fig.) exercer.

wife /waɪf/ n. (pl. **wives**) femme f., épouse f. ~**ly** a. d'épouse.

wig /wɪg/ n. perruque f.

wiggle /'wɪgl/ v.t./i. remuer; (hips) tortiller; (of worm) se tortiller.

wild /waɪld/ a. (-**er**, -**est**) sauvage; (sea, enthusiasm) déchaîné; (mad) fou; (angry) furieux. ● adv. (grow) à l'état sauvage. ~**s** n. pl. régions sauvages f. pl. **run** ~, (free) courir en liberté. ~**-goose chase**, fausse piste f. ~**ly** adv. violemment; (madly) follement.

wildcat /'waɪldkæt/ a. ~ **strike**, grève sauvage f.

wilderness /'wɪldənɪs/ n. désert m.

wildlife /'waɪldlaɪf/ n. faune f.

wile /waɪl/ n. ruse f., artifice m.

wilful /'wɪlfl/ a. (intentional, obstinate) volontaire.

will[1] /wɪl/ v. aux. **he** ~ **do/you** ~ **sing**/etc., (future tense) il fera/tu chanteras/etc. ~ **you have a coffee?**, voulez-vous prendre un café?

will[2] /wɪl/ n. volonté f.; (document) testament m. ● v.t. (wish) vouloir. **at** ~, quand or comme on veut. ~**power** n. volonté f. ~ **o.s. to do**, faire un effort de volonté pour faire.

willing /'wɪlɪŋ/ a. (help, offer) spontané; (helper) bien disposé. ~ **to**, disposé à. ~**ly** adv. (with pleasure) volontiers; (not forced) volontairement. ~**ness** n. empressement m. (**to do**, à faire); (goodwill) bonne volonté f.

willow /'wɪləʊ/ n. saule m.

willy-nilly /wɪlɪ'nɪlɪ/ adv. bon gré mal gré.

wilt /wɪlt/ v.i. (plant etc.) dépérir.

wily /'waɪlɪ/ a. (-**ier**, -**iest**) rusé.

win /wɪn/ v.t./i. (p.t. **won**, pres. p. **winning**) gagner; (victory, prize) remporter; (fame, fortune) acquérir, trouver. ● n. victoire f. ~ **round**, convaincre.

winc|e /wɪns/ v.i. se crisper, tressaillir. **without** ~**ing**, sans broncher.

winch /wɪntʃ/ n. treuil m. ● v.t. hisser au treuil.

wind[1] /wɪnd/ n. vent m.; (breath) souffle m. ● v.t. essouffler. **get** ~ **of**, avoir vent de. **in the** ~, dans l'air. ~**cheater**, (Amer.) ~**breaker** ns. blouson m. ~ **instrument**, instrument à vent m. ~**swept** a. balayé par les vents.

wind[2] /waɪnd/ v.t./i. (p.t. **wound**) (s')enrouler; (of path, river) serpenter. ~ (**up**), (clock etc.) remonter. ~ **up**, (end) (se) terminer. ~ **up in hospital**, finir à l'hôpital. ~**ing** a. (path) sinueux.

windfall /'wɪndfɔːl/ n. fruit tombé m.; (money: fig.) aubaine f.

windmill /'wɪndmɪl/ n. moulin à vent m.

window /'wɪndəʊ/ n. fenêtre f.; (glass pane) vitre f.; (in vehicle, train) vitre f.; (in shop) vitrine f.; (counter) guichet m. ~**-box** n. jardinière f. ~**-cleaner** n. laveur de carreaux m. ~**-dresser** n. étalagiste m./f. ~**-ledge** n. rebord de (la) fenêtre m.; ~**-shopping** n. lèche-vitrines m. ~**-sill** n. (inside) appui de (la) fenêtre m.; (outside) rebord de (la) fenêtre m.

windpipe /'wɪndpaɪp/ n. trachée f.

windscreen /'wɪndskriːn/, (Amer.) **windshield** /'wɪndʃiːld/ n. pare-brise m. invar. ~ **washer**, lave-glace m. ~ **wiper**, essuie-glace m.

windsurf|ing /'wɪndsɜːfɪŋ/ n. planche à voile f. ~**er** n. véliplanchiste m./f.

windy /'wɪndɪ/ a. (-**ier**, -**iest**) venteux. **it is** ~, il y a du vent.

wine /waɪn/ n. vin m. ~**-cellar** n. cave (à vin) f. ~**-grower** n. viticulteur m. ~**-growing** n. viticulture f.; a. viticole. ~ **list**, carte des vins f. ~**-tasting** n. dégustation de vins f. ~ **waiter**, sommelier m.

wineglass /'waɪnglɑːs/ n. verre à vin m.

wing /wɪŋ/ n. aile f. ~**s**, (theatre) coulisses f. pl. **under one's** ~, sous son aile. ~ **mirror**, rétroviseur extérieur m. ~**ed** a. ailé. ~**er** n. (sport) ailier m.

wink /wɪŋk/ v.i. faire un clin d'œil; (light, star) clignoter. ● n. clin d'œil m.; clignotement m.

winner /'wɪnə(r)/ n. (of game) gagnant(e) m. (f.); (of fight) vainqueur m.

winning /'wɪnɪŋ/ see win. ● a. (number, horse) gagnant; (team)

winter /'wɪntə(r)/ n. hiver m. ● v.i. hiverner. **~ry** a. hivernal.

wipe /waɪp/ v.t. essuyer. ● v.i. **~ up**, essuyer la vaisselle. ● n. coup de torchon or d'éponge m. **~ off** or **out**, essuyer. **~ out**, (destroy) anéantir; (remove) effacer.

wir|e /'waɪə(r)/ n. fil m.; (Amer.) télégramme m. **~e netting**, grillage m. **~ing** n. (electr.) installation électrique f.

wireless /'waɪəlɪs/ n. radio f.

wiry /'waɪərɪ/ a. (-ier, -iest) (person) nerveux et maigre.

wisdom /'wɪzdəm/ n. sagesse f.

wise /waɪz/ a. (-er, -est) prudent, sage; (look) averti. **~ guy**, (fam.) petit malin m. **~ man**, sage m. **~ly** adv. prudemment.

wisecrack /'waɪzkræk/ n. (fam.) mot d'esprit m., astuce f.

wish /wɪʃ/ n. (specific) souhait m., vœu m.; (general) désir m. ● v.t. souhaiter, vouloir, désirer (**to do**, faire); (bid) souhaiter. ● v.i. **~ for**, souhaiter. **I — he'd leave**, je voudrais bien qu'il parte. **best ~es**, (in letter) amitiés f. pl.; (on greeting card) meilleurs vœux m. pl.

wishful /'wɪʃfl/ a. **it's ~ thinking**, on se fait des illusions.

wishy-washy /'wɪʃɪwɒʃɪ/ a. fade.

wisp /wɪsp/ n. (of smoke) volute f.

wistful /'wɪstfl/ a. mélancolique.

wit /wɪt/ n. intelligence f.; (humour) esprit m.; (person) homme d'esprit m., femme d'esprit f. **be at one's ~'s** or **~s' end**, ne plus savoir que faire.

witch /wɪtʃ/ n. sorcière f. **~craft** n. sorcellerie f.

with /wɪð/ prep. avec; (having) à; (because of) de; (at house of) chez. **the man ~ the beard**, l'homme à la barbe. **fill**/etc. **~**, remplir/etc. de. **pleased/shaking**/etc. **~**, content/frémissant/ etc. de. **~ it**, (fam.) dans le vent.

withdraw /wɪð'drɔː/ v.t./i. (p.t. **withdrew**, p.p. **withdrawn**) (se) retirer. **~al** n. retrait m. **~n** a. (person) renfermé.

wither /'wɪðə(r)/ v.t./i. (se) flétrir. **~ed** a. (person) desséché.

withhold /wɪð'həʊld/ v.t. (p.t. **withheld**) refuser (de donner); (retain) retenir; (conceal, not tell) cacher (**from**, à).

within /wɪ'ðɪn/ prep. & adv. à l'intérieur (de); (in distances) à moins de. **~ a month**, (before) avant un mois. **~ sight**, en vue.

without /wɪ'ðaʊt/ prep. sans. **~ my knowing**, sans que je sache.

withstand /wɪð'stænd/ v.t. (p.t. **withstood**) résister à.

witness /'wɪtnɪs/ n. témoin m.; (evidence) témoignage m. ● v.t. être le témoin de, voir; (document) signer. **bear ~ to**, témoigner de. **~ box** or **stand**, barre des témoins f.

witticism /'wɪtɪsɪzəm/ n. bon mot m.

witt|y /'wɪtɪ/ a. (-ier, -iest) spirituel. **~iness** n. esprit m.

wives /waɪvz/ see wife.

wizard /'wɪzəd/ n. magicien m.; (genius: fig.) génie m.

wobbl|e /'wɒbl/ v.i. (of jelly, voice, hand) trembler; (stagger) chanceler; (of table, chair) branler. **~y** a. tremblant; branlant.

woe /wəʊ/ n. malheur m.

woke, woken /wəʊk, 'wəʊkən/ see wake[1].

wolf /wʊlf/ n. (pl. **wolves**) loup m. ● v.t. (food) engloutir. **cry ~**, crier au loup. **~-whistle** n. sifflement admiratif m.

woman /'wʊmən/ n. (pl. **women**) femme f. **~ doctor**, femme médecin f. **~ driver**, femme au volant f. **~ friend**, amie f. **~hood** n. féminité f. **~ly** a. féminin.

womb /wuːm/ n. utérus m.

women /'wɪmɪn/ see woman.

won /wʌn/ see win.

wonder /'wʌndə(r)/ n. émerveillement m.; (thing) merveille f. ● v.t. se demander (**if**, si). ● v.i. s'émerveiller (**at**, de); (reflect) songer (**about**, à). **it is no ~**, ce or il n'est pas étonnant (**that**, que).

wonderful /'wʌndəfl/ a. merveilleux. **~ly** adv. merveilleusement; (work, do, etc.) à merveille.

won't /wəʊnt/ = will not.

woo /wuː/ v.t. (woman) faire la cour à; (please) chercher à plaire à.

wood /wʊd/ n. bois m. **~ed** a. boisé. **~en** a. en or de bois; (stiff: fig.) raide, comme du bois.

woodcut /'wʊdkʌt/ n. gravure sur bois f.

woodland /'wʊdlənd/ n. région boisée f., bois m. pl.

woodpecker /'wʊdpekə(r)/ n. (bird) pic m., pivert m.

woodwind /'wʊdwɪnd/ n. (mus.)
bois m. pl.

woodwork /'wʊdwɜːk/ n. (craft, objects) menuiserie f.

woodworm /'wʊdwɜːm/ n. (larvae)
vers (de bois) m. pl.

woody /'wʊdɪ/ a. (wooded) boisé;
(like wood) ligneux.

wool /wʊl/ n. laine f. **~len** a. de
laine. **~lens** n. pl. lainages m. pl.
~ly a. laineux; (vague) nébuleux; n.
(garment: fam.) lainage m.

word /wɜːd/ n. mot m.; (spoken)·
parole f., mot m.; (promise) parole
f.; (news) nouvelles f. pl. ● v.t.
rédiger. **by ~ of mouth**, de vive
voix. **give/keep one's ~**, donner/
tenir sa parole. **have a ~ with**,
parler à. **in other ~s**, autrement
dit. **~ processor**, machine de traitement de texte f. **~ing** n. termes m.
pl.

wordy /'wɜːdɪ/ a. verbeux.

wore /wɔː(r)/ see wear.

work /wɜːk/ n. travail m.; (product,
book, etc.) œuvre f., ouvrage m.;
(building etc. work) travaux m. pl.
~s, (techn.) mécanisme m.; (factory)
usine f. ● v.t./i. (of person) travailler; (shape, hammer, etc.) travailler;
(techn.) (faire) fonctionner, (faire)
marcher; (land, mine) exploiter; (of
drug etc.) agir. **~ s.o.**, (make work)
faire travailler qn. **~-force** n. main-
d'œuvre f. **~ in**, (s')introduire. **~-
load** n. travail (à faire) m. **~ off**,
(get rid of) se débarrasser de. **~ out**
v.t. (solve) résoudre; (calculate) calculer; (elaborate) élaborer; v.i. (succeed) marcher; (sport) s'entraîner.
~-station n. poste de travail m. **~-
to-rule** n. grève du zèle f. **~ up** v.t.
développer; v.i. (to climax) monter
vers. **~ed up**, (person) énervé.

workable /'wɜːkəbl/ a. réalisable.

workaholic /wɜːkə'hɒlɪk/ n. (fam.)
bourreau de travail m.

worker /'wɜːkə(r)/ n. travailleu|r, -se
m., f.; (manual) ouvr|ier, -ière m., f.

working /'wɜːkɪŋ/ a. (day, lunch, etc.)
de travail. **~s** n. pl. mécanisme m. **~-
class**, classe ouvrière f. **~-class** a.
ouvrier. **in ~ order**, en état de
marche.

workman /'wɜːkmən/ n. (pl. **-men**)
ouvrier m. **~ship** n. maîtrise f.

workshop /'wɜːkʃɒp/ n. atelier m.

world /wɜːld/ n. monde m. ● a.
(power etc.) mondial; (record etc.)

du monde. **best in the ~**, meilleur
au monde. **~-wide** a. universel.

worldly /'wɜːldlɪ/ a. de ce monde,
terrestre. **~-wise** a. qui a l'expérience du monde.

worm /wɜːm/ n. ver m. ● v.t. **~
one's way into**, s'insinuer dans.
~-eaten a. (wood) vermoulu; (fruit)
véreux.

worn /wɔːn/ see wear. ● a. usé. **~-
out** a. (thing) complètement usé;
(person) épuisé.

worr|y /'wʌrɪ/ v.t./i. (s')inquiéter.
● n. souci m. **~ied** a. inquiet. **~ier**
n. inqu|et, -iète m., f.

worse /wɜːs/ a. pire, plus mauvais.
● adv. plus mal. ● n. pire m. **be ~
off**, perdre.

worsen /'wɜːsn/ v.t./i. empirer.

worship /'wɜːʃɪp/ n. (adoration)
culte m. ● v.t. (p.t. **worshipped**)
adorer. ● v.i. faire ses dévotions.
~per n. (in church) fidèle m./f.

worst /wɜːst/ a. pire, plus mauvais.
● adv. (**the**) **~**, (sing etc.) le plus
mal. ● n. **the ~ (one)**, (person,
object) le or la pire. **the ~ (thing)**,
le pire (**that**, que). **get the ~ of it**,
(be defeated) avoir le dessous.

worsted /'wʊstɪd/ n. worsted m.

worth /wɜːθ/ a. **be ~**, valoir. **it is ~
waiting**/etc., ça vaut la peine d'at-
tendre/etc. ● n. valeur f. **ten pence
~ of**, (pour) dix pence de. **it is ~
(one's) while**, ça (en) vaut la peine.
~less a. qui ne vaut rien.

worthwhile /wɜːθ'waɪl/ a. qui (en)
vaut la peine.

worthy /'wɜːðɪ/ a. (**-ier, -iest**) digne
(**of**, de); (laudable) louable. ● n.
(person) notable m.

would /wʊd, unstressed wəd/ v. aux.
he ~ do/you ~ sing/etc., (conditional tense) il ferait/tu chanterais/
etc. **he ~ have done**, il aurait fait. **I
~ come every day**, (used to) je
venais chaque jour. **I ~ like some
tea**, je voudrais du thé. **~ you come
here?**, voulez-vous venir ici? **he
~n't come**, il a refusé de venir. **~-
be** a. soi-disant.

wound[1] /wuːnd/ n. blessure f. ● v.t.
blesser. **the ~ed**, les blessés m. pl.

wound[2] /waʊnd/ see wind[2].

wove, woven /wəʊv, 'wəʊvn/ see
weave.

wow /waʊ/ int. mince (alors).

wrangle /'ræŋgl/ v.i. se disputer.
● n. dispute f.

wrap /ræp/ *v.t.* (*p.t.* **wrapped**). **~ (up)**, envelopper. ● *v.i.* **~ up**, (*dress warmly*) se couvrir. ● *n.* châle *m.* **~ped up in**, (*engrossed*) absorbé dans. **~per** *n.* (*of book*) jaquette *f.*; (*of sweet*) papier *m.* **~ping** *n.* emballage *m.*; **~ping paper**, papier d'emballage *m.*

wrath /rɒθ/ *n.* courroux *m.*

wreak /ri:k/ *v.t.* **~ havoc**, (*of storm etc.*) faire des ravages.

wreath /ri:θ/ *n.* (*pl.* **-s** /-ðz/) (*of flowers, leaves*) couronne *f.*

wreck /rek/ *n.* (*sinking*) naufrage *m.*; (*ship, remains, person*) épave *f.*; (*vehicle*) voiture accidentée ou delabrée *f.* ● *v.t.* détruire; (*ship*) provoquer le naufrage de. **~age** *n.* (*pieces*) débris *m. pl.*; (*wrecked building*) décombres *m. pl.*

wren /ren/ *n.* roitelet *m.*

wrench /rentʃ/ *v.t.* (*pull*) tirer sur; (*twist*) tordre; (*snatch*) arracher (**from**, à). ● *n.* (*tool*) clé *f.*

wrest /rest/ *v.t.* arracher (**from**, à).

wrestl|e /'resl/ *v.i.* lutter, se débattre (**with**, contre). **~er** *n.* lutteu|r, -se *m., f.*; catcheu|r, -se *m., f.* **~ing** *n.* lutte *f.* (**all-in**) **~ing**, catch *m.*

wretch /retʃ/ *n.* malheureu|x, -se *m., f.*; (*rascal*) misérable *m./f.*

wretched /'retʃid/ *a.* (*pitiful, poor*) misérable; (*bad*) affreux.

wriggle /'rɪgl/ *v.t./i.* (se) tortiller.

wring /rɪŋ/ *v.t.* (*p.t.* **wrung**) (*twist*) tordre; (*clothes*) essorer. **~ out of**, (*obtain from*) arracher à. **~ing wet**, trempé (jusqu'aux os).

wrinkle /'rɪŋkl/ *n.* (*crease*) pli *m.*; (*on skin*) ride *f.* ● *v.t./i.* (se) rider.

wrist /rɪst/ *n.* poignet *m.* **~-watch** *n.* montre-bracelet *f.*

writ /rɪt/ *n.* acte judiciaire *m.*

write /raɪt/ *v.t./i.* (*p.t.* **wrote**, *p.p.* **written**) écrire. **~ back**, répondre. **~ down**, noter. **~ off**, (*debt*) passer aux profits et pertes; (*vehicle*) considérer bon pour la casse. **~-off** *n.* perte totale *f.* **~ up**, (*from notes*) rédiger. **~-up** *n.* compte rendu *m.*

writer /'raɪtə(r)/ *n.* auteur *m.*, écrivain *m.* **~ of**, auteur de.

writhe /raɪð/ *v.i.* se tordre.

writing /'raɪtɪŋ/ *n.* écriture *f.* **~(s)**, (*works*) écrits *m. pl.* **in ~**, par écrit. **~-paper** *n.* papier à lettres *m.*

written /'rɪtn/ *see* write.

wrong /rɒŋ/ *a.* (*incorrect, mistaken*) faux, mauvais; (*unfair*) injuste; (*amiss*) qui ne va pas; (*clock*) pas à l'heure. **be ~**, (*person*) avoir tort (**to**, de); (*be mistaken*) se tromper. ● *adv.* mal. ● *n.* injustice *f.*; (*evil*) mal *m.* ● *v.t.* faire (du) tort à. **be in the ~**, avoir tort. **go ~**, (*err*) se tromper; (*turn out badly*) mal tourner; (*vehicle*) tomber en panne. **it is ~ to**, (*morally*) c'est mal de faire. **what's ~?**, qu'est-ce qui ne va pas? **what is ~ with you?**, qu'est-ce que vous avez? **~ly** *adv.* mal; (*blame etc.*) à tort.

wrongful /'rɒŋfl/ *a.* injustifié, injuste. **~ly** *adv.* à tort.

wrote /rəʊt/ *see* write.

wrought /rɔ:t/ *a.* **~ iron**, fer forgé *m.*

wrung /rʌŋ/ *see* wring.

wry /raɪ/ *a.* (**wryer, wryest**) (*smile*) désabusé, forcé. **~ face**, grimace *f.*

X

xerox /'zɪərɒks/ *v.t.* photocopier.

Xmas /'krɪsməs/ *n.* Noël *m.*

X-ray /'eksreɪ/ *n.* rayon X *m.*; (*photograph*) radio(graphie) *f.* ● *v.t.* radiographier.

xylophone /'zaɪləfəʊn/ *n.* xylophone *m.*

Y

yacht /jɒt/ *n.* yacht *m.* **~ing** *n.* yachting *m.*

yank /jæŋk/ *v.t.* tirer brusquement. ● *n.* coup brusque *m.*

Yank /jæŋk/ *n.* (*fam.*) Américain(e) *m.* (*f.*), Amerloque *m./f.*

yap /jæp/ *v.i.* (*p.t.* **yapped**) japper.

yard¹ /jɑ:d/ *n.* (*measure*) yard *m.* (= 0.9144 metre).

yard² /jɑ:d/ *n.* (*of house etc.*) cour *f.*; (*garden: Amer.*) jardin *m.*; (*for storage*) chantier *m.*, dépôt *m.*

yardstick /'jɑ:dstɪk/ *n.* mesure *f.*

yarn /jɑ:n/ *n.* (*thread*) fil *m.*; (*tale: fam.*) (longue) histoire *f.*

yawn /jɔ:n/ *v.i.* bâiller. ● *n.* bâillement *m.* **~ing** *a.* (*gaping*) béant.

year /jɪə(r)/ *n.* an *m.*, année *f.*; **school/ tax**/*etc.* **~**, année scolaire/fiscale/ *etc.* **be ten**/*etc.* **~s old**, avoir dix/*etc.*

ans. **~-book** n. annuaire m. **~ly** a. annuel; adv. annuellement.

yearn /jɜːn/ v.i. avoir bien or très envie (**for, to,** de). **~ing** n. envie f.

yeast /jiːst/ n. levure f.

yell /jel/ v.t./i. hurler. ● n. hurlement m.

yellow /'jeləʊ/ a. jaune; (cowardly: fam.) froussard. ● n. jaune m.

yelp /jelp/ n. (of dog etc.) jappement m. ● v.i. japper.

yen /jen/ n. (desire) grande envie f.

yes /jes/ adv. oui; (as answer to negative question) si. ● n. oui m. invar.

yesterday /'jestədɪ/ n. & adv. hier (m.).

yet /jet/ adv. encore; (already) déjà. ● conj. pourtant, néanmoins.

yew /juː/ n. (tree, wood) if m.

Yiddish /'jɪdɪʃ/ n. yiddish m.

yield /jiːld/ v.t. (produce) produire, rendre; (profit) rapporter; (surrender) céder. ● v.i. (give way) céder. ● n. rendement m.

yoga /'jəʊɡə/ n. yoga m.

yoghurt /'jɒɡət, Amer. 'jəʊɡərt/ n. yaourt m.

yoke /jəʊk/ n. joug m.

yokel /'jəʊkl/ n. rustre m.

yolk /jəʊk/ n. jaune (d'œuf) m.

yonder /'jɒndə(r)/ adv. là-bas.

you /juː/ pron. (familiar form) tu, pl. vous; (polite form) vous; (object) te, t'*, pl. vous; (polite) vous; (after prep.) toi, pl. vous; (polite) vous; (indefinite) on; (object) vous. (**to**) **~,** te, t'*, pl. vous; (polite) vous. **I gave ~ a pen,** je vous ai donné un stylo. **I know ~,** je te connais; je vous connais.

young /jʌŋ/ a. (**-er, -est**) jeune. ● n. (people) jeunes m. pl.; (of animals) petits m. pl. **~er** a. (brother etc.) cadet. **~est** a. **my ~est brother,** le cadet de mes frères.

youngster /'jʌŋstə(r)/ n. jeune m./f.

your /jɔː(r)/ a. (familiar form) ton, ta, pl. tes; (polite form, & familiar form pl.) votre, pl. vos.

yours /jɔːz/ poss. pron. (familiar form) le tien, la tienne, les tien(ne)s; (polite form, & familiar form pl.) le or la vôtre, les vôtres. **~ faithfully/sincerely,** je vous prie d'agréer/de croire en l'expression de mes sentiments les meilleurs.

yourself /jɔː'self/ pron. (familiar form) toi-même; (polite form) vous-même; (reflexive & after prep.) te, t'*;

vous. **~ves** pron. pl. vous-mêmes; (reflexive) vous.

youth /juːθ/ n. (pl. **-s** /-ðz/) jeunesse f.; (young man) jeune m. **~ club,** centre de jeunes m. **~hostel,** auberge de jeunesse f. **~ful** a. juvénile, jeune.

yo-yo /'jəʊjəʊ/ n. (pl. **-os**) (P.) yo-yo m. invar. (P.).

Yugoslav /'juːɡəslɑːv/ a. & n. Yougoslave (m./f.) **~ia** /-'slɑːvɪə/ n. Yougoslavie f.

yuppie /'jʌpɪ/ n. yuppie m.

Z

zany /'zeɪnɪ/ a. (**-ier, -iest**) farfelu.

zap /zæp/ v.t. (fam.) (kill) descendre; (comput.) enlever; (TV) zapper.

zeal /ziːl/ n. zèle m.

zealous /'zeləs/ a. zélé. **~ly** a. zèle.

zebra /'zebrə, 'ziːbrə/ n. zèbre m. **~ crossing,** passage pour piétons m.

zenith /'zenɪθ/ n. zénith m.

zero /'zɪərəʊ/ n. (pl. **-os**) zéro m. **~ hour,** l'heure H f.

zest /zest/ n. (gusto) entrain m.; (spice: fig.) piment m.; (of orange or lemon peel) zeste m.

zigzag /'zɪɡzæɡ/ n. zigzag m. ● a. & adv. en zigzag. ● v.i. (p.t. **zig-zagged**) zigzaguer.

zinc /zɪŋk/ n. zinc m.

Zionism /'zaɪənɪzəm/ n. sionisme m.

zip /zɪp/ n. (vigour) allant m. **~(-fastener),** fermeture éclair f. (P.). ● v.t. (p.t. **zipped**) fermer avec une fermeture éclair (P.). ● v.i. aller à toute vitesse. **Zip code,** (Amer.) code postal m.

zipper /'zɪpə(r)/ n. (Amer.) = **zip (-fastener).**

zither /'zɪðə(r)/ n. cithare f.

zodiac /'zəʊdɪæk/ n. zodiaque m.

zombie /'zɒmbɪ/ n. mort(e) vivant(e) m. (f.); (fam.) automate m.

zone /zəʊn/ n. zone f.

zoo /zuː/ n. zoo m.

zoolog|y /zəʊ'ɒlədʒɪ/ n. zoologie f. **~ical** /-ə'lɒdʒɪkl/ a. zoologique. **~ist** n. zoologiste m./f.

zoom /zuːm/ v.i. (rush) se précipiter. **~ lens,** zoom m. **~ off** or **past,** filer (comme une flèche).

zucchini /zuː'kiːnɪ/ n. invar. (Amer.) courgette f.

French Verb Tables

Notes: The conditional may be formed by substituting the following endings for those of the future: *ais* for *ai* and *as*, *ait* for *a*, *ions* for *ons*, *iez* for *ez*, *aient* for *ont*. The present participle is formed (unless otherwise indicated) by substituting *ant* for *ons* in the first person plural of the present tense (e.g. *finissant* and *donnant* may be derived from *finissons* and *donnons*). The imperative forms are (unless otherwise indicated) the same as the second persons singular and plural and the first person plural of the present tense. The second person singular does not take *s* after *e* or *a* (e.g. *donne*, *va*), except when followed by *y* or *en* (e.g. *vas-y*).

Regular verbs:

1. in *-er* (e.g. **donn|er**)
    Present. ~e, ~es, ~e, ~ons, ~ez, ~ent.
    Imperfect. ~ais, ~ais, ~ait, ~ions, ~iez, ~aient.
    Past historic. ~ai, ~as, ~a, ~âmes, ~âtes, ~èrent.
    Future. ~erai, ~eras, ~era, ~erons, ~erez, ~eront.
    Present subjunctive. ~e, ~es, ~e, ~ions, ~iez, ~ent.
    Past participle. ~é.

2. in *-ir* (e.g. **fin|ir**)
    Pres. ~is, ~is, ~it, ~issons, ~issez, ~issent.
    Impf. ~issais, ~issais, ~issait, ~issions, ~issiez, ~issaient.
    Past hist. ~is, ~is, ~it, ~îmes, ~îtes, ~irent.
    Fut. ~irai, ~iras, ~ira, ~irons, ~irez, ~iront.
    Pres. sub. ~isse, ~isses, ~isse, ~issions, ~issiez, ~issent.
    Past part. ~i.

3. in *-re* (e.g. **vend|re**)
    Pres. ~s, ~s, ~, ~ons, ~ez, ~ent.
    Impf. ~ais, ~ais, ~ait, ~ions, ~iez, ~aient.
    Past hist. ~is, ~is, ~it, ~îmes, ~îtes, ~irent.
    Fut. ~rai, ~ras, ~ra, ~rons, ~rez, ~ront.
    Pres. sub. ~e, ~es, ~e, ~ions, ~iez, ~ent.
    Past part. ~u.

Peculiarities of -er verbs:

In verbs in *-cer* (e.g. **commencer**) and *-ger* (e.g. **manger**), *c* becomes *ç* and *g* becomes *ge* before *a* and *o* (e.g. commença, commençons; mangea, mangeons).

In verbs in *-yer* (e.g. **nettoyer**), *y* becomes *i* before mute *e* (e.g. nettoie,

nettoierai). Verbs in *-ayer* (e.g. **payer**) may retain *y* before mute *e* (e.g. paye or paie, payerai or paierai).

In verbs in *-eler* (e.g. **appeler**) and in *-eter* (e.g. **jeter**), *l* becomes *ll* and *t* becomes *tt* before a syllable containing mute *e* (e.g. appelle, appellerai; jette, jetterai). In the verbs **celer, ciseler, congeler, déceler, démanteler, écarteler, geler, marteler, modeler** and **peler**, and in the verbs **acheter, crocheter, fureter, haleter** and **racheter**, *e* becomes *è* before a syllable containing mute *e* (e.g. cèle, cèlerai; achète, achèterai).

In verbs in which the penultimate syllable contains mute *e* (e.g. **semer**) or *é* (e.g. **révéler**), both *e* and *é* become *è* before a syllable containing mute *e* (e.g. sème, sèmerai; révèle). However, in the verbs in which the penultimate syllable containx *é*, *é* remains unchanged in the future and conditional (e.g. révéleral).

Irregular verbs

At least the first persons singular and plural of the present tense are shown. Forms not listed may be derived from these. Thought the base form of the imperfect, future, and present subjunctive may be irregular, the endings of these tenses are as shown in the regular verb section. Only the first person singular of these tenses is given in most cases. The base form of the past historic may also be irregular but the endings of this tense shown in the verbs below fall (with few exceptions) into the 'u' category, listed under **être** and **avoir**, and the 'i' category shown under **finir** and **vendre** in the regular verb section.

Only the first person singular of the past historic is listed in most cases. Additional forms appear throughout when these cannot be derived from the forms given or when it is considered helpful to list them. Only those irregular verbs judged to be the most useful are shown in the tables.

abbattre *as* BATTRE.
accueillir *as* CUEILLIR.
acquérir ● *Pres.* acquiers, acquérons, acquièrent. ● *Impf.* acquérais. ● *Past hist.* acquis. ● *Fut.* acquerrai. ● *Pres. sub.* acquière. ● *Past part.* acquis.
admettre *as* METTRE.
aller ● *Pres.* vais, vas, va, allons, allez, vont. ● *Fut.* irai. ● *Pres. sub.* aille, allions.
apercevoir *as* RECEVOIR.
apparaître *as* CONNAÎTRE.
appartenir *as* TENIR.
apprendre *as* PRENDRE.
asseoir ● *Pres.* assieds, asseyons, asseyent. ● *Impf.* asseyais. ● *Past hist.* assis. ● *Fut.* assiérai. ● *Pres. sub.* asseye. ● *Past part.* assis.
atteindre ● *Pres.* atteins, atteignons, atteignent. ● *Impf.* atteignais. ● *Past hist.* atteignis. ● *Fut.* atteindrai. ● *Pres. sub.* atteigne. ● *Past part.* atteint.
avoir ● *Pres.* ai, as, a, avons, avez, ont. ● *Impf.* avais. ● *Past hist.* eus, eut, eûmes, eûtes, eurent. ● *Fut.* aurai. ● *Pres. sub.* aie, aies, ait, ayons, ayez, aient. ● *Pres. part.* ayant. ● *Past part.* eu. ● *Imp.* aie, ayons, ayez.
battre ● *Pres.* bats, bat, battons, battez, battent.
boire ● *Pres.* bois, buvons, boivent. ● *Impf.* buvais. ● *Past hist.* bus. ● *Pres. sub.* boive, buvions. ● *Past part.* bu.
bouillir ● *Pres.* bous, bouillons, bouillent. ● *Impf.* bouillais. ● *Pres. sub.* bouille.

combattre *as* BATTRE.
commettre *as* METTRE.
comprendre *as* PRENDRE.
concevoir *as* RECEVOIR.
conclure ● *Pres.* conclus, concluons, concluent. ● *Past hist.* conclus. ● *Past part.* conclu.
conduire ● *Pres.* conduis, conduisons, conduisent. ● *Impf.* conduisais. ● *Past hist.* conduisis. ● *Pres. sub.* conduise. ● *Past part.* conduit.
connaître ● *Pres.* connais, connaît, connaissons. ● *Impf.* connaissais. ● *Past hist.* connus. ● *Pres. sub.* connaisse. ● *Past part.* connu.
construire *as* CONDUIRE.
contenir *as* TENIR.
contraindre *as* ATTEINDRE (except *ai* replaces *ei*).
contredire *as* DIRE, except ● *Pres.* vous contredisez.
convaincre *as* VAINCRE.
convenir *as* TENIR.
corrompre *as* ROMPRE.
coudre ● *Pres.* couds, cousons, cousent. ● *Impf.* cousais. ● *Past hist.* cousis. ● *Pres. sub.* couse. ● *Past part.* cousu.
courir ● *Pres.* cours, courons, courent. ● *Impf.* courais. ● *Past hist.* courus. ● *Fut.* courrai. ● *Pres. sub.* coure. ● *Past part.* couru.
couvrir ● *Pres.* couvre, couvrons. ● *Impf.* couvrais. ● *Pres. sub.* couvre. ● *Past part.* couvert.
craindre *as* ATTEINDRE (except *ai* replaces *ei*).
croire ● *Pres.* crois, croit, croyons, croyez, croient. ● *Impf.* croyais. ● *Past hist.* crus. ● *Pres. sub.* croie, croyions. ● *Past part.* cru.
croître ● *Pres.* crois, croît, croissons. ● *Impf.* croissais. ● *Past hist.* crûs. ● *Pres. sub.* croisse. ● *Past part.* crû, crue.

cueillir
- *Pres.* cueille, cueillons.
- *Impf.* cueillais.
- *Fut.* cueillerai.
- *Pres. sub.* cueille.

débattre *as* BATTRE.
décevoir *as* RECEVOIR.
découvrir *as* COUVRIR.
décrire *as* ÉCRIRE.
déduire *as* CONDUIRE.
défaire *as* FAIRE.
détenir *as* TENIR.
détruire *as* CONDUIRE.
devenir *as* TENIR.
devoir
- *Pres.* dois, devons, doivent.
- *Impf.* devais.
- *Past hist.* dus.
- *Fut.* devrai.
- *Pres. sub.* doive.
- *Past part.* dû, due.

dire
- *Pres.* dis, dit, disons, dites, disent.
- *Impf.* disais.
- *Past hist.* dis.
- *Past part.* dit.

disparaître *as* CONNAÎTRE.
dissoudre
- *Pres.* dissous, dissolvons.
- *Impf.* dissolvais.
- *Pres. sub.* dissolve.
- *Past part.* dissous, dissoute.

distraire *as* EXTRAIRE.
dormir
- *Pres.* dors, dormons.
- *Impf.* dormais.
- *Pres. sub* dorme.

écrire
- *Pres.* écris, écrivons.
- *Impf.* écrivais.
- *Past hist.* écrivis.
- *Pres. sub.* écrive.
- *Past part.* écrit.

élire *as* LIRE.
émettre *as* METTRE.
s'enfuir *as* FUIR.
entreprendre *as* PRENDRE.
entretenir *as* TENIR.
envoyer
- *Fut.* enverrai.

éteindre *as* ATTEINDRE.
être
- *Pres.* suis, es, est, sommes, êtes, sont.
- *Impf.* étais.
- *Past hist.* fus, futm fûmes, fûtes, furent.
- *Fut.* serai.
- *Pres. sub.* sois, soit, soyons, soyez, soient.
- *Pres. part.* étant.
- *Past part.* été.
- *Imp.* sois, soyons, soyez.

exclure *as* CONCLURE.
extraire
- *Pres.* extrais, extrayons.
- *Impf.* extrayais.
- *Pres. sub.* extraie.
- *Past part.* extrait.

faire
- *Pres.* fais, fait, faisons, faites, font.
- *Impf.* faisais.
- *Past hist.* fis.
- *Fut.* ferai.
- *Pres. sub.* fasse.
- *Past part.* fait.

falloir
- (Impersonal)
- *Pres.* faut.
- *Impf.* fallait.
- *Past hist.* fallut.
- *Fut.* faudra.
- *Pres. sub.* faille.
- *Past part.* fallu.

feindre *as* ATTEINDRE.
fuir
- *Pres.* fuis, fuyons, fuient.
- *Impf.* fuyais.
- *Past hist.* fuis.
- *Pres sub.* fuie.
- *Past part.* fui.

inscrire *as* ÉCRIRE.
instruire *as* CONDUIRE.
interdire *as* DIRE, except ● *Pres.* vous interdisez.
interrompre *as* ROMPRE.
intervenir *as* TENIR.
introduire *as* CONDUIRE.
joindre *as* ATTEINDRE (except *oi* replaces *ei*).
lire
- *Pres.* lis, lit, lisons, lisez, lisent.
- *Impf.* lisais.
- *Past hist.* lus.
- *Pres. sub.* lise.
- *Past part.* lu.

luire
- *Pres.* luis, luisons.
- *Impf.* luisais.
- *Past hist.* luisis.
- *Pres. sub.* luise.
- *Past part.* lui.

maintenir *as* TENIR.
maudire
- *Pres.* maudis, maudissons.
- *Impf.* maudissais.
- *Past hist.* maudis.
- *Pres. sub.* maudisse.
- *Past part.* maudit.

mentir *as* SORTIR (except en replaces or).
mettre
- *Pres.* mets, met, mettons, mettez. mettent.
- *Past hist.* mis.
- *Past part.* mis.

mourir
- *Pres.* meurs, mourons, meurent.
- *Impf.* mourais.
- *Past hist.* mourus.
- *Fut.* mourrai.
- *Pres sub.* meure, mourions.
- *Past part.* mort.

mouvoir
- *Pres.* meus, mouvons, meuvent.
- *Impf.* mouvais.
- *Fut.* mouvrai.
- *Pres. sub.* meuve, mouvions.

● *Past part.* mû, mue.

naître ● *Pres.* nais, naît, naissons. ● *Impf.* naissais. ● *Past hist.* naquis. ● *Pres. sub.* naisse. ● *Past part.* né.

nuire *as* LUIRE.

obtenir *as* TENIR.

offrir, ouvrir *as* COUVRIR.

omettre *as* METTRE.

paraître *as* CONNAÎTRE.

parcourir *as* COURIR.

partir *as* SORTIR (except *ar* replaces *or*).

parvenir *as* TENIR.

peindre *as* ATTEINDRE.

percevoir *as* RECEVOIR.

permettre *as* METTRE.

plaindre *as* ATTEINDRE (except *ai* replaces *ei*).

plaire ● *Pres.* plais, plaît, plaisons. ● *Impf.* plaisais. ● *Past hist.* plus. ● *Pres. sub.* plaise. ● *Past part.* plu.

pleuvoir (impersonal) ● *Pres.* pleut. ● *Impf.* pleuvait. ● *Past hist.* plut. ● *Fut.* pleuvra. ● *Pres. sub.* pleuve. ● *Past part.* plu.

poursuivre *as* SUIVRE.

pourvoir *as* VOIR, except ● *Fut.* pourvoirai.

pouvoir ● *Pres.* peux, peut, pouvons, pouvez, peuvent. ● *Impf.* pouvais. ● *Past hist.* pus. ● *Fut.* pourrai. ● *Pres. sub.* puisse. ● *Past part.* pu.

prédire *as* DIRE, except ● *Pres.* vous prédisez.

prendre ● *Pres.* prends, prenons, prennent. ● *Impf.* prenais. ● *Past hist.* pris. ● *Pres. sub.* prenne, prenions. ● *Past part.* pris.

prescrire *as* ÉCRIRE.

prévenir *as* TENIR.

prévoir *as* VOIR, except ● *Fut.* prévoirai.

produire *as* CONDUIRE.

prommettre *as* METTRE.

provenir *as* TENIR.

recevoir ● *Pres.* reçois, recevons, reçoivent. ● *Impf.* recevais. ● *Past hist.* reçus. ● *Fut.* recevrai.

● *Pres. sub.* reçoive, recevions. ● *Past part.* reçu.

reconduire *as* CONDUIRE.

reconnaître *as* CONNAÎTRE.

reconstruire *as* CONDUIRE.

recouvrir *as* COUVRIR.

recueillir *as* CUEILLIR..

redire *as* DIRE.

réduire *as* CONDUIRE.

refaire *as* FAIRE.

rejoindre *as* ATTEINDRE (except *oi* replaces *ei*).

remettre *as* METTRE.

renvoyer *as* ENVOYER.

repartir *as* SORTIR (except *ar* replaces *or*.

reprendre *as* PRENDRE.

reproduire *as* vCONDUIRE.

résoudre ● *Pres.* résous, résolvons. ● *Impf.* résolvais. ● *Past hist.* résolus. ● *Pres. sub.* résolve. ● *Past part.* résolu.

ressortir *as* SORTIR.

restreindre *as* ATTEINDRE.

retenir, revenir *as* TENIR.

revivre *as* vVIVRE.

revoir *as* VOIR.

rire ● *Pres.* ris, rit, rions, riez, rient. ● *Impf.* riais. ● *Past hist.* ris. ● *Pres. sub.* rie, riions. ● *Past part.* ri.

rompre *as* VENDRE (regular), except ● *Pres.* il rompt.

satisfaire *as* FAIRE.

savoir ● *Pres.* sais, sait, savons, savez, savent. ● *Impf.* savais. ● *Past hist.* sus. ● *Fut.* saurai. ● *Pres. sub.* sache, sachions. ● *Pres. part.* sachant. ● *Past part.* su. ● *Impt.* sache, sachons, sachez.

séduire *as* CONDUIRE.

sentir *as* SORTIR (except *en* replaces *or*).

servir ● *Pres.* sers, servons. ● *Impf.* servais. ● *Pres. sub.* serve.

sortir ● *Pres.* sors, sortons. ● *Impf.* sortais. ● *Pres. sub.* sorte.

souffrir *as* COUVRIR.

soumettre *as* METTRE.

soustraire *as* EXTRAIRE.

soutenir *as* TENIR.

541

suffire
- *Pres.* suffis, suffisons.
- *Impf.* suffisais.
- *Past hist.* suffis.
- *Pres. sub.* suffise.
- *Past part.* suffi.

suivre
- *Pres.* suis, suivons.
- *Impf.* suivais. ● *Past hist.* suivis. ● *Pres. sub.* suive. ● *Past part.* suivi.

surprendre *as* PRENDRE.
survivre *as* VIVRE.
taire
- *Pres.* tais, taisond. ● *Impf.* taisais. ● *Past hist.* tus. ● *Pres. sub.* taise. ● *Past part.* tu.

teindre *as* ATTEINDRE.
tenir
- *Pres.* tiens, tenons, tiennent. ● *Impf.* tenais.
- *Past hist.* tins, tint, tinmes, tintes, tinrent.
- *Fut.* tiendrai.
- *Pres. sub.* tienne.
- *Past part.* tenu.

traduire *as* CONDUIRE.
traire *as* EXTRAIRE.
transmettre *as* METTRE.
vaincre
- *Pres.* vaincs, vaine, vainquons.
- *Impf.* vain-quais.

valoir
- *Past hist.* vainquis.
- *Pres. sub.* vainque.
- *Past part.* vaincu.
- *Pres.* vaux, vaut, valons, valez, valent.
- *Impf.* valais. ● *Past hist.* valus. ● *Fut.* vaudrai. ● *Pres. sub.* vaille. ● *Past part.* valu.

venir *as* TENIR.
vivre
- *Pres.* vis, vit, vivons, vivez, vivent.
- *Impf.* vivais. ● *Past hist.* vécus. ● *Pres. sub.* vive. ● *Past part.* vécu.

voir
- *Pres.* vois, voyons, voient. ● *Impf.* voyais.
- *Past hist.* vis. ● *Fut.* verrai. ● *Pres. sub.* voie, voyions. ● *Past part.* vu.

vouloir
- *Pres.* veux, veut, voulons, voulez, veulent.
- *Impf.* voulais. ● *Past hist.* voulus. ● *Fut.* voudrai. ● *Pres. sub.* veuille, voulions. ● *Past part.* voulu. ● *Imp.* veuille, veuillons, veuillez.